CONSIDER PHILOSOPHY

BRUCE N. WALLER

Youngstown State University

Prentice Hall

Boston   New York   San Francisco   Mexico City   Montreal
Toronto   London   Madrid   Munich   Paris   Hong Kong
Singapore   Tokyo   Cape Town   Sydney

Editorial Director: Craig Campanella
Editor in Chief: Dickson Musslewhite
Publisher: Nancy Roberts
Editorial Project Manager: Kate Fernandes
Editorial Assistant: Nart Varoqua
Director Of Marketing: Brandy Dawson
Senior Marketing Manager: Laura Lee Manley
Managing Editor: Maureen Richardson
Project Manager: Robert Merenoff
Operations Specialist: Christina Amato
Cover Manager: Jayne Conte
Cover Designer: Suzanne Behnke
Cover Credit: fallen birch leaves © Fotolia / Fotolia X
Full-Service Project Management: Integra Software Services Pvt. Ltd.
Composition: Integra Software Services Pvt. Ltd.
Printer/Binder: Edwards Brothers
Cover Printer: Lehigh-Phoenix Color/Hagerstown
Text Font: 10/12 Goudy

Credits and acknowledgments borrowed from other sources and reproduced, with permission, in this textbook appear on pages.

Library of Congress Cataloging-in-Publication Data

Waller, Bruce N.,
   Consider philosophy/Bruce N. Waller. — 1st ed.
     p. cm.
Includes bibliographical references and index.
   ISBN-13: 978-0-205-64422-3 (alk. paper)
   ISBN-10: 0-205-64422-8 (alk. paper)
   1. Philosophy—Textbooks.   I. Title.
   B74.W25 2011
   100—dc22

                    2010023225

10 9 8 7 6 5 4 3 2 1

Prentice Hall
is an imprint of

PEARSON

www.pearsonhighered.com

A la Carte: ISBN 13: 978-0-205-01205-3
          ISBN 10:   0-205-01205-1

          ISBN 13: 978-0-205-64422-3
          ISBN 10:   0-205-64422-8

CONTENTS

PREFACE

Consider Philosophy is a problems-oriented approach to philosophy, which concentrates on questions that are of contemporary interest to both philosophers and students. However, the text also makes an extensive examination of the history and development of philosophical thought, using that history to make the problems clearer, to show why those basic problems remain significant, and to explore the many implications and connections of those problems. In order to bring out the full significance of the continuing issues and debates, the text places each issue in the widest possible context, making extensive use of the history of science, social history, political developments, and religious history to help students gain a better understanding of the philosophical questions as well as a clearer picture of how philosophy has influenced—and been influenced by—developments in other disciplines and in the larger culture. In addition, this approach helps in drawing connections among the various philosophical debates and positions: Students gain a better grasp of why conclusions drawn about the theory of knowledge also influence ideas and theories about the mind, ethics, free will, personal identity, and political philosophy; and why conclusions they reached when considering epistemology might be reconsidered under pressure of questions raised about free will, ethics, or the nature of mind.

While the text examines substantial philosophical issues and the serious continuing arguments surrounding them, it retains throughout a comfortable, conversational tone. Students are consistently addressed as intelligent inquirers, engaged in serious philosophical examination, who must make their own evaluations of arguments and theories and draw their own conclusions. Questions at the end of each chapter are designed to stimulate further thought and raise genuine open questions, rather than merely checking to see if students can "get the right answer." This is a very readable book for students from a wide variety of backgrounds, inviting them to participate fully in philosophical arguments and conversations. The text presents philosophy as a challenging and important enterprise, but one which is also intriguing and enjoyable.

The text contains extensive readings from both contemporary and historical sources (including readings from the ancient, medieval, Renaissance, modern and contemporary periods). While the readings are quite substantial, they are arranged in relation to specific questions and issues, so that students can approach these readings with a specific issue or debate in mind and thus a starting context that makes the readings easier to understand. In addition, the readings are often arranged in such a way that the writers are taking opposing positions on common questions: reading one essay helps students gain a better appreciation of the other essays in that section.

Every chapter contains extensive boxed material: to explain difficult concepts, enhance interest, and aid students in placing the philosophical issues in larger historical, social, and scientific contexts.

Learning aids—study questions, suggestions for additional reading and suggestions for online resources—are found in every chapter.

DISTINCTIVE FEATURES

- An opening chapter on how to argue effectively and congenially, while avoiding the pitfalls that undermine productive philosophical exploration and discussion.

- A conversational introduction to philosophical issues, that starts from the philosophical questions that are of most immediate interest—the existence of God, the nature of knowledge, the nature of mind, personal identity, free will, and ethical claims—and explores the historical and cultural contexts of those questions, the impact of contemporary scientific research on the issues, and the larger social implications.

- Presents arguments pro and con on each issue and each position, as well as primary source material from a variety of perspectives, and invites students to reach their own conclusions on these continuing controversies.

- Includes a wide range of primary texts—from Aristotle to Annette Baier, and from Martin Luther and Giovanni Pico della Mirandola to Stephen Gould and Richard Dawkins—placed in clear argumentative contexts, enabling students to understand and appreciate original sources and arguments.

- Discussion questions at the end of each chapter pose challenging open questions and draw out the larger implications of the debates—questions that stimulate class discussion and/or provide short written assignments.

- Special boxed material scattered through each chapter explains and enlivens the text material and places it in its historical and cultural setting.

- Respects students as genuine philosophical inquirers, who are capable of wrestling with serious philosophical questions and drawing their own conclusions.

- Learning aids—including suggestions for further reading and for Internet inquiry—at the end of each chapter. An end-of-book glossary presents the definitions of the key terms used in the book.

SUPPORT FOR INSTRUCTORS AND STUDENTS

- **myphilosophylab** is an interactive and instructive multimedia site designed to help students and instructors save time and improve results. It offers access to a wealth of resources geared to meet the individual teaching and learning needs of every instructor and student. Combining an ebook, video, audio, multimedia simulations, research support and assessment, MyPhilosophyLab engages students and gives them the tools they need to enhance their performance in the course. Please see your Pearson sales representative or visit www.myphilosophylab.com for more information.

- Instructor's Manual with Tests (0-205-64424-4): For each chapter in the text, this valuable resource provides a detailed outline, list of objectives, discussion questions, and suggested readings and videos. In addition, test questions in multiple-choice, true/false, fill-in-the-blank, and short answer formats are available for each chapter; the answers are page-referenced to the text. For easy access, this manual is available within the instructor section of MyPhilosophyLab for *Consider Philosophy*, or at www.pearsonhighered. com/irc.

- MyTest Test Generator (0-205-01199-3): This computerized software allows instructors to create their own personalized exams, edit any or all of the existing test questions, and add new questions. Other special features of this program include random generation of test questions, creation of alternate versions of the same test, scrambling question sequence, and test preview before printing. For easy access, this software is available within the instructor section of MyPhilosophyLab for *Consider Philosophy*, or at www.pearsonhighered.com/irc.

- PowerPoint Presentation Slides for Consider Philosophy (0-205-01198-5): These PowerPoint slides combine text and graphics for each chapter to help instructors convey anthropological principles in a clear and engaging way. For easy access, they are available within the instructor section of MyPhilosophyLab for *Consider Philosophy*, or at www.pearsonhighered.com/irc.

ACKNOWLEDGMENTS

Many people have been of enormous help in my work on this book—perhaps many without even realizing it. First, I am most fortunate to work in a department that is congenial, stimulating, and productive—and with colleagues eager to read, examine, and critique one's work, colleagues who listen attentively, thoughtfully, and cordially to even the wildest and weirdest ideas, and colleagues who are a constant source of new arguments and fascinating ideas. Special thanks to Julie Aultman, Chris Bache, Walter Carvin, Nancy Dawson, Z Kermani, Jeff Limbian, Vince Lisi, Sarah Lown, Martina Malvasi, Brendan Minogue, Mustansir Mir, Deborah Mower, Bernard Oakes, Gabriel Palmer-Fernandez, Charles Reid, Joseph Schonberger, Tom Shipka, Donna Sloan, Arnold Smith, Andrew Stypinski, Linda "Tess" Tessier, Alan Tomhave, Mark Vopat, and Victor Wan-Tatah. Being chair of the Philosophy and Religious Studies Department at Youngstown State University for the past four years—including the years when I was writing this book—has been, well, an interesting and challenging experience. It has always been clear to me that any talents I might have are not administrative; and my years as department chair have only confirmed that conviction. That we have muddled through my years as department chair without departmental disaster, and that I have still had time to continue writing, is due to several factors. First, the department faculty is wonderfully congenial, cooperative, and tolerant. Second, the former chair, Tom Shipka, set a good and productive course, and so we had a clear track to follow—and Tom has also been more than willing to offer guidance and counsel and aid on the many occasions when it was needed. Third, no department has ever been more fortunate in its department administrators: Joan Bevan, until her retirement, managed the complex and maddening machinery of departmental paperwork and academic red tape with remarkable efficiency and good cheer; and her successor, Mary Dillingham, has taken over the controls without the least glitch and kept everything moving smoothly with the same warm friendliness to faculty, staff, and students. I trust I am betraying no academic secrets when I say that a well-functioning academic department owes a great deal more to the competence of the department secretary/administrator than to any talents of the department chair; and our department has been blessed with two of the absolute best. They have been very ably assisted by wonderful hardworking student workers: Hannah Detec, James Hamilton, and Gina Ponzio. Finally, a department chair's life can be made relatively easy or absolutely horrific, depending on the goodwill, the leadership, and the integrity of the Dean and Provost. I have been very fortunate to have a Dean, Shearle Furnish, who is deeply supportive of our department and its activities, and does everything in his power to help us succeed in our goals (and who is aided by an associate dean, Jane Kestner, who knows absolutely everything about how the university functions and has the remarkable patience to explain budget lines, budget categories, and paperwork details to a department chair incapable of mastering any of it); and a Provost, Ikram Khawaja, who is genuinely dedicated to the flourishing of every department, who has a special affection for the Philosophy and Religious Studies department (it doesn't hurt that his daughter is a superb philosopher), and whose integrity is beyond question.

Many others have been of great help and inspiration in the course of very enjoyable conversations; among those are Homer Warren, Lauren Schroeder, Fred Alexander, Lia Ruttan, Richard White, Jack Raver, Paul Sracic, Charles Singler, Robyn Repko, and Stephen Flora. My philosophical debts to those philosophers whose work I have read and with whom I have discussed many of these issues are too profound and too numerous to list. My editor at Pearson, Nancy Roberts, and her very able special projects manager, Kate Fernandes, have been highly skilled, totally professional, and wonderfully supportive. My copy editor, George Jacob of Integra, has done a marvelous job of catching my many mistakes and turning rough copy into a polished final product.

My wife, Mary Newell Waller, has kept me informed on many issues and developments in psychology, through her professional interests and her work as a clinical psychologist; her constant support and affection is the essential foundation for all my work; and it was her stimulating question—"Why don't you write books that make money?"—that started me writing textbooks in the first place. My sons, Russell and Adam, are my great pride and joy. Russell is pursuing a Ph.D. in math at Florida State, and Adam is working on a Ph.D. in musical theory at Eastman: an academic father's dream. Russ is a splendid center fielder, Adam a cunning poker player. They are also warm, funny, kind, creative, and wonderful. And this despite childhoods in which they were constantly besieged by their father's strange questions about determinism and pragmatism and personal identity—questions which they tolerated with good cheer, even over their breakfast cereal; and which they often answered with remarkable insight. This book is dedicated to them, with love and gratitude.

BRUCE N. WALLER

CHAPTER 1

THINKING CRITICALLY AND CORDIALLY ABOUT PHILOSOPHY

WHAT IS PHILOSOPHY?

What is philosophy? Like most questions in philosophy, that's a disputed question. Philosophy has been studied and written for at least 2,500 years, perhaps longer; and no doubt people *thought* about philosophy for many centuries before that. During that time there have been many competing claims about what philosophy is, and the controversy continues. The question is complicated by the fact that for most of the historical development of philosophy, there was no clear distinction between philosophy and natural science, or between philosophy and religion, or between philosophy and magic (in the eighteenth century, the term for science was "natural philosophy," which distinguished it from traditional philosophical questions of metaphysics and ethics).

> Philosophy, though unable to tell us with certainty what is the true answer to the doubts it raises, is able to suggest many possibilities which enlarge our thoughts and free them from the tyranny of custom. Thus, while diminishing our feeling of certainty as to what things are, it greatly increases our knowledge as to what they may be; it removes the somewhat arrogant dogmatism of those who have never travelled into the region of liberating doubt, and it keeps alive our sense of wonder by showing familiar things in an unfamiliar aspect. *Bertrand Russell*

So what *is* philosophy? Literally, the word means *love* (philo) of *wisdom* (sophia). That's nice, but it probably doesn't get us much closer to answering the question. If we had asked the ancient Greeks, such as Plato, they would have given a clear and conclusive answer: Philosophy seeks wisdom about the *ultimate* reality, the *deeper* reality beyond mere appearance and opinion. Physics may tell us about atoms, and astronomers can observe the planets, but philosophers seek the deeper universal truths behind these appearances: the deep structure of the universe, the relation of God to the cosmos, the nature of the *substance* that underlies the mere appearance, the understanding of the *essential* rather than the accidental and the *universal* behind the particular. Impressive, but very few contemporary philosophers would make such exalted claims.

> Philosophy is a battle against the bewitchment of our intelligence by means of language. *Ludwig Wittgenstein*

At the other extreme, there are those who favor the "underlaborer" view of philosophy: Philosophers don't tell physicists the ultimate reality that lies beneath and beyond their research; rather, philosophers help physicists (and other scientists) by clearing away the verbal confusions; that is, philosophers clear away the verbal underbrush so that scientists can pursue their research. It's true that philosophers are often very interested in dealing with the confusions and problems and ambiguities inherent in language, and that is a useful enterprise. But what else does philosophy do?

> Philosophy, like all other fields, is unique. But the uniqueness of philosophy seems more impressive. Whereas historians, physicists, etc., generally agree about what constitutes their proper field of study, philosophers do not. Some philosophers have even maintained that there is no proper field of study for philosophers. This extreme position fortunately is not held by too many philosophers, but it illustrates perhaps the most distinctive feature of philosophy, namely that it leaves nothing unquestioned. This explains why philosophers do not accept any authority but their own reason. *Bernard Gert*

If we were trying to find defining characteristics of the philosophical enterprise, there are a few characteristics that stand out. First, philosophers—at least in principle—do not accept anything on authority, or on faith; or another way of putting it, there are no questions or challenges that are "off-limits" to philosophers. Does God exist? What is the nature of knowledge? Can we have genuine knowledge? Are there objective ethical truths? What is the nature of humans? Do we have free will? Are we morally responsible for our behavior? Are we different in kind from other animals? Questions are explored by means of rational argument; and arguments are offered, scrutinized, and criticized without fear or favor. Furthermore, the questions posed are often among the most basic questions we can ask: psychologists, physicists, historians, mathematicians, biologists, and anthropologists all pursue *knowledge*; but philosophers ask, what is the *nature* of knowledge, what *counts* as genuine knowledge, is the knowledge discovered by mathematicians different in kind from the knowledge attained by biologists?

But does philosophy actually find *answers*? That's a legitimate question. After all, philosophers have been asking many of the same questions for several thousand years, and there is *still* philosophical dispute about the right answers. For example, currently there are probably more *different* and competing philosophical views about free will than there were a thousand years ago, and there is vigorous dispute about which one is right. So in one sense, philosophers do go on asking the *same* questions; but in another sense, philosophers are always asking *new* questions, questions that are constantly changing. Consider the question of free will. When Aristotle asked that question, there was no science of psychology, biology was in its infancy, there was almost no knowledge of the brain, and powerful unseen forces often seemed in control of our fates. When philosophers asked that question in 1700, they were dealing with Newton's great discoveries and wondering whether Newtonian laws might apply not only to planets and rocks but also to humans and thoughts and choices. When the question was posed in 1900, we had to take account of the influence of evolution, and perhaps of unconscious forces. When we ask it today, we must consider what psychologists have learned about how situational cues (of which we are unaware) influence how we act, and what neurological science has taught us about the operations of the brain (which oftentimes are not conscious); when we ask that question in light of these new findings, it is a very different question from the question posed by Aristotle. That seems to be true for almost every major philosophical question: These questions are new and fresh and important for every generation. But precisely because these questions are constantly new, and must be explored by each generation in light of new discoveries and new conditions, it may be that for many of these questions there are no *permanent* answers. *Is* it the case that there are no final answers to philosophical questions? If so, does that mean that philosophers can never gain *knowledge*? Those are serious *philosophical* questions.

> To teach how to live with uncertainty, yet without being paralyzed by hesitation, is perhaps the chief thing that philosophy can do. *Bertrand Russell*

Socrates claimed that "the unexamined life is not worth living." I think he was wrong. Many people have lived very decent and worthwhile lives while never exploring basic philosophical questions, never examining or challenging the deep assumptions of their belief system, never wrestling with philosophical ideas. But those who never explore the challenges and puzzles and *disturbances* generated by philosophical questions miss an opportunity to live a deeper and richer life. You can live without philosophy, and certainly you can attain worldly success without exploring philosophy; but can you live as *well* if you never consider the fundamental philosophical questions? That's a philosophical question; ultimately, it's one you'll have to answer for yourself.

THINKING CRITICALLY AND PLAYING FAIR

Philosophy deals with *arguments*—nothing mysterious about that. You've probably come across an argument before; perhaps you've even participated in one. An argument attempts to establish a *conclusion*, and the argument gives reasons or *premises* in support of that conclusion. For example: "A thriving economy is essential for our well-being. Well-educated workers are necessary for a thriving economy. Therefore, we should provide strong support for public education." That is an argument, in which the last sentence is the *conclusion* ("We should provide strong support for public education") and the first two sentences are the *premises*. In evaluating that argument, we must do two separate and distinct things. First, we must decide whether the premises are *true*. Second, we have to decide whether the premises give sufficient support for the conclusion; that is, even if we *assume* that the premises are true, do they actually give us good reasons for the conclusion? Does the conclusion actually *follow from* the premises? Consider this argument: "You should wear purple tomorrow, because bloodthirsty extraterrestrials will invade the university tomorrow, and they will slaughter everyone who is not wearing purple." In this case, the conclusion does follow from the premises (the premises provide excellent reasons for wearing purple); but you might well have some doubts about the truth of the premises. And consider this argument: "Skiing is *not* a dangerous sport; after all, skiing is great exercise, and it gets you out in the fresh air, and it's also great fun." Even if the three reasons given (great exercise, fresh air, and great fun) are *true*, they don't give you good reasons for the *conclusion* that skiing is not dangerous. So, as you consider arguments, keep in mind that you must do *two* things: consider whether the *premises* are actually true; and also, consider whether the premises (whether true or false) provide good reasons for that specific conclusion.

Deductive and Inductive Arguments

An important distinction among arguments is the distinction between *deductive* arguments and *inductive* arguments. A *deductive* argument is one in which the conclusion is extracted from the premises by logical operations; in other words, the conclusion is already contained in the premises in some form, and the argument draws the conclusion out. For example, consider the argument: If the tavern is open, then Bruce is at the tavern; and the tavern is open; therefore, Bruce is at the tavern. By putting those premises together, the conclusion—Bruce is at the tavern—is a logical consequence; it can be extracted from those premises. Another way of thinking of deductive arguments is that they are based on *logical form*. Consider this argument: If the library is open, then Donna is at the library; and the library is open; therefore, Donna is at the library. Those are very different arguments (one concludes with Bruce at the tavern, the other places Donna in the library) but they have the same *logical form*: If A then B; A; therefore B. Of course, deductive arguments can come in *many* forms (an endless number): Either Bruce is at the library or Bruce is at the tavern; Bruce is not at the library; therefore, Bruce is at the tavern. All students are wealthy; Erica is a student; therefore, Erica is wealthy. All dogs are animals; some dogs have floppy ears; therefore, some animals have floppy ears. Because good deductive arguments use legitimate logical operations to *extract* conclusions from their premises, in good—that is, in *valid*—deductive arguments, the truth of the premises *guarantees* the truth of the conclusion.

The other major form of argument is *inductive*. Inductive arguments use the premises to *project* a conclusion that goes *beyond* the conclusion. For example, Bruce has been at the tavern every night for the past month; so probably Bruce will be at the tavern tomorrow night. That's a reasonable conclusion to draw, given the fact of Bruce's regular visits to the tavern. But note: Reasonable though it is, the conclusion goes *beyond* the premises, it can't just be *extracted* from the premises; for the premises have to do with Bruce's tavern visits in the *past* month, while the conclusion is about a tavern visit *tomorrow*. And that's not just because the conclusion is about something happening tomorrow. Suppose someone is wondering where Bruce was last night, and someone says: Well, Bruce was at the tavern every night for the previous two months; so probably he was at the tavern last night. That's an inductive argument: last night is not contained in the premises, which deal with the two months *prior* to last night. Like deductive arguments, inductive arguments come in many shapes and sizes. For example, we have interviewed 1,000 students at North State University, and 800 of them were opposed to capital punishment; so probably most of the students at North State University oppose capital punishment. In that inductive argument, the premises cover only 1,000 students, but the conclusion goes well beyond those premises to draw a (reasonable) conclusion about many times that number. As another example, we have tested this new drug on 10,000 patients, and we have had no adverse reactions; so probably this new drug is safe for everybody. Likewise, Sandra and Sarah like the same novels, the same music, the same clothes, the same jewelry, and the same poetry; so probably they'll also like the same movies. Because the conclusions of inductive arguments go *beyond* their premises (the conclusion is not just extracted *from* the premises, as in deductive arguments), an inductive argument with true premises cannot *guarantee* the truth of the conclusion (though a good inductive argument can make its conclusion highly *probable*). In contrast, if a *deductive* argument has true premises and the right logical form (when it is *valid*), then it *does* guarantee the truth of its conclusion. So inductive arguments and deductive arguments are very different sorts of arguments. Not that one is *better* than the other; both are very valuable; they're just *different*, and they serve different functions. Most of the philosophical arguments that are examined in this book are *deductive* arguments, though there is also a scattering of inductive arguments.

Thinking Critically and Cooperatively

Arguments can sometimes be heated and divisive—maybe you already knew that. But arguments don't *have* to be heated and angry. They can also be cooperative and friendly, especially when everyone works together to examine the arguments, and everyone carefully and thoughtfully considers and critiques the *arguments* rather than the *people* who gave the arguments, and when everyone is motivated to gain better understanding rather than scoring points or winning contests. Philosophy deals with arguments, and those arguments are often about deeply contested issues; but the arguments can also be thoughtful and friendly. And if studying philosophy helps you learn to argue intelligently, cheerfully, and cooperatively about difficult and divisive questions, then that alone will make the study of philosophy a very worthwhile enterprise.

Philosophy poses some difficult and controversial questions, and people often have very strong beliefs about those questions: beliefs that are among their most basic and cherished principles. Some people have a rule, that one should avoid discussions of politics and religion, because they are likely to stir up controversy and discord. Philosophy has no such rule: In the next chapter we shall examine the question of the existence of God, and before the end we'll look at some very controversial questions in political philosophy. And if that isn't enough to touch off some squabbles, we'll also take on questions about free will and basic questions of ethics.

You probably know from your own sad experience that people have strong feelings about such questions. Late-night dorm discussions can become heated when political issues are on the table, and even good friends can become a trifle hostile when their religious or ethical views are challenged. In an effort to prevent hostility, and to promote harmonious discussion of deep philosophical questions—even when the participants champion radically different positions—we'll start by considering a few basic rules of good argument, as well as noting a few argument pitfalls and delusions that should be avoided.

Philosophical issues are profoundly interesting, they touch on some of our deepest principles and convictions, and they often arouse strong passions. That's fine and good. They also provoke very spirited and fascinating argument, and that's also fine. But they can occasionally spark bitter and acrimonious exchanges, and that's not so good. It's none of my business if you want to engage in bitter fights with your friends. If you enjoy that sort of thing, perhaps you have a brilliant future in politics. But when discussing *philosophical* questions, it might be better to *try* to keep things calm and rational, and maybe even friendly. And that is simply because you will have a better chance of really appreciating the various philosophical positions and arguments if you do so calmly and reasonably, rather than in the heat of passion. (There's nothing wrong with the heat of passion, of course; in some circumstances it is delightful. It's just that passion can be something of a distraction in philosophical inquiry and debate.) There are some arguments that can be very tempting, and that often inflame passions, but that are a severe impediment to serious and insightful philosophical inquiry. Such arguments are *fallacious*; they commit *fallacies*.

A *fallacy* is simply a common argument *mistake*, or error. There are many different ways of going wrong in arguments, and some of them are so common that we have given them special names to aid in remembering those errors, recognizing them, and *avoiding* them. Though there are many more fallacies than can be covered here, there are some very common and particularly deceptive fallacies that you should learn to recognize, and that we'll examine in this chapter: the *irrelevant reason* fallacy (sometimes called the *red herring* fallacy); the *ad hominem* fallacy; the *appeal to authority* fallacy; and the *strawman* fallacy.

Irrelevant Reason Fallacy

> *Pat.*   The current U.S. laws make drinking illegal for young people who are 18 or 19 or 20; and those laws are fundamentally *unfair*. After all, the United States expects 18-year-olds to take on the *responsibilities* of full adults: for the U.S. makes 18-year-olds eligible for the military draft, and can require young people of that age to enter the military, risk their lives for their country, and perhaps even die for their country. That responsibility of being *obligated* to sacrifice your life for your country is a responsibility of *adults*, not children; after all, we would think it wrong to draft children. So if the government gives young people the *responsibilities* of adulthood at age 18, it is unfair and unjust to deny them the *rights* of adulthood—including the same right to drink that other adults enjoy.
>
> *Mike.*   No, you're wrong; denying the right to drink to people who are 18 is *not* a violation of their rights. After all, raising the legal drinking age to 21 resulted in a significant decrease in alcohol-related automobile deaths for young people aged 18 to 21. So these legal restrictions on the right to drink have saved lives, and they are *not* unfair.

> Mike's argument commits the fallacy of *irrelevant reason*. It may well be true that laws raising the legal drinking age have saved lives; and certainly saving lives is a wonderful thing. But that wonderful fact is *irrelevant* to the question Pat is raising: Is it *fair* to impose the *responsibilities* of adulthood on 18-year-olds while denying them the *rights and privileges* of adulthood?

The fallacy of *irrelevant reason* is the fallacy—as the name implies—of giving a reason that is *irrelevant* to the question at issue. For example, suppose you are sitting on the jury in a sensational and gruesome murder trial. The defendant, who has been charged with the murder, claims that this is a case of mistaken identity: The only witness against the defendant is an old man with weak eyesight who looked across a darkened street and saw the murder being committed and the murderer fleeing. This witness told the police that his eyesight is not very good, that the street was dark, that he did not get a good look at the murderer, and that he did not think he could identify the murderer. The witness remembered that the murderer appeared to be a young man wearing faded blue jeans, but he couldn't tell much else about him. A week later, in a lineup, he picked out a young man wearing blue jeans, and the witness said he thought the young man was the murderer he had seen. But in fact the only person in the lineup wearing faded blue jeans was the defendant; and the defendant's lawyer pointed out that probably the witness was only picking out a young man in faded blue jeans from the lineup, and not the murderer. The prosecutor, in his closing argument to the jury, emphasizes the brutal nature of this murder: "The victim was murdered in cold blood, while walking down the sidewalk, bothering no one. This quiet and peaceful man was murdered, so this cruel gunman could steal a few dollars. This was a vicious, coldhearted, cruel crime; and I ask you, the jury, to return a verdict of guilty." In this case, the prosecutor's argument commits the fallacy of irrelevant reason. The *question* at issue is not whether the crime was cruel—everyone agrees that it was—but whether the crime was committed *by the defendant*. The *irrelevant reason* offered by the prosecutor may well inflame the jury; and if they become really disturbed by the brutality of the murder, that irrelevant reason may lead them to conclude that the defendant is guilty: a conclusion that obviously is not justified by that argument. The murder *was* brutal, and that point easily catches our attention, and makes us forget that the *real* question is not whether the murder was brutal but whether the defendant did it.

> A nineteenth-century Devonshire jury found the defendant guilty of stealing hay, but added the following note to the judge:
>
> *We don't think the prisoner done it, but there's been a lot of hay taken*
> *hereabouts by someone.*

The irrelevant reason fallacy sometimes goes by a more colorful name: the *red herring* fallacy. The name apparently comes from British fox hunting: When the hunters finally grew tired of chasing a pack of hounds that were pursuing a terrified fox, they wanted to quickly round up the dogs and head back to the lodge for tea and crumpets. But the dogs, of course, were eager to continue their pursuit, and were not easy to catch. So the hunters would place cooked herring (herring is a fish with a very strong smell, and when it is cooked it turns red, and also becomes quite oily) in a cloth bag; the oil and the strong scent from the red herring would soak the bag, and then the hunters would drag the red herring across the trail of the fox. When the pursuing hounds hit the strong smell of the red herring, they would lose the scent of the fox and stop, so the hunters could easily catch the hounds. Thus the name of the *red herring* fallacy: a red herring (or irrelevant reason) is a reason that takes you *off* the trail of the real issue by distracting you with a dramatic point that may well be *true* but is not relevant to the current question.

The key to avoiding red herring fallacies is staying focused on *exactly* what question is being debated, *exactly* what conclusion the argument is supposed to be proving. In the case of the murder trial, the question at issue is whether the *defendant* committed the crime, *not* whether the murder itself was a brutal one: emphasizing the brutality of the crime is emphasizing an irrelevant reason, it is dragging a red herring across the trail of the argument. But in another context, the brutality of the murder may be *relevant*. Suppose that the defendant admits he did the crime, and now the issue is *not* whether the defendant did it, but what *punishment* is appropriate. In that case, noting the cruel brutality of the murder *would* be relevant. The moral of the story is important: Before you can determine whether a reason or argument is *relevant*, you must know exactly what the argument is supposed to establish (that is, you must know what *conclusion* the argument is supposed to prove). In a debate about whether we should have capital punishment, Joan argues that capital punishment is desirable because it is an effective deterrent: It influences some potential murderers not to commit murders. Joan's deterrence argument is *relevant* to that question. And note, it is *relevant* even if it turns out that Joan is wrong, and capital punishment is *not* an effective deterrent. The question of whether her claim is *relevant* is not a question of whether it is *true*; rather, it is a question of whether it *matters* if it's true (if Joan's claim is relevant to the conclusion that capital punishment is justified, then the *truth* of that claim would provide support for the conclusion; if her claim is *not* relevant, then it doesn't matter whether her claim is true: true or not, it won't give any support for the conclusion). Suppose instead we are arguing about whether there is a danger in capital punishment that we might sometimes execute *innocent* persons. If *that* is the issue, then Joan's claim that capital punishment is an effective deterrent would be an *irrelevant reason*. That is, from the fact that capital punishment is an effective deterrent, it does *not* follow that there is no danger of executing the innocent.

Whenever the public begins to complain about the high cost of prescription medicine, the Pharmaceutical Manufacturers Association—a public relations group for the drug companies—runs advertisements promoting the value of medications, such as a two-page color advertisement in the August 1993 issue of *Scientific American*, which featured a pleasant smiling woman, Phyllis, with her affectionate cat perched on her shoulder. The text of the advertisement goes like this:

> Ask Phyllis her opinion of the anti-stroke drug that lets her hold onto her independence and life savings. When medicines can help people like Phyllis avoid a stroke, that's obviously a good thing. What's not so apparent is how dramatically the same drugs reduce nursing home costs.
>
> Stroke often leaves survivors so disabled they require nursing home care, which now averages over $30,000 a year per patient. But drugs that reduce the risk of strokes are helping individuals and families avoid such a huge financial blow. And helping to hold down the nation's expenditures for nursing home care, estimated at $66 billion a year.
>
> America's health care crisis calls for this kind of cost-saving power. And new prescription drugs are our best hope for providing it.

Drugs that prevent strokes are wonderful, and helping Phyllis "hold onto her independence and life savings" is great. And certainly it's true that drugs that prevent strokes cost less than nursing homes. But all of that is *irrelevant* to the question that is under debate: Are the drug companies spending too much on advertising and raking in excessive profits and *overcharging* for the valuable life-saving drugs they produce. We all agree that such drugs can yield great benefits; but if the *question* is whether the drug companies are exploiting their monopolistic positions to charge excessive prices, then the benefits of the drugs are a red herring.

Ad Hominem Arguments

An *ad hominem* argument is, literally, an argument *to the person*; that is, an ad hominem argument is an argument that attacks a person. Not all ad hominem arguments commit the ad hominem *fallacy*. In fact, there are *many* times when it is useful and legitimate to verbally *attack* a person and point out flaws in his or her character or behavior: Don't believe that witness, he's a habitual liar; Don't loan money to Anita, she's a deadbeat and will never pay you back; Don't vote for Senator Scam, he's in the pocket of the oil industry; Don't ride with Sandra, she's a reckless and dangerous driver; Don't take a course from Bruce, his lectures are boring and his tests are impossible; Don't hire Alice, she's a crook who will steal from the cash register; Don't go out with Arthur, he's abusive and possessive and a cheater. In all of those cases, there is an attack on the person; but those attacks are relevant and legitimate. After all, before you ride with Sandra, it's useful to know that she's likely to place your life at risk; and if you are considering taking a course with Bruce, you might find it helpful to know that he is a terminally boring teacher. Thus, many ad hominem arguments are perfectly legitimate, and do *not* commit the ad hominem fallacy. But when you attack a person who is giving an *argument*, and you claim that the person's *argument* is bad because of something bad about the *arguer*, then that is an ad hominem *fallacy*. An ad hominem *fallacy* attempts to refute a person's *argument* by attacking the *person* giving that argument. An attack on a person giving an argument is *always* a fallacious way of trying to refute the argument. If I give an *argument*, then the argument must stand or fall on its own merits, and you don't need to know anything at all about the *source* of the argument in order to evaluate the argument itself. There's the argument: you can probe it, dissect it, challenge it, critique it. If it's a bad argument, point out its mistakes. For example, if I give an argument, and my argument commits the irrelevant reason fallacy, then there is nothing wrong with criticizing my fallacious argument. But focus on the *argument*, not the person who gave the argument. If I give an *argument*, it doesn't matter whether I'm drunk or sober, vicious or virtuous, kind or cruel, liberal or conservative, sincere or hypocritical, rich or poor. Suppose you are examining an *argument* in favor of higher taxes on the wealthy: Such taxes will stimulate the economy, the great gap between the wealthy and the rest of our society creates dissension, higher taxes are needed to improve our educational system and the wealthy are the ones who can best afford to pay, and so forth. Okay, there's the argument; have at it. You can attack the reasons given (you might try to establish that some of them are false); you could try to show that even if the reasons given are true, the conclusion that we should increase taxes on the wealthy doesn't really follow from those reasons. You might argue that some of the reasons given are *irrelevant* to the question at issue. But you can do all that without having any idea of whose argument it is; and in fact, it doesn't *matter* whose argument it is. It doesn't matter whether the argument came from Barack Obama or Sarah Palin or Albert Einstein or Osama bin Laden. It's still the same argument. Suppose that you learned the argument came from someone who is very wealthy, like Bill Gates; that wouldn't make the *argument* any better, because *nothing* about the argument is changed. Or suppose it came from George Washington. That would be an interesting historical fact, but it doesn't make any difference whatsoever in evaluating the argument. And if initially you thought it had been given by George Washington, but then you discovered it was actually given by Benedict Arnold, the *argument* would remain the same. It *doesn't matter* who is the source of the argument; and if you try to refute an *argument* by bringing up characteristics of the *arguer*—the arguer has a special interest, the arguer is biased, the arguer is stupid, the arguer is a hypocrite, the arguer has a criminal record, the arguer hates kittens—then you have committed the ad hominem *fallacy*.

Suppose that I give an *argument* for why you shouldn't drink and drive: it impairs your reflexes, it places yourself and others at increased risk of injury or death, it exposes you to potential legal action and a possible criminal record that won't look good on your job applications, and so forth. Later, you see me stagger out of the tavern, fumble with my keys, fall into my car, and weave off down the street sideswiping three other cars as I drive away. Then you would conclude that I am a hypocrite, and not to be trusted—and certainly not someone you want to ride with—and you would be exactly right. But if you *also* conclude that my *argument* against drinking and driving must be a bad one, then you have committed the ad hominem fallacy. *I* may be impaired, but that doesn't mean that my *argument* is impaired. My argument may be a great one, even if I myself fail to live up to it. Now suppose that the person you saw was my twin brother, who has a drinking problem; and that I *never* drink and drive. That would in no way *change* my argument, or rehabilitate my argument. Whether I am drunk or sober, sincere or hypocritical, my *argument* remains unchanged and unaffected.

> Argument is argument. You cannot help paying regard to their arguments, if they are good. If it were testimony, you might disregard it. Testimony is like an arrow shot from a long bow; the force of it depends on the strength of the hand that draws it. Argument is like an arrow from a crossbow, which has equal force though shot by a child. *Samuel Johnson*

So, ad hominem arguments against *arguers* commit the ad hominem fallacy. But obviously there are *other* contexts—when a person is *not* giving *argument*—where ad hominem arguments are legitimate and important. If Jill gives an *argument* against excessive use of alcohol, then her *argument* against alcohol abuse may be an excellent argument even if Jill drinks herself into oblivion every single night; and if you say, "Jill is a lush, so her argument against alcohol abuse is no good," then *you* have committed the ad hominem fallacy. But suppose instead that Jill is a heart surgeon, and one of your friends is thinking of having open heart surgery, and has selected Jill as his surgeon. In *that* case, it would be perfectly legitimate—and very important—to warn your friend *not* to have the surgery done by Jill: "Dr. Jill has a very serious drinking problem; you shouldn't let her operate on your ingrown toenail, much less on your heart." That is *not* an ad hominem fallacy. Jill is being attacked, but Jill is *not* giving argument. Or suppose someone asks whether you should take a philosophy class with Bruce, and you reply: "*Don't* take a class with Bruce! He is the most boring professor I've ever heard, he knows nothing about the subject, he's nasty and insulting to his students, and he always flunks at least 90 percent of the class." That's an ad hominem attack, but it is a legitimate and valuable ad hominem argument: Those are things you would want to know when deciding whether to take a class with Bruce. If Bruce were giving an *argument*, his personality problems wouldn't matter; but in this case, no *argument* is at issue, and the ad hominem attack is legitimate. Consider another example: Suppose that Alex is giving *testimony*, rather than argument. Testimony often occurs in court, of course; but that is not the only, nor even the most common, use of testimony. "I saw Sam pull the trigger" and "I saw Serina breaking the window" are cases of testimony that you might hear in court; "I saw Tony kissing Alyssa in the shadows outside Foley Hall" or "I heard Gina say she was planning to dump Dean" is the sort of testimony you might hear at lunch; "I have seen secret reliable information that Iraq has weapons of mass destruction" is the sort of testimony you might hear from a president; and "I was kidnapped by extraterrestrials and forced to participate in a three day sexual competition" is the sort of testimony you might hear on afternoon television. In all these cases, the testifier is asserting something on the basis of his or her own credibility or trustworthiness, *not* on the strength of his or her argument. The underlying implied support for the testimony is this: *Trust* me, take my word for it.

Consider this excellent example of a *legitimate* ad hominem argument that defense attorney F. Lee Bailey directed against Harflinger, a key prosecution witness:

Question.   (by Bailey): Mr. Harflinger, you have told us that when you came on for trial in the bomb possession case, that you attempted to win it by telling the jury that you weren't guilty, right?

Answer.   (by the prosecution witness, Alfred Harflinger): Yes, sir.

Question.   When you took the oath [in Harflinger's own trial], you took it knowing your were going to lie, right?

Answer.   I did.

Question.   There is hardly a con in the pen that doesn't want to hit the street, true?

Answer.   There are very few.

Question.   And if there are any that don't want to hit the street, you are not one of them?

Answer.   I am not.

Question.   You would like to get out tomorrow, right?

Answer.   Yes, sir.

Question.   And if you can accomplish it, you would get out very shortly, won't you, if you can accomplish it?

Answer.   If it is possible, I will do everything within my power.

Question.   I am sure that you will. Now, Mr. Harflinger, is it fair to say that when you lied to the jury in your own case, that you didn't really lose much sleep about the whole business, it didn't keep you awake at night, the fact that you had committed perjury, did it?

Answer.   No, sir.

Question.   Have you not in the course of your adult lifetime lied whenever necessary to protect yourself from any kind of harm, including imprisonment? . . . . You practice fraud and deceit whenever you have to, right?

Answer.   That is true. (From *For the Defense*, F. Lee Bailey, 1975)

Bailey's legitimate ad hominem attack should at the very least raise serious doubts about the *truthfulness* of any *testimony* given by *Alfred Harflinger*.

If that testifier has a long history of perjury, or a long record of being rather loose with the truth, or has a special interest or a special motive for lying, then it is perfectly legitimate to point that out: "Ladies and Gentlemen of the jury, you heard Mr. Prentiss *testify* that he saw the defendant murder Mr. Jones; but you should keep in mind that Mr. Prentiss has been convicted twice of perjury and three times for fraud, and that Mr. Prentiss appears to be strongly motivated by his desire to claim the ten thousand dollar reward that has been offered in this case. Mr. Prentiss is a liar and a crook; and in this case, he has a strong monetary motive for lying." That is a powerful ad hominem attack on the witness, but it is a *legitimate* ad hominem attack; and this is information that you, as a juror, would want to consider when you weigh the testimony given by Mr. Prentiss. Perhaps you can think of a few friends whose *testimony* you would be inclined to doubt; perhaps you can think of a few elected officials you would place in the same category. If Wayne is a nasty individual who loves to spread rumors and start fights and who has little regard for honesty, you should keep that in mind when he tells you that he saw your lover dancing cheek to cheek with an attractive stranger in a bar on the other side of town. "Wayne is a vicious liar" is a legitimate ad hominem attack against such testimony.

Ad hominem arguments against *arguments* are fallacious, while ad hominem arguments against *testifiers* are legitimate. Unfortunately, sometimes the important line between argument and testimony can be difficult to draw. In the murder trial of O. J. Simpson, Prosecutor Marcia Clark made the following remarks in her closing argument to the jury:

> I know what the ethical obligations are of a prosecutor. I took a cut in pay to join this office, because I believe in this job. I believe in doing it fairly and doing it right and I like the luxury of being a prosecutor. Because I have the luxury on any case of going to the judge and saying: "Guess what, Your Honor, dismiss it, it's not here."
>
> Ladies and Gentlemen [of the jury], I can come to you and I can say: "Don't convict, it's not here." . . . I can get up in the morning and look at myself in the mirror and say I tell you the truth, I will never ask for a conviction unless I should, unless the law says I must, unless he is proven guilty beyond a reasonable doubt on credible evidence.

At that point the defense attorneys intervened with an objection, claiming that Marcia Clark's statements were improper, because she was supposed to be giving *argument* to prove Simpson guilty, and instead she was improperly giving *testimony* about her own certainty that Simpson was guilty. Clark denied that she was giving testimony, insisting instead that she was strictly giving *argument* based on well-known principles of legal ethics.

If you were the judge in that case, how would you rule? Was Clark legitimately giving *argument*, or had she crossed the line into *testimony*?

The moral of the story is this: If I give a philosophical argument, it doesn't matter how nasty and vile and depraved I am; you still have to consider my arguments on their own merits, and an ad hominem attack on the source of that argument commits the ad hominem *fallacy*. So when you are considering *arguments* about tough and controversial questions in philosophy, resist the temptation to indulge in fallacious ad hominem attacks against your friends and classmates—or against your professor, for that matter. Philosophy is challenging and controversial enough without adding ad hominem fallacies to the mix. I'm not denying that a nice ad hominem attack on your philosophical opponent can sometimes be fun; but it poisons the atmosphere, undercuts intelligent discussion, and undermines attempts to critically and rationally examine philosophical issues. Try to find a better way to have fun—for example, by serious thoughtful inquiry into the deep questions of philosophy.

Strawman Fallacy

While ad hominem arguments in philosophy are *usually* fallacies, *Strawman* arguments are *always* fallacies, whether they are used in philosophy, politics, economics, or biology. They are fallacious in New York, and they are fallacious in Los Angeles, and they are fallacious from Edmonton to Baton Rouge, from Atlanta to Vancouver, in Nome as well as Miami. A *strawman* fallacy is the fallacy of distorting, or exaggerating, or misrepresenting your opponent's argument in order to make it easier to attack. If Joan gives an argument for the existence of God, and I treat her argument as if it is an argument for the existence of Zeus—and "refute" her argument by pointing out that God is supposed to be good, and Zeus did some rather nasty things—then that will be a hollow refutation, since I am refuting only a strawman distortion of her argument and not the real thing. If I give a prochoice argument in favor of a woman's right to an abortion, and you attack my position on the grounds that I favor the killing of newborns and infants up to the age of three, then you are attacking a distortion of my position. And it is still a distortion, even though there may be *some* prochoice advocate who approves of infanticide until age three: That is *not* the position of most in the prochoice movement, and that is a *distortion* of their view. It's much easier to attack the extreme and distorted position than attack the real position. That's why the strawman fallacy is so tempting, and why it fails to convince those on the other side whose positions are distorted. Likewise, if I attack your prolife position on the grounds that you want to ban not only abortion but also all forms of artificial birth control, then I am committing the strawman fallacy. True, there are a few in the prolife movement who see a ban on birth control as an important part of the prolife movement; but that is a more extreme position, and much easier to attack, than the main prolife view. Attacking that extreme position is attacking a strawman, and refuting that extreme position does not refute the position of most prolife advocates.

> When the Equal Rights Amendment (which would guarantee women equal economic and employment rights) was before Congress, television evangelist Pat Robertson led a campaign against the Amendment; and in one of his arguments against the amendment, he asserted that the goal of the Equal Rights Amendment is to encourage women to leave their husbands, kill their children, and practice witchcraft. That's a much easier target to attack than the actual Equal Rights Amendment; perhaps that's why Robertson used the distorted account in his arguments and in his fundraising.

The strawman fallacy not only plays havoc with intelligent discussion—you can't intelligently debate an issue if one side is misrepresenting the subject of the debate, or distorting the arguments given by the other side—but it also prevents people from giving honest serious consideration to opposing views. If you want to give sincere and open-minded consideration even to ideas and arguments you now oppose (and it's just *possible* that one or two of your beliefs could be wrong), then avoid the strawman fallacy; instead, adopt a *principle of charity* toward other views. You obviously don't have to agree with every philosophical theory or argument; in fact, you could not do so, since they are often in fundamental conflict. But most of the positions and arguments have been developed, refined, and defended over many years, and they usually have *some* good points; so if you think that a position you oppose is absurd—and has no redeeming qualities whatsoever, and that nothing could possibly be said in its favor—then perhaps you are looking at a strawman version of that position. You might wish to look at the position again, more open-mindedly and charitably. You may still not agree with it, but it might have *some* features that are worth appreciating. (To be perfectly honest, there may well be some philosophical positions that you find utterly ridiculous, no matter how kindly you consider them; but just be sure you are considering the real position, rather than some strawman substitute.)

If you want to enlarge your perspectives, shun the temptations of the strawman fallacy. If you want to convince your opponent that her position is mistaken, then avoid the temptations of the strawman fallacy; after all, you aren't likely to convince someone that her argument or theory is wrong by refuting a distortion of her actual position. But if you are absolutely sure that all your beliefs are exactly right, and you want to avoid ever changing your mind, then the strawman fallacy is a good way of preserving your beliefs against inconvenient challenges.

> In 2000, a major epidemiological study reported that air pollution from U. S. electric power plants is the cause of more than 30,000 American deaths every year. Ralph DiNicola, a spokesperson for First Energy Corporation, had this response: "It is one thing to stand on the sidelines and bark about what the problem is, and a totally different responsibility to produce reliable, affordable electricity in an environmentally responsible manner. While these people would like to grow food in their backyards, and pedal bicycles to power medical diagnostic equipment, that is not what the rest of the

world wants to do." And of course it is not what critics of electric power-generating plants want to do, either; but they do want those plants to take further steps to reduce pollution. The strawman attack fails to address that serious question, instead attacking a much more extreme and implausible view.

Appeal to Authority

If you want to know which planet in our solar system has the greatest mass, you would ask your astronomy professor, or maybe look it up in a reputable textbook or encyclopedia. That is a perfectly legitimate way of gaining knowledge, and one that we often use. That is a *legitimate* use of appeal to authority. If we are in doubt about which planet in our solar system has the greatest mass, and we call up Professor Sykes in the astronomy department, and she tells us that Jupiter has the greatest mass, then that is a legitimate way of settling the issue (and a lot less trouble than trying to weigh Jupiter). Such an appeal to authority is legitimate because it meets two essential conditions: First, Professor Sykes is an *expert*, an authority, in the *appropriate area*. If our question were about Civil War history, asking Professor Sykes would *not* be a legitimate appeal to authority. Second, this is a question on which authorities in the area have reached *general agreement*. Suppose we are arguing about who is the greatest basketball coach of all time, and we call up Coach Weiss, who is the head coach of one of the varsity basketball teams at the university. Coach Weiss may well be an expert on basketball and basketball coaches; but if Coach Weiss states that John Wooden was the greatest basketball coach of all time, that would *not* establish that John Wooden is the greatest basketball coach. For if we call ten other coaches, or sports-casters, or writers on basketball—each of whom is an expert on the subject—we may get ten different answers: one says John Wooden, another says Dean Smith, someone else favors John Thompson, and Red Auerbach, Phil Jackson, and Pat Summit also receive votes. In that case, there is obviously no general agreement among authorities, and so appeal to authority would be a *fallacy*. (Incidentally, an appeal to authority is an appeal to expert *testimony*; so if someone appeals to a supposed authority, it is legitimate to make ad hominem attacks against the integrity, the character, and the abilities of the "authority." For example, if the authority is a hired gun for some corporation, and is being paid large sums of money by that group, then it is legitimate to note that the authority may be biased and may be giving "expert testimony" that is not honest and not accurate. Or you might legitimately challenge the *credentials* and expertise of the supposed authority.)

Even when appeal to authority is *legitimate*, it is not *infallible*. There are many examples of genuine authorities being profoundly mistaken even when they are in agreement; for example:

"Stocks have reached what looks like a permanently high plateau." Irving Fisher, Professor of Economics at Yale University, October 17, 1929; one week prior to the stock market crash.

"I think there is a world market for about five computers." Thomas J. Watson, Chairman of the Board of IBM, 1943.

"Heavier-than-air flying machines are impossible." Lord Kelvin, physicist and president of the British Royal Society, 1895.

We can appeal to authority if we want to know whether Alexander the Great was one of Aristotle's students (he was), or how long Descartes lived in France; there are some experts on the history of philosophy, and those are questions on which those experts agree. But if we want to know whether Aristotle's virtue ethics is the *correct* view of ethics, or if

Descartes' rationalism is the best approach to understanding knowledge, then appeal to authority is *not* legitimate. Even if we accept the idea that there are experts on these issues, it is clear that these are *not* questions on which there is *general agreement* among the experts. The questions are fiercely debated among the most respected contemporary philosophers, as they were among the great figures in the history of philosophy. If we were selecting experts on social contract theory, it would be hard to select better ones than Thomas Hobbes, John Locke, and Jean Jacques Rousseau from philosophical history, with John Rawls, Jean Hampton, David Gauthier, and Martha Nussbaum in contemporary philosophy. But it would be a mistake to appeal to any of them to settle a question about the legitimacy of social contract theory, since their views are often in fundamental conflict with one another. So it's wonderful to read great philosophers, from the ancients to the contemporaries; and it's wonderful to consider their views, and think about them carefully, and give them honest attention; but accepting their positions as true *because* they are great philosophers would be a mistake: the mistake of committing the fallacy of appeal to authority.

For many centuries, the Catholic Church regarded Aristotle as a great authority; indeed, Catholic writers often referred to him simply as "The Philosopher." In that tradition, if Aristotle said something, that was enough: Aristotle was the authority, Aristotle said it, that settled it. But what a religion may choose to accept as authoritative doctrine is one thing; what philosophy accepts must be established by open argument, not by authoritative pronouncement. It's certainly worth noting the views of famous philosophers such as Plato, Aristotle, Descartes, Hume, and Kant—*not*, however, because they are famous authorities, but because they developed interesting positions and gave interesting *arguments* for their conclusions.

That doesn't cover all the fallacies (there is also the slippery slope fallacy, the fallacy of affirming the consequent, the false dilemma fallacy, the fallacy of appeal to popularity, and many more); and there is much more to say about what makes arguments bad *and* what makes arguments good. If you haven't already taken a course in logic or critical thinking, you might want to consider those courses when you are planning your schedule for next semester. But this should give you a good start on how to think about arguments and some nasty problems to avoid when you are engaged in arguments. Ad hominem and strawman fallacies are the most important ones to avoid in philosophical discussion. Such fallacies may inflame your opponents, but will certainly not convince them. And they make serious focused argument impossible by drawing attention away from the actual issue: the real position being debated, rather than the strawman distortion; or the actual *argument*, rather than the person giving the argument. *Argument* is the heart and soul of philosophy, and philosophical arguments deal with complex and often controversial issues. The main thing to keep in mind when arguing philosophical questions with your friends and classmates is a simple rule you probably learned in kindergarten: *play nice*.

READINGS

⇻ APOLOGY* ⇻
Plato

Plato (427–347 BCE) was one of the great philosophers of antiquity; so great was his influence, especially when joined with that of Aristotle (who was Plato's student, though he diverged from Plato on many issues), that the philosopher Alfred North Whitehead

---

*Translated by Benjamin Jowett.

claimed that "All philosophy is a footnote to Plato." That is an exaggeration, but not a ridiculous one. Plato posed many of the most basic philosophical questions of metaphysics, theory of knowledge, ethics, and political philosophy; and his "Socratic method" of trying to elucidate issues through a series of probing questions has had great influence on philosophical practice.

In the *Apology*, Plato speaks through the character of his own great teacher, Socrates. On trial before the Athenian Senate on charges of corrupting and confusing the minds of the youth of Athens, and of calling into doubt traditional beliefs (including beliefs about the gods), Socrates denies the charges and insists that instead he performs a valuable service to the state: He acts as a "gadfly," constantly questioning and probing, and exposing those who *think* they know the truth and those who *claim* to know the truth. Socrates is condemned to death, and in a later dialogue Plato recounts the calm and noble death of his teacher.

Men of Athens, I honor and love you; but I shall obey God rather than you, and while I have life and strength I shall never cease from the practice and teaching of philosophy, exhorting anyone whom I meet after my manner, and convincing him, saying: O my friend, why do you who are a citizen of the great and mighty and wise city of Athens, care so much about laying up the greatest amount of money and honor and reputation, and so little about wisdom and truth and the greatest improvement of the soul, which you never regard or heed at all? Are you not ashamed of this? And if the person with whom I am arguing says: Yes, but I do care; I do not depart or let him go at once; I interrogate and examine and cross-examine him, and if I think that he has no virtue, but only says that he has, I reproach him with undervaluing the greater, and overvaluing the less. And this I should say to everyone whom I meet, young and old, citizen and alien, but especially to the citizens, inasmuch as they are my brethren. For this is the command of God, as I would have you know; and I believe that to this day no greater good has ever happened in the state than my service to the God. For I do nothing but go about persuading you all, old and young alike, not to take thought for your persons and your properties, but first and chiefly to care about the greatest improvement of the soul. I tell you that virtue is not given by money, but that from virtue come money and every other good of man, public as well as private. This is my teaching, and if this is the doctrine which corrupts the youth, my influence is ruinous indeed. But if anyone says that this is not my teaching, he is speaking an untruth. Wherefore, O men of Athens, I say to you, do as Anytus bids or not as Anytus bids, and either acquit me or not; but whatever you do, know that I shall never alter my ways, not even if I have to die many times.

Men of Athens, do not interrupt, but hear me; there was an agreement between us that you should hear me out. And I think that what I am going to say will do you good: for I have something more to say, at which you may be inclined to cry out; but I beg that you will not do this. I would have you know that, if you kill such a one as I am, you will injure yourselves more than you will injure me. Meletus and Anytus will not injure me: they cannot; for it is not in the nature of things that a bad man should injure a better than himself. I do not deny that he may, perhaps, kill him, or drive him into exile, or deprive him of civil rights; and he may imagine, and others may imagine, that he is doing him a great injury: but in that I do not agree with him; for the evil of doing as Anytus is doing—of unjustly taking away another man's life—is greater far. And now, Athenians, I am not going to argue for my own sake, as you may think, but for yours, that you may not sin against the God, or lightly reject his boon by condemning me. For if you kill me you will not easily find another like me, who, if I may use such a ludicrous figure of speech, am a sort of gadfly, given to the state by the God; and the state is like a great and noble steed who is tardy in his motions owing to his very size, and requires to be stirred into life; I am that gadfly which God has given the state and all day long and in all places am always fastening upon you, arousing and persuading and reproaching you. And as you will not easily find another like me, I would advise you to spare me. I dare say that you may feel irritated at being suddenly awakened when you are caught napping; and you may think that if you were to strike me dead, as Anytus advises, which you easily might, then you would sleep on for the remainder of your lives, unless God in his care of you gives you another gadfly.

⇌ THE VALUE OF PHILOSOPHY* ⇌
Bertrand Russell

Bertrand Russell (1872–1970) was one of the most influential philosophers of the twentieth century. He was a powerful force in moving Anglo-American philosophy away from traditional metaphysical and speculative questions and more in the direction of careful logical and linguistic analysis. He was also a dedicated social reformer, who gave away his large inherited fortune because he believed it wrong to pass on wealth through inheritance. He was a leader in the nuclear disarmament movement and championed many social reforms. A brilliant writer, Russell won the Nobel Prize for Literature in 1950.

In "The Value of Philosophy," Russell argues for the value of philosophy when it is carried out using logic and careful language analysis. For Russell, the main value of philosophy comes from challenging some of our cherished assumptions and examining philosophical questions more critically, rather than in making speculative claims concerning the nature of "true reality," "the deeper essence," "ultimate truth," or God.

[I]f we are not to fail in our endeavour to determine the value of philosophy, we must first free our minds from the prejudices of what are wrongly called "practical" men. The "practical" man, as this word is often used, is one who recognizes only material needs, who realizes that men must have food for the body, but is oblivious of the necessity of providing food for the mind. If all men were well off, if poverty and disease had been reduced to their lowest possible point, there would still remain much to be done to produce a valuable society; and even in the existing world the goods of the mind are at least as important as the goods of the body. It is exclusively among the goods of the mind that the value of philosophy is to be found; and only those who are not indifferent to these goods can be persuaded that the study of philosophy is not a waste of time.

Philosophy, like all other studies, aims primarily at knowledge. The knowledge it aims at is the kind of knowledge which gives unity and system to the body of the sciences, and the kind which results from a critical examination of the grounds of our convictions, prejudices, and beliefs. But it cannot be maintained that philosophy has had any very great measure of success in its attempts to provide definite answers to its questions. If you ask a mathematician, a mineralogist, a historian, or any other man of learning, what definite body of truths has been ascertained by his science, his answer will last as long as you are willing to listen. But if you put the same question to a philosopher, he will, if he is candid, have to confess that his study has not achieved positive results such as have been achieved by other sciences. It is true that

this is partly accounted for by the fact that, as soon as definite knowledge concerning any subject becomes possible, this subject ceases to be called philosophy, and becomes a separate science. The whole study of the heavens, which now belongs to astronomy, was once included in philosophy; Newton's great work was called "the mathematical principles of natural philosophy." Similarly, the study of the human mind, which was a part of philosophy, has now been separated from philosophy and has become the science of psychology. Thus, to a great extent, the uncertainty of philosophy is more apparent than real: those questions which are already capable of definite answers are placed in the sciences, while those only to which, at present, no definite answer can be given, remain to form the residue which is called philosophy.

This is, however, only a part of the truth concerning the uncertainty of philosophy. There are many questions—and among them those that are of the profoundest interest to our spiritual life—which, so far as we can see, must remain insoluble to the human intellect unless its powers become of quite a different order from what they are now. Has the universe any unity of plan or purpose, or is it a fortuitous concourse of atoms? Is consciousness a permanent part of the universe, giving hope of indefinite growth in wisdom, or is it a transitory accident on a small planet on which life must ultimately become impossible? Are good and evil of importance to the universe or only to man? Such questions are asked by philosophy, and variously answered by various philosophers. But it would seem that, whether answers be otherwise discoverable or not, the answers

---

*Chapter 15 of Bertrand Russell, *The Problems of Philosophy* (1912).

suggested by philosophy are none of them demonstrably true. Yet, however slight may be the hope of discovering an answer, it is part of the business of philosophy to continue the consideration of such questions, to make us aware of their importance, to examine all the approaches to them, and to keep alive that speculative interest in the universe which is apt to be killed by confining ourselves to definitely ascertainable knowledge.

. . .

The value of philosophy is, in fact, to be sought largely in its very uncertainty. The man who has no tincture of philosophy goes through life imprisoned in the prejudices derived from common sense, from the habitual beliefs of his age or his nation, and from convictions which have grown up in his mind without the co-operation or consent of his deliberate reason. To such a man the world tends to become definite, finite, obvious; common objects rouse no questions, and unfamiliar possibilities are contemptuously rejected. As soon as we begin to philosophize, on the contrary, we find . . . that even the most everyday things lead to problems to which only very incomplete answers can be given. Philosophy, though unable to tell us with certainty what is the true answer to the doubts which it raises, is able to suggest many possibilities which enlarge our thoughts and free them from the tyranny of custom. Thus, while diminishing our feeling of certainty as to what things are, it greatly increases our knowledge as to what they may be; it removes the somewhat arrogant dogmatism of those who have never travelled into the region of liberating doubt, and it keeps alive our sense of wonder by showing familiar things in an unfamiliar aspect.

Apart from its utility in showing unsuspected possibilities, philosophy has a value—perhaps its chief value—through the greatness of the objects which it contemplates, and the freedom from narrow and personal aims resulting from this contemplation. The life of the instinctive man is shut up within the circle of his private interests: family and friends may be included, but the outer world is not regarded except as it may help or hinder what comes within the circle of instinctive wishes. In such a life, there is something feverish and confined, in comparison with which the philosophic life is calm and free. The private world of instinctive interests is a small one, set in the midst of a great and powerful world which must, sooner or later, lay our private world in ruins. Unless we can so enlarge our interests as to include the whole outer world, we remain like a garrison in a beleaguered fortress, knowing that the enemy prevents escape and that ultimate surrender is inevitable. In such a life there is no peace, but a constant strife between the insistence of desire and the powerlessness of will. In one way or another, if our life is to be great and free, we must escape this prison and this strife.

One way of escape is by philosophic contemplation. Philosophic contemplation does not, in its widest survey, divide the universe into two hostile camps—friends and foes, helpful and hostile, good and bad—it views the whole impartially. Philosophic contemplation, when it is unalloyed, does not aim at proving that the rest of the universe is akin to man. All acquisition of knowledge is an enlargement of the Self, but this enlargement is best attained when it is not directly sought. It is obtained when the desire for knowledge is alone operative, by a study which does not wish in advance that its objects should have this or that character, but adapts the Self to the characters which it finds in its objects. This enlargement of Self is not obtained when, taking the Self as it is, we try to show that the world is so similar to this Self that knowledge of it is possible without any admission of what seems alien. The desire to prove this is a form of self-assertion and, like all self-assertion, it is an obstacle to the growth of Self which it desires, and of which the Self knows that it is capable. Self-assertion, in philosophic speculation as elsewhere, views the world as a means to its own ends; thus it makes the world of less account than Self, and the Self sets bounds to the greatness of its goods. In contemplation, on the contrary, we start from the not-Self, and through its greatness the boundaries of Self are enlarged; through the infinity of the universe the mind which contemplates it achieves some share in infinity.

. . .

The true philosophic contemplation . . . finds its satisfaction in every enlargement of the not-Self, in everything that magnifies the objects contemplated, and thereby the subject contemplating. Everything, in contemplation, that is personal or private, everything that depends upon habit, self-interest, or desire, distorts the object, and hence impairs the union which the intellect seeks. By thus making a barrier between subject and object, such personal and private things become a prison to the intellect. The free intellect will see as God might see, without a here and now, without hopes and fears, without the trammels of customary beliefs and traditional prejudices, calmly, dispassionately, in the sole and exclusive desire of knowledge—knowledge as impersonal, as purely contemplative, as it is possible for man to attain. Hence also the free intellect will value more the abstract and universal knowledge into which the accidents of private history do not enter, than the knowledge brought by the senses, and dependent, as such knowledge must be, upon an exclusive and personal point of view and a body whose sense-organs distort as much as they reveal.

The mind which has become accustomed to the freedom and impartiality of philosophic contemplation will preserve something of the same freedom and impartiality in the world of action and emotion. It will view its purposes and desires as parts of the whole, with the absence of insistence that results from seeing them as infinitesimal fragments in a world of which all the rest is unaffected by any one man's deeds. The impartiality which, in contemplation, is the unalloyed desire for truth, is the very same quality of mind which, in action, is justice, and in emotion is that universal love which can be given to all, and not only

to those who are judged useful or admirable. Thus contemplation enlarges not only the objects of our thoughts, but also the objects of our actions and our affections: it makes us citizens of the universe, not only of one walled city at war with all the rest. In this citizenship of the universe consists man's true freedom, and his liberation from the thraldom of narrow hopes and fears.

Thus, to sum up our discussion of the value of philosophy; Philosophy is to be studied, not for the sake of any definite answers to its questions since no definite answers can, as a rule, be known to be true, but rather for the sake of the questions themselves; because these questions enlarge our conception of what is possible, enrich our intellectual imagination and diminish the dogmatic assurance which closes the mind against speculation; but above all because, through the greatness of the universe which philosophy contemplates, the mind also is rendered great, and becomes capable of that union with the universe which constitutes its highest good.

EXERCISES

For the following arguments, tell what *form* the argument is (such as ad hominem) and state whether it is legitimate or fallacious; the possibilities include: ad hominem fallacy, legitimate ad hominem, strawman (always a fallacy), irrelevant reason or red herring (always a fallacy), appeal to authority fallacy, and legitimate appeal to authority.

1. The new immigration bill proposed by the Republican House of Representatives would make it illegal for a soup kitchen to give food to a starving undocumented immigrant, and would make it illegal for a doctor to save the life of an undocumented immigrant child. Some people claim that this is a cruel measure that treats undocumented immigrants harshly. But it certainly is not a cruel measure, because the problem of illegal undocumented immigrants is a huge problem in this country. Illegal undocumented immigrants pose security risks, they hold down wages for other workers, and they place a huge burden on our social services. The number of undocumented immigrants in the United States is now in the millions, and the number continues to increase. Therefore, the measures required in this new immigration bill are not cruel to undocumented immigrants.

2. Some people are opposed to the planned missile defense system—the "star wars" system—that is designed to intercept and destroy any missiles that are launched against the United States. Those opponents of the system say it has never been tested effectively, that it would be very easy to overwhelm with dummy missiles, and that the real danger is not from missiles launched from outside the United States but instead from bombs smuggled into the United States. But those people who oppose the missile defense system don't live in the real world. They believe that we should never do anything to protect ourselves from attacks. They would just watch while missiles fall on our cities, and never fight back and do nothing to prevent it. Apparently, they think that the world is safe and peaceful, and the United States is not in any danger of attack from anyone.

3. Brad Staunton argues that we should allow more immigrants to enter this country as guest workers, and then—if they maintain a good work record and avoid any criminal activity—allow them to become U.S. citizens. Staunton argues that such a program will make it possible to better regulate the immigration process, make it easier to separate potential terrorists from legitimate workers, and provide jobs for people who desperately need work; and he

argues that we are a nation of immigrants, and we should not close the door on those who want to come to our country. Staunton points out that the inscription on our Statue of Liberty invites "the huddled masses, yearning to breathe free" to come to our country and join us, and not bringing in more eager immigrants makes us hypocrites. Well, Staunton's arguments sound good, except for one thing: Staunton owns a huge farm in northern California, and his real motive for wanting more immigrant workers is that he can hire cheap agricultural workers to harvest his crops. When you understand Staunton's real motives, then the flaws in his arguments become obvious.

4. Some people complain about the profits being raked in by the major oil companies: Exxon made a profit of $10 billion in the last quarter, and Chevron made $4 billion. They claim that the oil companies are making enormous and unfair profits, while we consumers are paying painfully high prices for gasoline. But no one should take their criticisms seriously. Apparently, they believe that people in the oil industry should work for free and that investors in Exxon and Chevron have no right to make a profit on their investment. They think that all profits are wrong and that no company should ever make a profit for its work. They apparently want to abolish capitalism altogether and do away with our free enterprise system.

5. Former president Bill Clinton argues that it is very important that we raise the minimum wage. He points out that the minimum wage has not been raised in years and that those who work for a minimum wage work full time for wages that leave them deep in poverty. He also notes that the salaries of CEOs are the highest in history, and he argues that it is fundamentally unfair for them to receive millions of dollars while some of their workers receive wages that leave them in poverty. Clinton also points out that if the minimum wage is increased, then workers will have more money to spend, and their spending will provide a needed boost for the economy. But you should keep in mind that Bill Clinton is a man who lied under oath about a sexual affair and who also lied to his wife and to the American people about his affair. It's clear that the man is a liar, and his argument for raising the minimum wage is worthless.

6. Sam has been offering to tutor students in Critical Thinking, for a fee of $20 per hour. But don't you hire Sam as a tutor! The fact is that Sam knows nothing whatsoever about critical thinking: It's true that he took a class in Critical Thinking, but he only attended three classes, and he had a severe hangover in those classes, and he flunked every exam. Also, Sam demands that everyone pay him in advance—and then he hardly ever shows up for the tutoring sessions, and he refuses to give the money back. And when he does show up for tutoring, he's usually dead drunk, and Sam gets nasty and abusive when he's drunk. On at least two occasions, he stole the Critical Thinking books of the students he was supposed to be tutoring and resold them at the book store. So Sam is *not* someone you want as a Critical Thinking tutor.

7. Felicia Standish argues that we should lower the legal age for buying tobacco products to 16. She points out that teenagers who really want to smoke are usually able to obtain cigarettes, and making that illegal encourages them to make a habit of breaking the law. Also, she argues that making tobacco legal only for those 18 and older leads younger teenagers to regard smoking as something adult, and thus makes it more appealing. But before you accept her arguments for lowering the legal age for tobacco, you should be aware that Ms. Standish is a major investor in Philip Morris, the world's leading cigarette manufacturer; so, the more teenagers who are hooked on cigarettes, the more money she makes. Ms. Standish's arguments are designed to increase her wealth rather than arrive at the truth.

8. Look, it is clear that U.S. oil companies are *not* price gouging American consumers with their high gasoline prices. Because, after all, we Americans have a love affair with our cars! We love to drive through the countryside with the windows open and smell the fresh air, high school kids love to cruise around town with their friends, we like to drive out to the mall and follow the home team on road trips and drive down to the beach during spring break. There's nothing better than turning up the radio, picking up a friend, and heading out on the road. So when you think of all the enjoyment we get out of driving, it's perfectly clear that U.S. oil companies are not overcharging us for gasoline.

9. Arthur claims that he saw Julie take $100 out of the cash register at work yesterday. But before you conclude that Julie is a thief, there are several things you should consider. First, Arthur was also working at that cash register, and it's quite possible that he took the money

himself and is now trying to direct the blame at Julie. Furthermore, at his last job, Arthur was fired because he stole merchandise from the store. Also, Arthur has a big-time gambling problem, and he has been losing a lot of money lately, and he's in desperate need of money to pay off his bookmaker. One more thing: Arthur hates Julie, because Julie got the promotion to manager that Arthur wanted. So you should think twice before you believe Arthur's accusation against Julie.

10. It is quite clear that high-sugar soft drinks are causing health problems and contributing to obesity among elementary and middle school children. The American Medical Association, the American Heart Association, the National Institute of Health, Harvard Medical School, and the Mayo Clinic have all agreed that children's consumption of these high-sugar drinks is a major cause of both obesity and health problems in school-age children.

11. There is concern about the current push to release patients from hospitals more rapidly. Patients undergoing heart surgery, mastectomies, and other major surgeries are sent home days earlier than they would have been a few years ago, and some people claim that such early hospital releases reduce the quality of patient care and pose a risk to patient health. But in fact the earlier releases do NOT pose any risk for patient health. Keeping patients in hospitals is enormously expensive, and every extra day in a hospital drives the cost of treatment higher and higher. We have to find ways of getting our health care costs under control, so that both insurance rates and government expenditures on health care can be kept to a reasonable level. Releasing hospital patients earlier is one way of reducing our high medical costs. So clearly the early release of patients does not threaten the health of patients.

12. Fifteen years ago in Cleveland, Gary Reece was convicted of assault and rape against Kim Croft, and Reece has been in prison for the past 15 years. There was no physical evidence against Reece. In fact, the only evidence against Reece was the testimony of Croft, who swore in the trial that Reece, one of her neighbors in an apartment complex, had forced his way into her apartment, stabbed her in the chest with a kitchen knife, and then raped her. But it turns out that Croft has some problems: She has a history of stabbing herself in the chest with knives and scissors in order to control others and frighten them into doing what she wants. Also, she claims that she died when she was attacked by Reece, and a voice came to her and told her she had to go back to life. The voice was Snow White's, and Snow White led her back from death to life. Certainly I feel sorry for Ms. Croft; but she is severely unstable and not trustworthy, and Reece never should have been convicted on her testimony.

13. Arnold Schwarzenegger is a world champion body builder, a successful movie actor—he was great in *Twins* with Danny DeVito—and a very successful politician who was elected Governor of California. He maintains that embryonic stem cell research is a very promising line of research that might provide cures for paralysis, Alzheimer's, and a number of nervous system disorders. Obviously, if Schwarzenegger thinks embryonic stem cell research is an important and promising area of medical research, then it must really be so.

14. The defendant is obviously guilty. After all, he is charged with burglary, and burglary is a very serious crime indeed: Burglars break into our homes and businesses and leave us all feeling terribly insecure and vulnerable. Think of how you would feel if you realized that someone had broken into your home while you and your family were asleep! So burglary not only deprives us of our possessions but also of our sense of security and safety within our own homes. Certainly, then, the right verdict in this case is guilty as charged.

15. Some people have questioned whether the new electronic computer voting systems are foolproof and honest, or whether they might be rigged to miscount votes and thus result in voting fraud. But the new voting systems are fast and efficient, and they are very easy for voters to use, they avoid long frustrating lines at voting booths, and they report the results in seconds and therefore do not require a long tedious process of hand counting paper ballots. So obviously the new electronic voting machines cannot be used to fraudulently rig elections.

16. Those who want to allow gay marriages favor a completely unreasonable policy. If they have their way, all churches would be required to recognize and perform gay marriages, and that would be a great attack on the freedom of religious groups to set their own rules. And they want to require that every priest and rabbi and minister be compelled to perform gay marriages whenever they are asked, and that would certainly limit the religious and personal freedom of those religious leaders. Those who favor gay marriage maintain that when a gay couple is married, all their family members would have to attend the service and give their

approval and blessing to the newly married couple, which would of course be an enormous violation of the rights of those who do not approve of such marriages. So when we look closely at the position of those who favor gay marriage, we see that it is a terrible violation of individual rights and religious freedom.

17. When you are charged with a crime, you have the legal right to have your lawyer present when you are questioned. There is no doubt that you do have that right: We asked Supreme Court Justices Souter and O'Connor and also Ronald Dworkin (who teaches constitutional law at New York University) and Alan Dershowitz (a professor of criminal law at Harvard Law School), and all of them affirmed that persons charged with crimes definitely have a legal right to have a lawyer present when they are questioned.

18. Look, how can we possibly find the defendant guilty? The only real evidence against him was the testimony of Seth Bridger, and there's no way you could put any faith in that guy's testimony. After all, Seth Bridger has been convicted twice of bank fraud, once of forgery, and three times of theft by deception. He's a long-time scam artist, and he makes his living by being an accomplished liar and cheat. Besides that, why is he testifying against the defendant? Just because he's a good citizen who wants to see justice done? Forget that. Seth Bridger worked out a deal with the District Attorney, and in exchange for testifying against the defendant, Seth is getting a greatly reduced sentence on his own fraud conviction. So he's getting paid off for his testimony! So obviously we can't trust a lying cheat like Seth Bridger.

19. Professor Wycliffe should be fired from North State University! Last year he accepted bribes from several students to pass them in his courses. An article he recently published as his own work was in fact plagiarized from someone else's writings. He has made racist remarks during his lectures, and over the past two years at least seven of his students have made complaints of sexual harassment against him. The man should be fired, and quickly.

20. Opponents of capital punishments sometimes claim that there is a danger that innocent people will be executed. But that is not really a danger. After all, our society is swamped with violent, vicious crimes, and we must have strong measures in response. Swift and severe punishment is essential to control crime and to properly express society's deep disgust with the most vicious and depraved criminal acts. So there is no real danger of executing the innocent.

21. Arthur Kraft has been arguing that the Olympic Games have become overcommercialized. He says that having all the manufacturers of soft drinks, cars, cameras, sportswear, and even junk foods promote themselves as "Official Sponsors of the Olympics" cheapens the games, and he argues that selling the rights to carry the Olympic torch across the country was a new low in crass commercialization of the Olympics. But Kraft's arguments against overcommercialization of the Olympics are not convincing: He himself is vice president of marketing for Belch Brewery, which makes Spring Mountain Beer, and Spring Mountain Beer advertises that it is "the favorite beer of America's Olympic athletes"!

22. When you are buying a new car battery, it's hard to know which car battery you should choose. But remember one thing: Chuck Yeager says that AC Delco batteries are the best you can buy; and Chuck Yeager is one of the greatest test pilots of all time. So AC Delco batteries must really be the best.

23. Bruce Waller says that there are bald eagles nesting in Mill Creek Park. He claims to have seen several bald eagles there, and further says that he saw one bald eagle sitting on a nest containing eggs. Well, Bruce probably does believe that he saw bald eagles in Mill Creek Park. But Bruce knows absolutely nothing about birds: He couldn't distinguish a bald eagle from a Canada goose, much less tell an eagle from a hawk. Plus his eyes are so bad, even if he knew what a bald eagle looked like, he still couldn't see an eagle well enough to identify it if the eagle were more than 10 feet away. While Bruce wouldn't lie about what he thought he saw, he does have a vivid imagination: Last year he was walking through Mill Creek Park and reported seeing a grizzly bear. It turned out to be just a large raccoon. So we should be very skeptical about Bruce's reports of seeing bald eagles in Mill Creek Park.

24. Some people claim that the United States should not have invaded Iraq, or at the very least should have waited until there was a broad-based coalition of countries willing to support military action against Iraq. But their position is ridiculous. Those people obviously believe we should never go to war under any circumstances, no matter how many times we are attacked. If they had their way, we would suffer terrorist strikes and attacks on our people and

make no response whatsoever. Their passive pacifism may sound good in theory, but in the harsh reality of our dangerous world such a policy would soon lead to our destruction.

25. William Bennett is the best-selling author of *The Book of Virtues*. Bennett argues in favor of the traditional virtues, such as honesty, thrift, patriotism, traditional family roles, and self-reliance: the values that Bennett and other social conservatives call "family values." But now we know that Bill Bennett is a high-stakes gambler, who has lost hundreds of thousands of dollars during gambling sprees at Atlantic City casinos. Well, blowing several hundred thousand dollars in casinos is not exactly practicing thrift, nor is it a great way to spend quality time with your family. So nobody should be fooled by "Blackjack Bill Bennett" and his arguments for "family values."

26. For several years there has been a profound controversy—involving medical professionals, patients, politicians, and ethicists—about active *euthanasia* (mercy killing) and physician-assisted suicide. But Dr. Willard Gaylin, a distinguished psychiatrist who is a former director of the Hastings Center for Applied Ethics, is widely recognized as an expert in the field of bioethics. Dr. Gaylin clearly and decisively asserts that active euthanasia is wrong, and he insists that no medical personnel can legitimately participate in such practices. That should settle the issue. When such an outstanding bioethicist as Dr. Gaylin says that active euthanasia is wrong, then it must really be wrong.

27. The Chairman of the Northeast Ohio Sierra club, Brian Ulm, has argued that we should not change the Endangered Species Act, because through the act we have been able to bring 267 species back from the brink of extinction, and the cost has not been excessive: He notes that fewer than one construction project in 200 is stopped because of enforcement of the Endangered Species Act; and he argues that it is not too great a price to pay for preserving species and environments for future generations. But Ulm's arguments shouldn't carry much weight: He is just the spokesperson for a bunch of environmental extremists who really don't care about economic progress and who are just sounding alarms so they can recruit more members and raise more money.

   For the remainder of the arguments, tell which arguments are *deductive* and which are *inductive*.

28. We have interviewed 1,200 U.S. college students, and 900 of them favored 18 as the legal age for the purchase of beer. Therefore, a substantial majority of all U.S. college students favor 18 as the legal age for the purchase of beer.

29. We should set 18 as the legal age for the purchase of alcoholic beverages. If people are old enough to vote, then they are certainly old enough to drink, and 18-year-olds are indeed old enough to vote.

30. We have carefully surveyed 500 registered voters, chosen at random from throughout Ohio, on whether they favor a law making it legal for ordinary citizens to carry concealed weapons. Of those surveyed, 320 opposed legalizing concealed weapons, 140 supported legalizing concealed weapons, and 40 were undecided or had no opinion. So, obviously most of the registered voters in Ohio are opposed to legalizing concealed weapons.

31. Mighty Casey is very likely to strike out. For the bases are loaded, and Casey struck out the last time he batted with the bases loaded, and he struck out the time before when he batted with the bases loaded; and, in fact, the two times before that he struck out when the bases were loaded.

32. Either the Chicago Cubs or the New York Mets will win the World Series. The New York Mets obviously will not win the series, since they have had lots of injuries, and their pitching and fielding have both been weak. So the Chicago Cubs will win the World Series.

33. In the last five World Series, the team that is at home for the first game has won the Series. Therefore, the Toronto Blue Jays are a good bet to win this World Series, since they are the home team for the first game.

34. All U.S. citizens have a right to vote in presidential elections. Joan Jakobovitz is a U.S. citizen; so Joan Jakobovitz has a right to vote in the presidential election.

35. Last semester there were 18 students in the Critical Thinking course who never missed a class, and they all passed the course. The semester before that, 16 students attended every class, and all of them passed. So if you attend every class this semester, you have a very good chance of passing the course.

36. Ladies and Gentlemen of the Jury, this is a simple case. Clearly Selena Skowron is not guilty of robbing the Detroit National Bank. The Detroit National Bank was robbed at noon on March 3, 2008. If Skowron was in Cleveland at noon on that day, then she could not be guilty of robbing the Detroit National Bank. And she certainly was in Cleveland at noon of that day, as was proven by the testimony of four reliable witnesses.

ADDITIONAL READING

For more on the question of what philosophy is, see *What Is Philosophy?* Edited by C. P. Ragland and Sarah Heidt (Yale University Press), it contains essays by six outstanding contemporary philosophers in answer to that question. The Dartmouth College Department of Philosophy Web site has a number of brief essays on "What is Philosophy"; go to www.dartmouth.edu/~phil/whatis. The Victoria University of Wellington—at www.victoria.ac.nz/phil/about/philosophy.aspx—has a nice collection of brief statements by philosophers concerning the nature of philosophy.

There are many excellent guides to critical thinking; among them are Theodore Schick, Jr., and Lewis Vaughn, *How to Think About Weird Things*, 3rd ed. (Boston, MA: McGraw-Hill, 2002); Bruce N. Waller, *Critical Thinking: Consider the Verdict*, 5th ed. (Upper Saddle River, NJ: Prentice-Hall, 2005); and Douglas Walton, *Fundamentals of Critical Argumentation* (New York: Cambridge University Press, 2006). There are also several very good Web resources: *The Reasoning Page* (which has a number of links, as well as some sample LSAT and MCAT exams) can be found at pegasus.cc.ucf.edu/~janzb/reasoning. Another excellent site, especially rich in links, is maintained by Tim van Gelder, at www.austhink.org

Doug Walton, *Ad Hominem Arguments* (Tuscaloosa, AL: University of Alabama Press, 1998), is a very thorough study of ad hominem arguments in all their forms.

For more on expert testimony (in relation to appeal to authority), see C. A. J. Coady, *Testimony: A Philosophical Study* (Oxford: Oxford University Press, 1992); Douglas Walton, *Appeal to Expert Opinion: Arguments from Authority* (University Park, PA: Penn State Press, 1997); and for a fascinating account of how "experts for hire" can be used to manipulate public opinion, see Sheldon Rampton and John Stauber, *Trust Us, We're Experts!* (New York: Tarcher/Putnam, 2001).

CHAPTER 2

PHILOSOPHICAL QUESTIONS ABOUT RELIGION

Does God exist? That is one of the oldest and most basic philosophical questions. But before we can consider answers to that question, we must ask for clarification: What God are you inquiring about? Obviously if one of your friends asks you, "Do you believe that God exists?" you have *some* sense of what your friend is asking. If you replied, "No, I don't think Zeus exists; I don't believe that there is a god named Zeus who lives on Mount Olympus with Hera, his wife," then your friend would assume you are joking. Your friend may not have a very clear idea of the defining features of this God whose existence is being queried; but whatever those features may be, Zeus will not fit them.

CONCEPTIONS OF GOD

> My friends often ask me, "Do you believe in the existence of God?" I think I am entitled to know the meaning of the terms used in this question before I answer it. My friends ought to explain to me what they mean by "believe," "existence" and "God," especially the last two, if they want an answer to their question. I confess I do not understand these terms; and whenever I cross-examine them I find that they do not understand them either. *Muhammad Iqbal*, from *Stray Reflections: The Private Notebook of Muhammad Iqbal*, 3rd ed. (Lahore: Iqbal Academy, 2006).

But when we get down to specifics, the question of exactly what God we are inquiring about can get a bit tricky. Suppose your friend pushes harder: "No, of course I don't mean does *Zeus* exist; and I'm not asking about Jupiter or Triton or Diana or Wotan, for that matter. I'm asking whether you believe that *God* exists: you know, the God Who created the universe, the God Who delivered the children of Israel out of bondage in Egypt, the God Who loves us as a father loves his children, the infinite God Who is completely self-sufficient and is all-powerful and all-knowing and infinitely present—that is, the God Who is omnipotent, omniscient, and omnipresent. Do you believe *that* God exists?"

That sounds like a fairly clear question, but it soon generates some serious difficulties. There's an old puzzle, one you probably heard when you were in high school: "Do you believe that God can do *anything*?" Yes, of course. "Well, could God make a stone so heavy that no one—not even God—could lift it?" Either way you answer, you are admitting that there is something beyond God's capabilities. In response to such a paradox, theologians typically answer that God can do everything that is *logically possible*, and an inability to do what is *not* logically possible does not imply a limit on God's abilities, but is rather a limit on what is rationally conceivable. It is *logically* impossible for an all-powerful being to make something that is beyond His *infinite* powers, just as it is logically impossible for God to make a square circle; but that doesn't show that God's powers are limited.

The demand that God make a stone so heavy that God himself can't lift it is logically incoherent. Does the same incoherence apply to the combination of God's characteristics specified by your friend: a *creator* God Who is perfect and totally self-sufficient and omniscient, omnipotent, and omnipresent, and Who becomes angry at pharaoh and *very* angry with the children of Israel when they worship a golden calf, and who loves us like a loving father and grieves when we do wrong? As Aristotle recognized, if God is eternally *perfect*, then obviously God cannot *change* (for if God changes, then either God *was* perfect and has now become imperfect; or God was imperfect, and has finally achieved perfection). If *perfection* undergoes change, then there's nowhere to go but down. But of course the Hebrew God changes His mind on a regular basis. He decides to create humankind, then gets disgusted and decides to destroy them; then He changes His mind again, and decides to save a few. He decides to deliver the children of Israel out of bondage; then changes His mind and decides to slay them all; then changes His mind again and decides to kill only a large portion of them. Furthermore, if God is totally self-sufficient, then God can have little interest in creating anything, much less a world and its stars and planets, including an Earth and all its species.

When we are trying to decide whether we "believe in God," we may be confused by two very different (and perhaps contradictory) concepts of God—the Hebraic and the Aristotelian. Those two conceptions of God have been run together in the Western tradition, but it is not at all clear that they can be combined into one consistent and coherent concept of God. Instead, attempts at combining the Hebraic and the Aristotelian concepts of God are similar to the *combination* of two high speed locomotives when both are racing at full throttle and suffer a head-on crash. Bits and pieces of both get mashed together, but it's tough to make one coherent locomotive out of the collision.

Spinoza, a great Jewish philosopher of the seventeenth century, recognized the problem: If God is *infinite*, then there can be only one substance, and there is *nothing* outside of God (so the notion of God creating something distinct from Himself is nonsense; and the notion of God being *angry* at people who are distinct from this infinite God is super nonsense). So if you asked Spinoza, "Do you believe in God?" then Spinoza would certainly answer yes; but Spinoza is dealing with a very different concept of God. In fact, some insist that Spinoza did not *really* "believe in God," because Spinoza's concept of God is so different from that held by most people.

Of course, one can say that the concept of God is mysterious and beyond our understanding; but it's hard to actually believe in something—or *not* believe in it, for that matter—if you don't know what it is. Do you really believe in the jabberwocky? Hard to say, if you have no idea what a jabberwocky is.

St. Thomas Aquinas was the most influential theologian in Catholic history, and one of his major efforts was to incorporate elements of Aristotelian thought into Christian theology (obviously Aquinas did not wish to take *everything* from Aristotle; but with a systematic philosopher such as Aristotle, it is very difficult to take some of the pieces without taking it all). It is not clear that Aristotle can be made compatible with the Hebraic concept of God, but Catholic theologians certainly made a heroic effort. The great medieval writer on Aristotle, however, was a Muslim scholar, Averroës (also known as ibn-Rushd), who lived from 1126 to 1198. Though Averroës was recognized in the Arabic world as a profound philosopher and scholar, the great era of Arabic speculative philosophy was ending around the time of his death, and thus the philosophical work of Averroës had limited influence on Muslim thought. However, his

> commentaries on Aristotle had enormous influence on Christian theologians—so great that Averroës became known as simply "the commentator," and his writings on Aristotle were taught in most European universities from around 1200 until the mid-seventeenth century.

So, before examining the question of whether God exists, it is important to note that there are actually *several* questions that could be on the table, depending on which conception of God is held. While of course there are many rival conceptions of God, there are three that tend to dominate in contemporary Western thought. One is the Judeo-Christian-Muslim conception of God. Obviously there are many variations within that view (e.g., Christians believe that God is composed of a mysterious Trinity, while Jews and Muslims reject that notion), but the basics are these: God is a *creator* God, Who made the world; God takes a *personal interest* in the world and particularly in its human inhabitants; God is very powerful, and perhaps also omniscient, but God is not infinite (for humans, at least, are distinct from God, and so there is something that is *not* God; and an infinite God must include *everything* with no limits); God has emotions (e.g., God feels love for at least some humans); and God is very special, but not perfect, because God can and does change (in particular, God can change His mind, and He goes through emotional changes as well: becomes angry, puts away his wrath, feels regret, and so forth).

> The idea of an infinite God which encompasses everything is expressed poetically by the Sufi poet Mahmūd Shabistarē:
>
> Know the world is a mirror from head to foot,
> In every atom are a hundred blazing suns.
> If you cleave the heart of one drop of water,
> A hundred pure oceans emerge from it.
> If you examine closely each grain of sand,
> A thousand Adams may be seen in it.
> In its members a gnat is like an elephant;
> In its qualities a drop of rain is like the Nile.
> The heart of a barleycorn equals a hundred harvests,
> A world dwells in the heart of a millet seed.
> In the wing of a gnat is the ocean of life,
> In the pupil of the eye a heaven.
>
> *Translated by E. H. Winfield, 1880*

The second profoundly influential conception of God was initially developed by Aristotle: Aristotle's God is an "unmoved mover," that may inspire and thus influence humans as well as the heavens by its godly perfection, but does not in any way intervene in the world (and certainly does not create the world) because Aristotle's God is perfect and perfectly self-sufficient, and thus has no interest in creating anything. In fact, Aristotle's God can hardly be said to have interests at all, and certainly not emotions—rather, this God spends eternity in perfect contemplation *of* contemplation. Because Aristotle's God is eternally perfect, He never changes at all. (Some Muslim and Jewish theologians, and many Christian theologians, have tried to combine Aristotle's concept of God with the Hebraic conception; whether they have enjoyed any success in this enterprise is a disputed question. But obviously, given the very different conceptions of God, reconciling them is not an easy task.)

The third conception of God is the one favored by Spinoza; and in some respects, it is similar to the Taoist conception of God. On this view God really is *infinite*; and therefore there can be only one substance, and that substance is God, and *everything* that exists is necessarily a part of God (nothing can exist outside of a genuinely *infinite* being); and there is a long and perhaps arduous process of development toward an ultimate perfect harmonious order of this One being (part of this process may involve recognizing that our individual existences are illusory, since we are all part of this One). In Islamic thought, this concept of God as the infinite unity of everything is strongly embraced by the Sufi tradition, and it was explicitly formulated by the great thirteenth-century Sufi theologian, Muhyî al-Dîn ibn Arabî.

If we are trying to decide "whether God exists," it is useful to keep in mind that such a question may be oversimplified; perhaps we should ask instead whether something exists that matches one of these specific conceptions of God (or some other conception). And of course if one *denies* the existence of God, it will be helpful to be clear on whether one is denying one of those conceptions, or all three, or some more general thesis about *any* divine or nonnatural element in the universe.

ARGUMENTS FOR THE EXISTENCE OF GOD

> The spacious firmament on high,
> With all the blue Ethereal Sky,
> And spangled Heavens, a shining Frame
> Their great Original proclaim.
> The unweary'd Sun, from Day to Day,
> Does his Creator's power display;
> And publishes to every land,
> The work of an Almighty Hand.
>
> Soon as the evening shades prevail,
> The Moon takes up the wondrous tale,
> And nightly to the listening earth
> Repeats the story of her birth:
> Whilst all the Stars that round her burn,
> And all the planets, in their turn,
> Confirm the tidings as they roll,
> And spread the truth from pole to pole.
>
> What though, in solemn silence, all
> Move round the terrestrial ball?
> What tho' nor real voice nor sound
> Amid their radiant orbs be found?
> In Reason's ear they all rejoice,
> And utter forth a glorious voice,
> For ever singing, as they shine,
> "The hand that made us is divine."
>
> *Joseph Addison, 1711*

Is there a God? Well, look around you: the trees, the mountains, the Earth, the Sun, the stars—and not only the stars in our galaxy but also the stars in many other galaxies. So where did it all come from? Scientists can tell us a great deal about the stars, the black holes, and the multitude of galaxies scattered about our inconceivably vast cosmos. But where did it all come from? Even if you trace it back to the "Big Bang," where did *that* come from? There has to be a beginning, there has to be something that started it all, that *created* everything: something beyond what science explains. Science tells us how it goes on; but where did it start? The creator, the *first* cause: That is God.

The Cosmological Argument

That ancient (it goes back at least to Plato) but still popular argument for the existence of God is called the *Cosmological* argument. Reason tells us that *something* must have made the stars, the planets, and the cosmos; and that something *must* be divine. Another version of the argument asks: Why does the world *continue* to exist? It must have something to sustain it, and that something is God. And a third version focuses on the existence of motion or energy in the cosmos: Once the initial motion is exerted, the process can continue; but the *first cause*, or the *initial mover*, must be God.

There are many objections to the cosmological argument, but this is the most common: The cosmological argument is based on observations *within* our universe—everything that happens *within* our observable universe has a cause—but it draws a conclusion about an event *outside* the universe (it draws a conclusion about the cause that *created* the universe or initially set it in motion). Extending principles based on observation within the universe to claims about what happened *before* the universe existed is an unjustified leap. It may be reasonable to conclude that there are causes for everything that happens in our universe; but what reason is there to go far beyond that, and claim that there is *also* a cause for the *entire system*? That claim goes far beyond our observational experience, and we can't reasonably draw conclusions about forces operating outside the system on the basis of our observations within the system. What we *observe* is a continuing world, not one with a starting point; so why not conclude—as the ancient Greeks, including Aristotle, concluded—that the world *has* no starting point, and has existed eternally (and thus requires no Creator). A second objection is perhaps more basic. The cosmological argument appeals to God as the first cause or creator of the cosmos, and offers that as a basic *explanation* for why the cosmos exists. But—this second objection goes—at best that is "explaining" the obscure by the more obscure. Saying that "God is whatever caused the whole thing" merely places a name on our ignorance; it doesn't *explain* anything.

The Ontological Argument

The *Ontological* argument for the existence of God is one that some people find charming, and others find exasperating. To some it seems a decisive proof for God's existence, while others regard it as pure philosophical trickery. It was first proposed by a theologian and philosopher who lived from 1033 to 1109: Anselm. The argument received little attention for several centuries, but was later offered in a revised version by Descartes, and it has been debated ever since. The argument, in its basic form, goes like this: Imagine a Being having all possible perfections, or as Anselm puts it, imagine "Something than which nothing greater can be conceived." Now, this maximally great Being that you are imagining: Does it exist? If you say that it does *not* exist, then there is something *greater* than the Being you have imagined; namely, something precisely like the great Being of your imagination *except* that *this* Being actually *exists*. For after all, an *existent* Super Being obviously is greater than a *nonexistent* Super Being. So if you genuinely think of the *greatest possible* Being, you immediately recognize that this is a Being Whose existence is *necessary*; for something *like* this Super Being that does *not* exist would not be "Something than which nothing greater can be conceived." Therefore, God is the one Being whose existence is *necessary*: You cannot genuinely think of God without recognizing that God *must* exist. Your very *thought* of God establishes the *necessary existence* of God. (Note, incidentally, that the ontological argument would work—if it works at all—only for the Aristotelian conception of a *perfect* God.)

Many people, on first encountering Anselm's ontological argument for the existence of God, find it an intriguing argument; but they are not convinced. They have a sense that *something* must be wrong with that argument: You can't prove the existence of God *that* easily, just by focusing on the *concept* of God. There must be a trick. It's like a magician drawing a rabbit out of an empty hat: rabbits can't be made and God can't be proved that easily.

The major criticism of the ontological argument claims that it goes wrong because it treats existence as a *characteristic*, like color or thickness. When you say that something *exists*, you are not naming another feature of that object. "Alice is tall, she is a brilliant philosopher, she has a warm smile and a kind heart, and she exists." That is not a sentence you would use (unless you were speaking in some very strange fictional context). Being tall is one of Alice's properties, but *existence* is not. Perhaps God exists, perhaps not; but God's existence is not simply an additional property of God, like God's omniscience: It is not a property at all. But like all the arguments presented here, you will have to decide for yourself whether the argument works.

The Design argument is sometimes called the *Teleological* argument for the existence of God. "Telos" is the Greek term for goal or purpose, and the Design argument is based on seeing the world as a product of God's purpose and design; thus the Design argument is an argument based in God's purposes, a goal-oriented or *teleological* argument.

The Argument from Design

While the ontological argument is of interest mainly to philosophers and theologians, the *Design* argument has a broader following. "Look at the marvelous design of a hand, of an eye; obviously there must be a designer, and that designer is God." This argument has occurred to many people, but the English philosopher William Paley (1743–1805) developed it in detail, so that it is often called "Paley's Argument from Design." Paley's version of the argument goes like this:

> Suppose I had found a watch upon the ground . . . When we come to inspect the watch, we perceive that its several parts are framed and put together for a purpose, e.g., that they are so formed and adjusted as to produce motion, and that motion so regulated as to point out the hour of the day. . . . This mechanism being observed . . . the inference we think is inevitable, that the watch must have had a maker . . . who completely comprehended its construction and designed its use.

Several decades following Paley's version of the design argument, Charles Darwin published *Origin of Species*. While Darwin did not put all advocates of the design argument to flight (there are currently proponents of "intelligent design" who wish to have their view taught in public schools), his work obviously poses a severe challenge for the design argument. If the process of natural selection can account for such marvelous structures as the hand or the eye, then the hypothesis of a "designer god" is not required. However, some of the strongest arguments against the argument from design were formulated by the great Scottish philosopher, David Hume, who was a contemporary of Paley's. In his *Dialogues Concerning Natural Religion*, Hume argues that if we take seriously the "watchmaker" argument, the most plausible hypothesis for the creator of this world would not be a God Who is omnipotent and omniscient, much less a God Who is omnibenevolent: After all, the world does contain some marvelous hands and eyes, but it also contains cancer cells that run wild, severe birth defects, terrible childhood diseases, and human windpipes that are easily choked (even a god of modest abilities could surely have designed a better windpipe). So from our observation of the "designed world," what conclusion should we draw about the Designer? Not that the Designer was the omnipotent caring God of the Judeo-Christian-Muslim tradition, but more likely—or at least just as plausibly—the designer was an apprentice god, who made this world as a first clumsy effort; or an old and feeble god, well past his world-making prime; or maybe the world was produced by a collection of gods, like a construction crew in which each worker has a limited specialty.

In his *Dialogues Concerning Natural Religion* criticism of the design argument, David Hume wrote: ". . . a man who follows your hypothesis is able, perhaps, to assert or conjecture that the universe sometime arose from something like design: But beyond that position he cannot ascertain one single circumstance, and is left afterwards to fix every point of his theology by the utmost license of fancy and hypothesis. This world, for aught he knows, is very faulty and imperfect, compared to a superior standard; and was only the first rude essay of some infant deity who afterwards abandoned it, ashamed of his lame performance: It is the work of some dependent, inferior deity, and is the object of derision to his superiors: It is the production of old age and dotage in some superannuated deity; and ever since his death has run on at adventures, from the first impulse and active force which it received from him."

Thomas Hardy (1840–1928), British novelist and poet, had a rather dark view of the world; and in one of his poems, he brings to life the idea—expressed by David Hume— that our less than perfect world might be the creation of a less than perfect God:

–"The Earth, sayest thou? The Human race?
By Me created? Sad its lot?
Nay: I have no remembrance of such place:
    Such world I fashioned not."—

–"O Lord, forgive me when I say
Thou spakest the word that made it all."—
"The Earth of men – let me bethink me . . . . Yea!
    I dimly do recall

"Some tiny sphere I built long back
(Mid millions of such shapes of mine)
So named . . . . It perished, surely—not a wrack
    Remaining, or a sign?

"It lost my interest from the first,
My aims therefor succeeding ill;
Haply it died of doing as it durst?"—
    "Lord, it existeth still."—

The Intuitive Argument

Though efforts to prove the existence of God never lose their popularity, the problems with those proofs have led some to a different sort of justification for belief in God. Rather than looking outwardly to cosmological or design proofs, they counsel an inward, intuitive, and introspective justification of belief in God. Walter Terence Stace, born in 1886, worked in the British Civil Service for 22 years while continuing to pursue his strong interest in theology and philosophy. At age 46 he retired from the British Civil Service, joined the philosophy department at Princeton University, and eventually became the leading advocate for the *Intuitive* proof for the existence of God. Stace insisted that such a proof was the *only* possible proof of God's existence, since any proof based on the facts of the natural order must inevitably fail to prove the existence of *God*:

> If I start from a natural fact, my inferential process, however long, can end only in another natural fact. A "first cause," simply by virtue of being a cause, would be a fact in the natural order. It is not denied that it might conceivably be possible to argue back from the present state of the world to an intelligent cause of some of its present characteristics—though I do not believe that any such argument is in fact valid. The point is that an intelligent cause of the material world, reached by any such inference, would be only another natural being, a part of the natural order. The point is that such a first cause *would not be God*.

So instead of any cosmological or design proof for the existence of God, Stace turns inward:

> . . . the argument for anything within the divine order must start from within the divine order. The divine order, however, is not far off. It is not beyond the stars. It is within us—as also within all other things. God exists in the eternal moment which is in every man, either self-consciously present and fully revealed, or buried, more or less deeply, in the unconscious. We express this in poetic language if we say that God is "in the heart." It is in the heart, then, that the witness of Him, the proof of Him, must lie, and not in any external circumstance of the natural order.

> *From Chapter 8 of Walter Terence Stace, Time and Eternity*
> *(Princeton, NJ: Princeton University Press, 1952)*

Stace is promoting a view that Blaise Pascal, the seventeenth-century mathematician and philosopher, would approve: "The heart has its reasons that the reason knows not of." But basing a proof of the existence of God on reasons "in the heart" seems a doubtful enterprise. Of course Stace himself may have powerful heartfelt intuitions of the divine that are convincing proof for *him*; but if this is supposed to be a general proof of God, it may fall short. Stace would insist, of course, that "God exists in the eternal moment which is in every man," but it seems clear that not every person has this powerful heartfelt experience of God. Stace can respond that the experience *is* present: "self-consciously present and fully revealed, or buried, more or less deeply, in the unconscious." But if it is "buried, more or less deeply, in the unconscious," then that's not much help. Stace confidently asserts that every person who is not conscious of the experience *must* have a buried *unconscious* version; but what evidence is there of such an *unconscious* experience? Is it confirmed by psychological experiment? Furthermore, the reliability of "intuitions" is deeply suspect: After all, "intuitions" come in many shapes and sizes, including racist and sexist and homophobic intuitions that have caused enormous suffering but offer very poor credentials for their truth or accuracy. Finally, even if I do experience an "intuition" of the divine presence, why should I suppose such an intuitive feeling to be an accurate guide? Perhaps this intuitive sense of divinity is caused by a deep genetic tendency toward hierarchy: Humans evolved in such a way that we naturally adapt to a hierarchical structure (with kings at the top, the nobility next, on down to the commoners and peasants; or a Pope at the top, cardinals next, priests somewhat lower, and everyone else at the bottom), and our "sense of divinity" is just a manifestation of that hierarchical tendency. Not that I think that is the true explanation for any intuitive sense of divinity, but it is at least as plausible as the supposition that it is implanted in us by God.

> If the provinces of faith and reason are not kept distinct by these boundaries, there will, in matters of religion, be no room for reason at all; and those extravagant opinions and ceremonies that are to be found in the several religions of the world will not deserve to be blamed. For, to this crying up of faith, in opposition to reason, we may, I think, in good measure ascribe those absurdities that fill almost all the religions which possess and

divide mankind. For men, having been principled with an opinion that they must not consult reason in the things of religion, however apparently contradictory to common sense and the very principles of all their knowledge, have let loose their fancies and natural superstition; and have been by them let into so strange opinions, and extravagant practices in religion, that a considerate man cannot but stand amazed at their follies, and judge them so far from being acceptable to the great and wise God, that he cannot avoid thinking them ridiculous, and offensive to a sober good man. So that in effect religion, which should most distinguish us from beasts, and ought peculiarly to elevate us, as rational creatures, above brutes, is that wherein men often appear most irrational and more senseless than beasts themselves. *John Locke (1632–1704), Essay Concerning Human Understanding (1690), Book IV, Chapter 18.*

PASCAL'S WAGER

What a chimera then is man! What a novelty! What a monster, what a chaos, what a contradiction, what a prodigy! Judge of all things, feeble earthworm, depository of truth, a sink of uncertainty and error, the glory and the shame of the universe. *Blaise Pascal*

Given the difficulty with traditional proofs for the existence of God, Blaise Pascal (1623–1662) proposed a new approach that now bears his name: *"Pascal's wager."* It is not really an argument for the existence of God, but instead an argument for why you should *believe* in God. First Pascal notes that the question of belief in God is forced upon you: If you decide not to choose, then by your indecision you are already *making* a choice *not* to believe. Since you *must* choose, Pascal urges the unbeliever to consider the odds, and make the best possible wager on four distinct possibilities. First, suppose that there is no God, and you believe there is no God. In that case, death ends all, and your advantage in having lived with a true belief of God's nonexistence doesn't give you any great benefit. Second, suppose there is no God, but you believe that there *is* a God. Again, death ends all, and you have lived with a false belief; but this false belief in God may well have helped you to live a better and more confident life than you would have lived *without* that belief. Third, suppose that you believe in God, and you're right! In that case, your winnings are enormous: an infinity of pure joy. Fourth, suppose that you do *not* believe in God, and you're *wrong*. Too bad. In fact, *infinitely* too bad, since you will suffer the tortures of the damned for all eternity. So, since you are compelled to wager, what is your best bet? If you wager on *nonbelief*, there is little to be gained and the possibility of infinite loss. If you wager on *belief*, there is little to be lost and the possibility of infinite gain. So, obviously you should choose to believe. Of course, it's not quite that simple: You can't just *choose* what you will believe (just *try* believing that a colony of woodland elves is living in your professor's office). Pascal is aware of that problem: He suggests that you go to church, participate in the services, surround yourself with believers, *act* like a believer, and eventually belief will come.

Emmanuel Levinas, a twentieth-century Jewish theologian and philosopher, maintained that questions of the existence of God, and even belief in God, were not the most important issues: "Faith is not a question of the existence or nonexistence of God. It is believing that love without reward is valuable."

Pascal's wager provokes strong reactions. Some see the suggestion of "gambling on belief in God" as disgusting, while others regard it as sound advice (of course, Pascal's wager would make no sense to those holding either Aristotle's or Spinoza's view of God). There is a bumper sticker which reads "If you don't believe in God—You'd better be right!" The message contains a dark threat: *Believe*, or suffer the consequences. But that makes God sound like a cosmic Mafia Godfather, who compels you to believe by "making you an offer you can't refuse." Also, the idea of worshiping God from fear of horrific punishment or hope of vast reward seems a shallow approach to religious understanding. Rabi'a was a spiritual teacher in the Sufi Muslim tradition, who once rushed through a marketplace carrying a torch in one hand and a jug of water in the other. When asked why she carried the torch and the water, she replied that she wanted to burn Paradise and put out the fires of Hell, so that people would do good acts from love of doing good, love of kindness, and love of God rather than from hope of reward or fear of punishment. Maybe the threat of hell will prevent some people from doing evil; but it does not seem a very promising path to either genuine moral behavior or religious enlightenment.

You yourself, if you surrender your judgment at any time to the blood-curdling declamations of the prophets, will want to desert our ranks. Only think what phantoms they can conjure up to overturn the tenor of your life and wreck your happiness with fear. And not without cause. For, if men saw that a term was set to their troubles, they would find strength in some way to withstand the hocus-pocus and intimidation of the prophets. As it is, they have no power of resistance, because they are haunted by the fear of eternal punishment after death. *Lucretius (99–55 B.C.E.), On the Nature of the Universe* (translated by R. E. Latham).

Spinoza was particularly disgusted by those who practiced virtue (though they lusted after evil) solely out of fear of eternal punishment. In a letter, he describes such a person thus: "I see in what mud this man sticks. He is one of those who would follow after his own lusts, if he were not restrained by the fear of hell. He abstains from evil actions and fulfils God's command like a slave against his will, and for his bondage he expects to be rewarded by God with gifts far more to his taste than Divine love, and great in proportion to his original dislike of virtue." *Letter XLIX*

THE PROBLEM OF EVIL

There are a number of arguments for the existence of God (in addition to Pascal's Wager argument for *belief* in the existence of God). Among arguments *against* the existence of God, one is by far the most famous: the argument from Evil. If we start from the supposition that God is omnipotent and omniscient, *and* that God is benevolent and loving, then how can there be *evil* in the world? Consider a small child suffering from a painful fatal disease. On the supposition that God exists, and God is loving, omniscient, and omnipotent, such suffering should never occur. Suffering might occur if God were not aware of it; but God is omniscient. It might occur if God knew but lacked the power to prevent it; but God is omnipotent. Or the suffering might occur if God were omnipotent and omniscient, but was indifferent to the child's suffering. But the existence of an omniscient, omnipotent, and loving God is inconsistent with the suffering of a child. Since in fact there is enormous suffering—millions of children die annually from starvation, disease, and violence, while storms, floods, earthquakes, and wars wreak havoc on millions more—that is strong evidence against the existence of a loving, omnipotent, and omniscient God.

> Tell me honestly, I challenge you—answer me: imagine that you are charged with building the edifice of human destiny, the ultimate aim of which is to bring people happiness, to give them peace and contentment at last, but that in order to achieve this it is essential and unavoidable to torture just one little speck of creation, that same little child beating her chest with her little fists, and imagine that this edifice, has to be erected on her unexpiated tears. Would you agree to be the architect under those conditions? Tell me honestly! *Fyodor Dostoyevsky, The Karmazov Brothers*, translated by Ignat Avsey (Oxford: Oxford University Press, 1994), i, Part 2, Book 5, Chapter 4. First published in 1879–1880.

This is an ancient problem. In the Hebraic scriptures, the story of Job is one of the most famous sources of the problem of evil. Job is a good and virtuous man, as God affirms in a conversation with Satan: "And the Lord said unto Satan, Hast thou considered my servant Job, that there is none like him in the earth, a perfect and an upright man, one that feareth God, and escheweth evil?" Satan responds that it is not surprising that Job worships God and lives a good life, considering all the wealth and blessings God has given Job. God then allows Satan to test Job by afflicting Job with terrible suffering. So Satan causes Job's family to be killed, all his wealth destroyed, and his body to be covered with painful sores. Ultimately Job cries out a question to God: Why have You treated me this way? Why are You allowing me to suffer so dreadfully? And God's answer is:

> Who is this that darkeneth counsel by words without knowledge? . . . Where wast thou when I laid the foundations of the earth? . . . Who laid the corner stones thereof, when the morning stars sang together? . . . Canst thou lift up thy voice to the clouds, that abundance of waters may cover thee? Canst thou send lightnings, that they may go, and say unto thee, Here we are?

Or in other words: Who are you to question God and God's ways, you puny worm?

> The American philosopher, Josiah Royce (1855–1916), offered this answer to the problem of evil:
>
> > God is not in ultimate essence another being than yourself. He is the Absolute Being. You truly are one with God, part of his life. He is the very soul of your soul. And so, here is the first truth: When you suffer, *your sufferings are God's sufferings*, not his external work, not his external penalty, not the fruit of his neglect, but identically his own personal woe. In you God himself suffers, precisely as you do, and has all your concern in overcoming this grief.
> >
> > The true question then is: Why does God thus suffer? The sole possible, necessary, and sufficient answer is, Because without suffering, without ill, without woe, evil, tragedy, God's life could not be perfected. This grief is not a physical means to an external end. It is a logically necessary and eternal constituent of the divine life. It is logically necessary the Captain of your salvation should be perfect through suffering. No outer nature compels him. He chooses this because he chooses his own perfect selfhood. He is perfect. His world is the best possible world. Yet all its finite regions know not only of joy but of defeat and sorrow, for thus alone, in the completeness of his eternity, can God in his wholeness be triumphantly perfect. *Josiah Royce, "The Problem of Job."*

The story of Job is fascinating, and the language magnificent; but it doesn't offer much of an answer to the problem of evil. In this story, God's answer to the problem of evil seems to be: You have no right to ask for an answer. Even if that's true, it's not much of an answer to the problem.

> Suppose that the world's author put the case to you before creation, saying: "I am going to make a world not certain to be saved, a world the perfection of which shall be conditional merely, the condition being that each several agent does its own "level best." I offer you the chance of taking part in such a world. Its safety, you see, is unwarranted. It is a real adventure, with real danger, yet it may win through. It is a social scheme of co-operative work genuinely to be done. Will you join the procession? Will you trust yourself and trust the other agents enough to face the risk?" There is a healthy buoyancy in most of us which such a universe would exactly fit. *William James, Pragmatism.*

So what answer is possible? One type of answer is to deny the starting supposition: that God is omnipotent, omniscient, and loving. Perhaps God is *indifferent* to us: Human suffering is beneath His concern. That solves the problem of evil, but in a way that few believers find attractive. Another alternative—and one that some find more attractive—is to deny that God is *omnipotent*. The American pragmatist philosopher William James (1842–1910) favored that position: God struggles against evil and suffering, and God is a strong steady ally in our struggle against evil, but God is *not* all powerful, and He cannot always banish evil. For James, this meant that the struggle between good and evil was a tough contest, and either side could win. Therefore, our own efforts against evil are vitally important, and might switch the tide of battle to the side of good. We aren't just idle spectators watching God win the inevitable victory for goodness; rather, we are an important part of a real struggle. That's a solution to the problem of evil—but few believers can accept that solution. Another solution, from the opposite direction, denies the existence of evil, the existence of suffering. We might *think* that there is genuine suffering in the world, but we are mistaken. But while that answer to the problem has some advocates, it is very difficult for most people to accept: One afternoon of severe headache or toothache is sufficient to convince most people that there is at least some genuine suffering in the world; and even a glimpse at the vast suffering brought about by disease, famine, drought, natural disaster, and war makes it difficult to count all suffering as illusion—indeed, anyone who made such an assertion would be morally suspect.

> As there is an infinity of possible universes in the Ideas of God, and as only one of them can exist, there must be a sufficient reason for God's choice, which determines him toward one rather than another. And this reason can be found only in the fitness, or the degrees of perfection, that these worlds contain, since each possible thing has the right to claim existence in proportion to the perfection it involves. *Leibniz, Monadology.*

The most promising and sophisticated responses to the problem of evil treat suffering as an essential element in the best possible world. That is, suffering is genuinely bad; but a world devoid of all suffering would not be, on the whole, as good or desirable as a world that contains suffering. Advocates of this type of answer often use the metaphor of a beautiful painting: If you focus narrowly on a small section of the painting, its dark colors may seem somber and uninspiring; but if you consider the entire canvas, you realize that the dark hues make the brilliant colors even more vivid, and that the dark colors are essential to the beauty of the entire painting: without them, the painting would not be quite so wonderful. The great seventeenth-century philosopher and mathematician and scientist Gottfried Wilhelm Leibniz put forward the most famous argument of this type. Leibniz insisted that a world in which humans are always happy, never suffer, and never make mistakes might be a *pleasant* world, but it would not be the *best of all possible* worlds. It would lack opportunities to develop and exercise virtue, it could not contain genuine free will (which must include the opportunity to make bad choices with bad consequences), it would give no opportunity for genuine moral development and moral triumph. A constantly pleasant world might be alright, but it would not be the *best of all possible* worlds, for it would lack free will and genuine virtue. In order to include the development of moral virtue, the exercise of free will, and the opportunity for moral and spiritual growth, God had to allow evil and suffering: Evil and suffering are *necessary* for such vitally important goods, and thus the presence of evil and suffering cannot be eliminated from the *best* of all possible worlds.

Leibniz is caricatured by Voltaire, in Voltaire's great satirical novel, *Candide*. In the novel, Candide and his friends (including Dr. Pangloss, who obviously represents Leibniz) lurch from disaster to disaster: they are captured by brutal pirates, sold into slavery, subjected to torture, and ravaged by awful diseases. But at every step, Dr. Pangloss solemnly assures everyone that this is undoubtedly the best of all possible worlds.

Picture the world as a perpetual spring break, with warm sunshine, the health and energy of youth, and free flowing fountains of cold fruity margaritas—without, of course, hangovers, sunburn, or sexually transmitted diseases. Not bad, obviously; and an omnipotent God could surely have shaped the world to those specifications. But—so this argument goes—God's purpose is *not* to make a world of indolent indulgence; rather, God designs the world as a setting in which humans can exercise genuine free will, can make themselves better, can develop genuine and enduring virtues, and can exercise the great virtues of kindness, compassion, courage, and benevolence. This perspective is expressed by the great American idealist philosopher Josiah Royce (1855–1916): "The triumph of the wise is no easy thing. Their lives are not light, but sorrowful. Yet they rejoice in their sorrow, not, to be sure, because it is mere experience, but because, for them, it becomes part of a strenuous whole of life." Free will is an essential element of virtue, and of genuine morality, and of being a full genuine *person*; but free will necessarily involves the opportunity to make *bad* decisions: decisions that harm yourself as well as others. And unless those mistakes and harms are *genuine*, it is not a real exercise of free will. If God only allowed you to make good choices, with good consequences, that would be like when you were a small child and you wanted to eat your candy; and your mother replied that you were free to eat your candy whenever you chose, so long as you chose to wait until after dinner. No doubt your mother's restriction was good for you; but it certainly didn't allow for much exercise of genuine free will.

While some find this a satisfactory solution to the problem of evil, others are more skeptical. Even if we grant that genuine free will is desirable, and that exercise of free will must leave room for bad choices with bad consequences, that still accounts for only a small fraction of the evil in the world—evil and suffering that a benevolent omnipotent God *could* prevent. What about natural disasters—floods, hurricanes, earthquakes, and tsunamis—that kill, injure, cause massive suffering, and seem to have no relation to the exercise of free will? Perhaps hardship and suffering offer opportunities to develop the virtues of fortitude and courage: What doesn't kill you makes you stronger. But even if that is true, it cannot account for the multitude of terrible childhood diseases that cause suffering and death, with no question of making the deceased sufferer "stronger" or more patient or more virtuous. And it is hardly clear that severe suffering is very effective in fostering courage and fortitude: It seems more likely to promote bitterness and helplessness. And while severe suffering does offer opportunities for the exercise of such virtues as generosity and benevolence, it seems that such virtues could be exercised sufficiently without the need for quite so *much* suffering. Furthermore, much suffering occurs without any increase in the virtues of kindness and benevolence; and sadly, such situations seem to promote selfishness as often as benevolence. There is surely enough suffering and hunger in Mexico and Latin

America to inspire our generosity; but it instead inspires the building of expensive large fences to keep the hungry out. Certainly the tsunami inspired generosity from people around the world for the victims; but it seems nonetheless that an omniscient and omnipotent God could have devised a less painful method of promoting generosity.

OCKHAM'S RAZOR

There is another common argument against the existence of God; and while it does not have a common name, we might label it the argument from simplicity, or perhaps the *Ockham's Razor* argument. Ockham's Razor is a principle proposed by the great medieval philosopher, William of Ockham (sometimes spelled *Occam*, and so sometimes called "Occam's Razor"). William of Ockham (1285–1349) insisted that in offering explanations, "entities should not be multiplied unnecessarily." That is, in explaining some phenomenon, you should not postulate the existence of any object or force beyond the *minimum* required for an adequate explanation. In other words, don't make explanations more complicated than necessary. I can give an easy explanation for why our streets have so many potholes toward the end of winter: It's because the pothole elves come out of hibernation late in winter, and they throw wild parties in the streets to celebrate awakening from their hibernation, and these elf parties, with their nonstop vigorous dancing, break down the street surface and cause potholes. My explanation covers the phenomenon or pothole proliferation quite effectively: More potholes simply require more elves. You aren't likely to buy my elf explanation; but why not? It accounts for the existence of potholes, so what's wrong? It *does* account for the existence of potholes, but we have available a much *simpler* explanation, involving the effects of water working into cracks and expanding as it turns into ice and cracking the pavement, and heavy cars and trucks rolling over the cracked pavement and causing larger breaks, which become larger and larger as more water runs in and freezes, and more cars and trucks break larger pieces of the surface pavement and gradually work down to destroy softer underlying material. In *that* explanation, you don't have to posit any *new* entities; rather, you note the combined effects of water, ice, and traffic—and those are things we already acknowledge to exist. My explanation adds a new and rather special entity: party-loving pothole elves. It's not that we *never* posit new entities in the course of our explanations: Scientists have posited the existence of black holes to explain astronomical phenomena, and strange subatomic particles to explain phenomena at the atomic level. But such explanations are acceptable only when no *simpler* or more *parsimonious* explanation is available.

> The principle of Ockham's Razor got its name from the claim that William of Ockham used his simplicity principle to "shave Plato's beard." The great ancient Greek philosopher, Plato, was very fond of explanations which involved the existence of special eternal "models" or "forms." How do we recognize that a circle is round? We compare it to the "form" or "ideal" of circleness, and that ideal is eternal and known only through special rational insight. How do we know that this object is a table? We compare it to the form of tableness. Ockham argued that Plato's explanations were flawed, because simpler explanations were available: thus, Ockham's simplicity principle eliminated Plato's excessive metaphysics (Plato's extravagant positing of special eternal "forms"); that is, *Ockham's Razor "shaved Plato's beard."*

Evolution certainly does not prove that God does not exist; and while many Christian fundamentalists—who believe in the *literal* truth of the Bible—worry that evolutionary explanations threaten their religious views, that is really not the main source for fear of evolution. After all, Biblical literalism has far more serious problems than evolution. Consider the story of Joshua and the Battle of Gibeon: Joshua and his warriors had their enemies on the run, but night was approaching and Joshua feared that his enemies would escape into the darkness. And God commanded: "Sun, stand thou still upon Gibeon . . . . And the sun stood still . . . until the people had avenged themselves upon their enemies." Note that God did not command the Earth to stop turning, but rather the Sun to stop moving. So if one insists on a literal interpretation of the Bible, one must reject the Copernican theory, and all of modern astronomy, and insist that the Earth is at the center of the universe, and stationary, and the Sun travels around the Earth. So if Biblical literalists— Christian fundamentalists—accept the Copernican theory, why should they object to Darwinian evolution?

> I had no intention to write atheistically. But I own that I cannot see as plainly as others do, and as I should wish to do, evidence of design and beneficence on all sides of us. There seems to me too much misery in the world. I cannot persuade myself that a beneficent and omnipotent God would have designedly created the Ichneumonidae with the express intention of their feeding within the living bodies of caterpillars, or that a cat should play with mice. *Charles Darwin, Letters.*

The threat posed by evolution is not so much to Biblical literalism, but instead to a certain view of the proper *role* of religion. If God is posited as an *explanation* of what we see in the world, then Darwin does pose a threat to God. Scientists can now offer all sorts of explanations for events we once thought could be explained only by the hypothesis of God. Once it was God Who held the Moon in place; now it's gravity. Once God sent comets as divine warnings; now they are explained by Newton's laws of motion. Once disease was a manifestation of God's wrath; now it's explained by germ theory. But some things remained inexplicable by science, and required the special intervention of a divine designer: the hand, the eye, the human mind. But Darwin—and the continued development of Darwinian biological science—accounted for all those with a *simpler* and more economical explanation, making use of a *natural* process of natural selection and not requiring the intervention of any special divine entity. Darwinian science doesn't prove the *nonexistence* of God, of course; but it does make God *superfluous.*

There is a famous story—I can't guarantee that it's *true*, but it is famous—of the French philosopher and scientist LaPlace and his meeting with Napoleon. LaPlace told Napoleon a great deal about the new developments in science, and of all the things that the scientific system could now explain. After listening awhile, Napoleon interrupted: "But where is God in your system?" "Sire," replied LaPlace, "We have no need for that hypothesis."

Science offers explanations that stay within the natural realm, and thus it can never adopt a divine cause as part of the explanation. Of course many scientists believe in God. But when a scientist attempts to offer a scientific explanation of how continental drift occurs, or why black holes exert enormous gravitational force, or what caused an outbreak of disease, then the scientist cannot appeal to nonnatural divine forces. It's a free country, and if you wish to claim that a recent outbreak of flu on campus was God's punishment of evil behavior by the students, you can do so; but such an "explanation" could never count as a *scientific* explanation. So religion doesn't work very well if it attempts to offer explanations that compete with those offered by science. When judged by the standard of Ockham's Razor, the religious explanation always falls short: It can never be as simple, because it adds a divine force to its explanations, and such explanations will thus be more complex than the explanations which do not invoke the divine factor. Thus, one argument against the existence of God is that *simpler* explanations are better, and explanations that deny the existence of God are therefore better than explanations and claims that assert God's existence.

DO SCIENCE AND RELIGION OCCUPY DIFFERENT SPHERES?

Religion cannot compete with science on scientific grounds; so rather than casting religion and science as competitors—as the Catholic Church did in its battle with Galileo, and as some contemporary Christian fundamentalists do in their battle with Darwin—some defenders of religion insist that religion and science occupy different and noncompeting spheres: Religion deals with the Supernatural, and science with the natural; or religion is based on faith, while science works from observation; or religion is the realm of fixed truths, while science is the realm of hypotheses and theories and explorations in which knowledge develops through changing models (religion rests on fixed principles and settled creeds and articles of faith, while in science the best theories are those which generate the most new unanswered questions); or religion is the realm of values, while science is the realm of natural fact. Of course, all of those contrasts are controversial (e.g., some scientists claim they can establish or discover values, while some—such as the fundamentalists—insist that religion does give us knowledge of the natural world: e.g., the knowledge that it was created by God, or that it is only a few thousand years old). And some reject the idea of separate spheres altogether. Still, the "different realms" model for avoiding conflict between science and religion is appealing to many. Indeed, that is what William of Ockham himself did: Theology, Ockham maintained, is not a science, but is instead a realm of faith and revelation. Ockham believed that both realms contain truths, but the truths of theology are a different set of truths, and discovered through a very different process, than the truths of science. This is a popular idea; for example, the pro-religion blogger and writer Andrew Sullivan states: "truth is not exhausted by empiricism or materialism. I do not believe, in short, that all truth rests on scientific premises and can be 'proven' by empirical or scientific methods. I believe science is one important, valuable and respectable mode of thinking about the whole. But there are truth questions it has not answered and cannot answer."

> The further the spiritual evolution of mankind advances, the more certain it seems to me that the path to genuine religiosity does not lie through the fear of life, and the fear of death, and blind faith, but through striving after rational knowledge. *Albert Einstein, Out of My Later Years*.

The view that religion and science occupy different spheres and answer different questions is illustrated by the Biblical account of the Garden of Eden. In the Genesis account, "God said, Let there the light: And there was light." And as the story continues, on the fourth day "God created great whales, and every living creature that moveth, which the waters brought forth abundantly, after their kind, and every winged fowl after his kind"; on the fifth day, God gets around to creating "cattle, and creeping things, and the beasts of the earth," and the next day God created Adam and Eve: "God created man in his own image, in the image of God created he him; male and female created he them." If we read the Genesis story as biology, we not only get bad biology but we also miss the real point of the story. The point is not about how or in what order whales, cattle, and creeping things came into existence; rather, the point is that we are all the children of Adam and Eve, that we are all (like Adam and Eve) made in the image of God. That is, each of us is of great importance, and each of us, every individual, must be considered special and entitled to full equal rights. Furthermore, whatever race or ethnic group or nationality, we are all brothers and sisters, all children of a common mother and father. The Genesis story expresses important moral principles about human relations; and it is more plausible and more inspiring as an ethical guide rather than a biology textbook.

Exactly how to differentiate the sphere of science from the sphere of religion is not always clear. According to the teachings of the Catholic Church, science deals with the material world, while questions about souls and divinity belong to religion (thus, the Catholic Church currently does not object to the Darwinian account of the evolution of the physical body, so long as the question of how bodies are ensouled remains the property of the religious sphere). Another way of drawing the distinction has to do with values: Science deals with matters of empirical fact, questions of what *is*; religion is the realm of values, and questions of what *ought* to be.

Whatever God hath revealed is certainly true; no doubt can be made of it. This is the proper object of faith; but whether it be a divine revelation or no, reason must judge; which can never permit the mind to reject a greater evidence to embrace what is less evident, nor allow it to entertain probability in opposition to knowledge and certainty. There can be no evidence that any traditional revelation is of divine original, in the words we receive it, and in the sense we understand it, so clear and so certain, as that of the principles of reason: and therefore nothing that is contrary to, and inconsistent with, the clear and self-evident dictates of reason has a right to be urged or assented to as a matter of faith. *John Locke, Essay Concerning Human Understanding*, 1690, Book IV, Chapter 18.

But the proposal to reconcile religion and science by giving each a distinctive and proper sphere also has its critics. Richard Dawkins, for example, rejects the two spheres approach:

> . . . it is completely unrealistic to claim . . . that religion keeps itself away from science's turf, restricting itself to morals and values. A universe with a supernatural presence would be a fundamentally and qualitatively different kind of universe from one without. The difference is, inescapably, a scientific difference. Religions make existence claims, and this means scientific claims.
>
> The same is true of many of the major doctrines of the Roman Catholic Church. The Virgin Birth, the bodily Assumption of the Blessed Virgin Mary, the Resurrection of Jesus, the survival of our own souls after death: these are all claims of a clearly scientific nature. Either Jesus had a corporeal father or he didn't. This is not a question of "values" or "morals," it is a question of sober fact.

And while Dawkins complains that religion crosses the boundary into scientific claims, others insist that scientists have a legitimate role in exploring values and must not leave such important questions to the sphere of religion. The biologist E. O. Wilson (in *Consilience*) writes:

> The empiricist argument, then, is that by exploring the biological roots of moral behavior, and explaining their material origins and biases, we should be able to fashion a wiser and more enduring ethical consensus than has gone before. The current expansion of scientific inquiry into the deeper processes of human thought makes this venture feasible. (p. 240)

So if we wish to keep science and religion in separate spheres, and keep each from invading the territory of the other, that may not be an easy task.

Certainly the same subject can be approached in different ways without being in conflict: Monet's paintings of water lilies would be of little use in a botany textbook; and the drawings in the botany text might have little value in an art museum. But whether the interests, claims, and spheres of science and religion can be so easily separated is a more controversial issue.

READINGS

⇒ GENESIS, EXODUS* ⇒

The passages below show some of the key characteristics of the Hebraic God (the accounts are common to the Jewish, Christian, and Muslim religious traditions). God is shown to be a *creator*, Who changes His mind ("it repententh me that I have made them," "the Lord repented of the evil which he thought to do unto his people") and is actively involved in world events.

THE FIRST BOOK OF MOSES CALLED GENESIS

Chapter 1

1. In the beginning God created the heaven and the earth.
2. And the earth was without form, and void; and darkness *was* upon the face of the deep. And the Spirit of God moved upon the face of the waters.
3. And God said, Let there be light: and there was light.
4. And God saw the light, that it *was* good: and God divided the light from the darkness.
5. And God called the light Day, and the darkness he called Night. And the evening and the morning were the first day.
6. And God said, Let there be a firmament in the midst of the waters, and let it divide the waters from the waters.
7. And God made the firmament, and divided the waters which *were* under the firmament from the waters which *were* above the firmament: and it was so.
8. And God called the firmament Heaven. And the evening and the morning were the second day.
9. And God said, Let the waters under the heaven be gathered together unto one place, and let the dry *land* appear: and it was so.
10. And God called the dry *land* Earth; and the gathering together of the waters called he Seas: and God saw that *it was* good.
11. And God said, Let the earth bring forth grass, the herb yielding seed, *and* the fruit tree yielding fruit after his kind, whose seed *is* in itself, upon the earth: and it was so.
12. And the earth brought forth grass, *and* herb yielding seed after his kind, and the tree yielding fruit, whose seed *was* in itself, after his kind: and God saw that *it was* good.
13. And the evening and the morning were the third day.
14. And God said, Let there be lights in the firmament of the heaven to divide the day from the night; and let them be for signs, and for seasons, and for days, and years:
15. And let them be for lights in the firmament of the heaven to give light upon the earth: and it was so.
16. And God made two great lights; the greater light to rule the day, and the lesser light to rule the night: *he made* the stars also.
17. And God set them in the firmament of the heaven to give light upon the earth,
18. And to rule over the day and over the night, and to divide the light from the darkness: and God saw that *it was* good.
19. And the evening and the morning were the fourth day.
20. And God said, Let the waters bring forth abundantly the moving creature that hath life, and fowl *that* may fly above the earth in the open firmament of heaven.
21. And God created great whales, and every living creature that moveth, which the waters brought forth abundantly, after their kind, and every winged fowl after his kind: and God saw that *it was* good.
22. And God blessed them, saying, Be fruitful, and multiply, and fill the waters in the seas, and let fowl multiply in the earth.
23. And the evening and the morning were the fifth day.
24. And God said, Let the earth bring forth the living creature after his kind, cattle, and creeping thing, and beast of the earth after his kind: and it was so.
25. And God made the beast of the earth after his kind, and cattle after their kind, and every thing that creepeth upon the earth after his kind: and God saw that *it was* good.
26. And God said, Let us make man in our image, after our likeness: and let them have dominion over the

---

*From the books of Genesis and Exodus, King James translations.

fish of the sea, and over the fowl of the air, and over the cattle, and over all the earth, and over every creeping thing that creepeth upon the earth.

27. So God created man in his *own* image, in the image of God created he him; male and female created he them.

28. And God blessed them, and God said unto them, Be fruitful, and multiply, and replenish the earth, and subdue it: and have dominion over the fish of the sea, and over the fowl of the air, and over every living thing that moveth upon the earth.

29. And God said, Behold, I have given you every herb bearing seed, which *is* upon the face of all the earth, and every tree, in the which *is* the fruit of a tree yielding seed; to you it shall be for meat.

30. And to every beast of the earth, and to every fowl of the air, and to every thing that creepeth upon the earth, wherein *there* is life, I *have given* every green herb for meat: and it was so.

31. And God saw every thing that he had made, and, behold, *it was* very good. And the evening and the morning were the sixth day.

Chapter 2

1. Thus the heavens and the earth were finished, and all the host of them.

2. And on the seventh day God ended his work which he had made; and he rested on the seventh day from all his work which he had made.

3. And God blessed the seventh day, and sanctified it: because that in it he had rested from all his work which God created and made.

. . .

22. And the LORD God said, Behold, the man is become as one of us, to know good and evil: and now, lest he put forth his hand, and take also of the tree of life, and eat, and live for ever:

23. Therefore the LORD God sent him forth from the garden of Eden, to till the ground from whence he was taken.

24. So he drove out the man; and he placed at the east of the garden of Eden Cherubims, and a flaming sword which turned every way, to keep the way of the tree of life.

. . .

Chapter 6

1. And it came to pass, when men began to multiply on the face of the earth, and daughters were born unto them.

2. That the sons of God saw the daughters of men that they *were* fair; and they took them wives of all which they chose.

3. And the LORD said, My spirit shall not always strive with man, for that he also *is* flesh: yet his days shall be an 100 and 20 years.

4. There were giants in the earth in those days; and also after that, when the sons of God came in unto the daughters of men, and they bare *children* to them, the same *became* mighty men which *were* of old, men of renown.

5. And God saw that the wickedness of man *was* great in the earth, and *that* every imagination of the thoughts of his heart *was* only evil continually.

6. And it repented the LORD that he had made man on the earth, and it grieved him at his heart.

7. And the LORD said, I will destroy man whom I have created from the face of the earth; both man, and beast, and the creeping thing, and the fowls of the air; for it repenteth me that I have made them.

. . .

Chapter 6 Exodus

1. Then the LORD said unto Moses, Now shalt thou see what I will do to Pharaoh: for with a strong hand shall he let them go, and with a strong hand shall he drive them out of his land.

2. And God spake unto Moses, and said unto him, I *am* the LORD:

3. And I appeared unto Abraham, unto Isaac, and unto Jacob, by *the name* of God Almighty, but by my name JEHOVAH was I not known to them.

4. And I have also established my covenant with them, to give them the land of Canaan, the land of their pilgrimage, wherein they were strangers.

5. And I have also heard the groaning of the children of Israel, whom the Egyptians keep in bondage; and I have remembered my covenant.

6. Wherefore say unto the children of Israel, I *am* the Lord, and I will bring you out from under the burdens of the Egyptians, and I will rid you out of their bondage, and I will redeem you with a stretched out arm, and with great judgments:

7. And I will take you to me for a people, and I will be to you a God: and ye shall know that I *am* the LORD your God, which bringeth you out from under the burdens of the Egyptians.

8. And I will bring you in unto the land, concerning the which I did swear to give it to Abraham, to Isaac, and to Jacob; and I will give it you for an heritage: I *am* the Lord.

. . .

Chapter 32

7. And the Lord said unto Moses, Go, get thee down; for thy people, which thou broughtest out of the land of Egypt, have corrupted *themselves*:

8. They have turned aside quickly out of the way which I commanded them: they have made them a molten calf, and have worshipped it, and have sacrificed thereunto, and said, These *be* thy gods, O Israel, which have brought thee up out of the land of Egypt.

9. And the LORD said unto Moses, I have seen this people, and, behold, it is a stiffnecked people:

10. Now therefore let me alone, that my wrath may wax hot against them, and that I may consume them: and I will make of thee a great nation.

11. And Moses besought the LORD his God, and said, *Lord*, why doth thy wrath wax hot against thy people, which thou hast brought forth out of the land of Egypt with great power, and with a mighty hand?

12. Wherefore should the Egyptians speak, and say, For mischief did he bring them out, to slay them in the mountains, and to consume them from the face of the earth? Turn from thy fierce wrath, and repent of this evil against thy people.

13. Remember Abraham, Isaac, and Israel, thy servants, to whom thou swarest by thine own self, and saidst unto them, I will multiply your seed as the stars of heaven, and all this land that I have spoken of will I give unto your seed, and they shall inherit *it* for ever.

14. And the Lord repented of the evil which he thought to do unto his people.

A THEOLOGICO-POLITICAL TREATISE
Benedict Spinoza

Benedict Spinoza (1632–1677) was a Jewish philosopher who lived in Amsterdam. He was excommunicated from the Jewish temple for beliefs that Jewish religious leaders regarded as heretical. He lived a simple life and earned a modest income grinding precision lenses for researchers. Though he spent most of his life in Amsterdam, he corresponded with people throughout Europe, and his reputation as a brilliant philosopher (who was also suspected of being a heretic) was widespread. During his lifetime, he allowed his major works to be read only by a select small group, believing that his writings generally would be misunderstood. Spinoza devoted his life to an attempt to understand God and God's relation to humans and to the world, and the ethical implications of this understanding of God. However, he was a fierce critic of popular religion, turning his critical wrath equally against Jewish, Christian, and Muslim religious views. As a result of those criticisms, he has sometimes been—during his own lifetime, and for many years after—wrongly thought to be an atheist. The following passage is taken from the "Preface" to *A Theologico-Political Treatise*, which Spinoza published under a fictitious name, correctly believing that the book would cause enormous controversy.

Men would never be superstitious, if they could govern all their circumstances by set rules, or if they were always favoured by fortune: but being frequently driven into straits where rules are useless, and being often kept fluctuating pitiably between hope and fear by the uncertainty of fortune's greedily coveted favours, they are consequently, for the most part, very prone to credulity. The human mind is readily swayed this way or that in times of doubt, especially when hope and fear are struggling for the mastery, though usually it is boastful, over-confident, and vain.

This as a general fact I suppose everyone knows, though few, I believe, know their own nature; no one can have lived in the world without observing that most people, when in prosperity, are so over-brimming with wisdom (however inexperienced they may be), that they take every offer of advice as a personal insult, whereas in adversity they know not where to turn, but beg and pray for counsel from every passer-by. No plan is then too futile, too absurd, or too fatuous for their adoption; the most frivolous causes will raise them to hope, or plunge them into despair—if anything happens during their fright which reminds them of some past good or ill, they think it portends a happy or unhappy issue, and therefore (though it may have proved abortive a hundred times before) style it a lucky or unlucky omen. Anything which excites their astonishment they believe to be a portent signifying the anger of the gods or of the Supreme Being, and, mistaking superstition for religion, account it impious not to avert the evil with prayer and sacrifice. Signs and wonders of this sort they conjure up perpetually, till one might think Nature as mad as themselves, they interpret her so fantastically.

Thus it is brought prominently before us, that superstition's chief victims are those persons who greedily covet temporal advantages; they it is, who (especially when they are in danger, and cannot help themselves) are wont with prayers and womanish tears to implore help from God: upbraiding Reason as blind, because she cannot show a sure path to the shadows they pursue, and rejecting human wisdom as vain; but believing the phantoms of imagination, dreams, and other childish absurdities, to be the very oracles of Heaven. As though God had turned away from the wise, and written His decrees, not in the mind of man but in the entrails of beasts, or left them to be proclaimed by the inspiration and instinct of fools, madmen, and birds. Such is the unreason to which terror can drive mankind!

Superstition, then, is engendered, preserved, and fostered by fear. . . .

I have often wondered, that persons who make a boast of professing the Christian religion, namely, love, joy, peace, temperance, and charity to all men, should quarrel with such rancorous animosity, and display daily towards one another such bitter hatred, that this, rather than the virtues they claim, is the readiest criterion of their faith. Matters have long since come to such a pass, that one can only pronounce a man Christian, Turk, Jew, or Heathen, by his general appearance and attire, by his frequenting this or that place of worship, or employing the phraseology of a particular sect—as for manner of life, it is in all cases the same. Inquiry into the cause of this anomaly leads me unhesitatingly to ascribe it to the fact, that the ministries of the Church are regarded by the masses merely as dignities, her offices as posts of emolument—in short, popular religion may be summed up as respect for ecclesiastics. The spread of this misconception inflamed every worthless fellow with an intense desire to enter holy orders, and thus the love of diffusing God's religion degenerated into sordid avarice and ambition. Every church became a theatre, where orators, instead of church teachers, harangued, caring not to instruct the people, but striving to attract admiration, to bring opponents to public scorn, and to preach only novelties and paradoxes, such as would tickle the ears of their congregation. This state of things necessarily stirred up an amount of controversy, envy, and hatred, which no lapse of time could appease; so that we can scarcely wonder that of the old religion nothing survives but its outward forms (even these, in the mouth of the multitude, seem rather adulation than adoration of the Deity), and that faith has become a mere compound of credulity and prejudices—aye, prejudices too, which degrade man from rational being to beast, which completely stifle the power of judgment between true and false, which seem, in fact, carefully fostered for the purpose of extinguishing the last spark of reason! Piety, great God! and religion are become a tissue of ridiculous mysteries; men, who flatly despise reason, who reject and turn away from understanding as naturally corrupt, these, I say, these of all men, are thought, O lie most horrible! to possess light from on High. Verily, if they had but one spark of light from on High, they would not insolently rave, but would learn to worship God more wisely, and would be as marked among their fellows for mercy as they now are for malice; if they were concerned for their opponents' souls, instead of for their own reputations, they would no longer fiercely persecute, but rather be filled with pity and compassion.

Furthermore, if any Divine light were in them, it would appear from their doctrine. I grant that they are never tired of professing their wonder at the profound mysteries of Holy Writ; still I cannot discover that they teach anything but speculations of Platonists and Aristotelians, to which (in order to save their credit for Christianity) they have made Holy Writ conform; not content to rave with the Greeks themselves, they want to make the prophets rave also; showing conclusively, that never even in sleep have they caught a glimpse of Scripture's Divine nature. The very vehemence of their admiration for the mysteries plainly attests, that their belief in the Bible is a formal assent rather than a living faith: and the fact is made still more apparent by their laying down beforehand, as a foundation for the study and true interpretation of Scripture, the principle that it is in every passage true and divine. Such a doctrine should be reached only after strict scrutiny and thorough comprehension of the Sacred Books (which would teach it much better, for they stand in need of no human fictions), and not be set up on the threshold, as it were, of inquiry.

. . .

This idea seems to have taken its rise among the early Jews who saw the Gentiles round them worshipping visible gods such as the sun, the moon, the earth, water, air, &c., and in order to inspire the conviction that such divinities were weak and inconstant, or changeable, told how they themselves were under the sway of an invisible God, and narrated their miracles, trying further to show that the God whom they worshipped arranged the whole of nature for their sole benefit: this idea was so pleasing to humanity that men go on to this day imagining miracles, so that they may believe themselves God's favourites, and the final cause for which God created and directs all things.

What pretension will not people in their folly advance! They have no single sound idea concerning either God or nature, they confound God's decrees with human decrees, they conceive nature as so limited that they believe man to be its chief part!

. . . [A]ll that God wishes or determines involves eternal necessity and truth, for we demonstrated that God's understanding is identical with His will, and that it is the same thing to say that God wills a thing, as to say that He understands it; hence, as it follows necessarily from the Divine nature and perfection that God understands a thing as it is, it follows no less necessarily that He wills it as it is. Now, as nothing is necessarily true save only by Divine decree, it is plain that the universal laws of nature are decrees of God following from the necessity and perfection of the Divine nature. Hence, any event happening in nature which contravened nature's universal laws, would necessarily also contravene the Divine decree, nature, and understanding; or if anyone asserted that God acts in contravention to the laws of nature, he, *ipso facto*, would be compelled to assert that God acted against His own nature—an evident absurdity. One might easily show from the same premises that the power and efficiency of nature are in themselves the Divine power and efficiency, and that the Divine power is the very essence of God, but this I gladly pass over for the present.

Nothing, then, comes to pass in nature in contravention to her universal laws, nay, everything agrees with them and follows from them, for whatsoever comes to pass, comes to pass by the will and eternal decree of God; that is, as we have just pointed out, whatever comes to pass, comes to pass according to laws and rules which involve eternal necessity and truth; nature, therefore, always observes laws and rules which involve eternal necessity and truth, although they may not all be known to us, and therefore she keeps a fixed and immutable order. Nor is there any sound reason for limiting the power and efficacy of nature, and asserting that her laws are fit for certain purposes, but not for all; for as the efficacy and power of nature, are the very efficacy and power of God, and as the laws and rules of nature are the decrees of God, it is in every way to be believed that the power of nature is infinite, and that her laws are broad enough to embrace everything conceived by the Divine intellect; the only alternative is to assert that God has created nature so weak, and has ordained for her laws so barren, that He is repeatedly compelled to come afresh to her aid if He wishes that she should he preserved, and that things should happen as He desires: a conclusion, in my opinion, very far removed from reason. Further, as nothing happens in nature which does not follow from her laws, and as her laws embrace everything conceived by the Divine intellect, and lastly, as nature preserves a fixed and immutable order; it most clearly follows that miracles are only intelligible as in relation to human opinions, and merely mean events of which the natural cause cannot be explained by a reference to any ordinary occurrence, either by us, or at any rate, by the writer and narrator of the miracle.

We may, in fact, say that a miracle is an event of which the causes cannot be explained by the natural reason through a reference to ascertained workings of nature; but since miracles were wrought according to the understanding of the masses, who are wholly ignorant of the workings of nature, it is certain that the ancients took for a miracle whatever they could not explain by the method adopted by the unlearned in such cases, namely, an appeal to the memory, a recalling of something similar, which is ordinarily regarded without wonder; for most people think they sufficiently understand a thing when they have ceased to wonder at it. The ancients, then, and indeed most men up to the present day, had no other criterion for a miracle; hence we cannot doubt that many things are narrated in Scripture as miracles of which the causes could easily be explained by reference to ascertained workings of nature.

⟹ **METAPHYSICS** ⟸

Aristotle

Aristotle (384–322 B.C.E.) was perhaps the greatest thinker of the ancient world, whose work in philosophy, theology, logic, biology, cosmology, and physics had an enormous effect for almost 2,000 years. He was a student of Plato and the teacher of Alexander the Great. Aristotle's concept of God is very different from the idea of God described in Genesis and

Exodus, though much of Aristotle's thought has been (with various degrees of success) incorporated into contemporary Western concepts of God. The following passage is from Aristotle's *Metaphysics*, Book XII.

There is, then, something which is always moved with an unceasing motion, which is motion in a circle; and this is plain not in theory only but in fact. Therefore the first heavens must be eternal. There is therefore also something which moves them. And since that which is moved and moves is intermediate, there is a mover which moves without being moved, being eternal, substance, and actuality. And the object of desire and the object of thought move in this way; they move without being moved. The primary objects of desire and of thought are the same. For the apparent good is the object of appetite, and the real good is the primary object of rational desire. But desire is consequent on opinion rather than opinion on desire; for the thinking is the starting-point. And thought is moved by the object of thought, and one side of the list of opposites is in itself the object of thought; and in this, substance is first, and in substance, that which is simple and exists actually. (The one and the simple are not the same; for 'one' means a measure, but 'simple' means that the thing itself has a certain nature.)

But the good, also, and that which is in itself desirable are on this same side of the list; and the first in any class is always best, or analogous to the best.

That the final cause may be something unmovable, is shown by the distinction of its meanings. For the final cause is (*a*) something for whose good the action is done, and (*b*) something at which the action aims; and of these the latter is unmovable though the former is not. The final cause, then, produces motion by being loved, and by that which it moves, it moves all other things. Now if something is moved it is capable of being otherwise than as it is. Therefore if the actuality of the heavens is primary motion, then in so far as they are in motion, in this *respect* they are capable of being otherwise,—in place, even if not in substance. But since there is something which moves while itself unmoved, existing actually, this can in no way be otherwise than as it is. For motion in space is the first of the kinds of change, and motion in a circle the first kind of spatial motion; and this the first mover *produces*. The first mover, then, of necessity exists; and in so far as it is necessary, it is good, and in this sense a first principle. For the necessary has all these senses—that which is necessary perforce because it is contrary to the natural impulse, that without which the good is impossible, and that which cannot be otherwise but is *absolutely* necessary.

On such a principle, then, depend the heavens and the world of nature. And its life is such as the best which we enjoy, and enjoy for but a short time. For it is ever in this state (which we cannot be), since its actuality is also pleasure. (And therefore are waking, perception, and thinking most pleasant, and hopes and memories are so because of their reference to these.) And thought in itself deals with that which is best in itself, and that which is thought in the fullest sense with that which is best in the fullest sense. And thought thinks itself because it shares the nature of the object of thought; for it becomes an object of thought in coming into contact with and thinking its objects, so that thought and object of thought are the same. For that which is *capable* of receiving the object of thought, i. e. the essence, is thought. And it is *active* when it *possesses* this object. Therefore the latter (possession) rather than the former (receptivity) is the divine element which thought seems to contain, and the act of contemplation is what is most pleasant and best. If, then, God is always in that good state in which we sometimes are, this compels our wonder; and if in a better this compels it yet more. And God *is* in a better state. And life also belongs to God; for the actuality of thought is life, and God is that actuality; and God's essential actuality is life most good and eternal. We say therefore that God is a living being, eternal, most good, so that life and duration continuous and eternal belong to God; for this *is* God.

. . .

It is clear then from what has been said that there is a substance which is eternal and unmovable and separate from sensible things. It has been shown also that this substance cannot have any magnitude, but is without parts and indivisible. For it produces movement through infinite time, but nothing finite has infinite power. And, while every magnitude is either infinite or finite, it cannot, for the above reason, have finite magnitude, and it cannot have infinite magnitude because there is no infinite magnitude at all. But it is also clear that it is impassive and unalterable; for all the other changes are posterior to change of place. It is clear, then, why the first mover has these attributes.

. . .

Our forefathers in the most remote ages have handed down to their posterity a tradition, in the form of a *myth*, that these substances are gods and that the divine encloses the whole of nature. The rest of the tradition has been added later in mythical form with a view to the persuasion of the multitude and to its legal and utilitarian expediency; they say these gods are in the form of men or like some of the other animals, and they say other things consequent on and similar to these which we have mentioned. But if we were to separate the first point from these additions and take it alone—that they thought the first substances to be gods, we must regard this as an inspired utterance, and reflect that, while probably each art and science has often been developed as far as possible and has again perished, these opinions have been preserved until the present, like relics of the ancient treasure. Only thus far, then, is the opinion of our ancestors and our earliest predecessors clear to us.

. . .

The nature of the divine thought involves certain problems; for while thought is held to be the most divine of things observed by us, the question what it must be in order to have that character involves difficulties. For if it thinks nothing, what is there here of dignity? It is just like one who sleeps. And if it thinks, but this depends on something else, then (as that which is its substance is not the act of thinking, but a potency) it cannot be the best substance; for it is through thinking that its value belongs to it. Further, whether its substance is the faculty of thought or the act of thinking, what does it think? Either itself or something else; and if something else, either the same always or something different. Does it matter, then, or not, whether it thinks the good or any chance thing? Are there not some things about which it is incredible that it should think? Evidently, then, it thinks that which is most divine and precious, and it does not change ; for change would be change for the worse, and this would be already a movement.

First, then, if 'thought' is not the act of thinking but a potency, it would be reasonable to suppose that the continuity of its thinking is wearisome to it. Secondly, there would evidently be something else more precious than thought, viz. that which is thought. For both thinking and the act of thought will belong even to one who has the worst of thoughts. Therefore if this ought to be avoided (and it ought, for there are even some things which it is better not to see than to see), the act of thinking cannot be the best of things. Therefore it must be itself, that thought thinks (since it is the most excellent of things), and its thinking is a thinking on thinking.

But evidently knowledge and perception and opinion and understanding have always something else as their object, and themselves only by the way. Further, if thinking and being thought are different, in respect of which does goodness belong to thought? For the act of thinking and the object of thought have not the same *essence*. We answer that in some cases the knowledge is the object. In the productive sciences (if we abstract from the matter) the substance in the sense of essence, and in the theoretical sciences the formula or the act of thinking, *is* the object. As, then, thought and the object of thought are not different in the case of things that have not matter, they will be the same, i.e. the divine thinking will be one with the object of its thought.

A further question is left—whether the object of the divine thought is composite; for if it were, thought would change in passing from part to part of the whole. We answer that everything which has not matter is indivisible. As human thought, or rather the thought of composite objects, is in a certain period of time (for it does not possess the good at this moment or at that, but its best, being something *different* from it, is attained only in a whole period of time), so throughout eternity is the thought which has *itself* for its object.

⇒ SUMMA THEOLOGICA ⇐
St. Thomas Aquinas

St. Thomas Aquinas (1226–1274) is widely acclaimed as one of the greatest European philosophers and theologians of the medieval period. His impact on Christian thought was enormous, and so great was his influence on the Catholic Church that for centuries he was simply known as "the theologian." It was Aquinas, more than anyone else, who endeavored to forge a synthesis between Hebraic-Christian religion and the work of the great Greek philosopher Aristotle. Aquinas wrote an enormous body of work, but his greatest work was *Summa Theologica*. In this passage, Aquinas offers his famous five proofs for the existence of God:

proofs that are still regarded as classics of their kind. The passage is taken from the Second and Revised Edition of *Summa Theologica,* and was translated by Fathers of the English Dominican Province, 1920.

First part, a, Question 2, Article 3

The existence of God can be proved in five ways.

The first and more manifest way is the argument from motion. It is certain, and evident to our senses, that in the world some things are in motion. Now whatever is in motion is put in motion by another, for nothing can be in motion except it is in potentiality to that towards which it is in motion; whereas a thing moves inasmuch as it is in act. For motion is nothing else than the reduction of something from potentiality to actuality. But nothing can be reduced from potentiality to actuality, except by something in a state of actuality. Thus that which is actually hot, as fire, makes wood, which is potentially hot, to be actually hot, and thereby moves and changes it. Now it is not possible that the same thing should be at once in actuality and potentiality in the same respect, but only in different respects. For what is actually hot cannot simultaneously be potentially hot; but it is simultaneously potentially cold. It is therefore impossible that in the same respect and in the same way a thing should be both mover and moved, i.e. that it should move itself. Therefore, whatever is in motion must be put in motion by another. If that by which it is put in motion be itself put in motion, then this also must needs be put in motion by another, and that by another again. But this cannot go on to infinity, because then there would be no first mover, and, consequently, no other mover; seeing that subsequent movers move only inasmuch as they are put in motion by the first mover; as the staff moves only because it is put in motion by the hand. Therefore it is necessary to arrive at a first mover, put in motion by no other; and this everyone understands to be God.

The second way is from the nature of the efficient cause. In the world of sense we find there is an order of efficient causes. There is no case known (neither is it, indeed, possible) in which a thing is found to be the efficient cause of itself; for so it would be prior to itself, which is impossible. Now in efficient causes it is not possible to go on to infinity, because in all efficient causes following in order, the first is the cause of the intermediate cause, and the intermediate is the cause of the ultimate cause, whether the intermediate cause be several, or only one. Now to take away the cause is to take away the effect. Therefore, if there be no first cause among efficient causes, there will be no ultimate, nor any intermediate cause. But if in efficient causes if is possible to go on to infinity, there will be no first efficient cause, neither will there be an ultimate effect, nor any intermediate efficient causes; all of which is plainly false. Therefore it is necessary to admit a first efficient cause, to which everyone gives the name of God.

The third way is taken from possibility and necessity, and runs thus. We find in nature things that are possible to be and not to be, since they are found to be generated, and to corrupt, and consequently, they are possible to be and not to be. But it is impossible for these always to exist, for that which is possible not to be at some time is not. Therefore, if everything is possible not to be, then at one time there could have been nothing in existence. Now if this were true, even now there would be nothing in existence, because that which does not exist only begins to exist by something already existing. Therefore, if at one time nothing was in existence, it would have been impossible for anything to have begun to exist; and thus even now nothing would be in existence—which is absurd. Therefore, not all beings are merely possible, but there must exist something the existence of which is necessary. But every necessary thing either has its necessity caused by another, or not. Now it is impossible to go on to infinity in necessary things which have their necessity caused by another, as has been already proved in regard to efficient causes. Therefore we cannot but postulate the existence of some being having of itself its own necessity, and not receiving it from another, but rather causing in others their necessity. This all men speak of as God.

The fourth way is taken from the gradation to be found in things. Among beings there are some more and some less good, true, noble and the like. But "more" and "less" are predicated of different things, according as they resemble in their different ways something which is the maximum, as a thing is said to be hotter according as it more nearly resembles that which is hottest; so that there is something which is truest, something best, something noblest and, consequently, something which is uttermost being; for those things that are greatest in truth are greatest in being, as it is written in Metaph. ii. Now the maximum in any genus is the cause of all in that genus; as fire, which is the maximum heat, is the cause of all hot things. Therefore there must also be something which is to all beings the cause of their being, goodness, and every other perfection; and this we call God.

The fifth way is taken from the governance of the world. We see that things which lack intelligence, such as natural bodies, act for an end, and this is evident from their acting always, or nearly always, in the same way, so as to obtain the best result. Hence it is plain that not fortuitously, but designedly, do they achieve their end. Now whatever lacks intelligence cannot move towards an end, unless it be directed by some being endowed with knowledge and intelligence; as the arrow is shot to its mark by the archer. Therefore some intelligent being exists by whom all natural things are directed to their end; and this being we call God.

⇒ THEODICY ⇐
Gottfried Wilhelm Leibniz

Gottfried Wilhelm Leibniz (1646–1716) was born in Leipzig and traveled widely in Europe throughout his life, associating with many influential people, proposing a number of large-scale cooperative research projects, studying and making contribution in almost every area of knowledge (he invented the calculus independently of Newton, and during roughly the same period), and writing a wide variety of works. He was one of the great metaphysicians, developing an elaborate system of "monads" to account for all the worldly phenomena; as the Oxford philosopher Austin Farrer once said of Leibniz's metaphysics: "His system is, if nothing else, a miracle of ingenuity, and there are moments when we are in danger of believing it." Much of that ingenuity can also be seen in his *Theodicy*, which still stands as the monumental philosophical work in the effort to answer the *problem of evil*. This reading is from *Theodicy: Essays on the Goodness of God, the Freedom of Man, and the Origin of Evil*, translated by E. M. Huggard (New Haven, CT: Yale University Press, 1952). The original work was published in 1710.

12. Use has ever been made of comparisons taken from the pleasures of the senses when these are mingled with that which borders on pain, to prove that there is something of like nature in intellectual pleasures. A little acid, sharpness or bitterness is often more pleasing than sugar; shadows enhance colours; and even a dissonance in the right place gives relief to harmony. We wish to be terrified by rope-dancers on the point of falling and we wish that tragedies shall well-nigh cause us to weep. Do men relish health enough, or thank God enough for it, without having ever been sick? And is it not most often necessary that a little evil render the good more discernible, that is to say, greater?

13. But it will be said that evils are great and many in number in comparison with the good: that is erroneous. It is only want of attention that diminishes our good, and this attention must be given to us through some admixture of evils. If we were usually sick and seldom in good health, we should be wonderfully sensible of that great good and we should be less sensible of our evils. But is it not better, notwithstanding, that health should be usual and sickness the exception? Let us then by our reflexion supply what is lacking in our perception, in order to make the good of health more discernible. Had we not the knowledge of the life to come, I believe there would be few persons who, being at the point of death, were not content to take up life again, on condition of passing through the same amount of good and evil, provided always that it were not the same kind: one would be content with variety, without requiring a better condition than that wherein one had been.

14. When one considers also the fragility of the human body, one looks in wonder at the wisdom and the goodness of the Author of Nature, who has made the body so enduring and its condition so tolerable. That has often made me say that I am not astonished men are sometimes sick, but that I am astonished they are sick so little and not always. This also ought to make us the more esteem the divine contrivance of the mechanism of animals, whose Author has made machines so fragile and so subject to corruption and yet so capable of maintaining themselves: for it is Nature which cures us rather than medicine. Now this very fragility is a consequence of the nature of things, unless we are to will that this kind of creature, reasoning and clothed in flesh and bones, be not in the world. But that, to all appearance, would be a defect which some philosophers of old would have called *vacuum formarum*, a gap in the order of species.

. . .

16. It must be confessed, however, that there are disorders in this life, which appear especially in the prosperity of sundry evil men and in the misfortune of many good people. . . .

. . .

17. But . . . the remedy is all prepared in the other life: religion and reason itself teach us that, and we must not murmur against a respite which the supreme wisdom has thought fit to grant to men for repentance. Yet these objections multiply on another side, when one considers salvation and damnation: for it appears strange that, even in the great future of eternity, evil should have the advantage over good, under the supreme authority of him who is the sovereign good, since there will be many that are called and few that are chosen or are saved.

. . .

19. Holding then to the established doctrine that the number of men damned eternally will be incomparably greater than that of the saved, we must say that the evil could not but seem to be almost as nothing in comparison with the good, when one contemplates the true vastness of the city of God. Coelius Secundus Curio wrote a little book, *De Amplitudine Regni Coelestis*, which was reprinted not long since; but he is indeed far from having apprehended the compass of the kingdom of heaven. The ancients had puny ideas on the works of God, and St. Augustine, for want of knowing modern discoveries, was at a loss when there was question of explaining the prevalence of evil. It seemed to the ancients that there was only one earth inhabited, and even of that men held the antipodes in dread: the remainder of the world was, according to them, a few shining globes and a few crystalline spheres. To-day, whatever bounds are given or not given to the universe, it must be acknowledged that there is an infinite number of globes, as great as and greater than ours, which have as much right as it to hold rational inhabitants, though it follows not at all that they are human. It is only one planet, that is to say one of the six principal satellites of our sun; and as all fixed stars are suns also, we see how small a thing our earth is in relation to visible things, since it is only an appendix of one amongst them. It may be that all suns are peopled only by blessed creatures, and nothing constrains us to think that many are damned, for few instances or few samples suffice to show the

advantage which good extracts from evil. Moreover, since there is no reason for the belief that there are stars everywhere, is it not possible that there may be a great space beyond the region of the stars? Whether it be the Empyrean Heaven, or not, this immense space encircling all this region may in any case be filled with happiness and glory. It can be imagined as like the Ocean, whither flow the rivers of all blessed creatures, when they shall have reached their perfection in the system of the stars. What will become of the consideration of our globe and its inhabitants? Will it not be something incomparably less than a physical point, since our earth is as a point in comparison with the distance of some fixed stars? Thus since the proportion of that part of the universe which we know is almost lost in nothingness compared with that which is unknown, and which we yet have cause to assume, and since all the evils that may be raised in objection before us are in this near nothingness, haply it may be that all evils are almost nothingness in comparison with the good things which are in the universe.

. . .

21. Evil may be taken metaphysically, physically and morally. *Metaphysical evil* consists in mere imperfection, *physical evil* in suffering, and *moral evil* in sin. Now although physical evil and moral evil be not necessary, it is enough that by virtue of the eternal verities they be possible. And as this vast Region of Verities contains all possibilities it is necessary that there be an infinitude of possible worlds, that evil enter into divers of them, and that even the best of all contain a measure thereof. Thus has God been induced to permit evil. . . .

23. Thence it follows that God wills *antecedently* the good and *consequently* the best. And as for evil, God wills moral evil not at all, and physical evil or suffering he does not will absolutely. Thus it is that there is no absolute predestination to damnation; and one may say of physical evil, that God wills it often as a penalty owing to guilt, and often also as a means to an end, that is, to prevent greater evils or to obtain greater good. The penalty serves also for amendment and example. Evil often serves to make us savour good the more; sometimes too it contributes to a greater perfection in him who suffers it, as the seed that one sows is subject to a kind of corruption before it can germinate: this is a beautiful similitude, which Jesus Christ himself used.

24. Concerning sin or moral evil, although it happens very often that it may serve as a means of obtaining good or of preventing another evil, it is not this that renders it a sufficient object of the divine will or a legitimate object of a created will. It must only be admitted or *permitted* in so far as it is considered to be a certain consequence of an indispensable duty: as for instance if a man who was determined not to permit another's sin were to fail of his own duty, or as if an officer on guard at an important post were to leave it, especially in time of danger, in order to prevent a quarrel in the town between two soldiers of the garrison who wanted to kill each other.

25. . . . But in relation to God nothing is open to question, nothing can be opposed to *the rule of the best*, which suffers neither exception nor dispensation. It is in this sense that God permits sin: for he would fail in what he owes to himself, in what he owes to his wisdom, his goodness, his perfection, if he followed not the grand result of all his tendencies to good, and if he chose not that which is absolutely the best, notwithstanding the evil of guilt, which is involved therein by the supreme necessity of the eternal verities. Hence the conclusion that God wills all good *in himself antecedently*, that he wills the best *consequently as an end*, that he wills what is indifferent, and physical evil, sometimes as a *means*, but that he will only permit moral evil as the *sine quo non* or as a hypothetical necessity which connects it with the best. Therefore the *consequent will* of God, which has sin for its object, is only *permissive*.

. . .

God wishes to save all men: that means that he would save them if men themselves did not prevent it, and did not refuse to receive his grace; and he is not bound or prompted by reason always to overcome their evil will. He does so sometimes nevertheless, when superior reasons allow of it, and when his consequent and decretory will, which results from all his reasons, makes him resolve upon the election of a certain number of men. He gives aids to all for their conversion and for perseverance, and these aids suffice in those who have good will, but they do not always suffice to give good will. Men obtain this good will either through particular aids or through circumstances which cause the success of the general aids. God cannot refrain from offering other remedies which he knows men will reject, bringing upon themselves all the greater guilt: but shall one wish that God be unjust in order that man may be less criminal? Moreover, the grace that does not serve the one may serve the other, and indeed always serves the totality of God's plan, which is the best possible

in conception. Shall God not give the rain, because there are low-lying places which will be thereby incommoded? Shall the sun not shine as much as it should for the world in general, because there are places which will be too much dried up in consequence? In short, all these comparisons, spoken of in these maxims that M. Bayle has just given, of a physician, a benefactor, a minister of State, a prince, are exceedingly lame, because it is well known what their duties are and what can and ought to be the object of their cares: they have scarce more than the one affair, and they often fail therein through negligence or malice. God's object has in it something infinite, his cares embrace the universe: what we know thereof is almost nothing, and we desire to gauge his wisdom and his goodness by our knowledge. What temerity, or rather what absurdity! The objections are on false assumptions; it is senseless to pass judgement on the point of law when one does not know the matter of fact. To say with St. Paul, *O altitudo divitiarum et sapientiae*, is not renouncing reason, it is rather employing the reasons that we know, for they teach us that immensity of God whereof the Apostle speaks. [Leibniz is referring to Paul's Epistle to the Romans, Chapter 11, verse 33: "O the depth of the riches both of the wisdom and knowledge of God! How unsearchable are his judgments, and his ways past finding out!"] But therein we confess our ignorance of the facts, and we acknowledge, moreover, before we see it, that God does all the best possible, in accordance with the infinite wisdom which guides his actions. It is true that we have already before our eyes proofs and tests of this, when we see something entire, some whole complete in itself, and isolated, so to speak, among the works of God. Such a whole, shaped as it were by the hand of God, is a plant, an animal, a man. We cannot wonder enough at the beauty and the contrivance of its structure. But when we see some broken bone, some piece of animal's flesh, some sprig of a plant, there appears to be nothing but confusion, unless an excellent anatomist observe it: and even he would recognize nothing therein if he had not before seen like pieces attached to their whole. It is the same with the government of God: that which we have been able to see hitherto is not a large enough piece for recognition of the beauty and the order of the whole. Thus the very nature of things implies that this order in the Divine City, which we see not yet here on earth, should be an object of our faith, of our hope, of our confidence in God. If there are any who think otherwise, so much the worse for them, they are malcontents in the State of the greatest and the best of all monarchs; and they are wrong not to take advantage of the examples he has given them of his wisdom and his infinite goodness, whereby he reveals himself as being not only wonderful, but also worthy of love beyond all things.

✦ "NON-OVERLAPPING MAGISTERIA" ✦
Stephen Jay Gould

Stephen Jay Gould was the Alexander Agassiz Professor of Zoology at Harvard University, until his recent death. He wrote many books, including his great work on evolutionary theory, *The Structure of Evolutionary Theory* (Cambridge, MA: Harvard University Press, 2002); and wonderful collections of scientific essays, dealing with many issues in biology as well as in other areas, such as *Ever Since Darwin* (New York: Norton, 1977) and *The Hedgehog, the Fox, and the Magister's Pox* (New York: Three Rivers Press, 2003). While he was an ardent opponent of "creationism" and "intelligent design" (especially of the movement to have such views taught in schools as science), he was sympathetic to religious views and often spoke to religious groups. "Non-Overlapping Magisteria," from which the following passage is taken, was published in *Skeptical Inquirer* (July/August, 1999): 55–61. It was originally published in Gould's *Leonardo's Mountain of Clams and the Diet of Worms* (New York: Harmony Books, 1998).

THERE IS NO BASIC CONFLICT BETWEEN RELIGION AND SCIENCE

Incongruous places often inspire anomalous stories. In early 1984, I spent several nights at the Vatican housed in a hotel built for itinerant priests . . . One day at lunch, the priests called me over to their table to pose a problem that had been troubling them. What, they wanted to know, was going on in America with all this talk about "scientific creationism"? One of the priests asked me: "Is evolution really in some kind of trouble; and, if so, what could such trouble be? I have always been taught that no doctrinal conflict exists between evolution and Catholic faith, and the evidence for evolution seems both utterly satisfying and entirely overwhelming. Have I missed something?"

A lively pastiche of French, Italian, and English conversation then ensued for half an hour or so, but the priests all seemed reassured by my general answer—"Evolution has encountered no intellectual trouble; no new arguments have been offered. Creationism is a home-grown phenomenon of American sociocultural history—a splinter movement (unfortunately rather more of a beam these days) of Protestant fundamentalists who believe that every word of the Bible must be literally true, whatever such a claim might mean." We all left satisfied, but I certainly felt bemused by the anomaly of my role as, a Jewish agnostic, trying to reassure a group of priests that evolution remained both true and entirely consistent with religious belief . . .

This story illustrates a cardinal point, frequently unrecognized but absolutely central to any understanding of the status and impact of the politically potent, fundamentalist doctrine known by its self-proclaimed oxymoron as "scientific creationism"—the claim that the Bible is literally true, that all organisms were created during six days of 24 hours, that the earth is only a few thousand years old, and that evolution must therefore be false. Creationism does not pit science against religion (as my opening stories indicate), for no such conflict exists. Creationism does not raise any unsettled intellectual issues about the nature of biology or the history of life. Creationism is a local and parochial movement, powerful only in the United States among Western nations, and prevalent only among the few sectors of American Protestantism that choose to read the Bible as an inerrant document, literally true in every jot and tittle.

I do not doubt that one could find an occasional nun who would prefer to teach creationism in her parochial school biology class, or an occasional rabbi who does the same in his yeshiva, but creationism based on biblical literalism makes little sense either to Catholics or Jews, for neither religion maintains any extensive tradition for reading the Bible as literal truth, other than illuminating literature based partly on metaphor and allegory (essential components of all good writing), and demanding interpretation for proper understanding. Most Protestant groups, of course, take the same position—the fundamentalist fringe notwithstanding.

The argument that I have just outlined . . . represents the standard of all major Western religions (and of Western science) today. (I cannot, through ignorance, speak of Eastern religions, though I suspect that the same position would prevail in most cases.) The *lack of conflict* between science and religion arises from a *lack of overlap* between their respective domains of professional expertise—science in the empirical constitution of the universe, and religion in the search for proper ethical values and the spiritual meaning of our lives. The attainment of wisdom in a full life requires extensive attention to both domains—for a great book tells us both that the truth can make us free, and that we will live in optimal harmony with our fellows when we learn to do justly, love mercy, and walk humbly.

In the context of this "standard" position, I was enormously puzzled by a statement issued by Pope John Paul II on October 22, 1996, to the Pontifical Academy of Sciences, the same body that had sponsored my earlier trip to the Vatican. In this document, titled "Truth Cannot Contradict Truth," the Pope defended both the evidence for evolution and the consistency of the theory with Catholic religious doctrine. Newspapers throughout the world responded with front-page headlines, as in *The New York Times* for October 25: "Pope Bolsters Church's Support for Scientific View of Evolution."

Now I know about "slow news days," and I do allow that nothing else was strongly competing for headlines at that particular moment. Still, I couldn't help feeling immensely puzzled by all the attention paid to the Pope's statement . . . The Catholic Church does not oppose evolution, and has no reason to do so. Why had the Pope issued such a statement at all? And why had the press responded with an orgy of worldwide front-page coverage? . . .

Clearly, I was out to lunch; something novel or surprising must lurk within the papal statement, but what could be causing all the fuss?—especially given . . . that the Catholic Church values scientific study, views science as no threat to religion in general or Catholic doctrine in particular, and has long accepted both the legitimacy of evolution as a field of study and the potential harmony of evolutionary conclusions with Catholic faith.

As a former constituent of Tip O'Neill, I certainly know that "all politics is local"—and that the Vatican undoubtedly had its own internal reasons, quite opaque to me, for announcing papal support of evolution in a major statement. Still, I reasoned that I must be missing some important key, and I felt quite frustrated. I then remembered the primary rule of intellectual life: When puzzled, it never hurts to read the primary documents—a rather simple and self-evident principle that has, nonetheless, completely disappeared from large sectors of the American experience.

I knew that Pope Pius XII (not one of my favorite figures in twentieth-century history, to-say the least) had made the primary statement in a 1950 encyclical entitled *Humani Generis*. I knew the main thrust of his message: Catholics could believe whatever science determined about the evolution of the human body, so long as they accepted that, at some, time of his choosing, God had infused the soul into such a creature. I also knew that I had no problem with this argument—for, whatever my private beliefs about souls, science cannot touch such a subject and therefore cannot be threatened by any theological position on such a legitimately and intrinsically religious issue. Pope Pius XII, in other words, had properly acknowledged and respected the separate domains of science and theology. Thus, I found myself in total agreement with *Humani Generis*—but I had never read the document in full (not much of an impediment to stating an opinion these days).

I quickly got the relevant writings from, of all places, the Internet . . . Having now read in full both Pope Pius's *Humani Generis* of 1950 and Pope John Paul's proclamation of October 1996, I finally understand why the recent statement seems so new, revealing, and worthy of all those headlines. And the message could not be more welcome for evolutionists, and friends of both science and religion.

The text of *Humani Generis* focuses on the *Magisterium* (or Teaching Authority) of the Church—a word derived not from any concept of majesty or unquestionable awe, but from the different notion of teaching, for *magister* means "teacher" in Latin. We may, I think, adopt this word and concept to express the central point of this essay and the principled resolution of supposed "conflict" or "warfare" between science and religion. No such conflict should exist because each subject has a legitimate magisterium, or domain of teaching authority—and these magisteria do not overlap (the principle that I would like to designate as NOMA, or "nonover-lapping magisteria"). The net of science covers the empirical realm: what is the universe made of (fact) and why does it work this way (theory). The net of religion extends over questions of moral meaning and value. These two magisteria do not overlap, nor do they encompass all inquiry (consider, for starters, the magisterium of art and the meaning of beauty). To cite the usual clichés, we get the age of rocks, and religion retains the rock of ages; we study how the heavens go, and they determine how to go to heaven.

This resolution might remain entirely neat and clean if the non-overlapping magisteria of science and religion stood far apart, separated by an extensive no-man's-land. But, in fact, the two magisteria bump right up against each other, inter-digitating in wondrously complex ways along their joint border. Many of our deepest questions call upon aspects of both magisteria for different parts of a full answer—and the sorting of legitimate domains can become quite complex and difficult. To cite just two broad questions involving both evolutionary facts and moral arguments: Since evolution made us the only earthly creatures with advanced consciousness, what responsibilities are so entailed for our relations with other species? What do our genealogical ties with other organisms imply about the meaning of human life?

Pius XII's *Humani Generis* (1950), a highly traditionalist document written by a deeply conservative man, faces all the "isms" and cynicisms that rode the wake of World War II and informed the struggle to rebuild human decency from the ashes of the Holocaust. The encyclical bears the subtitle "concerning some false opinions which threaten to undermine the foundation of Catholic doctrine," and begins with a statement of embattlement:

> Disagreement and error among men on moral and religious matters have always been a cause of profound sorrow to all good men, but above all to the true and loyal sons of the Church, especially today, when we see the principles of Christian culture being attacked on all sides.

. . . Pius presents his major statement on evolution near the end of the encyclical, in paragraphs 35 through 37. He accepts the standard model of nonoverlapping magisteria (NOMA) and begins by acknowledging that evolution lies in a difficult area where the domains press hard against each other. "It remains for Us now to speak about those questions which, although they pertain to the positive sciences, are nevertheless more or less connected with the truths of the Christian faith."

Pius then writes the well-known words that permit Catholics to entertain the evolution of the human body (a factual issue under the magisterium of science), so long as they accept the divine creation and infusion of the soul (a theological notion under the magisterium of religion).

> The Teaching Authority of the Church does not forbid that, in conformity with the present state of human sciences and sacred theology, research and discussions, on the part of men experienced in both fields, take place with regard to the doctrine of evolution, in as far as it inquires into the origin of the human body as coming from pre-existent and living matter—for the Catholic faith obliges us to hold that souls are immediately created by God.

I had, up to here, found nothing surprising in *Humani Generis*, and nothing to relieve my puzzlement about the novelty of Pope John's recent statement. But I read further and realized that Pius had said more about evolution, something I had never seen quoted, and something that made John Paul's statement most interesting indeed. In short, Pius forcefully proclaimed that while evolution may be legitimate in principle, the theory, in fact, had not been proven and might well be entirely wrong. One gets the strong impression, moreover, that Pius was rooting pretty hard for a verdict of falsity.

Continuing directly from the last quotation, Pius advises us about the proper study of evolution:

> However, this must be done in such a way that the reasons for both opinions, that is, those favorable and those unfavorable to evolution, be weighed and judged with the necessary seriousness, moderation and measure. . . . Some, however, rashly transgress this liberty of discussion, when they act as if the origin of the human body from preexisting and living matter were already completely certain and proved by the facts which have been discovered up to now and by reasoning on those facts, and as if there were nothing in the sources of divine revelation which demands the greatest moderation and caution in this question.

To summarize, Pius generally accepts the NOMA principle of nonoverlapping magisteria in permitting Catholics to entertain the hypothesis of evolution for the human body so long as they accept the divine infusion of the soul. But he then offers some (holy) fatherly advice to scientists about the status of evolution as a scientific concept: the idea is not yet proven, and you all need to be especially cautious because evolution raises many troubling issues right on the border of my magisterium. One may read this second theme in two rather different ways: either as a gratuitous incursion into a different magisterium, or as a helpful perspective from an intelligent and concerned outsider. As a man of goodwill, and in the interest of conciliation, I am content to embrace the latter reading.

In any case, this rarely quoted second claim (that evolution remains both un-proven and a bit dangerous)—and not the familiar first argument for the NOMA principle (that Catholics may accept the evolution of the body so long as they embrace the creation of the soul)—defines the novelty and the interest of John Paul's recent statement.

John Paul begins by summarizing Pius's older encyclical of 1950, and particularly by reaffirming the NOMA principle—nothing new here, and no cause for extended publicity:

> In his encyclical "Humani Generis" (1950) my predecessor Pius XII had already stated that there was no opposition between evolution and the doctrine of the faith about man and his vocation.

To emphasize the power of NOMA, John Paul poses a potential problem and a sound resolution: How can we possibly reconcile science's claim for physical continuity in human evolution with Catholicism's insistence that the soul must enter at a moment of divine infusion?

> With man, then, we find ourselves in the presence of an ontological difference, an ontological leap, one could say. However, does not the posing of such ontological discontinuity run counter to that physical continuity which seems to be the main thread of research into evolution in the field of physics and chemistry? Consideration of the method used in the various branches of knowledge makes it possible to reconcile two points of view which would seem irreconcilable. The sciences of observation describe and measure the multiple manifestations of life with increasing precision and correlate them with the time line. The moment of transition to the spiritual cannot be the object of this kind of observation.

The novelty and news value of John Paul's statement lies, rather, in his profound revision of Pius's second and rarely quoted claim that evolution, while conceivable in principle and reconcilable with religion, can cite little persuasive evidence in support, and may well be false. John Paul states—and I can only say amen, and thanks for noticing—that the half century between Pius surveying the ruins of World War II and his own pontificate heralding the dawn of a new millennium has witnessed such a growth of data, and such a refinement of theory, that evolution can no longer be doubted by people of goodwill and keen intellect:

> Pius XII added . . . that this opinion (evolution) should not be adopted as though it were a certain, proven doctrine . . . Today, almost half a century after the publication of the encyclical, new knowledge has led to the recognition of the theory of evolution as more than a hypothesis. It is indeed remarkable that this theory has been progressively accepted by researchers, following a series of discoveries in various fields of knowledge. The convergence, neither sought nor fabricated, of the results of work that was conducted independently is in itself a significant argument in favor of the theory.

In conclusion, Pius had grudgingly admitted evolution as a legitimate hypothesis that he regarded as only tentatively supported and potentially (as he clearly hoped) untrue. John Paul, nearly 50 years later, reaffirms the legitimacy of evolution under the NOMA principle—no news here—but then adds that additional data and theory have placed the factuality of evolution beyond reasonable doubt. Sincere Christians must now accept evolution not merely as a plausible possibility, but also as an effectively proven fact. In other words, official Catholic opinion on evolution has moved from "say it ain't so, but we can deal with it if we have to" (Pius's grudging view of 1950) to John Paul's entirely welcoming "it has been proven true; we always celebrate nature's factuality, and we look forward to interesting discussions of theological implications." I happily endorse this turn of events as gospel—literally good news. I may represent the magisterium of science, but I welcome the support of a primary leader from the other major magisterium of our complex lives. And I recall the wisdom of King Solomon: "As cold waters to a thirsty soul, so is good news from a far country" (Proverbs 25:25).

Just as religion must bear the cross of its hardliners, I have some scientific colleagues, including a few in prominent enough positions to wield influence by their writings, who view this rapprochement of the separate magisteria with dismay. To colleagues like me—agnostic scientists who welcome and celebrate the rapprochement, especially the Pope's latest statement—they say, "C'mon, be honest; you know that religion is addlepated, superstitious, old-fashioned BS. You're only making those welcoming noises because religion is so powerful, and we need to be diplomatic in order to buy public support for science." I do not think that many scientists hold this view, but such a position fills me with dismay—and I therefore end this essay with a personal statement about religion, as a testimony to what I regard as a virtual consensus among thoughtful scientists (who support the NOMA principle as firmly as the Pope does).

I am not, personally, a believer or a religious man in any sense of institutional commitment or practice. But I have great respect for religion, and the subject has always fascinated me, beyond almost all others (with a few exceptions, like evolution and paleontology). Much of this fascination lies in the stunning historical paradox that organized religion has fostered, throughout Western history, both the most unspeakable horrors and the most heartrending examples of human goodness in the face of personal danger. (The evil, I believe, lies in an occasional confluence of religion with secular power. The Catholic Church has sponsored its share of horrors, from Inquisition to liquidations—but only because this institution held great secular power during so much of Western history. When my folks held such sway, more briefly and in Old Testament times, we committed similar atrocities with the same rationales.)

I believe, with all my heart, in a respectful, even loving, concordant between our magisteria—the NOMA concept. NOMA represents a principled position on moral and intellectual grounds, not a merely diplomatic solution. NOMA also cuts both ways. If religion can no longer dictate the nature of factual conclusions residing properly within the magisterium of science, then scientists cannot claim higher insight into moral truth from any superior knowledge of the world's empirical constitution. This mutual humility leads to important practical consequences in a world of such diverse passions.

Religion is too important for too many people to permit any dismissal or denigration of the comfort still sought by many folks from theology. I may, for example, privately suspect that papal insistence on divine infusion of the soul represents a sop to our fears, a device for maintaining a belief in human superiority within an evolutionary world offering no privileged position to any creature. But I also know that the subject of souls lies outside the magisterium of science. My world cannot prove or disprove such a notion, and the concept of souls cannot threaten or impact my domain. Moreover, while I cannot personally accept the Catholic view of souls, I surely honor the metaphorical value of such a concept both for grounding moral discussion, and for expressing what we most value about human potentiality: our decency, our care, and all the ethical and intellectual struggles that the evolution of consciousness imposed upon us.

As a moral position (and therefore not as a deduction from my knowledge of nature's factuality), I prefer the "cold bath" theory that nature can be truly "cruel" and "indifferent" in the utterly inappropriate terms of our ethical discourse—because nature does not exist for us, didn't know we were coming (we are, after all, interlopers of the latest geological moment), and doesn't give a damn about us (speaking metaphorically). I regard such a position as liberating, not depressing, because we then gain the capacity to conduct moral discourse—and nothing could be more important—in our own terms, free from the delusion that we might read moral truth passively from nature's factuality.

But I recognize that such a position frightens many people, and that a more spiritual view of nature retains broad appeal (acknowledging the factuality of evolution, but still seeking some intrinsic meaning in human terms, and from the magisterium of religion). I do appreciate, for example, the struggles of a man who wrote to *The New York Times* on November 3, 1996, to declare both his pain and his endorsement of John Paul's statement:

> Pope John Paul II's acceptance of evolution touches the doubt in my heart. The problem of pain and suffering in a world created by a God who is all love and light is hard enough to bear, even if one is a creationist. But at least a creationist can say that the original creation, coming from the hand of God, was good, harmonious, innocent and gentle. What can one say about evolution, even a spiritual theory of evolution? Pain and suffering, mindless cruelty and terror are its means of creation. Evolution's engine is the grinding of predatory teeth upon the screaming, living flesh and bones of prey . . . If evolution be true, my faith has rougher seas to sail.

I don't agree with this man, but we could have a terrific argument. I would push the "cold bath" theory; he would (presumably) advocate the theme of inherent spiritual meaning in nature, however opaque the signal. But we would both be enlightened and filled with better understanding of these deep and ultimately unanswerable issues. Here, I believe, lies the greatest strength and necessity of NOMA, the non-overlapping magisteria of science and religion. NOMA permits—indeed enjoins—the prospect of respectful discourse, of constant input from both magisteria toward the common goal of wisdom. If human beings can lay claim to anything special, we evolved as the only creatures that must ponder and talk. Pope John Paul II would surely point out to me that his magisterium has always recognized this uniqueness, for John's gospel begins by stating *in principio erat verbum* —in the beginning was the word.

"YOU CAN'T HAVE IT BOTH WAYS: IRRECONCILABLE DIFFERENCES?"

Richard Dawkins

Richard Dawkins is the Charles Simonyi Professor of the Public Understanding of Science at Oxford University. His books include *A Devil's Chaplain* (Boston, MA: Houghton Mifflin, 2003); *Unweaving the Rainbow* (London: Penguin Books, 1998); *The Blind Watchmaker* (New York: Norton, 1986), which is his sustained attack on the design argument; and *The Selfish Gene*, 2nd ed. (Oxford: Oxford University Press, 1989). The following is from "You Can't Have it Both Ways: Irreconcilable Differences?" *Skeptical Inquirer* (July/August 1999): 62–64. It was originally published in the *Quarterly Review of Biology*, volume 72 (1997): 397–399. In this essay, Dawkins opposes any compromise with religious views, arguing that contemporary scientific explanations are fundamentally incompatible with traditional religious beliefs.

RELIGION AND SCIENCE CANNOT BE RECONCILED

A cowardly flabbiness of the intellect afflicts otherwise rational people confronted with long-established religions (though, significantly, not in the face of younger traditions such as Scientology or the Moonies). S. J. Gould, commenting in his *Natural History* column on the Pope's attitude to evolution, is representative of a dominant strain of conciliatory thought, among believers and nonbelievers alike:

> Science and religion are not in conflict, for their teachings occupy distinctly different domains . . . I believe, with all my heart, in a respectful, even *loving* concordat [my emphasis] . . .

Well, what are these two distinctly different domains, these "Non-overlapping Magisteria" which should snuggle up together in a respectful and loving concordat? Gould again:

> The net of science covers the empirical universe: what is it made of (fact) and why does it work this way (theory). The net of religion extends over questions of moral meaning and value.

Would that it were that tidy. In a moment I'll look at what the Pope actually says about evolution, and then at other claims of his church, to see if they really are so neatly distinct from the domain of science. First though, a brief aside on the claim that religion has some special expertise to offer us on moral questions. This is often blithely accepted even by the nonreligious, presumably in the course of a civilized "bending over backwards" to concede the best point your opponent has to offer—however weak that best point may be.

The question, "What is right and what is wrong?" is a genuinely difficult question which science certainly cannot answer. Given a moral premise or a priori moral belief, the important and rigorous discipline of secular moral philosophy can pursue scientific or logical modes of reasoning to point up hidden implications of such beliefs, and hidden inconsistencies between them. But the absolute moral premises themselves must come from elsewhere, presumably from unargued conviction. Or, it might be hoped, from religion—meaning some combination of authority, revelation, tradition and scripture.

Unfortunately, the hope that religion might provide a bedrock, from which our otherwise sand-based morals can be derived, is a forlorn one. In practice no civilized person uses scripture as ultimate authority for moral reasoning. Instead, we pick and choose the nice bits of scripture (like the Sermon on the Mount) and blithely ignore the nasty bits (like the obligation to stone adulteresses, execute apostates, and punish the grandchildren of offenders). The God of the Old Testament himself, with his pitilessly vengeful jealousy, his racism, sexism, and terrifying bloodlust, will not be adopted as a literal role model by anybody you or I would wish to know. Yes, *of course* it is unfair to judge the customs of an earlier era by the enlightened standards of our own. But that is precisely my *point*! Evidently, we have some alternative source of ultimate moral conviction which overrides scripture when it suits us.

That alternative source seems to be some kind of liberal consensus of decency and natural justice which changes over historical time, frequently under the influence of secular reformists. Admittedly, that doesn't sound like bedrock. But in practice we, including the religious among us, give it higher priority than scripture. In practice we more or less ignore scripture, quoting it when it supports our liberal consensus, quietly forgetting it when it doesn't. And, wherever that liberal consensus comes from, it is available to all of us, whether we are religious or not.

Similarly, great religious teachers like Jesus or Gautama Buddha may inspire us, by their good example, to adopt their personal moral convictions. But again we pick and choose among religious leaders, avoiding the bad examples of Jim Jones or Charles Manson, and we may choose good secular role models such as Jawaharlal Nehru or Nelson Mandela. Traditions too, however anciently followed, may be good or bad, and we use our secular judgment of decency and natural justice to decide which ones to follow, which to give up.

But that discussion of moral values was a digression. I now turn to my main topic of evolution, and whether the Pope lives up to the ideal of keeping off the scientific grass. His Message on Evolution to the Pontifical Academy of Sciences begins with some casuistical doubletalk designed to reconcile what John Paul is about to say with the previous, more equivocal pronouncements of Pius XII whose acceptance of evolution was comparatively grudging and reluctant. Then the Pope comes to the harder task of reconciling scientific evidence with "revelation."

> Revelation teaches us that [man] was created in the image and likeness of God. If the human body takes its origin from preexistent living matter, the spiritual soul is immediately created by God . . . Consequently, theories of evolution which, in accordance with the philosophies inspiring them, consider the mind as emerging from the forces of living matter, or as a mere epiphenomenon of this matter, are incompatible with the truth about man . . . With man, then, we find ourselves in the presence of an ontological difference, an ontological leap, one could say.

To do the Pope credit, at this point he recognizes the essential contradiction between the two positions he is attempting to reconcile:

> However, does not the posing of such ontological discontinuity run counter to that physical continuity which seems to be the main thread of research into evolution in the field of physics and chemistry?

Never fear. As so often in the past, obscurantism comes to the rescue:

> Consideration of the method used in the various branches of knowledge makes it possible to reconcile two points of view which would seem irreconcilable. The sciences of observation describe and measure the multiple manifestations of life with increasing precision and correlate them with the time line. The moment of transition to the spiritual cannot be the object of this kind of observation, which nevertheless can discover at the experimental level a series of very valuable signs indicating what is specific to the human being.

In plain language, there came a moment in the evolution of hominids when God intervened and injected a human soul into a previously animal lineage (When? A million years ago? Two million years ago? Between *Home erectus* and *Homo sapiens*? Between "archaic" *Homo sapiens* and *H. sapiens sapiens*?). The sudden injection is necessary, of course, otherwise there would be no distinction upon which to base Catholic morality, which is speciesist to the core. You can kill adult animals for meat, but abortion and euthanasia are murder because human life is involved.

Catholicism's "net" is not limited to moral considerations, if only because Catholic morals have scientific implications. Catholic morality demands the presence of a great gulf between *Homo sapiens* and the rest of the animal kingdom. Such a gulf is fundamentally anti-evolutionary. The sudden injection of an immortal soul in the time-line is an anti-evolutionary intrusion into the domain of science.

More generally it is completely unrealistic to claim, as Gould and many others do, that religion keeps itself away from science's turf, restricting itself to morals and values. A universe with a supernatural presence would be a fundamentally and qualitatively different kind of universe from one without. The difference is, inescapably, a scientific difference. Religions make existence claims, and this means scientific claims.

The same is true of many of the major doctrines of the Roman Catholic Church. The Virgin Birth, the bodily Assumption of the Blessed Virgin Mary, the Resurrection of Jesus, the survival of our own souls after death: these are all claims of a clearly scientific nature. Either Jesus had a corporeal father or he didn't. This is not a question of "values" or "morals," it is a question of sober fact. We may not have the evidence to answer it, but it is a scientific question, nevertheless. You may be sure that, if any evidence supporting the claim were discovered, the Vatican would not be reticent in promoting it.

Either Mary's body decayed when she died, or it was physically removed from this planet to Heaven. The official Roman Catholic doctrine of Assumption, promulgated as recently as 1950, implies that Heaven has a physical location and exists in the domain of physical reality—how else could the physical body of a woman go there? I am not, here, saying that the doctrine of the Assumption of the Virgin is necessarily false (although of course I think it is). I am simply rebutting the claim that it is outside the domain of science. On the contrary, the Assumption of the Virgin is transparently a scientific theory. So is the theory that our souls survive bodily death and so are all stories of angelic visitations, Marian manifestations, and miracles of all types.

There is something dishonestly self-serving in the tactic of claiming that all religious beliefs are outside the domain of science. On the one hand miracle stories and the promise of life after death are used to impress simple people, win converts, and swell congregations. It is precisely their scientific power that gives these stories their popular appeal. But at the same time it is considered below the belt to subject the same stories to the ordinary rigors of scientific criticism: these are religious matters and therefore outside the domain of science. But you cannot have it both ways. At least, religious theorists and apologists should not be allowed to get away with having it both ways. Unfortunately all too many of us, including nonreligious people, are unaccountably ready to let them get away with it.

I suppose it is gratifying to have the Pope as an ally in the struggle against fundamentalist creationism. It is certainly amusing to see the rug pulled out from under the feet of Catholic creationists such as Michael Behe. Even so, given a choice between honest-to-goodness fundamentalism on the one hand, and the obscurantist, disingenuous doublethink of the Roman Catholic Church on the other, I know which I prefer.

EXERCISES

1. In a criminal trial, the prosecution bears the *burden of proof*; that is, the prosecution must prove that the defendant is guilty, rather than the defendant being required to prove innocence. In the debate over the existence of God, which side has the burden of proof?

2. In *God's Trombones*, the poet James Weldon Johnson offers a poetic version of the Hebraic story of creation, beginning with a scene in which God says: "I'm lonely; I'll make me a world." The poetry is charming, but it raises some difficult theological questions. If God is perfect and complete, then God could hardly be *lonely*; but that leaves the question of *why* a perfect and self-sufficient God would create *anything*. Could an infinite, perfect, and self-sufficient God be a plausible candidate for Creator of the universe?

3. Consider the following positions: First, "God endowed us with the power of reason; obviously God wants us to use our reason to examine the vitally important questions concerning the nature of God and God's will. After all, we use reason when buying a car or investing in stocks or deciding on a college major; and the more important the decision, the more important it is to reason carefully about it. If we refuse to reason about religion, then we are likely to get taken by crooks and charlatans—and obviously there are a lot of them around who are posing as 'religious leaders' when their only goal is to get their hands in our pockets. Religious questions are vitally important, and it is vitally important that we use all our rational resources of reason in critically examining them." Second, "God's ways are beyond our understanding; our reason is nothing compared to God's infinite wisdom. Reason may be fine in the sciences, or in choosing which car to buy; but issues of religion are beyond reason, and only faith can guide us in the religious sphere. Thinking carefully and raising hard questions is not the right approach to a religious quest." How would you evaluate those opposing positions? Is there another alternative?

4. The philosopher/theologian Walter Terence Stace insists that:

   God is either known by revelation—that is to say, by intuition—or not at all. And revelation is not something which took place in the past. It takes place in every moment of time, and in every heart . . .

   If Stace is correct, is it then hopeless to try to convince anyone else of the existence of God? That is, would evangelism be futile? If he is correct, does real *argument* concerning the existence of God become impossible?

5. Does God *want* to be worshiped? Perhaps it is *appropriate* to worship God (that is, if God is all-powerful, all-loving, all-knowing, then maybe that sort of being is an appropriate object of worship); but could an all-powerful, completely self-sufficient being actually *want* to be worshiped? Could such a being have any *wants* at all? I want more money, and I want to be

better looking; but that implies that I am short of money and lacking in good looks. Surely God has no such inadequacies, no "wants" of any sort. Could God then *want* our worship? Could God *want* us to act well? Could God *want* us to follow the Ten Commandments?

6. If we think of God as a caring, loving God Who is also all-powerful, then the problem of evil is challenging. Does the problem of evil pose a serious problem for someone who holds the Aristotelian conception of God?

7. William James, the famous American philosopher and psychologist who lived at the end of the nineteenth century, wanted very much to believe in God. He felt that without belief in some eternal positive divine force, life would (for him) lose much of its importance and significance. After all, ultimately—in a few billion years—the Sun will burn out, the Earth will be lifeless; and all our struggles, accomplishments, and goals will be gone, utterly wiped out, there will be no memory of them; unless, that is, there is some special Consciousness that will give them eternal significance. For James, believing in such a divine force was a *useful* belief, that helps us (or at least helped him) live more confidently, successfully, and optimistically; that is, such a belief *works well*, and when a belief works well, and helps us live successfully, then that belief is *true*. For James, true beliefs aren't fixed ideals; rather, they are *tools* that guide us effectively. If this religious belief proves its worth as an effective tool that helps us to live well—that is, if we live better with the belief than without it—then the belief is *true* (according to James), in the only meaningful sense of being *true*. Like Pascal's wager, this is an argument for why we should *believe* in God; but for James, the payoff for that belief is not in heavenly bliss, but in practical psychological benefits in this immediate human animal life. Is that a satisfactory proof for the legitimacy of believing in God?

8. William James favors belief in God, but not belief in an Absolute all-powerful God. Rather, James favored belief in a God who is "but one helper . . . in the midst of all the shapers of the great world's fate." For James, this is the *healthiest* and most effective belief in God; and he poses this question:

> Suppose that the world's author put the case to you before creation, saying: "I am going to make a world not certain to be saved, a world the perfection of which shall be conditional merely, the condition being that each several agent does its own 'level best.' I offer you the chance of taking part in such a world. Its safety, you see, is unwarranted. It is a real adventure, with real danger, yet it may win through. It is a social scheme of co-operative work genuinely to be done. Will you join the procession? Will you trust yourself and trust the other agents enough to face the risk?"

In traditional conceptions of God as all-powerful, there is no question that ultimately God (and the good) will win over evil; James maintains that such a belief leads to a sense of helplessness: There is nothing we can really do to make a difference. But if the outcome is uncertain, then our efforts really do have an effect—an effect on a cosmic level! Strictly in terms of which belief "works better," how would you evaluate those alternatives?

9. William James maintained that belief in God was a very positive and useful—and thus *true*—belief that helps us live more confidently and successfully. But for James, the most useful belief was not belief in some Absolute All-Powerful God. Would belief in a powerful—but not *all*-powerful—God be a psychologically healthier belief than belief in an all-powerful God? Psychologically better than belief in no God?

A God that is less than all-powerful sounds strange to contemporary Western ears; after all, contemporary Jews, Christians, and Muslims share belief in an *omnipotent* God. If you are a believer in the traditional all-powerful God, would you be profoundly bothered if you discovered that God is *very* powerful, but not *all*-powerful?

ADDITIONAL READING

A good brief introduction to some of the key issues in philosophy of religion is presented by Brian Davies in *An Introduction to the Philosophy of Religion* (Oxford: Oxford University Press, 1982). John Hick, *Classical and Contemporary Readings in the Philosophy of Religion*, 2nd ed. (Englewood Cliffs, NJ: 1970), is a good general collection. Philip L. Quinn and

Charles Taliaferro, eds, *A Companion to Philosophy of Religion* (Oxford: Blackwell, 1997), is an outstanding collection of new essays on a wide range of issues. *Philosophy of Religion: Selected Readings*, 2nd ed., edited by Michael Peterson, William Hasker, Bruce Reichenbach, and David Basinger (Oxford: Oxford University Press, 2001), includes key essays on almost every major issue. *Philosophy of Religion: A Guide and Anthology*, edited by Brian Davies (Oxford: Oxford University Press, 2000), covers a number of topics and has very good sections on arguments for the existence of God. A very good collection of essays by contemporary writers is offered by Steven M. Cahn and David Shatz, eds, *Contemporary Philosophy of Religion* (Oxford: Oxford University Press, 1982); it focuses on contemporary writers, while *Readings in the Philosophy of Religion: An Analytic Approach*, 2nd ed., edited by Baruch A. Brody (Englewood Cliffs, NJ: Prentice-Hall, 1992), includes work ranging from Plato through Aquinas to Locke and Hume, as well as contemporary essays. A collection that features debates on key issues in philosophy of religion by major contemporary writers is Michael L. Peterson and Raymond J. Vanarragon, eds, *Contemporary Debates in the Philosophy of Religion* (Oxford: Blackwell, 2004).

While arguments for the existence of God go back at least to Plato (*The Laws*, Book X) and Aristotle (*Metaphysics*), the best known early systematic source of arguments for the existence of God is St. Thomas Aquinas, in his "Five Ways," in the *Summa Theologica*, Part I. Criticism of those arguments can be found in Hume's *Dialogues Concerning Natural Religion*, as well as in Section XI of Hume's *Inquiry Concerning Human Understanding*. Immanuel Kant's critique of traditional arguments for the existence of God can be found in the *Critique of Pure Reason* (see the chapter on "The Ideal of Pure Reason"). One of the best known twentieth-century critics of religious belief and arguments for the existence of God was Bertrand Russell. A systematic but difficult presentation of his views on religion can be found in his book on Leibniz: *A Critical Exposition of the Philosophy of Leibniz*, 2nd ed. (London: Allen & Unwin, 1937); more accessible accounts of Russell's views are found in his *Religion and Science* (London: Oxford University Press, 1935, paperback); and *Why I Am Not a Christian and Other Essays* (London: Allen & Unwin, 1957). J. J. C. Smart and J. J. Haldane conduct an extensive argument concerning the existence of God in *Atheism and Theism*, 2nd ed. (London: Blackwell, 2003).

The design argument has a long history, and it never seems to go away. Recently it has been revived by "creationists" and "intelligent design" theorists, who campaign to have the Biblical creation account or the thesis of a Designer God taught in public schools as a "scientific alternative" to Darwin's theory of natural selection. One of the better known critics of this view is Richard Dawkins; see his book, *The Blind Watchmaker* (London: Longman, 1986); and more recently, *A Devil's Chaplain: Reflections on Hope, Lies, Science, and Love* (Boston, MA: Houghton Mifflin, 2003). Another critic of intelligent design is Philip Kitcher; see his *Living with Darwin: Evolution, Design, and the Future of Faith* (Oxford: Oxford University Press, 2007). For a debate on intelligent design, based on a set of articles in *Natural History* Magazine (April 2002), go to http://www.actionbioscience.org/evolution/nhmag.html. The site contains papers favoring intelligent design as well as critiquing the view, and each author lists favorite Web links to other resources. Darwin's own views can be found in *The Autobiography of Charles Darwin* (London: Collins, 1958). Asa Gray, an American botanist who was a contemporary of Darwin's, argued that there was no conflict between natural theology and Darwinism. Gray's work can be found in *Darwinia*, edited by A. H. Dupree (Cambridge: Cambridge University Press, 1963). Kenneth R. Miller is a professor of biology at Brown University who follows the Christian religion; he explains his own reconciliation of his scientific and religious views in *Finding Darwin's God: A Scientist's Search for Common Ground Between God and Evolution* (New York: HarperCollins, 1999). Neil A. Manson has edited a superb collection of essays on the Design argument, both pro and con: *God and Design: The Teleological Argument and Modern Science* (London: Routledge, 2003).

For a very interesting and beautifully written view of the contrast between science and religion, as seen by a distinguished contemporary biologist, see the final chapter of E.O. Wilson's *Consilience*. Wilson summarizes the problem thus: "The essence of humanity's spiritual dilemma is that we evolved genetically to accept one truth and discovered another" (p. 264). Chet Raymo is a physicist-astronomer who tries to build bridges between the scientific and the spiritual; see his *Skeptics and True Believers: The Exhilarating Connection Between Science and Religion* (New York: Walker and Company, 1998).

The "problem of evil" is one of the most intractable in the philosophy of religion. There is a fascinating debate on the subject among three distinguished British philosophers: Antony Flew, R. M. Hare, and Basil Mitchell. It was first published in 1955, in *New Ideas in Philosophical Theology*, edited by Antony Flew and Alasdair MacIntyre (New York: The Macmillan Co.), and has been widely anthologized. A Christian response to the problem of evil is offered by Richard Swinburne, *Providence and the Problem of Evil* (Oxford: Oxford University Press, 1998). An interesting answer to the problem, proposed from the perspective of process theology, is offered by John B. Cobb and David Ray Griffin in *Process Theology: An Introductory Exposition* (Philadelphia, PA: Westminster Press, 1976), 69–75. Marilyn McCord Adams, *Horrendous Evils and the Goodness of God* (Ithaca, NY: Cornell University Press, 1999), offers a new slant on this ancient debate; and the anthology she edited with Robert Merrihew Adams—*The Problem of Evil* (Oxford: Oxford University Press, 1990)—is a good collection of contemporary essays on the issue. Another good collection of contemporary essays is *The Evidential Argument from Evil*, edited by Daniel Howard-Snyder (Bloomington, IN: Indiana University Press, 1996).

Pascal's Wager originates in Pascal's *Pensée*. An English translation is available by F. W. Trotter (New York: E. P. Dutton & Co., 1932), No. 233. William James discussed the argument in his essay "The Will to Believe," which formed part of *The Will to Believe and Other Essays in Popular Philosophy* (New York: Longmans, Green & Co.,1897) and is now available in *The Will to Believe and Other Essays in Popular Philosophy* (New York: Dover, 1957). Pascal's Wager is also the subject of a lively and interesting paper by William Lycan and George Schlesinger, "You Bet Your Life," which can be found in Joel Feinberg, ed., *Reason and Responsibility* (Belmont, CA: Wadsworth, 1989), 7th ed.; also in 8th, 9th, and 10th editions, and it has been anthologized elsewhere. *Gambling on God* (Lanham, MD: Rowman & Littlefield, 1994) is a good collection of articles on Pascal's Wager (Schlesinger restates the "You Bet Your Life" argument in this anthology).

Spinoza's *Ethics* is available in an excellent translation by R. H. M. Elwes. Originally done in 1883, the translation is now published in a Dover edition (New York: Dover, 1955) under the title *The Chief Works of Benedict de Spinoza*. Stuart Hampshire provides an excellent and very readable study of Spinoza's philosophy in his *Spinoza* (London: Penguin, 1951). A wonderful study of Spinoza's life and the era in which he lived is Lewis Samuel Feuer's *Spinoza and the Rise of Liberalism* (Boston, MA: Beacon Press, 1958).

The issue of direct experience of God is taken up by Michael Martin in *Atheism: A Philosophical Justification* (Philadelphia, PA: Temple University Press, 1990). For a more positive perspective, see William James, *Varieties of Religious Experience* (New York: Longmans, Green, and Co., 1923).

CHAPTER 3

WHAT CAN WE KNOW?

When we take the philosophical plunge, it seems natural enough to start by asking basic *metaphysical* questions: Questions about the ultimate nature of reality, the structure of the cosmos, and the existence of God. As the ancients developed a taste for philosophy, those are precisely the questions they posed: In ancient Greece, about 550 BC, Anaximander proposed a spherical model of the universe (with the Earth, naturally, at the center); and he claimed that the origin, starting point, and the guide of the cosmic process is the *Boundless* force which creates and governs the world.

> Out of those things whence is the generation of existing things, into them also does their destruction take place, as is right and due; for they make retribution and pay the penalty to one another for their offense, according to the ordering of time. *Anaximander*

Plato, in his deep reflections, insisted that the physical observable world is merely a poor copy of the transcendent pure Ideas that can only be known through reason. The great Hebrew king and sage Solomon taught that "there is nothing new under the Sun," and nothing really changes.

> All the rivers run into the sea; yet the sea is not full; unto the place from whence the rivers come, thither they return again. . . . The thing that hath been, it is that which shall be; and that which is done is that which shall be done: and there is no new thing under the sun. Is there any thing whereof it may be said, See, this is new? It hath been already of old time, which was before us. *Solomon, Ecclesiastes.*

Parmenides, the Greek philosopher of the fifth century BC, agreed: There is no motion, and no change, and everything "remains the same, . . . held fast in the bonds of limit by the power of necessity," and all the changes we suppose we observe are illusory. In contrast, Heraclitus—a Greek philosopher who was a contemporary of Parmenides— insisted that we "cannot step twice into the same river," for it (and everything else) is constantly changing: "Nothing endures but change." These are wonderful questions, certainly, and you may have passed some pensive hours exploring them: Is there a God? Are there many gods? Does everything change? Does nothing ever really change? Is the world of our senses and observations the ultimate reality, or is there a hidden deeper level of existence that is the true reality? Is time real? Is everything ultimately connected? Is the world just a collection of separate atoms? Is everything reducible to physical objects and physical laws? Is determinism true? Is all reality just ideas and thoughts? These metaphysical questions are fascinating, and it is hardly surprising that they charmed the ancients as indeed they charm many of us.

SKEPTICISM

Even as these great ancient philosophers and system builders were developing their views, there were also some who were *skeptical* about the possibility of answering such questions. Heraclitus might be considered a skeptic, since if everything is in constant flux, there is no possibility of gaining fixed knowledge.

> The most famous of the ancient skeptics were the *Pyrrhonians*, who took their name from their teacher and model Pyrrho of Elis. Indeed, *pyrrhonism* is still used to designate the belief in extreme skepticism, and those who hold such strong skeptical views are sometimes called *pyrrhonists*.

Socrates was famous for the "Socratic method" of posing questions, and he (reluctantly) acknowledged that he was perhaps the wisest man alive, because he *knew* that he did *not* know. But Socrates actually tended to use his probing questions to break down weaker positions and make progress toward real knowledge. The immediate follower of Socrates was Plato, the great classical philosopher who developed (what many regard as) rather extravagant metaphysical doctrines, positing a whole realm of transcendent *models* or *forms* or *Ideas* that can only be approached through special powers of pure reason, and are above and beyond what we can know through our faulty senses. But in the years following Plato—and perhaps in reaction to his rather flowery metaphysical doctrines—skeptics revived some of Socrates' arguments, and used them to promote genuine skepticism about the possibility of any real knowledge, whether gained by the senses or by reason. Among the ancient Romans, the *Pyrrhonian* school—followers of Pyrrho of Elis (who lived from approximately 360 to 270 BC)—promoted skeptical views. The moral they drew from their skepticism was that because we can never attain certain knowledge, our best path is to live quietly and modestly and seek peace of mind. Their conclusions were somewhat similar to those drawn many centuries later by the main character in Voltaire's wickedly satirical *Candide*: Candide quietly listens to all the metaphysical speculation of Dr. Pangloss (whom Voltaire models after the great metaphysician of his age, Leibniz), and concludes that perhaps it's true, or perhaps not; but in any case, "we must tend our garden": We must focus on practical work, and avoid metaphysical dreams.

Though skepticism did not disappear, it was largely eclipsed during the centuries of the medieval period. After all, the people of that age had the astronomy of Ptolemy, which gave a wonderful order to the majestic motions of the Sun, planets, and stars that orbit around our fixed Earth. And they had the physics of Aristotle, which explained the rising of heat and the falling of bricks and even the perfect spinning of the realm of fixed stars (the "fixed" stars were thought to be attached—"fixed"—to a great sphere which spun in place): They are all seeking their proper place in the great cosmic order. And then there was the authority of the Church—which did not look kindly on skeptics, treating them very harshly in this life while promising even worse in the next.

But in the sixteenth and seventeenth centuries there was a significant change in the approach to philosophical questions. Not that philosophers stopped asking the metaphysical questions about God and reality, of course; but rather, philosophers started to focus on questions that were in some ways even *more* basic. Instead of starting with questions about *what* do we know, the main questions became: *How* do we know? And even more basically: *Can* we know? *Can* we have genuine knowledge?

> *Epistemology* is the study of knowledge, and the conditions for knowledge. The word is based on the Greek word for knowledge, *episteme*.

Obviously these questions did not wait until the sixteenth and seventeenth centuries to be asked: As already noted, there were famous *skeptics* among the ancient Greeks and Romans, and many ancient philosophers—Aristotle is a clear example—were very interested in the conditions for gaining knowledge. But in the sixteenth and seventeenth centuries, these questions about knowledge—these *epistemological* questions about whether and how we gain knowledge—took on a special urgency. One source of that urgency, or perhaps a symptom of the urgency, was a widespread philosophical *skepticism*. Many people began to doubt whether real knowledge was possible at all.

> What a chimera then is man! What a novelty! What a monster, what a chaos, what a contradiction, what a prodigy! Judge of all things, imbecile worm of the earth, depository of truth, a sink of uncertainty and error; the pride and refuse of the universe!
>
> Who will unravel this tangle? Nature confutes the skeptics, and reason confutes the dogmatists. What then will you become, O men! Who try to find out by your natural reason what is your true condition? *Blaise Pascal, Pensées* (Pascal's notebooks, published in 1662, years after his death.)

Why was this such an age of skepticism? There were many reasons. For one thing, it was painfully obvious that there was a lot they did *not* know; and a lot of what people realized they did not know was very important stuff. Comets would occasionally make an appearance, totally disrupting the clockwork order of the heavens, the steady and reliable motion of the distant realm of fixed stars. Suddenly there would appear, in this orderly cycle of the heavens, a strange object with a long tail; it would appear, cross amidst the stars, and disappear as mysteriously as it had arrived. This severe disruption of the good cosmic order seemed to be a special messenger: a warning perhaps, or a signal of doom or disorder. But if a warning, was it a warning from God? And if it carried a message, the message seemed beyond our knowledge: and knowledge of such a warning, whether Divine or demonic, was knowledge that people really wanted—really wanted, but did not have. During this period, cities and towns were struck with terrible diseases: Diseases that decimated whole villages, killed entire families, and left large cities empty—with many of the inhabitants dead and the survivors fleeing for their lives from the pestilence.

> Father abandoned child, wife husband, one brother another; for this illness seemed to strike through the breath and sight. And so they died. And no one could be found to bury the dead for money or friendship. Members of a household brought their dead to a ditch as best they could, without priest, without divine offices. . . . Great pits were dug and piled high with the multitude of the dead. And they died by the hundreds both day and night. . . . I, Agnolo di Tura, called the Fat, buried my five children with my own hands. And there were also those who were so sparsely covered with earth that the dogs dragged them forth and devoured many bodies throughout the city. There was no one who wept for any death, for all awaited death. And so many died that all believed it was the end of the world. *Agnola di Tura, Siena.*

The Bubonic Plague, the dreadful Black Death, swept across Europe again and again.

> The violence of this disease was such that the sick communicated it to the healthy who came near them, just as a fire catches anything dry or oily near it. And it even went further. To speak to or go near the sick brought infection and a common death to the living; and moreover, to touch the clothes or anything else the sick had touched or worn gave the disease to the person touching. *Giovanni Boccaccio, translated by Richard Aldington.*

It would suddenly appear, ravage city after city for months, and then disappear. During the course of a few plague years, perhaps a quarter of all Europeans died—and some estimates made the death rate even higher. Months or years later it would return—and no one knew when it would come, or why, or how to avoid it.

The mood across Europe became very dark, and—not surprisingly—thoughts of death dominated. The theme of the *Danse Macabre* (or "Dance of Death") was popular, and illustrations in that distinctive style—in which skeletons, as messengers of death, interact with persons in all walks of life—were painted in churches and published as books. The two below, by the artist Hans Holbein, are from a collection he published in Lyons in 1538. They show a peddler and a Queen being abruptly seized by death. The common themes of Danse Macabre were that death could come at any time and that it was no respecter of persons.

The queen, Hans Holbein the younger, Danse Macabre, 1538, Germany (Alamy ID: B11GTT)

The peddler, Hans Holbein the younger, Danse Macabre, 1538, Germany (Alamy ID: B11KMR)

If comets and plagues weren't bad enough, the Church was breaking apart. In 1517, Martin Luther nailed his theses to the door of the Castle Church in Wittenberg (the church doors were regarded almost as a public bulletin board; the sixteenth-century equivalent, perhaps, of a blog), challenging the authority of the Catholic Church.

Luther's break with Catholicism allowed for no compromise, as indicated in the following passage:

> The world is unwilling to accept God as the true God, and the devil as the real devil, therefore it is compelled to endure their representative, namely the pope, who is the false vicar of God and the true vicar of the devil. The papacy is a government by which the wicked and those who despise God deserve to be ruled, for it is fitting that those who are unwilling to obey God of their own accord should be forced to obey a scoundrel. From P. Smith and H. Ballinger, *Conversations with Luther* (Boston, 1915).

Of course many others had hurled that challenge before, but they generally had not lasted long: Denounced as heretics, they were soon overpowered and killed. But Luther had the backing of the German princes, and the Protestant Reformation spread across Germany and other areas of central Europe, as other Protestant leaders—such as John Calvin, Huldreich Zwingli, and John Knox—spread the protest. So comets mystified, the Black Death terrified, and the old religious certainties crumbled. Who is right, Luther or the Pope? The destiny of your eternal soul might hang in the balance, and how could you know the right answer? And if you hesitated in making up your mind, the Black Death might claim you before you decided.

The Copernican Revolution

All that contributed to an atmosphere of skepticism—but there was another source for skepticism, and it was probably the most powerful skeptical force of all. If there is one thing that is certain, one fixed truth you can rely on, it is surely this: The Sun comes up in the morning, passes overhead, and goes down at night in its regular and predictable and orderly path around our Earth. You can stand there and watch as the steady old Sun rises in the East, tracks its path across the sky, and sets in the Western horizon. Of course it gradually shifts in its path: It crosses the sky at a much lower point in December than it does in June. But even that is orderly, predictable, and certain, as the path of the regular and reliable Sun shifts with the seasons. We awaken every morning on our solid, immovable Earth, and watch the Sun trace its path over our heads; at night, we can watch the glorious realm of the stars circling above us as well: Like our Sun every day, the realm of the stars orbits around our fixed Earth every night. The ways of comets, kings, and plagues may be mysterious and unpredictable, but the Sun and the stars give us one realm of fixed certainty. But then along comes Copernicus, and that last fixed truth is shattered. The astronomical system of the great ancient Greek astronomer Ptolemy had guided us for many centuries. We used the Ptolemaic system to mark our calendars, follow the phases of the moon, track the paths of the planets, navigate our ships, predict eclipses, and plant our crops. The Earth is at the center and is fixed and unmoving. The Sun orbits the Earth daily, along with the planets and the realm of fixed stars (fixed on a single great sphere that orbits around us); and beyond the fixed stars is of course the glorious realm of the heavenly hosts: the seraphims, the cherubims, all arranged in their ranks before the great throne of the perfect God.

> Perhaps you were taught in the first grade that centuries ago people believed that the Earth was flat and that Columbus was very brave to strike out across the ocean, because most people thought his ship would sail right off the edge of the flat Earth. Nonsense. The ancient Greek astronomer Ptolemy had devised the Ptoemaic astronomical system some 2,000 years before Columbus set sail; and in Ptolemy's system—which had long since been adopted by the Catholic Church, and was almost universally accepted—the Earth is a sphere at the center of the cosmos, with the moon, the Sun, the planets, and the realm of fixed stars all arranged in spherical patterns revolving around the Earthly sphere. As Columbus stated: "I have always read that the world, both land and water, was spherical, as the authority and researches of Ptolemy and all the others who have written on this subject demonstrate and prove, as do the eclipses of the moon."

And that's just the half of it. When we start to doubt that the Sun travels around a central and stationary Earth, we aren't just doubting an ancient astronomical belief. What is called into doubt is an enormous clockwork *system* of circles within circles: The fixed Earth is at the center, with the Moon, the Sun, and the planets in orbit around the Earth; and since the planets take somewhat irregular paths (that's why the Greeks named them *planets*, meaning *wanderers*) the orbits of the planets require spheres within spheres: There is a sphere for each planet, and then there is another smaller sphere that spins within that larger sphere, and the planet is attached to the smaller inner sphere (think of a bicycle traveling in a circle around you, and there is a light attached to the bicycle wheel, and all you can see is the light; the bicycle moves in a circle, while the light revolves in a smaller circle within that larger circle: The planets are like the light on the bicycle wheel, and that is why the planets seem to move in somewhat irregular paths).

When this majestic Ptolemaic clockwork was shattered by Copernicus, the Aristotelian physics that was wedded to the Ptolemaic system also collapsed. On the Aristotelian account, why does a stone fall toward Earth while hot sparks fly upward? And why do the fixed stars move in a circular motion around us? It is because each of those substances is *seeking its proper place*, or following its natural movement: the hot spark seeking its proper place by moving upward, while the stone naturally moves downward. In like manner, the realm of fixed stars spins in place, once daily. Being closest to the perfect God, it is the least changeable, but of course only God can be absolutely immutable; and so seeking to emulate God, the realm of the fixed stars makes the smallest possible change: It remains stationary, and turns in place. All of this we observe from our ideal vantage point: our stationary Earth, fixed in the very center of the whole system, which in the Christian adaptation of Aristotle becomes the perfect central point for the drama of salvation. But if we are flying and spinning through space on our orbit of the Sun, how could any element—whether fire, water, or earth—seek its proper place? And if the realm of fixed stars is no longer spinning in place to emulate God, then what *is* its purpose and goal? The great Ptolemaic-Aristotelian system of astronomy and physics were under a common threat from the Copernican revolution.

In our contemporary world of swift scientific change, theories are frequently challenged and often replaced. Einstein's relativity theory, then quantum mechanics, now string theory: Change seems to be the only scientific constant. But in the sixteenth century, the Ptolemaic-Aristotelian account of astronomy and physics wasn't just another in a series of theories; it was the *truth*, the final word. New details might be added, but no one imagined rejecting the basics of the Ptolemaic-Aristotelian theory that had dominated for almost 2,000 years.

> People give ear to an upstart astrologer who strove to show that the earth revolves, not the heavens of the firmament, the sun and the moon. . . . This fool wishes to reverse the entire scheme of astronomy; but sacred Scripture tell us that Joshua commanded the sun to stand still, not the earth. *Martin Luther, Table Talk*, 1540.

The challenge to Ptolemaic astronomy also called into question the theological system with which it had become closely linked. First of all—though this was not the major problem—there are obviously many Biblical passages which assert that the Earth is stationary and unmoving: In Psalm 93, King David asserts that "The Lord reigneth . . . the world also is stablished, that it cannot be moved." And in the Biblical account of Joshua's battle against the Amorites, Joshua asked the Lord to cause the Sun to stand still in the sky, that the Israelites might finish slaughtering their foes before darkness fell: "And the sun stood still . . . until the people had avenged themselves upon their enemies. . . . So the sun stood still in the midst of heaven, and hasted not to go down about a whole day. . . . For the Lord fought for Israel" (Joshua 10: 13–14)—not that the Earth stops spinning, but that the Sun pauses in its orbit around the Earth. But the conflict between the Copernican view and a few passages of Scripture was a comparatively minor problem, for the Copernican theory was in fundamental conflict with the entire Aristotelian/Ptolemaic/Christian cosmology that had been built up for centuries. According to the Copernican view, we are not the center of the universe, not center stage, where the drama of salvation is played out; and if each of those fixed stars is actually like our Sun (as Giordano Bruno died proclaiming), and at vast distances from us, with no end in sight (as telescopes would confirm in the next century), then where is God? Not so easy to find. And if the heavenly order is disrupted, might the secular hierarchy also be disrupted? The king and the nobility are no longer naturally at the top. The Church hierarchy—with the Pope at the top, down in order through the cardinals and bishops, and then the priests, with the lay people at the bottom following the teachings of their spiritual superiors—had already been challenged. When the fixed hierarchical celestial and spiritual orders were shaken, the reverberations were also felt in the secular order. The nobility rule in idle luxury, while the peasants labor in poverty; but is that really the fixed eternal order? Many began to question that tradition, and there were widespread peasant revolts; revolts that were ultimately crushed by the nobility with horrific savagery (a savagery blessed by both Protestant and Catholic authorities).

New philosophy calls all in doubt,
The element of fire is quite put out;
The sun is lost, and the earth, and no man's wit
Can well direct him where to look for it.
And freely men confess that this world's spent,
When in the planets, and the firmament
They seek so many new; then see that this
Is crumbled out again to his atomies.
'Tis all in pieces, all coherence gone;
All just supply, and all relation:
Prince, subject, Father, Son, are things forgot.

John Donne, *An Anatomy of the World*, 1611

Everything taught us that we are on a stationary Earth, and the Sun orbits around us. The Bible, the Church, the ancient astronomical authorities, and—above all—our own senses: They all taught us that the Earth is stationary while the Sun moves around us. And all were wrong. *We* are the ones hurtling through space and circling the Sun, rather than the other way around. And the reason the Sun *looks* like its moving is because *we* are *spinning*. But if we are wrong about *that*—about living on a fixed Earth, while the Sun circles overhead—then how could we ever be confident that we know *anything*?

The Copernican Revolution taught us two things. First, that our most cherished and obvious truths may in fact be *false*. And second, before we can draw a reliable observation about what we see, we must *take into account* the effect of our own observational position and faculties. The Sun *looks* like it's moving, but that's because we are spinning. The apple *looks* red, but perhaps that's because of the way our eyes process light. The room *feels* cold, but perhaps that's because I have a fever. The food *tastes* salty, but perhaps that is because I have an illness.

The result was that epistemology vaulted to the primary place in philosophy: Before we can ask what *really exists*, we have to consider whether we have any legitimate and reliable method for *knowing*; after all, we've now learned that we can believe we *know* with certainty things that are actually false. To find a method of gaining genuine reliable knowledge, we must take careful account of our own *perspective* and our own *powers* of gaining knowledge. Our senses have been shown to be sadly unreliable; maybe our powers of *reason* are not much better.

Skepticism was a common and reasonable response to the social, religious, astronomical, and common-sense chaos into which the world had plunged. The Church was split asunder, wars were almost constant, the threat of plague was ever present, astronomy was in turmoil, and the most basic common sense—we are stationary observers watching the Sun circling around us—was unreliable. Why should we have confidence in any claim of knowledge, whether common sense, sacred, or scientific? Indeed, skepticism was so widespread during this period that some Catholic leaders decided that if you can't beat them, maybe we should join them—or at least put skepticism to a righteous use. One of the great skeptics of the late sixteenth century was a Catholic theologian, Michel de Montaigne. He developed a battery of skeptical arguments to show that gaining knowledge—whether of the sacred or of the physical world—is beyond human powers; and he concluded that since you can never be confident that any of your views are right or that any road you have chosen will take you to a safe destination, you are better off just "staying where God put you," and not trying any new and inherently uncertain beliefs or paths. Therefore, since God saw fit to make you a Catholic, you should just stay Catholic, and not recklessly embrace new beliefs—and particularly you should not take the mad plunge into the abyss of Protestantism.

> "When I play with my cat, who knows if I am not a pastime to her more than she is to me?" *Michel de Montaigne (1533–1592), Essays*, Book II, Chapter 12.

DESCARTES

Some, like Montaigne, embraced skepticism; or if not quite embraced it, at least tried to make good use of it, and learn to live with it. But for most people, the desire for reliable knowledge is strong, and skepticism is not a comfortable resting place. Everything we had thought reliable—our observation that the Sun is moving over us, the Ptolemaic theory, the authority of the Church—had been called into question. Is it *possible* to build a reliable system of knowledge? How would you go about trying? Those were the questions René Descartes posed for himself; and in pursuing answers to those questions, Descartes brought about a major shift in the way philosophy was done. In fact, Descartes had a profound influence on the way we think about knowledge and the pursuit of knowledge—a profound influence that remains to this day, and that influences people who perhaps have never even heard of Descartes.

The first way in which Descartes shifted the focus was through the basic question he asked: Instead of *what* do we know, he asked *how* can we know? That is, before examining or constructing some catalog of what we know, we should first examine a more basic question: *How* do we gain knowledge? What process do we have to follow? How is it possible for us to be certain that we *know* something? *Is* that possible?

> Several years have now elapsed since I first became aware that I had accepted, even from my youth, many false opinions for true, and that consequently what I afterwards based on such principles was highly doubtful: and from that time I was convinced of the necessity of undertaking once in my life to rid myself of all the opinions I had adopted, and of commencing anew the work of building from the foundation, if I desired to establish a firm and abiding superstructure in the sciences. *Descartes, 1637.*

Second, Descartes—in his search for certain knowledge, and for the *method* or process for gaining real knowledge—turned to his *own capacity* for gaining knowledge: How can *I* be certain? He did not appeal to any *authority* to give him truth, whether the authority of the Church, or the King, or the Ancients. Descartes himself would be the judge of what counts as knowledge and of what method would yield knowledge.

Third, Descartes wanted to develop a *method* that would give him reliable knowledge *whenever* and *wherever* he used it, a method that others could use with equal success. Descartes certainly did not invent the scientific method of hypothesis testing; in fact, his method was very different from the scientific method. But he insisted that if knowledge were to be gained, there would have to be a reliable *method* of gaining it.

Certainty

Though Descartes made important changes in philosophical inquiry, there was one very important assumption that he shared with the earlier philosophical tradition: Genuine knowledge must be *certain*. The view that *genuine* knowledge must be absolutely *certain*— that there can be no element of doubt or contingency—is a view that traces its history back many centuries, at least to Plato. Your senses deceive you, observations are unreliable. If "seeing is believing," then we will wind up with a lot of false beliefs. That was the moral of Plato's myth of the cave.

In *The Republic*, Plato (using the voice of his great teacher, Socrates) described the human situation using an elaborate cave analogy. Suppose that we are all trapped inside a dimly lit cave; we are chained to a small ledge, jutting out from a great cliff deep in a cavern. The only light comes from a flickering fire, far below us. We cannot see the fire, but only the shadows it casts on the wall opposite us. Far below us—where we cannot see from our ledge—people walk in front of the fire, and they hold up various objects. But all that we can see is the shadows of the objects that flicker on the opposite wall. We have no idea we are in a cave, or that we are observing shadows; the cave and its shadows are the only reality we have ever experienced. Thus, we take the shadow world to be the real world; and so long as we concentrate our attention on the shadows, we will never gain any real knowledge of the truth. We may come to know a great deal about the shadow world, but we will never see the true world. Suppose that one of the prisoners escapes from his bonds, and finds his way out of the cave to the sunlit surface. At first he will be almost blinded by the bright light, and unable to see much of anything. But as his eyes adjust, he will come to understand that he was living in a world of shadows, and now he has seen the truth. If he tries to return to the cave and explain to his fellow captives about the true sunlit world, they will think he is a madman: Nothing in their shadowy experience equips them to understand the world outside the cave.

The moral of Plato's story is that we are like those persons trapped on the cavern ledge: We see the flickering shadows that reveal themselves to our senses, and take the shadows to be the reality. So long as we focus our attention on those shadows—and no matter how closely we observe them—we will never understand the genuine reality. The truth behind the shadowy appearances must be grasped by our powers of reason: Reason is the path to certain, eternal, universal truth. The flickering shadows that appear to our senses only distract us from the deep truths we find through the power of reason.

The Church adopted the same principle: Real knowledge must be certain and infallible. Reason is a gift from God, and reason can thus give us some knowledge of the nature of God; but reason is a limited resource (God gave us the special gift of reason, but we are certainly not omniscient). So we must rely on God's grace and revelation for certain, fixed, unchanging truth. The world of sensation and appearance is the Earthly world of sin, corruption, and change; turn your thoughts instead to the eternal stars, which remain changeless in their fixed orbit around our Earth of death and decay; and let the realm of the fixed stars remind you of the perfection of God, and the unchanging absolute truth that God grants us through the gifts of reason and special revelation.

While the Copernican revolution shook belief in the Ptolemaic world of unchanging fixed stars orbiting around a corruptible Earth at the center of the universe, it powerfully confirmed the problems and doubts attached to sensory observation. After all, what could be more obvious to our senses than our stationary observation of the Sun in its daily movement across the horizon? The Copernican revolution shook belief in many age-old ideas that had been regarded as certainties (such as the fundamental belief that the Earth is the unmoving center of the universe). While it led to widespread skepticism about all knowledge, it particularly undercut sensory knowledge.

Descartes and Reason

Descartes asserts that it is only the pure knowledge known by the resources of reason that can be totally reliable, and he uses the example of a lump of wax to illustrate that point. When I hold a lump of wax, and then pass it before the open fire, the ball of wax may change in its shape, become warm rather than cool, and take on a different color and texture; but though my senses observe completely different characteristics, I recognize through my rational powers that this is the same ball of wax. Thus, the model of genuine knowledge becomes knowledge we can gain through pure reason, without relying on our unreliable senses: knowledge such as the knowledge of mathematics and geometry. (Of course we can make a mathematical error, as all of us know to our sorrow; but such errors can be discovered and corrected by reason, and not by the fallible resources of sensory observation.) If a clever magician picks up two balls in her right hand and two more in her left hand, and then asks how many balls she is holding in both hands, my senses will tell me that she is holding four balls. If she now opens both hands to reveal five balls, or three, or none, I will applaud her clever trick and her skill at deceiving my senses. But no matter how many times she performs the trick, she will never convince me that two plus two does not equal four. Thus, what I know through pure reason—the truths of mathematics and geometry are good examples—is known with a level of certitude that rises far beyond what can be known through sensory observation: so far beyond that it seems a different sort of knowledge altogether. In fact, the philosophical tradition has divided knowledge into two distinct types: the *a priori* knowledge of pure reason (such as the truths of mathematics and geometry) and the *a posteriori* knowledge that is gained by experience (such as our knowledge of the weather, or of physics, or of astronomy). *A priori* knowledge is knowledge *prior* to experience; that is, knowledge that does not depend on experiential observation, but only on reason: the sort of knowledge that we can gain while sitting and reasoning in a darkened room. In contrast, *a posteriori* knowledge is knowledge that comes *from experience*, knowledge that *follows* from experience and is based on experience: *empirical* knowledge. The distinction between *a priori* and *a posteriori* knowledge has been challenged, especially since the mid-twentieth century; but it has played an important part in the history of philosophy. And in the philosophical tradition, *a priori* knowledge has usually been held in the highest esteem. All the way back to Plato, *a priori* knowledge was regarded as the highest knowledge, a knowledge that was immune to the confusions and deceptions of the senses: a knowledge that seemed to be universal, absolute, and permanent. The Ptolemaic theory might be replaced by the Copernican theory, but the *mathematics* that guided Ptolemy remains just as true for Copernicus. Observations might reveal the flaws in our system of astronomy or physics, but not in our system of mathematics.

Like the ancients, Descartes had great respect for the *a priori* truths of reason and mathematics, but he could not quite rest content with them. After all, mathematics had not been vanquished by the Copernican Revolution, and yet skepticism had become rampant. Furthermore, Descartes wasn't quite content with the contemplation of mathematical truth: He also wanted to know whether our senses can give us real knowledge of the physical world we observe: Can the senses ever be relied upon to yield genuine knowledge? And finally, Descartes was aware that even in mathematics and geometry we could make mistakes and fall into error. Impressive as mathematical truth may be, Descartes wanted to find a foundation that would support a whole body or *system* of reliable truth.

Descartes' Method of Doubt

Descartes was in search of a *method* that would reveal truth, and his search for a method was based on several fundamental assumptions. First, real truth must be *certain*. Second, if we are to have real *knowledge*, it is not enough that we happen to guess the truth, or hold true beliefs by lucky accident; rather, we must have a way of *knowing* that we know. Third, our knowledge must be established on a solid and certain *foundation*. And fourth, all our genuine knowledge must be *built up* from that solid foundation by steps that preserve the certainty at every step. To reach that goal, Descartes developed his *method of doubt*. Descartes proposed to take the very weapons of the extreme skeptics and turn them *against* the skeptics.

Descartes used all the tools and tricks of skepticism—and devised a few of his own—with the purpose of discovering some fixed, immovable, indubitable truth: some truth that *could not* be doubted, some truth that could not be shaken by the strongest skeptical assault.

If he could find such an indubitable, absolute, unshakable truth, then Descartes wanted to use it for two purposes. First, he wanted that truth to serve as a fixed and certain foundation, on which a system of certain truth could be safely constructed. And second, he wanted to study that indubitable truth to find any special identifying marks or characteristics of that truth; so that when he should encounter those marks in other inquiries, he would know he had again found certain truth; that is, so that he could *know* that he knows.

Descartes started by dismissing what most of us might regard as the best and most obvious candidates for indubitable truth: my immediate knowledge that I am sitting in a chair, that I have hands, that in my hands I am holding a book. Those are tempting starting points for beliefs that are certain. Descartes maintained that we should resist such temptations: Such beliefs are by no means as certain as we might suppose, and clearly are not *indubitable*. After all, you think it is certain that you are sitting in a chair reading a book that you hold in your hands. But perhaps you are having a very vivid dream (or since you are dreaming that you are reading your philosophy book, perhaps you regard this as a vivid nightmare). True enough, your dreams about reading philosophy books are not usually that vivid. But *some* of your dreams—those involving moonlight, soft breezes, warm sand, rippling surf (you can fill in your own dream memories)—have been very vivid indeed. Or perhaps you have been drugged, and you are experiencing a vivid hallucination. True, those scenarios hardly seem *likely*; but they are at least *possible*, and so you have not arrived at *indubitable* truth when you believe that you *know* that you are sitting in a chair reading a philosophy book. Descartes goes even further, proposing a "malevolent demon" with awesome powers who devotes all his enormous skills and strengths to deceiving you. If that were the case, perhaps even the mathematical truths that seem so evident to you could be products of demonic deception. Perhaps—to use the contemporary version of Descartes' evil demon argument—you are merely a "brain in a vat," whose thoughts are being manipulated by some evil scientist who is sitting at a keyboard typing in stimulation patterns to your brain. If your brain is stimulated by drugs, or by electrical stimulation, you can have vivid hallucinations that seem very real to you. Perhaps—as we learn more about the brain—someday someone could feed in a pattern of stimulation to your brain that would give you a strong sense that you had just worked out an elaborate logical or mathematical proof—though in fact your "reasoning" process is just as false as your sensations. If your mind/brain were under the control of such a devious thought-controlling scientist (or, in Descartes's example, under the control of a very powerful and malevolent and deceptive demon) would there still be *anything* you could know with certainty? That is, even under such extreme skeptical challenges and contrivances, is there anything that could escape doubt, anything we could still *know*, and *know* that we know?

If you have watched the science fiction film *The Matrix* you may find it much easier to imagine this scenario; in fact, the creators of the film acknowledge their debt to Descartes.

I Think, Therefore I Exist

Descartes' answer is that there *is* a bedrock certainty, an item of knowledge that each of us can confidently and assuredly *know*, no matter what wiles some powerful deceiver uses against us. And that absolutely certain and indubitable truth is: *I exist*, as a thinking thing. Even if some powerful malevolent demon exerts all its efforts to deceive me, it *cannot* deceive me about the indubitable fact that *I am thinking*, that *I am a thing which thinks*. Even if this powerful demon manages to muddle my thoughts, it remains the case that *I have thoughts*, that I am a being that is capable of thought, that I am a thinking being which *exists*. Descartes' conclusion has become a famous philosophical saying: "I think, therefore I am." Or as it is sometimes named, this is the famous *cogito*; that is, *cogito, ergo sum*: I think, therefore I am.

Descartes is careful not to overstate his exciting conclusion. He believes he has found a certainty: that he exists as a thinking thing. But at this initial stage, that is a very limited claim. He is not saying that he knows he exists as a human being, or that he has a brain or a body; rather, his claim is only that he knows of his own existence at this moment as a thing which thinks. Perhaps he is a physical object, like a brain; perhaps he is something purely ethereal; perhaps he exists only from moment to moment, and all his supposed "memories" are illusions. Nonetheless, Descartes has reached one indubitable rock bottom certainty: At whatever moment I think it, at that moment I *know* that I exist as a thinking thing.

> Archimedes, in order that he might draw the terrestrial globe out of its place, and transport it elsewhere, demanded only that one point should be fixed and immoveable; in the same way I shall have the right to conceive high hopes if I am happy enough to discover one thing only which is certain and indubitable. *Descartes, Meditation II*.

The Lasting Influence of Descartes

Okay, perhaps you don't think that's such an exciting discovery: It's not like discovering a new galaxy or a new cancer-fighting drug or a new species or a new mathematical proof. But for Descartes, in his age of extreme skepticism, it was a very exciting discovery indeed. Of course, if Descartes had thought that his "existence as a thinking thing" was the *only* thing he could rescue from skepticism, that might have tempered his enthusiasm. But having found a solid foundation of certainty from which to start, Descartes was confident he could then build up an extensive and impressive system of knowledge. Whether he was successful in that further project is obviously a disputed question. In fact, controversy arises at the very next step in Descartes' attempt to build up a system of knowledge:

> . . . in order to be able to remove it [doubt about his reasoning abilities], I must inquire whether there is a God as soon as the occasion presents itself; and if I find that there is a God, I must also inquire whether He may be a deceiver; for without a knowledge of these two truths I do not see that I can ever be certain of anything.

> *Descartes, Mediation III*

But although Descartes goes on to develop an argument for the existence of God (and of God as *not* being a deceiver) that he himself finds compelling, that argument obviously does not convince everyone. On that question, you can read Descartes' *Meditations* and decide for yourself. But whatever we conclude about the success or failure of Descartes' project to build up an extensive and reliable system of knowledge, there is little doubt that Descartes' impact on how we think about knowledge and skepticism has been profound, and that it is still felt centuries later.

Descartes' argument is fascinating, even if you are not completely convinced. After all, if you are setting out to prove that you are sitting in a chair, holding a pen in your hand, it seems a long way around to first prove that there is a God, and that God is no deceiver. And even if you think Descartes met with some success in proving that he himself exists as a thinking thing, you may have some doubts about all the rest of the justified beliefs he spins out of that starting point. But in many ways, it is not the arguments that Descartes gave that have proved most influential, but the assumptions he made in the course of his work: his foundationalism (all knowledge must be built up from a *foundation* of certainty), his insistence on certainty, and his fundamental belief that humans and human knowledge must be something special that is distinct from the grubby empirical world.

How do we gain knowledge? Descartes gives us the seductive image of the splendid, godlike, isolated, totally self-sufficient reasoner, sitting sublimely in his dressing gown before the fire, and reasoning his way to the pure ultimate indubitable deepest truths. That image is dear to those who—like Descartes—seek fixed and certain truths that can be discovered and reliably *known*, and known by my own individual rational powers. By what method can we reliably gain fixed *certain* knowledge? It is not so much Descartes' answers that shaped the subsequent debate, but the way he framed the question.

Whether one rejects or accepts Descartes' argument and method and assumptions, one element of his approach to philosophy had a profound and lasting impact. Descartes attempted to discover what we could know using our *own resources*; that is, using our rational powers (which Descartes deeply trusted), our senses (which he thought very limited and fallible), and perhaps also our own intuitions (which Descartes considered important). Rather than asking some *authority* what was true—whether the authority of the Ancients (like Aristotle or Plato) or the authority of the Church (or of Scripture)—Descartes sought out the answer for himself. Not that Descartes *rejected* the authority of the Church. Descartes may well have been a sincere believer; but in any case, challenging the authority of the Church would have been a reckless and dangerous act during that period—as Galileo and Giordano Bruno and many others learned to their sorrow—and Descartes was a very cautious man who desired a quiet, safe life. But in his philosophical work, though Descartes was careful to say positive things about the Church, he entrusted his inquiries to his own rational capacities. That trust in one's own ability to inquire, examine, and understand was a key feature of the *Enlightenment* Period which Descartes helped usher in. Even if you reached a *skeptical* conclusion, that skeptical conclusion was based on your *own* reasoning and evaluation, rather than acceptance of some authority. In pursuing philosophical inquiries, it is often helpful to read others who have explored some of the same questions—Descartes, for example. But your decision about the right conclusion must be your *own* conclusion, based on your own best efforts at exploring these questions. Whatever one thinks of Descartes' overall position, that is certainly an important part of Descartes' enduring legacy.

READINGS

⤞ MEDITATIONS 1 AND 2* ⤝
René Descartes

Descartes is often considered "the father of modern philosophy" for his strong emphasis on questions of *how* we can gain knowledge and what *methods* are reliable for gaining knowledge, as well as his strong reliance on his *own* capacities for reasoning and inquiring (rather than depending on some other source of *authority* for what can be known). In these opening *Meditations*, Descartes poses his extreme skeptical challenge, offers his own solution to that challenge, and defends his basic rationalist approach to knowledge.

MEDITATION I

Of The Things of Which We May Doubt

1. SEVERAL years have now elapsed since I first became aware that I had accepted, even from my youth, many false opinions for true, and that consequently what I afterward based on such principles was highly doubtful; and from that time I was convinced of the necessity of undertaking once in my life to rid myself of all the opinions I had adopted, and of commencing anew the work of building from the foundation, if I desired to establish a firm and abiding superstructure in the sciences. But as this enterprise appeared to me to be one of great magnitude, I waited until I had attained an age so mature as to leave me no hope that at any stage of life more advanced I should be better able to execute my design. On this account,

---

*From *Meditations on First Philosophy*, translated by John Veitch (1901).

I have delayed so long that I should henceforth consider I was doing wrong were I still to consume in deliberation any of the time that now remains for action. To-day, then, since I have opportunely freed my mind from all cares and am happily disturbed by no passions, and since I am in the secure possession of leisure in a peaceable retirement, I will at length apply myself earnestly and freely to the general overthrow of all my former opinions.

2. But, to this end, it will not be necessary for me to show that the whole of these are false—a point, perhaps, which I shall never reach; but as even now my reason convinces me that I ought not the less carefully to withhold belief from what is not entirely certain and indubitable, than from what is manifestly false, it will be sufficient to justify the rejection of the whole if I shall find in each some ground for doubt. Nor for this purpose will it be necessary even to deal with each belief individually, which would be truly an endless labor; but, as the removal from below of the foundation necessarily involves the downfall of the whole edifice, I will at once approach the criticism of the principles on which all my former beliefs rested.

3. All that I have, up to this moment, accepted as possessed of the highest truth and certainty, I received either from or through the senses. I observed, however, that these sometimes misled us; and it is the part of prudence not to place absolute confidence in that by which we have even once been deceived.

4. But it may be said, perhaps, that, although the senses occasionally mislead us respecting minute objects, and such as are so far removed from us as to be beyond the reach of close observation, there are yet many other of their informations (presentations), of the truth of which it is manifestly impossible to doubt; as for example, that I am in this place, seated by the fire, clothed in a winter dressing gown, that I hold in my hands this piece of paper, with other intimations of the same nature. But how could I deny that I possess these hands and this body, and withal escape being classed with persons in a state of insanity, whose brains are so disordered and clouded by dark bilious vapors as to cause them pertinaciously to assert that they are monarchs when they are in the greatest poverty; or clothed in gold and purple when destitute of any covering; or that their head is made of clay, their body of glass, or that they are gourds? I should certainly be not less insane than they, were I to regulate my procedure according to examples so extravagant.

5. Though this be true, I must nevertheless here consider that I am a man, and that, consequently, I am in the habit of sleeping, and representing to myself in dreams those same things, or even sometimes others less probable, which the insane think are presented to them in their waking moments. How often have I dreamt that I was in these familiar circumstances that I was dressed, and occupied this place by the fire, when I was lying undressed in bed? At the present moment, however, I certainly look upon this paper with eyes wide awake; the head which I now move is not asleep; I extend this hand consciously and with express purpose, and I perceive it; the occurrences in sleep are not so distinct as all this. But I cannot forget that, at other times I have been deceived in sleep by similar illusions; and, attentively considering those cases, I perceive so clearly that there exist no certain marks by which the state of waking can ever be distinguished from sleep, that I feel greatly astonished; and in amazement I almost persuade myself that I am now dreaming.

6. Let us suppose, then, that we are dreaming, and that all these particulars—namely, the opening of the eyes, the motion of the head, the forth-putting of the hands—are merely illusions; and even that we really possess neither an entire body nor hands such as we see. Nevertheless it must be admitted at least that the objects which appear to us in sleep are, as it were, painted representations which could not have been formed unless in the likeness of realities; and, therefore, that those general objects, at all events, namely, eyes, a head, hands, and an entire body, are not simply imaginary, but really existent. For, in truth, painters themselves, even when they study to represent sirens and satyrs by forms the most fantastic and extraordinary, cannot bestow upon them natures absolutely new, but can only make a certain medley of the members of different animals; or if they chance to imagine something so novel that nothing at all similar has ever been seen before, and such as is, therefore, purely fictitious and absolutely false, it is at least certain that the colors of which this is composed are real. And on the same principle, although these general objects, viz. a body, eyes, a head, hands, and the like, be imaginary, we are nevertheless absolutely necessitated to admit the reality at least of some other objects still more simple and universal than these, of which, just as of certain real colors, all those images of things, whether true and real, or false and fantastic, that are found in our consciousness (cogitatio), are formed.

7. To this class of objects seem to belong corporeal nature in general and its extension; the figure of extended things, their quantity or magnitude, and their number, as also the place in, and the time during, which they exist, and other things of the same sort.

8. We will not, therefore, perhaps reason illegitimately if we conclude from this that Physics, Astronomy, Medicine, and all the other sciences that have for their end the consideration of composite objects, are indeed of a doubtful character; but that Arithmetic, Geometry, and the other sciences of the same class, which regard merely the simplest and most general objects, and scarcely inquire whether or not these are really existent, contain somewhat that is certain and indubitable: for whether I am awake or dreaming, it remains true that two and three make five, and that a square has but four sides; nor does it seem possible that truths so apparent can ever fall under a suspicion of falsity or incertitude.

9. Nevertheless, the belief that there is a God who is all powerful, and who created me, such as I am, has, for a long time, obtained steady possession of my mind. How, then, do I know that he has not arranged that there should be neither earth, nor sky, nor any extended thing, nor figure, nor magnitude, nor place, providing at the same time, however, for the rise in me of the perceptions of all these objects, and the persuasion that these do not exist otherwise than as I perceive them? And further, as I sometimes think that others are in error respecting matters of which they believe themselves to possess a perfect knowledge, how do I know that I am not also deceived each time I add together two and three, or number the sides of a square, or form some judgment still more simple, if more simple indeed can be imagined? But perhaps Deity has not been willing that I should be thus deceived, for he is said to be supremely good. If, however, it were repugnant to the goodness of Deity to have created me subject to constant deception, it would seem likewise to be contrary to his goodness to allow me to be occasionally deceived; and yet it is clear that this is permitted.

10. Some, indeed, might perhaps be found who would be disposed rather to deny the existence of a Being so powerful than to believe that there is nothing certain. But let us for the present refrain from opposing this opinion, and grant that all which is here said of a Deity is, fabulous: nevertheless, in whatever way it be supposed that I reach the state in which I exist, whether by fate, or chance, or by an endless series of antecedents and consequents, or by any other

means, it is clear (since to be deceived and to err is a certain defect) that the probability of my being so imperfect as to be the constant victim of deception, will be increased exactly in proportion as the power possessed by the cause, to which they assign my origin, is lessened. To these reasonings I have assuredly nothing to reply, but am constrained at last to avow that there is nothing of all that I formerly believed to be true of which it is impossible to doubt, and that not through thoughtlessness or levity, but from cogent and maturely considered reasons; so that henceforward, if I desire to discover anything certain, I ought not the less carefully to refrain from assenting to those same opinions than to what might be shown to be manifestly false.

11. But it is not sufficient to have made these observations; care must be taken likewise to keep them in remembrance. For those old and customary opinions perpetually recur—long and familiar usage giving them the right of occupying my mind, even almost against my will, and subduing my belief; nor will I lose the habit of deferring to them and confiding in them so long as I shall consider them to be what in truth they are, viz, opinions to some extent doubtful, as I have already shown, but still highly probable, and such as it is much more reasonable to believe than deny. It is for this reason I am persuaded that I shall not be doing wrong, if, taking an opposite judgment of deliberate design, I become my own deceiver, by supposing, for a time, that all those opinions are entirely false and imaginary, until at length, having thus balanced my old by my new prejudices, my judgment shall no longer be turned aside by perverted usage from the path that may conduct to the perception of truth. For I am assured that, meanwhile, there will arise neither peril nor error from this course, and that I cannot for the present yield too much to distrust, since the end I now seek is not action but knowledge.

12. I will suppose, then, not that Deity, who is sovereignly good and the fountain of truth, but that some malignant demon, who is at once exceedingly potent and deceitful, has employed all his artifice to deceive me; I will suppose that the sky, the air, the earth, colors, figures, sounds, and all external things, are nothing better than the illusions of dreams, by means of which this being has laid snares for my credulity; I will consider myself as without hands, eyes, flesh, blood, or any of the senses, and as falsely believing that I am possessed of these; I will continue resolutely fixed in this belief, and if indeed by this means it be not in my power to arrive at the knowledge of truth, I shall at least do what is in my power, viz, suspend my judgment, and guard with settled purpose against giving my assent to what is false, and being imposed upon by this deceiver, whatever be his power and artifice. But this undertaking is arduous, and a certain indolence insensibly leads me back to my ordinary course of life; and just as the captive, who, perchance, was enjoying in his dreams an imaginary liberty, when he begins to suspect that it is but a vision, dreads awakening, and conspires with the agreeable illusions that the deception may be prolonged; so I, of my own accord, fall back into the train of my former beliefs, and fear to arouse myself from my slumber, lest the time of laborious wakefulness that would succeed this quiet rest, in place of bringing any light of day, should prove inadequate to dispel the darkness that will arise from the difficulties that have now been raised.

MEDITATION II

Of the Nature of the Human Mind; and That it is More Easily Known Than the Body

1. The Meditation of yesterday has filled my mind with so many doubts, that it is no longer in my power to forget them. Nor do I see, meanwhile, any principle on which they can be resolved; and, just as if I had fallen all of a sudden into very deep water, I am so greatly disconcerted as to be unable either to plant my feet firmly on the bottom or sustain myself by swimming on the surface. I will, nevertheless, make an effort, and try anew the same path on which I had entered yesterday, that is, proceed by casting aside all that admits of the slightest doubt, not less than if I had discovered it to be absolutely false; and I will continue always in this track until I shall find something that is certain, or at least, if I can do nothing more, until I shall know with certainty that there is nothing certain. Archimedes, that he might transport the entire globe from the place it occupied to another, demanded only a point that was firm and immovable; so, also, I shall be entitled to entertain the highest expectations, if I am fortunate enough to discover only one thing that is certain and indubitable.

2. I suppose, accordingly, that all the things which I see are false (fictitious); I believe that none of those objects which my fallacious memory represents ever existed; I suppose that I possess no senses; I believe that body, figure, extension, motion,

and place are merely fictions of my mind. What is there, then, that can be esteemed true? Perhaps this only, that there is absolutely nothing certain.

3. But how do I know that there is not something different altogether from the objects I have now enumerated, of which it is impossible to entertain the slightest doubt? Is there not a God, or some being, by whatever name I may designate him, who causes these thoughts to arise in my mind? But why suppose such a being, for it may be I myself am capable of producing them? Am I, then, at least not something? But I before denied that I possessed senses or a body; I hesitate, however, for what follows from that? Am I so dependent on the body and the senses that without these I cannot exist? But I had the persuasion that there was absolutely nothing in the world, that there was no sky and no earth, neither minds nor bodies; was I not, therefore, at the same time, persuaded that I did not exist? Far from it; I assuredly existed, since I was persuaded. But there is I know not what being, who is possessed at once of the highest power and the deepest cunning, who is constantly employing all his ingenuity in deceiving me. Doubtless, then, I exist, since I am deceived; and, let him deceive me as he may, he can never bring it about that I am nothing, so long as I shall be conscious that I am something. So that it must, in fine, be maintained, all things being maturely and carefully considered, that this proposition I am, I exist, is necessarily true each time it is expressed by me, or conceived in my mind.

4. But I do not yet know with sufficient clearness what I am, though assured that I am; and hence, in the next place, I must take care, lest perchance I inconsiderately substitute some other object in room [instead] of what is properly myself, and thus wander from truth, even in that knowledge (cognition) which I hold to be of all others the most certain and evident. For this reason, I will now consider anew what I formerly believed myself to be, before I entered on the present train of thought; and of my previous opinion I will retrench all that can in the least be invalidated by the grounds of doubt I have adduced, in order that there may at length remain nothing but what is certain and indubitable.

5. What then did I formerly think I was? Undoubtedly I judged that I was a man. But what is a man? Shall I say a rational animal? Assuredly not; for it would be necessary forthwith to inquire into what is meant by animal, and what by rational, and thus, from a single question, I should insensibly glide into others, and these more difficult than the first; nor do I now possess enough of leisure to warrant me in wasting my time amid subtleties of this sort. I prefer here to attend to the thoughts that sprung up of themselves in my mind, and were inspired by my own nature alone, when I applied myself to the consideration of what I was. In the first place, then, I thought that I possessed a countenance, hands, arms, and all the fabric of members that appears in a corpse, and which I called by the name of body. It further occurred to me that I was nourished, that I walked, perceived, and thought, and all those actions I referred to the soul; but what the soul itself was I either did not stay to consider, or, if I did, I imagined that it was something extremely rare and subtile, like wind, or flame, or ether, spread through my grosser parts. As regarded the body, I did not even doubt of its nature, but thought I distinctly knew it, and if I had wished to describe it according to the notions I then entertained, I should have explained myself in this manner: By body I understand all that can be terminated by a certain figure; that can be comprised in a certain place, and so fill a certain space as therefrom to exclude every other body; that can be perceived either by touch, sight, hearing, taste, or smell; that can be moved in different ways, not indeed of itself, but by something foreign to it by which it is touched and from which it receives the impression; for the power of self-motion, as likewise that of perceiving and thinking, I held as by no means pertaining to the nature of body; on the contrary, I was somewhat astonished to find such faculties existing in some bodies.

6. But as to myself, what can I now say that I am, since I suppose there exists an extremely powerful, and, if I may so speak, malignant being, whose whole endeavors are directed toward deceiving me? Can I affirm that I possess any one of all those attributes of which I have lately spoken as belonging to the nature of body? After attentively considering them in my own mind, I find none of them that can properly be said to belong to myself. To recount them were idle and tedious. Let us pass, then, to the attributes of the soul. The first mentioned were the powers of nutrition and walking; but, if it be true that I have no body, it is true likewise that I am capable neither of walking nor of being nourished. Perception is another attribute of the soul; but perception too is impossible without the body; besides, I have frequently, during sleep, believed that I perceived objects which I afterward observed I did not in reality perceive. Thinking is another attribute of the soul;

and here I discover what properly belongs to myself. This alone is inseparable from me. I am—I exist: this is certain; but how often? As often as I think; for perhaps it would even happen, if I should wholly cease to think, that I should at the same time altogether cease to be. I now admit nothing that is not necessarily true. I am therefore, precisely speaking, only a thinking thing, that is, a mind (mens sive animus), understanding, or reason, terms whose signification was before unknown to me. I am, however, a real thing, and really existent; but what thing? The answer was, a thinking thing.

7. The question now arises, am I aught besides? I will stimulate my imagination with a view to discover whether I am not still something more than a thinking being. Now it is plain I am not the assemblage of members called the human body; I am not a thin and penetrating air diffused through all these members, or wind, or flame, or vapor, or breath, or any of all the things I can imagine; for I supposed that all these were not, and, without changing the supposition, I find that I still feel assured of my existence. But it is true, perhaps, that those very things which I suppose to be nonexistent, because they are unknown to me, are not in truth different from myself whom I know. This is a point I cannot determine, and do not now enter into any dispute regarding it. I can only judge of things that are known to me: I am conscious that I exist, and I who know that I exist inquire into what I am. It is, however, perfectly certain that the knowledge of my existence, thus precisely taken, is not dependent on things, the existence of which is as yet unknown to me: and consequently it is not dependent on any of the things I can feign in imagination. Moreover, the phrase itself, I frame an image, reminds me of my error; for I should in truth frame one if I were to imagine myself to be anything, since to imagine is nothing more than to contemplate the figure or image of a corporeal thing; but I already know that I exist, and that it is possible at the same time that all those images, and in general all that relates to the nature of body, are merely dreams or chimeras. From this I discover that it is not more reasonable to say, I will excite my imagination that I may know more distinctly what I am, than to express myself as follows: I am now awake, and perceive something real; but because my perception is not sufficiently clear, I will of express purpose go to sleep that my dreams may represent to me the object of my perception with more truth and clearness. And, therefore, I know that nothing of all that I can embrace in imagination belongs to the knowledge which I have of myself, and that there is need to recall with the utmost care the mind from this mode of thinking, that it may be able to know its own nature with perfect distinctness.

8. But what, then, am I? A thinking thing, it has been said. But what is a thinking thing? It is a thing that doubts, understands, conceives, affirms, denies, wills, refuses; that imagines also, and perceives.

9. Assuredly it is not little, if all these properties belong to my nature. But why should they not belong to it? Am I not that very being who now doubts of almost everything; who, for all that, understands and conceives certain things; who affirms one alone as true, and denies the others; who desires to know more of them, and does not wish to be deceived; who imagines many things, sometimes even despite his will; and is likewise percipient of many, as if through the medium of the senses. Is there nothing of all this as true as that I am, even although I should be always dreaming, and although he who gave me being employed all his ingenuity to deceive me? Is there also any one of these attributes that can be properly distinguished from my thought, or that can be said to be separate from myself? For it is of itself so evident that it is I who doubt, I who understand, and I who desire, that it is here unnecessary to add anything by way of rendering it more clear. And I am as certainly the same being who imagines; for although it may be (as I before supposed) that nothing I imagine is true, still the power of imagination does not cease really to exist in me and to form part of my thought. In fine, I am the same being who perceives, that is, who apprehends certain objects as by the organs of sense, since, in truth, I see light, hear a noise, and feel heat. But it will be said that these presentations are false, and that I am dreaming. Let it be so. At all events it is certain that I seem to see light, hear a noise, and feel heat; this cannot be false, and this is what in me is properly called perceiving (sentire), which is nothing else than thinking.

10. From this I begin to know what I am with somewhat greater clearness and distinctness than heretofore. But, nevertheless, it still seems to me, and I cannot help believing, that corporeal things, whose images are formed by thought which fall under the senses, and are examined by the same, are known with much greater distinctness than that I know not what part of myself which is not imaginable; although, in truth, it may seem strange to say that I know and comprehend with greater distinctness

things whose existence appears to me doubtful, that are unknown, and do not belong to me, than others of whose reality I am persuaded, that are known to me, and appertain to my proper nature; in a word, than myself. But I see clearly what is the state of the case. My mind is apt to wander, and will not yet submit to be restrained within the limits of truth. Let us therefore leave the mind to itself once more, and, according to it every kind of liberty permit it to consider the objects that appear to it from without, in order that, having afterward withdrawn it from these gently and opportunely and fixed it on the consideration of its being and the properties it finds in itself, it may then be the more easily controlled.

11. Let us now accordingly consider the objects that are commonly thought to be the most easily, and likewise the most distinctly known, viz, the bodies we touch and see; not, indeed, bodies in general, for these general notions are usually somewhat more confused, but one body in particular. Take, for example, this piece of wax; it is quite fresh, having been but recently taken from the beehive; it has not yet lost the sweetness of the honey it contained; it still retains somewhat of the odor of the flowers from which it was gathered; its color, figure, size, are apparent (to the sight); it is hard, cold, easily handled; and sounds when struck upon with the finger. In fine, all that contributes to make a body as distinctly known as possible, is found in the one before us. But, while I am speaking, let it be placed near the fire—what remained of the taste exhales, the smell evaporates, the color changes, its figure is destroyed, its size increases, it becomes liquid, it grows hot, it can hardly be handled; and, although struck upon, it emits no sound. Does the same wax still remain after this change? It must be admitted that it does remain; no one doubts it, or judges otherwise. What, then, was it I knew with so much distinctness in the piece of wax? Assuredly, it could be nothing of all that I observed by means of the senses, since all the things that fell under taste, smell, sight, touch, and hearing are changed, and yet the same wax remains.

12. It was perhaps what I now think, viz, that this wax was neither the sweetness of honey, the pleasant odor of flowers, the whiteness, the figure, nor the sound, but only a body that a little before appeared to me conspicuous under these forms, and which is now perceived under others. But, to speak precisely, what is it that I imagine when I think of it in this way? Let it be attentively considered, and, retrenching all that does not belong to the wax, let us see what remains. There certainly remains nothing, except something extended, flexible, and movable. But what is meant by flexible and movable? Is it not that I imagine that the piece of wax, being round, is capable of becoming square, or of passing from a square into a triangular figure? Assuredly such is not the case, because I conceive that it admits of an infinity of similar changes; and I am, moreover, unable to compass this infinity by imagination, and consequently this conception which I have of the wax is not the product of the faculty of imagination. But what now is this extension? Is it not also unknown? for it becomes greater when the wax is melted, greater when it is boiled, and greater still when the heat increases; and I should not conceive clearly and according to truth, the wax as it is, if I did not suppose that the piece we are considering admitted even of a wider variety of extension than I ever imagined, I must, therefore, admit that I cannot even comprehend by imagination what the piece of wax is, and that it is the mind alone . . . which perceives it. I speak of one piece in particular; for as to wax in general, this is still more evident. But what is the piece of wax that can be perceived only by the mind? It is certainly the same which I see, touch, imagine; and, in fine, it is the same which, from the beginning, I believed it to be. But (and this it is of moment to observe) the perception of it is neither an act of sight, of touch, nor of imagination, and never was either of these, though it might formerly seem so, but is simply an intuition (inspectio) of the mind, which may be imperfect and confused, as it formerly was, or very clear and distinct, as it is at present, according as the attention is more or less directed to the elements which it contains, and of which it is composed.

13. But, meanwhile, I feel greatly astonished when I observe the weakness of my mind, and its proneness to error. For although, without at all giving expression to what I think, I consider all this in my own mind, words yet occasionally impede my progress, and I am almost led into error by the terms of ordinary language. We say, for example, that we see the same wax when it is before us, and not that we judge it to be the same from its retaining the same color and figure: whence I should forthwith be disposed to conclude that the wax is known by the act of sight, and not by the intuition of the mind alone, were it not for the analogous instance of human beings passing on in the street

below, as observed from a window. In this case I do not fail to say that I see the men themselves, just as I say that I see the wax; and yet what do I see from the window beyond hats and cloaks that might cover artificial machines, whose motions might be determined by springs? But I judge that there are human beings from these appearances, and thus I comprehend, by the faculty of judgment alone which is in the mind, what I believed I saw with my eyes.

14. The man who makes it his aim to rise to knowledge superior to the common, ought to be ashamed to seek occasions of doubting from the vulgar forms of speech: instead, therefore, of doing this, I shall proceed with the matter in hand, and inquire whether I had a clearer and more perfect perception of the piece of wax when I first saw it, and when I thought I knew it by means of the external sense itself, or, at all events, by the common sense (sensus communis), as it is called, that is, by the imaginative faculty; or whether I rather apprehend it more clearly at present, after having examined with greater care, both what it is, and in what way it can be known. It would certainly be ridiculous to entertain any doubt on this point. For what, in that first perception, was there distinct? What did I perceive which any animal might not have perceived? But when I distinguish the wax from its exterior forms, and when, as if I had stripped it of its vestments, I consider it quite naked, it is certain, although some error may still be found in my judgment, that I cannot, nevertheless, thus apprehend it without possessing a human mind.

15. But finally, what shall I say of the mind itself, that is, of myself? for as yet I do not admit that I am anything but mind. What, then! I who seem to possess so distinct an apprehension of the piece of wax, do I not know myself, both with greater truth and certitude, and also much more distinctly and clearly? For if I judge that the wax exists because I see it, it assuredly follows, much more evidently, that I myself am or exist, for the same reason: for it is possible that what I see may not in truth be wax, and that I do not even possess eyes with which to see anything; but it cannot be that when I see, or, which comes to the same thing, when I think I see, I myself who think am nothing. So likewise, if I judge that the wax exists because I touch it, it will still also follow that I am; and if I determine that my imagination, or any other cause, whatever it be, persuades me of the existence of the wax, I will still draw the same conclusion. And what is here remarked of the piece of wax, is applicable to all the other things that are external to me. And further, if the notion or perception of wax appeared to me more precise and distinct, after that not only sight and touch, but many other causes besides, rendered it manifest to my apprehension, with how much greater distinctness must I now know myself, since all the reasons that contribute to the knowledge of the nature of wax, or of any body whatever, manifest still better the nature of my mind? And there are besides so many other things in the mind itself that contribute to the illustration of its nature, that those dependent on the body, to which I have here referred, scarcely merit to be taken into account.

16. But, in conclusion, I find I have insensibly reverted to the point I desired; for, since it is now manifest to me that bodies themselves are not properly perceived by the senses nor by the faculty of imagination, but by the intellect alone; and since they are not perceived because they are seen and touched, but only because they are understood or rightly comprehended by thought, I readily discover that there is nothing more easily or clearly apprehended than my own mind. But because it is difficult to rid one's self so promptly of an opinion to which one has been long accustomed, it will be desirable to tarry for some time at this stage, that, by long continued meditation, I may more deeply impress upon my memory this new knowledge.

ON CERTAINTY*
Ludwig Wittgenstein

Wittgenstein (1889–1951) was one of the most influential philosophers of the twentieth century. Born in Vienna, he studied at Cambridge University with Bertrand Russell, and later taught there. His *Tractatus* had a powerful impact on the Vienna Circle, a group of philosophers and scientists who were attempting to develop a scientific/logical methodology for philosophy. His later works, especially his *Philosophical Investigations*, went in a rather different direction and strongly influenced the emerging analytic method in philosophy, which focused on close analysis of language as the means of solving (or often "dissolving") philosophical questions. *On Certainty* was the collection of ideas, pieced together by his editors, that Wittgenstein had sketched out toward the end of his life. The style—a collection of thoughts and ideas, often tentative, giving the sense of a work still in progress—is characteristic of his later work.

In *On Certainty*, Wittgenstein lodges an objection against an argument by a very influential early twentieth-century British philosopher, G. E. Moore. Moore attempted to fortify our commonsense beliefs (concerning the real existence of tables, chairs, and hands) against the claims of both skeptics and those "idealists" who maintain that the physical world is essentially illusory, since everything is actually just minds and ideas. Holding out a hand, Moore confidently asserts: "I know that this is a hand," *and* he insists that he knows the existence of his physical hand much better than he could possibly know any skeptical or idealist reason for doubting it. Therefore, since Moore knows that he does in fact have a physical hand, it follows that he is not a brain-in-a-vat, and thus he knows that skepticism is false. Wittgenstein responds that in everyday contexts, it might make perfectly good sense to affirm that I know I have a hand; but the skeptic's challenge operates in a very different *context*. Moore is using the context of commonsense everyday life, while the skeptic is exploring questions of what certainties could be relied upon under the most severe challenge. It is one thing to say "that is my hand" in ordinary circumstances, and something quite different when the context is one in which I am under the effect of some mind-altering drug, or when the mirrors in an arcade have left me confused and disoriented, or when I awaken—still groggy from anesthesia—having undergone an arm transplant after a severe accident and am not quite sure that I am in control of the five-fingered object I see down at the end of my arm. What is obviously true

*Edited by G. E. M. Anscombe and G. H. von Wright, translated by Denis Paul and G. E. M. Anscombe (Oxford: Basil Blackwell, 1969).

in one context may not be true in all contexts. Contextualists insist that the radical skeptical hypothesis is *not* part of the context of ordinary life, and thus in the ordinary context it *is* legitimate to assert that we know the truth of our ordinary beliefs; but (Wittgenstein argues) it is not legitimate for Moore to use the context of ordinary life when challenging the very different context of radical skepticism.

1. If you do know that here is one hand, we'll grant you all the rest.

When one says that such and such a proposition can't be proved, of course that does not mean that it can't be derived from other propositions; any proposition can be derived from other ones. But they may be no more certain than it is itself . . .

2. From its seeming to me—or to everyone—to be so, it doesn't follow that it is so.

What we can ask is whether it can make sense to doubt it.

3. If e.g. someone says "I don't know if there's a hand here" he might be told "Look closer".—This possibility of satisfying oneself is part of the language-game. Is one of its essential features.

4. "I know that I am a human being." In order to see how unclear the sense of this proposition is, consider its negation. At most it might be taken to mean "I know I have the organs of a human." (E.g. a brain which, after all, no one has ever yet seen.) But what about such a proposition as "I know I have a brain"? Can I doubt it? Grounds for doubt are lacking! Everything speaks in its favour, nothing against it. Nevertheless it is imaginable that my skull should turn out empty when it was operated on.

5. Whether a proposition can turn out false after all depends on what I make count as determinants for that proposition.

6. Now, can one enumerate what one knows (like Moore)? Straight off like that, I believe not.—For otherwise the expression "I know" gets misused. And through this misuse a queer and extremely important mental state seems to be revealed.

7. My life shews that I know or am certain that there is a chair over there, or a door, and so on.—I tell a friend e.g. "Take that chair over there", "Shut the door", etc. etc.

. . .

18. "I know" often means: I have the proper grounds for my statement. So if the other person is acquainted with the language-game, he would admit that I know. The other, if he is acquainted with the language-game, must be able to imagine how one may know something of the kind.

19. The statement "I know that here is a hand" may then be continued: "for it's my hand that I'm looking at". Then a reasonable man will not doubt that I know.—Nor will the idealist; rather he will say that he was not dealing with the practical doubt which is being dismissed, but there is a further doubt behind that one.—That this is an illusion has to be shewn in a different way.

20. "Doubting the existence of the external world" does not mean for example doubting the existence of a planet, which later observations proved to exist.—Or does Moore want to say that knowing that here is his hand is different in kind from knowing the existence of the planet Saturn? Otherwise it would be possible to point out the discovery of the planet Saturn to the doubters and say that its existence has been proved, and hence the existence of the external world as well.

21. Moore's view really comes down to this: the concept 'know' is analogous to the concepts 'believe', 'surmise', 'doubt', 'be convinced' in that the statement "I know . . ." can't be a mistake. And if that is so, then there can be an inference from such an utterance to the truth of an assertion. And here the form "I thought I knew" is being overlooked.—But if this latter is inadmissible, then a mistake in the assertion must be logically impossible too. And anyone who is acquainted with the language-game must realize this—an assurance from a reliable man that he knows cannot contribute anything.

22. It would surely be remarkable if we had to believe the reliable person who says "I can't be wrong"; or who says "I am not wrong".

23. If I don't know whether someone has two hands (say, whether they have been amputated or not) I shall believe his assurance that he has two hands, if he is trustworthy. And if he says he knows it, that can only signify to me that he has been able to make sure, and hence that his arms are e.g. not still concealed by coverings and bandages, etc. etc. My believing the trustworthy man stems from my admitting that it is possible for him to make sure. But someone who says that perhaps there are no physical objects makes no such admission.

24. The idealist's question would be something like: "What right have I not to doubt the existence of my hands?" (And to that the answer can't be: I know that they exist.) But someone who asks such a question is overlooking the fact that a doubt about existence only works in a language-game. Hence, that we should first have to ask: what would such a doubt be like?, and don't understand this straight off.

. . .

32. It's not a matter of Moore's knowing that there's a hand there, but rather we should not understand him if he were to say "Of course I may be wrong about this". We should ask "What is it like to make such a mistake as that?"—e.g. what's it like to discover that it was a mistake?

35. But can't it be imagined that there should be no physical objects? I don't know. And yet "There are physical objects" is nonsense. Is it supposed to be an empirical proposition?—And is this an empirical proposition: "There seem to be physical objects"?

. . .

37. But is it an adequate answer to the scepticism of the idealist, or the assurances of the realist, to say that "There are physical objects" is nonsense? For them after all it is not nonsense. It would, however, be an answer to say: this assertion, or its opposite is a misfiring attempt to express what can't be expressed like that. And that it does misfire can be shewn; but that isn't the end of the matter. We need to realize that what presents itself to us as the first expression of a difficulty, or of its solution, may as yet not be correctly expressed at all. Just as one who has a just censure of a picture to make will often at first offer the censure where it does not belong, and an investigation is needed in order to find the right point of attack for the critic.

. . .

52. This situation is thus not the same for a proposition like "At this distance from the sun there is a planet" and "Here is a hand" (namely my own hand). The second can't be called a hypothesis. But there isn't a sharp boundary line between them.

53. So one might grant that Moore was right, if he is interpreted like this: a proposition saying that here is a physical object may have the same logical status as one saying that here is a red patch.

54. For it is not true that a mistake merely gets more and more improbable as we pass from the planet to my own hand. No: at some point it has ceased to be conceivable.

This is already suggested by the following: if it were not so, it would also be conceivable that we should be wrong in every statement about physical objects; that any we ever make are mistaken.

55. So is the hypothesis possible, that all the things around us don't exist? Would that not be like the hypothesis of our having miscalculated in all our calculations?

56. When one says: "Perhaps this planet doesn't exist and the light-phenomenon arises in some other way", then after all one needs an example of an object which does exist. This doesn't exist,—as for example does. . . .

Or are we to say that certainty is merely a constructed point to which some things approximate more, some less closely? No. Doubt gradually loses its sense. This language-game just is like that.

And everything descriptive of a language-game is part of logic.

. . .

83. The truth of certain empirical propositions belongs to our frame of reference.

84. Moore says he knows that the earth existed long before his birth. And put like that it seems to be a personal statement about him, even if it is in addition a statement about the physical world. Now it is philosophically uninteresting whether Moore knows this or that, but it is interesting that, and how, it can be known. If Moore had informed us that he knew the distance separating certain stars, we might conclude from that that he had made some special investigations, and we shall want to know what these were. But Moore chooses precisely a case in which we all seem to know the same as he, and without being able to say how. I believe e.g. that I know as much about this matter (the existence of the earth) as Moore does, and if he knows that it is as he says, then I know it too.

. . .

105. All testing, all confirmation and disconfirmation of a hypothesis takes place already within a system. And this system is not a more or less arbitrary and doubtful point of departure for all our arguments: no, it belongs to the essence of what we call an argument. The system is not so much the point of departure, as the element in which arguments have their life.

. . .

111. "I know that I have never been on the moon." That sounds quite different in the circumstances which actually hold, to the way it would sound if a good many men had been on the moon, and some perhaps without knowing it. In this case one could give grounds for this knowledge. Is there not a relationship here similar to that between the general rule of multiplying and particular multiplications that have been carried out?

I want to say: my not having been on the moon is as sure a thing for me as any grounds I could give for it.

112. And isn't that what Moore wants to say, when he says he knows all these things?—But is his knowing it really what is in question, and not rather that some of these propositions must be solid for us?

113. When someone is trying to teach us mathematics, he will not begin by assuring us that he knows that a + b = b + a.

114. If you are not certain of any fact, you cannot be certain of the meaning of your words either.

115. If you tried to doubt everything you would not get as far as doubting anything. The game of doubting itself presupposes certainty.

116. Instead of "I know . . .", couldn't Moore have said: "It stands fast for me that . . ."? And further: "It stands fast for me and many others. . . ."

. . .

136. When Moore says he knows such and such, he is really enumerating a lot of empirical propositions which we affirm without special testing; propositions, that is, which have a peculiar logical role in the system of our empirical propositions.

. . .

151. I should like to say: Moore does not know what he asserts he knows, but it stands fast for him, as also for me; regarding it as absolutely solid is part of our method of doubt and enquiry.

152. I do not explicitly learn the propositions that stand fast for me. I can discover them subsequently like the axis around which a body rotates. This axis is not fixed in the sense that anything holds it fast, but the movement around it determines its immobility.

. . .

155. In certain circumstances a man cannot make a mistake. ("Can" is here used logically, and the proposition does not mean that a man cannot say anything false in those circumstances.) If Moore were to pronounce the opposite of those propositions which he declares certain, we should not just not share his opinion: we should regard him as demented.

. . .

185. It would strike me as ridiculous to want to doubt the existence of Napoleon; but if someone doubted the existence of the earth 150 years ago, perhaps I should be more willing to listen, for now he is doubting our whole system of evidence. It does not strike me as if this system were more certain than a certainty within it.

. . .

247. What would it be like to doubt now whether I have two hands? Why can't I imagine it at all? What would I believe if I didn't believe that? So far I have no system at all within which this doubt might exist.

248. I have arrived at the rock bottom of my convictions.

And one might almost say that these foundation-walls are carried by the whole house.

249. One gives oneself a false picture of doubt.

250. My having two hands is, in normal circumstances, as certain as anything that I could produce in evidence for it.

That is why I am not in a position to take the sight of my hand as evidence for it.

. . .

279. It is quite sure that motor cars don't grow out of the earth. We feel that if someone could believe the contrary he could believe everything that we say is untrue, and could question everything that we hold to be sure.

But how does this one belief hang together with all the rest? We should like to say that someone who could believe that does not accept our whole system of verification.

This system is something that a human being acquires by means of observation and instruction. I intentionally do not say "learns".

. . .

403. To say of man, in Moore's sense, that he knows something; that what he says is therefore unconditionally the truth, seems wrong to me.—It is the truth only inasmuch as it is an unmoving foundation of his language-games.

404. I want to say: it's not that on some points men know the truth with perfect certainty. No: perfect certainty is only a matter of their attitude.

405. But of course there is still a mistake even here.

406. What I am aiming at is also found in the difference between the casual observation "I know that that's a . . .", as it might be used in ordinary life, and the same utterance when a philosopher makes it.

407. For when Moore says "I know that that's . . ." I want to reply "you don't know anything!"—and yet I would not say that to anyone who was speaking without philosophical intention. That is, I feel (rightly?) that these two mean to say something different.

. . .

410. Our knowledge forms an enormous system. And only within this system has a particular bit the value we give it.

. . .

445. But if I say "I have two hands", what can I add to indicate reliability? At the most that the circumstances are the ordinary ones.

446. But why am I so certain that this is my hand? Doesn't the whole language-game rest on this kind of certainty?

Or: isn't this 'certainty' already presupposed in the language-game? Namely by virtue of the fact that one is not playing the game, or is playing it wrong, if one does not recognize objects with certainty.

. . .

481. When one hears Moore say "I *know* that's a tree," one suddenly understands those who think that that has by no means been settled.

The matter strikes one all at once as being unclear and blurred. It is as if Moore had put it in the wrong light.

It is as if I were to see a painting (say a painted stage set) and recognize what it represents from a long way off at once and without the slightest doubt. But now I step nearer: and then I see a lot of patches of different colours, which are all highly ambiguous and do not provide any certainty whatever.

482. It is as if "I know" did not tolerate a metaphysical emphasis.

483. The correct use of the expression "I know". Someone with bad sight asks me: do you believe that the thing we can see there is a tree? I reply "I *know* it is; I can see it clearly and am familiar with it."

. . .

495. One might simply say "O, rubbish!" to someone who wanted to make objections to the propositions that are beyond doubt. That is, not reply to him but admonish him.

. . .

498. The queer thing is that even though I find it quite correct for someone to say "Rubbish!" and so brush aside the attempt to confuse him with doubts at bedrock,—nevertheless, I hold it to be incorrect if he seeks to defend himself (using, e.g., the words "I know").

. . .

520. Moore has every right to say he knows there's a tree there in front of him. Naturally he may be wrong. (For it is *not* the same as with the utterance "I believe there is a tree there.") But whether he is right or wrong in this case is of no philosophical importance. If Moore is attacking those who say that one cannot really know such a thing, he can't do it by assuring them that *he* knows this and that. For one need not believe him. If his opponents had asserted that one could not *believe* this and that, then he could have replied: "I believe it."

521. Moore's mistake lies in this—countering the assertion that one cannot know that by saying "I do know it."

EXERCISES

1. The Copernican challenge to *Ptolemaic astronomy* had a shattering impact on the belief system of the sixteenth century. Can you think of any contemporary widespread belief or theory that would produce a comparable skeptical effect if it were called into question? That is, is there any basic belief that is as basic to our world view as the Ptolemaic view was to the people of the sixteenth century?

2. It may seem strange that *Reason* should hold such an exalted place in the philosophical tradition, from Plato through the eighteenth century (and for many philosophers, all the way to the present), in contrast to sensory experience, which is regarded somewhat suspiciously, or even scorned. After all, our senses often seem to us the best guide to knowledge: "Seeing is believing," as the old saying goes. In John's account, Doubting Thomas states that he will refuse to believe that Jesus rose from the dead, "Except I shall see in his hands the print of the nails, and put my finger into the print of the nails, and thrust my hand into his side." That is, Thomas required *sensory* proof; notably, Thomas did *not* say: I will not believe until I have *reasoned* carefully and concluded that Jesus rose from the dead. Why would the philosophical tradition place such great emphasis on the powers of reason, rather than on the senses?

3. In his quest to defeat skepticism and establish genuine knowledge, Descartes went in search of knowledge that was absolutely certain and beyond doubt; and he believed that all genuine knowledge would have to be built up from such a certain foundation. Do you agree with Descartes that, first, all genuine knowledge must be built up from a reliable *foundation*? (That is, if you claim to really *know* something, do you believe that you must be able to trace that knowledge claim back to some *foundation* of knowledge? Or could you have genuine knowledge that cannot be traced to some foundational base?) And second, do you agree with Descartes that genuine knowledge must have a basis in indubitable *certainty*? (That is, would it be possible to gain genuine knowledge even if we never gain absolute *certainty* about anything?)

4. Is there a single *method* of gaining knowledge? Or might some knowledge come from the use of one method, and other knowledge come from use of a completely different method? (For example, does all genuine knowledge have to be based on something like the scientific method?)

5. For many people, skepticism seems in fundamental conflict with religious belief; indeed, one term often used for those who question religious belief is "skeptic." And yet skepticism is often a prominent element of religion; as noted, Montaigne—in attempting to counter the Protestant Reformation—made use of skeptical arguments, to conclude that we could never have good grounds for claims of knowledge, and so we are better off "staying where God placed us" (in the Catholic Church) rather than stumbling around with no clear direction. And Biblical tradition often emphasizes the puny rational resources of humans in comparison to the great wisdom and power of God, with the implication being that humans are foolish—indeed, arrogant, and evil—when they try to rely on their own powers of reason to discover answers. For example, consider the book of Job. Job, who was a faithful and even exemplary servant of God, is treated very cruelly: All his children are killed, his great wealth is taken from him, and his body is afflicted with terrible agonizing diseases. Finally, Job had had enough, and he wants to know from God why He has allowed all these terrible things to occur: "Even today is my complaint bitter. . . . Oh that I knew where I might find him! That I might come even to his seat! I would order my cause before him, and fill my mouth with arguments. I would know the words which he would answer me, and understand what he would say to me." And so God does answer Job, but not to explain or give Job understanding. Quite the contrary. "The Lord answered Job out of the whirlwind, and said, Who is this that darkeneth counsel by words without knowledge? . . . Where was thou when I laid the foundations of the earth? declare, if thou hast understanding. Who hath laid the measures thereof, if thou knowest? . . . Whereupon are the foundations thereof fastened? Or who hath laid the corner stone thereof? . . . Shall he that contendeth with the Almighty instruct him?" Job quickly gets the point, as his answer shows: "Behold, I am vile; what shall I answer thee? I will lay mine hand upon my mouth. . . . I know that thou canst do everything, and that no thought can be withholden from thee. . . . Therefore have I uttered that I understood not: things too wonderful for me, which I knew not. . . . Wherefore I abhor myself, and repent in dust and ashes." The message is clear: The knowledge, power, and ways of God are beyond human understanding; humans can't know or understand, since their rational powers are too shabby; so follow God's rules, and don't question or try to understand. Is Judeo-Christian-Muslim religion fundamentally *skeptical* concerning human knowledge?

6. Discussions in contemporary epistemology often make reference to "the Gettier problem" or "Gettier cases," originally posed by Edwin Gettier. We *know* something when we have a *true justified belief*. I can't *know* that the Earth is the largest planet, because that's not *true*. I can't *know* something when I'm merely taking a wild guess that happens to be correct, because my belief lacks *justification*. And if I don't actually *believe* something is true then I can't *know* it. If all three conditions are met—I genuinely *believe* something that is *true*, and I have solid *justification* for my belief —then I have knowledge. Or so it seemed, until Gettier caused problems: You *believe* that Joan owns a yellow VW bug, and you are *justified* in that belief (you have seen her title and registration papers, and an hour ago you rode to school with her in her yellow bug), and it's *true* that she owns a yellow bug. However, shortly after arriving at school, Joan lost her car in a poker game; *but* five minutes ago her distant Uncle Fred died and left his yellow bug to Joan. So it's *true* that Joan owns a yellow bug, you believe it, and you have strong justification for that belief. But it seems implausible to say that you *know* Joan owns a yellow bug; after all, Joan doesn't know it herself. This is a weird case, certainly;

but the point is, there do seem to be cases when true justified beliefs do *not* qualify as genuine knowledge. And cases of this sort are called Gettier cases. In trying to resolve the "Gettier paradox," what do you think is the most plausible path? Should we simply reject the traditional account of knowledge as "true justified belief"? Should we place stronger conditions (e.g., stronger conditions on what counts as "justified")? Or what?

7. You have a seminar today, but you won't be penalized for missing the class; and you *know* that your seminar meets in Greenlaw Hall, Room 254, at 3 PM. Next week, you have the same seminar, but this time you must give a major presentation: If you are late your professor will flunk you and you will not graduate. On the contextualist view, you *know* the time and place for today's less important seminar; but next week, with *precisely the same evidence*, you might *not* know when and where the critically important seminar meeting will occur (because its greater importance changes the context). Does that seem plausible?

8. You will recall that one of Descartes' arguments for skepticism (in the first meditation), to show that he could be mistaken in believing that he is sitting in a chair before the fire, is that he could be *dreaming*. Ludwig Wittgenstein, a famous twentieth-century philosopher, wrote the following brief objection to Descartes' dream argument: "The argument 'I may be dreaming' is senseless for this reason: if I am dreaming, this remark is being dreamed as well—and indeed it is also being dreamed that these words have any meaning" (Wittgenstein, *On Certainty*, note 383). Is that a strong objection to Descartes' skeptical argument? Could Descartes answer that objection?

9. William K. Clifford (a British mathematician and philosopher of the late nineteenth century) wrote *The Ethics of Belief*, in which he argues vigorously for the view that it is wrong to believe *anything* without sufficient justification:

> Belief, that sacred faculty which prompts the decisions of our will, and knits into harmonious working all the compacted energies of our being, is ours not for ourselves, but for humanity. It is rightly used on truths which have been established by long experience and waiting toil, and which have stood in the fierce light of free and fearless questioning. Then it helps bind men together, and to strengthen and direct their common action. It is desecrated when given to unproved and unquestioned statements, for the solace and private pleasure of the believer; to add a tinsel splendour to the plain straight road of our life and display a bright mirage beyond it; or even to drown the common sorrows of our kind by a self-deception which allows them not only to cast down, but also to degrade us. Whoso would deserve well of his fellows in this matter will guard the purity of his belief with a very fanaticism of jealous care, least at any time it should rest on an unworthy object, and catch a stain which can never be wiped away. . . .

> To sum up: it is wrong always, everywhere, and for anyone, to believe anything upon insufficient evidence.

Would Descartes agree with Clifford? Would Moore? Would Wittgenstein? Would you?

ADDITIONAL READING

Descartes' *Meditations on First Philosophy* was originally published in 1641; a good English translation is offered by Hackett Publishing (Indianapolis, IN: 1979). Norman Kemp Smith's *New Studies in the Philosophy of Descartes* (London: Macmillan, 1963) is very good on Descartes; see also J. Cottingham, *Descartes* (Oxford: Blackwell, 1986), and Bernard Williams, *Descartes: The Project of Pure Enquiry* (Hammondsworth: Penguin, 1978). A careful assessment of Descartes' method of doubt is offered by Harry G. Frankfurt in *Demons, Dreamers, and Madmen: The Defense of Reason in Descartes's Meditations* (Indianapolis, IN: Bobbs-Merrill, 1970).

There are several excellent recent anthologies that focus on skepticism: Michael D. Roth and Glenn Ross, *Doubting: Contemporary Perspectives on Skepticsm* (Dordrecht: Kluwer Academic Publishers, 1990); *Skepticism: A Contemporary Reader*, edited by Keith DeRose and Ted A. Warfield (Oxford: Oxford University Press, 1999); *Skepticism*, edited by Ernest Sosa and Enrique Villanueva (Oxford: Blackwell Publishers, 2000), which contains major articles followed by critical responses and the authors' responses to critics; and *The Skeptics: Contemporary Essays*, edited by Steven Luper (Aldershot, UK: Ashgate, 2003).

Richard Foley has argued that we cannot defeat skepticism, but we can make it look less frightening; his views are developed in more detail in *Intellectual Trust in Oneself and Others* (Cambridge: Cambridge University Press, 2001); and Catherine Z. Elgin offers a very interesting review and critique of that book in *Philosophy and Phenomenological Research*, volume 68, number 3 (May 2004): 724–734.

For some of the most influential earlier essays on skepticism, see the first section of papers in Ernest Sosa and Jaegwon Kim, eds., *Epistemology: An Anthology* (Oxford: Blackwell, 2000). Another good collection of very influential essays on skepticism can be found in Part IV of *Knowledge: Readings in Contemporary Epistemology* (Oxford: Oxford University Press, 2000), edited by Sven Bernecker and Fred Dretske. A good survey of some major skeptical positions and their critics is offered in "Skepticism," by Peter Klein, in Paul K. Moser, ed., *The Oxford Handbook of Epistemology* (Oxford: Oxford University Press, 2002): 336–361. Another good overview of the issues is "Skepticism," by Michael Williams, in *The Blackwell Guide to Epistemology*, edited by John Greco and Ernest Sosa (Oxford: Blackwell Publishers, 1999): 35–69.

A recent development in attempts to deal with skepticism is "the semantic response," as developed by Hilary Putnam, "Brains in a Vat," in *Reason, Truth and History* (Cambridge: Cambridge University Press, 1981), 1–21; Fred Dretske, "The Epistemology of Belief," *Synthese*, volume 55 (1983): 3–19; and Donald Davidson, "A Coherence Theory of Truth and Knowledge," in A. R. Malachowski, ed., *Reading Rorty: Critical Responses to Philosophy and the Mirror of Nature (and Beyond)* (Oxford: Blackwell Publishers, 1990): 120–138. All are available in anthologies.

Keith DeRose, "Contextualism: An Explanation and Defense," in John Greco and Ernest Sosa, eds., *The Blackwell Guide to Epistemology* (Oxford: Blackwell Publishers, 1999) is a helpful examination and defense of contextualism, and is particularly good in tracing its origins and history. There is a good survey of contextualist thought in The Internet Encyclopedia of Philosophy; titled "Contextualism in Epistemology," it was written by Tim Black, and can be found at http://www.iep.utm.edu/c/contextu.htm. Several key papers on contextualism are contained in Part 9 of *Epistemology: An Anthology*, edited by Ernest Sosa and Jaegwon Kim (Oxford: Blackwell, 2000).

An excellent debate between Earl Conee (who criticizes contextualism) and Stewart Cohen (who champions contextualism) is contained in Chapter 2 of Matthias Steup and Ernest Sosa, eds., *Contemporary Debates in Epistemology* (Oxford: Blackwell Publishing, 2005).

Influential contextualist writings include Keith DeRose, "Contextualism and Knowledge Attributions," *Philosophy and Phenomenological Research*, volume 52 (1992): 913–929; Keith DeRose, "Solving the Skeptical Puzzle," *Philosophical Review*, volume 104 (1995): 1–52; Stewart Cohen, "Knowledge, Context and Social Standards," *Synthese*, volume 73 (1987): 3–26; and Peter Unger, "The Cone Model of Knowledge," *Philosophical Topics*, volume 14 (1986): 125–178.

One important version of contextualism places great emphasis on eliminating all "relevant alternatives" in order to establish genuine knowledge, a view favored by Fred I. Dretske in "The Pragmatic Dimension of Knowledge," contained in his *Perception, Knowledge and Belief: Selected Essays* (Cambridge: Cambridge University Press, 2000). Stewart Cohen developed an important version of relevant alternatives contexualism in "How to be a Fallibilist," *Philosophical Perspectives 2, Epistemology* (1988): 91–123. Other important papers along relevant alternatives lines are David Lewis, "Elusive Knowledge," *Australasian Journal of Philosophy*, volume 74, number 4 (1996): 549–567; and Gail Stine, "Skepticism, Relevant Alternatives, and Deductive Closure," *Philosophical Studies*, volume 29 (1976): 249–261.

Michael Williams offers a radical version of contextualism which denies that there are any facts at all independent of contexts; see his *Unnatural Doubts: Epistemological Realism and the Basis of Skepticism* (Princeton, NJ: Princeton University Press, 1996).

Helen E. Longino gives a feminist account of the strengths of contextualism, in her "Feminist Epistemology," which is Chapter 14 in *The Blackwell Guide to Epistemology*, edited by John Greco and Ernest Sosa (Oxford: Blackwell Publishers, 1999).

For more on the views of G. E. Moore and Ludwig Wittgenstein on "common sense," skepticism, and contextualism, see Avrum Stroll, *Moore and Wittgenstein on Certainty* (New York: Oxford University Press, 1994); and Rush Rhees, with D. Z Phillips, ed., *Wittgenstein's On Certainty* (Oxford: Blackwell, 2003). A good examination of G. E. Moore's views, along with his response to criticisms, is Paul Arthur Schilpp, *The Philosophy of G. E. Moore*, 3rd ed. (LaSalle, IL: Open Court, 1968).

An excellent overview of contemporary issues in epistemology is offered by the writers contributing to *The Oxford Handbook of Epistemology*, edited by Paul K. Moser (Oxford: Oxford University Press, 2002).

EpistemeLinks.Com covers many topics in philosophy, but it is particularly good in epistemology; go to http://www.epistemelinks.com. There are also a couple of excellent Web sites devoted to epistemology. See "The Epistemology Page," developed by Keith De Rose of Yale University, for very good material on contemporary epistemologists; it's at http://Pantheon.yale.edu/~kd47/e-page.htm. Also, a particularly entertaining site is "Certain Doubts: Devoted to Matters Epistemic," at http://el-prod.baylor.edu/certain_doubts/

CHAPTER 4

RATIONALISM, EMPIRICISM, KANT

Descartes was a pivotal figure in the history of epistemology. He certainly did not refute skepticism once and for all; skeptics, such as David Hume, continued to raise doubts concerning the possibility of knowledge (or at least doubts about many knowledge claims), and there are skeptics living today. Perhaps they aren't as common as in the years when Descartes was writing, but neither have they become an endangered philosophical species. But whatever Descartes' success in refuting skepticism, he had an enormous impact on the development of *rationalism*. *Rationalists* maintain that we *can* gain genuine knowledge, that genuine knowledge must be known with *certainty*, and that the key for gaining certain knowledge is the careful and methodical use of *reason*. While not everyone accepted Cartesian rationalism, it clearly marked one important path of philosophical inquiry into the nature of knowledge: a clear rationalist path that some followed, others modified, and still others rejected altogether.

RATIONALISM

Descartes emphasized the importance of individual *reason* in discovering truth; and he showed—at least to the satisfaction of most of his contemporaries—that reason could banish skepticism and establish a system of certain knowledge. Our senses might deceive us (after all, it still *appears* that we are on a stationary Earth while the Sun travels across the sky), but reason could be a reliable guide to discovering truth. This demonstration of the powers of reason won Descartes great fame. Such was his renown that the brilliant young Queen Christina of Sweden persuaded Descartes to take up residence at the royal castle and teach her philosophy. Unfortunately, that ended badly: Descartes preferred to rise very late in the morning, followed by thoughtful philosophical reflection in his dressing gown before a warm fire; the young and energetic Queen Christina insisted on starting her philosophy lessons at five in the morning, in the cold Swedish dawn of a poorly heated castle. Under such unaccustomed stress, Descartes developed pneumonia and died. But the fame of Descartes—and his apparent success in conquering skepticism through the use of his reason—inspired other philosophers to continue his rationalist quest. Mathematics and geometry were also clear examples of the successful methodical use of reason to discover certain truth, and Descartes' use of a *method* for finding truth suggested to others that *reason*—if it followed the right method—might reveal all the deeper truths about the universe (or at least all the truths worth knowing). Thus, the great Dutch Jewish philosopher Benedict Spinoza used reason to prove that the world is all one divine substance, comprehending all that exists. About the same time, the great German philosopher and mathematician Leibniz employed his own rationalist method to unlock the fundamental structure of the universe: a complex structure of distinct individual monads, kept in perfect harmony by God's guidance.

Certainly the rationalist metaphysical systems of Spinoza and Leibniz were impressive. Through pure reason, Leibniz had spun out an amazing metaphysical world of multiple independent monads. Unfortunately, Spinoza had used reason to draw out a very different metaphysical world of a single substance; and the rationalist method of Descartes had yielded yet another. Other rationalist metaphysicians were drawing their own metaphysical wonders—all based on reason, but all reaching different conclusions. These rationalist systems were awe-inspiring, and some rationalist philosophers—Leibniz among them—believed that they were on the edge of discovering a rational method that would unlock all the secrets of the universe. But the wonders of these rationalist metaphysical discoveries began to seem a bit too wonderful to some critics: Unfettered by any real test of the systems, rationalists were spinning out an amazing variety of metaphysical systems—metaphysical systems that were in fundamental conflict, with no clear way to choose among them. Every system was backed by the certainty of reason, and that rationally derived certainty was a feature that rationalists profoundly valued. But if pure reason could produce such diverse and even contradictory systems—Spinoza's rationalism proved that there could be only one substance, while Descartes was certain that the mental and the physical were two distinct and different substances, and Leibniz insisted on a vast array of distinct substances—could reason alone show us the truth?

Rationalists maintain that we can know essential truths through the power of pure reason, and that reason can reveal absolute universal certainties (and for rationalists, anything less than fixed certainty will not qualify as genuine truth). Can pure reason give us truth about the nature of the world around us? Can reason, unaided by sensory observation, tell us how many planets are there in our solar system, or which planet has the greatest mass? Can reason tell us the atomic structure of water? Can reason tell us that oxygen is essential for human life? There is dispute among rationalists about how to answer those questions; and there are at least three different answers that rationalists offer. First, some rationalists deny that reason, unaided by observation, can tell us the atomic structure of water or the number of planets in our solar system; but they would count such "observational" or empirical "knowledge" as insignificant: It deals only with appearances, and the true *deeper* reality of the *genuine* nature of things is revealed only to reason. "Knowledge" based on observations isn't real *knowledge* at all. A second rationalist response is to count observational knowledge as "knowledge," but only as a "lower form" of knowledge: a type of knowledge that is distinctly inferior to the knowledge of mathematics and geometry (and other knowledge gained by pure reason). Such empirical "knowledge" lacks the certainty and is lower in status and significance than the knowledge gained by pure reason. Third, some rationalists insist that the resources of pure reason—unaided by sensory observation—will eventually unlock the deep structure of the universe, and tell us how many planets there are, how many species, how many stars, and what the weather will be tomorrow (and what it was a million years ago). Obviously, we are not far enough along in our reasoning and deeper understanding to unlock such secrets *yet*; but (because, for example, we can use reason to understand the necessary nature of God, and then through reason we could understand the nature of the world that such a necessarily perfect God would create) it is *possible* for pure reason to ultimately provide such answers.

Rationalism played an important part in restoring belief in the powers of reason, following the period of widespread skepticism; and it played an important part in restoring confidence that humans could use their own faculties to discover truth (without abject dependence on faith or ancient authority). Still, rationalism does not carry the prestige it had in the golden age of rationalism, when Descartes, Spinoza, Leibniz, and others constructed their magnificent rationalist systems of metaphysics. Not that rationalism has disappeared: There are rationalists walking the Earth even as we speak. But they are not the dominant species they were in the seventeenth century.

There were two factors that challenged the dominance of rationalism. One, as already noted, was the development of competing metaphysical systems, each laying claim to certain truth discovered through pure reason. Of course, the rationalists did not believe they had perfect powers of reason, and so it was not too surprising that different reasoners might reach different conclusions (just as several people may reach different and conflicting answers to a mathematics or geometry problem). Still, the proliferation of different and conflicting metaphysical answers—all claiming to be based on the power of pure reason—did cause some to doubt the reliability of rationalist methodology. The second factor was even more decisive: The enormous success of scientists—particularly Isaac Newton—in developing elegant accounts of the world, using both reason *and* empirical observation.

God Said, Let Newton Be

It is almost impossible to exaggerate the impact of Isaac Newton on the late seventeenth and eighteenth centuries, and on into the twenty-first century. To appreciate Newton's significance, consider what the world was like in the decades before Newton. Terrible plagues continued to sweep through cities and regions, decimating them without warning and without apparent reason. The Church was split asunder, and religious fervor was provoking war rather than peace. Reason and observation seemed enemies, or at the very best they belonged to distinctly different realms: Reason tells us deep absolute necessary truths while observation is inherently questionable and tells us only about the world as it *happens* to be. Reason tells us the truths of geometry, in which intersecting lines form corresponding angles that are absolutely and *necessarily* equal. Observation tells us that two roads eventually intersect—but they might not have intersected, there is nothing necessary or absolute about their intersection. And while rationalism might satisfy the philosophical quest for absolute truth, the world of observational truth remained in a terrible mess. Copernican astronomy was widely accepted, but the result was that astronomy seemed permanently estranged from physics: Aristotelian physics was based on the idea of everything seeking its proper place, with heat rising toward the fixed stars and material objects seeking their proper Earthly realm; But now that the Earth is hurtling through space rather than acting as a stationary target, that model of physics had lost its foundation. The greatest astronomers (such as Johannes Kepler, whose astronomical studies were essential to Newton's work) often clung to the idea that astronomical principles could be established through pure *reason*—perhaps by rationally understanding the perfect mathematical harmony of the heavenly spheres—thus avoiding the uncertainty and contingency inherent in observational studies. The new Copernican system was impressive, but the random arrival of comets broke down the clockwork order of the entire system.

Into this confusion and uncertainty strode a scientific giant: Isaac Newton. Drawing on the work of Copernicus, Galileo, and Kepler, Newton devised some elegantly simple laws of motion that in one monumental step closed the divide between Earthly physics and heavenly astronomy: In the Newtonian system, exactly the same principles that explain why the Earth orbits the Sun also explain why the Moon orbits the Earth, and furthermore explain why a ball tossed into the air returns to Earth. Aristotelian physics and Copernican astronomy had been at war; Newton's system made physics and astronomy part of one seamless whole, all governed by a few elegantly simple mathematical laws. Not only was the split between astronomy and physics closed but also the split between mathematical reason and observation: Newton used careful empirical observation in establishing his principles of motion, but he showed how those observations could be part of an elegant mathematical system of basic principles of *all* motion, both on earth and in the heavens. A rock thrown on Earth falls in precisely the same way and following exactly the same laws that explain how the Earth itself and all the planets "fall" toward the Sun in their orbits. Newton himself always gave credit to Copernicus, Galileo, Kepler, and the other scientists who came before him—"If I have seen further it is by standing on the shoulders of Giants" (letter to Robert Hooke, 1675)—but to Newton's contemporaries, Newton seemed the great giant of science. The British poet, Alexander Pope, who was Newton's contemporary, summed up the general attitude toward Newton:

> Nature and Nature's laws lay hid in night:
> God said, Let Newton be! and all was light.

Newton's triumph had several important results. First, physics and astronomy were joined in one scientific system; and that led to the belief that ultimately all scientific knowledge might be unified into one great system (if not by means of a few simple unifying laws, like Newton's laws of motion, at least through allegiance to a common scientific method of research). Second, Newton showed that mathematics and empirical observation did not have to occupy different and opposing realms, but could exist harmoniously and even cooperatively: Pure mathematics and geometry could be applied to our observational findings and the result could be elegant mathematical principles that explain the workings of the world. And third, we might use such methods to discover truths about almost anything: astronomy and physics, obviously; but perhaps also biology; perhaps even psychology, and maybe ethics and politics. In any case, that seemed the most plausible approach. That was a radically different orientation from the old view: The world is largely a mystery that we have no capacity to understand, and no business trying. God had challenged Job with questions he could not answer: "Hast thou perceived the breadth of the earth? Declare if thou knowest it all. Where is the way where light dwelleth?" A post-Newtonian Job might well have replied: I don't know, but I know how to find out.

Newton's elegant laws of motion resulted in greatly increased confidence that through the combination of mathematical reasoning and careful observation, we could gain reliable knowledge: knowledge about the world around us and how it works, knowledge with a high degree of certainty, knowledge of our observable world that is clearly genuine knowledge. But the event that sealed the deal for empirical knowledge and the strength of empirical methods (combining mathematics with careful observation) actually occurred after Newton's death. Comets were the prime example of mysterious, inexplicable phenomena. No one could explain where they came from, why they appeared, or what they were. One thing that both Ptolemaic and Copernican astronomers could agree on: Comets played hell with the majestic clockwork of the heavens. They came and went with no rhyme or reason, they were the essence of mystery and unpredictability, they were the poster child for human ignorance. Since there was no possible natural explanation for them, they were regarded as divine messengers, perhaps divine warnings. But were they divine or demonic? Harbingers of doom or bearers of glad tidings? Comets were generally taken as mysterious disruptive signals of cataclysmic changes; and for most people—especially for kings and the nobility, with their precarious grip on power—change was not welcome. But an English astronomer, Edmund Halley, was inspired by Newton's theory to wonder whether comets might actually be natural and predictable phenomena that could be *explained* using Newton's principles. Halley studied the historical record of comet sightings, and he did the mathematical calculations using Newton's basic laws of motion; and he *predicted* the precise time, place, and path of a bright comet; and he was right. (The actual appearance of the comet was not until 1759, right on schedule, and in accordance with Halley's prediction using Newton's principles; but the fact that Halley could *make* such a plausible prediction using Newton's principles was itself very exciting; the actual arrival of the predicted comet confirmed the Newtonian revolution and the power of Newtonian science.) Comets— just like planets, moons, balls dropped from towers, and arrows shot into the air—all follow the same basic principles of motion; and if we do careful observations and exact calculations, we can understand and accurately predict their motion. Comets had seemed the ultimate mystery. Newtonian science solved that mystery.

The eighteenth century was the century following Newton's discoveries, and the century when Newton's principles were used to predict the precise appearance and path of a comet. An indication of the scientific confidence and excitement of the eighteenth century can be found in the comments of the great French mathematician *Jean d'Alembert*, in the year 1759 (the year Halley's comet reappeared as predicted):

> Our century is . . . the century of philosophy [including *natural* philosophy, which we would call science] par excellence. . . . The discovery and application of a new method of philosophizing, the kind of enthusiasm which accompanies discoveries, a certain exaltation of ideas which the spectacle of the universe produces in us—all these causes have brought about a lively fermentation of minds, spreading through nature in all directions like a river which has burst its dams.

If Newtonian science could unlock even the secrets of *comets*, it seemed reasonable to suppose that scientific inquiry might hold the key to all the mysteries. If we can use the methods of mathematical science to understand and predict the coming and going of comets, then surely there is *nothing* that can defy scientific explanation. Human behavior may be weird and erratic and apparently inexplicable; but certainly no more so than the behavior of comets. If the latter can be understood and predicted, then perhaps the former can be as well. In any case, science—in the Newtonian style of careful observation combined with mathematical calculation, and without submission to either divine or secular authority—seemed the most promising path to genuine and valuable knowledge.

EMPIRICISM

Everyone agrees that reason is important—indeed, essential—to discovering truth; and everyone agrees that our sensory faculties can deceive us. But the *empiricists* believe that rationalists place too *much* reliance on pure reason, and that rationalists set too severe a standard for truth. Truths that are certain are very nice; but some truths with a bit of uncertainty might also prove useful, according to the empiricists. In particular, the empiricists believe that while pure reason might give us truths of mathematics and geometry, to learn the truth about the world around us will require that we also use the evidence of our senses, that we make *empirical* observations and run experiments.

David Hume issued the great anti-metaphysical manifesto of radical empiricism:

> If we take in our hand any volume—of divinity or school metaphysics, for instance—let us ask, *Does it contain any abstract reasoning concerning quantity or number?* No. *Does it contain any experimental reasoning concerning matter of fact and existence?* No. Commit it then to the flames, for it can contain nothing but sophistry and illusion.
>
> *An Enquiry Concerning Human Understanding, 1748*

Some rationalists might insist that we can know the nature of the world around us *without* empirical sensory observations: Suppose that reason can tell us the characteristics that *must* be part of God's perfection, and reason could also reveal the essential characteristics (such as the harmony and the order) of a world that such a perfect God would create; then reason could reveal what the nature of the world *must* be like (and of course, if the world doesn't *appear* that way to us, that is only because of the limits of our senses in apprehending the true nature of the world). Empiricists don't buy it: If we want to know what the world is really like, we have to make observations and run experiments. If we run careful experiments and do close observations, then we can gain knowledge of the actual world outside our skins—and inside our skins, for that matter (e.g., William Harvey's 1619 discovery of the circulation of the blood). Of course we may make mistakes: Empirical knowledge is not infallible. But infallibility is not a necessary element of genuine knowledge. Rationalists tend to see sensory observation as inherently flawed, and a distraction from the deeper truth to be gained by pure reason; in contrast, empiricists regard sensory observation as a vital element of the process of gaining knowledge. Rationalism might proclaim that it had unlocked the deeper truths about what is genuinely real and beyond our powers of observation; but rationalists hadn't revealed any basic laws of motion, and they hadn't predicted the paths of comets. Empiricism—with its use of reason and mathematics and its great respect for careful empirical observation—became the dominant view.

Empiricism is the view that *experience* is the basis for all genuine knowledge. Reason is obviously of great use, but it must take its basic data from experience. The three great empiricists of the Enlightenment were John Locke, David Hume, and Bishop Berkeley (pronounced *Bark*ley). Though their views differed on many points, they shared two basic commitments: to *experience* as the essential foundation for knowledge; and to *rejection* of any metaphysical doctrines that could not be supported by experiential or experimental evidence. For example, is there an underlying necessary but unobservable *substance* for every entity? Empiricists reject such metaphysical claims as unsupported by empirical evidence.

John Locke

John Locke was born in 1632, 10 years before Newton. Newton published his revolutionary work, *Principia Mathematica*, in 1687; two years later, in 1689, John Locke published his empiricist manifesto, *Essay Concerning Human Understanding*. That is not to suggest that Locke's *Essay* is the philosophical result of Newton's work; in fact, Locke had been working on the *Essay* for many years, and much of it was written before the publication of Newton's *Principia*. But Locke's work captured the spirit of empiricism that was becoming dominant; and Locke stands as the clearest direct empiricist challenge to Descartes' rationalism.

. . . the unity, the simplicity, or the inseparability of all the attributes of God is one of the most important of the perfections which I understand him to have. And surely the idea of the unity of all his perfections could not have been placed in me by any cause which did not also provide me with the ideas of the other perfections; for no cause could have made me understand the interconnection and inseparability of the perfections without at the same time making me recognize what they were. . . .

It only remains for me to examine how I received this idea from God. For I did not acquire it from the senses; it has never come to me unexpectedly, as usually happens with the ideas of things that are perceivable by the senses. . . . And it was not invented by me either; for I am plainly unable either to take away anything from it or to add anything to it. The only remaining alternative is that it is innate in me, just as the idea of myself is innate in me.

And indeed it is no surprise that God, in creating me, should have placed this idea in me to be, as it were, the mark of the craftsman stamped on his work. *Descartes,* fourth Meditation

Descartes insisted we must turn away from misleading sensory impressions, seeking first the principles that we can know with certainty through pure reason. In stark contrast, John Locke argued that we cannot avoid starting with sensory input: All our ideas must ultimately come from experience. It is only through *experience* that we gain our original ideas of color, shape, and size. Having gained those ideas from experience, we can manipulate and combine them in various ways. One of the famous empiricist examples was of a *golden mountain*. Obviously I have never observed a golden mountain; but because I have the idea of gold and the idea of mountain—from my sensory observations—I can *combine* those ideas to yield the idea of a golden mountain. But such fanciful and imaginative exercises require initial building blocks of sensory experience (which give us our ideas of colors, mountains, and oceans) and without such basic sensory building blocks, we could never proceed further.

Descartes was convinced that reason could open the cosmos to our understanding: It could reveal to us the nature of God, of the human constitution, and (with a little help from the senses) the world around us. Locke was not so sure. Locke believed we could have knowledge, certainly; but he thought that our faculties might limit the range of our knowledge. We must start from our senses, and perhaps our senses have limits: There could be knowledge that we can never gain because of our limitations, particularly the limitations of our sensory abilities.

Let us then suppose the mind to be, as we say, white paper, void of all characters, without any ideas: how comes it to be furnished? Whence comes it by that vast store which the busy and boundless fancy of man has painted on it with an almost endless variety? Whence has it all the materials of reason and knowledge? To this I answer, in one word, from experience; in all that our knowledge is founded, and from that it ultimately derives itself. Our observation employed either about external sensible objects, or about the internal operations of our minds, perceived and reflected on by ourselves, is that which supplies our understandings with all the materials of thinking. These two are the fountains of knowledge, from whence all the ideas we have, or can naturally have, do spring. *John Locke, An Essay Concerning Human Understanding.*

Descartes believed we have "innate ideas": ideas that do not come from experience, but are instead inscribed in us by God (Descartes compared these to a "maker's mark" inscribed on a piece of pottery). For example, we have the idea of infinity; but—Descartes insisted—we could never have gained such an idea from our reasoning, since our reasoning capacity is obviously finite. Even more obviously (to Descartes), we could not have come to such an idea through our sensory experience. Therefore, it must have been implanted by God. In contrast, Locke maintained that the human consciousness is a "tabula rasa," a *blank slate*, on which our sensory experience must make the first marks; and all our ideas must ultimately be derived from experience (operated on by reason). Once we get the ideas, we can mix, match, sort, and expand; but we depend on our sensory experiences for our stock of ideas to manipulate.

The seventeenth-century dispute over innate ideas has waxed and waned over the successive centuries, but it has never quite disappeared, not even to this day. In ethics, some *intuitionists* believe that we have special immediate intuitive knowledge of right and wrong (or of ethical principles): You *know* that it is wrong to tell a lie or commit a murder, and you did not (intuitionists insist) gain that knowledge from experience; rather, you *know* it as soon as you think clearly about it. And this is not like a truth of mathematics that comes from reason, because you do not have to reason about it to recognize such basic moral principles. In contrast, of course, are those who doubt the existence of any such ethical intuitions, or who maintain that these "intuitions" are actually the result of our social conditioning, or who give some other account of their origin. But we'll return to that question later, in our discussion of ethics. A fierce rationalist/empiricist debate erupted in the late twentieth century, and it still reverberates. It was a debate over innate vs. learned structures of *language*; and the major adversaries were the rationalist linguist Noam Chomsky and the fiercely empiricist behavioral psychologist B. F. Skinner.

> A theory of linguistic structure that aims for explanatory adequacy incorporates an account of linguistic universals, and it attributes tacit knowledge of these universals to the child. It proposes, then, that the child approaches the data with the presumption that they are drawn from a language of a certain antecedently well-defined type, his problem being to determine which of the (humanly) possible languages is that of the community in which he is placed. Language learning would be impossible unless this were the case. The important question is: What are the initial assumptions concerning the nature of language that the child brings to language learning, and how detailed and specific is the innate schema (the general definition of "grammar") that gradually becomes more explicit and differentiated as the child learns the language? *Noam Chomsky, 1965.*

Chomsky maintains that language is too complex for children to learn from scratch in just a few years, and so we must be born with an innate theory or template for language development. (Chomsky does not believe those innate linguistic frameworks were implanted in us by God, but rather that they are a product of our evolutionary history; but however they got there, they are still innate, rather than learned.) In contrast, Skinner insists that we should not fall back on claims of innate ideas or innate theories until we have thoroughly examined the possibilities of acquiring language through learned experience.

> Nothing which could be called following a plan or applying a rule is observed when behavior is a product of the contingencies [of reinforcement] alone. To say that "the child who learns a language has in some sense constructed the grammar for himself" (Chomsky, 1959) is as misleading as to say that a dog which has learned to catch a ball has in some sense constructed the relevant part of the science of mechanics. Rules can be extracted from the reinforcing contingencies in both cases and once in existence they may be used as guides. The direct effect of the contingencies is of a different nature. *B. F. Skinner, 1966.*

The opening rounds of this continuing contemporary struggle between rationalists and empiricists were fought hundreds of years ago by Descartes and Locke.

David Hume

Rationalists—such as Descartes—maintain that *reason* is the fundamental source of knowledge. Reason is more reliable than our easily deceived senses, and it is our only path to deeper understanding of reality. The senses may tell us something of the changing characteristics of a piece of wax, but only reason can discover its deeper true nature: the *substance* that reason recognizes beneath the surface of the sensory impressions. Descartes wanted to discover truths that he could know with certainty, and reason—rather than sensory impressions—was his sure path to such truths. Of course reasoners can make mistakes: They can think too quickly, without considering all the essential factors. But Descartes was convinced that by following careful methodical reasoning processes, we could discover an enormous range of truth. Reason is so powerful and effective—when used judiciously and well—that there seem to be almost no limits to what we might ultimately discover and know through its marvelous powers. In contrast to Descartes and the rationalists, the *empiricists* place more emphasis on the importance of gaining ideas through experience, including sensory experience. The empiricists believe we can know a great deal; but because our understanding relies ultimately on our senses, and our senses may have limits, our knowledge may have limits. Dogs smell things that we do not. Perhaps other animals see and hear things we do not, and there might be senses with which we are totally unfamiliar. Therefore, there may be limits to our understanding, limits that are important to explore and recognize. Are our faculties (particularly our perceptual faculties) well suited to gathering knowledge? Does our sensory nature—and the limits of our senses— place limits on the sort of knowledge we can gain?

John Locke explored such questions, examining the possibility that our limited human faculties might place outer limits on the range and extent of our knowledge. But the person who took this question even more seriously was David Hume, and Hume concluded that such limits might well exist. That is *not* to suggest that we should give up on making empirical inquiries. We cannot know where our limits lie without pushing such inquiries as far as they can go, and even when we suppose that we have hit a limit we may discover another path or approach that will carry us further. But we should not arrogantly assume that our human capacities are sufficient to carry us to the ultimate ends of knowledge, nor should we suppose that perfect certainty is possible in all areas of knowledge.

Empiricists recognized that empirical knowledge claims were subject to error, and that there might be limits to what we can understand; but they were also confident that empirical research could make remarkable discoveries and find ways to correct our errors. If there were limits to our human understanding, those limits seemed very far away: There was much to discover, and we now had some excellent tools for making those discoveries. After all, this was the age of the glorious Newton, whose empirical inquiries—building on the work of Copernicus, Kepler, and Galileo—had revealed the laws of motion that govern the universe, from the Earth to the planets. And using Newton's laws, Halley predicted the coming and going of comets—those mysterious messengers which had seemed the least likely phenomena to yield to our powers of understanding. It was David Hume, the great Scottish empiricist, who reined in some of this exuberance.

Hume was an empiricist, and he recognized the importance of observation in gaining knowledge. But he was also acutely aware of both the limits of empirical knowledge and the gaps in our basic understanding. First, the limits: Reason and experience may tell us a good deal about how to accomplish our goals, what paths are most likely to lead us to our desired destination. But when it comes to the very basic questions of ethics, and the questions of what goals are *worthy* of pursuit, what destinations we *should* pursue, what sort of lives we *should* live, and what type of character we *should* develop; then—Hume insisted—reason can give us no answers. Reason and experience can tell us the best way of pursuing wealth; but they can tell us nothing about whether wealth is worth pursuing. This is obviously not a small gap in what we can know; after all, both Plato and Aristotle would have agreed that the questions of what is good, what is just, and how should we live are the most basic and important questions of all. Hume insisted that our most basic goals and values come from our feelings, our *passions*; and rather than reason telling us what passions, desires, and goals are worthwhile, the control runs in the opposite direction: "Reason is, and ought always to be, the slave of the passions." Reason and experience can tell us a great deal about what *is*, but it can never leap across the chasm from *is* to *ought*. Hume's claims about ethics are obviously controversial, and they have inspired both virulent critics and fervent defenders— and we'll examine both in later chapters.

Not only did Hume maintain that there were important *limits* (particularly in the area of ethics) on what we could know from either reason *or* experience, but he also insisted that there were profound *gaps* in our understanding of the basic nature of the world. First, we frequently speak confidently of knowing *causes*; but when we look closely, all that we really observe is one event regularly followed by another. A billiard ball strikes a second ball, and (we say) *causes* the second ball to move; a sword plunges into the heart, which *causes* the heart to stop beating, which in turn causes death; a flame touches powder, which causes the powder to explode, which in turn causes a cannon ball to speed through the barrel; and the cannon ball is ultimately caused to fall by the force of gravity. But in all these cases, what we observe is simply the regular pattern of one event followed by another. Of course we may delve deeper into the causal sequence: The heart stops beating, which causes the blood to stop circulating, which further causes loss of oxygen to the brain, which in turn causes brain cells to cease functioning, and this finally causes death. But in looking at greater depth and detail, what we see is still nothing more than the regular succession of events. That does not mean that we do not know that the flame causes the powder to ignite, or that a sword wound can cause the heart to stop beating; but what Hume is emphasizing is that when we *know* such causes, all we really know is a customary succession of events; and from the occurrence of the first, we come by custom to infer the second. But we should not suppose that we know something deeper about the nature of causality: Our causal conclusions are based on *custom* or *habit*, rather than on deep rational insight.

> The squirrel does not infer by induction that it is going to need stores next winter as well. And no more do we need a law of induction to justify our actions or our predictions. *Ludwig Wittgenstein, On Certainty.*

But there is also a second way in which our basic understanding is limited, and it poses a challenge even to our limited "one event customarily follows another" conception of causation. In all our understanding of the world, we rely on the principle that the future will be like the past. That is the principle that governs our use of *induction*, on which we base our knowledge of the world and what to expect from its operations. When we say that "stopping the heart causes death," that is based on the fact that in all the cases we have observed, stoppage of the heart is followed by death. But we don't confine ourselves to a statement about the past: that is, we do not say that "in all past cases stopping the heart caused death"; rather, when we say that "stopping the heart causes death," we mean that as a *universal* statement: Stopping the heart always leads to death, whether past, present, or *future*. But what *rational grounds* can we offer for supposing that the future will be like the past? How could we rationally justify our belief in induction: Our belief that patterns observed in the past will continue to hold in the future? We *could* say that in the past that belief proved accurate; but that simply drives the question back one step further: Why should we believe that the *past* success of inductive conclusions shows that they will work in the *future*? And in answering that question, if we reply that "it always worked in the past, so it will continue to work in the future," then we are not *answering* the question; instead, we are *begging* the question, by assuming exactly what we are supposed to be proving.

The twentieth-century philosopher Nelson Goodman posed this problem in a very clear form with (what he called) the "new riddle of induction." All the emeralds we have observed so far have been green, and so it seems reasonable to suppose that all emeralds have the property of being green, including all future emeralds. But perhaps instead of the property of being green, they have the property of being *grue*; that is, the property of being green until 2025, and then becoming blue. The "grue hypothesis" may seem rather silly; but note this: It has exactly the same support as the inductive hypothesis that all emeralds are (and will continue to be) *green*. That is, all our past observations of green emeralds support the grue hypothesis just as strongly as the green hypothesis. The *point* of Goodman's grue hypothesis is not to show that we have good support for the claim that all emeralds are grue, but rather to show that the problem of justifying induction is a serious problem indeed: If both the green and the grue claims are equally supported by induction, then induction is not a very strong foundation.

Causation and induction are the foundation of our empirical understanding of the world; and Hume argued that the causal and inductive foundation is a lot less solid than we had supposed. We had thought we could base our understanding of the world and its causal processes on good solid rational grounds; Hume concluded that rather than rationality, our guide to the world is *custom*, or the learned *habits* of belief and expectation: "Custom . . . is the great guide of human life." This is rather shocking. We believed we were being guided by our wonderful powers of reason; it turns out that we are just creatures of custom. Like mice taking a path through a maze that leads successfully to the cheese, we follow a path that guides us to our desired ends; but at the most fundamental level, we are no more guided by *reason* than is the successful mouse. We follow what has worked in the past, we follow the *custom* we have learned; but in doing so, we are not guided by reason. This following of custom is basic: more basic than reason, and it cannot be *justified* by reason. Hume himself was not deeply bothered by that. He thought our natural adherence to custom needed no rational justification. To the contrary, nature would have been silly to guide us by reason, since our rational faculties are rather weak, and we rarely make good use of even those limited rational powers. Hume counseled that in our day-to-day lives we are adequately guided by custom; and in our intellectual lives, a little skepticism is a useful corrective to our arrogance. But many others were profoundly bothered by Hume's conclusions; and one of them was Immanuel Kant.

IMMANUEL KANT

Hume had an enormous influence on those who followed him; sometimes because of the answers he gave, and just as often because of the questions and perplexities he raised. Immanuel Kant credited Hume with being the philosopher who "awakened me out of my dogmatic slumber." It seems obvious to us that events in our world are caused by other events; but where is the *proof* of that claim? How do we *know* that causation is universal? It was this perplexing question that shook Kant out of his "dogmatic slumber" and pushed him to develop his own remarkable philosophical system.

Kant acknowledged that Hume had posed a severe challenge for those who believe that reason can yield reliable knowledge of the world. Kant's response to that challenge was radical: In some ways, it called for a shift in our thinking as radical as that demanded by the Copernican Revolution. In fact, Kant claimed to have carried out the Copernican Revolution in philosophy. Think of what the Copernican Revolution did: It forced us to recognize that we are not privileged spectators of the world, but instead we are part of that world. We do not stand outside the solar system and make our observations, but must make our observations from *within* the system. So as we make our observations, we must *take account* of the effects of our own perspective; in particular, we must take account of the fact that *we are moving*, and that our own motion influences what we see. If we go out every night and watch the stars pass over our heads, we observe that they *shift* their positions as the seasons pass: just as the Sun shifts lower on the horizon in January and gradually shifts higher as the months pass, then shifting back lower as fall moves toward winter; likewise, the entire panorama of stars shifts as the seasons pass, and they all shift together. They all shift together, except for a few weird "stars" that "wander"; thus, the ancients called them *planets*, meaning that they do not consistently shift in the same pattern as all the stars, but instead seem to move in a rather jerky pattern, sometimes shifting more swiftly and at other times more slowly. Ptolemy assumed that we were making our observations from a fixed privileged *unmoving* position on Earth, and so the strange motion of the planets had to be due to the fact that the planets move on special spheres that are embedded within larger spheres: The planets move on turning spheres that are attached to the larger sphere circling around the fixed Earth. But Copernicus attributed this special planetary motion—the "retrograde motion of the planets"—not to some exotic motion of the planets themselves, but rather to the fact that *we* are moving as we make our observations from the moving Earth. In our orbits around the Sun, sometimes the Earth "catches up" with another planet and then passes it, which makes it *look* as if the planet is moving in a strange path. If we are to understand the motions of our solar system, we have to figure in our *own* motion. Kant—in his philosophical "Copernican revolution"—maintained that if we are to understand the world around us, we likewise must take account of our own *conceptual system*. Our categories and concepts force us to see the world in a certain way; and some of what we are seeing—like the retrograde motion of the planets—may be due to the categories, concepts, and perspectives we bring to our observation of the world, rather than being part of the world as it really is in itself. Kant distinguishes the *noumena* from the *phenomena*. *Noumena* denotes reality as it exists in itself, in its essence, independent of our observation of it; the *phenomena* are what we actually observe, our own perceptions of the world as colored and shaped by our perceptual and conceptual apparatus.

So how do we distinguish the phenomenal from the noumenal? That is, how can we determine the nature of the world as it is in itself, and distinguish that from the conceptual and perceptual apparatus we bring to our observations? To answer that question, Kant starts from some basic distinctions: First, the distinction between *analytic* and *synthetic* statements; and second, the distinction between knowledge that is *a priori* and knowledge that is *a posteriori*. An *analytic* statement is a statement that is true by definition, a statement in which the *predicate* is contained in the *subject*. For example, a frog is an animal: Part of the meaning of the subject term, "frog," is that it is an animal; the predicate, "animal," is contained in the subject. Therefore, this is an analytic truth. Circles are round: Again, part of the meaning of circle is that it is round; the predicate is contained in the subject, and it is an *analytic* truth; its truth can be determined by *analysis* of the subject and predicate terms. In synthetic statements, the predicate is *not* contained in the subject: The National Football League has 32 teams. That happens to be true, but it is a synthetic truth: Having 32 teams is not part of the definition of the National Football League. New York City is the largest city in the United States. Again, that is true, but it is a synthetic truth: Being the largest city is not part of the definition; at some point in the future, Los Angeles might be larger, and then that synthetic statement would be false. The Pacific Ocean is the largest ocean on Earth. That's true, but it's a synthetic truth, not an analytic truth: In fact, it was many years before we learned that the statement is true. The Earth is the largest planet in our solar system: That synthetic statement happens to be false.

Now consider the second distinction, between two types of knowledge: *a priori* and *a posteriori* knowledge. As discussed in the previous chapter, this is a distinction between *ways of knowing*. *A priori* knowledge is knowledge that we can gain purely through reason, without the need of observation. Analytic truths are known *a priori*, because they can be known to be true simply by analyzing the concepts: *Think* about the definition of circle, and you will know that circles are round; you don't have to go out and make observations of lots of different circles to discover that truth. (Unless you already *know* that circles are round, you wouldn't even know what to look for.) The other great examples of *a priori* truths come from mathematics and geometry. When two straight lines intersect, their opposite angles are equal. Two plus two equals four. Those are truths that you can know purely by *reasoning* about it, without ever having to go out and measure angles, and without checking to see if two balls added to two more balls actually totals up to four. Those truths are known *a priori*. In contrast, we learned that tomatoes are good to eat by eating tomatoes and observing the results. For many years, Europeans thought that tomatoes were deadly poisonous; and no matter how long they *reasoned* about it, they could never have discovered that tomatoes are not poisonous; that is an *a posteriori* truth, a truth that follows or depends on *experience* and observation. Or as we might also say, it is an *empirical* truth. Truths that are known *a posteriori* are common as dirt: Oxygen is necessary for human life; Jupiter is the largest planet in our solar system, penguins cannot fly; the Pacific Ocean is the largest ocean on Earth. All of those are synthetic statements that are known *a posteriori*. By empirical observation we learn something new about tomatoes: They are good to eat. We have *a posteriori* knowledge that oxygen is essential for human life: Being necessary for human life is not part of the *definition* of oxygen, but is instead something new that we learned about oxygen from *a posteriori* experience and experiment. So there is no trouble finding examples of *a posteriori* truths that are synthetic.

The interesting question—the question that fascinated Kant, and that still prompts debate—is this question: Are there any *synthetic* statements that can be known *a priori*? That is, can we have *a priori* knowledge of facts about the world, purely through the use of *reason*?

Think of something that is currently on one of the moons of Jupiter, something that *no one* has ever observed: It might be a rock, a cloud, a sheet of ice, or even some object unlike anything we have ever seen on Earth. Is there anything that you *know* about that unobserved object? You don't know its chemical structure, or its density; you don't know its color, its hardness, or its melting point. But is there *anything* you know about this object? Kant says that there is: You *know* that the object exists in *space* and in *time*. The object may be small or large, it may—like a cloud—change its shape; but it *must* have dimensions, it *must* exist in space. And it may be very old or very new, it may be long term or transient; but it also *must* exist in time.

At first glance, this hardly seems amazing. After all, if you ask me to describe a building, and I tell you that it exists in space and time, you will find that rather unhelpful. But Kant thinks it is very significant indeed: It is a synthetic statement *about the world*, and it is known *a priori*. True statements about the world are commonplace. Penguins cannot fly, Jupiter is the largest planet in our solar system, the Earth's atmosphere contains oxygen: All of those are true synthetic statements about the world, and we know them by observational experience (*a posteriori*). But that our unobserved object on one of Jupiter's moons exists *in space* and *in time*: that is, something we know *a priori*, without the benefit of experience; and it is a *synthetic* statement, not analytic. Of course, we've observed many other objects, and all of them existed in space and time. But note, the way we *know* that this unobserved object exists in space and time is *not* by generalizing from those observed cases: It is *not* known inductively. After all, suppose we observe several hundred penguins, of numerous types, and none of them can fly; then we are justified in thinking that it is very likely that *no* penguins can fly. But we are not *ruling out* the possibility of discovering flight-worthy penguins on some unexplored island. But knowing that our object on Jupiter's moon exists *in space* and *in time* is not like that: We *know* that the unknown object *must* exist in space and time. So, Kant concluded, there are synthetic *a priori* truths: truths *about the world* that we can know *purely by reason*.

But how can this be? How can reason, without the aid of empirical observation, tell us things about the world? And not only tell us things about the world but also tell us things about the world that are *necessarily true*? There is only one way such truths could be possible: They are truths that we *know* with *certainty* because they are part of our observation and conceptualization of the world. They are *built in* to our conceptual and observational capacities. Thus, there *are* some synthetic *a priori* truths: Truths known exclusively through reason that tell us facts about the world and are not analytic statements based on definition.

Why do the planets appear to *wander* in their paths? Because of the way we see them, from our moving observation post. Why does everything that we observe exist in space and time? Why does everything have a cause? Because these form part of our own conceptual and perceptual structure: We see the world through the lenses of space and time. They are part of our *phenomenal* world, but not part of the *noumena*; that is, they are an essential part of our observation and understanding—if we could somehow remove the space and time lenses, the world would appear to us as a disordered and incomprehensible "blooming buzzing confusion"—but they are not part of the world as it is in itself, independent of our observation and understanding of it. That does *not* mean, Kant insists, that space, time, and causality are mere illusions. To the contrary, they are an inescapable element of our empirical observable world. They are "empirically real, but transcendentally ideal"; that is, they are a genuine part of our empirical world; but from a God's eye view—from some ideal perspective which we cannot take—they are not part of the world.

This is Kant's effort to reconcile the insights of both empiricism and rationalism: to retain both Descartes' demand for certainty while recognizing Hume's empirical constraints on the limits of our knowledge. Kant's goal was to incorporate the remarkable developments of Newtonian empirical science (with its mechanistic, deterministic orientation) into a system which would also leave room for absolute certainties and the special powers of human reason and human will. Whether he was successful is a question that is still debated, and you will have to reach your own conclusion. But whether you follow the path laid out by Kant, or diverge sharply from his position, Kant's work marks an important crossroads in the history of thought. Kant pushed us to think much more carefully about how our own perspective and our own conceptual system shapes our understanding of the world.

READINGS

⇒ AN ENQUIRY CONCERNING HUMAN ⇒ UNDERSTANDING*
Of the Origin of Ideas
David Hume

David Hume (1711–1776) was born in Edinburgh and attended Edinburgh University. He attained great fame for his writings on philosophy, English history, and politics; and he is generally acknowledged to be one of the most insightful and influential philosophers of the modern era. He spent much of his adult life in Paris (during part of that time he held positions with the British ambassador in Paris) and was a very popular figure there (among his friends were Benjamin Franklin, the American ambassador to Paris). Hume's writings on religion were controversial, and during his lifetime the Scottish clergy referred to Hume as "the great infidel." In contrast, Hume's close friend and fellow Scot, the economist Adam Smith, said of him: "Upon the whole, I have always considered him, both in his lifetime and since his death, as approaching as nearly to the idea of a perfectly wise and virtuous man as perhaps the nature of human frailty will permit."

In this passage, Hume lays out the basics of his empiricist position, and uses the principles of empiricism to attack knowledge claims that lack an empirical or mathematical basis.

Everyone will readily allow that there is a considerable difference between the perceptions of the mind when a man feels the pain of excessive heat or the pleasure of moderate warmth, and when he afterwards recalls to his memory this sensation or anticipates it by his imagination. These faculties may mimic or copy the perceptions of the senses, but they never can entirely reach the force and vivacity of the original sentiment. The utmost we say of them, even when they operate with greatest vigor, is that they represent their object in so lively a manner that we could *almost* say we feel or see it. But, except the mind be disordered by disease or madness, they never can arrive at such a pitch of vivacity as to render these perceptions altogether undistinguishable. All the colors of poetry, however splendid, can never paint natural objects in such a manner as to make the description be taken for a real landscape. The most lively thought is still inferior to the dullest sensation.

---

*From *An Enquiry Concerning Human Understanding*, Sections 2 and 12 (originally published in 1758, though earlier versions were published several years before).

We may observe a like distinction to run through all the other perceptions of the mind. A man in a fit of anger is actuated in a very different manner from one who only thinks of that emotion. If you tell me that any person is in love, I easily understand your meaning and form a just conception of his situation, but never can mistake that conception for the real disorders and agitations of the passion. When we reflect on our past sentiments and affections, our thought is a faithful mirror and copies its objects truly, but the colors which it employs are faint and dull in comparison of those in which our original perceptions were clothed. It requires no nice discernment or metaphysical head to mark the distinction between them.

Here, therefore, we may divide all the perceptions of the mind into two classes or species, which are distinguished by their different degrees of force and vivacity. The less forcible and lively are commonly denominated "thoughts" or "ideas." The other species want a name in our language, and in most others; I suppose, because it was not requisite for any but philosophical purposes to rank them under a general term or appellation. Let us, therefore, use a little freedom and call them "impressions," employing that word in a sense somewhat different from the usual. By the term "impression," then, I mean all our more lively perceptions, when we hear, or see, or feel, or love, or hate, or desire, or will. And impressions are distinguished from ideas, which are the less lively perceptions of which we are conscious when we reflect on any of those sensations or movements above mentioned.

Nothing, at first view, may seem more unbounded than the thought of man, which not only escapes all human power and authority, but is not even restrained within the limits of nature and reality. To form monsters and join incongruous shapes and appearances costs the imagination no more trouble than to conceive the most natural and familiar objects. And while the body is confined to one planet, along which it creeps with pain and difficulty, the thought can in an instant transport us into the most distant regions of the universe, or even beyond the universe into the unbounded chaos where nature is supposed to lie in total confusion. What never was seen or heard of, may yet be conceived, nor is anything beyond the power of thought except what implies an absolute contradiction.

But though our thought seems to possess this unbounded liberty, we shall find upon a nearer examination that it is really confined within very narrow limits, and that all this creative power of the mind amounts to no more than the faculty of compounding, transposing, augmenting, or diminishing the materials afforded us by the senses and experience. When we think of a golden mountain, we only join two consistent ideas, "gold" and "mountain," with which we were formerly acquainted. A virtuous horse we can conceive, because, from our own feeling, we can conceive virtue; and this we may unite to the figure and shape of a horse, which is an animal familiar to us. In short, all the materials of thinking are derived either from our outward or inward sentiment; the mixture and composition of these belongs alone to the mind and will, or, to express myself in philosophical language, all our ideas or more feeble perceptions are copies of our impressions or more lively ones.

. . .

Here, therefore, is a proposition which not only seems in itself simple and intelligible, but, if a proper use were made of it, might render every dispute equally intelligible, and banish all that jargon which has so long taken possession of metaphysical reasonings and drawn disgrace upon them. All ideas, especially abstract ones, are naturally faint and obscure. The mind has but a slender hold of them. They are apt to be confounded with other resembling ideas; and when we have often employed any term, though without a distinct meaning, we are apt to imagine it has a determinate idea annexed to it. On the contrary, all impressions, that is, all sensations either outward or inward, are strong and vivid. The limits between them are more exactly determined, nor is it easy to fall into any error or mistake with regard to them. When we entertain, therefore, any suspicion that a philosophical terms is employed without any meaning or idea (as is but too frequent), we need but inquire, *from what impression is that supposed idea derived?* And if it be impossible to assign any, this will serve to confirm our suspicion. By bringing ideas in so clear a light, we may reasonably hope to remove all dispute which may arise concerning their nature and reality.

. . .

PART III

There is, indeed, a more *mitigated* skepticism or *academical* philosophy which may be both durable and useful, and which may, in part, be the result of this Pyrrhonism or *excessive* skepticism when its undistinguished doubts are, in some measure, corrected by common sense and reflection. The greater part of mankind are naturally apt to be affirmative and dogmatical in their opinions, and while they see objects only on one side and have no idea of any counterpoising argument, they throw themselves precipitately into the principles to which they are inclined, nor have they any indulgence for those who entertain opposite sentiments. To hesitate or balance perplexes their understanding, checks their passion, and suspends their actions. They are, therefore, impatient till they escape from a state which to them is so uneasy, and they think that they can never remove themselves far enough from it by the violence of their affirmations and obstinacy of their belief. But could such dogmatical reasoners become sensible of the strange infirmities of human understanding, even in its most perfect state and when most accurate and cautious in its determinations—such a reflection would naturally inspire them with more modesty and reserve, and diminish their fond opinion of themselves and their prejudice against antagonists. The illiterate may reflect on the disposition of the learned, who, amidst all the advantages of study and reflection, are commonly still diffident in their determinations. And if any of the learned be inclined, from their natural temper, to haughtiness and obstinacy, a small tincture of Pyrrhonism might abate their pride by showing them that the few advantages which they may have attained over their fellows are but inconsiderable if compared with the universal perplexity and confusion which is inherent in human nature. In general, there is a degree of doubt and caution and modesty which, in all kinds of scrutiny and decision, ought forever to accompany a just reasoner.

Another species of *mitigated* skepticism which may be of advantage to mankind, and which may be the natural result of the Pyrrhonian doubts and scruples, is the limitation of our inquiries to such subjects as are best adapted to the narrow capacity of human understanding. The *imagination* of man is naturally sublime, delighted with whatever is remote and extraordinary, and running, without control, into the most distant parts of space and time in order to avoid the objects which custom has rendered too familiar to it. A correct *judgment* observes a contrary method and, avoiding all distant and high inquiries, confines itself to common life and to such subjects as fall under daily practice and experience, leaving the more sublime topics to the embellishment of poets and orators or to the arts of priests and politicians. To bring us to so salutary a determination, nothing can be more serviceable than to be once thoroughly convinced of the force of the Pyrrhonian doubt and of the impossibility that anything but the strong power of natural instinct could free us from it. Those who have a propensity to philosophy will still continue their researches, because they reflect that, besides the immediate pleasure attending such an

occupation, philosophical decisions are nothing but the reflections of common life, methodized and corrected. But they will never be tempted to go beyond common life so long as they consider the imperfection of those faculties which they employ, their narrow reach, and their inaccurate operations. While we cannot give a satisfactory reason why we believe, after a thousand experiments, that a stone will fall or fire burn, can we ever satisfy ourselves concerning any determination which we may form with regard to the origin of worlds and the situation of nature from and to eternity?

This narrow limitation, indeed, of our inquiries is in every respect so reasonable that it suffices to make the slightest examination into the natural powers of the human mind, and to compare them with their objects, in order to recommend it to us. We shall then find what are the proper subjects of science and inquiry.

It seems to me that the only objects of the abstract sciences, or of demonstration, are quantity and number, and that all attempts to extend this more perfect species of knowledge beyond these bounds are mere sophistry and illusion. As the component parts of quantity and number are entirely similar, their relations become intricate and involved, and nothing can be more curious, as well as useful, than to trace, by a variety of mediums, their equality or inequality through their different appearances. But as all other ideas are clearly distinct and different from each other, we can never advance further, by our utmost scrutiny, than to observe this diversity and, by an obvious reflection, pronounce one thing not to be another. Or if there be any difficulty in these decisions, it proceeds entirely from the undeterminate meaning of words, which is corrected by juster definitions. That *the square of the hypotenuse is equal to the squares of the other two sides* cannot be known, let the terms be ever so exactly defined, without a train of reasoning and inquiry. But to convince us of this proposition, *that where there is no property there can be no injustice*, it is only necessary to define the terms and explain injustice to be a violation of property. This proposition is, indeed, nothing but a more imperfect definition. It is the same case with all those pretended syllogistical reasonings which may be found in every other branch of learning except the sciences of quantity and number; and these may safely, I think, be pronounced the only proper objects of knowledge and demonstration.

All other inquiries of men regard only matter of fact and existence, and these are evidently incapable of demonstration. Whatever *is* may *not be*. No negation of a fact can involve a contradiction. The nonexistence of any being, without exception, is as clear and distinct an idea as its existence. The proposition which affirms it not to be, however false, is no less conceivable and intelligible than that which affirms it to be. The case is different with the sciences, properly so called. Every proposition which is not true is there confused and unintelligible. That the cube root of 64 is equal to the half of 10 is a false proposition and can never be distinctly conceived. But that Caesar, or the angel Gabriel, or any being never existed may be a false proposition, but still is perfectly conceivable and implies no contradiction.

The existence, therefore, of any being can only be proved by arguments from its cause or its effect, and these arguments are founded entirely on experience. If we reason *a priori*, anything may appear able to produce anything. The falling of a pebble may, for aught we know, extinguish the sun, or the wish of a man control the planets in their orbits. It is only experience which teaches us the nature and bounds of cause and effect and enables us to infer the existence of one object from that of another. Such is the foundation of moral reasoning, which forms the greater part of human knowledge and is the source of all human action and behavior.

Moral reasonings are either concerning particular or general facts. All deliberations in life regard the former; as also all disquisitions in history, chronology, geography, and astronomy.

The sciences which treat of general facts are politics, natural philosophy, physics, chemistry, etc., where the qualities, causes, and effects of a whole species of objects are inquired into.

Divinity or theology, as it proves the existence of a deity and the immortality of souls, is composed partly of reasonings concerning particular, partly concerning general facts. It has a foundation in *reason* so far as it is supported by experience. But its best and most solid foundation is *faith* and divine revelation.

Morals and criticism are not so properly objects of the understanding as of taste and sentiment. Beauty, whether moral or natural, is felt more properly than perceived. Or if we reason concerning it and endeavor to fix the standard, we regard a new fact, to wit, the general taste of mankind, or some such fact which may be the object of reasoning and inquiry.

When we run over libraries, persuaded of these principles, what havoc must we make? If we take in our hand any volume—of divinity or school metaphysics, for instance—let us ask, *Does it contain any abstract reasoning concerning quantity or number?* No. *Does it contain any experimental reasoning concerning matter of fact and existence?* No. Commit it then to the flames, for it can contain nothing but sophistry and illusion.

⫸ AN ENQUIRY CONCERNING HUMAN ⫷ UNDERSTANDING*

Skeptical Doubts Concerning the Operations of The Understanding
David Hume

In this passage, Hume puts forward arguments that cast doubt on the *rational* grounds for inductive reasoning, and argues for a limited form of skepticism.

PART I

All the objects of human reason or inquiry may naturally be divided into two kinds, to wit, "Relations of Ideas," and "Matters of Fact." Of the first kind are the sciences of Geometry, Algebra, and Arithmetic, and, in short, every affirmation which is either intuitively or demonstratively certain. *That the square of the hypotenuse is equal to the square of the two sides* is a proposition which expresses a relation between these figures. *That three times five is equal to the half of thirty* expresses a relation between these numbers. Propositions of this kind are discoverable by the mere operation of thought, without dependence on what is anywhere existent in the universe. Though there never were a circle or triangle in nature, the truths demonstrated by Euclid would forever retain their certainty and evidence.

---

*From *An Enquiry Concerning Human Understanding* (originally published in 1758, though earlier versions were published several years before).

Matters of fact, which are the second objects of human reason, are not ascertained in the same manner, nor is our evidence of their truth, however great, of a like nature with the foregoing. The contrary of every matter of fact is still possible, because it can never imply a contradiction and is conceived by the mind with the same facility and distinctness as if ever so conformable to reality. *That the sun will not rise tomorrow* is no less intelligible a proposition and implies no more contradiction than the affirmation *that it will rise.* We should in vain, therefore, attempt to demonstrate its falsehood. Were it demonstratively false, it would imply a contradiction and could never be distinctly conceived by the mind.

It may, therefore, be a subject worthy of curiosity to inquire what is the nature of that evidence which assures us of any real existence and matter of fact beyond the present testimony of our senses or the records of our memory. This part of philosophy, it is observable, had been little cultivated either by the ancients or moderns; and, therefore, our doubts and errors in the prosecution of so important an inquiry may be the more excusable while we march through such difficult paths without any guide or direction. They may even prove useful by exciting curiosity and destroying that implicit faith and security which is the bane of all reasoning and free inquiry. The discovery of defects in the common philosophy, if any such there be, will not, I presume, be a discouragement, but rather an incitement, as is usual, to attempt something more full and satisfactory than has yet been proposed to the public.

All reasoning concerning matters of fact seem to be founded on the relation of *cause* and *effect.* By means of that relation alone we can go beyond the evidence of our memory and senses. If you were to ask a man why he believes any matter of fact which is absent, for instance, that his friend is in the country or in France, he would give you a reason, and this reason would be some other fact: as a letter received from him or the knowledge of his former resolutions and promises. A man finding a watch or any other machine in a desert island would conclude that there had once been men in that island. All our reasonings concerning fact are of the same nature. And here it is constantly supposed that there is a connection between the present fact and that which is inferred from it. Were there nothing to bind them together, the inference would be entirely precarious. The hearing of an articulate voice and rational discourse in the dark assures us of the presence of some person. Why? Because these are the effects of the human make and fabric, and closely connected with it. If we anatomize all the other reasonings of this nature, we shall find that they are founded on the relation of cause and effect, and that this relation is either near or remote, direct or collateral. Heat and light are collateral effects of fire, and the one effect may justly be inferred from the other.

If we would satisfy ourselves, therefore, concerning the nature of that evidence which assures us of matters of fact, we must inquire how we arrive at the knowledge of cause and effect.

I shall venture to affirm, as a general proposition which admits of no exception, that the knowledge of this relation is not, in any instance, attained by reasonings *a priori*, but arises entirely from experience, when we find that any particular objects are constantly conjoined with each other. Let an object be presented to a man of ever so strong natural reason and abilities—if that object be entirely new to him, he will not be able, by the most accurate examination of its sensible qualities, to discover any of its causes or effects. Adam, though his rational faculties may be supposed, at the very first, entirely perfect, could not have inferred from the fluidity and transparency of water that it would suffocate him, or from the light and warmth of fire that it would consume him. No object ever discovers, by the qualities which appear to the senses, either the causes which produced it or the effects which will arise from it; nor can our reason, unassisted by experience, ever draw any inference concerning real existence and matter of fact.

This proposition, *that causes and effects are discoverable, not by reason, but by experience,* will readily be admitted with regard to such objects as we remember to have once been altogether unknown to us, since we must be conscious of the utter inability which we then lay under of foretelling what would arise from them. Present two smooth pieces of marble to a man who has no tincture of natural philosophy; he will never discover that they will adhere together in such a manner as to require great force to separate them in a direct line, while they make so small a resistance to a lateral pressure. Such events as bear little analogy to the common course of nature are also readily confessed to be known only by experience, nor does any man imagine that the explosion of gunpowder or the attraction of a loadstone could ever be discovered by arguments *a priori.* In like manner, when an effect is supposed to depend upon an intricate machinery or secret structure of parts, we make no difficulty in attributing all our knowledge of it to experience. Who will assert that he can give the ultimate reason why milk or bread is proper nourishment for a man, not for a lion or tiger?

But the same truth may not appear at first sight to have the same evidence with regard to events which have become familiar to us from our first appearance in the world, which bear a close analogy to the whole course of nature, and which are supposed to depend on the simple qualities of objects without any secret structure of parts. We are apt to imagine that we could discover these effects by the mere operation of our reason without experience. We fancy that, were we brought on a sudden into this world, we could at first have inferred that one billiard ball would communicate motion to another upon impulse, and that we needed not have waited for the event in order to pronounce with certainty concerning it. Such is the influence of custom that where it is strongest it not only covers our natural ignorance but even conceals itself, and seems not to take place, merely because it is found in the highest degree.

But to convince us that all the laws of nature and all the operations of bodies without exception are known only by experience, the following reflections may perhaps suffice. Were any object presented to us, and were we required to pronounce concerning the effect which will result from it without consulting past observation, after what manner, I beseech you, must the mind proceed in this operation? It must invent or imagine some event which it ascribes to the object as its effect; and it is plain that this invention must be entirely arbitrary. The mind can never possibly find the effect in the supposed cause by the more accurate scrutiny and examination. For the effect is totally different from the cause, and consequently can never be discovered in it. Motion in the second billiard ball is a quite distinct event from motion in the first, nor is there anything in the one to suggest the smallest hint of the other. A stone or piece of metal raised into the air and left without any support immediately falls. But to consider the matter *a priori*, is there anything we discover in this situation which can beget the idea of a downward rather than an upward or any other motion in the stone or metal?

And as the first imagination or invention of a particular effect in all natural operations is arbitrary where we consult not experience, so must we also esteem the supposed tie or connection between the cause and effect which binds them together and renders it impossible that any other effect could result from the operation of that cause. When I see, for instance, a billiard ball moving in a straight line toward another, even suppose motion in the second ball should by accident be suggested to me as the result of their contact or impulse, may I not conceive that a hundred different events might as well follow from that cause? May not both these balls remain at absolute rest? May not the first ball return in a straight line or leap off from the second in any line or direction? All these suppositions are consistent and conceivable. Why, then, should we give the preference to one which is no more consistent or conceivable than the rest? All our reasonings *a priori* will never be able to show us any foundation for this preference. In a word, then, every effect is a distinct event from its cause. It could not, therefore, be discovered in the cause, and the first invention or conception of it, *a priori*, must be entirely arbitrary. And even after it is suggested, the conjunction of it with the cause must appear equally arbitrary, since there are always many other effects which, to reason, must seem fully as consistent and natural. In vain, therefore, should we pretend to determine any single event or infer any cause or effect without the assistance of observation and experience.

Hence we may discover the reason why no philosopher who is rational and modest has ever pretended to assign the ultimate cause of any natural operation, or to show distinctly the action of that power which produces any single effect in the universe. It is confessed that the utmost effort of human reason is to reduce the principles productive of natural phenomena to a greater simplicity, and to resolve the many particular effects into a few general causes, by means of reasonings from analogy, experience, and observation. But as to the causes of these general causes, we should in vain attempt their discovery, nor shall we ever be able to satisfy ourselves by any particular explication of them. These ultimate springs and principles are totally shut up from human curiosity and inquiry. Elasticity, gravity, cohesion of parts, communication of motion by impulse—these are probably the ultimate causes and principles which we shall ever discover in nature; and we may esteem ourselves sufficiently happy if, by accurate inquiry and reasoning, we can trace up the particular phenomena to, or near to, these general principles. The most perfect philosophy of the natural kind only staves off our ignorance a little longer, as perhaps the most perfect philosophy of the moral or metaphysical kind serves only to discover larger portions of it. Thus the observation of human blindness and weakness is the result of all philosophy, and meets us, at every turn, in spite of our endeavors to elude or avoid it.

Nor is geometry, when taken into the assistance of natural philosophy, ever able to remedy this defect or lead us into the knowledge of ultimate causes by all that accuracy of reasoning for which it is so justly celebrated. Every part of mixed mathematics proceeds upon the supposition that certain laws are established by nature in her operations, and abstract reasonings are employed either to assist experience in the discovery of these laws or to determine their influence in particular instances where it depends upon any precise degree of distance and quantity. Thus it is a law of motion, discovered by experience, that the moment or force of any body in motion is in the compound ratio or proportion of its solid contents and its velocity, and, consequently, that a small force may remove the greatest obstacle or raise the greatest weight if by any contrivance or machinery we can increase the velocity of that force so as to make it an overmatch for its antagonist. Geometry assists us in the application of this law by giving us the just dimensions of all the parts and figures which can enter into any species of machine, but still the discovery of the law itself is owing merely to experience; and all the abstract reasonings in the world could never lead us one step toward the knowledge of it. When we reason *a priori* and consider merely any object or cause as it appears to the mind, independent of all observation, it never could suggest to us the notion of any distinct object, such as its effect, much less show us the inseparable and inviolable connection between them. A man must be very sagacious who could discover by reasoning that crystal is the effect of heat, and ice of cold, without being previously acquainted with the operation of these qualities.

Part II

But we have not yet attained any tolerable satisfaction with regard to the question first proposed. Each solution still gives rise to a new question as difficult as the foregoing and leads us on to further inquiries. When it is asked, *What is the nature of all our reasonings concerning matter of fact?* the proper answer seems to be, That they are founded on the relation of cause and effect. When again it is asked, *What is the foundation of all our reasonings and conclusions concerning that relation?* it may be replied in one word, *experience*. But if we still carry on our sifting humor and ask, *What is the foundation of all conclusions from experience?* this implies a new question which may be of more difficult solution and explication. Philosophers that give

themselves airs of superior wisdom and sufficiency have a hard task when they encounter persons of inquisitive dispositions, who push them from every corner to which they retreat, and who are sure at last to bring them to some dangerous dilemma. The best expedient to prevent this confusion is to be modest in our pretensions and even to discover the difficulty ourselves before it is objected to us. By this means we may make a kind of merit of our very ignorance.

I shall content myself in this section with an easy task and shall pretend only to give a negative answer to the question here proposed. I say, then, that even after we have experience of the operations of cause and effect, our conclusions from that experience are *not* founded on reasoning or any process of the understanding. This answer we must endeavor both to explain and to defend.

It must certainly be allowed that nature has kept us at a great distance from all her secrets and has afforded us only the knowledge of a few superficial qualities of objects, while she conceals from us those powers and principles on which the influence of these objects entirely depends. Our senses inform us of the color, weight, and consistency of bread, but neither sense nor reason can ever inform us of those qualities which fit it for the nourishment and support of the human body. Sight or feeling conveys an idea of the actual motion of bodies, but as to that wonderful force or power which would carry on a moving body forever in a continued change of place, and which bodies never lose but by communicating it to others, of this we cannot form the most distant conception. But notwithstanding this ignorance of natural powers and principles, we always presume when we see like sensible qualities that they have like secret powers, and expect that effects similar to those which we have experienced will follow from them. If a body of like color and consistency with that bread which we have formerly eaten be presented to us, we make no scruple of repeating the experiment and foresee with certainty like nourishment and support. Now this is a process of the mind or thought of which I would willingly know the foundation. It is allowed on all hands that there is no known connection between the sensible qualities and the secret powers, and, consequently, that the mind is not led to form such a conclusion concerning their constant and regular conjunction by anything which it knows of their nature. As to past *experience*, it can be allowed to give *direct* and *certain* information of those precise objects only, and that precise period of time which fell under its cognizance: But why this experience should be extended to future times and to other objects which, for aught we know, may be only in appearance similar, this is the main question on which I would insist. The bread which I formerly ate nourished me; that is, a body of such sensible qualities was, at that time, endued with such secret powers. But does it follow that other bread must also nourish me at another time, and that like sensible qualities must always be attended with like secret powers? The consequence seems nowise necessary. At least, it must be acknowledged that there is here a consequence drawn by the mind that there is a certain step taken, a process of thought, and an inference which wants to be explained. These two propositions are far from being the same: *I have found that such an object has always been attended with such an effect*, and *I foresee that other objects which are in appearance similar will be attended with similar effects*. I shall allow, if you please, that the one proposition may justly be inferred from the other: I know, in fact, that it always is inferred. But if you insist that the inference is made by a chain of reasoning, I desire you to produce that reasoning. The connection between these propositions is not intuitive. There is required a medium which may enable the mind to draw such an inference, if indeed it be drawn by reasoning and argument. What that medium is I must confess passes my comprehension; and it is incumbent on those to produce it who assert that it really exists and is the original of all our conclusions concerning matter of fact.

This negative argument must certainly, in process of time, become altogether convincing if many penetrating and able philosophers shall turn their inquires this way, and no one be ever able to discover any connecting proposition or intermediate step which supports the understanding in this conclusion. But as the question is yet new, every reader may not trust so far to his own penetration as to conclude, because an argument escapes his inquiry, that therefore it does not really exist. For this reason it may be requisite to venture upon a more difficult task, and, enumerating all the branches of human knowledge, endeavor to show that none of them can afford such an argument.

All reasonings may be divided into two kinds, namely, demonstrative reasoning, or that concerning relations of ideas, and moral reasoning, or that concerning matter of fact and existence. That there are no demonstrative arguments in the case seems evident, since it implies no contradiction that the course of nature may change and that an object, seemingly like those which we have experienced, may be attended with different or contrary effects. May I not clearly and distinctly conceive that a body, falling from the clouds and which in all other respects resembles snow, has yet the taste of salt or feeling of fire? Is there any more intelligible proposition than to affirm that all the trees will flourish in December and January, and will decay in May and June? Now, whatever is intelligible and can be distinctly conceived implies no contradiction and can never be proved false by any demonstrative argument or abstract reasoning *a priori*.

If we be, therefore, engaged by arguments to put trust in past experience and make it the standard of our future judgment, these arguments must be probable only, or such as regard matter of fact and real existence, according to the division above mentioned. But that there is no argument of this kind must appear if our explication of that species of reasoning be admitted as solid and satisfactory. We have said that all arguments concerning existence are founded on the relation of cause and effect, that our knowledge of that relation is derived entirely from experience, and that all our experimental conclusions proceed upon the supposition that the future will be conformable to the past. To endeavor, therefore, the proof of this last supposition by probable arguments, or arguments regarding existence, must be evidently going in a circle and taking that for granted which is the very point in question.

In reality, all arguments from experience are founded on the similarity which we discover among natural objects, and by which we are induced to expect effects similar to those which we have found to follow from such objects. And though none but a fool or madman will ever pretend to dispute the authority of experience or to reject that great guide of human life, it may surely be allowed a philosopher to have so much curiosity at least as to examine the principle of human nature which gives this mighty authority to experience and makes us draw advantage from that similarity which nature has placed among different objects. From causes which appear similar, we expect similar effects. This is the sum of all our experimental conclusions. Now it seems evident that, if this conclusion were formed by reason, it would be as perfect at first, and upon one instance, as after ever so long a course of experience; but the case is far otherwise. Nothing is so like as eggs, yet no one, on account of this appearing similarity, expects the same taste and relish in all of them. It is only after a long course of uniform experiments in any kind that we attain a firm reliance and security with regard to a particular event. Now, where is that process of reasoning which, from one instance, draws a conclusion so different from that which it infers from a hundred instances that are nowise different from that single one? This question I propose as much for the sake of information as with an intention of raising difficulties. I cannot find, I cannot imagine any such reasoning. But I keep my mind still open to instruction if anyone will vouchsafe to bestow it on me.

Should it be said that, from a number of uniform experiments, we *infer* a connection between the sensible qualities and the secret powers, this, I must confess, seems the same difficulty, couched in different terms. The question still occurs, On what process of argument is this *inference* founded? Where is the medium, the interposing ideas which join propositions so very wide of each other? It is confessed that the color, consistency, and other sensible qualities of bread appear not of themselves to have any connection with the secret powers of nourishment and support; for otherwise we could infer these secret powers from the first appearance of these sensible qualities without the aid of experience, contrary to the sentiment of all philosophers, and contrary to plain matter of fact. Here, then, is our natural state of ignorance with regard to the powers and influence of all objects. How is this remedied by experience? It only shows us a number of uniform effects resulting from certain objects, and teaches us that those particular objects, at that particular time, were endowed with such powers and forces. When a new object endowed with similar sensible qualities is produced, we expect similar powers and forces, and look for a like effect. From a body of like color and consistency with bread, we expect like nourishment and support. But this surely is a step or progress of the mind which wants to be explained. When a man says, *I have found, in all past instances, such sensible qualities, conjoined with such secret powers,* and when he says, *similar sensible qualities will always be conjoined with similar secret powers,* he is not guilty of tautology, nor are these propositions in any respect the same. You say that the one proposition is an inference from the other; but you must confess that the inference is not intuitive, neither is it demonstrative. Of what nature is it then? To say it is experimental is begging the question. For all inferences from experience suppose, as their foundation, that the future will resemble the past and that similar powers will be conjoined with similar sensible qualities. If there be any suspicion that the course of nature may change, and that the past may be no rule for the future, all experience becomes useless and can give rise to no inference or conclusion. It is impossible, therefore, that

any arguments from experience can prove this resemblance of the past to the future, since all these arguments are founded on the supposition of that resemblance. Let the course of things be allowed hitherto ever so regular, that alone, without some new argument or inference, proves not that for the future it will continue so. In vain do you pretend to have learned the nature of bodies from your past experience. Their secret nature, and consequently all their effects and influence, may change without any change in their sensible qualities. This happens sometimes, and with regard to some objects. Why may it not happen always, and with regard to all objects? What logic, what process of argument secures you against this supposition? My practice, you say, refutes my doubts. But you mistake the purport of my question. As an agent, I am quite satisfied in the point; but as a philosopher who has some share of curiosity, I will not say skepticism, I want to learn the foundation of this inference. No reading, no inquiry has yet been able to remove my difficulty or give me satisfaction in a matter of such importance. Can I do better than propose the difficulty to the public, even though, perhaps, I have small hopes of obtaining a solution? We shall at least, by this means, be sensible of our ignorance, if we do not augment our knowledge.

I must confess that a man is guilty of unpardonable arrogance who concludes, because an argument has escaped his own investigation, that therefore it does not really exist. I must also confess that, though all the learned, for several ages, should have employed themselves in fruitless search upon any subject, it may still, perhaps, be rash to conclude positively that the subject must therefore pass all human comprehension. Even though we examine all the sources of our knowledge and conclude them unfit for such a subject, there may still remain a suspicion that the enumeration is not complete or the examination not accurate. But with regard to the present subject, there are some considerations which seem to remove all this accusation of arrogance or suspicion of mistake.

It is certain that the most ignorant and stupid peasants, nay infants, nay even brute beasts, improve by experience and learn the qualities of natural objects by observing the effects which result from them. When a child has felt the sensation of pain from touching the flame of a candle, he will be careful not to put his hand near any candle, but will expect a similar effect from a cause which is similar in its sensible qualities and appearance. If you assert, therefore, that the understanding of the child is led into this conclusion by any process of argument or ratiocination, I may justly require you to produce that argument, nor have you any pretense to refuse so equitable a demand. You cannot say that the argument is abstruse and may possibly escape your inquiry, since you confess that it is obvious to the capacity of a mere infant. If you hesitate, therefore, a moment or if, after reflection, you produce an intricate or profound argument, you, in a manner, give up the question and confess that it is not reasoning which engages us to suppose the past resembling the future, and to expect similar effects from causes which are to appearance similar. This is the proposition which I intended to enforce in the present section. If I be right, I pretend not to have made any mighty discovery. And if I be wrong, I must acknowledge myself to be indeed a very backward scholar, since I cannot now discover an argument which, it seems, was perfectly familiar to me long before I was out of my cradle.

⇒ PROLEGOMENA TO ANY FUTURE METAPHYSICS* ⇒
Immanuel Kant

Immanuel Kant (1724–1804) was a rather frail man who lived quietly, carried out his duties as a professor at the university at Königsberg, and never traveled more than a few miles from his birthplace. But even during his lifetime he was recognized as one of the great thinkers of his era, and "Kant Societies"—devoted to reading and studying his work—existed in many European cities.

Kant explored the basic question of *how* we gain knowledge, particularly *certain* knowledge; and he examined how our own methods of thinking and perceiving structure and shape our knowledge. Many of the most basic distinctions and questions that dominated philosophy over the following centuries were either proposed or elucidated by Kant.

PROLEGOMENA

Preamble on the Peculiarities of All Metaphysical Cognition

1. *Of the Sources of Metaphysics*

If it becomes desirable to formulate any cognition as science, it will be necessary first to determine accurately those peculiar features which no other science has in common with it, constituting its characteristics; otherwise the boundaries of all sciences become confused, and none of them can be treated thoroughly according to its nature.

The characteristics of a science may consist of a simple difference of object, or of the sources of cognition, or of the kind of cognition, or perhaps of all three conjointly. On this, therefore, depends the idea of a possible science and its territory.

First, as concerns the sources of metaphysical cognition, its very concept implies that they cannot be empirical. Its principles (including not only its maxims but its basic notions) must never be derived from experience. It must not be physical but metaphysical knowledge, viz., knowledge lying beyond experience. It can therefore have for its basis neither external experience, which is the source of physics proper, nor internal, which is the basis of empirical psychology. It is therefore *a priori* knowledge, coming from pure Understanding and pure Reason.

But so far Metaphysics would not be distinguishable from pure Mathematics; it must therefore be called pure philosophical cognition; . . .

2. *Concerning the Kind of Cognition Which Can Alone Be Called Metaphysical*

a. *Of the distinction between Analytical and Synthetical Judgments in general.*—The peculiarity of its sources demands that metaphysical cognition must consist of nothing but *a priori* judgments. But whatever be their origin, or their logical form, there is a distinction in judgments, as to their content, according to which they are either merely explicative, adding nothing to the content of the cognition, or expansive, increasing the given cognition: the former may be called analytical, the latter synthetical, judgments.

Analytical judgments express nothing in the predicate but what has been already actually thought in the concept of the subject, though not so distinctly or with the same (full) consciousness. When I say: All bodies are extended,

---

*Originally published in 1783.

I have not amplified in the least my concept of body, but have only analysed it, as extension was really thought to belong to that concept before the judgment was made, though it was not expressed. This judgment is therefore analytical. On the contrary, this judgment, All bodies have weight, contains in its predicate something not actually thought in the general concept of the body; it amplifies my knowledge by adding something to my concept, and must therefore be called synthetical.

b. *The Common Principles of all Analytical Judgments is the Law of Contradiction.*—All analytical judgments depend wholly on the law of Contradiction, and are in their nature *a priori* cognitions, whether the concepts that supply them with matter be empirical or not. For the predicate of an affirmative analytical judgment is already contained in the concept of the subject, of which it cannot be denied without contradiction. In the same way its opposite is necessarily denied of the subject in an analytical, but negative, judgment, by the same law of contradiction. Such is the nature of the judgments: all bodies are extended, and no bodies are unextended (i.e., simple).

For this very reason all analytical judgments are *a priori* even when the concepts are empirical, as, for example, Gold is a yellow metal; for to know this I require no experience beyond my concept of gold as a yellow metal: it is, in fact, the very concept, and I need only analyse it, without looking beyond it elsewhere.

c. *Synthetical Judgments require a different Principle from the Law of Contradiction.*—There are synthetical *a posteriori* judgments of empirical origin; but there are also others which are proved to be certain *a priori*, and which spring from pure Understanding and Reason. Yet they both agree in this, that they cannot possibly spring from the principle of analysis, viz., the law of contradiction, alone; they require a quite different principle, though, from whatever they may be deduced, they must be subject to the law of contradiction, which must never be violated, even though everything cannot be deduced from it. I shall first classify synthetical judgments.

1. *Empirical Judgments* are always synthetical. For it would be absurd to base an analytical judgment on experience, as our concept suffices for the purpose without requiring any testimony from experience. That body is extended, is a judgment established *a priori*, and not an empirical judgment.

For before appealing to experience, we already have all the conditions of the judgment in the concept, from which we have but to elicit the predicate according to the law of contradiction, and thereby to become conscious of the necessity of the judgment, which experience could not ever teach us.

2. *Mathematical Judgments* are all synthetical. This fact seems hitherto to have altogether escaped the observation of those who have analysed human reason; it even seems directly opposed to all their conjectures, though incontestably certain, and most important in its consequences. For as it was found that the conclusions of mathematicians all proceed according to the law of contradiction (as is demanded by all apodeictic certainly), men persuaded themselves that the fundamental principles were known from the same law. This was a great mistake, for a synthetical proposition can indeed be comprehended according to the law of contradiction, but only by presupposing another synthetical proposition from which it follows, but never in itself.

First of all, we must observe that all proper mathematical judgments are *a priori*, and not empirical, because they carry with them necessity, which cannot be obtained from experience. But if this be not conceded to me, very good; I shall confine my assertion to *pure Mathematics*, the very notion of which implies that it contains pure *a priori* and not empirical cognitions.

. . .

3. *A Remark on the General Division of Judgments into Analytical and Synthetical*

This division is indispensable, as concerns the critique of human understanding, and therefore deserves to be called classical, though otherwise it is of little use, but this is the reason why dogmatic philosophers, who always seek the sources of metaphysical judgments in Metaphysics itself, and not apart from it, in the pure laws of reason generally, altogether neglected this apparently obvious distinction. Thus the celebrated Wolf, and his acute follower Baumgarten, came to seek the proof of the principle of Sufficient Reason, which is clearly synthetical, in the principle of Contradiction. In Locke's Essay, however, I find an indication of my division. For in the fourth book (chap. iii. § 9. seq.), having discussed the various connexions of representations in judgments, and their sources, one of which he makes "identity and contradiction" (analytical judgments), and another the coexistence of representations in a subject, he confesses (§ 10) that our *a priori* knowledge of the latter is very narrow, and almost nothing. But in his remarks on this species of cognition, there is so little of what is definite, and reduced to rules, that we cannot wonder if no one, not even Hume, was led to make investigations concerning this sort of judgments. For such general and yet definite principles are not easily learned from other men, who have had them obscurely in their minds. We must hit on them first by our own reflexion, then we find them elsewhere, where we could not possibly have found them at first, because the authors themselves did not know that such an idea lay at the basis of their observations. Men who never think independently have nevertheless the acuteness to discover everything, after it has been once shown them, in what was said long since, though no one ever saw it there before.

4. *The General Question of the Prolegomena—Is Metaphysics at all Possible?*

Were a metaphysics, which could maintain its place as a science, really in existence; could we say, here is metaphysics, learn it, and it will convince you irresistibly and irrevocably of its truth? This question would be useless, and there would only remain that other question (which would rather be a test of our acuteness, than a proof of the existence of the thing itself), "How is the science possible, and how does reason come to attain it?" But human reason has not been so fortunate in this case. There is no single book to which you can point as you do to Euclid, and say: This is Metaphysics; here you may find the noblest objects of this science, the knowledge of a highest Being, and of a future existence, proved from principles of pure reason. We can be shown indeed many judgments, demonstrably certain, and never questioned; but these are all analytical, and rather concern the materials and the scaffolding for Metaphysics, than the extension of knowledge, which is our proper object in studying it. . . . Even supposing you produce synthetical judgments (such as the law of Sufficient Reason, which you have never proved, as you ought to, from pure reason *a priori*, though we gladly concede its truth), you lapse when they come to be employed for your principal object, into such doubtful assertions, that in all ages one Metaphysics has contradicted another, either in its assertions, or their proofs, and thus has itself destroyed its own claim to lasting assent. Nay, the very attempts to set up such a

science are the main cause of the early appearance of scepticism, a mental attitude in which reason treats itself with such violence that it could never have arisen save from complete despair of ever satisfying our most important aspirations. For long before men began to inquire into nature methodically, they consulted abstract reason, which had to some extent been exercised by means of ordinary experience; for reason is ever present, while laws of nature must usually be discovered with labor. So Metaphysics floated to the surface, like foam, which dissolved the moment it was scooped off. But immediately there appeared a new supply on the surface, to be ever eagerly gathered up by some, while others, instead of seeking in the depths the cause of the phenomenon, thought they showed their wisdom by ridiculing the idle labor of their neighbors.

The essential and distinguishing feature of pure mathematical cognition among all other *a priori* cognitions is, that it cannot at all proceed from concepts, but only by means of the construction of concepts. . . . As therefore in its judgments it must proceed beyond the concept to that which its corresponding visualisation contains, these judgments neither can, nor ought to, arise analytically, by dissecting the concept, but are all synthetical.

. . .

5. *The General Problem: How Is Knowledge from Pure Reason Possible?*

We have above learned the significant distinction between analytical and synthetical judgments. The possibility of analytical propositions was easily comprehended, being entirely founded on the law of Contradiction. The possibility of synthetical *a posteriori* judgments, of those which are gathered from experience, also requires no particular explanation; for experience is nothing but a continual synthesis of perceptions. There remain therefore only synthetical propositions *a priori*, of which the possibility must be sought or investigated, because they must depend upon other principles than the law of contradiction.

But here we need not first establish the possibility of such propositions so as to ask whether they are possible. For there are enough of them which indeed are of undoubted certainty, and as our present method is analytical, we shall start from the fact, that such synthetical but purely rational cognition actually exists; but we must now inquire into the reason of this possibility, and ask, *how* such cognition is possible, in order that we may from the principles of its possibility be enabled to determine the conditions of its use, its sphere and its limits. The proper problem upon which all depends, when expressed with scholastic precision, is therefore:

How are Synthetical Propositions a priori *possible?*

For the sake of popularity I have above expressed this problem somewhat differently, as an inquiry into purely rational cognition, which I could do for once without detriment to the desired comprehension, because, as we have only to do here with metaphysics and its sources, the reader will, I hope, after the foregoing remarks, keep in mind that when we speak of purely rational cognition, we do not mean analytical, but synthetical cognition.

Metaphysics stands or falls with the solution of this problem: its very existence depends upon it. Let any one make metaphysical assertions with ever so much plausibility, let him overwhelm us with conclusions, if he has not previously proved able to answer this question satisfactorily, I have a right to say: this is all vain baseless philosophy and false wisdom. You speak through pure reason, and claim, as it were to create cognitions *a priori* by not only dissecting given concepts, but also by asserting connexions which do not rest upon the law of contradiction, and which you believe you conceive quite independently of all experience; how do you arrive at this, and how will you justify your pretensions? . . .

The answer to this question, though indispensable, is difficult; and though the principal reason that it was not made long ago is, that the possibility of the question never occurred to anybody, there is yet another reason, which is this that a satisfactory answer to this one question requires a much more persistent, profound, and painstaking reflexion, than the most diffuse work on Metaphysics, which on its first appearance promised immortality to its author. And every intelligent reader, when he carefully reflects what this problem requires, must at first be struck with its difficulty, and would regard it as insoluble and even impossible, did there not actually exist pure synthetical cognitions *a priori.*

. . .

8. . . . "How is it possible to intuit [in a visual form] anything *a priori?*" An intuition [viz., a visual sense perception] is such a representation as immediately depends upon the presence of the object. Hence it seems impossible to intuit from the outset *a priori,* because intuition would in that event take

place without either a former or a present object to refer to, and by consequence could not be intuition. Concepts indeed are such that we can easily form some of them *a priori,* viz., such as contain nothing but the thought of an object in general; and we need not find ourselves in an immediate relation to the object. Take, for instance, the concepts of Quantity, of Cause, etc. But even these require, in order to make them understood, a certain concrete use—that is, an application to some sense-experience by which an object of them is given us. But how can the intuition of the object [its visualization] precede the object itself?

9. If our intuition [i.e., our sense-experience] were perforce of such a nature as to represent things as they are in themselves, there would not be any intuition *a priori,* but intuition would be always empirical. For I can only know what is contained in the object in itself when it is present and given to me. It is indeed even then incomprehensible how the visualising of a present thing should make me know this thing as it is in itself, as its properties cannot migrate into my faculty of representation. But even granting this possibility, a visualising of that sort would not take place *a priori,* that is, before the object were presented to me; for without this latter fact no reason of a relation between my representation and the object can be imagined, unless it depend upon a direct inspiration.

Therefore in one way only can my intuition anticipate the actuality of the object, and be a cognition *a priori,* viz.: if my intuition contains nothing but the form of sensibility, antedating in my subjectivity all the actual impressions through which I am affected by objects.

For that objects of sense can only be intuited according to this form of sensibility I can know *a priori.* Hence it follows: that propositions, which concern this form of sensuous intuition only, are possible and valid for objects of the senses; as also, conversely, that intuitions which are possible *a priori* can never concern any other things than objects of our senses.

10. Accordingly, it is only the form of sensuous intuition by which we can intuit things *a priori,* but by which we can know objects only as they appear to us (to our senses), not as they are in themselves; and this assumption is absolutely necessary if synthetical propositions *a priori* be granted as possible, or if, in case they actually occur, their possibility is to be comprehended and determined beforehand.

Now, the intuitions which pure mathematics lays at the foundation of all its cognitions and judgments which appear at once apodeictic and necessary are Space and Time. For mathematics must first have all its concepts in intuition, and pure mathematics in pure intuition, that is, it must construct them. If it proceeded in any other way, it would be impossible to make any headway, for mathematics proceeds, not analytically by dissection of concepts, but synthetically, and if pure intuition be wanting, there is nothing in which the matter for synthetical judgments *a priori* can be given. Geometry is based upon the pure intuition of space. Arithmetic accomplishes its concept of number by the successive addition of units in time; and pure mechanics especially cannot attain its concepts of motion without employing the representation of time. Both representations, however, are only intuitions; for if we omit from the empirical intuitions of bodies and their alterations (motion) everything empirical, or belonging to sensation, space and time still remain, which are therefore pure intuitions that lie *a priori* at the basis of the empirical. Hence they can never be omitted, but at the same time, by their being pure intuitions *a priori*, they prove that they are mere forms of our sensibility, which must precede all empirical intuition, or perception of actual objects, and conformably to which objects can be known *a priori*, but only as they appear to us.

11. The problem of the present section is therefore solved. Pure mathematics, as synthetical cognition *a priori*, is only possible by referring to no other objects than those of the senses. At the basis of their empirical intuition lies a pure intuition (of space and of time) which is *a priori*. This is possible, because the latter intuition is nothing but the mere form of sensibility, which precedes the actual appearance of the objects, in that it, in fact, makes them possible. Yet this faculty of intuiting *a priori* affects not the matter of the phenomenon (that is, the sense-element in it, for this constitutes that which is empirical), but its form, viz., space and time. Should any man venture to doubt that these are determinations adhering not to things in themselves, but to their relation to our sensibility, I should be glad to know how it can be possible to know the constitution of things *a priori*, viz., before we have any acquaintance with them and before they are presented to us. Such, however, is the case with space and time. But this is quite comprehensible as soon as both count for nothing more than formal conditions of our sensibility, while the objects count merely as phenomena; for then the form of the phenomenon, i.e., pure intuition, can by all means be represented as proceeding from ourselves, that is, *a priori*.

. . .

Remark I

Pure Mathematics, and especially pure geometry, can only have objective reality on condition that they refer to objects of sense. But in regard to the latter the principle holds good, that our sense representation is not a representation of things in themselves, but of the way in which they appear to us. Hence it follows, that the propositions of geometry are not the results of a mere creation of our poetic imagination, and that therefore they cannot be referred with assurance to actual objects; but rather that they are necessarily valid of space, and consequently of all that may be found in space, because space is nothing else than the form of all external appearances, and it is this form alone in which objects of sense can be given. Sensibility, the form of which is the basis of geometry, is that upon which the possibility of external appearance depends. Therefore these appearances can never contain anything but what geometry prescribes to them.

It would be quite otherwise if the senses were so constituted as to represent objects as they are in themselves. For then it would not by any means follow from the conception of space, which with all its properties serves to the geometer as an *a priori* foundation, together with what is thence inferred, must be so in nature. The space of the geometer would be considered a mere fiction, and it would not be credited with objective validity, because we cannot see how things must of necessity agree with an image of them, which we make spontaneously and previous to our acquaintance with them. But if this image, or rather this formal intuition, is the essential property of our sensibility, by means of which alone objects are given to us, and if this sensibility represents not things in themselves, but their appearances: we shall easily comprehend, and at the same time indisputably prove, that all external objects of our world of sense must necessarily coincide in the most rigorous way with the propositions of geometry; because sensibility by means of its form of external intuition, viz., by space, the same with which the geometer is occupied, makes those objects at all possible as mere appearances.

How Is the Science of Nature Possible?

14. Nature is the existence of things, so far as it is determined according to universal laws. Should nature signify the existence of things in themselves, we could never cognise it either *a priori* or *a posteriori*. Not *a priori*, for how can we know what belongs to things in themselves, since this never can be done by the dissection of our concepts (in analytical judgments)? We do not want to know what is contained in our concept of a thing (for the [concept describes what] belongs to its logical being), but what is in the actuality of the thing superadded to our concept, and by what the thing itself is determined in its existence outside the concept. Our understanding, and the conditions on which alone it can connect the determinations of things in their existence, do not prescribe any rule to things themselves; these do not conform to our understanding, but it must conform itself to them; they must therefore be first given us in order to gather these determinations from them, wherefore they would not be cognised *a priori*.

A cognition of the nature of things in themselves *a posteriori* would be equally impossible. For, if experience is to teach us laws, to which the existence of things is subject, these laws, if they regard things in themselves, must belong to them of necessity even outside our experience. But experience teaches us what exists and how it exists, but never that it must necessarily exist so and not otherwise. Experience therefore can never teach us the nature of things in themselves.

15. We nevertheless actually possess a pure science of nature in which are propounded, *a priori* and with all the necessity requisite to apodeictical propositions, laws to which nature is subject. I need only call to witness that propaedeutic [introduction] of natural science which, under the title of the universal Science of Nature, precedes all Physics (which is founded upon empirical principles). In it we have Mathematics applied to appearance, and also merely discursive principles (or those derived from concepts), which constitute the philosophical part of the pure cognition of nature. But there are several things in it, which are not quite pure and independent of empirical sources: such as the concept of *motion*, that of *impenetrability* (upon which

the empirical concept of matter rests), that of *inertia*, and many others, which prevent its being called a perfectly pure science of nature. Besides, it only refers to objects of the external sense, and therefore does not give an example of a universal science of nature, in the strict sense, for such a science must reduce nature in general, whether it regards the object of the external or that of the internal sense (the object of Physics as well as Psychology), to universal laws. But among the principles of this universal physics there are a few which actually have the required universality; for instance, the propositions that "substance is permanent," and that "every event is determined by a cause according to constant laws," etc. These are actually universal laws of nature, which subsist completely *a priori*. There is then in fact a pure science of nature, and the question arises, *How is it possible?*

16. The word "nature" assumes yet another meaning, which determines the object, whereas in the former sense it only denotes the conformity to law of the determinations of the existence of things generally. If we consider it *materialiter* (i.e., in the matter that forms its objects) "nature is the complex of all the objects of experience." And with this only are we now concerned, for besides, things which can never be objects of experience, if they must be cognised as to their nature, would oblige us to have recourse to concepts whose meaning could never be given *in concreto* (by any example of possible experience). Consequently we must form for ourselves a list of concepts of their nature, the reality whereof (i.e., whether they actually refer to objects, or are mere creations of thought) could never be determined. The cognition of what cannot be an object of experience would be hyperphysical, and with things hyperphysical we are here not concerned, but only with the cognition of nature, the actuality of which can be confirmed by experience, though it [the cognition of nature] is possible *a priori* and precedes all experience.

17. The former [aspect] of nature in this narrower sense is therefore the conformity to law of all the objects of experience, and so far as it is cognised *a priori*, their necessity conformity. But it has just been shown that the laws of nature can never be cognised *a priori* in objects so far as they are considered not in reference to possible experience, but as things in themselves. And our inquiry here extends not to things in themselves (the properties of which we pass by), but to things as objects of possible experience, and the complex of these is what we properly designate as nature. And now I ask, when the possibility of a cognition of nature *a priori* is in question, whether it is better to arrange the problem thus: How can we cognise *a priori* that things as objects of experience necessarily conform to law? or thus: How is it possible to cognise *a priori* the necessary conformity to law of experience itself as regards all its objects generally?

Closely considered, the solution of the problem, represented in either way, amounts, with regard to the pure cognition of nature (which is the point of the question at issue), entirely to the same thing. For the subjective laws, under which alone an empirical cognition of things is possible, hold good of these things, as objects of possible experience (not as things in themselves, which are not considered here). Either of the following statements means quite the same:

"A judgment of observation can never rank as experience without the law that whenever an event is observed, it is always referred to some antecedent, which it follows according to a universal rule."

"Everything, of which experience teaches that it happens, must have a cause."

It is, however, more commendable to choose the first formula. For we can *a priori* and previous to all given objects have a cognition of those conditions, on which alone experience is possible, but never of the laws to which things may in themselves be subject, without reference to possible experience. We cannot therefore study the nature of things *a priori* otherwise than by investigating the conditions and the universal (though subjective) laws, under which alone such a cognition as experience (as to mere form) is possible, and we determine accordingly the possibility of things, as objects of experience. For if I should choose the second formula, and seek the conditions *a priori*, on which nature as an object of experience is possible, I might easily fall into error, and fancy that I was speaking of nature as a thing in itself, and then move round in endless circles, in a vain search for laws concerning things of which nothing is given me.

Accordingly we shall here be concerned with experience only, and the universal conditions of its possibility which are given *a priori*. Thence we shall determine nature as the whole object of all possible experience. I think it will be understood that I here do not mean the rules of the observation of a nature that is already given, for these already presuppose experience. I do not mean how (through experience) we can study the laws of nature; for these would not then be laws *a priori*, and would yield us no pure science of nature; but [I mean to ask] how the conditions of the possibility of experience are at the same time the sources from which all the universal laws of nature must be derived.

18. In the first place we must state that, while all judgments of experience are empirical (i.e., have their ground in immediate sense-perception), vice versa, all empirical judgments are not judgments of experience, but, besides the empirical, and in general besides what is given to the sensuous intuition, particular, concepts must yet be superadded—concepts which have their origin quite *a priori* in the pure understanding, and under which every perception must be first of all subsumed and then by their means changed into experience.

Empirical judgments, so far as they have objective validity, are *judgments of experience*; but those which are only subjectively valid, I name mere *judgments of perception*. The latter require no pure concept of the understanding, but only the logical connexion of perception in a thinking subject. But the former always require, besides the representation of the sensuous intuition, particular *concepts originally begotten in the understanding*, which produce the objective validity of the judgment of experience.

All our judgments are at first merely judgments of perception; they hold good only for us (i.e., for our subject), and we do not till afterwards give them a new reference (to an object), and desire that they shall always hold good for us and in the same way for everybody else; for when a judgment agrees with an object, all judgments concerning the same object must likewise agree among themselves, and thus the objective validity of the judgment of experience signifies nothing else than its necessary universality of application. And conversely when we have reason to consider a judgment necessarily universal (which never depends upon perception, but upon the pure concept of the understanding, under which the perception is subsumed), we must consider it objective also, that is, that it expresses not merely a reference of our perception to a subject, but a quality of the object. For there would be no reason for the judgment of other men necessarily agreeing with mine, if it were not the unity of the object to which they all refer, and with which they accord; hence they must all agree with one another.

19. Therefore objective validity and necessary universally (for everybody) are equivalent terms, and

though we do not know the object in itself, yet when we consider a judgment as universal, and also necessary, we understand it to have objective validity. By this judgment we cognise the object (though it remains unknown as it is in itself) by the universal and necessary connexion of the given perceptions. As this is the case with all objects of sense, judgments of experience take their objective validity not from the immediate cognition of the object (which is impossible), but from the condition of universal validity in empirical judgments, which, as already said, never rests upon empirical, or, in short, sensuous conditions, but upon a pure concept of the understanding. The object always remains unknown in itself; but when by the concept of the understanding the connexion of the representations of the object, which are given to our sensibility, is determined as universally valid, the object is determined by this relation, and it is the judgment that is objective.

To illustrate the matter: When we say, "the room is warm, sugar sweet, and wormwood bitter,"— we have only subjectively valid judgments. I do not at all expect that I or any other person shall always find it as I now do; each of these sentences only expresses a relation of two sensations to the same subject, to myself, and that only in my present state of perception; consequently they are not valid of the object. Such are judgments of perception. Judgments of experience are of quite a different nature. What experience teaches me under certain circumstances, it must always teach me and everybody; and its validity is not limited to the subject nor to its state at a particular time. Hence I pronounce all such judgments as being objectively valid. For instance, when I say the air is elastic, this judgment is as yet a judgment of perception only—I do nothing but refer two of my sensations to one another. But, if I would have it called a judgment of experience, I require this connexion to stand under a condition, which makes it universally valid. I desire therefore that I and everybody else should always connect necessarily the same perceptions under the same circumstances.

20. We must consequently analyse experience in order to see what is contained in this product of the senses and of the understanding, and how the judgment of experience itself is possible. The foundation is the intuition of which I become conscious i.e., perception which pertains merely to the senses. But in the next place, there are acts of judging (which belong only to the understanding). But this judging may be twofold— first, I may merely compare perceptions and connect

them in a particular state of my consciousness; or, secondly, I may connect them in consciousness generally. The former judgment is merely a judgment of perception, and of subjective validity only: it is merely a connexion of perceptions in my mental state, without reference to the object. Hence it is not, as is commonly imagined, enough for experience to compare perceptions and to connect them in consciousness through judgment; there arises no universality and necessity, for which alone judgments can become objectively valid and be called experience.

Quite another judgment therefore is required before perception can become experience. The given intuition must be subsumed under a concept, which determines the form of judging in general relatively to the intuition, connects its empirical consciousness of intuition in consciousness generally, and thereby procures universal validity for empirical judgments. A concept of this nature is a pure *a priori* concept of the Understanding, which does nothing but determine for an intuition the general way in which it can be used for judgments. Let the concept be that of cause, then it determines the intuition which is subsumed under it, for example, that of air, relative to judgments in general, viz., the concept of air serves with regard to its expansion in the relation of antecedent to consequent in a hypothetical judgment. The concept of cause accordingly is a pure concept of the understanding, which is totally disparate from all possible perception, and only serves to determine the representation subsumed under it, relatively to judgments in general, and so to make a universally valid judgment possible.

Before, therefore, a judgment of perception can become a judgment of experience, it is requisite that the perception should be subsumed under some such a concept of the understanding; for instance, air ranks under the concept of causes, which determines our judgment about it in regard to its expansion as hypothetical. Thereby the expansion of the air is represented not as merely belonging to the perception of the air in my present state or in several states of mine, or in the state of perception of others, but as belonging to it necessarily. The judgment, "the air is elastic," becomes universally valid, and a judgment of experience, only by certain judgments preceding it, which subsume the intuition of air under the concept of cause and effect: and they thereby determine the perceptions not merely as regards one another in me, but relatively to the form of judging in general, which is here hypothetical, and in this way they render the empirical judgment universally valid.

If all our synthetical judgments are analysed so far as they are objectively valid, it will be found that they never consist of mere intuitions connected only (as is commonly believed) by comparison into a judgment; but that they would be impossible were not a pure concept of the understanding superadded to the concepts abstracted from intuition, under which concept these latter are subsumed, and in this manner only combined into an objectively valid judgment. . . .

21. . . . Experience consists of intuitions, which belongs to the sensibility, and of judgments, which are entirely a work of the understanding. But the judgments, which the understanding forms alone from sensuous intuitions, are far from being judgments of experience. For in the one case the judgment connects only the perceptions as they are given in the sensuous intuition, while in the other the judgments must express what experience in general, and not what the mere perception (which possesses only subjective validity) contains. The judgment of experience must therefore add to the sensuous intuition and its logical connexion in a judgment (after it has been rendered universal by comparison) something that determines the synthetical judgment as necessary and therefore as universally valid. This can be nothing else than that concept which represents the intuition as determined in itself with regard to one form of judgment rather than another, viz., a concept of that synthetical unity of intuitions which can only be represented by a given logical function of judgments.

22. The sum of the matter is this: the business of the senses is to intuit—that of the understanding is to think. But thinking is uniting representations in one consciousness. This union originates either merely relative to the subject, and is accidental and subjective, or is absolute, and is necessary or objective. The union of representations in one consciousness is judgment. Thinking therefore is the same as judging, or referring representations to judgments in general. Hence judgments are either merely subjective, when representations are referred to a consciousness in one subject only, and united in it, or objective, when they are united in a consciousness generally, that is, necessarily. The logical functions of all judgments are but various modes of uniting representations in consciousness. But if they serve for concepts, they are concepts of their necessary union in a consciousness, and so principles of objectively valid judgments. This union in a consciousness is either analytical, by identity, or synthetical, by the combination and addition of various representations one to another. Experience consists in the synthetical connexion of phenomena (perceptions) in consciousness, so far as this connexion is necessary. Hence the pure concepts of the understanding are those under which all perceptions must be subsumed before they can serve for judgments of experience, in which the synthetical unity of the perceptions is represented as necessary and universally valid.

EXERCISES

1. Descartes championed an *internalist* view: If we are to have genuine knowledge, we must be able to *know* that we know (or at least know that our beliefs are *justified*) by means of our own reflective capacities, without any *external* confirmation (for after all, once we go outside ourselves—to our observations, or some external authority, or whatever—we open ourselves to the possibility of being mistaken or misled or misinformed). In contrast to internalists, the *externalists* hold that justifying beliefs need not be a private process, but can instead rely on external sources: A belief may be justified by checking observations and results and calculations with others, perhaps with a broad community of observers and inquirers. The basic question is whether one can be *justified* in holding a belief, even if one cannot now call up any internal resources that would offer evidence for that belief. (That evidence need not be derived from pure reason; internalists would accept your remembered observations, or your memory of gaining the belief from some reputable source—such as an encyclopedia or a newspaper. But internalists insist that for a belief to be justified, the believer must currently have *internal* resources that provide the justification. If you would require an external source in order to justify your belief—the evidence of your senses, the confirmation of a friend, or the assurance of an authority—then you are not now *justified* in holding that belief. And if you cannot *give* an internal justification for your belief—for example, if you think you know that Jupiter is the largest planet, but you have no idea why you think that

belief is true; you can't remember learning it from any reliable source, or proving it by any calculation of your own—then your belief is *not justified*. Even if your belief happens to be true, you do not really *know* that it is true because *you* lack internal justification for your belief.) The internalist/externalist controversy is an active debate in contemporary epistemology. Which side strikes you as more plausible? Do you hold any beliefs for which you could not give some reasonable justification? If so, would you claim to *know* that any of those beliefs—which you cannot now internally justify—are beliefs that count as genuine *knowledge*? If you believe that such beliefs *cannot* count as knowledge, then you are an internalist; if you think they might qualify as knowledge, even though you cannot give an internal justification for your belief, then you are an externalist.

2. Of all your ideas, are there any you would consider plausible candidates to be *innate*?

3. John Dewey—the American pragmatist of the early twentieth century—criticized Kant for supposing that our conceptual categories are *permanent*. On that basis, Dewey insisted that Kant did not really carry out the Copernican Revolution in philosophy (as Kant claimed) because Kant could not give up the idea of fixed permanent principles and categories. Dewey viewed these categories as changing instruments that we *use* as tools—and modify, and sometimes replace—rather than as fixed principles of universal understanding. From your own perspective, is it more plausible to view such basic categories as fixed ways of thinking that all rational creatures must use, or as useful ways of thinking that are subject to modification and replacement?

4. Thomas Nagel, a leading contemporary British philosopher (who now teaches at New York University), made the following claim (in his fascinating book, *The View from Nowhere*, 1986, p. 98):

> Creatures who recognize their limited nature and their containment in the world must recognize both that reality may extend beyond our conceptual reach and that there may be concepts that we could not understand. The condition is met by a general concept of reality under which one's actual conception, as well as all possible extensions of that conception, falls as an instance. This concept seems to me adequately explained through the idea of a hierarchical set of conceptions, extending from those much more limited than one's own but contained in it to those larger than one's own but containing it—of which some are reachable by discoveries one might make but others, larger still, are not.

Does the claim made by Nagel assume Kant's distinction between *noumena* and *phenomena*? If one denied that distinction, would it still be possible to accept Nagel's claim? Would Kant accept Nagel's claim? Would Descartes? Would you?

5. A bridge collapses, or a person becomes ill, or your car won't start, or a tire goes flat. You believe that for *all* of those cases something *caused* them to happen; and even if you never discover the cause of Joe's illness or your flat tire, you believe there was a cause. "There must have been a cause," you would insist. How do you know there was a cause? Is it part of your conceptual system? Or would you claim to have *learned* it from observation? From reason?

ADDITIONAL READING

Plato's rationalism is evident in *The Republic*, available in many translations and editions; as well as in other dialogues: For example, see *Five Dialogues (Euthyphro, Apology, Crito, Meno, Phaedo* (Indianapolis, IN: Hackett, 1981). Descartes (discussed in the previous chapter; see the readings for that chapter) is of course the key modern rationalist. The other great rationalists of that period were Spinoza and Leibniz. A very interesting recent study of their relation is Matthew Stewart, *The Courtier and the Heretic: Leibniz, Spinoza, and the Fate of God in the Modern World* (New York: W. W. Norton & Company, 2006). Lewis Samuel Feuer, *Spinoza and the Rise of Liberalism* (Boston, MA: Beacon Press, 1958), is a fascinating examination of Spinoza's thought and the period and culture in which Spinoza lived.

Classical empiricist sources include Bishop Berkeley's *The Principles of Human Knowledge* and *Three Dialogues between Hylas and Philonous*; David Hume's *Treatise of Human Nature* (especially Book I, Part IV); and John Locke's *An Essay Concerning Human Understanding*. *Berkeley*, edited by G. J. Warnock (Hammondsworth: Penguin, 1953) is a very good account of Berkeley's position. On Hume, see *Hume's Theory of the External World* (Oxford: Clarendon Press, 1940), edited by H. H. Price; Norman Kemp Smith, *The Philosophy of David Hume* (London: Macmillan, 1964); and (a very clear and readable account) *Hume*, edited by Barry Stroud (London and Boston: Routledge & Kegan Paul, 1977). More recent empiricist views are represented by A. J. Ayer, *The Foundations of Empirical Knowledge* (London: Macmillan, 1940) and *The Problem of Knowledge* (Baltimore, MD: Penguin Books, 1956), and Carl G. Hempel, *Aspects of Scientific Explanation* (Free Press, 1965). A good introduction to and comparison of the major traditional epistemological views is Bruce Aune's *Rationalism, Empiricism, and Pragmatism: An Introduction* (New York: Random House, 1970).

Kant's key works on epistemology are *Critique of Pure Reason*, 2nd ed., translated by Norman Kemp Smith (London: Macmillan, 1964) and *Prolegomena to Any Future Metaphysics*, translated by Lewis White Beck (Indianapolis, IN: Bobbs-Merrill, 1950). Among the many excellent studies of Kantian epistemology are Richard Aquila, *Representational Mind: A Study of Kant's Theory of Knowledge* (Bloomington, IN: Indiana University Press, 1983); Jonathan Bennett, *Kant's Analytic* (Cambridge: Cambridge University Press, 1966); C. D. Broad, *Kant: An Introduction* (Cambridge: Cambridge University Press, 1978); Norman Kemp Smith, *A Commentary on Kant's Critique of Pure Reason*, 2nd ed. (London: Macmillan, 1923); and P. F. Strawson, *The Bounds of Sense* (London: Methuen, 1966).

A very interesting book on the origins of mathematics (that seeks the basic psychological sources of mathematics, and denies that mathematics is based in intuition or definition or pure *a priori* insight) is *Where Mathematics Comes from: How the Embodied Mind Brings Mathematics into Being*, edited by George Lakoff and Rafael E. Nunez (New York: Basic Books, 2000).

For more on the "rationalist-empiricist" conflict between Noam Chomsky and B. F. Skinner, see Skinner's *Verbal Behavior* (New York: Appleton-Century-Crofts, 1957) and *Contingencies of Reinforcement* (New York: Appleton-Century-Crofts, 1969); and Chomsky's "Review of Skinner's *Verbal Behavior*," in *Language*, 1959, volume 35: 26–58; and Chomsky's *Cartesian Linguistics* (New York: Harper & Row, 1966). For a response to Chomsky on behalf of Skinner, see Kenneth MacCorquodale, 1970, "On Chomsky's Review of Skinner's Verbal Behavior," *Journal of the Experimental Analysis of Behavior*, volume 13: 83–99.

There are a number of excellent essays introducing the internalism/externalism debate: Laurence Bonjour, "Internalism and Externalism," Chapter 7, in *The Oxford Handbook of Epistemology*, edited by Paul K. Moser (Oxford: Oxford University Press, 2002): 234–263; in *Knowledge: Readings in Contemporary Epistemology* (Oxford: Oxford University Press, 2000), edited by Sven Bernecker and Fred Dretske, see the editors' introductory essay for Part II, as well as the excellent set of articles that follow; and the editor's introductory essay— "Internalism and Externalism: A Brief Historical Introduction," in Hilary Kornblith's excellent anthology, *Epistemology: Internalism and Externalism* (Oxford: Blackwell Publishers, 2001). An extensive and valuable debate on internalism vs. externalism is found in Laurence BonJour and Ernest Sosa, *Epistemic Justification: Internalism v. Externalism, Foundations vs. Virtues* (Oxford: Blackwell Publishing, 2003), in which the authors develop their own views at length, each critiques the opposing position, and each replies to the other's objections. A briefer debate—between John Greco and Richard Feldman—makes up Chapter 9 of *Contemporary Debates in Epistemology*, edited by Matthias Steup and Ernest Sosa (Oxford: Blackwell Publishing, 2005). *Epistemology: An Anthology*, edited by Ernest Sosa and Jaegwon Kim (Oxford: Blackwell, 2000), contains a number of important essays. In

"Knowledge in Humans and Other Animals," *Philosophical Perspectives*, volume 13 (1999), edited by James E. Tomberlin: 327–346; Hilary Kornblith offers a strong argument for externalism, drawing very effectively on cognitive ethology research into what is known by animals other than humans. *Externalism and Self-Knowledge*, edited by Peter Ludlow and Norah Martin (Stanford, CA: CSLI Publications, 1998), is a collection of essays exploring some of the implications of externalism, particularly the implications for the nature of self-knowledge.

CHAPTER 5

CONTEMPORARY EPISTEMOLOGY

There is a long tradition which regards change as bad, permanence as good. This was especially strong in the Greeks. In Plato's *Republic*, the ideal state is ruled by the wise, with the support of strong soldiers commanded by the wise; the masses are kept in check by the soldiers, and their only virtue is to follow the orders of their superiors. Change is always to be avoided, for it is inevitably for the worse; and it proceeds downward from an Aristocracy of the wise, to a state governed by the wealthy (but not so wise), then slides lower to government by the masses in—shudder—a democracy, and finally declines into tyranny. "May no new thing arise": That may sound strange in our world of passionate desire for the latest fashion and the newest technology, but it was a common greeting or blessing for many cultures. What is fixed and permanent is good, and the winds of change usually blow ill.

> There is nothing more difficult to take in hand, more perilous to conduct, or more uncertain in its success, than to take the lead in the introduction of a new order of things. *Machiavelli, The Prince.*

PERMANENCE AND CHANGE

The same assumption has a long history in epistemology. For Plato, genuine truth must be absolute, unchanging, and eternal. Two thousand years later, Descartes was still operating from the same assumption: Genuine truth must be fixed and eternal. In the intervening years, the Catholic Church had been incorporating the Aristotelian concept of a perfect God—and therefore an *unchanging* God—into the Christian world view; and since the source of the most important truths is this immutable God, the *permanent* nature of truth was assumed. Empiricists might seek truth using different methods from those employed by rationalists, but both would agree that whatever truths were discovered must be permanent and unchanging.

Another fixed and unchanging element of our world, from the ancients through the medieval period and well into the seventeenth century, was the *fixity of species*. As Aristotle pointed out, the offspring of dogs may not look exactly like their parents, but they are still dogs. Sheep produce lambs, not kittens. And the children of human parents are humans, generation after generation. Following Aristotle's lead, the Church viewed the fixity of species as evidence of God's plan. Species are fixed and constant, just as God made them; any change would obviously be a corruption of God's design, and would certainly be for the worse.

But by the time of the Enlightenment—the seventeenth- and eighteenth-century period of Descartes and Spinoza, Locke and Hume—the attitude toward change was itself undergoing change. After all, there were revolutions in England, the United States, and France; and governments founded on revolutions are unlikely to reject all change as bad. The authority of Aristotle, Ptolemy, and Plato had been challenged, and their views were often rejected. If Aristotle had the best account of motion, then fine; but if Galileo and Newton could do better, then those new theories would be adopted, ancient authority notwithstanding. The Catholic Church remained very powerful, of course; but the Reformation had shown that it could be successfully challenged, and even religious doctrines could change—and at least according to the Protestants, they could change for the better.

This new attitude toward change extended even to the idea of species: Maybe species are not as fixed and permanent as we thought. Change could be adaptive and positive; after all, the evolution of species led to *us*, and that can't be such a bad thing. In the eighteenth century, especially in France, the idea of *evolution* became very intriguing. There were many factors contributing to the emerging popularity of the idea of species evolution (or of "transmutation," as it was commonly called at that time). First, obviously, was the fact that ancient and religious authorities—who insisted on the fixity of species—had lost much of their power. Aristotle was still a respected ancient philosopher, of course; but Newton was now the authority on physics and astronomy, with Aristotle a historical footnote. William Harvey was a better authority on the human body than Aristotle, and perhaps Aristotle's authoritative pronouncements on biology—including the fixity of the species—were ready to go the way of Aristotle's physics and Ptolemy's astronomy. Second, new studies in geology had shown that the Earth was much older than previously believed (certainly much older than the literal Biblical account would suggest), and that it had passed through many geological eras. Even more significant were discoveries of fossil remains from animals that no longer existed: animals now extinct. But if species were *fixed*, then the disappearance of animals was almost as problematic as their emergence. And if species could disappear, perhaps new ones could develop.

> Treason doth never prosper: what's the reason?
> For if it prosper, none dare call it treason.
>
> John Harrington (1561–1612), *Epigrams*

Third, change was in the air, and change was much more welcome. The British had undergone enormous changes—a revolution in which the King had been beheaded, a second "glorious revolution" in which a royal family was replaced, enormous shifts in governmental power (England was now governed more by the Parliament than by the King); and most of the British thought these were changes for the better. (Of course, most of those who thought the changes were for the better were the ones in power; most of those who disagreed were dead.) The American colonies were hot with revolutionary fervor, ready to throw off the old and venture into something new.

The Lamarckian theory of evolution was widely known and discussed and was part of fashionable French conversation and flirtation. Denis Diderot, the great philosopher and encyclopedist of the eighteenth century, wrote *D'Alembert's Dream*, in which D'Alembert, Doctor Bordeu, and Mademoiselle de L'Espinasse carry on a long conversation, at one point touching on the Larmarckian account of evolution:

D'Alembert.   If a distance of a few thousand leagues changes my species, what would a distance of a few thousand earth diameters do? And if everything is a universal flux, as the panorama of the universe demonstrates to me everywhere, what would the changes in a time span of a few million centuries produce here and elsewhere? Who knows what a thinking, feeling being is on Saturn? . . . Would the sentient and thinking being on Saturn have more sense than I do? If that's so, how unfortunate for the Saturnian! The more senses, the more needs.

> *Bordeu.*   He's right. The organs produce the needs and, conversely, the needs produce
> the organs. . . . Imagine a long sequence of people with no arms. Now assume a
> continuous effort, and you'll see the two sides of this pincer grow longer and
> longer, . . . and perhaps develop digits at their extremities, thus making new arms
> and hands. The original structure alters itself according to necessity or habitual
> functions. We walk and work so little, and we think so much, that I wouldn't deny
> the possibility that man might finish up as nothing but a head.
>
> *Mademoiselle de L'Espinasse.*   A head! Just a head! That's not much. I was hoping
> that with unrestrained love-making . . . you're putting all sorts of ridiculous
> ideas in my head.

And the French, in particular, were eager for radical change: "Mankind will not be free until the last king is strangled with the entrails of the last priest." This was not a slogan for those who were frightened of change. Monarchs ruled by divine right, and the royal line was fixed and could not be changed. Overthrowing a monarch is a corruption of God's plan, and would necessarily result in disaster. But by the eighteenth century, belief in the divine right and permanent rule of a royal line was widely doubted: Deposing permanent "fixed" monarchs sometimes led to positive results, rather than disaster. Maybe the evolution of "fixed species" could also be beneficial.

EVOLUTION

The dominant evolutionary theory of the late eighteenth and early nineteenth centuries was proposed by a scientist at the French Museum of Natural History: Jean Baptiste Pierre Antoine de Monet, Chevalier de Lamarck (1744–1829). Though he did not publish his book on transmutation until 1802, his ideas had long been widely known and discussed—but not widely accepted by the scientific community. In Lamarck's account, evolution proceeds through the inheritance of acquired characteristics. Industrious animals seeking tasty leaves from higher branches stretch their necks to reach higher for food. Perhaps under drought conditions, these animals and their descendants are forced to strain higher and higher to secure enough food to survive. Through these efforts, their necks stretch longer, and then longer still; and they pass on this *acquired characteristic* to their offspring. Their descendants continue the same active process, passing on to their offspring the acquired characteristic of even longer necks. As this process continues generation after generation, eventually the animals evolve into new long-necked animals, and thus the giraffe species has emerged.

Lamarck's model explained evolution in terms of purposiveness: New species evolve through the purposeful exertions of animals that then pass on the results of those purposive efforts to their progeny. Lamarck rejected fixity of species and embraced change, and that idea of progressive evolutionary change was popular among French intellectuals and revolutionaries; but it was frightening to those with a stake in maintaining the fixed order: the Church, the Monarchy, and the nobility. Most biologists of the period were not ready to renounce the ancient Aristotelian orthodoxy of fixed species; and even those who were willing to consider the radical idea of species change doubted that Lamarckian purposive evolution of acquired characteristics could adequately account for such change.

Half a century later, the stage was better prepared for evolutionary theory. The discovery of the remains of enormous dinosaurs established that species were not fixed and permanent, since *those* species had obviously become extinct. And the fossil record seemed to indicate that new species—that had not previously existed—emerged at different periods. Not everyone was ready to embrace an *evolutionary* account of species change; to the contrary, one of the more popular views (developed primarily by Adam Sedgwick, the first professor of geology at Cambridge) was that as the Earth changed through successive geological periods, God *created* new species that were *well-designed* for the new conditions. Thus God, as a benevolent and effective designer, made sure that each stage of creation was well matched with the geological era in which it existed—including, of course, the pinnacle of God's creation, the human species. But while maintaining the fixity of species and the special role of the Creator, Sedgwick also believed in *progress*: that change could be for the *better*: "I allow (as all geologists must) a kind of progressive development. For example, the first fish are below the reptiles and the first reptiles older than man." * But however change occurred, it no longer seemed so frightening. That was especially true in Britain, at least for the wealthy and influential who had greatly benefited from the changes wrought by the industrial revolution.

> Indeed, God became more than superfluous under Darwin's emerging view of origins— He became problematic. At the very least, the theory of evolution dispenses with the immediate need for a Creator to shape individual species, including humans. More critically, a natural-selection mechanism relying on cutthroat intraspecies competition to evolve new species struck Darwin as incompatible with any reasonable notion of benevolent divine action. *Edward J. Larson, Evolution, 2004: 69–70.*

While many former craftsmen and their families suffered terribly in the dangerous and polluted factories and mines of the industrial revolution, many powerful and influential people in Britain owed their wealth and position to the changes in social and working conditions wrought by the industrial revolution; and since they had prospered, they tended to look on change as positive progress rather than frightening disruption. Too bad about all those children who were living brutal short lives in the mines and factories; but that's just nature's way: It is essential in order for the best people—such as myself—to survive, succeed, and bring progress. Along the same lines, in the United States, the wealthy industrialists—such as Henry Ford and Andrew Carnegie—happily embraced what they mistakenly understood as Darwinism: The survival of the fittest (meaning, of course, the wealthiest), that produces progressive results and constant improvement through harsh measures, and with no pity for the weak.

Darwin

But of course it was precisely that *purposive* and *progressive* model of evolution—the Lamarckian model—that Darwin rejected. Darwin's theory of natural selection had nothing purposive about it. Individuals of the same species, by chance, are born with slightly different characteristics. When an individual is lucky enough to be born with characteristics that make the individual better adapted for survival in its environment, then that individual is more likely to survive and pass along its advantageous characteristic to its offspring; and over time, those with the advantageous characteristic for a given environmental niche may branch off to form a new species. Thus, new species tend to develop to fill new environmental niches—but not because of any *purpose*, either natural or divine. The new species do not form a line of *progress*, but only of opportunistic fit into openings offered by changing environmental conditions (including the development of other species). Such changes in the environment may afford opportunities for the successful development of both humans and of parasites that thrive in human bloodstreams; one is not "higher" or "more progressive" than the other, on Darwin's model of natural mechanistic selection.

---

*Adam Sedgwick in a letter to Louis Agassiz, 1845, in Elizabeth Cary Agassiz, ed., *Louis Agassiz: His Life and Correspondence* (Boston, MA: Houghton, Mifflin and Co., 1886). Cited in Edward Larson, *Evolution*, p. 37.

An influential contemporary perspective on knowledge marches under the banner of "evolutionary epistemology," and it takes its inspiration directly from Darwin's theory of natural selection. W. W. Bartley III is one of the advocates of evolutionary epistemology, and he describes the view thus:

> The highest creative thought, like animal adaptation, is the product of blind variation and selective retention. Growth of knowledge is achieved through variation and selective retention—or, to use Popper's phrase, conjecture and refutation. Science is, on this account, *utterly unjustified and unjustifiable*. It is a shot in the dark, a bold guess going beyond all evidence. The question of its justification is irrelevant: it is as irrelevant as any question about whether a particular mutation is justified. The issue, rather, is of the viability of the mutation—or the new theory. This question is resolved through exposing it to the pressures of natural selection—or attempted criticism and refutation. Survival in the process does not justify the survivor either: a species that survived for thousands of years may nonetheless become extinct. A theory that survived for generations may eventually be refuted—as was Newton's. There is *no* justification—*ever*. The process that began with unjustified variation ends in unjustified survivors.
>
> *"Philosophy of Biology versus Philosophy of Physics," 1987*

Like Copernicus and Newton before him, the impact of Darwin would be hard to overstate. Hard, but not impossible. The notion that Darwin opened the world of ideas to the attractiveness of *change* over permanence would be an overstatement. In fact, the relation probably was reversed: Openness to change made evolutionary theories—including the one proposed by Darwin—more readily embraced. Still, Darwin's influence was enormous. He was hardly the first to suggest the idea of evolution, but his evolutionary account placed biology—including *human* development—squarely within the mechanical world view that had been developing in physics and astronomy. He solidified the idea that change—rather than permanence—is standard, and even desirable. Darwin also strengthened the belief that scientific theory could apply to humans as simply one part of the natural world, rather than as special creatures existing in some privileged sphere; and Darwin's work took that belief into uncharted territory: not only do our physical bodies obey the same laws of gravity that govern stones and planets, and our hearts pump blood like any other mechanical pump, but indeed we are totally—body and mind, emotions and intellect—the product of a mechanical process no different from that which produced the other species. Any difference between humans and other species is a difference of degree, not a difference in kind.

PRAGMATISM

Obviously, not everyone accepted all of these ideas, and indeed there was widespread opposition to Darwin's theory. Even today—though the basics of Darwinian natural selection, combined with genetic theory, are almost universally accepted among biologists—there is significant popular opposition to Darwin's views. In addition, there were many philosophers who continued to insist that all genuine truth must be fixed and eternal, and that the goal of philosophy is to discover such immutable eternal absolute truths. But Darwin's theory— and the general acceptance of change—led some philosophers to take a very different view of the nature of truth and of knowledge and the pursuit of knowledge. The *pragmatists*, in particular, acknowledged the Darwinian influence on their thought. Their perspective on epistemology wholeheartedly embraced change and placed human thought and inquiry squarely within the natural world. In short, they adopted views that caused Descartes to turn in his grave and Plato to spin.

> The rejection of fixed and permanent certainties—such as the eternal truths of geometry—was an important step in the development of pragmatism, and it was also important in Einstein's development of his theory of relativity. Euclidean geometry was the poster child for absolute truth: we might doubt our sensory observations, but Euclidean geometry had reigned supreme and unchallenged for thousands of years, and it seemed to come straight from the immutable mind of God. In a world of change, Kant had regarded Euclidean geometry as a fixed point of certainty. But in the late nineteenth century, non-Euclidean geometrical systems were proposed, and they were fascinating to mathematicians, physicists, and philosophers. The great French mathematician, philosopher, and scientist Henri Poincaré stated that "One geometry cannot be more true than another; it can only be more convenient."(1902) Einstein's own rejection of "fixed certainties" was clearly expressed: "Notions which have proved useful in the ordering of things acquire such an authority over us that we forget their worldly origins, and accept them as irrevocable givens. They are then stamped as 'necessities of thought', 'a priori given', etc."(1916)

The first element adopted by the pragmatists was a firm commitment to humans as *part of* the world, *not* outside observers. We are not Platonic observers, trying to find eternal truths; nor Cartesian doubters, seeking absolute certainties; rather, we are animals that are trying to get along in the world. Our ideas and theories are not maps of God's mind nor eternal verities for our detached contemplation. They are *tools* that help us live and work successfully in our world. Like any other tool, an idea or theory must *prove its usefulness* for our tasks; it must guide us effectively, and enhance our ability to predict and control the useful but dangerous world in which we live. If a theory *works* for our purposes, then it is *true* for those purposes. A tool that was useful at one time may be replaced by a tool that now works better. For the pragmatists, that applies to *all* our ideas: Some of our ideas and theories have proved useful for a very long time; but that only means they have been very good tools for our purposes, *not* that they are eternal truths that map "the world as it truly is" or the "true ideals" or the "absolute truth" or the Kantian "noumena."

Pragmatists reject many of the traditional philosophical distinctions. They reject distinctions between *foundational* truths and the system built upon that foundation; between truths of reason (a priori) and empirical (a posteriori) truths; between analytic and synthetic statements; and between noumena and phenomena. All these are distinctions (according to the pragmatists) designed to establish a realm of fixed, absolute, foundational truths that are exempt from change or challenge. For pragmatists, there is no such special realm of truth. Instead, our belief systems and theories must be judged as *wholes*, not as distinct individual parts.

> The lore of our fathers is a fabric of sentences. In our hands it develops and changes, through more or less arbitrary and deliberate revisions and additions of our own, more or less directly occasioned by the continuing stimulation of our sense organs. It is a pale grey lore, black with fact and white with convention. But I have found no substantial reasons for concluding that there are any quite black threads in it, or any white ones. *Willard Van Orman Quine,* "Carnap and Logical Truth," *The Ways of Paradox.*

There is no *foundation* of scientific principles, basic observation statements, or fundamental geometrical axioms; rather, there is a *system* of belief, and when something goes wrong, changes can occur *anywhere* in the system. Of course, some of the basic ideas in the system are more *central* than others, and they are *less likely* to be revised when the system encounters problems; but even the most central beliefs—the "eternal" truths of geometry and mathematics, of space and time—*can* be revised, for none are regarded as privileged foundational truths.

> The trail of the human serpent is thus over everything. Truth independent; truth that we *find* merely; truth no longer malleable to human need; truth incorrigible, in a word: such truth exists indeed superabundantly—or is supposed to exist by rationalistically minded thinkers; but then it means only the dead heart of the living tree, and its being there means only that truth also has its paleontology and its "prescription," and may grow stiff with years of veteran service and petrified in men's regard by sheer antiquity. But how plastic even the oldest truths nevertheless really are has been vividly shown in our day by the transformation of logical and mathematical ideas. *William James, Pragmatism*, 1907.

Think of what actually happens (the pragmatists insist) when we make a prediction that *goes wrong*: not what some absolutist account says *should* happen, but what *actually* happens. I'm running an experiment in the chemistry lab, to see what happens when I heat helium in an airtight container, with no oxygen present. I turn on the Bunsen burner, expecting to see the pressure in the container increase; instead, the gas in the container flames brightly and then explodes. What do we conclude? Well, my experiment has just proved that combustion does not require oxygen! I've refuted one of the basic principles of chemistry; somebody get in touch with the Nobel Prize Committee! Well, hardly. What we conclude is that Bruce is a stupid klutz, who probably hooked up the wrong cylinder to the container. When we run such an experiment, there are *lots of things* involved: the chemical theory, the reliability of the experimenter, the quality of the materials used, and so on. We thought Bruce could manage this experiment effectively; but we were wrong, Bruce is so lousy in a chemistry lab that he screws up this simple experiment. Our belief in Bruce's competence is easily overturned in this case; after all, we didn't have that much confidence in him to begin with. And so *that* is the belief we change, *not* the central principles of chemical gas theory. But suppose our highly competent chemistry professor decides to show the class how the experiment is *supposed* to be done; and much to our surprise, her experiment produces the same explosion! That's a very different matter. It's easy to lose faith in Bruce's laboratory competence; but the competence of this professor, who has run chemistry labs for decades, and is a highly respected and widely published chemistry researcher: doubting *her* laboratory competence is something else entirely. *Now* we are likely to conclude that someone screwed up the labels on the cylinders, or perhaps that the chemical supply company made a dreadful mistake when filling the cylinders. But note: same result, very different conclusion. When something goes wrong, there are *lots* of places where adjustments are possible. If we now check the gas cylinders very carefully, but get the same surprising result, we might conclude that the glass container was somehow contaminated or flawed, so that oxygen seeped in. If we can find nothing wrong with the experimental procedure or the experimental apparatus, and competent scientific researchers continue to produce these surprising results, we will seek some special cause for this strange result: Perhaps this is what happens when the experiment is run at a very high altitude, or when the atmospheric pressure is extremely low and a severe storm is brewing. But if the experiment is repeated many times in many places, eventually we may be driven to revise some basic ideas in our chemical theory. The key pragmatist point is this: When we run a test or make a prediction, that involves an enormous body of knowledge and background assumptions, and they are tested as a coherent *whole*; and when things go wrong and revisions are called for, the revisions may occur *anywhere* in the system. The truths of geometry were once regarded as absolute and unchanging; but Einstein showed that an *alternative* geometrical system might prove to be a *better tool* in the context of special relativity.

The totality of our so-called knowledge or beliefs, from the most casual matters of geography and history to the profoundest laws of atomic physics or even of pure mathematics and logic, is a man-made fabric which impinges on experience only along the edges. Or, to change the figure, total science is like a field of force whose boundary conditions are experience. A conflict with experience at the periphery occasions readjustments in the interior of the field. Truth values have to be redistributed over some of our statements. Reevaluation of some statements entails reevaluation of others, because of their logical interconnections—the logical laws being in turn simply certain further statements of the system, certain further elements of the field. Having reevaluated one statement, we must reevaluate some others which may be statements logically connected with the first or may be the statements of logical connections themselves. But the total field is so underdetermined by its boundary conditions, experience, that there is much latitude of choice as to what statements to reevaluate in the light of any single contrary experience. . . . Any statement can be held true come what may, if we make drastic enough adjustments elsewhere in the system. . . . Conversely, by the same token, no statement is immune to revision. Revision even of the logical law of the excluded middle has been proposed as a means of simplifying quantum mechanics. *Willard Van Orman Quine, "Two Dogmas of Empiricism," 1951.*

When failed predictions or new experiences call for changes in our theoretical system, where are the changes made? Though the required changes can occur anywhere in the system—remember, on the pragmatist view, the entire *system* is involved in predictions and observations—the changes will typically be made in ways that require the minimum adjustment of the system as a whole. Suppose a respected entomologist returns from a journey to a South American rain forest, bringing with her a new species of beetle never before seen. In that case, we simply add a new beetle species to our biological system. That's an easy modification: We knew of X number of beetle species, and now we have X plus one; probably this new species belongs to a well-defined genus, and the new species fits snugly into its place in the system. But suppose instead that our biologist returns with the *medusa* of Greek mythology: a woman with fierce snakes growing out of her scalp instead of hair. We can't just add the medusa into our biological system, for it contradicts some of our basic biological principles: for a start, reptiles and primates are *very* different sorts of animals, one being cold-blooded and the other warm-blooded. And different species are *distinct*: They don't share common bodies. To accept the existence of a genuine medusa would require that we abandon just about everything we thought we knew about biology. No matter how well respected the biologist who exhibited such a monster, we would first believe that the biologist was trying to carry out a scientific fraud—perhaps a very clever fraud, if we can't discover the trick. Ultimately, we might accept the genuine existence of the medusa—if, for example, an expedition discovered an entire colony of medusa, with medusa infants and grandparents—but that acceptance would require an enormous body of evidence that could not be refuted: a *lot* more evidence than we need for a new species of beetle, where the changes required are easy.

Think back a moment to the controversy between the Copernican theory and the Ptolemaic theory. The Ptolemaic theory says that the Earth is at the center of the universe, and is fixed and unmoving; the Copernican theory places the Sun at the center, with the Earth (along with the other planets) revolving around the Sun. How do we settle this dispute? We obviously can't send up a spaceship to make observations; we don't even have telescopes (until some years later) to aid our observations. So what kind of experiment, using what we have at hand in the sixteenth century, could we run to answer this question? That's not easy, but the astronomers of the sixteenth century were very clever, and they devised a crucial test. The Ptolemaic theory says that the Earth is fixed, and does not move. The Copernican theory, by contrast, claims that every year the Earth moves in an enormous orbit, all the way around the Sun. So on November 1, we'll do a very careful reading of the angles among the stars; and six months later, on April 1, we'll do another very careful observation. According to the Ptolemaic theory, the readings should be: exactly the same, since the Earth has not moved from its fixed place at the center of the universe. But according to the Copernican theory, on April 1, the Earth will be a vast distance from where it was on November 1; indeed, it will be all the way over on the other side of the Sun! So according to the Copernican theory, we should see a *difference* in the angles between the stars, because of the dramatic difference in the position of the Earth from which we are taking our measurements. That is, the Copernican theory predicts that we will observe a *stellar parallax*, a difference in observed angle between two stars; the Ptolemaic theory predicts that we will *not* see a stellar parallax. So they did the great experiment: measured the angles, waited half a year, measured again. And they found: *no stellar parallax*! What did the Copernicans conclude? Okay, we were wrong, you guys win. No, of course not: Galileo, Bruno, and many other Copernicans were still convinced that Copernicus was right about the Earth traveling around the Sun; and so they concluded that one of their *other* beliefs was wrong—specifically, they decided that they had been *wrong* in their belief that the stars were relatively close to the planets; instead, they decided that the stars must be a great distance from the Earth and the other planets; thus, that when the Earth moves to the other side of the Sun the distance is so small relative to the distance to the stars that no difference in angle (no stellar parallax) would be observable. Some significant details of the Copernican theory had to be changed, but the theory as a *coherent whole* was consistent with all the observations.

This is a good illustration of how *coherence* theorists—as opposed to *foundationalists*— see human knowledge. Rather than starting from a foundation of fixed and absolutely certain rationally derived principles (as the rationalists favor) or a fixed foundational starting point of simple observations (as the empiricists require), the coherence theorists regard the whole body of knowledge as constantly under test. Both rationalists and empiricists sought a firm foundation for their systems of knowledge: Descartes, famously, in basic indubitable principles that could be known by pure reason; empiricists in basic observations that could be intersubjectively confirmed. Though they proposed *different* foundations, and they disagreed about exactly how firm and *certain* such foundations must be, they agreed on a basic point: A system of genuine knowledge must be built upon a reliable *foundation*. We start from some basic truths (whether from observation or reason) that are *most* reliable; and from there we build up our system of knowledge. The image is of a structure in which the basic foundation *must* be solid and reliable, and that image is almost irresistible.

But some epistemologists did resist it. The *coherence* theorists reject the picture of a system of knowledge built up from a foundation, and instead emphasize the coherence of the whole *system* of knowledge. On the coherence view, we *cannot* start from a certain foundation—whether discovered by reason or by empirical observation—and then build up our system of justified beliefs on that solid foundation; we cannot do so because none of our ideas and beliefs are that *isolated* and individual. They have meaning and significance only as part of a larger system of beliefs and theories and ideas and observations. If the knowledge system guides us well, the entire body of knowledge gains support; and if the system leads to mistakes or errors or false predictions, then adjustments can be made *anywhere* in the system (though we will usually make adjustments at points requiring the *least* overall change). Of course, the whole system could prove unwieldy, and we might decide there is a better system available: as, for example, when astronomers turned from the Ptolemaic to the Copernican system. But a mistaken prediction does not mean the collapse of the whole system. To the contrary, mistaken predictions can lead us to make valuable changes in the knowledge system: The Copernicans wrongly predicted the appearance of a stellar parallax; they were wrong, but that was a very fruitful mistake, since it led to a better understanding of the vast distances between our solar system and the other stars in our galaxy.

At almost the same time Darwin was writing *Origin of Species*, the British philosopher and reformer John Stuart Mill was writing his classic work, *On Liberty*. In that small volume, Mill gave the definitive justification for freedom of speech; and surely it was no accident that his arguments parallel those of his contemporary and countryman Darwin.

> . . . the peculiar evil of silencing the expression of an opinion is that it is robbing the human race, posterity as well as the existing generation—those who dissent from the opinion still more than those who hold it. If the opinion is right, they are deprived of the opportunity of exchanging error for truth; if wrong, they lose, what is almost as great a benefit, the clearer perception and livelier impression of truth procured by its collision with error.
>
> . . . There is the greatest difference between presuming an opinion to be true because, with every opportunity for contesting it, it has not been refuted, and assuming its truth for the purpose of not permitting its refutation. Complete liberty of contradicting and disproving our opinion is the very condition which justifies us in assuming its truth for purposes of action; and on no other terms can a being with human faculties have any rational assurance of being right.
>
> *John Stuart Mill (1806–1873), On Liberty, 1859*

That leads to another point that the pragmatists emphasize: *mistakes aren't so bad.* In Darwin's evolutionary theory of natural selection, there are many variations (mutations), and most of them are failures in their environment; but it is only through many variations, most of which fail, that the successful variations can have an opportunity to flourish. In similar manner, human animals will be most successful in discovering better knowledge tools and theories if they try many different theories and are not afraid to try theories that fail. Ideas and theories compete for survival. Bold hypotheses, testable theories, and lots of candidates: That's the best way to find what works best and what guides us best. By proposing new theories that open themselves up for failure, and subjecting those theories to hard tests, we can discover which theories are best adapted for our present environment. As the great twentieth-century philosopher of science Karl Popper stated: *"It is through the falsification of our suppositions that we actually get in touch with 'reality.' It is the discovery and elimination of our errors which alone constitute that 'positive' experience which we gain from reality."** Halley used Newton's theory to boldly predict the arrival of a comet. That prediction opened the theory to challenge, but that is also what makes the theory a valuable tool for human inquiry: It makes bold predictions, opens up new areas of inquiry, and suggests new experiments. Einstein correctly predicted, on the basis of his theory of relativity, that a star shift—never before observed—would be visible at the time of an eclipse; that was a daring prediction by a daring theory. Copernicans predicted the discovery of the stellar parallax. Their prediction was wrong—no stellar parallax was observed—but the Copernican theory nonetheless proved its value as a tool for human inquiry: It led to a much better grasp of the vast distances between our Sun and the other stars; and its prediction of a stellar parallax was eventually confirmed—centuries later, with much more sensitive measuring instruments than were available in the sixteenth century. Darwinian theorists predicted the discovery of discrete inheritance "traits," which were discovered and called "genes." And they predicted that the Earth would be found to be much older than the several score million years that most late nineteenth-century scientists estimated. Recognizing the immense time required for the evolutionary process to work, Darwin and other natural selection theorists made a bold prediction about the age of the Earth, and put their theory on the line: had they been wrong, their theory would have failed. But it is through such bold theories—which are often proposed without conclusive proof of their usefulness—that we evolve better theories; and our bold failures are an essential part of that process.

---

*Popper, "The Bucket and the Searchlight: Two Theories of Knowledge," in *Objective Knowledge: An Evolutionary Approach* (Oxford University Press, 1972), p. 360; emphasis in original.

Truth gains more even by the errors of one who, with due study and preparation, thinks for himself than by the true opinions of those who only hold them because they do not suffer themselves to think. *John Stuart Mill, On Liberty,* 1859.

If nothing could possibly count against a theory, that is not a sign of the *strength* of the theory, but of its sterility. "Creationism" is a good example. What bold predictions does creationism make? If any at all, perhaps it would predict that a benevolent omnipotent God would design a reasonably kind nature. But such a prediction would result in falsification of the theory, for as Darwin himself wrote (in a letter to the botanist Joseph Hooker), "What a book a Devil's chaplain might write on the clumsy, wasteful, blundering low and horridly cruel works of nature!" Of course the creationist has a ready answer to such problems: The ways of God are beyond our understanding. But that answer is too easy; it "saves the theory," but at the expense of making it predictively empty and of no use in guiding us to further discoveries. Creationism can't be proved false; not because it is a wonderful scientific tool, but because it is not a scientific tool at all: It makes no predictions, takes no chances, and offers no guidance to further inquiries. The problem is not that creationism cannot account for all the data; to the contrary, it can easily accommodate any data at all, and much too easily to function as a scientific theory. The hypothesis of an unfathomable God Who creates according to His own wishes can "explain" anything. But it doesn't lead us anywhere, doesn't reveal anything new, doesn't expose itself to predictions and tests, and opens no paths to new discoveries. Newton's theory enabled Halley to predict the path of a comet, and it is that capacity to make surprising and testable predictions that made his theory scientifically important. The Hebrew creation story is a wonderful and fascinating myth, and tells us a deeply moving story of how we are all brothers and sisters. But trying to turn it into a scientific theory twists it into a role it is ill-equipped to play.

Pragmatists reject the view that truth is a fixed and permanent achievement that matches or maps the way the world truly is. In fact, pragmatists have little use for any account of truth as "matching reality as it is in itself." Pragmatists insist that there is *no* getting away from our ideas, theories, and perceptions, that only through using such tools can we deal with the world. It is useless—worse than useless—to insist on some concept of truth that involves mapping the world "as it truly is, independent of our conception of it." Rather than "our theories are true just in case they accurately map the world as it is," pragmatists would say "our theories are true just in case they are effective tools that prove their worth by guiding us well."

Obviously, this pragmatist view has provoked harsh criticism. Some say it substitutes a crass, crude, "might makes right" account for the high standard that scientists and philosophers have long celebrated. Others have criticized the pragmatist view for a shallow "feel good" view of the world. Pragmatists fiercely deny those accusations, insisting that they are strawman distortions of their position. Consider the claim of environmental scientists that pollution-caused global warming poses a severe threat to our environment, to many endangered species, and indeed to the future of all humans. That's a very harsh view, and it's scary to think about. Doing something about it would require enormous effort and significant changes in our wasteful way of life. Many politicians and industrial leaders promote a very different account: Global warming is a fantasy, everything is going to be fine, all we need are small and painless adjustments. That is a more appealing view, certainly, at least short term; but it will have terrible long-term consequences, and prevent us from taking effective but costly steps to deal with the environmental crisis. The account given by environmental scientists is frightening, but ultimately it is a much better guide to effective action than its denial. Pragmatists insist that if you try to hold "feel good" views you will be led badly astray, because they *don't work.*

Consider a harsher case: the Nazi "system of belief" represented Jews as devious, greedy, and destructive, and promoted a doctrine of racial purity and Aryan supremacy. Thankfully, it was defeated, and the advocates of that view suffered severe consequences. But suppose the Nazis had triumphed—and in the darkest days of World War II, that was not a ridiculous supposition. Would their views then have been *true*? Of course, the Nazi ideology didn't lead *everyone* well: The suffering unleashed on the Jewish people, on the occupied countries, and on Russia was enormous. But suppose it had led the Nazis to their desired power over Europe, and the Nazis had managed to develop fearful weapons that no other country could match, and they had become the dominant world power. One might say that such a regime would not be *long-term* successful, even by their own hideous standards; but there are many sad examples of brutal regimes that for centuries held power over conquered peoples. To say that (had that happened) the Nazi ideology worked for Nazi purposes and thus the Nazi ideology is *true* (because it "guided them well") is not an easy conclusion to accept. Indeed, some might take it as a *reductio ad absurdum* of pragmatism.

Pragmatists make several responses to this sort of argument. First, a pragmatist might insist that this example interprets "guided them well" much too narrowly; the pragmatist standard is *not* that something is true if it guides a small subgroup to narrow and selfish benefits gained at the cost of enormous suffering for everyone else. Second, the pragmatist might argue that even for the small briefly advantaged subgroup, the brutal racist Nazi ideology was *not* really a useful guide. Promoting such an ideology stifles open inquiry, blocks thought, and destroys creativity: A brief glance at the remarkably bad art and architecture produced by the Third Reich should be sufficient evidence. And any system that holds the Jews to be universally vile and inferior will be twisted into knots in order to deny the evident talents and contributions of Albert Einstein, Sigmund Freud, Benedict Spinoza, Franz Kafka, Arthur Miller, Leonard Bernstein, Karl Marx, Ludwig Wittgenstein, Karl Popper, Paul Erdos, Georg Cantor, Jonas Salk, Richard Feynman, Niels Bohr, and Jesus of Nazareth. Or consider the racist system of slavery and Jim Crow laws that once held sway in sections of the United States. Obviously, some people *could and did* continue to believe in that system for many years. But even for the slave owners and racists who supposedly gained benefits, this was *not* a useful system. Running such a system of thought required twisting the interpretation of their religious texts, treating physical labor as degrading, promoting "genteel idleness" as virtue, and holding in place a brutal hierarchical system that deprived women of opportunities and rights while concentrating wealth in the hands of a few large plantation owners and choking off opportunities for everyone else. And a system that insists on the inherent inferiority of Nelson Mandela, Justice Thurgood Marshall, Barack Obama, Frederick Douglass, Tiger Woods, Bishop Desmond Tutu, Reverend Martin Luther King, Rosa Parks, Duke Ellington, Aretha Franklin, Oprah Winfrey, Charles Rangel, and General Colin Powell is a system requiring constant distortion and self-deceit in order to keep it functioning. That is not to compare the harm done to the slave-owning group with the enormous harm and injustice done to those enslaved; but—so this pragmatist answer notes—the harm done even to the supposed beneficiaries of this slave-holding ideology is enough to show that such repugnant systems of thought are not good tools or guides for *anyone*.

That second response to the pragmatist critique leads into a third. This is the response offered by one of the most famous and articulate champions of pragmatism in the late twentieth and early twenty-first centuries: Richard Rorty. When faced with such criticisms of pragmatism, Rorty bites the bullet:

> The idea of a universally shared source of truth called 'reason' or 'human nature' is, for us pragmatists, just the idea that such discussion [of what is best] *ought* to be capable of being made conclusive. We see this idea as a misleading way of expressing the hope, which we share, that the human race as a whole should gradually come together in a global community, a community which incorporates most of the thick morality of the European industrialized

democracies. It is misleading because it suggests that the aspiration to such a community is somehow built into every member of the biological species. This seems to us pragmatists like the suggestion that the aspiration to be an anaconda is somehow built into all reptiles, or that the aspiration to be an anthropoid is somehow built into all mammals. This is why we pragmatists see the charge of relativism as simply the charge that we see luck where our critics insist on seeing destiny. We think that the utopian world community envisaged by the Charter of the United Nations and the Helsinki Declaration of Human Rights is no more the *destiny* of humanity than is an atomic holocaust or the replacement of democratic governments by feuding warlords. If either of the latter is what the future holds, our species will have been unlucky, but it will not have been irrational. . . .

I do not know how to argue the question of whether it is better to see human beings in this biologistic way or to see them in a way more like Plato's or Kant's. So I do not know how to give anything like a conclusive argument for the view which my critics call 'relativism' and I prefer to call 'antifoundationalism' or 'antidualism'. It is certainly not enough for my side to appeal to Darwin and ask our opponents how they can avoid an appeal to the supernatural. That way of stating the issue begs many questions. It is certainly not enough for my opponents to say that a biologistic view strips human beings of their dignity and self-respect. That too begs most of the questions at issue. I suspect that all that either side can do is to restate its case over and over again, in context after context. The controversy between those who see both our species and our society as a lucky accident, and those who find an immanent teleology in both, is too radical to permit of being judged from some neutral standpoint.

Richard Rorty, Introduction to Philosophy and Social Hope

That is (Rorty might say), if you are looking for an absolutist justification of pragmatism—whether in the realm of epistemology or ethics—you are going to be profoundly disappointed.

When we come down to the basic contrast between pragmatists and their opponents, the argument may go something like this. Critics of pragmatism might say that pragmatism gets everything backwards: A theory isn't true because it works well and guides us effectively; rather it is a good guide *because it's true*. Pragmatists will respond that the traditional account adds a step that *does no work*, that is merely an empty title: It makes no sense to think of our theories "matching the world as it really is," as the old *correspondence* account of truth would have it. All we actually have when we evaluate our theories and beliefs is: Do they *lead us well*, are they *effective tools?* When we say something like, "This theory works really well, it opens new areas of exploration, it guides us to new discoveries; but is it *really true?*" then we are adding a question that adds nothing. Our *true* facts and theories are tools, not trophies. They do not show us God's eye view of the world, but show us ways of getting along as clever animals. No matter how sophisticated our system of knowledge—incorporating mathematics, quantum mechanics, and string theory—what we have are theories and models that *guide us well*, that improve our ability to make new discoveries and accurate predictions. Perhaps string theory is currently our *most useful* physics model, but it will someday—probably soon, given the rapid changes in theoretical physics—be replaced by a better account that will guide our research more effectively. If you like, you may say: As we move from Galileo's physics to Newton's, to Einstein's and then to quantum mechanics, and now to string theory, we are getting closer and closer to the *real truth*. But pragmatists would argue that this notion of the "real truth" is no more helpful than supposing that the change from a rough flint to a steel hand saw to a powerful circular saw is carrying us closer to the "true saw." In both cases, we are gaining better tools for our chosen tasks.

Charles Saunders Peirce was a leading pragmatist of the late nineteenth and early twentieth centuries; indeed, some consider him the father of pragmatism. Peirce favored the idea of "final truth" as an essential *ideal*: ". . . all the followers of science are fully persuaded that the processes of investigation, if only pushed far enough, will give one certain solution to every question to which they can be applied. . . . Different minds may set out with the most antagonistic views, but the progress of investigation carries them by a force outside of themselves to one and the same conclusion. This activity of thought by which we are carried, not where we wish, but to a foreordained goal, is like the operation of destiny. No modification of the point of view taken, no selection of other facts for study, no natural bent of mind even, can enable a man to escape the predestinate opinion. This great law is embodied in the conception of truth and reality. The opinion which is fated to be ultimately agreed to by all who investigate, is what we mean by the truth, and the object represented in this opinion is the real" ("How to Make Our Ideas Clear," 1878). However, most later pragmatists—especially William James—found even the notion of an "ultimate ideal" of final truth too strong, or at least not very helpful: "The 'absolutely' true, meaning what no farther experience will ever alter, is that ideal vanishing-point towards which we imagine all our temporary truths will some day converge. It runs on all fours with the perfectly wise man, and with the absolutely complete experience; and, if these ideals are ever realized, they will all be realized together. Meanwhile we have to live to-day by what truth we can get to-day, and be ready to-morrow to call it falsehood" (*William James, "Pragmatism,"* Lecture 6).

Pragmatism has its contemporary champions; but then, so do various forms of empiricism; and there are many who favor a more Kantian perspective, or even rationalism. Since at least the time of Newton, science (and the method of science) has dominated philosophical thought concerning the nature and development of knowledge. But even among those who regard science as the best model for knowledge, there is deep division concerning the actual nature of scientific practice: Does science proceed by proposing hypotheses that are confirmed? By proposing ambitious hypotheses that are ultimately falsified? By rejecting falsified hypotheses? By modifying those hypotheses? Does science confront the world through specific narrow claims, or through larger comprehensive systems? And of course there are those who maintain that science cannot discover all truths, and perhaps not even the most significant truths: maybe the truths of ethics are not discoverable through scientific methodologies. Or perhaps—others would argue—there are no truths of ethics *because* they cannot be scientifically established. Many of these are questions that will be examined in later chapters; and like the central issues of epistemology, many of these are questions that remain the subject of fierce philosophical dispute.

READINGS

⇥ PRAGMATISM: A NEW NAME FOR SOME ⇥ OLD WAYS OF THINKING

William James

William James (1842–1910) was a psychologist and philosopher who spent most of his career at Harvard University. *The Principles of Psychology* (1890) was his great contribution to the field of psychology. He also had a strong interest in religion throughout his life, and *The Will to Believe* (1897) contains his pragmatic approach to the question of religious belief. Though not the originator of pragmatism, through his books and public lectures he was probably the person most responsible for popularizing pragmatic philosophy. Though pragmatism has undergone significant changes in the century since James gave these lectures, the central elements of pragmatism—anti-foundationalism, judging theories and ideas by their usefulness, and the importance of "trying out" new ideas even if they fail—are clearly present in these lectures.

The pragmatic method is primarily a method of settling metaphysical disputes that otherwise might be interminable. Is the world one or many?—fated or free?—material or spiritual?—here are notions either of which may or may not hold good of the world; and disputes over such notions are unending. The pragmatic method in such cases is to try to interpret each notion by tracing its respective practical consequences. What difference would it practically make to anyone if this notion rather than that notion were true? If no practical difference whatever can be traced, then the alternatives mean practically the same thing, and all dispute is idle. Whenever a dispute is serious, we ought to be able to show some practical difference that must follow from one side or the other's being right. . . .

To attain perfect clearness in our thoughts of an object, then, we need only consider what conceivable effects of a practical kind the object may involve—what sensations we are to expect from it, and what reactions we must prepare. Our conception of these effects, whether immediate or remote, is then for us the whole of our conception of the object, so far as that conception has positive significance at all . . .

Pragmatism represents a perfectly familiar attitude in philosophy, the empiricist attitude, but it represents it, as it seems to me, both in a more radical and in a less objectionable form than it has ever yet assumed. A pragmatist turns his back resolutely and once for all upon a lot of inveterate habits dear to professional philosophers. He turns away from abstraction and insufficiency, from verbal solutions, from bad *a priori* reasons, from fixed principles, closed systems, and pretended absolutes and origins. He turns towards concreteness and adequacy, towards facts, towards action, and towards power. That means the empiricist temper regnant, and the rationalist temper sincerely given up. It means the open air and possibilities of nature, as against dogma, artificiality and the pretence of finality in truth . . .

Theories thus become instruments, not answers to enigmas, in which we can rest. We don't lie back upon them, we move forward, and, on occasion, make nature over again by their aid. Pragmatism unstiffens all our theories, limbers them up and sets each one at work. Being nothing essentially new, it harmonizes with many ancient philosophic tendencies. It agrees with nominalism for instance, in always appealing to particulars; with utilitarianism in emphasizing practical aspects; with positivism in its disdain for verbal solutions, useless questions, and metaphysical abstractions.

All these, you see, are *anti-intellectualist* tendencies. Against rationalism as a pretension and a method, pragmatism is fully armed and militant. But, at the outset, at least, it stands for no particular results. It has no dogmas, and no doctrines save its method. As the young Italian pragmatist Papini has well said, it lies in the midst of our theories, like a corridor in a hotel. Innumerable chambers open out of it. In one you may find a man writing an atheistic volume; in the next someone on his knees praying for faith and strength; in a third a chemist investigating a body's properties. In a fourth a system of idealistic metaphysics is being excogitated; in a fifth the impossibility of metaphysics is being shown. But they all own the corridor, and all must pass through it if they want a practicable way of getting into or out of their respective rooms.

No particular results then, so far, but only an attitude of orientation, is what the pragmatic method means. *The attitude of looking away from first things, principles, 'categories,' supposed necessities; and of looking towards last things, fruits, consequences, facts.* . . .

Riding now on the front of this wave of scientific logic Messrs. Schiller and Dewey appear with their pragmatistic account of what truth everywhere signifies. Everywhere, these teachers say, 'truth' in our ideas and beliefs means the same thing that it means in science. It means, they say, nothing but this, *that ideas (which themselves are but parts of our experience) become true just in so far as they help us to get into satisfactory relation with other parts of our experience,* to summarize them and get about among them by conceptual short-cuts instead of following the interminable succession of particular phenomena. Any idea upon which we can ride, so to speak; any idea that will carry us prosperously from any one part of our experience to any other part, linking things satisfactorily, working securely, simplifying, saving labor; is true for just so much, true in so far forth, true *instrumentally.* . . .

The observable process which Schiller and Dewey particularly singled out for generalization is the familiar one by which any individual settles into *new opinions*. The process here is always the same. The individual has a stock of old opinions already, but he meets a new experience that puts them to a strain. Somebody contradicts them; or in a reflective moment he discovers that they contradict each other; or he hears of facts with which they are incompatible; or desires arise in him which they cease to satisfy. The result is an inward trouble to which his mind till then had been a stranger, and from which he seeks to escape by modifying his previous mass of opinions. He saves as much of it as he can, for in this matter of belief we are all extreme conservatives. So he tries to change first this opinion, and then that (for they resist change very variously), until at last some new idea comes up which he can graft upon the ancient stock with a minimum of disturbance of the latter, some idea that mediates between the stock and the new experience and runs them into one another most felicitously and expediently.

This new idea is then adopted as the true one. It preserves the older stock of truths with a minimum of modification, stretching them just enough to make them admit the novelty, but conceiving that in ways as familiar as the case leaves possible. An *outrée* explanation, violating all our preconceptions, would never pass for a true account of a novelty. We should scratch round industriously till we found something less excentric. The most violent revolutions in an individual's beliefs leave most of his old order standing. Time and space, cause and effect, nature and history, and one's own biography remain untouched. New truth is always a go-between, a smoother-over of transitions. It marries old opinion to new fact so as ever to show a minimum of jolt, a maximum of continuity. We hold a theory true just in proportion to its success in solving this "problem of maxima and minima." But success in solving this problem is eminently a matter of approximation. We say this theory solves it on the whole more satisfactorily than that theory; but that means more satisfactorily to ourselves, and individuals will emphasize their points of satisfaction differently. To a certain degree, therefore, everything here is plastic.

The point I now urge you to observe particularly is the part played by the older truths. Failure to take account of it is the source of much of the unjust criticism leveled against pragmatism. Their influence is absolutely controlling. Loyalty to them is the first principle—in most cases it is the only principle; for by far the most usual way of handling phenomena so novel that they would make for a serious rearrangement of our preconceptions is to ignore them altogether, or to abuse those who bear witness for them.

You doubtless wish examples of this process of truth's growth, and the only trouble is their super-abundance. The simplest case of new truth is of course the mere numerical addition of new kinds of facts, or of new single facts of old kinds, to our experience—an addition that involves no alteration in the old beliefs. Day follows day, and its contents are simply added. The new contents themselves are not true, they simply *come* and *are*. Truth is *what we say about* them, and when we say that they have come, truth is satisfied by the plain additive formula.

But often the day's contents oblige a rearrangement. If I should now utter piercing shrieks and act like a maniac on this platform, it would make many of you revise your ideas as to the probable worth of my philosophy. 'Radium' came the other day as part of the day's content, and seemed for a moment to contradict our ideas of the whole order of nature, that order having come to be identified with what is called the conservation of energy. The mere sight of radium paying heat away indefinitely out of its own pocket seemed to violate that conservation. What to think? If the radiations from it were nothing but an escape of unsuspected 'potential' energy, pre-existent inside of the atoms, the principle of conservation would be saved. The discovery of 'helium' as the radiation's outcome, opened a way to this belief. So Ramsay's view is generally held to be true, because, altho it extends our old ideas of energy, it causes a minimum of alteration in their nature.

I need not multiply instances. A new opinion counts as 'true' just in proportion as it gratifies the individual's desire to assimilate the novel in his experience to his beliefs in stock. It must both lean on old truth and grasp new fact; and its success (as I said a moment ago) in doing this, is a matter for the individual's appreciation. When old truth grows, then, by new truth's addition, it is for subjective reasons. We are in the process and obey the reasons. That new idea is truest which performs most felicitously its function of satisfying our double urgency. It makes itself true, gets itself classed as true, by the way it works; grafting itself then upon the ancient body of truth, which thus grows much as a tree grows by the activity of a new layer of cambium.

Now Dewey and Schiller proceed to generalize this observation and to apply it to the most ancient parts of truth. They also once were plastic. They also were called true for human reasons. They also mediated between still earlier truths and what in those days were novel observations. Purely objective truth, truth in whose establishment the function of giving human satisfaction in marrying previous parts of experience with newer parts played no role whatever, is nowhere to be found. The reasons why we call things true is the reason why they *are* true, for 'to be true' *means* only to perform this marriage-function.

The trail of the human serpent is thus over everything. Truth independent; truth that we *find* merely; truth no longer malleable to human need; truth incorrigible, in a word; such truth exists indeed superabundantly—or is supposed to exist by rationalistically minded thinkers; but then it means only the dead heart of the living tree, and its being there means only that truth also has its paleontology and its 'prescription,' and may grow stiff-with years of veteran service and petrified in men's regard by sheer antiquity. But how plastic even the oldest truths nevertheless really are has been vividly shown in our day by the transformation of logical and mathematical ideas, a transformation which seems even to be invading physics. The ancient formulas are reinterpreted as special expressions of much wider principles, principles that our ancestors never got a glimpse of in their present shape and formulation. . . .

Pragmatism, on the other hand, asks its usual question. "Grant an idea or belief to be true," it says, "what concrete difference will its being true make in anyone's actual life? How will the truth be realized? What experiences will be different from those which would obtain if the belief were false? What, in short, is the truth's cash-value in experiential terms?"

The moment pragmatism asks this question, it sees the answer: *True ideas are those that we can assimilate, validate, corroborate and verify. False ideas are those that we cannot.* That is the practical difference it makes to us to have true ideas; that, therefore, is the meaning of truth, for it is all that truth is known-as.

This thesis is what I have to defend. The truth of an idea is not a stagnant property inherent in it. Truth *happens* to an idea. It *becomes* true, is *made* true by events. Its verity *is* in fact an event, a process: the process namely of its verifying itself, its veri-*fication*. Its validity is the process of its validation.

But what do the words verification and validation themselves pragmatically mean? They again signify certain practical consequences of the verified and validated idea. It is hard to find any one phrase that characterizes these consequences better than the ordinary agreement-formula—just such consequences being what we have in mind whenever we say that our ideas 'agree' with reality. They lead us, namely, through the acts and other ideas which they instigate, into or up to, or towards, other parts of experience with which we feel all the while—such feeling being among our potentialities—that the original ideas remain in agreement. The connexions and transitions come to us from point to point as being progressive, harmonious, satisfactory. This function of agreeable leading is what we mean by an idea's verification. Such an account is vague and it sounds at first quite trivial, but it has results which it will take the rest of my hour to explain.

Let me begin by reminding you of the fact that the possession of true thoughts means everywhere the possession of invaluable instruments of action; and that our duty to gain truth, so far from being a blank command from out of the blue, or a 'stunt' self-imposed by our intellect, can account for itself by excellent practical reasons.

The importance to human life of having true beliefs about matters of fact is a thing too notorious. We live in a world of realities that can be infinitely useful or infinitely harmful. Ideas that tell us which of them to expect count as the true ideas in all this primary sphere of verification, and the pursuit of such ideas is a primary human duty. The possession of truth, so far from being here an end in itself, is only a preliminary means towards other vital satisfactions. If I am lost in the woods and starved, and find what looks like a cow-path, it is of the utmost importance that I should think of a human habitation at the end of it, for if I do so and follow it, I save myself. The true thought is useful here because the house which is its object is useful. The practical value of true ideas is thus primarily derived from the practical importance of their objects to us. Their objects are, indeed, not important at all times. I may on another occasion have no use for the house; and then my idea of it, however verifiable, will be practically irrelevant, and had better remain latent. Yet since almost any object may some day become temporarily important, the advantage of having a general stock of *extra* truths, of ideas that shall be true of merely possible situations, is obvious. We store such extra truths away in our memories, and with the overflow we fill our books of reference. Whenever such an extra truth becomes practically relevant to one of our emergencies, it passes from cold-storage to do work in the world, and our belief in it grows active. You can say of it then either that 'it is useful because it is true' or that 'it is true because it is useful.' Both these phrases mean exactly the same thing, namely that here is an idea that gets fulfilled and can be verified. True is the name for whatever idea starts the verification-process, useful is the name for its completed function in experience. True ideas would never have been singled out as such, would never have acquired a class-name, least of all a name suggesting value, unless they had been useful from the outset in this way.

From this simple cue pragmatism gets her general notion of truth as something essentially bound up with the way in which one moment in our experience may lead us towards other moments which it will be worth while to have been led to. Primarily, and on the common-sense level, the truth of a state of mind means this function of *a leading that is worth while*. When a moment in our experience, of any kind whatever, inspires us with a thought that is true, that means that sooner or later we dip by that thought's guidance into the particulars of experience again and make advantageous connexion with them. This is a vague enough statement, but I beg you to retain it, for it is essential.

Our experience meanwhile is all shot through with regularities. One bit of it can warn us to get ready for another bit, can 'intend' or be 'significant of' that remoter object. The object's advent is the significance's verification. Truth, in these cases, meaning nothing but eventual verification, is manifestly incompatible with waywardness on our part. Woe to him whose beliefs play fast and loose with the order which realities follow in his experience: they will lead him nowhere or else make false connexions. . . .

'The true', to put it very briefly, is only the expedient in the way of our thinking, just as 'the right' is only the *expedient in the way of our behaving*. Expedient in almost any fashion; and expedient in the long run and on the whole of course; for what meets expediently all the experience in sight won't necessarily meet all farther experiences equally satisfactorily. Experience, as we know, has ways of *boiling over*, and making us correct our present formulas.

The 'absolutely' true, meaning what no farther experience will ever alter, is that ideal vanishing-point towards which we imagine that all our temporary truths will some day converge. It runs on all fours with the perfectly wise man, and with the absolutely complete experience; and, if these ideals are ever realized, they will all be realized together. Meanwhile we have to live to-day by what truth we can get to-day, and be ready to-morrow to call it falsehood. Ptolemaic astronomy, euclidean space, aristotelian logic, scholastic metaphysics, were expedient for centuries, but human experience has boiled over those limits, and we now call these things only relatively true, or true within those borders of experience. 'Absolutely' they are false; for we know that those limits were casual, and might have been transcended by past theorists just as they are by present thinkers. . . .

I have already insisted on the fact that truth is made largely out of previous truths. Men's beliefs at any time are so much experience *funded*. But the beliefs are themselves parts of the sum total of the world's experience, and become matter, therefore, for the next day's funding operations. So far as reality means experienceable reality, both it and the truths men gain about it are everlastingly in process of mutation—mutation towards a definite goal, it may be—but still mutation.

⇒+ "TRANSATLANTIC TRUTH" +⇐
Bertrand Russell

Bertrand Russell (1872–1970) was born into a wealthy and politically influential family, but gave away his substantial inherited wealth because he was morally opposed to inheritance, whether of titles or money. He wrote and lectured extensively, and held teaching positions in both the United States and in Great Britain (primarily at Cambridge University). Always controversial, in 1940 Russell was offered a position at City College in New York City; but the offer was then withdrawn, on the grounds that Russell (primarily due to his atheistic and pacifistic views) was a threat to public safety and morality. Russell was an outstanding writer (in 1950 he was awarded the Nobel Prize for Literature) and was also famous for his work in mathematics and philosophy. A very energetic and outspoken social reformer, Russell was a strong campaigner for nuclear disarmament (in 1961, at the age of 89, he was jailed for his participation in that campaign).

Russell was a powerful opponent of the idealism that dominated British and American philosophy at the end of the nineteenth century and a strong and steady advocate of empiricism. Though many of his views changed over his long and active life, he never wavered in his support of scientific empiricism, and he argued vigorously against any threats to that view; and Russell regarded pragmatism as a clear threat to empiricism. In this essay, he concentrates his fire on the pragmatist views of William James.

PART V

William James's Conception of Truth

'The history of philosophy', as William James observes, 'is to a great extent that of a certain clash of human temperaments.' In dealing with a temperament of such charm as his, it is not pleasant to think of a 'clash'; one does not willingly differ, or meet so much urbanity by churlish criticisms. Fortunately, a very large part of his book is concerned with the advocacy of positions which pragmatism shares with other forms of empiricism; with all this part of his book, I, as an empiricist, find myself, broadly speaking, in agreement.

. . .

'Pragmatism', says James, 'represents a perfectly familiar attitude in philosophy, the empiricist attitude, but it represents it, as it seems to me, both in a more radical and in a less objectionable form than it has ever yet assumed. A pragmatist turns his back resolutely and once for all upon a lot of inveterate habits dear to professional philosophers. He turns away from abstraction and insufficiency, from verbal solutions, from bad *a priori* reasons, from fixed principles, closed systems, and pretended absolutes and origins. He turns towards concreteness and adequacy, towards facts, towards action and towards power. That means the empiricist temper regnant and the rationalist temper sincerely given up. It means the open air and possibilities of nature, as against dogma, artificiality, and the pretence of finality in truth'.

. . .

The temper of mind here described is one with which I, for my part, in the main cordially sympathize. But I think there is an impression in the mind of William James, as of some other pragmatists, that pragmatism involves a more open mind than its opposite. As regards scientific questions, or even the less important questions of philosophy, this is no doubt more or less the case. But as regards the fundamental questions of philosophy—especially as regards what I consider *the* fundamental question, namely, the nature of truth—pragmatism is absolutely dogmatic.

The hypothesis that pragmatism is erroneous is not allowed to enter for the pragmatic competition; however well it may work, it is not to be entertained. To 'turn your back resolutely and once for all' upon the philosophy of others may be heroic or praiseworthy, but it is not undogmatic or open-minded. A modest shrinking from self-assertion, a sense that all our theories are provisional, a constant realization that after all the hypothesis of our opponents may be the right one—these characterize the truly empirical temper, but I do not observe that they invariably characterize the writings of pragmatists. Dogmatism in fundamentals is more or less unavoidable in philosophy, and I do not blame pragmatists for what could not be otherwise; but I demur to their claim to a greater open-mindedness than is or may be possessed by their critics. . . .

But it is time to return to the pragmatic method.

'The pragmatic method', we are told, 'is primarily a method of settling metaphysical disputes that otherwise might be interminable. Is the world one or many?—fated or free?—material or spiritual?—here are notions either of which may or may not hold good of the world; and disputes over such notions are unending. The pragmatic method in such cases is to try to interpret each notion by tracing its respective practical consequences. What difference would it practically make to anyone if this notion rather than that notion were true? If no practical difference whatever can be traced, then the alternatives mean practically the same thing, and all dispute is idle. Whenever a dispute is serious, we ought to be able to show some practical difference that must follow from one side or the other's being right.' And again: 'To attain perfect clearness in our thoughts of an object, then, we need only consider what conceivable effects of a practical kind the object may involve—what sensations we are to expect from it, and what reactions we must prepare. Our conception of these effects, whether immediate or remote, is then for us the whole of our conception of the object, so far as that conception has positive significance at all'

. . .

To this method, applied within limits and to suitable topics, there is no ground for objecting. On the contrary, it is wholesome to keep in touch with concrete facts, as far as possible, by remembering to bring our theories constantly into connection with them. The method, however, involves more than is stated in the extract which I quoted just now. It involves also the suggestion of the pragmatic criterion of truth: a belief is to be judged true in so far as the practical consequences of its adoption are good. . . .

The pragmatic theory of truth is the central doctrine of pragmatism, and we must consider it at some length. William James states it in various ways, some of which I shall now quote. He says: 'Ideas (which themselves are but parts of our experience) become true just in so far as they help us to get into satisfactory relation with other parts of our experience' . . . Again: 'Truth is *one species of good*, and not, as is usually supposed, a category distinct from good, and coordinate with it. *The true is the name of whatever proves itself to be good in the way of belief, and good, too, for definite, assignable reasons'* . . . That truth means 'agreement with reality' may be said by a pragmatist as well as by anyone else, but the pragmatist differs from others as to what is meant by 'agreement', and also (it would seem) as to what is meant by 'reality'. William James gives the following definition of 'agreement': 'To "agree" in the widest sense with a reality *can only mean to be guided either straight up to it or into its surroundings, or to be put into such working touch with it as to handle either it or something connected with it better than if we disagreed'. . . .* This language is rather metaphorical, and a little puzzling; it is plain, however, that 'agreement' is regarded as practical, not as merely intellectual. This emphasis on practice is, of course, one of the leading features of pragmatism.

In order to understand the pragmatic notion of truth, we have to be clear as to the basis of *fact* upon which truths are supposed to rest. Immediate sensible experience, for example, does not come under the alternative of *true* and *false*. 'Day follows day', says James, 'and its contents are simply added. The new contents themselves are not true, they simply *come and are*. Truth is *what we say about* them' . . . Thus when we are merely aware of sensible objects, we are not to be regarded as knowing any truth, although we have a certain kind of contact with reality. It is important to realize that the *facts* which thus lie outside the scope of truth and falsehood supply the material which is presupposed by the pragmatic theory. Our beliefs have to agree with matters of fact: it is an essential part of their 'satisfactoriness' that they should do so. James also mentions what he calls 'relations among purely mental ideas' as part of our

stock-in-trade with which pragmatism starts. He mentions as instances '1 and 1 make 2', 'white differs less from grey than it does from black', and so on. All such propositions as these, then, we are supposed to know for certain before we can get under way. As James puts it: 'Between the coercions of the sensible order and those of the ideal order, our mind is thus wedged tightly. Our ideas must agree with realities, be such realities concrete or abstract, be they facts or be they principles, under penalty of endless inconsistency and frustration' . . . Thus it is only when we pass beyond plain matters of fact and a *priori* truisms that the pragmatic notion of truth comes in. It is, in short, the notion to be applied to doubtful cases, but it is not the notion to be applied to cases about which there can be no doubt. And that there are cases about which there can be no doubt is presupposed in the very statement of the pragmatist position. 'Our account of truth', James tells us, 'is an account . . . of processes of leading, realized *in rebus*, and having only this quality in common, that they *pay*' . . . We may thus sum up the philosophy in the following definition: 'A truth is anything which it pays to believe.' Now, if this definition is to be useful, as pragmatism intends it to be, it must be possible to know that it pays to believe something without knowing anything that pragmatism would call a truth. Hence the knowledge that a certain belief pays must be classed as knowledge of a sensible fact or of a 'relation among purely mental ideas', or as some compound of the two, and must be so easy to discover as not to be worthy of having the pragmatic test applied to it. There is, however, some difficulty in this view. Let us consider for a moment what it means to say that the belief 'pays'. We must suppose that this means that the consequences of entertaining the belief are better than those of rejecting it. In order to know this, we must know what are the consequences of entertaining it, and what are the consequences of rejecting it; we must know also what consequences are good, what bad, what consequences are better, and what worse. Take, say, belief in the Roman Catholic Faith. This, we may agree, causes a certain amount of happiness at the expense of a certain amount of stupidity and priestly domination. Such a view is disputable and disputed, but we will let that pass. But then comes the question whether, admitting the effects to be such, they are to be classed as on the whole good or on the whole bad; and this question is one which is so difficult that our test of truth becomes practically useless. It is far easier, it seems to me, to settle the plain question of fact: 'Have Popes been always infallible?'

than to settle the question whether the effects of thinking them infallible are on the whole good. Yet this question, of the truth of Roman Catholicism, is just the sort of question that pragmatists consider specially suitable to their method.

The notion that it is quite easy to know when the consequences of a belief are good, so easy, in fact, that a theory of knowledge need take no account of anything so simple—this notion, I must say, seems to me one of the strangest assumptions for a theory of knowledge to make. Let us take another illustration. Many of the men of the French Revolution were disciples of Rousseau, and their belief in his doctrines had far-reaching effects, which make Europe at this day a different place from what it would have been without that belief. If, on the whole, the effects of their belief have been good, we shall have to say that their belief was true; if bad, that it was false. But how are we to strike the balance? It is almost impossible to disentangle what the effects have been; and even if we could ascertain them our judgment as to whether they have been good or bad would depend upon our political opinions. It is surely far easier to discover by direct investigation that the *Contract Social* is a myth than to decide whether belief in it has done harm or good on the whole.

Another difficulty which I feel in regard to the pragmatic meaning of 'truth' may be stated as follows: Suppose I accept the pragmatic criterion, and suppose you persuade me that a certain belief is useful. Suppose I thereupon conclude that the belief is true. Is it not obvious that there is a transition in my mind from seeing that the belief is useful to actually holding that the belief is true? Yet this could not be so if the pragmatic account of truth were valid. Take, say, the belief that other people exist. According to the pragmatists, to say 'it is true that other people exist' *means* 'it is useful to believe that other people exist'. But if so, then these two phrases are merely different words for the same proposition; therefore when I believe the one I believe the other. If this were so, there could be no transition from the one to the other, as plainly there is. This shows that the word 'true' represents for us a different idea from that represented by the phrase 'useful to believe', and that, therefore, the pragmatic definition of truth ignores, without destroying, the meaning commonly given to the word 'true', which meaning, in my opinion, is of fundamental importance, and can only be ignored at the cost of hopeless inadequacy. . . .

'On pragmatic principles', James says, we cannot reject any hypothesis if consequences useful to life flow from it' . . . He proceeds to point out that consequences useful to life flow from the hypothesis of the Absolute, which is therefore so far a true hypothesis. But it should be observed that these useful consequences flow from the hypothesis that the Absolute is a fact, not from the hypothesis that useful consequences flow from belief in the Absolute. But we cannot believe the hypothesis that the Absolute is a fact merely because we perceive that useful consequences flow from this hypothesis. What we can believe on such grounds is that this hypothesis is what pragmatists call 'true', i.e. that it is useful; but it is not from this belief that the useful consequences flow, and the grounds alleged do not make us believe that the absolute is a fact, which is the useful belief. In other words, the useful belief is that the Absolute is a fact, and pragmatism shows that this belief is what it calls 'true'. Thus pragmatism persuades us that belief in the Absolute is 'true', but does not persuade us that the Absolute is a fact. The belief which it persuades us to adopt is therefore not the one which is useful. In ordinary logic, if the belief in the Absolute is true, it follows that the Absolute is a fact. But with the pragmatist's meaning of 'true' this does not follow; hence the proposition which he proves is not, as he thinks, the one from which comforting consequences flow . . .

To sum up: while agreeing with the empirical temper of pragmatism, with its readiness to treat all philosophical tenets as 'working hypotheses', we cannot agree that when we say a belief is true we mean that it is a hypothesis which 'works', especially if we mean by this to take account of the excellence of its effects, and not merely of the truth of its consequences. If, to avoid disputes about words, we agree to accept the pragmatic definition of the word 'truth', we find that the belief that A exists may be 'true' even when A does not exist. This shows that the conclusions arrived at by pragmatism in the sphere of religion do not have the meaning which they appear to have, and are incapable, when rightly understood, of yielding us the satisfaction which they promise. The attempt to get rid of 'fact' turns out to be a failure, and thus the old notion of truth reappears. And if the pragmatist states that utility is to be merely a *criterion* of truth, we shall reply first, that it is not a useful criterion, because it is usually harder to discover whether a belief is useful than whether it is true; secondly, that since no *a priori* reason is shown why truth and utility should always go together, utility can only be shown to be a criterion at all by showing inductively that it accompanies truth in all known instances, which requires that we should already know in many instances what things are true. Finally, therefore, the pragmatist theory of truth is to be condemned on the ground that it does not 'work'.

⊨ RECONSTRUCTION IN PHILOSOPHY ⊨
John Dewey

John Dewey (1859–1952) was a dominant figure in American intellectual life during the first half of the twentieth century. His work in both educational theory and educational practice had enormous influence on the American system of education; his writings on politics and on political philosophy were widely read; and his work on ethics was also quite influential. He was perhaps the leading American "public intellectual" for several decades, and was consulted on a wide variety of topics, ranging from problems in public education to domestic politics to international affairs; had there been television news shows such as *Meet the Press,*" Dewey would have been a regular guest.

In the chapter included here, Dewey is writing as a leader of pragmatism, pressing points that are central to his pragmatist approach to epistemology—points that had great influence on later philosophers, such as W. V. O. Quine and Richard Rorty. Like other pragmatists, Dewey opposes the traditional distinction—drawn by both empiricists and rationalists—between reason and experience. Dewey insists that our understanding of the world requires both and that they are inextricably joined together. In particular, he rejects the common philosophical belief that philosophy must be a "quest for certainty," and that disciplines which might provide such certainties—such as pure mathematics—are somehow higher and distinct from other inquiries. For Dewey, the knowledge required for engineering is just as important as the knowledge of the pure mathematician; and the knowledge gained by the metalsmith is fully equal to the knowledge acquired by the theoretical physicist; and there is no line that divides one type of knowledge from another. Any distinction between "applied" knowledge and "theoretical" knowledge is rejected by Dewey, along with any idea that some area of knowledge is more fundamental or basic and that knowledge must be "built up" from a foundation of fundamental truths. Rather than taking sides between the rationalists and the empiricists, Dewey maintains that both start from false assumptions about the nature of knowledge, reason, and experience; and that these false assumptions result in false distinctions that hamstring our quest for workable understanding of ourselves and our world.

CHAPTER IV

Changed Conceptions of Experience and Reason

What is experience and what is Reason, Mind? What is the scope of experience and what are its limits? How far is it a sure ground of belief and a safe guide of conduct? Can we trust it in science and in behavior? Or is it a quagmire as soon as we pass beyond a few low material interests? Is it so shaky, shifting, and shallow that instead of affording sure footing, safe paths to fertile fields, it misleads, betrays, and engulfs? Is a Reason outside experience and above it needed to supply assured principles to science and conduct? In one sense, these questions suggest technical problems of abstruse philosophy; in another sense, they contain the deepest possible questionings regarding the career of man. They concern the criteria he is to employ in forming his beliefs; the principles *by* which he is to direct his life and the ends *to* which he is to direct it. Must man transcend experience by some organ of unique character that carries him into the superempirical? Failing this, must he wander sceptical and disillusioned? Or is human experience itself worth while in its purposes and its methods of guidance? Can it organize itself into stable courses or must it be sustained from without?

We know the answers of traditional philosophy. They do not thoroughly agree among themselves, but they agree that experience never rises above the level of the particular, the contingent, and the probable. Only a power transcending in origin and content any and all conceivable experience can attain to universal, necessary and certain authority and direction. The empiricists themselves admitted the correctness of these assertions. They only said that since there is no faculty of Pure Reason in the possession of mankind, we must put up with what we have, experience, and make the most possible out of it. They contented themselves with sceptical attacks upon the transcendentalist, with indications of the ways in which we might best seize the meaning and good of the passing moment; or like Locke, asserted that in spite of the limitation of experience, it affords the light needed to guide men's footsteps modestly in conduct. They affirmed that the alleged authoritative guidance by a higher faculty had practically hampered men.

It is the function of this lecture to show how and why it is now possible to make claims for experience as a guide in science and moral life which the older empiricists did not and could not make for it.

Curiously enough, the key to the matter may be found in the fact that the old notion of experience was itself a product of experience—the only kind of experience which was then open to men. If another conception of experience is now possible, it is precisely because the quality of experience as it may now be lived has undergone a profound social and intellectual change from that of earlier times. The account of experience which we find in Plato and Aristotle is an account of what Greek experience actually was. It agrees very closely with what the modern psychologist knows as the method of learning by trial and error as distinct from the method of learning by ideas. Men tried certain acts, they underwent certain sufferings and affections. Each of these in the time of its occurrence is isolated, particular—its counterpart is transient appetite and transient sensation. But memory preserves and accumulates these separate incidents. As they pile up, irregular variations get cancelled, common features are selected, reinforced and combined. Gradually a habit of action is built up, and corresponding to this habit there forms a certain generalized picture of an object or situation. We come to know or note not merely this particular which as a particular cannot strictly be known at all (for not being classed it cannot be characterized and identified) but to recognize it as man, tree, stone, leather—an individual of a certain kind, marked by a certain universal form characteristic of a whole species of thing. Along with the development of this common-sense knowledge, there grows up a certain regularity of conduct. The particular incidents fuse, and a *way* of acting which is general, as far as it goes, builds up. The skill develops which is shown by the artisan, the shoemaker, the carpenter, the gymnast, the physician, who have regular ways of handling cases. This regularity signifies, of course, that the particular case is not treated as an isolated particular, but as one of a kind, which therefore demands a *kind* of action. From the multitude of particular illnesses encountered, the physician in learning to class some of them as indigestion learns also to treat the cases of the class in a common or general way. He forms the rule of recommending a certain diet, and prescribing a certain remedy. All this forms what we call experience. It results, as the illustration shows, in a certain general insight and a certain organized ability in action.

But needless to insist, the generality and the organization are restricted and fallible. They hold, as Aristotle was fond of pointing out, usually, in most cases, as a rule, but not universally, of necessity, or as a principle. The physician is bound to make mistakes, because individual cases are bound to vary unaccountably: such is their very nature. The difficulty does not arise in a defective experience which is capable of remedy in some better experience. Experience itself, as such, is defective, and hence default is inevitable and irremediable. The only universality and certainly is in a region above experience, that of the rational and conceptual. As the particular was a stepping-stone to image and habit, so the latter may become a stepping-stone to conceptions and principles. But the latter leave experience behind, untouched; they do not react to rectify it. Such is the notion which still lingers in the contrast of "empirical" and "rational" as when we say that a certain architect or physician is empirical, not scientific in his procedures. But the difference between the classic and the modern notion of experience is revealed in the fact that such a statement is now a charge, a disparaging accusation, brought against *a* particular architect or physician. With Plato, Aristotle and the Scholastic, it was a charge against the callings, since they were modes of experience. It was an indictment of all practical action in contrast with conceptual contemplation.

The modern philosopher who has professed himself an empiricist has usually had a critical purpose in mind. Like Bacon, Locke, Condillac and Helvetius, he stood face to face with a body of beliefs and a set of institutions in which he profoundly disbelieved. His problem was the problem of attack upon so much dead weight carried uselessly by humanity, crushing and distorting it. His readiest way of undermining and disintegrating was by appealing to experience as a final test and criterion. In every case, active reformers were "empiricists" in the philosophical sense. They made it their business to show that some current belief or institution that claimed the sanction of innate ideas or necessary conceptions, or an origin in an authoritative revelation of reason, had in fact proceeded from a lowly origin in experience, and had been confirmed by accident, by class interest or by biased authority.

The philosophic empiricism initiated by Locke was thus disintegrative in intent. It optimistically took it for granted that when the burden of blind custom, imposed authority, and accidental associations was removed, progress in science and social organization would spontaneously take place. Its part was to help in removing the burden. The best way to liberate men from the burden was through a natural history of the origin and growth in the mind of the ideas connected with objectionable beliefs and customs. Santayana justly calls the psychology of this school a malicious psychology. It tended to identify the history of the formation of certain ideas with an account of the things to which the ideas refer—an identification which naturally had an unfavorable effect on the things. But Mr. Santayana neglects to notice the social zeal and aim latent in the malice. He fails to point out that this "malice" was aimed at institutions and traditions which had lost their usefulness; he fails to point out that to a large extent it was true of them that an account of their psychological origin was equivalent to a destructive account of the things themselves. But after Hume with debonair clarity pointed out that the analysis of beliefs into sensations and associations left "natural" ideas and institutions in the same position in which the reformers had placed "artificial" ones, the situation changed. The rationalists employed the logic of sensationalistic-empiricism to show that experience, giving only a heap of chaotic and isolated particulars, is as fatal to science and to moral laws and obligations as to obnoxious institutions; and concluded that "Reason" must be resorted to if experience was to be furnished with any binding and connecting principles. The new rationalistic idealism of Kant and his successors seemed to be necessitated by the totally destructive results of the new empirical philosophy.

Two things have rendered possible a new conception of experience and a new conception of the relation of reason to experience, or, more accurately, of the place of reason *in* experience. The primary factor is the change that has taken place in the actual nature of experience, its contents and methods, as it is actually lived. The other is the development of a psychology based upon biology which makes possible a new scientific formulation of the nature of experience. Let us begin with the technical side—the change in psychology. We are only just now commencing to appreciate how completely exploded is the psychology that dominated philosophy

throughout the eighteenth and nineteenth centuries. According to this theory, mental life originated in sensations which are separately and passively received, and which are formed, through laws of retention and association, into a mosaic of images, perceptions, and conceptions. The senses were regarded as gateways or avenues of knowledge. Except in combining atomic sensations, the mind was wholly passive and acquiescent in knowing. Volition, action, emotion, and desire follow in the wake of sensations and images. The intellectual or cognitive factor comes first and emotional and volitional life is only a consequent conjunction of ideas with sensations of pleasure and pain.

The effect of the development of biology has been to reverse the picture. Wherever there is life, there is behavior, activity. In order that life may persist, this activity has to be both continuous and adapted to the environment. This adaptive adjustment, moreover, is not wholly passive; is not a mere matter of the moulding of the organism by the environment. Even a clam acts upon the environment and modifies it to some extent. It selects materials for food and for the shell that protects it. It does something to the environment as well as has something done to itself. There is no such thing in a living creature as mere conformity to conditions, though parasitic forms may approach this limit. In the interests of the maintenance of life there is transformation of some elements in the surrounding medium. The higher the form of life, the more important is the active reconstruction of the medium. This increased control may be illustrated by the contrast of savage with civilized man. Suppose the two are living in a wilderness. With the savage there is the maximum of accommodation to given conditions; the minimum of what we may call hitting back. The savage takes things "as they are," and by using caves and roots and occasional pools leads a meagre and precarious existence. The civilized man goes to distant mountains and dams streams. He builds reservoirs, digs channels, and conducts the waters to what had been a desert. He searches the world to find plants and animals that will thrive. He takes native plants and by selection and cross-fertilization improves them. He introduces machinery to till the soil and care for the harvest. By such means he may succeed in making the wilderness blossom like the rose.

Such transformation scenes are so familiar that we overlook their meaning. We forget that the inherent power of life is illustrated in them. Note what a change this point of view entails in the traditional notions of experience. Experience becomes an affair primarily of doing. The organism does not stand about, Micawberlike, waiting for something to turn up. It does not wait passive and inert for something to impress itself upon it from without. The organism acts in accordance with its own structure, simple or complex, upon its surroundings. As a consequence the changes produced in the environment react upon the organism and its activities. The living creature undergoes, suffers, the consequences of its own behavior. This close connection between doing and suffering or undergoing forms what we call experience. Disconnected doing and disconnected suffering are neither of them experiences. Suppose fire encroaches upon a man when he is asleep. Part of his body is burned away. The burn does not perceptibly result from what he has done. There is nothing which in any instructive way can be named experience. Or again there is a series of mere activities, like twitchings of muscles in a spasm. The movements amount to nothing; they have no consequences for life. Or, if they have, these consequences are not connected with prior doing. There is no experience, no learning, no cumulative process. But suppose a busy infant puts his finger in the fire; the doing is random, aimless, without intention or reflection. But something happens in consequence. The child undergoes heat, he suffers pain. The doing and undergoing, the reaching and the burn, are connected. One comes to suggest and mean the other. Then there is experience in a vital and significant sense.

Certain important implications for philosophy follow. In the first place, the interaction of organism and environment, resulting in some adaptation which secures utilization of the latter, is the primary fact, the basic category. Knowledge is relegated to a derived position, secondary in origin, even if its importance, when once it is established, is overshadowing. Knowledge is not something separate and self-sufficing, but is involved in the process by which life is sustained and evolved. The senses lose their place as gateways of knowing to take their rightful place as stimuli to action. To an animal an affection of the eye or ear is not an idle piece of information about something indifferently going on in the world. It is an invitation and inducement to act in a needed way. It is a clue in behavior, a directive factor in adaptation of life in its surroundings. It is urgent not cognitive in quality. The whole controversy between empiricism and rationalism as to the intellectual worth of sensations is rendered strangely obsolete. The discussion of sensations belongs under the head of immediate stimulus and response, not under the head of knowledge.

As a *conscious* element, a sensation marks an interruption in a course of action previously entered upon. Many psychologists since the time of Hobbes have dwelt upon what they call the relativity of sensations. We *feel* or sense cold in transition from warmth rather than absolutely; hardness is sensed upon a background of less resistance; a color in contrast with pure light or pure dark or in contrast with some other hue. A continuously unchanged tone or color cannot be attended to or sensed. What we take to be such monotonously prolonged sensations are in truth constantly interrupted by incursions of other elements, and represent a series of excursions back and forth. This fact was, however, misconstrued into a doctrine about the nature of knowledge. Rationalists used it to discredit sense as a valid or high mode of knowing things, since according to it we never get hold of anything *in itself* or intrinsically. Sensationalists used it to disparage all pretence at absolute knowledge.

Properly speaking, however, this fact of the relativity of sensation does not in the least belong in the sphere of knowing. Sensations of this sort are emotional and practical rather than cognitive and intellectual. They are shocks of change, due to interruption of a prior adjustment. They are signals to redirections of action. Let me take a trivial illustration. The person who is taking notes has no sensation of the pressure of his pencil on the paper or on his hand as long as it functions properly. It operates merely as stimulus to ready and effective adjustment. The sensory activity incites automatically and unconsciously its proper motor response. There is a preformed physiological connection, acquired from habit but ultimately going back to an original connection in the nervous system. If the pencil-point gets broken or too blunt and the habit of writing does not operate smoothly, there is a conscious shock:—the feeling of something the matter, something gone wrong. This emotional change operates as a stimulus to a needed change in operation. One looks at his pencil, sharpens it or takes another pencil from one's pocket. The sensation operates as a pivot of readjusting behavior. It marks a break in the prior routine of writing and the beginning of some other mode of action. Sensations are "relative" in the sense of marking transitions in habits of behavior from one course to another way of behaving.

The rationalist was thus right in denying that sensations as such are true elements of knowledge. But the reasons he gave for this conclusion and the consequences he drew from it were all wrong. Sensations are not parts of *any* knowledge, good or bad, superior or inferior, imperfect or complete. They are rather provocations, incitements, challenges to an act of inquiry which is to *terminate* in knowledge. They are not ways of knowing things inferior in value to reflective ways, to the ways that require thought and inference, because they are not ways of knowing at all. They are stimuli to reflection and inference. As interruptions, they raise the questions: What does this shock mean? What is happening? What is the matter? How is my relation to the environment disturbed? What should be done about it? How shall I alter my course of action to meet the change that has taken place in the surroundings? How shall I readjust my behavior in response? Sensation is thus, as the sensationalist claimed, the beginning of knowledge, but only in the sense that the experienced shock of change is the necessary stimulus to the investigating and comparing which eventually produce knowledge.

When experience is aligned with the life-process and sensations are seen to be points of readjustment, the alleged atomism of sensations totally disappears. With this disappearance is abolished the need for a synthetic faculty of super-empirical reason to connect them. Philosophy is not any longer confronted with the hopeless problem of finding a way in which separate grains of sand may be woven into a strong and coherent rope—or into the illusion and pretence of one. When the isolated and simple existences of Locke and Hume are seen not to be truly empirical at all but to answer to certain demands of their theory of mind, the necessity ceases for the elaborate Kantian and Post-Kantian machinery of *a priori* concepts and categories to synthesize the alleged stuff of experience. The true "stuff" of experience is recognized to be adaptive courses of action, habits, active functions, connections of doing and undergoing; sensori-motor co-ordinations. Experience carries principles of connection and organization within itself. These principles are none the worse because they are vital and practical rather than epistemological. Some degree of organization is indispensable to even the lowest grade of life. Even an amoeba must have some continuity in time in its activity and some adaptation to its environment in space. Its life and experience cannot possibly consist in momentary, atomic, and self-enclosed sensations. Its activity has reference to its surroundings and to what goes before and what comes after. This organization intrinsic to life renders unnecessary a super-natural and super-empirical synthesis. It affords the basis and material for a positive evolution of intelligence as an organizing factor within experience.

Nor is it entirely aside from the subject to point out the extent in which social as well as biological organization enters into the formation of human experience. Probably one thing that strengthened the idea that the mind is passive and receptive in knowing was the observation of the helplessness of the human infant. But the observation points in quite another direction. Because of his physical dependence and impotency, the contacts of the little child with nature are mediated by other persons. Mother and nurse, father and older children, determine what experiences the child shall have; they constantly instruct him as to the meaning of what he does and undergoes. The conceptions that are socially current and important become the child's principles of interpretation and estimation long before he attains to personal and deliberate control of conduct. Things come to him clothed in language, not in physical nakedness, and this garb of communication makes him a sharer in the beliefs of those about him. These beliefs coming to him as so many facts form his mind; they furnish the centres about which his own personal expeditions and perceptions are ordered. Here we have "categories" of connection and unification as important as those of Kant, but empirical not mythological.

From these elementary, if somewhat technical considerations, we turn to the change which experience itself has undergone in the passage from ancient and medieval to modern life. To Plato, experience meant enslavement to the past, to custom. Experience was almost equivalent to established customs formed not by reason or under intelligent control but by repetition and blind rule of thumb. Only reason can lift us above subjection to the accidents of the past. When we come to Bacon and his successors, we discover a curious reversal. Reason and its bodyguard of general notions is now the conservative, mind-enslaving factor. Experience is the liberating power. Experience means the new, that which calls us away from adherence to the past, that which reveals novel facts and truths. Faith in experience produces not devotion to custom but endeavor for progress. This difference in temper is the more significant because it was so unconsciously taken for granted. Some concrete and vital change must have occurred in actual experience as that is lived. For, after all, the thought of experience follows after and is modelled upon the experience actually undergone.

When mathematics and other rational sciences developed among the Greeks, scientific truths did not react back into daily experience. They remained isolated, apart and super-imposed. Medicine was the art in which perhaps the greatest amount of positive knowledge was obtained, but it did not reach the dignity of science. It remained an art. In practical arts, moreover, there was no conscious invention or purposeful improvement. Workers followed patterns that were handed down to them, while departure from established standards and models usually resulted in degenerate productions. Improvements came either from a slow, gradual, and unacknowledged accumulation of changes or else from some sudden inspiration, which at once set a new standard. Being the result of no conscious method, it was fittingly attributed to the gods. In the social arts, such a radical reformer as Plato felt that existing evils were due to the absence of such fixed patterns as controlled the productions of artisans. The ethical purport of philosophy was to furnish them, and when once they were instituted, they were to be consecrated by religion, adorned by art, inculcated by education and enforced by magistrates so that alteration of them would be impossible.

It is unnecessary to repeat what has been so often dwelt upon as to the effect of experimental science in enabling man to effect a deliberate control of his environment. But since the impact of this control upon the traditional notion of experience is often overlooked, we must point out that when experience ceased to be empirical and became experimental, something of radical importance occurred. Aforetime man employed the results of his prior experience only to form customs that henceforth had to be blindly followed or blindly broken. Now, old experience is used to suggest aims and methods for developing a new and improved experience. Consequently experience becomes in so far constructively self-regulative. What Shakespeare so pregnantly said of nature, it is "made better by no mean, but nature makes that mean," becomes true of experience. We do not merely have to repeat the past, or wait for accidents to force change upon us. We *use* our past experiences to construct new and better ones in the future. The very fact of experience thus includes the process by which it directs itself in its own betterment.

Science, "reason" is not therefore something laid from above upon experience. Suggested and tested in experience, it is also employed through inventions in a thousand ways to expand and enrich experience. Although, as has been so often repeated, this self-creation and self-regulation of experience is still largely technological rather than truly artistic or human, yet what has been achieved contains the guaranty of the possibility of an intelligent administering of experience. The limits are moral and intellectual, due to defects in our good will and

knowledge. They are not inherent metaphysically in the very nature of experience. "Reason" as a faculty separate from experience, introducing us to a superior region of universal truths begins now to strike us as remote, uninteresting and unimportant. Reason, as a Kantian faculty that introduces generality and regularity into experience, strikes us more and more as superfluous—the unnecessary creation of men addicted to traditional formalism and to elaborate terminology. Concrete suggestions arising from past experiences, developed and matured in the light of the needs and deficiencies of the present, employed as aims and methods of specific reconstruction, and tested by success or failure in accomplishing this task of readjustment, suffice. To such empirical suggestions used in constructive fashion for new ends the name intelligence is given.

This recognition of the place of active and planning thought within the very processes of experience radically alters the traditional status of the technical problems of particular and universal, sense and reason, perceptual and conceptual. But the alteration is of much more than technical significance. For reason is experimental intelligence, conceived after the pattern of science, and used in the creation of social arts; it has something to do. It liberates man from the bondage of the past, due to ignorance and accident hardened into custom. It projects a better future and assists man in its realization. And its operation is always subject to test in experience. The plans which are formed, the principles which man projects as guides of reconstructive action, are not dogmas. They are hypotheses to be worked out in practice, and to be rejected, corrected and expanded as they fail or succeed in giving our present experience the guidance it requires. We may call them programmes of action, but since they are to be used in making our future acts less blind, more directed, they are flexible. Intelligence is not something possessed once for all. It is in constant process of forming, and its retention requires constant alertness in observing consequences, an open-minded will to learn and courage in re-adjustment.

In contrast with this experimental and re-adjusting intelligence, it must be said that Reason as employed by historic rationalism has tended to carelessness, conceit, irresponsibility, and rigidity—in short absolutism. A certain school of contemporary psychology uses the term "rationalization" to denote those mental mechanisms by which we unconsciously put a better face on our conduct or experience than facts justify. We excuse ourselves to ourselves by introducing a purpose and order into that of which we are secretly ashamed. In like fashion, historic rationalism has often tended to use Reason as an agency of justification and apologetics. It has taught that the defects and evils of actual experience disappear in the "rational whole" of things; that things *appear* evil merely because of the partial, incomplete nature of experience. Or, as was noted by Bacon, "reason" assumes a false simplicity, uniformity and universality, and opens for science a path of fictitious ease. This course results in intellectual irresponsibility and neglect:—irresponsibility because rationalism assumes that the concepts of reason are so self-sufficient and so far above experience that they need and can secure no confirmation in experience. Neglect, because this same assumption makes men careless about concrete observations and experiments. Contempt for experience has had a tragic revenge *in* experience; it has cultivated disregard for fact and this disregard has been paid for in failure, sorrow and war.

The dogmatic rigidity of Rationalism is best seen in the consequences of Kant's attempt to buttress an otherwise chaotic experience with pure concepts. He set out with a laudable attempt at restricting the extravagant pretensions of Reason apart from experience. He called his philosophy critical. But because he taught that the understanding employs fixed, *a priori*, concepts, in order to introduce connection into experience and thereby make known *objects* possible (stable, regular relationships of qualities), he developed in German thought a curious contempt for the living variety of experience and a curious overestimate of the value of system, order, regularity for their own sakes. More practical causes were at work in producing the peculiarly German regard for drill, discipline, "order" and docility.

But Kant's philosophy served to provide an intellectual justification or "rationalization" of subordination of individuals to fixed and ready-made universals, "principles," laws. Reason and law were held to be synonyms. And as reason came into experience from without and above, so law had to come into life from some external and superior authority. The practical correlate to absolutism is rigidity, stiffness, inflexibility of disposition. When Kant taught that some conceptions, and these the important ones, are *a priori*, that they do not arise in experience and cannot be verified or tested in experience, that without such ready-made injections into experience the latter is anarchic and chaotic, he fostered the spirit of absolutism, even though technically he denied the possibility of absolutes. His successors were true to his

spirit rather than his letter, and so they taught absolutism systematically. That the Germans with all their scientific competency and technological proficiency should have fallen into their tragically rigid and "superior" style of thought and action (tragic because involving them in inability to understand the world in which they lived) is a sufficient lesson of what may be involved in a systematical denial of the experimental character of intelligence and its conceptions.

By common consent, the effect of English empiricism was sceptical where that of German rationalism was apologetic; it undermined where the latter justified. It detected accidental associations formed into customs under the influence of self- or class-interest where German rational-idealism discovered profound meanings due to the necessary evolution of absolute reason. The modern world has suffered because in so many matters philosophy has offered it only an arbitrary choice between hard and fast opposites: Disintegrating analysis *or* rigid synthesis; complete radicalism neglecting and attacking the historic past as trivial and harmful, *or* complete conservation idealizing institutions as embodiments of eternal reason; a resolution of experience into atomic elements that afford no support to stable organization *or* a clamping down of all experience by fixed categories and necessary concepts—these are the alternatives that conflicting schools have presented.

They are the logical consequences of the traditional opposition of Sense and Thought, Experience and Reason. Common sense has refused to follow both theories to their ultimate logic, and has fallen back on faith, intuition or the exigencies of practical compromise. But common sense too often has been confused and hampered instead of enlightened and directed by the philosophies proffered it by professional intellectuals. Men who are thrown back upon "common sense" when they appeal to philosophy for some general guidance are likely to fall back on routine, the force of some personality, strong leadership or on the pressure of momentary circumstances. It would be difficult to estimate the harm that has resulted because the liberal and progressive movement of the eighteenth and earlier nineteenth centuries had no method of intellectual articulation commensurate with its practical aspirations. Its heart was in the right place. It was humane and social in intention. But it had no theoretical instrumentalities of constructive power. Its head was sadly deficient. Too often the logical import of its professed doctrines was almost anti-social in their atomistic individualism, anti-human in devotion to brute sensation. This deficiency played into the hands of the reactionary and obscurantist. The strong point of the appeal to fixed principles transcending experience, to dogmas incapable of experimental verification, the strong point of reliance upon *a priori* canons of truth and standards of morals in opposition to dependence upon fruits and consequences in experience, has been the unimaginative conception of experience which professed philosophic empiricists have entertained and taught.

A philosophic reconstruction which should relieve men of having to choose between an impoverished and truncated experience on one hand and an artificial and impotent reason on the other would relieve human effort from the heaviest intellectual burden it has to carry. It would destroy the division of men of good will into two hostile camps. It would permit the co-operation of those who respect the past and the institutionally established with those who are interested in establishing a freer and happier future. For it would determine the conditions under which the funded experience of the past and the contriving intelligence which looks to the future can effectually interact with each other. It would enable men to glorify the claims of reason without at the same time falling into a paralyzing worship of super-empirical authority or into an offensive "rationalization" of things as they are.

EXERCISES

1. "The search for truth is more precious than its possession" (Albert Einstein). Would you agree? Would a pragmatist agree? How would a pragmatist—perhaps—wish to rephrase that statement?

2. "Is pragmatism the true account of human knowledge? Is pragmatism (or anti-foundationalism) the best epistemological theory?" Suppose the pragmatist responds: "To settle that question, we must try pragmatist accounts, and try foundationalist accounts, and see which one works best." Does that pragmatist answer beg the question? That is, does it assume what it is supposed to be proving? Is there any alternative answer that the pragmatist could give?

3. In his discussion of rationalism and empiricism, William James asserts that the basic conflict between those two approaches "is to a great extent that of a certain clash of human temperaments" (*Pragmatism*, Lecture 1). That is, we do not favor the rationalist or the empiricist approach because we are convinced by strong arguments that one side is correct; rather, our *temperaments*—our basic orientations, our basic inclinations—mark us as either rationalist or empiricist, and then we *find* arguments to support the view we favor. Is James right about that? Think of your own view on rationalism, empiricism, and pragmatism: Does your "temperament" play a major role in determining which view you find more plausible?

4. What guides us well is true, according to the pragmatist. How broadly does that principle apply? William James uses that principle to justify belief in God: Believing in God helps us live better and more successfully, and thus it guides us well (according to James). Can the pragmatic principle (what guides us well is true) legitimately be applied to religious belief? *Must* a consistent pragmatist use the principle in judging religious beliefs?

5. A work of fiction can be wonderfully *coherent*, though it is clearly not *true*; is that a problem for the coherence view of epistemology?

6. Charles Sanders Peirce was a pragmatist who rejected the idea that simple direct truth can be known either empirically or rationally. But he insisted on the importance of a concept of *final truth*: that is, the set of beliefs on which scientific inquiry will *ultimately converge*. Is such a belief *useful*? Is it consistent with the pragmatist perspective?

7. William Butler Yeats, the great Irish poet and essayist, wrote that "Wisdom is a butterfly, and not a gloomy bird of prey." Would you agree? Would rationalists, empiricists, or pragmatists agree? Could some empiricists agree, and some disagree? Rationalists? Pragmatists?

ADDITIONAL READING

Knowledge: Readings in Contemporary Epistemology (Oxford: Oxford University Press, 2000), edited by Sven Bernecker and Fred Dretske, contains key contemporary essays by foundationalists and their critics. An excellent collection of important papers on foundationalism and coherence from the last several decades is *Epistemology: An Anthology*, edited by Ernest Sosa and Jaegwon Kim (Oxford: Blackwell, 2000). Laurence Bonjour, "The Dialectic of Foundationalism and Coherentism," in John Greco and Ernest Sosa, eds., *The Blackwell Guide to Epistemology* (Oxford: Blackwell Publishers, 1999), is a good survey of the foundationalist/coherentist controversy, though Bonjour ultimately sides with the foundationalists. Another good survey article is "Theories of Justification," by Richard Fumerton, which is Chapter 6 in *The Oxford Handbook of Epistemology*, edited by Paul K. Moser (Oxford: Oxford University Press, 2002).

A sustained attack on foundationalism is offered by Michael Williams, in *Groundless Belief: An Essay on the Possibility of Epistemology*, 2nd ed. (Princeton, NJ: Princeton University Press, 1999).

Several writers have advanced mixed theories, which involve some combination of foundationalism and coherentism. One of the most interesting of such theories is developed by Susan Haack, in *Evidence and Inquiry* (Oxford: Blackwell Publishers, 1993).

Laurence Bonjour's earlier coherence view, and his criticisms of foundationalism, can be found in *The Structure of Empirical Knowledge* (Cambridge, MA: Harvard University Press, 1985); his more recent foundationalist views are presented in *In Defense of Pure Reason* (London: Cambridge University Press, 1997).

N. R. Hanson's *Patterns of Discovery* (Cambridge: Cambridge University Press, 1958) used research in Gestalt psychology to challenge the traditional empiricist distinction between observation and theory. Willard van Orman Quine raised serious questions concerning the traditional distinctions between analytic and synthetic, between *a priori* and *a posteriori*, and between theory and observation. His work can be found in *From a Logical Point of View*, revised ed. (Cambridge, MA: Harvard University Press, 1961); *Word and Object* (Cambridge, MA: M.I.T. Press, 1960); *The Ways of Paradox and Other Essays* (New York: Random House, 1966); and *Ontological Relativity and Other Essays* (New York: Columbia University Press, 1969).

Historian Thomas Kuhn's fascinating and enormously influential *The Structure of Scientific Revolutions*, 2nd ed. (Chicago, IL: The University of Chicago Press, 1970) is a very readable book that should interest anyone who likes either science or history. An excellent examination of Kuhn's views—including Kuhn's response to some key criticisms—is *Criticism and the Growth of Knowledge*, edited by Imré Lakatos and Alan Musgrave (Cambridge: Cambridge University Press, 1970).

The French mathematician Henri Poincaré and the French scientist Pierre Duhem had significant influence on the development of views such as Kuhn's and Quine's. See Pierre Duhem's *The Aim and Structure of Physical Theory*, 2nd ed., translated by Philip P. Wiener (Princeton, NJ: Princeton University Press, 1954), originally published in Paris in 1914; and Henri Poincaré's *Science and Hypothesis*, first published in English in 1905, currently available in a 1952 Dover edition of that translation (New York: Dover Publications, 1952).

Karl Popper's work has been very influential both in science and philosophy. See *The Logic of Scientific Discovery* (London: Hutchinson, 1959); *Conjectures and Refutations* 3rd ed. (London: Routledge and Kegan Paul, 1969); and *Objective Knowledge: An Evolutionary Approach* (Oxford: Oxford University Press, 1972). An excellent book on Popper—containing a brief autobiography by Popper and Popper's response to various critics—is by Paul A. Schilpp, *The Philosophy of Karl Popper* (La Salle, IL: Open Court Publishing, 1974); this is a volume in Schilpp's superb series, The Library of Living Philosophers.

Ludwig Wittgenstein's work has had great influence on contemporary philosophy of language and epistemology. See particularly his *Philosophical Investigations* 3rd ed. (London: The Macmillan Company, 1958); and *On Certainty*, originally published by Basil Blackwell, 1969; available in paperback from Harper & Row (New York, 1972). *Wittgenstein's Poker*, by David Edmonds and John Eidinow, is the dramatic story of a brief confrontation between Wittgenstein and Popper in 1946, when Popper came to Cambridge to give a lecture that Wittgenstein attended. The book not only gives a nice account of their competing positions but also offers a superb study of the intellectual and historical background of their debate.

Wilfrid Sellars is not an easy read, but his work on epistemology and philosophy of science has had great influence. For a collection of some of his most important essays, see *Science, Perception and Reality* (London: Routledge and Kegan Paul, 1963). Nicholas Rescher, *The Coherence Theory of Truth* (Oxford: Clarendon Press, 1973), offers a strong alternative to the traditional correspondence account of truth. Thomas Nagel, *The View from Nowhere* (Oxford: Oxford University Press, 1986), offers a very insightful analysis of our tendency to suppose we can take a detached "purely objective" view of the world, independent of our own perspective, and the problems generated by that assumption.

Charles S. Peirce is the primary source for classical pragmatism. The best source for his work is a collection edited by Charles Hartshorne and Paul Weiss, *Collected Papers of Charles Sanders Peirce* (Cambridge, MA: The Belknap Press of Harvard University Press, 1965). There is also a good collection by Philip P. Weiner, entitled *Charles S. Peirce: Selected Writings*. Originally published by Doubleday in 1958, it is now available in a Dover Edition (New York: Dover, 1966). William James is perhaps the best known pragmatist, and his work is always interesting. His *Pragmatism* was originally published in 1907, and is available in many editions. See also *The Will to Believe and Other Essays in Popular Philosophy*, which was originally published in 1897 and is also widely available. John Dewey was well known as a pragmatist and public philosopher in the mid-twentieth century, writing extensively on philosophy, education, and political issues. Among his many books, see *Human Nature and Conduct* (New York: Henry Holt, 1922); *Reconstruction in Philosophy* (New York: Henry Holt, 1920); and especially *The Quest for Certainty*, the text of Dewey's Gifford Lectures in 1929, available as a Putnam Capricorn paperback (New York: G. P. Putnam's Sons, 1960).

Richard Rorty champions contemporary pragmatism, and his writings are always interesting as well as controversial. His spirited challenge to traditional correspondence views of knowledge can be found in *Philosophy and the Mirror of Nature* (Princeton, NJ: Princeton University Press, 1979); see also the three volumes of his Philosophical Papers, published by Cambridge University Press (Cambridge): *Objectivity, Relativism, and Truth*, 1991; *Essays on Heidegger and Others*, 1991; and *Truth and Progress*, 1998; as well as Rorty's *Philosophy and Social Hope* (London: Penguin, 1999). Another influential contemporary pragmatist— whose views differ from Rorty's on some interesting points—is Hilary Putnam; a good introduction to his work is *The Many Faces of Realism* (Chicago, IL: Open Court, 1987); see also his *Realism with a Human Face* (Cambridge, MA: Harvard University Press, 1990).

Cornel West is a very engaging writer, and his "prophetic pragmatism" is clearly presented in *The American Evasion of Philosophy: A Genealogy of Pragmatism* (Madison, WI: University of Wisconsin Press, 1987).

Evolutionary epistemology is a fascinating recent development in epistemology. An excellent introduction to the issues raised by this approach can be found in Gerard Radnitzky and W. W. Bartley, III, eds., *Evolutionary Epistemology, Theory of Rationality, and the Sociology of Knowledge* (La Salle, IL: Open Court, 1987).

An excellent site for information on Thomas Kuhn, including a brief biography and a number of links as well as papers on Kuhn's work, can be found at www.emory.edu/ EDUCATION/mfp/Kuhnsnap.html. An interesting RealAudio discussion of Kuhn's work from the NPR program Science Friday can be heard at www.sciencefriday.com/pages/1996/ Aug/hour2_081696.html

For information on pragmatism, visit www.pragmatism.org, the superb site of the Pragmatism Cybrary. Also visit radicalacademy.com/amphilosophy7a.htm. A good site on William James can be found at www.emory.edu/EDUCATION/mfp/james.html. It is part of the Welcome to the Middle Web site, which is a bit offbeat, but very entertaining.

Online, the Stanford Encyclopedia of Philosophy—http://plato.stanford.edu—is an excellent resource; see the articles on epistemology, as well as several articles under the heading "justification, epistemic." Keith DeRose maintains "The Epistemology Page," at http://pantheon.yale.edu/~kd47/e-page.htm. It is an interesting mix of recent articles in several areas of epistemology and good bibliographical resources, as well as a collection of course syllabi, ratings of graduate programs in epistemology, and even a few pictures of contemporary epistemologists.

CHAPTER 6

WHAT IS THE MIND?

What is the mind? Is it simply part of the body? Is it attached to the body? Is the mind a physical entity, or a special distinct mental substance? Does it operate like a complex machine, or is it something unique, perhaps even miraculous? Descartes was profoundly influential in epistemology because he took seriously the implications of the Copernican Revolution, and tried to deal with the powerful shock it delivered to our system of knowledge. Because Descartes took seriously the developing scientific system of his time, he is also a major figure in questions about the nature of human identity—in particular, on questions of whether we are a distinctive combination of *mind and body*.

MECHANISM AND THE MIND

It is not surprising that the seventeenth century produced deep concern about the mind as distinguished from the body. This was the period when the mechanistic view of the physical world really developed. Think of the world view that had dominated for 2,000 years, from Aristotle's ancient Greece straight through into the sixteenth century: the Aristotelian-Ptolemaic view of the universe. On that view, the world is a very orderly place, with the unmoving but corruptible Earth at the center, the Moon—with its changing phases—next, and then the planets and the Sun making their orbits around the Earth. Farther beyond is the realm of fixed stars, a giant sphere to which all the stars are attached; it spins in place, once daily, in its unchanging glory. And out beyond the fixed stars are the angelic hosts: the ranks of cherubims, then seraphims, on up to the angelic ophanim (who carry the throne of God), and ultimately to God Himself. (Aristotle, of course, had no Heavenly hosts except for God; but the Judeo-Christian version of the Aristotelian-Ptolemaic universe had no trouble finding the appropriate place for the ranks of angels.) The order is provided by distance from the perfect unchanging God: with God in His unchanging perfection at the top, the angelic hosts next in line, down to the realm of fixed stars which lies closest to the heavenly hosts, and thus changes the least (it merely spins in place), and on down to the "wandering" planets in their somewhat irregular orbits, then the Moon with its changing phases, all the way down to the Earth in its change and corruption. Aristotelian physics fits snugly with this Ptolemaic astronomy/cosmology. A stone falls to the Earth because it is made up of Earthly substance, and is seeking its proper place; smoke rises because its primary substance is air, and it seeks its proper place away from the Earthly substance. And the heavenly bodies—such as the planets—stay in their proper circular orbits because they are made up of a more perfect type of substance, that is also seeking to follow its proper path. The realm of fixed stars spins without changing its place because it seeks to emulate the perfection of God. The entire system is permeated with purposefulness, and ordered by the divine hierarchy.

   Copernicus challenges this model, giving a mathematical account of the motion of the planets around the Sun: an account that makes no reference to purposes or divine order, substituting instead a relatively simple model of cosmic motion. Then Galileo, a great supporter of the Copernican account, gave an account of the motion of objects in terms of inertia: Unless otherwise acted upon (by a force such as friction) objects simply continue on the path they are traveling, and no purposefulness of the moving objects enters the account. A very important addition to this essentially mechanistic model came from the English physician William Harvey, who in 1628 published an account of the circulation of the blood through the body propelled by the pumping of the heart. (The Muslim physician Ibn Nafis of the thirteenth century may well have given the first account of the circulation of the blood; but his work was unknown in Europe, and Harvey was the first European to describe the circulatory system.) All of this work was very familiar to Descartes. Descartes apparently sympathized with the Copernican model, though he was quite discreet about those sympathies: Galileo's experiences with the Inquisition had made it clear that publicly advocating the Copernican theory could be hazardous to your health. And Descartes was so impressed by William Harvey's work that he wrote a *Description of the Human Body* incorporating Harvey's account.

DESCARTES AND MIND–BODY DUALISM

Descartes was fascinated by the mechanistic developments in astronomy, physics, and biology, but also found them disturbing. In this mechanistic world—which, as Harvey had shown, clearly included the human body—what is the place of humans? Do we remain something special, or are we just one more part of this vast machinery? If the world, including ourselves, is one vast machine, does that leave room for human reason? Does it leave room for free will?

Obviously, people had long been asking the question of whether humans are distinctly different from the rest of the world: If humans are somehow immortal, that would certainly make us quite different; or perhaps human rational powers are so distinctive that they set us apart. But when the world around us started to look more and more like a great machine, with all its parts moving in clockwork order, the question of how humans fit into that machine—or perhaps did *not* fit, and somehow existed *apart*—became a very pressing issue. Descartes proposed an answer that still has its advocates, and still causes controversy, some four centuries later. And even those who do not consciously accept Descartes' proposed solution are often deeply influenced by the assumptions in Descartes' position.

When Descartes was seeking a fixed certainty with which he could defeat the forces of skepticism, he reached one indubitable clear and distinct certainty: I exist as a *thinking thing*:

> What then is it that I am? A thinking thing. What is a thinking thing? It is a thing that doubts, understands, affirms, denies, wills, abstains from willing, that also can be aware of images and sensations.

That is, I am a *mind*. Maybe I also have a body (later Descartes becomes quite confident that he does); but at this point, what I *know* is that I am a *mind*, a *thinking thing*.

For Descartes, what is *essential* to who I am is my *mind*:

> . . . I have a body with which I am very closely conjoined, yet since on the one hand I have a clear and distinct idea of myself in so far as I am only a thinking unextended thing, and on the other hand a distinct idea of the body, in so far as it is only an extended unthinking thing, it is certain t hat I am truly distinct from my body, and can exist without it.

Phineas Fletcher, a poet who was a contemporary of Descartes, expressed poetically the idea of the human mind being an altogether different type of material from the physical body, and of course being the supreme ruler of the body. In his elaborate poem *The Purple Island*, the *Prince* of the human island is the mind:

> The Islands Prince, of frame more than celestiall,
> Is rightly call'd th' all-seeing *Intellect*;
> All glorious bright, such nothing is terrestriall;
> Whose Sun-like face, and most divine aspect
>   No humane sight may ever hope descrie:
>   For when himself on's self reflects his eye,
> Dull or amaz'd he stands at so bright majestie.
>
>   . . . .
>
> His strangest body is not bodily,
> But matter without matter; never fill'd,
> Nor filling; though within his compasse high
> All heav'n and earth, and all in both are held;
>   Yet thousand heav'ns he could contain,
>   And still as empty as at first remain;
> And when he takes in most, readi'st to take again.

Of course, this idea of a mind (or perhaps soul) that is distinct from the physical body did not originate with Descartes. Plato, some 2,000 years earlier, used the image of a "disembodied soul" in some of his dialogues; and for Plato, the Reason was distinct from the bodily passions and sensations. But the great emphasis on mind–body differentiation really stems from Descartes and the seventeenth century. Descartes eventually concludes that he also *has* a body with which he is intimately connected—not merely as a pilot in a ship, but much more closely—but that nonetheless he is essentially *mind*, and his physical body is something different and distinct: Indeed, it is an entirely different sort of substance. The physical body has weight, shape, and size; but his *mind* (and its ideas) has none of those characteristics: it has no weight, no shape. Descartes believes that his mind is very closely connected with his brain, but his mind is *not* his brain: The brain is *physical* substance, while the *mental* substance of the mind is a different type of substance altogether. Somehow my physical body substance *interacts* with my mind substance: I hit my finger with a hammer, and my mind has the idea of intense pain; I pour beer into my body, and it obviously affects my mind; my mind has the idea of writing something and that causes my fingers to trudge about on the keyboard. So the mind and body interact—thought exactly how is not quite clear.

Advantages of Mind–Body Dualism

Descartes' mind–body dualism has obvious appeal. In the first place, it seems to fit our immediate beliefs about mind and body. Suppose you say, "Wow, I just had a great idea for my philosophy term paper!" and I reply, "Oh, really? How big is your idea? How much does it weigh? What color is it?" You might well be offended, and think I was making sport of you. Or you might think I was incredibly stupid. "Don't be silly," you might respond; "ideas don't have weight or size or color; you can't measure them with a tape measure or weigh them on a scale." Of course if you tell your roommate about your great idea for a term paper on mind–body interactionism, your roommate might reply with something like, "Wow, that's heavy, man." But your roommate is speaking metaphorically, not literally. Ideas can be good or bad, wise or stupid; but they can't *literally* be big or small, heavy or light. Those are characteristics that apply to the *physical* world, and not to the *mental* world of minds and ideas. Minds and ideas, bodies and the physical world: these seem to belong to two different realms. Along the same lines, it is easy for us to distinguish mental from physical abilities. Stephen Hawking, the brilliant cosmologist and physicist, is a brilliant mind locked in a body that has been devastated by amyotrophic lateral sclerosis (popularly known as Lou Gehrig's disease); Hawking's mind does remarkable work in theoretical physics, while his body is almost entirely paralyzed. And on the opposite track, you can perhaps think of several fabulous bodies that are attached to rather subpar minds. So the distinction between mind and body seems a perfectly natural distinction to draw.

Mind–body dualism is now a minority view among philosophers, though it is still advocated by some contemporary philosophers and even some contemporary neuropsychologists. C. E. M. Joad was a mid-twentieth-century philosopher who strongly favored mind–body dualism:

> . . . in addition to the body and brain, the composition of the living organism includes an immaterial element which we call mind; . . . this element, although it is in very close association with the brain, is more than a mere glow or halo surrounding the cerebral structure, the function of which is confined to reflecting the events occurring in the structure; . . . on the contrary, it is in some sense independent of the brain, and in virtue of its independence is able in part to direct and control the material constituents of the body, using them to carry out its purposes in relation to the external world of objects, much as a driver will make use of the mechanism of his motorcar. Mind so conceived is an active, dynamic, synthesizing force; it goes out beyond the sensations provided by external stimuli and arranges them into patterns, and it seems to be capable on occasion of acting without the provocation of bodily stimuli to set it in motion. It is, in other words, creative, that is, it carries on activities which even the greatest conceivable extension of our physiological knowledge would not enable us to infer from observing the brain.
>
> *How Our Minds Work*, 1947

The second advantage of mind–body dualism is that it gives us a very convenient way of thinking about personal immortality. "The River Jordan is chilly and cold, it chills the body, but not the soul," goes the old song. Our bodies are mortal, but our souls/minds are immortal.

The third advantage of mind–body dualism was one that Descartes must have felt very strongly: Mechanistic natural science is encroaching further and further into explanation of the natural world, and leaving less and less room for special human capacities. The world of Copernicus is not one in which humans act out their starring roles on a fixed and immobile center stage, with the glorious realms of planets and stars and angelic hosts revolving around us; it is instead a marvelous mechanical clockwork, in which our little planet circles in space. It's a marvelous machine, but still a machine. And William Harvey, with his explanation of the mechanical operations of the human body—the blood is pumped by the heart through a circuit of pipes in the body—extended this mechanical model to human beings along with many other animals. So where is the special distinctness of human beings? Where—in this vast machinery—is there room for free will? If the mind is a distinctive substance, different in kind from rocks, planets, hearts, and blood vessels, then there is no danger that the mechanization of the physical realm will encroach upon the very different world of minds, ideas, and wills.

Problems for Mind–Body Dualism and Interactionism

But Cartesian dualism has some problems, as well. First, there is the basic problem of Ockham's Razor, discussed in Chapter 2. This is the principle that in giving explanations, we "should not multiply entities beyond necessity"; that is, if we can explain phenomena with a *simpler* theory that posits *fewer* entities, then that simpler theory is—all else being equal—a better explanation than the more complex theory. *If* we can explain the world (including humans and human thought and behavior) through a theory that uses only physical objects and their properties, then that theory is clearly simpler (and by Ockham's Razor, therefore *better*) than a theory which adds another whole realm of special *mental* objects. Of course, the mind–body dualists will insist that theories denying the existence of special mental substance *cannot* adequately explain everything that dualist theories can explain: Monistic theories are explanatorily *inadequate* to explain all the mental phenomena we observe. And that remains a disputed question.

The second problem for mind–body dualism is one that has plagued Cartesian dualism since Descartes proposed his theory. As already noted, it seems obvious to most mind–body dualists (including Descartes) that there is *interaction* between the mind and the body. But the nature of that interaction is very difficult to understand, or even imagine. After all, consider the radical difference between mind and body. Mind—as the dualists insist—is totally *nonphysical*: it has no weight, no density, no *physical force* whatsoever. The physical, by contrast, is a totally different type of substance from the mental: it has weight, physical dimensions, exerts force, and so on. Suppose I have the mental *idea* that I wish to type this sentence on my keyboard: How does this idea, with no physical weight or force of any kind, *cause* my (purely physical) body to move? Descartes proposed that *perhaps* the interaction between mind and body occurred in the pineal gland, conveniently located at the base of the brain (the pineal gland was a good candidate: it was in the right spot, it was situated in such a way that very small amounts of energy might cause vibrations which could be transferred to the brain and thence to the rest of the nervous system, and—at the time Descartes was writing—biologists had not discovered any other function for the gland). It's a charming idea: Thoughts cause the pineal gland to vibrate slightly, and those vibrations reverberate in the brain, triggering responses in the nerves, which stimulate the muscles; and from that tiny tremor, enormous physical responses can be activated. It's a charming idea, but utterly hopeless as a way of explaining mind–body interaction. The problem, after all, is not how to transfer energy from the vibrations of the pineal gland to the brain, and from there to nerves and muscles; the problem is how to generate the original physical motion or physical force (no matter how small) from a mental substance with *no* physical force, no physical mass, and no *physical* characteristics or capacities whatsoever. And of course the problem is equally severe from the other direction: How can a physical event (such as the stimulation of the optic nerve) cause a totally *nonphysical* idea? Still, there are those who insist that if the amount of energy that must be generated is very very small, this basic difficulty can be avoided; this is the approach favored by the contemporary neuropsychologist John Eccles, who insists that only a tiny charge would be required, because the brain is finely tuned to respond to minute effects. But the generation of even that very small physical force still poses a challenge for mind–body interactionism.

Mind–body dualists have struggled with this problem for centuries, and the struggle continues. The problem for mind–body interactionists became even more severe when the principle of the conservation of energy was generally acknowledged as a fundamental principle of physical systems: the principle that the amount of energy in the total system is constant, though it can take many different forms. If the mind is—through some inexplicable process—generating energy into the physical system, then the fundamental law of conservation of energy is violated every time my thought that I want to type a sentence generates energy in my brain, or my pineal gland, or wherever it starts; indeed, the law is broken anytime *anyone* has a thought that is generated into action.

The perplexing question of how a mental (nonphysical) mind could generate a physical effect on the body has driven many to seek alternatives to mind–body interactionism.

Some of those alternatives may seem a bit strange. However, before you judge these theories too harshly, try this exercise: *Start* from the assumption that we have *both* a physical body/brain and a *non*physical mental substance (the mind); and assume also that such radically different substances *cannot* causally interact. Starting from those assumptions, how would you explain the *apparent* causal interaction of mind and body? When viewed from that perspective, there are some fascinating—and very creative—philosophical efforts at solving the quandary.

PREESTABLISHED HARMONY

The mind is purely nonphysical while the body–brain is physical, and thus there can be no direct *causal* interaction between them (those are the operating assumptions), though there certainly *appears* to be causal interaction (when, for example, I form the mental purpose of kicking a ball, and that is followed by the physical swinging of my leg and the propulsion of the ball). The great seventeenth-century Rationalist Gottfried Wilhelm Leibniz proposed this solution: rather than *interaction*, there is a *preestablished harmony* (sometimes called *parallelism*). Imagine two clocks, both of which keep perfect time: One is a beautiful old grandfather clock, that chimes out the hours; the other, a lovely little cuckoo clock, which marks the hours by sending forth a cute little cuckoo bird to chirp "cuckoo, cuckoo." Hour after hour and day following day you observe both clocks: As soon as the grandfather clock begins to toll the hours, the cuckoo bird immediately pops out of the clock. If you didn't know better, it would certainly *appear* to you that the chiming of the grandfather clock awakens the cuckoo bird and causes it to shoot from the clock and give voice. Of course if one or both of the clocks occasionally malfunctioned, and sometimes the cuckoo emerged first, sometimes it came out 15 minutes late, and sometimes not at all, then it would no longer appear that there is causal interaction. But so long as they stay exactly in time, the conclusion that they are causally connected would be almost irresistible. This is a wonderful solution to the mind–body problem: It solves the problem of how the mental and physical could interact (they do *not*); and it also accounts for the *appearance* of mind–body interaction. Of course it does require an amazing preestablished harmony: a perfect clockwork that harmonizes every mental and every physical act performed by every human in the entire range of human history. That's a harmony that makes the harmony of the planets look like child's play. But for an omnipotent and omniscient God—with powers far beyond our humble imagining—establishing such a magnificent harmony would be no challenge. (Actually, the harmony proposed by Leibniz may be even more complicated than that: Leibniz proposes that every object in the world is an independent *monad*, containing a representation of everything else in the world and thus guaranteeing their harmony; but still, an omnipotent God could manage it.) And Leibniz' solution does not make the world more complicated than necessary (it does not violate Ockham's Razor) because it appeals only to entities already acknowledged to exist (by Leibniz's contemporaries): minds, bodies, and an omnipotent God.

OCCASIONALISM

Another solution to the mind–body problem—not quite as elegant to my eye, but you can make your own evaluation—is *occasionalism*. In this model (still operating from the assumptions that there are both minds and bodies, and that they cannot causally interact), God intervenes on *every occasion* when you have a thought that you would like to kick a ball or lift your arm or move your fingers, or when a physical event *appears* to cause you to have an idea.

> But when one thinks about the idea of God, i.e., of an infinitely perfect and consequently all-powerful being, one knows that there is such a connection between His will and the motion of all bodies, that it is impossible to conceive that He wills a body to be moved and that this body not be moved. We must therefore say that only His will can move bodies if we wish to state things as we conceive them and not as we sense them. The motor force of bodies is therefore not in the bodies that are moved, for this motor force is nothing other than the will of God. Thus, bodies have no action; and when a ball that is moved collides with and moves another, it communicates nothing of its own, for it does not itself have the force it communicates to it. . . . But not only are bodies incapable of being the true causes of whatever exists: the most noble minds are in a similar state of impotence. They can know nothing unless God enlightens them. They can sense nothing unless God modifies them. They are incapable of willing anything unless God moves them. *Nicolas Malebranche, The Search After Truth*, Book 6, Part 2, Chapter 3 (translated by Thomas M. Lennon and Paul J. Oscamp).

You have the idea of kicking the ball toward the goal, and God intervenes to carry out the actual bodily physical operation. Even your thought of kicking the ball requires God's empowerment. That many *occasions* of active intervention would be rather taxing for you or me, but an omnipotent and omnipresent God can manage it effortlessly. Indeed, on this view God has *all* power—God is *omnipotent*—and so neither our thoughts nor our physical motions are caused by us: God is the *only* cause. Occasionalism eliminates the problem of how your *mind* can cause your *body* to move: it can't, because neither your mind *nor* your body can cause anything whatsoever. But occasionalism was not really designed to answer the problem of mind–body interactionism; rather, it is a system built on the idea of an omnipotent God Who holds *all* power, with no power other than the powers exercised by God. Occasionalism is just one of the implications of that system: Your mind experiences an idea of moving your hand, and you experience your hand moving, but neither the idea nor the physical motion were caused by you; like all events, they must be caused by God alone. In the West, the most famous advocate of occasionalism was Nicolas Malebranche, the great French metaphysician of the generation following Descartes. But the occasionalist view was championed centuries earlier by the great Sunni Muslim theologian Abu Hamid Muhammad ibn Muhammad al-Ghazali, who lived in Baghdad in the eleventh century; and like Malebranche, al-Ghazali based his occasionalism on God's omnipotence: no power exists outside of God, and no event occurs except by God's causation.

IDEALISM

Even with its problems, mind–body dualism still has its champions (most of them favor some form of mind–body interactionism, or alternatively some form of dualism that is less radical than the notion of two distinctly different mind and body *substances*). But the problems confronting dualism have pushed many toward a *monistic* solution to the mind–body problem. There is no problem of mind–body or physical–mental interaction, because there is actually just *one* type of substance, rather than two. So what is that one substance?

> But, say you, though the ideas themselves do not exist without the mind, yet there may be things *like* them, whereof they are copies or resemblances, which things exist without the mind in an unthinking substance. I answer, an idea can be like nothing but an idea; a color or figure can be like nothing but another color or figure. If we look but never so little into our thoughts, we shall find it impossible for us to conceive a likeness except only between our ideas. Again, I ask whether those supposed originals or external things, of which our ideas are the pictures or representations, be themselves perceivable or no? If they are, then they are ideas and we have gained our point; but if you say they are not, I appeal to anyone whether it be sense to assert a color is like something which is invisible; hard or soft, like something which is intangible; and so of the rest. *Bishop George Berkeley, Three Dialogues Between Hylas and Philonous, 1713.*

The great Irish philosopher Bishop Berkeley maintained that the one substance could only be *mental*: minds and their ideas. This view—all that exists is the mental world of minds and ideas, there is no physical substance that exists independently of minds—is called *idealism*. A better name might be *ideaism*; but that's a lot harder to say, so *idealism* is the name that stuck. But it's a bit confusing. *Idealist* in this sense (only mental substance exists) means something very different from our usual use of "idealist," which refers to someone with very high (perhaps unrealistically high) ideals.

> I do not pretend to be a setter-up of new notions. My endeavors tend only to unite and place in a clearer light that truth which was before shared between the vulgar and the philosophers, the former being of opinion that *those things they immediately perceive are the real things,* and the latter, that *the things immediately perceived are ideas which exist only in the mind.* Which two notions put together do, in effect, constitute the substance of what I advance. *Bishop George Berkeley, Three Dialogues Between Hylas and Philonous, 1713.*

Idealism (in Berkeley's sense) strikes many as obviously absurd. The famous Dr. Samuel Johnson, on first hearing of Berkeley's theory, supposedly kicked a rock down a hill, stating: "I refute it *thus.*" But when you examine the theory a bit more closely, *and* you consider some of the problems with competing theories (such as mind–body interactionism or preestablished harmony), then Berkeley's idealism has some genuine charms. In the first place, it avoids the big problem for mind–body dualism: the problem of how mental substance could causally interact with physical substance. It avoids the problem quite elegantly, by totally eliminating one of the substances, and thus eliminating the need for interaction of radically different types of substance.

Berkeley insists on a second big advantage: It is the *simplest* theory that can account for all the observed phenomena. Think about it for a moment: When you observe the world around you, and when you lift your arm or chop down a tree or—to use Samuel Johnson's case—kick a rock down a hill, what do you *actually experience?* Well, if you are kicking a rock, first you must have a visual sensation of a rock; then you must form the idea of kicking the rock, and *will* yourself to do so; that is followed by a sensation—perhaps a painful sensation—in your toe, as well as a sensation of moving your leg; and finally, you have the visual sensation of a rock tumbling down a hill. So you have a significant range of visual, purposeful, and kinesthetic ideas (your sensation of bodily movement), and perhaps some sensations of pain. But (Berkeley insists) *all* of these are *ideas in the mind.* Do you ever have an *experience* that is *not* an idea in your mind? You bump into a door: you have an experience of solidity, hardness, perhaps of sharp pain. But do you ever get *outside* those mental experiences and encounter something *nonmental?* Certainly not. Instead, on the basis of all these mental experiences and ideas, you imagine or hypothesize that there is something else, something *entirely different* from anything you have actually experienced, that was the *cause* of your painful experience. But (Berkeley argues) why should you propose such a wild, and wildly *extravagant*, theory? What you actually experience—and *all* that you experience—are thoughts, sensations, ideas: *mental* experiences. But then you claim, on the basis of this purely *mental* experience, that there exist *physical* objects that are *radically different* from all our experiences, a physical realm that is different in kind from the mental, physical substances that are different in every way from our experienced mental thoughts and ideas but which somehow *cause* those thoughts. But why propose such a strange and extravagant addition to our world? Why not instead confine ourselves to what we actually know and experience: the *mental* realm. On this idealist model, the world is made up exclusively of minds and ideas: no account of mental–physical interaction is required because there is only *one* type of substance. In Berkeley's famous phrase, *Esse est percipi*: To be is to be perceived.

Someone might object that this idealist account offers no explanation for the *continuity* and regularity of our experiences. You leave your bedroom in the morning in a hurry to reach your philosophy class on time; you attend class, eat lunch with some friends, go to an afternoon lab, play a couple of pickup basketball games, meet a friend for dinner, and late that night return to your room and find: everything exactly as you left it, including your desk, your bed, and your dirty clothes on the floor. But you haven't given a thought to your room since you left it 12 hours earlier; and certainly you have not thought constantly about your room and its contents. So what happened to the desk, the bed, and the dirty clothes while they were *not* ideas in your mind, nor in anyone else's mind? Did they all disappear, and spring back into existence when you began to think of them again? But if that were the case, why would they remain constant? Why should you have the same idea of a bed now that you had this morning? Why don't you instead have the idea of a huge four poster king-size bed, rather than the double bed that you had an idea of this morning and the *same* idea tonight? If there are *only* minds and ideas, why would we have the *same* ideas in the morning and evening? But Berkeley has a ready reply. It is *not* the case that the idea of your room ceased to exist during the period when *you* were not thinking of it; it continued to exist—and its continuity was maintained—because it is always an *idea in the mind of God*. After all, God is omniscient, and has an idea of *everything*, including your bed, your dresser, and the dirty socks you left on the floor. Some might suppose that this involves almighty God—Who created the stars and the planets—in too much mundane "busywork": keeping up with every tree, all the desks in your classroom, and even your dirty laundry. But Berkeley considers that a virtue of this theory, rather than a flaw; it reminds us that God is involved in every detail of our day-to-day existence.

MATERIALISM

Most mind–body dualists—such as Descartes—were very impressed by the remarkable advances in the physical sciences: the Copernican account of planetary motion, Harvey's account of how the pumping heart circulates the blood, and Galileo's research on trajectories. Science was making great advances in giving clear mechanical accounts of the world system, and deeper understanding of how this entire machine worked seemed to be coming from all corners.

> To be a machine, to feel, to think, to know how to distinguish good from bad, as well as blue from yellow, and to be but an animal, are therefore hardly contradictory. I believe that thought is so little incompatible with organized matter, that it seems to be one of its properties on a par with electricity, the faculty of motion, penetrability, extension, etc. *J. O. de la Mettrie, 1747.*

All this was exciting, and there were bright prospects for further scientific advances in physics, medicine, and astronomy: advances that might lessen the threat of disease and enhance our understanding of the world. But while they might be delighted with the advances in our mechanical understanding of the world, the dualists wanted to draw a line. The mechanical model might work for the planets, for cannon balls, and even for the human body: but there must be room for something distinct from that mechanical model, something that lies *beyond* mechanical motions, mechanical explanations, and mechanical predictions.

> The standard interpretation of Descartes' dualism is that it was designed to protect the mind or soul from encroachments by mechanical science. But another interpretation is possible: that Descartes developed his dualism not to protect the mind from physical science, but rather to allow the physical sciences scope for enlargement and development. In the seventeenth century, potential conflicts between science and religion were resolved by suppressing science (as the Church's treatment of Galileo had made painfully clear). Descartes, by setting mind–soul in a special category, radically distinct and different from the world of mechanical science, *could* be striving to guarantee a physical sphere where the work of mechanical science could enjoy free inquiry.

There must be room for the human *mind*, soul, or consciousness; something that can reason without mechanical compulsion, something with a consciousness that can rise above the physical, something with a power of free will that can transcend mechanism, perhaps something that can survive physical death. Bishop Berkeley thought that the mechanical model had already gone too far, and he saw idealism as a counter force: the essence of the world is mind, spirit, and idea, not mechanical processes.

> Leibniz offered this argument against a thorough mechanistic materialism (from Section 17 of the *Monadology*, 1714).
>
> > One is obliged to admit that *perception* and what depends upon it is *inexplicable on mechanical principles*, that is, by figures and motions. In imagining that there is a machine whose construction would enable it to think, to sense, and to have perception, one could conceive it enlarged while retaining the same proportions, so that one could enter into it, just like into a windmill. Supposing this, one should, when visiting within it, find only parts pushing one another, and never anything by which to explain a perception. Thus it is in the simple substance, and not in the composite or in the machine, that one must look for perception.

But while dualists such as Descartes and idealists like Berkeley wanted to place limits on mechanical explanation, others were eager to advance the mechanical model of explanation into new areas, in hope of the same success in understanding the human mind as Newton had achieved in astronomy and physics. This was the view favored by many French philosophers of the eighteenth century, who championed a radically mechanist/materialist view of the world.

> This animal [a bird] moves, is agitated, cries . . . ; it comes forth [from its shell], walks, flies, is irritated, flees, approaches, complains, suffers, loves, desires, enjoys: it feels everything that you feel; all your actions, it performs. Do you claim, with Descartes, that it is a purely imitative machine? But little children will laugh at you, and philosophers will reply that if this is a machine, you are another. If you admit that between you and the animal

the only difference is in organization, you will be sensible and reasonable and will do so in good faith, but it will be concluded against you that with inert matter disposed in a certain manner and impregnated with other inert matter, with heat and motion, there can be obtained sensibility, life, memory, self-consciousness, passions and thought. . . . [If you reject this materialist view] you will be sorry for yourself; you will perceive that in order not to admit of a simple supposition that explains everything, namely sensibility as a general attribute of matter or a product of the organization of matter, you renounce common sense and cast yourself into an abyss of mysteries, contradictions and absurdities. *Denis Diderot, "Conversation Between D'Alembert and Diderot," 1769.*

On this view—sometimes called "materialism," and sometimes called "physicalism"—there is no problem of mind–body interaction, because no distinct "mind" substance exists. Of course we have ideas and thoughts, but those are just physical events in the body—particularly in the brain and central nervous system.

. . . the content of his [Darwin's] work was so disruptive to traditional Western thought that we have yet to encompass it all. Arthur Koestler's campaign against Darwin, for example, rests upon a reluctance to accept Darwin's materialism and an ardent desire once again to invest living matter with some special property. . . . This, I confess, I do not understand. Wonder and knowledge are both to be cherished. Shall we appreciate any less the beauty of nature because its harmony is unplanned? And shall the potential of mind cease to inspire our awe and fear because several billion neurons reside in our skulls? *Stephen Jay Gould, "Darwin's Delay," in Ever Since Darwin.*

Resistance to materialism is always strong. After all, it's the last step toward a mechanistic view of humans, and that makes many people queasy, and lots more really angry.

"Materialism" is a confusing word, with a number of meanings and uses. In the discussion of mind–body views, the *materialist* holds that there is only one substance: the physical or *material* substance. Our minds are simply our brains, composed of a very complex arrangement of matter, and not some separate and distinct sort of substance. But "materialist" is also used to refer to someone who is concerned exclusively with the *material* aspects of life—big houses, fancy cars, and flashy clothes—and who has little or no interest in the arts, literature, family, the public welfare, or the good of others. But these are very different senses of "materialist." A "materialist" in the latter sense can believe in mind–body dualism; and the "materialist" (in the sense of someone who believes that humans are a single material-physical substance) may be devoted to music and poetry and good works, and care little for accumulating material wealth.

The distinguished biologist and historian of science Stephen Jay Gould maintained that Charles Darwin long delayed the publication of *The Origin of Species* because he dreaded the hostile reaction to his materialist/mechanist account of human development and of the human mind/brain. In his notebooks, Darwin wrote: "Love of the deity effect of organization, oh you materialist! . . . Why is thought being a secretion of brain, more wonderful than gravity a property of matter? It is our arrogance, our admiration of ourselves." Alfred R. Wallace, who independently developed a theory of natural selection at the same time that Darwin was working on his own account of natural selection, found the idea of mechanical evolution of humans—including the evolution of the special human mind—so disturbing that he concluded that all other life forms were the result of natural selection, but humans were the unique creation of God.

> I am concerned to deny that in the world there are non-physical entitities and non-physical laws. In particular I wish to deny the doctrine of psycho-physical dualism. . . .
>
> Popular theologians sometimes argue against materialism by saying that 'you can't put love in a test-tube'. Well you can't put a gravitational field in a test-tube . . . , but there is nothing incompatible with materialism . . . in the notion of a gravitational field.
>
> Similarly, even though love may elude test-tubes, it does not elude materialist metaphysics, since it can be analyzed as a pattern of bodily behaviour or, perhaps better, as the internal state of the human organism that accounts for this behaviour. *J. J. C. Smart,* "Materialism," 1963.

The visceral opposition to materialism notwithstanding, materialism has some distinct advantages. First, it has the advantage of simplicity: rather than two substances that somehow must interact (or at least *appear* to interact) materialism gets by with a single substance. And unlike idealism, materialism does not require divine intervention to keep our observed material world in steady continuity. Second, materialism is a *useful* theory that guides us effectively: It generates a wide and productive range of research in the behavioral, medical, and neuropsychological sciences. When you prescribe an antidepressant to your patient, you hope that the chemicals in the drug will affect the brain in such a way that depression is relieved; you are not hoping that the drug will affect the brain, and then in some mysterious way the changed brain state will generate happy ideas in a completely different nonbrain mental realm.

There are, of course, traditional objections to materialism. After all, useful as the materialist model may have proved to scientists, it is difficult to conceptualize our thoughts and ideas as simply "brain arrangements." My *thoughts* about capital punishment, politics, and poetry certainly *seem* to be something quite different from what someone would see by doing a brainscan while I'm thinking. But proponents of materialism are not moved by such arguments. After all, they reply, your intense feeling of heat when you drink a very hot cup of coffee doesn't match up very easily with the description of heat given by physicists, but that doesn't mean that their account of heat is wrong. Your study of the molecular structure of water will not give you the sensation of a cool drink on a summer day, but that is no reason to reject the molecular account. One of Wordsworth's poems opens with the line "My heart leaps up when I behold a rainbow in the sky." Newton's scientific account of the rainbow may not cause your heart to leap, but that doesn't mean Newton must be describing something other than what brought joy to Wordsworth.

DUAL-ASPECT THEORY

There does *seem* to be something special about thoughts and ideas and consciousness, and some have tried to find a way to keep that special category while avoiding all the problems with mind–body *dualism*. One interesting theory—developed centuries ago by Spinoza, but which still has its advocates—is the *dual-aspect* (sometimes called the *double-aspect*) theory. Spinoza believed there was only one substance, period. Everything is part of one whole: one infinite substance which has infinite attributes or "modes." But we can observe that substance *either* in its physical or its mental nature (if we reached a higher stage of understanding, we might also be able to observe other attributes which are now invisible to us). The relevant point here is that for Spinoza we are *both* physical and mental; these are simply different *perspectives* on the *same* substance.

The contemporary philosopher Daniel Dennett developed an account of distinctly different *stances* one could take toward the functioning of the brain, or, in this specific case, toward a chess-playing computer. While Dennett is not a dual-aspect theorist, his account does help to illustrate the type of perspective-taking emphasized by those favoring dual-aspect theory. Dennett offers the following example:

> Consider the case of the chess-playing computer, and the different stances one can choose to adopt in trying to predict and explain its behavior. First there is the *design stance*. If one knows exactly how the computer's program has been designed, . . . one can predict the computer's designed response to any move one makes. . . . The essential feature of the design stance is that we make predictions solely from knowledge of or assumptions about the system's design, often without making any examination of the innards of the particular object.
>
> Second, there is what we may call the *physical stance*. From this stance our predictions are based on the actual state of the particular system, and are worked out by applying whatever knowledge we have of the laws of nature. . . . Attempting to give a physical account or prediction of the chess-playing computer would be a pointless and herculean labor, but it would work in principle. One could predict the response it would make in a chess game by tracing out the effects of the input energies all the way through the computer until once more type was pressed against paper and a response was printed.
>
> There is a third stance one can adopt toward a system, and that is the *intentional stance*. This tends to be most appropriate when the system one is dealing with is too complex to be dealt with effectively from the other stances. In the case of the chess-playing computer one adopts this stance when one tries to predict its response to one's move by figuring out what a good or reasonable response would be, given the information the computer has about the situation. Here one assumes not just the absence of malfunction, but the rationality of the design or programming as well.
>
> *Daniel Dennett, "Mechanism and Responsibility," 1973*

Suppose you take a helicopter tour of the Grand Canyon, while I go through the Grand Canyon on a raft trip down the Colorado River. If we are both describing what we saw to a friend, we will give very different reports; but it would make no sense for her to say, "Yes, but which one is a description of the *real* Grand Canyon." They both are, from different perspectives. A recent version of the dual-aspect theory was proposed by Herbert Feigl, who offered the following example:

> If a brain physiologist were equipped with the knowledge and devices that may be available a thousand years hence, and could investigate my brain processes and describe them in full detail, then he could formulate his findings in neurophysiological language, and might even be able to produce a complete microphysical account in terms of atomic and subatomic concepts. . . . But, since in point of empirical fact, *I* am directly acquainted with the qualia of my own immediate experience, I happen to know (by acquaintance) what the neurophysiologist refers to when he talks about certain configurational aspects of my cerebral process.
>
> *Herbert Feigl, "The 'Mental' and the 'Physical,' " in Minnesota Studies in the Philosophy of Science, Volume II, edited by Herbert Feigl, Michael Scriven, and Grover Maxwell (Minneapolis: University of Minnesota Press, 1958): 370–497, 450*

The neurophysiologist and the thinking individual whose brain is examined may thus experience the *same thing*, but will experience very different aspects of it in distinctly different ways.

FUNCTIONALISM

What is a carburetor? We usually define it in terms of its *function* in an internal combustion engine: The carburetor is the part of the engine that mixes fuel with oxygen; that is the *function* the carburetor serves in the engine. But what is a carburetor *made* of? It could be made of many different things: metal or plastic or some combination of those; perhaps even glass or graphite. In different engines, carburetors might have a variety of shapes and sizes and be made of many different materials; but they would all be *functionally* defined as carburetors. In the context of the mind–body question, *functionalism* is the view that mental phenomena—such as thoughts and sensations—should not be identified with some specific physical part of the brain, but rather should be characterized *functionally*: that is, in terms of whatever carries out that function. Consider a mathematical calculation: in Joan, it might be carried out in a specific area of the left side of her brain, while in Robert it might occur on the corresponding right side, and in Henry—who suffered brain damage at an early age—another part of the brain might have taken over the function of mathematical calculations; and in some intelligent extraterrestrial, made of very different stuff, the same calculation might be performed by a different sort of material altogether; and in an intelligent computer or robot, the same function might be fulfilled using still different physical material and structure. Though functionalists typically favor a physicalist/materialist monistic view, it would be possible for a functionalist to hold that our mental operations are functionally accomplished by some ethereal nonphysical mentalistic substance. But since functionalists typically suppose that the mental operations will be carried out by some physical process, we will treat functionalism as a special variety of phyicalism/materialism. Even with that restriction, however, functionalism comes in a wide variety of flavors.

As a version of materialism, *functionalism* does not treat thoughts as *identical* with brain states; that is, functionalism is not a materialist *identity* theory which holds that thoughts are ultimately reducible to specific brain states. Functionalists regard the identity theory as too narrow. Obviously (to identity theorists), it is our human brains that are the sources of our thoughts and ideas. But if there are intelligent extraterrestrials with ideas and thoughts similar to those we have, the source of *their* thoughts might be something very different from human brains; indeed, they might be made of a different material altogether. Or consider a stroke victim who has suffered damage in part of her brain, but who has—through a lengthy rehabilitation process— "relearned" much that had been lost as a result of her stroke, and who now uses different parts of her brain to generate ideas that were once the product of the portion of her brain that was damaged.

While such examples give some support to functionalism, the main force behind the development of functionalism was the computer and its programming. We can run the same *program* on a number of very different computers, which may be made from a variety of materials. Though the computers may be quite different, the program will generate the same results from each. Likewise—functionalists theorized—the mind is like the programming *software*, while the brain is like the *hardware*. If we have several distinctly different computers running the same software program, all the similarly programmed computers will produce the same results, but the hardware generating those results will differ. Instead of seeing an operation in the program as *identical* with a physical operation in one of the computer systems, we should think of each computer performing the same *function*, though they may each perform that function using very different physical hardware. Rather than strict *identity* between a step in the program and a machine state, we should think of the relation between the hardware and the software (or between the brain and the body) as a specific functional relation, with the software functions perhaps being carried out in many different physical forms: perhaps in the grey matter of our brains, or perhaps in the circuit boards of a computer, or in some different material in intelligent extraterrestrials.

Functionalism has been a popular contemporary account of the mind–body relation, particularly among those who find the concept of "artificial intelligence"—intelligent thinking computers—appealing. But it has also generated fierce opposition; and most of its opponents are not mind–body dualists, but rather physicalists who maintain that functionalism undervalues the vitally important and incredibly complex operation of the thinking physical *brain*. A leading opponent of the functionalist position is John Searle, who uses a question and answer format to briefly state his basic *objection* to some aspects of the functionalist view while reaffirming his commitment to *physicalism*:

"Could a machine think?"
 The answer is, obviously, yes. We are precisely such machines.
 . . . "Could something think, understand, and so on *solely* in virtue of being a computer with the right sort of program? Could instantiating a program, the right program of course, by itself be a sufficient condition of understanding?"
 This I think is the right question to ask, . . . and the answer to it is no.
 "Why not?"
 Because the formal symbol manipulations by themselves don't have any intentionality; they are quite meaningless; they aren't even *symbol* manipulations, since the symbols don't symbolize anything. . . .
 "Could a machine think?" My own view is that *only* a machine could think, and indeed only very special kinds of machines, namely brains and machines that had the same causal powers as brains. And that is the main reason that strong AI [artificial intelligence] has had little to tell us about thinking, since it has nothing to tell us about machines. By its own definition, it is about programs, and programs are not machines. Whatever else intentionality is, it is a biological phenomenon, and it is as likely to be as causally dependent on the specific biochemistry of its origins as lactation, photosynthesis, or any other biological phenomenon.

 John R. Searle, "Minds, Brains, and Programs"

Some of the most basic criticisms of functionalism are based on our experience of (what philosophers call) *qualia*. "Qualia" is the special name for the *qualitative* content of such psychological experiences as emotions, sensations, and perceptions. Think of *what it feels like* to experience the perception of a brilliant red sunset, or to hear the howling notes of a saxophone, or to feel the sharp pain of striking your big toe on a large rock. Even if we could specify precisely what brain operations are activated in such experiences, that would not capture *what it feels like* to have those experiences: it would not capture the *qualia* of those experiences. Thomas Nagel offers one of the most famous examples: What is it *like* to be a bat, experiencing the size and shape of our world through echoing sound rather than through sight? Some day neuroscientists might discover and describe in detail the brain operations of the bat that functionally account for the bat's acoustic navigation; but that complete functional account would leave out something vital: what it *feels like* to be a bat, the *qualia* of bat experience. Thus, functionalism (and perhaps—some critics claim—*any* physicalist theory) will be fundamentally and fatally *incomplete*: It will be unable to completely account for the full qualitative mental experience.

This is a fierce and ongoing controversy, and defenders of functionalism offer a wide range of responses, while critics of functionalism offer a variety of other criticisms. At the very least, functionalism is an attempt to make mental events and states a "subject for science": taking them out of an inaccessible realm of inexplicable mystery and exposing them to scientific investigation. Whether that attempt is successful, and whether any such attempt could be successful, is a question for your further consideration.

EPIPHENOMENALISM

Another approach to the mind–body question is called *epiphenomenalism*. This is the view that the basic causal processes and thought operations are *physical* brain activities, and the brain generates—as a sort of by-product of its causal activity—our conscious thoughts and ideas and *sense* of causal willing; that is, the *mental* elements are not really part of the causal chain, but are instead by-products, *epiphenomena*. The theory of epiphenomenalism has been around for many years, but it had few champions until recent experiments in neuropsychology renewed interest in epiphenomenalism. In one key experiment, Benjamin Libet attached a device to experimental subjects that made it possible to detect a specific electrical change in the brain. Then he told the experimental subjects to flick their wrists whenever they chose. He also placed a large clock dial with a sweep hand in front of them, and had the subjects note the exact location of the sweep hand at the moment they *decided* to flick their wrists. It turned out that there was brain activity just over half a second before the subjects flicked their wrists; and this brain activity was initiated almost one-third of a second *before* the subjects *consciously willed* to flick their wrists! The experiment seemed to show that the subjects' actual choice to flick their wrists started in their brains, *before* the experience of conscious willing. The conscious sense of "willing" the wrist flick was not actually part of the causal process that moved the wrist; rather, the conscious experience was a *by-product* of activity that had already occurred (without consciousness) in the brain. The conscious willing is a symptom, not a cause. Just as fever doesn't cause infection, but rather indicates the presence of an infection, likewise the conscious willing doesn't cause the act, but is instead a symptom of the causation being initiated nonconsciously by the brain.

That doesn't imply that the epiphenomenal conscious activity—though not part of the *causal* system—is totally useless. Neuropsychologist Daniel Wegner suggests that the experience of conscious willing is a sort of feedback mechanism, that informs me (when I move my hand) that the act done was done *by* me, that it was not something done *to* me. If you pull my hand with a string, the absence of a *sense* of conscious willing tips me off that something outside me is controlling my movements. If we stimulate your brain in a specific way, we can make your hand move. But when that is done to experimental subjects, they do not experience such movements as their own. So a sense of conscious will tells me when a movement actually originates in *me*, with my brain, and not as a result of some external force. Conscious thought—according to this contemporary version of epiphenomenalism—doesn't play the *causal* role we had imagined, but it does perform a valuable feedback function.

CONSCIOUSNESS

Obviously Daniel Wegner's version of epiphenomenalism, with its marginal role for *conscious thought*, is a very controversial view. And in fact, the whole question of *consciousness* itself generates many questions and widespread controversy, starting with the very basic question of: *What is consciousness?*

As David Chalmers notes:

> Consciousness fits uneasily into our conception of the natural world. On the most common conception of nature, the natural world is the physical world. But on the most common conception of consciousness, it is not easy to see how it could be part of the physical world. So it seems that to find a place for consciousness within the natural order, we must either revise our conception of consciousness, or revise our conception of nature.
>
> *David J. Chalmers, "Consciousness and its Place in Nature," in S. Stich and F. Warfield, eds., Blackwell Guide to the Philosophy of Mind (Blackwell, 2003).*

Thomas Nagel believes that much of the difficulty in saying exactly what consciousness is comes from the fact that it is so basic to our experience: "Though we can describe certain of its [consciousness] features, and identify more specific types of mental phenomena as instances, it is so basic that it can't be defined in terms of anything else."* If you ask yourself, "what *is* consciousness," there is a sense that you *know* what it is; but if you try to make clear, even to yourself, just *what* consciousness is, then you can appreciate why it has generated so much philosophical questioning and inquiry. Questions about the nature of consciousness are among the most widely debated questions in contemporary philosophy of mind, and there is an enormous range of consciousness accounts—from "it's something basic to all our experience and somewhat mysterious" to "it is something fairly straightforward and nonmysterious," and from claims that "it is distinctive and nonmaterial" to claims that "it is simply part of our natural material world." Probably there is no other issue in contemporary philosophy that generates such a variety of radically differing theories, and on which there is less basic agreement.

Questions concerning the mind and body are basic to many other philosophical issues, including questions concerning personal identity, free will, and moral responsibility. All of those are issues that will be examined in the following chapters. It may be that your conclusion concerning the nature of mind and body will influence the theories you find plausible on those issues; or on the other hand, it may be that your conclusions on those later issues will lead you to draw new conclusions concerning the nature of mind, body, and consciousness.

READINGS

⟞ MEDITATION VI ⟝
René Descartes

In Chapter 3 we examined the first and second of Descartes' *Meditations*, in which Descartes attempts to refute skepticism and discover a n indubitable foundation of truth. This passage is from the final (sixth) Meditation, and at this point Descartes has satisfied himself that he does have an extensive system of reliable knowledge. Now he is turning his attention to gaining a clearer understanding of the nature of mind and body and their relation, and in this section he proposes his classic account of mind–body interactionism.

4. But I am accustomed to imagine many other objects besides that corporeal nature which is the object of the pure mathematics, as, for example, colors, sounds, tastes, pain, and the like although with less distinctness; and inasmuch as I perceive these objects much better by the senses, through the medium of which and of memory, they seem to have reached the imagination, I believe that, in order the more advantageously to examine them, it is proper I should at the same time examine what sense-perception is and inquire whether from those ideas that are apprehended by this mode of thinking (consciousness), I cannot obtain a certain proof of the existence of corporeal objects.

5. And, in the first place, I will recall to my mind the things I have hitherto held as true, because perceived by the sense, and the foundations upon which my belief in their truth rested; I will, in the second place, examine the reasons that afterward constrained me to doubt of them; and, finally, I will consider what of them I ought now to believe.

6. Firstly, then, I perceived that I had a head, hands, feet and other members composing that body which I considered as part, or perhaps even as the whole, of myself. I perceived further, that that body was placed among many other, by which it was capable of being affected in diverse ways, both beneficial and hurtful; and what was beneficial I remarked by a

---

*Thomas Nagel, "The Mind Wins!" *New York Review of Books*, March 4, 1993.

certain sensation of pleasure, and what was hurtful by a sensation of pain. And besides this pleasure and pain, I was likewise conscious of hunger, thirst, and other appetites, as well as certain corporeal inclinations toward joy, sadness, anger, and similar passions. And, out of myself besides the extension, figure, and motions of bodies, I likewise perceived in them hardness, heat, and the other tactile qualities, and, in addition, light, colors, odors, tastes, and sounds, the variety of which gave me the means of distinguishing the sky, the earth, the sea, and generally all the other bodies, from one another. And certainly, considering the ideas of all these qualities, which were presented to my mind, and which alone I properly and immediately perceived, it was not without reason that I thought I perceived certain objects wholly different from my thought, namely, bodies from which those ideas proceeded; for I was conscious that the ideas were presented to me without my consent being required, so that I could not perceive any object, however desirous I might be, unless it were present to the organ of sense; and it was wholly out of my power not to perceive it when it was thus present. And because the ideas I perceived by the senses were much more lively and clear, and even, in their own way, more distinct than any of those I could of myself frame by meditation, or which I found impressed on my memory, it seemed that they could not have proceeded from myself, and must therefore have been caused in me by some other objects; and as of those objects I had no knowledge beyond what the ideas themselves gave me, nothing was so likely to occur to my mind as the supposition that the objects were similar to the ideas which they caused. And because I recollected also that I had formerly trusted to the senses, rather than to reason, and that the ideas which I myself formed were not so clear as those I perceived by sense, and that they were even for the most part composed of parts of the latter, I was readily persuaded that I had no idea in my intellect which had not formerly passed through the senses. Nor was I altogether wrong in likewise believing that that body which, by a special right, I called my own, pertained to me more properly and strictly than any of the others; for in truth, I could never be separated from it as from other bodies; I felt in it and on account of it all my appetites and affections and in fine I was affected in its parts by pain and the titillation of pleasure, and not in the parts of the other bodies that were separated from it. But when I inquired into the reason why, from this I know not what sensation of pain, sadness of mind should follow, and why from the sensation of pleasure, joy should arise, or why this indescribable

twitching of the stomach, which I call hunger, should put me in mind of taking food, and the parchedness of the throat of drink, and so in other cases, I was unable to give any explanation, unless that I was so taught by nature; for there is assuredly no affinity, at least none that I am able to comprehend, between this irritation of the stomach and the desire of food, any more than between the perception of an object that causes pain and the consciousness of sadness which springs from the perception. And in the same way it seemed to me that all the other judgments I had formed regarding the objects of sense, were dictates of nature; because I remarked that those judgments were formed in me, before I had leisure to weigh and consider the reasons that might constrain me to form them.

7. But, afterward, a wide experience by degrees sapped the faith I had reposed in my senses; for I frequently observed that towers, which at a distance seemed round, appeared square, when more closely viewed, and that colossal figures, raised on the summits of these towers, looked like small statues, when viewed from the bottom of them; and, in other instances without number, I also discovered error in judgments founded on the external senses; and not only in those founded on the external, but even in those that rested on the internal senses; for is there aught more internal than pain? And yet I have sometimes been informed by parties whose arm or leg had been amputated, that they still occasionally seemed to feel pain in that part of the body which they had lost, —a circumstance that led me to think that I could not be quite certain even that any one of my members was affected when I felt pain in it. And to these grounds of doubt I shortly afterward also added two others of very wide generality: the first of them was that I believed I never perceived anything when awake which I could not occasionally think I also perceived when asleep, and as I do not believe that the ideas I seem to perceive in my sleep proceed from object external to me, I did not any more observe any ground for believing this of such as I seem to perceive when awake; the second was that since I was as yet ignorant of the author of my being or at least supposed myself to be so, I saw nothing to prevent my having been so constituted by nature as that I should be deceived even in matters that appeared to me to possess the greatest truth. And, with respect to the grounds on which I had before been persuaded of the existence of sensible objects, I had no great difficulty in finding suitable answers to them, for as nature seemed to incline me to many things from which reason made me averse, I thought that I ought not to confide much in its

teachings. And although the perceptions of the senses were not dependent on my will, I did not think that I ought on that ground to conclude that they proceeded from things different from myself, since perhaps there might be found in me some faculty, though hitherto unknown to me, which produced them.

8. But now that I begin to know myself better, and to discover more clearly the author or my being, I do not, indeed, think that I ought rashly to admit all which the senses seem to teach, nor, on the other hand, is it my conviction that I ought to doubt in general of their teachings.

9. And, firstly, because I know that all which I clearly and distinctly conceive can be produced by God exactly as I conceive one thing apart from another, in order to be certain that the one is different from the other, seeing they may at least be made to exist separately, by the omnipotence of God; and it matters not by what power this separation is made, in order to be compelled to judge them different; and, therefore, merely because I know with certitude that I exist, and because, in the meantime, I do not observe that aught necessarily belongs to my nature or essence beyond my being a thinking thing, I rightly conclude that my essence consists only in my being a thinking thing or a substance whose whole essence or nature is merely thinking. And although I may, or rather, as I will shortly say, although I certainly do possess a body with which I am very closely conjoined; nevertheless, because, on the one hand, I have a clear and distinct idea of myself, in as far as I am only a thinking and unextended thing, and as, on the other hand, I possess a distinct idea of body, in as far as it is only an extended and unthinking thing, it is certain that I, that is, my mind, by which I am what I am, is entirely and truly distinct from my body, and may exist without it.

10. Moreover, I find in myself diverse faculties of thinking that have each their special mode: for example I find I possess the faculties of imagining and perceiving, without which I can indeed clearly and distinctly conceive myself as entire, but I cannot reciprocally conceive them without conceiving myself, that is to say, without an intelligent substance in which they reside, for in the notion we have of them, or to use the terms of the schools in their formal concepts, they comprise some sort of intellection; whence I perceive that they are distinct from myself as modes are from things. I remark likewise certain other faculties, as the power of changing place, of assuming diverse figures, and the like, that cannot be conceived and cannot therefore exist, any more than the preceding, apart from a substance in which they inhere. It is very evident, however, that these faculties, if they really exist, must belong to some corporeal or extended substance, since in their clear and distinct concept there is contained some sort of extension, but no intellection at all. Further, I cannot doubt but that there is in me a certain passive faculty of perception, that is, of receiving and taking knowledge of the ideas of sensible things; but this would be useless to me, if there did not also exist in me, or in some other thing, another active faculty capable of forming and producing those ideas. But this active faculty cannot be in me in as far as I am but a thinking thing, seeing that it does not presuppose thought, and also that those ideas are frequently produced in my mind without my contributing to it in any way, and even frequently contrary to my will. This faculty must therefore exist in some substance different from me, in which all the objective reality of the ideas that are produced by this faculty is contained formally or eminently, as I before remarked; and this substance is either a body, that is to say, a corporeal nature in which is contained formally and in effect all that is objectively and by representation in those ideas; or it is God himself, or some other creature, of a rank superior to body, in which the same is contained eminently. But as God is no deceiver, it is manifest that he does not of himself and immediately communicate those ideas to me, nor even by the intervention of any creature in which their objective reality is not formally, but only eminently, contained. For as he has given me no faculty whereby I can discover this to be the case, but, on the contrary, a very strong inclination to believe that those ideas arise from corporeal objects, I do not see how he could be vindicated from the charge of deceit, if in truth they proceeded from any other source, or were produced by other causes than corporeal things: and accordingly it must be concluded, that corporeal objects exist. Nevertheless, they are not perhaps exactly such as we perceive by the senses, for their comprehension by the senses is, in many instances, very obscure and confused; but it is at least necessary to admit that all which I clearly and distinctly conceive as in them, that is, generally speaking all that is comprehended in the object of speculative geometry, really exists external to me.

11. But with respect to other things which are either only particular, as, for example, that the sun is of such a size and figure, etc., or are conceived with less clearness and distinctness, as light, sound, pain, and the like, although they are highly dubious and uncertain, nevertheless on the ground alone that God is no deceiver, and that consequently he has permitted no

falsity in my opinions which he has not likewise give me a faculty of correcting, I think I may with safety conclude that I possess in myself the means of arriving at the truth. And, in the first place, it cannot be doubted that in each of the dictates of nature there is some truth: for by nature, considered in general, I now understand nothing more than God himself, or the order and disposition established by God in created things; and by my nature in particular I understand the assemblage of all that God has given me.

12. But there is nothing which that nature teaches me more expressly or more sensibly than that I have a body which is ill affected when I feel pain, ands stands in need of food and drink when I experience the sensations of hunger and thirst, etc. And therefore I ought not to doubt but that there is some truth in these informations.

13. Nature likewise teaches me by these sensations of pain, hunger, thirst, etc., that I am not only lodged in my body as a pilot in a vessel, but that I am besides so intimately conjoined, and as it were intermixed with it, that my mind and body compose a certain unity. For if this were not the case, I should not feel pain when my body is hurt, seeing I am merely a thinking thing, but should perceive the wound by the understanding alone, just as a pilot perceives by sight when any part of his vessel is damaged; and when my body has need of food or drink, I should have a clear knowledge of this, and not be made aware of it by the confused sensations of hunger and thirst: for, in truth, all these sensations of hunger, thirst, pain, etc., are nothing more than certain confused modes of thinking, arising from the union and apparent fusion of mind and body.

14. Besides this, nature teaches me that my own body is surrounded by many other bodies, some of which I have to seek after, and others to shun. And indeed, as I perceive different sorts of colors, sounds, odors, tastes, heat, hardness, etc., I safely conclude that there are in the bodies from which the diverse perceptions of the senses proceed, certain varieties corresponding to them, although, perhaps, not in reality like them; and since, among these diverse perceptions of the senses, some are agreeable, and others disagreeable, there can be no doubt that my body, or rather my entire self, in as far as I am composed of body and mind, may be variously affected, both beneficially and hurtfully, by surrounding bodies.

15. But there are many other beliefs which though seemingly the teaching of nature, are not in reality so, but which obtained a place in my mind through a habit of judging inconsiderately of things. It may thus easily happen that such judgments shall contain error: thus, for example, the opinion I have that all space in which there is nothing to affect or make an impression on my senses is void: that in a hot body there is something in every respect similar to the idea of heat in my mind; that in a white or green body there is the same whiteness or greenness which I perceive; that in a bitter or sweet body there is the same taste, and so in other instances; that the stars, towers, and all distant bodies, are of the same size and figure as they appear to our eyes, etc. But that I may avoid everything like indistinctness of conception, I must accurately define what I properly understand by being taught by nature. For nature is here taken in a narrower sense than when it signifies the sun of all the things which God has given me; seeing that in that meaning the notion comprehends much that belongs only to the mind to which I am not here to be understood as referring when I use the term nature; as, for example, the notion I have of the truth, that what is done cannot be undone, and all the other truths I discern by the natural light without the aid of the body; and seeing that it comprehends likewise much besides that belongs only to body, and is not here any more contained under the name nature as the quality of heaviness, and the like, of which I do not speak, the term being reserved exclusively to designate the things which God has given to me as a being composed of mind and body. But nature taking the term in the sense explained, teaches me to shun what causes in me the sensation of pain, and to pursue what affords me the sensation of pleasure, and other things of this sort; but I do not discover that it teaches me, in addition to this, from these diverse perceptions of the senses, to draw any conclusions respecting external objects without a previous careful and mature consideration of them by the mind: for it is, as appears to me, the office of the mind alone, and not of the composite whole of mind and body, to discern the truth in those matters. Thus, although the impression a star makes on my eye is not larger than that from the flame of a candle, I do not, nevertheless, experience any real or positive impulse determining me to believe that the star is not greater that the flame; the true account of the matter being merely that I have so judged from my youth without any rational ground. And, though on approaching the fire I feel heat, and even pain on approaching it too closely, I have, however, from this no ground for holding that something resembling the heat I feel is in the fire, any more than that there is something similar to the pain; all that I have ground for believing is, that there is something in it, whatever it may be, which excites in me those sensations of heat or pain. So also, although there are spaces in which I find nothing to excite and affect my senses, I must not therefore conclude that those spaces contain in them no body; for I see that in this, as in many other similar matters, I have been accustomed to pervert the order of nature because these perceptions of the senses, although given me by nature merely to signify to my mind what things are beneficial and hurtful to the composite whole of which it is a part, and being sufficiently clear and distinct for that purpose, are nevertheless used by me as infallible rules by which to determine immediately the essence of the bodies that exist out of me, of which they can of course afford me only the most obscure and confused knowledge.

16. But I have already sufficiently considered how it happens that, notwithstanding the supreme goodness of God, there is falsity in my judgments. A difficulty, however, here presents itself, respecting the things which I am taught by nature must be pursued or avoided, and also respecting the internal sensations in which I seem to have occasionally detected error, and thus to be directly deceived by nature: thus, for example, I may be so deceived by the agreeable taste of some viand with which poison has been mixed, as to be induced to take the poison. In this case, however, nature may be excused, for it simply leads me to desire the viand for its agreeable taste, and not the poison, which is unknown to it; and thus we can infer nothing from this circumstance beyond that our nature is not omniscient; at which there is assuredly no ground for surprise, since, man being of a finite nature, his knowledge must likewise be of a limited perfection.

17. But we also not unfrequently err in that to which we are directly impelled by nature, as is the case with invalids who desire drink or food that would be hurtful to them. It will here, perhaps, be alleged that the reason why such persons are deceived is that their nature is corrupted; but this leaves the difficulty untouched, for a sick man is not less really the creature of God than a man who is in full health; and therefore it is as repugnant to the goodness of God that the nature of the former should be deceitful as it is for that of the latter to be so. And as a clock, composed of wheels and counter weights, observes not the less accurately all the laws of nature when it is ill made, and points out the hours incorrectly, than when it satisfies the desire of the maker in every respect; so likewise if the body of man be considered as a kind of machine, so made up and composed of bones, nerves, muscles, veins, blood, and skin, that although there were in it no mind, it would still exhibit the same motions which it at present manifests involuntarily, and therefore without the aid of

the mind, and simply by the dispositions of its organs, I easily discern that it would also be as natural for such a body, supposing it dropsical, for example, to experience the parchedness of the throat that is usually accompanied in the mind by the sensation of thirst, and to be disposed by this parchedness to move its nerves and its other parts in the way required for drinking, and thus increase its malady and do itself harm, as it is natural for it, when it is not indisposed to be stimulated to drink for its good by a similar cause; and although looking to the use for which a clock was destined by its maker, I may say that it is deflected from its proper nature when it incorrectly indicates the hours, and on the same principle, considering the machine of the human body as having been formed by God for the sake of the motions which it usually manifests, although I may likewise have ground for thinking that it does not follow the order of its nature when the throat is parched and drink does not tend to its preservation, nevertheless I yet plainly discern that this latter acceptation of the term nature is very different from the other: for this is nothing more than a certain denomination, depending entirely on my thought, and hence called extrinsic, by which I compare a sick man and an imperfectly constructed clock with the idea I have of a man in good health and a well made clock; while by the other acceptation of nature is understood something which is truly found in things, and therefore possessed of some truth.

18. But certainly, although in respect of a dropsical body, it is only by way of exterior denomination that we say its nature is corrupted, when, without requiring drink, the throat is parched; yet, in respect of the composite whole, that is, of the mind in its union with the body, it is not a pure denomination, but really an error of nature, for it to feel thirst when drink would be hurtful to it: and, accordingly, it still remains to be considered why it is that the goodness of God does not prevent the nature of man thus taken from being fallacious.

19. To commence this examination accordingly, I here remark, in the first place, that there is a vast difference between mind and body, in respect that body, from its nature, is always divisible, and that mind is entirely indivisible. For in truth, when I consider the mind, that is, when I consider myself in so far only as I am a thinking thing, I can distinguish in myself no parts, but I very clearly discern that I am somewhat absolutely one and entire; and although the whole mind seems to be united to the whole body, yet, when a foot, an arm, or any other part is cut off, I am conscious that nothing has been taken from my mind; nor can the faculties of willing, perceiving, conceiving, etc., properly be called its parts, for it is the same mind that is exercised all entire in willing, in perceiving, and in conceiving, etc. But quite the opposite holds in corporeal or extended things; for I cannot imagine any one of them how small soever it may be, which I cannot easily sunder in thought, and which, therefore, I do not know to be divisible. This would be sufficient to teach me that the mind or soul of man is entirely different from the body, if I had not already been apprised of it on other grounds.

20. I remark, in the next place, that the mind does not immediately receive the impression from all the parts of the body, but only from the brain, or perhaps even from one small part of it, viz, that in which the common sense is said to be, which as often as it is affected in the same way gives rise to the same perception in the mind, although meanwhile the other parts of the body may be diversely disposed, as is proved by innumerable experiments, which it is unnecessary here to enumerate.

21. I remark, besides, that the nature of body is such that none of its parts can be moved by another part a little removed from the other, which cannot likewise be moved in the same way by any one of the parts that lie between those two, although the most remote part does not act at all. As, for example, in the cord A,B,C,D, which is in tension, if its last part D, be pulled, the first part A, will not be moved in a different way than it would be were one of the intermediate parts B or C to be pulled, and the last part D meanwhile to remain fixed. And in the same way, when I feel pain in the foot, the science of physics teaches me that this sensation is experienced by means of the nerves dispersed over the foot, which, extending like cords from it to the brain, when they are contracted in the foot, contract at the same time the inmost parts of the brain in which they have their origin, and excite in these parts a certain motion appointed by nature to cause in the mind a sensation of pain, as if existing in the foot; but as these nerves must pass through the tibia, the leg, the loins, the back, and neck, in order to reach the brain, it may happen that although their extremities in the foot are not affected, but only certain of their parts that pass through the loins or neck, the same movements, nevertheless, are excited in the brain by this motion as would have been caused there by a hurt received in the foot, and hence the mind will necessarily feel pain in the foot, just as if it had been hurt; and the same is true of all the other perceptions of our senses.

22. I remark, finally, that as each of the movements that are made in the part of the brain by which the mind is immediately affected, impresses it with but a single sensation, the most likely supposition in the circumstances is, that this movement causes the mind to experience, among all the sensations which it is capable of impressing upon it; that one which is the best fitted, and generally the most useful for the preservation of the human body when it is in full health. But experience shows us that all the perceptions which nature has given us are of such a kind as I have mentioned; and accordingly, there is nothing found in them that does not manifest the power and goodness of God. Thus, for example, when the nerves of the foot are violently or more than usually shaken, the motion passing through the medulla of the spine to the innermost parts of the brain affords a sign to the mind on which it experiences a sensation, viz, of pain, as if it were in the foot, by which the mind is admonished and excited to do its utmost to remove the cause of it as dangerous and hurtful to the foot. It is true that God could have so constituted the nature of man as that the same motion in the brain would have informed the mind of something altogether different: the motion might, for example, have been the occasion on which the mind became conscious of itself, in so far as it is in the brain, or in so far as it is in some place intermediate between the foot and the brain, or, finally, the occasion on which it perceived some other object quite different, whatever that might be; but nothing of all this would have so well contributed to the preservation of the body as that which the mind actually feels. In the same way, when we stand in need of drink, there arises from this want a certain parchedness in the throat that moves its nerves, and by means of them the internal parts of the brain; and this movement affects the mind with the sensation of thirst, because there is nothing on that occasion which is more useful for us than to be made aware that we have need of drink for the preservation of our health; and so in other instances.

23. Whence it is quite manifest that, notwithstanding the sovereign goodness of God, the nature of man, in so far as it is composed of mind and body, cannot but be sometimes fallacious. For, if there is any cause which excites, not in the foot, but in some one of the parts of the nerves that stretch from the foot to the brain, or even in the brain itself, the same movement that is ordinarily created when the foot is ill affected, pain will be felt, as it were, in the foot, and the sense will thus be naturally deceived; for as the same movement in the brain can but impress the mind with the same sensation, and as this sensation is much more frequently excited by a cause which hurts the foot than by one acting in a different quarter, it is reasonable that it should lead the mind to feel pain in the foot rather than in any other part of the body. And if it sometimes happens that the parchedness of the throat does not arise, as is usual, from drink being necessary for the health of the body, but from quite the opposite cause, as is the case with the dropsical, yet it is much better that it should be deceitful in that instance, than if, on the contrary, it were continually fallacious when the body is well-disposed; and the same holds true in other cases.

24. And certainly this consideration is of great service, not only in enabling me to recognize the errors to which my nature is liable, but likewise in rendering it more easy to avoid or correct them: for, knowing that all my senses more usually indicate to me what is true than what is false, in matters relating to the advantage of the body, and being able almost always to make use of more than a single sense in examining the same object, and besides this, being able to use my memory in connecting present with past knowledge, and my understanding which has already discovered all the causes of my errors, I ought no longer to fear that falsity may be met with in what is daily presented to me by the senses. And I ought to reject all the doubts of those bygone days, as hyperbolical and ridiculous, especially the general uncertainty respecting sleep, which I could not distinguish from the waking state: for I now find a very marked difference between the two states, in respect that our memory can never connect our dreams with each other and with the course of life, in the way it is in the habit of doing with events that occur when we are awake. And, in truth, if someone, when I am awake, appeared to me all of a sudden and as suddenly disappeared, as do the images I see in sleep, so that I could not observe either whence he came or whither he went, I should not without reason esteem it either a specter or phantom formed in my brain, rather than a real man. But when I perceive objects with regard to which I can distinctly determine both the place whence they come, and that in which they are, and the time at which they appear to me, and when, without interruption, I can connect the perception I have of them with the whole of the other parts of my life, I am perfectly sure that what I thus perceive occurs while I am awake and not during sleep. And I ought not in the least degree to doubt of the truth of these presentations, if, after having called together all my senses, my memory, and my understanding for the purpose of examining them, no deliverance is given by any one of these faculties which is repugnant to that of any other: for since God is no deceiver, it necessarily follows that I am not herein deceived. But because the necessities of action frequently oblige us to come to a determination before we have had leisure for so careful an examination, it must be confessed that the life of man is frequently obnoxious to error with respect to individual objects; and we must, in conclusion, acknowledge the weakness of our nature.

⇒ Where Am I? ⇐
Daniel Dennett

Daniel Dennett (born 1942) is a widely read contemporary American philosopher, best known for his extensive work in the philosophy of mind and cognitive science. Austin B. Fletcher Professor of Philosophy and Director of the Center for Cognitive Studies at Tufts University, Dennett's many books include *Elbow Room: The Varieties of Free Will Worth Wanting* (Cambridge, Mass.: MIT Press, 1984); *The Intentional Stance* (Cambridge, MA: MIT Press, 1989); *Consciousness Explained* (Back Bay Books, 1991); *Darwin's Dangerous Idea* (New York: Simon and Schuster, 1995); *Kinds of Minds: Towards an Understanding of Consciousness* (Basic Books, 1997); *Brainchildren: Essay on Designing Minds* (Cambridge, Mass.: MIT Press, 1998); and *Freedom Evolves* (New York: Viking, 2003). In addition, the collection of papers and comments Dennett edited with Douglas Hofstadter, *The Mind's I*, is a fascinating collection of essays on philosophy of mind; anyone interested in the subject will find it a challenging treat for both the reason and the imagination. "Where Am I" is a delightful work of fiction that not only gives an interesting twist to the old "brain in the vat" skeptical argument but also provokes reflection on functionalism, materialism, the general relation of mind to body, and the question of computer intelligence.

Now that I've won my suit under the Freedom of Information Act, I am at liberty to reveal for the first time a curious episode in my life that may be of interest not only to those engaged in research in the philosophy of mind, artificial intelligence, and neuroscience but also to the general public.

Several years ago I was approached by Pentagon officials who asked me to volunteer for a highly dangerous and secret mission. In collaboration with NASA and Howard Hughes, the Department of Defense was spending billions to develop a Supersonic Tunneling Underground Device, or STUD. It was supposed to tunnel through the earth's core at great speed and deliver a specially designed atomic warhead "right up the Red's missile silos," as one of the Pentagon brass put it.

The problem was that in an early test they had succeeded in lodging a warhead about a mile deep under Tulsa. Oklahoma, and they wanted me to retrieve it for them. "Why me?" I asked. Well, the mission involved some pioneering applications of current brain research, and they had heard of my interest in brains and of course my Faustian curiosity and great courage and so forth . . . Well, how could I refuse? The difficulty that brought the Pentagon to my door was that the device I'd been asked to recover was fiercely radioactive, in a new way. According to monitoring instruments, something about the nature of the device and its complex interactions with pockets of material deep in the earth had produced radiation that could cause severe abnormalities in certain tissues of the brain. No way had been found to shield the brain from these deadly rays, which were apparently harmless to other tissues and organs of the body. So it had been decided that the person sent to recover the device should *leave his brain behind*. It would be kept in a safe place where it could execute its normal control functions by elaborate radio links. Would I submit to a surgical procedure that would completely remove my brain, which would then be placed in a life-support system at the Manned Spacecraft Center in Houston? Each input and output pathway, as it was severed, would be restored by a pair of microminiaturized radio transceivers, one attached precisely to the brain, the other to the nerve stumps in the empty cranium. No information would be lost, all the connectivity would be preserved. At first I was a bit reluctant. Would it

really work? The Houston brain surgeons encouraged me. "Think of it," they said, "as a mere *stretching* of the nerves. If your brain were just moved over an *inch* in your skull, that would not alter or impair your mind. We're simply going to make the nerves indefinitely elastic by splicing radio links into them."

I was shown around the life-support lab in Houston and saw the sparkling new vat in which my brain would be placed, were I go agree. I met the large and brilliant support team of neurologists, hematologists, biophysicists, and electrical engineers, and after several days of discussions and demonstrations, I agreed to give it a try. I was subjected to an enormous array of blood tests, brain scans, experiments, interviews, and the like. They took down my autobiography at great length, recorded tedious lists of my beliefs, hopes, fears, and tastes. They even listed my favorite stereo recordings and gave me a crash session of psychoanalysis.

The day for surgery arrived at last and of course I was anesthetized and remember nothing of the operation itself. When I came out of anesthesia, I opened my eyes, looked around, and asked the inevitable, the traditional, the lamentably hackneyed postoperative question: "Where am I?" The nurse smiled down at me. "You're in Houston," she said, and I reflected that this still had a good chance of being the truth one way or another. She handed me a mirror. Sure enough, there were the tiny antenae poling up through their titanium ports cemented into my skull.

"I gather the operation was a success," I said. "I want to go see my brain." They led me (I was a bit dizzy and unsteady) down a long corridor and into the life-support lab. A cheer went up from the assembled support team, and I responded with what I hoped was a jaunty salute. Still feeling lightheaded, I was helped over to the life-support vat. I peered through the glass. There, floating in what looked like ginger ale, was undeniably a human brain, though it was almost covered with printed circuit chips, plastic tubules, electrodes, and other paraphernalia. "Is that mine?" I asked. "Hit the output transmitter switch there on the side of the vat and see for yourself," the project director replied. I moved the switch to OFF, and immediately slumped, groggy and nauseated, into the arms of the technicians, one of whom kindly restored the switch to its ON position. While I recovered my equilibrium and composure, I thought to myself: "Well, here I am sitting on a folding chair, staring through a piece of plate glass at my own brain . . . . But wait," I said to myself, "shouldn't I have thought, `Here I am, suspended in a bubbling fluid, being stared at by my own eyes'?" I tried to think this latter thought. I tried to project it into the tank, offering it hopefully to my brain, but I failed to carry off the exercise with any conviction. I tried again. "Here am *I*, Daniel Dennett, suspended in a bubbling fluid, being stared at by my own eyes." No, it just didn't work. Most puzzling and confusing. Being a philosopher of firm physicalist conviction, I believed unswervingly that the tokening of my thoughts was occurring somewhere in my brain: yet, when I thought "Here I am," where the thought occurred to me was *here*, outside the vat, where I, Dennett, was standing staring at my brain.

I tried and tried to think myself into the vat, but to no avail. I tried to build up to the task by doing mental exercises. I thought to myself, "The sun is shining *over there*," five times in rapid succession, each time mentally ostending a different place: in order, the sunlit corner of the lab, the visible front lawn of the hospital, Houston, Mars, and Jupiter. I found I had little difficulty in getting my "there" 's to hop all over the celestial map with their proper references. I could loft a "there" in an instant through the farthest reaches of space, and then aim the next "there" with pinpoint accuracy at the upper left quadrant of a freckle on my arm. Why was I having such trouble with "here"? "Here in Houston" worked well enough, and so did "here in the lab," and even "here in this part of the lab," but "here in the vat" always seemed merely an unmeant mental mouthing. I tried closing my eyes while thinking it. This seemed to help, but still I couldn't manage to pull it off, except perhaps for a fleeting instant. I couldn't be sure. The discovery that I couldn't be sure was also unsettling. How did I know *where* I meant by "here" when I thought "here"? Could I *think* I meant one place when in fact I meant another? I didn't see how that could be admitted without untying the few bonds of intimacy between a person and his own mental life that had survived the onslaught of the brain scientists and philosophers, the physicalists and behaviorists. Perhaps I was incorrigible about where I *meant* when I said "here." But in my present circumstances it seemed that either I was doomed by sheer force of mental habit to thinking systematically false indexical thoughts or where a person is (and hence where his thoughts are tokened for purposes of semantic analysis) is not necessarily where his brain, the physical seat of his soul, resides. Nagged by confusion, I attempted to orient myself by falling back on a favorite philosopher's ploy. I began naming things.

"Yorick," I said aloud to my brain, "you are my brain. The rest of my body, seated in this chair, I dub 'Hamlet.' " So here we all are: Yorick's my brain, Hamlet's my body, and I am Dannett. *Now*, where am I? And when I think "where am I?" where's that thought tokened? Is it tokened in my brain, lounging about in the vat, or right here between my ears where it *seems* to be tokened? Or nowhere? Its *temporal* coordinates give me no trouble; must it not have spatial coordinates as well? I began making a list of the alternatives.

1. *Where Hamlet goes, there goes Dannett.* This principle was easily refuted by appeal to the familiar brain-transplant thought experiments so enjoyed by philosophers. If Tom and Dick switch brains, Tom is the fellow with Dick's former body—just ask him; he'll claim to be Tom, and tell you the most intimate details of Tom's autobiography. It was clear enough, then, that my current body and I could part company, but not likely that I could be separated from my brain. The rule of thumb that emerged so plainly from the thought experiments was that in a brain-transplant operation, one wanted to be the *doner*, not the recipient. Better to call such an operation a *body* transplant, in fact. So perhaps the truth was,

2. *Where Yorick goes, there goes Dennett.* This was not at all appealing, however. How could I be in the vat and not about to go anywhere, when I was so obviously outside the vat looking in and beginning to make guilty plans to return to my room for a substantial lunch? This begged the question I realized, but it still seemed to be getting at something important. Casting about for some support for my intuition, I hit upon a legalistic sort of argument that might have appealed to Locke.

Suppose, I argued to myself, I were now to fly to California, rob a bank, and be apprehended. In which state would I be tried: in California, where the robbery took place, or in Texas, where the brains of the outfit were located? Would I be a California felon with an out-of-state brain, or a Texas felon remotely controlling an accomplice of sorts in California? It seemed possible that I might beat such a rap just on the undecidability of that jurisdictional question, though perhaps it would be deemed an interstate, and hence Federal, offense. In any event, suppose I were convicted. Was it likely that California would be satisfied to throw Hamlet into the brig, knowing that Yorick was living the good life and luxuriously taking the waters in Texas? Would Texas incarcerate Yorick, leaving Hamlet free to take the next boat to Rio? This alternative appealed to me. Barring capital punishment or other cruel and unusual punishment, the state would be obliged to maintain the life-support system for Yorick though they might move him from Houston to Leavenworth, and aside from the unpleasantness of the opprobrium, I, for one, would not mind at all and would consider myself a free man under those circumstances. If the state has an interest in forcibly relocating persons in institutions, it would fail to relocate *me* in any institution by locating Yorick there. If this were true, is suggested a third alternative.

3. *Dennett is wherever he thinks he is.* Generalized, the claim was as follows: At any given time a person has a *point of view*, and the location the point of view (which is determined internally by the content of the point of view) is also the location of the person.

Such a proposition is not without its perplexities, but to me it seemed a step in the right direction. The only trouble was that it seemed to place one in a heads-I-win/tails-you-lose situation of unlikely infallibility as regards location. Hadn't I myself often been wrong about where I was, and at least as often uncertain? Couldn't one get lost? Of course, but getting lost *geographically* is not the only way one might get lost. If one were lost in the woods one could attempt to reassure oneself with the consolation that at least one knew where one was: one was right *here* in the familiar surroundings of one's own body. Perhaps in this case one would not have drawn one's attention to much to be thankful for. Still, there were worse plights imaginable, and I wasn't sure I wasn't in such a plight right now.

Point of view clearly had something to do with personal location, but it was itself an unclear notion. It was obvious that the content of one's point of view was not the same as or determined by the content of one's beliefs or thoughts. For example, what should we say about the point of view of the Cinerama viewer who shrieks and twists in his seat as the roller-coaster footage overcomes his psychic distancing? Has he forgotten that he is safely seated in the theater? Here I was inclined to say that the person is experiencing an illusory shift in point of view. In other cases, my inclination to call such shifts illusory was less strong. The workers in laboratories and

plants who handle dangerous materials by operating feedback-controlled mechanical arms and hands undergo a shift in point of view that is crisper and more pronounced than anything Cinerama can provoke. They can feel the heft and slipperiness of the containers they manipulate with their metal fingers. They know perfectly well where they are and are not fooled into false beliefs by the experience, yet it is as if they were inside the isolation chamber they are peering into. With mental effort, they can manage to shift their point of view back and forth, rather like making a transparent Necker cube or an Escher drawing change orientation before one's eyes. It does seem extravagant to suppose that in performing this bit of mental gymnastics, they are transporting *themselves* back and forth.

Still their example gave me hope. If I was in fact in the vat in spite of my intuitions, I might be able to train myself to adopt that point of view even as a matter of habit. I should dwell on images of myself comfortably floating in my vat, beaming volitions to that familiar body *out there*. I reflected that the ease or difficulty of this task was presumably independent of the truth about the location of one's brain. Had I been practicing before the operation, I might now be finding it second nature. You might now yourself try such a *trompe l'oeil*. Imagine you have written an inflammatory letter which has been published in the *Times*, the result of which is that the government has chosen to impound your brain for a probationary period of three years in its Dangerous Brain Clinic in Bethesda, Maryland. Your body of course is allowed freedom to earn a salary and thus to continue its function of laying up income to be taxed. At this moment, however, your body is seated in an auditorium listening to a peculiar account by Daniel Dennett of his own similar experience. Try it. Think yourself to Bethesda, and then hark back longingly to your body, far away, and yet *seeming* so near. It is only with long-distance restraint (yours? the government's?) that you can control your impulse to get those hands clapping in polite applause before navigating the old body to the rest room and a well-deserved glass of evening sherry in the lounge. The task of imagination is certainly difficult, but if you achieve your goal the results might be consoling.

Anyway, there I was in Houston, lost in thought as one might say, but not for long. My speculations were soon interrupted by the Houston doctors, who wished to test out my new prosthetic nervous system before sending me off on my hazardous mission. As I mentioned before, I was a bit dizzy at first, and not surprisingly, although I soon habituated myself to my new circumstances (which were, after all, well nigh indistinguishable from my old circumstances). My accommodation was not perfect, however, and to this day I continue to be plagued by minor coordination difficulties. The speed of light is fast, but finite, and as may brain and body move farther and farther apart, the delicate interaction of my feedback systems is thrown into disarray by the time lags. Just as one is rendered close to speechless by a delayed or echoic hearing of one's speaking voice so, for instance, I am virtually unable to track a moving object with my eyes whenever my brain and my body are more than a few miles apart. In most matters my impairment is scarcely detectable, though I can no longer hit a slow curve ball with the authority of yore. There are some compensations of course. Though liquor tastes as good as ever, and warms my gullet while corroding my liver, I can drink it in any quantity I please, without becoming the slightest bit inebriated, a curiosity some of my close friends may have noticed (though I occasionally have *feigned* inebriation, so as not to draw attention to my unusual circumstances). For similar reasons, I take aspirin orally for a sprained wrist, but if the pain persists I ask Houston to administer codeine to me *in vitro*. In times of illness the phone bill can be staggering.

But to return to my adventure. At length, both the doctors, and I were satisfied that I was ready to undertake my subterranean mission. And so I left my brain in Houston and headed by helicopter for Tulsa. Well, in any case, that's the way it seemed to me. That's how I would put it, just off the top of my head as it were. On the trip I reflected further about my earlier anxieties and decided that my first postoperative speculations had been tinged with panic. The matter was not nearly as strange or metaphysical as I had been supposing. Where was I? In two places, clearly: both inside the vat and outside it. Just as one can stand with one foot in Connecticut and the other in Rhode Island. I was in two places at once. I had become one of those scattered individuals we used to hear so much about. The more I considered this answer, the more obviously true it appeared. But, strange to say, the more true it appeared, the less important the question to which it could be the true answer seemed. A sad, but not unprecedented, fate for a philosophical question to suffer. This answer did not completely satisfy me, of course. There lingered some question to which I should have liked an answer, which was neither "Where are all my various and sundry parts?" nor "What is my current point of view?" Or at least there seemed to be such a question. For it did seem undeniable that in some sense I and not merely *most of me* was descending into the earth under Tulsa in search of an atomic warhead.

When I found the warhead, I was certainly glad I had left my brain behind, for the pointer on the specially built Geiger counter I had brought with me was off the dial. I called Houston on my ordinary radio and told the operation control center of my position and my progress. In return, they gave me instructions for dismantling the vehicle, based upon my onsite observations. I had set to work with my cutting torch when all of a sudden a terrible thing happened. I went stone deaf. At first I thought it was only my radio earphones that had broken, but when I tapped on my helmet, I heard nothing. Apparently the auditory transceivers had gone on the fritz. I could no longer hear Houston or my own voice, but I could speak, so I started telling them what had happened. In midsentence, I knew something else had gone wrong. My vocal apparatus had become paralyzed. Then my right hand went limp—another transceiver had gone. I was truly in deep trouble. But worse was to follow. After a few more minutes. I went blind. I cursed my luck, and then I cursed the scientists who had led me into this gave peril. There I was, deaf, dumb, and blind, in a radioactive hole more than a mile under Tulsa. Then the last of my cerebral radio links broke, and suddenly I was faced with a new and even more shocking problem: whereas an instant before I had been buried alive in Oklahoma, now I was disembodied in Houston. My recognition of my new status was not immediate. It took me several very anxious minutes before it dawned on me that my poor body lay several hundred miles away, with heart pulsing and lungs respiring, but otherwise as dead as the body of any heart-transplant donor, its skull packed with useless, broken electronic gear. The shift in perspective I had earlier found well nigh impossible now seemed quite natural. Though I could think myself back into my body in the tunnel under Tulsa, it took some effort to sustain the illusion. For surely it was an illusion to suppose I was still in Oklahoma. I had lost all contact with that body.

It occurred to me then, with one of those rushes of revelation of which we should be suspicious, that I had stumbled upon an impressive demonstration of the immateriality of the soul based upon physicalist principles and premises. For as the last radio signal between Tulsa and Houston died away, had I not changed location from Tulsa to Houston at the speed of light? And had I not accomplished this without any increase in mass? What moved from A to B at such speed was surely myself, or at any rate my soul or mind—the massless center of my being and home of my consciousness. My *point of view* had lagged somewhat behind, but I had already noted the indirect bearing of point of view on personal location. I could not see how a physicalist philosopher could quarrel with this except by taking the dire and counterintuitive route of banishing all talk of persons. Yet the notion of personhood was so well entrenched in everyone's world view, or so it seemed to me, that any denial would be as curiously unconvincing, as systematically disingenuous, as the Cartesian negation, "non sum."

The joy of philosophic discovery thus tided me over some very bad minutes or perhaps hours as the helplessness and hopelessness of my situation became more apparent to me. Waves of panic and even nausea swept over me, made all the more horrible by the absence of their normal body-dependent phenomenology. No adrenaline rush of tingles in the arms, no pounding heart, no premonitory salivation. I did feel a dread sinking feeling in my bowels at one point, and this tricked me momentarily into the false hope that I was undergoing a reversal or the process that landed me in this fix—a gradual undisembodiment. But the isolation and uniqueness of that twinge soon convinced me that it was simply the first of a plague of phantom body hallucinations that I, like any other amputee, would be all too likely to suffer.

My mood then was chaotic. On the one hand, I was fired up with elation of my philosophic discovery and was wracking my brain (one of the few familiar things I could still do), trying to figure out how to communicate my discovery to the journals; while on the other, I was bitter, lonely, and filled with dread and uncertainty. Fortunately, this did not last long, for my technical support team sedated me into a dreamless sleep from which I awoke, hearing with magnificent fidelity the familiar opening strains of my favorite Brahms piano trio. So that was why they had wanted a list of my favorite recordings! It did not take me long to realize that I was hearing the music without ears. The output from the stereo stylus was being fed through some fancy rectification circuitry directly into my auditory nerve. I was mainlining Brahms, an unforgettable experience for any stereo buff. At the end of the record it did not surprise me to hear the reassuring voice of the project director speaking into a microphone that was now my prosthetic ear. He confirmed my analysis of what had gone wrong and assured me that steps were being taken to

re-embody me. He did not elaborate, and after a few more recordings, I found myself drifting off to sleep. My sleep lasted, I later learned, for the better part of a year, and when I awoke, it was to find myself fully restored to my senses. When I looked into the mirror, though, I was a bit startled to see an unfamiliar face. Bearded and a bit heavier, bearing no doubt a family resemblance to my former face, and with the same look of spritely intelligence and resolute character, but definitely a new face. Further self-explorations of an intimate nature left me no doubt that this was a new body, and the project director confirmed my conclusions. He did not volunteer any information on the past history of my new body and I decided (wisely, I think in retrospect) not to pry. As many philosophers unfamiliar with my ordeal have more recently speculated, the acquisition of a new body leaves one's *person* intact. And after a period of adjustment to a new voice, new muscular strengths and weaknesses, and so forth, one's *personality* is by and large also preserved. More dramatic changes in personality have been routinely observed in people who have undergone extensive plastic surgery, to say nothing of sex-change operations, and I think no one contests the survival of the person in such cases. In any event I soon accommodated to my new body, to the point of being unable to recover any of its novelties to my consciousness or even memory. The view in the mirror soon became utterly familiar. That view, by the way, still revealed antennae, and so I was not surprised to learn that my brain had not been moved from its haven in the life-support lab.

I decided that good old Yorick deserved a visit. I and my new body, whom we might as well call Fortinbras, strode into the familiar lab to another round of applause from the technicians, who were of course congratulating themselves, not me. Once more I stood before the vat and contemplated poor Yorick, and on a whim I once again cavalierly flicked off the output transmitter switch. Imagine my surprise when nothing unusual happened. No fainting spell, no nausea, no noticeable change. A technician hurried to restore the switch to ON, but still I felt nothing. I demanded an explanation, which the project director hastened to provide. It seems that before they had even operated on the first occasion, they had constructed a computer duplicate of my brain, reproducing both the complete information-processing structure and the computational speed of my brain in a giant computer program. After the operation, but before they had dared to send me off on my mission to

Oklahoma, they had run this computer system and Yorick side by side. The incoming signals from Hamlet were sent simultaneously to Yorick's transceivers and to the computer's array of inputs. And the outputs from Yorick were not only beamed back to Hamlet, my body; they were recorded and checked against "Hubert" for reasons obscure to me. Over days and even weeks, the outputs were identical and synchronous, which of course did not *prove* that they had succeeded in copying the brain's functional structure, but the empirical support was greatly encouraging.

Hubert's input, and hence activity, had been kept parallel with Yorick's during my disembodied days. And now, to demonstrate this, they had actually thrown the master switch that put Hubert for the first time in on-line control of my body—not Hamlet, of course, but Fortinbras. (Hamlet, I learned, had never been recovered from its underground tomb and could be assumed by this time to have largely returned to the dust. At the head of my grave still lay the magnificent bulk of the abandoned device, with the word **STUD** emblazoned on its side in large letters—a circumstance which may provide archeologists of the next century with a curious insight into the burial rites of their ancestors.)

The laboratory technicians now showed me the master switch, which had two positions, labeled *B*, for Brian (they didn't know my brian's name was Yorick) and *H*, for Hubert. The switch did indeed point to *H*, and they explained to me that if I wished, I could switch it back to *B*. With my heart in my mouth (and my brain in its vat), I did this. Nothing happened. A click, that was all. To test their claim, and with the master switch now set at *B*, I hit Yorick's output transmitter switch on the vat and sure enough, I began to faint. Once the output switch was turned back on and I had recovered my wits, so to speak, I continued to play with the master switch, flipping it back and forth. I found that with the exception of the transitional click, I could detect no trace of a difference. I could switch in mid-utterance, and the sentence I had begun speaking under the control of Yorick was finished without a pause or hitch of any kind under the control of Hubert. I had a spare brain, a prosthetic device which might some day stand me in very good stead, were some mishap to befall Yorick. Or alternatively, I could keep Yorick as a spare and use Hubert. It didn't seem to make any difference which I chose, for the wear and tear and fatigue on my body did not have any debilitating

effect on either brain, whether or not it was actually causing the motions of my body, or merely spilling its output into thin air.

The one truly unsettling aspect of this new development was the prospect, which was not long in dawning on me, of someone detaching the spare—Hurbert or Yorick, as the case might be—from Fortinbras and hitching it to yet another body—some Johnny-come-lately Rosencrantz or Guildenstern. Then (if not before) there would be *two* people, that much was clear. One would be me and the other would be a sort of super-twin brother. If there were two bodies, one under the control of Hubert and the other being controlled by Yorick, then which would the world recognize as the true Dennett? And whatever the rest of the world decided, which one would be *me*? Would I be the Yorick-brained one, in virtue of Yorick's casual priority and former intimate relationship with the original Dennett body, Hamlet? That seemed a bit legalistic, a bit too redolent of the arbitrariness of consanguinity and the legal possession, to be convincing at the metaphysical level. For suppose that before the arrival of the second body on the scene, I had been keeping Yorick as the spare for years, and letting Hubert's output drive my body—that is, Fortinbras—all that time. The Hubert-Fortinbras couple would seem then by squatter's rights (to combat one legal intuition with another) to be true Dennett and the lawful inheritor of everything that was Dennett's. This was an interesting question, certainly, but not nearly so pressing as another question that bothered me. My strongest intuition was that in such an eventuality I would survive so long as *either* brain-body couple remained intact, but I had mixed emotions about whether I should want both to survive.

I discussed my worries with the technicians and the project director. The prospect of two Dennetts was abhorrent to me, I explained, largely for social reasons. I didn't want to be my own rival for the affections of my wife, nor did I like the prospect of the two Dennetts sharing my modest professor's salary. Still more vertiginous and distasteful, though, was the idea of knowing *that much* about another person, while he had the very same goods on me. How could we ever face each other? My colleagues in the lab argued that I was ignoring the bright side of the matter. Weren't there many things I wanted to do but, being only one person, had been unable to do? Now one Dennett could stay at home and be the professor and family man, while the other could strike out on a life of travel and adventure—missing the family of course, but happy in the knowledge that the other Dennett was keeping the home fires burning. I could be faithful and adulterous at the same time. I could even cuckold myself—to say nothing of other more lurid possibilities my colleagues were all too ready to force upon my overtaxed imagination. But my ordeal in Oklahoma (or was it Houston?) had made me less adventurous, and I shrank from this opportunity that was being offered (though of course I was never quite sure it was being offered to *me* in the first place).

There was another prospect even more disagreeable: that the spare, Hubert or Yorick as the case might be, would be detached from any input from Fortinbras and just left detached. Then, as in the other case, there would be two Dennetts, or at least two claimants to my name and possessions, one embodied in Fortinbras, and the other sadly, miserably disembodied. Both selfishness and altruism bade me take steps to prevent this from happening. So I asked that measures be taken to ensue that no one could ever tamper with the transceiver connections or the master switch without my (our? no *my*) knowledge and consent. Since I had no desire to spend my life guarding the equipment in Houston, it was mutually decided that all the electronic connections in the lab would be carefully locked. Both those that controlled the life-support system for Yorick and those that controlled the power supply for Hubert would be guarded with fail-safe devices, and I would take the only master switch, outfitted for radio remote control, with me wherever I went. I carry it strapped around my waist and—wait a moment—*here it is*. Every few months I reconnoiter the situation by switching channels. I do this only in the presence of friends, of course, for if the other channel were, heaven forbid, either dead or otherwise occupied, there would have to be somebody who had my interests at heart to switch, I'd be unable to control it. By the way, the two positions on the switch are intentionally unmarked, so I never have the faintest idea whether I am switching from Hubert to Yorick or vice versa. (Some of you may think that in this case I really don't know *who* I am, let alone where I am. But such reflections no longer make much of a dent on my essential Dennettness, on my own sense of who I am. If it is true that in one sense I don't know who I am then that's another one of your philosophical truths of underwhelming significance.)

In any case, every time I've flipped the switch so far, nothing has happened. *So let's give it a try.* . . .

"THANK GOD! I THOUGHT YOU'D NEVER FLIP THAT SWITCH!" You can't imagine how horrible it's been these last two weeks—but now you know; it's your turn in purgatory. How I've longed for this moment! You see, about two weeks ago—excuse me, ladies and gentlemen, but I've got to explain this to my . . . um, brother, I guess you could say, but he's just told you the facts, so you'll understand—about two weeks ago our two brains drifted just a bit out of synch. I don't know whether *my* brain is now Hubert or Yorick, any more than you do, but in any case, the two brains drifted apart, and of course once the process started, it snowballed, for I was in a slightly different receptive state for the input we both received, a difference that was soon magnified. In no time at all the illusion that I was in control of my body—our body—was completely dissipated. There was nothing I could do—no way to call you. YOU DIDN'T EVEN KNOW I EXISTED! It's been like being carried around in a cage, or better, like being possessed—hearing my own voice say things I didn't mean to say, watching in frustration as my own hands performed deeds I hadn't intended. You'd scratch our itches, but not the way I would have, and you kept me awake, with your tossing and turning. I've been totally exhausted, on the verge of a nervous breakdown, carried around helplessly by your frantic round of activities, sustained only by the knowledge that some day you'd throw the switch.

"Now it's your turn, but at least you'll have the comfort of knowing *I* know you're in there. Like an expectant mother, I'm eating—or at any rate tasting, smelling, seeing—for *two* now, and I'll try to make it easy for you. Don't worry. Just as soon as this colloquium is over, you and I will fly to Houston, and we'll see what can be done to get one of us another body. You can have a female—your body could be any color you like. But let's think it over. I tell you what—to be fair, if we both want this body, I promise I'll let the project director flip a coin to settle which of us gets to keep it and which then gets to choose a new body. That should guarantee justice, shouldn't it? In any case, I'll take care of you, I promise. These people are my witnesses.

"Ladies and gentlemen, this talk we have just heard is not exactly the talk *I* would have given, but I assure you that everything he said was perfectly true. And now if you'll excuse me, I think I'd—we'd—better sit down."

⚊ WHAT IS IT LIKE TO BE A BAT? ⚊

Thomas Nagel

Thomas Nagel is the University Professor of Philosophy at New York University. He is the author of *The View from Nowhere* (New York: Oxford University Press, 1986), *The Last Word* (New York: Oxford University Press, 1997), and many other very influential philosophical works. In this provocative and widely debated essay, Nagel argues that the goal of "reducing" consciousness to some brain structure is one that we could never achieve, and that indeed we would have—and could have—no clear notion of how to start such a project.

Consciousness is what makes the mind–body problem really intractable. Perhaps that is why current discussions of the problem give it little attention or get it obviously wrong. The recent wave of reductionist euphoria has produced several analyses of mental phenomena and mental concepts designed to explain the possibility of some variety of materialism, psychophysical identification, or reduction. But the problems dealt with are those common to this type of reduction and other types, and what makes the mind–body problem unique, and unlike the water–H_2O problem or the Turing machine–IBM machine problem or the lightning-electrical discharge problem or the gene–DNA problem or the oak tree–hydrocarbon problem, is ignored.

Every reductionist has his favorite analogy from modern science. It is most unlikely that any of these unrelated examples of successful reduction will shed light on the relation of mind to brain. But philosophers share the general human weakness for explanations of what is incomprehensible in terms suited for what is familiar and well understood, though entirely different. This has led to the acceptance of implausible accounts of the mental largely because they would permit familiar kinds of reduction. I shall try to explain why the usual examples do not help us to understand the relation between mind and body—why, indeed, we have at present no conception of what an explanation of the physical nature of a mental phenomenon would be. Without consciousness the mind–body problem would be much less interesting. With consciousness it seems hopeless. The most important and characteristic feature of conscious mental phenomena is very poorly understood. Most reductionist theories do not even try to explain it. And careful examination will show that no currently available concept of reduction is applicable to it. Perhaps a new theoretical form can be devised for the purpose, but such a solution, if it exists, lies in the distant intellectual future.

Conscious experience is a widespread phenomenon. It occurs at many levels of animal life, though we cannot be sure of its presence in the simpler organisms, and it is very difficult to say in general what provides evidence of it. (Some extremists have been prepared to deny it even of mammals other than man.) No doubt it occurs in countless forms totally unimaginable to us, on other planets in other solar systems throughout the universe. But no matter how the form may vary, the fact that an organism has conscious experience *at all* means, basically, that there is something it is like to *be* that organism. There may be further implications about the form of the experience; there may even (though I doubt it) be implications about the behavior of the organism. But fundamentally an organism has conscious mental states if and only if there is something that it is like to *be* that organism—something it is like *for* the organism.

We may call this the subjective character of experience. It is not captured by any of the familiar, recently devised reductive analyses of the mental, for all of them are logically compatible with its absence. It is not analyzable in terms of any explanatory system of functional states, or intentional states, since these could be ascribed to robots or automata that behaved like people though they experienced nothing. It is not analyzable in terms of the causal role of experiences in relation to typical human behavior—for similar reasons. I do not deny that conscious mental states and events cause behavior, nor that they may be given functional characterizations. I deny only that this kind of thing exhausts their analysis. Any reductionist program has to be based on an analysis of what is to be reduced. If the analysis leaves something out, the problem will be falsely posed. It is useless to base the defense of materialism on any analysis of mental phenomena that fails to deal explicitly with their subjective character. For there is no reason to suppose that a reduction which seems plausible when no attempt is made to account for consciousness can be extended to include consciousness. Without some idea, therefore, of what the subjective character of experience is, we cannot know what is required of physicalist theory.

While an account of the physical basis of mind must explain many things, this appears to be the most difficult. It is impossible to exclude the phenomenological features of experience from a reduction in the same way that one excludes the phenomenal features of an ordinary substance from a physical or chemical reduction of it—namely, by explaining them as effects on the minds of human observers . . . If physicalism is to be defended, the phenomenological features must themselves be given a physical account. But when we examine their subjective character it seems that such a result is impossible. The reason is that every subjective phenomenon is essentially connected with a single point of view, and it seems inevitable that an objective, physical theory will abandon that point of view.

Let me first try to state the issue somewhat more fully than by referring to the relation between the subjective and the objective, or between the *pour soi* and the *en soi*. This is far from easy. Facts about what it is like be an X are very peculiar, so peculiar that some may be inclined to doubt their reality, or the significance of claims about them. To illustrate the connection between subjectivity and a point of view, and to make evident the importance of subjective features, it will help to explore the matter in relation to an example that brings out clearly the divergence between the two types of conception, subjective and objective.

I assume we all believe that bats have experience. After all, they are mammals, and there is no more doubt that they have experience than that mice or pigeons or whales have experience. I have chosen bats instead of wasps or flounders because if one travels too far down the phylogenetic tree, people gradually shed their faith that there is experience there at all. Bats, although more closely related to us than those other species, nevertheless present a range of activity and a sensory apparatus so different from ours that the problem I want to pose is exceptionally vivid (though it certainly could be raised with other species). Even without the benefit of philosophical reflection, anyone who has spent some time in an enclosed space with an excited bat knows what it is to encounter a fundamentally *alien* form of life.

I have said that the essence of the belief that bats have experience is that there is something that it is like to be a bat. Now we know that most bats (the microchiroptera, to be precise) perceive the external world primarily by sonar, or echolocation, detecting the reflections, from objects within range, of their own rapid, subtly modulated, high-frequency shrieks. Their brains are designed to correlate the outgoing impulses with the subsequent echoes, and the information thus acquired enables bats to make precise discriminations of distance, size, shape, motion, and texture comparable to those we make by vision. But bat sonar, though clearly a form of perception, is not similar in its operation to any sense that we posses and there is no reason to suppose that it is subjectively like anything we can experience or imagine. This appears to create difficulties for the notion of what it is like to be a bat. We must consider whether any method will permit us to extrapolate to the inner life of the bat from our own case, and if not, what alternative methods there may be for understanding the notion.

Our own experience provides the basic material for our imagination, whose range is therefore limited. It will not help to try to imagine that one has webbing one one's arms, which enables one to fly around at dusk and dawn catching insects in one's mouth; that one has very poor vision, and perceives the surrounding world by a system of reflected high-frequency sound signals; and that one spends the day hanging upside down by one's feet in an attic. Insofar as I can imagine this (which is not very far), it tells me only what it would be like for *me* to behave as a bat behaves. But that is not the question. I want to know what it is like for a *bat* to be a bat. Yet if I try to imagine this, I am restricted to the resources of my own mind, and those resources are inadequate to the task. I cannot perform it either by imagining additions to my present experience, or by imagining segments gradually subtracted from it, or by imagining some combination of additions, subtractions, and modifications.

To the extent that I could look and behave like a wasp or a bat without changing my fundamental structure, my experiences would not be anything like the experiences of those animals. On the other hand, it is doubtful that any meaning can be attached to the supposition that I should possess the internal neurophysiological constitution of a bat. Even if I could by gradual degrees be transformed into a bat, nothing in my present constitution enables me to imagine what the experiences of such a future stage of myself thus metamorphosed would be like. The best evidence would come from the experiences of bats, if we only knew what they were like.

So if extrapolation from our own case is involved in the idea of what it is like to be a bat, the extrapolation must be incompletable. We cannot form more than a schematic conception of what it *is* like. For example, we may ascribe general *types* of experience on the basis of the animal's structure and behavior. Thus we describe bat sonar as a form of three-dimensional forward perception; we believe that bats feel some versions of pain, fear, hunger, and lust, and that they have other, more familiar types of perception besides sonar. But we believe that these experiences also have in each case a specific subjective character, which it is beyond our ability to conceive. And if there is conscious life elsewhere in the universe, it is likely that some of it will not be describable even in the most general experiential terms available to us. (The problem is not confined to exotic cases, however, for it exists between one person and another. The subject character of the experience of a person deaf and blind from birth is not accessible to me, for example, nor presumably is mine to him. This does not prevent us each from believing that the other's experience has such a subjective character.).

If anyone is inclined to deny that we can believe in the existence of facts like this whose exact nature we cannot possibly conceive, he should reflect that in contemplating the bats we are in much the same position that intelligent bats or Martians would occupy if they tried to form a conception of what it was like to be us. The structure of their own minds might make it impossible for them to succeed, but we know they would be wrong to conclude that there is not anything precise that it is like to be us: that only certain general types of mental state could be ascribed to us (perhaps perception and appetite would be concepts common to us both; perhaps not). We know they would be wrong to draw such a skeptical conclusion because we know what it is like to be us. And we know that while it includes an enormous amount of variation and complexity, and while we do not possess the vocabulary to describe it adequately, its subjective character is highly specific, and in some respects describable in terms that can be understood only by creatures like us. The fact that we cannot expect ever to accommodate in our language a detailed description of Martian or bat phenomenology should not lead us to dismiss as meaningless the claim that bats and Martians have experiences fully comparable in richness of detail to our own. It would be fine if someone were to develop

concepts and a theory that enabled us to think about those things; but such an understanding may be permanently denied to us by the limits of our nature. And to deny the reality or logical significance of what we can never describe or understand is the crudest form of cognitive dissonance.

This brings us to the edge of a topic that requires much more discussion than I can give it here: namely, the relation between facts on the one hand and conceptual schemes or systems of representation on the other. My realism about the subjective domain in all its forms implies a belief in the existence of facts beyond the reach of human concepts. Certainly it is possible for a human being to believe that there are facts which humans never *will* possess the requisite concepts to represent or comprehend. Indeed, it would be foolish to doubt this, given the finiteness of humanity's expectations. After all, there would have been transfinite numbers even if everyone had been wiped out by the Black Death before Cantor discovered them. But one might also believe that there are facts which *could* not ever be represented or comprehended by human beings, even if the species lasted forever—simply because our structure does not permit us to operate with concepts of the requisite type. This impossibility might even be observed by other beings, but it is not clear that the existence of such beings, or the possibility of their existence, is a precondition of the significance of the hypothesis that there are humanly inaccessible facts. (After all, the nature of beings with access to humanly inaccessible facts is presumably itself a humanly inaccessible fact). Reflection on what it is like to be a bat seems to lead us, therefore, to the conclusion that there are facts that do not consist in the truth of propositions expressible in a human language. We can be compelled to recognize the existence of such facts without being able to state or comprehend them.

I shall not pursue this subject, however. Its bearing on the topic before us (namely, the mind–body problem) is that it enables us to make a general observation about the subjective character of experience. Whatever may be the status of facts about what it is like to be a human being, or a bat, or a Martian, these appear to be facts that embody a particular point of view. I am not adverting here to the alleged privacy of experience to its possessor. The point of view in question is not one accessible only to a single individual. Rather it is a *type*. It is often possible to take up a point of view other than one's own, so the comprehension of such facts is not limited to one's own case. There is a sense in which phenomenological facts are perfectly objective: One person can know or say of another what the quality of the other's experience is. They are subjective, however, in the sense that even this objective ascription of experience is possible only for someone sufficiently similar to the object of ascription to be able to adopt his point of view—to understand the ascription in the first person as well as in the third, so to speak. The more different from oneself the other experience is, the less success one can expect with this enterprise. In our own case we occupy the relevant point of view, but we will have as much difficulty understanding our own experience properly if we approach it from another point of view as we would if we tried to understand the experience of another species without taking up *its* point of view.

This bears directly on the mind–body problem. For if the facts of experience—facts about what it is like *for* the experiencing organism—are accessible only from one point of view, then it is a mystery how the true character of experiences could be revealed in the physical operation of that organism. The latter is a domain of objective facts par excellence—the kind that can be observed and understood from many points of view and by individuals with differing perceptual systems. There are no comparable imaginative obstacles to the acquisition of knowledge about bat neurophysiology by human scientists, and intelligent bats or Martians might learn more about the human brain than we ever will.

This is not by itself an argument against reduction. A Martian scientist with no understanding of visual perception could understand the rainbow, or lightning, or clouds as physical phenomena, though he would never be able to understand the human concepts of rainbow, lightning, or cloud, or the place these things occupy in our phenomenal world. The objective nature of the things picked out by these concepts could be apprehended by him because, although the concepts themselves are connected with a particular point of view and a particular visual phenomenology, the things apprehended from that point of view are not: they are observable from the point of view but external to it; hence they can be comprehended from other points of view also, either by the same organisms or by others. Lightning has an objective character that is not exhausted by its visual appearance, and this can be investigated by a Martian without vision. To be precise, it has a *more* objective character than is revealed in its visual appearance. In speaking of the move from subjective to objective characterization, I wish to remain noncommittal

about the existence of an end point, the completely objective intrinsic nature of the thing, which one might or might not be able to reach. It may be more accurate to think of objectivity as a direction in which the understanding can travel. And in understanding a phenomenon like lightning, it is legitimate to go as far away as one can from a strictly human viewpoint.

In the cases of experience, on the other hand, the connection with a particular point of view seems much closer. It is difficult to understand what could be meant by the *objective* character of an experience, apart from the particular point of view from which its subject apprehends it. After all, what would be left of what it was like to be a bat if one removed the view point of the bat? But if experience does not have, in addition to its subjective character, an objective nature that can be apprehended from many different points of view, then how can it be supposed that a Martian investigating my brain might be observing physical processes which were my mental processes (as he might observe physical processes which were bolts of lightning), only from a different point of view? How, for the matter, could a human physiologist observe them from another point of view?

We appear to be faced with a general difficulty about psychophysical reduction. In other areas the process of reduction is a move in the direction of greater objectivity, toward a more accurate view of the real nature of things. This is accomplished by reducing our dependence on individual or species-specific points of view toward the object of investigation. We describe it not in terms of the impression it makes on our senses, but in terms of its more general effects and of properties detectable by means other than the human senses. The less it depends on a specifically human viewpoint, the more objective is our description. It is possible to follow this path because although the concepts and ideas we employ in thinking about the external world are initially applied from a point of view that involves our perceptual apparatus, they are used by us to refer to things beyond themselves—toward which we *have* the phenomenal point of view. Therefore we can abandon it in favor of another, and still be thinking about the same things.

Experience itself, however, does not seem to fit the pattern. The idea of moving from appearance to reality seems to make no sense here. What is the analogue in this case to pursuing a more objective understanding of the same phenomena by abandoning the initial subjective viewpoint toward them in favor of another that is more objective but concerns the same thing? Certainly it *appears* unlikely that we will get closer to the real nature of human experience by leaving behind the particularity of our human point of view and striving for a description in terms accessible to beings that could not imagine what it was like to be us. If the subjective character of experience is fully comprehensible only from one point of view, then any shift to greater objectivity—that is, less attachment to a specific viewpoint—does not take us nearer to the real nature of the phenomenon: It takes us farther away from it.

In a sense, the seeds of this objection to the reducibility of experience are already detectable in successful cases of reduction; for in discovering sound to be, in reality, a wave phenomenon in air or other media, we leave behind one viewpoint to take up another, and the auditory, human or animal viewpoint that we leave behind remains unreduced. Members of radically different species may both understand the same physical events in objective terms, and this does not require that they understand the phenomenal forms in which those events appear to the senses of members of the other species. Thus it is a condition of their referring to a common reality that their more particular viewpoints are not part of the common reality that they both apprehend. The reduction can succeed only if the species-specific viewpoint is omitted from what is to be reduced.

But while we are right to leave this point of view aside in seeking a fuller understanding of the external world, we cannot ignore it permanently, since it is the essence of the internal world, and not merely a point of view on it. Most of the neobehaviorism of recent philosophical psychology results from the effort to substitute an objective concept of mind for the real thing, in order to have nothing left over which cannot be reduced. If we acknowledge that a physical theory of mind must account for the subjective chapter of experience, we must admit that no presently available conception gives us a clue how this could be done. The problem is unique. If mental processes are indeed physical processes, then there is something it is like, intrinsically, to undergo certain physical processes. What it is for such a thing to be the case remains a mystery.

What moral should be drawn from these reflections, and what should be done next? It would be a mistake to conclude that physicalism must be false. Nothing is proved by the inadequacy of physicalist hypotheses that assume a faulty objective analysis of mind. It would be truer to say that physicalism is a position we cannot understand because we do not at present have any conception of how it might be true. Perhaps it will be thought unreasonable to require such a conception as a condition of understanding. After all, it might be said, the meaning of physicalism is clear enough: mental states are states of the body; mental events are physical events. We do not know *which* physical states and events they are, but that should not prevent us from understanding the hypothesis. What could be clearer than the words "is" and "are"?

But I believe it is precisely this apparent clarity of the word "is" that is deceptive. Usually, when we are told that X is Y we know *how* it is supposed to be true, but that depends on a conceptual or theoretical background and is not conveyed by the "is" alone. We know how both "X" and "Y" refer, and the kinds of things to which they refer, and we have a rough idea how the two referential paths might converge on a single thing, be it an object, a person, a process, an event or whatever. But when the two terms of the identification are very disparate it may not be so clear how it could be true. We may not have even a rough idea of how the two referential paths could converge, or what kind of things they might converge on, and a theoretical framework may have to be supplied to enable us to understand this. Without the framework, an air of mysticism surrounds the identification.

This explains the magical flavor of popular presentations of fundamental scientific discoveries, given out as propositions to which one must subscribe without really understanding them. For example, people are now told at an early age that all matter is really energy. But despite the fact that they know what "is" means, most of them never form a conception of what makes this claim true, because they lack the theoretical background.

At the present time the status of physicalism is similar to that which the hypothesis that matter is energy would have had if uttered by a pre-Socratic philosopher. We do not have the beginnings of a conception of how it might be true. In order to understand the hypothesis that a mental event is a physical event, we require more than an understanding of the word "is." The idea of how a mental and a physical term might refer to the same thing is lacking, and the usual analogies with theoretical identification in other fields fail to supply it. They fail because if we construe the reference of mental terms to physical events on the usual model, we either get a reappearance of separate subjective events as the effects through which mental reference to physical events is secured, or else we get a false account of how mental terms refer (for example, a causal behaviorist one). . . .

Very little work has been done on the basic question (from which mention of the brain can be entirely omitted) whether any sense can be made of experiences' having an objective character at all. Does it make sense, in other words, to ask what my experiences are *really* like, as opposed to how they appear to me? We cannot genuinely understand the hypothesis that their nature is captured in a physical description unless we understand the more fundamental idea that they *have* an objective nature (or that objective processes can have a subjective nature).

EXERCISES

1. Which would seem more impressive to you: A God that sets up a perfect preestablished harmony, never requiring intervention or a God that intervenes constantly and accurately, a billion times every second, whenever someone has a thought that "causes" a physical event, or vice versa? That is, do you think that the God of preestablished harmony or the Occasionalist God is most glorious?

2. Many dualists favor a separation of mind and body because then the mind can be identified with the soul, and the soul can survive the death of the physical body. But of course a mind–body dualist need not believe in a soul, nor in any sort of survival after death; that is, a dualist might maintain that the mind and body are distinct substances, but that both cease to exist when the body dies. But consider the question from the other direction: Could one consistently believe in an immortal *soul* while rejecting mind–body dualism? In particular, could a monist who takes a materialist view (as opposed to the idealist view) consistently believe in an immortal soul?

3. Descartes' theory of mind separates the mind and body into two distinct substances; and his theory of knowledge (his epistemology) insists on a starting point of fixed and indubitable certainty. If Descartes had adopted a different view of knowledge, do you think that would have resulted in a different mind–body view?

4. The development of computers has generated claims about "artificial intelligence." Some philosophers and artificial intelligence researchers have put forward a position known as "strong artificial intelligence," or "strong AI." Advocates of this position maintain that the crucial thing about thought is the programming. They hold that if a very powerful computer could be adequately programmed, then by virtue of that programming it would actually be thinking: perhaps not thinking in exactly the same way that humans think, since humans have different programming; but nonetheless genuinely thinking, and thinking as well or even better than humans do. John Searle is one of the leading opponents of strong AI: He adamantly opposes the idea that any computer could ever be programmed so that it would actually *think* or *reason*. A computer can sort material admirably well, but it can never really *think*, according to Searle. Some people may suppose that Searle's view is based on dualism: A computer is purely physical, and it cannot really think because only *minds* can think. But Searle insists that he is *not* a dualist, and he is *not* opposed to the idea that material machines can think:

   > My own view is that *only* a machine could think, and indeed only very special kinds of machines, namely brains and machines that had the same causal powers as brains. . . . Whatever else intentionality is, it is a biological phenomenon, and it is likely to be as causally dependent on the specific biochemistry of its origins as lactation, photosynthesis, or any other biological phenomena.

   In fact, Searle attempts to turn the table on his opponents, and charges the advocates of strong AI with being mind–body dualists:

   > Strong AI only makes sense given the dualistic assumption that, where the mind is concerned, the brain doesn't matter. In strong AI . . . what matters are programs, and programs are independent of their realization in machines. . . . The single most surprising discovery that I have made in discussing these issues is that many AI workers are quite shocked by my idea that actual human mental phenomena might be dependent on actual physical-chemical properties of actual human brains. But if you think about it a minute you can see that

I should not have been surprised; for unless you accept some form of dualism, the strong AI project hasn't got a chance. The project is to reproduce and explain the mental by designing programs, but unless the mind is not only conceptually but empirically independent of the brain you couldn't carry out the project, for the program is completely independent of any realization. Unless you believe that the mind is separable from the brain both conceptually and empirically—dualism in a strong form—you cannot hope to reproduce the mental by writing and running programs since programs must be independent of brains or any other particular forms of instantiation. If mental operations consist in computational programs on formal symbols, then it follows that they have no interesting connection with the brain; the only connection would be that the brain just happens to be one of the indefinitely many types of machines capable of instantiating the program. This form of dualism is not the traditional Cartesian variety that claims there are two sorts of *substances*, but it is Cartesian in the sense that it insists that what is specifically mental about the mind has no intrinsic connection with the actual properties of the brain.

John R. Searle, "Minds, Brains, and Programs," from The Behavioral and Brain Sciences, volume 3 (1980)

This is a continuing controversy between Searle and strong AI proponents. So if you're interested in artificial intelligence, what's your take on this issue? Is the strong AI program dualist, as Searle charges? Or is Searle's opposition to strong AI actually rooted in dualism, as some charge? Neither? Both? Or what? *Could* a computer ever be programmed to think?

5. One of the most interesting claims associated with mind–body dualism is that we have special "privileged access" to our own thoughts. Someone else might know my brain better than I (by means of a PET scan, for example); but no one else can know what I am thinking—or at least cannot know it with the special immediate knowledge and certainty that I have. Many people believe that claim to be true, and many others insist it is false; that's not my question. Do mind–body dualists (and of course *you* might or might not be included in that group) believe that we have privileged access to our own minds *because* they believe in mind–body dualism? Or do they believe in mind–body dualism because of their more basic belief that we have privileged access to our own minds (and mind–body dualism seems the best way to explain that)? That is, which came first: belief in mind–body dualism, or belief in privileged access to one's own mind?

6. Suppose you believe that others can have knowledge of your own mind, your own thoughts, that is at least as good as the knowledge you yourself possess. Would such a belief make it much more difficult to accept mind–body dualism?

7. Recently, researchers who are attempting—with some success—to find effective treatments for some severe forms of epilepsy have implanted tiny devices in the brains of patients, and used those devices to monitor minute electromechanical processes in the brain. In one *reported* experiment with some of those subjects (there is some question of whether the experiment actually occurred), researchers showed subjects a series of slides of beautiful vacation sites: beaches, mountains, waterfalls, and so on. The subjects were instructed to press a button when they chose to move to the next slide, and pressing the button would switch to the next picture. The button, however, was fake; it controlled nothing. Instead, specific forms of brain activity—associated with making a choice—that were measured by the implanted monitors were amplified and those brain waves triggered the change in the slides. The subjects reported the strange sensation that the slide projector was "predicting" their choice, just before the choice itself occurred. That is, the brain activity associated with choice occurred an instant *prior* to the consciousness of choice. *If* that is an accurate report of the experiment, what implications does it have for the mind–body question?

8. Searle would find Dennett's "Where Am I?" story charming, but impossible. If Dennett's brain were replaced by a computer—Searle would say—there would no longer exist a thinking Dennett. If the story told by Dennett ever *actually happened*, would that refute Searle?

9. What would it *be* like for *you*, if you—instead of being a human—were a *bat*? Does that question make sense?

ADDITIONAL READING

For a good general review of the "mind–body problem," see Keith Campbell's *Body and Mind* (New York: Doubleday Anchor, 1970); Jerome Shaffer's *The Philosophy of Mind* (Englewood Cliffs, NJ: Prentice-Hall, 1968) also examines the issue, and the many proposals that have been made to solve the problem. John O' Connor's *Modern Materialism: Readings on Mind–Body Identity* (New York: Harcourt, Brace & World, 1969) is a good collection of contemporary essays; another is David Rosenthal, ed., *Materialism and the Mind–Body Problem* (Englewood Cliffs, NJ: Prentice-Hall, 1971). The most famous contemporary attack on mind–body dualism is by Gilbert Ryle; his book, *The Concept of Mind* (London: Hutchinson, 1949), has influenced both philosophical and psychological theory.

Two good collections of papers on philosophy of mind, which include historical as well as contemporary writings, are B. Beakley and P. Ludlow, eds., *The Philosophy of Mind: Classical Problems, Contemporary Issues* (Cambridge, MA: MIT Press, 1992); and G. N. A. Vesey, *Body and Mind: Readings in Philosophy* (London: George Allen & Unwin, 1964). A superb collection (primarily of recent work) is *Philosophy sof Mind: A Guide and Anthology*, edited by John Heil (Oxford: Oxford University Press, 2004). Still another good anthology on the philosophy of mind is *The Nature of Mind*, edited by David M. Rosenthal (New York: Oxford University Press, 1991).

Herbert Feigl's version of dual-aspect theory can be found in Herbert Feigl, *The "Mental" and the "Physical"* (Minneapolis, MN: University of Minnesota Press, 1967); the essay which forms the heart of the book was originally published in 1958. John Searle's provocative work has stimulated much debate in both philosophy of mind and artificial intelligence. He tackles difficult issues, attacks popular positions, and writes with remarkable clarity. A good introduction to his recent work can be found in John R. Searle, *The Rediscovery of the Mind* (Cambridge, MA: MIT Press, 1992).

There is a vast and ever increasing literature on functionalism, both pro and con. An excellent introduction to the positions and issues involved, as well as a very extensive bibliography on the subject, is offered by Janet Levin in her Stanford Encyclopedia of Philosophy article on functionalism, which can be found at http://plato.stanford.edu/entries/functionalism.

A superb collection of essays concerning contemporary neuropsychology and mind–body (as well as free will) issues is contained in *The Volitional Brain: Towards a Neuroscience of Free Will*, edited by Benjamin Libet, Anthony Freeman, and Keith Sutherland (Exeter UK: Imprint Academic, 1999). Much of this is very difficult material, but the debates among the participants are fascinating, and the essays are generally of very high quality. There is an excellent and very readable book by a contemporary neuropsychologist defending his own version of epiphenomenalism: Daniel M. Wegner, *The Illusion of Conscious Will* (Cambridge, MA: The MIT Press, 2002). Another neuropsychologist who has written interesting and accessible books on issues related to philosophy of mind is Antonio R. Damasio; see *Descartes' Error: Emotion, Reason, and the Human Brain* (New York: G. P. Putnam's Sons, 1994); *Looking for Spinoza: Joy, Sorrow, and the Feeling Brain* (New York: Harcourt, 2003); and *The Feeling of What Happens: Body and Emotion in the Making of Consciousness* (New York: Harcourt, 1999). All of Damasio's books are in paperback, and are widely available. *Neurophilosophy: Toward a Unified Science of the Mind–Brain*, by Patricia Smith Churchland (Cambridge, MA: MIT Press, 1986) is an insightful examination of the implications of recent work in neuroscience for both philosophy of mind and philosophy of science. A philosophical book that pulls together contemporary work from many disciplines to offer a fresh perspective on the traditional mind–body problem is by Andy Clark: *Being There: Putting Brain, Body, and World Together Again* (Cambridge, MA: MIT Press, 1997).

The interactionist position championed by neuropscyologist John Eccles can be found in his book *The Human Psyche* (New York: Springer, 1980); see also his "Brain and Mind: Two or One?" in C. Blakemore and S. Greenfield, eds., *Mindwaves* (Oxford: Blackwell, 1987).

Frank Jackson develops his epiphenomenalist account in "Epiphenomenal Qualia," *The Philosophical Quarterly*, volume 32 (1982): 127–136.

A wonderful and entertaining collection of essays on philosophy of mind—including work by philosophers, novelists, and cognitive scientists—is *The Mind's I: Fantasies and Reflections on Self and Soul*, edited by Douglas R. Hofstadter and Daniel C. Dennett (New York: Basic Books, 1981); it is also available in a Bantam Books paperback edition (1982).

A particularly clear path into many tricky philosophy of mind issues is provided by George Graham in *Philosophy of Mind: An Introduction* (Oxford: Blackwell, 1993). Another good and clearly written guide to issues in the philosophy of mind is by Owen Flanagan, *Consciousness Reconsidered* (Cambridge, MA: MIT Press, 1992). Still another excellent introduction is by Paul M. Churchland, *Matter and Consciousness: A Contemporary Introduction to the Philosophy of Mind*, revised edition (Cambridge, MA: MIT Press, 1988).

Thomas Nagel's "What Is It Like to Be a Bat?" (included in the readings for this chapter) has prompted many responses. Peter M. S. Hacker, "Is There Anything It Is Like to Be a Bat?"*Philosophy*, volume 77 (2002): 157–174, uses Wittgenstein's "linguistic-therapeutic" method to argue that Nagel's case for the irreducibility of consciousness is based on linguistic mistakes.

David Chalmers has compiled a remarkably thorough, beautifully organized, and easily navigated bibliography of recent work on philosophy of mind (back to approximately 1950); many of the entries are annotated. Go to http://www.u.arizona.edu/~chalmers/biblio.html. His home page also contains a remarkable collection of hundreds of online papers (his own and many others), conveniently arranged by topic and easily available. In addition, there's a section of philosophical humor, and pictures of philosophers taken at various conferences—examine these at your own risk.

"A Field Guide to the Philosophy of Mind" is a very appealing Web site. Its best feature is an extensive and excellent set of "Guided Tours" to a wide variety of topics in philosophy of mind. The tours are clearly written, and they provide excellent guides to the history of the topic as well as current research. It can be found at http://host.uniroma3.it/progetti/kant/field/

The MIT Encyclopedia of Cognitive Sciences is also a very useful site; go to http:/cognet.mit.edu/MITECS/login.html

The "Wifilosofia" has an excellent and extensive set of Web links to papers, discussions, and sites related to philosophy of mind. Go to http://lgxserver.uniba.it/lei/mind/home.htm

www.Naturalism.org is an excellent site for papers, articles, and reviews of material on philosophy of mind (as well as other topics).

CHAPTER 7

PERSONAL IDENTITY

I love children's books. One of my favorite authors is Laura Joffe Numeroff, who wrote *If You Give a Mouse a Cookie* and *If You Give a Moose a Muffin*. Maybe you remember the stories: you give a moose a muffin, and he wants jam on it, and he has to go out for jam so he puts on his socks, but then he thinks about socks and he wants to make sock puppets, and the sock puppets lead to a play, and eventually back to another muffin. I think it's hilarious; but then, I'm easily entertained. There's another children's book that I particularly like: *The Runaway Bunny*, by Margaret Wise Brown; it was first published in 1942, and has remained a children's favorite ever since. It's about a little bunny who talks to his mother about running away, and his mother replies that she will run after him, "for you are my little bunny." And the little bunny thinks of running away by becoming a fish, and then a rock high on a mountain, and then a flower in a garden, a bird, a tree, a sailboat; and his mother assures him that she will come after him, no matter what, "for you are my little bunny." It's a very nice story, about the unconditional love of a mother for her child. And it's nice for children to hear this story, and to have the comfort of knowing that their parents love them *unconditionally*: no matter what mistakes I make, wrongs I commit, bad things I do, failures I have, my parents will still love me. It's psychologically wonderful; but it's philosophically perplexing.

It's nice to think that *I* will be loved unconditionally, but problems arise when we look closely at the identity of that "I." If I become a bunny, is there any sense in which I have an ongoing identity? If "I become a rock," or a flower or a sailboat, the rock, the flower, and the sailboat may be quite delightful, but none of them will be *me*. I may be a bit sketchy on the essential conditions for my personal identity; but whatever those conditions are, a rock is not likely to meet them.

This can raise problems for some accounts of a continuing afterlife. I have lustful desires, a fondness for gin, a passion for Chicago blues, and a deep skepticism concerning religious claims; and I'm selfish, short-tempered, and mean-spirited besides. Suppose that in the afterlife I suddenly have no lustful desires, no taste for gin, I prefer hymns to the blues, I have unwavering faith, and I am warmhearted, generous, and wonderfully patient. In that case, there may be *someone* living in angelic bliss, but I'm not so sure that someone is actually *me*.

There are some movies that are focused on the question of personal identity. For example, the movie *Sommersby* tells the story of a young man who returns from the Civil War— to his wife, his son, his farm, and his community. He had gone to war a newly married young man of only 18 or 19; three years later he returns a battle-scarred veteran of a fierce conflict. But is he really the same man, or an impostor? The wife accepts him as her husband, and some members of the community agree that this is the same man. But others disagree, claiming that this is someone else who is trying to take up the identity of another soldier—perhaps one who died in the war—so that he can claim the man's farm. The surface plot concerns whether this is the "same man" (in the sense of having the same DNA, the man born of a particular mother with a specific given name); but the underlying question is whether anyone who returns from such a terrible experience as a Civil War is the "same person" who left.

PRACTICAL IMPLICATIONS OF PERSONAL IDENTITY

Personal identity debates often have a substantial element of science fiction. But in trying to fix exactly what features determine identity, it is useful to imagine rather improbable scenarios, in order to separate out some factors that usually occur together. Our brains and the rest of our bodies are usually in close proximity to one another; but if we are trying to select the key element for determining identity, it may be useful to imagine them separated in special circumstances.

Religions often claim that their converts become "new persons"; in the evangelical Christian tradition, they are "born again." Perhaps the most famous case is that of St. Paul, who started by persecuting Christians (supposedly approving when they were stoned to death), but then—on the Road to Damascus—experienced a blinding light, from which God spoke to him and caused him to undergo a radical change; indeed, he even changed his name from Saul to Paul. But charming as the story is, it does not imply that following the Road to Damascus experience, there was literally a "new man." If God had struck Saul dead, and created a new individual on the spot to replace Saul, that would be an interesting story; but it would not be the story of Paul's *conversion* experience. In order for this to be the story of a *conversion*, Paul cannot literally be a *new* person, but rather the *same* person who has now undergone a remarkable change.

But even though the exploration of identity questions may involve some rather exotic scenarios, the question of personal identity has important practical implications. Consider a very realistic case. Joan suffers an abusive childhood, and at 15 she runs away from home to escape her violent, sexually aggressive stepfather. Living on the street, Joan falls in with a rather rough crowd. She develops a drug habit, and to support her habit she and her friends do some shoplifting, and then move on to some warehouse break-ins, but nothing violent. When they break into warehouses, Joan stands guard and signals if she sees anyone approaching. Joan has just turned 17, and one night while she is standing watch, two of her friends break into a warehouse. Joan sees a security guard approaching, and signals her friends to escape. But unknown to Joan, one of her friends has borrowed a pistol, and when the security guard shows up, Joan's friend panics and shoots him. The guard dies, and Joan is now guilty of first degree murder: She willingly participated in a crime in which a victim was killed, and that makes her guilty of murder. Joan is terribly shocked: she abhors violence, and had no idea her friend was armed. She leaves her friends, moves to another city, goes into drug rehab, finishes high school, goes to college, and becomes a first grade teacher in an inner city school. She dedicates her life to helping children succeed, she spends long hours after school doing free tutoring for neighborhood children, and she is honored as an outstanding teacher for her dedicated service. She marries and has four children, and her children have successful careers. Now at age 68 Joan is finally retired, and she splits her time between taking care of her beloved grandchildren and doing volunteer tutoring with inner city children. But there is no statute of limitations for murder, and a detective takes out the collected evidence from the unsolved murder that occurred more than half a century ago. With new forensic techniques, the evidence leads him to Joan. She is arrested, and charged with first degree murder. The 68-year-old Joan who is charged with murder has the same fingerprints and the same DNA as the 17-year-old girl, and Joan the retired grandmother remembers the night when a security guard was killed. But is Joan the grand-mother and tutor the *same person* as the young drug addict?

> Psychological continuity is obviously . . . a matter of degree. So long as we think that identity is a further fact, one of the things we're inclined to think is that it's all or nothing. . . . It's obvious on reflection that, to give an example, the relations between me now and me next year are much closer in every way than the relation between me now and me in twenty years. And the sorts of relations that I'm thinking of are relations of memory, character, ambition, intention—all of those. Next year I shall remember much more of this year than I will in twenty years. I shall have a much more similar character. I shall be carrying out more of the same plans, ambitions and, if that is so, I think there are various plausible implications for our moral beliefs and various possible effects on our emotions. . . . On the view which I'm sketching it seems to me much more plausible to claim that people deserve much less punishment, or even perhaps no punishment, for what they did many years ago as compared with what they did very recently. Plausible because the relations between them now and them many years ago when they committed the crime are so much weaker. *Derek Parfit*, 1974, "Brain Transplants and Personal Identity" (A dialogue with Godfrey Vesey).

Consider another example—sad, but not uncommon. Ruth is a brilliant economist, who is very proud of her broad knowledge of economics and her keen analytic ability for discovering and analyzing economic trends. She is widely respected in her field, and her research is superb; but she is also rather morose. Not really grumpy, but not a very happy person, either. She very rarely smiles, never laughs, and her usual expression is a frown. Those who know Ruth recognize her intellectual brilliance, but they are convinced that she has not had a very happy life. Ruth, being proud of her intellectual abilities, writes out a living will giving precise instructions concerning her treatment should she become unable to make her own decisions: Should she suffer a disease that leaves her mentally incompetent, she wants no treatment whatsoever, and she wants to be allowed to die from any infection that she develops. Unfortunately, what Ruth had feared comes to pass: She suffers from a disease that destroys her intellectual capacities and her memory and leaves her childlike in her reasoning ability. However, this intellectually impaired Ruth seems to be very happy: She frequently laughs, hums to herself, smiles constantly, and seems to take enormous pleasure in sorting blocks of various sizes and colors into piles. Ruth now develops an infection that could be easily treated with standard drugs; but left untreated, it will cause her death. In the living will Ruth wrote when she was intellectually sound, Ruth instructed that she wanted no treatment. But the nurses at the home where Ruth now lives are deeply disturbed: They believe that Ruth—as she presently is—is a very happy person, and that she would want to continue living. Is the brilliant Ruth who wrote the living will the *same person* as the Ruth who happily sorts blocks into piles? If so, then it seems that Ruth's living will should govern what happens; but if not, then it's not at all clear that the economist Ruth should be able to make life or death decisions for this very different person. So identity questions are much more than philosophers indulging their taste for science fiction; they are often serious questions with serious implications. Should we allow Ruth to die? Is it just to imprison Grandmother Joan for something done more than half a century ago by youthful Joan?

Some people suggest that philosophical examples place too much strain on our old workaday concept of personal identity. If you have a brain transplant, or if you transplant half your brain into another body: well, in such extraordinary circumstances you may have trouble determining identity; but in ordinary cases, in which brains don't get juggled from body to body, we have perfectly adequate standards for personal identity. But cases like Joan and Ruth may undermine such easy confidence. After all, neither Joan nor Ruth has a brain transplant, and neither of their stories is weird or unimaginable; to the contrary, they are all too believable. But even in such cases, problems of identity can prove very challenging.

Richard Double suggests that we go wrong because we want a sense of *absolute* identity that we cannot have, or at least, that we cannot have if we adopt the *materialist* view.

> Suppose that human beings consist entirely of their bodies and have no nonphysical minds. If so, then as the matter in our bodies gradually changes, so do we. Biologists know that living organisms constantly renew themselves as new molecules go into their living cells and replace the old molecules. After twenty years human beings will have almost entirely new molecules in their bodies. . . . This entails that *if persons are solely material*, as the materialists maintain, then a person cannot literally be the same person after twenty years. This is *not* to claim merely that we will have different beliefs, desires, and values. Rather, we will be *entirely different persons*. . . . The person who bears your name twenty years from now will not be *you*, but a replacement person who grew out of you—if materialism is true.

Richard Double, Beginning Philosophy, *p. 112*

PHYSICAL IDENTITY

So what *is* a workable standard for my continuing identity? One of the easiest, of course, is simple *bodily* identity. In traditional Jewish and Christian beliefs, the emphasis is on *bodily resurrection*: the graves will give up their dead. But on closer scrutiny, that standard for personal identity has some problems. If I lose an arm, am I still the same person? Two arms and two legs? Two arms and two legs, and I have a heart and lung and kidney and liver transplant: still the same person? Is there some specific point at which I would *lose* my identity? (For example, with the loss of no more than two limbs my identity is the same, but when a third limb is lost my identity goes with it.) Any such standard seems ridiculously arbitrary. Furthermore, we know that the cells making up our bodies die and are replaced constantly; would this mean that my identity is constantly shifting?

Suppose that Smith's brain is transplanted into the body of Jones. We tend to assume that Jones no longer exists (too bad for Jones) but there is no problem for Smith: Smith is still the same person, but with a new body. But the question of Smith surviving *as Smith* in this new and very different body may be more difficult than such thought examples make it seem. Consider the following passage from Bernard Williams:

> Suppose a magician is hired to perform the old trick of making the emperor and the peasant become each other. He gets the emperor and the peasant in one room, with the emperor on his throne and the peasant in the corner. What will count as success? Clearly not that after the smoke has cleared the old emperor should be in the corner and the old peasant on the throne. That would be a rather boring trick. The requirement is presumably that the emperor's body, with the peasant's personality, should be on the throne, and the peasant's body with the emperor's personality, in the corner. What does this mean? In particular, what has happened to the voices? The voice presumably ought to count as a bodily function; yet how would the peasant's gruff blasphemies be uttered in the emperor's cultivated tones, or the emperor's witticisms in the peasant's growl? A similar point holds for the features; the emperor's body might include the sort of face that just *could not* express the peasant's morose suspiciousness, the peasant's a face no expression of which could be taken for one of fastidious arrogance. These 'could's' are not just empirical—such expressions on these features might be unthinkable.

Bernard Williams, Problems of the Self, *pp. 11–12*

In science fiction accounts (and occasional cartoons), *brains* sometimes get transplanted; and in such cases, we tend to assume that it is the identity of the individual whose *brain* survives that keeps his or her identity. If my brain were transplanted into the body of Tiger Woods, I can imagine that *I* would now be able to drive a golf ball 300 yards, and that *I* would now be tall and good looking. But if the brain of Tiger Woods were transplanted into my body, Tiger would not win any more golf tournaments; and *I* would cease to exist. So, perhaps what is crucial for my continuing identity is the continuity of my *brain*. But that option doesn't work very well, either. After all, suppose that I were so severely brainwashed that I lost all my present memories and values, but my brain—now equipped with totally new thoughts, goals, values, and beliefs—continued humming along. My brain might still be there, but it's doubtful that I would be. Or suppose a severe blow erases all my memories and completely changes my personality, to the degree that I can't remember "who I am," and my old friends conclude "that's simply not the same person: he has a completely different personality." The brain continuity does not seem to guarantee continuity of individual identity.

SOULS AND PERSONAL IDENTITY

The dominant view of personal identity from the time of Plato until the seventeenth century was that personal identity is centered in the immaterial *soul*, and that the soul is a single indivisible substance. If ongoing personal identity is determined by the continuing indivisible presence of the soul, then we need not worry about bodily continuity or memory continuity: the soul can easily transcend both. But exactly how does continuity of my *soul* guarantee *my* continuing existence? Suppose that some new angel shows up in the afterlife, and this angelic individual has none of my memories, beliefs, or desires, and obviously does not have my body; but—supposedly—it is the continued existence of my *soul*. So far as I can see, that would not be much of a continued existence for *me*. It is no accident that those who make claims about "channeling" some person who is now in the afterlife (Elvis Presley had about a dozen channelers at last count) endeavor to establish those claims on the basis of memory or knowledge of the individual's earthly life or personality. (That's why, if you wish to make a few bucks in the channeling business, it's always safer to channel some member of an ancient lost tribe that is currently unknown.)

MEMORY AND IDENTITY

One of the first modern philosophers to think carefully about the question of personal identity was John Locke, and he proposed that the criterion for personal identity must be continuity of *memory*. That view has considerable plausibility. *Psychological* (rather than

My heart leaps up when I behold
A rainbow in the sky:
So was it when my life began;
So is it now I am a man;
So be it when I shall grow old,
  Or let me die!
The child is father of the Man;
And I could wish my days to be
Bound each to each by natural piety.

William Wordsworth

physical) standards for individual identity seem promising; and memory seems a better candidate than beliefs or values. After all, you may have undergone rather radical changes in your values and beliefs. Perhaps you grew up a Southern Baptist and have now become a Buddhist; or you once believed that eating meat was fine, and now you are a dedicated vegan.

Or you were once a strongly pro-union Democrat, and you are now a pro-business Republican. Those may well be substantial changes, but they are changes that happened to *you*. You are very different in values, perspective, and beliefs from when you were 14, but when you think back to that very different 14-year-old, your memories are still memories of *you*; and you can reflect on how much *you* have changed. So John Locke proposed this standard for personal identity: If you have a common store of *memories*, then you are still the same person.

But attractive as personal memory is as a standard for personal identity, it still has some problems.

Thomas Reid developed the philosophically famous example of the "brave soldier" to pose problems for the memory account of personal continuity.

> Suppose a brave officer to have been flogged when a boy at school for robbing an orchard, to have taken a standard from the enemy in his first campaign, and to have been made a general in advanced life; suppose, also, which must be admitted to be possible, that, when he took the standard, he was conscious of his having been flogged at school, and that, when made a general, he was conscious of his taking the standard, but had absolutely lost the consciousness of his flogging.
>
> These things being supposed, it follows, from Mr. Locke's doctrine, that he who was flogged at school is the same person who took the standard, and that he who took the standard is the same person who was made a general. Whence it follows, if there be any truth in logic, that the general is the same person with him who was flogged at school. But the general's consciousness does not reach so far back as his flogging; therefore, according to Mr. Locke's doctrine, he is not the person who was flogged. Therefore the general is, and at the same time is not, the same person with him who was flogged at school.

Thomas Reid, "Of Memory," Essays on the Intellectual Powers of Man, 1785.

You can recall many events from your years in high school, right? Some of them you might wish to forget, but the fact is you do remember them. So—by the common memory standard—the college student is identical with the high school person who also had those (more immediate) memories. That's fine, right? You have certainly undergone some changes since high school, but you are still the same individual. But imagine yourself 50 years from now, pleasantly reminiscing about your happy college days. That older person still has many of the same memories that you now have. But that older person has gotten a bit hazy about high school, and really can't remember much at all that happened prior to going to college. But now we've got a problem. The older person is identical with you as a college student; and the college student is identical with the high school person; but—by the memory standard—the older person is *not* identical with the high school person. But that's crazy. After all, if A (the high school person) is identical with B (the college person), and B is identical with C (the older person), then A *must* be identical with C. But according to the memory standard of identity, that is not the case. So if you want to hang onto the memory standard of identity, you will have to give up the basic *law of identity* (you would have to give up the claim that if X is identical with Y and Y is identical with Z, then X is also identical with Z). And most people think that is too high a price to pay for the memory account of personal identity.

Here's another problem for the memory account of personal identity. Our brains are divided into two hemispheres, and although each hemisphere tends to take on rather specialized tasks, it is possible for tasks formerly done by one section of the brain to be learned by other healthy sections (for example, in the case of those who have suffered strokes or localized brain injuries). If one hemisphere of your brain were severely damaged but the other hemisphere managed to soldier along effectively, taking over the essential activities formerly performed by the other hemisphere and retaining at least the bulk of your memories and beliefs, then it seems plausible to conclude that you are the same continuing individual. But suppose instead that one hemisphere of your brain were transplanted into one body, and the other hemisphere into another body, and that *both* hemispheres managed to function effectively, retaining most of your memories and beliefs. There would now be two of you; but those two would quickly diverge, having new experiences and collecting new memories and beliefs. If *both* of these two individuals—who are now quite different—claim to be identical to the earlier person who had both brain hemispheres, then we would be back to the same problem: Two very different individuals cannot both be identical with a single individual.

Science Fiction and Personal Identity Problems

Some of the most interesting quandaries for personal identity have involved full leaps into science fiction scenarios—which may be useful for probing carefully into our ideas about what *really* counts as personal identity. Suppose that we have devised a special scanning device that can scan you molecule by molecule, record the structure and location of every molecule in your body (including of course in your brain and nervous system), and then create an exact duplicate of you. We have tested this process extensively, and it works flawlessly. Evangeline has a scan done, and on the way home she is killed in a terrible auto accident. Using the scanning record, she is re-created, and she is certain that she is the same person—the same Evangeline—who recently stepped into the scanner; and all her friends agree. Eventually this technology is used for more extensive purposes: you want to go to Australia, but you don't want to endure a long flight. We scan you, transmit the data in electronic form to Australia, and you are "reconstituted" in Australia; as you experience it, you step into the scanner in Chicago, and seconds later you step out of a scanner in Sydney. (Of course the "original" in Chicago is instantaneously and painlessly destroyed; but you survive, and enjoy the sights of Sydney.) And once we have the technology in place, the same process will take you swiftly, painlessly, and safely for a holiday on one of the moons of Jupiter. So long as you are the *functional equivalent* of the individual who stepped into the scanner in Chicago, it seems easy enough to conclude that this individual in Sydney, or holidaying near Jupiter, is still you.

But suppose one day you step into the scanner, and the operator punches the wrong button. You were planning to go to Sydney today, Paris next month, Mumbai the month after that, and Moscow a couple of months later. But the operator gets confused, and sends your data to all four locations simultaneously (sort of like an e-mail that is sent to several recipients). Now you are in Sydney, but you are also in Paris, Mumbai, and Moscow. The four of you are momentarily identical; but you have very different experiences in these four locations (for example, suppose that all four of you fall deeply in love, but obviously with very different people—one falls in love with a student in Sydney, the second with a jazz pianist in Paris, the third with an artist in Moscow, the fourth with a merchant in Mumbai). Now the four of you have had very different experiences, and you become distinctly different people. And yet, all four claim to be identical with that person who stepped into the scanner in Chicago. Suppose all four of you decide to live permanently in your new locations. Ten years later, having had dramatically different lives during those 10 years, you are distinctly different persons. The "you" in Mumbai is very different from the "you" in Paris; and so you cannot *both* be identical with the person who once lived in Chicago, since you are not identical with each other. So psychological continuity—even continuity of memory—will not be enough to guarantee continuity of personal identity.

It gets worse. Here you are, living happily in Sydney, thinking back to when *you* lived in Chicago. So far as you know, there is one unique individual—you—who is the same person who once lived in Chicago. But the persons in Mumbai, Paris, and Moscow are thinking the same thing! So unknown to you—because these "duplicates" exist, without your knowledge—you are *not* the same person as the person who once lived in Chicago.

So maybe we can't settle personal identity questions merely by looking internally at our memories and continuing consciousness; instead, we can't be sure of personal identity until we know more about the world outside of us: Specifically, are there any *duplicates* walking around. But this pushes us into all manner of strange results. If a duplicate was made of me a few years ago, then at that time I lost my personal identity—without knowing or even suspecting it. And suppose that now, several years later, my duplicate is run over by a train: Do I suddenly *regain* my lost personal identity (even if I never suspected it was lost)?

BEYOND PERSONAL IDENTITY

This sort of puzzling case has led some contemporary philosophers to conclude that perhaps personal identity is not really as important as we traditionally thought. After all, even if I were not sure that my personal identity has been maintained (since I suspect that someone has secretly duplicated me), I would still have some very profound concerns about the future. For example, I—whether I am confident of my personal identity or *not*—am still very much and quite reasonably concerned that I not fall into the hands of some nefarious band that wishes to torture me. I am reasonably confident that I am the same person who studied philosophy at the University of North Carolina at Chapel Hill—I don't think it likely that I've been duplicated over the intervening years, and I have clear memories of my years in Chapel Hill; but if I am certain that five exact duplicates of me will be made tomorrow (complete with all my memories and beliefs) —then I am not at all sure that I will have retained my personal identity after tomorrow. But suppose that I somehow know that four out of the resulting six of "us" (myself and my five duplicates) will be captured by a terrible gang that will torture us; but by taking certain precautions today, I can prevent that from happening. Then, whether I—with my present personal identity—continue or not, I shall certainly be concerned to prevent four of those six individuals from being captured. Whether any one of them is *me*, all four will have a *continuity of experience* with me. So perhaps *that* is what I am really concerned about: it's not *personal identity* that concerns me, but *continuity* of experience.

STRAINS ON OUR ORDINARY CONCEPT OF PERSONAL IDENTITY

If we try to determine what our standard sense of "personal identity" would tell us about such cases, we will probably fail. Our standard concept of personal identity was designed to give us good service in ordinary cases, and in cases that stretch just a bit outside the ordinary. You are somewhat taller than you were when you were a freshman in high school, you know more than you knew then, and perhaps some of your beliefs have changed; but you are still the *same person* that you were in high school. When you go back home, and you happen to run into your freshman English teacher and your soccer coach, they may mention that you are taller; they may even speak of how proud they are of you ("we knew you would do well in college, from the excellent work you did in high school"); they might even exclaim—if you have grown much taller, or you've done a lot of weight lifting—"Why, I would hardly have recognized you." But there's no question that they are still talking about the same *you* who was once a freshman in high school. Even in cases where there might be some questions about personal identity, we can usually muddle along: When my grandfather's memory is entirely gone, and he cannot recognize any member of the family or even recall his own name, he is still—in some sense—the same individual who read stories to me when I was a child, and took me for walks in the woods; and I still go to visit *him*, rather than some other individual. But our conceptual system did not evolve to deal with cases of brain transplants and personal duplicating machines, and what we should say about personal identity in such cases cannot be settled by appeal to "our traditional meaning" of personal identity.

In fact, it's not clear that we have an adequate account of personal identity even for ordinary use; at least, that's the view of David Hume. Hume believed that our sense of personal identity develops from the easy transition among our ideas; but that transition is a matter of degree, not a clear marker of identity. Therefore, Hume maintained, "we have no just standard by which we can decide any dispute concerning the time when they [our bundle of ideas] acquire or lose a title to the name of identity." We can *decide* to define a standard for what counts as identity; but we are then (Hume would say) stipulating a definition of identity, not *identifying* an actual identity.

IDENTITY AND THE ONE

If you agree with Spinoza (or the Taoists or at least some versions of Buddhism) that the world is *One*, then you believe that all distinct individuals are an *illusion*. Some who suppose themselves to be Taoists claim to believe in individual reincarnation (in one of your past lives you were Napoleon, and before that you were the captain of a whaling ship that was lost in a storm off the New England coast, and before that you were a nun in an Italian convent, and so on). But, of course, individual reincarnation makes no sense on a genuine Taoist account, because all personal identity is submerged into the One. On that view, the question of personal identity is a question of why people mistakenly suppose that they have separate individual identities; and the notion of individual people being mistaken is also wrong. The question is more like: Why are there areas of confusion in the One Whole?

> Really now, just where do you leave off and the rest of the universe begin? Or where does the rest of the universe leave off and you begin? Once you can see the so-called "you" and the so-called "nature" as a continuous whole, then you can never again be bothered by such questions as whether it is you who are controlling nature or nature who is controlling you. *Raymond M. Smullyan,* "Is God a Taoist?"

THE NARRATIVE ACCOUNT OF PERSONAL IDENTITY

One way of trying to make sense of personal identity takes us away from brain transplants and imaginative scientific scenarios, and turns instead to our capacities as *story tellers*, as individuals who develop *narratives*—including narratives about ourselves and who we are. From this perspective on personal identity, our personal identity is not set by a specific body (which changes), or a set of memories (which also change). Rather, the only way to secure a genuine personal identity is to pull the strands of your life together in a personal narrative that unifies the changes as well as the continuities into a coherent narrative whole. The narrative can have some twists and turns; for example, one might have undergone a major conversion experience, or one's life might be forever altered by meeting a stranger on "some enchanted evening," or by enduring terrible trials (such as being caught up in a war). Your narrative need not be an action thriller; a relatively quiet life might have great integrity of purpose and value. We aren't just *given* a personal identity; rather, we actively *make* it by fitting the disparate parts into a purposive and cohesive narrative. The events of our life don't gain significance until we invest them with that significance: until we fit them into a pattern of purposive behavior. As the psychologist Jerome Bruner insists: "Self is a conceptual structure, a system for categorizing selected memories, for engendering expectations, for judging fitness, and so forth. The crucial cognitive activities involved in Self-construction seem much more like 'thinking' than 'memory'" (Jerome Bruner, "The 'Remembered' Self," 1994). The key point for those who favor the *narrative* account of personal identity is that we can't just *find* or discover or remember our personal identity, as a given object; rather, we must *make* our personal identity, by weaving the variety of our experiences into narrative coherence. And that narrative has great significance for us. Some even claim that a coherent narrative is essential in order for our lives to have meaning for us.

> Let me briefly note another property of Self as we encounter it in ourselves and others. It is "storied," or narrative, in structure. When you ask people what they are really like, they tell a great many stories involving the usual elements of narrative . . . : there is an *agent* engaged in *action* deploying certain *instruments* for achieving a *goal* in a particular *scene*, and somehow things have gone awry between these elements to produce *trouble*. The stories they tell, moreover, are genre-like: One encounters the hero-tale, . . . the tale of the victim, the love story, and so on. If one ever doubted Oscar Wilde's claim that life imitates art, reading biographies lessens the doubt. *Jerome Bruner, "The 'Remembered' Self," 1994.*

Narrative Truth

A serious question for advocates of narrative identity is the question of how *accurate* the narrative must be. We know that people can have vivid "memories" that are totally wrong: The tragic cases of "recovered memory" in which people "remembered" being sexually abused by persons practicing satanic rituals is a clear example. Can one construct a narrative out of a history that never happened? If I regard my years spent living under mushrooms with the woodland elves as the pivotal and defining years of my life, can that form a coherent narrative that will constitute my identity? Even if I take great delight in "remembering" my happy elf days, it's unlikely that such a narrative will be very effective, since it will constantly run up against counter evidence. But suppose that I am a very mediocre athlete who fantasized of athletic stardom, and over the years my fantasies have blurred into my genuine memories; now one of my most significant "memories" is of hitting three home runs as a high school baseball star to beat our crosstown rival. If I'm now living in Boston, all my high school friends are back in Iowa and I'll never see them again, and all my friends in Boston now believe that I was a high school baseball star, then this false memory—that I now believe really happened—may never be proved wrong. Can such a false belief form a core element of my narrative identity?

Psychologists who study memory are well aware of how inaccurate even our most graphic memories can be. However, they may regard inaccurate memories as sometimes having positive effects. Psychologists Michael Ross and Roger Buehler conclude their essay on "Creative Remembering" with this paragraph:

> In closing, we should emphasize that it is perfectly healthy and normal for people to create pasts that satisfy their current needs. Such creativity probably serves us well most of the time. . . . The past is a resource that people can use and adapt for current purposes. People can get

into trouble, however, when they underestimate the fallibility of their own memories. Perhaps the lesson of psychological research on memory is not that people should be less creative, but that they should be aware of the degree to which they author their own histories.

Ulric Neisser and Robyn Fivush, The Remembering Self, *1994, p. 231.*

The points made by Ross and Buehler are insightful, but they raise a basic question for narrative accounts of personal identity: If our life narratives are systematically inaccurate and distorted, can they serve effectively as grounds for marking our personal identity? As Daniel Dennett notes, "We are all, at times, confabulators, telling and retelling ourselves the story of our own lives, with scant attention to the question of truth" (Dennett, 1992).

Perhaps the accuracy doesn't matter quite as much as we might suppose; or perhaps there are other factors which are even more important than narrative accuracy. If we think of the unity of the self as analogous to the unity of a country, then the accuracy of the narrative may be much less important than the basic existence of the narrative itself, which draws disparate elements into one more or less coherent story. Think of the narrative that forms U.S. history, and which helps to define the United States as a country. (The people who launched the American Revolution are long gone, the country has changed its boundaries many times, and the U.S. Constitution has undergone numerous changes; an ongoing narrative may be the best candidate for defining the enduring country). A fundamental element of that narrative is that the United States was founded as a democracy, though that is not even remotely true. (Whatever else a democracy may be, it requires that all citizens have an equal or at least a significant voice in deciding how the country is governed; but after the United States won independence, only white males who were significant property holders were eligible to vote, and that was less than a third of the population. Women could not vote until 1920, and in many parts of the United States blacks were deprived of their right to vote until late in the twentieth century.) Another important element of the U.S. narrative is our support for democratic movements of oppressed people around the world; but in fact, our history—especially in Latin America and Mexico—has been a history of supporting brutal dictatorships ("Papa Doc" Duvalier in Haiti; Somoza in Nicaragua; Manuel Cabrera, General Jorge Ubico, Romeo Lucas Garcia, and Efrain Montt in Guatemala; General Carlos Romero and the PCN of El Salvador) against people's revolutionary movements. So like most countries, the U.S. narrative contains glaring falsehoods. Nonetheless, this narrative—perhaps including ideals we typically fail to live up to—helps to give a unifying identity to the country. In like manner, perhaps our personal narratives, including our faulty and self-serving "memories," can give some coherent form and unity to our sense of personal identity.

Our Modular Brain

That source of unity becomes especially important if our basic psychological and neuropsychological structure is made up of distinct *bundles* of psychological operations, which are neither necessarily well-coordinated nor even in effective *communication* with one another. As Daniel Dennett states (drawing on the research of Michael Gazzaniga and Julian Jaynes):

> . . . the normal mind is *not* beautifully unified, but rather a problematically yoked-together bundle of partly autonomous systems. All parts of the mind are not equally accessible to each other at all times. These modules or systems sometimes have internal communication problems which they solve by various ingenious and devious routes. . . . Sometimes talking and listening to yourself can have wonderful effects, not otherwise obtainable. All that is needed to make sense of this idea is the hypothesis that the modules of the mind have different capacities and ways of doing things, and are not perfectly interaccessible. Under such circumstances it could be true that the way to get yourself to figure out a problem is to tickle

your ear with it, to get that part of your brain which is best stimulated by *hearing* a question to work on the problem.

Daniel Dennett, "The Self as a Center of Gravity," in Self and Consciousness: Multiple Perspectives, *edited by F. Kessel, P. Cole, and D. Johnson (Hillsdale, NJ: Erlbaum, 1992).*

On this view, there is no given controller, no specific part that guides or directs the whole system; instead, specialized subsystems work together without any overall controller, though there often *appears* to be a central controller.

> [I]t is possible to regard instantaneous consciousness as a multiplicity, rather than a unity, and yet claim that it is "unified." The sense in which consciousness is "unified" is not a matter of *oneness*, but a matter of representational coherence. Such coherence . . . goes some way towards explaining how a self emerges from the multiple strands of representational activity in the brain. . . . It is reasonable to conjecture that schizophrenia is a disease which impairs the capacity of consciousness-making mechanisms to produce a coherent set of experiences. Instead, possibly as a result of desynchronization, these mechanisms operate in an autonomous fashion, producing experiences whose contents are disconnected and discontinuous with one another. This gives rise to the familiar symptoms of schizophrenia. In the case of delusions of thought insertion, for example, it is precisely because one part of the brain generates a thought that is representationally discontinuous with mental contents being produced elsewhere that the patient judges it to be alien, and hence disowns it. What we see here is a partial disintegration of the self, but not in the sense of the self failing to be a single thing—on the multitrack view it was never that in the first place—rather, in the sense that the many self-directed representations produced by the brain no longer hang together as a coherent system. *Gerard O'Brien and Jonathan Opie,* "The Multiplicity of Consciousness and the Emergence of the Self," *in Tilo Kircher and Anthony David, eds.,* The Self in Neuroscience and Psychiatry *(Cambridge: Cambridge University Press, 2003).*

When confronted with the question of who is the overall *supervisor*, Nicholas Humphrey and Daniel Dennett give this reply:

> The answer that is emerging from both biology and Artificial Intelligence is that complex systems can in fact function in what seems to be a thoroughly "purposeful and integrated" way simply by having *lots of subsystems doing their own thing* without any central supervision. Indeed, most systems on earth that appear to have central controllers (and are usefully described as having them) do not. The behavior of a termite colony provides a wonderful example of it. The colony as a whole builds elaborate mounds, gets to know its territory, organizes foraging expeditions, sends out raiding parties against other colonies, and so on. The group cohesion and coordination is so remarkable that hardheaded observers have been led to postulate the existence of a colony's "group soul". . . . Yet, in fact, all this group wisdom results from nothing other than myriads of individual termites, specialized in different castes, going about their individual business—influenced by each other, but quite uninfluenced by any master-plan.

Humphrey and Dennett, "Speaking for Our Selves," originally in Raritan: A Quarterly Review, *volume 9, number 1, Summer 1989.*

How are these various modules unified into a whole, if indeed they are? How do the modules of our brain at least *appear* to form a unified self? Perhaps the narrative model is the most promising way of dealing with the disunity. A false narrative is still a narrative, and it can be a coherent and unified narrative, its false elements notwithstanding. Such a narrative—not quite accurate, and not even perfectly coherent—may be the best we can do in establishing a unity, a "unified self," out of these diverse modules. As Dennett writes:

> . . . We are all virtuoso novelists, who find ourselves engaged in all sorts of behavior, more or less unified, but sometimes disunified, and we always put the best "faces" on it we can. We try to make all of our material cohere into a single good story. And that story is our autobiography.
>
> *Dennett, 1992.*

The traditional account of self-identity—at least since the time of John Locke—is based on some unifying element of self-consciousness (memory is a favorite candidate). But suppose that there is no underlying unity of self-consciousness and our consciousness is instead made up of a number of distinct psychological modules: modules that are not always in communication with one another. In that case, a unified identity will have to be constructed, rather than discovered; and narrative construction is one possible construction method.

> The narrative approach to self recognizes the importance of the appropriative activity of consciousness in the constitution of the self, but it goes further. It also recognizes that the appropriative process typically involves a story-line, where the self is the chief character in the drama or plot of a life, that other people have secondary roles to play, and that the physical and social world is the stage upon which the leading character—the self—plays his part. What is essential to the formation of such a self is to have a stable identity through time, which one constitutes by acting within the play in which one conceives oneself to be engaged.
>
> *John Barresi, "On Becoming a Person,"*
> Philosophical Psychology, *volume 12: 79–98.*

Narrative Accountability

The hypothesis of radically divided "bundles" or modules is one prompt for the narrative account of personal identity, but it is not the only one. Alasdair MacIntyre promotes a narrative account of personal identity as grounds for the *meaning* of life: "When someone complains—as do some of those who attempt or commit suicide—that his or her life is meaningless, he or she is often and perhaps characteristically complaining that the narrative of their life has become unintelligible to them, that it lacks any point, any movement towards a climax or a *telos*" (*After Virtue*, p. 203). But for MacIntyre, perhaps even more important is that the narrative account of life is essential for *accountability*: "To be the subject of a narrative that runs from one's birth to one's death is . . . to be accountable for the actions and experiences which compose a narratable life" (*After Virtue*, p. 203). Thus for MacIntyre, the narrative model is essential as an element of having moral responsibility for one's life and acts.

> All the world's a stage,
> And all the men and women merely players: They have their exits and their entrances;
> And one man in his time plays many parts. . . .
>
> *William Shakespeare,* As You Like It

You might have doubts about whether accountability and moral responsibility are well supported by the narrative model. After all, it may be possible to give a narrative account that emphasizes one's general helplessness in the face of disaster—possibly with a nod toward the stoicism with which one has borne such disasters. A fatalist might well think that his or her life is under the control of capricious fate—many ancient Greeks held this view—while still believing that one's life has a coherent narrative.

Ronald Dworkin, a well-known contemporary legal philosopher, makes use of the narrative model in explaining why some people might prefer to die even if they are suffering no pain and to make clear why some would not want to spend a long period at the end of their lives in a state of unconsciousness, tethered to a machine, even if there is no question of their suffering. He writes:

> In almost every case, someone who is permanently unconscious or incompetent was not born into that condition: the tragedy lies at the end of a life that someone has led in earnest. When we ask what would be best for him, we are not judging only his future and ignoring his past. We worry about the effect of his life's last stage on the character of his life as a whole, as we might worry about the effect of a play's last scene or a poem's last stanza on the entire creative work. . . .
>
> When patients remain conscious, their sense of integrity and of the coherence of their lives crucially affects their judgment about whether it is in their best interests to continue to live. Athletes, or others whose physical activity is at the center of their self-conception, are more likely to find a paraplegic's life intolerable. When Nancy B., the Canadian woman who won the right to have her respirator turned off, said that all she had in her life was television, she was not saying that watching television was painful, but that a wholly passive life, which watching television had come to symbolize, was worse than none. For such people, a life without the power of motion is unacceptable, not for reasons explicable in experiential terms, but because it is stunningly inadequate to the conception of self around which their own lives have so far been constructed. Adding decades of immobility to a life formerly organized around action will for them leave a narrative wreck, with no structure or sense, a life worse than one that ends when its activity ends.

Ronald Dworkin, Life's Dominion, *1993*

Consider Job, who becomes a puppet in a cosmic game played between God and Satan: a game in which Job has no control of the events or the outcome. Nonetheless, Job's life is one of the great narrative accounts of a human life; in this case, a human life tossed about by forces beyond Job's comprehension. A tragic narrative, as were many of the narratives described in ancient Greek drama, but no less a coherent narrative of a life.

So a narrative account may not involve quite the degree of autonomous control that some of its advocates—such as MacIntyre—suppose. But central to narrative accounts of personal identity is the view that personal identity is *not* a given, but is instead *constructed* out of elements that may not otherwise have any real unity. It is the *constructivist* model of personal identity that is emphasized by Jerome Bruner, a psychologist who regards narrative construction as essential for a sense of self:

> I begin by proposing boldly that, in effect, there is no such thing as an intuitively obvious and essential self to know, one that just sits there to be portrayed in words. Rather, we constantly construct and reconstruct a self to meet the needs of the situations we encounter, and do so with the guidance of our memories of the past and our hopes and fears for the future. Telling oneself about oneself is rather like making up a story about who and what we are, what has happened, and why we are doing what we are doing.
>
>   . . . .
>
> I have argued that it is through narrative that we create and recreate selfhood, that self is a product of our telling and not some essence to be delved for in the recesses of subjectivity. There is now evidence that without the capacity to make stories about ourselves, there would be no such thing as selfhood.

Jerome Bruner, "The Narrative Creation of Self," Making Stories: Law, Literature, Life *(Farrar, Straus and Giroux, 2002)*

Personal identity would seem to be the easiest of questions. After all, "who am I" is not a question that would seem to cause great problems. But like many philosophical questions, when we look more deeply and question carefully, the easy questions don't always have easy answers. That was a lesson taught by Socrates, and perhaps it is useful to be reminded of that lesson some 2500 years later.

READINGS

⇒ ESSAY CONCERNING HUMAN UNDERSTANDING ⇒
John Locke

John Locke (1632–1704) was a leader of the *empiricist* movement in modern philosophy and one of the greatest of the English philosophers. He emphasized the importance of experience and observation as the key to knowledge. He was also very influential in political philosophy, and his revisions of social contract theory had a large impact on political theory (including on the U.S. Constitution). On the question of *personal identity*, Locke's work was vitally important in framing the whole question for the Enlightenment period; and indeed, Locke posed the question of personal identity in a way which still influences the way we think about the issue. Even if you conclude that Locke's account of personal identity has some problems, you should still appreciate the rigor with which Locke sets up the issue. The following passage is from Book II of Locke's *Essay Concerning Human Understanding*.

Personal identity.—To find wherein personal identity consists, we must consider what *person* stands for; which, I think, is a thinking intelligent being, that has reason and reflection, and can consider itself as itself, the same thinking thing, in different times and places; which it does only by that consciousness which is inseparable from thinking, and as it seems to me essential to it; it being impossible for any one to perceive without perceiving that he does perceive. When we see, hear, smell, taste, feel, meditate, or will anything, we know that we do so. Thus it is always as to our present sensations and perceptions: and by this every one is to himself that which he calls *self*; it not being considered, in this case, whether the same self be continued in the same or diverse substances. For since consciousness always accompanies thinking and it is that that makes every one to be what he calls self, and thereby distinguishes himself from all other thinking things; in this alone consists personal identity, i.e., the sameness of a rational being: and as far as this consciousness can be extended backwards to any past action or thought, so far reaches the identity of that person; it is the same self now it was then; and it is by the same self with this present one that now reflects on it, that that action was done.

Consciousness makes personal identity.—But it is farther enquired, whether it be the same identical substance. This few would think they had reason to doubt of, if these perceptions, with their consciousness, always remained present in the mind, whereby the same thinking thing would be always consciously present, and, as would be thought, evidently the same to itself. But that which seems to make the difficulty is this, that this consciousness being interrupted always by forgetfulness, there being no moment of our lives wherein we have the whole train of all our past actions before our eyes in one view; but even the best memories losing the sight of one part whilst they are viewing another; and we sometimes, and that the greatest part of our lives, not reflecting on our past selves, being intent on our present thoughts, and in sound sleep having no thoughts at all, or at least, none with that consciousness which remarks our waking thoughts: I say, in all these cases, our consciousness being interrupted, and we losing the sight of our past selves, doubts are raised whether we are the same thinking thing, i.e., the same substance, or no. Which, however reasonable or unreasonable, concerns not *personal identity* at all: the question being what makes the same person, and not, whether it be the same identical substance which always thinks in the same person, which in this case matters not at all; different substances, by the same consciousness (where they do partake in it), being united into one person, as well as different bodies by the same life are united into one animal, whose identity is preserved, in that change of substances, by the unity of one continued life. For it being the same consciousness that makes a man be himself to himself, personal identity depends on that only, whether it be annexed only to one individual substance, or can be continued in a succession of several substances. For as far as any intelligent being can repeat the idea of any past action with the same consciousness it had of it at first, and with the same consciousness it has of any present action; so far it is the same personal self. For it is by the consciousness it has of its present thoughts and actions that it is *self to itself* now, and so will be the same self, as far as the same consciousness can extend to actions past or to come; and would be by distance of time, or change of substance, no more two persons, than a man be two men by wearing other clothes to-day than he did yesterday, with a long or short sleep between: the same consciousness uniting those distant actions into the same persons, whatever substances contributed to their production.

Personal identity in change of substances.—That this is so, we have some kind of evidence in our very bodies, all whose particles, whilst vitally united to this same thinking conscious self, so that we feel when they are touched, and are affected by and conscious of good or harm that happens to them, are a part of ourselves, i.e., of our thinking conscious self. Thus the limbs of his body are to every one a part of himself: he sympathizes and is concerned for them. Cut off a hand and thereby separate it from that consciousness we had of its heat, cold, and other affections, and it is then no longer a part of that which is himself, any more than the remotest part of matter. Thus we see the substance, whereof personal self consisted at one time, may be varied at another, without the change of personal identity; there being no question about the same person, though the limbs which but now were a part of it, be cut off.

Whether in the change of thinking substances.—But the question is, whether, if the same substance which thinks be changed, it can be the same person, or remaining the same, it can be different persons. As to the first part of the question, whether, if the same thinking substance (supposing immaterial substances only to think) be changed, it can be the same person, I answer, That cannot be resolved but by those who

know what kind of substances they are that do think; and whether the consciousness of past actions can be transferred from one thinking substance to another. I grant, were the same consciousness the same individual action, it could not; but it being but a present representation of a past action, why it may not be possible that that may be represented to the mind to have been, which really never was, will remain to be shown. And therefore, how far the consciousness of past actions is annexed to any individual agent, so that another cannot possibly have it, will be hard for us to determine, till we know what kind of action it is, that cannot be done without a reflex act of perception accompanying it, and how performed by thinking substances, who cannot think without being conscious of it. But that which we call the same consciousness, not being the same individual act, why one intellectual substance may not have represented to it as done by itself what it never did, and was perhaps done by some other agent; why, I say, such a representation may not possibly be without reality of matter of fact, as well as several representations in dreams are, which yet whilst dreaming we take for true, will be difficult to conclude from the nature of things. And that it never is so, will by us, till we have clearer views of the nature of thinking substances, be best resolved into the goodness of God, who, as far as the happiness or misery of any of his sensible creatures is concerned in it, will not by a fatal error of theirs transfer from one to another that consciousness which draws reward or punishment with it. How far this may be an argument against those who would place thinking in a system of fleeting animal spirits, I leave to be considered. But yet, to return to the question before us, it must be allowed that if the same consciousness (which, as has been shown, is quite a different thing from the same numerical figure or motion in body) can be transferred from one thinking substance to another, it will be possible that two thinking substances may make but one person. For the same consciousness being preserved, whether in the same or different substances, the personal identity is preserved.

As to the second part of the question, whether the same immaterial substance remaining, there may be two distinct persons; which question seems to me to be built on this, whether the same immaterial being, being conscious of the actions of its past duration, may be wholly stripped of all the consciousness of its past existence, and lose it beyond the power of ever retrieving again: and so, as it were, beginning a new account from a new period, have a consciousness that cannot reach beyond this new state. All those who hold pre-existence are evidently of this mind, since they allow the soul to have no remaining consciousness of what it did in that pre-existent state, either wholly separate from body, or informing any other body. So that personal identity reaching no farther than consciousness reaches, a pre-existent spirit not having continued so many ages in a state of silence, must needs make different persons. Suppose a Christian Platonist or Pythagorean should, upon God's having ended all his works of creation the seventh day, think his soul hath existed ever since, and should imagine it has revolved in several human bodies; as I once met with one who was persuaded his had been the soul of Socrates (how reasonably I will not dispute: this I know, that in the post he filled, which was no inconsiderable one, he passed for a very rational man; and the press has shown that he wanted not parts or learning)—would any one say that he, being not conscious of any of Socrates' actions or thoughts, could be the same person with Socrates? Let any one reflect upon himself, and conclude, that he has in himself an immaterial spirit, which is that which thinks in him, and, in the constant change of his body, keeps him the same, and is that which he calls himself: let him also suppose it to be the same soul that was in Nestor or Thersites, at the siege of Troy (for souls being, as far as we know anything of them, in their nature indifferent to any parcel of matter, the supposition has no apparent absurdity in it), but he now having no consciousness of any of the actions either of Nestor or Thersites, does or can he conceive himself the same person with either of them? Can he be concerned in either of their actions, attribute them to himself, or think them his own, more than the actions of any other man that ever existed? So that this consciousness not reaching to any of the actions of either of those men, he is no more one *self* with either of them, than if the soul or immaterial spirit that now informs him had been created and began to exist when it began to inform his present body, though it were never so true that the same spirit that informed Nestor's or Thersites' body were numerically the same that now informs his. For this would no more make him the same person with Nestor, than if some of the particles of matter that were once a part of Nestor were now a part of this man; the same immaterial substance, without the same consciousness, no more making the same person by being united to any body, than the same particle of matter, without consciousness, united to any body,

makes the same person. But let him once find himself conscious of any of the actions of Nestor, he then finds himself the same person with Nestor.

And thus we may be able, without any difficulty, to conceive the same person at the resurrection, though in a body not exactly in make or parts the same which he had here, the same consciousness going along with the soul that inhabits it. But yet the soul alone, in the change of bodies, would scarce to any one but to him that makes the soul the man, be enough to make the same man. For should the soul of a prince, carrying with it the consciousness of the prince's past life, enter and inform the body of a cobbler, as soon as deserted by his own soul, every one sees he would be the same person with the prince, accountable only for the prince's actions: but who would say it was the same man? The body too goes to the making of the man, and would, I guess, to everybody determine the man in this case, wherein the soul, with all its princely thoughts about it, would not make another man; but he would be the same cobbler to every one besides himself. I know that, in the ordinary way of speaking, the same person, and the same man, stand for one and the same thing. And indeed every one will always have a liberty to speak as he pleases, and to apply what articulate sounds to what ideas he thinks fit, and change them as often as he pleases. But yet, when we will enquire what makes the same *spirit*, *man*, or *person*, we must fix the ideas of spirit, man, or person, in our minds; and having resolved with ourselves what we mean by them, it will not be hard to determine in either of them, or the like, when it is the same, and when not.

Consciousness makes the same person.—But though the same immaterial substance or soul does not alone, wherever it be, and in whatsoever state, make the same man; yet it is plain, consciousness, as far as ever it can be extended, should it be to ages past, unites existences and actions, very remote in time, into the same person, as well as it does the existence and actions of the immediately preceding moment: so that whatever has the consciousness of present and past actions is the same person to whom they both belong. Had I the same consciousness that I saw the ark and Noah's flood, as that I saw an overflowing of the Thames last winter, or as that I write now, I could no more doubt that I that write this now, that saw the Thames overflowed last winter, and that viewed the flood at the general deluge, was the same *self*, place that self in what substance you please, than that I that write this am the same *myself* now whilst I write (whether I consist of all the same substance, material or immaterial, or no) that I was yesterday. For as to this point of being the same self, it matters not whether this present self be made up of the same or other substances, I being as much concerned and as justly accountable for any action was done a thousand years since, appropriated to me now by this self-consciousness, as I am for what I did the last moment.

Self depends on consciousness.—Self is that conscious thinking thing (whatever substance made up of, whether spiritual or material, simple or compounded, it matters not) which is sensible, or conscious of pleasure and pain, capable of happiness or misery, and so is concerned for itself, as far as that consciousness extends. Thus every one finds, that whilst comprehended under that consciousness, the little finger is as much a part of itself as what is most so. Upon separation of this little finger, should this consciousness go along with the little finger, and leave the rest of the body, it is evident the little finger would be the person, the same person; and self then would have nothing to do with the rest of the body. As in this case it is the consciousness that goes along with the substance, when one part is separate from another, which makes the same person, and constitutes this inseparable self: so it is in reference to substances remote in time. That with which the consciousness of this present thinking thing can join itself makes the same person, and is one self with it, and with nothing else; and so attributes to itself and owns all the actions of that thing as its own, as far as that consciousness reaches, and no farther; as every one who reflects will perceive.

Object of reward and punishment.—In this personal identity is founded all the right and justice of reward and punishment, happiness and misery being that for which every one is concerned for himself, not mattering what becomes of any substance not joined to or affected with that consciousness. For as is evident in the instance I gave but now, if the consciousness went along with the little finger when it was cut off, that would be the same self which was concerned for the whole body yesterday, as making a part of itself, whose actions then it cannot but admit as its own now. Though if the same body should still live, and immediately from the separation of the little finger have its own peculiar consciousness, whereof the little finger knew nothing, it would not at all be concerned for it, as a part of itself, or could own any of its actions, or have any of them imputed to him.

This may show us wherein personal identity consists, not in the identity of substance, but, as I have said, in the identity of consciousness, wherein if Socrates and the present mayor of Queenborough

agree, they are the same person. If the same Socrates waking and sleeping do not partake of the same consciousness, Socrates waking and sleeping is not the same person; and to punish Socrates waking for what sleeping Socrates thought, and waking Socrates was never conscious of, would be no more of right than to punish one twin for what his brother-twin did, whereof he knew nothing, because their outsides were so like that they could not be distinguished.

But yet possibly it will still be objected, Suppose I wholly lose the memory of some parts of my life, beyond the possibility of retrieving them, so that perhaps I shall never be conscious of them again; yet am I not the same person that did those actions, had those thoughts, that I was once conscious of, though I have now forgot them? To which I answer, That we must here take notice what the word *I* is applied to; which in this case, is the man only. And the same man being presumed to be the same person, *I* is easily here supposed to stand also for the same person. But if it be possible for the same man to have distinct incommunicable consciousness at different times, it is past doubt the same man would at different times make different persons; which, we see, is the sense of mankind in the solemnest declaration of their opinions, human laws not punishing the mad man for the sober man's actions, nor the sober man for what the mad man did, thereby making them two persons; which is somewhat explained by our way of speaking in English, when we say, such an one is 'not himself', or is 'beside himself,' in which phrases it is insinuated as if those who now or, at least, first used them, thought that self was changed, the selfsame person was no longer in that man.

Consciousness alone makes self.—Nothing but consciousness can unite remote existences into the same person; the identity of substance will not do it. For whatever substance there is, however framed, without consciousness there is no person: and a carcase may be a person, as well as any sort of substance be so without consciousness.

Could we suppose two distinct incommunicable consciousnesses acting the same body, the one constantly by day, the other by night; and, on the other side, the same consciousness acting by intervals two distinct bodies: I ask, in the first case, whether the day and the night man would not be two as distinct persons as Socrates and Plato; and whether, in the second case, there would not be one person in two distinct bodies, as much as one man is the same in two distinct clothings. Nor is it at all material to say, that this same and this distinct consciousness, in the cases above mentioned, is owing to the same and distinct immaterial substances, bringing it with them to those bodies. For granting that the thinking substance in man must be necessarily supposed immaterial, it is evident that immaterial thinking thing may sometimes part with its past consciousness, and be restored to it again, as appears in the forgetfulness men often have of their past actions; and the mind many times recovers the memory of a past consciousness which it had lost for twenty years together. Make these intervals of memory and forgetfulness to take their turns regularly by day and night, and you have two persons with the same immaterial spirit, as much as in the former instance two persons with the same body. So that self is not determined by identity or diversity of substance, which it cannot be sure of, but only by identity of consciousness.

Indeed it may conceive the substance whereof it is now made up to have existed formerly, united in the same conscious being: but, consciousness removed, that substance is no more itself, or makes no more a part of it, than any other substance; as is evident in the instance we have already given of a limb cut off, of whose heat or cold or other affections having no longer any consciousness, it is no more of a man's self than any other matter of the universe. In like manner it will be in reference to any immaterial substance, which is void of that consciousness whereby I am myself to myself: if there be any part of its existence which I cannot upon recollection join with that present consciousness whereby I am now myself, it is in that part of its existence no more *myself* than any other immaterial being. For whatsoever any substance has thought or done, which I cannot recollect, and by my consciousness make my own thought and action, it will no more belong to me, whether a part of me thought or did it, than if it had been thought or done by any other immaterial being anywhere existing.

I agree, the more probable opinion is, that this consciousness is annexed to, and the affection of, one individual immaterial substance.

But let men, according to their diverse hypotheses, resolve of that as they please. This every intelligent being, sensible of happiness or misery, must grant—that there is something that is *himself* that he is concerned for, and would have happy; that this self has existed in a continued duration more than one instant, and therefore it is possible may exist, as it has done, months and years to come, without any certain bounds to be set to its duration; and may be the same self, by the same consciousness, continued on for the future. And thus, by this consciousness, he finds himself to be the same self which did such or such an action some years since, by which he comes to be happy or miserable now. In all which account of self, the same numerical substance is not considered as making the same self: but the same continued consciousness, in which several substances may have been united, and again separated from it, which, whilst they continued in a vital union with that wherein this consciousness then resided, made a part of that same self. Thus any part of our bodies vitally united to that which is conscious in us, makes a part of ourselves; but upon separation from the vital union by which that consciousness is communicated, that which a moment since was part of ourselves, is now no more so than a part of another man's self is a part of me; and it is not impossible, but in a little time may become a real part of another person. And so we have the same numerical substance become a part of two different persons; and the same person preserved under the change of various substances. Could we suppose any spirit wholly stripped of all its memory or consciousness of past actions, as we find our minds always are of a great part of ours, and sometimes of them all; the union or separation of such a spiritual substance would make no variation of personal identity, any more than that of any particle of matter does. Any substance vitally united to the present thinking being is a part of that very same self which now is: anything united to it by a consciousness of former actions makes also a part of the same self, which is the same both then and now.

Person, a forensic term.—*Person*, as I take it, is the name for this self. Wherever a man finds what he calls *himself*, there, I think, another may say is the same person. It is a forensic term appropriating actions and their merit; and so belongs only to intelligent agents capable of a law, and happiness and misery. This personality extends itself beyond present existence to what is past, only by consciousness; whereby it becomes concerned and accountable, owns and imputes to itself past actions, just upon the same ground and for the same reason that it does the present. All which is founded in a concern for happiness, the unavoidable concomitant of consciousness; that which is conscious of pleasure and pain desiring that that self that is conscious should be happy. And therefore whatever past actions it cannot reconcile or appropriate to that present self by consciousness, it can be no more concerned in, than if they had never been done: and to receive pleasure or pain, i.e., reward or punishment, on the account of any such action, is all one as to be made happy or miserable in its first being without any demerit at all. And therefore, conformable to this, the apostle tells us, that at the great day, when every one shall 'receive according to his doings, the secrets of all hearts shall be laid open'. The sentence shall be justified by the consciousness all persons shall have that they *themselves*, in what bodies soever they appear, or what substances soever that consciousness adheres to, are the *same* that committed those actions, and deserve that punishment for them.

⇒ A Treatise of Human Nature ⇒
David Hume

David Hume (1711–1776) wrote profoundly influential work in almost every area of philosophy, and his impact on the empiricist branch of philosophical inquiry runs deep. In this passage (taken from *A Treatise of Human Nature*) concerning personal identity, Hume rejects the idea of an underlying "soul substance" that determines personal identity. In Hume's view, the self is only "a bundle" or collection of different perceptions; and the futile search for a definitive standard of personal identity is caused by verbal confusions.

There are some philosophers, who imagine we are every moment intimately conscious of what we call our SELF; that we feel its existence and its continuance in existence; and are certain, beyond the evidence of a demonstration, both of its perfect identity and simplicity. The strongest sensation, the most violent passion, say they, instead of distracting us from this view, only fix it the more intensely, and make us consider their influence on *self* either by their pain or pleasure. To attempt a farther proof of this were to weaken its evidence; since no proof can be deriv'd from any fact, of which we are so intimately conscious; nor is there any thing, of which we can be certain, if we doubt of this.

Unluckily all these positive assertions are contrary to that very experience, which is pleaded for them, nor have we any idea of *self*, after the manner it is here explain'd. For from what impression cou'd this idea be deriv'd? This question 'tis impossible to answer without a manifest contradiction and absurdity; and yet 'tis a question, which must necessarily be answer'd, if we wou'd have the idea of self pass for clear and intelligible. It must be some one impression, that gives rise to every real idea. But self or person is not any one impression, but that to which our several impressions and ideas are suppos'd to have a reference. If any impression gives rise to the idea of self, that impression must continue invariably the same, thro' the whole course of our lives; since self is suppos'd to exist after that manner. But there is no impression constant and invariable. Pain and pleasure, grief and joy, passions and sensations succeed each other, and never all exist at the same time. It cannot, therefore, be from any of these impressions, or from any other, that the idea of self is deriv'd; and consequently there is no such idea.

But farther, what must become of all our particular perceptions upon this hypothesis? All these are different, and distinguishable, and separable from each other, and may be separately consider'd, and may exist separately, and have no need of any thing to support their existence. After what manner, therefore, do they belong to self; and how are they connected with it? For my part, when I enter most intimately into what I call *myself*, I always stumble on some particular perception or other, of heat or cold, light or shade, love or hatred, pain or pleasure. I never can catch *myself* at any time without a perception, and never can observe any thing but the perception. When my perceptions are remov'd for any time, as by sound sleep; so long am I insensible of *myself*, and may truly be said not to exist. And were all my perceptions remov'd by death, and cou'd I neither think, nor feel, nor see, nor love, nor hate after the dissolution of my body, I shou'd be entirely annihilated, nor do I conceive what is farther requisite to make me a perfect non-entity. If any one upon serious and unprejudic'd reflexion, thinks he has a different notion of *himself*, I must confess I can reason no longer with him. All I can allow him is, that he may be in the right as well as I, and that we are essentially different in this particular. He may, perhaps, perceive something simple and continu'd, which he calls *himself*; tho' I am certain there is no such principle in me.

But setting aside some metaphysicians of this kind, I may venture to affirm of the rest of mankind, that they are nothing but a bundle or collection of different perceptions, which succeed each other with an inconceivable rapidity, and are in a perpetual flux and movement. Our eyes cannot turn in their sockets without varying our perceptions. Our thought is still more variable than our sight; and all our other senses and faculties contribute to this change; nor is there any single power of the soul, which remains unalterably the same, perhaps for one moment. The mind is a kind of theatre, where several perceptions successively make their appearance; pass, re-pass, glide away, and mingle in an infinite variety of postures and situations. There is properly no *simplicity* in it at one time, nor *identity* in different; whatever natural propension we may have to imagine that simplicity and identity. The comparison of the theatre must not mislead us. They are the successive perceptions only, that constitute the mind; nor have we the most distant notion of the place, where these scenes are represented, or of the materials, of which it is compos'd.

What then gives us so great a propension to ascribe an identity to these successive perceptions, and to suppose ourselves possest of an invariable and uninterrupted existence thro' the whole course of our lives? In order to answer this question, we must distinguish betwixt personal identity, as it regards our thought or imagination, and as it regards our passions or the concern we take in ourselves. The first is our present subject; and to explain it perfectly we must take the matter pretty deep, and account for that identity, which we attribute to plants and animals; there being a great analogy betwixt it, and the identity of a self or person.

We have a distinct idea of an object, that remains invariable and uninterrupted thro' a suppos'd variation of time; and this idea we call that of *identity* or *sameness*. We have also a distinct idea of several different objects existing in succession, and connected together by a close relation; and this to an accurate view affords as perfect a notion of *diversity*, as if there was no manner of relation among the objects. But tho' these two ideas of identity, and a succession of related objects be in themselves perfectly distinct, and even contrary, yet 'tis certain, that in our common way of thinking they are generally confounded with each other. That action of the imagination, by which we consider the uninterrupted and invariable object, and that by which we reflect on the succession of related objects, are almost the same to the feeling, nor is there much more effort of thought requir'd in the latter case than in the former. The relation facilitates the transition of the mind from one object to another, and renders its passage as smooth as if it contemplated one continu'd object. This resemblance is the cause of the confusion and mistake, and makes us substitute the notion of identity, instead of that of related objects. However at one instant we may consider the related succession as variable or interrupted, we are sure the next to ascribe to it a perfect identity, and regard it as invariable and uninterrupted. Our propensity to this mistake is so great from the resemblance above-mention'd, that we fall into it before we are aware; and tho' we incessantly correct ourselves by reflexion, and return to a more accurate method of thinking, yet we cannot long sustain our philosophy, or take off this bias from the imagination. Our last resource is to yield to it, and boldly assert that these different related objects are in effect the same, however interrupted and variable. In order to justify to ourselves this absurdity, we often feign some new and unintelligible principle, that connects the objects together, and prevents their interruption or variation. Thus we feign the continu'd existence of the perceptions of our senses, to remove the interruption; and run into the notion of a *soul*, and *self*, and *substance*, to disguise the variation. But we may farther observe, that where we do not give rise to such a fiction, our propension to confound identity with relation is so great, that we are apt to imagine something unknown and mysterious, connecting the parts, beside their relation; and this I take to be the case with regard to the identity we ascribe to plants and vegetables. And even when this does not take place, we still feel a propensity to confound these ideas, tho' we are not able fully to satisfy ourselves in that particular, nor find any thing invariable and uninterrupted to justify our notion of identity.

Thus the controversy concerning identity is not merely a dispute of words. For when we attribute identity, in an improper sense, to variable or interrupted objects, our mistake is not confin'd to the expression, but is commonly attended with a fiction, either of something invariable and uninterrupted, or of something mysterious and inexplicable, or at least with a propensity to such fictions. What will suffice to prove this hypothesis to the satisfaction of every fair enquirer, is to shew from daily experience and observation, that the objects, which are variable or interrupted, and yet are suppos'd to continue the same, are such only as consist of a succession of parts, connected together by resemblance, contiguity, or causation. For as such a succession answers evidently to our notion of diversity, it can only be by mistake we ascribe to it an identity; and as the relation of parts, which leads us into this mistake, is really nothing but a quality, which produces an association of ideas, and an easy transition of the imagination from one to another, it can only be from the resemblance, which this act of the mind bears to that, by which we contemplate one continu'd object, that the error arises. Our chief business, then, must be to prove, that all objects, to which we ascribe identity, without observing their invariableness and uninterruptedness, are such as consist of a succession of related objects.

In order to this, suppose any mass of matter, of which the parts are contiguous and connected, to be plac'd before us; 'tis plain we must attribute a perfect identity to this mass, provided all the parts continue uninterruptedly and invariably the same, whatever motion or change of place we may observe either in the whole or in any of the parts. But supposing some very *small* or *inconsiderable* part to be added to the mass, or subtracted from it; tho' this absolutely destroys the identity of the whole, strictly speaking; yet as we seldom think so accurately, we scruple not to pronounce a mass of matter the same, where we find so trivial an alteration. The passage of the thought from the object before the change to the object after it, is so smooth and easy, that we scarce perceive the transition, and are apt to imagine, that 'tis nothing but a continu'd survey of the same object.

There is a very remarkable circumstance, that attends this experiment; which is, that tho' the change of any considerable part in a mass of matter destroys the identity of the whole, yet we must measure the greatness of the part, not absolutely, but by its *proportion* to the whole. The addition or diminution of a mountain wou'd not be sufficient to produce a diversity in a planet; tho' the change of a very few inches wou'd be able to destroy the identity of some bodies. 'Twill be impossible to account for this, but by reflecting that objects operate upon the mind, and break or interrupt the continuity of its actions not according to their real greatness, but according to their proportion to each other: And therefore, since this interruption makes an object cease to appear the same, it must be the uninterrupted progress of the thought, which constitutes the identity.

This may be confirm'd by another phenomenon. A change in any considerable part of a body destroys its identity; but 'tis remarkable, that where the change is produc'd *gradually* and *insensibly* we are less apt to ascribe to it the same effect. The reason can plainly be no other, than that the mind, in following the successive changes of the body, feels an easy passage from the surveying its condition in one moment to the viewing of it in another, and at no particular time perceives any interruption in its actions. From which continu'd perception, it ascribes a continu'd perception, it ascribes a continu'd existence and identity to the object.

But whatever precaution we may use in introducing the changes gradually, and making them proportionable to the whole, 'tis certain, that where the changes are at last observ'd to become considerable, we make a scruple of ascribing identity to such different objects. There is, however, another artifice, by which we may induce the imagination to advance a step farther; and that is, by producing a reference of the parts to each other, and a combination to some *common end* or purpose. A ship, of which a considerable part has been chang'd by frequent reparations, is still consider'd as the same; nor does the difference of the materials hinder us from ascribing an identity to it. The common end, in which the parts conspire, is the same under all their variations, and affords an easy transition of the imagination from one situation of the body to another.

But this is still more remarkable, when we add a *sympathy* of parts to their *common end*, and suppose that they bear to each other, the reciprocal relation of cause and effect in all their actions and operations. This is the case with all animals and vegetables; where not only the several parts have a reference to some general purpose, but also a mutual dependance on, and connexion with each other. The effect of so strong a relation is, that tho' every one must allow, that in a very few years both vegetables and animals endure a *total* change, yet we still attribute identity to them, while their form, size, and substance are entirely alter'd. An oak, that grows from a small plant to a large tree, is still the same oak; tho' there be not one particle of matter, or figure of its parts the same. An infant becomes a man, and is sometimes fat, sometimes lean, without any change in his identity.

We may also consider the two following phenomena, which are remarkable in their kind. The first is, that tho' we commonly be able to distinguish pretty exactly betwixt numerical and specific identity, yet it sometimes happens, that we confound them, and in our thinking and reasoning employ the one for the other. Thus a man, who hears a noise, that is frequently interrupted and renew'd, says, it is still the same noise; tho' 'tis evident the sounds have only a specific identity or resemblance, and there is nothing numerically the same, but the cause, which produc'd them. In like manner it may be said without breach of the propriety of language, that such a church, which was formerly of brick, fell to ruin, and that the parish rebuilt the same church of free-stone, and according to modern architecture. Here neither the form nor materials are the same, nor is there any thing common to the two objects, but their relation to the inhabitants of the parish; and yet this alone is sufficient to make us denominate them the same. But we must observe, that in these cases the first object is in a manner annihilated before the second comes into existence; by which means, we are never presented in any one point of time with the idea of difference and multiplicity; and for that reason are less scrupulous in calling them the same.

Secondly, We may remark, that tho' in a succession of related objects, it be in a manner requisite, that the change of parts be not sudden nor entire, in order to preserve the identity, yet where the objects are in their nature changeable and inconstant, we admit of a more sudden transition, than wou'd otherwise be consistent with that relation. Thus as the nature of a river consists in the motion and change of parts; tho' in less than four and twenty hours these be totally alter'd; this hinders not the river from continuing the same during several ages. What is natural and essential to any thing is, in a manner, expected; and what is expected makes less impression, and appears of less moment, than what is unusual and extraordinary. A considerable change of the former kind seems really less to the imagination, than the most trivial alteration of the latter; and by breaking less the continuity of the thought, has less influence in destroying the identity.

We now proceed to explain the nature of *personal identity*, which has become so great a question in philosophy, especially of late years in *England*, where all the abstruser sciences are study'd with a peculiar ardour and application. And here 'tis evident, the same method of reasoning must be continu'd, which has so successfully explain'd the identity of plants, and animals, and ships, and houses, and of all the compounded and changeable productions either of art or nature. The identity, which we ascribe to the mind of man, is only a fictitious one, and of a like kind with that which we ascribe to vegetables and animal bodies. It cannot, therefore, have a different origin, but must proceed from a like operation of the imagination upon like objects.

But lest this argument shou'd not convince the reader; tho' in my opinion perfectly decisive; let him weigh the following reasoning, which is still closer and more immediate. 'Tis evident, that the identity, which we attribute to the human mind, however perfect we may imagine it to be, is not able to run the several different perceptions into one, and make

them lose their characters of distinction and difference, which are essential to them. 'Tis still true, that every distinct perception, which enters into the composition of the mind, is a distinct existence, and is different, and distinguishable, and separable from every other perception, either contemporary or successive. But, as, notwithstanding this distinction and separability, we suppose the whole train of perceptions to be united by identity, a question naturally arises concerning this relation of identity; whether it be something that really binds our several perceptions together, or only associates their ideas in the imagination. That is, in other words, whether in pronouncing concerning the identity of a person, we observe some real bond among his perceptions, or only feel one among the ideas we form of them. This question we might easily decide, if we wou'd recollect what has been already prov'd at large, that the understanding never observes any real connexion among objects, and that even the union of cause and effect, when strictly examin'd, resolves itself into a customary association of ideas. For from thence it evidently follows, that identity is nothing really belonging to these different perceptions, and uniting them together; but is merely a quality, which we attribute to them, because of the union of their ideas in the imagination, when we reflect upon them. Now the only qualities, which can give ideas an union in the imagination, are these three relations abovemention'd. These are the uniting principles in the ideal world, and without them every distinct object is separable by the mind, and may be separately consider'd, and appears not to have any more connexion with any other object, than if disjoin'd by the greatest difference and remoteness. 'Tis, therefore, on some of these three relations of resemblance, contiguity and causation, that identity depends; and as the very essence of these relations consists in their producing an easy transition of ideas; it follows, that our notions of personal identity, proceed entirely from the smooth and uninterrupted progress of the thought along a train of connected ideas, according to the principles above-explain'd.

The only question, therefore, which remains, is, by what relations this uninterrupted progress of our thought is produc'd, when we consider the successive existence of a mind or thinking person. And here 'tis evident we must confine ourselves to resemblance and causation, and must drop contiguity, which has little or no influence in the present case.

To begin with *resemblance*; suppose we cou'd see clearly into the breast of another, and observe that succession of perceptions, which constitutes his mind or thinking principle, and suppose that he always preserves the memory of a considerable part of past perceptions; 'tis evident that nothing cou'd more contribute to the bestowing a relation on this succession amidst all its variations. For what is the memory but a faculty, by which we raise up the images of past perceptions? And as an image necessarily resembles its object, must not the frequent placing of these resembling perceptions in the chain of thought, convey the imagination more easily from one link to another, and make the whole seem like the continuance of one object? In this particular, then, the memory not only discovers the identity, but also contributes to its production, by producing the relation of resemblance among the perceptions. The case is the same whether we consider ourselves or others.

As to *causation*; we may observe, that the true idea of the human mind, is to consider it as a system of different perceptions or different existences, which are link'd together by the relation of cause and effect, and mutually produce, destroy, influence, and modify each other. Our impressions give rise to their correspondent ideas; and these ideas in their turn produce other impressions. One thought chaces another, and draws after it a third, by which it is expell'd in its turn. In this respect, I cannot compare the soul more properly to any thing than to a republic or commonwealth, in which the several members are united by the reciprocal ties of government and subordination, and give rise to other persons, who propagate the same republic in the incessant changes of its parts. And as the same individual republic may not only change its members, but also its laws and constitutions; in like manner the same person may vary his character and disposition, as well as his impressions and ideas, without losing his identity. Whatever changes he endures, his several parts are still connected by the relation of causation. And in this view our identity with regard to the passions serves to corroborate that with regard to the imagination, by the making our distant perceptions influence each other, and by giving us a present concern for our past or future pains or pleasures.

As memory alone acquaints us with the continuance and extent of this succession of perceptions, 'tis to be consider'd, upon that account chiefly, as the source of personal identity. Had we no memory, we never shou'd have any notion of causation, nor consequently of that chain of causes and effects, which constitute our self or person. But having once acquir'd this notion of causation from the memory, we can extend the same chain of causes, and consequently the identity of our persons beyond our memory, and can comprehend times, and circumstances, and actions, which we have entirely forgot, but suppose in general to have existed. For how few of our past actions are there, of which we have any memory? Who can tell me, for instance, what were his thoughts and actions on the first of *January* 1715, the 11th of *March* 1719, and the 3d of *August* 1733? Or will he affirm, because he has entirely forgot the incidents of these days, that the present self is not the same person with the self of that time; and by that means overturn all the most establish'd notions of personal identity? In this view, therefore, memory does not so much *produce* as *discover* personal identity, by shewing us the relation of cause and effect among our different perceptions. 'Twill be incumbent on those, who affirm that memory produces entirely our personal identity, to give a reason why we can thus extend our identity beyond our memory.

The whole of this doctrine leads us to a conclusion, which is of great importance in the present affair, *viz.* that all the nice and subtile questions concerning personal identity can never possibly be decided, and are to be regarded rather as grammatical than as philosophical difficulties. Identity depends on the relations of ideas; and these relations produce identity, by means of that easy transition they occasion. But as the relations, and the easiness of the transition may diminish by insensible degrees, we have no just standard, by which we can decide any dispute concerning the time, when they acquire or lose a title to the name of identity. All the disputes concerning the identity of connected objects are merely verbal, except so far as the relation of parts gives rise to some fiction or imaginary principle of union, as we have already observ'd.

⇌ REASONS AND PERSONS ⇌
Derek Parfit

Derek Parfit is Research Fellow of All Souls College, Oxford; he has also taught at Harvard University and New York University. This passage is taken from his *Reasons and Persons* (Oxford: Clarendon Press, 1984).

When Derek Parfit speaks of the *reductionist* view, he is referring to the view that the facts of personal identity consist of more particular facts that can be described impersonally; for example, a reductionist might hold that personal identity consists in elements of psychological continuity, or the continued existence of sufficient specific portions of a living brain: personal identity can be *reduced* to such specific impersonal facts. (An example of a *non*reductionist view would be the view that our identity requires the continued existence of a special spiritual or mental substance; however, nonreductionists need not be dualists.) Parfit favors a psychological reductionist view of personal identity, but he goes on to argue that personal identity is not what really matters to us: the important thing is psychological continuity of experiences, *not* that those experiences belong to a particular continuing individual.

DIVIDED MINDS

Some recent medical cases provide striking evidence in favor of the Reductionist View. Human beings have a lower brain and two upper hemispheres, which are connected by a bundle of fibers. In treating a few people with severe epilepsy, surgeons have cut these fibers. The aim was to reduce the severity of epileptic fits, by confining their causes to a single hemisphere. This aim was achieved. But the operations had another unintended consequence. The effect, in the words of one surgeon, was the creation of "two separate spheres of consciousness."

This effect was revealed by various psychological tests. These made use of two facts. We control our right arms with our left hemispheres, and vice versa. And what is in the right halves of our visual fields we see with our left hemispheres, and vice versa. When someone's hemispheres have been disconnected, psychologists can thus present to this person two different written questions in the two halves of his visual field, and can receive two different answers written by this person's two hands.

Here is a simplified version of the kind of evidence that such tests provide. One of these people is shown a wide screen, whose left half is red and right half is blue. On each half in a darker shade are the words, "How many colors can you see?" With both hands the person writes, "Only one." The words are now changed to read: "Which is the only color that you can see?" With one of his hands the person writes "Red," with the other he writes "Blue."

If this is how this person responds, there seems no reason to doubt that he is having visual sensations—that he does, as he claims, see both red and blue. But in seeing red he is not aware of seeing blue, and vice versa. This is why the surgeon writes of "two separate spheres of consciousness." In each of his centers of consciousness the person can see only a single color. In one center, he sees red, in the other, blue.

The many actual tests, though differing in details from the imagined test that I have just described, show the same two essential features. In seeing what is in the left half of his visual field, such a person is quite unaware of what he is now seeing in the right half of his visual field, and vice versa. And in the center of consciousness in which he sees the left half of his visual field, and is aware of what he is doing with his left hand, this person is quite unaware of what he is doing with his right hand, and vice versa.

. . . The left hemisphere typically supports or "has" the linguistic and mathematical abilities of an adult, while the right hemisphere "has" these abilities at the level of a young child. But the right hemisphere, though less advanced in these respects, has greater abilities of other kinds, such as those involved in pattern recognition, or musicality. . . . It is also believed that, in a minority of people, there may be no difference between the abilities of the two hemispheres.

Suppose that I am one of this minority, with two exactly similar hemispheres. And suppose that I have been equipped with some device that can block communication between my hemispheres. Since this device is connected to my eyebrows, it is under my control. By raising an eyebrow I can divide my mind. . . .

It is worth restating other parts of the Reductionist View. I claim:

> Because we ascribe thoughts to thinkers, it is true that thinkers exist. But thinkers are not separately existing entities. The existence of a thinker just involves the existence of his brain and body, the doing of his deeds, the thinking of his thoughts, and the occurrence of certain other physical and mental events. We could therefore redescribe any person's life in impersonal terms. In explaining the unity of this life, we need not claim that it is the life of a particular person. We could describe what, at different times, was thought and felt and observed and done, and how these various events were interrelated. Persons would be mentioned here only in the descriptions of the *content* of many thoughts, desires, memories, and so on. Persons need not be claimed to be the thinkers of any of these thoughts.

These claims are supported by the case where I divide my mind. It is not merely true here that the unity of different experiences does not *need* to be explained by ascribing all of these experiences to me. The unity of my experiences, in each stream, *cannot* be explained in this way. There are only two alternatives. We might ascribe the experiences in each stream to a subject of experiences which is *not* me, and, therefore, not a person. Or, if we doubt the existence of such entities, we can accept the Reductionist explanation. At least in this case, this may now seem the best explanation. . . .

It is natural to believe that our identity is what matters. In my division, each half of my brain will be successfully transplanted into the very similar body of one of my two brothers. Both of the resulting people will be fully psychologically continuous with me, as I am now. What happens to me?

. . . Note that we could not *find out* what happens even if we could actually perform this operation. Suppose, for example, that I do survive as one of the resulting people. I would believe that I have survived. But I would know that the other resulting person falsely believes that he is me, and that he survived. Since I know this, I could not trust my own belief. I might be the resulting person with the false belief. And, since we both claim to be me, other people would have no reason to believe one claim rather than the other. Even if we performed this operation, we would therefore learn nothing.

Whatever happened to me, we could not discover what happened. This suggests a more radical answer to our question. It suggests that the Reductionist View is true. Perhaps there are not here different possibilities, each of which might be what happens, though we could never know which actually happens. Perhaps, when we know that each resulting person would have one half of my brain, and would be psychologically continuous with me, we know everything. What are we supposing when we suggest, for instance, that one of the resulting people might be me? What would make this the true answer?

I believe that there cannot be different possibilities, each of which might be the truth, unless we are separately existing entities, such as Cartesian Egos. If what I really am is one particular Ego, this explains how it could be true that one of the resulting people would be me. It could be true that it is in this person's brain and body that this particular Ego regained consciousness. . . .

The difficult question, for believers in Cartesian Egos, is whether I would survive at all. Since each of the resulting people would be psychologically continuous with me, there would be no evidence supporting either answer to this question. This argument retains its force, even if I am a Cartesian Ego.

As before, a Cartesian might object that I have misdescribed what would happen. He might claim that, if we carried out this operation, it would not in fact be true that *both* of the resulting people would be psychologically continuous with me. It might be true that one or the other of these people was psychologically continuous with me. In either of these cases, this person would be me. It might instead be true that neither person was psychologically continuous with me. In this case, I would not survive. In each of these three cases, we would learn the truth.

Whether this is a good objection depends on what the relation is between our psychological features and the states of our brains. As I have said, we have conclusive evidence that the carrier of psychological continuity is *not* indivisible. In the actual cases in which hemispheres have been disconnected, this produced two series of thoughts and sensations. These two streams of consciousness were both psychologically continuous with the original stream. Psychological continuity has thus, in several actual cases, taken a dividing form. This fact refutes the objection just given. It justifies my claim that, in the imagined case of My Division, both of the resulting people would be psychologically continuous with me. Since this is so, the Cartesian View can be advanced here only in the more dubious version that does not connect the Ego with any observable or introspectable facts. Even if I am such an Ego, I could never know whether or not I had survived. For Cartesians, this case is a problem with no possible solution.

Suppose that, for the reasons given earlier, we reject the claim that each of us is really a Cartesian Ego. And we reject the claim that a person is any other kind of separately existing entity, apart from his brain and body, and various mental and physical events. How then should we answer the question about what happens when I divide? . . .

On the Reductionist View, the problem disappears. . . . We know what this outcome is. There will be two future people, each of whom will have the body of one of my brothers, and will be fully psychologically continuous with me, because he has half of my brain. Knowing this, we know everything. I may ask, "But shall I be one of these two people, or the other, or neither?" But I should regard this as an empty question. Here is a similar question. In 1881 the French Socialist Party split. What happened? Did the French Socialist Party cease to exist, or did it continue to exist as one or other of the two new Parties? Given certain further details, this would be an empty question. Even if we have no answer to this question, we could know just what happened. . . .

What Matters When I Divide?

Some people would regard division as being as bad, or nearly as bad, as ordinary death. This reaction is irrational. We ought to regard division as being about as good as ordinary survival. As I have argued, the two "products" of this operation would be two different people. Consider my relation to each of these people. Does this relation fail to contain some vital element that is contained in ordinary survival? It seems clear that it does not. I would survive if I stood in this very same relation to only one of the resulting people. It is a fact that someone can survive even if half his brain is destroyed. And on reflection it was clear that I would survive if my whole brain was successfully transplanted into my brother's body. It was therefore clear that I would survive if half my brain was destroyed, and the other half was successfully transplanted into my brother's body. In the case that we are now considering, my relation to each of the resulting people thus contains everything that would be needed for me to survive as that person. It cannot be the *nature* of my relation to each of the resulting people that, in this case, causes it to fail to be survival. Nothing is *missing*. What is wrong can only be the duplication.

Suppose that I accept this, but still regard division as being nearly as bad as death. My reaction is now indefensible. I would be like someone who, when told of a drug that could double his years of life, regarded the taking of this drug as death. The only difference in the case of division is that the extra years are to run concurrently. This is an interesting difference. But it cannot mean that there are *no* years to run. We might say: "You will lose your identity. But there are at least two ways of doing this. Dying is one, dividing is another. To regard these as the same is to confuse two with zero. Double survival is not the same as ordinary survival. But this does not make it death. It is further away from death than ordinary survival." . . .

If it was put forward on its own, it would be difficult to accept the view that personal identity is not what matters. But I believe that, when we consider the case of division, this difficulty disappears. When we see *why* neither resulting person will be me, I believe that, on reflection, we can also see that this does not matter, or matters only a little.

The case of division supports part of the Reductionist View: the claim that our identity is not what matters. But this case does not support another Reductionist claim: that our identity can be indeterminate. If we abandon the view that identity is what matters, we can claim that there *is* an answer here to my question. Neither of the resulting people will be me. I am about to die. While we believed that identity is what matters, this claim implied, implausibly, that I ought to regard My Division as being nearly as bad as ordinary death. But the implausibility disappears if we claim instead that this way of dying is about as good as ordinary survival. . . .

. . . On the Non-Reductionist View, a person is a separately existing entity, distinct from his brain and body, and his experiences. On the best-known version of this view, a person is a Cartesian Ego. On the Reductionist View that I defend, persons exist. And a person is distinct from his brain and body, and his experiences. But persons are not separately existing entities. The existence of a person, during any period, just consists in the existence of his brain and body, and the thinking of his thoughts, and the doing of his deeds, and the occurrence of many other physical and mental events.

Since these views disagree about the nature of persons, they also disagree about the nature of personal identity over time. On the Reductionist View, personal identity just involves physical and psychological continuity. As I argued, both of these can be described in an impersonal way. These two kinds of continuity can be described without claiming that experiences are had by a person. A Reductionist also claims that personal identity is not what matters. Personal identity just involves certain kinds of connectedness and continuity, when these hold in a one-one form. These relations are what matter.

On the Non-Reductionist View, personal identity is what matters. And it does not just involve physical and psychological continuity. It is a separate further fact, which must, in every case, either hold completely, or not at all. Psychological unity is explained by ownership. The unity of consciousness at any time is explained by the fact that *several* experiences are being had by a person. And the unity of a person's life is explained in the same way. These several claims must, I have argued, stand or fall together. . . .

Some of the evidence [against the Non-Reductionist View] is provided by the actual cases of divided minds. Because their hemispheres have been disconnected, several people have two streams of consciousness, in each of which they are unaware of the other. We might claim that, in such a case, there are two different people in the same body. This treats such cases as being like the imagined case where I divide, which I review below. Our alternative is to claim, about these actual cases, that there is a single person with two streams of consciousness.

If we make this claim, how can we explain the unity of consciousness in each stream? We cannot explain this unity by claiming that the various different experiences in each stream are being had by the same person, or subject of experiences. This describes the two streams as if they were one. If we believe that the unity of consciousness must be explained by ascribing different experiences to a particular subject, we must claim that in these cases, though there is only a single person, there are two subjects of experiences. We must therefore claim that there are, in a person's life, subjects of experiences that are *not* persons. It is hard to believe that there really are such things. These cases are better explained by the Reductionist Psychological Criterion. This claims that, at any time, there is one state of awareness of the experiences in one stream of consciousness, and another state of awareness of the experiences in the other stream.

Though they raise this problem for the Non-Reductionist View, these cases of divided minds are only a small part of the evidence against this view. There is no evidence that the carrier of psychological continuity is something whose existence, like that of a Cartesian Ego, must be all-or-nothing. And there is much evidence that the carrier of this continuity is the brain. There is much evidence that our psychological features depend upon states and events in our brains. A brain's continued existence need not be all-or-nothing. Physical connectedness can be a matter of degree. And there are countless actual cases in which psychological connectedness holds only in certain ways, or to some reduced degree.

We have sufficient evidence to reject the Non-Reductionist View. The Reductionist View is, I claim, the only alternative. I considered possible third views, and found none that was both non-Reductionist and a view that we had sufficient reasons to accept. More exactly, though these other views differ in other ways, the plausible views do not deny a Reductionist's central claim. They agree that we are *not* separately existing entities, distinct from our brains and bodies, whose existence must be all-or-nothing. . . .

WHAT DOES MATTER—LIBERATION FROM THE SELF

The truth is very different from what we are inclined to believe. Even if we are not aware of this, most of us are Non-Reductionists. If we considered my imagined cases, we would be strongly inclined to believe that our continued existence is a deep further fact, distinct from physical and psychological continuity, and a fact that must be all-or-nothing. This belief is not true.

Is the truth depressing? Some may find it so. But I find it liberating, and consoling. When I believed that my existence was such a further fact, I seemed imprisoned in myself. My life seemed like a glass tunnel, through which I was moving faster every year, and at the end of which there was darkness. When I changed my view, the walls of my glass tunnel disappeared. I now live in the open air. There is still a difference between my life and the lives of other people. But the difference is less. Other people are closer. I am less concerned about the rest of my own life, and more concerned about the lives of others.

When I believed the Non-Reductionist View, I also cared more about my inevitable death. After my death, there will be no one living who will be me. I can now redescribe this fact. Though there will later be many experiences, none of these experiences will be connected to my present experiences by chains of such direct connections as those involved in experience-memory, or in the carrying out of an earlier intention. Some of these future experiences may be related to my present experiences in less direct ways. There will later be some memories about my life. And there may later be thoughts that are influenced by mine, or things done as the result of my advice. My death will break the more direct relations between my present experiences and future experiences, but it will not break various other relations. This is all there is to the fact that there will be no one living who will be me. Now that I have seen this, my death seems to me less bad.

═ AFTER VIRTUE ═
Alasdair MacIntyre

Alasdair MacIntyre (born in 1929 in Glasgow, Scotland) is O'Brien Senior Research Professor of Philosophy at the University of Notre Dame. He was a leader in the resurgence of virtue theory in ethics, and his communitarian views have been influential in political philosophy. In addition, MacIntyre's emphasis on *narrative* understanding of personal identity has been influential in several areas of thought. The following is excerpted from the best known of his many books, *After Virtue* (Notre Dame, IN: University of Notre Dame Press, 1981).

[Marx] wishes to present the narrative of human social life in a way that will be compatible with a view of that life as law-governed and predictable in a particular way. But it is crucial that at any given point in an enacted dramatic narrative we do not know what will happen next. The kind of unpredictability for which I argued in Chapter 8 is required by the narrative structure of human life, and the empirical generalisations and explorations which social scientists discover provide a kind of understanding of human life which is perfectly compatible with that structure.

This unpredictability coexists with a second crucial characteristic of all lived narratives, a certain teleological character. We live out our lives, both individually and in our relationships with each other, in the light of certain conceptions of a possible shared future, a future in which certain possibilities beckon us forward and others repel us, some seem already foreclosed and others perhaps inevitable. There is no present which is not informed by some image of some future and an image of the future which always presents itself in the form of a *telos*—or of a variety of ends or goals—towards which we are either moving or failing to move in the present. Unpredictability and teleology therefore coexist as part of our lives; like characters in a fictional narrative we do not know what will happen next, but none the less our lives have a certain form which projects itself towards our future. Thus the narratives which we live out have both an unpredictable and a partially teleological character. If the narrative of our individual and social lives is to continue intelligibly—and either type of narrative may lapse into unintelligibility—it is always both the case that there are constraints on how the story can continue *and* that within those constraints there are indefinitely many ways that it can continue.

A central thesis then begins to emerge: man is in his actions and practice, as well as in his fictions, essentially a story-telling animal. He is not essentially, but becomes through his history, a teller of stories that aspire to truth. But the key question for men is not about their own authorship; I can only answer the question 'What am I to do?' if I can answer the prior question 'Of what story or stories do I find myself a part?' We enter human society, that is, with one or more imputed characters—roles into which we have been drafted—and we have to learn what they are in order to be able to understand how others respond to us and how our responses to them are apt to be construed. It is through hearing stories about wicked stepmothers, lost children, good but misguided kings, wolves that suckle twin boys, youngest sons who receive no inheritance but must make their own way in the world and eldest sons who waste their inheritance on riotous living and go into exile to live with the swine, that children learn or mislearn both what a child and what a parent is, what the cast of characters may be in the drama into which they have been born and what the ways of the world are. Deprive children of stories and you leave them unscripted, anxious stutterers in their actions as in their words. Hence there is no way to give us an understanding of any society, including our own, except through the stock of stories which constitute its initial dramatic resources. Mythology, in its original sense, is at the heart of things. Vico was right and so was Joyce. And so too of course is that moral tradition from heroic society to its medieval heirs according to which the telling of stories has a key part in educating us into the virtues.

I suggested earlier that 'an' action is always an episode in a possible history: I would now like to make a related suggestion about another concept, that of personal identity. Derek Parfit and others have recently drawn our attention to the contrast between the criteria of strict identity, which is an all-or-nothing matter (*either* the Tichborne claimant *is* the last Tichborne heir; *either* all the properties of the last heir belong to the claimant *or* the claimant is not the heir—Leibniz's Law applies) and the psychological continuities of personality which are a matter of more or less. (Am I the same man at fifty as I was at forty in respect of memory, intellectual powers, critical responses? More or less.) But what is crucial to human beings as characters in enacted narratives is that, possessing only the resources of psychological continuity, we have to be able to respond to the imputation of strict identity. I am forever whatever I have been at any time for others—and I may at any time be called upon to answer for it—no matter how changed I may be now. There is no way of *founding* my identity—or lack of it—on the psychological continuity or discontinuity of the self. The self inhabits a character whose unity is given as the unity of a character. Once again there is a crucial disagreement with empiricist or analytical philosophers on the one hand and with existentialists on the other.

Empiricists, such as Locke or Hume, tried to give an account of personal identity solely in terms of psychological states or events. Analytical philosophers, in so many ways their heirs as well as their critics, have wrestled with the connection between those states and events and strict identity understood in terms of Leibniz's Law. Both have failed to see that a background has been omitted, the lack of which makes the problems insoluble. That background is provided by the concept of a story and of that kind of unity of character which a story requires. Just as a history is not a sequence of actions, but the concept of an action is that of a moment in an actual or possible history abstracted for some purpose from that history, so the characters in a history are not a collection of persons, but the concept of a person is that of a character abstracted from a history.

What the narrative concept of selfhood requires is thus twofold. On the one hand, I am what I may justifiably be taken by others to be in the course of living out a story that runs from my birth to my death; I am the *subject* of a history that is my own and no one else's, that has its own peculiar meaning. When someone complains—as do some of those who attempt or commit suicide—that his or her life is meaningless, he or she is often and perhaps characteristically complaining that the narrative of their life has become unintelligible to them, that it lacks any point, any movement towards a climax or a *telos*. Hence the point of doing any one thing rather than another at crucial junctures in their lives seems to such a person to have been lost.

To be the subject of a narrative that runs from one's birth one's death is, I remarked earlier, to be accountable far the actions and experiences, which compose a narratable life. It is, that is, to be open to being asked to give a certain kind of account of what one did or what happened to one or what one witnessed at any earlier point in one's life the time at which the question is posed. Of course someone may have forgotten or suffered brain damage or simply not attended sufficiently at the relevant times to be able to give the relevant account. But to say of someone under some one description ('The prisoner of the Chateau d'If') that he is the same person as someone characterised quite differently ('The Count of Monte Cristo') is precisely to say that it makes sense to ask him to give an intelligible narrative account enabling us to understand how he could at different times and different places be one and the same person and yet be so differently characterised. Thus personal identity is just that identity presupposed by the unity of the character which the unity of a narrative requires.

Without such unity there would not be subjects of whom stories could be told.

The other aspect of narrative selfhood is correlative: I am not only accountable, I am one who can always ask others for an account, who can put others to the question. I am part of their story, as they are part of mine. The narrative of any one life is part of an interlocking set of narratives. Moreover this asking for and giving of accounts itself plays an important part in constituting narratives. Asking you what you did and why, saying what I did and why, pondering the differences between your account of what I did and my account of what I did, and *vice versa*, these are essential constituents of all but the very simplest and barest of narratives. Thus without the accountability of the self those trains of events that constitute all but the simplest and barest of narratives could not occur; and without that same accountability narratives would lack that continuity required to make both them and the actions that constitute them intelligible.

It is important to notice that I am not arguing that the concepts of narrative or of intelligibility or of accountability are *more* fundamental than that of personal identity. The concepts of narrative, intelligibility and accountability presuppose the applicability of the concept of personal identity, just as it presupposes their applicability and just as indeed each of these three presupposes the applicability of the two others. The relationship is one of mutual presupposition. It does follow of course that all attempts to elucidate the notion of personal identity independently of and in isolation from the notions of narrative, intelligibility and accountability are bound to fail. As all such attempts have.

It is now possible to return to the question from which this enquiry into the nature of human action and identity started: In what does the unity of an individual life consist? The answer is that its unity is the unity of a narrative embodied in a single life. To ask 'What is the good for me?' is to ask how best I might live out that unity and bring it to completion. To ask 'What is the good for man?' is to ask what all answers to the former question must have in common. But now it is important to emphasise that it is the systematic asking of these two questions and the attempt to answer them in deed as well as in word which provide the moral life with its unity. The unity of a human life is the unity of a narrative quest. Quests sometimes fail, are frustrated, abandoned or dissipated into distractions; and human lives may in all these ways also fail. But the only criteria for success or failure in a human life as a whole are the criteria of success or failure in a narrated or to-be-narrated quest . . .

EXERCISES

1. If you believe that what is really essential for preservation of individual identity is *not* the continuity of the brain, but rather the continuity of memories and values and beliefs, does that imply that—to be consistent—you must favor a *functionalist* view of the mind?

2. Your family owns an old axe, a prized family possession: it has been in the family for over 300 years, generation after generation. Your forefathers brought it with them when they crossed the ocean to become colonists in New England. Of course, over the centuries the handle of the axe has been replaced at least a dozen times, and the head of the axe has been replaced three times; but it's still the same axe. Well, maybe not. After all, the axe consists of only two parts, the handle and the head; if both have been replaced many times, what you have is a new axe, not the same axe that was brought over in Colonial times.

   But now consider your old beater of a car: It was your dad's, and he drove it for years before giving it to you on your junior year in high school; and now you've had it for several years. Last year you replaced the brakes, and the year before that it was in a fender bender, and you replaced the hood and both front fenders and the front bumper. Your dad had the car for 10 years, and he got into several small scrapes, and had to replace various parts. The transmission was replaced just before you left for college; and the engine was replaced with a rebuilt engine the year before that; the car has new shocks, a new steering wheel, and new seats. In fact, when you start figuring it all up, you realize that at least 90 percent of your old car is not the original equipment. Is this still the same car your dad bought and drove? Suppose that 100 percent of the parts have been replaced, part by part, over many years; is it still the same car? When you tell a friend, "This is my dad's old car," are you telling the truth?

3. How accurate does a narrative account have to be in order to work as an account of personal identity? For example, I have now convinced myself that the reason I went into philosophy and not on to a brilliant career as a major league shortstop is because I had an injury to my elbow, when in fact, I just barely made my high school team, and could never hit a curve ball had my life depended on it. Can that form a key part of a workable narrative that establishes my personal identity?

4. Suppose that I committed a crime a week ago (I pretended to give the bank teller a check to cash, and then I grabbed some money from the bank teller's drawer and ran out the door). I used the stolen money to fly to Rio, and I spent it all in a glorious week of partying. I returned yesterday, and was perfectly duplicated: there are now six of us (five perfect copies and the original, with all the same thoughts, ideas, beliefs, memories, and precisely the same fingerprints and DNA). Today we are all apprehended. Should all of us be found guilty of bank robbery?

   Suppose only one of the six is caught and spends five years in jail for bank robbery. Then one of the other five is caught; should that second person also be sentenced to prison for bank robbery?

5. Derek Parfit finds *continuity* a quite adequate replacement for the notion of personal identity; indeed, he finds it preferable and comforting. Would you agree?

6. Are there key points on which Hume and MacIntyre *agree*? Could MacIntyre agree with Hume and still hold his narrative view of personal identity?

7. MacIntyre insists that our narrative accounts must encompass purposefulness: our basic goals and values. Without such purpose, MacIntyre thinks a coherent meaningful narrative is not possible. Do you agree? Imagine an individual who says, "Well, my life story (my life narrative) is basically just drifting with the tide, free as the breeze. No real goals, I just take life as it comes: easy come, easy go. Enjoy today, don't worry about tomorrow." (Perhaps "The Dude" in *The Big Lebowski* would be an example.) Could such a person have a coherent life narrative?

8. Advocates of narrative accounts of personal identity often insist that such narrative accounts must include a sense of *personal authorship*: the story of one's life must contain at least some fundamental elements of free *choice*.

   But is free choice an essential element of the narrative account of personal identity? In T. S. Eliot's poem, "The Love Song of J. Alfred Prufrock," Prufrock is giving a narrative account of his own life, and he implies that his life is essentially fixed by his *fate*, his *given character*, rather than his own free choice: "I am not Prince Hamlet, nor was meant to be; am an attendant lord. . . . " But there is little doubt that Prufrock regards this as a narrative that defines his essential personal identity. Would it be possible for someone who favors the narrative account of personal identity to consistently deny free will? Could one give a narrative account of one's own personal identity, while believing that the key elements of that narrative were *not* matters of choice, but were instead elements of one's destiny?

9. Could my life narrative establish my personal identity if at key points it contained a number of mistaken memories? Suppose, for example, that three of the most significant events of my life were scoring the winning goal in the state high school championship soccer match, winning the competition for best undergraduate philosophy paper during my university years, and spending a wild passionate night with a very attractive stranger in Rome. But it turns out that though I *believe* these were all my own experiences, in fact they are the product of my "wishful thinking": it was one of my friends who scored the winning goal, another student (whom I envied) who won the university competition, and my "memory" of the passionate night in Rome comes from a movie I watched. Could such a narrative establish my personal identity?

10. There is an old parlor trick—employed to great advantage by "psychic advisors"—that is very revealing; it is sometimes used in introductory psychology classes. Give everyone a slip of paper and ask them to write down a passage, and you will analyze their handwriting and draw up their personality profile; or alternatively, ask them to write the date, time, and location of their births, and you will give them a personality profile based on an analysis of their handwriting. After carrying out the detailed "analysis," you give each person a sheet of paper with his or her personality profile. The trick, of course, is that you give everyone exactly the same profile, as follows:

> You have a need for other people to like and admire you and yet you tend to be critical of yourself. While you have some personality weaknesses you are generally able to compensate for them. You have considerable unused capacity that you have not turned to your advantage. Disciplined and self-controlled on the outside, you tend to be worrisome and insecure on the inside. At times you have serious doubts as to whether you have made the right decision or done the right thing. You prefer a certain amount of change and variety and become dissatisfied when hemmed in by restrictions and limitations. You also pride yourself as an independent thinker and do not accept other's statements without satisfactory proof. But you have found it unwise to be too frank in revealing yourself to others.*

When given such a "profile," many people will insist that it fits them precisely, that it is an amazing result! The moral of the story, of course, is how easy it is to be taken in by fraudulent "pseudoscientific" claims. But what is also interesting is the nature of the "profile" which is embraced by so many people: It basically takes a number of characteristics and insists that you have at least part of two opposite characteristics: you are rather greedy, but you are also wonderfully generous and open-handed; you value stability, but you also cherish adventure and instability. Is the enthusiastic embracing of such incompatible elements evidence in favor of the "multiple bundles" model of our psychological structure?

ADDITIONAL READING

The classical sources for the problem of self-identity are John Locke, *Essay Concerning Human Understanding*, 2nd ed., Chapter 27, 1694; Bishop Joseph Butler, *The Anatomy of Religion*, first appendix, 1736; David Hume, *Treatise of Human Nature*, Book I, Part IV, 1739; and Thomas Reid, third essay in *Essays on the Intellectual Powers of Man*, 1785.

An excellent collection of influential essays on the subject of personal identity is *The Identities of Persons*, edited by Amélie Oksenberg Rorty (Berkeley, Cal.: University of

---

*This is taken from an online essay, "The Psychic Frauds?" by Jerome Burne, originally in *Focus*, November 1994; many of its elements were developed by Bertram Forer in 1943 for a classroom demonstration on research techniques.

California Press, 1976). *Personal Identity*, edited by Raymond Martin and John Barresi (Oxford: Blackwell Publishers, 2002), is another good collection. It opens with an excellent historical essay by the editors and contains important recent essays on the subject. Still another good collection is Henry Harris, ed., *Identity* (Oxford: Oxford University Press, 1995). An excellent volume of contemporary essays draws the connections between identity issues and ethical questions (especially questions concerning moral responsibility): *Identity, Character, and Morality*, edited by Owen Flanagan and Amélie Oksenberg Rorty (Cambridge, Mass: MIT Press, 1990). A very good anthology of feminist perspectives on personal identity is edited by Diana Tietjens Meyers, Alison Jaggar, and Virginia Held, *Feminists Rethink the Self* (Westview Press: 1997).

John R. Perry, *A Dialogue on Personal Identity and Immortality* (Indianapolis, Ind.: Hackett, 1978), is a very readable introduction to the question of personal identity, including discussion of many of the traditional problems associated with personal identity and application to the question of individual immortality. Also, John Perry's *Personal Identity* (Berkeley, Cal.: University of California Press, 1975) is an excellent anthology that brings together both classical and contemporary writings on the question of personal identity; Perry's introduction to the volume is a very helpful brief guide. Another good introduction to the issue of personal identity is Harold W. Noonan, *Personal Identity*, 2nd ed. (London: Routledge, 2003).

Derek Parfit, *Reasons and Persons* (Oxford: Clarendon Press, 1984), is one of the most influential contemporary books on identity. Christine M. Korsgaard, "Personal Identity and the Unity of Agency: A Kantian Response to Parfit," *Philosophy & Public Affairs*, volume 18, number 2 (Spring 1989): 101–132, argues that even if Parfit's arguments were correct, we would still have strong, practical, moral reasons for believing in the continuing personal identity of ourselves as rational agents. First, we require such a unity to be effective actors; and second, unity is "implicit in the *standpoint* from which you deliberate and choose," and having such a standpoint is essential for genuine deliberation. Thomas Nagel's "Brain Bisection and the Unity of Consciousness" is also well known. Originally published in 1971 in *Synthese*, volume 22, pp. 396–413, it is available in the collection of essays by Nagel entitled *Mortal Questions* (Cambridge: Cambridge University Press, 1979), as well as in several anthologies.

Bernard Williams is always fascinating and is one of the best philosophical writers; for his views on personal identity, see his *Problems of the Self* (Cambridge: Cambridge University Press, 1973).

Eric T. Olson argues for a *biological continuity* view of personal identity: "one survives just in case one's purely animal functions—metabolism, the capacity to breathe and circulate one's blood, and the like—continue." His book considers a variety of thought experiments, and poses some original ones as well: *The Human Animal: Personal Identity Without Psychology* (New York: Oxford University Press, 1997).

Among the most influential contemporary philosophers on personal identity are Sydney Shoemaker, *Self-Knowledge and Self-Identity* (Ithaca, N.Y.: Cornell University Press, 1963) and *Identity, Cause, and Mind* (Cambridge: Cambridge University Press, 1984); and Peter Van Inwagen, whose writings on the subject include *Material Beings* (Ithaca: Cornell University Press, 1990) and "What Do I Refer to When I Say 'I'?" in R. Gale, ed., *The Blackwell Guide to Metaphysics* (Oxford: Blackwell Publishers, 2002).

Personal Identity, by Sidney Shoemaker and Richard Swinburne (Oxford: Blackwell Publishing, 1984), offers sustained arguments and responses by Shoemaker (a materialist) and Swinburne (a dualist) on the questions surrounding personal identity.

Studies in psychopathology have stimulated difficult questions and interesting arguments concerning personal identity; see Mark T. Brown, "Multiple Personality and Personal Identity," *Philosophical Psychology*, volume 14 (2001): 435–448; Daniel Kolak, "Finding Our Selves: Identification, Identity and Multiple Personality," *Philosophical Psychology*, volume 6 (2001): 363–386; R. W. Sperry, "Hemisphere Deconnection and Unity in Conscious

Awareness," *American Psychologist*, volume 23, number 10 (1968); Roland Puccetti, "The Case for Mental Duality: Evidence from Split-Brain and Other Considerations," *Behavioral and Brain Sciences*, volume 4 (1981): 83–128, including commentaries; George Graham and G. Lynn Stephens, *When Self-Consciousness Breaks: Alien Voices and Inserted Thoughts* (Cambridge: MIT Press, 2000); and particularly George Graham and G. Lynn Stephens, eds., *Philosophical Psychopathology* (Cambridge, Mass.: MIT Press, 1994).

A leader in the development of narrative accounts of personal identity is Alasdair MacIntrye, in *After Virtue* (Notre Dame, Indiana: University of Notre Dame Press, 1981). Others employing this approach are Charles Taylor, *Sources of the Self: The Making of the Modern Identity* (Cambridge, Mass.: Harvard University Press, 1989); and Ronald Dworkin, *Life's Dominion* (New York: Knopf, 1993). The psychological research of D. P. McAdams has also been important to narrative accounts; see *The Stories We Live By: Personal Myths and the Making of the Self* (New York: William Morrow and Company, 1993). Another influential psychologist on this subject is Jerome Bruner: *Making Stories: Law, Literature, Life* (Farrar, Strauss and Giroux, 2002). A good anthology on this approach is Gary D. Fireman, Ted E. McVay, and Owen J. Flanagan, eds., *Narrative and Consciousness: Literature, Psychology, and the Brain* (New York: Oxford University Press, 2003). For psychological examinations of the narrative self, see John Baressi and T. Juckes, "Personology and the Narrative Interpretation of Lives," *Journal of Personality*, volume 65 (1997): 693–719; Jerome Bruner, *Acts of Meaning* (Cambridge, MA: Harvard University Press, 1990); Ulric Neisser and Robyn Fivush, eds., *The Remembering Self: Construction and Accuracy in the Self-Narrative* (Cambridge: Cambridge University Press, 1994); and Robyn Fivush and Catherine A. Haden, eds., *Autobiographical Memory and the Construction of a Narrative Self* (Mahwah, NJ: Lawrence Erlbaum, 2003).

A detailed account of one Buddhist approach to personal identity can be found in Steven Collins, *Selfless Persons: Imagery and Thought in Theravada Buddhism* (Cambridge: Cambridge University Press, 1982).

The Stanford Encyclopedia of Philosophy article on Personal Identity, by Eric T. Olson, is a good overview of the contemporary debate; it can be found at http://plato.stanford.edu/entries/identity~personal/.

For a very entertaining foray into personal identity issues, go to www.philosophers.net.com/games/ and click on "Staying Alive."

CHAPTER 8

FATALISM, DETERMINISM, AND FREE WILL

The ancient *stoic* philosopher Epictetus gave this advice to his followers:

> Remember that you are an actor in a drama of such sort as the author chooses—if short, then in a short one; if long, then in a long one. If it be his pleasure that you should enact a poor man, or a cripple, or a ruler, or a private citizen see that you act it well. For this is your business—to act well the given part, but to choose it belongs to another.
>
> *Epictetus*, The Enchiridion, *translated by Thomas W. Higginson*

FATALISM

Epictetus is teaching *fatalism*: the view that the key features and events of our lives (our births, our deaths, our major successes and failures, our *destinies*) are fixed by *fate*, and there is nothing whatsoever we can do to change our fate. You cannot choose your fate, but you can live out your fated existence with grace and dignity and patience. Epictetus was a great *stoic* teacher, and stoicism often accompanies fatalism. Stoics counsel us to remain steady and calm: don't get too excited at good fortune, and certainly you should not boast and crow over your victories; and likewise, accept your defeats and disappointments with an even temperament, with dignity, even with detachment. You cannot control the world, nor what happens to you. A fool may gain wealth and glory, while a wise and virtuous person suffers loss and defeat. Such things are a matter of fate, and beyond our control. But you can control your reaction to your success as well as to your failure, and live your part well, whatever part the fates select for you.

The ancient stoics—who were generally *fatalists*—offered the following metaphor. You are like a dog tied securely to a cart, and the cart is being pulled to market by two strong horses. Your fate is to go to the market, and there is absolutely nothing you can do to change your fate: bark and bite, pull with all your strength in the opposite direction, growl and howl, but you are going to market behind the cart. However, you can either trot along contentedly behind the cart, enjoying the warm spring sunshine, sniffing the flowers, and traveling with dignity and composure; or you can bite and kick and howl, and be dragged ignominiously in the dust behind the cart. Either way, you will reach your fated destination; but your manner of travel will be very different, depending on whether you accept your fate and live as best you can in accordance with that fate, or fight your fate and struggle vainly every step of the way.

> Ask not that events should happen as you wish, but let your will be that events should happen as they do, and you shall find peace.
>
> Epictetus, Enchiridion

There is a wonderful fatalistic story from the Islamic tradition that expresses the *inevitability* of fate and the *futility* of trying to escape your fate. There was a merchant who traveled to Baghdad with his servant. After arriving in Baghdad, he sent his servant to the marketplace to buy supplies. The servant returned, pale and terrified: while he was in the marketplace, he was jostled by an old woman; when he turned to look, the old woman was Death, and she glared at him. "Now lend me your horse," the servant pleads, "that I may ride to Samarra and escape my fate." The master lends the servant his horse, and the servant flees Baghdad as fast as the horse will run, on his way to Samarra. Later the master goes to the market to buy the supplies that his terrified servant had forgotten, and at the market he encounters Death. "Why did you glare at my servant?" asks the master. Death replies: "I didn't glare at him; that was an expression of surprise. I was surprised to see him here in Baghdad, for I have an appointment with him tonight in Samarra." So it matters not how swiftly you ride nor how shrewdly you plot your escape: your fate will be waiting for you, and you cannot avoid it.

Fatalism . . . holds that our actions do not depend upon our desires. Whatever our wishes may be, a superior power, or an abstract destiny, will overrule them, and compel us to act, not as we desire, but in the manner predestined. Our love of good and hatred of evil are of no efficacy, and though in themselves they may be virtuous, as far as conduct is concerned it is unavailing to cultivate them.

John Stuart Mill, An Examination of William Hamilton's Philosophy, *Chapter 26, 1867*

In ancient Greek drama, Oedipus is *fated* to slay his father (the king) and marry his mother (who is queen). His royal father, hearing this terrible prophesy, instructs a woodsman to take the infant Oedipus into the forest and slay him, thus circumventing fate. But the woodsman pities the infant, and instead sends Oedipus to a far country, where he is adopted by a couple whom he believes to be his parents. On getting word of the terrible murderous fate prophesied for him, Oedipus resolves to escape his fate, and so leaves his homeland for a distant country. On arriving in this new country, he gets into a struggle against a group of warriors, including the king. Oedipus fights bravely and slays them all. He meets with great success in his new country, soon is acclaimed king, and is wedded to the widowed queen. But of course all his stratagems are to no avail, for his real father and mother were—you guessed it—the king he killed and the queen he married.

Predestination is a religious doctrine favored by such theologians as Luther and Calvin (and perhaps Valla). It holds that God selects (predestines) each person for either salvation or damnation. Those selected for salvation receive the gift of God's grace, while those who do not receive that gift are damned; the choice is entirely up to God, God's choice is made before the individual humans are even born, and God's decision has nothing to do with the choices, works, or worth of the individuals.

Many people shudder at fatalism: your fate seems to stalk you and all your efforts and ideas are twisted into tricks used by fate for your own destruction. If fatalism is true, we are helpless and hopeless, and nothing we do has any real effect. We play our parts in the drama, as Epictetus says; but our lines and our lives are scripted. We can play the part well or ill, but we cannot change the script, cannot become different characters, and cannot rewrite the ending. On the other hand, some—such as Epictetus—see fatalism as comforting. Accept your fate, take what enjoyment you can from life, don't worry about what will happen because there is really nothing you can do about it anyway. Que será, será; what will be, will be. Don't worry, be happy.

> In Herman Melville's great tragic novel *Moby Dick*, it is Captain Ahab's fate to seek the great white whale; but it is a fate that Ahab embraces as his own, and he finds comfort in the fact that since his destiny is *fated*, even the gods cannot change his fate, nor change Ahab's iron nature, without the gods making *themselves* false. Thus Ahab's challenge, mocking the gods of fate and their powers:
>
> > Swerve me? Ye cannot swerve me, else ye swerve yourselves! man has ye there. Swerve me? The path to my fixed purpose is laid on iron rails, whereon my soul is grooved to run.

Fatalism is a very common view. In fact, for any monotheistic religion in which God is all-powerful and all-knowing, fatalism is a natural and almost inevitable element.

> The great Protestant leader John Calvin strongly affirmed the doctrine of predestination:
>
> > God preordained, for His own glory and the display of His attributes of mercy and justice, a part of the human race, without any merit of their own, to eternal salvation, and another part, in just punishment of their sin, to eternal damnation.
>
> This was, incidentally, the view that was prevalent in the American colonies in the seventeenth and early eighteenth centuries; and anyone who denied it —especially in the New England colonies—was regarded as a heretic and expelled from the colony, often after suffering torture.

After all, if God is the maker of all things and holds *all* power, and God knows all (including knowing every detail of your future long before you were born), then the story of your life was written when God created the world. As the great Persian astronomer and poet Omar Khayyám writes (in the rather loose Fitzgerald translation):

> With Earth's first clay They did the Last Man knead,
> And there of the Last Harvest sow'd the Seed;
> And the first Morning of Creation wrote
> What the Last Dawn of Reckoning shall read.

In the Jewish tradition, the classic story of Job is the story of a man who is but a pawn in a great cosmic struggle: Job lives a good life, follows God's commandments, practices virtue; and then—in a contest between God and Satan—Job's family is killed, all his property is destroyed or stolen, and his body is covered with terrible agonizing sores. When Job asks God for an explanation, God swiftly puts Job in his place: God created the world, and Job also, and God can do with them as He wishes, and no one has the right to question God's decisions:

> Then the Lord answered Job out of the whirlwind, and said, Who is this that darkeneth counsel by words without knowledge? . . . Where was thou when I laid the foundations of the earth? . . . Wilt thou also disannul my judgment? Wilt thou condemn me, that thou mayest be righteous? Has thou an arm like God? Or canst thou thunder with a voice like him?
>
> *Job, from chapters 38 and 40*

The Hebrew prophet Isaiah teaches the same doctrine:

> Woe unto him that striveth with his Maker! Let the potsherd strive with the potsherds of the earth. Shall the clay say to him that fashioneth it, What makest thou?
>
> *Isaiah, chapter 45, verse 9*

In the Christian tradition, this fatalistic element—while echoing the words of Isaiah—becomes even clearer in the teachings of Paul:

> Therefore hath he mercy on whom he will have mercy, and whom he will he hardeneth. Thou wilt say unto me, Why doth he yet find fault? For who hath resisted his will? Nay but, O man, who art thou that repliest against God? Shall the thing formed say to him that formed it, Why hast thou made me thus? Hath not the potter power over the clay, of the same lump to make one vessel unto honour, and another unto dishonour? What if God, willing to shew his wrath, and to make his power known, endured with much longsuffering the vessels of wrath fitted to destruction: And that he might make known the riches of his glory on the vessels of mercy, which he had afore prepared unto glory. . . .

> *Romans, chapter 9*

Desiderius Erasmus (1466–1536) was one of the most famous of the Renaissance scholars, and a contemporary of Martin Luther. Though he supported reform of the Catholic Church, he did not join the Protestants—at least in part because he opposed many of Martin Luther's views, particularly Luther's views on predestination. In this passage from *A Disquisition upon Free Will*, Erasmus claims that belief in the doctrine of predestination would do terrible harm:

> Let us then suppose that it is true . . . , as Luther has asserted, that whatever is done by us is done not by free will but by pure necessity; what is more inexpedient than to publish this paradox to the world? . . . What a door to impiety this pronouncement would open to countless mortals, if it were spread abroad in the world. . . . What weak man would keep up the perpetual and weary struggle against the flesh? What evil man would strive to amend his life? Who could persuade his soul to love with all his heart a God who prepared a hell flaming with eternal tortures where He may avenge on wretched men His own misdeeds, as if He delighted in human tortures? [Translated by Mary Martin McLaughlin]

So God fashions some for glory and some for destruction, and that is their fate, for no one can resist God's omnipotent will. Why does God do that? Don't ask. Who are you to question God? The potter can do as he pleases with the clay, and the clay has neither the right to complain nor the power to resist.

> Oh, Thou, who didst with pitfall and with gin
> Beset the Road I was to wander in!,
> Thou wilt not with Predestined Evil round
> Enmesh, and then impute my Fall to Sin!
> Oh, Thou, who Man of baser Earth didst make,
> And ev'n with Paradise devise the Snake:
>   For all the Sin the Face of wretched Man
> Is black with—Man's Forgiveness give—and take!
>
> *The Rubaiyat of Omar Khayyam, verses 87–88, translated by Edward Fitzgerald*

FATALISM AND DETERMINISM

Fatalism is a fascinating position, embraced by such diverse groups as ancient Greek dramatists, Roman Stoics, Jewish prophets, Muslim teachers, and Christian writers. Some, like the stoics, find it comforting; others—who picture death stalking the servant who is vainly riding toward Samarra to "escape his fate"—find it frightening, even spooky.

Fatalism is a common theme in literature, from the plays of Sophocles to the poetry of Omar Khayyám, and in the novels of Thomas Hardy and Theodore Dreiser. But interesting as fatalism is in its own right, it is also important to consider the relation between *fatalism* and *determinism*. Some hold that determinism and fatalism are identical: just two names for the same thing. Perhaps you will also reach that conclusion. But many determinists vehemently deny that they are *fatalists*, and it is important to consider whether determinism and fatalism are the same doctrine under different names or distinctly different positions.

Determinism is the view that everything that occurs in the world—every thought, every breeze, every planet, every galaxy, every leaf that falls, every ripple in every pool—is a product of causal laws affecting earlier states of the universe; that is, given the universe as it is at this moment in every detail, the operation of causal laws will determine the exact position of every detail of the universe at any subsequent time. Obviously, determinists do not believe that we *know* or can *predict* all future events in the universe: we do not know all the relevant causal laws, nor do we know the position of every object and force at this moment in the universe. But determinists maintain that it is more plausible to believe that every event in the world is uniquely determined by past events and the causal laws operating on the world, and that there is no point at which complete causality does not apply: all events, thoughts, and phenomena are ultimately explicable in terms of causal laws, even though it is unlikely we shall ever know all those laws.

So, is determinism really the same thing as fatalism? Though some claim that it is, there seem to be enormous differences between the two views. Fatalists care little for the details leading up to the fated event, while determinists regard the details as crucially important. Suppose it is your *fate* to die in a plane crash on a specified date. On that date you avoid airports, and absolutely refuse to get on any aircraft whatsoever; in fact, you decide to take no chances and remain safely in bed for the entire 24 hours of the fated date. But on the fated day, a jetliner crashes into your house, killing you and all the passengers. Or suppose you want to be even safer, and you arrange to be hidden deep in Carlsbad Caverns, where a surface plane crash would have no effect. But the persons who claim to be taking you to Carlsbad Caverns are instead vicious kidnappers, who tie you up and put you on their private jet to fly you to their hideout, where they plan to demand an enormous ransom for your safe return. But the plane develops engine trouble en route, and—well, you know the rest; you can't escape your fate, and all your efforts are foolish futility. In contrast, consider a determinist case. You won the county championship in the 1,600 meter run in your senior year in high school. Determinists would insist that your winning was a *determined* event; but among the key determining factors were your years of dedicated training. Had you not trained very hard, you would *not* have won the race. According to determinism, it was *determined* that you would get up at dawn, come rain or snow, and put in your training miles: it was determined by your own passion for running, your supportive family, the encouragement of your coach, and many other factors. The determining causes are very complex, and we certainly don't know all of them. Why did you train so hard, when other runners did not? Determinists would say there are determining *causes* for your fortitude and dedication—and many of those determining factors might be things you aren't even aware of (perhaps one cause was your beloved grandmother's praise when you worked so hard at weeding her flowerbed when you were eight years old; it helped to shape your fortitude for doing your best at any task you undertake). If you had not trained with such fortitude, you would not have won: your own training was a vital determining factor in your victory. But that you trained hard—and absolutely every other detail in your life and behavior—is the product of determined causal forces. It was not your *fate* to win the race. If you had *wanted* to do something else rather than run (play in a rock band, for example), you could have done that: determinism doesn't force you to do things that you try to avoid. But you deeply desired to win that race, and you trained very hard, and you have great fortitude: all those causal factors are determined, and together (along with many other causal factors we may not know, including genetic and social factors) they determined the result. Fatalism doesn't worry about any intervening causes; instead, some mysterious force of fate brings about a fated result, and your desires and efforts and dedication have nothing to do with that result. If you are *fated* to win the race, it doesn't matter whether you train or not. If winning the race is a result of *determined* causes, then prominent among those essential causes will be your hard training. For determinists, those causes—such as your dedicated training and your enduring desire to win—*are* essential causal factors; for fatalists, there are *no* key causal factors—the fated event just *happens*, prior events or details be damned.

> Fatalism is the thesis that some event must happen, and no further explanation, notably no causal explanation, is called for. Determinism, by contrast, is the reasonably science-minded thesis that whatever happens can be explained in terms of prior causes and standing conditions (facts, events, states of affairs, internal structures, and dispositions), plus the laws of nature.
>
> *Robert C. Solomon, "On Fate and Fatalism," 2003*

Consider the great fatalistic example from the stoics, described at the beginning of this chapter: you are like a dog tied to a wagon, and you are *fated* to go to market; but whether you trot along happily or resist as you are dragged through the dirt—that's totally up to you, those details of how you live your life as it proceeds toward its *fated destiny* are your choice, and you could choose either happy acquiescence or bitter frustration. But determinists see it very differently. Whether you trot along happily or bite, kick, and resist is *determined* by all sorts of complex psychological causes. Epictetus says that "this is your business—to act well the given part, but to choose it belongs to another." Determinists would agree that how you act is your business, but how you act—like everything else in the world—is the product of determining causal events. If Joe lives his life in a bitter, morose manner, while Joan lives happily and cheerfully and enthusiastically, that is not (according to determinists) something that they just *choose*, with no causes for their choices. Determinists insist that our characters and personalities and fortitude and cheerfulness and bitterness are *all* part of the determined process. For determinists, *everything* is determined by causal processes: winning the race is *caused*, but not fated; your hard training is *completely caused* and is itself a key causal element in the outcome of the race, but neither your training nor the race result is *fated*. And whether you are a gracious or an arrogantly obnoxious race winner, a cheerful or cantankerous teammate—all of that, every detail, is causally determined. Big events and small, the determinist fits them all into the causal pattern. Finally, fatalism embraces a sort of mysterious process in which the big events in your life (the fated events, such as your murder of your father, or the time of your death, or your great military victory) are set by some mysterious force (perhaps God, or the fates, or whatever) that seems to have no connection with any of the other events or causes that occur in the world. Determinism rejects such mysteries, insisting that *all* phenomena ultimately fit into the great causal process. Much of that causal process is *unknown* to determinists, but none of it is mysterious.

Of course you may reject both fatalism and determinism; many people do. But if the above argument is correct, then you are rejecting *two* views, rather than one view that happens to have two names.

DETERMINISM

Set fatalism aside for a moment and concentrate on determinism. Do you believe in determinism? If you are like most people, you answer *no*. But think about it for a moment. Suppose that you are sitting quietly in your dorm room or your apartment, or perhaps in an empty classroom, delightedly reading your philosophy textbook. The door to your room is open just a crack, and there seems to be no one around. As you read, the door slowly creaks open.

So, what happened? Why did the door slowly open? Perhaps there's a breeze in the hall. No, there's no breeze whatsoever. Maybe the furnace switched on and caused a draft, and the air current moved the door. No, no movement of air. Then perhaps it's just the force of gravity: the door wasn't hung level. No, the door is dead level. Alright, someone attached a very thin nylon filament and is playing a joke on us. No, nothing is attached to the door. Well, perhaps it's some vile terrorist gang, testing a new gamma ray on my door. No, we check for gamma rays and other strange weapons, and none are operative. In that case, maybe the room is haunted: some poor philosophy student of decades past who perished from terminal boredom while reading her philosophy text was disturbed by this discussion of determinism and fled the room.

Okay, notice what happened: a door opened, and we wondered why. What caused the door to open? We thought of all manner of possible causes, finally pushing into terrorist gamma rays and even ghosts. But one possibility was never suggested, one possibility struck you as so utterly implausible that you would believe in ghosts before admitting that possibility: the possibility that the movement of the door "just happened," and there was *no* cause whatsoever. So if a door opens, or a tree falls, or a computer crashes, we believe there *must* be a cause.

Tomorrow morning you go to your philosophy class, eager to see your warmhearted, kind, cheerful philosophy professor. "Good morning, Professor," you say. "Go to hell," is the reply. You are profoundly shocked, and you turn to a classmate, "What's the matter with Professor Jones? She's usually so nice. I said good morning to her, and she snarled at me and told me to go to hell." Maybe the book manuscript she's been working on got rejected. No, her book is going to be published, and the reviews have been excellent. Maybe she got rejected for tenure. No, she was tenured two years ago. Maybe she had a fight with her husband, or maybe one of her teenage kids wrecked the car. No, no problems at home. Maybe she's got a terrible hangover, and a splitting headache. No, she's a very moderate drinker, and her health is great. Maybe she's been brainwashed by extraterrestrials. Or, maybe she's been possessed by demons. But again, one option is never mentioned: there's no cause for this strange behavior; it just happened. No way. You would believe in extraterrestrial invasions or demon possession before believing that there was no cause whatsoever.

> It would be very singular that all nature, all the planets, should obey eternal laws, and that there should be a little animal about five foot high, who in contempt of these laws, could act as he pleases, solely according to his caprice. *Voltaire*

So what's the moral of this story (a story originally told by David Hume)? It's simple. Whatever you *say* when someone asks whether you are a determinist, in fact you *do* believe in determinism. Of course that's not a proof that determinism is *true*. But it does show that almost all of us strongly *believe* that determinism is true. That is, we believe that for *everything* that happens—whether a door closing or a tree falling, or someone snapping at us or our acing a philosophy exam—there is a sufficient *cause* for that event. We may not have any idea what that cause was; but we firmly believe that for *everything* that happens, there is a cause that led to that result. And that means we believe in determinism. We believe in determinism, not fatalism: We believe that everything that happens is part of a complex causal process, *not* the product of some "fickle hand of fate" that operates independently of the causal system. Determinism is not some scary exotic doctrine dreamed up by philosophers; instead (as David Hume argued), it is really just a commonsense belief that almost all of us hold, whether we *call* ourselves determinists or not.

It is hardly surprising that Hume enthusiastically embraced determinism. Hume lived in the era when Newton had recently given a clear deterministic account of the motion of the planets around the Sun, the Moon around the Earth, of balls dropped from a tower, and of cannonballs fired from a fortress; and Edmund Halley had used Newton's principles to determine the path of a comet—those strange celestial visitors that appeared to defy all order and predictability. Determinism seemed to be the right path, and the question was only what causal laws governed the rest of the world—including human behavior—as Newton's laws governed the motion of planets and comets and cannonballs. And in fact, determinism does seem a good guide to inquiry: if we believe that some things "just happen" and there is no cause, then we will not push hard to discover complex causal processes. If comets "just happen," then it is useless to seek understanding of how gravity shapes their complex orbits. If a terrible disease "just happens," with no cause, then in vain will medical researchers try to discover what caused you to get sick and how to prevent it from happening again. Most people benefit from penicillin, but it makes *you* terribly sick. We don't say, oh, that just happened; rather, we keep looking until we find what caused this different and special reaction in you, and so we discover—and learn to control—allergies. If becoming severely depressed "just happens," then we can never understand the causes that lead to this debilitating problem, and we can never find effective methods for treating and preventing depression. When an important event—like a disease epidemic, or a crime wave, or a flooded river—occurs, our belief that there *must* be a cause (a cause we can find if we look hard enough) is a very valuable belief. And that is another contrast with fatalism: if you are fated to die at a certain time, then it will be useless to seek causes of your death, or try to understand why it happened. It was your fate, and there is nothing more to say or discover.

Reactions to Determinism

Even if we carefully distinguish determinism from fatalism and acknowledge the usefulness of the determinist hypothesis for promoting research, many people strongly resist the doctrine of determinism; indeed, many people find it repulsive. Some object that determinism would deprive us of free will, others fear that determinism would eliminate all freshness, originality, and creativity: the world of determinism would be dull and dreary. And some worry that determinism would destroy moral responsibility. Concerns about determinism notwithstanding, it is a view embraced by a wide variety of people. Karl Marx was a determinist, and so was Albert Einstein; but it would be difficult to think of any other belief they share. While some favor determinism for religious reasons, others embrace determinism as an important element of scientific investigation. In B. F. Skinner's *Walden Two*, Frazier (who appears to be a stand-in for Skinner) says:

> I deny that freedom exists at all. I must deny it—or my program would be absurd. You can't have a science about a subject matter which hops capriciously about. Perhaps we can never *prove* that man isn't free; it's an assumption. But the increasing success of a science of behavior makes it more and more plausible. (p. 242)

In this passage, Skinner equates determinism with absence of freedom, and that's a question we'll be examining in Chapter 9. But the point here is that—for Skinner—advancing a *science* of human behavior requires that we operate from the assumption of determinism. So determinism can be held for many different reasons. What is implied by such deterministic beliefs is a subject of great debate; and that will be our next subject.

READINGS

"DIALOGUE ON FREE WILL"
Lorenzo de Valla

Lorenzo de Valla (1405–1457) was one of the greatest of the Italian humanist scholars of the fifteenth century, who generally favored the teachings of the early Church Fathers (such as Augustine) over the scholasticism of Thomas Aquinas. He spent much of his career as a respected scholar doing translations from other languages, as well as writing his own work, in the court of King Alfonso of Aragon. His "Dialogue on Free Will" was one of his most famous pieces, and it had enormous influence on the discussion of that issue over the next several centuries. In the dialogue, Lorenzo de Valla (represented by "Lor") first examines the question of God's foreknowledge, but then moves on to the much more problematic question of how God's *omnipotence* could be reconciled with human free will. Valla concludes that no answer is possible to that question (the answer is "food of the gods," and not knowledge that is given to mere mortals). There is some question of whether that conclusion is the actual conclusion favored by Valla, or whether it hints at an answer he dare not write for fear of condemnation by the Church. But you will have to reach your own conclusions about that. ("Ant" in the dialogue represents "Antonio," Lorenzo de Valla's imagined dialogue partner)

Lor. What do you ask me to explain to you?

Ant. Whether the foreknowledge of God stands in the way of free will and whether Boethius has correctly argued this question.

Lor. I shall attend to Boethius later; but if I satisfy you in this matter, I want you to make a promise.

Ant. What sort of a promise?

Lor. That if I serve you splendidly in this luncheon, you will not want to be entertained again for dinner.

Ant. What do you mean as lunch for me and what as dinner, for I do not understand?

Lor. That contented after discussing this one question, you will not ask for another afterward.

Ant. You say another? As if this one will not be sufficient and more! I freely promise that I will ask no dinner from you.

Lor. Go ahead then and get into the very heart of the question.

Ant. You advise well. If God foresees the future, it cannot happen otherwise than He foresaw. For example, if He sees that Judas will be a traitor, it is impossible for him not to become a traitor, that is, it is necessary for Judas to betray, unless—which should be far from us—we assume God to lack providence. Since He has providence, one must undoubtedly believe that mankind does not have free will in its own power; and I do not speak particularly of evil men, for as it is necessary for these to do

evil, so conversely it is necessary for the good to do good, provided those are still to be called good or evil who lack will or that their actions are to be considered right or wrong which are necessary and forced. And what now follows you yourself see: for God either to praise this one for justice or accuse that of injustice and to reward the one and punish the other, to speak freely, seems to be the opposite of justice, since the actions of men follow by necessity the foreknowledge of God. We should therefore abandon religion, piety, sanctity, ceremonies, sacrifices; we may expect nothing from Him, employ no prayers, not call upon his mercy at all, neglect to improve our mind, and, finally, do nothing except what pleases us, since our justice or injustice is foreknown by God. Consequently, it seems that either He does not foresee the future if we are endowed with will or He is not just if we lack free will. There you have what makes me inclined to doubt in this matter.

Lor. You have indeed not only pushed into the middle of the question but have even more widely extended it. You say God foresaw that Judas would be a traitor, but did He on that account induce him to betrayal? I do not see that, for, although God may foreknow some future act to be done by man, this act is not done by necessity because he may do it willingly. Moreover, what is voluntary cannot be necessary.

Ant. Do not expect me to give in to you so easily or to flee without sweat and blood.

Lor. Good luck to you; let us contend closely in hand-to-hand and foot-to-foot conflict. Let the decision be by sword, not spear.

Ant. You say Judas acted voluntarily and on that account not by necessity. Indeed, it would be most shameless to deny that he did it voluntarily. What do I say to that? Certainly this act of will was necessary since God foreknew it; moreover, since it was foreknown by Him, it was necessary for Judas to will and do it lest he should make the foreknowledge in any way false.

Lor. Still I do not see why the necessity for our volitions and actions should derive from God's foreknowledge. For, if foreknowing something *will be* makes it come about, surely knowing something *is* just as easily makes the same thing *be*. Certainly, if I know your genius, you would not say that something *is* because you *know* it is. For example, you know it is now day; because you know it is, is it on that account also day? Or, conversely, because it is day, do you for that reason know it is day?

Ant. Indeed, continue.

Lor. The same reasoning applies to the past. I know it was night eight hours ago, but my knowledge does not make [it] that it was night; rather I know it was night because it was night. Again, that I may come closer to the point, I know in advance that after eight hours it will be night, and will it be on that account? Not at all, but because it will be night for that reason I foreknew it; now if the foreknowledge of man is not the cause of something occurring, neither is the foreknowledge of God.

Ant. Believe me, that comparison deceives us; it is one thing to know the present and past, another to know the future. For when I know something is, it cannot be changed, as that day, which now is, cannot be made not to be. Also the past does not differ from the present, for we did not notice the day when it was past but while it was occurring as the present; I learned it was night not then when it *had passed* but when it was. And so for these times I concede that something *was*, or *is*, not because I know it but that I know it because it

is or *was*. But a different reasoning applies to the future because it is subject to change. It cannot be known for certain because it is uncertain. And, in order that we may not defraud God of foreknowledge, we must admit that the future is certain and on that account necessary; this is what deprives us of free will. Nor can you say what you said just now that the future is not preordained merely because God foresees it but that God foresees it because the future is preordained; you thus wound God by implying that it is necessary for him to foreknow the future.

Lor. You have come well armed and weaponed for the fight, but let us see who is deceived, you or I. First, however, I would meet this latter point where you say that, if God foresees the future because it is to be, He labors under the necessity to foresee the future. Indeed this should not be attributed to necessity but to nature, to will, to power, unless it is an attribute of weakness perchance that God cannot sin, cannot die, cannot give up His wisdom rather than an attribute of power and of divinity. Thus, when we said He is unable to escape foresight, which is a form of wisdom, we inflicted no wound on Him but did Him honor. So I shall not be afraid to say that God is unable to escape foreseeing what is to be. I come now to your first point: that the present and the past are unalterable and therefore knowable; that the future is alterable and therefore not capable of being foreknown. I ask if it can be changed that at eight hours from now night will arrive, that after summer there will be autumn, after autumn winter, after winter spring, after spring summer?

Ant. Those are natural phenomena always running the same course; I speak, however, of matters of the will.

Lor. What do you say of chance things? Can they be foreseen by God without necessity being imputed to them? Perchance today it may rain or I may find a treasure, would you concede this could be foreknown without any necessity?

Ant. Why should I not concede it? Do you believe I think so ill of God?

Lor. Make sure that you do not think ill when you say you think well. For if you concede in this case, why should you doubt in matters of the will, for both classes of events can happen in two different ways?

Ant.   The matter is not that way. For these chance things follow a certain nature of their own, and for this reason doctors, sailors, and farmers are accustomed to foresee much, since they reckon consequences out of antecedents, which cannot happen in affairs of the will. Predict which foot I will move first, and, whichever you have said, you will lie, since I shall move the other.

Lor.   I ask you, who was ever found so clever as this Glarea? He thinks he can impose on God like the man in Aesop who consulted Apollo whether the sparrow he held under his coat was dead for the sake of deceiving him. For you have not told me to predict, but God. Indeed, I have not the ability to predict whether there will be a good vintage, such as you ascribe to farmers. But by saying and also believing that God does not know which foot you will move first, you involve yourself in great sin.

Ant.   Do you think I affirm something rather than raise the question for the sake of the argument? Again you seem to seek excuses by your speech and, giving ground, decline to fight.

Lor.   As if I fought for the sake of victory rather than truth! Witness how I am driven from my ground; do you grant that God now knows your will even better than you yourself do?

Ant.   I indeed grant it.

Lor.   It is also necessary that you grant that you will do nothing other than the will decides.

Ant.   Of course.

Lor.   How then can He not know the action if He knows the will which is the source of the action?

Ant.   Not at all, for I myself do not know what I shall do even though I know what I have in my will. For I do not will to move this foot or that foot, in any case, but the other than He will have announced. And so, if you compare me with God, just as I do not know what I will do, so He does not know.

Lor.   What difficulty is there in meeting this sophism of yours? He knows that you are prepared to reply otherwise than He will say and that you will move the left first if the right is named by Him; whichever one He should say therefore, it is certain to Him what will happen.

Ant.   Yet which of the two will He say?

Lor.   Do you speak of God? Let me know your will and I will announce what will happen.

Ant.   Go ahead, you try to know my will.

Lor.   You will move the right one first.

Ant.   Behold, the left one.

Lor.   How have you shown my foreknowledge to be false, since I knew you would move the left one?

Ant.   But why did you say other than you thought?

Lor.   In order to deceive you by your own arts and to deceive the man willing to deceive.

Ant.   But God Himself would not lie nor deceive in replying, nor did you do rightly in replying for Another as He would not reply.

Lor.   Did you not tell me to "predict"? Therefore, I should not speak for God but for myself whom you asked.

Ant.   How changeable you are. A little while ago you were saying I told God to "predict," not you; now on the contrary you say the opposite. Let God reply which foot I will move first.

Lor.   How ridiculous, as if He would answer you!

Ant.   What? Can He not indeed reply truly if He wishes?

Lor.   Rather He can lie who is the Truth itself.

Ant.   What would He reply then?

Lor.   Certainly what you will do, but, you not hearing, He might say to me, He might say to one of those other people, He might say it to many; and, when He has done that, do you not think He will truly have predicted?

Ant.   Yea, indeed, He will have truly predicted, but what would you think if He predicted it to me?

Lor.   Believe me, you who thus lie in wait to deceive God, if you should hear or certainly know what He said you would do, either out of love or out of fear you would hasten to do what you knew was predicted by Him. But let us skip this which has nothing to do with foreknowledge. For it is one thing to foreknow and another to predict the future. Say whatever you have in mind about foreknowledge, but leave prediction out of it.

Ant.   So be it, for the things that I have said were spoken not so much for me as against you. I return from this digression to where I said it was necessary for Judas to betray, unless we entirely annul providence, because God foresaw it would be thus. So if it was possible for something to happen otherwise than it was foreseen, providence is destroyed; but if it is impossible, free will is destroyed, a thing no less unworthy to God than if we should cancel His providence. I, in what concerns me, would prefer Him to be less wise rather than less good. The latter would injure mankind; the other would not.

Lor. I praise your modesty and wisdom. When you are not able to win, you do not fight on stubbornly but give in and apply yourself to another defense, which seems to be the argument of what you set forth a while back. In reply to this argument, I deny that foreknowledge can be deceived as the consequence of the possibility that something might turn out otherwise than as it has been foreseen. For what prevents it from also being true that something can turn out otherwise than it will immediately happen? Something that can happen and something that will happen are very different. I can be a husband, I can be a soldier or a priest, but will I right away? Not at all. Though I can do otherwise than will happen, nevertheless I shall not do otherwise; and it was in Judas' power not to sin even though it was foreseen that he would, but he preferred to sin, which it was foreseen would happen. Thus foreknowledge is valid and free will abides. This will make a choice between two alternatives, for to do both is not possible, and He foreknows by His own light which will be chosen . . .

Ant. I will not object further, nor, since I smashed all my weapons, will I fight with tooth and nail as is said; but, if there is any other point through which you can explain it to me more amply and plainly persuade, I wish to hear it.

Lor. You covet the praise of wisdom and modesty again, since you are your true self. And so I will do as you ask because I was doing it anyway of my own will. For what has been said so far is not what I had decided to say but what need of defense itself demanded. Now attend to what persuades me and perhaps it will even persuade you that foreknowledge is no impediment to free will. However, would you prefer me to touch on this subject briefly or to explain it more clearly at greater length?

Ant. It always seems to me, indeed, that those who speak lucidly speak most briefly, while those who speak obscurely, though in the fewest words, are always more lengthy. Besides, fulness of expression has itself a certain appropriateness and aptness for persuasion. Wherefore, since I asked you from the start that this matter be more lucidly stated by you, you should not doubt my wishes; nevertheless, do whatever is more agreeable to you. For I would never put my judgment ahead of yours.

Lor. Indeed, it is of importance to me to follow your wish, and whatever you think more convenient I do also. Apollo, who was so greatly celebrated among the Greeks, either through his own nature or by concession of the other gods, had foresight and knowledge of all future things, not only those which pertained to men but to the gods as well; thus, if we may believe the tradition, and nothing prevents our accepting it just for the moment, Apollo rendered true and certain prophecies about those consulting him. Sextus Tarquinius consulted him as to what would happen to himself. We may pretend that he replied, as was customary, in verse as follows:

An exile and a pauper you will fall,
Killed by the angry city.

To this Sextus: "What are you saying, Apollo? Have I deserved thus of you that you announce me a fate so cruel, that you assign me such a sad condition of death? Repeal your response, I implore you, predict happier things; you should be better disposed toward me who so royally endowed you." In reply Apollo: "Your gifts, O youth, certainly are agreeable and acceptable to me; in return for which I have rendered a miserable and sad prophecy, I wish it were happier, but it is not in my power to do this. I know the fates, I do not decide them; I am able to announce Fortune, not change her; I am the index of destinies, not the arbiter; I would reveal better things if better things awaited. Certainly this is not my fault who cannot prevent even my own misfortune that I foresee. Accuse Jupiter, if you will, accuse the fates, accuse Fortune whence the course of events descends. The power and decision over the fates are seated with them; with me, mere foreknowledge and prediction. You earnestly besought an oracle; I gave it. You inquired after the truth; I was unable to tell a lie. You have come to my temple from a far distant region, and I ought not to send you away without a reply. Two things are most alien to me: falsehood and silence." Could Sextus justly reply to this speech: "Yea, indeed, it is your fault, Apollo, who foresee my fate with your wisdom, for, unless you had foreseen it, this would not be about to happen to me"?

Ant.   Not only would he speak unjustly but he should never reply thus.

Lor.   How then?

Ant.   Why do you not say?

Lor.   Should he not reply in this way: "Indeed, I give thanks to you, holy Apollo, who have neither deceived me with falsehood nor spurned me in silence. But this also I ask you to tell me: Why is Jupiter so unjust, so cruel, to me that he should assign such a sad fate to me, an undeserving, innocent worshiper of the gods"?

Ant.   Certainly I would reply in this way if I were Sextus, but what did Apollo reply to him?

Lor.   "You call yourself undeserving and innocent, Sextus? You may be sure that the crimes that you will commit, the adulteries, betrayals, perjuries, the almost hereditary arrogance are to blame." Would Sextus then reply this way: "The fault for my crimes must rather be assigned to you, for it is necessary for me, who you foreknow will sin, to sin"?

Ant.   Sextus would be mad as well as unjust if he replied in that way.

Lor.   Do you have anything that you might say on his behalf?

Ant.   Absolutely nothing.

Lor.   If therefore Sextus had nothing which could be argued against the foreknowledge of Apollo, certainly Judas had nothing either which might accuse the foreknowledge of God. And, if that is so, certainly the question by which you said you were confused and disturbed is answered.

Ant.   It is indeed answered and, what I scarcely dared to hope, fully solved, for the sake of which I both give you thanks and have, I would say, an almost immortal gift. What Boethius was unable to show me you have shown.

Lor.   And now I shall try to say something about him because I know you expect it and I promised to do it.

Ant.   What are you saying about Boethius? It will be agreeable and pleasant to me.

Lor.   We may follow the line of the fable we started. You think Sextus had nothing to reply to Apollo; I ask you what would you say to a king who refused to offer an office or position to you because he says you would commit a capital offense in that function.

Ant.   "I would swear to you, King, by your most strong and faithful right hand that I will commit no crime in this magistracy."

Lor.   Likewise perhaps Sextus would say to Apollo, "I swear to you, Apollo, that I will not commit what you say."

Ant.   What does Apollo answer?

Lor.   Certainly not in the way the king would, for the king has not discovered what the future is, as God has. Apollo therefore might say: "Am I a liar, Sextus? Do I not know what the future is? Do I speak for the sake of warning you, or do I render a prophecy? I say to you again, you will be an adulterer, you will be a traitor, you will be a perjurer, you will be arrogant and evil."

Ant.   A worthy speech by Apollo! What was Sextus able to muster against it?

Lor.   Does it not occur to you what he could argue in his own defense? Is he with a meek mind to suffer himself to be condemned?

Ant.   Why not, if he is guilty?

Lor.   He is not guilty but is predicted to be so in the future. Indeed, I believe that if Apollo announced this to you, you would flee to prayer, and pray not to Apollo but to Jupiter that he would give you a better mind and change the fates.

Ant.   That I would do, but I would be making Apollo a liar.

Lor.   You speak rightly, because if Sextus cannot make him a liar, he employs prayers in vain. What should he do? Would he not be offended, angered, burst forth in complaints? "Thus, Apollo, am I unable to restrain myself from offenses, am I unable to accept virtue, do I not avail to reform the mind from wickedness, am I not endowed with free will?"

Ant.   Sextus speaks bravely and truly and justly. What does the god reply?

Lor.   "That is the way things are, Sextus. Jupiter as he created the wolf fierce, the hare timid, the lion brave, the ass stupid, the dog savage, the sheep mild, so he fashioned some men hard of heart, others soft, he generated one given to evil, the other to virtue, and, further, he gave a capacity for reform to one and made another incorrigible. To you, indeed, he assigned an evil soul with no resource for reform. And so both you, for your inborn character, will do evil, and Jupiter, on account of your actions and their evil effects, will punish sternly, and thus he has sworn by the Stygian swamp it will be."

Ant.   At the same time that Apollo neatly excuses himself, he accuses Jupiter the more, for I am more favorable to Sextus than Jupiter. And so he might best protest justly as follows: "And why is it my crime rather than Jupiter's? When I am not allowed to do anything except evil, why does Jupiter condemn me for his own crime? Why does he punish me without guilt? Whatever I do, I do not do it by free will but of necessity. Am I able to oppose his will and power?"

Lor. This is what I wished to say for my proof. For this is the point of my fable, that, although the wisdom of God cannot be separated from His power and will, I may by this device of Apollo and Jupiter separate them. What cannot be achieved with one god may be achieved with two, each having his own proper nature—the one for creating the character of men, the other for knowing—that it may appear that providence is not the cause of necessity but that all this whatever it is must be referred to the will of God.

Ant. See, you have thrown me back into the same pit whence you dug me; this doubt is like that which I set forth about Judas. There necessity was ascribed to the foreknowledge of God, here to the will; what difference is it how you annul free will? That it is destroyed by foreknowledge, you indeed deny, but you say it is by divine will, by which the question goes back to the same place.

Lor. Do I say that free will is annulled by the will of God?

Ant. Is it not implied unless you solve the ambiguity?

Lor. Pray who will solve it for you?

Ant. Indeed I will not let you go until you solve it.

Lor. But that is to violate the agreement, and not content with luncheon you demand dinner also.

Ant. Is it thus you have defrauded me and coerced me through a deceitful promise? Promises in which deceit enters do not stand, nor do I think I have received luncheon from you if I am forced to vomit up whatever I have eaten, or, to speak more lightly, you send me away no less hungry than you received me.

Lor. Believe me, I didn't want to make you promise in such a way that I would cheat you, for what advantage would there have been to me, since I not even have been allowed to give you luncheon? Since you received it willingly and since you gave me thanks for it, you are ungrateful if you say you were forced by me to vomit it or that I send you away as hungry as you came. That is asking for dinner, not luncheon, and wanting to find fault with

luncheon and to demand that I spread before you ambrosia and nectar, the food of the gods, not men. I have put my fish and fowl from my preserves and wine from a suburban hill before you. You should demand ambrosia and nectar from Apollo and Jupiter themselves.

Ant. Are not ambrosia and what you call nectar poetic and fabulous things? Let us leave this emptiness to the empty and fictitious gods, Jupiter and Apollo. You have given luncheon from these preserves and cellars; I ask dinner from the same.

Lor. Do you think I am so rude that I would send away a friend coming to me for dinner? But since I saw how this question was likely to end, I consulted my own interests back there and compelled you to promise that afterward you would not exact from me anything besides the one thing that was asked. Therefore, I proceed with you not so much from right as from equity. Perhaps you will obtain this dinner from others which, if friendship can be trusted, is not entirely in my possession.

Ant. I will give you no further trouble lest I seem ungrateful to a benefactor and distrustful of a friend; but, still, from whom do you suggest I seek this out?

Lor. If I were able, I would not send you away for dinner, but I would go there for dinner together with you.

Ant. Do you suppose no one has these divine foods, as you call them?

Lor. Why should I not think so. Have you not read the words of Paul about the two children of Rebecca and Isaac? There he said:

For the children being not yet born, neither having done any good or evil, that the purpose of God according to election might stand, not of works, but of him that calleth; it was said unto her, The elder shall serve the younger. As it is written, Jacob have I loved, but Esau have I hated. What shall we say then? Is there unrighteousness with God? God forbid. For he saith to Moses, I will have mercy on whom I will have mercy, and I will have compassion on whom I will have compassion. So then it is not of him that willeth, nor of him that runneth, but of God that showeth mercy. For the scripture saith unto Pharaoh, Even for this same purpose have I raised thee up, that

I might show my power in thee, and that my name might be declared throughout all the earth. Therefore hath he mercy on whom he will have mercy, and whom he will he hardeneth. Thou wilt say then unto me, Why doth he yet find fault? For who hath resisted his will? Nay but, O man, who art thou that repliest against God? Shall the thing formed say to him that formed it, Why hast thou made me thus? Hath not the potter power over the clay, of the same lump to make one vessel unto honor, and another unto dishonor? [Rom. 9:11–21 (King James Version)].

And a little later, as if the excessive splendor of the wisdom of God darkened his eyes, he proclaimed (Rom. 11: 33): "O the depth of the riches both of the wisdom and knowledge of God! how unsearchable are his judgments, and his ways past finding out!" For if that vessel of election who, snatched up even to the third heaven, heard the secret words which man is not permitted to speak, nevertheless was unable to say or even to perceive them, who at length would hope that he could search out and comprehend? Carefully notice, however, free will is not said to be impeded in the same way by the will of God as by foreknowledge, for the will has an antecedent cause which is seated in the wisdom of God. Indeed the most worthy reason may be adduced as to why He hardens this one and shows mercy to that, namely, that He is most wise and good. For it is impious to believe otherwise than that, being absolutely good, He does rightly.

BONDAGE OF THE WILL
Martin Luther

Martin Luther (1483–1546) was the brash, earthy, combative, and outspoken leader of the Protestant Reformation. In one of the most famous conflicts of the Reformation, Desiderius Erasmus (a famous philosopher and theologian of the Reformation era) squared off with Luther in a dispute over free will. Erasmus was a leader of the movement for reform in the Catholic Church, and it was widely expected that Erasmus would join the Protestant Reformation in its rejection of the Pope and the hierarchy—and corruption—of the Catholic Church. But although Erasmus favored reform of the Church, he opposed revolution, working instead for more modest reform efforts from within. Furthermore, Erasmus was never really comfortable with the views of Luther: Erasmus welcomed the influence of Greek philosophy—and the views of Plato and Aristotle—on Christianity, while Luther regarded all such additions as corruptions. Erasmus tried to stay on good terms with both the Catholic authorities and his many friends among the Protestants, but as the conflict became more heated, it became clear that he could not remain in the middle: The Catholic Church demanded that he make public his rejection of Protestantism (or face arrest—and probably death—for heresy). Erasmus agreed to write a piece—*A Disquisition upon Free Will* (De Libero Arbitrio Diatribe), sometimes translated as *Diatribe on Free Will*, published in 1524—attacking Protestant theology; and he chose an issue that was important to both himself and to Luther, but also an issue on which he thought he could offer mild criticisms of Protestant views and propose a compromise: the issue of free will. Even in his attack on Luther's views, Erasmus offers an olive branch, and is willing to compromise: "For my part I prefer moderation," Erasmus writes, and he proposes "this moderate solution" that leaves room for good works and some limited human free will, though all power still belongs to God. In contrast with the moderate and restrained defense of free will offered by Erasmus, Luther offers no compromises and takes no prisoners in his passionate denial of free will and his powerful defense of predestination. The following passage is excerpted from Luther's *Bondage of the Will*, 1525; the translation is by Henry Cole.

. . .

These statements of yours are without Christ, without the Spirit, and more cold than ice, so that the beauty of your eloquence is really deformed by them. Perhaps a fear of the popes and those tyrants extorted them from you, their miserable vassal, lest you should appear to them a perfect atheist. But what they assert is this: that there is ability in us; that there is a striving with all our powers; that there is mercy in God; that there are ways of gaining that mercy; that there is a God, by nature just, and most merciful, etc. But if a man does not know what these powers are, what they can do or in what they are to be passive, what their efficacy or what their inefficacy is, what can such an one do? What will you set him about doing?

"It is irreligious, curious, and superfluous," you say, "to wish to know whether our own will does anything in those things which pertain unto eternal salvation, or whether it is wholly passive under the work of grace." But here you say the contrary: that it is Christian piety to "strive with all the powers"; and that "without the mercy of God the will is ineffective."

Here you plainly assert that the will does something in those things which pertain unto eternal salvation, when you speak of it as striving; and again you assert that it is passive when you say that without the mercy of God it is ineffective. Though, at the same time, you do not define how far that doing, and being passive, is to be understood—thus designedly keeping us in ignorance how far the mercy of God extends, and how far our own will extends; what our own will is to do, in that which you enjoin, and what the mercy of God is to do. Thus that prudence of yours carries you along; by which you are resolved to hold with neither side and to escape safely through Scylla and Charybdis, in order that, when you come into the open sea and find yourself overwhelmed and confounded by the waves, you may have it in your power to assert all that you now deny, and deny all that you now assert. . . .

In this book, therefore, I will push you, and the Sophists together, until you shall define to me the power of free will and what it can do; and I hope I shall so push you (Christ willing) as to make you heartily repent that you ever published your *Diatribe*.

This, therefore, is also essentially necessary and wholesome for Christians to know: that God foreknows nothing by contingency, but that He foresees, purposes, and does all things according to His immutable, eternal, and infallible will. By this thunderbolt free will is thrown prostrate and utterly dashed to pieces. Those, therefore, who would assert free will must either deny this thunderbolt, or pretend not to see it, or push it from them. But, before I establish this point by any arguments of my own, and by the authority of Scripture, I will first set it forth in your words.

Are you not then the person, friend Erasmus, who just now asserted that God is by nature just and by nature most merciful? If this be true, does it not follow that He is *immutably* just and merciful? That as His nature is not changed to all eternity, so neither His justice nor His mercy? And what is said concerning His justice and His mercy must be said also concerning His knowledge, His wisdom, His goodness; His will, and His other attributes. If therefore these things are asserted religiously, piously, and wholesomely concerning God, as you say yourself, what has come to you that, contrary to your own self, you now assert that it is irreligious, curious, and vain to say that God foreknows of necessity? You openly declare that the immutable *will* of God is to be known, but you forbid the knowledge of His immutable *prescience*. Do you believe that He foreknows against His will or that He wills in ignorance? If, then, He foreknows, willing, His will is eternal and immovable, because His nature is so; and, if He wills, foreknowing, His knowledge is eternal and immovable, because His nature is so. . . .

"Who," you say, "will endeavour to amend his life?" I answer, "No man! No man can!" For your self-amenders without the Spirit, God regardeth not, for they are hypocrites. But the Elect, and those that fear God, will be amended by the Holy Spirit; the rest will perish unamended. Nor does Augustine say that the works of *none*, nor that the works of *all* are crowned, but the works of *some*. Therefore there will be *some* who shall amend their lives.

"Who will believe," you say, "that he is loved of God?" I answer, "No man will believe it! No man can!" But the Elect shall believe it; the rest shall perish without believing it, filled with indignation and blaspheming, as you here describe them. Therefore there will be *some* who shall believe it.

And as to your saying that "by these doctrines the floodgate of iniquity is thrown open unto men"—be it so. They pertain to that leprosy of evil to be borne, spoken of before. Nevertheless, by the same doctrines, there is thrown open to the Elect, and to them that fear God, a gate unto righteousness—an entrance into heaven, a way unto God! But if, according to your advice, we should refrain from these doctrines, and should hide from men this Word of God, so that each, deluded by a false persuasion of salvation, should never learn to fear God, and should never be humbled, in order that through this fear he might come to grace and love; then, indeed, we should shut up your floodgate to purpose! For in the room of it, we should throw open to ourselves and to all, wide gates, nay, yawning chasms and sweeping tides, not only unto iniquity, but unto the depths of hell! Thus we should not enter into heaven ourselves, and them that were entering in we should hinder. . . .

God has promised certainly His grace to the humbled: that is, to the self-deploring and despairing. But a man cannot be thoroughly humbled until he comes to know that his salvation is utterly beyond his own powers, counsel, endeavours, will, and works, and absolutely depending on the will, counsel, pleasure, and work of another, that is, of God only. For if, as long as he has any persuasion that he can do even the least thing himself towards his own salvation, he retain a confidence in himself and do not utterly despair in himself, so long he is not humbled before God; but he proposes to himself some place, some time, or some work, whereby he may at length attain unto salvation. But he who hesitates not to depend wholly upon the good will of God, he totally despairs in himself, chooses nothing for himself, but waits for God to work in him; and such a one is the nearest unto grace. . . .

These things, therefore, are openly proclaimed for the sake of the Elect; that, being by these means humbled and brought down to nothing, they might be saved. The rest resist this humiliation; nay, they condemn the teaching of self-desperation; they wish to have left a little something that they may do themselves. These secretly remain proud, and adversaries to the grace of God. This, I say, is one reason: that those who fear God, being humbled, might know, call upon, and receive the grace of God. . . .

This is the highest degree of faith—to believe that He is merciful, who saves so few and damns so many; to believe Him just, who according to His own will makes us necessarily damnable, that He may seem, as Erasmus says, "to delight in the torments of the miserable, and to be an object of hatred rather than of love." If, therefore, I could by any means comprehend how that same God can be merciful and just who carries the appearance of so much wrath and iniquity, there would be no need of faith. But now, since that cannot be comprehended, there is room for exercising faith, while such things are preached and openly proclaimed: in the same manner as, while God kills, the faith of life is exercised in death. . . .

As to the other paradox you mention, that "whatever is done by us is not done by free will but from mere necessity." Let us briefly consider this, lest we should suffer anything most perniciously spoken to pass by unnoticed. Here then, I observe, that if it be proved that our salvation is apart from our own strength and counsel, and depends on the working of God alone (which I hope I shall clearly prove hereafter, in the course of this discussion), does it not evidently follow that when God is not present with us to work in us, everything that we do is evil, and that we of necessity do those things which are of no avail unto salvation? For if it is not we ourselves, but God only, that works salvation in us, it must follow . . . that we do nothing unto salvation *before* the working of God in us. . . .

But again, on the other hand, when God works in us, the *will*, being changed and sweetly breathed on by the Spirit of God, desires and acts, not from *compulsion*, but *responsively*, from pure willingness, inclination, and accord; so that it cannot be turned another way by anything contrary, nor be compelled or overcome even by the gates of hell; but it still goes on to desire, crave after, and love that which is good; even as before it desired, craved after, and loved that which was evil. This, again, experience proves. How invincible and unshaken are holy men, when, by violence and other oppressions, they are only compelled and irritated the more to crave after good! Even as fire is rather fanned into flames than extinguished by the wind. So that neither is there here any willingness, or free will, to turn itself into another direction, or to desire anything else, while the influence of the Spirit and grace of God remain in the man.

In a word, if we be under the god of this world, without the operation and Spirit of God, we are led captives by him at his will, as Paul saith. So that we cannot will anything but that which he wills. For he is that "strong man armed," who so keepeth his palace that those whom he holds captive are kept in peace, that they might not cause any motion or feeling against him; otherwise the kingdom of Satan, being divided against itself, could not stand; whereas Christ affirms it does stand. And all this we do willingly and desiringly, according to the nature of *will*: for if it were forced, it would be no longer *will*. For compulsion is (so to speak) *unwillingness*. But if the "stronger than he" come and overcome him, and take us as His spoils, then, through the Spirit, we are His servants and captives (which is the royal liberty), that we may desire and do, willingly, what He wills.

Thus the human will is, as it were, a beast between the two. If God sit thereon, it wills and goes where God will: as the Psalm saith, "I am become as it were a beast before thee, and I am continually with thee." If Satan sit thereon, it wills and goes as Satan will. Nor is it in the power of its own will to choose, to which rider it will run, nor which it will seek; but the riders themselves contend, which shall have and hold it. . . .

I shall here draw this book to a conclusion, prepared if it were necessary to pursue this discussion still further. Though I consider that I have now abundantly satisfied the godly man, who wishes to believe the truth without making resistance. For if we believe it to be true that God foreknows and foreordains all things; that He can be neither deceived nor hindered in His Prescience and Predestination; and that nothing can take place but according to His will (which reason herself is compelled to confess), then, even according to the testimony of reason herself, there can be no free will in man, in angel, or in any creature!

⋙ Enquiry Concerning the Human Understanding ⋙
David Hume

David Hume (1711–1776) develops the classic arguments for *determinism* as well as for the *compatibilist* view that free will (or "liberty") is compatible with determinism (or "necessity"). Actually, Hume does not argue for determinism, but rather argues that everyone already *believes* in determinism, that belief in determinism is quite reasonable, and that only verbal confusions keep people from recognizing and acknowledging their belief in determinism. Hume pushes beyond simply claiming that determinism is *compatible* with free will, arguing that determinism is essential for genuine freedom: To the extent that determinism breaks down, free will is compromised. The passage that follows is "Of Liberty and Necessity," a section of Hume's *Enquiry Concerning the Human Understanding*, published in 1748.

PART I

It might reasonably be expected, in questions which have been canvassed and disputed with great eagerness since the first origin of science and philosophy, that the meaning of all the terms, at least, should have been agreed upon among the disputants, and our inquiries, in the course of two thousand years, been able to pass from words to the true and real subject of the controversy. For how easy may it seem to give exact definitions of the terms employed in reasoning, and make these definitions, not the mere sound of words, the object of future scrutiny and examination? But if we consider the matter more narrowly, we shall be apt to draw a quite opposite conclusion. From this circumstance alone, that a controversy has been long kept on foot and remains still undecided, we may presume that there is some ambiguity in the expression, and that the disputants affix different ideas to the terms employed in the controversy. For as the faculties of the mind are supposed to be naturally alike in every individual—otherwise nothing could be more fruitless than to reason or dispute together—it were impossible, if men affix the same ideas to their terms, that they could so long form different opinions of the same subject, especially when they communicate their views and each party turn themselves on all sides in search of arguments which may give them the victory over their antagonists. It is true, if men attempt the discussion of questions which lie entirely beyond the reach of human capacity, such as those concerning the origin of worlds or the economy of the intellectual system or region of spirits, they may long beat the air in their fruitless contests and never arrive at any determinate conclusion. But if the question regard any subject of common life and experience, nothing, one would think, could preserve the dispute so long undecided, but some ambiguous expressions which keep the antagonists still at a distance and hinder them from grappling with each other.

This has been the case in the long-disputed question concerning liberty and necessity, and to so remarkable a degree that, if I be not much mistaken, we shall find that all mankind, both learned and ignorant, have always been of the same opinion with regard to this subject, and that a few intelligible definitions would immediately have put an end to the whole controversy. I own that this dispute has been so much canvassed on all hands, and has led philosophers into such a labyrinth of obscure sophistry, that it is no wonder if a sensible reader indulge his ease so far as to turn a deaf ear to the proposal of such a question from which he can expect neither instruction nor entertainment. But the state of the argument here proposed may, perhaps, serve to renew his attention, as it has more novelty, promises at least some decision of the controversy, and will not much disturb his ease by any intricate or obscure reasoning.

I hope, therefore, to make it appear that all men have ever agreed in the doctrine both of necessity and of liberty, according to any reasonable sense which can be put on these terms, and that the whole controversy has hitherto turned merely upon words. We shall begin with examining the doctrine of necessity.

It is universally allowed that matter, in all its operations, is actuated by a necessary force, and that every natural effect is so precisely determined by the energy of its cause that no other effect, in such particular circumstances, could possibly have resulted from it. The degree and direction of every motion is, by the laws of nature, prescribed with such exactness that a living creature may as soon arise from the shock of two bodies, as motion, in any other degree or direction than what is actually produced by it. Would we, therefore, form a just and precise idea of *necessity*, we must consider whence that idea arises when we apply it to the operation of bodies.

It seems evident that, if all the scenes of nature were continually shifted in such a manner that no two events bore any resemblance to each other, but every object was entirely new, without any similitude to whatever had been seen before, we should never, in that case, have attained the least idea of necessity or of a connection among these objects. We might say, upon such a supposition, that one object or event has followed another, not that one was produced by the other. The relation of cause and effect must be utterly unknown to mankind. Inference and reasoning concerning the operations of nature would, from that moment, be at an end; and the memory and senses remain the only canals by which the knowledge of any real existence could possibly have access to the mind. Our idea, therefore, of necessity and causation arises entirely from the uniformity observable in the operations of nature, where similar objects are constantly conjoined together, and the mind is determined by custom to infer the one from the appearance of the other. These two circumstances form the whole of that necessity which we ascribe to matter. Beyond the constant *conjunction* of similar objects and the consequent *inference* from one to the other, we have no notion of any necessity of connection.

If it appears, therefore, that all mankind have ever allowed, without any doubt or hesitation, that these two circumstances take place in the voluntary actions of men and in the operations of mind, it must follow that all mankind have ever agreed in the doctrine of necessity, and that they have hitherto disputed merely for not understanding each other.

As to the first circumstance, the constant and regular conjunction of similar events, we may possibly satisfy ourselves by the following considerations. It is universally acknowledged that there is a great uniformity among the actions of men, in all nations and ages, and that human nature remains still the same in its principles and operations. The same motives always produce the same actions; the same events follow from the same causes. Ambition, avarice, self-love, vanity, friendship, generosity, public spirit—these passions, mixed in various degrees and distributed through society, have been, from the beginning of the world, and still are, the source of all the actions and enterprises which have ever been observed among mankind. Would you know the sentiments, inclinations, and course of life of the Greeks and Romans? Study well the temper and actions of the French and English: you cannot be much mistaken in transferring to the former *most* of the observations which you have made with regard to the latter. Mankind are so much the same, in all times and places, that history informs us of nothing new or strange in this particular. Its chief use is only to discover the constant and universal principles of human nature by showing men in all varieties of circumstances and situations, and furnishing us with materials from which we may form our observations and become acquainted with the regular springs of human action and behavior. These records of wars, intrigues, factions, and revolutions are so many collections of experiments by which the politician or moral philosopher fixes the principles of his science, in the same manner as the physician or natural philosopher becomes acquainted with the nature of plants, minerals, and other external objects, by the experiments which he forms concerning them. Nor are the earth, water, and other elements examined by Aristotle and Hippocrates more like to those which at present lie under our observation than the men described by Polybius and Tacitus are to those who now govern the world.

Should a traveler, returning from a far country, bring us an account of men wholly different from any with whom we were ever acquainted, men who were entirely divested of avarice, ambition, or revenge, who knew no pleasure but friendship, generosity, and public spirit, we should immediately, from these circumstances, detect the falsehood and prove him a liar with the same certainty as if he had stuffed his narration with stories of centaurs and dragons, miracles and prodigies. And if we would explode any forgery in history, we cannot make use of a more convincing argument than to prove that the actions ascribed to any person are directly contrary to the course of nature, and that no human motives, in such circumstances, could ever induce him to such a conduct. The veracity of Quintus Curtius is as much to be suspected when he describes the supernatural courage of Alexander by which he was hurried on singly to attack multitudes, as when he describes his supernatural force and activity by which he was able to resist them. So readily and universally do we acknowledge a uniformity in human motives and actions as well as in the operations of body.

Hence, likewise, the benefit of that experience acquired by long life and a variety of business and company, in order to instruct us in the principles of human nature and regulate our future conduct as well as speculation. By means of this guide we mount up to the knowledge of men's inclinations and motives from their actions, expressions, and even gestures, and again descend to the interpretation of their actions from our knowledge of their motives and inclinations. The general observations, treasured up by a course of experience, give us the clue of human nature and teach us to unravel all its intricacies. Pretexts and appearances no longer deceive us. Public declarations pass for the specious coloring of a cause. And though virtue and honor be allowed their proper weight and authority, that perfect disinterestedness, so often pretended to, is never expected in multitudes and parties, seldom in their leaders, and scarcely even in individuals of any rank or station. But were there no uniformity in human actions, and were every experiment which we could form of this kind irregular and anomalous, it were impossible to collect any general observations concerning mankind, and no experience, however accurately digested by reflection, would ever serve to any purpose. Why is the aged husbandman more skillful in his calling than the young beginner, but because there is a certain uniformity in the operation of the sun, rain, and earth toward the production of vegetables, and experience teaches the old practitioner the rules by which this operation is governed and directed?

We must not, however, expect that this uniformity of human actions should be carried to such a length as that all men, in the same circumstances, will always act precisely in the same manner, without making any allowance for the diversity of characters, prejudices, and opinions. Such a uniformity, in every particular, is found in no part of nature. On the contrary, from observing the variety of conduct in different men we are enabled to form a greater variety of maxims which still suppose a degree of uniformity and regularity.

Are the manners of men different in different ages and countries? We learn thence the great force of custom and education, which mold the human mind from its infancy and form it into a fixed and established character. Is the behavior and conduct of the one sex very unlike that of the other? It is thence we become acquainted with the different characters which nature has impressed upon the sexes, and which she preserves with constancy and regularity. Are the actions of the same person much diversified in the different periods of his life from infancy to old age? This affords room for many general observations concerning the gradual change of our sentiments and inclinations, and the different maxims which prevail in the different ages of human creatures. Even the characters which are peculiar to each individual have a uniformity in their influence, otherwise our acquaintance with the persons, and our observations of their conduct, could never teach us their dispositions or serve to direct our behavior with regard to them.

I grant it possible to find some actions which seem to have no regular connection with any known motives and are exceptions to all the measures of conduct which have ever been established for the government of men. But if we would willingly know what judgment should be formed of such irregular and extraordinary actions, we may consider the sentiments commonly entertained with regard to those irregular events which appear in the course of nature and the operations of external objects. All causes are not conjoined to their usual effects with like uniformity. An artificer who handles only dead matter may be disappointed of his aim, as well as the politician who directs the conduct of sensible and intelligent agents.

The vulgar, who take things according to their first appearance, attribute the uncertainty of events to such an uncertainty in the causes as makes the latter often fail of their usual influence, though they meet with no impediment in their operation. But philosophers, observing that almost in every part of nature there is contained a vast variety of springs and principles which are hid by reason of their minuteness or remoteness, find that it is at least possible the contrariety of events may not proceed from any contingency in the cause but from the secret operation of contrary causes. This possibility is converted into certainty by further observation, when they remark that, upon an exact scrutiny, a contrariety of effects always betrays a contrariety of causes and proceeds from their mutual opposition. A peasant can give no better reason for the stopping of any clock or watch than to say that it does not commonly go right. But an artist easily perceives that the same force in the spring or pendulum has always the same influence on the wheels, but fails of its usual effect perhaps by reason of a grain of dust which puts a stop to the whole movement. From the observation of several parallel instances philosophers form a maxim that the connection between all causes and effects is equally necessary, and that its seeming uncertainty in some instances proceeds from the secret opposition of contrary causes.

Thus, for instance, in the human body, when the usual symptoms of health or sickness disappoint our expectation, when medicines operate not with their wonted powers, when irregular events follow from any particular cause, the philosopher and physician are not surprised at the matter, nor are ever tempted to deny, in general, the necessity and uniformity of those principles by which the animal economy is conducted. They know that a human body is a mighty complicated machine, that many secret powers lurk in it which are altogether beyond our comprehension, that to us it must often appear very uncertain in its operations, and that, therefore, the irregular events which outwardly discover themselves can be no proof that the laws of nature are not observed with the greatest regularity in its internal operations and government.

The philosopher, if he be consistent, must apply the same reasonings to the actions and volitions of intelligent agents. The most irregular and unexpected resolutions of men may frequently be accounted for by those who know every particular circumstance of their character and situation. A person of an obliging disposition gives a peevish answer; but he has the toothache, or has not dined. A stupid fellow discovers an uncommon alacrity in his carriage; but he has met with a sudden piece of good fortune. Or even when an action, as sometimes happens, cannot be particularly accounted for, either by the person himself or by others, we know, in general, that the characters of men are to a certain degree inconstant and irregular. This is, in a manner, the constant character of human nature, though it be applicable, in a more particular manner, to some persons who have no fixed rule for their conduct, but proceed in a continual course of caprice and inconstancy. The internal principles and motives may operate in a uniform manner, notwithstanding these seeming irregularities—in the same manner as the winds, rains, clouds, and other variations of the weather are supposed to be governed by steady principles, though not easily discoverable by human sagacity and inquiry.

Thus it appears not only that the conjunction between motives and voluntary actions is as regular and uniform as that between the cause and effect in any part of nature, but also that this regular conjunction has been universally acknowledged among mankind and has never been the subject of dispute either in philosophy or common life. Now, as it is from past experience that we draw all inferences concerning the future, and as we conclude that objects will always be conjoined together which we find to have always been conjoined, it may seem superfluous to prove that this experienced uniformity in human actions is a source whence we draw *inferences* concerning them. But in order to throw the argument into a greater variety of lights, we shall also insist, though briefly, on this latter topic.

The mutual dependence of men is so great in all societies that scarce any human action is entirely complete in itself or is performed without some reference to the actions of others, which are requisite to make it answer fully the intention of the agent. The poorest artificer who labors alone expects at least the protection of the magistrate to insure him the enjoyment of the fruits of his labor. He also expects that when he carries his goods to market and offers them at a reasonable price, he shall find purchasers and shall be able, by the money he acquires, to engage others to supply him with those commodities which are requisite for his subsistence. In proportion as men extend their dealings and render their intercourse with others more complicated, they always comprehend in their schemes of life a greater variety of voluntary actions which they expect, from the proper motives, to co-operate with their own. In all these conclusions they take their measures from past experience, in the same manner as in their reasonings concerning external objects, and firmly believe that men, as well as all the elements, are to continue in their operations the same that they have ever found them. A manufacturer reckons upon the labor of his servants for the execution of any work as much as upon the tools which he employs, and would be equally surprised were his expectations disappointed. In short, this experimental inference and reasoning concerning the actions of others enters so much into human life that no man, while awake, is ever a moment without employing it. Have we not reason, therefore, to affirm that all mankind have always agreed in the doctrine of necessity, according to the foregoing definition and explication of it?

Nor have philosophers ever entertained a different opinion from the people in this particular. For, not to mention that almost every action of their life supposes that opinion, there are even few of the speculative parts of learning to which it is not essential. What would become of *history* had we not a dependence on the veracity of the historian according to the experience which we have had of mankind? How could *politics* be a science if laws and forms of government had not a uniform influence upon society? Where would be the foundation of *morals* if particular characters had no certain or determinate power to produce particular sentiments, and if these sentiments had no constant operation on actions? And with what pretense could we employ our *criticism* upon any poet or polite author if we could not pronounce the conduct and sentiments of his actors either natural or unnatural to such characters and in such circumstances? It seems almost impossible, therefore, to engage either in science or action of any kind without acknowledging the doctrine of necessity, and this *inference* from motives to voluntary action, from characters to conduct.

And, indeed, when we consider how aptly *natural* and *moral* evidence link together and form only one chain of argument, we shall make no scruple to allow that they are of the same nature and derived from the same principles. A prisoner who has neither money nor interest discovers the impossibility of his escape as well when he considers the obstinacy of the jailer as the walls and bars with which he is surrounded, and in all attempts for his freedom chooses rather to work upon the stone and iron of the one than upon the inflexible nature of the other. The same prisoner, when conducted to the scaffold, foresees his death as certainly from the constancy and fidelity of his guards as from the operation of the ax or wheel. His mind runs along a certain train of ideas: the refusal of the soldiers to consent to his escape; the action of the executioner; the separation of the head and body; bleeding, convulsive motions, and death. Here is a connected chain of natural causes and voluntary actions, but the mind feels no difference between them in passing from one link to another, nor is less certain of the future event than if it were connected with the objects present to the memory or senses by a train of causes cemented together by what we are pleased to call a "physical" necessity. The same experienced union has the same effect on the mind, whether the united objects be motives, volition, and actions, or figure and motion. We may change the names of things, but their nature and their operation on the understanding never change.

Were a man whom I know to be honest and opulent, and with whom I lived in intimate friendship, to come into my house, where I am surrounded with my servants, I rest assured that he is not to stab me before he leaves it in order to rob me of my silver standish; and I no more suspect this event than the falling of the house itself, which is new and solidly built and founded.—*But he may have been seized with a sudden and unknown frenzy.*—So may a sudden earthquake arise, and shake and tumble my house about my ears. I shall, therefore, change the suppositions. I shall say that I know with certainty that he is not to put his hand into the fire and hold it there till it be consumed. And this event I think I can foretell with the same assurance as that, if he throw himself out of the window and meet with no obstruction, he will not remain a moment suspended in the air. No suspicion of an unknown frenzy can give the least possibility to the former event which is so contrary to all the known principles of human nature. A man who at noon leaves his purse full of gold on the pavement at Charing Cross may as well expect that it will fly away like a feather as that he will find it untouched an hour after. Above one-half of human reasonings contain inferences of a similar nature, attended with more or less degrees of certainty, proportioned to our experience of the usual conduct of mankind in such particular situations.

I have frequently considered what could possibly be the reason why all mankind, though they have ever, without hesitation, acknowledged the doctrine of necessity in their whole practice and reasoning, have yet discovered such a reluctance to acknowledge it in words, and have rather shown a propensity, in all ages, to profess the contrary opinion. The matter, I think, may be accounted for after the following manner. If we examine the operations of body and the production of effects from their causes, we shall find that all our faculties can never carry us further in our knowledge of this relation than barely to observe that particular objects are *constantly conjoined* together, and that the mind is carried, by a *customary transition*, from the appearance of the one to the belief of the other. But though this conclusion concerning human ignorance be the result of the strictest scrutiny of this subject, men still entertain a strong propensity to believe that they penetrate further into the powers of nature and perceive something like a necessary connection between the cause and the effect. When, again, they turn their reflections toward the operations of their own minds and *feel* no such connection of the motive and the action, they are thence apt to suppose that there is a difference between the effects which result from material force and those which arise from thought and intelligence. But being once convinced that we know nothing further of causation of any kind than merely the *constant conjunction* of objects and the consequent *inference* of the mind from one to another, and finding that these two circumstances are universally allowed to have place in voluntary actions, we may be more easily led to own the same necessity common to all causes. And though this reasoning may contradict the systems of many philosophers in ascribing necessity to the determinations of the will, we shall find, upon reflection, that they dissent from it in words only, not in their real sentiments. Necessity, according to the sense in which it is here taken, has never yet been rejected, nor can ever, I think, be rejected by any philosopher. It may only, perhaps, be pretended that the mind can perceive in the operations of matter some further connection between the cause and effect, and a connection that has not place in the voluntary actions of intelligent beings. Now, whether it be so or not can only appear upon examination, and it is incumbent on these philosophers to make good their assertion by defining or describing that necessity and pointing it out to us in the operations of material causes.

It would seem, indeed, that men begin at the wrong end of this question concerning liberty and necessity when they enter upon it by examining the faculties of the soul, the influence of the understanding, and the operations of the will. Let them first discuss a more simple question, namely, the question of body and brute unintelligent matter, and try whether they can there form any idea of causation and necessity, expect that of a constant conjunction of objects and subsequent inference of the mind from one to another. If these circumstances form, in reality, the whole of that necessity which we conceive in matter, and if these circumstances be also universally acknowledged to take place in the operations of the mind, the dispute is at an end; at least, must be owned to be thenceforth merely verbal. But as long as we will rashly suppose that we have some further idea of necessity and causation in the operations of external objects, at the same time that we can find nothing further in the voluntary actions of the mind, there is no possibility of bringing the question to any determinate issue while we proceed upon so erroneous a supposition. The only method of undeceiving us is to

mount up higher, to examine the narrow extent of science when applied to material causes, and to convince ourselves that all we know of them is the constant conjunction and inference above mentioned. We may, perhaps, find that it is with difficulty we are induced to fix such narrow limits to human understanding, but we can afterwards find no difficulty when we come to apply this doctrine to the actions of the will. For as it is evident that these have a regular conjunction with motives and circumstances and character, and as we always draw inferences from one to the other, we must be obliged to acknowledge in words that necessity which we have already avowed in every deliberation of our lives and in every step of our conduct and behavior.

But to proceed in this reconciling project with regard to the question of liberty and necessity—the most contentious question of metaphysics, the most contentious science—it will not require many words to prove that all mankind have ever agreed in the doctrine of liberty as well as in that of necessity, and that the whole dispute, in this respect also, has been hitherto merely verbal. For what is meant by liberty when applied to voluntary actions? We cannot surely mean that actions have so little connection with motives, inclinations, and circumstances that one does not follow with a certain degree of uniformity from the other, and that one affords no inference by which we can conclude the existence of the other. For these are plain and acknowledged matters of fact. By liberty, then, we can only mean *a power of acting or not acting according to the determinations of the will*; that is, if we choose to remain at rest, we may; if we choose to move, we also may. Now this hypothetical liberty is universally allowed to belong to everyone who is not a prisoner and in chains. Here then is no subject of dispute.

Whatever definition we may give of liberty, we should be careful to observe two requisite circumstances: *first*, that it be consistent with plain matter of fact; *secondly*, that it be consistent with itself. If we observe these circumstances and render our definition intelligible, I am persuaded that all mankind will be found of one opinion with regard to it.

It is universally allowed that nothing exists without a cause of its existence, and that chance, when strictly examined, is a mere negative word and means not any real power which has anywhere a being in nature. But it is pretended that some causes are necessary, some not necessary. Here then is the advantage of definitions. Let anyone *define* a cause without comprehending, as a part of the definition, a *necessary connection* with its effect, and let him show distinctly the origin of the idea expressed by the definition, and I shall readily give up the whole controversy. But if the foregoing explication of the matter be received, this must be absolutely impracticable. Had not objects a regular conjunction with each other, we should never have entertained any notion of cause and effect; and this regular conjunction produces that inference of the understanding which is the only connection that we can have any comprehension of. Whoever attempts a definition of cause exclusive of these circumstances will be obliged either to employ unintelligible terms or such as are synonymous to the term which he endeavors to define. And if the definition above mentioned be admitted, liberty, when opposed to necessity, not to constraint, is the same thing with chance, which is universally allowed to have no existence.

Part II

There is no method of reasoning more common, and yet none more blamable, than in philosophical disputes to endeavor the refutation of any hypothesis by a pretense of its dangerous consequences to religion and morality. When any opinion leads to absurdity, it is certainly false; but it is not certain that an opinion is false because it is of dangerous consequence. Such topics, therefore, ought entirely to be forborne as serving nothing to the discovery of truth, but only to make the person of an antagonist odious. This I observe in general, without pretending to draw any advantage from it. I frankly submit to an examination of this kind, and shall venture to affirm that the doctrines both of necessity and liberty, as above explained, are not only consistent with morality, but are absolutely essential to its support.

Necessity may be defined two ways, conformably to the two definitions of *cause* of which it makes an essential part. It consists either in the constant conjunction of like objects or in the inference of the understanding from one object to another. Now necessity, in both these senses (which, indeed, are at bottom the same), has universally, though tacitly, in the schools, in the pulpit, and in common life been allowed to belong to the will of man, and no one has ever pretended to deny that we can draw inferences concerning human actions, and that those inferences are founded on the experienced union of like actions, with like motives, inclinations, and circumstances. The only particular in which anyone can differ is that either perhaps he will refuse to give the name of

necessity to this property of human actions—but as long as the meaning is understood I hope the word can do no harm—or that he will maintain it possible to discover something further in the operations of matter. But this, it must be acknowledged, can be of no consequence to morality or religion, whatever it may be to natural philosophy or metaphysics. We may here be mistaken in asserting that there is no idea of any other necessity or connection in the actions of the body, but surely we ascribe nothing to the actions of the mind but what everyone does and must readily allow of. We change no circumstance in the received orthodox system with regard to the will, but only in that with regard to material objects and causes. Nothing, therefore, can be more innocent at least than this doctrine.

All laws being founded on rewards and punishments, it is supposed, as a fundamental principle, that these motives have a regular and uniform influence on the mind and both produce the good and prevent the evil actions. We may give to this influence what name we please; but as it is usually conjoined with the action, it must be esteemed a *cause* and be looked upon as an instance of that necessity which we would here establish.

The only proper object of hatred or vengeance is a person or creature endowed with thought and consciousness; and when any criminal or injurious actions excite that passion, it is only by their relation to the person, or connection with him. Actions are, by their very nature, temporary and perishing; and where they proceed not from some *cause* in the character and disposition of the person who performed them, they can neither redound to his honor if good, nor infamy if evil. The actions themselves may be blamable; they may be contrary to all the rules of morality and religion; but the person is not answerable for them and, as they proceeded from nothing in him that is durable and constant and leave nothing of that nature behind them, it is impossible he can, upon their account, become the object of punishment or vengeance. According to the principle, therefore, which denies necessity and, consequently, causes, a man is as pure and untainted, after having committed the most horrid crime, as at the first moment of his birth, nor is his character anywise concerned in his actions, since they are not derived from it; and the wickedness of the one can never be used as a proof of the depravity of the other.

Men are not blamed for such actions as they perform ignorantly and casually, whatever may be the consequences. Why? But because the principles of these actions are only momentary and terminate in them alone. Men are less blamed for such actions as they perform hastily and unpremeditatedly than for such as proceed from deliberation. For what reason? But because a hasty temper, though a constant cause or principle in the mind, operates only by intervals and infects not the whole character. Again, repentance wipes off every crime if attended with a reformation of life and manners. How is this to be accounted for? But by asserting that actions render a person criminal merely as they are proofs of criminal principles in the mind; and when, by an alteration of these principles, they cease to be just proofs, they likewise cease to be criminal. But, except upon the doctrine of necessity, they never were just proofs, and consequently never were criminal.

It will be equally easy to prove, and from the same arguments, that *liberty*, according to that definition above mentioned, in which all men agree, is also essential to morality, and that no human actions, where it is wanting, are susceptible of any moral qualities or can be the objects of approbation or dislike. For as actions are objects of our moral sentiment so far only as they are indications of the internal character, passions, and affections, it is impossible that they can give rise either to praise or blame where they proceed not from these principles, but are derived altogether from external violence . . .

EXERCISES

1. Is determinism an optimistic or a pessimistic belief?

2. You are a physician; would determinism be a useful assumption in your practice?

3. In traditional fatalism, what happens to you—your *fate*—has little connection with your efforts, your acts, your desires, your values, and your character. When it comes to fate, your efforts don't matter: you are in the hands of something much more powerful. You can rest in Baghdad or ride as fast as you can go toward Samarra, but your fate will be waiting at the fated hour. You may stay at home or flee to a distant country, but if—like Oedipus—your *fate* is to kill your father and marry your mother, then your fate cannot be avoided. You can embrace your fate or flee it, await your fate with courage and fortitude or with fear and dread, but you cannot change your fate: your fate operates independently of all your hopes, plans, powers, and efforts. But by the time of the Renaissance, at least some writers had developed a rather different concept of fate. Rather than fate being an *external* force, your fate is set by your given *character*—by some character trait, typically a character *flaw*—that the fated person cannot or will not change. Thus, Lorenzo de Valla describes the *fate* of Sextus Tarquinius in terms of the incorrigible *character* of Sextus:

   > Jupiter as he created the wolf fierce, the hare timid, the lion brave, the ass stupid, the dog savage, the sheep mild, so he fashioned some men hard of heart, others soft, he generated one given to evil, the other to virtue, and further, he gave a capacity for reform to one and made another incorrigible. To you, indeed, he assigned an evil soul with no resource for reform. And so both you, for your inborn character, will do evil, and Jupiter, on account of your actions and their evil effects, will punish sternly. . . .

   So it is Sextus' *fate* to do evil; but that fate is brought about by Sextus' own vicious character, which Sextus has no desire to change (that also being part of the way Jupiter fashioned him). When fatalism becomes *internalized* in that manner, is it still distinguishable from determinism?

4. William James says that free will (and nondeterminism) is a doctrine of *hope*, and that is its major significance; in contrast, many behavioral scientists—such as B. F. Skinner—claim that determinism is an important methodological principle, that is, it is a very useful operating assumption when doing psychological research. In both cases, the question of determinism is linked to the question of whether it is *useful* or *beneficial* to believe in determinism. Is that a legitimate approach to the question of determinism?

5. Although the debate usually centers around the question of *determinism*, many philosophers (and psychologists) insist that *determinism* is not the important issue. Perhaps at the subatomic level, there is *randomness*, as some physicists believe. But (these philosophers say) randomness at the level of subatomic particles has little to do with the question of free will; after all, when you think of free will, you aren't thinking of the undetectable random motion

of inconceivably small microscopic particles, but of *macroscopic* acts of willing that make an observable difference in our acts. The question is one of *naturalism*, not determinism. That is, the question is whether *all* our behavior ultimately can be *explained* in terms of causal factors such as heredity and environmental conditioning and social influences. *Is* naturalism the real issue for free will, rather than determinism?

6. Psychologists have found that people who believe in *fate*—that is, people who believe that they *cannot control* the major events in their lives, cannot control their future course—are more likely to become depressed than those who believe that their future is essentially of their own making. Assuming that psychologists are right about that, would that finding have any relevance for the question of whether fatalism is *true*?

7. Suppose that you believe (as Calvin and Luther believed) in *predestination*; that is, you believe that every individual is *predestined* by God (long before the person is born) for either damnation or salvation. Would it still make sense for you to *preach* or make other efforts to convert people to the path of salvation? Would it make sense for *you* (a believer in predestination) to *try* to live a life of righteousness?

8. Napoleon, the French general and emperor whose military exploits are legendary, was a fatalist. Does that surprise you? That is, does it surprise you that someone who is very active and ambitious should be a fatalist? If you became absolutely convinced that the major events in your life (including your marriage, your major victories and defeats and joys and sorrows, and your death) were *fated*, would that change the way you live?

9. The great fatalistic poet Omar Khayyám has this advice:

> Perplext no more with human or divine,
> Tomorrow's tangle to the winds resign,
>   And lose your fingers in the tresses of
> The Cypress-slender Minister of wine. . . .
>
> Yesterday this day's madness did prepare;
> Tomorrow's silence, triumph, or despair:
>   Drink! For you know not whence you came, nor why:
> Drink! For you know not why you go, nor where.

Is that good fatalistic advice: enjoy yourself, because there's nothing you can do anyway? That is, *if* you believe in fatalism, would you agree with Omar Khayyám?

10. Obviously, Luther and Erasmus have views that are fundamentally different. If you were trying to put your finger on the *key* difference between Luther and Erasmus (maybe a difference that is even deeper than their differences on free will, a difference that perhaps *underlies* their differences on the question of free will), what do you think that difference would be?

ADDITIONAL READINGS

Good clear brief introductions to questions about determinism, free will, and moral responsibility have been written by Robert Kane, *A Contemporary Introduction to Free Will* (Oxford: Oxford University Press, 2005); and by Thomas W. Clark, *Encountering Naturalism: A Worldview and Its Uses* (Center for Naturalism, 2007). Kane is also the editor of the *Oxford Handbook of Free Will* (Oxford: Oxford University Press, 2002), which contains excellent articles on a variety of issues related to free will; and a good anthology, *Free Will* (Oxford: Blackwell, 2002). There are many excellent free will anthologies; perhaps the best small collection is edited by Gary Watson: *Free Will* (Oxford: Oxford University Press, 1982). A good recent anthology is edited by Laura W. Ekstrom, *Agency and Responsibility* (Boulder, Col.: Westview Press, 2001); another very good recent collection is *Philosophical Perspectives 14, Action and Freedom, 2000*, edited by James E. Tomberlin (Oxford: Blackwell, 2000).

Robert C. Solomon, "On Fate and Fatalism," *Philosophy East and West*, volume 53, number 4 (October 2003): 435–454, is an interesting account of fatalism, though Solomon's account of fatalism—weaving it into a narrative model—is a bit unorthodox. An excellent book-length study of fatalism is Mark H. Bernstein, *Fatalism* (Lincoln: University of Nebraska Press, 1992).

The Bondage of the Will (available in several editions and translations) was Martin Luther's passionate argument for a strict predestination view: God chooses some for grace, and others for damnation, and there is nothing whatsoever that any human can do about it.

The classic presentation of both determinism and compatibilism is David Hume, *An Inquiry Concerning Human Understanding*, section 8, and his *Treatise of Human Nature*, Book II, Part III. Thomas Hobbes developed an earlier similar account (1651) in *Leviathan*, Chapter 2. A more recent argument for compatibilism can be found in A. J. Ayer, "Freedom and Necessity," in his *Philosophical Essays* (London: Macmillan, 1954).

Philosophers who deny the existence of free will altogether (generally because they favor determinism and believe determinism and free will are incompatible) include Baron D'Holbach (1770) and Arthur Schopenhauer, *Essay on the Freedom of the Will* (first published in 1841, reissued by New York: Liberal Arts Press, 1960). More recently, John Hospers has denied free will (making extensive use of Freudian psychology in his arguments); see "What Means This Freedom," in Sidney Hook, ed., *Determinism and Freedom in the Age of Modern Science* (New York: New York University Press, 1958). Interesting contemporary denials of free will are offered by Ted Honderich, *How Free Are You?* (Oxford: Oxford University Press, 1993) and by Derk Pereboom, *Living Without Free Will* (Cambridge: Cambridge University Press, 2001). B. F. Skinner, in *Beyond Freedom and Dignity* (New York: Alfred A. Knopf, 1971), as well as in his utopian novel *Walden Two* (first published in 1948; available in paperback ed., New York: Macmillan, 1976), is often thought to be rejecting free will altogether. In fact, his writings reject *libertarian* free will (and moral responsibility), but he strongly champions compatibilist free will.

For a remarkably clear and insightful guide to the issues surrounding the free will debate (and also for a very creative addition to that debate), see two books by Richard Double: *The Non-Reality of Free Will* (New York: Oxford University Press, 1991) and *Metaphilosophy and Free Will* (New York: Oxford University Press, 1996).

A superb website on free will, determinism, fatalism, and moral responsibility—also containing a number of excellent links and beautifully organized—is Ted Honderich's Determinism and Freedom Philosophy Website, at www.ucl.ac.uk/~uctytho/dfwIntroIndex.htm. A very nice collection of online papers on free will (and many other topics related to philosophy of mind) has been compiled by David Chalmers and David Bourget and is available at http://consc.net/mindpapers/5.4. Naturalism.org at www.naturalism.org/freewill.htm offers a number of excellent papers and reviews on issues related to free will. A very interesting website is the Garden of Forking Paths: A Free Will/Moral Responsibility Blog; it contains good discussions and a variety of excellent papers and can be found at *gfp.typepad.com*. Unfortunately, the site is no longer active, but it still contains excellent material. A new and active site for discussions of free will is Flickers of Freedom, at http://agencyandresponsibility.typepad.com/flickers-of-freedom/.

CHAPTER 9

IS FREE WILL COMPATIBLE WITH DETERMINISM?

At the end of the previous chapter we were looking at reasons why people strongly *object* to determinism, and among those reasons are: Determinism destroys creativity and freshness; determinism destroys free will; and determinism destroys moral responsibility. These questions will lead us deep into the disputed issues of free will and moral responsibility— questions that have provoked controversy for well over 2,000 years and that are just as fascinating today as they were to Plato and Aristotle.

DOES DETERMINISM DESTROY CREATIVITY?

King Solomon, in *Ecclesiastes*, drew a sad picture of a world where nothing is new, nothing is original:

> Vanity of vanities, saith the Preacher, vanity of vanities; all is vanity. . . . All the rivers run into the sea; yet the sea is not full; unto the place from whence the rivers come, thither they return again. . . . The thing that hath been, it is that which shall be; and that which is done is that which shall be done; and there is no new thing under the sun.

Ecclesiastes, Chapter 1

That is the picture often painted of a determined world: Determinism would destroy freshness, eliminate creativity, and leave the world a stale, sterile, and boring place, with nothing new under the sun.

> On the prephilosophical level my conviction tends rather toward the old primitive notion of fate, Moira, of Homer and the tragic poets; but Homeric Moira is a very different thing from Newtonian or neo-Newtonian determinism, and my recoil from the latter is due to its dreary prospect of a stale and routine world from which surprise and genuine novelty may ultimately be banished. *William Barrett, "Determinism and Novelty," 1958*

That is a very common objection to determinism; and even some who have believed determinism to be true have accepted— and regretted—that dire consequence of living in a determined cosmos. Omar Khayyám certainly embraces determinism, but seems to agree that determinism means the end of anything genuinely new, original, and unique:

> And fear not lest Existence closing *your*
> Account, should lose, or know the type no more;
> The Eternal Sáki from that Bowl has pour'd
> Millions of Bubbles like us, and will pour.
>   (Edward Fitzgerald translation)

> Free-will pragmatically means *novelties in the world*, the right to expect that in its deepest elements as well as in its surface phenomena, the future may not identically repeat and imitate the past. . . . It holds up improvement as at least possible; whereas determinism assures us that our whole notion of possibility is born of human ignorance, and that necessity and impossibility between them rule the destinies of the world. *William James, Pragmatism*, Lecture 3, 1907

But is determinism really such a deadly threat to creativity and originality? An omniscient God would know the end of the drama before it plays out, just as an architect may know what a building will look like long before it is actually constructed; but in both cases the events of the Earthly drama may be genuinely new and original, just as the building will still be new when it is built. And if we take a more secular, naturalistic view of determinism, then *no one* knows what tomorrow will bring, much less what will occur in the next year or next century: it will be genuinely new and original. When Edison invented the electric light bulb, it was a genuinely new thing. Suppose you are a jazz musician, who is deeply influenced by your training in classical music as well as by your deep love of jazz. Then, you might develop a new and original sound of complex blues, perhaps working out jazz arrangements of works by Bach (as the Modern Jazz Quartet did). A musicologist might well trace the causal influences that shaped your music (learning to play Bach in your classical training, listening to the music of Duke Ellington, and so forth); but discovering that causal history—indeed, discovering, *all* the wonderfully diverse causes that came together to *completely determine* your special musical work—would not change the fact that your music was wonderfully creative, fresh, original, and *new*.

> I do not think that either heredity or environment, or these two forces together, fully account for the behavior of Hosea, Zarathustra, Jeremiah, the Buddha, Socrates, Jesus, Muhammad, and Saint Francis of Assisi. I believe that these "great souls" did have the freedom to take spiritual action that has no traceable source. I also believe that there is a spark of this creative spiritual power in every human being. *Arnold Toynbee*, "Great Expectations," in Harvey Wheeler, ed., *Beyond the Punitive Society* (San Francisco: W. H. Freeman and Co., 1973)

Newton came up with a remarkable *new* and *original* account of physics and astronomy; but he acknowledged that his original creation had been strongly influenced by many scientists who went before him: "If I have seen farther than others, then it is because I stood on the shoulders of giants." And among those giants were Copernicus, Kepler, and Galileo. Newton combined their work with his mathematical research, and the result was something remarkably *new* and creative. And the fact that we can trace the *causes* of his work and the influences that shaped his work in no way diminishes the originality and creativity of Newton's theory. Paul Klee and Wassily Kandinsky—two of the most original artists of the twentieth century—were profoundly influenced by both "primitive" art (especially African tribal art) and by the work of the great post-impressionist Paul Gauguin, as well as by the creative atmosphere of the Bauhaus studio where they both worked. But their acknowledgment of their profound debts to those rich positive influences does not make their work less original or less wonderful. Prior to those (and many other) influences coming together to shape the unique creative talents of Klee and Kandinsky, there was *no work* anywhere in the cosmos that was like theirs: They produced something "genuinely new under the Sun." Of course there were causes that came together to shape their work; but that combination of causes had never before existed, and the resulting work was fresh and original.

But the foe of determinism may respond: that's not enough. I don't want to be just *part* of the creative process, the place where all these causes join; I want to be the *ultimate* creator. The determinist is likely to respond: You want to be God, the first cause, the unmoved mover. Get *over* it, already. You actually do things, make things, create things, have original ideas, and produce original theories, poems, songs, and paintings. Of course, there are *causes* for your work, just as there are causes for who you are. You have your grandfather's nose, your grandmother's eyes, your mother's chin, and your father's high cheekbones; but it's still your own new and unique face. Your ideas, beliefs, and artistic inclinations were shaped by your family, your community, your trip to the Metropolitan Museum, the movies you've seen, your third grade art teacher, your high school orchestra teacher, and your college poetry professor—and countless others. But this unique combination of influences produced—even *determined*, when we add up all the myriad influences—a wonderful creative person whose work is genuinely original. So what's your problem? Do you want to be totally free of any outside influences? Perhaps dropped full-grown on a desert island? Or perhaps you think that only by living in a bubble, free of all outside influence, could you really be free and original. But that makes no sense. In that case, you wouldn't write music or poems, make scientific discoveries, or have wonderful new ideas; to the contrary, you would be a miserable isolated animal, with no language and no appreciation of music, art, or poetry. *Of course*, there are influences that shaped you: genetic, cultural, and environmental. But they shaped a unique and original person who has original ideas and creates original work. You, your work, and your ideas are *determined* by past events and causal laws (or so the determinist will insist); but you are still original and new, as those causal influences came together in a new and original way.

By analyzing the genetic and individual histories responsible for our behavior, we may learn how to be more original. The task is not to think of new forms of behavior but to create an environment in which they are likely to occur. *B. F. Skinner*, "A Lecture on Having a Poem," in *Cumulative Record*, 3rd ed. (New York: Appleton-Century-Crofts).

Some people will find that enough; others will not: They will insist that *genuine* originality and creativity require that one be the *ultimate* and *undetermined* source. Here is a conflict that runs very deep: perhaps deeper than philosophical argument can plumb. William James would say we have reached bedrock, that we have reached a basic difference in *attitude* or *temperament*. Our *temperaments* (according to James) are not conclusions based on evidence, but rather are basic orientations that influence what we *count* as evidence: Each person's temperament "loads the evidence for him one way or the other." From one basic perspective or "temperament," determinism looks attractive and empowering: We can understand the causes and use that understanding to make the world better (in ways that we are *determined* to pursue, but which are no less important). From the other perspective, determinism robs us of our ultimate responsibility and dignity, of our genuine creativity.

Everything is determined, the beginning as well as the end, by forces over which we have no control. It is determined for the insect as well as the star. Human beings, vegetables, or cosmic dust, we all dance to a mysterious tune, intoned in the distance by an invisible piper. *Albert Einstein*

DOES DETERMINISM DESTROY FREE WILL?

Is determinism compatible with genuine creativity and originality? That remains a deeply divisive issue, but it is not nearly so divisive as the next question: Is determinism compatible with *free will*?

For many people, that question is absurdly simple: They find it perfectly obvious that if determinism is true—if *everything* we do and think is *determined* by past causal forces—then we cannot have free will.

Hard Determinism

If you believe that determinism is true *and* that it is strictly incompatible with free will, then you are a *hard determinist*. Hard determinists hold that because determinism is true, there is no human free will. That doesn't mean we cannot actually *do* things, and make things happen; and certainly it does not mean that we are zombies. Hard determinists do not deny that we make plans, reason, choose, feel affection, and carry out projects; rather, they insist that *all* of those activities are completely determined by our past causal history, and so although we may *act*, we do not act *freely*. My desire to accumulate wealth may be my own desire, and acting on that desire may be my own goal; but the desire and the acts that result from it are the determined product of a causal history that stretches far back beyond my birth: a causal history I obviously do not control, and that I cannot escape (the desires are my *own*, and any wish to stifle such desires would also be the product of a determined and inevitable causal history). Determinism is true, and therefore free will is an illusion.

Hard determinists *may* find that depressing; but more often they find it exhilarating. Forget the mysteries of free will; now we can recognize the causal factors that are at work everywhere—not only for planets and comets but also for human behavior and social systems. And if we can understand the causes, then we can also understand how to change things for the better. If there is crime in our community, then don't attribute it to inexplicable *free will*; instead, look for the *causes* of crime, and *fix* them. If people are not working as hard as they should, don't lament their poor exercise of free will; rather, look for the *causes* of their laziness, and then you can work out how to change it to industriousness. If our society is rife with poverty and depression, look for the causes and you can change the society for the better. When we understand the *causes* of disease—poor nutrition, polluted environments, bad sanitation, and so on—then we can *change* those causes and reduce disease. And when we understand the causes of social and individual human problems, we can change those causes and produce improvements. Of course, *that* we desire to change those causes is also a product of our fortunate determined histories, but that doesn't alter the fact that we do want to make those changes and that our causal history has given us the resources to make those changes. Belief in free will blocks the path to those effective reform processes.

B. F. Skinner, the behavioral psychologist who championed determinism and denied free will, wrote in the concluding paragraph of *Beyond Freedom and Dignity*:

> An experimental analysis shifts the determination of behavior from autonomous man to the environment—an environment responsible both for the evolution of the species and for the repertoire acquired by each member. . . . Environmental contingencies now take over functions once attributed to autonomous man, and certain questions arise. Is man then "abolished"? Certainly not as a species or as an individual achiever. It is the autonomous inner man who is abolished, and that is a step forward. But does man not then become merely a victim or passive observer of what is happening to him? He is indeed controlled by his environment, but we must remember that it is an environment largely of his own making. The evolution of a culture is a gigantic exercise in self control. . . . A scientific view of man offers exciting possibilities. We have not yet seen what man can make of man.
>
> *B. F. Skinner*, Beyond Freedom and Dignity, *pp. 205–206*

On this view, determinism does away with mystery and opens the door to understanding and changing and improving our environment and our lives and our society.

> All men are born ignorant of the causes of things, that all have the desire to seek for what is useful to them, and that they are conscious of such desire. Herefrom it follows, first, that men think themselves free inasmuch as they are conscious of their volitions and desires, and never even dream, in their ignorance, of the causes which have disposed them so to wish and desire. *Spinoza, Ethics*, Part 1, Appendix

Hard determinists acknowledge that we often *feel* as if we are acting freely, and feel that there is nothing controlling our choices and behavior. But—they would say—that is only because we fail to take note of the causal forces that actually guide and control us. You act from your own desire, and it seems to you that you act independently of determining causes. But where did your desire come from? If you resist your desire (you desire chocolate chip cookies, but you are on a diet), then what is the origin of that desire to resist the chocolate chip cookie desire? Of course the desire is your *own*, it is in you (it's not like someone is holding a gun to your head). But if you think carefully, you'll realize that all of your psychological states (and your rational reflections) have *causes*: you did *not* create them out of nothingness. We usually don't pay much attention to the causes, and thus we suppose that they are not acting upon us, that our acts originate from our special power of *free will*. But just because we don't know all the causes, that doesn't mean the causes aren't there. Arthur Schopenhauer—a determinist philosopher of the nineteenth century—expressed this hard determinist rejection of free will quite eloquently:

> Let us imagine a man who, while standing on the street, would say to himself: "It is six o'clock in the evening, the working day is over. Now I can go for a walk, or I can go to the club; I can also climb up the tower to see the sun set; I can go to the theater; I can visit this friend or that one; indeed, I also can run out of the gate, into the wide world, and never return. All of this is strictly up to me, in this I have complete freedom. But still I shall do none of these things now, but with just as free a will I shall go home to my wife." This is exactly as if water spoke to itself: "I can make high waves (yes! in the sea during a storm), I can rush down hill (yes! in the river bed), I can plunge down foaming and gushing (yes! in the waterfall), I can rise freely as a stream of water into the air (yes! in the fountain), I can, finally, boil away and disappear (yes! at a certain temperature); but I am doing none of these things now, and am voluntarily remaining quiet and clear in the reflecting pond."
>
> *Arthur Schopenhauer*, Essay on the Freedom of the Will, 1841;
> *translated by Konstantine Kolenda*

It is easy to *imagine* that we have free will, the hard determinist would say; all that is required is that we remain ignorant of the vast complex system of causes of our behavior.

Most hard determinists see free will as a pernicious illusion and determinism as a path to understanding and improvement. Perhaps it is not surprising that most hard determinists regard determinism as a positive good and free will as an impediment they are happy to discard. After all, if they thought of determinism as stifling and horrific—something, as Dostoyevsky asserts, that would turn man into a ridiculous player piano, deprived of all dignity and originality—then it is unlikely that they would embrace hard determinism.

Soft Determinism (Compatibilism)

It seems obvious to many that if determinism is true, then there can be no free will. Indeed, that seemed obvious to the ancient *atomists*, who maintained that everything is made up of atoms; but then—fearing the loss of free will—some atomists proposed that some special atoms (those in humans) could *swerve*. Most atoms followed predetermined courses, but some atoms in humans were capable of swerving out of that determined path; and that swerve—that break in the general deterministic pattern—allows for human free will.

But for many philosophers, it has *not* seemed obvious that determinism would eliminate free will. In fact, the most widely held contemporary view among philosophers is probably *compatibilism*: the view that determinism is *compatible* with free will. Compatibilism has a long history, and its earliest proponents were probably theologians. It's not surprising that religious thinkers should wrestle with this problem—particularly religious thinkers from the Judaeo-Christian-Muslim tradition. Think for a moment of the concept of God that emerged from that tradition (with considerable help from Aristotle). While the earliest Hebraic concept of God was hardly one of a monotheistic, all-knowing, all-powerful God (after all, this God is a *jealous* God Who gets quite angry when his chosen people worship His divine competitors; and he is hardly all-knowing, since Moses is able to remind Him of factors He had neglected to consider), by the medieval period these theologians had assimilated Aristotle's notion of a single omniscient and omnipotent deity into their conception of God. But this Judeo-Christian-Muslim God had another feature which Aristotle's God did not: This God also hands out rewards of heavenly bliss and punishments of eternal torment. That leads to an obvious problem: Since God is *all*-knowing, He *knows* that we will be vile (or that we will be among the elect and be virtuous) long before we are born; and since God is *all*-powerful, all power resides in God and we have no power to make ourselves. As Martin Luther, the leader of the Protestant Reformation, states:

> God foreknows nothing by contingency, but that He foresees, purposes, and does all things according to His immutable, eternal, and infallible will. By this thunderbolt free will is thrown prostrate and utterly dashed to pieces. Those, therefore, who would assert free will must either deny this thunderbolt, or pretend not to see it, or push it from them.
>
> *Martin Luther,* The Bondage of the Will, *translated by Henry Cole*

And John Calvin, the other great Reformation leader, agrees:

> Predestination, by which God adopts some to the hope of life and adjudges others to eternal death, no one, desirous of the credit of piety, dares absolutely to deny. . . . This foreknowledge extends to the whole world and to all the creatures. Predestination we call the eternal decree of God, by which He hath determined in Himself what He would have to become of every individual of mankind. For they are not all created with a similar destiny; but eternal life is foreordained for some, and eternal damnation for others. Every man, therefore, being created for one or the other of these ends, we say, he is predestinated either to life or to death.
>
> *John Calvin, from* Institutes of the Christian Religion, *translated by John Allen*

Thus, God *knows* (long before I was even born) that I will be a vile and unrepentant sinner; and indeed God *makes* me in this way; and yet God *punishes* me with eternal torture for the way He made me and for the way He knew I would act. Martin Luther recognized this problem quite clearly:

> This is the highest degree of faith—to believe that He is merciful, who saves so few and damns so many; to believe Him just, who according to His own will, makes us necessarily damnable, that He may seem, as Erasmus says, "to delight in the torments of the miserable, and to be an object of hatred rather than of love." If, therefore, I could by any means comprehend how that same God can be merciful and just, who carries the appearance of so much wrath and iniquity, there would be no need of faith. But now, since that cannot be comprehended, there is room for exercising faith. . . .
>
> The Bondage of the Will, *translated by Henry Cole*

While Luther and Calvin were willing to say that this is inexplicable, and that (with our puny minds) we should not try to understand God's mysterious ways (but should just accept it through faith), most theologians had a difficult time accepting that answer.

> Reason is the greatest enemy that faith has: it never comes to the aid of spiritual things, but—more frequently than not—struggles against the divine Word, treating with contempt all that emanates from God. *Martin Luther, Table Talk, 1569*

Their alternative answer was basically compatibilism: True, our characters, desires, and reason are given to us by God, and they *determine* how we will act. If my character causes me to seek God, then I gain salvation; if my character causes me to seek wickedness, but I also have the character trait of wishing to repent and *reform*, then I will also gain salvation; and if I have a character and desires that seek evil, with no capacity for reform, then I will follow my wicked desires and be damned. God, of course, assigns all these characters (for His own inscrutable reasons), and knows what we will do; but we still follow our *own* desires, and thus we act freely. When I wish to do evil, and freely follow my own desires to do evil, then my evil acts come from my own free choice. Thus, free will is *compatible* with determinism and determined characters.

Hume's Compatibilism

While theologians were probably the first to promote compatibilism, the classic source for compatibilist arguments—and certainly the best early advocate of compatibilism—was David Hume. Hume (as noted in the previous chapter) was a strong champion of determinism; but he also believed fervently in free will (or as he called it, liberty). Indeed, Hume not only believed that determinism is *compatible* with free will; he also insisted that determinism is *essential* for free will.

It's easy to get mixed up by all the words, terms, and definitions, Hume argued; but when we clear away the verbal confusions, there is really no dispute about the nature of free behavior. When are you acting freely? When you are able to do what *you want to do*. If you are imprisoned, or in chains, or someone holds a gun to your head, or you are paralyzed, then you are *not free*. But when you are doing *as you wish*, then you are acting freely. Don't let all the philosophical flummery fool you. There's no mystery about freedom, and about the freedom we desire; it's the freedom to act on our *own* desires, and have those acts be effective. If you desire to drink a beer, and you walk down to the tavern and polish off a tall cool one, then you are acting freely. If you desire to drink a beer, but the state prevents you from drinking a beer because you are under 21, then the state has placed a restriction on your freedom. It may well be *determined* that you have a taste for beer (perhaps it was determined by your early conditioning, or your environment, or whatever); but that does not make your desire for beer any less your *own*, and it does not undercut your freedom when you stroll into the tavern and drink a beer.

To see the compatibility between determinism and freedom more clearly, imagine an even more basic deterministic scenario. Suppose you are a devoted *fanatical* fan of the Chicago Cubs (is there any other kind?), and you love to cheer for the Cubs, you regard Wrigley Field as a holy shrine and you passionately pull for your dear Cubbies. You have an opportunity to go to a Cubs game at Wrigley, with seats right behind the Cubs dugout; and so, of course, you *eagerly* go. Are you going *freely*? "Of course I'm going freely," you would answer; "I'm going because I dearly love the Cubs and dearly love to go to Cubs games along with the rest of the faithful. No one has to *force* me to go to a Cubs game. I *want* to go, and I go freely. In fact, I am *never* so free as when I'm at a Cubs game." Now suppose someone replies: "No, you are *not* going freely; you only think you are. In fact, we have discovered—as a result of all the recent research on gene mapping—that those who (like yourself) are *passionate* Cubs fans have the *Cubs fan gene*, or CFG. You are a Cubs fan because you are *genetically determined* to be a Cubs fan. You *think* you are acting freely when you go to a Cubs game, but in fact your behavior is *genetically determined*, and your attendance at a Cubs game is not a *free* act at all." You might reasonably reply: "Look, I'm a Cubs fan, and go to Cubs games and cheer myself hoarse because that's what *I want to do*. I don't care if the reason I like the Cubs is genetic, or the environment of the Chicago neighborhood I grew up in, or the fact that my favorite childhood toy was Cubby Bear, who had a nifty Cubs hat on his head and was wearing a Cubs uniform. *Why* am I a Cubs fan? Leave that for the psychologists to figure out. All I know is that I certainly *am* a Cubs fan, and when I go to Cubs game I *act freely*, from my *own choice*."

Now of course a "Cubs fan gene" is quite ridiculous; but the moral of this silly story is important. Even if your desires and behavior were *genetically determined*, that would *not* undercut your free choices and free will. So, if we assume that your character and behavior are *determined* by all manner of factors (your early childhood, the influence of your friends and community, the courses you take, the books you read, your genetic inheritance, and a combination of many other causes) nothing in that determined history destroys your freedom. *Of course* your desires, wishes, preferences, and character were shaped by your complex history (you didn't honestly think you *made* or *chose* the processes that shaped you; after all, who would be doing the choosing and shaping?); but that still leaves you free to follow your *own* preferences and make your *own* choices based on those preferences (so long as you are not imprisoned, threatened, or bound). Thus, you can act freely.

Hume goes even further. Determinism is not just *compatible* with acting freely, it is *required* for free acts. To the degree that determinism fails to hold, our freedom suffers. Though that claim may seem paradoxical, Hume insists it is simple truth. Suppose that instead of determinism, things occasionally happened by *chance*. You wanted to go to a Cubs game, that was the direction your determined desires were taking you; but suddenly you find yourself—as chance intervenes—at the Aquarium instead. That certainly wouldn't seem like an infusion of freedom; to the contrary, such a random thwarting of your desires would undercut your exercise of your own free (but determined) choices. When you go to a Cubs game because you love the Cubs and you therefore choose to attend a Cubs game, then you're acting freely. But if your choice, based on your own desire, were to go to a Cubs game, but chance frequently took over, and you could never be sure that your desired choice would take you where you choose to go, then free choices and free behavior would be impossible. You are driving toward Wrigley Field, following your own desires, and chance intervenes and takes you out across Lake Michigan. That might increase your excitement, but it would certainly diminish your exercise of free choice. So (Hume argued), chance is the enemy of genuine freedom rather than an ally.

Hierarchical Compatibilism

On David Hume's view, free will is simple:

> By liberty, then, we can only mean *a power of acting or not acting according to the determinations of the will*; that is, if we choose to remain at rest, we may; if we choose to move, we also may. Now this hypothetical liberty is universally allowed to belong to everyone who is not a prisoner and in chains. Here then is no subject of dispute.

But in fact, there is more room for dispute than Hume acknowledges. After all, there are times when we "act according to the determinations of the will," when we act as we *choose*, but it is not at all clear that we are acting freely. Consider the smoker who is desperately trying to quit: She smokes a cigarette because she certainly *wants* to smoke, she chooses to smoke. No one holds a gun to her head and she is not in chains. But it is not at all clear that she is acting freely; and indeed, she is likely to vehemently affirm that she is *not* acting freely. Hume is right that prisons and chains can deprive us of freedom; but chains are not always made of heavy steel: they may be chains of addiction or internal compulsion that we recognize as causing our *own* choices but which nonetheless deprive us of freedom. My choice to smoke is my *own*, but it hardly feels like an exercise of freedom.

Recognizing this problem, *hierarchical* compatibilists add another level to the analysis of free will. On the hierarchical view, you are acting *freely* if you can act as you *wish* to do. You're a Cubs fan, and you like going to Cubs games, and you go to Cubs games of your own free choice: You are not bound in chains and carried to a Cubs game against your wishes. You are then acting freely. But suppose that as you consider it, you realize that although you are indeed a dedicated Cubs fan, you now wish that you were *not* a Cubs fan: You have suffered much when your beloved Cubs blew the lead in the ninth inning, when they collapsed at the end of the pennant race, and when they discovered new and maddening methods for snatching defeat from the jaws of victory. And you think to yourself: I would be a much happier, healthier, and psychologically more stable person if I did not want to cheer for the Cubs; I *wish* I did not care about baseball, and loved sailing, birdwatching, or playing tennis instead. Of course, you still *do* love the Cubs (you can't just change your deep desires by wishing they would go away, as many jilted lovers and nicotine addicts will bear witness); and you act *freely*, following your own desires, when you cheer for the Cubs. But (as Harry Frankfurt, a leading hierarchical compatibilist, would say) you do not have free *will*, because you do not have the *will* that you wish to have. The desire to cheer for the Cubs is your own, but it is *not* a desire that you reflectively approve; it is *not* a desire that you affirm at a higher or deeper level, not a desire with which you identify.

Consider another example. Suppose that Pat (fill in whatever gender you prefer) is the great love of your life: you passionately desire Pat, Pat haunts your thoughts and dreams, you long for Pat in the night and fantasize about Pat in the day. But Pat is the "false lover" of song and story, who treats you like dirt: lies to you, cheats on you, and generally makes your life a living hell. You still love Pat, and long to be with Pat; but you fervently, deeply, and reflectively wish that you could rid yourself of this destructive desire for Pat. In that case you act *freely* when you go in search of Pat (you are acting on your *own* desire), but you certainly do not have the *free will* that you want, for your desires are not the desires you want and approve. If, on the other hand, you deeply desire Pat, and you *deeply approve* of your desire for Pat (you know that Pat will make your life miserable, but you deeply approve of being a tragic figure with a ruined life) then you are acting freely *and* you have free *will*. As Frankfurt says, you have everything you could want in the way of free will.

Frankfurt's most famous example is the "willing addict": Suppose that Joe is addicted to drugs, and will act on that overwhelming desire for drugs. In that case, Joe may be acting *freely* when he takes drugs (he is acting on his own desire); but this "freedom" may not feel very free. If Joe experimented with drugs and became a drug addict before he realized what was happening, and now understands that this is an addictive desire he cannot shake, then Joe may feel terribly trapped by his own powerful desire that he fervently wishes he did not have. In that case (Frankfurt says), Joe is an *unwilling addict*. But suppose that Joe strongly and reflectively *approves* of his addictive desire for drugs; he likes being an addict, he wants to remain an addict, and if he felt his addictive desire for drugs weakening, he would make every effort to restore that desire to its full strength. In that case, Joe is a *willing addict*: He has the will that he reflectively approves, and he enjoys *free will* (in Frankfurt's use of that phrase).

In short, on the *hierarchical* compatibilist view, Hume doesn't go quite far enough. It's not enough to act as you *wish* to act, as you *desire* to act (for though you may not be controlled by iron chains, you may be controlled by desires that feel alien and coercive to you: desires that you do not approve, even though they are your own). Control by external chains is terrible; but control by *internal* chains of desires you despise might be even worse, and is certainly not an exercise of *free will*. So the hierarchical compatibilist pushes Hume's analysis a step further: You must be free to act on your own desires, and those desires must be desires that you *reflectively and deeply approve*.

Challenges to Hierarchical Compatibilism Suppose you can effectively follow your own desires (you are not in chains), *and* those desires are desires of which you deeply, decisively, and reflectively approve (they are not *alien* desires, like an unwanted addiction, but desires that are your own and approved by you). In that case, are you fully free?

Perhaps. But attributing full freedom to "willing addicts" makes some folks a bit queasy. Frankfurt's willing addict may be acting on his own desires, and those may be desires of which he deeply approves; but the path he is "freely" following is one that leads to his own destruction. Could anyone *freely* follow such a disastrous and destructive route?

When we focus narrowly on the *willing* addict's choice to take drugs, it may appear to be a free choice; but seen from a broader perspective, problems appear. Consider how one takes the path to *willing* addiction. *Unwilling* addiction is easy enough: I experiment with powerful drugs, believing that I can control *them*, they won't control *me*—"I just use them recreationally; I can stop anytime I wish." But ultimately I discover, to my deep regret, that the drugs have mastered me, and I cannot resist my detested desire for them: They are destroying my relationships, robbing me of the goals and values I profoundly cherish (my goal of becoming a competitive marathoner, my hopes of establishing loving and trusting relationships, my deep values of helping others and making the world a better place). At that point my drug use is *not* free, just as the hierarchical theorist insists. But suppose that as my drug addictive life continues, all those hopes, dreams, and affections shrivel up, and now I am left with only my drug addiction: Without that, I would have *nothing at all*. If I lost my desire for drugs, I would have no desires remaining and my life would be totally empty. At this point, I cling to my drug addiction, I deeply approve of it, and I deeply desire to be a drug addict. But this deep, desperate, and single-minded devotion to drug addiction hardly seems like *free* behavior, and the *willing* drug addict does not seem a good example of *free* will.

Consider Sarah, who is captured and brutally enslaved. Sarah hates her enslavement, struggles valiantly against it, and takes every opportunity to escape from her brutal captors. Obviously Sarah is *not* free, as hierarchical compatibilists agree. But years pass, and Sarah's harsh treatment slowly erodes her courage: Her escape efforts are brutally punished and her resistance results in even harsher treatment; as her struggles lessen, so does the harshness of her conditions. Gradually Sarah's spirit is broken and she acquiesces in her slavery; and the more she accepts her enslavement, the less she suffers. Eventually, Sarah gives up all hope of freedom and embraces her servitude: She has become a willing slave, who finds enslavement the most tolerable and least frightening way to live. She cannot imagine breaking her bonds; instead, her deepest desire is to serve her master faithfully and well. Sarah the willing slave may live more comfortably and peacefully than Sarah the rebellious slave; but her willing embrace of slavery has not made her more *free*. The *unwilling* slave is not free; but the *willing* slave, whose savage treatment has extinguished all hope and desire for freedom, has not gained free will. If anything, Sarah the willing slave is even *less* free, even *further* from genuine freedom.

Or so, critics of hierarchical compatibilism might argue. Champions of hierarchical compatibilism will bite the bullet and insist that though it may sound paradoxical, the willing slave and the willing addict really *are* free, really *do* have free will. Gerald Dworkin, a leading advocate of hierarchical compatibilism, insists that:

> a person who wishes to be restricted in various ways, whether by the discipline of the monastery, regimentation of the army, or even by coercion, is not, on that account alone, less autonomous. . . . In my conception, the autonomous person can be a tyrant or a slave, a saint or a sinner, a rugged individualist or champion of fraternity, a leader or follower.
>
> *Dworkin 1988, p. 18, 29*

We have arrived at a pivotal point in the debate over free will. Hierarchical compatibilists count the willing slave and the willing addict as free, while others would regard them as the very antithesis of free will: The *willing* slave is even further from freedom than the *unwilling* slave. This is an ongoing controversy, and you will have to draw your own conclusions. But there are no shortcut answers to resolving this standoff. It won't work to argue that the brutal circumstances of the willing slave and the willing addict have robbed them of the power of reason, and therefore deprived them of freedom (since reason is essential for freedom). After all, the willing addict may have retained significant rational powers: He may be quite clever and able to carry out very elaborate and intricate plans in order to obtain the drugs he desires. This may be even more evident for the willing slave, who may—in her deep zeal to serve her master—carry out very extensive rational plans for designing and constructing a new mansion for her master's pleasure. Some religions regard total enslavement to God's will as the highest and most glorious good; and advocates of such views (such as John Calvin) have written elaborate philosophical treatises arguing in favor of such profound religious enslavement, while others have composed hymns honoring such perfect enslavement: "Trust and obey, for there's no other way," as one hymn writer puts it. In this view, the highest freedom may be to become an unquestioning, faithful, and profoundly willing slave to God's will. God commands Abraham to sacrifice his beloved son to honor God, and Abraham obeys without question or hesitation. Abraham is hailed as a hero of faith, an example to be exalted and followed. Can such willing enslavement to God's will count as genuine freedom?

Or consider someone who seems enslaved by greed: Ebeneezer Scrooge was a greedy man who deeply and reflectively approved of his greed. When reproached for his deep and all-consuming commitment to accumulating wealth, Scrooge retorts: "What then? Even if I have grown so much wiser, what then?" He seems not unlike some contemporary unscrupulous chief executives who are willing to sacrifice honor, integrity, family, friends, and decency for greater wealth; who are, we might judge, "willing slaves" to wealth, though often its pursuit makes them bitter, lonely, and unhappy. But both the Christmas Carol Scrooge and the more contemporary versions are often highly intelligent and perhaps even deeply reflective: They are willing to sacrifice everything for gain, as the willing addict sacrifices everything for drugs; but though we may question their values, their shrewd intelligence may remain intact and keen.

Rationalist Compatibilism

Can the willing slave and the willing drug addict be genuinely free? The *rationalist* compatibilist answer is *No*. Indeed, it is precisely such examples that lead *rationalist* compatibilists to insist that a vital element is missing from the hierarchical compatibilist account of freedom. For rationalist compatibilists, that missing element is not just intelligence or even the ability to think carefully and profoundly. Rather, what rationalist compatibilists require is the capacity to *reason correctly*.

> Leibniz was also an advocate of the rationalist compatibilist view, as shown in this passage from his abridged version of *The Theodicy* (1710):
>
> > it is . . . true liberty, and the most perfect, to be able to use one's free will for the best, and to always exercise this power, without ever being turned aside either by external force or by internal passions, the first of which causes slavery of the body, the second, slavery of the soul. There is nothing less servile, and nothing more in accordance with the highest degree of freedom, than to be always led toward the good, and always by one's own inclination, without any constraint and without any displeasure.
>
> Nicolas Malebranche, a contemporary of Leibniz who shared his rationalist outlook, takes a similar view of genuine freedom:
>
> > . . . a man who is perfectly free . . . knows perfectly that it is only God who is his good, or the true cause of the pleasures which he enjoys. . . . He wants to stop only with the enjoyment of

> the sovereign good: he wills to sacrifice all others to it; no pleasure is stronger than his
> enlightenment. . . . For when one loves God, one is perfect; when one enjoys him, one is
> happy; and when one loves him with pleasure, one is happy and perfect all at once.
>
> And for Malebranche (as for Leibniz) this undeviating desire to love and worship God
> is "the most perfect liberty" [*Treatise on Nature and Grace*, Discourse III, "On Liberty,"
> 1680 (translated by Patrick Riley)].

As Susan Wolf states it, genuine freedom and responsibility requires "the ability to be in touch with the True and the Good. In other words, what makes responsible beings special is their ability to recognize good values as opposed to bad ones and to act in a way that expresses appreciation of this recognition" (Wolf, *Freedom Within Reason*, p. 77).

Rationalist compatibilists have an easy solution to the problem of the willing addict. The willing addict is *not* free and responsible, because a life of drug addiction is *not* the right sort of life for humans: Devotion to drugs means that one favors something other than what is genuinely good, that one lacks "the ability to be in touch with the True and the Good." And only when one follows the *true* path for the *right* reasons is one acting with genuine freedom.

> David Hume, Harry Frankfurt, and Susan Wolf are all *compatibilists*; that is, they all
> agree that determinism is *compatible* with free will. But they diverge on what they
> think is required for genuine free will. On Hume's *simple* compatibilist view, you are
> free when you are "not in chains"; that is, you are free when you are not being coerced,
> when you are following your own desires. Frankfurt considers that inadequate. After
> all, your own desires—such as your addictive desire for drugs—may be experienced as
> alien and coercive. Thus, Frankfurt's *hierarchical* compatibilism goes deeper: The
> exercise of free will requires that you be able to follow your own wishes and desires, but
> you must also (at a higher level) *approve* of your desires and acknowledge them as your
> own. Susan Wolf's *rationalist* compatibilism sets still stronger requirements for genuine
> free will. According to Wolf, to have genuine free will you must reflectively choose the
> *right* path for the *right reason*.

The rationalist compatibilist view may seem very demanding; and indeed, it is. But rationalist compatibilism has some points in its favor. Suppose that you are taking a pleasant evening walk, enjoying the night breezes and the sounds of the crickets, frogs, and whippoorwills. The path on which you are traveling, however, has a nasty feature of which you are ignorant: It ends abruptly in a steep drop into a rocky chasm, a drop that causes severe injury to hikers who are unaware of this feature. If you plunge into the chasm in the darkness and break your leg, we would hardly say that you "freely chose" the path leading to disaster. Your ignorance of the true nature of the path undercut your genuine freedom. Stumbling in ignorance along a dangerous path is not real freedom: Real freedom consists in taking the *right* path because you *know* that path is good.

Rationalist compatibilism has its charms, but it also carries some substantial baggage: It requires that there be a True and Good, a fixed, objective, and universal standard for what is genuinely right. Furthermore, rationalist compatibilism makes true freedom as rare as it is wonderful: Only when we are doing the right thing and following the true path—because we rationally recognize the True and Good—are we acting freely. That leaves a lot of *unfree* behavior and it raises a difficult question: When I do *not* follow the right path for the right reason (for example, if I commit a theft or some other bad act) then rationalist compatibilism implies that I am *not* acting freely, and thus cannot be held responsible. It would seem to follow that when I do good, I am free and responsible and deserve credit for my good actions; but when I do bad things then I am not acting freely and do not deserve blame. That result has some charms, certainly; but it seems somewhat paradoxical, to say the least.[1]

Another implication of rationalist compatibilism is that it confines genuinely free acts to a very narrow and rigid path. You are acting freely only when your acts "track the True and Good." Deviate from that specific prescribed path, and your acts are no longer free. For some people, this seems a very reasonable result. As Susan Wolf states, "Why would one want the ability to pass up the apple when to do so would merely be unpleasant or arbitrary?" (1990, p. 55). The only thing that is *truly* desirable and *genuinely* worthwhile is following the True and the Good, and following that path is genuine freedom.

> The goal, to put it bluntly, is the True and the Good. The freedom we want is the freedom to find it. But such a freedom requires not only that we, as agents, have the right sorts of abilities—the abilities, that is, to direct and govern our actions by our most fundamental selves. It requires as well that the world cooperate in such a way that our most fundamental selves have the opportunity to develop into the selves they ought to be. *Susan Wolf,* "Asymmetrical Freedom," 1980.

To suppose that a better account of genuine freedom must involve the ability to deviate from the True path is like supposing that a train is better because it can occasionally jump the tracks. Krishnamurti agrees with Susan Wolf: A truly *enlightened* mind "simply cannot have choice," for it must invariably follow "the path of truth" (Jiddu Krishnamurti, *Total Freedom: The Essential Krishnamurti* New York: HarperCollins, 1996). But some regard such a narrow path as too constraining, whatever its claim to truth and rationality. The great Russian novelist Fyodor Dostoyevsky is willing to abandon even truth and reason if they restrict his opportunity to take new and different paths:

> What he [humanity] wants to preserve is precisely his noxious fancies and vulgar trivialities, if only to assure himself that men are still men . . . and not piano keys simply responding to the laws of nature. . . .
>
> But even if man was nothing but a piano key, even if this could be demonstrated to him mathematically—even then, he wouldn't come to his senses but would pull some trick out of sheer ingratitude, just to make his point. . . .
>
> Now, you may say that this too can be calculated in advance . . . and that the very possibility of such a calculation would prevent it, so that sanity would prevail. Oh no! In that case man would go insane on purpose, just to be immune from reason. (*Notes from Underground*).

Certainly Susan Wolf doesn't think humans are just "piano keys"; but in contrast to Dostoyevsky—who fervently wants to preserve "his noxious fancies" and "vulgar trivialities" in order to avoid a single narrow path—Wolf finds the true single path profoundly appealing. Like Wolf, some religious people apparently long for a state of perfect submission to God, in which they would never wish to deviate from the path of righteousness; indeed, some picture Heaven as a place where the saints (or the "saved," or the "elect") will find it absolutely impossible to desire anything evil or act in any imperfect way, because they will be in the compelling immediate presence of God; and that will be the state of highest unswerving single narrow path freedom. Like Dostoyevsky (and in contrast to Wolf), the poet e e cum-

[1]Susan Wolf, In "Asymmetrical Freedom," recognizes this problem and she proposes her own solution. Whether her answer works remains a controversial question.

mings finds the narrow path of reason too narrow and celebrates irrational impulses that lead us far from the single path that is dictated by Reaon:

Wholly to be a fool when spring is in the world my blood approves;
Kisses are a better fate than wisdom. . . .

Whether Wolf's powerful version of Reason is essential for genuine freedom and whether following a narrow rational path is the true path of freedom are questions that still deeply divide many philosophers, and you will have to reach your own conclusions.

READINGS

⟨ PRAGMATISM ⟩

William James

William James (1842–1910) was a psychologist and philosopher, who published *The Principles of Psychology* (1890), as well as *The Will to Believe* (1897), *Pragmatism* (1907), and *The Meaning of Truth* (1909). James was a leader in the development of American *pragmatism*, which emphasized that the *truth* of our ideas must be established in terms of how well they *work* for us and successfully guide us. This passage is excerpted from *Pragmatism*, and that book was the basic text of a series of popular lectures James delivered in Boston and New York in 1906 and 1907. James is here applying his pragmatic analysis to the question of free will and focusing on the practical *benefits* of belief in free will.

Let me take up another well-worn controversy, *the free-will problem*. Most persons who believe in what is called their free-will do so after the rationalistic fashion. It is a principle, a positive faculty or virtue added to man, by which his dignity is enigmatically augmented. He ought to believe it for this reason. Determinists, who deny it, who say that individual men originate nothing, but merely transmit to the future the whole push of the past cosmos of which they are so small an expression, diminish man. He is less admirable, stripped of this creative principle. I imagine that more than half of you share our instinctive belief in free-will, and that admiration of it as a principle of dignity has much to do with your fidelity.

But free-will has also been discussed pragmatically, and, strangely enough, the same pragmatic interpretation has been put upon it by both disputants. You know how large a part questions of *accountability* have played in ethical controversy. To hear some persons, one would suppose that all that ethics aims at is a code of merits and demerits. Thus does the old legal and theological leaven, the interest in crime and sin and punishment abide with us. 'Who's to blame? whom can we punish? whom will God punish?'—these preoccupations hang like a bad dream over man's religious history.

So both free-will and determinism have been inveighed against and called absurd, because each, in the eyes of its enemies, has seemed to prevent the 'imputability' of good or bad deeds to their authors. Queer antinomy this! Free-will means novelty, the grafting on to the past of something not involved therein. If our acts were predetermined, if we merely transmitted the push of the whole past, the free-willists say, how could we be praised or blamed for anything? We should be 'agents' only, not 'principals,' and where then would be our precious imputability and responsibility?

But where would it be if we *had* free-will? rejoin the determinists. If a 'free' act be a sheer novelty, that comes not *from* me, the previous me, but *ex nihilo*, and simply tacks itself on to me, how can I, the previous I, be responsible? How can I have any permanent *character* that will stand still long enough for praise or blame to be awarded? The chaplet of my days tumbles into a cast of disconnected beads as soon as the thread of inner necessity is drawn out by the preposterous indeterminist doctrine. Messrs. Fullerton and McTaggart have recently laid about them doughtily with this argument.

It may be good *ad hominem*, but otherwise it is pitiful. For I ask you, quite apart from other reasons, whether any man, woman or child, with a sense for realities, ought not to be ashamed to plead such principles as either dignity or imputability. Instinct and utility between them can safely be trusted to carry on the social business of punishment and praise. If a man does good acts we shall praise him, if he does bad acts we shall punish him—anyhow, and quite apart from theories as to whether the acts result from what was previous in him or are novelties in a strict sense. To make our human ethics revolve about the question of 'merit' is a piteous unreality—God alone can know our merits, if we have any. The real ground for supposing free-will is indeed pragmatic, but it has nothing to do with this contemptible right to punish which has made such a noise in past discussions of the subject.

Free-will pragmatically means *novelties in the world*, the right to expect that in its deepest elements as well as in its surface phenomena, the future may not identically repeat and imitate the past. That imitation *en masse* is there, who can deny? The general 'uniformity of nature' is presupposed by every lesser law. But nature may be only approximately uniform; and persons in whom knowledge of the world's past has bred pessimism (or doubts as to the world's good character, which become certainties if that character be supposed eternally fixed) may naturally welcome free-will as a *melioristic* doctrine. It holds up improvement as at least possible; whereas determinism assures us that our whole notion of possibility is born of human ignorance, and that necessity and impossibility between them rule the destinies of the world.

Free-will is thus a general cosmological theory of *promise*, just like the Absolute, God, Spirit or Design.

Taken abstractly, no one of these terms has any inner content, none of them gives us any picture, and no one of them would retain the least pragmatic value in a world whose character was obviously perfect from the start. Elation at mere existence, pure cosmic emotion and delight, would, it seems to me, quench all interest in those speculations, if the world were nothing but a lubberland of happiness already. Our interest in religious metaphysics arises in the fact that our empirical future feels to us unsafe, and needs some higher guarantee. If the past and present were purely good, who could wish that the future might possibly not resemble them? Who could desire free-will? Who would not say, with Huxley, "let me be wound up every day like a watch, to go right fatally, and I ask no better freedom." 'Freedom' in a world already perfect could only mean freedom to *be worse*, and who could be so insane as to wish that? To be necessarily what it is, to be impossibly aught else, would put the last touch of perfection upon optimism's universe. Surely the only *possibility* that one can rationally claim is the possibility that things may be *better*. That possibility, I need hardly say, is one that, as the actual world goes, we have ample grounds for desiderating.

Free-will thus has no meaning unless it be a doctrine of *relief*. As such, it takes its place with other religious doctrines. Between them, they build up the old wastes and repair the former desolations. Our spirit, shut within this courtyard of sense-experience, is always saying to the intellect upon the tower: 'Watchman, tell us of the night, if it aught of promise bear,' and the intellect gives it then these terms of promise.

⇒ "FREEDOM OF THE WILL AND THE CONCEPT ⇒ OF A PERSON"
Harry G. Frankfurt

Harry G. Frankfurt, Professor Emeritus of Philosophy at Princeton University, is one of the leading contemporary advocates of compatibilism and his *hierarchical* version of compatibilism has been a major influence on the current debate concerning free will. This essay— "Freedom of the Will and the Concept of a Person," *Journal of Philosophy*, volume 68 (1971)—is a key source for Frankfurt's version of hierarchical compatibilism.

It is my view that one essential difference between persons and other creatures is to be found in the structure of a person's will. Human beings are not alone in having desires and motives, or in making choices.

They share these things with the members of certain other species, some of whom even appear to engage in deliberation and to make decisions based upon prior thought. It seems to be peculiarly characteristic of humans, however, that they are able to form what I shall call "second-order desires" or "desires of the second order."

Besides wanting and choosing and being moved *to do* this or that, men may also want to have (or not to have) certain desires and motives. They are capable of wanting to be different, in their preferences and purposes, from what they are. Many animals appear to have the capacity for what I shall call "first-order desires" or "desires of the first order," which are simply desires to do or not to do one thing or another. No animal other than man, however, appears to have the capacity for reflective self-evaluation that is manifested in the formation of second-order desires.

I

. . .

Consider first those statements of the form "A wants to X" which identify first-order desires— that is, statements in which the term "to X" refers to an action. A statement of this kind does not, by itself, indicate the relative strength of A's desire to X. It does not make it clear whether this desire is at all likely to play a decisive role in what A actually does or tries to do. For it may correctly be said that A wants to X even when his desire to X is only one among his desires and when it is far from being paramount among them. Then it may be true that A wants to X when he strongly prefers to do something else instead; and it may be true that he wants to X despite the fact that, when he acts, it is not the desire to X that motivates him to do what he does. On the other hand, someone who states that A wants to X may mean to convey that it is this desire that is motivating or moving A to do what he is actually doing and that A will in fact be moved by this desire (unless he changes his mind) when he acts.

It is only when it is used in the second of these ways that, given the special usage of "will" that I propose to adopt, the statement identifies A's will. To identify an agent's will is either to identify the desire (or desires) by which he is motivated in some action he performs or to identify the desire (or desires) by which he will or would be motivated when or if he acts. An agent's will, then, is identical with one or more of his first-order desires. But the notion of the will, as I am employing it, is not coextensive with the notion of first-order desires. It is not the notion of something that merely inclines an agent in some degree to act in a certain way. Rather, it is the notion of an *effective* desire—one that moves the will or would move a

person all the way to action. Thus the notion of the will is not coextensive with the notion of what an agent intends to do. For even though someone may have a settled intention to do X, he may nonetheless do something else instead of doing X because, despite his intention, his desire to do X proves to be weaker or less effective than some conflicting desire.

Now consider those statements of the form "A wants to X" which identify second-order desires— that is, statements in which the term "to X" refers to a desire of the first order. There are also two kinds of situation in which it may be true that A wants to want to X. In the first place, it might be true of A that he wants to have a desire to X despite the fact that he has a univocal desire, altogether free of conflict and ambivalence, to refrain from X-ing. Someone might want to have a certain desire, in other words, but univocally want that desire to be unsatisfied.

Suppose that a physician engaged in psychotherapy with narcotics addicts believes that his ability to help his patients would be enhanced if he understood better what it is like for them to desire the drug to which they are addicted. Suppose that he is led in this way to want to have a desire for the drug. If it is a genuine desire that he wants, then what he wants is not merely to feel the sensations that addicts characteristically feel when they are gripped by their desires for the drug. What the physician wants, insofar as he wants to have a desire, is to be inclined or moved to some extent to take the drug.

It is entirely possible, however, that, although he wants to be moved by a desire to take the drug, he does not want this desire to be effective. He may not want it to move him all the way to action. He need not be interested in finding out what it is like to take the drug. And insofar as he now wants only to *want* to take it, and not to *take* it, there is nothing in what he now wants that would be satisfied by the drug itself. He may now have, in fact, an altogether univocal desire *not* to take the drug; and he may prudently arrange to make it impossible for him to satisfy the desire he would have if his desire to want the drug should in time be satisfied.

It would thus be incorrect to infer, from the fact that the physician now wants to desire to take the drug, that he already does desire to take it. His second-order desire to be moved to take the drug does not entail that he has a first-order desire to take it. If the drug were now to be administered to him, this might satisfy no desire that is implicit in his desire to want to take it. While he wants to want to take the drug, he may have *no* desire to take it; it may be that *all* he wants is to taste the desire for it. That is, his desire to have a certain desire that he does not have may not be a desire that his will should be at all different than it is.

Someone who wants only in this truncated way to want to X stands at the margin of preciosity, and the fact that he wants to want to X is not pertinent to the identification of his will. There is, however, a second kind of situation that may be described by "A wants to want X"; and when the statement is used to describe a situation of this second kind, then it does pertain to what A wants his will to be. In such cases the statement means that A wants the desire to X to be the desire that moves him effectively to act. It is not merely that he wants the desire to X to be among the desires by which, to one degree or another, he is moved or inclined to act. He wants this desire to be effective—that is, to provide the motive in what he actually does. Now when the statement that A wants to want to X is used in this way, it does entail that A already has a desire to X. It could not be true both that A wants the desire to X to move him into action and that he does not want to X. It is only if he does want to X that he can coherently want the desire to X not merely to be one of his desires but, more decisively, to be his will.

Suppose a man wants to be motivated in what he does by the desire to concentrate on his work. It is necessarily true, if this supposition is correct, that he already wants to concentrate on his work. This desire is now among his desires. But the question of whether or not his second-order desire is fulfilled does not turn merely on whether the desire he wants is one of his desires. It turns on whether this desire is, as he wants it to be, his effective desire or will. If, when the chips are down, it is his desire to concentrate on his work that moves him to do what he does, then what he wants at that time is indeed (in the relevant sense) what he wants to want. If it is some other desire that actually moves him when he acts, on the other hand, then what he wants at that time is not (in the relevant sense) what he wants to want. This will be so despite the fact that the desire to concentrate on his work continues to be among his desires.

II

Someone has a desire of the second order either when he wants simply to have a certain desire or when he wants a certain desire to be his will. In situations of the latter kind, I shall call his second-order desires "second-order volitions" or "volitions of the second order." Now it is having second-order volitions, and not having second-order desires generally, that I regard as essential to being a person. It is logically possible, however unlikely, that there should be an agent with second-order desires but with no volitions of the second order. Such a creature, in my view, would not be a person. I shall use the term "wanton" to refer to agents who have first-order desires but who are not persons because, whether or not they have desires of the second order, they have no second-order volitions.

The essential characteristic of a wanton is that he does not care about his will. His desires move him to do certain things, without its being true of him either that he wants to be moved by those desires or that he prefers to be moved by other desires. The class of wantons includes all non-human animals that have desires and all very young children. Perhaps it also includes some adult human beings as well. In any case, adult humans may be more or less wanton; they may act wantonly, in response to first-order desires concerning which they have no volitions of the second order, more or less frequently.

The fact that a wanton has no second-order volitions does not mean that each of his first-order desires is translated heedlessly and at once into action. He may have no opportunity to act in accordance with some of his desires. Moreover, the translation of his desires into action may be delayed or precluded either by conflicting desires of the first order or by the intervention of deliberation. For a wanton may possess and employ rational faculties of a high order. Nothing in the concept of a wanton implies that he cannot reason or that he cannot deliberate concerning how to do what he wants to do. What distinguishes the rational wanton from other rational agents is that he is not concerned with the desirability of his desires themselves. He ignores the question of what his will is to be. Not only does he pursue whatever course of action he is most strongly inclined to pursue, but he does not care which of his inclinations is the strongest.

Thus a rational creature, who reflects upon the suitability to his desires of one course of action or another, may nonetheless be a wanton. In maintaining that the essence of being a person lies not in reason but in will, I am far from suggesting that a creature without reason may be a person. For it is only in virtue of his rational capacities that a person is capable of becoming critically aware of his own will and of forming volitions of the second order. The structure of a person's will presupposes, accordingly, that he is a rational being.

The distinction between a person and a wanton may be illustrated by the difference between two narcotics addicts. Let us suppose that the physiological condition accounting for the addiction is the same in both men, and that both succumb inevitably to their periodic desires for the drug to which they are addicted. One of the addicts hates his addiction and always struggles desperately, although to no avail, against its thrust. He tries everything that he thinks might enable him to overcome his desires for the drug. But these desires are too powerful for him to withstand, and invariably, in the end, they conquer him. He is an unwilling addict, helplessly violated by his own desires.

The unwilling addict has conflicting first-order desires: he wants to take the drug, and he also wants to refrain from taking it. In addition to these first-order desires, however, he has a volition of the second order. He is not a neutral with regard to the conflict between his desire to take the drug and his desire to refrain from taking it. It is the latter desire, and not the former, that he wants to constitute his will; it is the latter desire, rather than the former, that he wants to be effective and to provide the purpose that he will seek to realize in what he actually does.

The other addict is a wanton. His actions reflect the economy of his first-order desires, without his being concerned whether the desires that move him to act are desires by which he wants to be moved to act. If he encounters problems in obtaining the drug or in administering it to himself, his responses to his urges to take it may involve deliberation. But it never occurs to him to consider whether he wants the relations among his desires to result in his having the will he has. The wanton addict may be an animal, and thus incapable of being concerned about his will. In any event he is, in respect of his wanton lack of concern, no different from an animal.

The second of these addicts may suffer a first-order conflict similar to the first-order conflict suffered by the first. Whether he is human or not, the wanton may (perhaps due to conditioning) both want to take the drug and want to refrain from taking it. Unlike the unwilling addict, however, he does not prefer that one of his conflicting desires should be paramount over the other; he does not prefer that one first-order desire rather than the other should constitute his will. It would be misleading to say that he is neutral as to the conflict between his desires, since this would suggest that he regards them as equally acceptable. Since he has no identity apart from his first-order desires, it is true neither that he prefers one to the other nor that he prefers not to take sides.

It makes a difference to the unwilling addict, who is a person, which of his conflicting first-order desires wins out. Both desires are his, to be sure; and whether he finally takes the drug or finally succeeds in refraining from taking it, he acts to satisfy what is in a literal sense his own desire. In either case he does something he himself wants to do, and he does it not because of some external influence whose aim happens to coincide with his own but because of his desire to do it. The unwilling addict identifies himself, however, through the formation of a second-order volition, with one rather than with the other of his conflicting first-order desires. He makes one of them more truly his own and, in so doing, he withdraws himself from the other. It is in virtue of this identification and withdrawal, accomplished through the formation of a second-order volition, that the unwilling addict may meaningfully make the analytically puzzling statements that the force moving him to take the drug is a force other than his own, and that it is not of his own free will but rather against his will that this force moves him to take it.

The wanton addict cannot or does not care which of his conflicting first-order desires wins out. His lack of concern is not due to his inability to find a convincing basis for preference. It is due either to his lack of the capacity for reflection or to his mindless indifference to the enterprise of evaluating his own desires and motives. There is only one issue in the struggle to which his first-order conflict may lead: whether the one or the other of his conflicting desires is the stronger. Since he is moved by both desires, he will not be altogether satisfied by what he does no matter which of them is effective. But it makes no difference to *him* whether his craving or his aversion gets the upper hand. He has no stake in the conflict between them and so, unlike the unwilling addict, he can neither win nor lose the struggle in which he is engaged. When a *person* acts, the desire by which he is moved is either the will he wants or a will he wants to be without. When a *wanton* acts, it is neither.

III

There is a very close relationship between the capacity for forming second-order volitions and another capacity that is essential to persons—one that has often been considered a distinguishing mark of the human condition. It is only because a person has volitions of the second order that he is capable both of enjoying and of lacking freedom of the will. The concept of a person is not only, then, the concept of a type of entity that has both first-order desires and volitions of the second order. It can also be construed as the concept of a type of entity for whom the freedom of its will may be a problem. This concept excludes all wantons, both infrahuman and human, since they fail to satisfy an essential condition for the enjoyment of freedom of the will. And it excludes those supra-human beings, if any, whose wills are necessarily free.

Just what kind of freedom is the freedom of the will? This question calls for an identification of the special area of human experience to which the concept of freedom of the will, as distinct from the concepts of other sorts of freedom, is particularly germane. In dealing with it, my aim will be primarily to locate the problem with which a person is most immediately concerned when he is concerned with the freedom of his will.

According to one familiar philosophical tradition, being free is fundamentally a matter of doing what one wants to do. Now the notion of an agent who does what he wants to do is by no means an altogether clear one: both the doing and the wanting, and the appropriate relation between them as well, require elucidation. But although its focus needs to be sharpened and its formulation refined, I believe that this notion does capture at least part of what is implicit in the idea of an agent who *acts* freely. It misses entirely, however, the peculiar content of the quite different idea of an agent whose *will* is free.

We do not suppose that animals enjoy freedom of the will, although we recognize that an animal may be free to run in whatever direction it wants. Thus, having the freedom to do what one wants to do is not a sufficient condition of having a free will. It is not a necessary condition either. For to deprive someone of his freedom of action is not necessarily to undermine the freedom of his will. When an agent is aware that there are certain things he is not free to do, this doubtless affects his desires and limits the range of choices he can make. But suppose that someone, without being aware of it, has in fact lost or been deprived of his freedom of action. Even though he is no longer free to do what he wants to do, his will may remain as free as it was before. Despite the fact that he is not free to translate his desires into actions or to act according to the determinations of his will, he may still form those desires and make those determinations as freely as if his freedom of action had not been impaired.

When we ask whether a person's will is free we are not asking whether he is in a position to translate his first-order desires into actions. That is the question of whether he is free to do as he pleases. The question of the freedom of his will does not concern the relation between what he does and what he wants to do. Rather, it concerns his desires themselves. But what question about them is it?

It seems to me both natural and useful to construe the question of whether a person's will is free in close analogy to the question of whether an agent enjoys freedom of action. Now freedom of action is (roughly, at least) the freedom to do what one wants to do. Analogously, then, the statement that a person enjoys freedom of the will means (also roughly) that he is free to want what he wants to want. More precisely, it means that he is free to will what he wants to will, or to have the will he wants. Just as the question about the freedom of an agent's action has to do with whether it is the action he wants to perform, so the question about the freedom of his will has to do with whether it is the will he wants to have.

It is in securing the conformity of his will to his second-order volitions, then, that a person exercises freedom of the will. And it is in the discrepancy between his will to his second-order volitions, or in his awareness that their coincidence is not his own doing but only a happy chance, that a person who does not have this freedom feels its lack. The unwilling addict's will is not free. This is shown by the fact that it is not the will he wants. It is also true, though in a different way, that the will of the wanton addict is not free. The wanton addict neither has the will he wants nor has a will that differs from the will he wants. Since he has no volitions of the second order, the freedom of his will cannot be a problem for him. He lacks it, so to speak, by default.

People are generally far more complicated than my sketchy account of the structure of a person's will may suggest. There is as much opportunity for ambivalence, conflict, and self-deception with regard to desires of the second order, for example, as there is with regard to first-order desires. If there is an unresolved conflict among someone's second-order desires, then he is in danger of having no second-order volition; for unless this conflict is resolved, he has no preference concerning which of his first-order desires is to be his will. This condition, if it is so severe that it prevents him from identifying himself in a sufficiently decisive way with *any* of his conflicting first-order desires, destroys him as a person. For it either tends to paralyze his will and to keep him from acting at all, or it tends to remove him from his will so that his will operates without his participation. In both cases he becomes, like the unwilling addict though in a different way, a helpless bystander to the forces that move him.

Another complexity is that a person may have, especially if his second-order desires are in conflict, desires and volitions of a higher order than the second. There is no theoretical limit to the length of the series of desires of higher and higher orders; nothing except common sense and, perhaps, a saving fatigue prevents an individual from obsessively refusing to identify himself with any of his desires until he forms a desire of the next higher order. The tendency to generate such a series of acts of forming desires, which would be a case of humanization run wild, also leads toward the destruction of a person.

It is possible, however, to terminate such a series of acts without cutting it off arbitrarily. When a person identifies himself *decisively* with one of his first-order desires, this commitment "resounds" throughout the potentially endless array of higher orders. Consider a person who, without reservation or conflict, wants to be motivated by the desire to concentrate on his work. The fact that his second-order volition to be moved by this desire is a decisive one means that there is no room for questions concerning the pertinence of desires or volitions of higher orders. Suppose the person is asked whether he wants to want to want to concentrate on his work. He can properly insist that this question concerning a third-order desire does not arise. It would be a mistake to claim that, because he has not considered whether he wants the second-order volition he has formed, he is indifferent to the question of whether it is with this volition or with some other that he wants his will to accord. The decisiveness of the commitment he has made means that he has decided that no further question about his second-order volition, at any higher order, remains to be asked. It is relatively unimportant whether we explain this by saying that this commitment implicitly generates an endless series of confirming desires of higher orders, or by saying that the commitment is tantamount to a dissolution of the pointedness of all questions concerning higher orders of desire.

Examples such as the one concerning the unwilling addict may suggest that volitions of the second order, or of higher orders, must be formed deliberately and that a person characteristically struggles to ensure that they are satisfied. But the conformity of a person's will to his higher-order volitions may be far more thoughtless and spontaneous than this. Some people are naturally moved by kindness when they want to be kind, and by nastiness when they want to be nasty, without any explicit forethought and without any need for energetic self-control. Others are moved by nastiness when they want to be kind and by kindness when they intend to be nasty, equally without forethought and without active resistance to these violations of their higher-order desires. The enjoyment of freedom comes easily to some. Others must struggle to achieve it.

IV

My theory concerning the freedom of the will accounts easily for our disinclination to allow that this freedom is enjoyed by the members of any species inferior to our own. It also satisfies another condition that must be met by any such theory, by making it apparent why the freedom of the will should be regarded as desirable. The enjoyment of a free will means the satisfaction of certain desires of the second or of higher orders—whereas its absence means their frustration. The satisfactions at stake are those which accrue to a person of whom it may be said that his will is his own. The corresponding frustrations are those suffered by a person of whom it may be said that he is estranged from himself, or that he finds himself a helpless or a passive bystander to the forces that move him.

A person who is free to do what he wants to do may yet not be in a position to have the will he wants. Suppose, however, that he enjoys both freedom of action and freedom of the will. Then he is not only free to do what he wants to do; he is also free to want what he wants to want. It seems to me that he has, in that case, all the freedom it is possible to desire or to conceive. There are other good things in life, and he may not possess some of them. But there is nothing in the way of freedom that he lacks.

It is far from clear that certain other theories of the freedom of the will meet these elementary but essential conditions: that it be understandable why we desire this freedom and why we refuse to ascribe it to animals. Consider, for example, Roderick Chisholm's quaint version of the doctrine that human freedom entails an absence of causal determination. Whenever a person performs a free action, according to Chisholm, it's a miracle. The motion of a person's hand, when the person moves it, is the outcome of a series of physical causes; but some event in this series, "and presumably one of those that took place within the brain, was caused by the agent and not by any other events". A free agent has, therefore, "a prerogative which some would attribute only to God: each of us, when we act, is a prime mover unmoved".

This account fails to provide any basis for doubting that animals of subhuman species enjoy the freedom it defines. Chisholm says nothing that makes it seem less likely that a rabbit performs a miracle when it moves its leg than that a man does so when he moves his hand. But why, in any case, should anyone *care* whether he can interrupt the natural order of causes in the way Chisholm describes? Chisholm offers no reason for believing that there is a discernible difference between the experience of a man who miraculously initiates a series of causes when he moves his hand and a man who moves his hand without any such breach of the normal causal sequence. There appears to be no concrete basis for preferring to be involved in the one state of affairs rather than in the other.

It is generally supposed that, in addition to satisfying the two conditions I have mentioned, a satisfactory theory of the freedom of the will necessarily provides an analysis of one of the conditions of moral responsibility. The most common recent approach to the problem of understanding the freedom of the will has been, indeed, to inquire what is entailed by the assumption that someone is morally responsible for what he has done. In my view, however, the relation between moral responsibility and the freedom of the will has been very widely misunderstood. It is not true that a person is morally responsible for what he has done only if his will was free when he did it. He may be morally responsible for having done it even though his will was not free at all.

A person's will is free only if he is free to have the will he wants. This means that, with regard to any of his first-order desires, he is free either to make that desire his will or to make some other first-order desire his will instead. Whatever his will, then, the will of the person whose will is free could have been otherwise; he could have done otherwise than to constitute his will as he did. It is a vexed question just how "he could have done otherwise" is to be understood in contexts such as this one. But although this question is important to the theory of freedom, it has no bearing on the theory of moral responsibility. For the assumption that a person is morally responsible for what he has done does not entail that the person was in a position to have whatever will he wanted.

This assumption *does* entail that the person did what he did freely, or that he did it of his own free will. It is a mistake, however, to believe that someone acts freely only when he is free to do whatever he wants or that he acts of his own free will only if his will is free. Suppose that a person has done what he wanted to do, that he did it because he wanted to do it, and that the will by which he was moved when he did it was his will because it was the will he wanted. Then he did it

freely and of his own free will. Even supposing that he could have done otherwise, he would not have done otherwise; and even supposing that he could have had a different will, he would not have wanted his will to differ from what it was. Moreover, since the will that moved him when he acted was his will because he wanted it to be, he cannot claim that his will was forced upon him or that he was a passive bystander to its constitution. Under these conditions, it is quite irrelevant to the evaluation of his moral responsibility to inquire whether the alternatives that he opted against were actually available to him.

In illustration, consider a third kind of addict. Suppose that his addiction has the same physiological basis and the same irresistible thrust as the addictions of the unwilling and wanton addicts, but that he is altogether delighted with his condition. He is a willing addict, who would not have things any other way. If the grip of his addiction should somehow weaken, he would do whatever he could to reinstate it; if his desire for the drug should begin to fade, he would take steps to renew its intensity.

The willing addict's will is not free, for his desire to take the drug will be effective regardless of whether or not he wants this desire to constitute his will. But when he takes the drug, he takes it freely and of his own free will. I am inclined to understand his situation as involving the overdetermination of his first-order desire to take the drug. This desire is his effective desire because he is physiologically addicted. But it is his effective desire also because he wants it to be. His will is outside his control, but, by his second-order desire that his desire for the drug should be effective, he has made this will his own. Given that it is therefore not only because of his addiction that his desire for the drug is effective, he may be morally responsible for taking the drug.

My conception of the freedom of the will appears to be neutral with regard to the problem of determinism. It seems conceivable that it should be causally determined that a person is free to want what he wants to want. If this is conceivable, then it might be causally determined that a person enjoys a free will. There is no more than an innocuous appearance of paradox in the proposition that it is determined, ineluctably and by forces beyond their control, that certain people have free wills and that others do not. There is no incoherence in the proposition that some agency other than a person's own is responsible (even *morally* responsible) for the fact that he enjoys or fails to enjoy freedom of the will. It is possible that a person should be morally responsible for what he does of his own free will and that some other person should also be morally responsible for his having done it.

On the other hand, it seems conceivable that it should come about by chance that a person is free to have the will he wants. If this is conceivable, then it might be a matter of chance that certain people enjoy freedom of the will and that certain others do not. Perhaps it is also conceivable, as a number of philosophers believe, for states of affairs to come about in a way other than by chance or as the outcome of a sequence of natural causes. If it is indeed conceivable for the relevant states of affairs to come about in some third way, then it is also possible that a person should in that third way come to enjoy the freedom of the will.

⇌ "ASYMMETRICAL FREEDOM" ⇌
Susan Wolf

Susan Wolf is professor of philosophy at the University of North Carolina at Chapel Hill. She defends a *rationalist compatibilist* account of free will, insisting that genuine freedom requires doing the *right thing* for the *right reasons*; and the implications she draws from her view are both very interesting and rather surprising. Her *Freedom within Reason* (New York: Oxford University Press, 1990) is a particularly clear and intriguing development of her views. This passage is from her "Asymmetrical Freedom," *Journal of Philosophy*, volume 77 (March 1980).

In order for a person to be morally responsible, two conditions must be satisfied. First, he must be a free agent—an agent, that is, whose actions are under his own control. For if the actions he performs are not up to him to decide, he deserves no credit or discredit for doing what he does. Second, he must be a moral agent—an agent, that is, to whom moral claims apply. For if the actions he performs can be neither right nor wrong, then there is nothing to credit or discredit him with. I shall call the first condition, *the condition of freedom*, and the second, *the condition of value*. Those who fear that the first condition can never be met worry about the problem of free will. Those who fear that the second condition can never be met worry about the problem of moral skepticism. Many people believe that the condition of value is dependent on the condition of freedom—that moral prescriptions make sense only if the concept of free will is coherent. In what follows, I shall argue that the converse is true—that the condition of freedom depends on the condition of value. Our doubts about the existence of true moral values, however, will have to be left aside.

I shall say that an agent's action is *psychologically determined* if his action is determined by his interests— that is, his values or desires—and his interests are determined by his heredity or environment. If all our actions are so determined, then the thesis of psychological determinism is true. This description is admittedly crude and simplistic. A more plausible description of psychological determination will include among possible determining factors a wider range of psychological states. There are, for example, some beliefs and emotions which cannot be analyzed as values or desires and which clearly play a role in the psychological explanations of why we act as we do. For my purposes, however, it will be easier to leave the description of psychological determinism uncluttered. The context should be sufficient to make the intended application understood.

Many people believe that if psychological determinism is true, the condition of freedom can never be satisfied. For if an agent's interests are determined by heredity and environment, they claim, it is not up to the agent to have the interests he has. And if his actions are determined by his interests as well, then he cannot but perform the actions he performs. In order for an agent to satisfy the condition of freedom, then, his actions must not be determined by his interests, or his interests must not be determined by anything external to himself. They therefore conclude that the condition of freedom requires the absence of psychological determinism. And they think this is what we mean to express when we state the condition of freedom in terms of the requirement that the agent "could have done otherwise."

Let us imagine, however, what an agent who satisfied this condition would have to be like. Consider first what it would mean for the agent's actions not to be determined by his interests—for the agent, in other words, to have the ability to act despite his interests. This would mean, I think, that the agent has the ability to act against everything he believes in and everything he cares about. It would mean, for example, that if the agent's son were inside a burning building, the agent could just stand there and watch the house go up in flames. Or that the agent, though he thinks his neighbor a fine and agreeable fellow, could just get up one day, ring the doorbell, and punch him in the nose. One might think such pieces of behavior should not be classified as actions at all—that they are rather more like spasms that the agent cannot control. If they are actions, at least, they are very bizarre, and an agent who performed them would have to be insane. Indeed, one might think he would have to be insane if he had even the ability to perform them. For the rationality of an agent who could perform such irrational actions as these must hang by a dangerously thin thread.

So let us assume instead that his actions are determined by his interests, but that his interests are not determined by anything external to himself. Then of any of the interests he happens to have, it must be the case that he does not have to have them. Though perhaps he loves his wife, it must be possible for him not to love her. Though perhaps he cares about people in general, it must be possible for him not to care. This agent, moreover, could not have reasons for his interests—at least no reasons of the sort we normally have. He cannot love his wife, for example, because of the way his wife is—for the way his wife is is not up to him to decide. Such an agent, presumably, could not be much committed to anything; his interests must be something like a matter of whim. Such an agent must be able not to care about his own life as well. An agent who didn't care about these things, one might think, would have to be crazy. And again, one might think he would have to be crazy if he had even the ability not to care.

In any case, it seems, if we require an agent to be psychologically undetermined, we cannot expect him to be a moral agent. For if we require that his actions not be determined by his interests, then *a fortiori* they cannot be determined by his moral interests. And if we require that his interests not be determined by anything else, then *a fortiori* they cannot be determined by his moral reasons.

When we imagine an agent who performs right actions, it seems, we imagine an agent who is rightly determined: whose actions, that is, are determined by the right sorts of interests, and whose interests are determined by the right sorts of reasons. But an agent who is not psychologically determined cannot

perform actions that are right in this way. And if his actions can never be appropriately right, then in not performing right actions, he can never be wrong. The problem seems to be that the undetermined agent is so free as to be free *from moral reasons*. So the satisfaction of the condition of freedom seems to rule out the satisfaction of the condition of value.

This suggests that the condition of freedom was previously stated too strongly. When we require that a responsible agent "could have done otherwise" we cannot mean that it was not determined that he did what he did. It has been proposed that "he could have done otherwise" should be analyzed as a conditional instead. For example, we might say that "he could have done otherwise" means that he would have done otherwise, if he had tried. Thus the bank robber is responsible for robbing the bank, since he would have restrained himself if he had tried. But the man he locked up is not responsible for letting him escape, since he couldn't have stopped him even if he had tried.

Incompatibilists, however, will quickly point out that such an analysis is insufficient. For an agent who would have done otherwise if he had tried cannot be blamed for his action if he could not have tried. The compatibilist might try to answer this objection with a new conditional analysis of "he could have tried." He might say, for example, that "he could have tried to do otherwise" be interpreted to mean he would have tried to do otherwise, if he had chosen. But the incompatibilist now has a new objection to make: namely, what if the agent could not have chosen?

It should be obvious that this debate might be carried on indefinitely with a proliferation of conditionals and a proliferation of objections. But if an agent is determined, no conditions one suggests will be conditions that an agent could have satisfied.

Thus, any conditional analysis of "he could have done otherwise" seems too weak to satisfy the condition of freedom. Yet if "he could have done otherwise" is not a conditional, it seems too strong to allow the satisfaction of the condition of value. We seem to think of ourselves one way when we are thinking about freedom, and to think of ourselves another way when we are thinking about morality. When we are thinking about the condition of freedom, our intuitions suggest that the incompatibilists are right. For they claim that an agent can be free only insofar as his actions are not psychologically determined. But when we are thinking about the condition of value, our intuitions suggest that the compatibilists are right. For they claim that an agent can be moral only insofar as his actions are psychologically determined. If our intuitions require that both these claims are right, then the concept of moral responsibility must be incoherent. For then a free agent can never be moral, and a moral agent can never be free.

In fact, however, I believe that philosophers have generally got our intuitions wrong. There is an asymmetry in our intuitions about freedom which has generally been overlooked. As a result, it has seemed that the answer to the problem of free will can lie in only one of two alternatives: Either the fact that an agent's action was determined is always compatible with his being responsible for it, or the fact that the agent's action was determined will always rule his responsibility out. I shall suggest that the solution lies elsewhere—that both compatibilists and incompatibilists are wrong. What we need in order to be responsible beings, I shall argue, is a suitable combination of determination and indetermination.

When we try to call up our intuitions about freedom, a few stock cases come readily to mind. We think of the heroin addict and the kleptomaniac, of the victim of hypnosis, and the victim of a deprived childhood. These cases, I think, provide forceful support for our incompatibilist intuitions. For of the kleptomaniac it may well be true that he would have done otherwise if he had tried. The kleptomaniac is not responsible because he could not have tried. Of the victim of hypnosis it may well be true that he would have done otherwise if he had chosen. The victim of hypnosis is not responsible because he could not have chosen.

The victim of the deprived childhood who, say, embezzles some money, provides the most poignant example of all. For this agent is not coerced nor overcome by an irresistible impulse. He is in complete possession of normal adult faculties of reason and observation. He seems, indeed, to have as much control over his behavior as we have of ours. He acts on the basis of his choice, and he chooses on the basis of his reasons. If there is any explanation of why this agent is not responsible, it would seem that it must consist simply in the fact that his reasons are determined.

These examples are all peculiar, however, in that they are examples of people doing bad things. If the agents in these cases were responsible for their actions, this would justify the claim that they deserve to be blamed. We seldom look, on the other hand, at examples of agents whose actions are morally good. We rarely ask whether an agent is truly responsible if his being responsible would make him worthy of praise.

There are a few reasons why this might be so which go some way in accounting for the philosophers'

neglect. First, acts of moral blame are more connected with punishment than acts of moral praise are connected with reward. So acts of moral blame are likely to be more public, and examples will be readier to hand. Second, and more important, I think, we have stronger reasons for wanting acts of blame to be justified. If we blame someone or punish him, we are likely to be causing him some pain. But if we praise someone or reward him, we will probably only add to his pleasures. To blame someone undeservedly is, in any case, to do him an injustice. Whereas to praise someone undeservedly is apt to be just a harmless mistake. For this reason, I think, our intuitions about praise are weaker and less developed than our intuitions about blame. Still, we do have some intuitions about cases of praise, and it would be a mistake to ignore them entirely.

When we ask whether an agent's action is deserving of praise, it seems we do not require that he could have done otherwise. If an agent does the right thing for just the right reasons, it seems absurd to ask whether he could have done the wrong. "I cannot tell a lie," "He couldn't hurt a fly" are not exemptions from praiseworthiness but testimonies to it. If a friend presents you with a gift and says "I couldn't resist," this suggests the strength of his friendship and not the weakness of his will. If one feels one "has no choice" but to speak out against injustice, one ought not to be upset about the depth of one's commitment. And it seems I should be grateful for the fact that if I were in trouble, my family "could not help" but come to my aid.

Of course, these phrases must be given an appropriate interpretation if they are to indicate that the agent is deserving of praise. "He couldn't hurt a fly" must allude to someone's gentleness—it would be perverse to say this of someone who was in an iron lung. It is not admirable in George Washington that he cannot tell a lie, if it is because he has a tendency to stutter that inhibits his attempts. "He could not have done otherwise" as it is used in the context of praise, then, must be taken to imply something like "because he was too good." An action is praiseworthy only if it is done for the right reasons. So it must be only in light of and because of these reasons that the praiseworthy agent "could not help" but do the right thing.

But when an agent does the right thing for the right reasons, the fact that, having the right reasons, he *must* do the right should surely not lessen the credit he deserves. For presumably the reason he cannot do otherwise is that his virtue is so sure or his moral commitment so strong.

One might fear that if the agent really couldn't have acted differently, his virtue must be *too* sure or his commitment *too* strong. One might think, for example, that if someone literally couldn't resist buying a gift for a friend, his generosity would not be a virtue—it would be an obsession. For one can imagine situations in which it would be better if the agent did resist—if, for example, the money that was spent on the gift was desperately needed for some other purpose. Presumably, in the original case, though, the money was not desperately needed—we praise the agent for buying a gift for his friend rather than, say, a gift for himself. But from the fact that the man could not resist in this situation it doesn't follow that he couldn't resist in another. For part of the explanation of why he couldn't resist in this situation is that in this situation he has no reason to try to resist. This man, we assume, has a generous nature—a disposition, that is, to perform generous acts. But, then, if he is in a situation that presents a golden opportunity, and has no conflicting motive, how could he act otherwise?

One might still be concerned that if his motives are determined, the man cannot be truly deserving of praise. If he cannot help but have a generous character, then the fact that he is generous is not up to him. If a man's motives are determined, one might think, then *he* cannot control them, so it cannot be to his credit if his motives turn out to be good. But whether a man is in control of his motives cannot be decided so simply. We must know not only whether his motives are determined, but how they are determined as well.

We can imagine, for example, a man with a generous mother who becomes generous as a means of securing her love. He would not have been generous had his mother been different. Had she not admired generosity, he would not have developed this trait. We can imagine further that once this man's character had been developed, he would never subject it to question or change. His character would remain unthinkingly rigid, carried over from a childhood over which he had no control. As he developed a tendency to be generous, let us say, he developed other tendencies—a tendency to brush his teeth twice a day, a tendency to avoid the company of Jews. The explanation for why he developed any one of these traits is more or less the same as the explanation for why he has developed any other. And the explanation for why he has retained any one of these tendencies is more or less the same as the explanation for why he has retained any other. These tendencies are all, for him, merely habits which he has never thought about breaking. Indeed, they are habits which, by hypothesis, it was determined he would never

think about breaking. Such a man, perhaps, would not deserve credit for his generosity, for his generosity might be thought to be senseless and blind. But we can imagine a different picture in which no such claim is true, in which a generous character might be determined and yet under the agent's control.

We might start again with a man with a generous mother who starts to develop his generosity out of a desire for her love. But his reasons for developing a generous nature need not be his reasons for retaining it when he grows more mature. He may notice, for example, that his generous acts provide an independent pleasure, connected to the pleasure he gives the person on whom his generosity is bestowed. He may find that being generous promotes a positive fellow feeling and makes it easier for him to make friends than it would otherwise be. Moreover, he appreciates being the object of the generous acts of others, and he is hurt when others go to ungenerous extremes. All in all, his generosity seems to cohere with his other values. It fits in well with his ideas of how one ought to live.

Such a picture, I think, might be as determined as the former one. But it is compatible with the exercise of good sense and an open frame of mind. It is determined, because the agent does not create his new reasons for generosity any more than he created his old ones. He does not *decide* to feel an independent pleasure in performing acts of generosity, or decide that such acts will make it easier for him to make friends. He discovers that these are consequences of a generous nature—and if he is observant and perceptive, he cannot help but discover this. He does not choose to be the object of the generous acts of others, or to be the victim of less generous acts of less virtuous persons. Nor does he choose to be grateful to the one and hurt by the other. He cannot help but have these experiences—they are beyond his control. So it seems that what reasons he *has* for being generous depends on what reasons there *are*.

If the man's character is determined in this way, however, it seems absurd to say that it is not under his control. His character is determined on the basis of his reasons, and his reasons are determined by what reasons there are. What is not under his control, then, is that generosity be a virtue, and it is only because he realizes this that he remains a generous man. But one cannot say for *this* reason that his generosity is not praiseworthy. This is the best reason for being generous that a person could have.

So it seems that an agent can be morally praiseworthy even though he is determined to perform the action he performs. But we have already seen that an agent cannot be morally blameworthy if he is determined to perform the action he performs. Determination, then, is compatible with an agent's responsibility for a good action, but incompatible with an agent's responsibility for a bad action. The metaphysical conditions required for an agent's responsibility will vary according to the value of the action he performs.

The condition of freedom, as it is expressed by the requirement that an agent could have done otherwise, thus appears to demand a conditional analysis after all. But the condition must be one that separates the good actions from the bad—the condition, that is, must be essentially value-laden. An analysis of the condition of freedom that might do the trick is:

> He could have done otherwise if there had been good and sufficient reason.

where the "could have done otherwise" in the analysis is not a conditional at all. For presumably an action is morally praiseworthy only if there are no good and sufficient reasons to do something else. And an action is morally blameworthy only if there are good and sufficient reasons to do something else. Thus, when an agent performs a good action, the condition of freedom is a counterfactual: though it is required that the agent would have been able to do otherwise *had there been* good and sufficient reason to do so, the situation in which the good-acting agent actually found himself is a situation in which there was no such reason. Thus, it is compatible with the satisfaction of the condition of freedom that the agent in this case could not actually have done other than what he actually did. When an agent performs a bad action, however, the condition of freedom is not a counterfactual. The bad-acting agent does what he does in the face of good and sufficient reasons to do otherwise. Thus the condition of freedom requires that the agent in this case could have done otherwise in just the situation in which he was actually placed. An agent, then, can be determined to perform a good action and still be morally praiseworthy. But if an agent is to be blameworthy, he must unconditionally have been able to do something else.

It may be easier to see how this analysis works, and how it differs from conditional analyses that were suggested before, if we turn back to the case in which these previous analyses failed—namely, the case of the victim of a deprived childhood.

We imagined a case, in particular, of a man who embezzled some money, fully aware of what he was doing. He was neither coerced nor overcome by an irresistible impulse, and he was in complete possession of normal adult faculties of reason and observation. Yet it seems he ought not to be blamed for committing his crime, for, from his point of view, one cannot reasonably expect him to see anything wrong with his action. We may suppose that in his childhood he was given no love—he was beaten by his father, neglected by his mother. And that the people to whom he was exposed when he was growing up gave him examples only of evil and selfishness. From his point of view, it is natural to conclude that respecting other people's property would be foolish. For presumably no one had ever respected his. And it is natural for him to feel that he should treat other people as adversaries.

In light of this, it seems that this man shouldn't be blamed for an action we know to be wrong. For if we had had his childhood, we wouldn't have known it either. Yet this agent seems to have as much control over his life as we are apt to have over ours: he would have done otherwise, if he had tried. He would have tried to do otherwise, if he had chosen. And he would have chosen to do otherwise, if he had had reason. It is because he couldn't have had reason that this agent should not be blamed.

Though this agent's childhood was different from ours, it would seem to be neither more not less binding. The good fortune of our childhood is no more to our credit than the misfortune of his is to his blame. So if he is not free because of the childhood he had, then it would appear that we are not free either. Thus it seems no conditional analysis of freedom will do—for there is nothing internal to the agent which distinguishes him from us.

My analysis, however, proposes a condition that is not internal to the agent. And it allows us to state the relevant difference: namely that, whereas our childhoods fell within a range of normal decency, his was severely deprived. The consequence this has is that he, unlike us, could not have had reasons even though there were reasons around. The problem is not that his reason was functioning improperly, but that his data were unfortuitously selective: Since the world for him was not suitably cooperating, his reason cannot attain its appropriate goal.

The goal, to put it bluntly, is the True and the Good. The freedom we want is the freedom to find it. But such a freedom requires not only that we, as agents, have the right sorts of abilities—the abilities, that is, to direct and govern our actions by our most fundamental selves. It requires as well that the world cooperate in such a way that our most fundamental selves have the opportunity to develop into the selves they ought to be.

If the freedom necessary for moral responsibility is the freedom to be determined by the True and the Good, then obviously we cannot know whether we have such a freedom unless we know, on the one hand, that there *is* a True and a Good and, on the other, that there *are* capacities for finding them. As a consequence of this, the condition of freedom cannot be stated in purely metaphysical terms. For we cannot know which capacities and circumstances are necessary for freedom unless we know which capacities and circumstances will enable us to form the *right* values and perform the *right* actions. Strictly speaking, I take it, the capacity to reason is not enough—we need a kind of sensibility and perception as well. But these are capacities, I assume, that most of us have. So when the world co-operates, we are morally responsible.

I have already said that the condition of freedom cannot be stated in purely metaphysical terms. More specifically, the condition of freedom cannot be stated in terms that are value-free. Thus, the problem of free will has been misrepresented insofar as it has been thought to be a purely metaphysical problem. And, perhaps, this is why the problem of free will has seemed for so long to be hopeless.

That the problem should have seemed to be a purely metaphysical problem is not, however, unnatural or surprising. For being determined by the True and the Good is very different from being determined by one's garden variety of causes, and I think it not unnatural to feel as if one rules out the other. For to be determined by the Good is not to be determined by the Past. And to do something because it is the right thing to do is not to do it because one has been taught to do it. One might think, then, that one can be determined only by one thing or the other. For if one is going to do whatever it is right to do, then it seems one will do it whether or not one has been taught to do, then it seems one will do it whether or not it is right.

In fact, however, such reasoning rests on a category mistake. These two explanations do not necessarily compete, for they are explanations of different kinds. Consider, for example, the following situation: you ask me to name the capital of Nevada, and I reply "Carson City." We can explain why I give the answer I do give in either of the following ways: First, we can point out that when I was in the fifth grade I had to memorize the capitals of the fifty states. I was taught to believe that Carson City was the capital of Nevada, and was subsequently positively reinforced for doing so. Second,

we can point out that Carson City *is* the capital of Nevada, and that this was, after all, what you wanted to know. So on the one hand, I gave my answer because I was taught. And on the other, I gave my answer because it was right.

Presumably, these explanations are not unrelated. For if Carson City were not the capital of Nevada, I would not have been taught that it was. And if I hadn't been taught that Carson City was the capital of Nevada, I wouldn't have known that it was. Indeed, one might think that if the answer I gave weren't right, I *couldn't* have given it because I was taught. For no school board would have hired a teacher who got such facts wrong. And if I hadn't been taught that Carson City was the capital of Nevada, perhaps I couldn't have given this answer because it was right. For that Carson City is the capital of Nevada is not something that can be known a priori.

Similarly, we can explain why a person acts justly in either of the following ways: First, we can point out that he was taught to act justly, and was subsequently positively reinforced for doing so. Second, we can point out that it is right to act justly, and go on to say why he knows this is so. Again, these explanations are likely to be related. For if it weren't right to act justly, the person may well not have been taught that it was. And if the person hadn't been taught that he ought to act justly, the person may not have discovered this on his own. Of course, the explanations of both kinds in this case will be more complex than the explanations in the previous case. But what is relevant here is that these explanations are compatible: that one can be determined by the Good and determined by the Past.

In order for an agent to be morally free, then, he must be capable of being determined by the Good. Determination by the Good is, as it were, the goal we need freedom to pursue. We need the freedom *to* have our actions determined by the Good, and the freedom to be or to become the sorts of persons whose actions will continue to be so determined. In light of this, it should be clear that no standard incompatibilist views about the conditions of moral responsibility can be right, for, according to these views, an agent is free only if he is the sort of agent whose actions are not causally determined at all. Thus, an agent's freedom would be incompatible with the realization of the goal for which freedom is required. The agent would be, in the words, though not in the spirit, of Sartre, "condemned to be free"—he could not both be free and realize a moral ideal.

Thus, views that offer conditional analyses of the ability to do otherwise, views that, like mine, take freedom to consist in the ability *to be determined* in a particular way, are generally compatibilist views. For insofar as an agent *is* determined in the right way, the agent can be said to be acting freely. Like the compatibilists, then, I am claiming that whether an agent is morally responsible depends not on whether but on how that agent is determined. My view differs from theirs only in what I take the satisfactory kind of determination to be.

However, since on my view the satisfactory kind of determination is determination by reasons that an agent ought to have, it will follow that an agent can be both determined and responsible only insofar as he performs actions that he ought to perform. If an agent performs a morally bad action, on the other hand, then his actions can't be determined in the appropriate way. So if an agent is ever to be responsible for a bad action, it must be the case that his action is not psychologically determined at all. According to my view, then, in order for both moral praise and moral blame to be justified, the thesis of psychological determinism must be false.

Is it plausible that this thesis is false? I think so. For though it appears that some of our actions are psychologically determined, it appears that others are not. It appears that some of our actions are not determined by our interests, and some of our interests are not determined at all. That is, it seems that some of our actions are such that no set of psychological facts are sufficient to explain them. There are occasions on which a person takes one action, but there seems to be no reason why he didn't take another.

For example, we sometimes make arbitrary choices—to wear the green shirt rather than the blue, to have coffee rather than tea. We make such choices on the basis of no reason—and it seems that we might, in these cases, have made a different choice instead.

Some less trivial and more considered choices may also be arbitrary. For one may have reasons on both sides which are equally strong. Thus, one may have good reasons to go to graduate school and good reasons not to; good reasons to get married, and good reasons to stay single. Though we might want, in these cases, to choose on the basis of reasons, our reasons simply do not settle the matter for us. Other psychological events may be similarly undetermined, such as the chance occurrence of thoughts and ideas. One is just struck by an idea, but for no particular reason—one might as easily have had another idea or no idea at all. Or one simply forgets an appointment

one has made, even though one was not particularly distracted by other things at the time.

On retrospect, some of the appearance of indetermination may turn out to be deceptive. We decide that unconscious motives dictated a choice that seemed at the time to the arbitrary. Or a number of ideas that seemed to occur to us at random reveal a pattern too unusual to be the coincidence we thought. But if some of the appearances of indetermination are deceptive, I see no reason to believe that all of them should be.

Let us turn, then, to instances of immoral behavior, and see what the right kind of indetermination would be. For indetermination, in this context, is indetermination among some number of fairly particular alternatives—and if one's alternatives are not of the appropriate kind, indetermination will not be sufficient to justify moral blame. It is not enough, for example, to know that a criminal who happened to rob a bank might as easily have chosen to hold up a liquor store instead. What we need to know, in particular, is that when an agent performs a wrong action, he could have performed the right action for the right reasons instead. That is, first, the agent could have had the interests that the agent ought to have had, and second, the agent could have acted on the interests on which he ought to have acted.

Corresponding to these two possibilities, we can imagine two sorts of moral failure: the first corresponds to a form of negligence, the second to a form of weakness. Moral negligence consists in a failure to recognize the existence of moral reasons that one ought to have recognized. For example, a person hears that his friend is in the hospital, but fails to attend to this when planning his evening. He doesn't stop to think about how lonely and bored his friend is likely to be—he simply reaches for the *TV Guide* or for his novel instead. If the person could have recognized his friend's sorry predicament, he is guilty of moral negligence. Moral weakness, on the other hand, consists in the failure to act on the reasons that one knows one ought, for moral reasons, to be acting on. For example, a person might go so far as to conclude that he really ought to pay his sick friend a visit, but the thought of the drive across town is enough to convince him to stay at home with his book after all. If the person could have made the visit, he is guilty of moral weakness.

There is, admittedly, some difficulty in establishing that an agent who performs a morally bad action satisfies the condition of freedom. It is hard to know whether an agent who did one thing could have done another instead. But presumably we decide such questions now on the basis of statistical evidence—and, if, in fact, these actions are not determined, this is the best method there can be. We decide, in other words, that an agent could have done otherwise if others in his situation have done otherwise, and these others are like him in all apparently relevant ways. Or we decide that an agent could have done otherwise if he himself has done otherwise in situations that are like this one in all apparently relevant ways.

It should be emphasized that the indetermination with which we are here concerned is indetermination only at the level of psychological explanation. Such indetermination is compatible with determination at other levels of explanation. In particular, a sub-psychological, or psychological, explanation of our behavior may yet be deterministic. Some feel that if this is the case, the nature of psychological explanations of our behavior cannot be relevant to the problem of free will. Though I am inclined to disagree with this view, I have neither the space nor the competence to argue this here.

Restricting the type of explanation in question appropriately, however, it is a consequence of the condition of freedom I have suggested that the explanation for why a responsible agent performs a morally bad action must be, at some level, incomplete. There must be nothing that made the agent perform the action he did, nothing that prevented him from performing a morally better one. It should be noted that there may be praiseworthy actions for which the explanations are similarly incomplete. For the idea that an agent who could have performed a morally bad action actually performs a morally good one is no less plausible than the idea that an agent who could have performed a morally good action actually performs a morally bad one. Presumably, an agent who does the right thing for the right reasons deserves praise for his action whether it was determined or not. But whereas indetermination is compatible with the claim that an agent is deserving of praise, it is essential to the justification of the claim that an agent is deserving of blame.

Seen from a certain perspective, this dealing out of praise and blame may seem unfair. In particular, we might think that if it is truly undetermined whether a given agent in a given situation will perform a good action or a bad one, then it must be a matter of chance that the agent ends up doing what he does. If the action is truly undetermined, then it is not determined by the agent himself. One might think that in this case the agent has no more control over the moral quality of his action than does anything else.

However, the fact that it is not determined whether the agent will perform a good action or a bad one does not imply that which action he performs can properly be regarded as a matter of chance. Of course, in some situations an agent might choose to make it a matter of chance. For example, an agent struggling with the decision between fulfilling a moral obligation and doing something immoral that he very much wants to do might ultimately decide to let the toss of a coin settle the matter for him. But, in normal cases, the way in which the agent makes a decision involves no statistical process or randomizing event. It appears that the claim that there is no complete explanation of why the agent who could have performed a better action performed a worse one or of why the agent who could have performed a worse action performed a better one rules out even the explanation that it was a matter of chance.

In order to have control over the moral quality of his actions, an agent must have certain requisite abilities—in particular, the abilities necessary to see and understand the reasons and interests he ought to see and understand and the abilities necessary to direct his actions in accordance with these reasons and interests. And if, furthermore, there is nothing that interferes with the agent's use of these abilities—that is, no determining cause that prevents him from using them and no statistical process that, as it were, takes out of his hands the control over whether or not he uses them—then it seems that these are all the abilities that the agent needs to have. But it is compatible with the agent's having these abilities and with there being no interferences to their use that it is not determined whether the agent will perform a good action or a bad one. The responsible agent who performs a bad action fails to exercise these abilities sufficiently, though there is no complete explanation of why he fails. The responsible agent who performs a good action does exercise these abilities—it may or may not be the case that it is determined that he exercise them.

The freedom required for moral responsibility, then, is the freedom to be good. Only this kind of freedom will be neither too much nor too little. For then the agent is not so free as to be free from moral reasons, nor so unfree as to make these reasons ineffective.

EXERCISES

1. It is dusk on a cold winter's evening. You are walking home, and you hear a cry: A small child has been playing, all alone, on a frozen lake; the ice gave way, and the child plunged into the icy water, and is now hanging on to the edge of the ice. No one else is near. You drop your books and run to the lake and then out onto the ice toward the child. You can hear the ice cracking as you crawl to the hole where the child is holding on, but you reach the child and pull him from the frozen water. As you carry the child from the ice, an ambulance arrives and a crowd gathers. The child is rushed into the ambulance and taken to the hospital, but he's fine. A police officer pats you on the shoulder: "That was a courageous act; you saved that child's life, but you could have easily lost your own. If you hadn't rescued that child when you did, he would have died. You're a real hero. Why did you do it?" "I had to," you reply. "I couldn't let that child die, even if there was a risk to myself. There's no way I could have left the child there without trying to save him. I couldn't have done anything else." *If* that is true, and—being *who you are*—you *could not* have done anything else, did you act freely?

2. I'm on a diet, trying to lose a few pounds. This afternoon I go to a department meeting and someone has brought a big plate of rich warm chocolate brownies, covered with creamy fudge frosting. I eat four of them. Obviously, no one forces me to do so: I eat them because I dearly love gooey chocolate fudge brownies. But I feel bad about it even as I wolf down the brownies, and I deeply regret my brownie indulgence. I really wish I did not have such a craving for chocolate. Did I act freely in eating the brownies?

3. You *love* playing tennis: It is by far your favorite sport, your favorite recreation. You play almost every day—you would rather play tennis than go to the beach, or go on a cruise, or just about anything. You play tennis because you *enjoy* playing tennis, and you are very *glad* that you enjoy playing tennis: you consider it good, wholesome, healthy exercise. It certainly seems that you are acting *freely* when you play tennis.

   Suppose that we could trace your love of tennis to your early childhood environment: Your parents bought you a teddy bear stuffy with a soft tennis racquet when you were an infant; they gave you a small tennis racquet when you were a toddler and cheered when you swung it; they strongly encouraged your tennis playing and gave you lots of praise when you played. They didn't forbid you to play soccer—you played some when you were 10—but it was clear that they weren't very interested: They never missed your tennis matches, but hardly ever attended your soccer games. Would being able to trace the social *causes* of your love of tennis lessen your freedom?

   Suppose that instead of early childhood conditioning, we discover that you have the "tennis gene": There is a special gene that causes everyone who has it to love tennis (you inherited it from your parents, who have both tested positive for the tennis gene). Some people who do not have the tennis gene also love tennis; but *all* persons who have the tennis gene passionately love tennis. Would that in any way lessen your freedom when you play tennis, the sport you dearly love?

   Consider another scenario: The United States Tennis Association is concerned that not enough young athletes are choosing tennis as their favorite sport. So they have hired a nefarious chemist to come up with a potion that causes anyone who drinks it to passionately love tennis. (Okay, this requires a bit of imagination, but you can manage it; after all, lots of people believe in "love potions" that causes people to fall in love; this is just a *special* love potion, that causes people to fall in love with tennis.) Last year you were a passionate soccer player, and a good one; but after one of your matches, the U.S. Tennis Association slipped their love potion into your Gatorade, and after drinking it you developed a deep and permanent passion for tennis (and you now have little interest in playing soccer). Still, you now play tennis because you fervently love to play tennis. Are you acting freely?

4. Susan Wolf insists that genuine freedom requires a "True and Good," that we can accurately track. In contrast, the existentialist philosopher Jean-Paul Sartre maintains that if there were objective values that would *deprive* us of real freedom. What is the source of this fundamental conflict? Why do they reach such different conclusions?

5. You have examined Luther's vehement attack on Erasmus' account of free will; what do you suppose Luther's response would be to the account of free will offered by William James? What might be Luther's response to Susan Wolf's (very different) view of free will?

ADDITIONAL READING

William Barrett claims that determinism destroys any genuine novelty or creativity; see William Barrett, *Irrational Man* (New York: Random House, 1958); and William Barrett, "Determinism and Novelty," in Sidney Hook, ed., *Determinism and Freedom in the Age of Modern Science* (New York: Collier Macmillan, 1958). Psychologist B. F. Skinner argues that belief in determinism can be beneficial in enhancing creativity; see his "Lecture on Having a Poem," in *Cumulative Record*, 3rd ed. (New York: Appleton-Century-Crofts, 1972).

The position of "hierarchical compatibilism" is championed by Harry G. Frankfurt. Frankfurt developed his views in a number of essays, all of them collected in *The Importance of What We Care About* (Cambridge: Cambridge University Press, 1988). Another excellent hierarchical compatibilist source is Gerald Dworkin's *The Theory and Practice of Autonomy* (Cambridge: Cambridge University Press, 1988).

Rationalist compatibilism is presented most effectively by Susan Wolf, in *Freedom within Reason* (New York: Oxford University Press, 1990). John Martin Fischer has developed an interesting form of compatibilism, which emphasizes a somewhat more limited power of rational control; a good account of his views can be found in a collection of his essays: *My Way: Essays on Moral Responsibility* (Oxford: Oxford University Press, 2006).

An excellent anthology, containing original essays on the issue of alternative possibilities (and whether alternative possibilities are required for free will and moral responsibility), is David Widerker and Michael McKenna, *Moral Responsibility and Alternative Possibilities* (Burlington, Vermont: Ashgate, 2003).

An attempt to find some common ground between libertarian and compatibilist views is made by Bruce N. Waller, in "A Metacompatibilist Account of Free Will: Making Compatibilists and Incompatibilists More Compatible," *Philosophical Studies*, volume 112, number 2/3 (2003): 209–224.

Daniel Dennett has written two very entertaining and readable books that take a compatibilist view on free will: *Elbow Room* (Cambridge, Mass.: Bradford Books, 1985) and *Freedom Evolves* (New York: Viking, 2003). P. F. Strawson's "Freedom and Resentment" was originally published in 1962; it is now widely anthologized, including in the excellent Gary Watson anthology, *Free Will* (Oxford: Oxford University Press, 1982). Strawson's essay has been a very influential compatibilist view, arguing that we simply can't get along without our basic concepts of freedom and responsibility, whatever scientists might discover about determinism.

CHAPTER 10

ARE WE MORALLY RESPONSIBLE?

LIBERTARIAN FREE WILL

Libertarians believe that *if* determinism were true, then there would be no free will; but they hold that there is at least some small space that is exempt from determinism. In some cases, libertarians hold that this power of making choices that are not determined by any causal laws or causal history makes us very special, even godlike. The Renaissance philosopher Giovanni Pico Della Minrandola claimed that God granted humans the special power of free will so that we might literally make ourselves gods, as expressed in the following passage (in which Mirandola imagines God speaking to humanity):

> The nature of all other beings is limited and constrained within the bounds of laws prescribed by Us. Thou, constrained by no limits, in accordance with thine own free will, in whose hand We have placed thee, shalt ordain for thyself the limits of thy nature. We have set thee at the world's center that thou mayest from thence more easily observe whatever is in the world. We have made thee neither of heaven nor of earth, neither mortal nor immortal, so that with freedom of choice and with honor, as though the maker and molder of thyself, thou mayest fashion thyself in whatever shape thou shalt prefer. Thou shalt have the power to degenerate into the lower forms of life, which are brutish. Thou shalt have the power, out of thy soul's judgment, to be reborn into the higher forms, which are divine.*

Roderick Chisholm, a contemporary American philosopher, took a similar position, though perhaps not quite so imaginatively:

> If we are responsible . . . then we have a prerogative which some would attribute only to God; each of us, when we really act, is a prime mover unmoved. In doing what we do, we cause certain events to happen, and nothing and no one, except we ourselves, causes us to cause those events to happen. (1975, p. 395)

This *libertarian* model of free will is probably the view most people have when they think of free will. It's a godlike, rugged individualism, swashbuckling version of free will: "*I* am the master of my fate, *I* am the captain of my soul," and *nothing* determines what I do or don't do except *my free choice*—*my* choice, not determined or constrained by *anything*.

Appealing as the view is for many people, it involves some serious problems. The first problem is immediately obvious: dramatic and inspiring as this version of free will may be, it just doesn't seem to be *true*. This image of ourselves making choices that are miraculously free of all influence doesn't match up very well with what we learn from psychology, biology, and sociology. If you walk into the dining room and find that the main course is roasted poodle with rice, you are likely to feel both physically and morally disgusted, while

---

*Giovanni Pico della Mirandola, "Oration on the Dignity of Man," translated by Paul O. Kristeller, in *The Renaissance Philosophy of Man*, ed., Ernst Cassirer, Paul O. Kristeller, and John H. Randall (Chicago: University of Chicago Press, 1948), 224–225.

in many Eastern cultures that would be a very appealing meal. In like manner, if the dining hall serves bacon and pork sausage with your breakfast eggs, most American students will attack breakfast with gusto; but in many Middle Eastern cultures, such a breakfast dish would evoke the same moral and physical disgust that you felt for a meal of roasted dog. Obviously, some people reject their cultural traditions—I know a Texan who grew up on barbecued beef who is now a fervent vegan—but that doesn't change the fact that our cultures exert enormous influence on us, and those influences were not freely chosen. (You didn't *choose* to find roasted dog disgusting.) Think of your sexual inclinations. Some people suggest that we *choose* to be homosexual or heterosexual, but such claims are ridiculous. If you think back to your adolescent years, you probably recall that profound stirring of sexual desire; and you certainly didn't say to yourself, "hmm, shall I choose to be sexually attracted to boys, or girls, or both?" So where did those strong specific sexual inclinations come from? Were they genetically programmed, or were they a product of your early conditioning history, or some combination of the two? I don't know. But I know they didn't develop because you *chose* them. Think of your tastes and values. You love Bluegrass music, or jazz, or perhaps Mozart; but did you *choose* that musical preference? You love baseball; but when did you *choose* to like baseball? You believe strongly in democracy and free speech, and your commitment to democracy is one of your strongest values; but did you choose that value? And consider the many experiments carried out by social psychologists. In one famous experiment (devised by A. M. Isen and P. F. Levin, 1972), some experimental subjects "accidentally" found a dime in a phone booth, while other subjects did not. As each subject left the phone booth, one of the experimenters walked by carrying some papers (the experimental subjects didn't know this person was part of the experiment) and dropped the papers. The subjects who had found a dime almost all stopped to help pick up the papers, while most of the subjects who had not found the dime walked on by. Those who found the dime and stopped to help would sincerely say that they "freely chose" to help, that *nothing* influenced their choice. Yet clearly, a small silly influence like finding a dime had a large impact on their "free choice"—an impact they did not recognize. When we think about it carefully, we realize that there are enormous influences on our character, behavior, and "choices," influences that stretch far back into a very influential early childhood environment we often cannot even remember, influences perhaps from a genetic makeup of which we are largely ignorant, and influences (like finding a dime) that we wrongly suppose have no impact on us. So is there really any room left for these "totally free and uninfluenced" choices?

Early libertarians—such as the Renaissance philosopher Pico Della Mirandola— imagined that we could totally "make ourselves," free of all outside influence: that God had given humans a special gift that empowered them to take "whatever place, whatever form, and whatever functions you shall desire." But as time went on and science developed, it became clear that we were being shaped by many forces throughout the course of our lives, and that our choices were not made independently of such influences. Contemporary libertarians tend to make the area of free choice much *smaller* and more specific. We don't "make ourselves," but we can—in some very special circumstances—make choices that are remarkable *exceptions* to the causal forces that generally operate.

Our demand for freedom must reckon with a universe that is marked by order and regularity. Life is like a game of bridge. The cards in the game are given to us. We do not select them. They are traced to past Karma but we are free to make any call as we think fit and lead any suit. Only we are limited by the rules of the game. We are more free when we start the game than later on when the game has developed and our choices become restricted. But till the very end there is always a choice. A good player will see possibilities which a bad one does not. The more skilled a player the more alternatives does he perceive. A good hand may be cut to pieces by unskillful play and the bad play need not be attributed to the frowns of fortune. Even though we may not like the way in which the cards are shuffled, we like the game and we want to play. Sometimes wind and tide may prove too strong for us and even the most noble may come down. The great souls find profound peace in the consciousness that the stately order of the world, now lovely and luminous, now dark and terrible, in which man finds his duty and destiny, cannot be subdued to known aims. It seems to have a purpose of its own of which we are ignorant. Misfortune is not fate but providence. *Sarvepalli Radhakrishnan*, "Karma and Freedom," 1932

The best-known statement of the contemporary libertarian position is by C. A. Campbell, who narrows down acts of free will to a very small scope. For Campbell, our power of free will is a special creative power and it comes into play only in very special circumstances: When our strongest desire or inclination is in *conflict* with our moral principles and our belief about what we *should* do. For example, suppose that I have a strong desire to cheat someone (I am selling my old car to a stranger, and I could hide all the defects in the car, collect a lot more than the car is worth, and be long gone before the stranger realizes he has been cheated; and I *really want* that money); but I recognize and believe that cheating this person would be *morally wrong* (I believe it is wrong to treat others in a way that I would not wish to be treated, and cheating others fits that description). In this case, there is a conflict between my strongest *desire* (for the money) and my *moral obligation*; and (according to Campbell) it is *exclusively* in those situations that the power of *contra-causal free will* comes into play. In those special circumstances, I have the power to make or withhold the *effort of will* required to *rise to duty*, overcome my strongest desire, and act morally. It is *entirely* up to me whether I exert the necessary effort of will. In choosing to exert or withhold the willpower required to overcome my desire and act morally, I make a choice that is quite remarkable: *my choice*, and my choice alone, determines which way things happen, which way the world goes. Campbell is *not* saying that *if* my desires had been different, or I had a different moral upbringing, or circumstances were otherwise than they are, *then* I could have chosen differently. According to Campbell, in these special circumstances (desire versus duty) I can literally choose *either way*, and *nothing* (nothing in my past, or my genes, or my circumstances) determines which way I will choose; *nothing* determines my choice of exerting or withholding an effort of will except *my choosing*. That's why Campbell calls it *contra-causal free will*: This special effort of free will is not controlled by any past causes, it operates *independently* of the entire causal history of the world and the genetic and conditioning history of myself.

Contra-causal free will is a very special power. As noted earlier, Roderick Chisholm characterizes it as godlike:

> We have a prerogative which some would attribute only to God: each of us, when we really act, is a prime mover unmoved. In doing what we do, we cause certain events to happen, and nothing and no one, except we ourselves, causes us to cause those events to happen.

Campbell believes that contra-causal free will is a very special power—he emphasizes that it is a special *creative* power—but he wants to keep its exercise to a minimum. In that respect, he agrees with most contemporary libertarians, who recognize that powerful biological, psychological, and sociological causes can account for a large part of our character and behavior, but want to preserve some small but vital niche that is free of such determining factors.

While Campbell and Chisholm have no qualms about making this special area of free will *nonnatural* or even divine, most contemporary libertarians balk at attributing such miracle-working powers to humans. If we ask where to find this special small area of *non*determined but natural (*neither* miraculous nor mysterious) libertarian free will, contemporary libertarians offer a variety of answers. Robert Kane locates it in an area of quantum indeterminacy that is somehow amplified into human action. Randolph Clarke has suggested that our causal capacity doesn't by itself cause the free event, but instead strengthens or supports an existing tendency and helps make it effective. Carl Ginet locates free action in the actor's strong *sense* that he or she is directly causing or producing some result, while Hugh McCann finds the essential element of free action in the *conscious intent* to make a decision. All of these views are interesting, and they are all quite elaborate and complex—considerably more complex than can be covered in this survey.

In contrast to most contemporary libertarians—who want to sharply restrict the area in which free will operates—the *existentialists* move in the opposite direction, expanding the scope of free action well beyond what most people would consider free.

Nothing in your life just *happens* to you; rather, you *choose* it. Or so Sartre insists:

> There are no *accidents* in a life; a community event which suddenly bursts forth and involves me in it does not come from the outside. If I am mobilized in a war, this war is *my* war; it is in my image and I deserve it. I deserve it first because I could always get out of it by my suicide or by desertion; these ultimate possibilities are those which must always be present for us when there is a question of envisaging a situation. For lack of getting out of it, I have *chosen* it. *Being and Nothingness*, 1943

Existentialism takes its name from the famous existentialist credo: Existence precedes essence. That is, our essence is not defined prior to our existence; instead, we define our *own* essences, we *make ourselves* by our choices. And there are no guides for those choices, no limits, no boundaries: We are *totally* free. As Jean Paul Sartre puts it:

> Everything is indeed permitted if God does not exist, and man is in consequence forlorn, for he cannot find anything to depend upon either within or outside himself. He discovers forthwith, that he is without excuse. For if indeed existence precedes essence, one will never be able to explain one's action by reference to a given and specific human nature, in other words, there is no determinism—man is free, man *is* freedom. Nor, on the other hand, if God does not exist, are we provided with any values or commands that could legitimize our behavior. Thus we have neither behind us, nor before us in a luminous realm of values, any means of justification or excuse. We are left alone, without excuse. That is what I mean when I say that man is condemned to be free. Condemned, because he did not create himself, yet is nevertheless at liberty, and from the moment that he is thrown into this world he is responsible for everything he does.*

Thus, we have complete responsibility for ourselves and what we *make* of ourselves and who we *choose* to be.

Man is a being who is what he is not and is not what he is. In him existence precedes his essence. Or better, man's essence is freedom itself, the choice of making his essence what he will. For himself he decides what is right and what is wrong, from his own point of view. His task is to make himself and to help prepare the definition of what man will have been. *Hazel Barnes, An Existentialist Ethics*

---

*Jean-Paul Sartre, "Existentialism is a Humanism," in W. Kaufmann, ed., *Existentialism from Dostoyevsky to Sartre* (New Arena Library: New York, 1975), p. 352. First published in 1946.

Existentialism is a bold, brash, dramatic free will theory. It goes *beyond* "I am the captain of my fate, I am the master of my soul." For existentialists, I am the *maker* of my soul through my own free godlike choices. Existentialism has its charms, but it also has its problems. The key problem is this: It is very difficult to make any sense whatsoever of what it could possibly be to "make yourself" by your *own* choices. Obviously the choices you make have a profound influence on your life and your character. Your choice to go to college instead of looking for work; your choice to attend a large state university, or a small private college; your choice to major in sociology, or secondary education, or civil engineering; your choice to renounce your family's religion and become a Taoist; the choice to leave your unhappy marriage. Such choices are important, and they shape our lives and our characters. But who is making those choices? In Sartre's scheme, we make these self-defining choices before we have values, preferences, ideals, and characters. We are pure existential points, and the choices we make set the course of how the lines of our character will be drawn. But how is it possible to choose without values, convictions, and preferences? It doesn't seem to be *my* choice at all, but instead just a random, capricious event. I can understand making a choice that reflects my own values and deep preferences, and I can understand making a choice to reject some of the values I have previously held (because I have changed and now favor a conflicting value scheme). But what would it be like to make a choice *before* I have any values, direction, or preferences? Who is doing the choosing? Sartre would reply that there are two basic categories of being. Things that do not have the power of free will, that lack the power of genuine self-making, are in the category of "being-in-itself"; such objects—houses, planets, stones, and hamsters— have their own *given* natures. In contrast, we self-conscious beings who are capable of free self-making choice are in the metaphysical category of "being-for-itself," being that defines its *own* character. But while that gives a name to the problem, it tells us nothing of *how* this "being-for-itself" could "choose itself," could choose its own values and path before it has any character or values to form the basis of its choices.

While the problem is most obvious in Sartre, the problem of how we can be in *control* of libertarian choices—these special nondetermined choices that occur in the special realm of free will—is a problem confronting all libertarian theories. The free choice obviously must be *my* choice, but it also cannot just be the product of who I am: it cannot come from my causal history, my character, my circumstances, or my values. For *compatibilists*, free choices are those that come from my character and my own values; but that is not enough for libertarians. They insist that these special libertarian choices must *not* be the product of my character and values; but if they are not, in what sense are they *my* choices at all? If I find myself making a choice to do something that is not closely associated with my own values, that is likely to seem more like a symptom of madness than an act of free will. If I am a strong pro-union social democrat, and I find myself suddenly "freely choosing" to vote for candidates who oppose those positions, that is more likely to feel like demon possession than free will. Of course, I might come to change my political views; but if *I* am changing my beliefs and values, then I can trace the causal and deliberative process that resulted in such changes. If the changes occur through some special free choice that is not the product of my character, I may have difficulty acknowledging it as *my* choice at all.

Many libertarians emphasize the feeling of freedom—or the special introspective awareness of freedom—as significant or even conclusive evidence that we have a special power of free will. Sartre claims that deep down we all *know* that we have free will, but acknowledging this profound responsibility requires more courage than many people have, and therefore many people *deny* this deep knowledge of freedom and live in "bad faith." Carl Ginet counts the strong phenomenal sense of freely acting as the very essence of free will. And C. A. Campbell places great reliance on the personal *introspective* observation that it is really up to me to choose whether to exert or withhold an effort of will: "no one while functioning as a moral agent can help believing that he enjoys free will. Theoretically he may be completely convinced by Determinist arguments, but when actually confronted with a personal situation of conflict between duty and desire, he is quite certain that it lies with him here and now whether or not he will rise to duty." When dealing with critics of contra-causal free will, Campbell asserts that "Reflection upon the act of moral decision as apprehended from the inner standpoint would force him [the critic] to recognise a . . . *creative activity*; in which . . . nothing determines the act save the agent's doing of it." But how reliable is such introspective evidence? Our "inner feelings" don't have a great record of reliability: that deep feeling you thought was pure eternal love turned out to be pure lust, as you swiftly recognized when you woke up next to the object of your feeling the next morning; and I may be sincerely convinced that I am totally over Mona, and don't care for her in the least, and have no feelings for her at all, while all my friends know perfectly well that I am still mad about her. And we need hardly mention the deep intuitive feeling of certainty held by men in various periods and cultures that it is wrong for women to hold positions of authority, and the deep intuitive certainty that many have felt for a variety of conflicting religious beliefs.

In addition to the everyday doubts we have about our "introspective evidence," some recent neuropsychological and social psychological research raises severe challenges for any libertarian theory that relies on deep introspective knowledge of free choice. Social psychologists have devised a wide range of ingenious experiments that reveal the powerful but unrecognized influence of the *situations* in which we make our choices, and they have shown that even very trivial factors—such as finding small change in a phone booth, being encouraged to hurry, or experiencing a pleasant smell—can have profound effects on our choices and behavior. As illustrated by the dime experiment mentioned earlier, obviously, finding a dime is a trivial factor; but the point is that even a trivial factor, which *introspectively* one would be unlikely to recognize as influencing one's choice to help, had a profound effect on the choices made by the subjects. In fact, social psychologists have consistently found that subtle situational factors have a much greater effect on our choices and behavior than does "underlying character." The common belief that our choices come from deep within us (rather than from the situations in which we find ourselves) is regarded by social psychologists as a widespread introspective mistake: what social psychologists have labeled the "fundamental attribution error." Perhaps social psychologists are mistaken, but their research poses a significant challenge for those who place their faith in an introspectively known experience of free choice.

While social psychology challenges libertarian introspection from one direction, contemporary neuropsychological research threatens on another front. Not so long ago we could only speculate about brain activity; with the technological resources now available, we can actually observe brain activity while a person is talking, thinking, acting, and choosing. In a famous experiment carried out by Benjamin Libet, subjects were asked to freely choose when they would perform a simple movement of the hand, and note (by watching a large sweeping hand on a clock face) exactly when they had made the choice. Libet discovered that about half a second *before* they *consciously* willed to move their hands, brain activity could be detected that would signal their choices. That is, the *brain* activates choice *before* we are *consciously aware* of making a choice. The moral of that story is plain (according to most neuropsychologists): Our *conscious experience of willing* (that some libertarians insist gives us our best evidence of contra-causal free will) is an effect of brain activities that occur *before* the conscious willing. That is, the experience of conscious willing is *not* the special contra-causal force that causes our free acts; rather, it is merely a *side-effect* of the *nonconscious* brain activity, and that nonconscious brain activity is doing the real causal work. Or as philosophers and psychologists might say, experiences of *conscious* willing are *epiphenomena*: They are *caused by* the actual nonconscious willing that occurs in our brains, but they are not themselves part of that causal process. The real causes of our choices occur *without* our conscious awareness.

Benjamin Libet (the neuropsychologist who devised the famous experiment described here) insists that there is still room for a special power of free will. Libet maintains that in the very brief interval between when one becomes *conscious* of willing and the actual acting, there is an opportunity to *freely* exercise *veto power* over our acts. The scenario might run like this: Cain chooses to strike Abel (the cause of that choice is in Cain's brain, and Cain is not immediately conscious of it). Cain's (unconscious brain-generated) choice then becomes *conscious* to Cain. But then there is a *very* brief moment *before* Cain actually raises his hand to strike, and in *that moment* Cain could *veto* his choice to strike; and it is in that *veto power* that our special capacity of free will is exercised. But what if that conscious exercise of veto power were itself preceded by *non*conscious brain activity that caused the veto? The time involved is so brief that we have not devised a way to test whether that is the case; but *if* the veto choice were itself the result of nonconscious brain activity, then for *Libet* that would eliminate the possibility of free will.

The actual choice occurs *nonconsciously* in the brain, and the conscious experience is an aftereffect of the real cause: According to these neuropsychologists, the real choice occurs nonconsciously in the brain while the conscious experience merely informs us that our own brains caused an act (that is, when I "consciously choose" to move my arm that conscious *feeling* of free choice informs me that the arm movement resulted from my own activity, and was not the result of some external force moving my arm). Just as a fever is a symptom of infection rather than the cause of illness, the introspective experience of conscious willing is a *symptom* of choice, not the choice itself.

Pointing to will as a force in a person that causes the person's action is the same kind of explanation as saying that God has caused an event. This is a stopper that trumps any other explanation but that still seems not to explain anything at all in a predictive sense. Just as we can't tell what God is going to do, we can't predict what the will is likely to do. *Daniel Wegner, The Illusion of Conscious Will*

Not surprisingly, there are many who are very uncomfortable with this neuropsychological account of our conscious experience of free will. John Searle, a leading philosopher of mind, argues that the neuropsychological account runs counter to the most plausible evolutionary explanation. Why would such a complex conscious sense of free will evolve if it is not really involved in causing our free choices? Why would evolution play such a nasty trick on us? As Searle describes it, on this neuropsychological account, one:

> has the experience of free will, but there is no genuine free will at the neurobiological level. I think most neurobiologists would feel that this is probably how the brain actually works, that we have the experience of free will but it is illusory; because the neuronal processes are causally sufficient to determine subsequent states of the brain, assuming there are no outside stimulus inputs or effects from the rest of the body. But this result is intellectually very unsatisfying because it gives us a form of epiphenomenalism. It says that our experience of freedom plays no causal or explanatory role in our behavior. It is a complete illusion, because our behavior is entirely fixed by the neurobiology that determines the muscle contractions. On this view evolution played a massive trick on us. Evolution gives us the illusion of freedom, but it is nothing more than that—an illusion.

John Searle, p. 62 of *Freedom and Neurobiology*

So why would evolution play "a massive trick on us"?

Neuropsychologists answer: it doesn't. Our experience of freedom doesn't *cause* our choices, but it does perform an important function: It signals to us that the action we have initiated—the moving of our arm or hand—is our *own* behavior, that it comes from our *own* choices rather than being the product of some outside force. If your arm moves because it is pulled by a rope (or even because of a sudden seizure) that is a very different experience from the experience of freely choosing to move your arm. Your conscious "free choice" experience is an important feedback mechanism that informs you that the movement of your body was initiated *by you* (that's the explanation favored by neuropsychologist Daniel Wegner). Your movement is initiated nonconsciously, but it is still your *own* movement rather than caused by some external force. Evolution didn't play a dirty trick in giving us a conscious sense of free choice; rather, it gave us a useful tool for distinguishing our own motions from those initiated outside of us. If some philosophers insist on misinterpreting that useful conscious experience as a special power of free will that consciously produces our choices, that's not the fault of evolution.

Unable to fully understand how and why some individuals are able to demonstrate self-control in the face of very trying circumstances, we have attributed such behavior to willpower, to some supernatural entity, or to an underlying personality trait. These ways of thinking about the problem have unfortunately retarded understanding and discouraged research. A vicious tautology or circularity has been created. The person who succeeds in demonstrating self-control by resisting a major temptation—for example, the heavy smoker who quits cold turkey—is often described as having willpower. How do we know that he has willpower? Well, he quit smoking, didn't he? This circular route of observing a self-regulative behavior, inferring willpower, and then using the latter to "explain" the former is an all too frequent journey in self-control discussions. We have not gotten beyond the behavior to be explained. Moreover, this tautology discourages further inquiries into the factors affecting self-control. *Michael Mahoney and Carl Thoresen, Behavioral Self-Control* 1974, pp. 20–21.

Whether some form of libertarian theory can deal with the challenges posed by contemporary psychology is a question that remains open; certainly there is no shortage of libertarians willing to try. As Samuel Johnson said, "All theory counts against freedom, and all experience counts for it." Belief in the experience of contra-causal free will is very strong, and libertarian free will remains one of the free will candidates, along with the various forms of compatibilism.

WHAT ABOUT MORAL RESPONSIBILITY?

There are several distinctly different concepts of "responsibility," and before tackling the tough question of *moral* responsibility, it is important to distinguish *moral* responsibility from the other varieties. *Moral responsibility* is the responsibility linked with *just deserts*: punishment and reward, praise and blame. To say that someone is *morally responsible* for an act is to judge that punishing or rewarding that person is morally justified.

A second sense of responsibility is *causal* responsibility. To say that Joe is *causally responsible* for something is simply to say that Joe *caused* it. Primitive cultures sometimes run causal responsibility together with moral responsibility: "He that smiteth a man, so that he die, shall be surely put to death" (Exodus 21:12); "He that killeth a man, he shall be put to death" (Leviticus 24:21). An eye for an eye: Cause a death, and you are morally responsible, you justly deserve to die. It's a simple code, but it purchases its simplicity at the price of ignoring the difference between causal responsibility and moral responsibility. If I suffer a seizure which causes me to jerk my car onto the sidewalk and kill a pedestrian, then I am causally responsible; but few would count me as *morally* responsible. And if Jill strikes Jeff with a beer bottle because Jill is receiving messages from her radio that Jeff is a vicious extraterrestrial who will destroy the world if he is not knocked unconscious, then Jill is *causally* responsible for the knot on Jeff's head, but her *moral* responsibility is very doubtful. (Even one who is so hardhearted as to think Jill *is* morally responsible and deserving of punishment must realize that judging Jill *morally* responsible is a further step beyond knowing that she is *causally* responsible; and that is enough to establish the distinction.)

The distinction between causal responsibility and moral responsibility is fairly obvious, but another sense of responsibility is more confusing. The twentieth-century British legal philosopher H. L. A. Hart called this third type of responsibility *role* responsibility. Role responsibility is the responsibility for a role or an office. If you are the treasurer of an organization, you have the *role* responsibility for managing its finances. Suppose you do a lousy job as treasurer: the accounts are a mess; or even worse, you steal some of the organization's funds. Your *role* responsibility is not in doubt; but your *moral* responsibility may be. For example, someone might say: "It's true, Jennifer 'misappropriated' our funds; she was a truly *awful* treasurer. But we really shouldn't *blame* her: Jennifer has developed a terrible gambling addiction, and she couldn't control her excessive gambling, and that is what drove her to take the funds." Or alternatively: "Jennifer failed in her role responsibility as our treasurer, but she doesn't deserve blame (she's not *morally* responsible), because she developed early onset Alzheimer's while serving as treasurer, and she's no longer capable of remembering how to keep the financial records." Perhaps you think Jennifer really *is* morally responsible, and deserves full blame for her failure; but the point is, that will be a *further* judgment, *beyond* the fact that Jennifer is *role* responsible. If we all agree that Jennifer is *role* responsible, but there remains a dispute about whether she is *morally* responsible, then it is clear that role responsibility is not the same as moral responsibility. The same point applies if we are considering whether role responsible Jennifer justly deserves *reward* (is *morally* responsible) for doing a great job as our treasurer. Suppose that someone says: "Jennifer doesn't deserve any special award; it's true, she did a great job as treasurer, but her sister— who is a brilliant accountant—actually did all the work." Or—to take a rather implausible case—suppose someone offers this objection to giving Jennifer special credit: "True, Jennifer did a great job as our treasurer; but she doesn't deserve any special credit, because she was blessed with the treasurer *gene*, and anyone with that special genetic endowment automatically does a great job in the role of treasurer; Jennifer is just *lucky* to have the right genes for the job, and so she doesn't *justly deserve* any special recognition." Again, maybe you think Jennifer *is* morally responsible, and *does* deserve the reward (whether her genes had anything to do with it or not). But still, that claim about Jennifer's moral responsibility is a *different* claim than the agreed upon claim that she has *role* responsibility.

If we extend Hart's concept of *role* responsibility, we can consider having role responsibility for one's own life. This is *my* life, and *I* am in charge of managing it; and if I want your advice, I'll ask for it. Of course there are those who do *not* wish to take role responsibility for their own lives: perhaps some who embrace the controlled and regimented life of the military or the monastery prefer to have others managing their lives for them. But most people wish to take role responsibility for their own lives: They want to make their own choices, live according to their own judgments, ideas, and plans. (Psychologists tell us that in *most* cases it is psychologically healthy to have a strong sense of being in control of one's own life, acts, and choices, of taking role responsibility for how one lives one's life; the sense that one *cannot* exercise effective control over how one lives is often associated with severe depression.) So generally, taking role responsibility for your own life is a good thing, and it is something most of us want to do. If someone else tries to manage our lives for us, we strongly resent it: "Don't tell me how to live my life! This is *my* life, and it's *my* (role) responsibility to live it." No doubt there are scores of people who could manage my life better than I do; but that doesn't alter the fact that I do *not* want such management. But just as the treasurer's role responsibility for her office did not make her *morally* responsible, likewise your role responsibility for your own life does not make you *morally* responsible for whether you live it well or ill.

Consider our fiercely independent friend Sam. He makes his own decisions, hates interference, and there is no doubt that he is *role* responsible for his own life. But judging him *morally* responsible is a very different matter. Sam makes some big mistakes and unfortunate choices: He falls in with a bad crowd, starts reading philosophy books, and winds up *majoring* in philosophy. One might argue: "Sure, Sam made his *own* choices, he had full *role* responsibility; but it's not fair to *blame* him for his bad management of his own life. After all, his mother is a passionate philosopher, his favorite uncle loved philosophy, his beloved grandfather was a dedicated philosopher, his formative years were spent in philosophical discussions from morning till night, and his favorite stuffy was a soft fuzzy Socrates bear; and given all the philosophers in his family, maybe he has a genetic predisposition toward philosophy. It's sad that he chose such an unfortunate path, but when you understand all the influences that shaped his character, then it doesn't make sense to *blame* him for becoming a philosopher." Someone might argue that Sam *is* morally responsible for his life and his choices (certainly libertarians would think so); but that will require *further* argument, beyond merely noting that Sam is *role* responsible. It may be *wrong* to suppose that Sam is role responsible but not morally responsible, but it is not conceptually incoherent: you can make *sense* of that claim, even if you think it is false. And that's enough to establish a difference between role responsibility and moral responsibility for one's own life.

When people speak of *taking* responsibility, they are obviously speaking of taking *role* responsibility. You can *take* responsibility for a role or office, often by volunteering or just claiming it: "I'll take responsibility for organizing our picnic," or "I'll be treasurer, if no one else wants to be," or "How I run my life is up to *me*, so stop interfering." (Obviously you can't take responsibility for any office whatsoever. You can't *take* responsibility for being president of the United States; to gain that office, you must win—or steal—an election. But there are plenty of roles and offices you can take just by volunteering for them.) In contrast, you can't just take *moral* responsibility by volunteering for it. Think back to our friend Jennifer, who did such a great job as treasurer. If someone says: "Sure, Jennifer did fine as treasurer; but she doesn't deserve any special credit or reward, because her brilliant sister did all the work"; then it would be silly for Jennifer to reply, "No, I *do* deserve special credit, because I *claim* moral responsibility, I *take* moral responsibility." Or suppose Jennifer does a lousy job, and her friend Tamara comes to her defense: "Don't blame Jennifer for the treasurer mess; the blame should go to me instead, because I claim the moral responsibility." We might respond: "That's nice, Tamara; you're a loyal friend to Jennifer. But no, you can't just *claim* the moral responsibility for the mess. That's not the way moral responsibility works."

Politicians often make use of the ambiguity of "responsibility." When something goes badly wrong with government operations—there is corruption, or incompetence, or dishonesty—the governor or president goes on television, strikes a strong and sincere pose, and says: "I take full responsibility for the problems in this administration." Of course he or she then hastens to say, "I had nothing to do with the problems, I didn't personally do anything wrong; but still, I *take responsibility* for what happened." But that's really just a clever way of *avoiding* blame while looking noble: I nobly acknowledge my *role* responsibility ("*I* am President") while ducking any *moral* responsibility (I shouldn't be *blamed*). Note how often politicians say, "I take responsibility" and how *seldom* they say, "I'm to blame, I justly deserve your condemnation."

The multiple meanings of "responsibility" are one source of confusion when trying to get clear on moral responsibility. A second source of problems is the double meaning of: It was my *fault*. We often use "it was Joe's *fault*" in the sense of "Joe is to *blame*, Joe deserves punishment, Joe is morally responsible." In fact, that is such a common usage that it sounds odd to say: "It was Joe's fault, but Joe doesn't deserve blame." But when we think more carefully about our faults, questions soon arise about whether we deserve blame for acts that stem from *our* faults. David is a coward, and his cowardly acts—stemming from his own cowardly character—cause harm to those in his group. Certainly that reveals a *fault* in David, and we might well say that the harm caused was due to *David's fault*. But was David *morally responsible* for his character flaw and the bad behavior resulting from it? Suppose that David had been subjected to severe torture that broke his spirit and robbed him of courage. (Psychological research has shown that placing animals—whether dogs or humans—in situations in which they are subjected to repeated episodes of prolonged inescapable pain produces "learned helplessness," and the tortured subjects eventually become severely depressed, offer no resistance, and stop making any effort to escape.) Under such treatment, David becomes a coward; and so would you and I. David is certainly *flawed*. He now has serious character faults, and his cowardly acts stem from his cowardly character. But it is not at all clear that he *deserves blame* for his cowardly character or craven behavior. The problem is easier to see in David; but the same point applies for Frank, whose flawed character resulted not from a month of torture but from a childhood filled with years of abuse. Frank may well have severe faults; but to say that his bad acts are "his fault" in the sense that Frank is *morally responsible* for those acts is subject to serious question. David was very unlucky to fall into the hands of the vile people who tortured him; and Frank was unlucky in his early childhood (obviously Frank didn't *choose* to be subjected to an abusive childhood). But unless we somehow *choose ourselves*, we are all the lucky or unlucky products of a good or bad formative history. Our faults and our virtues are our own, but the basic fairness of moral responsibility judgments are not settled simply by looking at those faults and virtues. Or perhaps that does settle things: David is unlucky to have been tortured into cowardice, but he *is* now a coward, that is his *own* character, and he should be held morally responsible for the flawed behavior that results. However one decides that question, the point is that there *is* a question there to decide, and "being at fault" is not the same thing as deserving blame.

With these distinctions in hand, we can look more closely at *moral* responsibility and the conditions for being genuinely *morally* responsible. It is often supposed that once the question about free will is settled, the question of moral responsibility automatically goes along with it. Thus, psychiatrist Willard Gaylin states unequivocally that "Freedom demands responsibility; autonomy demands culpability" (Gaylin 1983, p. 338). But that connection has not been so obvious for everyone. Martin Luther, for example, denied that we have free will, but insisted that we *are* morally responsible for our wicked characters and richly deserve eternal punishment for our sins. And it seems entirely possible to go the other direction: affirming free will but denying moral responsibility. For example, think back to the case of the "happy slave" whose brutal treatment has extinguished any desire for escape and who deeply desires to remain a slave, and strongly approves of her desire for slavery (perhaps because her brutal treatment has robbed her of her sense of worth, and she now believes that her abject character is best suited for slavery). Some philosophers count this unfortunate individual as having free will (she is free to follow her desire for slavery, and she deeply approves of her desire to be a slave); but even if one counts this happy slave as having free will, it is something very different to suppose that she is *morally responsible* for her morally repugnant embrace of slavery (when we consider the brutal treatment that made her a willing slave, it is hard to imagine that she *deserves blame*—is morally responsible—for her acquiescence in slavery).

If we existentially "make ourselves" through our own free choices—not shaped by our causal and environmental history—that might establish adequate grounds for moral responsibility (though there remains the vexing question of *how* we could "make ourselves" prior to *being* ourselves). Or perhaps some more moderate libertarian theory can ground moral responsibility. But if instead we are *compatibilists* on the question of free will, it is not so clear that such compatibilist free will is sufficient for moral responsibility. Suppose that I am a thoroughly vile individual, cold and greedy: Think of Ebeneezer Scrooge, pre-ghosts. Charles Dickens, who created this infamous character, paints his portrait in clear strokes. Scrooge resolutely follows his path of greed, and employs his fortitude as well as his keen intelligence to accumulate ever more wealth. Many compatibilists would insist that is all we need to know: Scrooge has free will, *and* he richly *deserves blame* for his miserly character and behavior. But when Dickens shows us the cruel process that shaped Scrooge's character, he still appears to be acting freely, but *some* may have doubts about Scrooge's moral responsibility (doubts about whether it is fair and just to *blame* Scrooge). An early life of harsh poverty marked Scrooge with a deep fear of the cruel treatment that often befalls the impoverished: "there is nothing on which it [the world] is so hard as poverty," Scrooge states. Scrooge's lost love, Belle, offers a searching and sad description of what Scrooge becomes: "You fear the world too much. . . . All your other hopes have merged into the hope of being beyond the chance of its sordid reproach. I have seen your nobler aspirations fall off one by one, until the master passion, Gain, engrosses you." But Scrooge looks on his character and ambition and reflectively approves: " 'What then?' he retorted. 'Even if I have grown so much wiser, what then?' " Scrooge is following his own deep desires, and he reflectively and decisively approves of this "master passion." As compatibilists, there is not much more we could ask in the way of free will (unless we are willing to embrace the narrow path of rationalist compatibilism). But when we reflect on the harsh environment that shaped Scrooge's harsh character, does that raise questions concerning the fairness of *blaming* Scrooge? If so, then those questions drive a wedge between compatibilist free will and moral responsibility, and establishing moral responsibility will require something *more* than establishing compatibilist free will.

Strong Feelings and Moral Responsibility

The relation between free will and moral responsibility may pose some puzzles; but for many people, there is no doubt whatsoever about moral responsibility, *whatever* one's verdict on the nature of free will. We just *know* we are morally responsible: We *feel* it in our own guilt, and in our profound sense that basic *justice* demands blame or punishment for wrongdoing. No doubt there is a visceral feeling of moral responsibility, tit for tat. David Hume regards such feelings not so much as *evidence* of moral responsibility as instead an indication that the emotional reaction is so strong as to not require proof:

> The mind of man is so formed by nature that, upon the appearance of certain characters, dispositions, and actions, it immediately feels the sentiment of approbation or blame; nor are there any emotions more essential to its frame and constitution. . . . These sentiments are not to be controlled or altered by any philosophical theory or speculation whatsoever. Hume, Enquiry, Section VIII

Do our strong retributive feelings count as evidence for moral responsibility? That will be a central question in our examination of ethics: What role can *feelings* or emotions legitimately play in our judgments, especially in our judgments concerning ethics (and more particularly, in the present case, in our judgments concerning *moral responsibility* and just deserts)? If we can make any judgments at all concerning ethical issues, then it's clear that in at least *some* cases our strong feelings should be trumped by our reflective judgment. In fact, we generally do not take such feelings as offering very good evidence. The "feeling" of racism was profound in this country, but it was an egregiously wrong feeling if *anything* is wrong. It led to monstrous and almost unbelievable acts: slaveholders such as Thomas Jefferson keeping their *own children* as slaves; some even *sold* their own children away from their mothers, "selling them South" to work in the sugarcane fields of southern Louisiana, where the brutal working conditions and widespread malaria condemned them to a miserable life and an early death. The *feeling* in favor of "retributive justice" is very strong; indeed, even if one believes that retributive justice and moral responsibility are false, that will not eradicate that feeling: If someone harms you, you will *feel* a visceral desire to strike back even if you believe that it would be wrong to act on that desire. But then, we often feel desires we consider it best not to act upon (I'm sure your wicked imagination can fill in the details). Whether the feeling of moral responsibility is one of those feelings that should yield to reflection is an open question; but in any case, arguments from strong feelings are a rather slender reed to support such an important doctrine as moral responsibility. Of course, if feelings about moral responsibility are absolutely dominating, and reasoned reflection can have no force against them, then raising doubts about moral responsibility will merely be an intellectual diversion that will have no real effect. But when we think of other very deep feelings—the feelings that women could never hold positions of authority, that a state must be ruled by a powerful king, and so on—then it is clear that at least some deep feelings that were once widely held can, thankfully, be rejected and even eliminated. That is not to suggest, of course, that strong emotional belief in moral responsibility is the moral equivalent of such vile emotions as racism and sexism. But the point is that strong feelings often *can* change over the course of time; and it's possible that the strong visceral feelings concerning moral responsibility might be capable of modification—in any case, the real question is not whether we *have* such strong feelings, but rather whether we *should* be guided by them. Some strong feelings are wonderful: the natural affection most people feel toward babies is a good example; you can probably think of some other strong feelings you approve, such as those celebrated by e e cummings:

> Wholly to be a fool while spring is in the world
> my blood approve; kisses are a better fate than wisdom,
> Lady, I swear by all flowers.

Some strong feelings are very bad: racism is a clear case. No doubt feelings are important, and they may well be the mainspring of our ethical lives. But sorting out which feelings to foster and which ones to reduce or, if possible, eliminate will require something in addition to feelings. Perhaps feelings of moral responsibility *could* be eliminated, or at least mitigated; or at the very least, people might come to realize that this *ineradicable* feeling is one we should not act upon or use as policy. Or perhaps not. But prior to that question is the question of whether we should *try*. Certainly we have learned to limit our strike back emotions and the behavior that stems from them: If you are struck by someone who suffers a sudden seizure, the blow may hurt just as much as if it were intentional, and your immediate feeling may be for retaliation; but when you understand the cause, you judge it unfair to strike back, and even your desire to strike back may disappear. Whether better understanding of the causes of character and behavior *could* or *should* lead to a more general judgment against moral responsibility sentiments and acts remains a disputed question.

The questions of free will and moral responsibility are among the most important as well as the most perplexing issues in philosophy. This should not surprise us. Our concepts of free will and moral responsibility were shaped many centuries ago, at a time when biological studies were in their stumbling infancy, brain research could not even be contemplated, and the scientific study of psychology was nonexistent. Now we are living through an explosion of research into how genetics influences behavior, the actual functioning of brain processes (which are very different from what we had imagined), and the many subtle ways that our behavior is shaped and influenced by a multitude of factors. It is increasingly difficult to believe in a "will" that is somehow independent of or *transcends* all those factors. Can we work out a coherent account of free will that is consistent with our contemporary psychological and biological research? And considering what we now know about the complex causes of human character and behavior, can we make sense of traditional notions of just deserts and moral responsibility? When we consider the psychological, sociological, and biological sources of human behavior, is it *fair* to punish people for their misdeeds? There is no more difficult, disputed, or important question in philosophy; and such questions of what is *fair* and *just* lead smoothly into the next chapters: What is the nature of our *ethical* judgments, principles, and commitments?

READINGS

"ORATION ON THE DIGNITY OF MAN"
Giovanni Pico della Mirandola

Giovanni Pico della Mirandola (1463–1494) was a young Italian nobleman who came to Rome in 1486. There he posted 900 theses and invited scholars to a public debate on those issues to be held in January of 1487. He composed an opening speech—the "Oration on the Dignity of Man" —which he apparently planned to use as his opening remarks in the debate. Unfortunately for Pico della Mirandola, the Catholic Church examined the 900 theses and declared that many of them were heretical, and thus banned the debate. Though he tried to defend his views, it only made matters worse. He fled to France, but was soon arrested. Eventually freed, he returned to Italy and settled in Florence, under the protection of the powerful Medici family; and he lived there until his death, probably a victim of arsenic poisoning, in 1494. In this key passage from "Oration on the Dignity of Man," Mirandola develops a dramatic *libertarian* account of human free will, in which humans have the power to make themselves into almost any form they choose—even, apparently, into godlike form.

THE DIGNITY OF MAN

I have read, reverend Fathers, in the works of the Arabs, that when Abdala the Saracen was asked what he regarded as most to be wondered at on the world's stage, so to speak, he answered that there was nothing to be seen more wonderful than man. To this opinion may be added the saying of Hermes [Trismegistus]: "A great miracle, Asclepius, is man." But when I thought about the reason for these statements, I was not satisfied by the many remarkable qualities which were advanced as arguments by many men—that man is the intermediary between creatures, the intimate of higher beings and the king of lower beings, the interpreter of nature by the sharpness of his senses, by the questing curiosity of his reason, and by the light of his intelligence, the interval between enduring eternity and the flow of time, and, as the Persians say, the nuptial bond of the world, and by David's testimony, a little lower than the angels. Great indeed as these attributes are, they are not the principal ones, those, that is, which may rightfully claim the privilege of the highest admiration. For why should we not admire the angels themselves and the most blessed choirs of heaven more? At last I seem to have understood why man is the most fortunate creature and thus worthy of all admiration, and what precisely is the place allotted to him in the universal chain, a place to be envied not only by the beasts, but also by the stars, and the Intelligences beyond this world. It is an incredible and wonderful thing. And why not? For this is the very reason why man is rightly called and considered a great miracle and a truly marvellous creature. But hear what this place is, Fathers, and courteously grant me the favour of listening with friendly ears.

Now the Highest Father, God the Architect, according to the laws of His secret wisdom, built this house of the world, this world which we see, the most sacred temple of His divinity. He adorned the region beyond the heavens with Intelligences, He animated the celestial spheres with eternal souls, and He filled the excrementary and filthy parts of the lower world with a multitude of animals of all kinds. But when His work was finished, the Artisan longed for someone to reflect on the plan of so great a creation, to love its beauty, and to admire its magnitude. When, therefore, everything was completed, as Moses and the *Timaeus* testify, He began at last to consider the creation of man. But among His archetypes there was none from which He could form a new offspring, nor in His treasure houses was there any inheritance which He might bestow upon His new son, nor in the tribunal seats of the whole world was there a place where this contemplator of the universe might sit. All was now filled out; everything had been apportioned to the highest, the middle, and the lowest orders. But it was not in keeping with the paternal power to fail, as though exhausted, in the last act of creation; it was not in keeping with His wisdom to waver in a matter of necessity through lack of a design; it was not in keeping with His beneficent love that the creature who was to praise the divine liberality with regard to others should be forced to condemn it with respect to himself. Finally the Great Artisan ordained that man, to whom He could give nothing belonging only to himself, should share in common whatever properties had been peculiar to each of the other creatures. He received man, therefore, as a creature of undetermined nature, and placing him in the middle of the universe, said this to him: "Neither an established place, nor a form belonging to you alone, nor any special function have We given to you, O Adam, and for this reason, that you may have and possess, according to your desire and judgment, whatever place, whatever form, and whatever functions you shall desire. The nature of other creatures, which has been determined, is confined within the bounds prescribed by Us. You, who are confined by no limits, shall determine for yourself your own nature, in accordance with your own free will, in whose hand I have placed you. I have set you at the centre of the world, so that from there you may more easily survey whatever is in the world. We have made you neither heavenly nor earthly, neither mortal nor immortal, so that, more freely and more honourably the moulder and maker of yourself, you may fashion yourself in whatever form you shall prefer. You shall be able to descend among the lower forms of being, which are brute beasts; you shall be able to be reborn out of the judgment of your own soul into the higher beings, which are divine."

O sublime generosity of God the Father! O highest and most wonderful felicity of man! To him it was granted to have what he chooses, to be what he wills. At the moment when they are born, beasts bring with them from their mother's womb, as Lucilius says, whatever they shall possess. From the beginning or soon afterwards, the highest spiritual beings have been what they are to be for all eternity. When man came into life, the Father endowed him with all kinds of seeds and with the germs of every way of life. Whatever seeds each man cultivates will grow and bear fruit in him. If these seeds are vegetative, he will be like a plant; if they are sensitive, he will become like the beasts; if they are rational, he will become like a heavenly creature; if intellectual, he will be an angel and a son of God. And if, content with the lot of no created being, he withdraws into the centre of his own oneness, his spirit, made one with God in the solitary darkness of the Father, which is above all things, will surpass all things.

Who then will not wonder at this chameleon of ours, or who could wonder more greatly at anything else? For it was man who, on the ground of his mutability and of his ability to transform his own nature, was said by Asclepius of Athens to be symbolized by Prometheus in the mysteries.

⊷ SELFHOOD AND GODHOOD ⊷
C. A. *Campbell*

C. A. Campbell (1897–1974) was a Scottish philosopher who taught at the University of Glasgow. In **Selfhood and Godhood** (London: Routledge, 1957)—from which the following passage is taken—Campbell develops one of the best-known libertarian positions of the twentieth century. Campbell's libertarian view (in contrast to that of the existentialists) is very modest: He is willing to grant that there are causal factors shaping most aspects of our lives, but he insists on preserving one small but vitally important area of special creative "contra-causal" (nondetermined) free will.

1. It is something of a truism that in philosophic enquiry the exact formulation of a problem often takes one a long way on the road to its solution. In the case of the Free Will problem I think there is a rather special need of careful formulation. For there are many sorts of human freedom; and it can easily happen that one wastes a great deal of labour in proving or disproving a freedom which has almost nothing to do with the freedom which is at issue in the traditional problem of Free Will. . . .

Fortunately we can at least make a beginning with a certain amount of confidence. It is not seriously disputable that the kind of freedom in question is the freedom which is commonly recognised to be in some sense a precondition of moral responsibility.

Clearly, it is on account of this integral connection with moral responsibility that such exceptional importance has always been felt to attach to the Free Will problem. But in what precise sense is free will a precondition of moral responsibility, and thus a postulate of the moral life in general? This is an exceedingly troublesome question; but until we have satisfied ourselves about the answer to it, we are not in a position to state, let alone decide, the question whether 'Free Will' in its traditional, ethical, significance is a reality.

Our first business, then, is to ask, exactly what kind of freedom is it which is required for moral responsibility? And as to method of procedure in this inquiry, there seems to me to be no real choice. I know of only one method that carries with it any hope of success; viz. the critical comparison of those acts for which, on due reflection, we deem it proper to attribute moral praise or blame to the agents, with those acts for which, on due reflection, we deem such judgments to be improper. The ultimate touchstone, as I see it, can only be our moral consciousness as it manifests itself in our more critical and considered moral judgments. . . .

2. The first point to note is that the freedom at issue (as indeed the very name 'Free *Will* Problem' indicates) pertains primarily not to overt acts but to inner acts. The nature of things has decreed that, save in the case of one's self, it is only overt acts which one can directly observe. But a very little reflection serves to show that in our moral judgments upon others their overt acts are regarded as significant only in so far as they are the expression of inner acts. We do not consider the acts of a robot to be morally responsible acts; nor do we consider the acts of a man to be so save in so far as they are distinguishable from those of a robot by reflecting an inner life of choice. Similarly, from the other side, if we are satisfied (as we may on occasion be, at least in the case of ourselves) that a person has definitely elected to follow a course which he believes to be wrong, but has been prevented by external circumstances from translating his inner choice into an overt act, we still regard him as morally blameworthy. Moral freedom, then, pertains to *inner* acts.

The next point seems at first sight equally obvious and uncontroversial; but, as we shall see, it has awkward implications if we are in real earnest with it (as almost nobody is). It is the simple point that the act must be one of which the person

judged can be regarded as the *sole* author. It seems plain enough that if there are any *other* determinants of the act, external to the self, to that extent the act is not an act which the *self* determines, and to that extent not an act for which the self can be held morally responsible. The self is only part-author of the act, and his moral responsibility can logically extend only to those elements within the act (assuming for the moment that these can be isolated) of which he is the *sole* author.

The awkward implications of this apparent truism will be readily appreciated. For, if we are mindful of the influences exerted by heredity and environment, we may well feel some doubt whether there is any act of will at all of which one can truly say that the self is sole author, sole determinant. No man has a voice in determining the raw material of impulses and capacities that constitute his hereditary endowment, and no man has more than a very partial control of the material and social environment in which he is destined to live his life. Yet it would be manifestly absurd to deny that these two factors do constantly and profoundly affect the nature of a man's choices. That this is so we all of us recognise in our moral judgments when we 'make allowances', as we say, for a bad heredity or a vicious environment, and acknowledge in the victim of them a diminished moral responsibility for evil courses. Evidently we do *try*, in our moral judgments, however crudely, to praise or blame a man only in respect of that of which we can regard him as *wholly* the author. And evidently we do recognise that, for a man to be the author of an act in the full sense required for moral responsibility, it is not enough merely that he 'wills' or 'chooses' the act: since even the most unfortunate victim of heredity or environment does, as a rule, 'will' what he does. It is significant, however, that the ordinary man, though well enough aware of the influence upon choices of heredity and environment, does not feel obliged thereby to give up his assumption that moral predicates *are* somehow applicable. Plainly he still believes that there is *something* for which a man is morally responsible, something of which we can fairly say that he is the sole author. *What is this something?* To that question common-sense is not ready with an explicit answer—though an answer is, I think, implicit in the line which its moral judgments take. I shall do what I can to give an explicit answer later in this lecture. Meantime it must suffice to observe that, if we are to be true to the deliverances of our moral consciousness, it is very difficult to deny that *sole* authorship is a necessary condition of the morally responsible act.

Thirdly we come to a point over which much recent controversy has raged. We may approach it by raising the following question. Granted an act of which the agent is sole author, does this 'sole authorship' suffice to make the act a morally free act? We may be inclined to think that it does, until we contemplate the possibility that an act of which the agent is sole author might conceivably occur as a necessary expression of the agent's nature; the way in which, e.g. some philosophers have supposed the Divine act of creation to occur. This consideration excites a legitimate doubt; for it is far from easy to see how a person can be regarded as a proper subject for moral praise or blame in respect of an act which he *cannot help* performing—even if it be his own 'nature' which necessitates it. Must we not recognise it as a condition of the morally free act that the agent 'could have acted otherwise' than he in fact did? It is true, indeed, that we sometimes praise or blame a man for an act about which we are prepared to say, in the light of our knowledge of his established character, that he 'could no other'. But I think that a little reflection shows that in such cases we are not praising or blaming the man strictly for what he does *now* (or at any rate we ought not to be), but rather for those past acts of his which have generated the firm habit of mind from which his *present* act follows 'necessarily'. In other words, our praise and blame, so far as justified, are really retrospective, being directed not to the agent *qua* performing *this* act, but to the agent *qua* performing those past acts which have built up his present character, and in respect to which we presume that he *could* have acted otherwise, that there really *were* open possibilities before him. These cases, therefore, seem to me to constitute no valid exception to what I must take to be the rule, viz. that a man can be morally praised or blamed for an act only if he could have acted otherwise. . . .

3. Let me, then, briefly sum up the answer at which we have arrived to our question about the kind of freedom required to justify moral responsibility. It is that a man can be said to exercise free will in a morally significant sense only in so far as his chosen act is one of which he is the sole cause or author, and only if—in the straightforward, categorical sense of the phrase—he 'could have chosen otherwise'.

I confess that this answer is in some ways a disconcerting one. Disconcerting, because most of us, however objective we are in the actual conduct of our thinking, would *like* to be able to believe that moral responsibility is real: whereas the freedom required for moral responsibility, on the analysis we have given, is certainly far more difficult to establish than the freedom required on the analyses we found ourselves obliged to reject. If, e.g. moral freedom entails only that I could have acted otherwise *if* I had chosen otherwise, there is no real 'problem' about it at all. I am 'free' in the normal case where there is no external obstacle to prevent my translating the alternative choice into action, and not free in other cases. Still less is there a problem if all that moral freedom entails is that I could have acted otherwise *if* I had been a differently constituted person, or been in different circumstances. Clearly I am *always* free in *this* sense of freedom. But . . . these so-called 'freedoms' fail to give us the preconditions of moral responsibility, and hence leave the freedom of the traditional free-will problem, the freedom that people are really concerned about, precisely where it was. . . .

5. That brings me to the second, and more constructive, part of this lecture. From now on I shall be considering whether it is reasonable to believe that man does in fact possess a free will of the kind specified in the first part of the lecture. If so, just how and where within the complex fabric of the volitional life are we to locate it?—for although free will must presumably belong (if anywhere) to the volitional side of human experience, it is pretty clear from the way in which we have been forced to define it that it does not pertain simply to volition as such; not even to all volitions that are commonly dignified with the name of 'choices'. It has been, I think, one of the more serious impediments to profitable discussion of the Free Will problem that Libertarians and Determinists alike have so often failed to appreciate the comparatively narrow area within which the free will that is necessary to 'save' morality is required to operate. It goes without saying that this failure has been gravely prejudicial to the case for Libertarianism. I attach a good deal of importance, therefore, to the problem of locating free will correctly within the volitional orbit. Its solution forestalls and annuls, I believe, some of the more tiresome clichés of Determinist criticism.

We saw earlier that Common Sense's practice of 'making allowances' in its moral judgments for the influence of heredity and environment indicates Common Sense's conviction, both that a just moral judgment must discount determinants of choice over which the agent has no control, and also (since it still accepts moral judgments as legitimate) that *something* of moral relevance survives which can be regarded as genuinely self-originated. We are now to try to discover what this 'something' is. And I think we may still usefully take Common Sense as our guide. Suppose one asks the ordinary intelligent citizen *why* he deems it proper to make allowances for X, whose heredity and/or environment are unfortunate. He will tend to reply, I think, in some such terms as these: that X has more and stronger temptations to deviate from what is right than Y or Z, who are normally circumstanced, so that he must put forth a *stronger moral effort* if he is to achieve the same level of external conduct. The intended implication seems to be that X is just as morally praiseworthy as Y or Z *if* he exerts an equivalent moral effort, even though he may not thereby achieve an equal success in conforming his will to the 'concrete' demands of duty. And this implies, again, Common Sense's belief that *in moral effort* we have something for which a man is responsible *without qualification*, something that is *not* affected by heredity and environment but depends *solely* upon the self itself.

Now in my opinion Common Sense has here, in principle, hit upon the one and only defensible answer. Here, and here alone, so far as I can see, in the act of deciding whether to put forth or withhold the moral effort required to resist temptation and rise to duty, is to be found an act which is free in the sense required for moral responsibility; an act of which the self is sole author, and of which it is true to say that 'it could be' (or, after the event, 'could have been') 'otherwise'. Such is the thesis which we shall now try to establish.

6. The species of argument appropriate to the establishment of a thesis of this sort should fall, I think, into two phases. First, there should be a consideration of the evidence of the moral agent's own inner experience. What *is* the act of moral decision, and what does it imply, from the standpoint of the actual participant? Since there is no way of knowing the act of moral decision— or for that matter any other form of activity— except by actual participation in it, the evidence of the subject, or agent, is on an issue of this kind of palmary importance. It can hardly, however, be taken as in itself conclusive. For even if that evidence should be overwhelmingly to the effect that moral decision does have the characteristics required by moral freedom, the question is bound to be raised—and in view of considerations from other quarters pointing in a contrary direction is *rightly* raised—Can we *trust* the evidence of inner experience? That brings us to what will be the second phase of the argument. We shall have to go on to show, if we are to make good our case, that the extraneous considerations so often supposed to be fatal to the belief in moral freedom are in fact innocuous to it.

In the light of what was said in the last lecture about the self's experience of moral decision as a *creative* activity, we may perhaps be absolved from developing the first phase of the argument at any great length. The appeal is throughout to one's own experience in the actual taking of the moral decision in the situation of moral temptation. 'Is it possible', we must ask, 'for anyone so circumstanced to *dis*believe that he could be deciding otherwise?' The answer is surely not in doubt. When we decide to exert moral effort to resist a temptation, we feel quite certain that we *could* withhold the effort; just as, if we decide to withhold the effort and yield to our desires, we feel quite certain that we *could* exert it—otherwise we should not blame ourselves afterwards for having succumbed. It may be, indeed, that this conviction is mere self-delusion. But that is not at the moment our concern. It is enough at present to establish that the act of deciding to exert or to withhold moral effort, as we know it from the inside in actual moral living, belongs to the category of acts which 'could have been otherwise'.

Mutatis mutandis, the same reply is forthcoming if we ask, 'Is it possible for the moral agent in the taking of his decision to *dis*believe that he is the *sole* author of that decision?' Clearly he cannot disbelieve that it is *he* who takes the decision. That, however, is not in itself sufficient to enable him, on reflection, to regard himself as *solely* responsible for the act. For his 'character' as so far formed might conceivably be a factor in determining it, and no one can suppose that the constitution of his 'character' is uninfluenced by circumstances of heredity and environment with which *he* has nothing to do. But as we pointed out in the last lecture, the very essence of the moral decision as it is experienced is that it is a decision whether or not to *combat* our strongest desire, and our strongest desire *is* the expression in the situation of our character as so far formed. Now clearly our character cannot be a factor in determining the decision whether or not to *oppose* our character. I think we are entitled to say, therefore, that the act of moral decision is one in which the self is for itself not merely 'author' but 'sole author'.

7. We may pass on, then, to the second phase of our constructive argument; and this will demand more elaborate treatment. Even if a moral agent *qua* making a moral decision in the situation of 'temptation' cannot help believing that he has free will in the sense at issue—a moral freedom between real alternatives, between genuinely open possibilities—are there, nevertheless, objections to a freedom of this kind so cogent that we are bound to distrust the evidence of 'inner experience'?

   I begin by drawing attention to a simple point whose significance tends, I think, to be underestimated. If the phenomenological analysis we have offered is substantially correct, no one while functioning as a moral agent can help believing that he enjoys free will. Theoretically he may be completely convinced by Determinist arguments, but when actually confronted with a personal situation of conflict between duty and desire he is quite certain that it lies with him here and now whether or not he will rise to duty. It follows that if Determinists could produce convincing theoretical arguments against a free will of this kind, the awkward predicament would ensue that man has to deny as a theoretical being what he has to assert as a practical being. Now I think the Determinist ought to be a good deal more worried about this than he usually is. He seems to imagine that a strong case on general theoretical grounds is enough to prove that the 'practical' belief in free will, even if inescapable for us as practical beings, is mere illusion. But in fact it proves nothing of the sort. There is no reason whatever why a belief that we find ourselves obliged to hold *qua* practical beings should be required to give way before a belief which we find ourselves obliged to hold *qua* theoretical beings; or, for that matter, *vice versa*. All that the theoretical arguments of Determinism can prove, unless they are reinforced by a refutation of the phenomenological analysis that supports Libertarianism, is that there is a radical conflict between the theoretical and the practical sides of man's nature, an antinomy at the very heart of the self. And this is a state of affairs with which no one can easily rest satisfied. I think therefore that the Determinist ought to concern himself a great deal more than he does with phenomenological analysis, in order to show, if he can, that the assurance of free will is not really an inexpugnable element in man's practical consciousness. There is just as much obligation upon him, convinced though he may be of the soundness of his theoretical arguments, to expose the errors of the Libertarian's phenomenological analysis, as there is upon us, convinced though we may be of the soundness of the Libertarian's phenomenological analysis, to expose the errors of the Determinist's theoretical arguments.

8. However, we must at once begin the discharge of our own obligation. The rest of this lecture will be devoted to trying to show that the arguments which seem to carry most weight with Determinists are, to say the least of it, very far from compulsive. . . .

   These arguments can, I think, be reduced in principle to no more than two: first, the argument from 'predictability'; second, the argument from the alleged meaninglessness of an act supposed to be the self's act and yet not an expression of the self's character. Contemporary criticism of free will seems to me to consist almost exclusively of variations on these two themes. I shall deal with each in turn.

9. On the first we touched in passing at an earlier stage. Surely it is beyond question (the critic urges) that when we know a person intimately we can foretell with a high degree of accuracy how he will respond to at least a large number of practical situations. One feels safe in predicting that one's dog-loving friend will not use his boot to repel the little mongrel that comes yapping at his heels; or again that one's wife will not pass with incurious eyes (or indeed pass at all) the new hat-shop in the city. So to behave would not be (as we say) 'in character'. But, so the criticism runs, you with your doctrine of 'genuinely open possibilities', of a free will by which the self can diverge from its own character, remove all rational basis from such prediction. You require us to make the absurd supposition that the success of countless predictions of the sort in the past has been mere matter of chance. If you *really* believed in your theory, you would not be surprised if tomorrow

your friend with the notorious horror of strong drink should suddenly exhibit a passion for whisky and soda, or if your friend whose taste for reading has hitherto been satisfied with the sporting columns of the newspapers should be discovered on a fine Saturday afternoon poring over the works of Hegel. But of course you *would* be surprised. Social life would be sheer chaos if there were not well-grounded social expectations; and social life is not sheer chaos. Your theory is hopelessly wrecked upon obvious facts.

Now whether or not this criticism holds good against some versions of Libertarian theory I need not here discuss. It is sufficient if I can make it clear that against the version advanced in this lecture, according to which free will is localised in a relatively narrow field of operation, the criticism has no relevance whatsoever.

Let us remind ourselves briefly of the setting within which, on our view, free will functions. There is X, the course which we believe we ought to follow, and Y, the course towards which we feel our desire is strongest. The freedom which we ascribe to the agent is the freedom to put forth or refrain from putting forth the moral effort required to resist the pressure of desire and do what he thinks he ought to do.

But then there is surely an immense range of practical situations—covering by far the greater part of life—in which there is no question of a conflict within the self between what he most desires to do and what he thinks he ought to do? Indeed such conflict is a comparatively rare phenomenon for the majority of men. Yet over that whole vast range there is nothing whatever in our version of Libertarianism to prevent our agreeing that character determines conduct. In the absence, real or supposed, of any 'moral' issue, what a man chooses will be simply that course which, after such reflection as seems called for, he deems most likely to bring him what he most strongly desires; and that is the same as to say the course to which his present character inclines him.

Over by far the greater area of human choices, then, our theory offers no more barrier to successful prediction on the basis of character than any other theory. For where there is no clash of strongest desire with duty, the free will we are defending has no business. There is just nothing for it to do.

But what about the situations—rare enough though they may be—in which there *is* this clash

and in which free will does therefore operate? Does our theory entail that there at any rate, as the critic seems to suppose, 'anything may happen'?

Not by any manner of means. In the first place, and by the very nature of the case, the range of the agent's possible choices is bounded by what he thinks he ought to do on the one hand, and what he most strongly desires on the other. The freedom claimed for him is a freedom of decision to make or withhold the effort required to do what he thinks he ought to do. There is no question of a freedom to act in some 'wild' fashion, out of all relation to his characteristic beliefs and desires. This so-called 'freedom of caprice', so often charged against the Libertarian, is, to put it bluntly, a sheer figment of the critic's imagination, with no *habitat* in serious Libertarian theory. Even in situations where free will does come into play it is perfectly possible, on a view like ours, given the appropriate knowledge of a man's character, to predict within certain limits how he will respond.

But 'probable' prediction in such situations can, I think, go further than this. It is obvious that where desire and duty are at odds, the felt 'gap' (as it were) between the two may vary enormously in breadth in different cases. The moderate drinker and the chronic tippler may each want another glass, and each deem it his duty to abstain, but the felt gap between desire and duty in the case of the former is trivial beside the great gulf which is felt to separate them in the case of the latter. Hence it will take a far harder moral effort for the tippler than for the moderate drinker to achieve the same external result of abstention. So much is matter of common agreement. And we are entitled, I think, to take it into account in prediction, on the simple principle that the harder the moral effort required to resist desire the less likely it is to occur. Thus in the example taken, most people would predict that the tippler will very probably succumb to his desires, whereas there is a reasonable likelihood that the moderate drinker will make the comparatively slight effort needed to resist them. So long as the prediction does not pretend to more than a measure of probability, there is nothing in our theory which would disallow it.

I claim, therefore, that the view of free will I have been putting forward is consistent with predictability of conduct on the basis of character over a very wide field indeed. And I make the further claim that that field will cover all the situations in life concerning which there is any empirical evidence that successful prediction is possible.

10. Let us pass on to consider the second main line of criticism. This is, I think, much the more illuminating of the two, if only because it compels the Libertarian to make explicit certain concepts which are indispensable to him, but which, being desperately hard to state clearly, are apt not to be stated at all. The critic's fundamental point might be stated somewhat as follows:

'Free will as you describe it is completely unintelligible. On your own showing no *reason* can be given, because there just *is* no reason, why a man decides to exert rather than to withhold moral effort, or *vice versa*. But such an act—or more properly, such an "occurrence"—it is nonsense to speak of as an act of a *self*. If there is nothing in the self's character to which it is, even in principle, in any way traceable, the self has nothing to do with it. Your so-called "freedom", therefore, so far from supporting the self's moral responsibility, destroys it as surely as the crudest Determinism could do.'

If we are to discuss this criticism usefully, it is important, I think, to begin by getting clear about two different senses of the word 'intelligible'.

If, in the first place, we mean by an 'intelligible' act one whose occurrence is in principle capable of being inferred, since it follows necessarily from something (though we may not know in fact from what), then it is certainly true that the Libertarian's free will is unintelligible. But that is only saying, is it not, that the Libertarian's 'free' act is not an act which follows necessarily from something! This can hardly rank as a *criticism* of Libertarianism. It is just a description of it. That there can be nothing unintelligible in *this* sense is precisely what the Determinist has got to *prove*.

Yet it is surprising how often the critic of Libertarianism involves himself in this circular mode of argument. Repeatedly it is urged against the Libertarian, with a great air of triumph, that on his view he can't say *why* I now decide to rise to duty, or now decide to follow my strongest desire in defiance of duty. Of course he can't. If he could he wouldn't *be* a Libertarian. To 'account for' a 'free' act is a contradiction in terms. A free will is *ex hypothesi* the sort of thing of which the request for an *explanation* is absurd. The assumption that an explanation must be in principle possible for the act of moral decision deserves to rank as a classic example of the ancient fallacy of 'begging the question'.

But the critic usually has in mind another sense of the word 'unintelligible'. He is apt to take it for granted that an act which is unintelligible in the *above* sense (as the morally free act of the Libertarian undoubtedly is) is unintelligible in the *further* sense that we can attach no meaning to it. And this is an altogether more serious matter. If it could really be shown that the Libertarian's 'free will' were unintelligible in this sense of being meaningless, that, for myself at any rate, would be the end of the affair. Libertarianism would have been conclusively refuted.

But it seems to me manifest that this can *not* be shown. The critic has allowed himself, I submit, to become the victim of a widely accepted but fundamentally vicious assumption. He has assumed that whatever is meaningful must exhibit its meaningfulness to those who view it from the standpoint of external observation. Now if one chooses thus to limit one's self to the rôle of external observer, it is, I think, perfectly true that one can attach no meaning to an act which is the act of something we call a 'self' and yet follows from nothing in that self's character. But then *why should we* so limit ourselves, when what is under consideration is a subjective activity? For the apprehension of subjective acts there is *another* standpoint available, that of *inner experience*, of the practical consciousness in its actual functioning. If our free will should turn out to be something to which we can attach a meaning from *this* standpoint, no more is required. And no more ought to be expected. For I must repeat that only from the inner standpoint of living experience *could* anything of the nature of 'activity' be directly grasped. Observation from without is in the nature of the case impotent to apprehend the active *qua* active. We can from without observe sequences of states. If into these we read activity (as we sometimes do), this can only be on the basis of what we discern in ourselves from the inner standpoint. It follows that if anyone insists upon taking his criterion of the meaningful simply from the standpoint of external observation, he is really deciding in advance of the evidence that the notion of activity, and *a fortiori* the notion of a free will, is 'meaningless'. He looks for the free act through a medium which is in the nature of the case incapable of revealing it, and then, because inevitably he doesn't find it, he declares that it doesn't exist!

But if, as we surely ought in this context, we adopt the inner standpoint, then (I am suggesting) things appear in a totally different light. From the inner standpoint, it seems to me plain, there is no difficulty whatever in attaching meaning to an act which is the self's act and which nevertheless does not follow from the self's character. So much I claim has been established by the phenomenological analysis, in this and the previous lecture, of the act of moral decision in face of moral temptation. It is thrown into particularly clear relief where the moral decision is to make the moral effort required to rise to duty. For the very function of moral effort, as it appears to the agent engaged in the act, is to enable the self to act against the line of least resistance, against the line to which his character as so far formed most strongly inclines him. But if the self is thus conscious here of *combating* his formed character, he surely cannot possibly suppose that the act, although his own act, *issues from* his formed character? I submit, therefore, that the self knows very well indeed—from the inner standpoint—what is meant by an act which is the *self's* act and which nevertheless does not follow from the self's *character*.

What this implies—and it seems to me to be an implication of cardinal importance for any theory of the self that aims at being more than superficial—is that the nature of the self is for itself something more than just its character as so far formed. The 'nature' of the self and what we commonly call the 'character' of the self are by no means the same thing, and it is utterly vital that they should not be confused. The 'nature' of the self comprehends, but is not without remainder reducible to, its 'character'; it must, if

we are to be true to the testimony of our experience of it, be taken as including *also* the authentic creative power of fashioning and re-fashioning 'character'.

The misguided, and as a rule quite uncritical, belittlement, of the evidence offered by inner experience has, I am convinced, been responsible for more bad argument by the opponents of Free Will than has any other single factor. How often, for example, do we find the Determinist critic saying, in effect, '*Either* the act follows necessarily upon precedent states, *or* it is a mere matter of chance and accordingly of no moral significance'. The disjunction is invalid, for it does not exhaust the possible alternatives. It seems to the critic to do so only because he *will* limit himself to the standpoint which is proper, and indeed alone possible, in dealing with the physical world, the standpoint of the external observer. If only he would allow himself to assume the standpoint which is not merely proper for, but necessary to, the apprehension of subjective activity, the inner standpoint of the practical consciousness in its actual functioning, he would find himself obliged to recognise the falsity of his disjunction. Reflection upon the act of moral decision as apprehended from the inner standpoint would force him to recognise a *third* possibility, as remote from chance as from necessity, that, namely, of *creative activity*, in which (as I have ventured to express it) nothing determines the act save the agent's doing of it.

. . .

⇒⇜ "MORAL LUCK" ⇒⇜
Thomas Nagel

Thomas Nagel is a professor of philosophy and law at New York University. His work often follows Kantian lines, but he is perhaps best known for raising serious philosophical perplexities to which he offers at most only tentative solutions. The philosophically famous essay on moral luck, printed below, is a good example. Among Nagel's major works are *The Possibility of Altruism* (Princeton: Princeton University Press, 1970); *Mortal Questions*, which contains the essay "Moral Luck" (Cambridge: Cambridge University Press, 1979); and *The View from Nowhere* (Oxford: Oxford University Press, 1986). All of Nagel's works are delightful to read; the questions they raise, however, are not easy to answer.

Kant believed that good or bad luck should influence neither our moral judgment of a person and his actions, nor his moral assessment of himself.

> The good will is not good because of what it effects or accomplishes or because of its adequacy to achieve some proposed end; it is good only because of its willing, i.e., it is good of itself. And, regarded for itself, it is to be esteemed incomparably higher than anything which could be brought about by it in favor of any inclination or even of the sum total of all inclinations. Even if it should happen that, by a particularly unfortunate fate or by the niggardly provision of a stepmotherly nature, this will should be wholly lacking in power to accomplish its purpose, and if even the greatest effort should not avail it to achieve anything of its end, and if there remained only the good will (not as a mere wish but as the summoning of all

the means in our power), it would sparkle like a jewel in its own right, as something that had its full worth in itself. Usefulness or fruitlessness can neither diminish nor augment this worth.

He would presumably have said the same about a bad will: whether it accomplishes its evil purposes is morally irrelevant. And a course of action that would be condemned if it had a bad outcome cannot be vindicated if by luck it turns out well. There cannot be moral risk. This view seems to be wrong, but it arises in response to a fundamental problem about moral responsibility to which we possess no satisfactory solution.

The problem develops out of the ordinary conditions of moral judgment. Prior to reflection it is intuitively plausible that people cannot be morally assessed for what is not their fault, or for what is due to factors beyond their control. Such judgment is different from the evaluation of something as a good or bad thing, or state of affairs. The latter may be present in addition to moral judgment, but when we blame someone for his actions we are not merely saying it is bad that they happened, or bad that he exists: we are judging *him*, saying he is bad, which is different from his being a bad thing. This kind of judgment takes only a certain kind of object. Without being able to explain exactly why, we feel that the appropriateness of moral assessment is easily undermined by the discovery that the act or attribute, no matter how good or bad, is not under the person's control. While other evaluations remain, this one seems to lose its footing. So a clear absence of control, produced by involuntary movement, physical force, or ignorance of the circumstances, excuses what is done from moral judgment. But what we do depends in many more ways than these on what is not under our control—what is not produced by a good or a bad will, in Kant's phrase. And external influences in this broader range are not usually thought to excuse what is done from moral judgment, positive or negative.

Let me give a few examples, beginning with the type of case Kant has in mind. Whether we succeed or fail in what we try to do nearly always depends to some extent on factors beyond our control. This is true of murder, altruism, revolution, the sacrifice of certain interests for the sake of others—almost any morally important act. What has been done, and what is morally judged, is partly determined by external factors. However jewel-like the good will may be in its own right, there is a morally significant difference between rescuing someone from a burning building and dropping him from a twelfth-storey window while trying to rescue him. Similarly, there is a morally

significant difference between reckless driving and manslaughter. But whether a reckless driver hits a pedestrian depends on the presence of the pedestrian at the point where he recklessly passes a red light. What we do is also limited by the opportunities and choices with which we are faced, and these are largely determined by factors beyond our control. Someone who was an officer in a concentration camp might have led a quiet and harmless life if the Nazis had never come to power in Germany. And someone who led a quiet and harmless life in Argentina might have become an officer in a concentration camp if he had not left Germany for business reasons in 1930.

I shall say more later about these and other examples. I introduce them here to illustrate a general point. Where a significant aspect of what someone does depends on factors beyond his control, yet we continue to treat him in that respect as an object of moral judgment, it can be called moral luck. Such luck can be good or bad. And the problem posed by this phenomenon, which led Kant to deny its possibility, is that the broad range of external influences here identified seems on close examination to undermine moral assessment as surely as does the narrower range of familiar excusing conditions. If the condition of control is consistently applied, it threatens to erode most of the moral assessments we find it natural to make. The things for which people are morally judged are determined in more ways than we at first realize by what is beyond their control. And when the seemingly natural requirement of fault or responsibility is applied in light of these facts, it leaves few pre-reflective moral judgments intact. Ultimately, nothing or almost nothing about what a person does seems to be under his control.

Why not conclude, then, that the condition of control is false—that it is an initially plausible hypothesis refuted by clear counter-examples? One could in that case look instead for a more refined condition which picked out the *kinds* of lack of control that really undermine certain moral judgments, without yielding the unacceptable conclusion derived from the broader condition, that most or all ordinary moral judgments are illegitimate.

What rules out this escape is that we are dealing not with a theoretical conjecture but with a philosophical problem. The condition of control does not suggest itself merely as a generalization from certain clear cases. It seems *correct* in the further cases to which it is extended beyond the original set. When we undermine moral assessment by considering new ways in which control is absent, we are not just discovering what *would* follow given the general hypothesis, but are actually being persuaded that in itself the absence of control is relevant in these cases too. The erosion of moral judgment emerges not as the absurd consequence of an over-simple theory, but as a natural consequence of the ordinary idea of moral assessment, when it is applied in view of a more complete and precise account of the facts. It would therefore be a mistake to argue from the unacceptability of the conclusions to the need for a different account of the conditions of moral responsibility. The view that moral luck is paradoxical is not a *mistake*, ethical or logical, but a perception of one of the ways in which the intuitively acceptable conditions of moral judgment threaten to undermine it all.

Moral luck is like this because while there are various respects in which the natural objects of moral assessment are out of our control or influenced by what is out of our control, we cannot reflect on these facts without losing our grip on the judgments.

There are roughly four ways in which the natural objects of moral assessment are disturbingly subject to luck. One is the phenomenon of constitutive luck—the kind of person you are, where this is not just a question of what you deliberately do, but of your inclinations, capacities, and temperament. Another category is luck in one's circumstances—the kind of problems and situations one faces. The other two have to do with the causes and effects of action: luck in how one is determined by antecedent circumstances, and luck in the way one's actions and projects turn out. All of them present a common problem. They are all opposed by the idea that one cannot be more culpable or estimable for anything than one is for that fraction of it which is under one's control. It seems irrational to take or dispense credit or blame for matters over which a person has no control, or for their influence on results over which he has partial control. Such things may create the conditions for action, but action can be judged only to the extent that it goes beyond these conditions and does not just result from them.

Let us first consider luck, good and bad, in the way things turn out. Kant, in the above-quoted passage, has one example of this in mind, but the category covers a wide range. It includes the truck driver who accidentally runs over a child, the artist who abandons his wife and five children to devote himself to painting, and other cases in which the possibilities of success and failure are even greater. The driver, if he is entirely without fault, will feel terrible about his role in the event, but will not have to reproach himself. Therefore this example of agent-regret is not yet a case of *moral* bad luck. However, if the driver was guilty of even a minor degree of negligence—failing to have his brakes checked recently, for example—then if that negligence contributes to the death of the child, he will not merely feel terrible. He will blame himself for the death. And what makes this an example of moral luck is that he would have to blame himself only slightly for the negligence itself if no situation arose which required him to brake suddenly and violently to avoid hitting a child. Yet the *negligence* is the same in both cases, and the driver has no control over whether a child will run into his path.

The same is true at higher levels of negligence. If someone has had too much to drink and his car swerves on to the sidewalk, he can count himself morally lucky if there are no pedestrians in its path. If there were, he would be to blame for their deaths, and would probably be prosecuted for manslaughter. But if he hurts no one, although his recklessness is exactly the same, he is guilty of a far less serious legal offence and will certainly reproach himself and be reproached by others much less severely. To take another legal example, the penalty for attempted murder is less than that for successful murder—however similar the intentions and motives of the assailant may be in the two cases. His degree of culpability can depend, it would seem, on whether the victim happened to be wearing a bullet-proof vest, or whether a bird flew into the path of the bullet—matters beyond his control.

Finally, there are cases of decision under uncertainty—common in public and in private life. Anna Karenina goes off with Vronsky, Gauguin leaves his family, Chamberlain signs the Munich agreement, the Decembrists persuade the troops under their command to revolt against the czar, the American colonies declare their independence from Britain, you introduce two people in an attempt at match-making. It is tempting in all such cases to feel that some decision must be possible, in the light of what is known at the time, which will make reproach unsuitable no matter how things turn out. But this is not true; when someone acts in such ways he takes his life, or his moral position, into his hands, because how things turn out determines what he has done. It is possible *also* to assess the decision from the point of view of what could be known at the time, but this is not the end of the story. If the Decembrists had succeeded in overthrowing Nicholas I in 1825 and establishing a constitutional regime, they would be heroes. As it is, not only did they fail and pay for it, but they bore some responsibility for the terrible punishments meted out to the troops who had been persuaded to follow them. If the American Revolution had been a bloody failure resulting in greater repression, then Jefferson, Franklin and Washington would still have made a noble attempt, and might not even have regretted it on their way to the scaffold, but they would also have had to blame themselves for what they had helped to bring on their compatriots. (Perhaps peaceful efforts at reform would eventually have succeeded.) If Hitler had not overrun Europe and exterminated millions, but instead had died of a heart attack after occupying the Sudetenland, Chamberlain's action at Munich would still have utterly betrayed the Czechs, but it would not be the great moral disaster that has made his name a household word.

In many cases of difficult choice the outcome cannot be foreseen with certainty. One kind of assessment of the choice is possible in advance, but another kind must await the outcome, because the outcome determines what has been done. The same degree of culpability or estimability in intention, motive, or concern is compatible with a wide range of judgments, positive or negative, depending on what happened beyond the point of decision. The *mens rea* which could have existed in the absence of any consequences does not exhaust the grounds of moral judgment. Actual results influence culpability or esteem in a large class of unquestionably ethical cases ranging from negligence through political choice.

That these are genuine moral judgments rather than expressions of temporary attitude is evident from the fact that one can say *in advance* how the moral verdict will depend on the results. If one negligently leaves the bath running with the baby in it, one will realize, as one bounds up the stairs toward the bathroom, that if the baby has drowned one has done something awful, whereas if it has not one has merely been careless. Someone who launches a violent revolution against an authoritarian regime knows that if he fails he will be responsible for much suffering that is in vain, but if he succeeds he will be justified by the outcome. I do not mean that *any* action can be retroactively justified by history. Certain things are so bad in themselves, or so risky, that no results can make them all right. Nevertheless, when moral judgment does depend on the outcome, it is objective and timeless and not dependent on a change of standpoint produced by success or failure. The judgment after the fact follows from an hypothetical judgment that can be made beforehand, and it can be made as easily by someone else as by the agent.

From the point of view which makes responsibility dependent on control, all this seems absurd. How is it possible to be more or less culpable depending on whether a child gets into the path of one's car, or a bird into the path of one's bullet? Perhaps it is true that what is done depends on more than the agent's state of mind or intention. The problem then is, why is it not irrational to base moral assessment on what people do, in this broad sense? It amounts to holding them responsible for the contributions of fate as well as for their own—provided they have made some contribution to begin with. If we look at cases of negligence or attempt, the pattern seems to be that overall culpability corresponds to the product of mental or intentional fault and the seriousness of the outcome. Cases of decision under uncertainty are less easily explained in this way, for it seems that the overall judgment can even shift from positive to negative depending on the outcome. But here too it seems rational to subtract the effects of occurrences subsequent to the choice, that were merely possible at the time, and concentrate moral assessment on the actual decision in light of the probabilities. If the object of moral judgment is the *person*, then to hold him accountable for what he has done in the broader sense is akin to strict liability, which may have its legal uses but seems irrational as a moral position.

The result of such a line of thought is to pare down each act to its morally essential core, an inner act of pure will assessed by motive and intention. Adam Smith advocates such a position in *The Theory of Moral Sentiments*, but notes that it runs contrary to our actual judgments.

> But how well soever we may seem to be persuaded of the truth of this equitable maxim, when we consider it after this manner, in abstract, yet when we come to particular cases, the actual consequences which happen to proceed from any action, have a very great effect upon our sentiments concerning its merit or demerit, and almost always either enhance or diminish our sense of both. Scarce, in any one instance, perhaps, will our sentiments be found, after examination, to be entirely regulated by this rule, which we all acknowledge ought entirely to regulate them.

Joel Feinberg points out further that restricting the domain of moral responsibility to the inner world will not immunize it to luck. Factors beyond the agent's control, like a coughing fit, can interfere with his decisions as surely as they can with the path of a bullet from his gun. Nevertheless the tendency to cut down the scope of moral assessment is pervasive, and does not limit itself to the influence of effects. It attempts to isolate the will from the other direction, so to speak, by separating out constitutive luck. Let us consider that next.

Kant was particularly insistent on the moral irrelevance of qualities of temperament and personality that are not under the control of the will. Such qualities as sympathy or coldness might provide the background against which obedience to moral requirements is more or less difficult, but they could not be objects of moral assessment themselves, and might well interfere with confident assessment of its proper object—the determination of the will by the motive of duty. This rules out moral judgment of many of the virtues and vices, which are states of character that influence choice but are certainly not exhausted by dispositions to act deliberately in certain ways. A person may be greedy, envious, cowardly, cold, ungenerous, unkind, vain, or conceited, but *behave* perfectly by a monumental effort of will. To possess these vices is to be unable to help having certain feelings under certain circumstances, and to have strong spontaneous impulses to act badly. Even if one controls the impulses, one still has the vice. An envious person hates the greater success of others. He can be morally condemned as envious even if he congratulates them cordially and does nothing to denigrate or spoil their success. Conceit, likewise, need not be displayed. It is fully present in someone who cannot help dwelling with secret satisfaction on the superiority of his own achievements, talents, beauty, intelligence, or virtue. To some extent such a quality may be the product of earlier choices; to some extent it may be amenable to change by current actions. But it is largely a matter of constitutive bad fortune. Yet people are morally condemned for such qualities, and esteemed for others equally beyond control of the will: they are assessed for what they are *like*.

To Kant this seems incoherent because virtue is enjoined on everyone and therefore must in principle be possible for everyone. It may be easier for some than for others, but it must be possible to achieve it by making the right choices, against whatever temperamental background. One may want to have a generous spirit, or regret not having one, but it makes no sense to condemn oneself or anyone else for a quality which is not within the control of the will. Condemnation implies that you should not be like that, not that it is unfortunate that you are.

Nevertheless, Kant's conclusion remains intuitively unacceptable. We may be persuaded that these moral judgments are irrational, but they reappear involuntarily as soon as the argument is over. This is the pattern throughout the subject.

The third category to consider is luck in one's circumstances, and I shall mention it briefly. The things we are called upon to do, the moral tests we face, are importantly determined by factors beyond our control. It may be true of someone that in a dangerous situation he would behave in a cowardly or heroic fashion, but if the situation never arises, he will never have the chance to distinguish or disgrace himself in this way, and his moral record will be different.

A conspicuous example of this is political. Ordinary citizens of Nazi Germany had an opportunity to behave heroically by opposing the regime. They also had an opportunity to behave badly, and most of them are culpable for having failed this test. But it is a test to which the citizens of other countries were not subjected, with the result that even if they, or some of them, would have behaved as badly as the Germans in like circumstances, they simply did not and therefore are not similarly culpable. Here again one is morally at the mercy of fate, and it may seem irrational upon reflection, but our ordinary moral attitudes would be unrecognizable without it. We judge people for what they actually do or fail to do, not just for what they would have done if circumstances had been different.

This form of moral determination by the actual is also paradoxical, but we can begin to see how deep in the concept of responsibility the paradox is embedded. A person can be morally responsible only for what he does; but what he does results from a great deal that he does not do; therefore he is not morally responsible for what he is and is not responsible for. (This is not a contradiction, but it is a paradox.)

It should be obvious that there is a connection between these problems about responsibility and control and an even more familiar problem, that of freedom of the will. That is the last type of moral luck I want to take up, though I can do no more within the scope of this essay than indicate its connection with the other types.

If one cannot be responsible for consequences of one's acts due to factors beyond one's control, or for antecedents of one's acts that are properties of temperament not subject to one's will, or for the circumstances that pose one's moral choices, then how can one be responsible even for the stripped-down acts of the will itself, if *they* are the product of antecedent circumstances outside of the will's control?

The area of genuine agency, and therefore of legitimate moral judgment, seems to shrink under this scrutiny to an extensionless point. Everything seems to result from the combined influence of factors, antecedent and posterior to action, that are not within the agent's control. Since he cannot be responsible for them, he cannot be responsible for their results—though it may remain possible to take up the aesthetic or other evaluative analogues of the moral attitudes that are thus displaced.

It is also possible, of course, to brazen it out and refuse to accept the results, which indeed seem unacceptable as soon as we stop thinking about the arguments. Admittedly, if certain surrounding circumstances had been different, then no unfortunate consequences would have followed from a wicked intention, and no seriously culpable act would have been performed; but since the circumstances were *not* different, and the agent *in fact* succeeded in perpetrating a particularly cruel murder, *that* is what he did, and that is what he is responsible for. Similarly, we may admit that if certain antecedent circumstances had been different, the agent would never have developed into the sort of person who would do such a thing; but since he *did* develop (as the inevitable result of those antecedent circumstances) into the sort of swine he is, and into the person who committed such a murder, *that* is what he is blameable for. In both cases one is responsible for what one actually does—even if what one actually does depends in important ways on what is not within one's control. This compatibilist account of our moral judgments would leave room for the ordinary conditions of responsibility—the absence of coercion, ignorance, or involuntary movement—as part of the determination of what someone has done—but it is understood not to exclude the influence of a great deal that he has not done.

The only thing wrong with this solution is its failure to explain how skeptical problems arise. For they arise not from the imposition of an arbitrary external requirement, but from the nature of moral judgment itself. Something in the ordinary idea of what someone does must explain how it can seem necessary to subtract from it anything that merely happens—even though the ultimate consequence of such subtraction is that nothing remains. And something in the ordinary idea of knowledge must explain why it seems to be undermined by any influences on belief not within the control of the subject—so that knowledge seems impossible without an impossible foundation in autonomous reason. But let us leave epistemology aside and concentrate on action, character, and moral assessment.

The problem arises, I believe, because the self which acts and is the object of moral judgment is threatened with dissolution by the absorption of its acts and impulses into the class of events. Moral judgment of a person is judgment not of what happens to him, but of him. It does not say merely that a certain event or state of affairs is fortunate or unfortunate or even terrible. It is not an evaluation of a state of the world, or of an individual as part of the world. We are not thinking just that it would be better if he were different, or did not exist, or had not done some of the things he has done. We are judging *him*, rather than his existence or characteristics. The effect of concentrating on the influence of what is not under his control is to make this responsible self seem to disappear, swallowed up by the order of mere events.

What, however, do we have in mind that a person must *be* to be the object of these moral attitudes? While the concept of agency is easily undermined, it is very difficult to give it a positive characterization. That is familiar from the literature on Free Will.

I believe that in a sense the problem has no solution, because something in the idea of agency is incompatible with actions being events, or people being things. But as the external determinants of what someone has done are gradually exposed, in their effect on consequences, character, and choice itself, it becomes gradually clear that actions are events and people things. Eventually nothing remains which can be ascribed to the responsible self, and we are left with nothing but a portion of the larger sequence of events, which can be deplored or celebrated, but not blamed or praised.

Though I cannot define the idea of the active self that is thus undermined, it is possible to say something about its sources. There is a close connexion between our feelings about ourselves and our feelings about others. Guilt and indignation, shame and contempt, pride and admiration are internal and external sides of the same moral attitudes. We are unable to view ourselves simply as portions of the world, and from inside we have a rough idea of the boundary between what is us and what is not, what we do and what happens to us, what is our personality and what is an accidental handicap. We apply the same essentially internal conception of the self to others. About ourselves we feel pride, shame, guilt, remorse—and agent-regret. We do not regard our actions and our characters merely as fortunate or unfortunate episodes—though they may also be that. We cannot *simply* take an external evaluative view of ourselves—of what we most essentially are and what we do. And this remains true even when we have seen that we are not responsible for our own existence, or our nature, or the choices we have to make, or the circumstances that give our acts the consequences they have. Those acts remain ours and we remain ourselves, despite the persuasiveness of the reasons that seem to argue us out of existence.

It is this internal view that we extend to others in moral judgment—when we judge *them* rather than their desirability or utility. We extend to others the refusal to limit ourselves to external evaluation, and we accord to them selves like our own. But in both cases this comes up against the brutal inclusion of humans and everything about them in a world from which they cannot be separated and of which they are nothing but contents. The external view forces itself on us at the same time that we resist it. One way this occurs is through the gradual erosion of what we do by the subtraction of what happens.

The inclusion of consequences in the conception of what we have done is an acknowledgment that we are part of the world, but the paradoxical character of moral luck which emerges from this acknowledgment shows that we are unable to operate with such a view, for it leaves us with no one to be. The same thing is revealed in the appearance that determinism obliterates responsibility. Once we see an aspect of what we

or someone else does as something that happens, we lose our grip on the idea that it has been done and that we can judge the doer and not just the happening. This explains why the absence of determinism is no more hospitable to the concept of agency than is its presence—a point that has been noticed often. Either way the act is viewed externally, as part of the course of events.

The problem of moral luck cannot be understood without an account of the internal conception of agency and its special connection with the moral attitudes as opposed to other types of value. I do not have such an account. The degree to which the problem has a solution can be determined only by seeing whether in some degree the incompatibility between this conception and the various ways in which we do not control what we do is only apparent. I have nothing to offer on that topic either. But it is not enough to say merely that our basic moral attitudes toward ourselves and others are determined by what is actual; for they are also threatened by the sources of that actuality, and by the external view of action which forces itself on us when we see how everything we do belongs to a world that we have not created.

⇌ Elbow Room ⇌
Daniel C. Dennett

Daniel C. Dennett is the Austin B. Fletcher Professor of Philosophy and Director of the Center for Cognitive Studies at Tufts University, and the author of *Darwin's Dangerous Idea* (New York: Simon & Schuster, 1995); *Elbow Room* (Cambridge, Mass.: The MIT Press, 1984), from which the following selection is excerpted; *Freedom Evolves* (New York: Viking, 2003); and many other works in philosophy of mind and cognitive science. In this passage, Dennett defends moral responsibility from arguments (such as Thomas Nagel's) that seek to undermine moral responsibility on the basis of *luck*: that is, from arguments insisting that because luck plays such an important role in our lives it undercuts claims of moral responsibility.

Luck is a curious concept. When we are told that something that happened was just luck, we should ask ourselves: luck as opposed to what? We know it would be superstitious to believe that "there actually is such a thing as luck"—something a rabbit's foot might or might not bring—but we nevertheless think there is an unsuperstitious and unmisleading way of characterizing events and properties as *merely* lucky. The contrast can be brought out with a thought experiment.

Suppose the United States and Russia were to agree that henceforth they would settle all disagreements and

conflicts by tossing a coin in Geneva. Each country was to designate a contestant for the great international toss-up. Who should represent us? I expect someone would hit upon the idea, both democratic and grandiose, of a national coin-tossing tournament, engaging every man, woman and child in a systematic elimination. The winner, of course, would be the ideal representative to send to Geneva: America's luckiest citizen, someone who had just won twenty-eight consecutive coin tosses without a single loss! Surely that person would stand a much better chance of winning in

Geneva than some citizen just chosen at random? If there were such a thing as luck—that is, if luck were a projectible property of people or things—then this imagined tournament would be a fine luck distiller or amplifier. But of course (unless we are very much mistaken) luck isn't like that; luck is *mere* luck, not a genuine, projectible endowment.

The winner of the imagined tournament would be lucky indeed (in the "safe," unsuperstitious sense). "I guess I was just lucky," the winner ought to say, but not: "I guess I am just a lucky person." For there is really no such thing (we think) as being lucky in general, being reliably lucky; there is only being lucky on particular occasions. But the winner would probably find it very difficult not to feel chosen or special or in some other way magically singled out for favor. The lucky survivors of disasters—shipwrecks and mining accidents—typically cannot forego drawing extravagant conclusions from the fact that *they* survived while others perished. The winner of our tournament, then, would be strongly tempted to believe that luck was something real, a force in nature that was running his way.

Someone might even feel *responsible* for winning the tournament—as if he had actually done something to deserve all the attention. Suppose, just to heighten the illusion, that the winner was unaware of the existence of the tournament. So far as he knew, he had simply started calling coin tosses a few weeks ago and had had an almost unbelievable string of wins—twenty-eight in a row without a loss. He would no doubt either begin to wonder about the fairness of the coins used or become devoutly superstitious. Of course those of us in the know would not be tempted by that line of thought; we would know that even if there is no such thing as luck, such a tournament is guaranteed to produce a winner (some winner or other) just so long as it takes place.

Now is there an illusion of personal responsibility in those of us who take ourselves to be the captains of our destiny analogous to the illusion of responsibility or prowess engendered in our tournament winner? Surely anyone who, winning such a tournament, takes credit for it, or anticipates future success on the basis of past experience, is simply making a mistake. Might we similarly be just wrong in thinking we—some of us, in any case—are genuinely responsible for our acts?

There is a sense in which we are all, like the winner of the coin-tossing tournament, extraordinarily lucky to be here in the winner's circle. Not a single one of *our* ancestors suffered the misfortune of dying childless! When one thinks of all the millions of generations of predecessors knocked out in the early rounds of the natural selection tournament, it must seem that the odds against *our* existing are astronomical.

The big difference between us and the winner of the coin-tossing tournament is that while we cannot take personal credit for the success of our ancestors, our genes can. The contest our genes have won was a test of genuine prowess. You have to be good at something (in fact, good at things in general) to get through to the round that is playing today. The person who wins a selective tournament in a game of skill *is* likely to do much better than the randomly chosen person in subsequent contests; skill, unlike luck, is projectible. And since the skills of self-control and deliberation have been put to a fairly severe test over the eons, there is a real basis in fact for our having high expectations about the deliberative skill, and more generally the capacity for self-control, of our fellow human beings. If you weren't very well equipped in that department, you wouldn't have made it to this round of the tournament. Of course some unfortunates, though born of skilled self-controllers, are defective, through no fault of their own. We do not consider them responsible. They are excused. But we do expect a lot from the rest of us, and for good reason. We are not just lucky; we are skilled.

The relation between skill and luck is complex. It is a maxim of athletes that the luck tends to average out, and that the best players are those who are well equipped to capitalize on lucky opportunities. After all, if you are not even capable of throwing a basketball seventy feet, you cannot ever avail yourself of the occasional desperate opportunities to heave a lucky, game-winning toss. Moreover, the better you are, the less luck you need, and the less your successes count as merely lucky. Why? Because the better you are, the more control you have over your performance. When the star basketball player shoots ten consecutive baskets in a game, we don't call it luck; if I were to get ten in a row, we would certainly call it luck. The star is not so good as to be beyond the reach of luck altogether, but for him, the threshold for what counts as luck is considerably higher. We expect more of him. Similarly then, if someone is skilled at self-improvement, such success in this line as he may achieve is not attributable to his luck on each occasion, but to his skill. We expect more of him. *Noblesse oblige*, as the saying goes.

But still, one may be tempted to say, there are two sorts of differences in an agent's circumstances that are merely matters of luck: how much initial strength or talent or character one is lucky enough to be born with, and how many lucky breaks one encounters during one's period of self-creation. One way or the other, it seems, these factors must conspire to defeat any self-styled agent's claim of personal responsibility for his own character. Let us look at these one at a time.

Suppose—what certainly seems to be true—that people are born with noticeably different cognitive endowments and propensities to develop character traits; some people have long lines of brilliant (or hot-blooded, or well-muscled) ancestors, for instance, and seem to have initial endowments quite distinct from those of their contemporaries. Is this "hideously unfair"—to use a phrase of Williams . . .—or is this bound to lead to something hideously unfair? Not necessarily.

Imagine a footrace in which the starting line was staggered: those with birthdays in January start a yard ahead of those born in February, and eleven yards ahead of those born in December. Surely no one can help being born in one month rather than another. Isn't this manifestly unfair? Yes, if the race is a hundred yard dash. No, if it's a marathon. In a marathon such a relatively small initial advantage would count for nothing, since one can reliably expect other fortuitous breaks to have even greater effects. In fact, in a large marathon the best runners are typically seeded and given a considerable head start, but I have never heard anyone complain that this is unfair. A good runner who starts at the back of the pack, if he is really good enough to deserve winning, will probably have plenty of opportunity to overcome the initial disadvantage. Some may doubt that this is fair, in spite of its current acceptance. They must agree, however, that the arbitrary birthday system just described is fairer. Is it fair enough not to be worth worrying about? Of course. After all, luck averages out in the long run.

Do we have any reason, however, to believe that the process of moral development or acquisition of agenthood is more like a marathon than a sprint? Yes, we have such evidence in abundance. For one thing, moral development is not a race at all, with a single winner and everyone else ranked behind, but a process that apparently brings people sooner or later to a sort of plateau of development—not unlike the process of learning your native language, for instance. Some people reach the plateau swiftly and easily, while others need compensatory effort to overcome initial disadvantages in one way or another.

But everyone comes out more or less in the same league. When people are deemed "good enough" their moral education is over, and except for those who are singled out as defective—retarded or psychopathic, for instance—the citizenry is held to be composed of individuals of roughly equivalent talents, insofar as the demands of such citizenship are commonly held to average out. Is this, the common wisdom, a big mistake? We can address the question by trying to envisage better policies, again in the simpler domain of sports.

Imagine trying to change the rules of basketball in the following way: if the referees decide that a particular basket was just a lucky shot, they disallow the points, and if they notice that bad luck is dogging one of the teams, they give that team compensatory privileges. A perfectly pointless effort at reform, of course, which would not appeal to anybody's sense of fairness. In sports we accept luck, and are content to plan and strive while making due allowance for luck—which is, after all, the same for everyone; no one actually *has more luck* than anyone else, even though some *have been* lucky enough to start off with more talent. But that is fair too, we think. We don't suppose that the only fair contest is between perfectly matched opponents; the strength of one may defeat the finesse of the other, or vice versa. Roughly comparable overall prowess is all we demand. And if on some particular occasion the particular strengths of one count for more than the particular strengths of the other, that is "too bad" for the latter, but not at all unfair.

When the talented succeed, it is not because they are lucky, but because they are talented. Ah, but they are lucky to be talented in the first place! Not always. Some talented performers are made, not born; some have diligently trained for hours every day for years on end to achieve their prowess, and in the process have denied themselves many delights and opportunities that we less skilled performers have enjoyed. Ah, but they were lucky to be born with the gumption and drive required to develop their skill in training themselves. Not always. Some aren't born with that temperament, but learn it from a wise teacher or coach. Ah, but then they are lucky to have the intelligence required to comprehend the lesson of that good coach. (After all, not all the players are capable of being inspired by him.) And, of course, they are lucky to have been born in the town where that fine coach works his miracles. Moreover, they are lucky not to have been born blind, and lucky not to have been struck by lightning on their way to school. In fact, as already remarked, they are astronomically lucky to have ever been born at all!

As this petulant little dialogue exhibits, there is a tendency to treat "lucky" and "unlucky" as complementary and exhaustive, leaving no room for skill at all. On this view nothing in principle could count as skill or the result of skill. This is a mistake. Once one recognizes that there is elbow room for skill in between lucky success and unlucky failure, the troubling argument that seems to show that no one could ever be responsible evaporates. Luck averages out and skill will tell in the end. Once in a while, to be sure, luck plays too large a role, but anyone who thinks that all losses are explicable *in the end* as due to bad luck, and all victories as due to good luck, simply misuses the concept of luck. . . .

We are all the "gifted" ones. That is, I take it that all my readers are members, like me, in the community of reason-givers and considerers. We are all gifted with the powers of deliberation, or we wouldn't be here (in the adult world of books and readers). Some of our friends and relations aren't here; some of them are infants, and some of them are, through no fault of their own, infantile or otherwise incapable of reason. A few of them *may* be culpable for their unfortunate state—for instance, a few may have quite knowingly ruined their brains with drugs or alcohol, but now that they are incapacitated, they are excused from further responsibility. We take steps to keep them out of circumstances where they might do serious mischief to themselves or to others.

We gifted ones are good at deliberation and self-control, and so we expect a good deal of each other in these regards. On the basis of those expectations we place gifted ones in positions of trust and responsibility, and then we *count on them* to do the right thing. And since they are gifted, when they do the right thing we don't call it luck. The better they are, in fact, the less of a role there is for sheer luck in the outcome of their deliberations.

We are not totally responsible for being responsible, of course, any more than the star player is totally beyond luck. After all, a mugger might leap out of an alley and brain me tomorrow. I would then be unlucky enough to lose my status as a responsible citizen through no fault or error of my own. But if that would be most unlucky, my not having met with a mugger to date is not just a matter of luck; I am quite good at staying out of trouble. The fact is that all of us responsible agents are well enough designed so that we tend to avoid circumstances where the odds are high that we will lose our prowess and hence our status as responsible citizens. We take care of ourselves. We are systematic status-preservers, but of course sometimes we fall on hard times. Sometimes the unexpectable and unavoidable happens. Then we are unlucky.

We can imagine (just barely, I think) a being who went through a lifetime of "correct" decision making, but always just by sheer luck, never thanks to skill. At every turn, this being just happened to turn the right way, away from the gallows, away from calumny and disgrace. One unlucky misstep, and boom—condemned to a lifetime of disgrace. But that is not the way we are.

"There but for the grace of God go I." . . . A very curious sentiment. It is often repeated in our own times with an even more curious meaning: indeed I could be so unlucky; I may yet suffer some such misfortune. But it would take an extraordinarily unlikely conspiracy of accidents to turn *me* into (say) a murderer—while quite a likely, normal, everyday turn of events could make all the difference to a tough young hoodlum who has so far stayed out of serious trouble only by the skin of his teeth. The day someone happens to make the mistake of insulting him is the day his life of violent crime begins. If the sort of temptation that would turn him into a murderer were to flash before my eyes, however, I would almost certainly resist it. If I failed to resist it, I would have no one but myself to blame. I am supposed to be good at resisting such temptations—and in fact most of them are child's play. I'm so good at them, *I don't even notice them as opportunities*. Consider fine chess players, who never even notice the stupid move opportunities . . . It is not just luck that keeps them from making the "patzer" plays.

If the hoodlum is a patzer at life (and he is), this is too bad for him, and it *may* be just his bad luck that he is so bad at decision making. We do make allowances, however. We set the threshold of expectations lower for patzers. For children, for instance. We keep them out of situations in which their juvenile powers of deliberation might lead them into horrible, regrettable errors. What counts as luck for them is something that would not count as luck for us adults.

⇒ "UNEVEN STARTS AND JUST DESERTS" ⇒
Bruce N. Waller

Bruce N. Waller, the author of this book, teaches philosophy at Youngstown State University. The following essay—originally published as "Uneven Starts and Just Deserts," *Analysis*, volume 49, number 4, October 1989—critiques arguments given by Dennett (and others) in defense of moral responsibility and argues that belief in moral responsibility distracts us from the best path to nurturing successful satisfying free behavior.

In life's race, the different results people achieve are due to "uneven starts". Since people start unequally—at starting points not of their own choosing or making—they are not morally responsible (do not justly deserve blame or credit) for the finish. This uneven starts position is stated elegantly by John Rawls:

> It seems to be one of the fixed points of our considered judgments that no one deserves his place in the distribution of native endowments, any more than one deserves one's initial starting place in society. The assertion that a man deserves the superior character that enables him to make the effort to cultivate his abilities is equally problematic; for his character depends in large part upon fortunate family and social circumstances for which he can claim no credit . . .

Rawls's claim that uneven starts undermine just deserts has recently been attacked on two fronts. Daniel Dennett . . . and George Sher . . . offer distinct but similar defences of just deserts, and each develops a spirited challenge to the uneven starts claims.

For both Dennett and Sher, the crucial point is that even if starting points are not precisely even, still in at least some cases what we do—what we accomplish—really does depend on our own efforts. While not every accomplishment is open to everyone (I could never be a jockey) there are still avenues of success open to most (if not quite all) of us, and it is up to us what we do with those open possibilities. Thus—according to Dennett and Sher—we can justly claim to deserve the fruits of our success (and perhaps also the bitter fruits of our failures). There *are* differences in starting points, but those differences do not eliminate moral responsibility.

Dennett challenges the uneven start basis for denying moral responsibility thus:

> . . . one may be tempted to say, there are two sorts of differences in an agent's circumstances that are merely matters of luck: how much initial strength or talent or character one is lucky enough to be born with, and how many lucky breaks one encounters during one's period of self-creation. One way or the other, it seems, these factors must conspire to defeat any self-styled agent's claim of personal responsibility for his own character. . . .
>
> Suppose—what certainly seems to be true—that people are born with noticeably different cognitive endowments and propensities to develop character traits. . . . Is this 'hideously unfair' . . . or is this bound to lead to something hideously unfair? Not necessarily.

Dennett then offers an insidiously charming example to show why such differences in starting points and subsequent lucky breaks do not vitiate just deserts and moral responsibility:

> Imagine a footrace in which the starting line was staggered: those with birthdays in January start a yard ahead of those born in February, and eleven yards ahead of those born in December. Surely no one can help being born in one month rather than another. Isn't this markedly unfair? Yes, if the race is a hundred yard dash. No, if it's a marathon. In a marathon such a relatively small initial advantage would count for nothing, since one can reliably expect other fortuitous breaks to have even greater effects. . . . Is it fair enough not to be worth worrying about? Of course. After all, luck averages out in the long run. . . .

It seems churlish to poke at Dennett's delightful example; but in truth the effects of small initial differences on long range character development are not at all analogous to staggered starting positions in a marathon. Initial differences in life's race are more often amplified than cancelled out. The initially more alert individual engages in exploratory activities that are reinforced, and thus becomes increasingly inquisitive; the eager student is positively reinforcing for her teacher and receives extra attention; the lad who steals a few coins is a suspect when other coins are lost; the better player sharpens skills and develops stamina in competition, while her less talented teammate's skills and stamina and confidence gradually erode on the bench. The small gap widens. Not always, of course; I am not claiming a slippery slope down which the initially disadvantaged inexorably slide. Subsequent influences—later "racing luck"—sometimes overbalance initial disadvantages. But small initial differences should not be lightly dismissd as making little or no difference in the essentially 'fair and equal' marathon race of life. Rather than Dennett's equal-luck marathon, a better analogy might be a horse race on a muddy track, in which the slow starters are additionally handicapped by the mud kicked onto them by the early speed.

Sher develops an argument similar to Dennett's. He, like Dennett, grants that such differences exist; and he also attempts to neutralize such differences in order to preserve claims of just deserts and moral responsibility. But Sher does not appeal merely to "racing luck"; rather, he offers specific suggestions for how such initial differences can be overcome. Sher suggests that an individual with less effort-making ability can negate that disadvantage by greater vigilance or by taking special steps to increase motivation and avoid distractions. And he later extends that claim to 'other differences in initial ability as well':

> Even if M is initially stronger or more intelligent than N, this difference will only entail that M does not deserve what he has achieved relative to N if the difference between them has made it impossible for N to achieve as much as M. However, differences in strength, intelligence, and other native gifts are rarely so pronounced as to have this effect. The far more common effect of such differences is merely to make it more *difficult* for the less talented person to reach a given level of attainment. He must work harder, husband his resources more carefully, plan more shrewdly, and so on . . .

That is an appealing scenario: the slow tortoise uses his greater perseverance to nose out the speedier hare, the weak rabbit outwits the powerful bear, the player of modest talents excels through practice and effort. Such stories are heart-warming and even inspiring, but usually they are also false. The less talented are *not* likely to develop greater diligence and perseverance, for those qualities are the conditioned product of successful past efforts, and those who are initially less talented are likely to experience fewer successes and consequently less positive reinforcement for their efforts. Thus less talent is more often linked to lethargy than to perseverance. In similar fashion, less talent is not likely to be offset by greater shrewdness; to the contrary, the more talented have

more opportunities to learn game strategy. Shrewd play is a function of playing time, which is likely to be a function of initial talent.

Both Dennett and Sher treat individual characteristics as if they were handed out one at a time by lottery. In fact, talents and abilities (as well as faults and liabilities) have a cumulative effect. Rather than the hare's speed being offset by the tortoise's endurance, the speedy hare is likely to be a more successful racer and thus a more positively reinforced and frequent racer, and thus also better-conditioned.

It is a mistake to suppose that 'luck averages out', that weaknesses in one capacity are balanced by other strengths, and that claims of moral responsibility and just deserts can thus be justified. However, it is *not* a mistake to tell our children the story of the gritty tortoise nosing out the indolent hare, and it is not a mistake to emphasize that disadvantaged starting points can be and sometimes are overcome. That is important for two reasons: first, it helps overcome any lingering fears of fatalism. There is sometimes fear that determinism (or naturalism) makes us helpless pawns of our early environmental-genetic influences. But that is certainly not the inevitable result that many people fear. *If* one strongly desires to break away from the influences and habits of one's early conditioning, then quite often—through effort and planning—one can actually do so. The individual who feels stifled by lack of education can take steps to correct that situation, and (usually) by effort and work the individual can remedy educational deficiencies and achieve the education he or she desires. So one need not feel *trapped* by one's conditioning-environmental history. However, the capacity to work hard to overcome such deficiencies, the intelligence to plan an educational program, the perseverance to carry it out, and—especially—the original desire to gain an education: all of that is the complex product of environmental conditioning-contingencies (the uneven start) for which one is *not* morally responsible. Strenuous efforts really can make things happen. It does not follow that one is *morally responsible* for the effort or its effects.

The second reason that it is important to emphasize what can be accomplished by those who 'really try'—even against bad luck and initial disadvantages—is that emphasis on the possibility of achievements may foster those achievements. Such verbal encouragement should not be overemphasized. Inspiring bedtime stories are no substitute for the early experience of well-ordered, interesting, and progressively more difficult tasks at which individuals can succeed through exerting modest effort. Early effort-enhancing experiences are the key to developing perseverance (and repeated early failure is the key to later lethargy). Still, inspiring stories and encouraging words have their uses. One of my childhood favourites was the story of Dick Whittington, who rose from poverty to become 'thrice Lord Mayor of London town', using only his wits, his hard work, and his lucky mouse-chasing cat. It's a good children's story, with a useful message: if you keep trying, luck will come your way; and through pluck and wit and a bit of luck, one may overcome enormous obstacles and make a great success. The story is a good one, despite the fact that in actuality childhood poverty is likely to produce lethargy, as early deprivation results in early failures and thus the extinguishing of effort-making behaviour and the deadening of desires and dreams. Still, we should continue telling the story of Dick Whittington. Children who have the good fortune to hear it may be somewhat more likely to develop perseverance. But we should not draw the wrong moral from the story. People can succeed through pluck and effort and wit; and if one has the good fortune to develop such characteristics (through hearing the right bedtime stories and experiencing the right early successes) then one really can accomplish things and achieve important goals. Such worthwhile accomplishments do not, however, justly deserve special credit or reward, since the means of achieving them (perseverance and intelligence) are the result of one's good luck.

In sum, there is every reason to promote (compatibilist) free will and the importance of individual effort. We *can* make things happen, and those who have the good fortune to learn that lesson are more likely to make successful efforts. But such compatibilist freedom does not establish moral responsibility. Whether the result is diligent accomplishment or lethargic failure, the influence of uneven starts and unequal racing lanes undercuts credit and blame.

EXERCISES

1. Years ago, the U.S. Supreme Court effectively placed a moratorium on capital punishment, while it examined the issue. After executions in the United States resumed, John Spenkelink was the first person executed in the state of Florida. Spenkelink had been a reasonably well-behaved boy until the age of 11, when he returned home from school to discover the body of his father, a suicide victim, whom John had idolized. After that John started skipping school, getting into trouble, eventually dropping out of school and drifting around the South. He committed a series of petty crimes, and ultimately he killed a fellow drifter in an argument. Shortly before his execution, Spenkelink stated: "Man is what he chooses to be. He chooses that for himself." Even after his tragic life and while awaiting his execution, Spenkelink affirmed that he had acted from free choice. Considering the entire story of John Spenkelink, does his story *support* or *undermine* the case for moral responsibility?

2. The research of neuropsychologists (such as Benjamin Libet and Daniel Wegner) indicates that when we have the experience of making a *conscious free choice*, the choice process has already originated in our brains without our being conscious of it. *If* that neuropsychological account is true, then when you make a "conscious choice," are you choosing *freely*? Would that neuropsychological evidence pose a challenge for a *compatibilist* view of free will?

3. Benjamin Libet says there is room for a *conscious veto* of our nonconscious brain activity. There is a period of a little more than one tenth of a second between the nonconscious willing and the actual muscular movement caused by that nonconscious brain activity; and Libet suggests that the very brief interval allows the conscious mind to *veto* the nonconscious will:

   The role of conscious free will would be, then, not to initiate a voluntary act, but rather to *control* whether the act takes place. We may view the unconscious initiatives for voluntary actions as 'bubbling up' in the brain. The conscious will then selects which of these initiatives may go forward to an action and which ones to veto and abort, with no act appearing.

Benjamin Libet, "Do We Have Free Will?" in The Volitional Brain: Towards a Neuroscience of
Free Will, *edited by Benjamin Libet, Anthony Freeman, and Keith Sutherland (Thorverton,
Exeter: Imprint Academic, 1999).*

There are some problems with this suggestion (for example, would the conscious veto have to be the product of our nonconscious brain behavior, etc.); but suppose that Libet's suggestion works. Would such a microsecond veto be enough for free will? Is it needed for free will? If such conscious control of the nonconscious brain is impossible, could we still act freely? Could we still be morally responsible?

4. Jay and Ray are twin brothers, and they have very similar characters. They graduate from high school with decent but not spectacular records, they were both fairly good athletes who were starters at defensive end in their senior years, and they each have one minor speeding ticket and no other problems. Neither is a strong leader, but they fit in well with their group. Both decide to join the army, and they go through basic training together. As luck would have it, Jay is assigned to a unit that helps to build roads, schools, and clinics in an earthquake stricken area of Bangladesh. The work of the unit is appreciated by the local citizens, and the unit commander encourages all members of the unit to help the people there and treat them with respect. Jay follows the leadership of his commander and the pattern established by the entire unit, and he performs good work that makes a significant contribution to restoring the lives of the people in that devastated region. Ray, on the other hand, is assigned to a military police unit in Iraq, and he becomes a prison guard at Abu Ghraib prison. Like Jay, he follows the leadership of his commander and the pattern established by others in his unit; but in this case, Ray is involved in torturing and abusing the prisoners and detainees held at the prison. Ray doesn't really like what he is doing, but he goes along with it.

With very similar characters, values, and abilities, Jay and Ray wind up going in very different directions: Ray is charged with basic violations of the rights of prisoners, is convicted and spends several months in jail, and then is kicked out of the army. Jay receives a commendation for his humanitarian work helping the people of Bangladesh. It seems very likely that if their assignments had been reversed, Ray would have received the commendation while Jay would have wound up in prison: Jay was lucky in his assignment, and Ray was unlucky. Do they justly deserve the reward and punishment they receive for what they did?

5. John Doris favors a "situationist" view; that is, he believes that psychological research has demonstrated that the key determinant of our behavior is not our character or virtue or moral principles, but the specific situation we are in. Doris concludes that with our situationist understanding in hand, we should focus our moral attention on avoiding bad situations (rather than relying on moral virtue or ethical principle):

> Imagine that a colleague with whom you have had a long flirtation invites you to dinner, offering enticement of interesting food and elegant wine, with the excuse that you are temporarily orphaned while your spouse is out of town. Let's assume the obvious way to read this text is the right one, and assume further that you regard the infidelity that may result as an ethically undesirable outcome. . . . You might think that there is little cause for concern; you are, after all, an upright person, and a spot of claret never did anyone a bit of harm. On the other hand, if you take the lessons of situationism to heart, you avoid the dinner like the plague, because you know that you are not able to confidently predict your behavior in a problematic situation on the basis of your antecedent values. You do not doubt that you sincerely value fidelity; you simply doubt your ability to act in conformity with this value once the candles are lit and the wine begins to flow. Relying on character once in the situation is a mistake, you agree; the way to achieve the ethically desirable result is to recognize that situational pressures may all too easily overwhelm character and avoid the dangerous situation.

John M. Doris, Lack of Character *(Cambridge: Cambridge University Press, 2002), p. 147.*

Suppose that someone should conclude that we are *still* morally responsible for our behavior; but the key exercise of moral responsibility consists in choosing to *avoid* (or not) the situations that are morally perilous. Would you agree with that conclusion?

6. In the Biblical account, the children of Israel are held in slavery in Egypt for many years. At one point Pharaoh apparently considers freeing them, but God "hardened Pharaoh's heart" and thus Pharaoh refused to free the Israeli slaves. Most of us, surely, would say that what Pharaoh did was *morally wrong*: It is wrong to hold slaves in bondage. But if Almighty God *hardened* Pharaoh's heart, then it is difficult to suppose that Pharaoh acted with *free will*. So *is* free will necessary for performing morally wrong (and morally right) acts? *If* you still believe that free will is essential for acting wrongly or rightly, how would you explain away this apparent counterexample?

7. Your friend Saul is the world's greatest procrastinator. If a term paper is due Wednesday at 8 a.m, he *never* starts it before Tuesday night. More likely he will plead for an extension, and start the paper Wednesday afternoon. His ethics term paper is due November 15. On the first day of October, you find Saul at his desk with stacks of ethics books around him, while he works furiously at his keyboard. Looking at the monitor, you discover Saul is on page 12 of the ethics paper that is not due for another six weeks.

> You are amazed. "What got into you? That paper isn't due for weeks yet. You *never* work on anything until the very last minute. What's the deal?"
>
> "Nothing happened," Saul replies; "I just exercised my free will and chose to write my term paper punctually, and not procrastinate."
>
> "Yeah, sure," you reply. "I bet your parents threatened to cut off your funds if you flunked another course. Or maybe the dean called you in for a stern lecture. Or I know, your coach read you the riot act about your low grades. No, I've got it: Allison said she was dumping you if you don't shape up and get your act together. That's got to be it, right?"
>
> "No, nothing like that. I know I have a tendency to procrastinate. And I was sorely tempted to put this paper off until the last minute. But this time I simply chose to do otherwise. It was an act of free will; nothing else has changed; that's the only explanation I can give."
>
> Would you find that a plausible explanation? Or would you suppose that there must be something that your friend Saul is not telling you? And what does your answer say about your own view of free will?

8. If psychologists accepted Campbell's libertarian view of free will, would that mean that psychology could *never* be a complete science? That there would always be human behavior that would remain completely beyond scientific psychological explanation?

9. Suppose that you reject moral responsibility: You believe that you are never *morally responsible* for any good or bad deed (you may be *causally* responsible, or *role* responsible, but— according to your beliefs—you are never morally responsible). Suppose that you do something that you consider a morally bad act (a friend has confided a special secret to you, and you have betrayed her confidence after promising never to tell anyone); could you (given your denial of moral responsibility) *sincerely apologize* for your bad act?

10. Suppose that careful studies have convinced you that the *best* way of rehabilitating criminals and preventing future criminal acts is by sending prisoners to very pleasant and comfortable prisons, where they live in attractive quarters, enjoy interesting entertainment, eat good food, attend interesting classes, and have plenty of enjoyable recreational opportunities; that these pleasant prison facilities are much more effective rehabilitation environments than are the harsh, ugly, crowded facilities of our contemporary prisons (and suppose, also, that the costs of the pleasant prisons are comparable to those of our current harsh prisons). Perhaps you think that's ridiculous: that pleasant prisons could never provide effective rehabilitation. That's not the issue. *Suppose* that you were convinced that such pleasant prisons *would* provide the best rehabilitation. Would you favor sending criminals to the pleasant facilities?

ADDITIONAL READINGS

For a fascinating libertarian account of free will from the Italian Renaissance, see Giovanni Pico della Mirandola, "The Dignity of Man" (sometimes titled "Oration on the Dignity of Man"); it is available in several renaissance anthologies. C. A. Campbell's *On Selfhood and Godhood* (London: George Allen & Unwin, 1957) is the classic modern libertarian argument. Peter van Inwagen's *An Essay on Free Will* (Oxford: Clarendon Press, 1983) has been a very influential contemporary defense of libertarian free will. Robert Kane has developed a sophisticated and fascinating contemporary defense of libertarian free will, in *Free Will and Values* (Albany: SUNY Press, 1985) and *The Significance of Free Will* (Oxford: Oxford University Press, 1996). Two other influential sources for incompatibilist views of free will are William James, "The Dilemma of Determinism," (1884, available in a number of anthologies); and Jean-Paul Sartre, *Being and Nothingness* (New York: Philosophical Library, 1956). A very thorough and subtle treatment of libertarian free will that sorts out a variety of libertarian positions is Randolph Clarke's *Libertarian Accounts of Free Will* (New York: Oxford University Press, 2003).

Some very good anthologies that focus primarily on moral responsibility include John Martin Fischer, ed., *Moral Responsibility* (Ithaca, N.Y.: Cornell University Press, 1986); Ferdinand Schoeman, ed., *Responsibility, Character, and the Emotions: New Essays in Moral Psychology* (Cambridge: Cambridge University Press, 1987); and John Christman, ed., *The Inner Citadel: Essays on Individual Autonomy* (New York: Oxford University Press, 1989). For an anthology that collects the key historical writings on free will and responsibility, as well as many important legal essays on the subject, see Herbert Morris, ed., *Freedom and Responsibility* (Stanford, Cal.: Stanford University Press, 1961).

A number of recent books consider the questions of free will and moral responsibility in light of recent research in biology and psychology. John M. Doris, in *Lack of Character: Personality and Moral Behavior* (Cambridge: Cambridge University Press, 2002), organizes and reviews several decades of psychological research (particularly social psychology research) and draws out in detail and depth its philosophical implications in the areas of free will and moral responsibility. One of the most interesting and important books written on free will is by a neuropsychologist, Daniel M. Wegner. *The Illusion of Conscious Will* (Cambridge, Mass.: Bradford Books) is a very readable book that draws out the implications of decades of neuropsychological research, and its often surprising results. A superb collection of essays—and commentary—on the implications of contemporary neuroscience for questions of free will can be found in *The Volitional Brain: Towards a Neuroscience of Free Will*, edited by Benjamin Libet, Anthony Freeman, and Keith Sutherland (Thorverton, Exeter: Imprint Academic). Albert R. Mele offers a substantive account of free will and moral responsibility, together with a detailed critique of recent neuropsychological research, in *Free Will and Luck* (New York: Oxford University Press, 2006); and a more extensive critique of some of that research in *Effective Intentions: The Power of Conscious Will* (New York: Oxford University Press, 2009). Bruce N. Waller, *The Natural Selection of Autonomy* (Albany: SUNY Press, 1998) uses recent research in biology and psychology in an attempt to uncover some of the motives common to both libertarian and compatibilist views of free will, and to attack traditional justifications for moral responsibility.

H. L. A. Hart draws a very important distinction between role responsibility and moral responsibility in *Punishment and Responsibility: Essays in the Philosophy of Law* (London: Oxford University Press, 1968).

A superb collection of essays on the issues surrounding punishment and just deserts is edited by Jeffrie G. Murphy, *Punishment and Rehabilitation*, 2nd ed. (Belmont, Cal.: Wadsworth, 1985). Among other excellent articles, Murphy's anthology contains the definitive contemporary defense of "the right to be punished": Herbert Morris, "Persons and

Punishment," originally published in 1968. A more recent article in favor of the right to be punished is by Andrew Oldenquist, "An Explanation of Retribution," in *The Journal of Philosophy*, 1988, volume 85: 464–478. For a more popular presentation of that view, see an article by C. S. Lewis, "The Humanitarian Theory of Punishment," in *Undeceptions* (London: Curtis Brown, 1970).

For an excellent debate between two outstanding philosophers who examine these questions carefully, give fair and honest consideration to their opponents' views, and offer their own conclusions with style and strength, see Jeffrie G. Murphy and Jean Hampton, *Forgiveness and Mercy* (Cambridge: Cambridge University Press, 1988). A marvelous discussion of these issues by four insightful participants in this ongoing debate is by John Martin Fischer, Robert Kane, Derk Pereboom, and Manuel Vargas: *Four Views on Free Will* (Malden, MA: Blackwell Publishing, 2007).

CHAPTER 11

ETHICS: REASON AND EMOTION

Sam and Will are volunteers for the "Meals on Wheels" program: Every weekday morning at 11 they rush from their intro to philosophy class and report to the meals on wheels center, where they each drive a truck and make deliveries of hot meals to people around the city—people who are very elderly, or disabled, and who would otherwise not have a nutritious hot meal during the day. They finish their runs about 2 and then rush back to campus for afternoon labs. They have no ulterior motives: They aren't trying to pad their graduate school applications, or impress the beautiful woman who manages the program, or curry favor with some elderly disabled person who might remember them in her will. Both Sam and Will are very good at what they do: They always have a smile and a few minutes of friendly conversation with the recipients of the meals (and since most of these people are quite isolated, the warm social interaction is perhaps even more important than the hot meals). Both are much loved by the meal recipients, and they are both exemplary volunteers: Both started their volunteer work during their freshman year, and are now seniors; and during those four years they have never missed a single day of volunteer work. Four years, 15 hours every week, 52 weeks every year: always with a smile and a kind word, Sam and Will have done much to improve the lives of the people on their routes.

One day late in their senior year they arrive early to their introduction to philosophy class—filled with eager anticipation of an exciting discussion of free will—and fall into conversation about their four years of volunteer work. "You know," Sam says, "I've really enjoyed college, especially this philosophy class. It's been great, lots of good friends, and I'm going to miss it when I graduate and move away. But what I'll miss most is the three hours every day with the meals on wheels program. I've never done anything I enjoy so much: people are so happy to see you, and with just a few minutes you can brighten up their whole day. It makes them happy, and that makes me happy. It's been wonderful."

Will smiled, but shook his head. "You and I have very different ideas about how to be happy. I've enjoyed college, but I'm ready to move on; and one of the main things I'm glad to be moving on from is that meals on wheels work. Don't misunderstand: It was certainly the right thing for me to do, and I don't regret it. I had the time available, and I'm very good at helping people and making them feel better, and I firmly believe it was my moral duty to perform that work, and to do it to the best of my abilities. And so I did it, and I followed my duty to help others in need, but enjoyment had nothing to do with it. I'm just glad it's over."

Sam was amazed. "Moral duty! Moral duty never even occurred to me! I enjoyed every minute of it, and never considered it a moral duty. Helping those in need, and seeing their sorrow turn to pleasure—I can't think of anything that would give me more joy. I don't suppose I ever really reflected on whether I was following some moral rule, much less doing my moral duty."

"If you want joy," Will replied, "let me take you surfing or skiing. Delivering meals to shut-ins, that's an important duty; but it's strictly duty, no joy involved."

Suppose that Sam and Will did an equally good job in their meals on wheels volunteer work. Obviously, if Will delivered the meals with a frown and never a kind word, while Sam was always smiling and friendly, then Sam did a much better job than Will. (And if Sam found great joy in the work while Will did not, it's likely that, in *fact*, Sam did the work in a much friendlier manner. But *suppose* that in fact they were *equally* friendly and warm and cordial, and did an equally good job.) In that case, which one would you consider *morally superior*?

This is not a question of judging one virtuous and the other evil. By my lights, they are both impressive: 15 hours of volunteer service every week during your college career is no small contribution. And it's not a question of handing out awards: neither Sam nor Will was in it for glory. But take a minute and think about your *own* conclusion: Even if you judge both of them quite good—that is, let's assume for the moment that helping others in need is a *good* and virtuous act—does one seem to you significantly *better* on the moral scale?

That question is at the heart of some basic divisions in ethics. From one perspective, Sam is clearly the morally superior individual. Sam does good because he *enjoys* doing good: "his heart is in the right place," or "Sam is a good-hearted person," we might say. Sam doesn't need moral rules to push him to do good; he delights in doing good and helping others, he has a *character* or nature that rejoices in doing good. When you are learning to hit a baseball, you may try to follow rules that your coach gives you: Keep your right foot stationary, and pivot sharply on the ball of your foot. At that stage, your efforts at hitting a baseball are likely to be weak. But once the mechanics have become deeply ingrained and feel natural, you no longer think of the rules, and your swing becomes much more effective. So it is with moral behavior: You might need rules as a novice moral actor, but when the moral behavior seems natural and feels right to you, then you are far superior as a moral person.

This view has a long and distinguished history. Aristotle taught that through proper education and practice we become virtuous—that is, we do the right thing out of habit and inclination: We don't strain and struggle to live well and virtuously, but find such a pattern of life natural and satisfying. Anyone who has a strong desire to act badly (or lacks the desire to act well) had the misfortune of bad early training in virtue. A similar perspective can be found in various religious texts. King David, in the first of the Psalms, writes, "Blessed is the man that walketh not in the counsel of the ungodly, . . . but his delight in is in the law of Lord. . . . " Following the moral law as a *duty* is good; but living according to the law because you take delight in what is good is much better. St. Augustine brought the same idea into the Christian tradition: "Love God, and do as you wish." That is, if you genuinely love God (Who for Augustine is the very essence of goodness) you will naturally *want* to do good. This view is even more deeply rooted in the Taoist tradition. At a higher level of enlightenment, one realizes that we are all interconnected; harming another is harming myself, and kindnesses done for others are naturally felt to be good.

> All this talk of goodness and duty, these perpetual pin-pricks unnerve and irritate the hearer. You had best study how it is that Heaven and Earth maintain their eternal course, that the sun and moon maintain their light, the stars their serried ranks, the birds and beasts their flocks, the trees and shrubs their station. Thus you too should learn to guide your steps by Inward Power, to follow the course that the Way of Nature sets; and soon you will no longer need to go round laboriously advertising goodness and duty.

On this view of morality, the ideal moral actor is one who *enjoys* moral behavior, for whom good moral deeds come *naturally* and easily, and who requires neither careful reflection on moral law to know what is good nor special effort to *do* virtuous acts of kindness and generosity.

On one side, then, is the view that—at least for the ideal moral person—acting virtuously is easy and natural (or at least it does not require careful *rational* deliberation); in stark contrast is the view that moral acts require special effort: the moral path is narrow and difficult, and staying the course is *never* easy. No one expressed this view more clearly than the sixteenth-century philosopher and theologian Michel de Montaigne:

> The easy, gentle, and sloping path . . . is not the path of true virtue. It demands a rough and thorny road. (Essays, book 11, 1580)

And no one presented this view more forcefully and uncompromisingly than Immanuel Kant, whose fiercely rationalistic view of ethics leaves no space whatsoever for emotions.

KANTIAN RATIONALIST ETHICS

A major stimulus for Kant's rationalist approach was his dedication to answering the fundamentally opposed position championed by David Hume. Hume maintained that there is no place for reason in the basic operations of ethics. Ethics is an area of emotion, dealing with what we find agreeable and disagreeable, with our sympathies and desires. Reason can play only a subordinate role: Once our feelings have set the basic goal, reason can help us discover the best means of reaching that goal; and reason can tell us whether our factual judgments are false (e.g., if we are arguing about whether capital punishment *deters* acts of murder, reason may be of assistance in answering that question; but if instead we are asking whether capital punishment is *just* and morally legitimate, reason is useless). At the basic level of setting our values, Hume insisted that: "Reason is, and ought only to be the slave of the passions, and can never pretend to any other office than to serve and obey them." Hume held that when it comes to genuine questions of basic values, we are moved by our feelings; and reason is out of the picture: " 'Tis not contrary to reason to prefer the destruction of the whole world to the scratching of my finger." Fortunately, we generally have feelings that are socially beneficial: "The mind of man is so formed by nature that upon the appearance of certain characters, dispositions, and actions, it immediately feels the sentiment of approbation or blame. . . . The characters which engage our approbation are chiefly such as contribute to the peace and security of human society. . . . " Indeed, Hume believed that nature was wise to place such important motives in our sentiments and feelings, rather than depending on our *reason*; for our powers of reason are limited and unreliable, and if reason were the foundation of morality then morality would be built on a very shaky foundation. Sentiments may not be perfectly reliable, but they are better than reason.

David Hume's view that ethics must be grounded in feelings has recently received support from neuropsychological research. As Antonio R. Damasio, a neuropsychology researcher, has recently written:

> The elimination of emotion and feeling from the human picture entails an impoverishment of the subsequent organization of experience. If social emotions and feelings are not properly deployed, and if the relation between social situations and joy and sorrow breaks down, the individual cannot categorize the experience of events in his autobiographical memory record according to the emotion/feeling mark that confers "goodness" or "badness" upon those experiences. That would preclude any subsequent level or construction of the notions of goodness and badness, namely the reasoned cultural construction of what *ought* to be considered good or bad, given its good or bad effects. *Looking for Spinoza*, p. 159

Kant was appalled by Hume's account of ethics (just as he similarly recoiled from Hume's account of knowledge, or rather Hume's account of our *lack* of knowledge). For Kant, sentiments and feelings are notoriously unreliable, changeable, and uncertain; and for most of us, our experiences bear out Kant's evaluation. You find the great love of your life in June, and in September, you can't imagine what charms you ever saw in that person. Perhaps the feelings which "contribute to the peace and security of human society" are more constant; but when we think of how easily corrupt politicians can inflame desires for socially destructive wars, we may well doubt the strength and reliability of such feelings. And of course there are others feelings—such as feelings of racism and sexism—that are profoundly *destructive* to "the peace and security of human society." Not only are feelings notoriously unreliable, they are also *not* universal. I trust that most of us feel strongly that discrimination against women is a terrible wrong; but sadly there are societies in which the *feeling* that women should always be subordinate is both strong and strongly approved (as indeed it was in our own society for many years). And for Kant, ethical principles *must* be universal, not relative to cultures. There is another factor that is probably the most important for Kant: *feelings* are not distinctively *human*. When you come home from college, your dog goes into ecstasy—and we say, quite naturally and correctly, that "Rover is certainly happy to see you," and that he will be sad when he sees you leaving at the airport. But for Kant, ethics is a distinctively *human* phenomenon, and so it must be based on what is distinctively *human*: our power of reason, and particularly our power of abstract reasoning from *principle*.

Are our *feelings* a helpful or even essential moral guide, or instead an impediment to the moral life? Kant regarded feelings as totally unreliable; even worse, a hindrance to the rational understanding of ethics and an obstacle to principled ethical behavior:

> . . . as to moral feeling, this supposed special sense, the appeal to it is indeed superficial when those who cannot *think* believe that *feeling* will help them out, even in what concerns general laws: and besides, feelings which naturally differ infinitely in degree cannot furnish a uniform standard of good and evil, nor has any one a right to form judgments for others by his own feelings . . .

> *Kant*, Fundamental Principles of the Metaphysics of Ethics

The poet, Percy Bysshe Shelley, defends the opposite perspective:

> The great secret of morals is love; or a going out of our own nature, and an identification of ourselves with the beautiful which exists in thought, action, or person not our own. . . . The great instrument of moral good is the imagination. . . .

> *Percy Bysshe Shelley*, A Defense of Poetry, *1821*

But is it really possible for pure reason to discover objective ethical truths? Kant insists that it is. And for Kant, such ethical truths must have some impressive characteristics. First, they must be *categorical*. That is, they are not merely *conditional* principles, such as *if* you want to be healthy, you should eat lots of fruits and vegetables, or *if* you want to be respected, you should tell the truth. There are no *ifs* in categorical truths: "Tell the truth," and "Keep your promises"; *not* "Tell the truth *if* it doesn't get you in trouble," or "Keep your promises *if* it is convenient." Second, they must be *universal*: they apply always and everywhere and to everyone. The feature of universality means that such truths *must* be the product of *reason*; they are not derived from experience or observation or experiment. We know the laws of gravity from *experience* and empirical observation and experiment, and so we have good reason to think they apply in *our* universe; but in some *other* universe (maybe there are parallel universes, or maybe God created several other universes), there might be *no* gravitational force. That's easy to imagine. But we cannot imagine a universe in which two plus two does not equal four. We can imagine a universe in which every time you combine two apples with two more apples the result is five apples (in this new universe, whenever four apples get together a fifth is spontaneously generated); but we cannot imagine the *experience* of two plus two equaling five, because that is *not* something learned from experience, but instead—as a *universal* truth—must be derived from *reason*.

Kant's ethics is an example of a *deontological* theory of ethics. "Deontological" comes from the Greek "deon," meaning that which is *binding*, in particular a *binding* duty. According to deontologists, the nature of ethical rules is to *bind* you to your duty; and that binding is *not* dependent on consequences. You are duty bound to keep your promise, even if a better offer comes along. And you are duty bound, whether the *consequences* are pleasant or painful. Duty is not based on what is pleasant or beneficial or advantageous, but rather upon the nature of the obligation itself. Though Kant's rationalist view of ethics is the best known deontological theory, it is not the only one: theological voluntarism (the divine command theory of ethics) is another deontological theory. On the divine command theory, a law is morally binding because God commands it. The consequences of following God's law—whether pleasant or painful—are irrelevant.

Kant insists that when we reason carefully, we can rationally discover a fundamental true ethical principle, which Kant calls *the categorical imperative*: Always act in such a way that you could will that your act should be a universal law. Can you will that *you* should be cheated? Well, maybe. Perhaps you're a masochist, who likes suffering abuse. But that way of thinking is too narrow and particular; think universal. Don't think about the diagonals that I draw on the board: *those* may not have equal opposite angles; rather, think of *ideal* diagonals, the way you do in geometry, or in mathematics. If I have two cookies in my left hand, and two more in my right, and then I put them together, then I may or may not have four cookies: perhaps the cookie monster was lurking nearby, and as soon as the four cookies came together, he grabbed three; or perhaps cookies have the special power of spontaneous generation, and as soon as you put four cookies together, they produce two *additional* cookies in some wonderful mysterious manner. In that case, two cookies plus two cookies would yield six cookies. But that would *not* alter the fact that two plus two is four: no experimental or experiential result whatsoever could possibly change that mathematical fact. (You may recall from earlier chapters that knowledge of that type—which is *not* derived from experience—is called *a priori* knowledge.) So getting back to Kant's ethics: Perhaps *you* could will that you be cheated and treated with contempt; but we're not thinking of the *particular* you, with your specific psychological problems; rather, we are thinking of you as a *person*, as someone who is *capable* of reasoning, capable of rationally discovering and following principles, of autonomously *choosing* to follow the moral law. Your gender, your ethnic group, your loyalty to the Chicago Cubs, and your taste for chocolate chip cookies: None of those things really matter. Think of yourself as one who has the characteristics of a *moral actor*: one who has the power of *Reason* and the power of *Will*. Having *those* characteristics makes you very special, whatever other accidental characteristics you happen to have. And *as* a rational autonomous moral being, you *cannot* consistently will that *you* be treated contemptuously or dishonestly: That would contradict your very nature. But of course, there is *no morally significant difference* between you and other persons: You may differ in ethnic group, gender, wealth, and even intelligence, but so long as you all share the essential moral characteristic of being *rational moral agents*, you share the same morally relevant features. Suppose, then, that someone says: It would be wrong for someone to cheat *me*, but there is nothing wrong with me cheating someone else. That is just as absurd (Kant argues) as supposing that the opposite angles between *these* intersecting lines are equal, but that doesn't apply to another *identical* set of intersecting lines; it would be like saying "Two plus two is four for *me*, but not necessarily for *you*." Simple consistency requires that we treat others as *we ourselves* would wish to be treated: that our actions should always be such that we could will that *everyone* act that way, including the actions of others toward us.

Thus by a purely rational process, similar to working out a geometrical proof, we arrive at a categorical ethical principle: Kant's *categorical imperative*, which demands we always act in such a way that we could will that our acts should be a universal law. Kant certainly did not invent that principle: It is very similar to "the golden rule" of ethics, that you should "Do unto others as you would have them do unto you," or (as stated in the Jewish tradition) "That which is hateful to you, do not unto others." But Kant believes that he can establish that principle purely through reason, without relying on emotion, revelation, or observation. Kant offers another statement of his categorical imperative, which he regards as an equivalent formulation: Always treat all persons as ends in themselves, and never as merely means to your ends. That doesn't mean you can't hire someone to design your website or wire your house; but it does mean that you must treat them respectfully, honestly, and justly—you obviously cannot cheat them, much less enslave them.

Kantian ethics is an ethics of pure reason. If Sam does acts of kindness because he *likes* helping others and takes joy in bringing them joy, then Kant would regard Sam's acts as pleasant and agreeable, but as having *no moral worth*:

> . . . there are many minds so sympathetically constituted that, without any other motive of vanity or self-interest, they find a pleasure in spreading joy around them and can take delight in the satisfaction of others so far as it is their own work. But I maintain that in such a case an action of this kind, however proper, however amiable it may be, has nevertheless no true moral worth, but is on a level with other inclinations. . . .

Kant, Fundamental Principles of the Metaphysics of Morals

The poet Ogden Nash (in a somewhat whimsical poem entitled "Kind of an Ode to Duty") writes:

O Duty,
Why hast thou not the visage of a sweetie or a cutie?

And for most of us—as well as for Aristotle—it would be wonderful if our *duties* had the charms of our desires. If my duty to visit my sick friend were as attractive as my desire to spend the afternoon at the beach, then duty would be a delight. It would be like steamed broccoli having the delightful taste of a hot fudge sundae.

But Kant sees it differently. If duty always matched our desire—if duty had "the visage of a cutie or a sweetie," rather than the stern demeanor of moral demand—then we would merely do right by inclination, rather than through the force and dedication of our wills. And for Kant, acting from inclination has no moral worth at all. For Kant, our uniquely human will power enables us to overcome desire and follow the demands of the rational moral law, and it is that power which sets humans apart from the mechanical world and gives us our special status.

For Kant emotion has no place whatsoever in ethics; even actions motivated by generous emotions such as affection and sympathy have no positive *moral* worth, but instead stand in the way of *genuine* moral acts, which must be carried out purely from the *rational* recognition of the *duty* to follow the moral law:

> . . . if nature has put little sympathy in the heart of this or that man; if he . . . is by temperament cold and indifferent to the sufferings of others, . . . would he not still find in himself a source from whence to give himself a far higher worth than that of a good-natured temperament could be? Unquestionably. It is just in this that the moral worth of the character is brought out which is incomparably the highest of all, namely, that he is beneficent, not from inclination, but from duty.

Kant, Fundamental Principles of the Metaphysics of Morals

If we must do our rationally recognized moral duty with *no* aid from feelings and inclinations, then what is the motive or force that moves us to do our stern duty and follow the moral law? The answer to that question adds the final piece to Kant's moral theory. We do our moral duty strictly from an act of *will*, which cannot be traced to our feelings or wishes or our causal history; the power of *will* to follow the moral law, together with the power of *reason* to recognize the moral law, is what sets us apart from the determined world of Newtonian physics, and sets us apart from the grubby material world: it makes us special, almost godlike.

The struggle between reason and emotion is a familiar one, found not only in philosophy but also in literature. William Wordsworth, the great English poet of the late eighteenth and early nineteenth centuries, took the side of feelings:

> One impulse from a vernal wood
> May teach you more of man,
> Of moral evil and of good,
> That all the sages can.
> Sweet is the lore which Nature brings;
> Our meddling intellect
> Mis-shapes the beauteous forms of things:—
> We murder to dissect.
>
> Enough of Science and of Art;
> Close up those barren leaves;
> Come forth, and bring with you a heart
> That watches and receives.

Kant represents rationalist ethics in its purest and most severe form. There is a profound contrast between Hume's emphasis on feelings and sympathies and Kant's pure rationalism: the one side tends to see moral behavior as a natural phenomenon; the other views moral behavior as requiring almost godlike powers. Hume finds it plausible to seek natural explanations for the development of morality; Kant does not. The former thinks it plausible that some behavior by nonhuman animals might qualify as moral; the latter thinks that absurd. The former tends to emphasize emotions and natural sympathies as the mainspring of ethics; the latter typically sees *reason* and the following of principle as the essential condition for ethical acts.

UTILITARIAN ETHICS

Kant insists that genuine ethical acts require following ethical principles discovered purely through reason; and in contrast, Hume argues that reason has no basic role in ethics, because ethics is a realm of feelings and passions. Another major ethical perspective that differs in significant respects from both of these is the *utilitarian* view. Though utilitarians base their theory on feelings, they tend to think of ethics as a much more rational enterprise than Hume does. And like Kant, utilitarians emphasize the importance of careful reasoning; however, the sort of reasoning favored by the utilitarians is very different from that demanded by the Kantian view. For utilitarians, the basic goal is to *maximize pleasure* and *minimize suffering*. Reasoning is useful in helping us discover the best means to that end, but reason does *not* establish that pleasure is good and suffering is bad: utilitarians tend to regard *that* as an obvious fact.

Utilitarian ethics is available in a wide variety of versions: If you look through the philosophy journals, you will find more different types of utilitarian theory than coffee choices at an upscale coffee shop. But the *basic* idea of utilitarian ethics is fairly simple: the right act is the act that produces the *best consequences overall* (including consequences for *everyone*, and including also the *long-term* consequences). For most utilitarians, the consequences to be sought are the *greatest possible balance of pleasure over suffering*; however, there are also "ideal" utilitarians who want to maximize not pleasure, but "the good." And there are also *preference* utilitarians who want to satisfy as many *preferences* as possible (even if some of those preferences have bad outcomes, such as a preference for smoking). And there are other varieties, too numerous to mention.

Kantians tend to find the utilitarian view deeply offensive, even repulsive: a corruption of ethics and a betrayal of ethical ideals. Kantians regard those who deny ethical objectivity as the enemy; but the utilitarians—who reduce the sublimity of ethical ideals to grubby calculations of maximizing pleasure—are despised as traitors. Kant saw legitimate morality as the precise opposite of the utilitarian calculation: "Morality is not properly the doctrine of how we may make ourselves happy, but how we may make ourselves worth of happiness" (Kant, 1788, *Critique of Practical Ethics*).

"I don't know why we are here, but I'm pretty sure that it is not in order to enjoy ourselves." *Ludwig Wittgenstein, 1889–1951*

If you're looking for an ethical theory with splendid ideals, absolute principles, and a conception of human ethical behavior that somehow transcends the grubby world of our day-to-day animal existence, then utilitarianism is probably not your kind of ethical theory. On the other hand, if you like your ethics as practical as possible, with careful attention to the society and circumstances we live in, then you may find utilitarian theory quite appealing. Utilitarianism doesn't start with God's commandments or appeals to pure Reason; rather, utilitarians start from a very unremarkable observation: Animals (including humans) like pleasure and dislike suffering. And so our ethical goals should be obvious: Act in the way that produces the greatest balance of pleasure over suffering for everyone involved. (If you think that suffering is good, because it gives us spiritual depth, or that pleasure is bad, because it distracts us from the deeper meaning of life, then utilitarian theory will hold few charms for you.) Should I tell a lie? Well, probably not; after all, we know from bitter experience that telling lies often causes a good deal of suffering. However, in *some* circumstances telling a lie may well be the *right* thing to do (e.g., when hiding escaped slaves from slave catchers). If you want to know what act is right, don't look for ethical ideals or absolute rules; rather, *look carefully* at the situation, and think carefully about what act *in these circumstances* is most likely to produce the greatest *overall* balance of pleasure over suffering.

Utilitarian ethics is an example of a *teleological* theory of ethics. "Teleological" comes from the Greek word "telos," meaning *end* or *goal*. Such theories are sometimes called *consequentialist* theories, since they base ethical rules and judgments on the *consequences*. Roughly, an act is judged good if it produces good *consequences*, if it has good *results*, or if it is productive of worthwhile *ends*. Utilitarian ethics (the right act is the act that produces the greatest benefits for everyone) is the dominant consequentialist view; but egoism (the right act is the one that produces the greatest benefits for the individual egoist) is also consequentialist. The contrast between tele-ological and deontological (duty-based) theories is one of the most fundamental divides in ethical theory. Deontologists basically believe that consequences don't matter in ethics (or at least are not of *primary* importance); teleologists believe that consequences are the *only* things that matter.

Some people like utilitarian ethics because it's an ethical theory that focuses on prac-tical consequences rather than absolute ideals; other people hate utilitarianism, for exactly the same reasons. But love it or hate it, utilitarian ethics should *not* be thought of as a short-sighted, live-for-the-moment, think-only-of-yourself view of ethics. That is a gross distor-tion of utilitarian theory. First, utilitarianism is *not* a self-centered, selfish view. When calculating the right thing to do, you should certainly weigh your own pleasure and suffer-ing in the balance; but you must *not*—as a good utilitarian—count your *own* pleasures and pains more than those of others. If a small reduction in your own individual pleasure would result in significantly greater pleasure for others, then you are *morally obligated* to do the act which would benefit others (even if it places you at a disadvantage). And in deciding what you should do, you must consider not just *immediate* pleasures and pains, but also long-term benefits and problems. Smoking is pleasant; but a good utilitarian weighs not only the immediate pleasurable benefits for herself, but also the long-term risks of horrific and painful forms of cancer, as well as the hazard posed to others by second-hand smoke. A night of heavy drinking involves substantial immediate pleasure; but weighing in tomor-row's hangover, not to mention your unhappiness at blowing your ethics exam and the long-term suffering that could result from liver damage, a thoughtful utilitarian may conclude that such drunken pleasure is overbalanced by future suffering. Don't ask whether heavy drinking is "wrong in itself," the utilitarian would say; if heavy drinking gives pleasure, then it is *good* to that extent. But when we weigh up *all* the pleasures and pains involved, we may well conclude that heavy drinking is *not* a good choice.

Utilitarians hold that our basic moral obligation is to strive for maximum pleasure and minimum suffering for everyone; but within that general framework, there are some signifi-cant disputes among utilitarians. First, do some pleasures count for more than others? That is, when making utilitarian calculations to determine which act is right (which act will produce the greatest balance of pleasure over suffering), should we give more weight to some pleasures than to others, or should all pleasures count equally? Should we consider *quality* of pleasures, in addition to *quantity*? Jeremy Bentham, the great nineteenth-century British reformer and philosopher who was the father of modern utilitarian ethics, adamantly rejected any distinc-tions among qualities of pleasures: "Pushpin is as good as poetry," Bentham insisted (or in con-temporary terms, video games are as good as poetry). You take pleasure in listening to Mozart and Bach, while my favorite music is by Britney Spears. Obviously, you have much more sophisticated and educated musical tastes, and you can hear and appreciate musical subtleties that are totally lost on me; but so long as we gain equal quantities of pleasure from our musi-cal preferences, Bentham will count those pleasures as equal. (Of course, if I quickly get bored listening to Britney, while you gain long-term pleasure from Bach, we will *not* gain equal quantities of pleasure. But if my pleasure in Britney remains as strong as your pleasure in Bach, then Bentham weighs them the same.) John Stuart Mill was the leader of the next generation of utilitarians following Bentham, but he disagreed with Bentham on that key point: Mill insisted that *qualities* of pleasures must *also* be considered in utilitarian calculations: "It is better to be a human being dissatisfied than a pig satisfied; better to be Socrates dissatisfied than a fool satisfied." Mill believed that those who could appreciate the *higher quality* pleasures would not trade those pleasures for a greater *quantity* of lower quality pleasures; and that such calculations should be part of utilitarian judgments.

Adding judgments of the *quality* of pleasures to the utilitarian calculus raises a basic question: How do we *rank* the quality of pleasures? It's tough enough to measure quantity, but measuring quality raises even greater difficulties. In Elizabethan England, an evening spent attending a Shakespeare play was regarded as a rather low form of pleasure, while an evening of playing cards was rated higher quality; today, most people would reverse that quality judgment. Mill claimed that in evaluating the quality of two forms of pleasure, only those who could appreciate *both* were qualified to judge. But finding such judges may be difficult: There are lots of people who find pleasure in stock-car racing, and others who delight in the music of Mozart; but people who can enjoy *both* and give a reliable judgment on which pleasure is of *higher quality* may be rare.

A second division among utilitarians is between *act* and *rule* utilitarians. Act utilitarianism is the standard utilitarian position: The right act is the specific act that produces the greatest balance of pleasure over suffering for everyone. If telling a lie yields a greater balance of pleasure over suffering than telling the truth, then telling the lie is not just morally acceptable, it is morally *required*. Rule utilitarians believe that utilitarian calculations must weigh in the larger benefits of having such *practices* as promise-keeping; and that those *practices* make it necessary to suspend act-utilitarian calculations. Think of our practice of promise-keeping. If you *promise* to meet me for lunch, then I can make plans on that basis: refuse other luncheon offers, travel across town to meet you, make reservations at a restaurant, and maybe buy a new outfit. But in order to make such planning effective, I must be able to *rely* on you to keep your promise. Of course, if some emergency comes up—you're in a bad auto accident on your way to the restaurant, or you must rush a close friend to the hospital—then you are legitimately excused from your luncheon promise: Allowing such excuses is part of our *practice* of promise-keeping. But suppose that there's no emergency; instead, you simply get a better offer. You're on your way to meet me for lunch, and a much more attractive and engaging person invites you to lunch. You weigh up the pleasures and pains for all involved: If you break your promise to me, I'll be disappointed; but that's balanced out by the fact that if you have to pass up this much more attractive luncheon opportunity in order to have a boring lunch with me, then *you* will be disappointed. When you add in the disappointment suffered by this attractive person whose luncheon invitation you decline, and factor in the great pleasure both you and this new person would enjoy at lunch, then it's obvious that the greatest balance of pleasure over suffering would result from breaking your promise. So by act-utilitarian calculations, you should break your promise; indeed, you are *morally obligated* to break your promise. But if people went around breaking promises whenever a more attractive alternative emerged, then *promises* would be worthless. If "I promise to meet you for lunch" merely means "I'll meet you for lunch unless something better comes along," then our practice of promising can no longer serve its function: It will no longer enable us to make confident plans.

So, *if* we think that the promising *practice* is valuable and beneficial, then we must *not* honor our promises only when utilitarian calculations are in their favor. Rather, we must treat promise-keeping as something we do even if the utilitarian calculations are *against* it. *Rule*-utilitarians argue that we should weigh *practices*—such as promise-keeping—by utilitarian standards, determining whether having the practice and its rules is likely to produce a greater balance of pleasure over suffering than not having the practice. But if our utilitarian calculations favor the practice, then adopting that practice will mean that when we are operating *within* the practice, we must follow the rules of that practice rather than making utilitarian calculations (because only by following the practice procedures, and suspending utilitarian calculations when operating within the practice, can we make the practice *work*). If we want to enjoy the utilitarian benefits of the promise-keeping practice, then we must follow the *rules* of that practice. Thus rule-utilitarians favor some exceptions to the strict case by case utilitarian calculations favored by act-utilitarians.

Criticisms of Utilitarianism

Utilitarian ethics remains a popular ethical theory, but it has its critics. As already noted, Kantians see utilitarian ethics as a fundamental corruption of the entire ethical enterprise: Focusing ethics on the maximization of *pleasure* reduces ethics from the sublime to the trivial. And there are other interesting critiques. One of the most basic criticisms is that utilitarianism is *psychologically false*: It is just not true that humans regard maximizing pleasure and minimizing suffering as the greatest good. Climbing a very challenging mountain often involves terrible suffering in brutally harsh conditions; perhaps we could give some sort of account that would represent such a severe enterprise as the pursuit of pleasure, but the account is likely to seem contrived and implausible. Even clearer examples can be found in the efforts of dedicated revolutionaries to overthrow governments they regard as illegitimate. Nelson Mandela's courageous stand against the brutal apartheid regime of South Africa, and his willingness to suffer many years in the harsh prisons of that regime, cannot plausibly be represented as the pursuit of pleasure and the avoidance of suffering. Behavioral psychologists provide strong support for this line of criticism.

> Behavioral psychologists, such as B. F. Skinner, noted that the key to happiness is *not* in gaining benefits or rewards, but rather in *how* those benefits are gained. If you work hard at a task, and you are rewarded by the progress you are making, and ultimately rewarded or reinforced by completing the task well, then you gain the enjoyment of the reward *as well as* a strengthened tendency to work hard and work well, and the work itself becomes enjoyable. On the other hand, if the benefits or pleasures or "rewards" you receive are unrelated to your own efforts—you work hard, but with little reward; or you receive rewards for doing nothing—the long-term result will be lethargy, boredom, and depression. Thus, for behavioral psychologists, utilitarianism focuses too much on merely "maximizing pleasure"; it should instead focus on the pattern by which pleasures/ reinforcers are received, and what pattern of reinforcement shapes energetic efforts and sustained interest. As Skinner states:
>
> > The greatest good of the greatest number may be the greatest bore, and the Utilitarians lost their case just because they neglected the reinforcing contingencies which build the condition we describe by saying that we are happy.
>
> *B. F. Skinner, "The Ethics of Helping People," 1975*

Behavioral studies show that when we experience pleasures that are unrelated to our own efforts, the result is often lethargy and depression. We like *doing* things that are positively reinforced, we like *doing* things that *result* in feelings of pleasure and satisfaction; but pleasures disconnected from our efforts are *not* psychologically healthy for human animals. The pleasure is important as a *reinforcer* for the behavior we perform; but what we really value (and what the pleasurable reinforcement shapes) is commitment to the acts that resulted in pleasure. You certainly gain pleasure from playing soccer; but it is the soccer playing you value, not the pleasure that results from playing. If someone offered to stimulate your brain so that you felt the *pleasure* you experience when you play soccer, but on the condition that you stop *playing* soccer, you would not find that an attractive offer.

> Think of someone—yourself, if you can—facing an important self-defining decision. If you are a woman with a chance to begin a demanding career that intrigues you, but only by sacrificing time with your young children, which choice do you make? Or, if you are a law-school graduate with an offer from an established firm, do you reject it for a less challenging offer that is more likely—but by no means certain—to lead to a political

career later? Or, if you are a Jew, should you abandon your comfortable life in Los Angeles and emigrate to Israel to identify yourself firmly with that nation's fate? People do not make momentous decisions like these by trying to predict how much pleasure each choice might bring. *Ronald Dworkin, Life's Dominion,* p. 205

This line of criticism is developed further in a famous thought experiment contrived by Robert Nozick, a late twentieth century American philosopher. Imagine a "pleasure machine": As you enter the machine, it wipes out your memory of having entered the machine; so far as you can tell, you are in the real world. In this machine you will experience great success and enormous pleasure: You will write great novels and win the Nobel Prize for literature; you will quarterback the Green Bay Packers to six straight Super Bowl victories; you will spend wild sultry nights on warm beaches with—well, I'm sure your imagination can fill in the details. You have perfect confidence in the operators of the machine (they won't run some ghastly experiment on you once you're locked inside); and you are to suppose that none of your family or friends will miss you or worry about you or be harmed by your absence. Would you enter the pleasure machine? Perhaps for a day, maybe even for a long weekend; but would you be willing to spend your life there? Tempting, but few will choose to go inside. It's not just the *fantasy* or *feeling* that you want; rather, you want to actually *make things happen* in the world, have an effect on *reality*. But if you refuse the opportunity to spend your life in the pleasure machine, then it's clear that maximizing your pleasure and minimizing your suffering is *not* your main goal. If that's the case, then the basic premise of utilitarian theory is threatened.

Even if you have doubts about utilitarian ethics as a personal ethical theory, you may find it useful at a larger social level. And in fact, that's how utilitarian ethics was originally developed: as a guide for *social* ethics, a guide to justice in the larger public sphere. Specifically, utilitarianism developed as an ethical system for *social reformers* who wanted to make important changes in their society. Think of early nineteenth century England, at the height of the industrial revolution: the harsh world of great extremes described by Charles Dickens. A few people have enormous wealth, and live lives of luxury: a huge house in London, a vast country estate for the summer, a large stable of horses for fox hunting and for pulling splendid carriages, closets crammed with tailored suits and finely crafted shoes, and dinners with a dozen courses and a wine for each course. But many endure bleak lives of poverty and desperation, with no place to sleep, little to eat, and no access to health care. Children go into smoky dangerous factories and mines before dawn, and stay there until well after dark, every day, day after day, until they die at an early age; there is no public education, and no chance to escape these terrible circumstances. Even the crudest utilitarian calculations make it obvious that when Lord Mustard has two huge houses while many people lack even one small cottage; when he eats enormous rich meals while others go hungry; when he holds an enormous estate just for his fox hunting, while others starve for lack of a little land for farming; then the system is not maximizing pleasure and minimizing suffering. Or to take a more contemporary case: When thousands live in luxury with huge homes and vacation condos and private jets, while millions live in poverty and are denied access to basic health care, then a quick utilitarian calculation shows that such a system is *not* the best possible system for improving life for *everyone*. Which will be more likely to produce a greater balance of pleasure over suffering: building a new luxurious wing onto the 16 bedroom mansion of a Walton heir, or building a dozen small comfortable homes for the homeless? That utilitarian calculation doesn't require great mathematical skill. So perhaps utilitarian ethics is less effective for the details of our ethical lives, but works well as a rough hammer to pound away at the most obvious injustices in our society. And that is how one of the leading contemporary utilitarians, the animal rights advocate Peter Singer, uses utilitarian ethics: Does the pleasure you gain from eating pale veal outweigh the suffering of a small calf kept confined and isolated in a small pen and then shipped to a slaughterhouse? Whatever the limitations of utilitarian ethics, it has the power to push us to think hard about the ethical dimensions of our lives and our society.

READINGS

⊰ A TREATISE OF HUMAN NATURE ⊰
David Hume

David Hume (1711–1776) was probably the greatest of the classical empiricist philosophers, and in this passage from *A Treatise of Human Nature* (1738) he rejects any rationalist account of ethics, insisting that ethics is based on our feelings and emotions, and that it *cannot* be derived from reason. Just as Hume posed the great challenge to the rationalist view of knowledge, he likewise is the great opponent of rationalism in ethics.

OF THE INFLUENCING MOTIVES OF THE WILL

Nothing is more usual in philosophy, and even in common life, than to talk of the combat of passion and reason, to give the preference to reason, and to assert that men are only so far virtuous as they conform themselves to its dictates. Every rational creature, 'tis said, is oblig'd to regulate his actions by reason; and if any other motive or principle challenge the direction of his conduct, he ought to oppose it, 'till it be entirely subdu'd, or at least brought to a conformity with that Superior principle. On this method of thinking the greatest part of moral philosophy, ancient and modern, seems to be founded; nor is there an ampler field, as well for metaphysical arguments, as popular declamations, than this suppos'd pre-eminence of reason above passion. The eternity, invariableness, and divine origin of the former have been display'd to the best advantage: The blindness, unconstancy, and deceitfulness of the latter have been as strongly insisted on. In order to shew the fallacy of all this philosophy, I shall endeavour to prove *first*, that reason alone can never be a motive to any action of the will; and *secondly*, that it can never oppose passion in the direction of the will.

The understanding exerts itself after two different ways, as it judges from demonstration or probability; as it regards the abstract relations of our ideas, or those relations of objects, of which experience only gives us information. I believe it scarce will be asserted, that the first species of reasoning alone is ever the cause of any action. As its proper province is the world of ideas, and as the will always places us in that of realities, demonstration and volition seem, upon that account, to be totally remov'd, from each other. Mathematics, indeed, are useful in all mechanical operations, and arithmetic in almost every art and profession: But 'tis not of themselves they have any influence. Mechanics are the art of regulating the motions of bodies *to some design'd end or purpose*; and the reason why we employ arithmetic in fixing the proportions of numbers, is only that we may discover the proportions of their influence and operation. A merchant is desirous of knowing the sum total of his accounts with any person: Why? but that he may learn what sum will have the same *effects* in paying his debt, and going to market, as all the particular articles taken together. Abstract or demonstrative reasoning, therefore, never influences any of our actions, but only as it directs our judgment concerning causes and effects; which leads us to the second operation of the understanding.

'Tis obvious, that when we have the prospect of pain or pleasure from any object, we feel a consequent emotion of aversion or propensity, and are carry'd to avoid or embrace what will give us this uneasiness or satisfaction. 'Tis also obvious, that this emotion rests not here, but making us cast our view on every side, comprehends whatever objects are connected with its original one by the relation of cause and effect. Here then reasoning takes place to discover this relation; and according as our reasoning varies, our actions receive a subsequent variation. But 'tis evident in this case, that the impulse arises not from reason, but is only directed by it. 'Tis from the prospect of pain or pleasure that the aversion or propensity arises towards any object: And these emotions extend themselves to the causes and effects of that object, as they are pointed out to us by reason and experience. It can never in the least concern us to know, that such objects are causes, and such others effects, if both the causes and effects be indifferent to us. Where the objects themselves do not affect us, their connexion can never give them any influence; and 'tis plain, that as reason is nothing but the discovery of this connexion, it cannot be by its means that the objects are able to affect us.

Since reason alone can never produce any action, or give rise to volition, I infer, that the same faculty is as incapable of preventing volition, or of disputing the preference with any passion or emotion. This consequence is necessary. 'Tis impossible reason cou'd have the latter effect of preventing volition, but by giving an impulse in a contrary direction to our passion; and that impulse, had it operated alone, wou'd have been able to produce volition. Nothing can oppose or retard the impulse of passion, but a contrary impulse; and if this contrary impulse ever arises from reason, that latter faculty must have an original influence on the will, and must be able to cause, as well as hinder any act of volition. But if reason has no original influence, 'tis impossible it can withstand any principle, which has such an efficacy, or ever kept the mind in suspence a moment. Thus it appears, that the principle, which opposes our passion, cannot be the same with reason, and is only call'd so in an improper sense. We speak not strictly and philosophically when we talk of the combat of passion, and can never pretend to any other office than to serve and obey them. As this opinion may appear somewhat extraordinary, it may not be improper to confirm it by some other considerations.

A passion is an original existence, or, if you will, modification of existence, and contains not any representative quality, which renders it a copy of any other existence or modification. When I am angry, I am actually possest with the passion, and in that emotion have no more a reference to any other object, than when I am thirsty, or sick, or more than five foot high. 'Tis impossible, therefore, that this passion can be oppos'd by, or be contradictory to truth and reason; since this contradiction consists in the disagreement of ideas, consider'd as copies, with those objects, which they represent.

What may at first occur on this head, is, that as nothing can be contrary to truth or reason, except what has a reference to it, and as the judgments of our understanding only have this reference, it must follow, that passions can be contrary to reason only so far as they are *accompany'd* with some judgment or opinion. According to this principle, which is so obvious and natural, 'tis only in two senses, that any affection can be call'd unreasonable. First, When a passion, such as hope or fear, grief or joy, despair or security, is founded on the supposition of the existence of objects, which really do not exist. Secondly, When in exerting any passion in action, we chuse means insufficient for the design'd end, and deceive ourselves in our judgment of causes and effects. Where a passion is neither founded on false suppositions, nor chuses means insufficient for the end, the understanding can neither justify nor condemn it. 'Tis not contrary to reason to prefer the destruction of the whole world to the scratching of my finger. 'Tis not contrary to reason for me to chuse my total ruin, to prevent the least uneasiness of an *Indian* or person wholly unknown to me. 'Tis as little contrary to reason to prefer even my own acknowleg'd lesser good to my greater, and have a more ardent affection for the former than the latter. A trivial good may, from certain circumstances, produce a desire superior to what arises from the greatest and most valuable enjoyment; nor is there any thing more extraordinary in this, than in mechanics to see one pound weight raise up a hundred by the advantage of its situation. In short, a passion must be accompany'd with some false judgment, in order to its being unreasonable; and even then 'tis not the passion, properly speaking, which is unreasonable, but the judgment.

The consequences are evident. Since a passion can never, in any sense, be call'd unreasonable, but when founded on a false supposition, or when it chuses means insufficient for the design'd end, 'tis impossible, that reason and passion can ever oppose each other, or dispute for the government of the will and actions. The moment we perceive the falshood of any supposition, or the insufficiency of any means our passions yield to our reason without any opposition. I may desire any fruit as of an excellent relish; but whenever you convince me of my mistake, my longing ceases. I may will the performance of certain actions as means of obtaining any desir'd good; but as my willing of these actions is only secondary, and founded on the supposition, that they are causes of the propos'd effect; as soon as I discover the falshood of that supposition, they must become indifferent to me. . . .

MORAL DISTINCTIONS NOT DERIV'D FROM REASON

Those who affirm that virtue is nothing but a conformity to reason; that there are eternal fitnesses and unfitnesses of things, which are the same to every rational being that considers them; that the immutable measures of right and wrong impose an obligation, not only on human creatures, but also on the Deity himself: All these systems concur in the opinion, that morality, like truth, is discern'd merely by ideas, and by their juxta-position and comparison. In order, therefore, to judge of these systems, we need only consider, whether it be possible, from reason alone, to distinguish betwixt moral good and evil, or whether there must concur some other principles to enable us to make that distinction.

If morality had naturally no influence on human passions and actions, 'twere in vain to take such pains to inculcate it; and nothing would be more fruitless than that multitude of rules and precepts with which all moralists abound. Philosophy is commonly divided into *speculative* and *practical*; and as morality is always comprehended under the latter division, 'tis supposed to influence our passions and actions, and to go beyond the calm and indolent judgments of the understanding. And this is confirm'd by common experience, which informs us, that men are often govern'd by their duties, and are deter'd from some actions by the opinion of injustice, and impell'd to others by that of obligation.

Since morals, therefore, have an influence on the actions and affections, it follows, that they cannot be deriv'd from reason; and that because reason alone, as we have already prov'd, can never have any such influence. Morals excite passions, and produce or prevent actions. Reason of itself is utterly impotent in this particular. The rules of morality, therefore, are not conclusions of our reason. . . .

But can there be any difficulty in proving, that vice and virtue are not matters of fact, whose existence we can infer by reason? Take any action allow'd to be vicious: Wilful murder, for instance. Examine it in all lights, and see if you can find that

matter of fact, or real existence, which you call *vice*. In which-ever way you take it, you find only certain passions, motives, volitions and thoughts. There is no other matter of fact in the case. The vice entirely escapes you, as long as you consider the object. You never can find it, till you turn your reflexion into your own breast, and find a sentiment of disapprobation, which arises in you, towards this action. Here is a matter of fact; but 'tis the object of feeling, not of reason. It lies in yourself, not in the object. So that when you pronounce any action or character to be vicious, you mean nothing, but that from the constitution of your nature you have a feeling or sentiment of blame from the contemplation of it. Vice and virtue, therefore, may be compar'd to sounds, colours, heat and cold, which, according to modern philosophy, are not qualities in objects, but perceptions in the mind: And this discovery in morals, like that other in physics, is to be regarded as a considerable advancement of the speculative sciences; tho', like that too, it has little or no influence on practice. Nothing can be more real, or concern us more, than our own sentiments of pleasure and uneasiness; and if these be favourable to virtue, and unfavourable to vice, no more can be requisite to the regulation of our conduct and behaviour.

I cannot forbear adding to these reasonings an observation, which may, perhaps, be found of some importance. In every system of morality, which I have hitherto met with, I have always remark'd, that the author proceeds for some time in the ordinary way of reasoning, and establishes the being of a God, or makes observations concerning human affairs; when of a sudden I am surpriz'd to find, that instead of the usual copulations of propositions, *is*, and *is not*, I meet with no proposition that is not connected with an *ought*, or an *ought not*. This change is imperceptible; but is, however, of the last consequence. For as this *ought*, or *ought not*, expresses some new relation or affirmation, 'tis necessary that it shou'd be observ'd and explain'd; and at the same time that a reason should be given, for what seems altogether inconceivable, how this new relation can be a deduction from others, which are entirely different from it. But as authors do not commonly use this precaution, I shall presume to recommend it to the readers; and am persuaded, that this small attention wou'd subvert all the vulgar systems of morality, and let us see, that the distinction of vice and virtue is not founded merely on the relations of objects, nor is perceiv'd by reason.

FUNDAMENTAL PRINCIPLES OF THE METAPHYSICS OF MORALS

Immanuel Kant

Immanuel Kant (1724–1804) champions a system of ethics based entirely on rationalism—in short, he takes the view that is diametrically opposed to the position favored by Hume. Kant maintains that there are absolute universal moral principles that can be known purely through reason and that—contrary to Hume—emotions have nothing whatsoever to do with *genuine* ethical behavior, which must be based on reasoned application of rules. The following is excerpted from Kant's *Fundamental Principles of the Metaphysic of Morals*, 1785, and (the very last section) from *The Critique of Practical Reason*, 1788, translated by Thomas K. Abbott.

TRANSITION FROM THE COMMON RATIONAL KNOWLEDGE OF MORALITY TO THE PHILOSOPHICAL

Nothing can possibly be conceived in the world, or even out of it, which can be called good, without qualification, except a good will. Intelligence, wit, judgement, and the other talents of the mind, however they may be named, or courage, resolution, perseverance, as qualities of temperament, are undoubtedly good and desirable in many respects; but these gifts of nature may also become extremely bad and mischievous if the will which is to make use of them, and which, therefore, constitutes what is called character, is not good. It is the same with the gifts of fortune. Power, riches, honour, even health, and the general well-being and contentment with one's condition which is called happiness, inspire pride, and often presumption, if there is not a good will to correct the influence of these on the mind, and with this also to rectify the whole principle of acting and adapt it to its end. The sight of a being who is not adorned with a single feature of a pure and good will, enjoying unbroken prosperity, can never give pleasure to an impartial rational spectator. Thus a good will appears to constitute the indispensable condition even of being worthy of happiness.

A good will is good not because of what it performs or effects, not by its aptness for the attainment of some proposed end, but simply by virtue of the volition; that is, it is good in itself, and considered by itself is to be esteemed much higher than all that can be brought about by it in favour of any inclination, nay even of the sum total of all inclinations. Even if it should happen that, owing to special disfavour of fortune, or the niggardly provision of a step-motherly nature, this will should wholly lack power to accomplish its purpose, if with its greatest efforts it should yet achieve nothing, and there should remain only the good will (not, to be sure, a mere wish, but the summoning of all means in our power), then, like a jewel, it would still shine by its own light, as a thing which has its whole value in itself. Its usefulness or fruitfulness can neither add nor take away anything from this value. It would be, as it were, only the setting to enable us to handle it the more conveniently in common commerce, or to attract to it the attention of those who are not yet connoisseurs, but not to recommend it to true connoisseurs, or to determine its value.

There is, however, something so strange in this idea of the absolute value of the mere will, in which no account is taken of its utility, that notwithstanding the thorough assent of even common reason to the idea, yet a suspicion must arise that it may perhaps really be the product of mere high-flown fancy, and that we may have misunderstood the purpose of nature in assigning reason as the governor of our will. Therefore we will examine this idea from this point of view.

In the physical constitution of an organized being, that is, a being adapted suitably to the purposes of life, we assume it as a fundamental principle that no organ for any purpose will be found but what is also the fittest and best adapted for that purpose. Now in a being which has reason and a will, if the proper object of nature were its conservation, its welfare, in a word, its happiness, then nature would have hit upon a very bad arrangement in selecting the reason of the creature to carry out this purpose. For all the actions which the creature has to perform with a view to this purpose, and the whole rule of its conduct, would be far more surely prescribed to it by instinct, and that end would have been attained thereby much more certainly than it ever can be by reason. Should reason have been communicated to this favoured creature over and above, it must only have served it to contemplate the happy constitution of its nature, to admire it, to congratulate itself thereon, and to feel thankful for it to the beneficent cause, but not that it should subject its desires to that weak and delusive guidance and meddle bunglingly with the purpose of nature. In a word, nature would have taken care that reason should not break forth into practical exercise, nor have the presumption, with its weak insight, to think out for itself the plan of happiness, and of the means of attaining it. Nature would not only have taken on herself the choice of the ends, but also of the means, and with wise foresight would have entrusted both to instinct.

And, in fact, we find that the more a cultivated reason applies itself with deliberate purpose to the enjoyment of life and happiness, so much the more does the man fail of true satisfaction. And from this circumstance there arises in many, if they are candid enough to confess it, a certain degree of misology, that is, hatred of reason, especially in the case of those who are most experienced in the use of it, because after calculating all the advantages they derive, I do not say from the invention of all the arts of common luxury, but even from the sciences (which seem to them to be after all only a luxury of the understanding), they find that they have, in fact, only brought more trouble on their shoulders, rather than gained in happiness; and they end by envying, rather than despising, the more common stamp of men who keep closer to the guidance of mere instinct and do not allow their reason much influence on their conduct. And this we must admit, that the judgement of those who would very much lower the lofty eulogies of the advantages which reason gives us in regard to the happiness and satisfaction of life, or who would even reduce them below zero, is by no means morose or ungrateful to the goodness with which the world is governed, but that there lies at the root of these judgements the idea that our existence has a different and far nobler end, for which, and not for happiness, reason is properly intended, and which must, therefore, be regarded as the supreme condition to which the private ends of man must, for the most part, be postponed.

For as reason is not competent to guide the will with certainty in regard to its objects and the satisfaction of all our wants (which it to some extent even multiplies), this being an end to which an implanted instinct would have led with much greater certainty; and since, nevertheless, reason is imparted to us as a practical faculty, i.e., as one which is to have influence on the will, therefore, admitting that nature generally in the distribution of her capacities has

adapted the means to the end, its true destination must be to produce a will, not merely good as a means to something else, but good in itself, for which reason was absolutely necessary. This will then, though not indeed the sole and complete good, must be the supreme good and the condition of every other, even of the desire of happiness. Under these circumstances, there is nothing inconsistent with the wisdom of nature in the fact that the cultivation of the reason, which is requisite for the first and unconditional purpose, does in many ways interfere, at least in this life, with the attainment of the second, which is always conditional, namely, happiness. Nay, it may even reduce it to nothing, without nature thereby failing of her purpose. For reason recognizes the establishment of a good will as its highest practical destination, and in attaining this purpose is capable only of a satisfaction of its own proper kind, namely that from the attainment of an end, which end again is determined by reason only, notwithstanding that this may involve many a disappointment to the ends of inclination.

We have then to develop the notion of a will which deserves to be highly esteemed for itself and is good without a view to anything further, a notion which exists already in the sound natural understanding, requiring rather to be cleared up than to be taught, and which in estimating the value of our actions always takes the first place and constitutes the condition of all the rest. In order to do this, we will take the notion of duty, which includes that of a good will, although implying certain subjective restrictions and hindrances. These, however, far from concealing it, or rendering it unrecognizable, rather bring it out by contrast and make it shine forth so much the brighter.

To be beneficent when we can is a duty; and besides this, there are many minds so sympathetically constituted that, without any other motive of vanity or self-interest, they find a pleasure in spreading joy around them and can take delight in the satisfaction of others so far as it is their own work. But I maintain that in such a case an action of this kind, however proper, however amiable it may be, has nevertheless no true moral worth, but is on a level with other inclinations, e.g., the inclination to honour, which, if it is happily directed to that which is in fact of public utility and accordant with duty and consequently honourable, deserves praise and encouragement, but not esteem. For the maxim lacks the moral import, namely, that such actions be done from duty, not from inclination. Put the case that the mind of that philanthropist were clouded by sorrow of his own, extinguishing all sympathy with the lot of others, and that, while he still has the power to benefit others in distress, he is not touched by their trouble because he is absorbed with his own; and now suppose that he tears himself out of this dead insensibility, and performs the action without any inclination to it, but simply from duty, then first has his action its genuine moral worth. Further still; if nature has put little sympathy in the heart of this or that man; if he, supposed to be an upright man, is by temperament cold and indifferent to the sufferings of others, perhaps because in respect of his own he is provided with the special gift of patience and fortitude and supposes, or even requires, that others should have the same—and such a man would certainly not be the meanest product of nature—but if nature had not specially framed him for a philanthropist, would he not still find in himself a source from whence to give himself a far higher worth than that of a good-natured temperament could be? Unquestionably. It is just in this that the moral worth of the character is brought out which is incomparably the highest of all, namely, that he is beneficent, not from inclination, but from duty.

It is in this manner, undoubtedly, that we are to understand those passages of Scripture also in which we are commanded to love our neighbour, even our enemy. For love, as an affection, cannot be commanded, but beneficence for duty's sake may; even though we are not impelled to it by any inclination—nay, are even repelled by a natural and unconquerable aversion. This is practical love and not pathological—a love which is seated in the will, and not in the propensions of sense—in principles of action and not of tender sympathy; and it is this love alone which can be commanded.

The second proposition is: That an action done from duty derives its moral worth, not from the purpose which is to be attained by it, but from the maxim by which it is determined, and therefore does not depend on the realization of the object of the action, but merely on the principle of volition by which the action has taken place, without regard to any object of desire. It is clear from what precedes that the purposes which we may have in view in our actions, or their effects regarded as ends and springs of the will, cannot give to actions, any unconditional or moral worth. In what, then, can their worth lie, if it is not to consist in the will and in reference to its expected effect? It cannot lie anywhere but in the principle of the will without regard to the ends which can be attained by the action. For the will stands between its a priori principle, which is formal, and its a posteriori spring, which is material, as between two roads, and as

it must be determined by something, in that it must be determined by the formal principle of volition when an action is done from duty, in which case every material principle has been withdrawn from it.

The third proposition, which is a consequence of the two preceding, I would express thus: Duty is the necessity of acting from respect for the law. I may have inclination for an object as the effect of my proposed action, but I cannot have respect for it, just for this reason, that it is an effect and not an energy of will. Similarly I cannot have respect for inclination, whether my own or another's; I can at most, if my own, approve it; if another's, sometimes even love it; i.e., look on it as favourable to my own interest. It is only what is connected with my will as a principle, by no means as an effect—what does not subserve my inclination, but overpowers it, or at least in case of choice excludes it from its calculation—in other words, simply the law of itself, which can be an object of respect, and hence a command. Now an action done from duty must wholly exclude the influence of inclination and with it every object of the will, so that nothing remains which can determine the will except objectively the law, and subjectively pure respect for this practical law, and consequently the maxim that I should follow this law even to the thwarting of all my inclinations.

Thus the moral worth of an action does not lie in the effect expected from it, nor in any principle of action which requires to borrow its motive from this expected effect. For all these effects—agreeableness of one's condition and even the promotion of the happiness of others—could have been also brought about by other causes, so that for this there would have been no need of the will of a rational being; whereas it is in this alone that the supreme and unconditional good can be found. The pre-eminent good which we call moral can therefore consist in nothing else than the conception of law in itself, which certainly is only possible in a rational being, in so far as this conception, and not the expected effect, determines the will. This is a good which is already present in the person who acts accordingly, and we have not to wait for it to appear first in the result.

But what sort of law can that be, the conception of which must determine the will, even without paying any regard to the effect expected from it, in order that this will may be called good absolutely and without qualification? As I have deprived the will of every impulse which could arise to it from obedience to any law, there remains nothing but the universal conformity of its actions to law in general, which alone is to serve the will as a principle, i.e., I am never to act otherwise than so that I could also will that my maxim should become a universal law. Here, now, it is the simple conformity to law in general, without assuming any particular law applicable to certain actions, that serves the will as its principle and must so serve it, if duty is not to be a vain delusion and a chimerical notion. The common reason of men in its practical judgements perfectly coincides with this and always has in view the principle here suggested. Let the question be, for example: May I when in distress make a promise with the intention not to keep it? I readily distinguish here between the two significations which the question may have: Whether it is prudent, or whether it is right, to make a false promise? The former may undoubtedly be the case. I see clearly indeed that it is not enough to extricate myself from a present difficulty by means of this subterfuge, but it must be well considered whether there may not hereafter spring from this lie much greater inconvenience than that from which I now free myself, and as, with all my supposed cunning, the consequences cannot be so easily foreseen but that credit once lost may be much more injurious to me than any mischief which I seek to avoid at present, it should be considered whether it would not be more prudent to act herein according to a universal maxim and to make it a habit to promise nothing except with the intention of keeping it. But it is soon clear to me that such a maxim will still only be based on the fear of consequences. Now it is a wholly different thing to be truthful from duty and to be so from apprehension of injurious consequences. In the first case, the very notion of the action already implies a law for me; in the second case, I must first look about elsewhere to see what results may be combined with it which would affect myself. For to deviate from the principle of duty is beyond all doubt wicked; but to be unfaithful to my maxim of prudence may often be very advantageous to me, although to abide by it is certainly safer. The shortest way, however, and an unerring one, to discover the answer to this question whether a lying promise is consistent with duty, is to ask myself, "Should I be content that my maxim (to extricate myself from difficulty by a false promise) should hold good as a universal law, for myself as well as for others? and should I able to say to myself. "Every one may make a deceitful promise when he finds himself in a difficulty from which he cannot otherwise extricate himself?" Then I presently become aware that while I can will the lie, I can by no means will that lying should be a universal law. For

with such a law there would be no promises at all, since it would be in vain to allege my intention in regard to my future actions to those who would not believe this allegation, or if they over hastily did so would pay me back in my own coin. Hence my maxim, as soon as it should be made a universal law, would necessarily destroy itself.

I do not, therefore, need any far-reaching penetration to discern what I have to do in order that my will may be morally good. Inexperienced in the course of the world, incapable of being prepared for all its contingencies, I only ask myself: Canst thou also will that thy maxim should be a universal law? If not, then it must be rejected, and that not because of a disadvantage accruing from it to myself or even to others, but because it cannot enter as a principle into a possible universal legislation, and reason extorts from me immediate respect for such legislation. I do not indeed as yet discern on what this respect is based (this the philosopher may inquire), but at least I understand this, that it is an estimation of the worth which far outweighs all worth of what is recommended by inclination, and that the necessity of acting from pure respect for the practical law is what constitutes duty, to which every other motive must give place, because it is the condition of a will being good in itself, and the worth of such a will is above everything.

Conclusion

Two things fill the mind with ever new and increasing admiration and awe, the oftener and the more steadily we reflect on them: the starry heavens above and the moral law within. I have not to search for them and conjecture them as though they were veiled in darkness or were in the transcendent region beyond my horizon; I see them before me and connect them directly with the consciousness of my existence. The former begins from the place I occupy in the external world of sense, and enlarges my connection therein to an unbounded extent with worlds upon worlds and systems of systems, and moreover into limitless times of their periodic motion, its beginning and continuance. The second begins from my invisible self, my personality, and exhibits me in a world which has true infinity, but which is traceable only by the understanding, and with which I discern that I am not in a merely contingent but in a universal and necessary connection, as I am also thereby with all those visible worlds. The former view of a countless multitude of worlds annihilates as it were my importance as an animal creature, which after it has been for a short time provided with vital power, one knows not how, must again give back the matter of which it was formed to the planet it inhabits (a mere speck in the universe). The second, on the contrary, infinitely elevates my worth as an intelligence by my personal-ity, in which the moral law reveals to me a life independent of animality and even of the whole sensible world, at least so far as may be inferred from the destination assigned to my existence by this law, a destination not restricted to conditions and limits of this life, but reaching into the infinite.

⇒ "THE CONSCIENCE OF HUCKLEBERRY FINN" ⇐
Jonathan Bennett

Jonathan Bennett (born 1930) taught philosophy at the University of Cambridge, the University of British Columbia, and Syracuse University. He has published influential books in a number of philosophical areas. This essay, "The Conscience of Huckleberry Finn," was originally published in *Philosophy*, volume 49 (1974): 123–134. It has been widely reprinted, both for the wonderful and engaging style of the writing and for the rich philosophical content of the work. Bennett offers a very careful but readable contemporary analysis of the basic conflict between the Kantian rationalist approach to ethics and the Humean ethical emphasis on the emotions.

I

In this paper, I shall present not just the conscience of Huckleberry Finn but two others as well. One of them is the conscience of Heinrich Himmler. He became a Nazi in 1923; he served drably and quietly, but well, and was rewarded with increasing responsibility and power. At the peak of his career he held many offices and commands, of which the most powerful was that of leader of the S.S.—the principal police force of the Nazi regime. In this capacity, Himmler commanded the whole concentration-camp system, and was responsible for the execution of the so-called "final solution of the Jewish problem." It is important for my purposes that this piece of social engineering should be thought of not abstractly but in concrete terms of Jewish families being marched to what they think are bathhouses, to the accompaniment of loud-speaker renditions of extracts from *The Merry Widow* and *Tales of Hoffmann*, there to be choked to death by poisonous gases. Altogether, Himmler succeeded in murdering about four and a half million of them, as well as several million gentiles, mainly Poles and Russians.

The other conscience to be discussed is that of the Calvinist theologian and philosopher Jonathan Edwards. He lived in the first half of the eighteenth century, and has a good claim to be considered America's first serious and considerable philosophical thinker. He was for many years a widely renowned preacher and Congregationalist minister in New England; in 1748 a dispute with his congregation led him to resign (he couldn't accept their view that unbelievers should be admitted to the Lord's Supper in the hope that it would convert them); for some years after that he worked as a missionary, preaching to Indians through an interpreter; then in 1758 he accepted the presidency of what is now Princeton University, and within two months died from a small-pox inoculation. Along the way he wrote some first-rate philosophy; his book attacking the notion of free will is still sometimes read. Why I should be interested in Edwards' *conscience* will be explained in due course.

I shall use Heinrich Himmler, Jonathan Edwards, and Huckleberry Finn to illustrate different aspects of a single theme, namely the relationship between *sympathy* on the one hand and *bad morality* on the other.

II

All that I can mean by a "bad morality" is a morality whose principles I deeply disapprove of. When I call a morality bad, I cannot prove that mine is better; but when I here call any morality bad, I think you will agree with me that it is bad; and that is all I need.

There could be dispute as to whether the springs of someone's actions constitute a *morality*. I think, though, that we must admit that someone who acts in ways which conflict grossly with our morality may nevertheless have a morality of his own—a set of principles of action which he sincerely assents to, so that for him the problem of acting well or rightly or in obedience to conscience is the problem of conforming to *those* principles. The problem of conscientiousness can arise as acutely for a bad morality as for any other: Rotten principles may be as difficult to keep as decent ones.

As for "sympathy" I use this term to cover every sort of fellow-feeling, as when one feels pity over someone's loneliness, or horrified compassion over his pain, or when one feels a shrinking reluctance to act in a way which will bring misfortune to someone else. These *feelings* must not be confused with *moral judgments*. My sympathy for someone in distress may lead me to help him, or even to think that I ought to help him; but in itself it is not a judgment about what I ought to do but just a *feeling* for him in his plight. We shall get some light on the difference between feelings and moral judgments when we consider Huckleberry Finn.

Obviously, feelings can impel one to action, and so can moral judgments; and in a particular case sympathy and morality may pull in opposite directions. This can happen not just with bad moralities, but also with good ones like yours and mine. For example, a small child, sick and miserable, clings tightly to his mother and screams in terror when she tries to pass him over to the doctor to be examined. If the mother gave way to her sympathy, that is to her feeling for the child's misery and fright, she would hold it close and not let the doctor come near; but don't we agree that it might be wrong for her to act on such a feeling? Quite generally, then, anyone's moral principles may apply to a particular situation in a way which runs contrary to the particular thrusts of fellow-feeling that he has in that situation. My immediate concern is with sympathy in relation to bad morality, but not because such conflicts occur only when the morality is bad.

Now, suppose that someone who accepts a bad morality is struggling to make himself act in accordance with it in a particular situation where his sympathies pull him another way. He sees the struggle as one between doing the right, conscientious thing, and acting wrongly and weakly, like the mother who won't let the doctor come near her sick, frightened baby. Since we don't accept this person's morality, we may see the situation very differently, thoroughly disapproving of the action he regards as the right one, and endorsing the action which from his point of view constitutes weakness and backsliding.

Conflicts between sympathy and bad morality won't always be like this, for we won't disagree with every single dictate of a bad morality. Still, it can happen in the way I have described, with the agent's right action being our wrong one, and vice versa. That is just what happens in a certain episode in Chapter 16 of *The Adventures of Huckleberry Finn*, an episode which brilliantly illustrates how fiction can be instructive about real life.

III

Huck Finn has been helping his slave friend Jim to run away from Miss Watson, who is Jim's owner. In their raft-journey down the Mississippi river, they are near to the place at which Jim will become legally free. Now let Huck take over the story:

> Jim said it made him all over trembly and feverish to be so close to freedom. Well I can tell you it made me all over trembly and feverish, too, to hear him, because I begun to get it through my head that he *was* most free—and who was to blame for it? Why, *me*. I couldn't get that out of my conscience, no how nor no way. . . . It hadn't ever come home to me, before, what this thing was that I was doing. But now it did; and it stayed with me, and scorched me more and more. I tried to make out to myself that *I* warn't to blame, because *I* didn't run Jim off from his rightful owner; but it warn't no use, conscience up and say, every time: "But you knowed he was running for his freedom, and you could a paddled ashore and told somebody." That was so—I couldn't get around that, no way. That was where it pinched. Conscience says to me: "What had poor Miss Watson done to you, that you could see her nigger go off right under your eyes and never say one single word? What did that poor old woman do to you, that you could treat her so mean? . . ." I got to feeling so mean and miserable I most wished I was dead.

Jim speaks of his plan to save up to buy his wife, and then his children, out of slavery; and he adds that if the children cannot be bought he will arrange to steal them. Huck is horrified:

> Thinks I, this is what comes of my not thinking. Here was this nigger which I had as good as helped to run away, coming right out flat-footed and saying he would steal his children—children that belonged to a man I didn't even know; a man that hadn't ever done me no harm.
>
> I was sorry to hear Jim say that, it was such a lowering of him. My conscience got to stirring me up hotter than ever, until at last I says to it: "Let up on me—it ain't too late, yet—I'll paddle ashore at first light, and tell." I felt easy, and happy, and light as a feather, right off. All my troubles was gone.

This is bad morality all right. In his earliest years Huck wasn't taught any principles, and the only one he has encountered since then are those of rural Missouri, in which slave-owning is just one kind of ownership and is not subject to critical pressure. It hasn't occurred to Huck to question those principles. So the action, to us abhorrent, of turning Jim in to the authorities presents itself *clearly* to Huck as the right thing to do.

For us, morality and sympathy would both dictate helping Jim to escape. If we felt any conflict, it would have both these on one side and something else on the other—greed for a reward, or fear of punishment. But Huck's morality conflicts with his sympathy, that is, with his unargued, natural feeling for his friend. The conflict starts when Huck sets off in the canoe towards the shore, pretending that he is going to reconnoiter, but really planning to turn Jim in:

> As I shoved off, [Jim] says: "Pooty soon I'll be a-shout'n for joy, en I'll say, it's all on accounts o' Huck I's a free man ... Jim won't ever forgit you, Huck, you's de bes' fren' Jim's ever had; en you's de *only* fren' old Jim's got now."
>
> I was paddling off, all in a sweat to tell on him; but when he says this, it seemed to kind of take the tuck all out of me. I went along slow then, and I warn't right down certain whether I was glad I started or whether I warn't. When I was fifty yards off, Jim says:
>
> "Dah you goes, de ole true Huck; de on'y white genlman dat ever kep' his promise to ole Jim." Well, I just felt sick. But I says, I *got* to do it—I can't get *out* of it.

In the upshot, sympathy wins over morality. Huck hasn't the strength of will to do what he sincerely thinks he ought to do. Two men hunting for runaway slaves ask him whether the man on his raft is black or white:

> I didn't answer up prompt. I tried to, but the words wouldn't come. I tried, for a second or two, to brace up and out with it, but I warn't man enough—hadn't the spunk of a rabbit. I see I was weakening; so I just give up trying, and up and says: "He's white."

So Huck enables Jim to escape, thus acting weakly and wickedly—he thinks. In this conflict between sympathy and morality, sympathy wins.

One critic has cited this episode in support of the statement that Huck suffers "excruciating moments of wavering between honesty and respectability." That is hopelessly wrong, and I agree with the perceptive comment on it by another critic, who says:

> The conflict waged in Huck is much more serious: He scarcely cares for respectability and never hesitates to relinquish it, but he does care for honesty and gratitude—and both honesty and gratitude

require that he should give Jim up. It is not, in Huck, honesty at war with respectability but love and compassion for Jim struggling against his conscience. His decision is for Jim and hell: a right decision made in the mental chains that Huck never breaks. His concern for Jim is and remains *irrational*. Huck finds many reasons for giving Jim up and none for stealing him. To the end Huck sees his compassion for Jim as a weak, ignorant, and wicked felony.

That is precisely correct—and it can have that virtue only because Mark Twain wrote the episode with such unerring precision. The crucial point concerns *reasons*, which all occur on one side of the conflict. On the side of conscience we have principles, arguments, considerations, ways of looking at things:

> "It hadn't ever come home to me before what I was doing"
> "I tried to make out that I warn't to blame"
> "Conscience said 'But you knowed ... '—I couldn't get around that"
> "What had poor Miss Watson done to you?"
> "This is what comes of my not thinking"
> " ... children that belonged to a man I didn't even know."

On the other side, the side of feeling, we get nothing like that. When Jim rejoices in Huck, as his only friend, Huck doesn't consider the claims of friendship or have the situation "come home" to him in a different light. All that happens is: "When he says this, it seemed to kind of take the tuck all out of me. I went along slow then, and I warn't right down certain whether I was glad I started or whether I warn't." Again, Jim's words about Huck's "promise" to him don't give Huck any *reason* for changing his plan: In his morality promises to slaves probably don't count. Their effect on him is of a different kind: "Well, I just felt sick." And when the moment for final decision come, Huck doesn't weigh up pros and cons: he simply *fails* to do what he believes to be right—he isn't strong enough, hasn't "the spunk of a rabbit." This passage in the novel is notable not just for its finely wrought irony, with Huck's weakness of will leading him to do the right thing, but also for its masterly handling of the difference between general moral principles and particular unreasoned emotional pulls.

IV

Consider now another case of bad morality in conflict with human sympathy: the case of the odious Himmler.

Here, from a speech he made to some S.S. generals, is an indication of the content of his morality:

> What happens to a Russian, to a Czech, does not interest me in the slightest. What the nations can offer in the way of good blood of our type, we will take, if necessary by kidnapping their children and raising them here with us. Whether nations live in prosperity or starve to death like cattle interests me only in so far as we need them as slaves to our *Kultur*; otherwise it is of no interest to me. Whether 10,000 Russian females fall down from exhaustion while digging an antitank ditch interests me only in so far as the antitank ditch for Germany is finished.

But has this a moral basis at all? And if it has, was there in Himmler's own mind any conflict between morality and sympathy? Yes there was. Here is more from the same speech:

> I also want to talk to you quite frankly on a very grave matter . . . I mean . . . the extermination of the Jewish race. . . . Most of you must know what it means when 100 corpses are lying side by side, or 500, or 1,000. To have stuck it out and at the same time—apart from exceptions caused by human weakness—to have remained decent fellows, that is what has made us hard. This is a page of glory in our history which has never been written and is never to be written.

Himmler saw his policies as being hard to implement while still retaining one's human sympathies—while still remaining a "decent fellow." He is saying that only the weak take the easy way out and just squelch their sympathies, and is praising the stronger and more glorious course of retaining one's sympathies while acting in violation of them. In the same spirit, he ordered that when executions were carried out in concentration camps, those responsible "are to be influenced in such a way as to suffer no ill effect in their character and mental attitude." A year later he boasted that the S.S. had wiped out the Jews

> without our leaders and their men suffering any damage in their minds and souls. The danger was considerable, for there was only a narrow path between the Scylla of their becoming heartless ruffians unable any longer to treasure life, and the Charybdis of their becoming soft and suffering nervous breakdowns.

And there really can't be any doubt that the basis of Himmler's policies was a set of principles which constituted his morality—a sick, bad, wicked *morality*. He described himself as caught in "the old tragic conflict between will and obligation." And when his physician Kersten protested at the intention to destroy the Jews, saying that the suffering involved was "not to be contemplated," Kersten reports that Himmler replied:

> He knew that it would mean much suffering for the Jews . . . "It is the curse of greatness that it must step over dead bodies to create new life. Yet we must . . . cleanse the soil or it will never bear fruit. It will be a great burden for me to bear."

This, I submit, is the language of morality.

So in this case, tragically, bad morality won out over sympathy. I am sure that many of Himmler's killers did extinguish their sympathies, becoming "heartless ruffians" rather than "decent fellows"; but not Himmler himself. Although his policies ran against the human grain to a horrible degree, he did not sandpaper down his emotional surfaces so that there was no grain there, allowing his actions to slide along smoothly and easily. He did, after all, bear his hideous burden, and even paid a price for it. He suffered a variety of nervous and physical disabilities, including nausea and stomach-convulsions, and Kersten was doubtless right in saying that these were "the expression of a psychic division which extended over his whole life."

This same division must have been present in some of those officials of the Church who ordered heretics to be tortured so as to change their theological opinions. Along with the brutes and cold careerists, there must have been some who cared, and who suffered from the conflict between their sympathies and their bad morality.

V

In the conflict between sympathy and bad morality, then, the victory may go to sympathy as in the case of Huck Finn, or to morality as in the case of Himmler.

Another possibility is that the conflict may be avoided by giving up, or not ever having, those sympathies which might interfere with one's principles. That seems to have been the case with Jonathan Edwards. I am afraid that I shall be doing an injustice to Edwards' many virtues, and to his great intellectual energy and inventiveness; for my concern is only with the worst thing about him—namely his morality, which was worse than Himmler's.

According to Edwards, God condemns some men to an eternity of unimaginably awful pain, though he arbitrarily spares others—"arbitrarily" because none deserve to be spared:

> Natural men are held in the hand of God over the pit of hell; they have deserved the fiery pit, and

are already sentenced to it; and God is dreadfully provoked, his anger is as great toward them as to those that are actually suffering the executions of the fierceness of his wrath in hell . . . ; the devil is waiting for them, hell is gaping for them, the flames gather and flash about them, and would fain lay hold on them . . . ; and . . . there are no means within reach that can be any security to them . . . All that preserves them is the mere arbitrary will, and uncovenanted unobliged forebearance of an incensed God.

Notice that he says "they have deserved the fiery pit." Edwards insists that men *ought* to be condemned to eternal pain; and his position isn't that this is right because God wants it, but rather that God wants it because it is right. For him, moral standards exist independently of God, and God can be assessed in the light of them (and of course found to be perfect). For example, he says:

They deserve to be cast into hell; so that . . . justice never stands in the way, it makes no objection against God's using his power at any moment to destroy them. Yes, on the contrary, justice calls aloud for an infinite punishment of their sins.

Elsewhere, he gives elaborate arguments to show that God is acting justly in damning sinners. For example, he argues that a punishment should be exactly as bad as the crime being punished; God is infinitely excellent; so any crime against him is infinitely bad; and so eternal damnation is exactly right as a punishment—it is infinite, but, as Edwards is careful also to say, it is "no more than infinite."

Of course, Edwards himself didn't torment the damned; but the question still arises of whether his sympathies didn't conflict with his *approval* of eternal torment. Didn't he find it painful to contemplate any fellow-human's being tortured for ever? Apparently not:

The God that holds you over the pit of hell, much as one holds a spider or some loathsome insect over the fire, abhors you, and is dreadfully provoked; . . . he is of purer eyes than to bear to have you in his sight; you are ten thousand times so abominable in his eyes as the most hateful venomous serpent is in ours.

When God is presented as being as misanthropic as that, one suspects misanthropy in the theologian. This suspicion is increased when Edwards claims that "the saints in glory will . . . understand how terrible the sufferings of the damned are; yet . . . will not be sorry for [them]." He bases this partly on a view of human nature whose ugliness he seems not to notice:

The seeing of the calamities of others tends to heighten the sense of our own enjoyments. When the saints in glory, therefore, shall see the doleful state of the damned, how will this heighten their sense of the blessedness of their own state . . . When they shall see how miserable others of their fellow-creatures are . . . ; when they shall see the smoke of their torment, . . . and hear their dolorous shrieks and cries, and consider that they in the mean time are in the most blissful state, and shall surely be in it to all eternity; how they will rejoice!

I hope this is less than the whole truth! His other main point about why the saints will rejoice to see the torments of the damned is that it is *right* that they should do so:

The heavenly inhabitants . . . will have no love nor pity to the damned . . . [This will not show] a want of spirit of love in them . . . ; for the heavenly inhabitants will know that it is not fit that they should love [the damned] because they will know then, that God has no love to them, nor pity for them.

The implication that *of course* one can adjust one's feelings of pity so that they conform to the dictates of some authority—doesn't this suggest that ordinary human sympathies played only a small part in Edwards' life?

VI

Huck Finn, whose sympathies are wide and deep, could never avoid the conflict in that way; but he is determined to avoid it, and so he opts for the only other alternative he can see—to give up morality altogether. After he has tricked the slave-hunters, he returns to the raft and undergoes a peculiar crisis:

I got aboard the raft, feeling bad and low, because I knowed very well I had done wrong, and I see it warn't no use for me to try to learn to do right; a body that don't get *started* right when he's little, ain't got no show—when the pinch comes there ain't nothing to back him up and keep him to his work, and so he gets beat. Then I thought a minute, and says to myself, hold on—s'pose you'd a done right and give Jim up; would you feel better than what you do now? No, says I, I'd feel bad—I'd feel just the same way I do now. Well, then, says I, what's the use you learning to do right, when it's troublesome to do right and ain't no trouble to do wrong, and the wages is just the same? I was stuck. I couldn't answer that. So I reckoned I wouldn't bother no more about it, but after this always do whichever come handiest at the time.

Huck clearly cannot conceive of having any morality except the one he has learned—too late, he thinks—from his society. He is not entirely a prisoner of that morality, because he does after all reject it; but for him that is a decision to relinquish morality as such; he cannot envisage revising his morality, altering its content in face of the various pressures to which it is subject, including pressures from his sympathies. For example, he does not begin to approach the thought that slavery should be rejected on moral grounds, or the thought that what he is doing is not theft because a person cannot be owned and therefore cannot be stolen.

The basic trouble is that he cannot or will not engage in abstract intellectual operations of any sort. In chapter 33 he finds himself "feeling to blame, somehow" for something he knows he had no hand in; he assumes that this feeling is a deliverance of conscience; and this confirms him in his belief that conscience shouldn't be listened to:

> It don't make no difference whether you do right or wrong, a person's conscience ain't got no sense, and just goes for him *anyway*. If I had a yaller dog that didn't know no more than a person's conscience does, I would poison him. It takes up more than all of a person's insides, and yet ain't no good, nohow.

That brisk, incurious dismissiveness fits well with the comprehensive rejection of morality back on the raft. But this is a digression.

On the raft, Huck decides not to live by principles, but just to do whatever "comes handiest at the time"—always acting according to the mood of the moment. Since the morality he is rejecting is narrow and cruel, and his sympathies are broad and kind, the results will be good. But moral principles are good to have, because they help to protect one from acting badly at moments when one's sympathies happen to be in abeyance. On the highest possible estimate of the role one's sympathies should have, one can still allow for principles as embodiments of one's best feelings, one's broadest and keenest sympathies. On that view, principles can help one across intervals when one's feelings are at less than their best, i.e. through periods of misanthropy or meanness or self-centeredness or depression or anger.

What Huck didn't see is that one can live by principles and yet have ultimate control over their content. And one way such control can be exercised is by checking of one's principles in the light of one's sympathies. This is sometimes a pretty straightforward matter. It can happen that a certain moral principle

becomes untenable—meaning literally that one cannot hold it any longer—because it conflicts intolerably with the pity or revulsion or whatever that one feels when one sees what the principle leads to. One's experience may play a large part here: Experiences evoke feelings, and feelings force one to modify principles. Something like this happened to the English poet Wilfred Owen, whose experiences in the First World War transformed him from an enthusiastic soldier into a virtual pacifist. I can't document his change of conscience in detail; but I want to present something which he wrote about the way experience can put pressure on morality.

The Latin poet Horace wrote that it is sweet and fitting (or right) to die for one's country—*dulce et decorum est pro patria mori*—and Owen wrote a fine poem about how experience could lead one to relinquish that particular moral principle. He describes a man who is too slow donning his gas mask during a gas attack—"As under a green sea I saw him drowning," Owen says. The poem ends like this:

> In all my dreams before my helpless sight
> He plunges at me, guttering, choking, drowning.
> If in some smothering dreams, you too could pace
> Behind the wagon that we flung him in,
> And watch the white eyes writhing in his face,
> His hanging face, like a devil's sick of sin;
> If you could hear, at every jolt, the blood
> Come gargling from the froth-corrupted lungs,
> Bitter as the cud
> Of vile, incurable sores on innocent tongues,—
> My friend, you would not tell with such high zest
> To children ardent for some desperate glory,
> The old Lie: Dulce et decorum est
> Pro patria mori.

There is a difficulty about drawing from all this a moral for ourselves. I imagine that we agree in our rejection of slavery, eternal damnation, genocide, and uncritical patriotic self-abnegation; so we shall agree that Huck Finn, Jonathan Edwards, Heinrich Himmler, and the poet Horace would all have done well to bring certain of their principles under severe pressure from ordinary human sympathies. But then we can say this because we can say that all those are bad moralities, whereas we cannot look at our own moralities and declare them bad. This is not arrogance: It is obviously incoherent for someone to declare the system of moral principles that he *accepts* to be *bad*, just as one cannot coherently say of anything that one *believes* it but it is *false*.

Still, although I can't point to any of my beliefs and say "That is false," I don't doubt that some of my beliefs *are* false; and so I should try to remain open to correction. Similarly, I accept every single item in my morality—that is inevitable—but I am sure that my morality could be improved, which is to say that it could undergo changes which I should be glad of once I had made them. So I must try to keep my morality open to revision, exposing it to whatever valid pressures there are—including pressures from my sympathies.

I don't give my sympathies a blank check in advance. In a conflict between principle and sympathy, principles ought sometimes to win. For example, I think it was right to take part in the Second World War on the allied side; there were many ghastly individual incidents which might have led someone to doubt the rightness of his participation in that war; and I think it would have been right for such a person to keep his sympathies in a subordinate place on those occasions, not allowing them to modify his principles in such a way as to make a pacifist of him.

Still, one's sympathies should be kept as sharp and sensitive and aware as possible, and not only because they can sometimes affect one's principles or one's conduct or both. Owen, at any rate, says that feelings and sympathies are vital even when they can do nothing but bring pain and distress. In another poem he speaks of the blessings of being numb in one's feelings: "Happy are the men who yet before they are killed/Can let their veins run cold," he says. These are the ones who do not suffer from any compassion which, as Owen puts it, "makes their feet/Sore on the alleys cobbled with their brothers." He contrasts these "happy" ones, who "lose all imagination," with himself and others "who with a thought besmirch/Blood over all our soul." Yet the poem's verdict goes against the "happy" ones. Owen does not say that they will act worse than the others whose souls are besmirched with blood because of their keen awareness of human suffering. He merely says that they are the losers because they have cut themselves off from the human condition:

> By choice they made themselves immune
> To pity and whatever moans in man
> Before the last sea and the hapless stars;
> Whatever mourns when many leave these shores;
> Whatever shares
> The eternal reciprocity of tears.

Utilitarianism
John Stuart Mill

John Stuart Mill (1806–1873) was one of the most important British philosophers of the nineteenth century, whose work was influential—and indeed, remains very influential—in ethics, logic, and political theory. Mill was also a political reformer, who was dedicated to many important social causes (such as improving and expanding public education in Great Britain, and reducing poverty and improving working conditions)—particularly the cause of promoting opportunities and equality for women. Jeremy Bentham was a close friend of Mill's father, and Bentham was the leading advocate of utilitarian ethics for that generation. Though Mill proposes a number of significant revisions to Bentham's earlier version of utilitarian ethics, Mill is a passionate defender of the utilitarian approach to ethical theory. The reading is excerpted from the seventh edition of Mill's *Utilitarianism* (1879); the original edition was published in 1861.

The creed which accepts as the foundation of morals, Utility, or the Greatest Happiness Principle, holds that actions are right in proportion as they tend to promote happiness, wrong as they tend to produce the reverse of happiness. By happiness is intended pleasure, and the absence of pain; by unhappiness, pain, and the privation of pleasure. To give a clear view of the moral standard set up by the theory, much more requires to be said; in particular, what things it includes in the ideas of pain and pleasure; and to what extent this is left an open question. But these supplementary explanations do not affect the theory of life on which this theory of morality is grounded—namely, that pleasure, and freedom from pain, are the only things desirable as ends; and that all desirable things (which are as numerous in the utilitarian as in any other scheme) are desirable either for the pleasure inherent in themselves, or as means to the promotion of pleasure and the prevention of pain.

Now, such a theory of life excites in many minds, and among them in some of the most estimable in feeling and purpose, inveterate dislike. To suppose that life has (as they express it) no higher end than pleasure—no better and nobler object of desire and pursuit—they designate as utterly mean and groveling; as a doctrine worthy only of swine, to whom the followers of Epicurus were, at a very early period, contemptuously likened; and modern holders of the doctrine are occasionally made the subject of equally polite comparisons by its German, French and English assailants.

When thus attacked, the Epicureans have always answered, that it is not they, but their accusers, who represent human nature in a degrading light; since the accusation supposes human beings to be capable of no pleasures except those of which swine are capable. If this supposition were true, the charge could not be gainsaid, but would then be no longer an imputation, for if the sources of pleasure were precisely the same to human beings and to swine, the rule of life which is good enough for the one would be good enough for the other. The comparison of the Epicurean life to that of beasts is felt as degrading, precisely because a beast's pleasures do not satisfy a human being's conceptions of happiness. Human beings have faculties more elevated than the animal appetites, and when once made conscious of them, do not regard anything as happiness which does not include their gratification. I do not, indeed, consider the Epicureans to have been by any means faultless in drawing out their scheme of consequences from the utilitarian principle. To do this in any sufficient manner, many Stoic, as well as Christian elements require to be included. But there is no known Epicurean theory of life which does not assign to the pleasures of the intellect, of the feelings and imagination, and of the moral sentiments, a much higher value as pleasures than to those of mere sensation. It must be admitted, however, that utilitarian writers in general have placed the superiority of mental over bodily pleasures chiefly in the greater permanency, safety, uncostliness, &c., of the former—that is, in their circumstantial advantages rather than in their intrinsic nature. And on all these points utilitarians have fully proved their case; but they might have taken the other, and, as it may be called, higher ground, with entire consistency. It is quite compatible with the principle of utility to recognise the fact, that some

kinds of pleasure are more desirable and more valuable than others. It would be absurd that while, in estimating all other things, quality is considered as well as quantity, the estimation of pleasures should be supposed to depend on quantity alone.

If I am asked, what I mean by difference of quality in pleasures, or what makes one pleasure more valuable than another, merely as a pleasure, except its being greater in amount, there is but one possible answer. Of two pleasures, if there be one to which all or almost all who have experience of both give a decided preference, irrespective of any feeling of moral obligation to prefer it, that is the more desirable pleasure. If one of the two is, by those who are competently acquainted with both, placed so far above the other that they prefer it, even though knowing it to be attended with a greater amount of discontent, and would not resign it for any quantity of the other pleasure which their nature is capable of, we are justified in ascribing to the preferred enjoyment a superiority in quality, so far outweighing quantity as to render it, in comparison, of small account.

Now it is an unquestionable fact that those who are equally acquainted with, and equally capable of appreciating and enjoying, both, do give a most marked preference to the manner of existence which employs their higher faculties. Few human creatures would consent to be changed into any of the lower animals, for a promise of the fullest allowance of a beast's pleasures; no intelligent human being would consent to be a fool, no instructed person would be an ignoramus, no person of feeling and conscience would be selfish and base, even though they should be persuaded that the fool, the dunce, or the rascal is better satisfied with his lot than they are with theirs. They would not resign what they possess more than he, for the most complete satisfaction of all the desires which they have in common with him. If they ever fancy they would, it is only in cases of unhappiness so extreme, that to escape from it they would exchange their lot for almost any other, however undesirable in their own eyes. A being of higher faculties requires more to make him happy, is capable probably of more acute suffering, and is certainly accessible to it at more points, than one of an inferior type; but in spite of these liabilities, he can never really wish to sink into what he feels to be a lower grade of existence. We may give what explanation we please of this unwillingness; we may attribute it to pride, a name which is given indiscriminately to some of the most and to some of the least estimable feelings of which mankind are capable; we may refer it to the love of liberty and personal independence, an appeal to which was with the Stoics one of the most effective means for the inculcation of it; to the love of power, or to the love of excitement, both of which do really enter into and contribute to it: but its most appropriate appellation is a sense of dignity, which all human beings possess in one form or other, and in some, though by no means in exact, proportion to their higher faculties, and which is so essential a part of the happiness of those in whom it is strong, that nothing which conflicts with it could be, otherwise than momentarily, an object of desire to them. Whoever supposes that this preference takes place at a sacrifice of happiness— that the superior being, in anything like equal circumstances, is not happier than the inferior— confounds the two very different ideas, of happiness, and content. It is indisputable that the being whose capacities of enjoyment are low, has the greatest chance of having them fully satisfied; and a highly endowed being will always feel that any happiness which he can look for, as the world is constituted, is imperfect. But he can learn to bear its imperfections, if they are at all bearable; and they will not make him envy the being who is indeed unconscious of the imperfections, but only because he feels not at all the good which those imperfections qualify. It is better to be a human being dissatisfied than a pig satisfied; better to be Socrates dissatisfied than a fool satisfied. And if the fool, or the pig, is of a different opinion, it is because they only know their own side of the question. The other party to the comparison knows both sides.

It may be objected, that many who are capable of the higher pleasures, occasionally, under the influence of temptation, postpone them to the lower. But this is quite compatible with a full appreciation of the intrinsic superiority of the higher. Men often, from infirmity of character, make their election for the nearer good, though they know it to be the less valuable; and this no less when the choice is between two bodily pleasures, than when it is between bodily and mental. They pursue sensual indulgences to the injury of health, though perfectly aware that health is the greater good. It may be further objected, that many who begin with youthful enthusiasm for everything noble, as they advance in years sink into indolence and selfishness. But I do not believe that those who undergo this very common change, voluntarily choose the lower description of pleasures in preference to the higher. I believe that before they devote themselves exclusively to the one, they have already become incapable of the other. Capacity for the nobler feelings is in most natures a very tender plant, easily killed, not only by hostile influences, but by mere want of sustenance; and in the majority of young persons it speedily dies away if the occupations to which their position in life has devoted them, and the society into which it has thrown them, are not favourable to keeping that higher capacity in exercise. Men lose their high aspirations as they lose their intellectual tastes, because they have not time or opportunity for indulging them; and they addict themselves to inferior pleasures, not because they deliberately prefer them, but because they are either the only ones to which they have access, or the only ones which they are any longer capable of enjoying. It may be questioned whether any one who has remained equally susceptible to both classes of pleasures, ever knowingly and calmly preferred the lower; though many, in all ages, have broken down in an ineffectual attempt to combine both.

From this verdict of the only competent judges, I apprehend there can be no appeal. On a question which is the best worth having of two pleasures, or which of two modes of existence is the most grateful to the feelings, apart from its moral attributes and from its consequences, the judgment of those who are qualified by knowledge of both, or, if they differ, that of the majority among them, must be admitted as final. And there needs be the less hesitation to accept this judgment respecting the quality of pleasures, since there is no other tribunal to be referred to even on the question of quantity. What means are there of determining which is the acutest of two pains, or the intensest of two pleasurable sensations, except the general suffrage of those who are familiar with both? Neither pains nor pleasures are homogeneous, and pain is always heterogeneous with pleasure. What is there to decide whether a particular pleasure is worth purchasing at the cost of a particular pain, except the feelings and judgment of the experienced? When, therefore, those feelings and judgment declare the pleasures derived from the higher faculties to be preferable in *kind*, apart from the question of intensity, to those of which the animal nature, disjoined from the higher faculties, is susceptible, they are entitled on this subject to the same regard.

I have dwelt on this point, as being a necessary part of a perfectly just conception of Utility or Happiness, considered as the directive rule of human conduct. But it is by no means an indispensable condition to the acceptance of the utilitarian standard; for that standard is not the agent's own greatest happiness, but the greatest amount of happiness altogether; and if it may possibly be doubted whether a noble character is always the happier for its nobleness, there can be no doubt that it makes other people happier, and that the world in general is immensely a gainer by it. Utilitarianism, therefore, could only attain its end by the general cultivation of nobleness of character, even if each individual were only benefited by the nobleness of others, and his own, so far as happiness is concerned, were a sheer deduction from the benefit. But the bare enunciation of such an absurdity as this last, renders refutation superfluous.

According to the Greatest Happiness Principle, as above explained, the ultimate end, with reference to and for the sake of which all other things are desirable (whether we are considering our own good or that of other people), is an existence exempt as far as possible from pain, and as rich as possible in enjoyments, both in point of quantity and quality; the test of quality, and the rule for measuring it against quantity, being the preference felt by those who, in their opportunities of experience, to which must be added their habits of self-consciousness and self-observation, are best furnished with the means of comparison. This, being, according to the utilitarian opinion, the end of human action, is necessarily also the standard of morality; which may accordingly be defined, the rules and precepts for human conduct, by the observance of which an existence such as has been described might be, to the greatest extent possible, secured to all mankind; and not to them only, but, so far as the nature of things admits, to the whole sentient creation. . . .

I must again repeat, what the assailants of utilitarianism seldom have the justice to acknowledge, that the happiness which forms the utilitarian standard of what is right in conduct, is not the agent's own happiness, but that of all concerned. As between his own happiness and that of others, utilitarianism requires him to be as strictly impartial as a disinterested and benevolent spectator. In the golden rule of Jesus of Nazareth, we read the complete spirit of the ethics of utility. To do as one would be done by, and to love one's neighbour as oneself, constitute the ideal perfection of utilitarian morality. As the means of making the nearest approach to this ideal, utility would enjoin, first, that laws and social arrangements should place the happiness, or (as speaking practically it may be called) the interest, of every individual, as nearly as possible in harmony with the interest of the whole; and secondly, that education and opinion, which have so vast a power over human character, should so use that power as to establish in the mind of every individual an indissoluble association between his own happiness and the good of the whole; especially between his own happiness and the practice of such modes of conduct, negative and positive, as regard for the universal happiness prescribes: so that not only he may be unable to conceive the possibility of happiness to himself, consistently with conduct opposed to the general good, but also that a direct impulse to promote the general good may be in every individual one of the habitual motives of action, and the sentiments connected therewith may fill a large and prominent place in every human being's sentient existence. If the impugners of the utilitarian morality represented it to their own minds in this its true character, I know not what recommendation possessed by any other morality they could possibly affirm to be wanting to it: what more beautiful or more exalted developments of human nature any other ethical system can be supposed to foster, or what springs of action, not accessible to the utilitarian, such systems rely on for giving effect to their mandates.

EXERCISES

1. Imagine someone who has *no* desire to help others, but who recognizes that the *moral law* requires offering help, and who then exerts will power and provides the morally required help. Kant would consider this person morally good (and far superior to one who helps from a pleasant *desire* to help others). Now suppose that there is someone who has a *strong desire* to torture little children, but who recognizes that the *moral law* prohibits torturing children, and who then exerts will power and *refrains* from torturing children. Would Kant regard such a person as morally superior to a person who does not torture children because he feels disgusted at the thought of torturing children? Or to rephrase the question: *Must* Kant, in order to be consistent, regard the person who must use will power to *refrain* from such torture as morally superior?

2. Kant insists that we must always treat others as ends in themselves, never as merely means to our ends. That means that it is alright to *hire* someone to build my house: I am hiring them as a means to my goal of having a house built, but (so long as I treat them honestly and respectfully as full persons) I am not treating them *merely* as a means to my ends. Suppose that we adopt a program of "guest workers," in which people from other countries (which would mean, primarily, people from poor Latin American countries) would be allowed to come to this country and work, but would *not* be allowed to become citizens, and would be required to leave after their work is done. Would such a policy violate Kant's categorical imperative to always treat others as ends in themselves?

3. Kant formulates two versions of his *categorical imperative*, though he claims that they are merely different formulations of the same principle. Would it be *possible* for someone to *consistently* hold the first imperative (always act in such a way that you could will that your act should be a universal law) but *deny* the second imperative (always treat others as ends-in-themselves, and never merely as means)?

4. Antonio R. Damasio is a neuropsychologist with a strong interest in the implications of neuropsychological research for questions of philosophy and ethics. In his *Descartes' Error* (New York: G. P. Putnam's Sons, 1994), Damasio describes the 1848 case of Phineas Gage, a pleasant, congenial, hard working, and very responsible man who suffered a severe brain injury that impaired his capacity to feel emotions. Though his intellectual abilities appeared to remain intact, Gage soon abandoned the positive moral life he had previously lived, becoming abrasive, impulsive, and violent.

   It's difficult to know exactly what happened to Gage, given the fact that his injury occurred over 150 years ago. But *suppose* that this (and other cases Damasio discusses) indicates that when people's emotional capacities are impaired, they generally become incapable of behaving morally. Kant, you remember, maintains that genuine moral behavior does not depend on emotions or feelings. Would such cases refute Kant? Would they provide *any* grounds for doubting Kant's position? How might Kant try to explain such cases?

5. Thomas Nagel, a contemporary Kantian, insists that it would be *irrational* to question our basic moral principles because of some finding in the social sciences: "Someone who abandons or qualifies his basic methods of moral reasoning on historical or anthropological grounds alone is nearly as irrational as someone who abandons a mathematical belief on other than mathematical grounds. . . . Moral considerations occupy a position in the system of thought that makes it illegitimate to subordinate them completely to anything else." According to Nagel, our mathematical system has its own system of justification and proof; therefore, if someone gave an anthropological account of how our mathematical system originated, that would not give us reason to reject our mathematical beliefs. Likewise, moral reasoning also has its own system of justification; and if someone gave a well-supported anthropological account of our moral principles, that should not cause us to question our moral system; for example, if an anthropologist proved that our cooperative ethical principles had their origins in tribal conflict, that would not be grounds for doubting our ethical views. Do you agree with Nagel? Can you imagine any findings in psychology or anthropology or biology that would cause you to abandon your *basic* approach to moral reasoning? (Of course, if scientists proved to us that trees have complex emotions and intricate systems of reasoning and felt agony when their branches were pruned, that would surely cause us to change *some* of our ethical beliefs: We would begin to consider our treatment of trees an ethical issue. But that wouldn't change our *basic* approach to ethical reasoning; rather, it would just enlarge the boundaries of ethical consideration.) Could *any* discovery in biology, psychology, or anthropology give us good grounds for changing our basic approach to ethics? Or, are Nagel and Kant right in maintaining that *no* scientific discovery could give us good grounds for revising our basic methods of ethical thinking?

6. You have very reliable information that a gang of terrorists is hiding in a small town in New Hampshire (don't worry about *how* you know this; you just know it). These terrorists are masters of secrecy and disguise, and you have no way of discovering who they are, and no way of isolating the town to make sure they do not leave. The gang is planning to release a poison gas that will kill thousands of people in a Midwestern city. The only way to prevent

this attack is to carpet bomb the small New Hampshire town, killing everyone there including the terrorists, but also including several hundred innocent people who have no idea there are terrorists in their midst. Would you be morally justified in bombing the town?

Do you have your answer? Look carefully at *how* you reached your answer. Were you guided by reason? Feelings? Both? Or what?

7. You are a member of the university chamber orchestra, which is on a weeklong spring concert tour through several Southern cities. One of your friends, J, is not along on the tour. J is not your dearest friend in the world, but is certainly a good friend. J's lover, K, is also on the tour. J and K have been lovers for over a year, and it seems to be a serious relationship; you wouldn't be surprised if they married next year after they graduate. You and K both play viola in the chamber orchestra, and you've spent a lot of time together on this trip. It's spring, the birds are singing, the bees are buzzing, and after a long cold winter it's great to be soaking up the warmth in the sunny South. As the week wears on, you realize you have become strongly attracted to K, and K apparently feels a reciprocal attraction. You have a private room at the hotel where you are staying, and if you ordered a bottle of champagne and invited K up to your room to watch a movie—well, the outcome is not difficult to imagine. Both you and K are very discreet, and it's unlikely J would learn about it. Would it be *wrong* to have a fling with K? Now compare the process you followed for answering Questions 6 and 7. Did you follow the same process in both cases? Or did you use different methods? Did your feelings play a larger role in one case than in the other?

Suppose someone says: "The first type of case must be answered using reason; but the second case is better handled through feelings." Would that make sense? Or do all ethical decisions require the same type of process (if feelings are important for one ethical question, then must they be important for all ethical questions)?

8. Psychologist Jonathan Haidt, in an article entitled "The Emotional Dog and Its Rational Tail" —*Psychological Review*, volume 108, number 4 (2001): 814–834, argues that "moral reasoning is rarely the direct cause of moral judgment"; instead, the moral decision is made immediately (or "intuitively"), and then moral reasoning is used to *justify* that decision. In Haidt's view, most moral reasoning occurs *after* the moral decision has already been made; we imagine that our moral decisions are based on reasoning, when in fact the reasoning comes along after the moral decision occurred. Typically, according to Haidt, the reasoning is used to *defend* our moral decision, not to *make* or *cause* the moral judgment. This is an area of psychological research in which there is still considerable controversy; but suppose for a moment that Haidt is correct. How much support would that give for Hume's view of ethics? Would it cause a major problem for the Kantian rationalist position? *If* someone claimed that this was strong evidence against the Kantian view, how might a Kantian respond?

9. "Feeding the hungry because you hope to gain reward—either an award as 'outstanding all-round student at North State University,' or treasure in heaven—is morally empty. Feeding the hungry because you believe it is your duty (and you do your duty, but you take no joy in it) is morally minimal. Feeding the hungry because you share their sorrow and rejoice in their comfort is to become a genuinely moral person." Would you agree or disagree?

10. Consider the statement in question 9. Would a utilitarian say that those are differences that make no difference, that the act is morally equivalent in all three cases? *Must* a utilitarian take that view?

11. "Acting morally is like swinging a golf club. When it seems easy, natural, and comfortable, then you know you have it right." Is that true? What would Kant think of that statement?

12. "Anyone who genuinely and profoundly *understands* what is right and what is wrong would never be tempted to do wrong." Is that true?

13. One objection to utilitarian ethics is that it turns everything into an ethical issue: If I spend an evening at a baseball game, but would have derived more pleasure from going to a concert, then I have committed a moral wrong. Nothing is exempt from moral evaluation. Is that a fair criticism?

14. One evening you get a call from the hospital. Your beloved old philosophy professor Ruth Zeno is near death and wishes to talk with you. You rush to the hospital. The attending physician confirms that Professor Zeno is indeed in her last hours. When you enter the room, your professor is there alone. She grasps your hand warmly and whispers to you that

she has a last request. From her bedside table she pulls out an old shoebox. She opens it, and you discover that it is stuffed with hundred-dollar bills. "There is almost half a million dollars in here," your professor says.

> "I have no relatives, no debts, no special obligations. The money is rightly mine, saved little by little during the course of my life. All the taxes have been paid. I want you to take this money and build a monument to my favorite racehorse, Run Dusty Run, in the infield at Pimlico racetrack. I'm certain the officials at Pimlico will give their permission. Run Dusty Run was my favorite racehorse. He wasn't a super horse, and few people remember him. But I cashed a nice bet on him once in Miami, and I loved that horse. He wasn't super fast, but he was always dead game, and he raced his heart out. I want you to take this money—no one else even knows the money exists—and spend every cent of it building a monument for Run Dusty Run. Hire a sculptor, and build a beautiful bronze monument in his honor. No tricks, okay? Don't put the money in a savings account, draw out the interest for 50 years, and then finally build the monument. And don't spend just 10 grand on the monument and use the rest for something else. Use all the money, as swiftly as possible, to build a monument to Run Dusty Run. I don't have long to live, and I need your answer quickly." Professor Zeno reaches over with her bony fingers and grasps your arm tightly, and her voice becomes raspy. "You were my favorite student, and I have always considered you a friend. Will you promise me, now, that you will spend the money and build the monument according to my wishes?"

Well, it seems a rather silly request. But then your dear old philosophy professor was always a rather strange bird, and you know that she dearly loved playing the ponies. And though her body is swiftly failing, her mind still seems to be clear and sharp. "Okay," you reply. "I promise. I'll build the monument exactly as you wish." Your professor smiles and relaxes her grip on your arm, and after a short conversation about the nature of time—always her favorite philosophical question—she slips into a quiet sleep, and within a few minutes her breathing stops. The doctor comes in and pronounces her dead.

You take the shoebox, filled with half a million bucks, leave the hospital, and head back to your apartment. "Where am I going to find a sculptor who does monuments for racehorses?" you think to yourself. And then some other thoughts cross your mind. "Nobody else knows about this money. I'm the only one who knows it exists, and I'm the only one who knows about Professor Zeno's weird request. Of course I should keep my promise . . . Or I *guess* I should keep my promise . . . Or really, *should* I keep the promise?"

"Certainly it can't matter any more to Professor Zeno. She's dead. If there is an afterlife, and she's sitting in heaven, then she's already as happy as she can possibly be, and one monument more or less won't change that. If she's in hell, then she's got more to worry about than a stupid monument. And if there's no afterlife, and she's simply dead and gone, then nothing I nor anyone else does will matter to her in the least. It's highly unlikely that Run Dusty Run will be happy about having a monument built in his honor. And as for the horseplayers at Pimlico, all they care about is trying to pick the winner of the next race. You could build an exact replica of the Taj Mahal on the infield of the track, and most of them wouldn't even notice. On the other hand, there's lots of wonderful things that could be done with half a million dollars. It could endow several generous scholarships at Professor Zeno's university. Or maybe add a much needed burn unit at the city hospital. Or start a lead-screening program in the city, and save many children from lead poisoning. That would be nice. We could call it the Zeno Scholarship, or the Zeno Burn Center. Those would be wonderful ways to use the money, ways that would really help people. In fact, it's hard to think of a more useless way to spend the money than by building that stupid monument.

"Of course, I did promise Professor Zeno, and I would be breaking my promise. But what's the harm in that? Professor Zeno certainly won't mind. And no one else will ever know about the promise (I can just say Professor Zeno instructed that the money be used for scholarships for needy philosophy students). So it's not like anyone will lose confidence in promising or the practice of promise-keeping. Of course I will know I broke my promise, but that won't make me feel guilty. Instead, I'll feel great about using Professor Zeno's money for a really good purpose. In fact, I would probably feel more guilty if I wasted the money on the stupid monument.

So when I think about it carefully, it seems clear that I ought to break the deathbed promise I made to Professor Zeno."

Do you agree with that conclusion?

It seems likely the student promiser in this case is an act-utilitarian. But what about your answer? Is it based on act-utilitarian ethics? Rule-utilitarian ethics? Kantian ethics? None of the above? (This question is loosely based on an example from the utilitarian ethicist, J. J. C. Smart.)

15. There is a spot open in Professor Ponder's film class. Your friends who have taken Professor Ponder's class all rave about it: "I really learned to appreciate the artistic potential of films by taking Professor Ponder's class. Before taking the class I liked almost every movie I saw. Now that I have learned from Professor Ponder how to understand and appreciate the fine nuances of the art of film-making, most of the movies I once enjoyed now strike me as stupid and amateurish. But because of my new appreciation of film, I now deeply enjoy a few great movies that otherwise I could never have appreciated. I have gained a depth of enjoyment from those few wonderful films I never dreamed you could get from watching a movie. Of course, it's very rare now that I enjoy going to the movies—most movies I see now strike me as dreadful, even painful to watch. But on the few occasions when I watch a really good movie—wow, that's a great experience. Take Professor Ponder's class: It will change forever your experience of going to the movies." If you think that is likely to be your own result from taking Professor Ponder's class, would you sign up? Does your answer support or does it challenge Mill's *quality of pleasure* version of utilitarianism?

16. Could a utilitarian who favors Mill's *qualitative* version of utilitarianism still be an egalitarian?

17. Kai Nielsen, a contemporary Canadian philosopher, notes that on some occasions the results of our consequentialist (utilitarian) calculations may conflict with our moral "common sense"; and Nielsen asserts that: "Given the comprehensiveness, plausibility, and overall rationality of consequentialism, it is not unreasonable to override even a deeply felt moral conviction if it does not square with such a theory. . . . ." Would you agree?

18. In Fall 2003, the Canadian Bar Association was formulating a new code of ethics. One of the issues they were considering was whether lawyers should be barred from sleeping with their clients. The code of ethics for doctors and psychologists prohibits sexual contact between professional and client/patient; should lawyers adopt the same principle?

The Canadian ethical code for lawyers requires that lawyers must always keep their clients' interests paramount. Also, lawyers acknowledge that at least sometimes clients are deeply dependent on their lawyers, and are very vulnerable, so there may exist a significant imbalance of power between lawyer and client. With those things in mind, the Canadian Bar Association considered four options. One, they could simply ignore the issue in the new code of ethics. Two, they could prohibit sexual relations in which the lawyer "takes advantage" of the client, by exploiting a difference in power. Three, they could prohibit sexual relations except when a consensual sexual relationship already exists *prior* to the lawyer/client relationship. Or four, they could prohibit *all* sexual relations between lawyer and client.

The Canadian Bar Association asked for advice in dealing with this issue. So give them your advice: What rule should they adopt? One of the four? Some other rule?

In making your recommendation, did you roughly follow one of the ethical models (utilitarian, rationalist, or Humean) that we have discussed? Did you use a combination of those methods?

19. It might seem that Kantians and utilitarians would usually reach the same conclusion on ethical issues, though by very different routes. For example, both are likely to condemn most cases of lying, though for quite different reasons. But in some cases their conclusions may be radically different. Suppose we are trying to make an ethical decision about who would be the best candidate for *non*therapeutic medical research. (*Therapeutic* research is an experimental procedure done because the physician judges it to be the best available treatment for this patient; for example, if I am suffering from a fatal disease for which no proven cure exists, and a new experimental treatment shows promise for perhaps saving my life, then my physician might recommend the experimental treatment for *therapeutic* purposes, as the best hope of curing me. Of course in carrying out the experimental treatment,

my physician may gain valuable knowledge about the new treatment, but the primary purpose is treating me, not gaining knowledge. In contrast, *non*therapeutic research is research—often performed on healthy subjects—that is designed primarily to gain knowledge, not to provide benefits for the experimental subject. For example, if we are testing a new arthritis drug to determine how humans metabolize it and what side effects it will produce in humans, we typically test the drug first on a small group of healthy subjects: subjects not suffering from arthritis. Later, of course, we shall also test the drug on arthritis patients; but in the early stages of testing on arthritis patients, the primary purpose will be to gain knowledge, not to provide therapy—though of course we hope there are some therapeutic benefits.) So suppose we are doing *non*therapeutic research on a powerful new drug that we *hope* will be effective in treating arthritis, and that we *fear* may have side effects and possibly pose some risks (we *believe* those risks are not severe—but we've never tested the drug on humans, so we aren't certain of that). From an *ethical* standpoint, who would be the best research subject? (This is not a question of who would give us the most *reliable* results, but rather who would it be most *ethically* acceptable to place at risk in carrying out this valuable medical experiment.) (This question is based on a Hans Jonas article concerning medical research.)

The utilitarian might say: Pick research subjects who are old and feeble, and who don't have long to live in any case. That way if something goes wrong, and the subject dies, at least we will not have killed someone who had many more years to live. Or do the experiment on someone dying of cancer: Their life expectancy is short anyway. (Obviously utilitarians might disagree, but this would not be an implausible answer for a utilitarian to give.)

The Kantian, in contrast, will probably say: Pick research subjects who are bright, alert, interested in scientific research, and dedicated to the goals of medical science. That way you are selecting people who are not being used as mere objects for research, but rather people who can identify with the purposes of the research (the Kantian insists that we must always treat people as ends-in-themselves, and that principle is more important than any consequences). For the Kantian, the *best* (ethically best) research subject would be the researcher herself: She obviously *identifies* with the research, agrees with the goal of the research, and is not being used as an object for someone else's purposes.

Is this a case in which Kantians and utilitarians must disagree? *Could* a utilitarian consistently favor selecting the younger, healthier medical personnel? Is this a case where ethical theory should trump "intuition" or "common sense"? Could there be such a case?

ADDITIONAL READING

Among general works on ethics, Peter Singer's edited work, *A Companion to Ethics* (Oxford: Blackwell Publishers, 1991), is a superb guide to many topics in ethical theory as well as applied ethics. An excellent collection of readings is edited by Hugh LaFollette: *The Blackwell Guide to Ethical Theory* (Oxford: Blackwell Publishers, 2000). Another collection of outstanding contemporary articles is Stephen Darwall, Allan Gibbard, and Peter Railton, eds., *Moral Discourse and Practice* (Oxford: Oxford University Press, 1997).

A superb ethics website is Ethics Update, run by Lawrence M. Hinman, Professor of Philosophy at the University of San Diego. It is a very comprehensive and easily navigated site with excellent links. It also offers a wide range of very good case studies, a nice collection of video lectures on ethics, and a great variety of papers on ethics (including a number of classic sources that are available online at the site). For almost any topic on ethics (especially applied ethics), this is a great place to start your internet inquiries. Go to http://ethics.sandiego.edu.

Stephen Darwall, formerly John Dewey Distinguished University Professor of philosophy at the University of Michigan and now the Andrew Downey Orrick Professor of Philosophy at Yale, has made the lecture notes for several of his classes available at his home page: www-personal.umich.edu/~sdarwall. The site contains excellent material on Hobbes, Hume, Kant, Bentham, and Mill.

David Hume has two classic works on ethics and emotions (though both works also contain much more). The first is *A Treatise of Human Nature*, originally published in 1738. A good edition is by L. A. Selby-Bigge (Oxford: Clarendon Press, 1978). The second is *An Inquiry Concerning Human Understanding*, originally published in 1751. A good edition is L. A. Selby-Bigge's *Hume's Enquiries*, 2nd ed. (Oxford: Clarendon Press, 1902).

Ty's David Hume Homepage is at http://www.cpm/ehime-u.ac.jp/AkamacHomePage/Akamac_E-text_Links/Hume.html. It is well organized, and contains extensive links.

Among Kant's classic works on ethics are *Groundwork of the Metaphysic of Morals*, translated by H. J. Paton, as *The Moral Law* (London: Hutchinson, 1953); *Critique of Practical Reason*, translated by L. W. Beck (Indianapolis: Bobbs-Merrill, 1977); and *Religion Within the Limits of Reason Alone*, translated by T. M. Greene and H. H. Hudson (New York: Harper and Row, 1960).

Excellent works on Kant's ethics include Lewis White Beck, *A Commentary on Kant's Critique of Practical Reason* (Chicago: University of Chicago Press, 1960); and Onora O'Neill, *Constructions of Reason: Explorations of Kant's Practical Philosophy* (Cambridge: Cambridge University Press, 1989). A fascinating brief challenge to Kant's ethical system is Rae Langton's "Maria von Herbert's Challenge to Kant," which can be found in Peter Singer, ed., *Ethics* (Oxford: Oxford University Press, 1994).

Many outstanding contemporary philosophers follow—to at least some degree—the Kantian tradition in ethics. A small sample would include Kurt Baier, *The Moral Point of View* (Ithaca, NY.: Cornell University Press, 1958); Stephen Darwall, *Impartial Reason* (Ithaca, NY: Cornell University Press, 1983); Alan Donagan, *The Theory of Morality* (Chicago: University of Chicago Press, 1977); and Thomas Nagel, *The View from Nowhere* (New York: Oxford University Press, 1986).

Kantian ethics can seem cold and austere. For a more engaging experience of Kantian ethics, try some essays by Thomas E. Hill, Jr., who is clearly a Kantian, but writes with grace, charm, and clarity on a variety of ethical issues. See his essays in *Respect, Pluralism, and Justice: Kantian Perspectives* (Oxford: Oxford University Press, 2000); and *Human Welfare and Moral Worth: Kantian Perspectives* (Oxford: Oxford University Press, 2002).

An excellent site for material on Immanuel Kant is "Kant on the Web," at www.hkbu.edu.hk/~ppp/Kant.html. It has very good links, including links to valuable information on teaching Kant's ethics.

The classic utilitarian writings are Jeremy Bentham, *An Introduction to the Principles of Morals and Legislation* (London, 1823) and John Stuart Mill, *Utilitarianism* (London, 1863). Perhaps the most influential contemporary utilitarian, and certainly one of the most readable, is Peter Singer. His *Writings on an Ethical Life* (New York: HarperCollins, 2000) is the work of a philosopher thinking carefully about ethical obligations, and also striving to live his life by the right ethical standards. Whatever one thinks of Singer's views—he holds very controversial positions on abortion, animal rights, the obligations of the affluent toward those who are less fortunate, and euthanasia, and has been the target of more protests than any other contemporary philosopher—not even his fiercest critics deny that Singer takes living ethically very seriously, and his *Writings on an Ethical Life* shows a dedicated utilitarian wrestling honestly with tough ethical questions. See also Singer's *Practical Ethics* (Cambridge: Cambridge University Press, 1979) for Singer's views on a variety of ethical issues.

For a critique of utilitarian ethics, see Samuel Scheffler, *The Rejection of Consequentialism* (Oxford: Clarendon Press, 1982). An excellent debate on utilitarian ethics can be found in J. J. C. Smart and Bernard Williams, *Utilitarianism: For and Against* (Cambridge: Cambridge University Press, 1973).

Michael Stocker, "The Schizophrenia of Modern Ethical Theories," *Journal of Philosophy*, volume 73 (1976): 453–466, offers a pointed critique of consequentialist views;

an interesting response is by Peter Railton, "Alienation, Consequentialism, and the Demands of Morality," *Philosophy and Public Affairs*, volume 13, number 2 (1984): 134–171. Bernard Williams' influential criticisms of utilitarianism can also be found in "Persons, Character, and Morality," in Bernard Williams, *Moral Luck* (Cambridge: Cambridge University Press, 1981). Elinor Mason, "Do Consequentialists Have One Thought Too Many?" *Ethical Theory and Moral Practice*, volume 2 (1999): 243–261, responds to some of the arguments by Williams and Stocker. Robert Nozick's pleasure machine argument (directed against one form of utilitarianism, and discussed by Railton) is found in *Anarchy, State, and Utopia* (New York: Basic Books, 1974), starting on page 42. A response to Nozick—along with other interesting essays on utilitarianism—can be found in Fred Feldman, *Utilitarianism, Hedonism, and Desert* (Cambridge: Cambridge University Press, 1997); see especially the essay "Two Questions About Pleasure."

Robert E. Goodin, "Utility and the Good," chapter 20 in Peter Singer, ed., *A Companion to Ethics* (Oxford: Blackwell, 1991): 241–248, offers a particularly clear account of the view that utilitarianism is best considered as a guide to public and legislative (rather than personal) ethics. See also Philip Pettit, "Consequentialism," pp. 230–240 in the same volume, for an excellent brief examination of contemporary consequentialism.

Michael Slote's conception of "satisficing consequentialism" can be found in "Satisficing Consequentialism," *Proceedings of the Aristotelian Society*, volume 58 (1984): 139–163; and *Common-Sense Morality and Consequentialism* (London: Routledge and Kegan Paul, 1985).

Among the many excellent anthologies on consequentialism and utilitarianism are Amartya Sen and Bernard Williams, eds., *Utilitarianism and Beyond* (Cambridge: Cambridge University Press, 1982); Samuel Scheffler, ed., *Consequentialism and Its Critics* (Oxford: Clarendon Press, 1988); Philip Pettit, *Consequentialism* (Aldershot, Hants: Dartmouth, 1993); Brad Hooker, Elinor Mason, and Dale E. Miller, eds., *Morality, Rules, and Consequences: A Critical Reader* (Lanham, Md.: Rowman & Littlefield, 2000); and Stephen Darwall, *Consequentialism* (Malden, Mass.: Blackwell, 2003).

Three Methods of Ethics: A Debate, edited by Marcia W. Baron, Philip Pettit, and Michael Slote (New York: Oxford University Press, 1993) is a well-argued debate among thoughtful and capable champions of Kantian, consequentialist, and virtue ethics.

Walter Sinnott-Armstrong provides an excellent account of contemporary consequentialism in the online *Stanford Encyclopedia of Philosophy*; go to http://plato.stanford.edu/entries/consequentialism.

For more information on utilitarianism, there are several interesting sites. http://www.laits.utexas.edu/poltheory/cuws/ is the Classical Utilitarianism website. It offers a variety of classic utilitarian writings, as well as some more recent papers. www.utilitarian.org/one.html is a site that promotes practical application of utilitarian principles. www.utilitarianism.com has a good collection of links to websites related to utilitarian ethics.

CHAPTER 12

ETHICAL THEORIES

DIVINE COMMAND THEORY OF ETHICS

In the book of *Exodus*, God delivers His famous ten commandments to the children of Israel; the eighth of those commandments is Thou shalt not steal. Okay, most would agree: Stealing is not a good thing. But if you are a believer in the God Who issued those commandments, consider this question: Did God command us not to steal because stealing is wrong? Or, is stealing wrong *because* God commanded us not to do it? That is, did God order us not to steal because God in His wisdom recognized the moral wrongness of stealing? Or, does stealing *become* wrong only because God commands us not to steal? Perhaps you've never thought about it quite like that; take a moment and consider it.

> The *Divine Command theory* of ethics is also called *theological voluntarism*, so called because it makes ethics depend entirely on what God wills, on God's voluntary choice. Something is good because God wills it, *not* because God recognizes it to be good. On this view, God's will or God's command is the whole of ethics: A law or principle is right if and only if it is willed or commanded by God.

For most people, the former answer is much more plausible: God commands us not to steal, because God in His great wisdom *knows* that it is wrong to steal, and thus commands us to follow the morally right path. But for some people, this raises serious problems: If God commands us not to steal because He recognizes that stealing is wrong, that implies there is a moral law *independent* of God, a moral law that God—as a moral being—*must* follow. But that runs counter to the idea of a majestic God Who creates *everything* (including the moral law) and Who is under *no* constraints. Martin Luther, the leader of the Protestant Reformation, vehemently rejected the idea of God being bound by principles of justice other than His own will: "What becomes of the power of the Potter to make what vessel He will, if He is controlled by merits and rules, and is not allowed to make as He would, but is required to make as He should?" (Martin Luther, *The Bondage of the Will*) This conception of God glorifies the power and greatness of God, contrasting God's glory with humankind's vile unworthiness. From this perspective, it is not surprising that God's moral law should sometimes appear strange and arbitrary to humans: Our role is not to *understand* God's ethical rules (the ways of God are far beyond our pathetic capacities) but only to *obey* them.

> "I do not feel obliged to believe that the same God who has endowed us with sense, reason, and intellect has intended us to forgo their use." *Galileo Galilei*

On the Divine Command view of ethics, it makes no sense to question whether God's moral laws are *good* or *just*; for there are no other moral standards to judge them by. What God commands *is* morally good, period. The deeply disturbing story of Abraham and Isaac seems to be written from a Divine Command perspective: God commands Abraham to

> Take now thy son, thine only son Isaac, whom thou lovest, and get thee into the land of Moriah; and offer him there for a burnt offering upon one of the mountains which I will tell thee of.

Abraham unquestioningly carries his son to the sacrificial altar, binds him, and takes up his knife to cut his throat. From the Divine Command perspective, God's cruel commandment is morally right, and Abraham's unquestioning obedience to that command is morally good. But that illustrates the fundamental problem for Divine Command ethics: Such ethical rules can be terribly arbitrary (one day God commands Thou shalt not kill, and killing is morally wrong; the next day God commands that Abraham kill Isaac, and killing becomes morally right). And from the Divine Command perspective, it would make no sense for Abraham to say: "Such a cruel command could *not* have come from God, for God is a God of justice." It makes no sense, because in the Divine Command account of ethics, there can be no judgments of *justice* other than what God commands.

> "A man's ethical behavior should be based effectually on sympathy, education, and social ties and needs; no religious basis is necessary. Man would indeed be in a poor way if he had to be restrained by fear of punishment and hope of reward after death." *Albert Einstein*, in *New York Times Magazine*, 9/11/1930

Suppose someone claims that "God commands us to make war on our neighboring state," or "God commands us to enslave all those of Italian descent." Before rushing into war or adopting slavery, we would want to be certain that these commandments actually come from *God*, and not someone merely claiming to speak for God. But if we are trying to decide whether these are *genuine* commandments from God, wouldn't a good test be whether the proposed commandments are *just*, whether they are *ethically sound?* That test is precisely what the Divine Command theory makes impossible.

So on the Divine Command theory of ethics, ethical principles will be—at least to our understanding—*arbitrary*. But that leads to a second objection to the Divine Command theory of ethics: It makes *human* ethical acts *impossible*. On the Divine Command model, we cannot attempt to *understand* what is right and wrong, and we cannot carefully deliberate about our moral obligations; rather, moral acts must consist entirely in the unreasoning adherence to arbitrary rules. Slavishly following rules is *not* acting ethically. One who unthinkingly follows another's moral dictates—whether that other is divine or mortal—is an automaton rather than an ethical *actor*.

> The divine command theory insists that whatever God commands is right. On that view, trying to evaluate God's commandments in the light of reason is hopeless, perhaps blasphemous. Thus many who favor the divine command theory reject all claims of *reason*, even regarding reliance on reason as profoundly wicked. Martin Luther, a fervent advocate of divine command ethics, offers a good example of such a view:
>
> > Reason is the devil's greatest whore; by nature and manner of being she is a noxious whore . . . who ought to be trodden underfoot and destroyed, and her wisdom. Martin Luther, Sermon at Wittenberg

There are those who claim there could be no ethics without God. From the Divine Command perspective on ethics, that is obviously true. But there are important objections to the Divine Command theory of ethics; and if we reject that theory, then ethics is *not* dependent on divine decree. For most, it will seem more plausible to judge claims that a commandment comes from God by its compliance with ethical principles, rather than attempting to base all ethical principles on divine commandments. That is not to suggest, of course, that religion has nothing to do with ethics. Some religions and religious teachers offer significant moral guidance: Jesus of Nazareth, for example, taught that the highest good is to provide food for the hungry, shelter for the homeless, and comfort for the afflicted; and that the greedy desire to accumulate great wealth is an impediment to living a good moral life, or indeed a good and satisfying life at all. Martin Luther King appealed to religious principles and religious teachings—we are all brothers and sisters, all equal, all children of God—to combat the racism and discrimination that was long dominant in the United States. But it is more reasonable to suppose that those are legitimate religious teachings (or divinely inspired) *because* they provide good moral guidance, rather than supposing that what is morally good is *whatever* is commanded by God. And from this perspective, you can evaluate the ethical teachings of Jesus quite independently of your judgment of his divinity.

RELATIVISM

Relativism comes in several varieties. Some philosophers use "relativism" to mean the view that all ethical principles are true or false only *relative* to a given system, and that the systems (or the basic principles of each system) cannot be proven or disproven; that is, all ethical systems are ultimately *nonobjective*. For example, given a basic egalitarian system of ethics, you can make all manner of true statements and logical connections *within* that system; but if you encounter a radically *different* system (such as an aristocratic or elitist system, which starts from the principle that some people are inherently better than others), then you cannot say that one system is true and the other false. Ultimately, all legitimate ethical claims are *system-relative*. That is one meaning of "relativism" in ethics; but it's rather confusing, because "relativism" has other meanings as well. A more convenient and more common term for that form of relativism is ethical *nonobjectivism*; and that's the term we'll use. Ethical nonobjectivism is an important view that will be closely examined in a later chapter. But for the moment, let's consider two other senses of "relativism."

"Relativism" is a very confusing term that is used in a variety of ways. It is sometimes used to mean that "all ethical judgments are relative," in the sense that *no* ethical judgments are genuinely *objective*; that is, *ultimately* there are *no objective moral truths*. In this sense of the term, "relativism" is a type of *ethical nonobjectivism*. A second, and very different, use of "relativism" is the *descriptive* use of the term by *sociologists* and *anthropologists*. "Sociological relativism" is simply the obvious and well-documented view that different cultures have different value systems: the dominant value system in contemporary Boston is not the value system that was in place in colonial times; and the value system in contemporary Boston is not the value system that is prevalent in the mountainous tribal regions of Afghanistan. *Sociological relativism* makes no judgment about whether that is a good or a bad thing, or about whether we *should* follow the rules and traditions of our culture; rather, it only notes the observable fact that different cultures do have different value systems. *Cultural relativism* is the view that what is morally *right*—what we *should* do—— is follow the rules and practices of the culture in which we live: the ethical rules of each culture are *ethically correct* within that culture, and it is ethically *wrong* to violate the ethical principles of the culture in which one is living.

Sociological relativism is the view that different cultures sometimes have different values. This claim is hardly controversial: The values held by tribal groups in the rugged mountains of Pakistan are quite different from the prevalent values in suburban Toronto; the values of an Amish community in rural Pennsylvania are not the same as the values held along the Miami Gold Coast. *Cultural relativism*, however, is a very different view, and it is considerably more controversial. Cultural relativists hold that ethical principles hold only *within* a given culture; the ethical principles and cultural practices of each culture are right *within* that culture; and ethical principles apply only within a culture, they are *culturally relative* rather than universal. However, *within* each culture, the culture's ethical principles are *right*.

Darius, after he had got the kingdom, called into his presence certain Greeks who were at hand, and asked "What he should pay them to eat the bodies of their fathers when they died?" To which they answered, that there was no sum that would tempt them to do such a thing. He then sent for certain Indians, of the race called Callatians, men who eat their fathers, and asked them, while the Greeks stood by . . . "What he should give them to burn the bodies of their fathers at their decease?" The Indians exclaimed aloud, and bade him forebear such language. Such is men's wont herein; and Pindar was right, in my judgment, when he said, "Custom is the king o'er all." *Herodotus*, 485–425 BCE (translated by George Rawlinson).

Cultural relativism has its charms and its benefits. It is a useful reminder that cultural practices are often quite complex, and outsiders should be very cautious in judging those practices and values without a thorough understanding of the culture. A practice that may look cruel to an outsider may serve an important function within the culture. For example, in a society based on hunting, the adults may eat more than their share, leaving the children somewhat hungry; but rather than an indication of cruelty to the children, this practice is based on the harsh necessities of their way of life: The hunters must keep up their strength in order to pursue game; and if they do not have sufficient strength for the chase, then the whole family will soon starve.

One reason for respecting cultural diversity rests on the observation that community membership, participation, and shared symbolism are important sources of human happiness and health, apart from any validity of the symbols with reference to science or to reality. *Kate Brown and Andrew Jameton*, "Culture, Healing, and Professional Obligations: Commentary," *Hastings Center Report* (1993).

Sociologists and anthropologists offer wise reminders that we should be very cautious about engaging in cultural reform, especially of cultures other than our own. Cultures are complex, and what may appear small and innocuous changes can turn out to be profoundly destructive. Though the Inuit of northern Canada had survived with a strong working culture for many traditions in a harsh climate, they appeared to be living hard lives in bitter conditions, and their children had little opportunity for formal education; with misguided concern for their well-being, the Canadian government made major "reforms" in the lives of these nomadic hunting tribes: housing them in small permanent buildings, giving them food, and cutting them off from their traditional way of life and the culture associated with it. The result was the destruction of their knowledge base and their sense of purpose and order and the promotion of helplessness; the eventual outcome was cultural breakdown, dependency, widespread depression, and alcoholism. And while "reform movements" always claim noble motives, many outsider "cultural reforms" are in fact designed for exploitation rather than benefit. The U.S. cultural "reform" for American Indians was designed to drive them off lands wanted by Whites and move them to regions of marginal land where they would be weakened; and the "cultural reform" of the "Indian schools" in the United States and Canada was designed not to reform but to destroy the indigenous cultures, by taking the children away and forbidding them to learn native languages or customs. "Cultural reform" in central America was designed to force peasants off their lands, so that those farming areas could be turned into vast plantations for large international corporations, and the peasants—who were once small independent self-sustaining farmers—turned into virtual slaves for those plantations. Violently imposed "cultural reform" in the Middle East may be motivated more by theft of oil than cultural improvement.

Cultural relativism may be useful in reminding us of the complex nature of cultures, and the perils of judging them from the outside; but as an ethical theory, it encounters some significant problems. The first of those problems, in our wonderfully multicultural world, is that often we simultaneously live in *many* cultures: The culture of your college may be quite different from the culture of your home town; the culture of your local neighborhood—particularly if it has a strong ethnic identity—may be quite distinct from the larger culture of your city or region, and of course your region may have a culture that is quite different from the larger culture of the nation. Being a good cultural relativist will be tough. If you are an Orthodox Jew living in North Carolina—where eating barbecued pork is almost a sacrament—should you (by cultural relativist principles) eat pork? Which "cultural rules" should you follow when they are in conflict?

An even more severe problem for cultural relativism is that it morally condemns all efforts at cultural reform. When Martin Luther King struggled against U.S. racism, his acts were (by cultural relativist standards) *morally wrong*, because the cultural tradition was strongly racist. When Susan B. Anthony battled for the rights of women, she was battling against a deeply entrenched cultural tradition, and so her reform efforts violated cultural relativist ethics. When Gandhi campaigned against the ancient Indian tradition of strict castes and the terribly mistreated "untouchables," he was (for cultural relativists) a moral reprobate. Any ethical theory that automatically condemns all efforts at ethical improvement is an ethical theory that has serious shortcomings.

Even if we reject the basic ethical theory of cultural relativism, there are important points to be learned from those who have held such views: Cultures are complex, and should be treated with caution and respect; cultural identity is of great importance for our social and psychological well-being. Thus, some anthropologists—such as Clifford Geertz and Elvin Hatch—champion "anti-antirelativism." They note that often those who are strongly *opposed* to relativism (the "antirelativists") hold simplistic absolutist views that condemn and interfere with other cultures without understanding their value and their complexity, and the results are often catastrophic. But recognizing the value of culture, and the danger of interfering in cultural practices, does not mean that we must regard all cultural practices as morally legitimate within that culture. If you say *tomato*, and I say *tomahto*, and what I call an elevator you call a lift, that is charming; if you like spices and I prefer bland, that's no problem. But if your culture endorses slavery, or maintains that women have no rights, or believes that homosexuals should be killed, then those are *not* differences that can be regarded with benign tolerance. Even if we conclude that attempts by outsiders to *reform* the culture would do more harm than good, we may still judge those cultural practices as egregiously wrong.

EGOISM

Like relativism, "egoism" describes two very different theories; and again like relativism, one of those theories is *descriptive*, while the other is *prescriptive*. Sociological relativism, you remember, is the sociological thesis that different cultures have different values. That's a *descriptive* claim. It makes a factual claim about the world, it *describes* (correctly or incorrectly) the way the world is. In contrast, *cultural* relativism is *prescriptive*: It claims that right and wrong are *relative to culture*, that we *should* follow the rules and practices of the culture in which we live. Likewise, egoism comes in two distinct varieties. *Psychological* egoism is a *descriptive* theory, which claims that in *fact* all people act strictly for their *own benefit*; in other words, it is a psychological theory that claims that everyone is fundamentally *selfish*. *Ethical egoism* is a *prescriptive* theory, asserting that all people *should* seek exclusively their own interests, that selfishness is a virtue. It is obviously possible to be a psychological egoist while rejecting ethical egoism; that is, you might believe that everyone *is* selfish, but regard that as ethically unfortunate, since you believe people *should not* be selfish. And from the other direction, you might be an ethical egoist and believe that people *should* look out only for number one, but believe that in fact people do *not* act with sufficient selfishness (Ayn Rand seems to hold some such view). If you are *both* a psychological and an ethical egoist, you probably regard the world as a wonderful place: *Everyone* always lives as they morally *should* because everyone invariably acts selfishly.

Egoism is a term used for two very different claims, and with two very different meanings. *Psychological egoism* is a claim about the psychological nature of human beings: the claim that all humans always act selfishly. Psychological egoism passes no moral judgment on selfishness; it's like saying that all humans are mammals: that's not a moral judgment, but a claim about the biological nature of humans. The plausibility or implausibility of psychological egoism is a question for psychologists and biologists, not ethicists. *Ethical egoism* means something else entirely: it does *not* claim that all humans *are* selfish, but asserts instead that everyone *should* be selfish; that selfishness is morally good, and unselfish behavior is morally bad.

When viewed from a certain angle, psychological egoism can seem obvious, even beyond question. After all, it is clear that we often pursue our own interests, and counterexamples can be explained away: What about my good friend Jennifer, who gave up her long awaited trip to the beach to sit in my hospital room and read to me after my auto accident? Well, obviously, Jennifer is the sort of person who takes more pleasure in reading to her friends than in going to the beach. But what about Joe, who used the money he had saved for a new car to aid the victims of Hurricane Katrina and spent his spring break volunteering at a shelter in New Orleans? Joe found greater satisfaction in helping those people than he would have found from a new car, so clearly he was still acting selfishly. Okay, what about my dear old Mother, who spent long sleepless nights cooling my fevered brow and taking care of me? Well, your mom was doing what she selfishly wanted to do: She wanted to care for you more than she wanted to rest. So Jennifer, Joe, and your Mom were acting selfishly after all. But such easy "explanations" for every case should raise our suspicions. After all, *psychological* egoism is supposed to be an empirical *descriptive* thesis: a claim about the world, *not* merely a stipulative definition. So what *would* count as an unselfish act? If the psychological egoist claims that such acts are not *possible*, that *nothing* would count, then psychological egoism is no longer a claim about the world at all, but only a special definition.

Suppose I claim that no penguins can fly. That's a real claim about the world and what exists (and does not exist) in the world; and it is easy to state what would prove that claim *false*. Show me an aerodynamic penguin soaring through the air, and I'll give up my claim. But suppose you show me a penguin—confirmed as a penguin by careful DNA analysis, the offspring of two perfectly respectable flightless penguins—that flies gracefully, soaring about like a seagull; and I *refuse* to give up my claim: "That's not a real penguin," I say, "because no real penguin can fly." At that point my claim is no longer an empirical factual claim about penguins, but rather a special *definition* of penguinness. Likewise, if *nothing* could count as an *unselfish* act, the claim that everyone acts selfishly is no longer a factual claim about human behavior, but instead a special and rather strange *definition* or stipulation. And indeed it *is* a rather strange definition. After all, when people do things out of kindness and concern for others and find it *satisfying* to act generously, then we normally count those as acts of *generosity*, not selfishness. Of course, if I do generous deeds only because I want to win an award for generosity, or because I want to earn my Boy Scout merit badge for generosity, or only because I believe that God will give me vast rewards in return for my small acts of kindness, then there would be legitimate doubts about whether my behavior is genuinely generous rather than selfish. But when the only motive is helping others in need and one finds such generous acts deeply satisfying, that is a standard example of generosity, not selfishness; and it requires a contorted special definition of "selfishness" to categorize such acts as selfish.

At first glance, psychological egoism may seem to be a tough-minded realism, but it doesn't hold up well under close scrutiny. We are a profoundly social and socially dependent species, and our survival—especially of our young—requires extensive mutual support and cooperation; thus, it would be very surprising if individually we were as exclusively self-interested as psychological egoists claim. But what about the *prescriptive* hypothesis of *ethical* egoism: the view that all people *should* act for their own selfish interests? How plausible is that?

Ethical egoism certainly has its charms. After all, there is a certain appeal about a view that tells you that when you act selfishly, never help your friends nor anyone else, and seek *only* what is of benefit to you and you alone, then you are actually acting *virtuously*. That would be like discovering that hot fudge sundaes are a health food. "I've got mine, and I'm going to keep getting as much as I can get, and the concerns and needs and suffering of others don't matter." Obviously, there are people who act that way; but why should anyone suppose that they are acting morally or living virtuous lives?

What grounds could one give for supposing that ethical egoism is the correct ethical theory? Most ethical egoists fall back on asserting that we always *do* act selfishly; but as already noted, that confuses the *descriptive* thesis of psychological egoism with the *prescriptive* claim of *ethical* egoism. Even if psychological egoism were a plausible *descriptive* theory, that would provide no prescriptive support.

Disengagement is absolutely necessary to enjoyment: and a person may have so steady and fixed an eye upon his own interest, whatever he places it in, as may hinder him from *attending* to many gratifications within his reach, which others have their minds *free* and *open* to. Over-fondness for a child is not generally thought to be for its advantage: and, if there be any guess to be made from appearances, surely that character we call selfish is not the most promising for happiness. Such a temper may plainly be, and exert itself in a degree and manner which may give unnecessary and useless solicitude and anxiety, in a degree and manner which may prevent obtaining the means and materials of enjoyment, as well as the making use of them. Immoderate self-love, does very ill consult its own interest: and how much soever a paradox it may appear, it is certainly true, that even from self-love we should endeavour to get over all inordinate regard to, and consideration of ourselves. *Joseph Butler (1692–1752), Sermon XI, Fifteen Sermons*

The most common justification for *ethical* egoism is a crude sort of *social Darwinism*: When everyone strives for individual gain, showing no pity for the weak, then those special strongest, most talented individuals will rise to the top and make the world—and our species—better; the weaker and unfit will be weeded out. So, a pitiless selfishness is the best path to individual success for the strongest and most talented, and the success of those stronger individuals is natural and right. Nature is cruel, but it is that cruel process—nature red in tooth and claw—that makes us better and puts the best people at the top. This is a view that has charms for those who enjoy great success: It frees them of any obligation to share with those who are less fortunate, and it affirms their right to a position at the top—and it helps them forget that their success may have come more from inherited wealth, a privileged early environment and education, and supportive family and community connections than from their own outstanding individual qualities. (Jim Hightower, former Texas Commissioner of Agriculture, used to say of George Bush that "He was born on third base, and now he thinks he hit a triple.") If you, individually, make a great scientific discovery, you must use the vast store of scientific knowledge gained over many generations with the support of the entire society; and your education, which enabled you to make the discovery, was the cooperative work of the entire society that provided and educated your teachers, published the books you studied, and maintained the social and economic and knowledge structure that made it all possible. There have been many brilliant individual scientists, but very few of them were raised by wolves, and none made their discoveries without the benefits of the supportive society in which they lived.

SOCIAL CONTRACT ETHICS

Perhaps we don't find ethical truths, nor reason our way to them, nor get them handed down by God; rather we *make* them ourselves. This is basically the *social contract* view of ethics: There is no ethics other than what we *make* as a social system of rules that is socially enforced. This type of view is sometimes called the *constructivist* approach to ethics: Ethics is not a natural phenomenon, not something we discover, not something handed to us or intuited or deduced by rational processes; rather it is something *we construct*, as social animals in need of a system of rules to control our behavior with one another.

Social Contract Ethics refers to ethical systems in which the principles and rules of ethics are set by general enforced *agreement* among those who live under those rules. Though social contract ethics comes in a variety of forms, the basic idea is this: The rules of ethics are rules that *we make*. Social contract theorists sometimes believe that we have ethical feelings or inclinations *prior* to or independently of the social contract, but all hold that the basic principles of ethics are *constructed* by human agreement and consent. Thus social contract ethics is sometimes called a *constructivist* view of ethics: ethics is *made*, not discovered.

Social contract theory is primarily a political theory, and it has played a prominent role in Western political thought. But it also contains an ethical theory that parallels the political account. Why should we obey the laws of our government? Not because a divinely anointed king commands them, but because we have agreed to them. We *contracted* to follow the laws, because we consider it in our interest to do so. A legitimate government (according to this view) governs only by the *consent* or agreement of the governed. Likewise, we agree to follow the ethical rules because we agree or contract with others to abide by a set of rules, from our own self-interest. Without a social contract, there is no legitimate government and no legitimate laws. And in the ethical version of social contract theory, without an agreed-upon contract there are no ethical rules: Rules of ethics exist only because we *make* them and agree with others to follow them.

> Our societies are based on the mammalian plan: the individual strives for personal reproductive success foremost and that of his immediate kin secondarily; further grudging cooperation represents a compromise struck in order to enjoy the benefits of group membership. *Sociobiologist E. O. Wilson*

Thomas Hobbes, a British philosopher of the seventeenth century, is the key modern source for social contract theory. The idea had been around long before Hobbes (the ancient Greeks proposed some social contract ideas), but it was Hobbes who developed social contract theory in detail. Hobbes starts his account with humans living in the *state of nature*, in which there is a war of all against all, "of every man, against every man." In this state of nature, there is a "continual fear and danger of violent death," and our lives are "solitary, poor, nasty, brutish, and short." In the state of nature, you must be constantly on your guard against others, and always be ready to strike the first blow. The person you encounter might *look* harmless, but he or she is always a potential threat, and so you must disable or kill that possible foe in order to prevent a later attack. And even if you are the strongest and most feared individual, you will also live a short brutish life of continual fear; for you must sleep, and then even your weakest foe can kill you. And indeed, if you are strong and dangerous, you will be a particularly attractive target in your slumber, since all those around you will fear future attacks.

> Social contract *practices* were developed in very complex and impressive form by the Iroquois Confederation, starting approximately 1450; and the Iroquois social contract also influenced the social contract model of government drawn up by the 13 American colonies following the American Revolution.

In such circumstances, even the strongest would be glad to sign a nonaggression pact: If you won't attack me, then I won't attack you. That is, we all realize that we would be better off agreeing not to rob and kill others if we can get a guarantee—enforced by the whole society—that we ourselves will not be harmed by others. And *that* is the basic idea of social contract ethics: We *agree*, for our *own self-interests*, to follow some basic moral rules: Essentially, we agree not to harm others in our society on the condition that they will also refrain from harming us. That may be a rather minimal ethics, but note this: It is an ethics constructed with *no* appeal to generous impulses, ethical intuitions, divine commandments, rational principles, or warm and fuzzy feelings. To the contrary, Hobbes starts from the view that human nature is brutal and selfish. In the state of nature, without social rules and constraints, we fight and kill and pillage. Our *natural* state is nasty and brutish. But even starting from this dark, harsh, pessimistic view of humankind, Hobbes is able to show that social cooperation in accordance with enforced rules is advantageous: adopting and following some basic moral rules is to our own selfish advantage. Thus, a moral system can be justified with *no* appeal to divine law or natural virtue or human generosity.

> A rather harsh view of the social contract was set forth by Herbert George Wells, in *Love and Mr. Lewisham*, 1899:
>
> > The Social Contract is nothing more or less than a vast conspiracy of human beings to lie to and humbug themselves and one another for the general Good. Lies are the mortar that bind the savage individual man into the social masonry.

Of course, humans never lived such brutal, solitary lives. We are profoundly social, and our young require extensive protection and care, and it is only by social cooperation that we humans—comparatively weak and slow and lacking sharp claws for attack or a bony exoskeleton for defense—were able to survive and raise our offspring. But Hobbes is not offering a historical or anthropological account of the development of human society and ethical systems. Rather, he is arguing that even from the harshest and narrowest self-interest perspective, we can still create a system of ethical rules that we will each accept as reasonable and advantageous. Of course, these aren't the rules I would choose if I got to draw them up all by myself. I would favor some rules such as I get to cheat, rob, and assault others whenever I wish, but no one can cheat, rob, or assault me. I might think those rules are peachy, but obviously no one else would agree to them. But if we all get together as intelligent self-interested individuals, we can *construct* and agree on general rules—*no one* is allowed to cheat, rob, assault, or kill anyone else in the society—that we each find reasonable and advantageous. That is, as each of us tries to get the best deal he or she can get, we can reach an agreement that each of us will consider worthwhile.

In the late twentieth century, John Rawls took social contract ethics to a new level. Social contract theorists had pushed the idea of a social contract to show that even narrowly self-interested individuals could find good reasons to support a system of moral rules. Rawls used social contract theory to establish standards for a *just* and *fair* society. Instead of thinking about what rules you would adopt if you were sitting down with others to draw up a social contract, think about what rules you would adopt if you did not know who *you* were. Imagine that you are drawing up the rules for the society you will be living in, but you must draw up those rules before you know anything about what sort of person you will be in that society. You know that you will be a human, with the standard desires, fears, needs, and vulnerabilities. But you have no idea about your race, gender, or ethnic group; you don't know whether you will be robustly healthy or severely disabled, whether you will be smart or stupid, industrious or lethargic, religious or skeptical, liberal or conservative. You don't know whether you will like philosophy or physics or poetry, whether you will have great musical genius or a tin ear, whether you will be able to run fast, slow, or not at all. And you don't know whether you will be born into a wealthy family in this society, or born into the poorest family. Under those circumstances—behind what Rawls calls the "veil of ignorance"—what rules would you adopt for this society you will enter? I might be tempted to make a rule that only white male heterosexual philosophers can be rulers; but then I recall that I might be a black woman lesbian physicist, and decide that such a rule would not be such a great idea. I might consider a rule that only my religion—which, after all, is the true religion—can be practiced; but then I remember that I might hold different religious views in this new society, and then I would be deprived of religious liberty. So from behind the veil of ignorance, with no knowledge of your particular characteristics or situation, what societal rules would you favor? I would want freedom of speech and freedom of religion; for while it might be great fun to suppress the speech and religion of those I oppose, it would be much worse to be the one whose speech and beliefs are suppressed—and that might be my situation. I would want genuine opportunities for developing my talents and abilities—and so (since I might be the poorest kid in the society) I would insist that everyone have an opportunity for an excellent education. And I might go further. I don't know if I'll be rich or poor in this new society. Certainly, it would be nice to live in a mansion with 20 bedrooms, eating luxurious multicourse dinners; but it would be awful to be homeless and hungry. So recognizing the possibility of being one of the poorest people in this new society, I might insist on a rule that *everyone* gets decent housing and sufficient food before *anyone* gets luxuries.

A practice is just if it is in accordance with the principles which all who participate in it might reasonably be expected to propose or to acknowledge before one another when they are similarly circumstanced and required to make a firm commitment in advance without knowledge of what will be their peculiar condition, and thus when it meets standards which the parties could accept as fair should occasion arise for them to debate its merits. Regarding the participants themselves, once persons knowingly engage in a practice which they acknowledge to be fair and accept the benefits of doing so, they are bound by the duty of fair play to follow the rules when it comes their turn to do so, and this implies a limitation on their pursuit of self-interest in particular cases. *John Rawls, A Theory of Justice* (1971)

So here's the basic idea of Rawls' version of social contract theory: Consider what kind of society and what kinds of ethical rules you would favor if you could strip yourself of all prejudices and biases and special interests (think of what you would favor from behind the *veil of ignorance*), and you will arrive at standards and rules and policies that are *genuinely fair*. Think of when you were a kid, and you had a delicious pizza to divide up among six hungry friends. How could you make sure the division was fair? Just make sure that the person cutting the pizza into slices gets *last choice*; or alternatively, assign the pizza slices randomly, so the person slicing the pizza doesn't know which slice she will get. In that case, the pizza slices might not be identical, but everyone will agree that the process was *fair*. Take a look at our own society: Would you be willing to roll the dice and take a chance on being the person who is worst off in our society? If not, that raises serious questions about whether our society is fair and just. So social contract theory, especially in the hands of contemporary social contract theorists such as Rawls, can be a very useful tool for pushing us to look hard at what rules and social structures are genuinely just.

Social contract ethics has it charms and its advocates, but it also has its critics. The point of social contract ethics is to show that even purely self-interested individuals can find good reasons for adopting and following a moral system. One of the main criticisms of social contract ethics is precisely that foundation of narrow *individualism*. Of course, social contract ethicists don't suppose we are actually just narrowly self-interested individuals: Even the most adamant social contract theorist is well aware of having been raised in a family and a community, and being long dependent on their nurturing and protection. Still, social contract theory posits the purely self-interested individual as the basic starting point of ethical theory, and thus (the critics of social contract ethics argue) social contract ethics entrenches the idea that as ethical agents we *start* from a position of strict individual self-interest. Critics of social contract ethics maintain that such a starting point fatally distorts our ethical perspective: Ethics starts at home, and social contract ethics neglects and devalues that essential ethical domain.

Martha Nussbaum is a powerful critic of social contract theory, and one of her strongest criticisms is that the very logic of social contract ethics marginalizes the severely disabled:

> the idea [basic to social contract theory] is that people will get together with others and contract for basic political principles only in certain circumstances, circumstances in which they can expect mutual benefit and in which all stand to gain from the cooperation. To include in the initial situation people who are unusually expensive or who can be expected to contribute far less than most to the well-being of the group . . . would run contrary to the logic of the whole exercise. If people are making a cooperative arrangement for mutual advantage, they will want to get together with those from cooperation with whom they may expect to gain, not those who will demand unusual and expensive attention without contributing anything much to the social product, thus depressing the level of society's well-being. (Nussbaum, p. 104)

Social contract ethics (say its critics) is an ethics for *strangers*, an ethics for the impersonal marketplace or legislature. Obviously, we need ethics in the marketplace and legislature; indeed, given the high level of financial and governmental corruption, it's clear that we need a good deal more ethical reflection in those spheres. But ethics doesn't start in the impersonal marketplace; it is developed and sustained in caring relationships within families and among friends. And relations with friends and family are very different from those of the marketplace. Social contract ethics is an ethics for individuals in a competitive setting: a market type of setting, in which everyone is working to maximize his or her own advantage. Our relation with our friends and family is very different: a relationship of support and nurturing and cooperation rather than competition and contracts. Occasionally a mother "goes on strike," or parents demand that children sign a "contract" not to drink or engage in sexual intercourse or use drugs. The news media give such cases considerable attention, but only because they are so *different* from the norm of loving rather than contractual family relations. When families must resort to contracts, it is a sign of a dysfunctional family, in which marketplace rules provide a poor substitute for relations of cooperative mutual affection. When you and your lover start bargaining to settle differences and counting who owes what favor to whom, then you know that the affectionate basis of your relationship is in serious jeopardy. And it is in the family, and later in relations with friends and lovers, that we develop the capacity for cooperation and affection that forms the essential foundation for ethical behavior. Whatever the benefits of the market, that is *not* where you developed your essential capacity for ethical behavior; to the contrary, the ability to form cooperative social contract relationships requires at least a minimally decent ethical upbringing. Sociopaths are not good partners for social contracting. If we treat the social contract as the central element of ethics, then we must devalue, deny, or ignore the very different ethical relationships among friends and family.

A second criticism of social contract ethics is closely related to the first. Ethics is for rough equals: those who pose threats and can reciprocate benefits and maintain agreements. But small children are not rough equals, and neither are the frail elderly. A large and very important part of our lives is spent as vulnerable children, as nurturing parents of small children, as weakened elderly persons, and as caregivers for aged loved ones. To base an ethical system on only one dimension of our lives—our lives as competent adults in impersonal interaction with other adults—results in an ethical system that is blind to some of the most important aspects of our lives.

The final criticism of social contract ethics is implicit in the first two, and is perhaps the most basic: Social contract ethics conceptualizes humans as radically individual self-interested independent operators, and thus it is based on a profoundly *false* view of human behavior and human needs. We don't start as atomic individuals, but rather as members of social groups; and we don't start as tough fighters but as very vulnerable small persons. The model implies that our "natural" state is as isolated individuals; but of course we are a profoundly social species (being placed in solitary confinement is a very harsh form of punishment, which can have long-term debilitating psychological effects). Those who favor social contract ethics will respond that it is *not* a psychological or sociological theory, but instead an account of how we could justify ethics with the minimum material to work from: Even if we *were* harshly impersonal self-seeking individuals with no commitment to family or community, we could *still* justify a substantive set of ethical principles. Critics still insist that social contract ethics paints a very misleading picture of the whole ethical enterprise as it involves human social animals, and that it ignores or obscures some vital elements of our ethical lives.

CARE ETHICS

Proponents of *care ethics* are prominent among the critics of social contract ethics, and that is hardly surprising. Social contract ethics starts from the assumption of radically independent self-interested individuals, while care ethicists believe that such a starting point turns ethics upside down. Ethics (the care ethicists insist) is rooted in care, affection, and personal relationships. Ethical rules have their place, especially in the impersonal interactions of our social lives: in the marketplace, the halls of the legislature, the courtroom, the city planning commission, driving along city streets. But the foundation and heart of ethics is in our relations of care and friendship and affection, among our families and friends and lovers.

> Care ethics is sometimes called *feminist* ethics, but "care ethics" is probably a better name. In the first place, some of the leading care ethicists have been men (such as Lawrence Blum), and many women philosophers reject care ethics (Christine Korsgaard is a major contemporary advocate of the Kantian view, which is in fundamental conflict with care ethics). And though obviously not all women are feminists, and men certainly can be supporters of feminism, there is clearly potential for confusion. A second reason for preferring the name "care ethics" is that a number of strong feminist writers are vigorously opposed to the idea of any distinctively "feminist" ethics; for example, Jean Grimshaw:
>
>> If ethical concerns and priorities arise from different forms of social life, then those which have emerged from a social system in which women have so often been subordinate to men must be suspect. Supposedly 'female' values are not only the subject of little agreement among women: they are also deeply mired in conceptions of 'the feminine' which depend on the sort of polarization between 'masculine' and 'feminine' which has itself been so closely related to the subordination of women. There is no autonomous realm of female values, or of female activities which can generate 'alternative' values to those of the public sphere; and any conception of a 'female ethic' which depends on these ideas cannot, I think, be a viable one

The difference between care ethics and the impersonal Kantian or social contract or utilitarian ethics can be seen in the contrasting views of two psychologists researching moral development: Lawrence Kohlberg and Carol Gilligan. Kohlberg was the lead researcher for a long-term study of moral development, tracing the moral views of a number of children as they matured through adolescence, their college-age years, and on into the next decade. The research focused on a story about a man named Heinz, whose sick wife desperately needed a rare and expensive drug. Heinz could not afford to buy the drug, and the pharmacist would not give it to him; what should Heinz do? Over the years the research subjects gave their reactions to this story, and told what they thought Heinz should do, and why.

> "Care ethics" is not easily defined, as it designates a large group of ethical theorists who differ on various details of their views. While the following are perhaps not *defining* characteristics of care ethics, they are views that are widely shared among this group: Personal relations—that cannot be adequately captured by abstract universal rules—are a very important part of ethics; many important ethical issues are *situated*, and the details of the situation are of vital importance in determining what act is right (if we try to decide what is right by thinking of the people involved as abstract entities, then we will neglect important ethical considerations); feelings of affection and care are the vital starting points of ethics, and questions of how such feelings are nurtured and sustained are important ethical questions.

Kohlberg was primarily interested in levels or *stages* of moral development, and his research revealed such stages: as children, most subjects considered only their own interests, progressing toward concern for others, moving on to recognition of the importance of rules, and—for some subjects—finally reaching a recognition of rationally derived universal principles of justice. Subjects reached various stages of moral development, but Kohlberg noted that women were significantly less likely than men to reach the highest stage. Why were women less likely to reach the highest stages of moral development, in which they could understand the preeminence of abstract universal ethical rules? Kohlberg hypothesized that their moral development might be stunted by spending less time in the impersonal surroundings of business and the larger world, and more time dealing with issues related to family and close friends in a smaller and more intimate community. Psychologist Carol Gilligan, who had worked with Kohlberg on the research project, saw it differently. Rather than asking why women failed to reach the highest stage of moral development, she questioned Kohlberg's basic model that placed impersonal universal principle at the pinnacle of ethics. The care ethic approach is a *different* orientation to ethics, Gilligan argued, rather than an *inferior* perspective. Care ethics places greater emphasis on maintaining and preserving relationships and community and on looking at individual relationships and individual needs rather than focusing on universal laws. From the perspective of universal ethical rules and principles, personal details are irrelevant distractions. From the care ethics perspective, personal details are of vital importance. At the level of family and friends, we are dealing with specific people and unique relationships rather than generic "members of the kingdom of ends" or "anyone capable of feeling pleasure or pain" or "all who agree to the social contract." In Kohlberg's study with the Heinz case, women were more interested than men in looking at alternative approaches, finding a way that would work for everyone, learning more of the details, seeking a solution for this *particular* problem.

For all their differences, the major ethical traditions—Kantian, utilitarian, social contract—start from the assumption that *rules* are the basis of ethics. Care ethics challenges that basic perspective. There is nothing wrong with impersonal rules; they may be quite useful in the public marketplace and in other contexts in which we are dealing with strangers, and where personal relationships are not an issue. But for care ethicists, the heart and foundation of morality is found in care and affection, rather than impersonal universal abstract rules. From the care ethics perspective, an ethics of rules and principles sadly distorts much of ethics; indeed, it undervalues or even ignores the core of ethics on which the rest is constructed.

Many moral theories . . . employ the assumption that to increase the utility of individuals is a good thing to do. But if asked *why* it is a good thing to increase utility, or satisfy desire, or produce pleasure, or *why* doing so counts as a good reason for something, it is very difficult to answer. The claim is taken as a kind of starting assumption for which no *further* reason can be given. It seems to rest on a view that people seek pleasure, or that we can recognize pleasure as having more intrinsic value. But if women recognize quite different assumptions as more likely to be valid, that would certainly be of importance to ethics. We might then take it as one of our starting assumptions that creating good relations of care and concern and trust between ourselves and our children, and creating social arrangements in which children will be valued and well cared for, are more important than maximizing individual utilities. And the moral theories that might be compatible with such assumptions might be very different from those with which we are familiar. *Virginia Held*, "Feminism and Moral Theory," in Eva Feder Kittay and Diana T. Meyers, eds., *Women and Moral Theory* (Totowa, N. J.: Rowman & Littlefield, 1987), p. 126.

Your best friend flunked her organic chemistry final, her dream of medical school is in serious jeopardy, and she is very upset. You go to her with comforting words and a shoulder to cry on, and spend the evening trying to cheer her up. Suppose someone asks, "Why did you spend the evening comforting Julie?" "Because she's my best friend, and I care deeply about her," you would reply; *not* "Because by utilitarian calculations I determined that comforting Julie would yield the maximum balance of pleasure over pain," and *not* because of some Kantian or social contract rule that "All persons in sorrow should be comforted." You comforted her from *friendship* and affection, not from duty. If you had to think about what *rule* you should follow or make utilitarian calculations, that is not a sign of moral superiority, but instead reveals weakness in your morally basic affection and commitment to your friend. (Obviously, Kant would see this very differently, regarding your act as moral *only* if you acted strictly from *duty* and not from affection; but care ethicists see that as a terrible distortion and diminishing of ethical reality.) In fact, if Julie thinks you are spending the evening with her out of *duty* rather than *friendship*, that will destroy much of the value of your presence. In the marketplace we may need abstract rules: the rules that social contracts and Kantian rationalism and utilitarianism can provide. But squeezing *all* of morality into a rule-governed box will—from the care ethics perspective—leave much of morality out, including the very foundations of morality and many of its most valuable elements. If you provide care for your children from a sense of duty, then that's better than nothing; but it falls far short of care given from love and affection and will not provide the basic support and nurturing required for healthy childhood psychological development. If you relate to your loved ones by rule, then something has been lost. When your relationship becomes one of "whose turn is it to do this, who owes what to the other," then that relationship is heading for the rocks. That's fine for your business relationships, maybe even for politics; but not for personal relations. Our social structures may become large enough to require rules, but the ethical starting point is personal relationships, and the nurturing and strengthening of those relationships. That—rather than impersonal rules or social contracts—is the essential foundation and starting point of ethics.

Nell Noddings, a philosopher and educator, gives the following characterization of the care ethics approach (often followed by women) toward moral issues:

> Women, perhaps the majority of women, prefer to discuss moral problems in terms of concrete situations. They approach moral problems not as intellectual problems to be solved by abstract reasoning but as concrete human problems to be lived and to be solved in living . . . .
>
> Faced with a hypothetical moral dilemma, women often ask for more information. It is not the case, certainly, that women cannot arrange principles hierarchically and derive conclusions logically. It is more likely that they see this process as peripheral to or even irrelevant to moral conduct. They want more information, I think, in order to form a picture. Ideally, they need to talk to the participants, to see their eyes and facial expressions, to size up the whole situation. Moral decisions are, after all, made in situations; they are qualitatively different from the solution to geometry problems. Women . . . give reasons for their acts, but the reasons point to feelings, needs, situational conditions, and their sense of personal ideal rather than universal principles and their application.

Nell Noddings, Caring: A Feminine Approach to Ethics & Moral Education (*Berkeley: University of California Press, 1984), p. 96*

Kantian ethics provides the clearest contrast to care ethics. Suppose that one of Harshad's closest friends is in the hospital, and Harshad knows he is feeling lonely and perhaps a bit frightened, and could really use an encouraging visit. Harshad goes to visit his friend because he deeply values his friend and his friendship, and because he *cares* about his friend and it is important to Harshad to relieve his friend's distress and cheer him up. But now consider a second case: Jill's friend is in the hospital, and is distressed, but Jill does not *want* to go visit her and bring comfort and companionship and support; Jill finds hospital visits uncomfortable, and she just received a low grade on her term paper, and she really doesn't want to see *anyone* right now, friend or not. But Jill believes it is her *duty* to visit her friend, and so Jill makes the visit, complete with flowers and magazines and good cheer. The Kantian finds Jill's act to be ethically exemplary: It is an act done from rational reflection on duty and general moral principle, and *not* from inclination or affection, and that is the Kantian ideal. For the Kantian, Harshad's affection-based act fails to qualify as an ethical act at all. The care ethicist believes that Jill has acted ethically, but that her act is a lower quality substitute for an act done from genuine concern and affection: Harshad's is the better approach to ethical behavior (at least in the important sphere of personal relations). For the care ethicist, consideration of ethical rules may be useful when affectionate impulses are absent and may be essential in the public realm of impersonal interaction; but the act guided by affection and valued personal relationships is the essential ethical foundation. This obviously doesn't mean that we should always follow our immediate feelings, even in our dealings with loved ones. My affection for my child might make me feel very unhappy when I have to take him for a vaccination shot that my child finds painful and frightening, and my immediate affectionate impulse is to skip the vaccination. But my concern for my child and my careful consideration of the overall risks and benefits may overrule my immediate wish to protect my child from short-term distress. And if you are in an abusive relationship, that may be a time when your affection should be withdrawn. Such cases do not show that care ethics is inadequate; it only indicates that caring need not rule out intelligent reflection.

Is the care ethics emphasis on affection and personal relationships an improvement over more impersonal ethical theories—Kantian, utilitarian, social contract—with their emphasis on universal rules? That is a subject of intense debate, and you will have to draw your own conclusions. But carefully considering and comparing the various theories may help you make your own choice, and give you a better understanding of the view you favor as well as those you reject. And there are some other ethical theories still to consider— those are the subject of the next chapter.

READINGS

⇒ "GOD AND HUMAN ATTITUDES" ⇒
James Rachels

James Rachels taught philosophy at the University of Alabama at Birmingham and wrote a number of very influential works in ethics. His *Created from Animals: The Moral Implications of Darwinism* (Oxford: Oxford University Press, 1990) is a very readable and insightful study of the implications of Darwinism. In the passage below, Rachels not only rejects the Divine Command view of ethics but also goes much further: He argues that any ethical view that bases ethical principles on God's commandments would make human ethical behavior *impossible*.

Kneeling down or groveling on the ground, even to express your reverence for heavenly things, is contrary to human dignity.

Kant

It is necessarily true that God (if He exists) is worthy of worship. Any being who is not worthy of worship cannot be God, just as any being who is not omnipotent, or who is not perfectly good, cannot be God. This is reflected in the attitudes of religious believers who recognize that, whatever else God may be, He is a being before whom men should bow down. Moreover, He is unique in this; to worship anyone or anything else is blasphemy. In this paper I shall present an a priori argument against the existence of God which is based on the conception of God as a fitting object of worship. The argument is that God cannot exist, because no being could ever *be* a fitting object of worship.

However, before I can present this argument, there are several preliminary matters that require attention. The chief of these, which will hopefully have some independent interest of its own, is an examination of the concept of worship. In spite of its great importance this concept has received remarkably little attention from philosophers of religion; and when it has been treated, the usual approach is by way of referring to God's awesomeness or mysteriousness: to worship is to "bow down in silent awe" when confronted with a being that is "terrifyingly mysterious." But neither of these notions is of much help in understanding worship. Awe is certainly not the same thing as worship; one can be awed by a performance of *King Lear*, or by witnessing an eclipse of the sun or an earthquake, or by meeting one's favourite film-star, without worshiping any of these things. And a great many things are both terrifying and mysterious that we have not the slightest inclination to worship— I suppose the Black Plague fits that description for many people. The account of worship that I will give will be an alternative to those which rely on such notions as awesomeness and mysteriousness.

Consider McBlank, who worked against his country's entry into the Second World War, refused induction into the army, and was sent to jail. He was active in the "ban the bomb" movements of the fifties; he made speeches, wrote pamphlets, led demonstrations, and went back to jail. And finally, he has been active in opposing the war in Vietnam. In all of this he has acted out of principle; he thinks that all war is evil and that no war is ever justified. I want to make three observations about McBlank's pacifist commitments.

(a) One thing that is involved is simply his recognition that certain facts are the case. History is full of wars; war causes the massive destruction of life and property; in war men suffer on a scale hardly matched in any other way; the large nations now have weapons which, if used, could destroy the human race; and so on. These are just facts which any normally informed man will admit without argument. (b) But of course they are not *merely* facts, which people recognise to be the case in some indifferent manner. They are facts that have special importance to human beings. They form an ominous and threatening backdrop to people's lives—even though for most people they are a backdrop only. But not so for McBlank. He sees the accumulation of these facts as having radical implications for his conduct; he behaves in a very different way from the way he would behave were it not for these facts. His whole style of life is different; his conduct is altered, not just in its details, but in its pattern. (c) Not only is his overt behaviour affected; so are his ways of thinking about the world and his place in it. His *self-image* is different. He sees himself as a member of a race with an insane history of self-destruction. He is an opponent of militarism just as he is a father or a musician. When some existentialists say that we "create ourselves" by our choices, they may have something like this in mind.

Thus, there are at least three things that determine McBlank's role as an opponent of war: first, his recognition that certain facts are the case; second, his taking these facts as having important implications for his conduct; and third, his self-image as living his life (at least in part) in response to these facts. My first thesis about worship is that the worshiper has a set of beliefs about God which function in the same way as McBlank's beliefs about war.

First, the worshiper believes that certain things are the case: that the world was created by an all-powerful, all-wise being who knows our every thought and action; that this being, called God, cares for us and regards us as his children; that we are made by him in order to return his love and to live in accordance with his laws; and that, if we do not live in a way pleasing to him, we may be severely punished. Now these beliefs are certainly not shared by all reasonable people; on the contrary, many thoughtful persons regard them as nothing more than mere fantasy. But these beliefs are accepted by religious people, and that is what is important here. I do not say that this particular set of beliefs is definitive of religion in general, or of Judaism or Christianity in particular; it is meant only as a sample of the sorts of belief typically held by religious people in the West. They are, however, the sort of beliefs about God that are required for the business of worshiping God to make any sense.

Second, like the facts about warfare, these are not merely facts which one notes with an air of indifference; they have important implications for one's conduct. An effort must be made to discover God's will both for people generally and for oneself in particular; and to this end, the believer consults the church authorities and the theologians, reads the scripture, and prays. The degree to which this will alter his overt behaviour will depend, first, on exactly what he decides God would have him do, and second, on the extent to which his behaviour would have followed the prescribed pattern in any case.

Finally, the believer's recognition of these "facts" will influence his self-image and his way of thinking about the world and his place in it. The world will be regarded as made for the fulfilment of divine purposes; the hardships that befall men will be regarded either as "tests" in some sense or as punishments for sin; and most important, the believer will think of himself as a "Child of God" and of his conduct as reflecting either honour or dishonour upon his Heavenly Father. . . .

Worship is something that is *done,* but it is not clear just *what* is done when one worships: Other actions; such as throwing a ball or insulting one's neighbour, seem transparent enough. But not so with worship: when we celebrate Mass in the Roman Catholic Church, for example, what are we doing (apart from eating a wafer and drinking wine)? Or when we sing hymns in a protestant church, what are we doing (other than merely singing songs)? What is it that makes these acts acts of *worship?* One obvious point is that these actions, and others like them, are ritualistic in character; so, before we can make any progress in understanding worship, perhaps it will help to ask about the nature of ritual.

First we need to distinguish the ceremonial form of a ritual from what is supposed to be accomplished by it. Consider, for example, the ritual of investiture for an English Prince. The Prince kneels; the Queen (or King) places a crown on his head; and he takes an oath: "I do become your liege man of life and limb and of earthly worship, and faith and trust I will bear unto thee to live and die against all manner of folks." By this ceremony the Prince is elevated to his new station; and by this oath he acknowledges the commitments which, as Prince,

he will owe the Queen. In one sense the ceremonial form of the ritual is quite unimportant: it is possible that some other procedure might have been laid down, without the point of the ritual being affected in any way. Rather than placing a crown on his head, the Queen might break an egg into his palm (that could symbolise all sorts of things). Once this was established as the procedure to be followed, it would do as well as the other. It would still be the ritual of investiture, so long as it was understood that by the ceremony a Prince is created. The performance of a ritual, then, is in certain respects like the use of language: in speaking, sounds are uttered and, thanks to the conventions of the language; something is said, or affirmed or done, etc.: and in a ritual performance, a ceremony is enacted and, thanks to the conventions associated with the ceremony, something is done, or affirmed, or celebrated, etc.

How are we to explain the point of the ritual of investiture? We might explain that certain parts of the ritual symbolise specific things, for example that the Prince kneeling before the Queen symbolises his subordination to her (it is not, for example, merely to make it easier for her to place the crown on his head). But it is essential that, in explaining the point of the ritual as a whole, we include that a Prince is being created, that he is henceforth to have certain rights in virtue of having been made a Prince, and that he is to have certain duties which he is now acknowledging, among which are complete loyalty and faithfulness to the Queen, and so on. If the listener already knows about the complex relations between Queens, Princes, and subjects, then all we need to tell him is that a Prince is being installed in office; but if he is unfamiliar with this social system, we must tell him a great deal if he is to understand what is going on.

So, once we understand the social system in which there are Queens, Princes, and subjects, and therefore understand the role assigned to each within that system, we can sum up what is happening in the ritual of investiture in this way: someone is being made a Prince, and he is accepting that role with all that it involves. (Exactly the same explanation could be given, *mutatis mutandis,* for the marriage ceremony.)

The question to be asked about the ritual of worship is what analogous explanation can be given of it. The ceremonial form of the ritual may vary according to the customs of the religious community; it may involve singing, drinking wine, counting beads, sitting with a solemn expression on one's face, dancing, making a sacrifice, or what-have-you. But what is the point of it?

As I have already said, the worshiper thinks of himself as inhabiting a world created by an infinitely wise, infinitely powerful, perfectly good God; and it is a world in which he, along with other men, occupies a special place in virtue of God's intentions. This gives him a certain role to play: the role of a "Child of God." My second thesis about worship is that in worshiping God one is acknowledging and accepting this role, and that this is the primary function of the ritual of worship. Just as the ritual of investiture derives its significance from its place within the social system of Queens, Princes, and subjects, the ritual of worship gets its significance from an assumed system of relationships between God and men. In the ceremony of investiture, the Prince assumes a role with respect to the Queen and the citizenry; and in worship, a man affirms his role with respect to God.

Worship presumes the superior status of the one worshiped. This is reflected in the logical point that there can be no such thing as mutual or reciprocal worship, unless one or the other of the parties is mistaken as to his own status. We can very well comprehend people loving one another or respecting one another, but not (unless they are misled) worshiping one another. This is because the worshiper necessarily assumes his own inferiority; and since inferiority is an asymmetrical relation, so is worship. (The nature of the "superiority" and "inferiority" involved here is of course problematic; but on the account I am presenting it may be understood on the model of superior and inferior positions within a social system. More on this later.) This is also why *humility* is necessary on the part of the worshiper. The role to which he commits himself is that of the humble servant, "not worthy to touch the hem of His garment." Compared to God's gloriousness, "all our righteousnesses are as filthy rags" (Isaiah 64: 6). So, in committing oneself to this role, one is acknowledging God's greatness and one's own relative worthlessness. This humble attitude is not a mere embellishment of the ritual: on the contrary, worship, unlike love or respect, *requires* humility. Pride is a sin, and pride before God is incompatible with worshiping him.

On the view that I am suggesting, the function of worship as "glorifying" or "praising" God, which is usually taken to be its primary function, may be regarded as derivative from the more fundamental nature of worship as commitment to the role of God's Child. "Praising" God is giving him the honour and respect due to one in his position of eminence, just as one shows respect and honour in giving fealty to a King.

In short, the worshiper is in this position: He believes that there is a being, God, who is the perfectly good, perfectly powerful, perfectly wise Creator of the Universe; and he views himself as the "Child of God," made for God's purposes and responsible to God for his conduct. And the ritual of worship, which may have any number of ceremonial forms according to the customs of the religious community, has as its point the acceptance of, and commitment to, one's role as God's Child, with all that this involves. If this account is accepted, then there is no mystery as to the relation between the act of worship and the worshiper's other activity. Worship will be regarded not as an isolated act taking place on Sunday morning, with no necessary connection to one's behaviour the rest of the week, but as a ritualistic expression of and commitment to a role which dominates one's whole way of life.

An important feature of roles is that they can be violated; we can act and think consistently with a role, or we can act and think inconsistently with it. The Prince can, for example, act inconsistently with his role as Prince by giving greater importance to his own interests and welfare than to the Queen's; in this case, he is no longer her "liege man." And a father who does not attend to the welfare of his children is not acting consistently with his role as a father (at least as that role is defined in our society), and so on. The question that I want to raise now is, What would count as violating the role to which one is pledged in virtue of worshiping God?

In Genesis there are two familiar stories, both concerning Abraham, that are relevant here. The first is the story of the near-sacrifice of Isaac. We are told that Abraham was "tempted" by God, who commanded him to offer Isaac as a human sacrifice. Abraham obeyed without hesitation: he prepared an altar, bound Isaac to it, and was about to kill him until God intervened at the last moment, saying "Lay not thine hand upon the lad, neither do thou any thing unto him; for now I know that thou fearest God, seeing thou hast not withheld thy son, thine only son from me" (Genesis 22: 12). So Abraham passed the test. But how could he have failed? What was his "temptation"? Obviously, his temptation was to disobey God; God had ordered him to do something contrary to both his wishes and his sense of what would otherwise be right and wrong. He could have defied God; but he did not—he subordinated himself, his own desires and judgments, to God's command, even when the temptation to do otherwise was strongest.

It is interesting that Abraham's record in this respect was not perfect. We also have the story of him bargaining with God over the conditions for saving Sodom and Gomorrah from destruction. God had said that he would destroy those cities because they were so wicked; but Abraham gets God to agree that if fifty righteous men can be found there, then the cities will be spared. Then he persuades God to lower the number to forty-five, then forty, then thirty, then twenty, and finally ten. Here we have a different Abraham, not servile and obedient, but willing to challenge God and bargain with him. However, even as he bargains with God, Abraham realises that there is something radically inappropriate about it: he says, "Behold now, I have taken upon me to speak unto the Lord, which am but dust and ashes . . . O let not the Lord be angry . . . " (Genesis 18: 27, 30).

The fact is that Abraham could not, consistently with his role as God's subject, set his own judgment and will against God's. The author of Genesis was certainly right about this. We cannot recognise any being *as God,* and at the same time *set* ourselves against him. The point is not merely that it would be imprudent to defy God, since we certainly can't get away with it; rather, there is a stronger, logical point involved—namely, that if we recognise any being *as God,* then we are committed, in virtue of that recognition, to obeying him.

To see why this is so, we must first notice that "God" is not a proper name like "Richard Nixon" but a title like "President of the United States" or "King." Thus, "Jehovah is God" is a nontautological statement in which the title "God" is assigned to Jehovah, a particular being—just as "Richard Nixon is President of the United States" assigns the title "President of the United States" to a particular man. This permits us to understand how statements like "God is perfectly wise" can be logical truths, which is highly problematic if "God" is regarded as a proper name. Although it is not a logical truth that any particular being is perfectly wise, it nevertheless is a logical truth that if any being is God (i.e. if any being properly holds that title) then that being is perfectly wise. This is exactly analogous to saying: although it is not a logical truth that Richard Nixon has the authority to veto congressional legislation, nevertheless it is a logical truth that if Richard Nixon is President of the United States then he has that authority.

To bear the title "God," then, a being must have certain qualifications. He must, for example, be all-powerful and perfectly good in addition to being perfectly wise. And in the same vein, to apply the title "God" to a being is to recognise him as one to be obeyed. The same is true, to a lesser extent, of "King"—to recognise anyone as King is to acknowledge that he occupies a place of authority and has a claim on one's allegiance as his subject. And to recognise any being as God is to acknowledge that he has *unlimited* authority, and an unlimited claim on one's allegiance. Thus, we might regard Abraham's reluctance to defy Jehovah as grounded not only in his fear of Jehovah's wrath, but as a logical consequence of his acceptance of Jehovah *as God.* Camus was right to think that "From the moment that man submits God to moral judgment, he kills Him in his own heart." What a man can "kill" by defying or even questioning God is not the being that (supposedly) *is* God, but *his own conception of that being as God.* That God is not to be judged, challenged, defied, or disobeyed, is at bottom a truth of logic; to do any of these things is incompatible with taking him as One to be worshiped.

So the idea that any being could be *worthy* of worship is much more problematical than we might have at first imagined. For in admitting that a being is worthy of worship we would be recognising him as having an unqualified claim on our obedience. The question, then, is whether there could be such an unqualified claim. It should be noted that the description of a being as all-powerful, all-wise, etc., would not automatically settle the issue; for even while admitting the existence of such an awesome being we might still question whether we should recognise him as having an unlimited claim on our obedience.

In fact, there is a long tradition in moral philosophy, from Plato to Kant, according to which such a recognition could never be made by a moral agent. According to this tradition, to be a moral agent is to be an autonomous or self directed agent; unlike the precepts of law or social custom, moral precepts are imposed by the agent upon himself, and the penalty for their violation is, in Kant's words, "self-contempt and inner abhorrence." The virtuous man is therefore identified with the man of integrity, i.e. the man who acts according to precepts which he can, on reflection, conscientiously approve in his own heart. Although this is a highly individualistic approach to morals, it is not thought to invite anarchy because men are regarded as more or less reasonable and as desiring what we would normally think of as a decent life lived in the company of other men.

On this view, to deliver oneself over to a moral authority for directions about what to do is simply incompatible with being a moral agent. To say "I will follow so-and-so's directions no matter what they are and no matter what my own conscience would otherwise direct me to do" is to opt out of moral thinking altogether; it is to abandon one's role as a moral agent. And it does not matter whether "so and so" is the law, the customs of one's society, or God. This does not, of course, preclude one from seeking advice on moral matters, and even on occasion following that advice blindly, trusting in the good judgment of the adviser. But this is to be justified by the details of the particular case, e.g. that you cannot in that case form any reasonable judgment of your own due to ignorance or inexperience in dealing with the types of matters involved. What is precluded is that a man should, while in possession of his wits, adopt this style of decision-making (or perhaps we should say this style of *abdicating* decision-making) as a general strategy of living, or abandon his own best judgment in any case where he can form a judgment of which he is reasonably confident.

What we have, then, is a conflict between the role of worshiper, which by its very nature commits one to total subservience to God, and the role of moral agent, which necessarily involves autonomous decision-making. The point is that the role of worshiper takes precedence over every other role which the worshiper's has—when there is any conflict, the worshiper's commitment to God has priority over any other commitments which he might have. But the first commitment of a moral agent is to do what in his own heart he thinks is right. Thus the following argument might be constructed:

a.   If any being is God, he must be a fitting object of worship.

b.   No being could possibly be a fitting object of worship, since worship requires the abandonment of one's role as an autonomous moral agent.

c.   Therefore, there cannot be any being who is God. . . .

The above argument will probably not persuade anyone to abandon belief in God—arguments rarely do—and there are certainly many more points which need to be worked out before it can be known whether this argument is even viable. Yet it does raise an issue which is clear enough. Theologians are already accustomed to speaking of theistic belief and commitment as taking the believer "beyond morality," and I think they are right. The question is whether this should not be regarded as a severe embarrassment.

⇌ New Perspectives on Old-Time Religion ⇌
George N. Schlesinger

George Schlesinger taught philosophy at the University of North Carolina at Chapel Hill, and wrote extensively on philosophy of religion, philosophy of science, the philosophy of time, and metaphysics. Schlesinger defends the plausibility of at least a modest version of the divine command theory, basing his defense on the concept of religious devotion and trust.

In an influential article Patrick Nowell-Smith has advanced the claim that religious morality is basically flawed and therefore may appropriately be labelled as 'infantile morality'. He cites Hobbes's phrase 'God who by right, that is by irresistible power, commandeth all things', which he finds repugnant since it equates God's right with his might. In Nowell-Smith's opinion—an opinion shared by most philosophers—for an act to qualify as a moral act, the agent has to perform it because of the intrinsic desirability of that act, and not because of fear of retribution or expectation of reward, or because of any other ulterior motive.

Nowell-Smith explains that the reason why religious morality is essentially infantile is that, first of all, just as a little boy may refrain from pulling his sister's hair not because it hurts her, but because Mummy forbids it (and he is aware that defying her may have painful consequences), so a religious person will refrain from wicked acts not because of their inherent wickedness, but because they violate a Divine command. Secondly, to a child morality is nothing but a curb on his own volition; he is not yet capable of understanding why he must not do certain things he would very much like to do, and so is forced to submit blindly to parental authority. The same is true in religion:

> It is the total surrender of the *will* that is required: Abraham must be prepared to sacrifice Isaac at God's command, and I take this to mean that we must be prepared to sacrifice our most deeply felt concerns if God should require us to do so. If we dare ask why, the only answer is 'Have faith'; and faith is an essentially heteronomous idea, for it is not a reasoned trust in someone in whom we have good grounds for reposing trust; it is blind faith, utter submission of our own reason and will.

However, a genuinely moral person does not act contrary to his will. His conduct is based on an understanding of what is desirable and what is repugnant. Such an understanding generates the will to act in compliance with the rules of morality, which amount to the required safeguards for proper conduct, ensuring the avoidance of what is bad and the doing of what is good.

Other philosophers, using similar arguments, have gone further to draw the radical conclusion that theism must be false. J. Rachels, for instance, has emphasized that a genuine moral agent is essentially autonomous. However, obedience to divine commands requires the surrendering of one's role as an autonomous moral agent. Religious morality is thus incompatible with genuine morality. Hence Rachels constructs the following compact deductive argument for atheism:

a. If any being is God, he must be a fitting object of worship.
b. No being could possibly be a fitting object of worship, since worship requires the abandonment of one's role as an autonomous moral agent.
c. Therefore, there cannot be any being who is God.

The theist is capable, of course, of defending himself against these attacks. It is interesting to see, however, whether he can do so even if he grants these philosophers all their presuppositions about the nature of ethics. Thus let us not question the assumption that there exists a more or less agreed-upon set of rules that constitutes morality, and that no justification is required to show that these rules are universally binding. Furthermore, we shall also accept it as obvious that an agent who does not act autonomously is at best practising an inferior kind of morality and

possibly no morality at all. However, we should not grant any views about religious precepts unless they are reasonable. Now, concerning the question as to what religious morality is, one cannot hope to arrive at the right answer with the aid of any kind of a priori reasoning; it is essential that we acquaint ourselves with the relevant religious teachings. For example, one of the most basic ideas concerning the end to which a pious person must strive, and one that has been emphasized by all religious teachers, is that an individual is to serve God because of the immeasurably great fulfilment and felicity all acts of piety are bound to bestow upon their practitioners. To obey the precepts of religion out of fear of Divine might is an attitude typical of a novice, who as yet has only a very crude understanding of the significance of a God-centred life. Upon a fuller realization of the nature of piety, a person acquires much loftier sentiments and his reverent acts are informed by a spirit of love and of longing for Divine communion. The service of the true worshipper is accompanied by a sense of spiritual self-enhancement and deep fulfilment that is the natural outcome of acts of love and joy. To cite but one of the many expressions of this idea:

> As the love of God is man's highest happiness and blessedness, and the aim of all human actions, it follows that he alone lives by the Divine law who loves God not from fear of punishment, or from love of any other object . . . but solely because he has knowledge of God.

It seems therefore sufficient to point out that he who refrains from doing evil for no other reason than his fear of Divine retribution is practising not merely an inferior kind of morality, but, in the view of virtually all religious authorities, also an inferior kind of religion. On the other hand, such a person is still much to be preferred to a complete non-believer, since he has already ascended the first important rung on the ladder leading to salvation, and even if he should rise no further, he—unlike the latter—will at least have the proper restraints to keep him from actually engaging in any wrongdoing.

Once our attention has been drawn to what constitutes a fully realized religious attitude, we are bound to see the mistake of describing all those who obey Divine commands as people who suspend their human autonomy, totally and blindly submitting their will to carry out, robot-like, and in complete ignorance of the whys and wherefores, whatever they are required to do. Suppose a person to whom I owe a very large debt of gratitude, and whom I love and admire greatly, informs me one day that it is imperative for him to get to Washington today, and in view of the airline strike and his inability to drive, he asks me to drive him there. Let us also suppose that because of my anxiety to please my benefactor, I at once cancel all my appointments for the day, inform my son that I shall not attend the school play in which he acts the title role, and so on, and without asking any questions drive to Washington. I do not believe that many would insist that it would have been nobler on my part if, instead of taking off in total ignorance of the purpose of our trip, I had first demanded to be reassured, by being given a full account of what my cherished friend proposed to do in Washington, that there was sufficient reason for this journey.

Also I believe that it would be nonsensical to describe me as one who has acted robot-like, blindly renouncing my autonomy to the will of another. Admittedly I have no idea of the nature of my benefactor's business in the capital, but that is quite irrelevant. What I do know for sure—and this is really what matters—is that he feels his presence is urgently required there, and also that he is a highly judicious person whom I have reason to trust and love. Thus, if I am a decent individual, I shall welcome this opportunity to do something which is beyond any doubt a service to him. Not only are all feelings of being coerced and of surrendering my autonomy totally out of place, but on the contrary I should be expected to be gratified with having made the clear-eyed and fully self-determined decision to carry out my benefactor's wish as promptly and smoothly as possible without subjecting him to an unbecoming interrogation. In a similar fashion, a pious person senses no pressure to which he has to surrender, and feels no coercion, but quite the opposite, will eagerly seek out the opportunity to engage in what to him amounts to the loftiest of all human activities, namely, serving God.

. . .

⇒ "THE GOOD SIDE OF RELATIVISM" ⇒
Elvin Hatch

Elvin Hatch is a professor in the Department of Anthropology at the University of California at Santa Barbara. While he argues for some advantages in the relativistic position, he is primarily concerned to challenge *anti*-relativism. Hatch sees dangers in universalist approaches to ethics, and he believes that such approaches often fail to understand cultures that diverge from Western values.

ETHICAL CULTURAL RELATIVISM HAS SOME ADVANTAGES

The efflorescence of ethical relativism among American anthropologists took place in the 1930s and 1940s, when Benedict and Herskovits were its most notable proponents. Their relativism combined two principles. The first was an attitude of skepticism in relation to Western values, for they held that Western standards with respect to such matters as sexuality and work are historically conditioned and do not warrant elevation to the status of universal principles. The second was the value of tolerance, inasmuch as they held that people everywhere ought to be free to live as they choose.

Opposition to this form of relativism was evident almost from the start, however, and by the 1950s some of the leading anthropologists in this country were speaking out against it. World War II stimulated some of this reaction, for it was difficult for people in the United States not to think in terms of universal or ultimate values in the face of the events taking place then. The intellectual climate for nearly two decades following the war also included a number of powerful images which seemed to speak against relativism. These were images about the end of colonialism, opportunities for economic development in underdeveloped countries, and the seemingly universal desirability of Western technology. Thus during the postwar years, such leading figures in anthropology as Ralph Linton, Robert Redfield, and Alfred Kroeber were critical of moral relativism, while a variety of philosophers underlined the flaws in the ethical reasoning of Benedict and Herskovits. Strong opposition has continued to the present, and today ethical relativism is more often attacked than embraced; I am not sure that anyone now is willing fully to endorse the version of relativism that was articulated by its major proponents in American anthropology in the 1930s.

It is in this context that I want to offer a defense of ethical relativism. This will be a very limited defense, and I do not propose reinstating the theories of either Benedict or Herskovits. But I believe that in our rush to distance ourselves from the moral and philosophical difficulties of their ideas, we may give up too much, and, indeed, we may fail to see the legacy of their thought continuing in other ethical theories today. In any event, it is important for us to keep sight of the issues that they were concerned with.

I need to be clear that I accept that there are situations in which ethical relativism is untenable, for it may lead to moral neutrality and inaction in situations that are intolerable. Ethical relativism is mistaken when it calls for us to be non-judgmental in relation to such issues as political executions, genocide, genital mutilations, honor killings, and the like. The recent executions of Ken Saro-Wiwa and others in Nigeria, which received international attention at the time this essay was first drafted, are a case in point. A strict relativist might argue that a moral response by the West is ethically unwarranted, yet how can we not respond? Again, how can we not express value judgments in regard to the reports of rape and mass killing in parts of the former Yugoslavia? But ethical relativism is not a simple, unitary scheme that can be dismissed by a single argument, for it is a complex notion made up of a variety of features which need to be evaluated individually. A corollary is that most anthropologists are ethical relativists in some respects and nonrelativists in others.

Underlying my defense of relativism—or my interest in looking on its good side—is my recognition that at the time of writing, the United States seems to be experiencing a cultural shift to the right, or at least the cultural right has gained significant ground in the national political arena. We see concerted attacks on multiculturalism in the schools and universities, for example, and on multilingualism, immigrants, and affirmative action. These pressures—which have never been absent in the United States, but which appear to be stronger now than they have been in recent memory—stimulate us to take another look at relativism. The philosophical questions raised by it do not exist independently of a context of real-world affairs, and as those affairs change, we see the elements making up that complex of features called relativism in a different light. Put simply, our judgments about ethical relativism are historically situated.

The Paradox of Ethical Relativism

The place to begin is with what I will call the paradox of ethical relativism. On one hand, the theory is mistaken to the extent that it denies the very possibility of making moral judgments across cultures or of developing a framework of human rights; but on the other hand, the problems that the relativists of the Boasian tradition were concerned with have not gone away. One of these is the problem of establishing reasonable and general grounds for making moral judgments about the actions of others, and another is a strong tendency among the more powerful peoples of the world to use their own standards, or standards favorable to them, in their relations with others. What standards are appropriate for us to use, how do we defend them, and how can we know that they will hold up to the scrutiny of those who do not share our perspective, now or in the future? No moral theory that has been advanced in opposition to relativism has been sufficiently convincing that it clearly stands above the rest as the winning alternative; consequently we cannot forge ahead with confidence in making moral judgments or establishing universal standards and a body of human rights. Whenever a set of standards is proposed, I feel myself being pulled back by a nagging sense of doubt. I have yet to see a general ethical theory that I personally find convincing. The paradox of ethical relativism is that we can't live with it, but it isn't clear how to avoid the skepticism which underlies it.

This paradox has helped structure the debate over the question of moral judgments and human rights, which is suggested by the fact that ethical relativism occupies such a prominent place in the literature on universal standards. Much of this literature takes relativism as its starting point or as its main foil. . . . It is as if we cannot conceive the one—the search for general moral principles or human rights (whether they are based on utilitarian principles, Kantian rights-based theory, or any other ground)—outside the context of the other. Adapting a Derridian argument, the question of human rights and general standards of ethical judgment are never a mere "presence," something to be established in their own right, but exist only in relation to their opposite, which is relativism.

I have mentioned my sense of skepticism about attempts to establish general moral standards, and the ethical relativism that underlies the paradox that I cite is a form of skepticism. What is more, the moral theories of such Boasians as Benedict and Herskovits had an important skeptical component, although not all forms of relativism in the anthropological literature did so. For example, skepticism seems to have played no part in the relativism of Malinowski, whose position rested on the principle that other cultures are successful or functional, which in turn assumed a universal standard of good. For example, his analysis of magic contained the message that missionaries and colonial administrators should not undermine the magical beliefs of other peoples because these rituals enabled the individual to cope with his or her anxieties and therefore to be more effective with the task at hand. Malinowski's relativism rested not on a form of skepticism, but on a version of utilitarian theory whereby the practical benefits of institutions served as a standard for making value judgments. For Malinowski, the institutions of non-Western societies are appropriate given the conditions in which those peoples live, and Western values regarding such matters as sexuality and marriage do not constitute universal standards.

The relativism that was incubated in Boasian anthropology adopted a skeptical attitude toward cross-cultural standards of all kinds, including Malinowski's utilitarianism. The Boasians would have been justified in accusing Malinowski of accepting this standard uncritically: it needed better philosophical grounding than he provided, and one even wonders how much care he gave to these matters. And this problem is still with us: the failure to arrive at a moral theory that is generally accepted and that will serve as an intellectual basis for universal human rights is notable.

I disagree with Benedict and Herskovits to the extent that they held that warrantable judgments across cultural boundaries can never be made, if only because the failure to act is itself an action that may have unacceptable consequences for other people—consequences which are unacceptable to us. But I agree with Benedict's and Herskovits's version of relativism on several other counts. The first is their basic skepticism: we do not have a set of moral principles that are rationally warranted, generally acceptable among those who are informed on these issues, and universally applicable. While there are situations in which we are compelled to take a moral stand, the grounds which warrant our doing so will necessarily be ad hoc and limited. I also agree with the connection that they made between skepticism and tolerance: when we do not find good reason to make judgments about the actions or ways of life of other people, we ought to show tolerance toward them, and we should do so on the basis of the moral principles that people ought to be free to live as they choose.

One might argue that any ethical theory might call for tolerance in situations in which it lacks adequate reasons to respond otherwise. And it seems to me that, to the extent that it does, that theory *incorporates* relativism. Ethical relativism is espoused even among the ethical theorists who reject it. But my argument goes even further, for I am suggesting that, at this point at least, no ethical theory which seeks to establish general standards of value is fully compelling. Consequently we are faced with the paradox of relativism: we have no moral theory to replace it with, yet there are situations in which the failure to take a moral stand other than tolerance is clearly unacceptable.

The Issue of Culpability

Relativism may have at least a tacit presence even in cases in which we decide that moral judgments are warranted, for to judge that the actions of the Other are intolerable is to raise the additional question of what went wrong: who or what was responsible for the actions that we find objectionable? To put this another way, moral judgments may take place at two levels. The first concerns the events that we want to evaluate, and here the issue is to find adequate grounds for making value judgments about those events; the second concerns the human agents involved, and here the question is their responsibility for these matters. It is important that relativism is an issue at both levels. I turn here to the second level, the question of culpability, and the work of Edward Tylor is illustrative.

Tylor was not a relativist at the first level, of course, for he ranked human societies by reference to degrees of moral perfection, and, in principle, evaluations were to be made on the basis of how effective the institutions were in promoting human happiness and physical well-being. Yet a form of relativism appeared at the second level, for he argued that savage societies should not be judged according to European standards of thought. Savages were not as intelligent as Europeans—they did not have the intellectual capacity to draw the same moral conclusions from experience that Europeans did; hence their institutions should be understood according to their standards of reason and not one's own. The implication was that the people of the lower societies were not culpable for their moral mistakes. Like children, they didn't know better. This was a form of relativism in that a society's standards of justice, say, were relative to the level of the people's intelligence, and institutions that were appropriate for societies at one level, that of the Tasmanians, say, were not appropriate for societies at another level, such as Britain. To state this another way, while Tylor faulted the institutions of lower societies, he held that the individual's actions should not be judged by reference to the standards of a higher civilization.

We find a similar division between the two levels of moral judgment in the work of Ruth Benedict. What stimulated Elgin Williams's criticism of her *Patterns of Culture* in 1947 was that Penguin had just issued a new, twenty-five-cent edition of her book, making it readily accessible, as Williams said, to the common man. The book was now available on book racks in drug stores and dime stores across the country. Williams showed that while the formal argument of Benedict's book was one of relativism and tolerance— she explicitly argued that all cultures were equally valid—in another sense the book was profoundly nonrelativistic, for it offered a plethora of value judgments. And Williams applauded her for it. For example, Benedict described war as an asocial, destructive trait; she preferred the nonviolent marital relations of the Zuni to the jealous outbursts of the Plains; and she favored the lack of a sense of sin among the Zuni to the guilt complexes that were associated with Puritanism.

We find similar departures from relativism elsewhere in Benedict's work, including her discussions of what she called the bereavement situation, or the cultural patterns associated with a person's death. She distinguished between realistic and nonrealistic ways of handling death and grief. The Pueblo peoples of the Southwest, she said, handled death in a realistic fashion, for the individual's behavior was directed toward the loss itself and toward getting past the trauma with as little disruption as possible. By contrast the Navajo were nonrealistically preoccupied with contamination. They had a strong fear of pollution from the dead and of the dangers posed by the possibility of the ghost's return.

These cases reveal Benedict abandoning her relativism, but it reappeared at another level. For example, while she looked unfavorably on Plains warfare and while she regarded Navajo reactions to death as nonrealistic, an implicit message was that the people themselves should not be faulted. Yet her grounds for denying their culpability were different from those that underlay Tylor's thinking. It was not that the people didn't know better, but that they adhered to cultural traditions which largely governed their lives: to a significant degree, the individual's actions were a product of cultural conditioning. While Tylor granted agency to other peoples but absolved them of culpability because of their low intelligence, Benedict held that all people were equally intelligent but denied their blameworthiness on the grounds of enculturation. In other words, the individual's culpability should not be judged by reference to standards that derive from outside his or her culture.

This reveals how our assumptions about culture, society, and human behavior influence the kinds of value judgments we make, and it suggests the critical importance of being clear about these matters in our own minds when developing moral judgments. This also reveals the importance of separating the two levels of moral evaluation. Consider the recent executions in Nigeria. It is one thing to condemn the Nigerian government's actions, but quite another to assign moral responsibility. Ethical, political, and legal judgments may be made at both levels, but the reasoning is different in the two cases, and the paradox of relativism applies to both. It is conceivable that one could favor the imposition of sanctions against the Nigerian government in order to bring about a change in its policies, while still accepting that the people who were behind the executions were not morally culpable since they were acting reasonably given the cultural meanings that underlay their behavior.

It is not only ethical relativism that operates at both levels, for other ethical theories do so as well, such as when they take into account, say, what Benedict referred to as cultural conditioning. And when they absolve the individual of blame on these grounds, then they are employing the relativistic principle whereby the individual's actions should be judged by reference to the historically variable standards within the culture, not by external ones.

Tolerance and Skepticism

The Boasian relativists may be faulted for being less critical than they should have been with regard to the question of making moral arguments. First, they were patently inconsistent. On one hand, they held that moral standards are historically conditioned, the same as pottery designs or folk tales—like all cultural features, values differ from society to society, and therefore we are not justified in making cross-cultural judgments. But on the other hand, the Boasians proceeded to do exactly what they asserted should not be done, which was to advance a universal moral standard. This was the standard of tolerance, whereby we ought not be judgmental about cultural differences; we ought to allow people to live as they choose.

Second, it was a mistake for them to assume that the means for arriving at universally valid moral principles should be by a comparative study of cultures. The question of values is a philosophical matter and not an empirical one. True, judgments of reality (as distinct from judgments of value) do enter legitimately into the application of value standards, inasmuch as the empirical facts of the case need to be understood before a standard of value may be applied to a given situation. But the process of arriving at value standards is a rational and not an empirical matter and cannot be approached by a comparative study of cultures. Indeed, if the Boasians had been consistent about using the comparative method, then surely they would have had to give up the call for tolerance, since intolerance is more likely the norm around the world.

Yet in spite of its difficulties, there is something to recommend the call for tolerance, which is grounded on the notion that people ought to be free to live as they choose. But the idea needs to be framed differently from the way the Boasians conceptualized it. In place of the straightforward principle that we ought to be tolerant of other ways of life, we should substitute the more limited principle that we ought to do so in the absence of persuasive arguments that would enable us to make moral judgments. Tolerance ought to constitute the default mode of thought governing our ethical judgments today. For example, we ought to be nonjudgmental in relation to culinary styles and modes of dress and about people's life goals and their treatment of one another—we should, that is, unless we see persuasive reasons to react otherwise. If we are not tolerant in such situations, then our actions necessarily will be arbitrary and will contravene the moral principle of freedom, whereby people should be able to live as they choose. This notion of relativism as default is crucial: the nonjudgmentalism that we associate with relativism is an attitude that does not come easily to most Americans, perhaps to most people throughout the world. Certainly it does not come easily to the religious right in the United States or to many members of the present U.S. Congress.

If we retain the Boasian call for tolerance as our default, what about Boasian skepticism? How may we fit that into our thinking? The Boasian relativists were not as consistently skeptical as it might appear, as Elgin Williams's criticisms of Benedict reveal. The principle that we should extract from Benedict—a principle that she herself was not very careful with, as Williams has shown—is the importance of maintaining a highly critical attitude in relation to the standards that we use in making value judgments. We

need not remain skeptical to the point of denying the possibility of making any valid judgments, but we should submit our evaluations to severe scrutiny. And we do not need to resort to such obvious examples as the moral beliefs of the religious right to make this case, for anthropology itself provides illustrations. This point is crucial: even well-meaning, sympathetic, and informed people may be faulted for their failure to be as cautiously skeptical as they should.

I appreciate that it doesn't take relativism to make us aware of unwarranted judgments about other people, for surely any scholarly ethical theory today recognizes the subtleties of ethnocentrism. Yet the limited form of relativism that I urge suggests that an attitude of skepticism should be our first reflex in the face of moral judgments.

I want to illustrate the subtleties of ethnocentrism and the importance of a basic skepticism in relation to moral judgments by examining the work of the late Ernest Gellner. His *Reason and Culture* is about rationality, not ethics, but the central argument of the book has important implications for ethical relativism. At one level, he rejected universal rationality, for he accepted that reason does not stand outside of culture. And he held that in an important sense, modern science is an irrational endeavor, as criticisms of the Popperian philosophy of science have shown. But Gellner accepted universal rationality at another level, for Western thought, he argued, is demonstrably better than that of other peoples. What sets Western rationality apart is that it gets better results, regardless of its truth-value. He wrote,

> The astonishing and unquestionable power of the [Western] technology born of [Western] rational inquiry is such that the majority of mankind—and in particular those men eager to increase their wealth and/or power—are eager to emulate it.

What are the characteristics of this new, Western form of thought, this rationally unwarranted rationality which is conquering the world? It is a fusion of two seemingly contradictory philosophical theories, Western rationalism and Western empiricism. This form of thought is empiricist in that it takes experience as the arbiter of competing ideas, but this empiricism is under the control of rationalism.

Drawing on Weber's analysis of the history of Western society, Gellner went on to describe Western rationality as a way of life, or lifestyle, which permeates much of Western society and culture. For example, it is manifest in the modern economy, which operates according to judgments about efficiency and cost-effectiveness. Gellner is clear that not all spheres of society or culture are fully dominated by the rationalist ideal, for in many spheres—etiquette might be one example—rules "have no rhyme or reason". Even more to the point, morality itself, he said, cannot be justified by pragmatic considerations the way science and economic production can.

Gellner's valorization of Western rationality stopped short of defending Western values in general, but I suggest that his privileging of Western rationality helps to normalize certain forms of thinking, and in doing so may have harmful ethical consequences. An example would be the use of highly rational, highly empirical, but highly value-laden economic models derived from the West for development programs in other parts of the world. Gellner's response to this criticism might be that it ignores a key part of his argument, which is the importance of the judgments of non-Western peoples. It is *their* demand for the products of Western rationality—medicines, new crop forms, tape recorders, television, rifles, missiles—that confirms the universality of Western forms of thought. And if an economic order is imposed on them that they do not want, then their judgments should be respected. Yet it is extremely difficult to circumscribe those things which are genuinely desired by the Other and to distinguish them from the things that are forced upon them because of asymmetries of privilege, prestige, and power. Gellner's thinking was insufficiently skeptical.

Consider the case of Appalachia. The Tennessee Valley Authority was created by an act of Congress in 1933, and its initial purpose was the planning and development of the entire Tennessee River Basin, which was considered underdeveloped and poverty-stricken. Dams would be built to improve navigation and flood control and to produce hydroelectric power, conservation programs would be implemented, and both agricultural and industrial development would be introduced. According to David Whisnant, the TVA began as a progressive, idealistic, democratic, comprehensive effort to improve the region. Its idealistic goals were soon subverted by powerful business interests, particularly after the dams were completed in 1944. But even if the original goals had not been subverted, Whisnant argues, the TVA would have been destructive. The leading figures in the organization believed that by instituting rational, apolitical, disinterested economic and social engineering, the project would succeed in improving the lives of these backward people. In brief, the project was founded on a set of cultural assumptions of the dominant society,

assumptions about development and the virtues of bringing a people with an aberrant way of life into the mainstream. Whisnant writes,

> Beneath the vast technological superstructure of TVA I perceived a substructure of cultural values and assumptions that controlled the agency more surely than the geomorphology of the Tennessee River Valley itself.

This kind of normalization is manifest in another characteristic of the relationship between Appalachia and the larger society, which is the tendency of the latter to perceive the Appalachian people as backward and impoverished. It is unquestionable that the people of that region do suffer impoverishment, which is evident, for example, in the figures on health care and education. But granting that, nevertheless, the *perception*, by mainstream, middle-class Americans, of the Appalachians' backwardness and impoverishment is a result of something else as well. For one thing, there has been a "systematic denigration" of the local population as a way to justify such programs as the TVA. The portrayal of Appalachia as backward has served the interests of certain individuals and agencies of the dominant society. For another, and more to the point here, some Appalachian patterns are seen as backward from the point of view of mainstream, middle-class America. The emotional forms of religious service among the congregations that proliferate in Appalachia are illustrative. These are perceived by the dominant society as manifestations of a gullible people. Similarly, one Appalachian pattern is a form of economic life whereby the people depend heavily on the informal economic sector (such as subsistence gardening and labor and food exchanges); they are jacks of all trades, and they tend to avoid long-term job commitments and regular employment. Tom Plaut argues that while there are many studies of the culture of Appalachia, very little work has been done on the "rationalist, achievement-oriented, 'scientific' culture" that is overwhelming the region. This "scientific" culture "has levelled, bleached, and bled out a rich variety of human ways of being that have stood in its path". Plaut sees the way of life of the Appalachians as meritorious in its own right.

Earlier I said that it is sometimes difficult to distinguish between those features of Western society which the Other truly wants and those which are forced on them. I suggest that one aspect of this problem is that mainstream Westerners tend to engage in a kind of metonymic thinking in conceiving the relationship between Us and the Other, for technology serves as a trope for representing a more general relationship among societies. For example, the success of such Western forms of technology as tape recorders, electric guitars, and rifles provides a model for thinking about the relationship between the Western economy and that of the Other. We tend to elide the distinction between specific forms of technology and, say, the value of economic efficiency and the work ethic. The theme of skepticism that we find in the work of Benedict and Herskovits retains its significance today.

Conclusion

The emergence of relativism at about the turn of this century was associated with a Copernican shift in both the Western worldview and the Western sense of self-identity. Western thought about where our civilization stood in the total gamut of human societies underwent profound change, and this took place in part in the context of Boasian anthropology and was one aspect of the emerging relativistic perspective. Whereas earlier, anthropologists imagined their own societies to be at the pinnacle of development, the Boasian worldview had it that the West occupied a very equivocal position, for while it may have enjoyed greater material power than other peoples, it did not enjoy moral superiority. This facet of relativism was crucial, and it remains a central legacy, regardless of how we may feel about the possibility of establishing general ethical standards or universal human rights. What is more, the efforts today to develop a warranted body of human rights are framed by this principle, for we now assume that the views of non-Western peoples ought to weigh as heavily as the views of Westerners in establishing general standards. So the very search for universal human rights today rests upon a relativistic foundation. Even the ethical theories which reject relativism reflect the Copernican shift that the Boasians helped to achieve.

⇌ LEVIATHAN ⇌
Thomas Hobbes

Thomas Hobbes (1588–1679) was not the first social contract theorist, but he was the first to formulate the theory in detail and offer extended arguments in its favor. Hobbes believed that a powerful ruler—a "great leviathan"—was necessary in order to prevent a vicious and chaotic "war of all against all"; and since we can all see the personal advantage of escaping the brutal and warlike conditions of the "state of nature," we all find it reasonable to sacrifice a portion of our liberty in order to gain protection. Though Hobbes was a strong supporter of the monarchy, he rejected the divine right of kings. That made him unpopular with both sides during the English Revolution, and he moved to France to escape danger. When Charles II was restored to the throne, Hobbes returned to England and became a great favorite at the court.

OF THE NATURALL CONDITION OF MANKIND, AS CONCERNING THEIR FELICITY, AND MISERY

Nature hath made men so equall, in the faculties of body, and mind; as that though there bee found one man sometimes manifestly stronger in body, or of quicker mind then another; yet when all is reckoned together, the difference between man, and man, is not so considerable, as that one man can thereupon claim to himselfe any benefit, to which another may not pretend, as well as he. For as to the strength of body, the weakest has strength enough to kill the strongest, either by secret machination, or by confederacy with others, that are in the same danger with himself.

And as to the faculties of the mind, (setting aside the arts grounded upon words, and especially that skill of proceeding upon generall, and infallible rules, called Science; which very few have, and but in few things; as being not a native faculty, born with us; nor attained, (as Prudence,) while we look after somewhat els,) I find yet a greater equality amongst men, than that of strength. For Prudence, is but Experience; which equall time, equally bestowes on all men, in those things they equally apply themselves unto. That which may perhaps make such equality incredible, is but a vain conceit of ones owne wisdome, which almost all men think they have in a greater degree, than the Vulgar; that is, than all men but themselves, and a few others, whom by Fame, or for concurring with themselves, they approve. For such is the nature of men, that howsoever they may acknowledge many others to be more witty, or more eloquent, or more learned; Yet they will hardly believe there be many so wise as themselves: For they see their own wit at hand, and other mens at a distance. But this proveth rather that men are in that point equall, than unequall. For there is not ordinarily a greater signe of the equall distribution of any thing, than that every man is contented with his share.

From this equality of ability, ariseth equality of hope in the attaining of our Ends. And therefore if any two men desire the same thing, which neverthelesse they cannot both enjoy, they become enemies; and in the way to their End, (which is principally their owne conservation, and sometimes their delectation only) endeavour to destroy, or subdue one another. And from hence it comes to passe, that where an Invader hath no more to feare, than an other mans single power; if one plant, sow, build, or possesse a convenient Seat, others may probably be expected to come prepared with forces united, to dispossesse, and deprive him, not only of the fruit of his labour, but also of his life, or liberty. And the Invader again is in the like danger of another.

And from this diffidence of one another, there is no way for any man to secure himselfe, so reasonable, as Anticipation; that is, by force, or wiles, to master the persons of all men he can, so long, till he see no other power great enough to endanger him: And this is no more than his own conservation requireth, and is generally allowed. Also because there be some, that taking pleasure in contemplating their own power in the acts of conquest, which they pursue farther than their security requires; if others, that otherwise would be glad to be at ease within modest bounds, should not by invasion increase their power, they would not be able, long time, by standing only on their defence, to subsist. And by consequence, such augmentation of dominion over men, being necessary to a mans conservation, it ought to be allowed him.

Againe, men have no pleasure, (but on the contrary a great deale of griefe) in keeping company, where there is no power able to over-awe them all. For every man looketh that his companion should value him, at the same rate he sets upon himselfe: And upon all signes of contempt, or undervaluing, naturally endeavours, as far as he dares (which amongst them that have no common power, to keep them in quiet, is far enough to make them destroy each other,)

to extort a greater value from his contemners, by dommage; and from others, by the example.

So that in the nature of man, we find three principall causes of quarrell. First, Competition; Secondly, Diffidence, Thirdly, Glory.

The first, maketh men invade for Gain; the second, for Safety; and the third, for Reputation. The first use Violence, to make themselves Masters of other mens persons, wives, children, and cattell; the second, to defend them; the third, for trifles, as a word, a smile, a different opinion, and any other signe of undervalue, either direct in their Persons, or by reflexion in their Kindred, their Friends, their Nation, their Profession, or their Name.

Hereby it is manifest, that during the time men live without a common Power to keep them all in awe, they are in that condition which is called Warre; and such a warre, as is of every man, against every man. For WARRE, consisteth not in Battell onely, or the act of fighting; but in a tract of time, wherein the Will to contend by Battell is sufficiently known: and therefore the notion of *Time*, is to be considered in the nature of Warre; as it is in the nature of Weather. For as the nature of Foule weather, lyeth not in a showre or two of rain; but in an inclination thereto of many dayes together: So the nature of War, consisteth not in actuall fighting; but in the known disposition thereto, during all the time there is no assurance to the contrary. All other time is PEACE.

Whatsoever therefore is consequent to a time of Warre, where every man is Enemy to every man; the same is consequent to the time, wherein men live without other security, than what their own strength, and their own invention shall furnish them withall. In such condition, there is no place for Industry; because the fruit thereof is uncertain; and consequently no Culture of the Earth; no Navigation, nor use of the commodities that may be imported by Sea; no commodious Building; no Instruments of moving, and removing such things as require much force; no Knowledge of the face of the Earth; no account of Time; no Arts; no Letters; no Society; and which is worst of all, continuall feare, and danger of violent death; And the life of man, solitary, poore, nasty, brutish, and short.

It may seem strange to some man, that has not well weighed these things; that Nature should thus dissociate, and render men apt to invade, and destroy one another: and he may therefore, not trusting to this Inference, made from the Passions, desire perhaps to have the same confirmed by Experience. Let him therefore consider with himselfe, when taking a journey, he armes himselfe, and seeks to go well accompanied; when going to sleep, he locks his dores; when even in his house he locks his chests; and this when he knows there bee Lawes, and publike Officers, armed, to revenge all injuries shall bee done him; what opinion he has of his fellow subjects, when he rides armed; of his fellow Citizens, when he locks his dores; and of his children and servants, when he locks his chests. Does he not there as much accuse mankind by his actions, as I do by my words? But neither of us accuse mans nature in it. The Desires, and other Passions of man, are in themselves no Sin. No more are the Actions, that proceed from those Passions, till they know a Law that forbids them: which till Lawes be made they cannot know: nor can any Law be made, till they have agreed upon the Person that shall make it.

It may peradventure be thought, there was never such a time, nor condition of warre as this; and I believe it was never generally so, over all *the* world: but there are many places, where they live so now. For the savage people in many places of *America*, except the government of small Families, the concord whereof dependeth on naturall lust, have no government at all; and live at this day in that brutish manner, as I said before. Howsoever, it may be perceived what manner of life there would be, where there were no common Power to feare; by the manner of life, which men that have formerly lived under a peacefull government, use to degenerate into, in a civil Warre.

But though there had never been any time, wherein particular men were in a condition of warre one against another; yet in all times, Kings, and Persons of Soveraigne authority, because of their Independency, are in continuall jealousies, and in the state and posture of Gladiators; having their weapons pointing; and their eyes fixed on one another; that is, their Forts, Garrisons, and Guns upon the Frontiers of their Kingdomes; and continuall Spyes upon their neighbours; which is a posture of War. But because they uphold thereby, the Industry of their Subjects; there does not follow from it, that misery, which accompanies the Liberty of particular men.

To this warre of every man against every man, this also is consequent; that nothing can be Unjust. The notions of Right and Wrong, Justice and Injustice have there no place. Where there is no common Power, there is no Law: where no Law, no Injustice.

Force, and Fraud, are in warre the two Cardinall vertues. Justice, and Injustice are none of the Faculties neither of the Body, not Mind. If they were, they might be in a man that were alone in the world, as well as his Senses, and Passions. They are Qualities, that relate to men in Society, not in Solitude. It is consequent also to the same condition, that there be no Propriety, no Dominion, no *Mine* and *Thine* distinct; but onely that to be every mans that he can get; and for so long, as he can keep it. And thus much for the ill condition, which man by meer Nature is actually placed in; though with a possiblity to come out of it, consisting partly in the Passions, partly in his Reason.

The Passions that encline men to Peace, are Feare of Death; Desire of such things as are necessary to commodious living, and a Hope by their Industry to obtain them. And Reason suggesteth convenient Articles of Peace, upon which men may be drawn to agreement. These Articles, are they, which otherwise are called the Lawes of Nature: whereof I shall speak more particularly, in the two following Chapters.

OF THE FIRST AND SECOND NATURALL LAWES, AND OF CONTRACTS

The Right of Nature, which Writers commonly call *Jus Naturale*, is the Liberty each man hath, to use his own power, as he will himselfe, for the preservation of his own Nature; that is to say, of his own Life; and consequently, of doing any thing, which in his own Judgement, and Reason, hee shall conceive to be the aptest means thereunto.

By LIBERTY, is understood, according to the proper signification of the word, the absence of externall Impediments: which Impediments, may oft take away part of a mans power to do what hee would; but cannot hinder him from using the power left him, according as his judgement, and reason shall dictate to him.

A LAW OF NATURE, (*Lex Naturalis*,) is a Precept, or generall Rule, found out by Reason, by which a man is forbidden to do, that, which is destructive of his life, or taketh away the means of preserving the same; and to omit, that, by which he thinketh it may be best preserved. For though they that speak of this subject, use to confound *Jus*, and *Lex*, Right and Law, yet they ought to be distinguished; because RIGHT, consisteth in liberty to do, or to forbeare; Whereas LAW, determineth, and bindeth to one of them: so that Law, and Right, differ as much, as

Obligation, and Liberty; which in one and the same matter are inconsistent.

And because the condition of Man, (as hath been declared in the precedent Chapter) is a condition of Warre of every one against every one; in which case every one is governed by his own Reason; and there is nothing he can make use of, that may not be a help unto him, in preserving his life against his enemyes; It followeth, that in such a condition, every man has a Right to every thing; even to one anothers body. And therefore, as long as this naturall Right of every man to every thing endureth, there can be no security to any man, (how strong or wise soever he be,) of living out the time, which Nature ordinarily alloweth men to live. And consequently it is a precept, or generall rule of Reason, *That every man, ought to endeavour Peace, as farre as he has hope of obtaining it; and when he cannot obtain it, that he may seek, and use, all helps, and advantages of Warre*. The first branch of which Rule, containeth the first, and Fundamentall Law of Nature; which is, *to seek Peace, and follow it*. The Second, the summe of the Right of Nature; which is, *By all means we can, to defend our selves*.

From this Fundamentall Law of Nature, by which men are commanded to endeavour Peace, is derived this second Law; *That a man be willing, when others are so too, as farre-forth, as for Peace, and defence of himselfe he shall think it necessary, to lay down this right to all things; and be contented with so much liberty against other men, as he would allow other men against himselfe*. For as long as every man holdeth this Right, of doing any thing he liketh; so long are all men in the condition of Warre. But if other men will not lay down their Right, as well as he; then there is no Reason for any one, to devest himselfe of his: For that were to expose himselfe to Prey, (which no man is bound to) rather than to dispose himselfe to Peace. This is that Law of the Gospell; *Whatsoever you require that others should do to you, that do ye to them*. And that Law of all men, *Quod tibi fieri non vis, alteri ne feceris*. *[Do not unto others what you do not want done to yourself.]*

To *lay downe* a mans Right to any thing, is to *devest* himselfe of the *Liberty*, of hindring another of the benefit of his own Right to the same. For he that renounceth, or passeth away his Right, giveth not to any other man a Right which he had not before; because there is nothing to which every man had not Right by Nature: but onely standeth out of his way, that he may enjoy his own originall Right, without hindrance from him; not without hindrance from another. So that the effect which redoundeth to one man, by another mans defect of Right, is but so much diminution of impediments to the use of his own Right originall.

OF OTHER LAWES OF NATURE

From that law of Nature, by which we are obliged to transferre to another, such Rights, as being retained, hinder the peace of Mankind, there followeth a Third; which is this, *That men performe their Covenants made*: without which, Covenants are in vain, and but Empty words; and the Right of all men to all things remaining, wee are still in the condition of Warre.

. . .

And in this law of Nature, consisteth the Fountain and Originall of JUSTICE. For where no Covenant hath preceded, there hath no Right been transferred, and every man has right to every thing; and consequently, no action can be Unjust. But when a Covenant is made, then to break it is *Unjust*; And the definition of INJUSTICE, is no other than *the not Performance of Covenant*. And whatsoever is not Unjust, *is Just*.

⇒ "TWO FACES OF CONTRACTARIAN THOUGHT" ⇐

Jean Hampton,

Jean Hampton was Professor of Philosophy at the University of California, Davis. She wrote on issues in ethics, justice, and political philosophy, and her work on the social contract tradition was particularly influential. Her books include *Hobbes and the Social Contract Tradition* (Cambridge: Cambridge University Press, 1988) and (with Jeffrie Murphy) *Forgiveness and Mercy* (Cambridge: Cambridge University Press, 1988). In this essay, Hampton scrutinizes the basic assumption of *individualism* inherent in social contract ethics.

SOCIAL CONTRACT THEORY: INADEQUATE ACCOUNT OF ETHICS

Although Hobbes's masterpiece *Leviathan* is primarily concerned with presenting a contract argument for the institution of a certain kind of state (one with an absolute sovereign), if one looks closely, one also sees a sketch of a certain kind of contractarian approach to morality, which has profoundly influenced contemporary moral theorists such as Gauthier.

Hobbes's approach to morality does not assume there are natural moral laws or natural rights that we discern through the use of our reason or intuition. It is not an approach that assumes there is a naturally good object in the world (such as Aristotle's *Summum Bonum*) that moral action serves and that people ought to pursue. It is not an approach that explains moral action as "natural," for example, as action generated by powerful other-regarding sentiments; Hobbes did not believe that such sentiments were very important or powerful in human life. And it is not an approach that justifies morality as a set of laws commanded by God—although Hobbes believed that his moral imperatives were *also* justified as commands of God. Using his contractarian method, he seeks to define the nature and authority of moral imperatives by reference to the desires and reasoning abilities of human beings, so that regardless of their religious commitments, all people will see that they have reason to act morally. So without repudiating the divine origin of the laws, Hobbes invokes contract language in order to develop an entirely *human* justification of morality. . . .

Let me simply state here the features of what I take to be the Hobbesian moral theory. . . .

1. What is valuable is what a person desires, not what he ought to desire (for no such prescriptively powerful object exists); and rational action is action that achieves or maximizes the satisfaction of desire (where it is a fact that the desire for self-preservation is our primary desire, and that human beings are, by and large, mutually unconcerned).

2. Moral action is rational for a person to perform if and only if such action advances his interests.

3. Morality is, in part, a body of causal knowledge about what human actions lead to peace, an end which it is common knowledge people desire and which they can all share, so that such actions are rational for them and "mutually agreeable." (This precept rests on the Hobbesian belief that people

are not self-sufficient, and that they are roughly equal in strength and mental ability.)

4. Peace producing action is only individually rational to perform (hence only moral action) when there is a convention in the community that people perform such action (so that I know that if I behave cooperatively, then others will do so too, and vice versa). These conventions comprise the institution of morality in our society. The rationality of performance is, however, subject to two provisos:

    Proviso 1: In order to be moral, an action must be not only peace producing and performed in the knowledge that others are willing to do so, but also an action that involves no net loss for the agent.

    Proviso 2: Human beings are not, as a group, rational enough to be able to institute moral conventions, and hence must create a sovereign who can use his power to generate them.

5. Defining justice or equitable treatment in situations of conflict is done by considering what principles of justice the people involved "could agree to" or "what they would be unreasonable to reject," where the reasonableness of rejection is determined by a calculation comparing the benefits and costs of accepting an arbitrator's resolution with the benefits and costs of resorting to violence to resolve the conflict. An impartial judge, therefore, arbitrates according to the principle "to each according to his threat advantage in war."

. . . Let us reflect, for a moment, on the interesting features and strengths of a moral theory with this structure. Consider, first of all, that the Hobbesian approach relies on a very strong conception of individuality. According to Hobbes, cooperative social interaction is presented neither as inevitable nor as something that people value for its own sake, but rather as something that asocially defined individuals find instrumentally valuable given their primary (nonsocially defined) desires. To think that cooperative behavior needs to be encouraged and justified, so that we must be *persuaded* to behave socially toward one another, is to believe that, even if society has some affect on us, it does not determine our fundamental or "intrinsic" nature as human beings, which is a nature that "dissociates us, and renders us apt to invade and destroy one another" (*Leviathan* 13, 10, 62).

Moreover, notice that there are two quite different ways in which this moral contractarian theory uses the notion of agreement. Features 2 and 3 capture the idea that the behavior enjoined by Hobbes's laws of nature is "agreeable," that is, that such action helps to secure the most-desired objects and/or states of affairs for each individual. Feature 5 captures the idea for which moral contractarians are famous; namely, that certain features of morality (e.g., fair resolution of conflict) can be understood as the *object* of agreement. However, there is connection, in Hobbes's theory, between the latter way of using agreement and the former. To resolve conflicts via the use of arbitrators and agreement procedures is to resolve them peacefully and with much less cost to the parties than more violent resolution procedures. Hobbes commends the use of arbitrators as individually rational for disputants, and warns the arbitrators that their usefulness to the disputants depends on the extent to which their peaceful resolution is more acceptable than going to war to resolve the dilemma. It is therefore conducive to self preservation to use a cooperative agreement procedure to resolve conflict, so that defining moral behavior through agreement is itself, for Hobbes, a mutually agreeable—that is, mutually self-preserving—behavior.

But perhaps most important of all, we should appreciate that all five features of Hobbes's moral view fit into a moral theory that is committed to the idea that morality is a *human-made institution,* which is justified only to the extent that it effectively furthers human interests. That is, Hobbes seeks to explain the *existence* of morality in society by appealing to the convention-creating activities of human beings, while arguing that the *justification* of morality in any human society depends upon how well its moral conventions serve individuals' desires.

In fact, there is a connection between Hobbes's contractarian approach to the state and this approach to morality. His decision to justify absolute sovereignty by reference to what people "could agree to" in a prepolitical society is an attempt to explain and legitimate the state's authority by appealing neither to God nor to any natural features of human beings that might be thought to explain the subordination of some to others, but solely to the needs and desires of the people who will be subjects of political realms. In the same manner, he insists that existing moral rules have power over us because they are social conventions for behavior (where Hobbes would also argue

that these conventions only exist because of the power of the sovereign).

But Hobbes does not assume that existing conventions are, in and of themselves, justified. By considering "what we *could* agree to" if we had the chance to reappraise and redo the cooperative conventions in our society, we are able to determine the extent to which our present conventions are "mutually agreeable" and so *rational* for us to accept and act on. So Hobbes's moral theory invokes both actual agreements (i.e., conventions) and hypothetical agreements (which involve considering what conventions would be "mutually agreeable") at different points in his theory; the former are what he believes our moral life consists of; the latter are what he believes our moral life *should* consist of—that is, what our actual moral life should model. The contractarian methodology is useful in defining and justifying morality for one who believes that morality is man-made because considering what moral laws "people could agree to" (as well as what laws they have agreed to) is a way of confirming *that* morality is man-made, and a way of appraising how well the present institution serves the powerful self-regarding interests that virtually all of us have.

Note that this way of cashing out the language of hypothetical agreement makes the agreement-talk only a kind of metaphor, and not a device that reveals, in and of itself, the nature of morality or justice. What rational agents could all agree to is the securing of an object and/or state of affairs, the benefits of which they could all share and for which there is a rational argument using premises that all rational agents would take as a basis for deliberation. Hence, to determine what these agents "could all agree to," one must perform a deduction of practical reason, something that Hobbes believes he has done in Chapters 14 and 15 of *Leviathan.*

Hence, the notion of contract or agreement does not do justificational work *by itself* in the Hobbesian moral theory. What we "could agree to" has moral force for Hobbes not because make-believe promises in hypothetical worlds have any binding force, but because this sort of agreement is a device that *reveals* the way in which the agreed-upon outcome is rational for all of us. The justificational force of this kind of contract theory is therefore carried within, but derived from sources other than, the contract or agreement in the theory.

. . .

There are no free giveaways or free rides on Hobbes's theory; you get what it is in your interest to get and what it is in others' interest to let you have. The results of this kind of thinking are not, I think, very attractive. Contemporary Hobbesians like Gauthier try to accept the self-interested underpinnings of the theory but dress up or deny the conclusions that Hobbes claims they force one to draw. I have attempted to suggest in these remarks that Hobbes is right to insist on them. I suspect that if Gauthier or other theorists sympathetic to the structure of Hobbesian theory long for "nicer" principles of morality and justice than those that Hobbes develops they need to find a non-Hobbesian foundation for them. And as I now discuss, there are signs that Gauthier himself suspects this is so.

Consider what many have found a particularly ugly side to Hobbesian morality: its radical individualism. Recall that the people in Hobbes's or Gauthier's contracting world are fully developed, asocially defined individuals. But when *Leviathan* was originally published some readers were shocked by the idea that the nature of our ties to others was interest-based. Aristotelian critics contended that Hobbes's theory goes too far in trying to represent us as radically separate from others. Their worries are also the worries of many twentieth-century critics. Do not our ties to our mothers and fathers, our children and our friends define, at least in part, who we are? Isn't it true that our distinctive tastes, projects, interests, characteristics, and skills are defined by and created within a social context? So how can a moral theory that does not take this into account be an accurate representation of our moral life? It would seem that we *must* bring into our moral theory noninstrumental ties with others that are not based on our affections because it is through such ties that we *become* individuals. . . .

Hobbes would either not understand or else resist the claims of our social definition. But Gauthier, a member of our place and time, accepts them, and this has strange consequences for his moral theory. Gauthier is moved by the criticism that it is unfair to use allocation procedures such as the market, to distribute goods in circumstances where the society permits—even encourages—one class of people to prevent development in another class of people of those talents that allow one to do well in a system using that allocation procedure. Thus, he suggests that we see his contract on the fair terms of cooperation not as an agreement among determinate, already defined, individuals, but as an agreement at a hypothetical

"Archimedean Point" among "protopeople"—people who have a certain genetic endowment and who are concerned to select principles that will structure their society such that they will develop well:

> The principles chosen from the Archimedean point must therefore provide that each person's expected share of the fruits of social interaction be related, not just to what he actually contributes, since his actual contribution may reflect the contingent permissions and prohibitions found in any social structure, but *to the contributions he would make* in that social structure most favorable to the actualization of his capacities and character traits, and to the fulfillment of his preferences, provided that this structure is a feasible alternative meeting the other requirements of the Archimedean choice. (My emphasis)

No longer does Gauthier's contract talk presume fully determinate individuals, and no longer is the object of any contract a principle for the resolution of conflict among individuals. Now the contract methodology is used to choose principles that are "for" the structuring of the social system that plays a profound role in structuring individuals. Like Rawls, Gauthier is declaring that the first order of moral business is the definition of social justice.

This is not a benign addition to Gauthier's Hobbesian moral theory: it is an addition that essentially destroys its character as a Hobbesian theory. Of course, it undermines the individualism of the original Hobbesian theory; many will think that this is no great loss. But it was that individualism that much of the rest of the theory presupposed. Consider, for example, that a Hobbesian theory answers the "Why be moral?" question with the response, "Because it is in your interest to be so." But that answer no longer makes sense in a contract theory designed to pursue the nature of social justice using protopeople. Suppose the results of that theory call for a more egalitarian distribution of resources and opportunities open to talents that society will attempt to develop in all its members. If I am a white male in a society that accords white males privileged opportunities to develop talents that will allow them to earn well, then why is it rational for me to pursue a restructuring of social institutions in which this is no longer true?

Indeed, given that their development has already taken place, *why is it even rational for adult minority members or females to support this restructuring?* All of these people are already "made." Restructuring the social world such that it does a fairer job of creating future generations of individuals is a costly and other-regarding enterprise. Why should these determinate individuals be rational to undertake it, given its cost, unless they just happened to be affected by sympathy for other members of their race or caste or sex, and so enjoyed the struggle? But the nontuistic perspective Gauthier encourages his bargainers to take encourages them to discount any benefits to others from their actions. So assuming the Hobbesian/Gauthierian theory of rationality, what it would be rational for "proto-me" to agree to in some extrasocietal bargain seems to have little bearing on what it is rational for *determinate-me* to accept now.

It is because the self-interest of *determinate* individuals does not seem sufficient to explain the commitment to the results of a bargain among *protopeople* that one wonders whether Gauthier's eventual interest in defining fair principles for the development of individual talents in a social system betrays a commitment to the intrinsic value of the individuals themselves. And it is the idea that individuals have intrinsic value that is missing from the Hobbesian approach. It has not been sufficiently appreciated, I believe, that by answering the "Why be moral?" question by invoking self-interest in the way that Hobbes does, one makes not only cooperative action, but the human beings with whom one will cooperate merely of *instrumental value*, and this is an implicit feature of Hobbes's moral theory that is of central importance. Now Hobbes is unembarrassed by the fact that in his view, "The *Value*, or WORTH of a man, is as of all other things, his Price; that is to say, so much as would be given for the use of his Power: and therefore is not absolute; but a thing dependent on the need and judgement of another" (*Leviathan* 10, 16, 42). But this way of viewing people is not something that we, or even Gauthier, can take with equanimity. In the final two chapters of his book, Gauthier openly worries about the fact that the reason why we value moral imperatives on this Hobbesian view is that they are instrumentally valuable to us in our pursuit of what we value. But note *why* they are instrumentally valuable: in virtue of our physical and intellectual weaknesses that make it impossible for us to be self-sufficient, we need the cooperation of others to prosper. If there were some way that we could remedy our weaknesses and become self-sufficient, for example, by becoming a superman or superwoman, or by using a Ring of Gyges to make ourselves invisible and so steal from the stores of others with impunity, then it seems we would no longer value or respect moral constraints because they would no longer be useful to us—unless we happened to like the idea. But in this case sentiment, rather than reason, would motivate kind treatment. And without such sentiment, people would simply be "prey" for us.

Even in a world in which we are not self-sufficient, the Hobbesian moral theory gives us no reason to respect those with whom we have no need of cooperating, or those whom we are strong enough to dominate, such as old people, or the handicapped, or retarded children whom we do not want to rear, or people from other societies with whom we have no interest in trading. And I would argue that this shows that Hobbesian moral contractarianism fails in a very serious way to capture the nature of morality. *Regardless* of whether or not one can engage in beneficial cooperative interactions with another, our moral intuitions push us to assent to the idea that one owes that person respectful treatment simply in virtue of the fact that he or she is a *person*. It seems to be a feature of our moral life that we regard a human being, whether or not she is instrumentally valuable, as always intrinsically valuable. Indeed, to the extent that the results of a Hobbesian theory are acceptable, this is because one's concern to cooperate with someone whom one cannot dominate leads one to behave in ways that mimic the respect one ought to show her simply in virtue of her worth as a human being. . . .

⇒ "What Do Women Want in a Moral Theory?" ⇐
Annette Baier

Annette Baier was Distinguished Service Professor of Philosophy at the University of Pittsburgh until her recent retirement to her native New Zealand. All her work, including the essay reprinted here, is readable and interesting, while maintaining the highest standards of philosophical rigor and argumentation. In this essay, she examines elements that have often been omitted or undervalued in moral philosophy and considers the best means of including them.

WOMEN HAVE A DISTINCTIVE ETHICAL PERSPECTIVE

When I finished reading Carol Gilligan's *In a Different Voice*, I asked myself the obvious question for a philosopher reader: what differences should one expect in the moral philosophy done by women, supposing Gilligan's sample of women to be representative and supposing her analysis of their moral attitudes and moral development to be correct? Should one expect women to want to produce moral theories, and if so, what sort of moral theories? How will any moral theories they produce differ from those produced by men?

Obviously one does not have to make this an entirely a priori and hypothetical question. One can look and see what sort of contributions women have made to moral philosophy. Such a look confirms, I think, Gilligan's findings. What one finds is a bit different in tone and approach from the standard sort of the moral philosophy as done by men following in the footsteps of the great moral philosophers (all men). . . . I hear the voice Gilligan heard, made reflective and philosophical. What women want in moral philosophy is what they are providing. And what they are providing seems to me to confirm Gilligan's theses about women. . . .

Although we find out what sort of moral philosophy women want by looking to see what they have provided, if we do that for moral theory, the answer we get seems to be 'none'. None of the contributions to moral philosophy by women really counts as a moral theory, nor is seen as such by its author. . . .

The paradigm examples of moral theories—those that are called by their authors 'moral theories'—are distinguished not by the comprehensiveness of their internally coherent account but by the *sort* of coherence which is aimed at over a fairly broad area. Their method is not the mosaic method but the broad brushstroke method. Moral theories, as we know them, are, to change the art form, vaults rather than walls—they are not built by assembling painstakingly made brick after brick. In *this* sense of theory—a fairly tightly systematic account of a large area of morality, with a keystone supporting all the rest—women moral philosophers have not yet, to my knowledge, produced moral theories or claimed that they have. . . .

What key concept or guiding motif might hold together the structure of a moral theory hypothetically produced by a reflective woman, Gilligan-style, who has taken up moral theorizing as a calling? What would be a suitable central question, principle, or concept to structure a moral theory which might accommodate those moral insights which women tend to have more readily than men, and to answer those moral questions which, it seems, worry women more than men? I hypothesized that the women's theory, expressive mainly of women's insights and concerns, would be an ethics of love, and this hypothesis seems to be Gilligan's too, since she has gone on from *In a Different Voice* to write about the limitations of Freud's understanding of love as women know it. But presumably women theorists will be like enough to men to want their moral theory to be acceptable to all, *so* acceptable both to reflective women and to reflective men. Like any good theory, it will need not to ignore the partial truth of previous theories. It must therefore accommodate both the insights men have more easily than women and those women have more easily than men. It should swallow up its predecessor theories. . . . So women theorists will need to connect their ethics of love with what has been the men theorists' preoccupation, namely, obligation.

The great and influential moral theorists have in the modern era taken *obligation* as the key and the problematic concept, and have asked what justifies treating a person as morally bound or obliged to do a particular thing. Since to be bound is to be unfree, by making obligation central one at the same time makes central the question of the justification of coercion, of forcing or trying to force someone to act in a particular way. The concept of obligation as justified limitation of freedom does just what one wants a good theoretical concept to do—to divide up the field (as one looks at different ways one's freedom may be limited, freedom in different spheres, different sorts and versions and levels of justification) and at the same time to hold the subfields together. There must in a theory be some generalization and some speciation or diversification, and a good rich key concept guides one both in recognizing the diversity and in recognizing the unity in it. The concept of obligation has served this function very well for the area of morality it covers, and so we have some fine theories about that area. But as Aristotelians and Christians, as well as women, know, there is a lot of morality *not* covered by that concept, a lot of very great importance even for the area where there are obligations.

This is fairly easy to see if we look at what lies behind the perceived obligation to keep promises. Unless there is some good moral reason why someone should assume the responsibility of rearing a child to be *capable* of taking promises seriously, once she understands what a promise is, the obligation to obey promises will not effectively tie her, and any force applied to punish her when she breaks promises or makes fraudulent ones will be of questionable justice. Is there an *obligation* on someone to make the child into a morally competent promisor? If so, on whom? Who has failed in his or her obligations when, say, war orphans who grew up without parental love or any other love arrive at legal adulthood very willing to be untrue to their word? Who failed in what obligation in all those less extreme cases of attempted but unsuccessful moral education? . . . The liberal version of our basic moral obligations tends to be fairly silent on who has what obligations to new members of the moral community, and it would throw most theories of the justification of obligations into some confusion if the obligation to rear one's children lovingly were added to the list of obligations. Such evidence as we have about the conditions in which children do successfully 'learn' the morality of the community of which they are members suggests that we cannot substitute 'conscientiously' for 'lovingly' in this hypothetical extra needed obligation. But an obligation to love, in the strong sense needed, would be an embarrassment to the theorist, given most accepted versions of 'ought implies can'. . . .

Reliance on a recognized obligation to turn oneself into a good parent or else to avoid becoming a parent would be a problematic solution. Good parents tend to be the children of good parents, so this obligation would collapse into the obligation to avoid parenthood unless one expected to be a good parent. That, given available methods of contraception, may itself convert into the obligation, should one expect not to be a good parent, to sexual abstinence, or sterilization, or resolute resort to abortion when contraception fails. The conditional obligation to abort, and in effect also the conditional obligation to sterilization, falls on the women. There may be conditions in which the rational moral choice is between obligatory sexual abstinence and obligatory sterilization, but obligatory abortion, such as women in China now face, seems to me a moral monster. . . .

No liberal moral theorist, as far as I know, is advocating obligatory abortion or obligatory sterilization when necessary to prevent the conception of children whose parents do not expect to love them. My point rather is that they escape this conclusion only by avoiding the issue of what is to ensure that new members of the moral community do get the loving care they need to become morally competent persons. Liberal moral theories assume that women either will provide loving maternal care, or will persuade their mates to provide loving paternal care, or when pregnant will decide for abortion, encouraged by their freedom-loving men. These theories, in other words, exploit the culturally encouraged maternal instinct and/or the culturally encouraged docility of women. The liberal system would receive a nasty spanner in its works should women use their freedom of choice as regards abortion to choose *not* to abort, and then leave their newborn children on their fathers' doorsteps. That would test liberal morality's ability to provide for its own survival.

At this point it may be objected that every moral theory must make some assumptions about the natural psychology of these on whom obligations are imposed. Why shouldn't the liberal theory count on a continuing sufficient supply of good loving mothers, as it counts on continuing self-interest and, perhaps, on a continuing supply of pugnacious men who are able and willing to become good soldiers, without turning any of these into moral *obligations*? Why waste moral resources recognizing as obligatory or as virtuous what one can count on getting without moral pressure? If, in the moral economy, one can get enough good mothers and good warriors 'for free', why not gladly exploit what nature and cultural history offer? I cannot answer this question fully here, but my argument does depend upon the assumption that a decent morality will *not* depend for its stability on forces to which it gives no moral recognition. Its account books should be open to scrutiny, and there should be no unpaid debts, no loans with no prospect of repayment. I also assume that once we are clear about these matters and about the interdependencies involved, our principles of justice will not allow us to recognize either a special obligation on every woman to initiate the killing of the foetus she has conceived, should she and her mate be, or think they will be, deficient in parental love, or a special obligation on every young man to kill those his elders have labelled enemies of his country. Both such 'obligations' are prima facie suspect, and difficult to make consistent with any of the principles supposedly generating obligations in modern moral theories. I also assume that, on reflection, we will not want to recognize as *virtues* the character traits of women and men which lead them to supply such life and death services 'for free.' Neither maternal servitude, nor the resoluteness needed to kill off one's children to prevent their growing up unloved, nor the easy willingness to go out and kill, when ordered to do so by authorities seems to me to be a character trait a decent morality will encourage by labelling it a virtue. But the liberals' morality must somehow encourage such traits if its stability depends on enough people showing them. There is, then, understandable motive for liberals' avoidance of the question of whether such qualities are or are not morally approved of, and of whether or not there is any obligation to act as one with such character traits would act.

It is symptomatic of the bad faith of liberal morality as understood by many of those who defend it that issues such as whether to fight or not to fight, to have or not to have an abortion, or to be or not to be an unpaid maternal drudge are left to individual conscience. Since there is no coherent guidance liberal morality can give on these issues, which clearly are *not* matters of moral indifference, liberal morality tells each of us, 'the choice is yours', hoping that enough will choose to be self-sacrificial life providers and self-sacrificial death dealers to suit the purposes of the rest. . . .

Granted that the men's theories of obligation need supplementation, to have much chance of integrity and coherence, and that the women's hypothetical theories will want to cover obligation as well as love, then what concept brings them together? My tentative answer is—the concept of appropriate trust, oddly neglected in moral theory. This concept also nicely mediates between reason and feeling, those tired old candidates for moral authority, since to trust is neither quite to believe something about the trusted nor necessarily to feel any emotion towards them—but to have a belief-informed and action-influencing attitude. To make it plausible that the neglected concept of appropriate trust is a good one for the enlightened moral theorist to make central, I need to show, or begin to show, how it could include obligation, indeed shed light on obligations and their justification, as well as include love, the other moral concerns of Gilligan's women, and many of the topics women moral philosophers have chosen to address, mosaic fashion. I would also need to show that it could connect all of these in a way which holds out promise both of synthesis and of comprehensive moral coverage. A moral theory which looked at the conditions for proper trust *of* all the various sorts we show, and at what sorts of reasons justify inviting such trust, giving it, and meeting it, would, I believe, not have to avoid turning its gaze on the conditions for the survival of the practices it endorses, *so* it could

avoid that unpleasant choice many current liberal theories seem to have—between incoherence and bad faith. I do not pretend that we will easily agree once we raise the questions I think we should raise, but at least we may have a language adequate to the expression of both men's and women's moral viewpoints.

My trust in the concept of trust is based in part on my own attempts to restate and consider what is right and what wrong with men's theories, especially Hume's, which I consider the best of the lot. I have found myself reconstructing his account of the artifices of justice as an account of the progressive enlargement of a climate of trust, and have found that a helpful way to see it. It has some textual basis, but is nevertheless a reconstruction, and one I have found, immodestly, an improvement. So it is because I have tried the concept and explored its dimensions a bit— the variety of goods we may trust others not to take from us, the sort of security or insurance we have when we do, the sorts of defences or potential defences we lay down when we trust, the various conditions for reasonable trust of various types—that I am hopeful about its power as a theoretical, and not just an exegetical, tool. I also found myself needing to use it when I made a brief rash attempt at that women's topic, caring (invited in by a male philosopher, I should say). I am reasonably sure that trust does generalize some central moral features of the recognition of binding obligations and moral virtues and of loving, as well as of other important relations between persons, such as teacher-pupil, confider-confidante, worker to co-worker in the same cause, and professional to client. Indeed it is fairly obvious that love, the main moral phenomenon women want attended to, involves trust, so I anticipate little quarrel when I claim that, if we had a moral theory spelling out the conditions for appropriate trust and distrust, that would include a morality of love in all its variants—parental love, love of children for their parents, love of family members, love of friends, of lovers in the strict sense, of co-workers, of one's country and its figureheads, of exemplary heroines and heroes, of goddesses and gods.

Love and loyalty demand maximal trust of one sort, and maximal trustworthiness, and in investigating the conditions for maximal trust and maximal risk we must think about the ethics of love. More controversial may be my claim that the ethics of obligation will also be covered. I see it as covered because to recognize a set of obligations is to trust some group of persons to instil them, to demand that they be met, possibly to levy sanctions if they are not, and this is to trust persons with very significant coercive power over others. Less coercive but still significant power is possessed by those shaping our conception of the virtues and expecting us to display them, approving when we do, disapproving and perhaps shunning us when we do not. Such coercive and manipulative power over others requires justification, and is justified only if we have reason to trust those who have it to use it properly and to use the discretion which is always given when trust is given in a way which serves the purpose of the whole system of moral control, and not merely self-serving or morally improper purposes. Since the question of the justification of coercion becomes, at least in part, the question of the wisdom of trusting the coercers to do their job properly, the morality of obligation, in as far as it reduces to the morality of coercion, is covered by the morality of proper trust. Other forms of trust may also be involved, but trusting enforcers with the use of force is the most problematic form of trust involved.

The coercers and manipulators are, to some extent, all of us, so to ask what our obligations are and what virtues we should exhibit is to ask what it is reasonable to trust us to demand, expect, and contrive to get from one another. It becomes, in part, a question of what powers we can in reason trust ourselves to exercise properly. But self-trust is a dubious or limit case of trust, so I prefer to postpone the examination of the concept of proper self-trust at least until proper trust of others is more clearly understood. Nor do we distort matters too much if we concentrate on those cases where moral sanctions and moral pressure and moral manipulation are not self-applied but applied to others, particularly by older persons to younger persons. Most moral pressuring that has any effect goes on in childhood and early youth. Moral sanctions may continue to be applied, formally and informally, to adults, but unless the criminal courts apply them it is easy enough for adults to ignore them, to brush them aside. It is not difficult to become a sensible knave, and to harden one's heart so that one is insensible to the moral condemnation of one's victims and those who sympathize with them. Only if the pressures applied in the morally formative stage have given one a heart that rebels against the thought of such ruthless independence of what others think will one see any reason *not* to ignore moral condemnation, not to treat it as mere powerless words and breath. Condemning sensible knaves is as much a waste of breath as arguing with them—all we can sensibly do is to try to protect children against their influence, and ourselves against their knavery. Adding to the

criminal law will not be the way to do the latter, since such moves will merely challenge sensible knaves to find new knavish exceptions and loopholes, not protect us from sensible knavery. Sensible knaves are precisely those who exploit us without breaking the law. So the whole question of when moral pressure of various sorts, formative, reformative, and punitive, ought to be brought to bear by whom is subsumed under the question of whom to trust when and with what, and for what good reasons.

In concentrating on obligations, rather than virtues, modern moral theorists have chosen to look at the cases where more trust is placed in enforcers of obligations than is placed in ordinary moral agents, the bearers of the obligations. In taking, as contractarians do, contractual obligations as the model of obligations, they concentrate on a case where the very minimal trust is put in the obligated person, and considerable punitive power entrusted to the one to whom the obligation is owed (I assume here that Hume is right in saying that when we promise or contract, we formally subject ourselves to the penalty, in case of failure, of never being trusted as a promisor again). This is an interesting case of the allocation of trust of various sorts, but it surely distorts our moral vision to suppose that *all* obligations, let alone all morally pressured expectations we impose on others, conform to that abnormally coercive model. It takes very special conditions for it to be safe to trust persons to inflict penalties on other persons, conditions in which either we can trust the penalizers to have the virtues necessary to penalize wisely and fairly, or else we can rely on effective threats to keep unvirtuous penalizers from abusing their power—that is to say, rely on others to coerce the first coercers into proper behaviour. But that reliance too will either be trust or will have to rely on threats from coercers of the coercers of coercers, and so on. Morality on this model becomes a nasty, if intellectually intriguing, game of mutual mutually corrective threats. The central question of who should deprive whom of what freedom soon becomes the question of whose anger should be dreaded by whom (the theory of obligation), supplemented perhaps by an afterthought on whose favour should be courted by whom (the theory of the virtues).

Undoubtedly some important part of morality does depend in part on a system of threats and bribes, at least for its survival in difficult conditions when normal goodwill and normally virtuous dispositions may be insufficient to motivate the conduct required for the preservation and justice of the moral network of relationships. But equally undoubtedly life will be nasty, emotionally poor, and worse than brutish (even if longer), if that is all morality is, or even if that coercive structure of morality is regarded as the backbone, rather than as an available crutch, should the main support fail. For the main support has to come from those we entrust with the job of rearing and training persons so that they can be trusted in various ways, some trusted with extraordinary coercive powers, some with public decision-making powers, all trusted as parties to promise, most trusted by some who love them and by one or more willing to become co-parents with them, most trusted by dependent children, dependent elderly relatives, sick friends, and so on. A very complex network of a great variety of sorts of trust structures our moral relationships with our fellows, and if there is a *main* support to this network it is the trust we place in those who respond to the trust of new members of the moral community, namely, children, and prepare them for new forms of trust.

A theory which took as its central question 'Who should trust whom with what, and why?' would not have to forgo the intellectual fun and games previous theorists have had with the various paradoxes of morality—curbing freedom to increase freedom, curbing self-interest the better to satisfy self-interest, not aiming at happiness in order to become happier. For it is easy enough to get a paradox of trust to accompany or, if I am right, to generalize the paradoxes of freedom, self-interest, and hedonism. To trust is to make oneself or to let oneself be more vulnerable than one might have been to harm from others—to give them an opportunity to harm one, in the confidence that they will not take it, because they have no good reason to. Why would one take such a risk? For risk it always is, given the partial opaqueness to us of the reasoning and motivation of those we trust and with whom we cooperate. Our confidence may be, and quite often is, misplaced. That is what we risk when we trust. If the best reason to take such a risk is the expected gain in security which comes from a climate of trust, then in trusting we are always giving up security to get greater security, exposing our throats so that others become accustomed to not biting. A moral theory which made proper trust its central concern could have its own categorical imperative, could replace obedience to self-made laws and freely chosen restraint on freedom with security-increasing sacrifice of security, distrust in the promoters of a climate of distrust, and so on.

Such reflexive use of one's central concept, negative or affirmative, is an intellectually satisfying activity which is bound to have appeal to those system lovers who want to construct moral theories, and it may help them design their theory in an intellectually pleasing manner. But we should beware of becoming hypnotized by our slogans or of sacrificing truth to intellectual elegance. Any theory of proper trust should not *prejudge* the question of when distrust is proper. We might find more objects of proper distrust than just the contributors to a climate of reasonable distrust, just as freedom should be restricted not just to increase human freedom but to protect human life from poisoners and other killers. I suspect, however, that all the objects of reasonable distrust are more reasonably seen as falling into the category of ones who contribute to a decrease in the scope of proper trust than can all who are reasonably coerced be seen as themselves guilty of wrongful coercion. Still, even if all proper trust turns out to be for such persons and on such matters as will increase the scope or stability of a climate of reasonable trust, and all proper distrust for such persons and on such matters as increase the scope of reasonable distrust, overreliance on such nice reflexive formulae can distract us from asking all the questions about trust which need to be asked if an adequate moral theory is to be constructed around that concept. These questions should include when to *respond* to trust with *un*trustworthiness, when and when not to invite trust, as well as when to give and refuse trust. We should not assume that promiscuous trustworthiness is any more a virtue than is undiscriminating distrust. It is appropriate trustworthiness, appropriate trustingness, appropriate encouragement to trust which will be virtues, as will be judicious untrustworthiness, selective refusal to trust, discriminating discouragement of trust.

Women are particularly well placed to appreciate these last virtues, since they have sometimes needed them to get into a position even to consider becoming moral theorizers. The long exploitation and domination of women by men depended on men's trust in women and women's trustworthiness to play their allotted role and so to perpetuate their own and their daughters' servitude. However keen women now are to end the lovelessness of modern moral philosophy, they are unlikely to lose sight of the cautious virtue of appropriate distrust or of the tough virtue of principled betrayal of the exploiters' trust.

Gilligan's girls and women saw morality as a matter of preserving valued ties to others, of preserving the conditions for that care and mutual care without which human life becomes bleak, lonely, and after a while, as the mature men in her study found, not self-affirming, however successful in achieving the egoistic goals which had been set. The boys and men saw morality as a matter of finding workable traffic rules for self-assertors, so that they might not needlessly frustrate one another and so that they could, should they so choose, cooperate in more positive ways to mutual advantage. Both for the women's sometimes unchosen and valued ties with others and for the men's mutual respect as sovereigns and subjects of the same minimal moral traffic rules (and for their more voluntary and more selective associations of profiteers), trust is important. Both men and women are concerned with cooperation, and the dimensions of trust–distrust structure the different cooperative relations each emphasize. The various considerations which arise when we try to defend an answer to any question about the appropriateness of a particular form of cooperation with its distinctive form of trust or distrust, that is, when we look into the terms of all sorts of cooperation, at the terms of trust in different cases of trust, at what are fair terms and what are trust-enhancing and trust-preserving terms, are suitably many and richly interconnected. A moral theory (or family of theories) that made trust its central problem could do better justice to men's and women's moral intuitions than do the going men's theories. Even if we don't easily agree on the answer to the question of who should trust whom with what, who should accept and who should meet various sorts of trust, and why, these questions might enable us better to reason morally together than we can when the central moral questions are reduced to those of whose favour one must court and whose anger one must dread.

EXERCISES

1. In Plato's *Euthyphro*, Socrates puts the following question to Euthyphro:
   > We are agreed that the gods love piety because it is pious, and that it is not pious because they love it. Is this not so?

   To phrase a similar question in more contemporary terms, we might say: "We are agreed that God loves just acts because they are just, and they are *not* just simply because God loves them, right?" If you agree that God's love of justice is determined by the goodness of justice (rather than God's will determining what counts as just), does that in any way diminish the power or the majesty of God?

2. The classic case of theological voluntarism is the story of Abraham and Isaac, told in Chapter 22 of Genesis. God commands Abraham to kill Isaac, Abraham's beloved son, as an offering to God; and without questioning, Abraham obeys God's command: "Abraham built an altar there, and laid the wood in order, and bound Isaac his son, and laid him on the altar upon the wood. And Abraham stretched forth his hand, and took the knife to slay his son." Thus, if God commands Abraham to kill Isaac, then killing Isaac becomes morally good—at least from the theological voluntarism perspective. However, Kierkegaard—a Danish theologian/philosopher of the mid-nineteenth century—interprets the story differently: Abraham, in *choosing* to follow God's terrible command, moves *beyond* all considerations of ethics, beyond all understanding, beyond reason: He *transcends* ethics. Thus (according to Kierkegaard), Abraham does not adopt an ethic of theological voluntarism, but instead moves beyond ethics altogether through his act of faith. Is that a more plausible interpretation of the story?

3. "We should always follow God's commandments, no matter what: Whatever God commands is right. But the way we know God's commandments is through *reason*, for reason is God's special gift to humankind. If a command is irrational—such as the command to kill a child—then we know it does not come from God." If someone took that position, would it still count as a divine command theory?

4. The Western culture in which most of us live generally approves of eating meat. But many persons within that culture belong to groups that oppose eating at least some forms of meat: Jainists oppose all meat eating, Muslims and Jews abhor pork. If I am a relativist living in Texas, and am also a Jainist, and I refuse to eat barbecued ribs, have I done something wrong? Would I be doing something wrong—from a cultural relativist perspective—whether I refused ribs or not?

5. In the United States, abortion was once widely condemned and was also illegal. Now abortion is widely accepted (though of course a minority fiercely opposes elective abortion).

If you were a dedicated cultural relativist, at what point would you think abortion has changed from wrong to right? When a majority of U.S. citizens favored legalized abortion? When the Supreme Court ruled on *Roe* v. *Wade*? Or when?

6. Execution of juveniles is almost universally condemned as a severe violation of human rights: It is legally permitted only in Somalia and the United States. Would it be legitimate for other countries to exert pressure on the United States to reform its cultural practice of capital punishment of juveniles? Would such pressure be effective, or counterproductive?

7. Social contract theory is often used to justify punishing those who violate the law (they have accepted the benefits, but have broken their agreement to abide by the social contract, and thus the other parties to the contract can legitimately penalize those violators). Jeffrie Murphy has argued that in our society—where there is enormous disparity in wealth and also huge differences in opportunity (as evidenced by the contrast between urban ghetto schools and suburban schools)—the social contract cannot be used to justify punishment. At least the social contract cannot justify punishing property crimes committed by those in the lowest socioeconomic class, since persons in such circumstances would not likely agree to a contract that would leave them so severely disadvantaged. Of course, there might be other arguments for the justice of punishment; but does Murphy's argument effectively undermine the *social contract* basis for punishment in societies like our own?

8. Social contract theorists generally believe that our moral rules are made, rather than discovered. The rules are what we draw up or agree to in our social contract. Yet a number of social contract theorists—John Locke, for example—also believe that there are objective moral truths, factually true moral principles that are just as true as the principles of math or physics. Are those beliefs fundamentally inconsistent, or can they be reconciled? In fact, the U.S. Declaration of Independence obviously contains a social contract view of government, but it starts with the famous pronouncement of *self-evident* ethical truths that do not wait upon social contracts: "We hold these truths to self-evident: That all men are created equal, and are endowed by their Creator with certain inalienable rights." Is that a *consistent* or a *contradictory* position?

9. Martha Nussbaum, a contemporary critic of social contract theory, argues that social contract theory requires treating "people of unusual need or impairment" as second-class citizens. Is this an implication of social contract theory? Is there any form of social contract theory that could avoid that criticism? That is, could social contract theory be suitably modified to avoid treating such people as second-class citizens, or is that an inevitable part of the theory?

10. Suppose someone suggested that "care ethics" is important in the home and among family and friends, but that an ethics of justice must govern our larger and more impersonal ethical lives. What do you think would be Annette Baier's response?

11. Social contract ethics and care ethics are generally regarded as conflicting moral views; would it be possible to combine them? (*Not* by compartmentalizing them: social contract ethics for the public sphere, care ethics for the private sphere of family and friends; but by genuinely *combining* them, joining them into a coherent whole? Or are they fundamentally at odds?)

12. You are a physician at a tissue match laboratory. Ben Thomas makes an appointment to be tested. Ben's daughter, Rebecca, is 25. Rebecca has lost most of the functioning in her kidneys as a result of a severe blow suffered in a bicycle accident. She requires dialysis twice a week, and her health is poor. A kidney transplant would very likely restore her to full health, and she is on a waiting list for a kidney; but the list is long, and Rebecca's chances of getting a kidney are small. Because relatives have the best chance of having a close tissue match (and thus greatly reducing the likelihood of the patient's body rejecting the transplanted kidney), Ben hopes his kidney will be a close match. Ben is in good health, with two healthy kidneys, and if there is a good match, he plans to donate one of his kidneys to Rebecca (an increasingly common procedure). Since Rebecca is on the waiting list for a kidney transplant, you already have complete data on her; you just need to run tests on Ben.

   You run the tests, as Ben requests, and unfortunately the tests show that Ben is not a good tissue match, and cannot contribute a kidney to Rebecca. But the tests also show something else that neither you nor Ben had anticipated: Ben is not the biological father of Rebecca. Should you tell Ben this additional information? What factors or principles should you weigh in making your decision? Does Ben have a right to this information? Would *care* theorists and Kantians be likely to reach very different conclusions on this issue? *Must* they reach different conclusions?

13. Consider the question of "physician-assisted suicide," currently much debated. Those who favor physician-assisted suicide believe that the terminally ill should be able to ask for and receive assistance from their doctors in ending their own lives at the time when they choose to die (the state of Oregon currently allows physician-assisted suicide). Those who oppose physician-assisted suicide believe that doctors should never aid patients in ending their lives, but should instead provide comfort measures until the patient dies naturally. Would a Kantian and a care ethicist be likely to reach different conclusions on the issue of legalizing physician-assisted suicide? Would they *necessarily* reach different conclusions? Might two care ethicists hold differing views on this issue?

ADDITIONAL READING

Plato's *Euthyphro* (available in a number of translations and editions) remains the classic source for the argument against theological voluntarism. Kai Nielsen, *Ethics without God* (London: Pemberton Press; and Buffalo, N.Y.: Prometheus Books, 1973), is perhaps the best and clearest contemporary argument against basing ethics on religion. A very sophisticated and interesting opposing view—that argues for the importance of religious considerations in ethics—can be found in George N. Schlesinger, *New Perspectives on Old-Time Religion* (Oxford: Clarendon Press, 1988). A brief argument for how ethics might be based on religion is given by Jonathan Berg, "How Could Ethics Depend on Religion?" in Peter Singer, ed., *A Companion to Ethics* (Oxford: Blackwell, 1991). Philip L. Quinn develops a detailed and sophisticated defense of theological voluntarism in "Divine Command Theory," in Hugh LaFollette, ed., *The Blackwell Guide to Ethical Theory* (Oxford: Blackwell Publishers, 2000). There are two excellent anthologies on the subject: Paul Helm, ed., *Divine Commands and Morality* (Oxford: Oxford University Press, 1981) and G. Outka and J. P. Reeder, Jr., eds., *Religion and Morality: A Collection of Essays* (Garden City/New York: Anchor/Doubleday, 1973).

Psychological egoism was defended by Thomas Hobbes in *Leviathan*, and ethical egoism was promoted by Bernard de Mandeville in *The Fable of the Bees, or Private Vices, Public Benefits* (London, 1723). Mandeville's book is better written and better argued than the more popular contemporary defense of ethical egoism by the novelist Ayn Rand in *The Virtue of Selfishness* (New York: New American Library, 1961). The classic critique of egoism is by Bishop Joseph Butler, *Fifteen Sermons upon Human Nature*, 1726 (Sermon Eleven in particular). Another excellent critique (among many) of psychological egoism is by C. D. Broad, "Egoism as a Theory of Human Motives," in *Ethics and the History of Philosophy* (New York: Humanities Press, 1952). For arguments against ethical egoism, see (among many) Laurence Thomas, "Ethical Egoism and Psychological Dispositions," *American Philosophical Quarterly*, volume 17 (1980). Thomas Nagel's superb book, *The Possibility of Altruism* (Oxford: Clarendon Press, 1970) might also be useful in this context.

The anthropologist Ruth Benedict, in *Patterns of Culture* (New York: Penguin, 1934), was a major advocate of cultural relativism. Mary Midgley, *Heart and Mind* (New York: St. Martin's Press, 1981), offers a well-crafted critique of cultural relativism. For a more sophisticated version of relativism, and a defense of that view, see Gilbert Harman, *Explaining Value and Other Essays in Moral Philosophy* (Oxford: Clarendon Press, 2000). For a clear and fascinating debate on moral relativism versus moral objectivism, by two outstanding contemporary philosophers, see Gilbert Harman and Judith Jarvis Thomson, *Moral Relativism and Moral Objectivity* (Oxford: Blackwell, 1996). More on Gilbert Harman's relativism can be found in his "Moral Relativism Defended," *The Philosophical Review*, volume 84 (1975): 3–22; and *The Nature of Morality: An Introduction to Ethics* (New York: Oxford University Press, 1977). Steven Darwall critiques Harman's relativism in "Harman and Moral

Relativism," *The Personalist*, volume 58 (1977): 199–207. Hugh LaFollette, "The Truth in Ethical Relativism," *Journal of Social Philosophy*, volume 22, number 1 (Spring, 1991): 146–154, offers a spirited defense of "rational relativist ethics." Steven Lukes, a sociologist who writes very insightfully about philosophical issues, examines relativism and its implications in *Moral Relativism* (New York: Picador, 2008).

Nicholas Sturgeon criticizes the "argument from disagreement" (the argument that cultural disagreement provides support for *normative* cultural relativism) in "Moral Disagreement and Moral Relativism," *Social Philosophy and Policy*, volume 20 (1994): 80–115. James A. Ryan recasts the argument and defends it from Sturgeon's criticisms in "Moral Relativism and the Argument from Disagreement," *Social Philosophy and Policy*, volume 34 (2003): 377–386.

Herbert Feigl presents a strong argument that our most basic value principles are "relative," in the sense that no real argument can be given for or against them, and disagreements at that level cannot be rationally resolved; see his "Validation and Vindication," in C. Sellars and J. Hospers, eds., *Readings in Ethical Theory* (New York: Appleton-Century-Crofts, 1952); and " 'De Principiis non Disputandum . . . ?' On the Meaning and the Limits of Justification," in Max Black, ed., *Philosophical Analysis* (Ithaca, New York: Cornell University Press, 1950).

A good anthology—containing works by both philosophers and anthropologists— is Michael Krausz, ed., *Relativism: Interpretation and Conflict* (Notre Dame: University of Notre Dame Press, 1989). Another excellent collection is by Paul K. Moser and Thomas L. Carson, eds., *Moral Relativism: A Reader* (New York: Oxford University Press, 2001).

A review of recent work on moral relativism, primarily examining work by philosophers, is Robert M. Stewart and Lynn L. Thomas, "Recent Work on Ethical Relativism," *American Philosophical Quarterly*, volume 28 (April, 1991): 85–100.

The extensive bioethical literature on cross-cultural issues includes A. Surbone, "Letter from Italy: Truth Telling to the Patient," *Journal of the American Medical Association*, volume 268 (1992): 1661–1662; N. S. Jecker, J. A. Carrese, and R. A. Pearlman, "Caring for Patients in Cross-Cultural Settings," *Hastings Center Report*, volume 25 (1995): 6–14; and Bernard Freedman, "Offering Truth: One Ethical Approach to the Uninformed Cancer Patient," in G. E. Henderson, N. M. P. King, R. P., Strauss, S. E. Estroff, and L. R. Churchill, eds., *The Social Medicine Reader* (Durham, N.C.: Duke University Press, 1997): 333–340.

A strong and broad argument against relativism can be found in Ruth Macklin, *Against Relativism: Cultural Diversity and the Search for Ethical Universals in Medicine* (New York: Oxford University Press, 1999). For arguments opposing Macklin's position (on at least some points), see Elvin Hatch, *Theories of Man and Culture* (New York: Columbia University Press, 1973), *Culture and Morality: The Relativity of Values in Anthropology* (New York: Columbia University Press, 1983), and "The Good Side of Relativism," *Journal of Anthropological Research*, volume 53 (1997): 371–381. One of the strongest recent spokespersons for a position that is not quite relativism, but rather an attack on the arguments of those who *attack* relativism, can be found in the work of anthropologist Clifford Geertz; see "Anti Anti-Relativism," *American Anthropologist*, volume 86, number 2 (June, 1984): 263–278; reprinted in Michael Krausz, ed., *Relativism: Interpretation and Conflict* (Notre Dame: University of Notre Dame Press, 1989); and also Clifford Geertz, *Available Light: Anthropological Reflections on Philosophical Topics* (Princeton, N.J.: Princeton University Press, 2000).

Merrilee H. Salmon, "Ethical Considerations in Anthropology and Archaeology, or Relativism and Justice for All," *Journal of Anthropological Research*, volume 53 (1997): 47–63, argues that anthropologists' respect for other cultures should not lead them to ethical relativism, and that values promoted by anthropologists—such as the value of preserving archaeological sites—indicate belief in values that go beyond the values of individual cultures. John J. Tilley, in "Cultural Relativism," *Human Rights Quarterly*, volume 22 (2000): 501–547, critiques a number of arguments for normative cultural relativism and argues in favor of ethical universalism.

One issue of the *Journal of Anthropological Research*, volume 53 (1997) is devoted to relativism, pluralism, and human rights. Among the authors included in the special issue are Elizabeth M. Zechenter ("In the Name of Culture: Cultural Relativism and the Abuse of the Individual," pp. 319–347), a trenchant critic of ethical cultural relativism who describes in detail some of the "cultural practices" that have resulted in "a long history of abysmal treatment of women" and argues that cultural relativist ethics undermines the movement toward basic human rights and thus causes enormous suffering; Carole Nagengast ("Women, Minorities, and Indigenous Peoples: Universalism and Cultural Relativity," pp. 349–369) fully recognizes the genuine difficulties in dealing with both cultural practices and individual rights, and her thoughtful and informative essay scrupulously avoids shallow slogans and inadequate solutions; and Ellen Messer ("Pluralist Approaches to Human Rights," pp. 293–317) combines broad and insightful knowledge of both anthropology and ethics in her argument for a pluralist approach to human rights that avoids both ethical relativism and the simplistic universalization of Western individualist values. See also Ellen Messer, "Anthropology and Human Rights," *Annual Review of Anthropology*, volume 22 (1993): 221–249.

The classic sources for social contract theory are Thomas Hobbes' *Leviathan*, John Locke's *Second Treatise on Government*, and Jean-Jacques Rousseau's *Social Contract (Du Contrat Social)*. Hobbes' *Leviathan* is available from Bobbs-Merrill (Indianapolis: 1958); it was originally published in 1651. Locke's *Second Treatise on Government* was originally published in 1690; an accessible edition is Indianapolis: Bobbs-Merrill, Library of Liberal Arts, 1952. Rousseau's *Social Contract* was originally published in 1762; it can be found in an edition edited by R. Masters (New York: St. Martin's Press, 1978).

Discussions of social contract theory tradition include Jean Hampton, *Hobbes and the Social Contract Tradition* (Cambridge: Cambridge University Press, 1986); and Patrick Riley, *Will and Political Legitimacy: A Critical Exposition of Social Contract Theory in Hobbes, Locke, Rousseau, Kant, and Hegel* (Cambridge, Mass.: Harvard University Press, 1982). A powerful and wide-ranging critique of social contract theory is offered by Martha C. Nussbaum, in *Frontiers of Justice: Disability, Nationality, Species Membership* (Cambridge, MA: Harvard University Press, 2006).

Probably the best known philosophical book of the late twentieth century presented an updated version of social contract theory: John Rawls, *A Theory of Justice* (London: Oxford University Press, 1971). For comments on the book, see *A Theory of Justice and Its Critics*, edited by Chandran Kukathas and Philip Petit (Polity, 1990), as well as *The Idea of a Political Liberalism*, edited by Victoria Davion and Clark Wolf (Rowman and Littlefield, 2000). David Gauthier's version of contractarian theory can be found in *Morals by Agreement* (Oxford: Oxford University Press, 1986) and *Moral Dealing* (Ithaca, N.Y.: Cornell University Press, 1990). For discussion and critique of Gauthier's theory, see Peter Vallentyne, ed., *Contractarianism and Rational Choice* (New York: Cambridge University Press, 1991).

For social contract theory and other topics, visit Paul Leighton's website at www.paulsjusticepage.com. Professor Leighton is a criminologist and sociologist at Eastern Michigan University, and his interests are wide ranging. Carol Gilligan, *In a Different Voice: Psychological Theory and Women's Development* (Cambridge, Mass: Harvard University Press, 1982), had a powerful impact on the contemporary development of care ethics. Nel Noddings' work has been influential in both philosophy and education; see her *Caring: A Feminine Approach to Ethics and Moral Education* (Berkeley, Cal.: University of California Press, 1984); and *Educating Moral People: A Caring Alternative to Character*

Education (New York: Teachers College Press, 2002). Annette C. Baier is a clear and cogent writer on this topic, who is particularly insightful in placing care ethics in a larger philosophical perspective. See her *Moral Prejudices* (Cambridge, Mass.: Harvard University Press, 1994). Among the best advocates of care ethics is Lawrence A. Blum, *Friendship, Altruism and Morality* (London: Routledge & Kegan Paul, 1980). Viginia Held's edited collection, *Justice and Care* (Boulder, Colorado: Westview Press, 1995), is an excellent collection of essays on the subject. A very good and wide-ranging anthology is Eva Feder Kittay and Diana T. Meyers, eds., *Women and Moral Theory* (Totowa, N. J.: Rowman & Littlefield, 1987).

Among the excellent sites on care ethics/feminist ethics is the Feminist Theory Web site, at www.cddc.vt.edu/feminism/eth.html..

CHAPTER 13

ARE THERE OBJECTIVE ETHICAL TRUTHS?

"I don't care *who* you are, you just *know* the difference between right and wrong." That's a common saying and a common belief, and a view favored by a significant number of ethicists. Our basic knowledge of ethical truths—of what we *should* and should *not* do—requires no deep rational deliberation: it is knowledge we have *intuitively* and immediately.

> *Intuitionism* is the view that there are ethical truths that we can recognize and know as soon as we concentrate carefully upon them: such ethical truths are *self-evident*. Knowing such ethical truths is not a process of deductive reasoning; rather, they are known by direct, immediate, and conclusive internal perception, and this internal perception is a special cognitive power.

INTUITIONISM

Murder is wrong. If you think hard about it, you can come up with strong reasons for *why* murder is wrong: Kantian reasons based on universal laws, utilitarian reasons based on maximizing pleasure and minimizing suffering, and social contract reasons based on what sort of agreement rational self-interested contractors would favor. But whatever the arguments you give for why murder is wrong, none of them will be as strong as your basic *intuition* that murder is wrong. You may have considerable confidence in the strength of your arguments against murder; but whatever the strength of those arguments, you *know* that murder is wrong, and you *knew* that murder is wrong long before you heard any argument against it. If I offer you an argument for why murder is a good thing, you may find it interesting to examine that argument and try to discover its flaws; but you already know the argument is flawed, because you *know* the conclusion is *false*. You *know* that murder is wrong, and you know that with more certainty than you know the soundness of any ethical argument. Your basic source of ethical knowledge is not argument, reason, nor authority; rather, it is your fundamental *intuition* of ethical truth.

> The sense of obligation to do, or the rightness of, an action of a particular kind is absolutely underivative or immediate. . . . We recognize, for instance, that this performance of a service to X, who has done us a service, just in virtue of its being the performance of a service to one who has rendered a service to the would-be agent, ought to be done by us. This apprehension is immediate, in precisely the sense in which a mathematical apprehension is immediate, e.g., the apprehension that this three-sided figure, in virtue of

> its being three-sided, must have three angles. Both apprehensions are immediate in the sense that in both insight into the nature of the subject leads us to recognize its possession of the predicate; and it is only stating this fact from the other side to say that in both cases the fact apprehended is self-evident. *H. A. Prichard, "Does Moral Philosophy Rest on a Mistake?" 1912*

Note that these basic ethical intuitions are not *feelings*, not even very *strong* feelings. Having grown up near New Orleans, I have strong *feelings* about the New Orleans Saints; but those aren't moral intuitions. Perhaps you have experienced powerful feelings of sexual desire, and maybe even acted on them; but whether you judge those feelings to have been fortunate or unfortunate, you didn't confuse them with moral intuitions. If you put chocolate sauce on your broccoli, I may have a strong feeling of disgust; but it's not a moral intuition of moral wrongness. If you torture a child, I will also have a strong feeling of disgust and revulsion, but something more, something distinctly different: an *intuition* that what you are doing is *morally wrong*.

> The following proposition seems to me in a high degree probable—namely, that any animal whatever, endowed with well-marked social instincts, the parental and filial affections being here included, would inevitably acquire a moral sense or conscience, as soon as its intellectual powers had become as well, or nearly as well developed, as in man. . . .
>
> It may be well first to premise that I do not wish to maintain that any strictly social animal, if its intellectual faculties were to become as active and as highly developed as in man, would acquire exactly the same moral sense as ours. In the same manner as various animals have some sense of beauty, though they admire widely different objects, so they might have a sense of right and wrong, though led by it to follow widely different lines of conduct. If, for instance, to take an extreme case, men were reared under precisely the same conditions as hive-bees, there can be no doubt that our unmarried females would, like the worker-bees, think it a sacred duty to kill their brothers, and mothers would strive to kill their fertile daughters; and no one would think of interfering. Nevertheless, the bee, or any other social animal, would gain in our supposed case, as it appears to me, some feeling of right or wrong, or a conscience. *Charles Darwin, The Descent of Man, 2nd ed., 1875*

That is the fundamental characteristic of *intuitionist* ethics: Ultimately our ethical knowledge is derived from ethical *intuitions* that we immediately recognize as true and decisive. But there are some differences in the intuitionist details. Exactly what do we intuit? Some intuitionists believe we intuit the rightness or wrongness of particular *acts*. H. A. Prichard held that we must look very carefully at each situation, learn as much about it as possible and view it as objectively as we can, and *then* consult our intuitions concerning what act is right in that situation. But most intuitionists have maintained that our intuitions operate on a higher, more principled level. One particularly influential intuitionist was W. D. Ross, who held that we intuit several basic ethical *principles* or truths: We know, *intuitively*, that we should keep our promises, return favors done to us, and help others when we can. When we get to *specific cases*, we may have much less certainty. Suppose you have promised to help a friend move next Saturday morning, and another person—who last month spent an entire weekend helping *you* move—is moving at exactly the same time, and you can help only one. *Probably* your duty to keep your promise is stronger, but it's hard to be certain of that. But whatever you decide about your specific obligation in a complex situation, there is *no doubt whatsoever* that you *do* have an obligation to keep your promise *and* an obligation to return a favor. Those basic obligatory principles are what we intuit, and what we know with certainty, according to Ross. There's uncertainty when we try to apply them to specific cases, but there is no uncertainty about our intuitive knowledge of those principles. I *know* it is right to keep my promise even when some other obligation outweighs it. In that case, I *still* know that it is right to keep promises: that doesn't change. How do you know that promise-keeping is right? Look to your *own intuitive experience*, and you will recognize that you have this basic intuitive knowledge.

Where do such intuitions come from? Intuitionists are less certain about that. Perhaps they are instilled in us by God. But the fact that we can't explain their origins is no reason for doubting their existence; after all, I don't understand how my visual apparatus works, but I don't doubt that I can see or that I can gain knowledge through my power of sight.

What if I introspect, and find no intuitive knowledge that promise-keeping is right? You're in denial, the intuitionist would reply; look closely, you'll see it. But no, I really have no such intuition. The intuitionist is likely to conclude that you are being dishonest. But perhaps you are a moral monster, who lacks these basic moral insights; or possibly you have ignored your moral intuitions for so long, constantly doing what you *knew* was wrong, that you have finally lost the ability to recognize these basic intuitions. But for most people (the intuitionist will insist) the existence of basic moral intuitions is clear and compelling. If a few people are blind to moral intuitions, that doesn't count against their existence.

Suppose I experience these strong intuitions, but am not sure that they are guides to moral *truth*. After all, many people have had what they considered clear moral intuitions that we now consider egregiously wrong: that it is our moral obligation to kill "witches," or "infidels"; that one who accidentally kills another deserves to die; that an insult to my "honor" must be punished by death; that those whose skin is a different color must be treated as inferior; that women should never hold positions of authority. Of course the intuitionists will insist that those were not real moral intuitions, but beliefs that were mistakenly taken to be genuine intuitions. But the problem is, if we can be *mistaken* about our moral intuitions, then how do we know when we have discovered a *genuine* moral intuition? What are their distinguishing marks? Obviously, it cannot be that they are *widely believed* to be obvious intuitively given moral truths, for we have just looked at horribly false beliefs that met *that* condition.

As a boy growing up on a small farm, I thought the treatment of farm animals was often horribly cruel, and it seemed immediately obvious to me that it was wrong to treat animals in that manner. As I grew older, I adopted the dominant view of my rural farming community: Animal suffering is unfortunate, but it's not a moral issue; farm animals are merely objects for the benefit and use of humans; it is obvious, when we look at it clearly, that humans are the only real moral beings, and there is nothing wrong with nonhuman animals suffering for our benefit. At different points in my life, both views seemed intuitively obvious. Intuitionists who agree with my "mature" view would say that my childhood intuitions were clouded by my feelings, and as I grew older I was able to see the intuitive truth more clearly. Intuitionists who favor my childhood view would claim that the childhood intuition was pure and accurate, but was ultimately obscured by the strong cultural values that overwhelmed my intuitions. Is there any way of telling which is the *authentic* intuition, and which is the impostor?

> "When choosing between two evils, I always like to try the one I've never tried before."
> *Mae West, 1892–1980*

One suggestion is that we accept the intuitions of the "best people" as our guide. W. D. Ross insists that

We have no more direct way of access to the facts about rightness and goodness and about what things are right or good, than by thinking about them; the moral convictions of thoughtful and well-educated people are the data of ethics just as sense perceptions are the data of a natural science. Just as some of the latter have to be rejected as illusory, so have some of the former; but as the latter are rejected only when they are in conflict with other more accurate sense perceptions, the former are rejected only when they are in conflict with other convictions which stand better the test of reflection. The existing body of moral convictions of the best people is the cumulative product of the moral reflection of many generations, which has developed an extremely delicate power of appreciation of moral distinctions; and this the theorist cannot afford to treat with anything other than the greatest respect. The verdicts of the moral consciousness of the best people are the foundation on which he must build. . . . *

But how do we identify those "best people"? In the antebellum South, many people might have considered the slave-holding owners of the great plantations as the "best people": they were very powerful, they were leaders of the region, and they were among the best educated (their sons often went to the best New England universities). But now we regard them as shining examples of profound moral blindness, rather than moral exemplars. If we say that the "best people" are those with the true intuitions, then we are only spinning in a circle. If we use some other standard—the correct intuitions are those that promote overall utility, or that can be defended by reason, or that promote human flourishing—then we are abandoning intuitionism in favor of some other theory, such as Kantian rationalism or utilitarianism. Intuitionism has immediate and broad appeal as an ethical theory, but careful scrutiny reveals some serious problems with trying to use it as an ethical guide.

VIRTUE ETHICS

We have examined a wide variety of ethical theories, ranging from Kantian rationalism to care ethics, from social contract ethics to utilitarianism to intuitionism. Though there are important differences and basic conflicts among those theories, all of them start from the same basic question: What should I do, how should I act, and what act is right or wrong? They may answer that question differently, but all take that as the basic question in ethics. *Virtue* ethics starts with a different question: What sort of *person* do I want to be; or alternatively, what is the *best life* for a human being?

> *Virtue ethics* focuses ethical theory away from the question of what act is right, turning instead to the question of what sort of human life is genuinely worthwhile and what sort of person do I want to be. Virtue ethics emphasizes the development of character, as well as the conditions that shape a virtuous character and a genuinely good and satisfying life.

When deciding whether to cheat someone, a utilitarian might ask whether such an act would produce the greatest balance of pleasure over suffering, and a Kantian would ask if it is the sort of act I could will as a universal law. A virtue theorist asks instead: Do I really want to be a cheat, untrustworthy, and underhanded? Is a life of deceit really a good life? You might be tempted to answer: I'm not going to live a *life* of deceit; this is just one case, and I'm only cheating today. Tomorrow I'll be very honest, a model of integrity. The virtue theorist finds that absurd. What you practice is what you become. Don't suppose you can cheat your way through college, and then become a person of integrity after graduation; that you can lie and cheat, but that deep down you are *really* a trustworthy person. That makes as much sense as saying that although I never exercise, avoid even brisk walking, and live on junk food, deep down I am really an excellent marathon

*W. D. Ross, pp. 46–7.

runner. Supposedly St. Augustine prayed, "Lord, give me chastity and continence, but not just now." That is, I wish to be virtuous, but I don't want to start practicing virtue until later. Virtue theorists don't buy it. You make yourself and your character by your choices and your behavior. You can no more *choose* one day to be an honest person than you can show up at the start of the Boston Marathon and *choose* to be an excellent marathoner.

> "Virtue consists, not in abstaining from vice, but in not desiring it." *George Bernard Shaw, Maxims for Revolutionists*

So—virtue theorists advise—rather than focusing on what *act* you *ought* to do, think about what sort of *person* you really want to be. Virtue theory pushes ethical inquiry into deep waters: Making good moral decisions involves careful reflection on how you want to live your life, what sort of person you wish to be, and what sort of life you consider genuinely worthwhile. Before you fall into a pattern of choices that will shape a character and life you do not genuinely approve, stop and reflect carefully about what kind of life and character you truly value. What sort of character, career, and accomplishments could you look back on in your old age and honestly say, "I have lived a good life"? Think carefully about it, rather than drifting into habits and patterns that will carry you along like a rudderless ship, eventually reaching a destination and fixed character that you find profoundly disappointing. T. S. Eliot, in "The Love Song of J. Alfred Prufrock," captures in verse the terrible self-appraisal of Prufrock, who looks back over his life with deep regret. Prufrock has lived a life of drifting indecision, decisions and revisions and trivialities: "I have measured out my life with coffee spoons," never daring to set a firm course and follow it. The result is a harsh accounting of himself as he grows old:

> I have seen the moment of my greatness flicker,
> And I have seen the eternal footman hold my coat, and snicker,
> And in short, I was afraid.

So if you think of ethics as the shallow unreflective process of following basic social norms, virtue theory cautions you to think more carefully.

> "The good of man is the active exercise of his soul's faculties in conformity with excellence or virtue . . . . Moreover this activity must occupy a complete lifetime; for one swallow dos not make spring, nor does one fine day; and similarly one day or a brief period of happiness does not make a man supremely blessed and happy." *Aristotle, Nicomachean Ethics*

Virtue theory asks what acts will contribute to a *good life*, rather than what acts are right. But what *is* the good life for humans? Answering that question poses a challenge for virtue theorists. Aristotle answered that the good life is the genuinely *happy* life, but he meant happy in a special sense: Genuine happiness is *eudaimonia*, which for Aristotle involves living in accordance with the highest or best or most distinctive part of our nature (and for Aristotle, of course, the *highest* part of our nature is our power of *reason*). Other virtue theorists have offered other standards for what counts as a genuinely good life: A leading contemporary virtue theorist Rosalind Hursthouse characterizes the good life as one of distinctively human *flourishing*, analogous to the flourishing of a specific plant or animal. But however virtue theorists answer the question of what counts as a *good life*, what they all have in common is the view that what we are seeking is the good life for *humans*: that is, not the good life as some abstract ideal, but the good life for human beings as rational social animals. That requires carefully examining the nature of humans and the conditions under which humans can live successfully. Trying to determine what sort of life is *best* for humans: That is a task for psychologists, sociologists, anthropologists, biologists, city planners, economists, and philosophers; indeed, virtue theorists regard it as *the* task, the most basic question of all.

ETHICAL NONOBJECTIVISM

Virtue theorists believe that the right act is the act which shapes a *good life*. Kantians believe that the right act is the act that can be rationally justified as universal law. Utilitarians maintain that the right act is the one that promotes the greatest happiness. Their sharp differences notwithstanding, what they *share* is the belief that there *is* a right act. In answering the question of "what *should* I do," you can get it right, and you can also get it wrong, just as you can get the right or wrong answer on your physics exam, or working out a problem in mathematics, or in answering a question on a quiz show. In contrast, ethical *nonobjectivists* reject the belief that there are any *objective facts* in ethics. We may feel strongly about ethical issues, we may struggle for them, and we may passionately support them; but there are no ethical *facts* to settle our dispute.

> The presumed objectivity of moral judgments thus being a chimera, there can be no moral truth in the sense in which this term is generally understood. The ultimate reason for this is, that the moral concepts are based upon emotions, and that the contents of an emotion fall entirely outside the category of truth. *Edward Westermarck, 1906*

Though it is possible to interpret David Hume differently, most see Hume as the standard bearer for nonobjectivism. According to Hume, when we get to the level of genuine basic value questions, there is no objective fact, and no reasoning process can settle such questions: " 'Tis not contrary to reason to prefer the destruction of the whole world to the scratching of my finger," Hume asserted.

> *Ethical nonobjectivism* is the view that there is no *objective factual basis* for ethical statements: if you say that stealing is wrong, or that all persons should be treated as ends-in-themselves rather than means, then you are making claims that ultimately have no objective factual support.

That is not to say that there is no reasoning in ethics. If we *agree* that it is ethically desirable to provide food and shelter for the hungry and homeless, then we can devote our rational powers to working out the best means of accomplishing that ethical goal. And if we *agree* that it is morally wrong to cause suffering for nonessential purposes, then we can use reason to examine the implications of that principle for our treatment of farm animals. That is, *given* agreement on ethical goals and principles, we can use reason to work out policies and implications. Furthermore, if I hold erroneous factual beliefs, then correcting those errors may result in changes in my moral judgments. For example, if I mistakenly believe that dogs are complicated mechanical devices, and that they have no nervous systems and cannot feel pain, then I would also believe that beating a dog is morally no worse than beating a wind-up toy. But if you correct my misconception about dogs, and explain to me that dogs do indeed feel pain, then I will see the beating of a dog as a moral wrong. But if our disagreement is over some genuine moral value—I see nothing wrong with inflicting very cruel painful treatment on nonhuman animals, and you believe it to be a serious moral wrong—then (according to the nonobjectivist) there is no room for rational dispute, because there are no objective facts to argue about. If you can find some other *basic* ethical principle that I hold that is *inconsistent* with my views about the treatment of nonhuman animals, then there may be room for rational deliberation. But if we have reached fundamental ethical principles and beliefs and commitments, then we have reached a level at which objective facts are nonexistent, and disagreements cannot be rationally resolved.

Emotivism is one special type of ethical nonobjectivism. Emotivism is the view that what *appear* to be statements about ethics (what appear to be genuine ethical claims) are not actually *statements* at all: they are instead disguised *imperatives* (that order you *not* to steal) or they are *expressions* of emotional reaction (that express emotional disgust at stealing or emotional approval of honesty). According to emotivists, there are no genuine ethical statements at all, so obviously there are no objectively true statements about ethics. Though emotivism was a popular position among nonobjectivists in the mid-twentieth century, it currently has few advocates.

The Argument from Diversity

The most common argument for moral nonobjectivism is the *argument from diversity*. Different cultures, eras, and individuals hold very different moral views. In some cultures, eating animals is regarded as morally legitimate, while in others it is regarded as morally wrong. In some cultures free speech is strongly valued, while in others it is condemned. Perhaps there is even more disagreement at the individual level: One sees capital punishment as a barbaric wrong, another sees the same act as a basic requirement of justice; one sees homosexual acts as a moral abomination, another regards homosexual relations as perfectly legitimate. Given this enormous diversity of views, how can we plausibly suppose that there are objective moral facts to guide our moral deliberations? If there were moral facts, wouldn't we expect to find greater consensus?

Those who reject ethical nonobjectivism have at least two different replies to the argument from diversity. First, some people suggest that there is greater ethical agreement than might appear at first sight. Consider the abortion controversy, one of the most heated disputes in contemporary society. Even there, we may find more agreement than disagreement. Both sides agree that it is wrong to kill babies (though, of course, there is disagreement about whether a tiny clump of cells with no nervous system but with the capacity to some day develop into a baby should be counted as a baby); and both sides agree that women should have the right of control over their own bodies (though one side believes that fetal rights trump the woman's right of personal control). And often the ethical disagreement turns not on an *ethical* issue at all, but instead on some other question: In the fierce dispute over capital punishment, one key disagreement is over whether capital punishment is an effective deterrent, and that is a sociological rather than an ethical dispute (since both sides agree that deterring crime is a morally good thing).

Second, even though there *are* genuine differences on questions of ethical principle, that doesn't prove that there is no ethical *truth*. After all, most of us believe that there *are* objective facts and objective truths in science, although we realize that there are genuine disputes about scientific questions. Under the influence of religious dogma, some people believe that the universe is only a few thousand years old; but that disagreement does not convince most of us that there are no scientific facts about the multibillion year age of our universe. Likewise, under the influence of some religious doctrines, there are those who deny that women are entitled to equal rights; but that disagreement does not prove that there are no objective ethical facts about the rights of women. (Perhaps no objective moral facts exist; but the existence of diversity in moral beliefs does not establish their nonexistence, just as diversity of opinion in contemporary physics does not establish that no objective facts exist in the field of physics.)

The Argument from Queerness

A more sophisticated argument for moral nonobjectivism was offered by the twentieth-century British philosopher John L. Mackie. Mackie called it the "argument from queerness," and it is sometimes called the "argument from simplicity." The foundation of Mackie's argument is a basic principle of explanation: The "principle of parsimony," which states that all other things being equal, the *simpler* explanation is better; that is, the explanation which assumes the fewest entities is the better explanation. The principle has come to be called "Ockham's razor," after the fourteenth-century philosopher and theologian William of Ockham (sometimes spelled "Occam"), who made great use of the principle in his arguments. The principle can be stated in several ways: "Entities are not to be multiplied without necessity," or "What can be done with fewer assumptions is done in vain with more." The basic idea is a simple one: If you let me assume extra entities in my explanations or theories, then I can "explain" anything; but simpler, thriftier explanations will be much more plausible. Adding elves, ghosts, and miracles to my explanatory system makes explanations much easier, but such explanations violate the principle of Ockham's Razor, and their excessive complexity renders them unreasonable and ineffective.

From Ockham's Razor to Mackie's simplicity argument for ethical nonobjectivism is an easy step. If we can explain all the ethical phenomena *without* positing objective moral facts, then we will have a simpler and—following the principle of parsimony—a *better* explanation than any explanation that adds the complexity of moral facts. Mackie adds an interesting twist to that argument: Moral facts (Mackie argues) are not just *additional* entities; they are also very *strange* and special entities with queer properties (that's why Mackie calls this the argument from queerness). They are queer, because although they exist independently of us (they are *objective facts*, and thus exist independently of our recognition of them), they *also* (and this is the special property) invariably command our approval and motivate us to pursue them when we recognize them. Mackie considers that a definitive property of a morally good fact: If I acknowledge that something is in fact morally good, but I have no interest whatsoever in promoting, preserving, or pursuing that good, then you can conclude that I did not really understand or appreciate the moral fact of its goodness.

In answer to Mackie's simplicity argument, the defender of moral objectivism might admit that moral facts *are* complex, but that no simpler explanation is available that will account for the observed phenomena of moral behavior. Like contemporary physics, moral objectivism is not a simple theory; but it's the simplest theory that will adequately account for morality. There have, however, been efforts to give simpler accounts of morality. Michael Ruse, a contemporary biologist and philosopher, offers an evolutionary account of morality that makes no appeal to special moral facts:

> We are what we are because we are recently evolved from savannah-dwelling primates. Suppose that we had evolved from cave-dwellers, or some such thing. We might have had as our highest principle of moral obligation the imperative to eat each others' faeces. Not simply the desire, but the obligation.

> *Michael Ruse,* Taking Darwin Seriously *(Oxford: Basil Blackwell, 1986), p. 263.*

Whatever one concludes about the adequacy of such an evolutionary biology account of morality, it is clear that this is a simpler account: It appeals only to biological principles, without adding a special category of moral facts. Psychologists also offer an account of moral development and behavior, without appealing to objective moral facts. Think back to your childhood. It's kindergarten playtime, and you are happily playing with a bright red shiny fire engine, complete with bell and a nifty ladder that goes up and down. Susie is also attracted to the new toy, and she grabs it away from you. Your screams of protest quickly bring a powerful adult onto the scene, who returns the toy to you and reprimands Susie. "No, Susie, he had it first, it's not nice to grab things away from others." Well, this is a delightful result, certainly. But a few minutes later this powerful adult returns to the scene: "You've been playing with the fire engine for quite a while. Wouldn't you like to let Susie play with it now?" No, actually you would not; you would much prefer to retain possession of the fire engine, and you wish that Susie were being swallowed by a boa constrictor. However, young as you are, you realize that this powerful adult is not really asking whether you *want* to share the fire engine, but telling you that you *must* give Susie a turn. You could make a stand, scream "MINE" as loud as you can, and take a death grip on the fire engine. But you've tried that before, and it didn't work very well. You wound up sitting in timeout with no fire engine, feeling bitter and helpless. So you try a different path: You graciously share the fire engine with that damned Susie, and maybe you'll get to continue playing with it—you can ring the bell while she operates the ladder—and your splendid behavior might get you an extra cookie at snack time. Best of all, you feel that you are sharing from your *own choice*: rather than bitter and powerless, you feel powerful and in control, and virtuous as well. So at a very early age you learn that "treat others as you would like to be treated" offers substantial benefits. Of course in kindergarten you don't recognize that as a moral principle, but your social environment has shaped you to act along those lines. When later you are taught that as a principle of ethics, you are predisposed to see it as an obvious or even intuitive truth. Society works hard at internalizing such rules in its members; after all, social cooperation is essential for a functioning society, and that social cooperation works a lot better if members of society have internalized rules of social cooperation, rather than following them due to external force. This may or may not be an adequate account of morality, but like the biological account it requires no objective moral facts, and thus it gets high marks by the standard of Ockham's principle of simplicity. Are these simpler theories adequate accounts of morality? That's a much debated question, and you will have to draw your own conclusions.

CONTEMPORARY MORAL REALISM

In response to powerful contemporary attacks on moral objectivity, contemporary *moral realists* have developed new approaches to defending moral objectivism. Contemporary *moral realists* maintain that the question of objective moral facts is not quite as straightforward as Mackie and other nonobjectivists suggest. Consider the contest between those who affirm and those who deny the existence of objective moral facts: It's not like the straightforward conflict between those who affirm and those who deny the existence of the Loch Ness Monster. Is there some strange reclusive sea creature in the depths of Loch Ness? Some small colony of sea animals we had thought were long extinct, but that somehow survived in that Scottish lake? I doubt it, but maybe I'm wrong. If some reputable scientific expedition fishes Nessie out of Loch Ness, shows her on television, and she is thoroughly examined and pronounced genuine by expert marine biologists, then that establishes the existence of Nessie and her family. I will be surprised, along with most members of the scientific community. However, there's nothing about the discovery of Nessie that would call for a major change in the biological sciences. We have a niche ready for Nessie: *If* such creatures exist, they are a species that we had thought extinct, and we simply switch that species from extinct to endangered. We would have to determine how an adequate breeding population could have survived so long in that environment, but that's a question biologists could readily tackle. But (returning to an example from the Chapter 5 discussion of epistemology) suppose that instead of Nessie, some team of biologists returns from an expedition deep into an unexplored rain forest, bringing along a family of Medusa: fierce humanlike creatures with very aggressive snakes growing out of their scalps rather than hair. We had always thought the Medusa were a mythological creation, and now we discover they are real biological beings. That would be a very different situation. We have a biological niche ready for Nessie, however unlikely we think that it will be filled. But in our contemporary system of biological science, there is *no* space available for the Medusa. A mammal that is also part reptile would destroy our system of biology: To take only the most obvious problem, how could there be a creature that is both warm-blooded and cold-blooded? Accepting the Medusa would mean not just modifications or additions to our system of biology, but the substitution of a radically different system.

So what's the moral of this long story about Loch Ness monsters and mythological creatures? The moral realists say that the contest between moral realists and moral nonobjectivists is like the situation of finding the Medusa, rather than like finding Nessie. That is, the conflict between moral realists and moral nonobjectivists is not simply a fight about whether we should add another set of objects—objective moral facts—to our list of things that exist in the world; rather, the conflict is between basic systemic views of morality. In such a conflict, we must consider not only questions of simplicity but also questions of the overall benefits of each system, the relative advantages of adopting the competing world views. Does a system that allows objective moral facts work better overall than a system that denies such facts? Which system will guide us better, which system is the most promising in terms of producing useful results, and which system offers the best chance of progress in understanding morality? Those are very complicated systemic questions, and simplicity is only one of many considerations that must be weighed when comparing the theories. There is no single experiment that will decide the issue (say the moral realists); instead, both systems (the realist and the nonobjectivist) must be developed and utilized by their respective advocates, and eventually we will get a sense of which system works best. But it's still much too early (the realists argue) to make any decision on their overall merits.

What evidence would strengthen the case for the system of moral realism? Suppose that when people think coolly, calmly, and reflectively about ethical issues, there emerges a growing consensus concerning ethical judgments. In that case, the moral realism view might well prove the most straightforward and workable explanation for this emerging consensus of ethical belief: The consensus develops *because* everyone is coming to recognize the same objective moral facts. Does such a consensus emerge from calm rational reflection? Perhaps. After all, almost everyone who thinks calmly about it concludes that it is wrong to discriminate against others on the basis of race, gender, or sexual orientation; that genocide is wrong; that people should be free to hold and express their own views; that slavery is wrong. That is not to say that *everyone*, or even *almost* everyone, has embraced those moral claims. But obviously not everyone thinks coolly, calmly, and deliberately about those issues: Nationalistic rhetoric, patriotic fervor, religious indoctrination, oppressive tradition, and rank prejudice all militate against calm reflective consideration, and for many people the ability to think calmly and carefully about ethical issues is held hostage by such constraints, passions, and pressures. But when people can set aside such forces, and think calmly and carefully, there does seem to be an emerging consensus on some basic ethical principles. If so, then perhaps the best explanation for that emerging consensus is the common recognition of objective moral facts.

> "According to the account on offer [moral realism] it is right that I give to famine relief just in case I have a reason to give to famine relief, and I have such a reason just in case, if I were in idealized conditions of reflection—well-informed, cool, calm and collected— I would desire to give to famine relief. And the same is true of you." *Michael Smith*

Or maybe there's a better explanation, that does not posit objective moral facts. But the moral realist insists that the best way of judging between these radically different realist and nonobjectivist perspectives is by allowing them to compete, and then seeing which system guides us to better ethical understanding. Maybe the moral realist system will prove best, and maybe it will not; but—the moral realists argue—moral realism is a plausible working hypothesis, and it's too early to tell which perspective will finally prove more successful. The moral realist hypothesis is still a contender.

This is not your grandmother's moral realism. When she told you it is wrong to tell a lie, she was not proposing that as a plausible hypothesis, but as absolute fact. But contemporary moral realism does offer one line of defense against contemporary moral nonobjectivists. Whether you find such a tentative moral realism satisfactory, or you favor some more robust form of moral realism, or a moderate sort of constructivism, or perhaps some form of care ethics, or you embrace stark moral *non*objectivism, that is a question you can mull over for yourself; indeed, you might find yourself mulling over it for quite a long time, and there are worse topics for mulling.

READINGS

⚊ THE RIGHT AND THE GOOD ⚊
W. D. Ross

W. D. Ross (1877–1971) taught at Oxford University and is probably the best known and most influential contemporary advocate of ethical intuitionism. This passage is taken from *The Right and the Good* (1930).

When a plain man fulfils a promise because he thinks he ought to do so, it seems clear that he does so with no thought of its total consequences, still less with any opinion that these are likely to be the best possible. He thinks in fact much more of the past than of the future. What makes him think it right to act in a certain way is the fact that he has promised to do so—that and, usually, nothing more. That his act will produce the best possible consequences is not his reason for calling it right. What lends colour to the theory [utilitarianism] we are examining, then, is not the actions (which form probably a great majority of our actions) in which some such reflection as 'I have promised' is the only reason we give ourselves for thinking a certain action right, but the exceptional cases in which the consequences of fulfilling a promise (for instance) would be so disastrous to others that we judge it right not to do so. It must of course be admitted that such cases exist. If I have promised to meet a friend at a particular time for some trivial purpose, I should certainly think myself justified in breaking my engagement if by doing so I could prevent a serious accident or bring relief to the victims of one. And the

supporters of the view we are examining hold that my thinking so is due to my thinking that I shall bring more good into existence by the one action than by the other. A different account may, however, be given of the matter, an account which will, I believe, show itself to be the true one. It may be said that besides the duty of fulfilling promises I have and recognize a duty of relieving distress, and that when I think it right to do the latter at the cost of not doing the former, it is not because I think I shall produce more good thereby but because I think it the duty which is in the circumstances more of a duty. This account surely corresponds much more closely with what we really think in such a situation. If, so far as I can see, I could bring equal amounts of good into being by fulfilling my promise and by helping some one to whom I had made no promise, I should not hesitate to regard the former as my duty. Yet on the view that what is right is right because it is productive of the most good I should not so regard it.

There are two theories, each in its way simple, that offer a solution of such cases of conscience. One is the view of Kant, that there are certain duties of perfect obligation, such as those of fulfilling promises, of paying debts, of telling the truth, which admit of no exception whatever in favour of duties of imperfect obligation, such as that of relieving distress. The other is the view of, for instance, Professor Moore and Dr Rashdall, that there is only the duty of producing good, and that all 'conflicts of duties' should be resolved by asking 'by which action will most good be produced?' But it is more important that our theory fit the facts than that it be simple, and the account we have given above corresponds (it seems to me) better than either of the simpler theories with what we really think, viz. that normally promise-keeping, for example, should come before benevolence, but that when and only when the good to be produced by the benevolent act is very great and the promise comparatively trivial, the act of benevolence becomes our duty.

In fact the theory of 'ideal utilitarianism', if I may for brevity refer so to the theory of Professor Moore, seems to simplify unduly our relations to our fellows. It says, in effect, that the only morally significant relation in which my neighbours stand to me is that of being possible beneficiaries by my action. They do stand in this relation to me, and this relation is morally significant. But they may also stand to me in the relation of promisee to promiser, of creditor to debtor, of wife to husband, of child to parent, of friend to friend, of fellow countryman to fellow countryman, and the like; and each of these relations is the foundation of a prima-facie duty, which is more or less incumbent on me according to the circumstances of the case. When I am in a situation, as perhaps I always am, in which more than one of these prima-facie duties is incumbent on me, what I have to do is to study the situation as fully as I can until I form the considered opinion (it is never more) that in the circumstances one of them is more incumbent than any other; then I am bound to think that to do this prima-facie duty is my duty *sans phrase* in the situation.

I suggest 'prima-facie duty' or 'conditional duty' as a brief way of referring to the characteristic (quite distinct from that of being a duty proper) which an act has, in virtue of being of a certain kind (e.g. the keeping of a promise), of being an act which would be a duty proper if it were not at the same time of another kind which is morally significant. Whether an act is a duty proper of actual duty depends on *all* the morally significant kinds it is an instance of. The phrase 'prima-facie duty' must be apologized for, since (1) it suggests that what we are speaking of is a certain kind of duty, whereas it is in fact not a duty, but something related in a special way to duty. Strictly speaking, we want not a phrase in which duty is qualified by an adjective, but a separate noun. (2) 'Prima' facie suggests that one is speaking only of an appearance which a moral situation presents at first sight, and which may turn out to be illusory; whereas what I am speaking of is an objective fact involved in the nature of the situation, or more strictly in an element of its nature, though not, as duty proper does, arising from its *whole* nature. I can, however, think of no term which fully meets the case.

. . .

There is nothing arbitrary about these prima-facie duties. Each rests on a definite circumstance which cannot seriously be held to be without moral significance. Of prima-facie duties I suggest, without claiming completeness or finality for it, the following division.

(1) Some duties rest on previous acts of my own. These duties seem to include two kinds, (*a*) those resting on a promise or what may fairly be called an implicit promise, such as the implicit undertaking not to tell lies which seems to be implied in the act of entering into conversation (at any rate by civilized men), or of writing books that purport to be history and not fiction. These may be called the duties of fidelity. (*b*) Those resting on a previous wrongful act. These may be called the duties of reparation. (2) Some rest on previous acts of other men, i.e. services done by them to me. These may be loosely described as the duties of gratitude. (3) Some rest on the fact or possibility of a distribution of pleasure or happiness (or of the means thereto) which is not in accordance with the merit of the persons concerned; in such cases there arises a duty to upset or prevent such a distribution. These are the duties of justice. (4) Some rest on the mere fact that there are other beings in the world whose condition we can make better in respect of virtue, or of intelligence, or of pleasure. These are the duties of beneficence. (5) Some rest on the fact that we can improve our own condition in respect of virtue or of intelligence. These are the duties of self-improvement. (6) I think that we should distinguish from (4) the duties that may be summed up under the title of 'not injuring others'. No doubt to injure others is incidentally to fail to do them good; but it seems to me clear that non-maleficence is apprehended as a duty distinct from that of beneficence, and as a duty of a more stringent character. It will be noticed that this alone among the types of duty has been stated in a negative way. An attempt might no doubt be made to state this duty, like the others, in a positive way. It might be said that it is really the duty to prevent ourselves from acting either from an inclination to

harm others or from an inclination to seek our own pleasure, in doing which we should incidentally harm them. But on reflection it seems clear that the primary duty here is the duty not to harm others, this being a duty whether or not we have an inclination that if followed would lead to our harming them; and that when we have such an inclination the primary duty not to harm others gives rise to a consequential duty to resist the inclination. The recognition of this duty of non-maleficence is the first step on the way to the recognition of the duty of beneficence; and that accounts for the prominence of the commands 'thou shalt not kill', 'thou shalt not commit adultery', 'thou shalt not steal', 'thou shalt not bear false witness', in so early a code as the Decalogue. But even when we have come to recognize the duty of beneficence, it appears to me that the duty of non-maleficence is recognized as a distinct one, and as prima facie more binding. We should not in general consider it justifiable to kill one person in order to keep another alive, or to steal from one in order to give alms to another.

The essential defect of the 'ideal utilitarian' theory is that it ignores, or at least does not do full justice to, the highly personal character of duty. If the only duty is to produce the maximum of good, the question who is to have the good—whether it is myself, or my benefactor, or a person to whom I have made a promise to confer that good on him, or a mere fellow man to whom I stand in no such special relation—should make no difference to my having a duty to produce that good. But we are all in fact sure that it makes a vast difference.

. . .

It is necessary to say something by way of clearing up the relation between prima-facie duties and the actual or absolute duty to do one particular act in particular circumstances. If, as almost all moralists except Kant are agreed, and as most plain men think, it is sometimes right to tell a lie or to break a promise, it must be maintained that there is a difference between prima-facie duty and actual or absolute duty. When we think ourselves justified in breaking, and indeed morally obliged to break, a promise in order to relieve some one's distress, we do not for a moment cease to recognize a prima-facie duty to keep our promise, and this leads us to feel, not indeed shame or repentance, but certainly compunction, for behaving as we do; we recognize, further, that it is our duty to make up somehow to the promisee for the breaking of the promise. We have to distinguish from the characteristic of being our duty that of tending to be our duty. Any act that we do contains various elements in virtue of which it falls under various categories. In virtue of being the breaking of a promise, for instance, it tends to be wrong; in virtue of being an instance of relieving distress it tends to be right. Tendency to be one's duty may be called a parti-resultant attribute, i.e. one which belongs to an act in virtue of some one component in its nature. *Being* one's duty is a toti-resultant attribute, one which belongs to an act in virtue of its whole nature and of nothing less than this. This distinction between parti-resultant and toti-resultant attributes is one which we shall meet in another context also.

Another instance of the same distinction may be found in the operation of natural laws. *Qua* subject to the force of gravitation towards some other body, each body tends to move in a particular direction with a particular velocity; but its actual movement depends on *all* the forces to which it is subject. It is only by recognizing this distinction that we can preserve the absoluteness of laws of nature, and only by recognizing a corresponding distinction that we can preserve the absoluteness of the general principles of morality. But an important difference between the two cases must be pointed out. When we say that in virtue of gravitation a body tends to move in a certain way, we are referring to a causal influence actually exercised on it by another body or other bodies. When we say that in virtue of being deliberately untrue a certain remark tends to be wrong, we are referring to no causal relation, to no relation that involves succession in time, but to such a relation as connects the various attributes of a mathematical figure. And if the word 'tendency' is thought to suggest too much a causal relation, it is better to talk of certain types of act as being prima facie right or wrong (or of different persons as having different and possibly conflicting claims upon us), than of their tending to be right or wrong.

Something should be said of the relation between our apprehension of the prima-facie rightness of certain types of act and our mental attitude towards particular acts. It is proper to use the word 'apprehension' in the former case and not in the latter. That an act, *qua* fulfilling a promise, or *qua* effecting a just distribution of good, or *qua* returning services rendered, or *qua* promoting the good of others, or *qua* promoting the virtue or insight of the agent, is prima facie right, is self—evident; not in the sense that it is evident from the beginning of our lives, or as soon as we attend to the proposition for the first time, but in the sense that when we have reached sufficient mental maturity and have given sufficient attention to the proposition it is evident without any need of proof, or of evidence beyond itself. It is self-evident just as a mathematical axiom, or the validity of a form of inference, is evident. The moral order expressed in these propositions is just as much part of the fundamental nature of the universe (and, we may add, of any possible universe in which there were moral agents at all) as is the spatial or numerical structure expressed in the axioms of geometry or arithmetic. In our confidence that these propositions are true there is involved the same trust in our reason that is involved in our confidence in mathematics; and we should have no justification for trusting it in the latter sphere and distrusting it in the former. In both cases we are dealing with propositions that cannot be proved, but that just as certainly need no proof.

· · ·

Our judgements about our actual duty in concrete situations have none of the certainty that attaches to our recognition of the general principles of duty. A statement is certain, i.e. is an expression of knowledge, only in one or other of two cases: when it is either self-evident, or a valid conclusion from self-evident premisses. And our judgements about our particular duties have neither of these characters. (1) They are not self-evident. Where a possible act is seen to have two characteristics, in virtue of one of which it is prima facie right, and in virtue of the other prima facie wrong, we are (I think) well aware that we are not certain whether we ought or ought not to do it; that whether we do it or not, we are taking a moral risk. We come in the long run, after consideration, to think one duty more pressing than the other, but we do not feel certain that it is so. And though we do not always recognize that a possible act has two such characteristics, and though there *may* be cases in which it has not, we are never certain that any particular possible act has not, and therefore never certain that it is right, nor certain that it is wrong. For, to go no further in the analysis, it is enough to point out that any particular act will in all probability in the course of time contribute to the bringing about of good or of evil for many human beings, and thus have a prima-facie rightness or wrongness of which we know nothing. (2) Again, our judgements about our particular duties are not logical conclusions from self-evident premisses. The only possible premisses would be the general principles stating their prima-facie rightness or wrongness *qua* having the different characteristics they do have; and even if we could (as we cannot) apprehend the extent to which an act will tend on the one hand, for example, to bring about advantages for our benefactors, and on the other hand to bring about disadvantages for fellow men who are not our benefactors, there is no principle by which we can draw the conclusion that it is on the whole right

or on the whole wrong. In this respect the judgement as to the rightness of a particular act is just like judgement as to the beauty of a particular natural object or work of art. A poem is, for instance, in respect of certain qualities beautiful and in respect of certain others not beautiful; and our judgement as to the degree of beauty it possesses on the whole is never reached by logical reasoning from the apprehension of its particular beauties or particular defects. Both in this and in the moral case we have more or less probable opinions which are not logically justified conclusions from the general principles that are recognized as self-evident.

· · ·

The general principles of duty are obviously not self-evident from the beginning or our lives. How do they come to be so? The answer is, that they come to be self-evident to us just as mathematical axioms do. We find by experience that this couple of matches and that couple make four matches, that this couple of balls on a wire and that couple make four balls: and by reflection on these and similar discoveries we come to see that it is of the nature of two and two to make four. In a precisely similar way, we see the prima-facie rightness of an act which would be the fulfilment of a particular promise, and of another which would be the fulfilment of another promise, and when we have reached sufficient maturity to think in general terms, we apprehend prima-facie rightness to belong to the nature of any fulfilment of promise. What comes first in time is the apprehension of the self-evident prima-facie rightness of an individual act of a particular type. From this we come by reflection to apprehend the self-evident general principle of prima-facie duty. From this, too, perhaps along with the apprehension of the self-evident prima-facie rightness of the same act in virtue of its having another characteristic as well, and perhaps in spite of the apprehension of its prima-facie wrongness in virtue of its having some third characteristic, we come to believe something not self-evident at all, but an object of probable opinion, viz. that this particular act is (not prima facie but) actually right.

· · ·

In what has preceded, a good deal of use has been made of 'what we really think' about moral questions; a certain theory has been rejected because it does not agree with what we really think. It might be said that this is in principle wrong; that we should not be content to expound what our present moral consciousness tells us but should aim at a criticism of our existing moral consciousness in the light of theory. Now I do not doubt that the moral consciousness of men has in detail undergone a good deal of modification as regards the things we think right, at the hands of moral theory. But if we are told, for instance, that we should give up our view that there is a special obligatoriness attaching to the keeping of promises because it is self-evident that the only duty is to produce as much good as possible, we have to ask ourselves whether we really, when we reflect, *are* convinced that this is self-evident and whether we really *can* get rid of our view that promise-keeping has a bindingness independent of productiveness of maximum good. In my own experience I find that I cannot, in spite of a very genuine attempt to do so; and I venture to think that most people will find the same, and that just because they cannot lose the sense of special obligation, they cannot accept as self-evident, or even as true, the theory which would require them to do so. In fact it seems, on reflection, self-evident that a promise, simply as such, is something that prima facie ought to be kept, and it does *not*, on reflection, seem self-evident that production of maximum good is the only thing that makes an act obligatory. And to ask us to give up at the bidding of a theory our actual apprehension of what is right and what is wrong seems like asking people to repudiate their actual experience of beauty, at the bidding of a theory which says 'only that which satisfies such and such conditions can be beautiful'. If what I have called our actual apprehension is (as I would maintain that it is) truly an apprehension, i.e. an instance of knowledge, the request is nothing less than absurd.

I would maintain, in fact, that what we are apt to describe as 'what we think' about moral questions contains a considerable amount that we do not think but know, and that this forms the standard by reference to which the truth of any moral theory has to be tested, instead of having itself to be tested by reference to any theory. I hope that I have in what precedes indicated what in my view these elements of knowledge are that are involved in our ordinary moral consciousness.

It would be a mistake to found a natural science on 'what we really think', i.e. on what reasonably thoughtful and well-educated people think about the subjects of science before they have studied them scientifically. For such opinions are interpretations, and often misinterpretations, of sense-experience; and the man of science must appeal from these to sense-experience itself, which furnishes his real data. In ethics no such appeal is possible. We have no more direct way of access to the facts about rightness and goodness and about what things are right or good, than by thinking about them; the moral convictions of thoughtful and well-educated people are the data of ethics just as sense-perceptions are the data of a natural science. Just as some of the latter have to be rejected as illusory, so have some of the former; but as the latter are rejected only when they are in conflict with other more accurate sense-perceptions, the former are rejected only when they are in conflict with other convictions which stand better the test of reflection. The existing body of moral convictions of the best people is the cumulative product of the moral reflection of many generations, which has developed an extremely delicate power of appreciation of moral distinctions; and this the theorist cannot afford to treat with anything other than the greatest respect. The verdicts of the moral consciousness of the best people are the foundation on which he must build; though he must first compare them with one another and eliminate any contradictions they may contain.

⇒ THE NICOMACHEAN ETHICS ⇐
Aristotle

For some 2,000 years—from ancient Greece to the Enlightenment—Aristotle was the greatest influence on Western philosophy. In addition to his views concerning the nature and existence of God, the structure of the universe, and the means of gaining knowledge, Aristotle also wrote extensively and influentially on ethics; and his *virtue theory* approach to ethics dominated ethical thought for many centuries. For Aristotle, the focus is not on what *act* I should or should not perform, but on what sort of *person* I really want to be, and on how to become such a person. And in deciding what sort of person I *really* want to be, Aristotle counsels that we must carefully examine what is the *genuinely* good and truly happy life for a human being. Contemporary virtue theorists have developed Aristotle's ideas in some new directions, but the fundamental questions of virtue ethics were posed by Aristotle many centuries ago.

NICOMACHEAN ETHICS BOOK 1

7

Let us again return to the good we are seeking, and ask what it can be. It seems different in different actions and arts; it is different in medicine, in strategy, and in the other arts likewise. What then is the good of each? Surely that for whose sake everything else is done. In medicine this is health, in strategy victory, in architecture a house, in any other sphere something else, and in every action and pursuit the end; for it is for the sake of this that all men do whatever else they do. Therefore, if there is an end for all that we do, this will be the good achievable by action, and if there are more than one, these will be the goods achievable by action. So the argument has by a different course reached the same point; but we must try to state this even more clearly. Since there are evidently more than one end, and we choose some of these (e.g., wealth, flutes, and in general instruments) for the sake of something else, clearly not all ends are final ends; but the chief good is evidently something final. Therefore, if there is only one final end, this will be what we are seeking, and if there are more than one, the most final of these will be what we are seeking. Now we call that which is in itself worthy of pursuit more final than that which is worthy of pursuit for the sake of something else, and that which is never desirable for the sake of something else more final than the things that are desirable both in themselves and for the sake of that other thing, and therefore we call final without qualification that which is always desirable in itself and never for the sake of something else.

Now such a thing happiness, above all else, is held to be; for this we choose always for self and never for the sake of something else, but honour, pleasure, reason, and every virtue we choose indeed for themselves (for if nothing resulted from them we should still choose each of them), but we choose them also for the sake of happiness, judging that by means of them we shall be happy. Happiness, on the other hand, no one chooses for the sake of these, nor, in general, for anything other than itself.

From the point of view of self-sufficiency the same result seems to follow; for the final good is thought to be self-sufficient. Now by self-sufficient we do not mean that which is sufficient for a man by himself, for one who lives a solitary life, but also for parents, children, wife, and in general for his friends and fellow citizens, since man is born for citizenship.

But some limit must be set to this; for if we extend our requirement to ancestors and descendants and friends' friends we are in for an infinite series. Let us examine this question, however, on another occasion; the self-sufficient we now define as that which when isolated makes life desirable and lacking in nothing; and such we think happiness to be; and further we think it most desirable of all things, without being counted as one good thing among others—if it were so counted it would clearly be made more desirable by the addition of even the least of goods; for that which is added becomes an excess of goods, and of goods the greater is always more desirable. Happiness, then, is something final and self-sufficient, and is the end of action.

Presumably, however, to say that happiness is the chief good seems a platitude, and a clearer account of what it is is still desired. This might perhaps be given, if we could first ascertain the function of man. For just as for a flute-player, a sculptor, or an artist, and, in general, for all things that have a function or activity, the good and the 'well' is thought to reside in the function, so would it seem to be for man, if he has a function. Have the carpenter, then, and the tanner certain functions or activities, and has man none? Is he born without a function? Or as eye, hand, foot, and in general each of the parts evidently has a function, may one lay it down that man similarly has a function apart from all these? What then can this be? Life seems to be common even to plants, but we are seeking what is peculiar to man. Let us exclude, therefore, the life of nutrition and growth. Next there would be a life of perception, but it also seems to be common even to the horse, the ox, and every animal. There remains, then, an active life of the element that has a rational principle; of this, one part has such a principle in the sense of being obedient to one, the other in the sense of possessing one and exercising thought. And, as 'life of the rational element' also has two meanings, we must state that life in the sense of activity is what we mean; for this seems to be the more proper sense of the term. Now if the function of man is an activity of soul which follows or implies a rational principle, and if we say 'a so-and-so' and 'a good so-and-so' have a function which is the same in kind, e.g. a lyre, and a good lyre-player, and so without qualification in all cases, eminence in respect of goodness being added to the name of the function (for the function of a lyre-player is to play the lyre, and that of a good lyre-player is to do so well): if this is the case, and we state the function of man to be a certain kind of life, and this to be an activity or actions of the soul implying a rational principle, and the function of a good man to be the good and noble performance of these, and if any action is well performed when it is performed in accordance with the appropriate excellence: if this is the case, human good turns out to be activity of soul in accordance with virtue, and if there are more than one virtue, in accordance with the best and most complete.

But we must add 'in a complete life.' For one swallow does not make a summer, nor does one day; and so too one day, or a short time, does not make a man blessed and happy.

. . .

NICHOMACHEAN ETHICS BOOK II

1

Virtue, then, being of two kinds, intellectual and moral, intellectual virtue in the main owes both its birth and its growth to teaching (for which reason it requires experience and time), while moral virtue comes about as a result of habit, whence also its name (ethike) is one that is formed by a slight variation from the word ethos (habit). From this it is also plain that none of the moral virtues arises in us by nature; for nothing that exists by nature can form a habit contrary to its nature. For instance the stone which by nature moves downwards cannot be habituated to move upwards, not even if one tries to train it by throwing it up ten thousand times; nor can fire be habituated to move downwards, nor can anything else that by nature behaves in one way be trained to behave in another. Neither by nature, then, nor contrary to nature do the virtues arise in us; rather we are adapted by nature to receive them, and are made perfect by habit.

Again, of all the things that come to us by nature we first acquire the potentiality and later exhibit the activity (this is plain in the case of the senses; for it was not by often seeing or often hearing that we got these senses, but on the contrary we had them before we used them, and did not come to have them by using them); but the virtues we get by first exercising them, as also happens in the case of the arts as well. For the things we have to learn before we can do them, we learn by doing them, e.g. men become builders by building and lyre-players by playing the lyre; so too we become just by doing just acts, temperate by doing temperate acts, brave by doing brave acts.

This is confirmed by what happens in states; for legislators make the citizens good by forming habits in them, and this is the wish of every legislator, and those who do not effect it miss their mark, and it is in this that a good constitution differs from a bad one.

Again, it is from the same causes and by the same means that every virtue is both produced and destroyed, and similarly every art; for it is from playing the lyre that both good and bad lyre-players are produced. And the corresponding statement is true of builders and of all the rest; men will be good or bad builders as a result of building well or badly. For if this were not so, there would have been no need of a teacher, but all men would have been born good or bad at their craft. This, then, is the case with the virtues also; by doing the acts that we do in our transactions with other men we become just or unjust, and by doing the acts that we do in the presence of danger, and being habituated to feel fear or confidence, we become brave or cowardly. The same is true of appetites and feelings of anger; some men become temperate and good-tempered, others self-indulgent and irascible, by behaving in one way or the other in the appropriate circumstances. Thus, in one word, states of character arise out of like activities. This is why the activities we exhibit must be of a certain kind; it is because the states of character correspond to the differences between these. It makes no small difference, then, whether we form habits of one kind or of another from our very youth; it makes a very great difference, or rather all the difference.

. . .

Actions, then, are called just and temperate when they are such as the just or the temperate man would do; but it is not the man who does these that is just and temperate, but the man who also does them as just and temperate men do them. It is well said, then, that it is by doing just acts that the just man is produced, and by doing temperate acts the temperate man; without doing these no one would have even a prospect of becoming good.

But most people do not do these, but take refuge in theory and think they are being philosophers and will become good in this way, behaving somewhat like patients who listen attentively to their doctors, but do none of the things they are ordered to do. As the latter will not be made well in body by such a course of treatment, the former will not be made well in soul by such a course of philosophy.

5

Next we must consider what virtue is. Since things that are found in the soul are of three kinds—passions, faculties, states of character, virtue must be one of these. By passions I mean appetite, anger, fear, confidence, envy, joy, friendly feeling, hatred, longing, emulation, pity, and in general the feelings that are accompanied by pleasure or pain; by faculties the things in virtue of which we are said to be capable of feeling these, e.g. of becoming angry or being pained or feeling pity; by states of character the things in virtue of which we stand well or badly with reference to the passions, e.g. with reference to anger we stand badly if we feel it violently or too weakly, and well if we feel it moderately; and similarly with reference to the other passions.

Now neither the virtues nor the vices are passions, because we are not called good or bad on the ground of our passions, but are so called on the ground of our virtues and our vices, and because we are neither praised nor blamed for our passions (for the man who feels fear or anger is not praised, nor is the man who simply feels anger blamed, but the man who feels it in a certain way), but for our virtues and our vices we are praised or blamed.

Again, we feel anger and fear without choice, but the virtues are modes of choice or involve choice. Further, in respect of the passions we are said to be moved, but in respect of the virtues and the vices we are said not to be moved but to be disposed in a particular way.

For these reasons also they are not faculties; for we are neither called good nor bad, nor praised nor blamed, for the simple capacity of feeling the passions; again, we have the faculties by nature, but we are not made good or bad by nature; we have spoken of this before. If, then, the virtues are neither passions nor faculties, all that remains is that they should be states of character. Thus we have stated what virtue is in respect of its genus.

6

We must, however, not only describe virtue as a state of character, but also say what sort of state it is. We may remark, then, that every virtue or excellence both brings into good condition the thing of which it is the excellence and makes the work of that thing be done well; e.g. the excellence of the eye makes both the eye and its work good; for it is by the excellence of the eye that we see well. Similarly the excellence of the horse makes a horse both good in itself and good

at running and at carrying its rider and at awaiting the attack of the enemy. Therefore, if this is true in every case, the virtue of man also will be the state of character which makes a man good and which makes him do his own work well.

How this is to happen we have stated already, but it will be made plain also by the following consideration of the specific nature of virtue. In everything that is continuous and divisible it is possible to take more, less, or an equal amount, and that either in terms of the thing itself or relatively to us; and the equal is an intermediate between excess and defect. By the intermediate in the object I mean that which is equidistant from each of the extremes, which is one and the same for all men; by the intermediate relatively to us that which is neither too much nor too little—and this is not one, nor the same for all. For instance, if ten is many and two is few, six is the intermediate, taken in terms of the object; for it exceeds and is exceeded by an equal amount; this is intermediate according to arithmetical proportion. But the intermediate relatively to us is not to be taken so; if ten pounds are too much for a particular person to eat and two too little, it does not follow that the trainer will order six pounds; for this also is perhaps too much for the person who is to take it, or too little—too little for Milo, too much for the beginner in athletic exercises. The same is true of running and wrestling. Thus a master of any art avoids excess and defect, but seeks the intermediate and chooses this—the intermediate not in the object but relatively to us.

If it is thus, then, that every art does its work well—by looking to the intermediate and judging its works by this standard (so that we often say of good works of art that it is not possible either to take away or to add anything, implying that excess and defect destroy the goodness of works of art, while the mean preserves it; and good artists, as we say, look to this in their work), and if, further, virtue is more exact and better than any art, as nature also is, then virtue must have the quality of aiming at the intermediate. I mean moral virtue; for it is this that is concerned with passions and actions, and in these there is excess, defect, and the intermediate. For instance, both fear and confidence and appetite and anger and pity and in general pleasure and pain may be felt both too much and too little, and in both cases not well; but to feel them at the right times, with reference to the right objects, towards the right people, with the right motive, and in the right way, is what is both intermediate and best, and this is characteristic of virtue.

Similarly with regard to actions also there is excess, defect, and the intermediate. Now virtue is concerned with passions and actions, in which excess is a form of failure, and so is defect, while the intermediate is praised and is a form of success; and being praised and being successful are both characteristics of virtue. Therefore virtue is a kind of mean, since, as we have seen, it aims at what is intermediate.

Again, it is possible to fail in many ways (for evil belongs to the class of the unlimited, as the Pythagoreans conjectured, and good to that of the limited), while to succeed is possible only in one way (for which reason also one is easy and the other difficult—to miss the mark easy, to hit it difficult); for these reasons also, then, excess and defect are characteristic of vice, and the mean of virtue.

For men are good in but one way, but bad in many. Virtue, then, is a state of character concerned with choice, lying in a mean, i.e. the mean relative to us, this being determined by a rational principle, and by that principle by which the man of practical wisdom would determine it. Now it is a mean between two vices, that which depends on excess and that which depends on defect; and again it is a mean because the vices respectively fall short of or exceed what is right in both passions and actions, while virtue both finds and chooses that which is intermediate. Hence in respect of its substance and the definition which states its essence virtue is a mean, with regard to what is best and right an extreme.

But not every action nor every passion admits of a mean; for some have names that already imply badness, e.g. spite, shamelessness, envy, and in the case of actions adultery, theft, murder; for all of these and suchlike things imply by their names that they are themselves bad, and not the excesses or deficiencies of them. It is not possible, then, ever to be right with regard to them; one must always be wrong. Nor does goodness or badness with regard to such things depend on committing adultery with the right woman, at the right time, and in the right way, but simply to do any of them is to go wrong. It would be equally absurd, then, to expect that in unjust, cowardly, and voluptuous action there should be a mean, an excess, and a deficiency; for at that rate there would be a mean of excess and of deficiency, an excess of excess, and a deficiency of deficiency. But as there is no excess and deficiency of temperance and courage because what is intermediate is in a sense an extreme, so too of the actions we have mentioned there is no mean nor any excess and deficiency, but however they are done they are wrong; for in general there is

neither a mean of excess and deficiency, nor excess and deficiency of a mean.

. . .

9

That moral virtue is a mean, then, and in what sense it is so, and that it is a mean between two vices, the one involving excess, the other deficiency, and that it is such because its character is to aim at what is intermediate in passions and in actions, has been sufficiently stated. Hence also it is no easy task to be good. For in everything it is no easy task to find the middle, e.g. to find the middle of a circle is not for every one but for him who knows; so, too, any one can get angry—that is easy—or give or spend money; but to do this to the right person, to the right extent, at the right time, with the right motive, and in the right way, that is not for every one, nor is it easy; wherefore goodness is both rare and laudable and noble.

Hence he who aims at the intermediate must first depart from what is the more contrary to it, as Calypso advises—

Hold the ship out beyond that surf and spray. For of the extremes one is more erroneous, one less so; therefore, since to hit the mean is hard in the extreme, we must as a second best, as people say, take the least of the evils; and this will be done best in the way we describe. But we must consider the things towards which we ourselves also are easily carried away; for some of us tend to one thing, some to another; and this will be recognizable from the pleasure and the pain we feel. We must drag ourselves away to the contrary extreme; for we shall get into the intermediate state by drawing well away from error, as people do in straightening sticks that are bent.

Now in everything the pleasant or pleasure is most to be guarded against; for we do not judge it impartially. We ought, then to feel towards pleasure as the elders of the people felt towards Helen, and in all circumstances repeat their saying; for if we dismiss pleasure thus we are less likely to go astray. It is by doing this, then, (to sum the matter up) that we shall best be able to hit the mean.

But this is no doubt difficult, and especially in individual cases; for it is not easy to determine both how and with whom and on what provocation and how long one should be angry; for we too sometimes praise those who fall short and call them good-tempered, but sometimes we praise those who get angry and call them manly. The man, however, who deviates little from goodness is not blamed, whether he do so in the direction of the more or of the less, but only the man who deviates more widely; for he does not fail to be noticed. But up to what point and to what extent a man must deviate before he becomes blameworthy it is not easy to determine by reasoning, any more than anything else that is perceived by the senses; such things depend on particular facts, and the decision rests with perception. So much, then, is plain, that the intermediate state is in all things to be praised, but that we must incline sometimes towards the excess, sometimes towards the deficiency; for so shall we most easily hit the mean and what is right.

. . .

NICOMACHEAN ETHICS BOOK X

1

After these matters we ought perhaps next to discuss pleasure. For it is thought to be most intimately connected with our human nature, which is the reason why in educating the young we steer them by the rudders of pleasure and pain; it is thought, too, that to enjoy the things we ought and to hate the things we ought has the greatest bearing on virtue of character. For these things extend right through life, with a weight and power of their own in respect both to virtue and to the happy life, since men choose what is pleasant and avoid what is painful, and such things, it will be thought, we should least of all omit to discuss, especially since they admit of much dispute. For some say pleasure is the good, while others, on the contrary, say it is thoroughly bad—some no doubt being persuaded that the facts are so, and others thinking it has a better effect on our life to exhibit pleasure as a bad thing even if it is not; for most people (they think) incline towards it and are the slaves of their pleasures, for which reason they ought to lead them in the opposite direction, since thus they will reach the middle state. But surely this is not correct. For arguments about matters concerned with feelings and actions are less reliable than facts: and so when they clash with the facts of perception they are despised, and discredit the truth as well; if a man who runs down pleasure is once seen to be aiming at it, his inclining towards it is thought to imply that it is all worthy of being aimed at; for most people are not good at drawing distinctions. True arguments seem, then, most useful, not only with a view to knowledge, but with a view to life also; for since they harmonize with the facts they are believed, and so they stimulate those who understand them to live according to them.

. . .

Now since activities differ in respect of goodness and badness, and some are worthy to be chosen, others to be avoided, and others neutral, so, too, are the pleasures; for to each activity there is a proper pleasure. The pleasure proper to a worthy activity is good and that proper to an unworthy activity bad; just as the appetites for noble objects are laudable, those for base objects culpable. But the pleasures involved in activities are more proper to them than the desires; for the latter are separated both in time and in nature, while the former are close to the activities, and so hard to distinguish from them that it admits of dispute whether the activity is not the same as the pleasure. (Still, pleasure does not seem to be thought or perception—that would be strange; but because they are not found apart they appear to some people the same.) As activities are different, then, so are the corresponding pleasures. Now sight is superior to touch in purity, and hearing and smell to taste; the pleasures, therefore, are similarly superior, and those of thought superior to these, and within each of the two kinds some are superior to others.

Each animal is thought to have a proper pleasure, as it has a proper function; viz. that which corresponds to its activity. If we survey them species by species, too, this will be evident; horse, dog, and man have different pleasures, as Heraclitus says 'asses would prefer sweepings to gold'; for food is pleasanter than gold to asses. So the pleasures of creatures different in kind differ in kind, and it is plausible to suppose that those of a single species do not differ. But they vary to no small extent, in the case of men at least; the same things delight some people and pain others, and are painful and odious to some, and pleasant to and liked by others. This happens, too, in the case of sweet things; the same things do not seem sweet to a man in a fever and a healthy man—nor hot to a weak man and one in good condition. The same happens in other cases. But in all such matters that which appears to the good man is thought to be really so. If this is correct, as it seems to be, and virtue and the good man as such are the measure of each thing, those also will be pleasures which appear so to him, and those things pleasant which he enjoys. If the things he finds tiresome seem pleasant to some one, that is nothing surprising; for men may be ruined and spoilt in many ways; but the things are not pleasant, but only pleasant to these people and to people in this condition. Those which are admittedly disgraceful plainly should not be said to be pleasures, except to a perverted taste; but of those that are thought to be good what kind of pleasure or what pleasure should be said to be that proper to man? Is it not plain from the corresponding activities? The pleasures follow these. Whether, then, the perfect and supremely happy man has one or more activities, the pleasures that perfect these will be said in the strict sense to be pleasures proper to man, and the rest will be so in a secondary and fractional way, as are the activities.

6

Now that we have spoken of the virtues, the forms of friendship, and the varieties of pleasure, what remains is to discuss in outline the nature of happiness, since this is what we state the end of human nature to be. Our discussion will be the more concise if we first sum up what we have said already. We said, then, that it is not a disposition; for if it were it might belong to some one who was suffering the greatest misfortunes. If these implications are unacceptable, and we must rather class happiness as an activity, as we have said before, and if some activities are necessary, and desirable for the sake of something else, while others are so in themselves, evidently happiness must be placed among those desirable in themselves, not among those desirable for the sake of something else; for happiness does not lack anything, but is self-sufficient. Now those activities are desirable in themselves from which nothing is sought beyond the activity. And of this nature virtuous actions are thought to be; for to do noble and good deeds is a thing desirable for its own sake.

Pleasant amusements also are thought to be of this nature; we choose them not for the sake of other things; for we are injured rather than benefited by them, since we are led to neglect our bodies and our property. But most of the people who are deemed happy take refuge in such pastimes, which is the reason why those who are ready-witted at them are highly esteemed at the courts of tyrants; they make themselves pleasant companions in the tyrants' favourite pursuits, and that is the sort of man they want. Now these things are thought to be of the nature of happiness because people in despotic positions spend their leisure in them, but perhaps such people prove nothing; for virtue and reason, from which good activities flow, do not depend on despotic position; nor, if these people, who have never tasted pure and generous pleasure, take refuge in the bodily pleasures, should these for that reason be thought more desirable; for boys, too, think the things that are valued among themselves are the best. It is to be expected, then, that, as different things seem valuable to boys and to men, so they should to bad men and to

good. Now, as we have often maintained, those things are both valuable and pleasant which are such to the good man; and to each man the activity in accordance with his own disposition is most desirable, and, therefore, to the good man that which is in accordance with virtue. Happiness, therefore, does not lie in amusement; it would, indeed, be strange if the end were amusement, and one were to take trouble and suffer hardship all one's life in order to amuse oneself. For, in a word, everything that we choose we choose for the sake of something else—except happiness, which is an end. Now to exert oneself and work for the sake of amusement seems silly and utterly childish. But to amuse oneself in order that one may exert oneself, as Anacharsis puts it, seems right; for amusement is a sort of relaxation, and we need relaxation because we cannot work continuously. Relaxation, then, is not an end; for it is taken for the sake of activity.

The happy life is thought to be virtuous; now a virtuous life requires exertion, and does not consist in amusement. And we say that serious things are better than laughable things and those connected with amusement, and that activity of the better of any two things—whether it be two elements of our being or two men—is the more serious; but the activity of the better is ipso facto superior and more of the nature of happiness. And any chance person—even a slave—can enjoy the bodily pleasures no less than the best man; but no one assigns to a slave a share in happiness—unless he assigns to him also a share in human life. For happiness does not lie in such occupations, but, as we have said before, in virtuous activities.

7

If happiness is activity in accordance with virtue, it is reasonable that it should be in accordance with the highest virtue; and this will be that of the best thing in us. Whether it be reason or something else that is this element which is thought to be our natural ruler and guide and to take thought of things noble and divine, whether it be itself also divine or only the most divine element in us, the activity of this in accordance with its proper virtue will be perfect happiness. That this activity is contemplative we have already said.

Now this would seem to be in agreement both with what we said before and with the truth. For, firstly, this activity is the best (since not only is reason the best thing in us, but the objects of reason are the best of knowable objects); and secondly, it is the most continuous, since we can contemplate truth more continuously than we can do anything. And we think happiness has pleasure mingled with it, but the activity of philosophic wisdom is admittedly the pleasantest of virtuous activities; at all events the pursuit of it is thought to offer pleasures marvellous for their purity and their enduringness, and it is to be expected that those who know will pass their time more pleasantly than those who inquire. And the self-sufficiency that is spoken of must belong most to the contemplative activity. For while a philosopher, as well as a just man or one possessing any other virtue, needs the necessaries of life, when they are sufficiently equipped with things of that sort the just man needs people towards whom and with whom he shall act justly, and the temperate man, the brave man, and each of the others is in the same case, but the philosopher, even when by himself, can contemplate truth, and the better the wiser he is; he can perhaps do so better if he has fellow-workers, but still he is the most self-sufficient. And this activity alone would seem to be loved for its own sake; for nothing arises from it apart from the contemplating, while from practical activities we gain more or less apart from the action. And happiness is thought to depend on leisure; for we are busy that we may have leisure, and make war that we may live in peace. Now the activity of the practical virtues is exhibited in political or military affairs, but the actions concerned with these seem to be unleisurely. Warlike actions are completely so (for no one chooses to be at war, or provokes war, for the sake of being at war; any one would seem absolutely murderous if he were to make enemies of his friends in order to bring about battle and slaughter); but the action of the statesman is also unleisurely, and—apart from the political action itself—aims at despotic power and honours, or at all events happiness, for him and his fellow citizens—a happiness different from political action, and evidently sought as being different. So if among virtuous actions political and military actions are distinguished by nobility and greatness, and these are unleisurely and aim at an end and are not desirable for their own sake, but the activity of reason, which is contemplative, seems both to be superior in serious worth and to aim at no end beyond itself, and to have its pleasure proper to itself (and this augments the activity), and the self-sufficiency, leisureliness, unweariedness (so far as this is possible for man), and all the other attributes ascribed to the supremely happy man are evidently those connected with this activity, it follows that this will be the complete happiness of man, if it be allowed a complete term of life (for none of the attributes of happiness is incomplete).

But such a life would be too high for man; for it is not in so far as he is man that he will live so, but in so far as something divine is present in him; and by so much as this is superior to our composite nature is its activity superior to that which is the exercise of the other kind of virtue. If reason is divine, then, in comparison with man, the life according to it is divine in comparison with human life. But we must not follow those who advise us, being men, to think of human things, and, being mortal, of mortal things, but must, so far as we can, make ourselves immortal, and strain every nerve to live in accordance with the best thing in us; for even if it be small in bulk, much more does it in power and worth surpass everything. This would seem, too, to be each man himself, since it is the authoritative and better part of him. It would be strange, then, if he were to choose not the life of his self but that of something else. And what we said before will apply now; that which is proper to each thing is by nature best and most pleasant for each thing; for man, therefore, the life according to reason is best and pleasantest, since reason more than anything else is man. This life therefore is also the happiest.

8

But in a secondary degree the life in accordance with the other kind of virtue is happy; for the activities in accordance with this befit our human estate. Just and brave acts, and other virtuous acts, we do in relation to each other, observing our respective duties with regard to contracts and services and all manner of actions and with regard to passions; and all of these seem to be typically human. Some of them seem even to arise from the body, and virtue of character to be in many ways bound up with the passions. Practical wisdom, too, is linked to virtue of character, and this to practical wisdom, since the principles of practical wisdom are in accordance with the moral virtues and rightness in morals is in accordance with practical wisdom. Being connected with the passions also, the moral virtues must belong to our composite nature; and the virtues of our composite nature are human; so, therefore, are the life and the happiness which correspond to these. The excellence of the reason is a thing apart; we must be content to say this much about it, for to describe it precisely is a task greater than our purpose requires. It would seem, however, also to need the external equipment but little, or less than moral virtue does. Grant that both need the necessaries, and do so equally, even if the statesman's work is the more concerned with the body and things of that sort; for there will be little difference there; but in what they need for the exercise of their activities there will be much difference. The liberal man will need money for the doing of his liberal deeds, and the just man too will need it for the returning of services (for wishes are hard to discern, and even people who are not just pretend to wish to act justly); and the brave man will need power if he is to accomplish any of the acts that correspond to his virtue, and the temperate man will need opportunity; for how else is either he or any of the others to be recognized? It is debated, too, whether the will or the deed is more essential to virtue, which is assumed to involve both; it is surely clear that its perfection involves both; but for deeds many things are needed, and more, the greater and nobler the deeds are. But the man who is contemplating the truth needs no such thing, at least with a view to the exercise of his activity; indeed they are, one may say, even hindrances, at all events to his contemplation; but in so far as he is a man and lives with a number of people, he chooses to do virtuous acts; he will therefore need such aids to living a human life.

But that perfect happiness is a contemplative activity will appear from the following consideration as well. We assume the gods to be above all other beings blessed and happy; but what sort of actions must we assign to them? Acts of justice? Will not the gods seem absurd if they make contracts and return deposits, and so on? Acts of a brave man, then, confronting dangers and running risks because it is noble to do so? Or liberal acts? To whom will they give? It will be strange if they are really to have money or anything of the kind. And what would their temperate acts be? Is not such praise tasteless, since they have no bad appetites? If we were to run through them all, the circumstances of action would be found trivial and unworthy of gods. Still, every one supposes that they live and therefore that they are active; we cannot suppose them to sleep like Endymion. Now if you take away from a living being action, and still more production, what is left but contemplation? Therefore the activity of God, which surpasses all others in blessedness, must be contemplative; and of human activities, therefore, that which is most akin to this must be most of the nature of happiness.

This is indicated, too, by the fact that the other animals have no share in happiness, being completely deprived of such activity. For while the whole life of the gods is blessed, and that of men too in so far as some likeness of such activity belongs to them, none of the other animals is happy, since they in no way share in contemplation. Happiness extends, then, just so far as contemplation does, and those to whom contemplation more fully belongs are more truly happy, not as a mere concomitant but in virtue of the contemplation; for this is in itself precious. Happiness, therefore, must be some form of contemplation.

But, being a man, one will also need external prosperity; for our nature is not self-sufficient for the purpose of contemplation, but our body also must be healthy and must have food and other attention. Still, we must not think that the man who is to be happy will need many things or great things, merely because he cannot be supremely happy without external goods; for self-sufficiency and action do not involve excess, and we can do noble acts without ruling earth and sea; for even with moderate advantages one can act virtuously (this is manifest enough; for private persons are thought to do worthy acts no less than despots—indeed even more); and it is enough that we should have so much as that; for the life of the man who is active in accordance with virtue will be happy. Solon, too, was perhaps sketching well the happy man when he described him as moderately furnished with externals but as having done (as Solon thought) the noblest acts, and lived temperately; for one can with but moderate possessions do what one ought. Anaxagoras also seems to have supposed the happy man not to be rich nor a despot, when he said that he would not be surprised if the happy man were to seem to most people a strange person; for they judge by externals, since these are all they perceive. The opinions of the wise seem, then, to harmonize with our arguments. But while even such things carry some conviction, the truth in practical matters is discerned from the facts of life; for these are the decisive factor. We must therefore survey what we have already said, bringing it to the test of the facts of life, and if it harmonizes with the facts we must accept it, but if it clashes with them we must suppose it to be mere theory. Now he who exercises his reason and cultivates it seems to be both in the best state of mind and most dear to the gods. For if the gods have any care for human affairs, as they are thought to have, it would be reasonable both that they should delight in that which was best and most akin to them (i.e. reason) and that they should reward those who love and honour this most, as caring for the things that are dear to them and acting both rightly and nobly. And that all these attributes belong most of all to the philosopher is manifest. He, therefore, is the dearest to the gods. And he who is that will presumably be also the happiest; so that in this way too the philosopher will more than any other be happy.

9

If these matters and the virtues, and also friendship and pleasure, have been dealt with sufficiently in outline, are we to suppose that our programme has reached its end? Surely, as the saying goes, where there are things to be done the end is not to survey and recognize the various things, but rather to do them; with regard to virtue, then, it is not enough to know, but we must try to have and use it, or try any other way there may be of becoming good. Now if arguments were in themselves enough to make men good, they would justly, as Theognis says, have won very great rewards, and such rewards should have been provided; but as things are, while they seem to have power to encourage and stimulate the generous-minded among our youth, and to make a character which is gently born, and a true lover of what is noble, ready to be possessed by virtue, they are not able to encourage the many to nobility and goodness. For these do not by nature obey the sense of shame, but only fear, and do not abstain from bad acts because of their baseness but through fear of punishment; living by passion they pursue their own pleasures and the means to them, and the opposite pains, and have not even a conception of what is noble and truly pleasant, since they have never tasted it. What argument would remould such people? It is hard, if not impossible, to remove by argument the traits that have long since been incorporated in the character; and perhaps we must be content if, when all the influences by which we are thought to become good are present, we get some tincture of virtue.

Now some think that we are made good by nature, others by habituation, others by teaching. Nature's part evidently does not depend on us, but as a result of some divine causes is present in those who are truly fortunate; while argument and teaching, we may suspect, are not powerful with all men, but the soul of the student must first have been cultivated by means of habits for noble joy and noble hatred, like earth which is to nourish the seed. For he who lives as passion directs will not hear argument that dissuades him, nor understand it if he does; and how can we persuade one in such a state to change his ways? And in general passion seems to yield not to argument but to force. The character, then, must somehow be there already with a kinship to virtue, loving what is noble and hating what is base.

But it is difficult to get from youth up a right training for virtue if one has not been brought up under right laws; for to live temperately and hardily is not pleasant to most people, especially when they are young. For this reason their nurture and occupations should be fixed by law; for they will not be painful when they have become customary. But it is surely not enough that when they are young they should get the right nurture and attention; since they must, even when they are grown up, practise and be habituated to them, we shall need laws for this as well, and generally speaking to cover the whole of life; for most people obey necessity rather than argument, and punishments rather than the sense of what is noble.

This is why some think that legislators ought to stimulate men to virtue and urge them forward by the motive of the noble, on the assumption that those who have been well advanced by the formation of habits will attend to such influences; and that punishments and penalties should be imposed on those who disobey and are of inferior nature, while the incurably bad should be completely banished. A good man (they think), since he lives with his mind fixed on what is noble, will submit to argument, while a bad man, whose desire is for pleasure, is corrected by pain like a beast of burden. This is, too, why they say the pains inflicted should be those that are most opposed to the pleasures such men love.

However that may be, if (as we have said) the man who is to be good must be well trained and habituated, and go on to spend his time in worthy occupations and neither willingly nor unwillingly do bad actions, and if this can be brought about if men live in accordance with a sort of reason and right order, provided this has force,—if this be so, the paternal command indeed has not the required force or compulsive power (nor in general has the command of one man, unless he be a king or something similar), but the law has compulsive power, while it is at the same time a rule proceeding from a sort of practical wisdom and reason. And while people hate men who oppose their impulses, even if they oppose them rightly, the law in its ordaining of what is good is not burdensome.

In the Spartan state alone, or almost alone, the legislator seems to have paid attention to questions of nurture and occupations; in most states such matters have been neglected, and each man lives as he pleases, Cyclops-fashion, 'to his own wife and children dealing law'. Now it is best that there should be a public and proper care for such matters; but if they are neglected by the community it would seem right for each man to help his children and friends towards virtue, and that they should have the power, or at least the will, to do this.

⇒ ETHICS: INVENTING RIGHT AND WRONG ⇒
J. L. Mackie

J. L. Mackie (1917–1981) was an Australian philosopher, who taught at the University of Sydney and finished his career at Oxford University. He is best known for his work in ethics and his powerful critique of ethical objectivism, as well as his writings on philosophy of religion and the problem of evil. His books include *Hume's Moral Theory* (New York: Routledge, 1980); *The Miracle of Theism: Arguments for and Against the Existence of God* (Oxford: Oxford University Press, 1982); and *Ethics: Inventing Right and Wrong* (Hammondsworth, U.K.: Penguin, 1977), from which the following reading is taken.

9. THE ARGUMENT FROM QUEERNESS

Even more important, however, and certainly more generally applicable, is the argument from queerness. This has two parts, one metaphysical, the other epistemological. If there were objective values, then they would be entities or qualities or relations of a very strange sort, utterly different from anything else in the universe. Correspondingly, if we were aware of them, it would have to be by some special faculty of moral perception or intuition, utterly different from our ordinary ways of knowing everything else. These points were recognized by Moore when he spoke of non-natural qualities, and by the Intuitionists in their talk about a 'faculty of moral intuition.' Intuitionism has long been out of favour, and it is indeed easy to point out its implausibilities. What is not so often stressed, but is more important, is that the central thesis of intuitionism is one to which any objectivist view of values is in the end committed: intuitionism merely makes unpalatably plain what other forms of objectivism wrap up. Of course the suggestion that moral judgements are made or moral problems solved by just sitting down and having an ethical intuition is a travesty of actual moral thinking. But, however complex the real process, it will require (if it is to yield authoritatively prescriptive conclusions) some input of this distinctive sort, either premisses or forms of argument or both. When we ask the awkward question, how we can be aware of this authoritative prescriptivity, of the truth of these distinctively ethical premises or of the cogency of this distinctively ethical pattern of reasoning, none of our ordinary accounts of sensory perception or introspection or the framing and confirming of explanatory hypotheses or inference or logical construction or conceptual analysis, or any combination of these, will provide a satisfactory answer; 'a special sort of intuition' is a lame answer, but it is the one to which the clear-headed objectivist is compelled to resort.

. . .

Plato's Forms give a dramatic picture of what objective values would have to be. The Form of the Good is such that knowledge of it provides the knower with both a direction and an overriding motive; something's being good both tells the person who knows this to pursue it and makes him pursue it. An objective good would be sought by anyone who was acquainted with it, not because of any contingent fact that this person, or every person, is so constituted that he desires this end, but just because the end has to-be-pursuedness somehow built into it. Similarly, if there were objective principles of right and wrong, any wrong (possible) course of action would have not-to-be-doneness somehow built into it. Or we should have something like Clarke's necessary relations of fitness between situations and actions, so that a situation would have a demand for such-and-such and action somehow built into it.

The need for an argument of this sort can be brought out by reflection on Hume's argument that 'reason'—in which at this stage he includes all sorts of knowing as well as reasoning—can never be an 'influencing motive of the will'. Someone might object that Hume has argued unfairly from the lack of influencing power (not contingent upon desires) in ordinary objects of knowledge and ordinary reasoning, and might maintain that values differ from natural objects precisely in their power, when known, automatically to influence the will. To this Hume could, and would need to, reply that this objection involves the postulating of value entities or value features of quite a different order from anything else with which we are acquainted, and of a corresponding faculty with which to detect them. That is, he would have to supplement his explicit argument with what I have called the argument from queerness.

Another way of bringing out this queerness is to ask, about anything that is supposed to have some objective moral quality, how this is linked with its natural features. What is the connection between the natural fact that an action is a piece of deliberate cruelty—say, causing pain just for fun—and the moral fact that it is wrong? It cannot be an entailment, a logical or semantic necessity. Yet it is not merely that the two features occur together. The wrongness must somehow be 'consequential' or 'supervenient'; it is wrong because it is a piece of deliberate cruelty. But just what *in the world* is signified by this 'because'? And how do we know the relation that it signifies, if this is something more than such actions being socially condemned, and condemned by us too, perhaps through our having absorbed attitudes from our social environment? It is not even sufficient to postulate a faculty which 'sees' the wrongness: something must be postulated which can see at once the natural features that constitute the cruelty, and the wrongness, and the mysterious consequential link between the two. Alternatively, the intuition required might be the perception that wrongness is a higher-order property belonging to certain natural properties; but what is this belonging of properties to other properties, and how can we discern it? How much simpler and more comprehensible the situation would be if we could replace the moral quality with some sort of subjective response which could be causally related to the detection of the natural features on which the supposed quality is said to be consequential.

⇒ "Realism" ⇒
Michael Smith

Michael Smith is the McCosh Professor of Philosophy at Princeton. He has written extensively in defense of the moral realist approach to ethics. The passage here is taken from his essay "Realism," in Peter Singer, ed., *A Companion to Ethics* (Oxford: Blackwell Publishers, 1991).

Imagine that you are giving the baby a bath. As you do, it begins to scream uncontrollably. Nothing you do seems to help. As you watch it scream, you are overcome with a desire to drown the baby in the bathwater. Certainly you may now be *motivated* to drown the baby. (You may even actually drown it.) But does the mere fact that you have this desire, and are thus motivated, mean that you have a *reason* to drown the baby?

One commonsensical answer is that, since the desire is not *worth* satisfying, it does not provide you with such a reason; that, in this case, you are motivated to do something you have *no* reason to do. However, the standard picture seems utterly unable to accept this answer. After all, your desire to drown the baby need be based on no false belief. As such, it is entirely beyond rational criticism—or so that standard picture tells us.

The problem, here, is that the standard picture gives no special privilege to what we would want if we were 'cool, calm and collected' (to use a flippant phrase). Yet we seem ordinarily to think that not being cool, calm and collected may lead to all sorts of irrational emotional outbursts. Having those desires that we would have if we were cool, calm and collected thus seems to be an independent rational ideal. When cool, calm and collected, you would wish for the baby not to be drowned, no matter how much it

screams, and no matter how overcome you may be, in your uncool, uncalm and uncollected state, with a desire to drown it. This is why you have no reason to drown the baby.

Perhaps we have already said enough to reconcile the objectivity of moral judgement with its practicality. Judgements of right and wrong are judgements about what we have reason to do and reason not to do. But what sort of fact is a fact about what we have reason to do? The preceding discussion suggests an answer. It suggests that facts about what we have reason to do are not facts about what we *do* desire, as the standard picture would have it, but are rather facts about what we *would* desire if we were in certain idealized conditions of reflection; if, say, we were well-informed, cool, calm and collected. According to this account then, I have a reason to give to famine relief in my particular circumstances just in case, if I were in such idealized conditions of reflection, I would desire that, even when in my particular circumstances, I give to famine relief. And this sort of fact may certainly be the object of a belief.

Moreover, this account of what it is to have a reason makes it plain why the standard picture of human psychology is wrong to insist that beliefs and desires are altogether distinct; why, on the contrary, having certain beliefs, beliefs about that we have reason to do, does make it rational for us to have certain desires, desires to do what we believe we have reason to do.

In order to see this, suppose I believe that I would desire to give to famine belief if I were cool, calm and collected—i.e. more colloquially, I believe I have a reason to give to famine relief—but, being uncool, uncalm and uncollected, I don't desire to give to famine relief. Am I rationally criticizable for not having the desire? I surely am. After all, from my own point of view my beliefs and desires form a more coherent, and thus a rationally preferable, package if I do in fact desire to do what I believe I would desire to do if I were cool, calm and collected. This is because, since it is an independent rational ideal to have the desires I would have if I were cool, calm and collected, so, from my own point of view, if I believe that I would have a certain desire under such conditions and yet fail to have it, then my beliefs and desires fail to meet this ideal. To believe that I would desire to give to famine relief if I were cool, calm and collected, and yet to fail to desire to give to famine relief, is thus to manifest a commonly recognizable species of rational failure.

If this is right, then it follows that, contrary to the standard picture of human psychology, there is in fact no problem at all in supposing that I may have genuine *beliefs* about what I have reason to do, where having those beliefs makes it rational for me to have the corresponding *desires*. And if there is no problem at all in supposing that this may be so, then there is no problem in reconciling the practicality of moral judgement with the claim that moral judgements express our beliefs about the reasons we have.

However, this doesn't yet suffice to solve the problem facing the moral realist. For moral judgements aren't *just* judgements about the reasons we have. They are judgements about the reasons we have *where those reasons are supposed to be determined entirely by our circumstances*. As I put it earlier, people in the same circumstances face the same moral choice: if they did the same action then either they both acted rightly (they both did what they had reason to do) or they both acted wrongly (they both did what they had reason not to do). Does the account of what it is to have a reason just given entail that this is so?

Suppose our circumstances are identical, and let's ask whether it is right for each of us to give to famine relief: that is, whether we each have a reason to do so. According to the account on offer it is right that I give to famine relief just in case I have a reason to give to famine relief, and I have such a reason just in case, if I were in idealized conditions

of reflection—well-informed, cool, calm and collected—I would desire to give to famine relief. And the same is true of you. If our circumstances are the same then, supposedly, we should both have such a reason or both lack such a reason. But do we?

The question is whether, if we were well-informed, cool, calm and collected we would tend to *converge* in the desires we have. Would we converge or would there always be the possibility of some non-rationally-explicable difference in our desires *even under such conditions*? The standard picture of human psychology now returns to centre-stage. For it tells us that there is *always* the possibility of some non-rationally-explicable difference in our desires even under such idealized conditions of reflection. This is the residue of the standard picture's conception of desire as a psychological state that is beyond rational criticism.

If this is right then the moral realist's attempt to combine the objectivity and the practicality of moral judgement must be deemed a failure. We are forced to accept that there is a *fundamental relativity* in the reasons we have. What we have reason to do is relative to what we would desire under certain idealized conditions of reflection, and this may differ from person to person. It is not wholly determined by our circumstances, as moral facts are supposed to be.

Many philosophers accept the standard picture's pronouncement on this point. But accepting there is such a fundamental relativity in our reasons seems altogether premature to me. It puts the cart before the horse. For surely moral practice is itself the forum in which we will *discover* whether there is a fundamental relativity in our reasons.

After all, in moral practice we attempt to change people's moral beliefs by engaging them in rational argument: i.e. by getting their beliefs to approximate those they would have under more idealized conditions of reflection. And sometimes we succeed. When we succeed, other things being equal, we succeed in changing their desires. But if we accept that there is a fundamental relativity in our reasons then we can say, in advance, that this procedure will never result in a massive *convergence* in moral beliefs; for we know in advance that there will never be a convergence in the desires we have under such idealized conditions of reflection. Or rather, and more accurately, if there is a fundamental relativity in our reasons then it follows that any convergence we find in our moral beliefs, and thus in our desires, must be entirely contingent. It could in no way be explained by, or suggestive of, the fact that the desires that emerge have some *privileged* rational status.

My question is: 'Why accept this?' Why not think, instead, that if such a converagence emerged in moral practice then that would itself suggest that these particular moral beliefs, and the corresponding desires, *do* enjoy a privileged rational status? After all, something like such a convergence in mathematical practice lies behind our conviction that mathematical claims enjoy a privileged rational status. So why not think that a like convergence in moral practice would show that moral judgements enjoy the same privileged rational status? At this point, the standard picture's insistence that there is a fundamental relativity in our reasons begins to sound all too much like a hollow dogma.

The kind of moral realism described here endorses a conception of moral facts that is a far cry from the picture presented at the outset: moral facts as queer facts about the universe whose recognition necessarily impacts upon our desires. Instead, the realist has eschewed queer facts about the universe in favour of a more 'subjectivist' conception of moral facts. This emerged in the realist's analysis of what it is to have a reason. The realist's point, however, is that such a conception of moral facts may make them subjective only in the innocuous sense that they are facts about what we would *want* under certain idealized conditions of reflection, where wants are, admittedly, a kind of psychological state enjoyed by subjects. But moral facts remain objective insofar as they are facts about what *we*, not just *you* or *I*, would want under such conditions. The existence of a moral fact—say, the rightness of giving to famine relief in certain circumstances—requires that, under idealized conditions of reflection, rational creatures would *converge* upon a desire to give to famine relief in such circumstances.

Of course, it must be agreed on all sides that moral argument has not yet produced the sort of convergence in our desires that would make the idea of a moral fact—a fact about the reasons we have entirely determined by our circumstances—look plausible. But neither has moral argument had much of a history in times in which we have been able to engage in free reflection unhampered by a false biology (the Aristotelian tradition) or a false belief in God (the Judeo-Christian tradition). It remains to be seen whether sustained moral argument can elicit the requisite convergence in our moral beliefs, and corresponding desires, to make the idea of a moral fact look plausible. The kind of moral realism described here holds out the hope that it will. Only time will tell.

⟻ "PHILOSOPHY AND SOCIAL HOPE" ⟼
Richard Rorty

Richard Rorty (1931–2007) was a professor at Princeton, the University of Virginia, and Stanford. Among his many important books are *Philosophy and the Mirror of Nature* (Princeton: Princeton University Press, 1979); *Contingency, Irony, and Solidarity* (Cambridge: Cambridge University Press, 1989), a very readable book that ranges through literature, social theory, and philosophy—Chapter 9, "Solidarity," contains interesting elements of his views of ethics; *Truth and Progress: Philosophical Papers,* volume 3 (Cambridge: Cambridge University Press, 1998); and *Philosophy and Social Hope* (London: Penguin Books, 1999). Rorty was one of the best known and most controversial philosophers of the late twentieth century, and his views—particularly his rejection of ethical objectivism—were widely denounced. Though sometimes called a relativist, Rorty prefers the title *antifoundationalist*, or alternatively, *pragmatist.* In this passage, excerpted from *Philosophy and Social Hope*, Rorty defends his denial of objective moral truth and argues that ethical nonobjectivism is not the disaster that some have imagined.

THERE ARE NO TRUTHS ABOUT VALUES

. . . Philosophers are called 'relativists' when they do not accept the Greek distinction between the way things are in themselves and the relations which they have to other things, and in particular to human needs and interests.

Philosophers who, like myself, eschew this distinction must abandon the traditional philosophical project of finding something stable which will serve as a criterion for judging the transitory products of our transitory needs and interests. This means, for example, that we cannot employ the Kantian distinction between morality and prudence. We have to give up on the idea that there are unconditional, transcultural moral obligations, obligations rooted in an unchanging, ahistorical human nature . . . .

The philosopher whom I most admire, and of whom I should most like to think of myself as a disciple, is John Dewey. Dewey was one of the founders of American pragmatism. He was a thinker who spent 60 years trying to get us out from under the thrall of Plato and Kant. Dewey was often denounced as a relativist, and so am I. But of course we pragmatists never call *ourselves* relativists. Usually, we define ourselves 'anti-Platonists' or 'antimetaphysicians' or 'antifoundationalists'. Equally, our opponents almost never call themselves 'Platonists' or 'metaphysicians' or 'foundationalists'. They usually call themselves defenders of common sense, or of reason.

Predictably, each side in this quarrel tries to define the terms of the quarrel in a way favourable to itself. Nobody wants to be called a Platonist, just as nobody wants to be called a relativist or an irrationalist. We so-called 'relativists' refuse, predictably, to admit that we are enemies of reason and common sense. We say that we are only criticizing some antiquated, specifically philosophical, dogmas. But, of course, what we call dogmas are exactly what our opponents call common sense. Adherence to these dogmas is what they call being rational. So discussion between us and our opponents tends to get bogged down in, for example, the question of whether the slogan 'truth is correspondence to the intrinsic nature of reality' expresses common sense, or is just a bit of outdated Platonist jargon.

In other words, one of the things we disagree about is whether this slogan embodies an obvious truth which philosophy must respect and protect, or instead simply puts forward one philosophical view among others. Our opponents say that the correspondence theory of truth is so obvious, so self-evident, that it is merely perverse to question it. We say that this theory is barely intelligible, and of no particular importance—that it is not so much a theory as a slogan which we have been mindlessly chanting for centuries. We pragmatists think that we might stop chanting it without any harmful consequences.

One way to describe this impasse is to say that we so-called 'relativists' claim that many of the things which common sense thinks are found or discovered are really made or invented. Scientific and moral truths, for example, are described by our opponents as 'objective', meaning that they are in some sense out there waiting to be recognized by us human beings. . . .

They think of us as saying that what was previously thought to be objective has turned out to be merely subjective . . . .

Our opponents like to suggest that to abandon that vocabulary is to abandon rationality—that to be rational consists precisely in respecting the distinctions between the absolute and the relative, the found and the made, object and subject, nature and convention, reality and appearance. We pragmatists reply that if that were what rationality was, then no doubt we are, indeed, irrationalists. But of course we go on to add that being an irrationalist in *that* sense is not to be incapable of argument. We irrationalists do not foam at the mouth and behave like animals. We simply refuse to talk in a certain way, the Platonic way. The views we hope to persuade people to accept cannot be stated in Platonic terminology. So our efforts at persuasion must take the form of gradual inculcation of new ways of speaking, rather than of straightforward argument within old ways of speaking.

To sum up what I have said so far: We pragmatists shrug off charges that we are 'relativists' or 'irrationalists' by saying that these charges presuppose precisely the distinctions we reject. If we have to describe ourselves, perhaps it would be best for us to call ourselves anti-dualists. This does not, of course, mean that we are against what Derrida calls 'binary oppositions': dividing the world up into the good Xs and the bad non-Xs will always be an indispensable tool of inquiry. But we are against a certain *specific* set of distinctions, the Platonic distinctions. We have to admit that these distinctions have become part of Western common sense, but we do not regard this as a sufficient argument for retaining them . . . .

So far I have been sketching the pragmatists' attitude towards their opponents, and the difficulties they encounter in avoiding the use of terms whose use would beg the question at issue between them and their opponents. Now I should like to describe in somewhat more detail how human inquiry looks from a pragmatist point of view—how it looks once one stops describing it as an attempt to correspond to the intrinsic nature of reality, and starts describing it as an attempt to serve transitory purposes and solve transitory problems.

Pragmatists hope to break with the picture which, in Wittgenstein's words, 'holds us captive'—the Cartesian–Lockean picture of a mind seeking to get in touch with a reality outside itself. So they start with a Darwinian account of human beings as animals doing their best to cope with the environment—doing their best to develop tools which will enable them to enjoy more pleasure and less pain. Words are among the tools which these clever animals have developed.

There is no way in which tools can take one out of touch with reality. No matter whether the tool is a hammer or a gun or a belief or a statement, tool-using is part of the interaction of the organism with its environment. To see the employment of words as the use of tools to deal with the environment, rather than as an attempt to represent the intrinsic nature of that environment, is to repudiate the question of whether human minds are in touch with reality—the question asked by the epistemological sceptic. No organism, human or non-human, is ever more or less in touch with reality than any other organism. The very idea of 'being out of touch with reality' presupposes the un-Darwinian, Cartesian picture of a mind which somehow swings free of the causal forces exerted on the body. The Cartesian mind is an entity whose relations with the rest of the universe are representational rather than causal. So to rid our thinking of the vestiges of Cartesianism, to become fully Darwinian in our thinking, we need to stop thinking of words as representations and to start thinking of them as nodes in the causal network which binds the organism together with its environment.

Seeing language and inquiry in this biologistic way . . . permits us to discard the picture of the human mind as an interior space within which the human person is located. As the American philosopher of mind Daniel Dennett has argued, it is only this picture of a Cartesian Theatre which makes one think that there is a big philosophical or scientific problem about the nature of the origin of consciousness. We should substitute a picture of an adult human organism as one whose behaviour is so complex that it can be predicted only by attributing intentional states—beliefs and desires—to the organism. On this account, beliefs and desires are not prelinguistic modes of consciousness, which may or may not be expressible in language. Nor are they names of immaterial events. Rather, they are what in philosophical jargon are called 'sentential attitudes'—that is to say, dispositions on the part of organisms, or of computers, to assert or deny certain sentences. To attribute beliefs and desires to non-users of language (such as dogs, infants and thermostats) is, for us pragmatists, to speak metaphorically.

Pragmatists complement this biologistic approach with Charles Sanders Peirce's definition of a belief as a habit of action. On this definition, to ascribe a belief to someone is simply to say that he or she will tend to behave as I behave when I am willing to affirm the truth of a certain sentence. We ascribe beliefs to things

which use, or can be imagined to use, sentences, but not to rocks and plants. This is not because the former have a special organ or capacity—consciousness—which the latter lack, but simply because the habits of action of rocks and plants are sufficiently familiar and simple that their behaviour can be predicted without ascribing sentential attitudes to them.

On this view, when we utter such sentences as 'I am hungry' we are not making external what was previously internal, but are simply helping those around to us to predict our future actions. Such sentences are not used to report events going on within the Cartesian Theatre which is a person's consciousness. They are simply tools for coordinating our behaviour with those of others. This is not to say that one can 'reduce' mental states such as beliefs and desires to physiological or behavioural states. It is merely to say that there is no point in asking whether a belief represents reality, either mental reality or physical reality, accurately. That is, for pragmatists, not only a bad question, but the root of much wasted philosophical energy.

The right question to ask is, 'For what purposes would it be useful to hold that belief?' This is like the question, 'For what purposes would it be useful to load this program into my computer?' On the Putnamesque view I am suggesting, a person's body is analogous to the computer's hardware, and his or her beliefs and desires are analogous to the software. Nobody knows or cares whether a given piece of computer software represents reality accurately. What we care about is whether it is the software which will most efficiently accomplish a certain task. Analogously, pragmatists think that the question to ask about our beliefs is not whether they are about reality or merely about appearance, but simply whether they are the best habits of action for gratifying our desires.

On this view, to say that a belief is, as far as we know, true, is to say that no alternative belief is, as far as we know, a better habit of acting. When we say that our ancestors believed, falsely, that the sun went around the earth, and that we believe, truly, that the earth goes round the sun, we are saying that we have a better tool than our ancestors did. Our ancestors might rejoin that their tool enabled them to believe in the literal truth of the Christian Scriptures, whereas ours does not. Our reply has to be, I think, that the benefits of modern astronomy and of space travel outweigh the advantages of Christian fundamentalism. The argument between us and our medieval ancestors should not be about which of us has got the universe right. It should be about the point of holding views about the motion of heavenly bodies, the ends to be achieved by the use of certain tools. Confirming the truth of Scripture is one such aim, space travel is another.

Another way of making this last point is to say that we pragmatists cannot make sense of the idea that we should pursue truth for its own sake. We cannot regard truth as a goal of inquiry. The purpose of inquiry is to achieve agreement among human beings about what to do, to bring about consensus on the ends to be achieved and the means to be used to achieve those ends. Inquiry that does not achieve coordination of behaviour is not inquiry but simply wordplay. To argue for a certain theory about the microstructure of material bodies, or about the proper balance of powers between branches of government, is to argue about what we should do: how we should use the tools at our disposal in order to make technological, or political, progress. So, for pragmatists there is no sharp break between natural science and social science, nor between social science and politics, nor between politics, philosophy and literature. All areas of culture are parts of the same endeavour to make life better. There is no deep split between theory and practice, because on a pragmatist view all so-called 'theory' which is not wordplay is always already practice.

To treat beliefs not as representations but as habits of action, and words not as representations but as tools, is to make it pointless to ask, 'Am I discovering or inventing, making or finding?' There is no point in dividing up the organisms' interaction with the environment in this way. Consider an example. We normally say that a bank account is a social construction rather than an object in the natural world, whereas a giraffe is an object in the natural world rather than a social construction. Bank accounts are made, giraffes are found. Now the truth in this view is simply that if there had been no human beings there would still have been giraffes, whereas there would have been no bank accounts. But this causal independence of giraffes from humans does not mean that giraffes are what they are apart from human needs and interests.

On the contrary, we describe giraffes in the way we do, as giraffes, because of our needs and interests. We speak a language which includes the word 'giraffe' because it suits our purposes to do so. The same goes for words like 'organ', 'cell', 'atom', and so on—the names of the parts out of which giraffes are made, so to speak. All the descriptions we give of things are descriptions suited to our purposes. No sense can be made, we pragmatists argue, of the claim

that some of these descriptions pick out 'natural kinds'—that they cut nature at the joints. The line between a giraffe and the surrounding air is clear enough if you are a human being interested in hunting for meat. If you are a language-using ant or amoeba, or a space voyager observing us from far above, that line is not so clear, and it is not clear that you would need or have a word for 'giraffe' in your language. More generally, it is not clear that any of the millions of ways of describing the piece of space time occupied by what we call a giraffe is any closer to the way things are in themselves than any of the others. Just as it seems pointless to ask whether a giraffe is really a collection of atoms, or really a collection of actual and possible sensations in human sense organs, or really something else, so the question, 'Are we describing it as it really is?' seems one we never need to ask. All we need to know is whether some competing description might be more useful for some of our purposes.

The relativity of descriptions to purposes is the pragmatist's principal argument for his antirepresentational view of knowledge—the view that inquiry aims at utility for us rather than an accurate account of how things are in themselves. Because every belief we have must be formulated in some language or other, and because languages are not attempts to copy what is out there, but rather tools for dealing with what is out there, there is no way to divide off 'the contribution to our knowledge made by the object' from 'the contribution to our knowledge made by our subjectivity'. Both the words we use and our willingness to affirm certain sentences using those words and not others are the products of fantastically complex causal connections between human organisms and the rest of the universe. There is no way to divide up this web of causal connections so as to compare the relative amount of subjectivity and of objectivity in a given belief. There is no way, as Wittgenstein has said, to come between language and its object, to divide the giraffe in itself from our ways of talking about giraffes. As Hilary Putnam, the leading contemporary pragmatist, has put it: 'elements of what we call "language" or "mind" penetrate so deeply into reality that the very project of representing ourselves as being "mappers" of something "language-independent" is fatally compromised from the start'.

The Platonist dream of perfect knowledge is the dream of stripping ourselves clean of everything that comes from inside us and opening ourselves without reservation to what is outside us. But this distinction between inside and outside, as I have said earlier, is one which cannot be made once we adopt a biologistic view. If the Platonist is going to insist on that distinction, he has got to have an epistemology which does not link up in any interesting way with other disciplines. He will end up with an account of knowledge which turns its back on the rest of science. This amounts to making knowledge into something supernatural, a kind of miracle.

The suggestion that everything we say and do and believe is a matter of fulfilling human needs and interests might seem simply a way of formulating the secularism of the Enlightenment—a way of saying that human beings are on their own, and have no supernatural light to guide them to the Truth. But of course the Enlightenment replaced the idea of such supernatural guidance with the idea of a quasi-divine faculty called 'reason'. It is this idea which American pragmatists and post-Nietzschean European philosophers are attacking. What seems most shocking about their criticisms of this idea is not their description of natural science as an attempt to manage reality rather than to represent it. Rather, it is their description of moral choice as always a matter of compromise between competing goods, rather than as a choice between the absolutely right and the absolutely wrong.

Controversies between foundationalists and antifoundationalists on the theory of knowledge look like the sort of merely scholastic quarrels which can safely be left to the philosophy professors. But quarrels about the character of moral choice look more important. We stake our sense of who we are on the outcome of such choices. So we do not like to be told that our choices are between alternative goods rather than between good and evil. When philosophy professors start saying that there is nothing either absolutely wrong or absolutely right, the topic of relativism begins to get interesting. The debates between the pragmatists and their opponents, or the Nietzscheans and theirs, begin to look too important to be left to philosophy professors. Everybody wants to get in on the act.

This is why philosophers like myself find ourselves denounced in magazines and newspapers which one might have thought oblivious of our existence. These denunciations claim that unless the youth is raised to believe in moral absolutes, and in objective truth, civilization is doomed. Unless the younger generation has the same attachment to firm moral principles as we have, these magazine and newspaper articles say, the struggle for human freedom and human decency will be over. When we philosophy teachers read this sort of article, we find ourselves being told that we have enormous power over the future of mankind. For all it will take to overturn centuries of moral progress, these articles suggest, is a generation which accepts the doctrines of moral relativism, accepts the views common to Nietzsche and Dewey . . . .

Critics of moral relativism think that unless there is something absolute, something which shares God's implacable refusal to yield to human weakness, we have no reason to go on resisting evil. If evil is merely a lesser good, if all moral choice is a compromise between conflicting goods, then, they say, there is no point in moral struggle. The lives of those who have died resisting injustice become pointless. But to us pragmatists moral struggle is continuous with the struggle for existence, and no sharp break divides the unjust from the imprudent, the evil from the inexpedient. What matters for pragmatists is devising ways of diminishing human suffering and increasing human equality, increasing the ability of all human children to start life with an equal chance of happiness. This goal is not written in the stars, and is no more an expression of what Kant called 'pure practical reason' than it is of the Will of God. It is a goal worth dying for, but it does not require backup from supernatural forces.

The pragmatist view of what opponents of pragmatism call 'firm moral principles' is that such principles are abbreviations of past practices—way of summing up the habits of the ancestors we most admire. For example, Mill's greater-happiness principle and Kant's categorical imperative are ways of reminding ourselves of certain social customs—those of certain parts of the Christian West, the culture which has been, at least in words if not in deeds, more egalitarian than any other. The Christian doctrine that all members of the species are brothers and sisters is the religious way of saying what Mill and Kant said in nonreligious terms: that considerations of family membership, sex, race, religious creed and the like should not prevent us from trying to do unto others as we would have them do to us—should not prevent us from thinking of them as people like ourselves, deserving the respect which we ourselves hope to enjoy.

But there are other firm moral principles than those which epitomize egalitarianism. One such principle is that dishonour brought to a woman of one's family must be paid for with blood. Another is that it would be better to have no son than to have one who is homosexual. Those of us who would like to put a stop to the blood feuds and the gaybashing produced by these firm moral principles call such principles 'prejudices' rather than 'insights'. It would be nice if philosophers could give us assurance that the principles which we approve of, like Mill's and Kant's, are 'rational' in a way that the principles of the blood-revengers and the gaybashers are not. But to say that they are more rational is just another way of saying that they are more universalistic—that they treat the differences between women of one's own family and other women, and the difference between gays and straights, as relatively insignificant. But it is not clear that failure to mention particular groups of people is a mark of rationality.

To see this last point, consider the principle 'Thou shalt not kill'. This is admirably universal, but is it more or less rational than the principle 'Do not kill unless one is a soldier defending his or her country, or is preventing a murder, or is a state executioner, or a merciful practioner of euthanasia'? I have no idea whether it is more or less rational, and so do not find the term 'rational' useful in this area. If I am told that a controversial action which I have taken has to be defended by being subsumed under a universal, rational principle, I may be able to dream up such a principle to fit the occasion, but sometimes I may only be able to say, 'Well, it seemed like the best thing to do at the time, all things considered.' It is not clear that the latter defence is less rational than some universal-sounding principle which I have dreamed up *ad hoc* to justify my action. It is not clear that all the moral dilemmas to do with population control, the rationing of health care, and the like—should wait upon the formulation of principles for their solution.

As we pragmatists see it, the idea that there must be such a legitimating principle lurking behind every right action amounts to the idea that there is something like a universal, super-national court of law before which we stand. We know that the best societies are those which are governed by laws rather than by the whim of tyrants or mobs. Without the rule of law, we say, human life is turned over to emotion and to violence. This makes us think that there must be a sort of invisible tribunal of reason administering laws which we all, somewhere deep down inside, recognize as binding upon us. Something like this was Kant's understanding of moral obligation. But, once again, the Kantian picture of what human beings are like cannot be reconciled with history or with biology. Both teach us that the development of societies ruled by laws rather than men was a slow, late, fragile, contingent, evolutionary achievement . . . .

Someone who adopts the anti-Kantian stance . . . and is asked to defend the thick morality of the society with which she identifies herself will not be able to do so by talking about the rationality of her moral views. Rather, she will have to talk about the various concrete advantages of her society's practices over those of other societies. Discussion of the relative advantages of different thick moralities will, obviously, be as inconclusive as discussion of the relative superiority of a beloved book or person over another person's beloved book or person.

The idea of a universally shared source of truth called 'reason' or 'human nature' is, for us pragmatists, just the idea that such discussion *ought* to be capable of being made conclusive. We see this idea as a misleading way of expressing the hope, which we share, that the human race as a whole should gradually come together in a global community, a community which incorporates most of the thick morality of the European industrialized democracies. It is misleading because it suggests that the aspiration to such a community is somehow built into every member of the biological species. This seems to us pragmatists like the suggestion that the aspiration to be an anaconda is somehow built into all reptiles, or that the aspiration to be an anthropoid is somehow built into all mammals. This is why we pragmatists see the charge of relativism as simply the charge that we see luck where our critics insist on seeing destiny. We think that the utopian world community envisaged by the Charter of the United Nations and the Helsinki Declaration of Human Rights is no more the *destiny* of humanity than is an atomic holocaust or the replacement of democratic governments by feuding warlords. If either of the latter is what the future holds, our species will have been unlucky, but it will not have been irrational. It will not have failed to live up to its moral obligations. It will simply have missed a chance to be happy.

I do not know how to argue the question of whether it is better to see human beings in this biologistic way or to see them in a way more like Plato's or Kant's. So I do not know how to give anything like a conclusive argument for the view which my critics call 'relativism' and which I prefer to call 'antifoundationalism' or 'antidualism'. It is certainly not enough for my side to appeal to Darwin and ask our opponents how they can avoid an appeal to the supernatural. That way of stating the issue begs many questions. It is certainly not enough for my opponents to say that a biologistic view strips human beings of their dignity and their self-respect. That too begs most of the questions at issue. I suspect that all that either side can do is to restate its case over and over again, in context after context. The controversy between those who see both our species and our society as a lucky accident, and those who find an immanent teleology in both, is too radical to permit of being judged from some neutral standpoint.

EXERCISES

1. I have come into possession of a small but lovely drawing by Michelangelo. (Never mind how I came to possess this drawing. Let's just agree that I own it fair and square, and that I did not gain possession of it by theft or deceit or fraud. The drawing is legitimately my own.) I have decided to paste the drawing over my dart board and use it as a target. You may think this quite stupid (even if I don't care for the drawing, it is obviously worth an enormous sum of money). That's not the issue. The question is this: Would I be doing anything *morally wrong* by destroying the drawing in this frivolous manner?

2. Suppose we find that some of our most basic and common moral "intuitions" can be traced deep into our evolutionary history: our history as weak and vulnerable primates who must live in close social groups for protection from fierce predators. If we made such a discovery, would that *weaken* or *strengthen* (or have no effect on) the claim that our "intuitions" are sources of genuine objective knowledge about moral truths?

3. I have lived a dissolute life for many years: a life devoted to excessive eating, heavy drinking, laziness, deceitfulness, and pettiness. At age 45, I awaken one morning in the gutter, painfully sober after a three-day binge, and I resolve to change my ways and pursue virtue. Could I become a virtuous person within an hour? A week? A month? A year? Ever?

4. The dramatist George Bernard Shaw claimed that "Virtue consists, not in abstaining from vice, but in not desiring it." Would Aristotle agree? Would *you* agree?

5. The great Hebrew prophet Jeremiah posed this question for God (*Jeremiah*, Book 12): "Wherefore doth the way of the wicked prosper? Wherefore are all they happy that deal very treacherously?" If God were a virtue theorist, how might God reply to Jeremiah's question? *If it is true that "the way of the wicked prosper," would that refute virtue theory?*

6. Stephen M. Cahn once posed a challenge for virtue theory: He gave an example of a fictitious person, Fred (whom Cahn claims is similar to several actual people he has known) who is deceitful, arrogant, and rather lucky; and who gains a reputation for virtuous character, even though he is thoroughly unscrupulous. Fred (according to Cahn) "enjoys great pleasure," and certainly appears to be happy. Can you think of anyone (a public figure, or someone you know) who is similar to Fred, and whom you would regard as *genuinely* happy? If you can, does that count against virtue theory? If you cannot, is that a point in favor of virtue theory? If there are *many* people like Fred, then that will be a severe threat to virtue theory; but if there are only a very few like Fred—and though they are happy, they were very *lucky*, and it was very improbable that they would be happy—would that pose problems for virtue theory?

7. You are a physician, specializing in the treatment of kidney disease. One of your patients, Alan Durkin, is a relative—a cousin, the two of you share grandparents. Alan is two years younger than you, you have known him since childhood, and you are friends. Alan is not one of your closest friends, but (in addition to now seeing him as your patient for the last three years) you see one another at weddings and funerals and other large family gatherings, maybe two or three times a year. Alan is 45, and his kidney disease has become progressively worse, and now his kidneys have failed to the point that he requires dialysis twice weekly, and soon his need for dialysis will increase to every other day. He can continue with dialysis for some time, and his condition is not immediately life threatening—but a successful kidney transplant would greatly improve his quality of life. Alan is on the waiting list for a kidney transplant, but because his dialysis treatments are relatively successful in purifying his blood, Alan is not a high-priority transplant candidate. Given the acute shortage of organs available for transplant, you know Alan will not soon receive one of the precious kidneys. But as Alan's physician, you could fudge the data just a little bit—no one would know, and by making Alan's condition look somewhat worse, you could easily bump him higher on the list and greatly improve his chances of receiving a transplant within the next year or so. Of course if you do that, then someone who actually is in greater need for a kidney transplant will be passed over in favor of your cousin Alan. Should you fudge the data, or not?

   In attempting to answer that question, which ethical perspective—Kantian, feelings-based, utilitarian, virtue, social contract, or care—is most useful to you?

8. You are a biology professor at the University of Wisconsin. You teach at the medical school, and you are well-known for your research: Your laboratory has carried out a number of important

studies on various drugs. You are approached by ZQZ Pharmaceuticals. They would like you to run a test on the "off-label" effectiveness of one of their drugs, Zeitelban. Zeitelban has been approved for the treatment of stomach ulcers, but recently some doctors have used it for treatment of high blood pressure (after noticing that ulcer patients treated with Zeitelban sometimes experienced a reduction in blood pressure readings). Such "off-label" treatments are perfectly legal; the problem is, the drug has not really been tested for treatment of hypertension (high blood pressure), and we don't know if it actually works for that. True, a few doctors noticed that their patients who were taking Zeitelban experienced lower blood pressure. But we have no idea whether that was caused by the Zeitelban or by something else. Perhaps when their stomach ulcers cleared up that caused them to feel better, reduced their tense worrying about ulcers, and that reduction in tension caused lower blood pressure. Or maybe the patients started eating less because of their stomach problems, and they lost some weight and that caused the reduction in blood pressure. Or maybe they stopped smoking, and that was the cause. Without a controlled experiment, we have no idea whether Zeitelban is effective in treating hypertension. Furthermore, since Zeitelban was not tested initially for the treatment of hypertension, we don't know whether it causes problems for patients using it for long-term treatment of hypertension. The initial tests, which led the FDA to approve the drug, were for short-term use with stomach ulcer patients. But treatment of hypertension would involve long-term use, and there might be side-effects that the earlier tests did not detect: It could be that Zeitelban will cause special problems, even serious dangers, for patients who use it long term. So ZQZ Pharmaceuticals wants you to run a long-term controlled study on the effectiveness of Zeitelban for the treatment of hypertension. This will be a very large study, and they will pay you very generously to direct the study. Also, with the money they pay for the study you can hire a number of medical students and graduate students at the University, to help you part-time and perhaps full-time in the summer; and they will also be paid well (and frankly, many of them could really use the money). And the grant will also pay for much needed laboratory equipment, the latest and best. And since this is a major megabucks grant, the University of Wisconsin will be very happy about it: The Dean will probably take you to lunch and lavish praise upon you.

No problems so far. This could be a worthwhile study, and it might provide information that would aid in the treatment of hypertension, and thus improve the lives of many people; and it will make your students very happy, since they will make some much-needed extra income. But there's one catch: ZQZ Pharmaceuticals is paying for the study, and they want control over the publication of any results. They want the right to read any research report *before* it is published, and they want the right to *veto* publication of your research findings. That is, if your research shows that Zeitelban is useless in the treatment of hypertension, or—even worse—reveals a harmful side effect that earlier studies had not detected, then ZQZ Pharmaceuticals can prevent the publication of your results; indeed, ZQZ Pharmaceuticals can require you not to discuss those results with anyone, nor publicize those results in any way. So if your research indicated that use of Zeitelban might cause kidney failure—a potentially lethal side effect—you would be prohibited from publishing that result. Or if your study showed that Zeitelban was useless in treating hypertension, but the data from a separate study made by some other laboratory indicated that Zeitelban might be an effective hypertension drug, then ZQZ Pharmaceuticals could veto the publication of your results and allow the publication of the other study. Under that condition—ZQZ Pharmaceuticals has veto rights to the publication of your study—would you agree to run the study?

Suppose that you want to refuse to run the study under those conditions: You would tell ZQZ Pharmaceuticals that you are turning down their megabucks study grant. You are discussing it with one of your fellow researchers, and she wants to accept the grant and run the study. "Look," she says, "I understand your concerns about the publication veto. I feel the same way: I don't like it. But let's be realistic. If we turn down this research contract, they won't have any trouble at all finding another researcher who *will* run the study, and will accept the veto condition; and that researcher may not be quite as good as we are, so the study might not be quite as careful. And that researcher's students will get the money, rather than our students. So the study is going to be run anyway, with the veto condition. Refusing the research contract will just mean that our students won't get the research funding, and the study may not be done as well as we could do it. So what will your principled refusal really accomplish? Nothing. At least nothing good. So I say: let's take the contract, and accept the veto power of ZQZ Pharmaceuticals."

What do you think of your colleague's argument? How would that argument look from the perspectives of virtue theory, utilitarian ethics, Humean ethics, and Kantian ethics?

Perhaps you have decided you should accept the research contract; perhaps you've decided that you shouldn't. Suppose that you *have* decided to accept the contract (maybe ZQZ Pharmaceuticals agreed to drop the veto requirement). The representative from ZQZ Pharmaceuticals drops by with a bottle of champagne to celebrate this wonderful new research partnership between ZQZ Pharmaceuticals and your laboratory, and hands you an envelope. "Look, we at ZQZ Pharmaceuticals consider you part of our family, and we want you to share in any success our company has. These are stock options on ZQZ Pharmaceuticals stock. Your study will be complete and ready for release next September 15; these are stock options on one million dollars worth of ZQZ Pharmaceuticals stock. These options allow you to purchase ZQZ Pharmaceuticals stock at its September 1 price; and you can exercise the option anytime between September 15 and September 30. It's a pleasure having you as a member of the ZQZ Pharmaceuticals family!" Well, you know what this stock option means. If your research shows that Zeitelban is not effective in treating hypertension, then the value of ZQZ Pharmaceuticals stock will not rise, and your stock option will be worthless. But if your research shows that Zeitelban *is* safe and effective in treating hypertension, then Zeitelban will be widely sold for hypertension, and ZQZ Pharmaceuticals will make a fortune in profits (there are *huge* numbers of hypertension patients), and the stock price will rise dramatically—and your stock option will be worth a *lot* of money. (Suppose ZQZ Pharmaceuticals stock was at $20 a share on September 1; on September 15, after release of your favorable research on Zeitelban, the stock soars to $40 a share. You can buy a million dollars worth of ZQZ stock at the September 1 price, and immediately sell it for double what you paid: a neat little profit of one millions dollars, with absolutely no risk. (Actually, you would just take the stock option to your broker, and your broker would give you a check for one million dollars.) Sounds peachy. But you know what is really going on: ZQZ Pharmaceuticals is not doing this out of simple kindness; rather, they are giving you a huge incentive to do a study that shows Zeitelban to be very effective and very safe (the better the drug, the more your stock option is worth). Of course, you are a highly principled researcher, and you would snever let that influence you, right? But is it ethically legitimate for you to accept the stock option?

9. Your friend Joe is a warm and friendly person, who is quick to provide aid and comfort to his distressed friends, and who is well known for being a peacemaker among his friends (he prevents fights, and he is often successful at reconciling conflicts among his friends). Joe, however, never reflects on his ethical principles or ethical beliefs. It's not that Joe is stupid; it's just that reflective consideration of ethics is something he has never done. When Joe comforts a friend in distress, or prevents a fight, or patches up a conflict; would you count him as acting ethically? Would you count Sam—a chimpanzee who is similar to Joe in comforting friends and preventing conflicts, and who likewise never reflects on his ethical principles or beliefs—as acting ethically?

10. Even when we get all the details straight, there remain basic differences about whether it is wrong to destroy a human embryo in doing stem cell research. Is this a problem of conflicting intuitions? The same for capital punishment: blood requires blood versus it is always wrong to purposefully take a human life, and two wrongs don't make a right. At this basic level of disagreement, is there still room for rational argument?

11. In the dispute between objectivists and nonobjectivists, who should have the burden of proof? The nonobjectivist, since she is denying what seems to many quite obvious? Or the objectivist, who is trying to establish the existence of moral truths, something positive? Placing the burden of proof is very important. For example, if I am charged with a crime, the *prosecution* is making the claim that I committed the crime, and the prosecution bears the burden of proving it. I don't have to prove my innocence, and that's obviously a good thing. If the burden of proof were reversed, then you could be convicted of all sorts of crimes you did not commit. Where were you on August 25, at 4 a.m., when the State Street

Convenience Store was robbed? You say you were home asleep; but can you *prove* that's where you were? Can you prove you did not commit the robbery? Of course not. Fortunately, you don't have to prove you are innocent. The prosecution has the burden of proving you are guilty. So in the case of objectivism versus nonobjectivism: Who has the burden of proof?

12. Astronomers maintain that black holes exist in our galaxy. A black hole results when a massive star implodes, and all its mass is compressed into a very small volume. This produces an object so dense, and with such powerful gravitational force, that no light can escape. Therefore, you can't really "see" a black hole; but by making careful observations of the motions of other objects in the vicinity of the black hole, we can reasonably conclude that a black hole exists: It is the *best explanation* for those motions. Likewise, you don't really "see" a moral fact; but by observing the convergent conclusions and behavior of people who think calmly and carefully about a moral issue, we can conclude that a moral fact exists: It is the *best explanation* for that convergent movement. Is that a good analogy?

13. If you discovered that your fiancée had views that were the polar opposite of yours on the question of whether ethics is objective or nonobjective, would that cause you to think twice about your wedding plans?

ADDITIONAL READING

Among the most important and influential intuitionist writings are G. E. Moore, *Principia Ethica* (New York: Cambridge, 1959); H. A. Prichard, *Moral Obligation* (Oxford: Clarendon Press, 1949); W. D. Ross, *The Right and the Good* (Oxford: Clarendon Press, 1930); W. D. Ross, *Foundations of Ethics* (Oxford: Clarendon Press, 1939); and D. D. Raphael, *The Moral Sense* (London: Oxford University Press, 1957).

Jan Garrett's guide to W. D. Ross is an excellent resource on this leading intuitionist. You can find it at www.wku.edu/~jan.garrett/ethics/rossethc.htm>.

Aristotle's *Nicomachean Ethics* is the classic source for virtue ethics, and it is widely available in printed versions as well as online. It is still the subject of extensive debate and commentary, both in philosophy and theology (so important is Aristotle to Catholic theology that he is often referred to simply as "the philosopher"), and remains the starting point for discussions of virtue ethics.

Elizabeth Anscombe, "Modern Moral Philosophy," *Philosophy*, volume 33 (1958): 1–19, was very important in reviving contemporary interest in virtue theory. Alasdair MacIntyre's *After Virtue* (South Bend, Ind.: University of Notre Dame Press, 1981) is an influential and widely-read book on virtue ethics, and it makes interesting claims concerning the necessity of a supportive culture for a successful virtue tradition; see also MacIntyre's more recent *Dependent Rational Animals: Why Human Beings Need the Virtues* (Chicago and La Salle, Illinois: Open Court, 1999). Edmund Pincoffs is another important contemporary virtue theorist; see his *Quandaries and Virtues* (Lawrence, Kansas: University of Kansas Press, 1986).

Joel Kupperman is an excellent writer in the virtue ethics tradition; see his "Character and Ethical Theory," *Midwest Studies in Philosophy*, volume 13 (1988): 115–125; and *Character* (New York: Oxford University Press, 1991). An intriguing brief case for virtue theory is presented by novelist and philosopher Iris Murdoch, in *The Sovereignty of Good* (New York: Schocken Books, 1971), though Murdoch's work encompasses a great deal more than a defense of virtue theory.

There are several important recent books on virtue ethics. Rosalind Hursthouse, *On Virtue Ethics* (Oxford: Oxford University Press, 1999), attempts to develop a contemporary version of Aristotle's biologically-oriented virtue ethics. Michael Slote, *Morals from Motives* (Oxford: Oxford University Press, 2001), emphasizes the virtue of caring. Philippa Foot, *Natural Goodness* (Oxford: Clarendon Press, 2001) is the work of an ethicist who has been particularly influential in the development of virtue ethics; see also her *Virtues and Vices* (Oxford: Blackwell, 1978).

Three Methods of Ethics: A Debate, edited by Marcia W. Baron, Philip Pettit, and Michael Slote (New York: Oxford University Press, 1993) is a focused and fascinating exchange among outstanding advocates of Kantian, consequentialist, and virtue approaches to ethics.

Among the excellent anthologies on virtue ethics are Roger Crisp and Michael Slote, *Virtue Ethics* (Oxford: Oxford University Press, 1997); Daniel Statman, *Virtue Ethics* (Washington, D.C.: Georgetown University Press, 1997); Stephen Darwall, *Virtue Ethics* (Oxford: Blackwell, 2003); and R. Kruschwitz and R. Roberts, *The Virtues: Contemporary Essays on Moral Character* (Belmont, Cal.: Wadsworth, 1987), which contains an extensive bibliography.

There are several online discussions of virtue ethics. See Virtue Ethics in the online Stanford Encyclopedia of Philosophy, at http://plato.stanford.edu/entries/ethics-virtue; also, virtue ethics in *The Internet Encyclopedia of Philosophy*, at http://www.iep.utm.edu/v/virtue.htm; and Aristotle and Virtue Ethics at Lawrence Hinman's Ethics Updates, at http://ethics.sandiego.edu. Helpful discussions and lectures on virtue theory can be found at Jan Garrett's Home Page, at www.wku.edu/~jan.garrett/ethics/virtthry.htm.

Contemporary research in "situationist" social psychology—indicating that the situation or environment often has a much greater influence on behavior than does character—has been used to challenge some of the basic assumptions of virtue theory ethics. Gilbert Harman, "Moral Philosophy Meets Social Psychology: Virtue Ethics and the Fundamental Attribution Error," *Proceedings of the Aristotelian Society*, volume 99 (1999): 315–332, offers a critique of virtue theory along those lines. John M. Doris, *Lack of Character: Personality and Moral Behavior* (Cambridge: Cambridge University Press, 2002), is an excellent and very readable book that reviews the relevant psychological research and develops a provocative and well-argued position on the importance of that research for ethics and our understanding of moral behavior.

Nafsika Athanassoulis, in "A Response to Harman: Virtue Ethics and Character Traits," *Proceedings of the Aristotelian Society*, volume 100 (2000): 216–221, offers an alternative explanation of the psychological research cited by Harman. Harman responds to Athanassoulis in "The Nonexistence of Character Traits," *Proceedings of the Aristotelian Society*, volume 100 (2000): 223–226. Another response to Harman is by James Montmarquet, "Moral Character and Social Science Research," *Philosophy*, volume 78 (2003): 355–368.

There have been a variety of virtue ethics responses to the situationist challenge. Gopal Sreenivasan, "Errors About Errors: Virtue Theory and Trait Attribution," *Mind*, volume 111 (January 2002): 47–68, attacks the legitimacy of the experiments supporting situationist psychology. Rachana Kamtekar, "Situationism and Virtue Ethics on the Content of Our Character," *Ethics*, volume 114 (April 2004): 458–491, argues that even if the situationist research is true, that does not undercut the importance of virtue ethics; rather, the intelligent virtue ethics response is "to identify the factors in one's environment that support the behavior one wants and then to see to the preservation of those factors." Christian Miller, "Social Psychology and Virtue Ethics," *The Journal of Ethics*, volume 7 (2003): 365–392, claims that while the relevant social psychology experiments may show that virtue traits are not fully functional for most people, that is consistent with at least the moderate or weak possession of important virtue traits; and even if very few people are strongly or even moderately virtuous, that is not a refutation of virtue theory. Maria Merritt, "Virtue Ethics and Situationist Personality Psychology," *Ethical Theory and Moral Practice*, volume 3 (2000): 365–383, agrees that psychological research undercuts the Aristotelian virtue tradition, but argues that it does not threaten a different and more plausible account of virtue ethics.

A number of contemporary philosophers have argued against moral objectivity, including A. J. Ayer, *Language, Truth and Logic* (London: Gollancz, 1970), and C. L. Stevenson, who wrote *Ethics and Language* (New Haven: Yale University Press, 1944) and *Facts and Values* (New Haven: Yale University Press, 1963). Another influential contemporary nonobjectivist is Gilbert Harman, *The Nature of Morality* (Oxford: Oxford University Press, 1977). A particularly strong case for nonobjectivism is made by John Mackie, in *Ethics: Inventing Right and Wrong* (Hammondsworth: Penguin, 1977). One of the strongest nonobjectivist writers is Herbert Feigl. See his "Validation and Vindication," in Carl Sellars and John Hospers, eds., *Readings in Ethical Theory* (New York: Appleton-Century-Crofts, 1952), and " 'De Principiis non Disputandum . . . ?' On the Meaning and the Limits of Justification," in Max Black, ed., *Philosophical Analysis* (Ithaca, New York: Cornell University Press, 1950). An interesting recent version of nonobjectivism has been proposed by Simon Blackburn; see his *Essays on Quasi-Realism* (Oxford: Oxford University Press, 1993).

Geoff Sayre-McCord, ed., *Essays on Moral Realism* (Ithaca, N.Y.: Cornell University Press, 1988) is a superb anthology, bringing together many of the best papers on moral realism. Another excellent anthology—that discusses moral realism and a great deal more—is David Copp and David Zimmerman, eds., *Morality, Reason and Truth: New Essays on the Foundations of Ethics* (Totowa, N. J.: Rowman & Allanheld, 1984). One of the best and clearest accounts of moral realism is a paper by Peter Railton: *The Philosophical Review*, volume 95 (1986): 163–207. An excellent book length study of moral realism is David O. Brink's *Moral Realism and the Foundations of Ethics* (Cambridge: Cambridge University Press, 1989).

There is an interesting survey of moral realist views in a paper by M. Y. Chew, available at www.bu.edu/wcp/Papers/TEth/TEthChew.htm. For a brief biography of Michael Smith (a leading writer on moral realism), an extensive list of his publications and an excellent selection of recent papers and works in progress that are available online, go to http://www.princeton.edu/~msmith/.

CHAPTER 14

POLITICAL PHILOSOPHY

Questions of political philosophy are among the oldest questions in philosophy. That is hardly surprising. We are profoundly social animals, and questions about how to live in groups and how to govern such groups are among the most basic questions we can ask. Some 2500 years ago, Plato wrote *The Republic* to give a model of his ideal state: The philosophers (who are of course the wisest) would be the rulers; they would be supported by the soldiers; and the great mass of people (whom Plato considered unfit to govern themselves or anything else) would follow the orders of the philosopher-kings, enforced by the loyal soldiers.

Few people would today favor Plato's model (some of my best friends are philosophers, but I wouldn't want to make them philosopher-kings); but questions of what form of government is best, what *justifies* any form of government, what is the proper relation between the government and the governed, what rights do (or should) citizens have, and what should be the *goal* of government: These are important questions, and all are debated vigorously.

JUSTIFICATION OF GOVERNMENT

A traditional justification for government was divine right: The royal family rules because the king is God's appointed, God's ordained. Thus, if you rebel against the king, you are not only rebelling against earthly authority but also rebelling against God.

> Kings are justly called gods, for that they exercise a manner or resemblance of divine power upon earth: for if you will consider the attributes of God, you shall see how they agree in the person of a king. God hath power to create or destroy, make or unmake at his pleasure, to give life or send death, to judge all and to be judged nor accountable to none; to raise low things and to make high things low at his pleasure, and to God are both souls and body due. And the like power have kings: they make and unmake their subjects, they have power of raising and casting down, of life and death, judges over all their subjects and in all causes and yet accountable to none but God only. *King James I, 1609*

The divine right theory has few contemporary followers, but its demise left a vacuum. If rulers are not divinely sanctioned, then by what right do they rule? By what right can governments govern? What obligation do I have to follow the laws established by the government of the country in which I live? By what right can that government compel me to follow those laws?

> . . . we must . . . be very careful not to despise or violate that authority of magistrates, full of venerable majesty, which God has established by the weightiest decrees, even though it may reside with the most unworthy men, who defile it as much as they can with their own wickedness. For, if the correction of unbridled despotism is the Lord's to avenge, let us not at once think it is instructed to us, to whom no command has been given except to obey and suffer. *John Calvin*, a leader of the Protestant Reformation in Europe

Many people have been frightened of government—and not without cause. After all, governments can take your money (through taxes or fines), can appropriate your property (through eminent domain or—if you are dealing with a king or a tax collector—simply by seizure), can take your liberty (by throwing you into prison), can restrict your freedom (by imposing or forbidding a religion, by censoring what you can read, or restricting where you can travel—for example, the U.S. government forbids its citizens from traveling to Cuba), can draft you into its army and compel you to fight its wars (whether you consider those wars just or unjust), and can take your life (through capital punishment). That's a lot of power. When the American colonies had won their independence from Great Britain, they still feared government power. That's not surprising. As just one example, British citizens could be "pressed" into active duty on British warships: "press gangs" would roam through a district, capturing able bodied men (ages 18 to 55) and forcing them onto ships which might be at sea for years. Once on board, those who resisted were severely flogged; those who continued to resist were hanged. If you can imagine starting your spring break with strawberry daiquiris on a Florida beach and ending it scrubbing the decks of a British frigate on its way to the other side of the world, then you can imagine the concern that was felt for the power of the state. Of course, the government can and often does provide substantial benefits as well: police and fire protection, monitoring of food and drugs for safety, building of highways, aid in emergencies, public education, and—in most countries—universal medical care. But the dangers of governmental abuse of power are real.

"That government is best which governs least." This quotation has been attributed to Thomas Jefferson, but Thomas Paine was probably the original source; it was explicitly approved by Henry David Thoreau. But even if you agree with that view, you still have the question of how to justify any governing *at all*. By what right does my government dictate to me about anything, however minimal? Or another way of framing that question: Do I have an *obligation* to follow the laws and rules set forth by my government? Of course, my government may well have the power to *force* me to follow its laws—or at the very least, to make things very unpleasant for me if I do not. But brute force obviously does not confer moral legitimacy. Do I have a *moral obligation* to follow the laws of my country?

That question must be asked more carefully before we can examine possible answers, because it can mean two distinctly different things. First, do I have an obligation to follow *all* the rules and laws laid down by my government, *without exception*? And second, the quite different question: Do I have a *general* obligation to follow the laws of my country? In the second case, there may or may not be *exceptions* to that general principle; but before we can consider whether there are exceptions to the general obligation, we must consider whether there is any obligation *whatsoever*.

One answer is rather easy: There is *no* right of government. A government may have the *power* to force us to do things—follow laws, pay taxes, and fight in its armies—but it has no *right* to compel such compliance. That is the view of the *anarchists*, who deny the legitimacy of all government powers. Anarchism poses the basic challenge to the idea of governmental authority: What right does a government have to impose its laws on *me*? It won't help to say, well, you live in the country, so you must follow its laws: That begs the question. After all, the anarchist is well aware that she lives on a patch of Earth claimed by a particular governmental authority; the question is, *why* should that government have any authority over *her?* Obviously the government may be able to bring enormous force against her, and lock her up or even kill her if she refuses to accept its authority; but that will not answer the question of what *justification* the country has for requiring her to obey its laws.

At one time the standard answer was divine right. Moses comes down from Mount Sinai with the Ten Commandments, but also with word that God has chosen him and his family to rule the Israelites. The Egyptian Pharaohs cut out the middle man: They ruled by divine right because they *were* divine. The Romans split the difference: They ruled by divine right, because their ancestors were gods. In Europe, from the medieval period through the Renaissance and through most of the eighteenth century, royalty ruled by divine right, and the priesthood played a prominent role in crowning the new king or queen as God's anointed ruler of the secular realm (this tight relationship between the church and the royal rulers was the reason for the famous rallying cry of the French Revolution: "Mankind will not be free until the last king is strangled with the entrails of the last priest.") But by the seventeenth century, divine right was under challenge as grounds for governmental legitimacy, and *social contract* theory was emerging to replace it.

The basic idea of the social contract model is that governmental legitimacy derives from the *consent* of the governed. But before turning to the contract model, consider some other efforts to establish an obligation of citizens to generally obey the laws and regulations of their government. That is the question that political philosophers and political scientists call the question of *political obligation:* Do I have a *general obligation* to follow the laws of my government? Note that this is *not* a question of how to determine whether the government of the country is *just* or legitimate. After all, suppose you are an American colonist and a British citizen living under British rule, and you think your government is fundamentally unjust. You might still believe that so long as the government is in place, and provides some benefits, you have a *general* obligation to follow its laws. Also, the question of political obligation is not the question of whether you have an absolute obligation to follow *all* the laws of your government. For example, many civil rights activists believed that it would be *wrong*—and certainly *not* obligatory—to follow racist segregation laws; but still believed in a *general* obligation to follow the laws of the country.

So, *if* we have a general *political obligation* to follow the laws and rules of the country in which we live, what is the source of that obligation? Some theorists (such as the legal philosopher H. L. A. Hart) attempt to ground that obligation in the rules of *fair play:* You receive the benefits of living under a government, so it is only fair that you also accept the rules and obligations, and thus carry a fair share of the burdens in return for accepting the benefits. But it's not clear that this model takes us very far; after all, if you live in the country, you inevitably receive the benefits of living in that society, but it is not clear that you incur reciprocal obligations. Suppose that someone plants flowers along the street which you drive; you inevitably receive the benefit of the beautiful flowers, but do you also have an obligation to pay something to the flower planter, or take a turn with the weeding? It might be nice if you helped out, but are you obligated to do so?

Another noncontract attempt to establish the obligation of citizens to obey governmental rules is in terms of *community* or *association:* It compares life in a political state to life in a family or community. You didn't *choose* your family, nor the community into which you were born; but most of us believe we have special family obligations to siblings and parents, even though we never consented to take on those obligations. An advocate of this view, John Horton, claims that:

> . . . a polity is, like the family, a relationship into which we are mostly born: and . . . the obligations which are constitutive of the relationship do not stand in need of moral justification in terms of a set of basic moral principles or some comprehensive moral theory.

John Horton, 1992, p. 150

I have obligations to my family simply because it is *my* family, and consent does not enter into it. In like manner, I have obligations to my country—including the general obligation to obey its laws—because it is *my* country, not because I gave explicit or even implicit consent, and not because of benefits received. However, the comparison between the family and the state may seem a bit forced: While many people feel great affection for their country, the affection seems quite different from the close and intimate relations we have with members of our families. Furthermore, my general obligation to obey the laws of my country is supposed to apply even if I lose any affectionate regard for or sense of identification with my country; and even if my affection for and sense of identification with my country remains intact, it is not clear that such affection can provide grounds for an obligation to obey its laws. If my ethnic background is Italian, I may feel a special affection and sense of identification with Italy; but I feel no obligation to obey its laws.

The Social Contract

Though there are other models for governmental legitimacy and the political obligation of citizens, the social contract model remains dominant. The idea of a *social contract* conferring legitimacy on government has been around a long time. In the Platonic dialogue, the *Crito*, Socrates argues that he must accept the death penalty imposed by the city-state of Athens, because he has accepted the benefits of living under its government and thus has accepted the "contract" to obey its laws and decrees. The earliest and most dramatic instance of the actual formation of a social contract is the great Iroquois Confederation. Historians debate its date of origin, but there is general agreement that by the mid-fifteenth century it was a complex representative democracy, with an elaborate constitution, and that the Iroquois League was a very important factor in the struggles among the French, the British, and the American colonists. Indeed, there is considerable evidence that the ideas of the Iroquois League influenced the development of the U.S. Constitution.

Government, like dress, is the badge of lost innocence; the palaces of kings are built on the ruins of the bowers of paradise. For, were the impulses of conscience clear, uniform, and irresistibly obeyed, man would need no other lawgiver; but that not being the case, he finds it necessary to surrender up a part of his property to furnish means for the protection of the rest; and this he is induced to do by the same prudence which in every other case, advises him out of two evils to choose the least. *Thomas Paine, Common Sense, 1776*

In political philosophy, the key source of classical social contract theory is Thomas Hobbes' great book, *Leviathan*. Hobbes starts by imagining life in a "state of nature," in which there is no government, no enforced rules, people live in a war of "all against all," and life is "solitary, poor, nasty, brutish, and short." In such a situation, all of us can see the advantage of contracting together to establish a government that will protect us from attacks, and that will enforce rules against murder and theft and assault. Even the strongest would see the advantage of such an agreement: In the state of nature the strong may have great opportunity to rob and pillage, but they are vulnerable when asleep—and everyone must sleep. Indeed, the strong would be especially vulnerable when asleep, because those of us who are weaker would be in fear of them and would try to eliminate that threat. In the state of nature there are no laws, no rules, and no break from the constant and horrific struggle. And so you would agree—from your own self-interest—to give up the right to attack others, and follow rules and laws that protect others, on the condition that others would agree to follow the same rules and not attack you. And in order to enforce those laws, Hobbes believed we would require a "Great Leviathan," or central power, that would have the power to enforce the laws. So why do we have an obligation to follow the laws? Because we *consent* to follow the laws, since we recognize it is in our interest to do so. Or if we don't *actually* consent (you didn't sign a form when you turned 16 that assented to the government and agreed to follow its laws), it is reasonable to suppose that you *would* consent to follow the rules of a government that protects you. We can *presume* your consent, because it would be *reasonable* for you to agree to the social contract: You're a reasonable person, and you recognize that living under the social contract is to your advantage.

No man is good enough to govern another man without that other's consent.
Abraham Lincoln, 1854

Hobbes' social contract may appear a rather conservative document: We agree to accept the government's rules, and thus the government has a right to compel our compliance. But when Hobbes first proposed his social contract form of government, it was a radical idea: The legitimacy of the government requires the *consent of the governed*. And that idea includes the belief that if people decide their government is *not* satisfactory, they have the right to overthrow it. For Hobbes, people should exercise that right *very* cautiously; after all, even a very bad government is better than the brutal and dangerous state of nature. Hobbes lived through the horrors of the English Civil War, and he had a profound fear of social and political chaos. Hobbes also believed that in the absence of a powerful ruler to "overawe" everyone, people would seek their own selfish ends, using whatever brutal means were at their disposal. Thus for Hobbes, the powerful authority and force of a ruler was an essential check on the vile, selfish, and brutal tendencies of the ruled; and the overthrow of a ruling government could only be justified in the most extreme circumstances: when the government was so bad that life under its power was actually worse than the "nasty, brutish, and short" life that would be briefly lived in the state of nature.

John Locke (1632–1704) also favored social contract theory, but his model of the social contract was quite different from that offered by Hobbes. For Locke, the state of nature is not a state of "war of all against all," for without a government people can still recognize the "Law of Nature" that is prescribed by God: We all equally belong to God, and thus no one has the right to harm others, for that would be harming God's possessions. Since human nature is not so hopelessly brutal as in Hobbes, the state of nature is not so bad; and since the state of nature is not so bad, we are not quite so desperate to escape the state of nature, and not so frightened of overthrowing a government and returning—at least temporarily—to a state of nature. Thus those who are thinking about entering into a social contract will be inclined to hold out for a better deal: They certainly are not eager to give up all power to a "great leviathan," who can rule over them with almost no restraints. Under Locke's model, if the government doesn't promote our welfare, then we have every right to overthrow it and institute a better one; and though of course we should not pursue such a course lightly, neither should we be terrified of doing so. The American Revolution was greatly influenced by Locke's social contract ideas, and key parts of the Declaration of Independence sound almost as if they were written by Locke:

> We hold these truths to be self-evident, that all men are created equal, that they are endowed by their Creator with certain unalienable Rights, that among these are Life, Liberty and the pursuit of Happiness.–That to secure these rights, Governments are instituted among Men, deriving their just powers from the consent of the governed,–That whenever any Form of Government becomes destructive of these ends, it is the Right of the People to alter or abolish it, and to institute new Government, laying its foundation on such principles and organizing its powers in such form, as to them shall seem most likely to effect their Safety and Happiness.

This is certainly a social contract model, but it has moved quite a distance from Hobbes. For Hobbes, if the government protects your life, that's about as much as you have any right to expect. The colonial revolutionaries placed much stronger demands on government legitimacy: It must protect one's life, certainly; but it must also promote liberty and enhance our pursuit of happiness.

Jean-Jacques Rousseau (1712–1778) also proposed a form of social contract theory, though his was quite different from that of either Hobbes or Locke. Rousseau starts from the belief that humans are naturally good: that (in stark contrast to the view of Hobbes) in a state of nature humans would live simply, peacefully and cooperatively. But as society becomes larger and more complex, humans face the danger of tyranny from their fellow humans. Since Rousseau regards freedom as the highest good, he is unwilling to compromise that freedom for security (as Hobbes recommends); and so he seeks a way of reconciling state authority with individual freedom. For Rousseau, the answer lies in forging a "general will," in which all the citizens share common ideals of cooperation and equality, and thus each citizen can freely join others in creating a society that reflects the values and goals of all. Rousseau's model is an optimistic championing of impressive ideals, but it has also come in for severe criticism: Does it ultimately require that each individual submerge himself or herself in the values of the whole? Does it leave room for dissent about basic values? Rousseau seemed to believe in a natural rational universal order—which reflects the goodness of the Creator. But if one is skeptical of values that will be universally acknowledged, then Rousseau's social contract model faces difficulties.

Can the social contract model—that bases political obligation on the "consent of the governed"—provide an adequate foundation for a general political obligation to obey the laws of the country? That remains a vexed question in political philosophy.

OBEYING OR DISOBEYING THE LAW

Suppose that we accept some social contract account of our *general* obligation to obey the laws of our government; that is, suppose that there is some general *political obligation*. There remains the question of how far that obligation extends: Do I have an obligation to follow *all* the laws of my government? What if my government passes a law—such as the fugitive slave act, which requires that I aid slave catchers in capturing escaped slaves, and forbids me from helping escaped slaves; or more recently, a law forbidding me from giving food to a hungry person who happens to be in this country illegally—that I find morally objectionable? Do I have an obligation to obey laws that are in conflict with my own basic values?

Even *if* one believes that there is a strong obligation to obey the legitimately passed laws of one's country, it is hard to maintain that one must *always* follow such laws, no matter what. After all, even if you believe that the fugitive slave act was a law passed in a lawful democratic manner, you might certainly believe that it is *morally wrong* to aid in the capturing of escaped slaves (as the law required citizens to do), and that it would be morally wrong to comply with that law. To suppose that one must always follow the laws of one's country, no matter what, is to give up all independent moral judgment (it is the political equivalent of the divine command theory of ethics). Ronald Dworkin, a distinguished contemporary political philosopher, states this point clearly:

> Someone who believes that it would be deeply wrong to deny help to an escaped slave who knocks at his door, and even worse to turn him over to the authorities, thinks that the Fugitive Slave Act requires him to behave in an immoral way. His personal integrity, his conscience, forbids him to obey. Soldiers drafted to fight in a war they deem wicked are in the same position. . . . Almost everyone would agree, I think, that people in this position do the right thing, given their convictions, if they break the law. Of course, violence and terrorism cannot be justified in this way. If someone's conscience will not let him obey some law, neither should it let him kill or harm innocent people. But it is hard to think of

any other qualifications a working theory would have to recognize here. It could not, for example, add the further and tempting qualification that a citizen must have exhausted the normal political process so long as this offers any prospect of reversing the political decision he opposes. Integrity-based disobedience is typically a matter of urgency. The Northerner who is asked to hand over a slave to the slavecatcher, even the schoolchild asked once to salute the flag, suffers a final loss if he obeys, and it does not much help him if the law is reversed soon afterward.

Ronald Dworkin, pp. 107–108, A Matter of Principle

It is of course possible to submerge one's identity into one's country, and affirm that "whatever is ordered by my country is right, and I should do it"; but then you are no longer an autonomous moral individual, and that's a rather high price to pay. That doesn't mean, obviously, that I should refuse to follow every law that I think is mistaken. I think traffic would move better if we all drove on the left side of the road rather than the right; but I am not morally compromised by driving on the right-hand side. A law requiring me to betray fugitive slaves is a very different law indeed.

LIBERAL AND CONSERVATIVE

Recall those lines quoted earlier from the U.S. Declaration of Independence: "We hold these truths to be self-evident, that all men are created equal, that they are endowed by their Creator with certain unalienable Rights, that among these are Life, Liberty and the pursuit of Happiness.–That to secure these rights, Governments are instituted among Men, deriving their just powers from the consent of the governed."

What does that imply? Government should promote liberty and support our pursuit of happiness; but it does *not* tell us what happiness path we should pursue: That choice is up to us. That is the classic liberal model of government, as defended by John Stuart Mill in *On Liberty:* The government supports whatever idea of happiness any of its citizens wish to pursue (so long as that pursuit does not interfere with the right of *others* to pursue *their* idea of happiness); but it does *not* favor one idea of happiness, or one idea of the good life, over others. The choice of how best to pursue your happiness is up to you; the government simply guarantees and protects your liberty to pursue your own chosen path.

When political philosophers discuss the difference between *liberal* and *conservative* views, they are using those terms rather differently from the way they are used in contemporary politics. Though this is somewhat oversimplified, *contemporary* liberals basically believe in a stronger role for government, while conservatives want to minimize the role of government. For example, liberals are more likely to favor a universal health care plan backed by government resources, a strong food and drug safety policy in which government inspectors would carefully monitor food and drug safety, monitoring of workplace safety, and careful government regulation of banks and financial institutions to prevent corruption and to protect consumers against deceptive lending practices. Contemporary conservatives are less likely to favor such government programs, or at the very least they wish to minimize them. The *traditional* use of "liberal" and "conservative" is quite different (and it is that traditional use that we are discussing in this section). On the traditional use of the terms, the "liberal" believes that government should be *neutral* on how you wish to live your life (whether you should be religious, what religion you should follow, what values you should hold), and promote and protect only those values that enhance your right to choose your *own* preferred way of life; while the traditional "conservative" maintains that government should actively promote a *good* way of life (including the *right* values and perhaps the *true* religion). To distinguish these two different uses of "liberal" and "conservative," we'll follow the standard practice of referring to the traditional use of "liberal" and "conservative" as "classical liberal" and "classical conservative."

The classical liberal model is certainly not value free. It champions some very specific values: freedom of speech, freedom of religion, freedom of association, and tolerance. That is, it champions values that are essential if people are to be free to pursue their own goals and values and lives. On this model, you are free to pursue any religion you wish, or none at all, so long as you do not harm others nor interfere in their pursuit of their own beliefs or rejection of beliefs; and the government leaves that up to each citizen, showing neither favor nor disfavor toward any religion. Obviously—on the classical liberal model—the government cannot compel you to follow a state-approved religion, nor prevent you from following a religion that it regards as wrong, nor require that you hold any religious belief whatsoever as a condition of full citizenship. But neither should it promote a particular religious perspective—for example, by posting the Ten Commandments in courthouses—because the government is supposed to remain *neutral* about the best way of pursuing happiness and the good life: That is a question each citizen has the right to answer for herself, and the only interest of the government is protecting that right from interference.

> It does me no injury for my neighbor to say that there are twenty gods or no god. It neither picks my pocket nor breaks my leg. *Thomas Jefferson*

The same applies to freedom of speech: Citizens must be free to hear and express and promote whatever ideas they wish, for only through such freedom can we discover what ideas best fit with our own ideas of happiness. So long as you don't harm or interfere with others, you should be able to carry out your *own* pursuit of happiness: whether that is cautious or reckless, gay or straight, religious or nonreligious, drunk or sober.

> If a man does not keep pace with his companions, perhaps it is because he hears a different drummer. Let him step to the music which he hears, however measured or far away. *Henry David Thoreau, Walden, 1854*

In contrast to the classical liberal model, the classical conservative perspective believes that citizens should be given more guidance—and even some restrictions—on how to pursue their own happiness. Experimenting with new paths to happiness is more likely to cause harm than good, and citizens should be encouraged, perhaps even required, to follow traditional paths that have been tested and found to be valuable. We have learned, through long years of experience, that some ways of life have better outcomes and contribute more positively to the good of the society; and that traditional wisdom is worthy of honor and should not be cast aside in favor of dubious life and belief experiments that are likely to lead down unfortunate paths.

> It is generally accepted that some shared morality, that is, some common agreement about what is right and wrong, is an essential element in the constitution of any society. Without it, there would be no cohesion. *Lord Patrick Devlin, The Enforcement of Morals, 1965*

Like the classical conservatives, the *communitarians* also believe that society should promote a specific value framework; but they offer a very different justification. Communitarians maintain that the social fabric requires some common deep values. Holding the society together as a functioning cooperative whole needs a more substantive value framework than merely promoting individual liberty; it needs deeper values that give all members of the society a shared sense of community and shared identity and shared ends. For communitarians, it's not so much a matter of promoting values that have been proved true by time and tradition, but rather of *maintaining* and sustaining a common value framework that strengthens cooperative ties among the diverse members of the society.

POSITIVE AND NEGATIVE LIBERTY

The classical liberal model sees government as a protector and promoter of *individual liberty*. But what does it mean to promote individual liberty? There are two different answers to that question that result in different views of the role of government. Both sides in this deep dispute believe that a basic role of government is the promotion of individual liberty, but they disagree about what that involves. The *negative* liberty perspective sees the role of government as protection against *interference* in individual liberty: The liberty to be protected is the liberty to be *left alone* to do as you wish. If someone tries to harm you, or someone interferes with your acts when you are neither harming nor posing a threat to others, then government should intervene to protect you; otherwise, you're on your own.

The American people may be mistaken as to men and measures, but we are confident that in principle, they will all assent to the doctrine of equality. We feel confident of their unanimous support, when we say that all the members of the community should have, so far as society is concerned, equal chances. But equal chances imply equal starting points. Nobody, it would seem, could pretend that where the points of departure were unequal the chances could be equal. Do the young man inheriting ten thousand pounds, and the one whose inheritance is merely the gutter, start even? Have they equal chances? It may be said both are free to rise as high as they can,—one starting with ten thousand pounds in advance, and the other starting with the gutter. But it might as well be said the chances of the eldest son of the Duke of Newcastle, and those of the eldest son of one of the lowest of the Duke's tenants, are equal, since both unquestionably are free to rise as high as they can,—one starting with a dukedom in advance, and the other with nothing. But to pretend this is mere jesting. *Orestes Brownson*, "The Laboring Class," 1840

From the *positive* liberty perspective, this noninterference approach is not the best way of promoting liberty. After all, we often need more than just *noninterference* in order to effectively pursue our freely chosen paths. Suppose, for example, that your chosen value is writing a novel or making a scientific discovery. If you have no resources for obtaining a decent education, then such options are closed to you; and the closing off of preferred paths is a severe impediment to your real freedom. Indeed, there are *many* paths that are closed to us if we have no way of gaining a sound education; in fact, without such educational opportunities, many free paths will not just be closed to us, but will actually be invisible. That being the case, most countries that value liberty offer every citizen, rich or poor, an opportunity for a good education; and to the extent that such educational opportunities are *not* offered, or are not offered to all, or are severely substandard, we can conclude that the society does *not* really value liberty for all, no matter what slogans it may chant.

Not only is one's freedom extended by education, it is also restricted by "mis-education"—by the inculcation of ideas and attitudes which reconcile one to existing circumstances or channel one's choices in certain specific directions. This will be partly a matter of direct and conscious manipulation, as in the form of political propaganda or commercial advertising, but partly a matter also of the unconscious acceptance of the prejudices and thought-patterns of one's own community. Consequently one's ability to make choices will require an ability to question and criticize the dominant attitudes; and that too is an ability which has to be fostered by the right kind of education. *Richard Norman, Free and Equal* (Oxford: Oxford University Press, 1987), 48–49

And of course a decent education is not the only basic need for maximizing liberty. Lack of decent health care is also a severe restriction on one's liberty: If lack of good health care, or inadequate nutrition, or a toxic environment leaves you chronically ill or severely fatigued, then the possibility of living a life rich in freedom is severely curtailed. Thus again, countries that genuinely value individual freedom and opportunity for everyone make sure that all their citizens have opportunities for a good education, good health care, and adequate nutrition. Imagine someone who has been deprived of the opportunity for a good education, who has suffered from disease complications that could have been easily prevented by good basic health care, and who has lacked access to adequate wholesome food during his entire life; and now, when he turns 21, we say: Happy birthday; now go and enjoy your full liberty, pursue your own freely chosen path; we'll make sure no one interferes with your full exercise of freedom. That would sound more like a cruel taunt than a genuine invitation to enjoy a free life.

We are so accustomed to great social and economic inequalities that it is easy to become dulled to them. But if everyone matters just as much as everyone else, it is appalling that the most effective social systems we have been able to devise permit so many people to be born into conditions of harsh deprivation which crush their prospects for leading a decent life, while many others are well provided for from birth, come to control substantial resources, and are free to enjoy advantages vastly beyond the conditions of mere decency. The mutual perception of these material inequalities is part of a broader inequality of social status, personal freedom, and self-respect. Those with high income, extensive education, inherited wealth, family connections, and genteel employment are served and in many cultures treated deferentially by those who have none of these things. One cannot ignore the difficulties of escaping from this situation, but that is no reason not to dislike it. *Thomas Nagel, Equality and Partiality* (New York: Oxford University Press, 1991), p. 64

READINGS

⇒ "ON THE ORIGIN OF INEQUALITY" ⇐
Jean-Jacques Rousseau

Though born in Geneva, Jean-Jacques Rousseau (1712–1778) spent most of his life in France and is regarded as a French philosopher. Rousseau was a prominent and influential literary figure during the revolutionary turmoil of the eighteenth century, and his ideas influenced the French Revolution. This passage is from "A Discourse on a Subject Proposed by the Academy of Dijon: What Is the Origin of Inequality Among Men, and Is It Authorised by Natural Law?" (which is commonly known simply as "On the Origin of Inequality"). Written in 1754, this translation is by G. D. H. Cole.

A section from Thomas Hobbes' *Leviathan*, the classic source for social contract theory, can be found in Chapter 12. Rousseau offers a very different model of the social contract, which results from his dramatically different picture of the "state of nature," as well as his profound commitment to maintaining individual freedom while living within the constraints of government.

THE SECOND PART

THE first man who, having enclosed a piece of ground, bethought himself of saying *This is mine*, and found people simple enough to believe him, was the real founder of civil society. From how many crimes, wars and murders, from how many horrors and misfortunes might not any one have saved mankind, by pulling up the stakes, or filling up the ditch, and crying to his fellows, "Beware of listening to this impostor; you are undone if you once forget that the fruits of the earth belong to us all, and the earth itself to nobody." But there is great probability that things had then already come to such a pitch, that they could no longer continue as they were; for the idea of property depends on many prior ideas, which could only be acquired successively, and cannot have been formed all at once in the human mind. Mankind must have made very considerable progress, and acquired considerable knowledge and industry which they must also have transmitted and increased from age to age, before they arrived at this last point of the state of nature. Let us then go farther back, and endeavour to unify under a single point of view that slow succession of events and discoveries in the most natural order.

Man's first feeling was that of his own existence, and his first care that of self-preservation. The produce of the earth furnished him with all he needed, and instinct told him how to use it. Hunger and other appetites made him at various times experience various modes of existence; and among these was one which urged him to propagate his species—a blind propensity that, having nothing to do with the heart, produced a merely animal act. The want once gratified, the two sexes knew each other no more; and even the offspring was nothing to its mother, as soon as it could do without her.

Such was the condition of infant man; the life of an animal limited at first to mere sensations, and hardly profiting by the gifts nature bestowed on him, much less capable of entertaining a thought of forcing anything from her. But difficulties soon presented themselves, and it became necessary to learn how to surmount them: the height of the trees, which prevented him from gathering their fruits, the competition of other animals desirous of the same fruits, and the ferocity of those who needed them for their own preservation, all obliged him to apply himself to bodily exercises. He had to be active, swift of foot, and vigorous in fight. Natural weapons, stones and sticks, were easily found: he learnt to surmount the obstacles of nature, to contend in case of necessity with other animals, and to dispute for the means of subsistence even with other men, or to indemnify himself for what he was forced to give up to a stronger.

In proportion as the human race grew more numerous, men's cares increased. The difference of soils, climates and seasons, must have introduced some differences into their manner of living. Barren years, long and sharp winters, scorching summers which parched the fruits of the earth, must have demanded a new industry. On the seashore and the banks of rivers, they invented the hook and line, and became fishermen and eaters of fish. In the forests they made bows and arrows, and became huntsmen and warriors. In cold countries they clothed themselves with the skins of the beasts they had slain. The lightning, a volcano, or some lucky chance acquainted them with fire, a new resource against the rigours of winter: they next learned how to preserve this element, then how to reproduce it, and finally how to prepare with it the flesh of animals which before they had eaten raw.

This repeated relevance of various beings to himself, and one to another, would naturally give rise in the human mind to the perceptions of certain relations between them. Thus the relations which we denote by the terms, great, small, strong, weak, swift, slow, fearful, bold, and the like, almost insensibly compared at need, must have at length produced in him a kind of reflection, or rather a mechanical prudence, which would indicate to him the precautions most necessary to his security.

The new intelligence which resulted from this development increased his superiority over other animals, by making him sensible of it. He would now endeavour, therefore, to ensnare them, would play them a thousand tricks, and though many of them might surpass him in swiftness or in strength, would in time become the master of some and the scourge of others. Thus, the first time he looked into himself, he felt the first emotion of pride; and, at a time when he scarce knew how to distinguish the different orders of beings, by looking upon his species as of the highest order, he prepared the way for assuming preeminence as an individual.

Other men, it is true, were not then to him what they now are to us, and he had no greater intercourse with them than with other animals; yet they were not neglected in his observations. The conformities, which he would in time discover between them, and between himself and his female, led him to judge of others which were not then perceptible; and finding that they all behaved as he himself would have done in like circumstances, he naturally inferred that their manner of thinking and acting was altogether in conformity with his own. This important truth, once deeply impressed on his mind, must have induced him, from an intuitive feeling more certain and much more rapid than any kind of reasoning, to pursue the rules of conduct, which he had best observe towards them, for his own security and advantage.

Taught by experience that the love of well-being is the sole motive of human actions, he found himself in a position to distinguish the few cases, in which mutual interest might justify him in relying upon the assistance of his fellows; and also the still fewer cases in which a conflict of interests might give cause to suspect them. In the former case, he joined in the same herd with them, or at most in some kind of loose association, that laid no restraint on its members, and lasted no longer than the transitory occasion that formed it. In the latter case, every one sought his own private advantage, either by open force, if he thought himself strong enough, or by address and cunning, if he felt himself the weaker.

In this manner, men may have insensibly acquired some gross ideas of mutual undertakings, and of the advantages of fulfilling them: that is, just so far as their present and apparent interest was concerned: for they were perfect strangers to foresight, and were so far from troubling themselves about the distant future, that they hardly thought of the morrow. If a deer was to be taken, every one saw that, in order to succeed, he must abide faithfully by his post: but if a hare happened to come within the reach of any one of them, it is not to be doubted that he pursued it without scruple, and, having seized his prey, cared very little, if by so doing he caused his companions to miss theirs.

It is easy to understand that such intercourse would not require a language much more refined than that of rooks or monkeys, who associate together for much the same purpose. Inarticulate cries, plenty of gestures and some imitative sounds, must have been for a long time the universal language; and by the addition, in every country, of some conventional articulate sounds (of which, as I have already intimated, the first institution is not too easy to explain) particular languages were produced; but these were rude and imperfect, and nearly such as are now to be found among some savage nations.

Hurried on by the rapidity of time, by the abundance of things I have to say, and by the almost insensible progress of things in their beginnings, I pass over in an instant a multitude of ages; for the slower the events were in their succession, the more rapidly may they be described.

These first advances enabled men to make others with greater rapidity. In proportion as they grew enlightened, they grew industrious. They ceased to fall asleep under the first tree, or in the first cave that afforded them shelter; they invented several kinds of implements of hard and sharp stones, which they used to dig up the earth, and to cut wood; they then made huts out of branches, and afterwards learnt to plaster them over with mud and clay. This was the epoch of a first revolution, which established and distinguished families, and introduced a kind of property, in itself the source of a thousand quarrels and conflicts. As, however, the strongest were probably the first to build themselves huts which they felt themselves able to defend, it may be concluded that the weak found it much easier and safer to imitate, than to attempt to dislodge them: and of those who were once provided with huts, none could have any inducement to appropriate that of his neighbour; not indeed so much because it did not belong to him, as because it could be of no use, and he could not make himself master of it without exposing himself to a desperate battle with the family which occupied it.

The first expansions of the human heart were the effects of a novel situation, which united husbands and wives, fathers and children, under one roof. The habit of living together soon gave rise to the finest feelings known to humanity, conjugal love and paternal affection. Every family became a little society, the more united because liberty and reciprocal attachment were the only bonds of its union. The sexes, whose manner of life had been hitherto the same, began now to adopt different ways of living. The women became more sedentary, and accustomed themselves to mind the hut and their children, while the men went abroad in search of their common subsistence. From living a softer life, both sexes also began to lose something of their strength and ferocity: but if individuals became to some extent less able to encounter wild beasts separately, they found it, on the other hand, easier to assemble and resist in common.

The simplicity and solitude of man's life in this new condition, the paucity of his wants, and the implements he had invented to satisfy them, left him a great deal of leisure, which he employed to furnish himself with many conveniences unknown to his fathers: and this was the first yoke he inadvertently imposed on himself, and the first source of the evils he prepared for his descendants. For, besides continuing thus to enervate both body and mind, these conveniences lost with use almost all their power to please, and even degenerated into real needs, till the want of them became far more disagreeable than the possession of them had been pleasant. Men would have been unhappy at the loss of them, though the possession did not make them happy.

We can here see a little better how the use of speech became established, and insensibly improved in each family, and we may form a conjecture also concerning the manner in which various causes may have extended and accelerated the progress of language, by making it more and more necessary. Floods or earthquakes surrounded inhabited districts with precipices or waters: revolutions of the globe tore off portions from the continent, and made them islands. It is readily seen that among men thus collected and compelled to live together, a common idiom must have arisen much more easily than among those who still wandered through the forest of the continent. Thus it is very possible that after their first essays in navigation the islanders brought over the use of speech to the continent: and it is at least very probable that communities and languages were first established in islands, and even came to perfection there before they were known on the mainland.

Everything now begins to change its aspect. Men, who have up to now been roving in the woods, by taking to a more settled manner of life, come gradually together, form separate bodies, and at length in every country arises a distinct nation, united in character and manners, not by regulations or laws, but by uniformity of life and food, and the common influence of climate. Permanent neighbourhood could not fail to produce, in time, some connection between different families. Among young people of opposite sexes, living in neighbouring huts, the transient commerce required by nature soon led, through mutual intercourse, to another kind not less agreeable, and more permanent. Men began now to take the difference

between objects into account, and to make comparisons; they acquired imperceptibly the ideas of beauty and merit, which soon gave rise to feeling of preference. In consequence of seeing each other often, they could not do without seeing each other constantly. A tender and pleasant feeling insinuated itself into their souls, and the least opposition turned it into an impetuous fury: with love arose jealousy; discord triumphed, and human blood was sacrificed to the gentlest of all passions.

As ideas and feelings succeeded one another, and heart and head were brought into play, men continued to lay aside their original wildness; their private connections became every day more intimate as their limits extended. They accustomed themselves to assemble before their huts round a large tree; singing and dancing, the true offspring of love and leisure, became the amusement, or rather the occupation, of men and women thus assembled together with nothing else to do. Each one began to consider the rest, and to wish to be considered in turn; and thus a value came to be attached to public esteem. Whoever sang or danced best, whoever was the handsomest, the strongest, the most dexterous, or the most eloquent, came to be of most consideration; and this was the first step towards inequality, and at the same time towards vice. From these first distinctions arose on the one side vanity and contempt and on the other shame and envy: and the fermentation caused by these new leavens ended by producing combinations fatal to innocence and happiness.

As soon as men began to value one another, and the idea of consideration had got a footing in the mind, every one put in his claim to it, and it became impossible to refuse it to any with impunity. Hence arose the first obligations of civility even among savages; and every intended injury became an affront; because, besides the hurt which might result from it, the party injured was certain to find in it a contempt for his person, which was often more insupportable than the hurt itself.

Thus, as every man punished the contempt shown him by others, in proportion to his opinion of himself, revenge became terrible, and men bloody and cruel. This is precisely the state reached by most of the savage nations known to us: and it is for want of having made a proper distinction in our ideas, and see how very far they already are from the state of nature, that so many writers have hastily concluded that man is naturally cruel, and requires civil institutions to make him more mild; whereas nothing is more gentle than man in his primitive state, as he is placed by nature at an equal distance from the stupidity of brutes, and the fatal ingenuity of civilised man. Equally confined by instinct and reason to the sole care of guarding himself against the mischiefs which threaten him, he is restrained by natural compassion from doing any injury to others, and is not led to do such a thing even in return for injuries received. For, according to the axiom of the wise Locke, *There can be no injury, where there is no property.*

But it must be remarked that the society thus formed, and the relations thus established among men, required of them qualities different from those which they possessed from their primitive constitution. Morality began to appear in human actions, and every one, before the institution of law, was the only judge and avenger of the injuries done him, so that the goodness which was suitable in the pure state of nature was no longer proper in the new-born state of society. Punishments had to be made more severe, as opportunities of offending became more frequent, and the dread of vengeance had to take the place of the rigour of the law. Thus, though men had become less patient, and their natural compassion had already suffered some diminution, this period of expansion of the human faculties, keeping a just mean between the indolence of the primitive state and the petulant activity of our egoism, must have been the happiest and most stable of epochs. The more we reflect on it, the more we shall find that this state was the least subject to revolutions, and altogether the very best man could experience; so that he can have departed from it only through some fatal accident, which, for the public good, should never have happened. The example of savages, most of whom have been found in this state, seems to prove that men were meant to remain in it, that it is the real youth of the world, and that all subsequent advances have been apparently so many steps towards the perfection of the individual, but in reality towards the decrepitude of the species.

So long as men remained content with their rustic huts, so long as they were satisfied with clothes made of the skins of animals and sewn together with thorns and fish-bones, adorned themselves only with feathers and shells, and continued to paint their bodies different colours, to improve and beautify their bows and arrows and to make with sharp-edged stones fishing boats or clumsy musical instruments; in a word, so long as they undertook only what a single person could accomplish, and confined themselves to such arts as did not require the joint labour of several hands, they lived free, healthy, honest and happy lives, so long as their nature allowed, and so they continued to enjoy the pleasures of mutual and independent intercourse. But from the moment one man began to stand in need of the help of another; from the moment it appeared advantageous to any one man to have enough provisions for two, equality disappeared, property was introduced, work became indispensable, and vast forests became smiling fields, which man had to water with the sweat of his brow, and where slavery and misery were soon seen to germinate and grow up with the crops.

· · ·

The cultivation of the earth necessarily brought about its distribution; and property, once recognised, gave rise to the first rules of justice; for, to secure each man his own, it had to be possible for each to have something. Besides, as men began to look forward to the future, and all had something to lose, every one had reason to apprehend that reprisals would follow any injury he might do to another. This origin is so much the more natural, as it is impossible to conceive how property can come from anything but manual labour: for what else can a man add to things which he does not originally create, so as to make them his own property? It is the husbandman's labour alone that, giving him a title to the produce of the ground he has tilled, gives him a claim also to the land itself, at least till harvest, and so, from year to year, a constant possession which is easily transformed into property. When the ancients, says Grotius, gave to Ceres the title of Legislatrix, and to a festival celebrated in her honour the name of Thesmophoria, they meant by that that the distribution of lands had produced a new kind of right: that is to say, the right of property, which is different from the right deducible from the law of nature.

In this state of affairs, equality might have been sustained, had the talents of individuals been equal, and had, for example, the use of iron and the consumption of commodities always exactly balanced each other, but, as there was nothing to preserve this balance, it was soon disturbed; the strongest did most work; the most skilful turned his labour to best account; the most ingenious devised methods of diminishing his labour: the husbandman wanted more iron, or the smith more corn, and, while both laboured equally, the one gained a great deal by his work, while the other could hardly support himself. Thus natural inequality unfolds itself insensibly with that of combination, and the difference between men, developed by their different circumstances, becomes more sensible and permanent in its effects, and begins to have an influence, in the same proportion, over the lot of individuals.

Matters once at this pitch, it is easy to imagine the rest. I shall not detain the reader with a description of the successive invention of other arts, the development of language, the trial and utilisation of talents, the inequality of fortunes, the use and abuse of riches, and all the details connected with them which the reader can easily supply for himself. I shall confine myself to a glance at mankind in this new situation.

Behold then all human faculties developed, memory and imagination in full play, egoism interested, reason active, and the mind almost at the highest point of its perfection. Behold all the natural qualities in action, the rank and condition of every man assigned him; not merely his share of property and his power to serve or injure others, but also his wit, beauty, strength or skill, merit or talents: and these being the only qualities capable of commanding respect, it soon became necessary to possess or to affect them.

It now became the interest of men to appear what they really were not. To be and to seem became two totally different things; and from this distinction sprang insolent pomp and cheating trickery, with all the numerous vices that go in their train. On the other hand, free and independent as men were before, they were now, in consequence of a multiplicity of new wants, brought into subjection, as it were, to all nature, and particularly to one another; and each became in some degree a slave even in becoming the master of other men: if rich, they stood in need of the services of others; if poor, of their assistance; and even a middle condition did not enable them to do without one another. Man must now, therefore, have been perpetually employed in getting others to interest themselves in his lot, and in making them, apparently at least, if not really, find their advantage in promoting his own. Thus he must have been sly and artful in his behaviour to some, and imperious and cruel to others; being under a kind of necessity to ill-use all the persons of whom he stood in need, when he could not frighten them into compliance, and did not judge it his interest to be useful to them. Insatiable ambition, the thirst of raising their respective fortunes, not so much from real want as from the desire to surpass others, inspired all men with a vile propensity to injure one another, and with a secret jealousy, which is the more dangerous, as it puts on the mask of benevolence, to carry its point with greater security. In a word, there arose rivalry and competition on the one hand, and conflicting interests on the other, together with a secret desire on both of profiting at the expense of others. All these evils were the first effects of property, and the inseparable attendants of growing inequality.

Before the invention of signs to represent riches, wealth could hardly consist in anything but lands and cattle, the only real possessions men can have. But, when inheritances so increased in number and extent as to occupy the whole of the land, and to border on one another, one man could aggrandise himself only at the expense of another; at the same time the supernumeraries, who had been too weak or too indolent to make such acquisitions, and had grown poor without sustaining any loss, because, while they saw everything change around them, they remained still the same, were obliged to receive their subsistence, or steal it, from the rich; and this soon bred, according to their different characters, dominion and slavery, or violence and rapine. The wealthy, on their part, had no sooner begun to taste the pleasure of command, than they disdained all others, and, using their old slaves to acquire new, thought of nothing but subduing and enslaving their neighbours; like ravenous wolves, which, having once tasted human flesh, despise every other food and thenceforth seek only men to devour.

Thus, as the most powerful or the most miserable considered their might or misery as a kind of right to the possessions of others, equivalent, in their opinion, to that of property, the destruction of equality was attended by the most terrible disorders. Usurpations by the rich, robbery by the poor, and the unbridled passions of both, suppressed the cries of natural compassion and the still feeble voice of justice, and filled men with avarice, ambition and vice. Between the title of the strongest and that of the first occupier, there arose perpetual conflicts, which never ended but in battles and bloodshed. The new-born state of society thus gave rise to a horrible state of war; men thus harassed and depraved were no longer capable of retracing their steps or renouncing the fatal acquisitions they had made, but, labouring by the abuse of the faculties which do them honour, merely to their own confusion, brought themselves to the brink of ruin.

· · ·

It is impossible that men should not at length have reflected on so wretched a situation, and on the calamities that overwhelmed them. The rich, in particular, must have felt how much they suffered by a constant state of war, of which they bore all the expense; and in which, though all risked their lives, they alone risked their property. Besides, however speciously they might disguise their usurpations, they knew that they were founded on precarious and false titles; so that, if others took from them by force what they themselves had gained by force, they would have no reason to complain. Even those who had been enriched by their own industry, could hardly base their proprietorship on better claims. It was in vain to repeat, "I built this well; I gained this spot by my industry." Who gave you your standing, it might be answered, and what right have you to demand payment of us for doing what we never asked you to do? Do you not know that numbers of your fellow-creatures are starving, for want of what you have too much of? You ought to have had the express and universal consent of mankind, before appropriating more of the common subsistence than you needed for your own maintenance. Destitute of valid reasons to justify and sufficient strength to defend himself, able to crush individuals with ease, but easily crushed himself by a troop of bandits, one against all, and incapable, on account of mutual jealousy, of joining with his equals against numerous enemies united by the common hope of plunder, the rich man, thus urged by necessity, conceived at length the profoundest plan that ever entered the mind of man: this was to employ in his favour the forces of those who attacked him, to make allies of his adversaries, to inspire them with different maxims, and to give them other institutions as favourable to himself as the law of nature was unfavourable.

With this view, after having represented to his neighbours the horror of a situation which armed every man against the rest, and made their possessions as burdensome to them as their wants, and in which no safety could be expected either in riches or in poverty, he readily devised plausible arguments to make them close with his design. "Let us join," said he, "to guard the weak from oppression, to restrain the ambitious, and secure to every man the possession of what belongs to him: let us institute rules of justice and peace, to which all without exception may be obliged to conform; rules that may in some measure make amends for the caprices of fortune, by subjecting equally the powerful and the weak to the observance of reciprocal obligations. Let us, in a word, instead of turning our forces against ourselves, collect them in a supreme power which may govern us by wise laws, protect and defend all the members of the association, repulse their common enemies, and maintain eternal harmony among us".

Far fewer words to this purpose would have been enough to impose on men so barbarous and easily seduced; especially as they had too many disputes among themselves to do without arbitrators, and too much ambition and avarice to go long without masters. All ran headlong to their chains, in hopes of securing their liberty; for they had just wit enough to perceive the advantages of political institutions, without experience enough to enable them to foresee the dangers. The most capable of foreseeing the dangers were the very persons who expected to benefit by them; and even the most prudent judged it not inexpedient to sacrifice one part of their freedom to ensure the rest; as a wounded man has his arm cut off to save the rest of his body.

Such was, or may well have been, the origin of society and law, which bound new fetters on the poor, and gave new powers to the rich; which irretrievably destroyed natural liberty, eternally fixed the law of property and inequality, converted clever usurpation into unalterable right, and, for the advantage of a few ambitious individuals, subjected all mankind to perpetual labour, slavery and wretchedness. It is easy to see how the establishment of one community made that of all the rest necessary, and how, in order to make head against united forces, the rest of mankind had to unite in turn. Societies soon multiplied and spread over the face of the earth, till hardly a corner of the world was left in which a man could escape the yoke, and withdraw his head from beneath the sword which he saw perpetually hanging over him by a thread. Civil right having thus become the common rule among the members of each community, the law of nature maintained its place only between different communities, where, under the name of the right of nations, it was qualified by certain tacit conventions, in order to make commerce practicable, and serve as a substitute for natural compassion, which lost when applied to societies, almost all the influence it had over individuals, and survived no longer except in some great cosmopolitan spirits, who, breaking down the imaginary barriers that separate different peoples, follow the example of our Sovereign Creator, and include the whole human race in their benevolence.

But bodies politic, remaining thus in a state of nature among themselves, presently experienced the inconveniences which had obliged individuals to forsake it; for this state became still more fatal to these great bodies than it had been to the individuals of whom they were composed. Hence arose national wars, battles, murders, and reprisals, which shock nature and outrage reason; together with all those horrible prejudices which class among the virtues the honour of shedding human blood. The most distinguished men hence learned to consider cutting each other's throats a duty; at length men massacred their fellow-creatures by thousands without so much as knowing why, and committed more murders in a single day's fighting, and more violent outrages in the sack of a single town, than were committed in the state of nature during whole ages over the whole earth. Such were the first effects which we can see to have followed the division of mankind into different communities. But let us return to their institutions.

I know that some writers have given other explanations of the origin of political societies, such as the conquest of the powerful, or the association of the weak. It is, indeed, indifferent to my argument which of these causes we choose. That which I have just laid down, however, appears to me the most natural for the following reasons. First: because, in the first case, the right of conquest, being no right in itself, could not serve as a foundation on which to build any other; the victor and the vanquished people still remained with respect to each other in the state of war, unless the vanquished, restored to the full possession of their liberty, voluntarily made choice of the victor for their chief. For till then, whatever capitulation may have been made being founded on violence, and therefore *ipso facto* void, there could not have been on this hypothesis either a real society or body politic, or any law other than that of the strongest. Secondly: because the words *strong* and *weak* are, in the second case, ambiguous; for during the interval between the establishment of a right of property, or prior occupancy, and that of political government, the meaning of these words is better expressed by the terms *rich* and *poor*: because, in fact, before the institution of laws, men had no other way of reducing their equals to submission, than by attacking their goods, or making some of their own over to them. Thirdly: because, as the poor had nothing but their freedom to lose, it would have been in the highest degree absurd for them to resign voluntarily the only good they still enjoyed, without getting anything in exchange: whereas the rich having feelings, if I may so express myself, in every part of their possessions, it was much easier to harm them, and therefore more necessary for them to take precautions against it; and, in short, because it is more reasonable to suppose a thing to have been invented by those to whom it would be of service, than by those whom it must have harmed.

Government had, in its infancy, no regular and constant form. The want of experience and philosophy prevented men from seeing any but present inconveniences, and they thought of providing against others only as they presented themselves. In spite of the endeavours of the wisest legislators, the political state remained imperfect, because it was little more than the work of chance; and, as it had begun ill, though time revealed its defects and suggested remedies, the original faults were never repaired. It was continually being patched up, when the first task should have been to get the site cleared and all the old materials removed, as was done by Lycurgus at Sparta, if a stable and lasting edifice was to be erected. Society consisted at first merely of a few general conventions, which every member bound himself to observe; and for the performance of covenants the whole body went security to each individual. Experience only could show the weakness of such a constitution, and how easily it might be infringed with impunity, from the difficulty of convicting men of faults, where the public alone was to be witness and judge: the laws could not but be eluded in many ways; disorders and inconveniences could not but multiply continually, till it became necessary to commit the dangerous trust of public authority to private persons, and the care of enforcing obedience to the deliberations of the people to the magistrate. For to say that chiefs were chosen before the confederacy was formed, and that the administrators of the laws were there before the laws themselves, is too absurd a supposition to consider seriously.

It would be as unreasonable to suppose that men at first threw themselves irretrievably and unconditionally into the arms of an absolute master, and that the first expedient which proud and unsubdued men hit upon for their common security was to run headlong into slavery. For what reason, in fact, did they take to themselves superiors, if it was not in order that they might be defended from oppression, and have protection for their lives, liberties and properties, which are, so to speak, the constituent elements of their being? Now, in the relations between man and man, the worst that can happen is for one to find himself at the mercy of another, and it would have been inconsistent with common-sense to begin by bestowing on a chief the only things they wanted his help to preserve. What equivalent could he offer them for so great a right? And if he had presumed to exact it under pretext of defending them, would he not have received the answer recorded in the fable. "What more can the enemy do to us?" It is therefore beyond dispute, and indeed the fundamental maxim of all political right, that people have set up chiefs to protect their liberty, and not to enslave them. *If we have a prince*, said Pliny to Trajan, *it is to save ourselves from having a master.*

Politicians indulge in the same sophistry about the love of liberty as philosophers about the state of nature. They judge, by what they see, of very different things, which they have not seen; and attribute to man a natural propensity to servitude, because the slaves within their observation are seen to bear the yoke with patience; they fail to reflect that it is with liberty as with innocence and virtue; the value is known only to those who possess them, and the taste for them is forfeited when they are forfeited themselves. . . .

An unbroken horse erects his mane, paws the ground and starts back impetuously at the sight of the bridle; while one which is properly trained suffers patiently even whip and spur: so savage man will not bend his neck to the yoke to which civilised man submits without a murmur, but prefers the most turbulent state of liberty to the most peaceful slavery. We cannot therefore, from the servility of nations already enslaved, judge of the natural disposition of mankind for or against slavery; we should go by the prodigious efforts of every free people to save itself from oppression. . . .

⇒ "RESISTANCE TO CIVIL GOVERNMENT" ⇐
Henry David Thoreau

Henry David Thoreau (1817–1862) is best known for *Walden*, his account of the time he spent living as simply and independently as he could, in a small hut on the shore of Walden Pond. He was a fierce advocate of free individual thought and action, and he detested government interference in aspects of his life he believed should be left to his own choices. He was also strongly opposed to slavery, and a harsh critic of the U.S. invasion of Mexico, which Thoreau considered an act of imperialist bullying with the primary purpose of extending the area of slavery. Thoreau's "Resistance to Civil Government," which he wrote in 1849, was at least partially inspired by his experience of being arrested and jailed because he refused to pay a tax that he believed was primarily used to support the War against Mexico (a war he believed to be morally wrong). It is a classic defense of the right of the individual to refuse to follow the laws of his or her country when those laws are regarded as violating the conscience (or values or principles) of the individual.

After all, the practical reason why, when the power is once in the hands of the people, a majority are permitted, and for a long period continue, to rule, is not because they are most likely to be in the right, nor because this seems fairest to the minority, but because they are physically the strongest. But a government in which the majority rule in all cases cannot be based on justice, even as far as men understand it. Can there not be a government in which majorities do not virtually decide right and wrong, but conscience?—in which majorities decide only those questions to which the rule of expediency is applicable? Must the citizen ever for a moment, or in the least degree, resign his conscience to the legislator? Why has every man a conscience, then? I think that we should be men first, and subjects afterward. It is not desirable to cultivate a respect for the law, so much as for the right. The only obligation which I have a right to assume, is to do at any time what I think right. It is truly enough said, that a corporation has no conscience; but a corporation of conscientious men is a corporation *with* a conscience. Law never made men a whit more just; and, by means of their respect for it, even the well-disposed are daily made the agents of injustice. A common and natural result of an undue respect for law is, that you may see a file of soldiers, colonel, captain, corporal, privates, powder-monkeys and all, marching in admirable order over hill and dale to the wars, against their wills, aye, against their common sense and consciences, which makes it very steep marching indeed, and produces a palpitation of the heart. They have no doubt that it is a damnable business in which they are concerned; they are all peaceably inclined. Now, what are they? Men at all? or small moveable forts and magazines, at the service of some unscrupulous man in power? . . .

How does it become a man to behave toward this American government to-day? I answer that he cannot without disgrace be associated with it. I cannot for an instant recognize that political organization as *my* government which is the *slave's* government also.

All men recognize the right of revolution; that is, the right to refuse allegiance to and to resist the government, when its tyranny or its inefficiency are great and unendurable. But almost all say that such is not the case now. But such was the case, they think, in the Revolution of '75. If one were to tell me that this was a bad government because it taxed certain foreign commodities brought to its ports, it is most probable that I should not make an ado about it, for I can do without them: all machines have their friction; and possibly this does enough good to counterbalance the evil. At any rate, it is a great evil to make a stir about it. But when the friction comes to have its machine, and oppression and robbery are organized, I say, let us not have such a machine any longer. In other words, when a sixth of the population of a nation which has undertaken to be the refuge of liberty are slaves, and a whole country is unjustly overrun and conquered by a foreign army, and subjected to military law, I think that it is not too soon for honest men to rebel and revolutionize. What makes this duty the more urgent is the fact, that the country so overrun is not our own, but ours is the invading army. . . .

It is not a man's duty, as a matter of course, to devote himself to the eradication of any, even the most enormous wrong; he may still properly have other concerns to engage him; but it is his duty, at least, to wash his hands of it, and, if he gives it no thought longer, not to give it practically his support. If I devote myself to other pursuits and contemplations, I must first see, at least, that I do not pursue them sitting upon another man's shoulders. I must get off him first, that he may pursue his contemplations too. See what gross inconsistency is tolerated. I have heard some of my townsmen say, "I should like to have them order me out to help put down an insurrection of the slaves, or to march to Mexico,—see if I would go"; and yet these very men have each, directly by their allegiance, and so indirectly, at least, by their money, furnished a substitute. The soldier is applauded who refuses to serve in an unjust war by those who do not refuse to sustain the unjust government which makes the war; is applauded by those whose own act and authority he disregards and sets at nought; as if the State were penitent to that degree that it hired one to scourge it while it sinned, but not

to that degree that it left off sinning for a moment. Thus, under the name of order and civil government, we are all made at last to pay homage to and support our own meanness. After the first blush of sin, comes its indifference; and from immoral it becomes, as it were, *un*moral, and not quite unnecessary to that life which we have made.

The broadest and most prevalent error requires the most disinterested virtue to sustain it. The slight reproach to which the virtue of patriotism is commonly liable, the noble are most likely to incur. Those who, while they disapprove of the character and measures of a government, yield to it their allegiance and support, are undoubtedly its most conscientious supporters, and so frequently the most serious obstacles to reform. Some are petitioning the State to dissolve the Union, to disregard the requisitions of the President. Why do they not dissolve it themselves,—the union between themselves and the State,—and refuse to pay their quota into its treasury? Do not they stand in the same relation to the State, that the State does to the Union? And have not the same reasons prevented the State from resisting the Union, which have prevented them from resisting the State?

How can a man be satisfied to entertain an opinion merely, and enjoy *it*? Is there any enjoyment in it, if his opinion is that he is aggrieved? If you are cheated out of a single dollar by your neighbour, you do not rest satisfied with knowing that you are cheated, or with saying that you are cheated, or even with petitioning him to pay you your due; but you take effectual steps at once to obtain the full amount, and see that you are never cheated again. Action from principle,—the perception and the performance of right,—changes things and relations; it is essentially revolutionary, and does not consist wholly with any thing which was. It not only divides states and churches, it divides families; aye, it divides the *individual*, separating the diabolical in him from the divine.

Unjust laws exist: shall we be content to obey them, or shall we endeavor to amend them, and obey them until we have succeeded, or shall we transgress them at once? Men generally, under such a government as this, think that they ought to wait until they have persuaded the majority to alter them. They think that, if they should resist, the remedy would be worse than the evil. But it is the fault of the government itself that the remedy is worse than the evil. It makes it worse. Why is it not more apt to anticipate and provide for reform? Why does it not cherish its wise minority? Why does it cry and resist before it is hurt? Why does it not encourage its citizens to be on the alert to point out its faults, and *do* better than it would have them? Why does it always crucify Christ, and excommunicate Copernicus and Luther, and pronounce Washington and Franklin rebels?

One would think, that a deliberate and practical denial of its authority was the only offence never contemplated by government; else, why has it not assigned its definite, its suitable and proportionate penalty? If a man who has no property refuses but once to earn nine shillings for the State, he is put in prison for a period unlimited by any law that I know, and determined only by the discretion of those who placed him there; but if he should steal ninety times nine shillings from the State, he is soon permitted to go at large again.

If the injustice is part of the necessary friction of the machine of government, let go, let it go: perchance it will wear smooth,—certainly the machine will wear out. If the injustice has a spring, or a pulley, or a rope, or a crank, exclusively for itself, then perhaps you may consider whether the remedy will not be worse than the evil; but if it is of such a nature that it requires you to be the agent of injustice to another, then, I say, break the law. Let your life be a counter friction to stop the machine. What I have to do is to see, at any rate, that I do not lend myself to the wrong which I condemn.

As for adopting the ways which the State has provided for remedying the evil, know not of such ways. They take too much time, and a man's life will be gone. I have other affairs to attend to. I came into this world, not chiefly to make this a good place to live in, but to live in it, be it good or bad. A man has not every thing to do, but something; and because he cannot do *every thing*, it is not necessary that he should do *something* wrong. It is not my business to be petitioning the governor or the legislature any more than it is theirs to petition me; and, if they should not hear my petition, what should I do then? But in this case the State has provided no way: its very Constitution is the evil. This may seem to be harsh and stubborn and unconciliatory; but it is to treat with the utmost kindness and consideration the only spirit that can appreciate or deserves it. So is all change for the better, like birth and death which convulse the body.

I do not hesitate to say, that those who call themselves abolitionists should at once effectually withdraw their support, both in person and property, from the government of Massachusetts, and not wait till they constitute a majority of one, before they suffer the right to prevail through them. I think that it is enough if they have God on their side, without waiting for the other one. Moreover, any man more right than his neighbors, constitutes a majority of one already. . . .

Under a government which imprisons any unjustly, the true place for a just man is also a prison. The proper place to-day, the only place which Massachusetts has provided for her freer and less desponding spirits, is in her prisons, to be put out and locked out of the State by her own act, as they have already put themselves out by their principles. It is there that the fugitive slave, and the Mexican prisoner on parole, and the Indian come to plead the wrongs of his race, should find them; on that separate, but more free and honorable ground, where the State places those who are not *with* her but *against* her,—the only house in a slave-state in which a free man can abide with honor. If any think that their influence would be lost there, and their voices no longer afflict the ear of the State, that they would not be as an enemy within its walls, they do not know by how much truth is stronger than error, nor how much more eloquently and effectively he can combat injustice who has experienced a little in his own person. Cast your whole vote, not a strip of paper merely, but your whole influence. A minority is powerless while it conforms to the majority; it is not even a minority then; but it is irresistible when it clogs by its whole weight. If the alternative is to keep all just men in prison, or give up war and slavery, the State will not hesitate which to choose. If a thousand men were not to pay their tax-bills this year, that would not be a violent and bloody measure, as it would be to pay them, and enable the State to commit violence and shed innocent blood. This is, in fact, the definition of a peaceable revolution, if any such is possible. If the tax-gatherer, or any other public officer, asks me, as one has done, "But what shall I do?" my answer is, "If you really wish to do anything, resign your office." When the subject has refused allegiance, and the officer has resigned his office, then the revolution is accomplished. But even suppose blood should flow. Is there not a sort of blood shed when the conscience is wounded? Through this wound a man's real manhood and immortality flow out, and he bleeds to an everlasting death. I see this blood flowing now.

. . .

⊷ ON LIBERTY ⊷
John Stuart Mill

John Stuart Mill (1806–1873) was born in London, and was certainly the best known English philosopher of the nineteenth century. His work on economics, political philosophy, ethics, logic, and the rights of women were widely read during the nineteenth century and—particularly his writings on ethics and political philosophy—are still very influential. Mill's major works include *A System of Logic* (London, 1843); *Principles of Political Economy* (London, 1848); *On Liberty* (London, 1859); *Utilitarianism* (London, 1863); *An Examination of Sir William Hamilton's Philosophy* (London, 1865); and *The Subjection of Women* (London, 1869). His development and refinement of utilitarian ethical theory insures his place in the history of ethics, and his small treatise *On Liberty* (London, 1859)—which Mill himself thought the most likely of his books to endure, and from which the reading below is excerpted—is a perennially popular defense of freedom of thought.

INTRODUCTORY

The struggle between Liberty and Authority is the most conspicuous feature in the portions of history with which we are earliest familiar, particularly in that of Greece, Rome, and England. But in old times this contest was between subjects, or some classes of subjects, and the Government. By liberty, was meant protection against the tyranny of the political rulers. The rulers were conceived (except in some of the popular governments of Greece) as in a necessarily antagonistic position to the people whom they ruled. They consisted of a governing One, or a governing tribe or caste, who derived their authority from inheritance or conquest, who, at all events, did not hold it at the pleasure of the governed, and whose supremacy men did not venture, perhaps did not desire, to contest, whatever precautions might be taken against its oppressive exercise. Their power was regarded as necessary, but also as highly dangerous; as a weapon which they would attempt to use against their subjects, no less than against external enemies. To prevent the weaker members of the community from being preyed upon by innumerable vultures, it was needful that there should be an animal of prey stronger than the rest, commissioned to keep them down. But as the king of the vultures would be no less bent upon preying on the flock than any of the minor harpies, it was indispensable to be in a perpetual attitude of defense against his beak and claws. The aim, therefore, of patriots was to set limits to the power which the ruler should be suffered to exercise over the community; and this limitation was what they meant by liberty. It was attempted in two ways. First, by obtaining a recognition of certain immunities, called political liberties or rights, which it was to be regarded as a breach of duty in the ruler to infringe, and which,

if he did infringe, specific resistance, or general rebellion, was held to be justifiable. A second, and generally a later expedient, was the establishment of constitutional checks, by which the consent of the community, or of a body of some sort, supposed to represent its interests, was made a necessary condition to some of the more important acts of the governing power. To the first of these modes of limitation, the ruling power, in most European countries, was compelled, more or less, to submit. It was not so with the second; and, to attain this, or when already in some degree possessed, to attain it more completely, became everywhere the principal object of the lovers of liberty. And so long as mankind were content to combat one enemy by another, and to be ruled by a master, on condition of being guaranteed more or less efficaciously against his tyranny, they did not carry their aspirations beyond this point.

A time, however, came, in the progress of human affairs, when men ceased to think it a necessity of nature that their governors should be an independent power, opposed in interest to themselves. It appeared to them much better that the various magistrates of the State should be their tenants or delegates, revocable at their pleasure. In that way alone, it seemed, could they have complete security that the powers of government would never be abused to their disadvantage. By degrees this new demand for elective and temporary rulers became the prominent object of the exertions of the popular part, wherever any such part existed; and superseded, to a considerable extent, the previous efforts to limit the power of rulers. As the struggle proceeded for making the ruling power emanate from the periodical choice of the ruled, some persons began to think that too much importance had been attached to the limitation of the power itself. *That* (it might seem) was a resource against rulers whose interests were habitually opposed to those of the people. What was now wanted was, that the rulers should be identified with the people; that their interest and will should be the interest and will of the nation. The nation did not need to be protected against its own will. There was no fear of its tyrannizing over itself. Let the rulers be effectually responsible to it, promptly removable by it, and it could afford to trust them with power of which it could itself dictate the use to be made. Their power was but the nation's own power, concentrated, and in a form convenient for exercise. This mode of thought, or rather perhaps of feeling, was common among the last generation of European liberalism, in the Continental section of which it still apparently predominates. Those who admit any limit to what a government may do, except in the case of such governments as they think ought not to exist, stand out as brilliant exceptions among the political thinkers of the Continent. A similar tone of sentiment might by this time have been prevalent in our own country, if the circumstances which for a time encouraged it, had continued unaltered.

But, in political and philosophical theories, as well as in persons, success discloses faults and infirmities which failure might have concealed from observation. The notion, that the people have no need to limit their power over themselves, might seem axiomatic, when popular government was a thing only dreamed about, or read of as having existed at some distant period of the past. Neither was that notion necessarily disturbed by such temporary aberrations as those of the French Revolution, the worst of which were the work of an usurping few, and which, in any case, belonged, not to the permanent working of popular institutions, but to a sudden and convulsive outbreak against monarchical and aristocratic despotism. In time, however, a democratic republic came to occupy a large portion of the earth's surface, and made itself felt as one of the most powerful members of the community of nations; and elective and responsible government became subject to the observations and criticisms which wait upon a great existing fact. It was now perceived that such phrases as "self-government," and "the power of the people over themselves," do not express the true state of the case. The "people" who exercised; and the "self-government" spoken of is not the government of each by himself, but of each by all the rest. The will of the people, moreover, practically means the will of the most numerous or the most active *part* of the people; the majority, or those who succeed in making themselves accepted as the majority; the people, consequently, *may* desire to oppress a part of their number; and precautions are as much needed against this as against any other abuse of power. The limitation, therefore, of the power of government over individuals loses none of its importance when the holders of power are regularly accountable to the community, that is, to the strongest party therein. This view of things, recommending itself equally to the intelligence of thinkers and to the inclination of those important classes in European society to whose real or supposed interests democracy is adverse, has had no difficulty in establishing itself; and in political speculations "the tyranny of the majority" is now generally included among the evils against which society requires to be on its guard.

Like other tyrannies, the tyranny of the majority was at first, and is still vulgarly, held in dread, chiefly as operating through the acts of the public authorities. But reflecting persons perceived that when society is itself the tyrant—society collectively, over the separate individuals who compose it—its means of tyrannizing are not restricted to the acts which it may do by the hands of its political functionaries. Society can and does execute its own mandates: and if it issues wrong mandates instead of right, or any mandates at all in things with which it ought not to meddle, it practices a social tyranny more formidable than many kinds of political oppression, since, though not usually upheld by such extreme penalties, it leaves fewer means of escape, penetrating much more deeply into the details of life, and enslaving the soul itself. Protection, therefore, against the tyranny of the magistrate is not enough: there needs protection also against the tyranny of the prevailing opinion and feeling; against the tendency of society to impose, by other means than civil penalties, its own ideas and practices as rules of conduct on those who dissent from them; to fetter the development, and, if possible, prevent the formation, of any individuality not in harmony with its ways, and compel all characters to fashion themselves upon the model of its own. There is a limit to the legitimate interference of collective opinion with individual independence: and to find that limit, and maintain it against encroachment, is as indispensable to a good condition of human affairs, as protection against political despotism.

But though this proposition is not likely to be contested in general terms, the practical question, where to place the limit—how to make the fitting adjustment between individual independence and social control—is a subject on which nearly everything remains to be done. All that makes existence valuable to any one, depends on the enforcement of restraints upon the actions of other people. Some rules of conduct, therefore, must be imposed, by law in the first place, and by opinion on many things which are not fit subjects for the operation of law. What these rules should be, is the principal question in human affairs; but if we except a few of the most obvious cases, it is one of those which least progress has been made in resolving. No two ages, and scarcely any two countries, have decided it alike; and the decision of one age or country is a wonder to another. Yet the people of any given age and country no more suspect any difficulty in it, than if it were a subject on which mankind had always been agreed. The rules which obtain among themselves appear to them self-evident and self-justifying. This all but universal illusion is one of the examples of the magical influence of custom, which is not only, as the proverb says, a second nature, but is continually mistaken for the first. The effect of custom, in preventing any misgiving respecting the rules of conduct which mankind impose on one another, is all the more complete because the subject is one on which it is not generally considered necessary that reasons should be given, either by one person to others, or by each to himself. People are accustomed to believe, and have been encouraged in the belief by some who aspire to the character of philosophers, that their feelings, on subjects of this nature, are better than reasons, and render reasons unnecessary. The practical principle which guides them to their opinions on the regulation of human conduct, is the feeling in each person's mind that everybody should be required to act as he, and those with whom he sympathizes, would like them to act. No one, indeed, acknowledges to himself that his standard of judgment is his own liking; but an opinion on a point of conduct, not supported by reasons, can only count as one person's preference; and if the reasons, when given are a mere appeal to a similar preference felt by other people, it is still only many people's liking instead of one. To an ordinary man, however, his own preference, thus supported, is not only a perfectly satisfactory reason, but the only one he generally has for any of his notions of morality, taste, or propriety, which are not expressly written in his religious creed; and his chief guide in the interpretation even of that. Men's opinions, accordingly, on what is laudable or blameable, are affected by all the multifarious causes which influence their wishes in regard to the conduct of others, and which are as numerous as those which determine their wishes on any other subject. Sometimes their reason—at other times their prejudices or superstitions: often their social affections, not seldom their antisocial ones, their envy or jealousy, their arrogance or contemptuousness: but most commonly, their desires or fears for themselves—their legitimate or illegitimate self-interest. Wherever there is an ascendant class, a large portion of the morality of the country emanates from its class interests, and its feelings of class superiority. The morality between Spartans and Helots, between planters and negroes, between princes and subjects, between nobles and roturiers, between men and women, has been for the most part the creation of these class interests and feelings: and the sentiments thus generated, react in turn upon the moral feelings of the members of the ascendant class, in their relations among themselves. Where, on the other hand, a class, formerly ascendant, has lost its ascendancy, or where its ascendancy is unpopular, the prevailing moral sentiments frequently bear the impress of an impatient dislike of superiority. Another grand determining principle of the rules of conduct, both in act and forbearance, which have been enforced by law or opinion, has been the servility of mankind towards the supposed preferences or aversions of their temporal masters, or of their gods. This servility, though essentially selfish, is not hypocrisy; it gives rise to perfectly genuine sentiments of abhorrence; it made men burn magicians and heretics. Among so many baser influences, the general and obvious interests of society have of course had a share, and a large one, in the direction of the moral sentiments: less, however, as a matter of reason, and on their own account, than as a consequence of the sympathies and antipathies which grew out of them: and sympathies and antipathies which had little or nothing to do with the interests of society, have made themselves felt in the establishment of moralities with quite as great force.

The likings and dislikings of society, or of some powerful portion of it, are thus the main thing which has practically determined the rules laid down for general observance, under the penalties of law or opinion. And in general, those who have been in advance of society in thought and feeling, have left this condition of things unassailed in principle, however they may have come into conflict with it in some of its details. They have occupied themselves rather in inquiring what things society ought to like or dislike, than in questioning whether its likings or dislikings should be a law to individuals. They preferred endeavoring to alter the feelings of mankind on the particular points on which they were themselves heretical, rather than make common cause in defense of freedom, with heretics generally. The only case in which the higher ground has been taken on principle and maintained with consistency, by any but an individual here and there, is that of religious belief: a case instructive in many ways, and not least so as forming a most striking instance of the fallibility of what is called the moral sense: for the *odium theologicum*, in a sincere bigot, is one of the most unequivocal cases of moral feeling. Those who first broke the yoke of what called itself the Universal Church, were in general as little willing to permit difference of religious opinion as that church itself. But when the heat of the conflict was over, without giving a complete victory to any party, and each church or sect was reduced to limit its hopes to retaining possession of the ground it already occupied; minorities, seeing that they had no chance of becoming majorities, were under the necessity of pleading to those whom they could not convert, for permission to differ. It is accordingly on this battle-field, almost solely, that the rights of the individual against society have been asserted on broad grounds of principle, and the claim of society to exercise authority over dissentients, openly controverted. The great writers to whom the world owes what religious liberty it possesses, have mostly asserted freedom of conscience as an indefeasible right, and denied absolutely that a human being is accountable to others for his religious belief. Yet so natural to mankind is intolerance in whatever they really care about, that religious freedom has hardly anywhere been practically realized, except where religious indifference, which dislikes to have its peace disturbed by theological quarrels, has added its weight to the scale. In the minds of almost all religious persons, even in the most tolerant countries, the duty of toleration is admitted with tacit reserves. One person will bear with dissent in matters of church government, but not of dogma; another can tolerate everybody, short of a Papist or a Unitarian; another, every one who believes in revealed religion; a few extend their charity a little further, but stop at the belief in a God and in a future state. Wherever the sentiment of the majority is still genuine and intense, it is found to have abated little of its claim to be obeyed.

In England, from the peculiar circumstances of our political history, though the yoke of opinion is perhaps heavier, that of law is lighter, than in most other countries of Europe; and there is considerable jealousy of direct interference, by the legislative or the executive power, with private conduct; not so much from any just regard for the independence of the individual, as from the still subsisting habit of looking on the government as representing an opposite interest to the public. The majority have not yet learnt to feel the power of the government their power, or its opinions their opinions. When they do so, individual liberty will probably be as much exposed to invasion from the government, as it already is from public opinion. But, as yet, there is a considerable amount of feeling ready to be called forth against any attempt of the law to control individuals in things in which they have not hitherto been accustomed to be controlled by it; and this with very little discrimination as to whether the matter is, or is not, within the legitimate sphere of legal control; insomuch that the feeling, highly salutary on the whole, is perhaps quite as often misplaced as well grounded in the particular instances of its application. There is, in fact, no recognized principle by which the propriety or impropriety of government interference is customarily tested. People decide according to their personal preferences. Some, whenever they see any good to be done, or evil to be remedied, would willingly instigate the government to undertake the business; while others prefer to bear almost any amount of social evil, rather than add one to the departments of human interests amenable to governmental control. And men range themselves on one or the other side in any particular case, according to this general direction of their sentiments; or according to the degree of interest which they feel in the particular thing which it is proposed that the government should do, or according to the belief they entertain that the government would, or would not, do it in the manner they prefer; but very rarely on account of any opinion to which they consistently adhere, as to what things are fit to be done by a government. And it seems to me that in consequence of this absence of rule or principle, one side is at present as often wrong as the other; the interference of government is, with about equal frequency, improperly invoked and improperly condemned.

The object of this Essay is to assert one very simple principle, as entitled to govern absolutely the dealings of society with the individual in the way of compulsion and control, whether the means used be physical force in the form of legal penalties, or the moral coercion of public opinion. That principle is, that the sole end for which mankind are warranted, individually or collectively, in interfering with the liberty of action of any of their number, is self-protection. That the only purpose for which power can be rightfully exercised over any member of a civilized community, against his will, is to prevent harm to others. His own good, either physical or moral, is not a sufficient warrant. He cannot rightfully be compelled to do or forbear because it will be better for him to do so, because it will make him happier, because, in the opinions of others, to do so would be wise, or even right. These are good reasons for remonstrating with him, or reasoning with him, or persuading him, or entreating him, but not for compelling him, or visiting with any evil in case he do otherwise. To justify that, the conduct from which it is desired to deter him, must be calculated to produce evil to some one else. The only part of the conduct of any one, for which he is amenable to society, is that which concerns others. In the part which merely concerns himself, his independence is, of right, absolute. Over himself, over his own body and mind, the individual is sovereign. . . .

But there is a sphere of action in which society, as distinguished from the individual, has, if any, only an indirect interest; comprehending all that portion of a person's life and conduct which affects only himself, or if it also affects others, only with their free, voluntary, and undeceived consent and participation. When I say only himself, I mean directly, and in the first instance: for whatever affects himself, may affect others through himself; and the objection which may be grounded on this contingency will receive consideration in the sequel. This, then, is the appropriate region of human liberty. It comprises, first, the inward domain of consciousness; demanding liberty of conscience, in the most comprehensive sense; liberty of thought and feeling; absolute freedom of opinion and sentiment on all subjects, practical or speculative, scientific, moral, or theological. The liberty of expressing and publishing opinions may seem to fall under a different principle, since it belongs to that part of the conduct of an individual which concerns other people; but, being almost of as much importance as the liberty of thought itself, and resting in great part on the same reasons, is practically inseparable from it. Secondly, the principle requires liberty of tastes and pursuits; of framing the plan of our life to suit our own character; of doing as we like, subject to such consequences as may follow: without impediment from our fellow creatures, so long as what we do does not harm them, even though they should think our conduct foolish, perverse, or wrong. Thirdly, from this liberty of each individual, follows the liberty, within the same limits, of combination among individuals; freedom to unite, for any purpose not involving harm to others: the persons combining being supposed to be of full age, and not forced or deceived.

No society in which these liberties are not, on the whole, respected, is free, whatever may be its form of government; and none is completely free in which they do not exist absolute and unqualified. The only freedom which deserves the name, is that of pursuing our own good in our own way, so long as we do not attempt to deprive others of theirs, or impede their efforts to obtain it. Each is the proper guardian of his own health, whether bodily, or mental and spiritual. Mankind are greater gainers by suffering each other to live as seems good to themselves, than by compelling each to live as seems good to the rest.

⊰ "Liberty and Justice" ⊰
Eric Mack

Eric Mack is Professor of Philosophy at Tulane University and a member of the Murphy Institute of Political Economy. A strong advocate of libertarian political thought and a sturdy critic of positive liberty positions, he has published widely on property rights, distributive justice, and philosophy of law.

In the following articles, Eric Mack argues in favor of the libertarian system of "rugged individualism," while Hugh LaFollette critiques that view and champions a more cooperative and mutually supportive society. A fundamental dispute between the two is which model is actually more protective and supportive of individual liberty; and central to that debate is the distinction between positive and negative rights. Mack insists on limiting rights to the negative variety: basically, rights of noninterference. LaFollette favors a broader account that also includes positive rights: rights to resources that enhance one's opportunity to exercise liberty.

LIBERTY AND JUSTICE

My thesis in this essay is that a coherent and attractive program for decentralization and participation on the one hand and for justice on the other hand can be found in the implementation of what I will call, alternatively, a Lockean or libertarian theory of rights. Since the central value expressed in such a theory of rights is respect for the liberty of persons, I shall be arguing that respect for liberty carries with it decentralization, participation, and justice. The emphasis in the first section on decentralization and participation serves to highlight the central role of free market institutions and transactions in any likely society in which persons' Lockean rights are respected. In such a society political institutions and practices will be replaced by forms of voluntary association. And market transactions and relationships are paradigmatically voluntary. Although I would argue that full implementation of persons' rights would require that the State itself be abolished, for present purposes we can image the State as continuing on the scene in nightwatchman form. That is, we shall image a State which is successfully restricted to protecting the Lockean rights of individuals. In the following section, I defend the conception of liberty (and the conception of coercion) that has been employed in this essay and show the congruence between respect for liberty and respect for just holdings. In this section the value of liberty, specifically the wrongness of inflicting coercion upon people, is shown to underlie the entitlement conception of just holdings.

Lockean Rights and Market Relationships

According to the Lockean or libertarian view of rights, each person possesses a natural moral right to life and liberty—i.e., a moral right to freedom from coercion of his person or of his activity. Each person possesses these rights against all other men and correlatively each person is under a natural moral obligation not to coerce any other person. Furthermore, persons may acquire property rights to various external objects—to fields, tools, and so on—by laboring upon or producing them or by acquiring them by voluntary transfer from parties who (until the transfer) respectively had rights to them. Whatever the philosophical difficulties connected with clarifying and defending these Lockean claims, their general import is clear enough. As Locke puts it, each man is by nature "absolute lord of his own person and possessions".

. . .

We can imagine what could be called a premarket Lockean society. Trade and contractual rights and obligations do not exist. Each (surviving) person is propertied and self-sufficient. Here we have the epitome of economic and social decentralization. Each exercises his lordship over his own domain and does just as he sees fit with it, coordinating his actions with those of others only in the negative sense of not interfering with their comparable lordship. To enjoy liberty is not to enjoy everything or even everything worth enjoying. Rather, to enjoy liberty is to stand in a certain relationship to other persons. It is to be free of disruptions caused by other persons in the ongoing activities which constitute one's life.

Although no one is obligated to do so, it is tremendously in persons' interests to move away from the type of social and economic isolation that would characterize a premarket society. Typically, there are many things within a person's domain—e.g., his labor or some of the products he has produced—which he would be eager to exchange for things within the domain of another who is himself eager for such an exchange. Most such exchanges lead to the possibility and desirability of additional exchanges. Similarly persons may agree, not so much to exchanges, but to engage in various joint activities, partying, churchgoing, etc. Voluntary agreements or permissions lower or relocate the initial fences between persons and do so on terms which are preferred over the status quo by all the parties involved. It would be tedious to list all the ways in which business, unions, fraternal societies, charitable organizations, and so on, might appear within the vast, multilayered web of associations which free agreement among individuals would produce—at least when individuals are secure in their domains and secure in their expectations that the rights generated by agreement, both simple and complex, will be respected.

Of course, two societies which were equally the product of such a complex of agreements and voluntary coordinations might be quite different—the differences being traceable to variations in culture and aesthetics, in technological levels and natural resources, and in the reflections of these and other factors in personal and individual preferences. But a central feature of any such contractual society would be the production of goods and services "for the market"—i.e., the production by firms, cooperatives, individuals or whatever of goods and services for the purpose of sale to other parties. Wanting what they can get in exchange for goods and services, producers will tend to provide those goods and services for which the demand is strongest and will tend to utilize in their production those resources which are least in demand. Hence the tendency toward efficiency in production for the market. Although the market will be central to all societies in which persons' Lockean rights are respected and persons do not live as self-supporting hermits, we should not think that all the associations and coordinations among individuals in such a society will be, in an interesting sense, economic.

With respect to decentralization, the Lockean market society seems to capture whatever is desirable about premarket decentralization, while including other dimensions of decentralization. Each individual remains free to maintain a premarket isolation, no matter how discomforting this is to him or how annoying it is to those who would have him engage in various social roles. Of course, it would be a rare person who, without having previously entered social relations, would have the skills and resources available for a commodious, isolated life. But what remains crucial is that no one is ever *coerced* into cooperation with others and each person retains throughout his life (complexities arising from long-term contractual relationships aside) the freedom to separate himself from the doings of others, i.e., a freedom to secede from some particular or all associations. All decisions about any single person's life and property are centered in that given person. Similarly, whenever a decision is made about the disposition of the lives, activities, or properties of more than one party—a decision about an exchange or some coordinated activity—the decision is centered in just those individuals whose persons or property are involved. Nobody whose life or property is not involved has any say whatsoever. Thus, decision-making is radically decentralized, not by any political decree, but rather by respecting the moral injunction: Do not cross the boundaries defined by persons' rights. Given the Lockean conception of rights, this injunction rules out participation in the sense of having a say in the doings of society at large. . . .

Negative Liberty and Entitlement

A good deal of resistance to the thesis presented previously will stem from dissatisfaction with the conception of coercion and the correlative conception of (negative) liberty which I employ. There are also likely to be doubts about making the demand that coercion be eschewed or, correlatively, that liberty be respected, the supreme social–political principle. In response to these dissatisfactions and

doubts, I present, in a very abbreviated fashion, a two-stage argument. First I provide a more precise specification of coercion which shows that the acts which are impermissible turn out to be coercive (violations of liberty) and the acts which have been deemed permissible turn out to be noncoercive (nonviolations of liberty). Second, I argue that the demand for noncoercion as specified, i.e., respect for liberty, should be accepted as the supreme social principle.

Characteristic of dissatisfaction with the conceptions of coercion and liberty which I use is this argument offered by James Sterba. Comparing Social Security taxation of persons with cases of hiring for low wages, he writes:

> . . . how can requiring a person to pay $500.00 into a social security program under threat of greater financial loss infringe upon the person's liberty when requiring a person to take a job paying $500.00 less under threat of greater financial loss does not infringe upon the person's liberty? Surely it would seem that if one requirement restricts a person's liberty, the other will also.

The implications of such arguments are that liberty can be denied in more ways than are recognized by the libertarian and that it may be necessary and proper, even in the name of liberty itself, to limit the liberties held dear by libertarians in order to thwart the denial of liberties not recognized by them.

There is both a short and a long answer to Sterba's argument. The short answer is that in the first case what is threatened is the deprivation of something to which the threatened party has a right, while in the second case what is "threatened" (by whom?) is that no employer is around who will offer more of his money to the job-seeker than is currently being offered. This is why the Social Security case involves treating a person objectionably while the job-seeker case does not. But this short answer does not differentiate between the case in terms of liberty (or coercion). To get an answer in terms of coercion one must argue that to be deprived of, or to be threatened with the nonconsensual deprivation of, justly held possessions (the Social Security case) is to be coerced, is to suffer a violation of liberty, while not to be offered what are some other party's justly held possessions is not to be coerced, is not to suffer a violation of liberty. That is, one deepens the (short) property rights answer into an answer in terms of coercion (or liberty) by showing that person A can be so related to an object that to deprive him of it without his consent is to coerce him and that it is in virtue of being so related to an object that A is entitled to (has a right to) it. Hence, if A is entitled to an object, then his being nonconsensually deprived of it is coercive. This deepening of the property rights answer into the answer in terms of coercion will also show why the demand for noncoercion encompasses the demand that persons' just holdings (their entitlements) be respected.

In very brief form the argument runs as follows: The just acquisition of object O by person A involves an intentional investment by A of his time and effort which results in O's becoming an instrument of A's (ongoing though, perhaps, intermittent) purposes. Since coercion involves nonconsensual interference with/into an agent's purposeful activity, an agent's being nonconsensually deprived of what he has justly acquired is coercive. In contrast, failure to provide someone with some object, service, etc., does not involve such interference with/into his activity with that (possible) instrument of activity. It is one thing not to provide another with the means for certain activities and quite another thing to intervene into his (ongoing) activity. If A justly holds O, B can acquire O noncoercively only with A's consent. Otherwise B will acquire O by nonconsensually depriving another party (A) of what is already an instrument of that party's (ongoing) purposes. On this sort of basis I claim that failure to provide a person with some object never is coercive, never is a violation of liberty, while depriving a person of what he has acquired as an instrument of his purposes (without depriving another of an acquired instrument of his purposes) is always coercive, is always a violation of liberty.

In Sterba's Social Security case a person is genuinely threatened with a coercive act, i.e., with an intervention into his purposeful activity or with a nonconsensual deprivation of something which he has (noncoercively) made an instrument of his purposeful activity. But in Sterba's job-seeker case no comparable intervention or disruption is "threatened". It is not as though the job-seeker has had an offer of a better-paying job his acceptance of which has been disrupted or blocked. The job-seeker's complaint is not that he has suffered some intervention but rather that he has not been offered a certain opportunity by, say, some employer.

The person who is required to participate in Social Security is coerced because he is threatened with a coercive act. That is, he is threatened with interference into his ongoing purposeful activity either in the form of an imposed loss in his capacity to move his body as and where he sees fit or an imposed loss in his capacity to utilize some other object which is an instrument of his purposes. We can say that he is threatened with being deprived of something to which he has a right (something to which he is morally entitled) because he is being threatened with a deprivation which would be coercive. It is the coerciveness of a person's loss of (capacity to use) an object which makes it wrongful for another to impose that loss. And it is because others are obligated not to impose that loss that the person who would suffer the coercive loss has a right to the object involved. An agent's right to any object rests on his being so related to it that nonconsensually depriving him of it constitutes coercion. Hence, it is the demand for noncoercion, for each person's liberty being respected, which underlies each person's moral titles (including each person's moral title to his own body, which can be seen as necessarily an instrument of his purposes). Insofar as justice is the condition of persons' possessing that to which they respectively are entitled, the call for liberty is also a call for justice.

On the entitlement view, each person is entitled to what he intentionally acquires from nature and from others in voluntary transfers or through voluntary mutual endeavors and which he has not abandoned or traded away. A person is entitled to whatever holdings result from economic activity in which he exercises his Lockean rights and violates no one's Lockean rights. If the holdings of each member of some group are the result of such a rights-respecting process, then the distribution of holdings within the group is just. If members of this group were to have engaged in different rights-respecting economic moves, e.g., different voluntary exchanges or different use of their resources, a different distribution of holdings would have been produced. And had that distribution, in fact, been produced by rights-respecting procedures, then it would have been just. For, what distribution is just depends upon how persons, individually and cooperatively, have exercised their respective rights. But a just distribution can only arise when people are left free to exercise these rights. So the strategy for producing distributive justice must be the procedural strategy of leaving people free to engage in (any) rights-respecting economic activities. Although economically free persons might choose to be economic hermits (i.e., to remain in premarket Lockean relationships) or might agree to economic communalism, it is likely that most individuals and communes will not choose to be communally related to others. Rather, they will opt for instances of economic interaction and association which will generate a complex market-centered society. Thus, the very social system which recommends itself to us in terms of decentralization and participation and in terms of liberty recommends itself to us in terms of justice.

This program of liberty and justice turns on the view that the only rights which individuals possess against one another—other than the special rights that are traceable to specific, concrete, and noncoerced agreements—are rights against interference. However, it is often asserted, e.g., in Peter Singer's "Rights and the Market," that in some way this conception of rights faultily ignores the fact that we are "social beings". If we were but to attend to this fact a different moral perspective would be forthcoming. Now, if we take the claim that we are social beings as indicative of some sort of radical organicism, then it is clear that such a different moral perspective is called for. We are each really just parts of a greater, living, striving whole whose well-being is the morally relevant issue. And so on. But, short of this sort of organicism, what is the relevance, faultily missed by the libertarian, of the fact that we live in communities (some politically better than others), that we interact along all sorts of dimensions, that we often see ourselves through the eyes of others, or whatever? After all, the libertarian theorist himself focuses upon the manifold interactions among persons for the purpose of answering the normative question, Which are permissible and which are impermissible? As do competing theorists, he focuses upon all the claimed or recognized rights and obligations and offers a theory about which of them are well-founded.

The vagueness of the "social beings" gambit appears in Singer's own statement of its relevance.

> If we reject the idea of independent individuals and start with people living together in a community, it is by no means obvious that rights must be restricted to rights against interference. When people live together, they may be born into, grow up with, and live in, a web of rights and obligations which include obligations to help others in need, and rights to be helped oneself when in need.

First, we might pause at the contrast between "independent individuals" and "people living together in a community." Second, we should note that one need not reject the idea of independent individuals and so on in order to realize that "it is by no means obvious that rights must be restricted to rights against interference." This libertarian thesis is not obvious—but that does not mean that it is false. Third, it indeed "may be" that when people live together there is a web of well-founded rights and obligations of a positive sort. Whether there is, of course, is a matter of philosophical debate. Furthermore, supposing that there are certain well-founded positive rights and obligations among individuals, the next question is, on what are they founded? For on the libertarian view such webs of rights and obligations among individuals do arise in the formation of voluntary social relationships. The challenge posed by libertarian theory to other theories is for them to indicate a plausible basis for positive rights and obligations other than (or in addition to) the contractual basis. This challenge is not met by reminding us that people live together in communities.

But should liberty (and with it justice-as-entitlement) be accepted as the supreme social-political principle? In its demanding version this question requires nothing less than a full philosophical grounding for the natural right against coercion. It seems that such a grounding would focus on the need to recognize each person's status as a moral end-in-himself. It would see the obligation not to coerce as a moral side-constraint on our actions toward others which proceeds from the fact that all persons are morally on an equal footing as purposive beings whose lives have value, while there is no overarching value which can justify the subordination of one person's life or activity to the purposes of others. The general fact that for each person his life is a separate and ultimate value is recognized in human interaction by respect for liberty, i.e., by not subordinating anyone's life or any portion or aspect thereof to anyone else's ends.

In *Anarchy, State and Utopia*, Robert Nozick cites, as the notions and contentions that motivate the natural rights (against coercion) point of view, the "principle that individuals are ends and not merely means; they may not be sacrificed or used for the achieving of other ends without their consent," and the views that, "To use a person . . . does not sufficiently respect and take account of the fact that he is a separate person, that his is the only life he has," and "that there are different individuals with separate lives and so no one may be sacrificed for others. . . . " And in characterizing the ideal of negative liberty, Isaiah Berlin says,

> To threaten a man with persecution unless he submits to a life in which he exercises no choices of his goals; to block before him every door but one, no matter how noble the prospect upon which it opens, or how benevolent the motives of those who arrange this, is *to sin against the truth that he is a man, a being with a life of his own to live.*

But it cannot be the (mere) fact of the separateness of persons or the (mere) fact that each has only his own life that underlies persons' rights (i.e., the wrongfulness of coercing persons). For these facts might be seen as calling for a program of remaking and unifying all persons into one great social sponge. What underlies rights must, at least in part, be the value, desirability, or rightness of persons being separate beings, each having his own life and living it. One could only *sin* against a person's being a being with a life of his own to live if his having and living his own life is what ought to be.

We should not forget that in choosing a supreme social-political principle we are choosing a principle which is to be backed by the police power of legal institutions. Awareness of the philosophical difficulty of establishing the existence of duties so fundamental that police power may properly be brought against individuals to further compliance should dispose us favorably to modest ascriptions of social-political duties. Similarly, a recognition of the disvalue of bringing police power to bear against individuals and of the disvalue of whatever contributes to a propensity to bring this power to bear should dispose

us toward modest ascriptions of duty. It is, then, an attractive feature of the principle of negative liberty that it requires only that persons not coerce—that they leave their neighbors in peace. Justice-as-entitlement requires only that persons not deprive others of what they have noncoercively acquired. Yet, compliance with these modest requirements has the strong justice-like consequence that all parties to all exchanges and mutual endeavors benefit (at least in their own eyes). No one ever benefits by imposing a cost, in loss of freedom of movement or loss of legitimately acquired holdings, on anyone else. No one is ever required to suffer an invasion of his person, liberty, or property for the sake of that moment's version of vital social interests.

Finally, to endorse freedom from coercion (and, therefore, justice-as-entitlement) as the supreme social-political principle is not to forgo interest in the realization of other values. Rather, values such as efficiency, social and economic mobility, a relatively high correlation between deserts and rewards, and steady improvement in the general standard of living are among the values which libertarians see as *consequences* of liberty (and the justice involved in liberty). Indeed, no social goal (not to mention private goals) is precluded by the recognition of respect for negative liberty as the supreme principle. Persons remain free to pursue as ardently as they desire any social ideal whatsoever and are only constrained in the means which they may employ in these pursuits. Unlike alternative principles, the enshrinement of liberty does not impose upon any individual the goals of others. It merely envisions for each a respect for, and an immunity for, his own peaceful pursuits.

"WHY LIBERTARIANISM IS MISTAKEN"
Hugh LaFollette

Hugh LaFollette holds the Marie and Leslie E. Cole Chair in Ethics at the University of South Florida. In addition to editing a number of important works in ethics (including the *Oxford Handbook for Practical Ethics* and the *Blackwell Guide to Ethical Theory*), he has written several books and a number of very influential articles in applied ethics (many of which have been widely reprinted).

In "Why Libertarianism Is Mistaken," LaFollette disputes Mack's claim that liberty is best promoted and protected by libertarian individualism, arguing that if our goal is genuine promotion of the broadest possible liberty for everyone, then we must take positive steps to provide genuine opportunities for exercising liberty; without such support, many people will lack the necessary means for making effective choices and pursuing their own goals and actually enjoying liberty.

Why Libertarianism Is Mistaken

Taxing the income of some people to provide goods or services to others, even those with urgent needs, is unjust. It is a violation of the wage earner's rights, a restriction of his freedom. At least that is what the libertarian tells us. I disagree. Not all redistribution of income is unjust; or so I shall argue.

Libertarianism has experienced a noticeable re-emergence in the past few years. F. A. Hayek, Milton Friedman, and Robert Nozick have given new intellectual impetus to the movement while a growing concern for personal autonomy has provided personal ground for the sowing of the idea. Yet even though this theory is prima facie plausible and demands serious reassessment of the concepts of liberty and property, it ultimately fails. Once we admit, as the libertarian does, that the state justifiably takes on certain functions, for example, police protection of persons and property, there is no rational basis for believing that the state is unjustified in redistributing tax revenue. We cannot stop, as the libertarian suggests, with the minimal state of classical liberal philosophy. I will not, in this paper, say exactly how far beyond the minimal state we should go. I only argue that libertarianism is not a moral option. On the surface this conclusion seems meager, yet its implications are far-reaching. By eliminating a previously plausible and popular conception of distributive justice, we will narrow the alternatives. By identifying a major flaw in libertarianism, we will secure direction in our search for an adequate theory.

After briefly describing libertarianism I will argue that the theory is guilty of internal incoherence: the theory falls prey to the very objection it offers against competing theories. Then I will consider . . . possible libertarian replies to my argument. Each, I will claim, fails to disarm my internal objection. After concluding my argument, I will speculate on the roles freedom and property should play in an adequate theory of distributive justice.

A Description of Libertarianism

Central to libertarianism is the claim that individuals should be free from the interference of others. Personal liberty is the supreme moral good. Hence, one's liberty can justifiably be restricted only if he consents to the restriction. Any other restriction, including taxing incomes for purposes of redistribution, is unjust. Or the libertarian may couch his theory in the language of rights: each individual has natural negative rights to at least life, liberty, and property. No one can justifiably harm him, restrict his freedom, or take his property—that is, no one can violate his rights—without his consent. Moreover, these are general (*in rem*) rights; they apply, so to speak, against the whole world. And since rights invariably have correlative duties, all the people in the world have the duty not to interfere with the right holder's life, liberty, and property. Each person possesses these rights simply in virtue of his humanity—he does not have to *do* anything to obtain this moral protection. The possession of rights does not depend upon the consent of others. They are essential moral constituents of personhood.

However, we should note that these two ways of speaking seem to amount to the same thing for the libertarian. Libertarian theorists often move back and forth between talk of negative rights and talk of liberty. I suspect that is because they ultimately see rights and liberty as equivalent or because they hold a theory of rights which is grounded in personal liberty. That is, the libertarian might say, the *reason* we have all and only libertarian rights (absolute negative rights to life, liberty, property, etc.) is that these rights protect individual liberty. Hence, on both models liberty is fundamental.

Libertarianism also contends that in certain prescribed circumstances there can be positive *in personam* rights, that is, that individual X has a positive right to, say, $1,000 and someone else Y has a positive duty to give X that money. These positive rights, however, are not natural rights; they are not possessed by all persons just because they are persons. They can arise only consensually. For example, if A promises B that he will serve as a lifeguard at B's swimming pool, then B has a right against A and A has a duty to B—a duty to guard those in B's pool. But unless A so consents, he has no positive duties to B, or to anyone else for that matter. Consequently, for the libertarian, there are no general positive duties and no general positive rights. There are only *alleged* general positive rights; claims to such rights (or of such duties) are mistaken. For if there were positive general duties we would have to violate negative general rights to satisfy them. For example, suppose everyone had a positive general right to life; then everyone would have rights (entitlements) *to* those goods necessary to stay alive, e.g., food to eat. But food, or the money to buy it, doesn't grow on trees (or, if it does, the trees are owned). Those who own the food or the money have negative rights protecting their possession of these things. And negative general rights, for the libertarian, are absolute. There are no circumstances in which these rights can be justifiably overridden, in which one's liberty can be justifiably limited without his consent. Hence, X's rights to property (or life or liberty) can never be overridden for the benefit of others (to satisfy the alleged positive rights of others). X can choose to charitably give his property to someone, or he can voluntarily give someone a positive right to his property. Nevertheless, morally he cannot be forced–either by legal sanctions or moral rules–to give up his life, liberty, or property. This moral/legal prohibition insures that an individual's liberty cannot be restricted in any way without his consent.

Thus we see two important features of libertarianism. First, the primary purpose of negative general rights is the protection of individual liberty, to insure that no one's life is restricted without his consent. Or as Nozick puts it: "Side constraints [which are equivalent to negative general rights] upon action reflect the underlying Kantian principle that individuals are ends and not merely means; they cannot be sacrificed or used for the achieving of other ends without their consent. . . . [These constraints] reflect the fact of our separate existences. They reflect the fact that no moral balancing act can take place among us." Secondly, the libertarian holds that a sufficient reason to reject any alleged moral rule or principle of distributive justice is that rule or principle restricts someone's freedom without his consent. . . .

Libertarianism, though morally austere, has a certain plausibility. Each of us wants to be able to live his own life, to be free from the unnecessary interference of others. We want, in Kant's words, to be ends in ourselves and not mere means for others. But just because a theory is plausible does not mean that it is correct. Libertarianism, I think, can be shown to be mistaken. I will argue that negative general rights fail to protect individual liberty the way the libertarian suggests. Since the protection of liberty is the express purpose of these libertarian rights, the theory fails. My argument will also show that even the libertarian must hold that one should not reject a moral rule or principle of distributive justice simply because it permits (or requires) non-consensual limitations on freedom. Once this failure is exposed there appears to be no good reason for denying that there are at least some positive general duties and probably some positive general rights. How many and how extensive these duties or rights are is another question.

Libertarianism Limits Liberty

The problem with libertarianism can be seen once we recognize the limitations that negative rights (libertarian constraints) themselves place on individual liberty. Suppose, for example, that I am the biggest and strongest guy on the block. My size is a natural asset, a physical trait I inherited and then developed. But can I use my strength and size any way I please? No! At least not morally. Though I am physically capable of pummeling the peasants, pillaging property, and ravishing women, I am not morally justified in doing so. My freedom is restricted without my consent. I didn't make a contract with the property owners or the women; I didn't promise not to rap, rob, or rape. Just the same, morally I cannot perform these actions and others can justifiably prohibit me from performing them.

Consequently, everyone's life is not, given the presence of negative general rights and negative general duties, free from the interference of others. The "mere" presence of others imposes duties on each of us; it limits everyone's freedom. In fact, these restrictions are frequently extensive. For example, in the previously described case I could have all of the goods I wanted; I could take what I wanted, when I wanted. To say that such actions are morally or legally impermissible significantly limits my freedom, and my "happiness," without my consent. Of course I am not saying these restrictions are bad. Obviously they aren't. But it does show that the libertarian fails to achieve his major objective, namely, to insure that an individual's freedom cannot be limited without his consent. The libertarian's own moral constraints limit each person's freedom without consent.

This is even more vividly seen when we look at an actual historical occurrence. In the nineteenth century American slaveholders were finally legally coerced into doing what they were already morally required to do: free their slaves. In many cases this led to the slave owners' financial and social ruin: they lost their farms, their money, and their power. Of course they didn't agree to their personal ruin; they didn't agree to this restriction on their freedom. Morally they didn't have to consent; it was a remedy long overdue. Even the libertarian would agree. The slaveholders' freedom was justifiably restricted by the presence of other people; the fact that there were other persons limited their acceptable alternatives. But that is exactly what the libertarian denies. Freedom, he claims, cannot be justifiably restricted without consent. In short, the difficulty is this: the libertarian talks as if there can be no legitimate non-consensual limitations on freedom, yet his very theory involves just such limitations. Not only does this appear to be blatantly inconsistent, but even if he could avoid this inconsistency, there appears to be no principled way in which he can justify only his theory's non-consensual limitations on freedom.

This theoretical difficulty is extremely important. First, the libertarian objections against redistribution programs (like those practiced in the welfare state) are weakened, if not totally disarmed. His ever-present objection to these programs has always been that they are unjust because they are non-consensual limitations on freedom. However, as I have shown, libertarian constraints themselves demand such limitations. Therefore, that cannot be a compelling reason for rejecting welfare statism unless it is also a compelling reason for rejecting libertarianism.

Secondly, once we see that justice demands certain non-consensual limitations on someone (X's) freedom, there seems to be no good reason for concluding (and good reason not to conclude) that X's freedom can be limited only by negative general duties. There seems to be no reason, for example, for concluding that X's freedom to make $1 million should not be restricted to aid other people, e.g., to give some workers enough funds to help them escape the de facto slavery in which they find themselves.

Think of it this way. Liberty, for the libertarian, is negative in nature. An individual's liberty is restricted whenever (and only if) his potential actions are restricted. This is essentially a Hobbesian view of liberty. So imagine with Hobbes and some libertarians that individuals are seen as initially being in a state of perfect freedom. In such a state, Hobbes claims, "nothing can be just. Right and wrong have there no place." To introduce right and wrong of any sort is to put moral limitations on individual freedom. To that extent, everyone's freedom is restricted. Each person has an external impediment–a moral rule which can be coercively enforced–against doing some action A (and actions relevantly like A). Therefore, to introduce negative general rights and duties, as the libertarian does, is to admit that there are non-consensual limitations on freedom. And these limits–as I argued–are sometimes significant and far-reaching. They arise–and this is crucial–without consent; each person has them simply because he is a person. Now if one's freedom can be limited without consent by negative rights, then it is unreasonable to hold that these are the only limitations on freedom which can legitimately arise without consent. This is particularly apparent when we realize that in a number of cases the limitations on freedom imposed by negative duties are more–even much more–than limitations which would be imposed if some claims of positive rights or duties were recognized. For example, forcing a slaveholder to free his slaves would limit his freedom

more than would a law forcing him to pay ten percent of his salary to educate and provide health care for his slaves. Or forcing Hitler to not take over the world (in other words, forcing him to recognize others' negative rights) would limit his freedom more extensively than would forcing him to support, by his taxes, some governmental welfare program. Yet the libertarian concludes that redistribution of income is unjust since it limits the taxed person's liberty without his consent. If redistribution is unjust for that reason, then so are libertarian constraints. Libertarian constraints also limit personal liberty without consent.

The libertarian might attempt to immediately avoid my conclusion by claiming that there is a principled difference between redistribution of income and libertarian constraints such that the former is *never* a justified restriction of liberty while the latter is always justified. For although both do limit personal liberty without consent, he might argue, libertarian constraints only restrict liberty in order to protect individual rights. And it is the protection of personal rights which justifies these, and only these, non-consensual restrictions on liberty.

However, this reply won't do. For as I have stated, any libertarian conception of rights is itself grounded in–justified by reference to–personal liberty. Or, as Eric Mack puts it, they are grounded in the right not be coerced. Hence, given my preceding argument, there is no principled way that concerns for personal liberty could generate *only* libertarian rights and duties, since negative rights restrict liberty as much as, or more than, would some positive rights or duties. Consequently, appeals to personal rights cannot provide the libertarian with a principled basis for distinguishing between types of non-consensual limitations on liberty.

We have uncovered a very telling incoherence. We have taken the main libertarian weapon against welfare statism and turned it on itself. The once-so-sharp sword is seen to have two sides. Instead of menacing the enemy, the sword only frustrates its wielder. As everyone knows, two-edged swords cut both ways. The libertarian is unable to support his conception of the minimal state. At least some redistribution of tax monies is justified.

Possible Libertarian Replies

"Liberty" Is Normative, not Descriptive   The libertarian might object to this argument by claiming that I have misunderstood his use of the word

"liberty." "Liberty" is not, he might argue, a purely descriptive term. On a purely descriptive model of liberty, anything which restricts an individual's options would be a restriction of his liberty. Hence, negative rights would be a restriction of individual liberty. But not just any restriction of someone's option is a restriction of his liberty. Prohibitions of unjust actions are surely not limitations of freedom. For example, a person does not have the liberty to knife someone even though he physically might be able to do it. In short, individuals have liberty to do only those things which are just. Consequently, "liberty" should be seen as a normative term such that if A has the liberty to do X then not only is no one prohibiting him from doing it, but it is also morally permissible that he do it. "Therefore," the libertarian might conclude, "your objection fails since negative duties do not really limit individual liberty. It is not just that people kill each other, so prohibitions against killing are not limitations of freedom."

This linguistic proposal is intriguing since "liberty" clearly does have a positive emotive force which suggests ethical overtones. My own hunch, though, is that `liberty' should be maintained as a descriptive term. That is, "liberty" is, and should be maintained as, a value-neutral term which merely states that there are limitations, without any judgment as to their propriety. For although we all have some tendencies to vacillate between the descriptive and normative senses of the term, it seems clear that its basic sense is descriptive. It is only after we identify liberty descriptively that we are able to distinguish between just and unjust restrictions on it. For the purposes of this paper, however, I need not belabor the point. For even the acceptance of this linguistic proposal cannot patch up the libertarian's deflated case. For if "liberty" is a normative term in the way proposed, then we could not know if something is a restriction of liberty until we knew if the restrained action is just. For example, we would not know that taxing a millionaire's money and distributing it to the needy was a violation of the millionaire's liberty until we knew if it was just to so tax him. Hence, the claim that A has the liberty to do X (spend his millions any way he pleases) could not be a *reason* for believing that some action (taxing the millions) is unjust. The justificatory relationship on this model would be exactly opposite. We would have reason to believe that A had the liberty to do X only if we already knew that it was just that he do it.

Consequently, the protection of individual liberty cannot be the purpose of (or consequence of) negative rights since the determination that someone had the liberty to do X depends upon the determination that he has the right to do it. For example, one would have the liberty to bequeath property P to Z only if he had the right of bequeathal. Yet the libertarian wants to ground such rights in personal liberty. Therefore, even if this linguistic proposal were acceptable, the libertarian's stated purpose of negative rights would be undermined. He would no longer be able to argue for stringent negative rights on the grounds that they protect individual liberties. Nor would he be able to reject other principles of distributive justice on grounds that they limited individual liberty without consent.

Liberty Should Be Maximized The libertarian might attempt another tack. "Admittedly negative rights limit individual freedom. There has never been any doubt about that. What the libertarian demands is that everyone have maximum personal liberty with equal liberty consistent for all." However, this popular statement of libertarianism fails to soften my objection. The maximum amount of liberty with equal liberty for all is absolute liberty–a state in which there are no legal or moral prohibitions of any kind. (Notice that this is a Hobbesian state of nature.) In such a state there are no prohibitions and everyone is equally free from prohibitions. The libertarian, I suspect, would disagree. Although in such a state people would *ideally* have equal liberty, the libertarian would probably contend that because some people would take advantage of the situation and deprive others of their liberty, people so situated would not, in fact, have equal liberty. In other words, though liberty is ideally maximal, it would not be prudentially maximal.

There are three problems with this reply. First, on this view there would no longer be absolute prohibitions against restriction of liberty. Liberty could be justifiably restricted; it would not be an absolute good. True, it is only liberty which overrides liberty. Nevertheless, to say that one species of liberty overrides another is to say that there is something about one of them (liberty$_1$) which makes it morally more potent than the other (liberty$_2$). This something–e.g., good consequences following the action–which makes liberty$_1$ more potent, must be something other than liberty. Otherwise, there would be no rational basis for preferring liberty$_1$ over liberty$_2$. This implies that this other feature (e.g., good consequences) is more important than liberty or that liberty is morally good only when it has this (or some other) specific feature. Thus, liberty would be neither absolute nor supreme.

Secondly, if the libertarian concern *is* with maximizing liberty, then there would no longer be absolute rights to liberty. Instead, liberty would be a goal, an end-state to be maximized. And, as Robert Nozick realizes (he makes his point in the language of rights), "This . . . would require us to violate someone's rights when doing so minimizes the total (weighted) amount of violations of rights in the society." That is why he rejects such an option. An individual's liberty could be justifiably protected only if certain empirical statements (about whether the requisite action maximized liberty) were true. Hence, negative rights would be neither theoretically nor practically absolute. And to deny that they are absolute is to deny libertarianism.

Thirdly, if liberty must be *exactly* equal, as the rebuttal suggests, then we would have to have an extremely repressive government (a police state with constant electronic surveillance, etc.). Otherwise some people's (but not all people's) rights would be violated by murders, muggers, etc. Consequently, if the demand were on maximizing liberty, a Hobbesian state of liberty would be chosen; if the emphasis were on equality of liberty, then something like a police state would be chosen.

In other words, any reference to maximal or equal liberty indicates only a formal criterion of justice which fails to distinguish between alternative determinations of what counts as maximal or equal liberty.

Individuals Tacitly Consent to Libertarianism The libertarian could attempt another reply by appealing to the notion of implied or tacit consent. "You have correctly identified my criterion for justifiably restricting personal freedom," he might say. "An individual must consent to any restriction. Consent, however, need not be explicitly offered. An individual can, merely by his action, tacitly consent to some limitations of his freedom." The libertarian then might go on to conjecture that by seeking interaction with others, all individuals tacitly agree to respect others' liberty in certain specified ways, namely, those ways protected by negative general rights.

There are, however, several difficulties with this reply. Initially there is the difficult question of how to adequately describe some action(s) such that it does indicate tacit consent. And no matter how one describes such an action, undoubtedly someone in the

world would fail to perform it—yet the libertarian would still assume that person had a duty not to violate libertarian constraints. We could also note that the notion of tacit consent normally implies that such consent is like explicit consent, it is just that it is not verbally offered. That suggests that A cannot be said to have tacitly consented to X, if, when he is explicitly asked if he so consents, he (A) denies it. Yet surely there would be at least one person in the world who would vehemently deny that he had consented to the presence of all and only negative general rights. Hence, there would be no basis for claiming that A is morally or legally required to do X. Still the libertarian would want to contend that A could not justifiably kill others, steal their property, etc.

Secondly, it is highly implausible to think that all people would consent—explicitly or implicitly—to all and only libertarian constraints. Robert Nozick, for example, recognizes this when he emphatically rejects the principle of fairness. If a rule of tacit consent could undergird negative general rights, then it could also justify at least some governmental redistribution programs. We don't, however, need to cite Nozick here; we can simply make the obvious claim that people would choose something other than libertarianism. They would at least opt for a system which also gave them sufficient goods (or the ready opportunity to obtain them) to stay alive. . . . The rebuttal fails.

. . .

Conclusion and Speculation

My argument is completed. I have argued that libertarianism is untenable. I have challenged . . . possible replies to my argument. I would like to end with some rather brief speculation on the direction an adequate theory of justice must go. My speculation emerges from the previous arguments. I have shown that neither property nor liberty (as defined by the libertarian) should be seen as the only social good; singling these out as the only social values is unreasonable. Instead, these should be seen as two values among many, all competing for recognition.

Property, as I have said, is important. But how important? Well, it should be apparent that an individual cannot be alive without some property, or at least some goods to use; neither can a person have any real options without goods to work on. In addition, there is some force to the Hegelian claim that individuals need property with which to "identify" themselves, and there is the Jeffersonian point that property seems to be necessary for the protection of civil liberty. These might suggest that everyone is entitled to some minimum of goods, and that that minimum is protected by negative rights. Beyond this minimum? That's a difficult question.

And what of liberty? Surely it is important. Just as surely it is not all-important. But in some societies, say, rather affluent ones, it (e.g., political and civil liberties) may be the highest (but even here not the only) value. The libertarian's claim that it is is mistaken.

EXERCISES

1. Suppose that you live under a well-functioning democracy, with full voter participation in making the laws; but the majority of your fellow citizens democratically pass a law that you find morally offensive (for example, a law forbidding anyone from providing medical care to illegal immigrants). Do you have an obligation to obey that law? Does the fact that the law was passed democratically make the obligation to obey the law *stronger*, or is that irrelevant? (You might believe that democratically passed laws carry stronger obligation, but *still* believe that you should *not* obey that law.)

2. You are serving on a jury, and the defendant is charged with growing and distributing marijuana. There is strong evidence that the defendant did in fact grow marijuana (she grew it in her basement, using artificial light), and she gave small amounts—about an ounce each—to several of her friends. However, she never grew a large amount of marijuana, and there is no evidence that she ever sold marijuana. In fact, the defendant is undergoing radiation treatment for cancer, and smoking marijuana helps her control the nausea that often accompanies that treatment; and the friends to whom she gives marijuana are all people undergoing similar treatments, whom she met at the clinic. What the defendant is doing is against the law. However, *suppose* you believe that the laws against marijuana are stupid and wrong and an infringement on individual liberty and that you strongly believe that persons undergoing cancer treatment should be allowed to use marijuana in order to gain relief from nausea. But also you have no doubt that the defendant is guilty under the law. Would it be legitimate for you to refuse to vote for the defendant's conviction, and instead vote not guilty? Would it be morally *obligatory* for you to vote not guilty?

3. This question is based on an example developed by M. B. E. Smith, a contemporary political philosopher. Suppose that you are driving along a lonely stretch of highway in the desert, and ahead there is a stop sign. There is no cross road, and no good reason to stop: The state was planning to build another road crossing the road you are driving on, and the state erected the stop sign, and the law says that you *should stop* at that stop sign; but the state never got around to actually building the other road, so there is no approaching traffic to worry about. Since you frequently drive along this stretch of highway, you are well aware that there is no crossroad. Still, the law is the law: You are legally mandated to stop at the stop sign. The question is this: Do you have an *obligation* to stop? Obviously, stopping would not violate your conscience or your basic principles: It's not like a law requiring you to help in the capture of fugitive slaves. And you believe the government that passed this law and erected this stop sign is *legitimate* (even though in this case, it may have done something rather silly). So: Do you have an obligation to stop?

4. Thomas Jefferson believed that the essential foundation of democratic government is in private businesses: the shopkeeper who owns and operates her own shop, the farmer who owns his own land and runs his own farm. According to Jefferson, this independent management of a business —making your own decisions, reaping the benefits of your own labor and ingenuity—gives you a stake in the future of the country as well as experience in making your own decisions, and both are vital to the democratic process. In our contemporary economic system, Jefferson's values seem rather quaint: Small family farms cannot compete with huge agribusinesses, and so have largely disappeared; small businesses typically either fail or get bought out by huge corporations; and the local shopkeepers have been displaced by gargantuan retail chains. We now live in an economy of concentrated wealth, enormous and powerful corporations, and top–down management style in which most workers have few opportunities for significant independent decision-making; in this economy, is there any workable substitute for the practice of independent decision-making and individual responsibility that ownership of small businesses and farms provided to past generations?

5. Suppose you are living under a social contract model of government—as in the United States, for example—but you have lived in circumstances that you would be very unlikely to accept as legitimate social contract terms: You are born into a community in which crime is common, there are frequent shootings, and there is little police protection (indeed, you are much more likely to be bullied or even abused by the police than protected by them); your school is unsafe, and the facilities are sadly inadequate; you have little access to health care; your prospects of finding a job that pays a living wage are very poor. Would you—from a social contract perspective—be under *less* obligation to obey the law than would be someone who has excellent police and fire protection, good schools, excellent medical resources, and good job opportunities?

6. Consider the classical liberal political philosophy: We should protect and promote those values that promote free discussion and the free opportunity to choose and pursue one's own preferred way of life (so long as that way of life does not harm others); but the state should *not* promote values that favor one way of life over others. *If* you favor such a liberal view, what specific values would you *promote?* Using that standard, which values do you think would generate the most controversy (that is, which values would cause the most dispute about whether they should or should not be promoted by the liberal state)?

7. Economists generally agree that lack of adequate marketplace regulation—particularly lack of regulation of banks and investment firms—was a major cause of the severe economic problems (home foreclosures, bankruptcies, bank failures, massive job losses, etc.) that became evident in late 2008. If economists are correct in that assessment, does that have any implications for the debate between Mack and LaFollette?

8. John's great-great-grandfather made a fortune in the U.S. slave trade; that fortune was invested carefully, and it continued to grow as it passed from John's great-grandfather to his grandfather to his father, and now to John. John now has great wealth, which is the result of careful investments of several generations of his family, but the original investment capital came from trading in slaves. Is *John's* wealth legitimate?

9. Sarah is a brilliant biochemistry researcher, and she discovers and patents a new drug that is effective in treating arthritis. Because arthritis is a very common disease, Sarah's new drug will be worth hundreds of millions of dollars in sales. Sarah was educated in public schools, she went to a state university for both her undergraduate and graduate studies, and her research was based on discoveries made and research techniques developed by hundreds of scientists that came before: Her discoveries would not have been possible without her excellent education, and without the vast body of knowledge built up by earlier generations of scientists who were trained and supported by our society. Does our society have a legitimate claim on some of the proceeds from the new drug that Sarah developed, or is Sarah entitled to keep all the money she makes from selling that drug?

10. Of the ethical theories and theorists considered in earlier chapters, which ones would be most congenial to Eric Mack? Which would be most compatible with Hugh LaFollette's views?

ADDITIONAL READING

Isaiah Berlin is the main source for the distinction between positive and negative liberty; see *Four Essays on Liberty* (New York: Oxford University Press, 1969). An excellent biography of Berlin is by Michael Ignatieff, *Isaiah Berlin: A Life* (New York: Vintage, 2000). A good collection of essays on Berlin's work is Mark Lilla, Ronald Dworkin and Robert B. Silvers, eds., *The Legacy of Isaiah Berlin* (New York: New York Review of Books; London: Granta, 2001).

For a history of political thought, there are many choices. Among the best resources are Ian Hampsher-Monk, *A History of Political Thought: Major Political Thinkers from Hobbes to Marx* (Oxford: Blackwell, 1992); and a two-volume study by Janet Coleman, *A History of Political Thought: From Ancient Greece to Early Christianity* and *A History of Political Thought: From the Middle Ages to the Renaissance*.

Thomas Hobbes' *Leviathan*, John Locke's *Second Treatise on Government*, and Jean-Jacques Rousseau's *Social Contract (Du Contrat Social)* are the classic sources for social contract theory. Hobbes' *Leviathan* is available from Bobbs-Merrill (Indianapolis, 1958); it was originally published in 1651. Locke's *Second Treatise on Government* was originally published in 1690; an accessible edition is Indianapolis: Bobbs-Merrill, Library of Liberal Arts, 1952. Rousseau's *Social Contract* was originally published in 1762; it can be found in an edition edited by R. Masters (New York: St. Martin's Press, 1978).

Interesting critiques of social contract theory, from a feminist perspective, are offered by Christine DiStefano, *Configurations of Masculinity* (Ithaca, NY: Cornell University Press, 1991); Virginia Held, *Feminist Morality* (Chicago: The University of Chicago Press, 1993); and Carole Pateman, *The Sexual Contract* (Stanford: Stanford University Press, 1988).

John Rawls offers a contemporary version of social contract theory, with an emphasis on questions of justice and fairness, in *A Theory of Justice* (London: Oxford University Press, 1971). For comments on the book, see *A Theory of Justice and Its Critics*, edited by Chandran Kukathas and Philip Pettit (Polity, 1990), as well as *The Idea of a Political Liberalism*, edited by Victoria Davion and Clark Wolf (Rowman and Littlefield, 2000). David Gauthier's contemporary contractarian theory is found in *Morals by Agreement* (Oxford: Oxford University Press, 1986).

For social contract theory and other topics, visit Paul Leighton's website at www.paulsjusticepage.com. A good resource for more information on John Rawls can be found at Policy Library, at www.policylibrary.com/rawls.

One of the great contrasts in modern political thought is between liberalism and conservatism. Immanuel Kant is a classical source for modern liberalism. His political writings can be found in *Political Writings*, edited by Hans Reiss (Cambridge: Cambridge University Press, 1996). John Stuart Mill's *On Liberty* is a major work in this tradition, and many good editions are widely available. Perhaps the best known contemporary philosopher in the liberal tradition is John Rawls; see the additional resources suggestions above and in Chapter 12, and also his *Political Liberalism* (New York: Cambridge University Press, 1993). Ronald Dworkin is another major figure in contemporary liberal philosophy; see his *Taking Rights Seriously* (Cambridge, Mass.: Harvard University Press, 1977); *A Matter of Principle* (Cambridge, Mass.: Harvard University Press, 1985); *Law's Empire* (Cambridge, Mass.: Harvard University Press, 1986); and *Freedom's Law* (Cambridge, Mass.: Harvard University Press, 1996). The classic source for conservative thought is Edmund Burke: Among his vast output of writings, one of the most readable is *Reflections on the Revolution in France*, available in many editions. More recent conservative writers include Michael Oakeshott, *Rationalism in Politics and Other Essays* (London: Methuen, 1962), and Milton Friedman, *Capitalism and Freedom* (Chicago: University of Chicago Press, 1962).

For the contrast between liberal individualism and communitarian views, see *The Communitarian Challenge to Liberalism*, edited by E. F. Paul, F. D. Miller, Jr. and J. Paul (Cambridge: Cambridge University Press, 1996). Alasdair MacIntyre's *After Virtue* (London: Duckworth, 1981) is a widely read philosophical essay that champions the communitarian view. Among the many excellent books on feminist political theory are J. B. Landes, ed., *Feminism, the Public and the Private* (Oxford: Oxford University Press, 1998), and G. Bock and S. James, eds., *Beyond Equality and Difference: Citizenship, Feminist Politics and Female Subjectivity* (London: Routledge, 1992).

An excellent anthology on the issue of "political obligation"—the general duty to obey the laws of one's country—is William A. Edmundson, ed., *The Duty to Obey the Law: Selected Philosophical Readings* (Lanham, MD: Rowman & Littlefield Publishers, 1999).

There are some superb Internet resources for political philosophy. One of my favorites—which contains a particularly good set of links—is maintained by the University of British Columbia Library, and can be found at http://www.library.ubc.ca/poli/theory.html. Another very good site, which is organized very effectively and has extensive links, is maintained by the Department of Political Science at University of Pisa; visit http://lgxserver.

uniba.it/lei/filpol/filpole/homepage.htm. The online Stanford Encyclopedia of Philosophy is an excellent site; you can search for almost any topic in political philosophy, or almost any influential political philosopher, from ancient to contemporary; visit http://plato. stanford.edu/ (and see especially "Political Obligation," by Richard Dagger and "Contractarianism," by Ann Cudd). The Internet Encyclopedia of Philosophy is also very good, at http://www.iep.utm.edu/. Wikipedia, "the free encyclopedia," is a good source for biographies, especially of contemporary philosophers; it's at http://en.wikipedia.org/wiki.

GLOSSARY

Ad hominem argument: "Ad hominem" literally means "to the person." An ad hominem argument is an argument that focuses on a person (or group of people), typically attacking the person. For example, "Joe is a liar," "Sandra is a hypocrite," "Republicans are coldhearted." Ad hominem arguments are *fallacious* only when they attack the source of an *argument* in order to discredit the argument; for example, "Joe's argument against drinking and driving doesn't carry much weight, because Joe himself is a lush." When *not* attacking the source of an *argument*, ad hominem arguments do *not* commit the ad hominem *fallacy*, and can often be valuable and legitimate arguments. For example, an ad hominem attack on someone giving *testimony* ("Don't believe Sally's testimony, she's a notorious liar") is relevant, and *not* an ad hominem fallacy; likewise, it is a legitimate use of ad hominem argument (*not* an ad hominem *fallacy*) if you are attacking a job applicant ("Don't hire Bruce, he's a crook"), a politician ("Don't vote for Sandra, she's in the pocket of the tobacco industry"), and in many other circumstances ("Don't go out with Bill, he's a cheat and a creep").

Analytic statement: A statement that is "true by definition"; that is, a statement in which the predicate is contained in the subject (what the predicate term says about or attributes to the subject is part of the meaning or definition of the subject). For example, "An equilateral triangle has three sides."

Anarchist: One who rejects all claims of government legitimacy.

A posteriori: Knowledge that comes from experience and observation; empirical knowledge.

Appeal to authority: Any attempt to establish a claim by appealing to an expert or to someone who supposedly has special expertise. If the authority to whom the appeal is made is a genuine expert or authority in the *relevant area*, and there is *consensus* among authorities, then appeal to authority is legitimate; otherwise it is fallacious.

A priori: Knowledge gained "prior to" or independently of experience; knowledge based on pure reason.

Argument: Reasons offered in support of a conclusion.

Argument from diversity: The argument against ethical objectivism based on the great diversity and conflict among the ethical systems of different individuals as well as different societies.

Argument from queerness: The argument (devised by J. L. Mackie) against ethical objectivism, claiming that the positing of objective moral facts violates the principle of Ockham's Razor, because simpler explanations of the same phenomena can be given without appeal to such very strange (queer) entities as moral facts.

Care ethics: The ethical theory that emphasizes personal (as opposed to impersonal marketplace) relationships as the basis of ethics, focusing less on establishing and following rules and more on preserving relationships and nurturing; regards family and community as the starting point of ethics, rather than independent individuals.

Categorical imperative: In Kant's ethical system, the basic ethical principle that is known through reason and applies universally and unconditionally. The principle is formulated in two ways that Kant regards as basically equivalent: Always act in such a way that you could will your act as a universal law; and always treat others as ends-in-themselves, and never merely as means to an end.

Causal responsibility: The key factor in bringing some result into effect (which may depend on context); distinguished from moral responsibility.

Coherence theory: The epistemological view that knowledge claims always occur as part of a larger system, and that the system as a whole must be tested for its effectiveness, rather than testing specific claims in isolation; systems work as wholes, and no part can be considered foundational.

Communitarian: The view that social cohesion of communities and countries requires a shared value framework.

Compatibilism: The view that determinism is *compatible* with free will and moral responsibility; there is no conflict between free will and determinism.

Conclusion: What an argument aims at proving; the statement that is supposedly proved by the premises of an argument.

Consequentialist ethics: Any ethical system (including but not limited to utilitarianism) that makes the goodness or badness of an act depend upon the consequences it produces, rather than the principle it falls under.

Conservative, classical: The view that government should promote established value systems, that have proven their worth by their long endurance, and that keep the country on a steady course; changes in the basic values contribute to disorder, and should be discouraged.

Constructivism: The view that ethical principles are made (constructed) by society, rather than discovered (for example, social contract theory).

Contextualism: The epistemological view that holds that beliefs are justified or unjustified relative to the *context* in which they occur and the uses that are made of them; that is, claims are not true (and beliefs are not justified) by some fixed and absolute standard, but only relative to context.

Correspondence theory: The epistemological view that a theory or claim is true if and only if it accurately corresponds to, matches, or maps the world as it actually exists.

Cosmological argument: An argument for the existence of God, based on the claim that the very existence of the universe (the cosmos) requires something that brought it into existence, since it could not have come into existence without a cause, and that ultimate cause must be God.

Deductive argument: An argument which claims that its premises provide conclusive proof of its conclusion; an argument that claims to extract its conclusion from its premises by logical operations.

Deontological ethics: A rule-based system of ethics that emphasizes the importance of following ethical rules, rather than achieving desirable goals or producing the best consequences.

Design argument: An argument for the existence of God based on the claim that observation of the world shows evidence that it was created by an intelligent and purposeful Designer, and only God could carry out such a design; sometimes called the teleological argument.

Determinism: The view that everything that happens, in every detail, is the inevitable result of the state of the world at any given time and the full set of causal laws.

Divine command theory of ethics (also known as theological voluntarism): The view that ethical principles are established only and entirely by God's commands and decrees.

Dual-aspect theory: The mind–body view that the mind and body (or mind and brain) make up a single substance, but that substance can be viewed from either the physical or the mental perspective.

Dualism: Any theory of the mind that claims that the mind and body are distinct and different substances.

Egoism, ethical: The ethical theory that holds that each individual should (is morally obligated to) seek only his or her own benefit.

Egoism, psychological: The empirical psychological claim that in fact every human seeks only his or her own benefit.

Emotivism: A special version of ethical nonobjectivism, which claims that "statements" concerning ethics are not factual claims at all, but instead are disguised imperatives or expressions of emotional reaction.

Empiricism: The view that some important elements of knowledge can only be gained through sensory observation; or (the stronger claim) that *all* our knowledge is ultimately based on sensory observation.

Epiphenomenalism: The view that ideas and thoughts are caused by brain activity, but they do not themselves cause any physical events; rather, they are "side effects" or symptoms of physical brain activity.

Ethical nonobjectivism: The view that there are no objective ethical truths.

Ethical objectivism: The view that ethical claims are objectively true or false.

Existentialism: The philosophical view that "existence precedes essence"; that is, that all people make themselves by their own choices, are totally and unavoidably free to make themselves without restrictions or restraints, and are morally responsible for the resulting character and for all choices and behavior.

Externalism: In contrast to *internalism*, the view that confirmation of the truth of our beliefs may require reference to resources outside our own immediate thoughts and reasons.

Fallacy: An argument error; usually a standard or common argument error.

Fatalism: The view that the most significant life events—such as one's death, triumphs, defeats—are controlled by a special power, and that human efforts can have no influence over those events.

Foundationalism: The epistemological view that all knowledge must be built up from a secure foundation, and that the foundation must be established independently.

Functionalism: The view that the contents of the mind—its thoughts, ideas, and consciousness—should be regarded as functional units that might be generated or produced by many different "hardware" arrangements, which would be functionally equivalent so long as they produced the same thought process.

Hard determinism: The view that determinism is true and that determinism is incompatible with free will and moral responsibility (because all our behavior is determined, we are not free and we are not morally responsible).

Hierarchical compatibilism: The position that we are free and morally responsible when we reflectively approve (at a higher level) of our desires, even though those desires may be determined.

Idealism: The view that everything that exists is mental; there are no physical bodies, no material objects; the world consists entirely of minds and ideas.

Identity theory: The view that mind and brain are identical; thoughts and ideas are identical with brain processes, they are one and the same thing.

Inductive argument: An argument that claims its premises make its conclusion *probable*, but not certain (the conclusion goes beyond what is contained in the premises).

Interactionism: A version of dualist theory that claims that the mind and body, though different substances, can interact and directly influence each other.

Internalism: The epistemological position that in order to genuinely know something, one must be able to be certain of that knowledge through an examination of one's own ideas and reasons, without requiring any *external* verification.

Intuitionism: In ethics, the view that ethical truths (such as basic ethical principles, or the rightness or wrongness of a specific act) are known through special intuitive powers, and are known directly and immediately.

Irrelevant reason fallacy: An argument that uses premises that have no bearing on the conclusion, but only distract from the real issue. Also known as the *red herring* fallacy.

Kantian ethics (rationalist ethics): A system of ethics that derives its rules from reason, and insists that its rules must be universal.

Liberal, classical: The view that government should give individuals the freedom to pursue their own ideas and experiments concerning their values and their ways of living, promoting only the values required to allow such diversity to flourish (such as freedom of speech and freedom of religion).

Libertarian (Free Will): The view that genuine free will and moral responsibility require the power to make choices that are not the product of our determined history; and that we infact have such power.

Libertarian (Political): The view that the role of government should be kept to an absolute minimum almost exclusively focused on protection of the country from foreign invasion or attack. Government should not be involved in insuring the safety of drugs, regulating the marketplace, licensing physicians, providing public education, or promoting any form of social welfare (such as social security).

Materialism: The view that everything that exists is material (or physical); there is no nonphysical mind stuff, no souls nor spirits.

Moral realism: In contemporary ethical theory, the view that the existence of objective moral facts is a plausible hypothesis that may be proven true.

Moral responsibility: The responsibility that justifies praise and blame and other forms or special or unequal treatment for one's behavior; the responsibility that supports claims and ascriptions of just deserts.

Myth: A story that expresses a deeper claim of truth than its literal meaning.

Narrative identity: An account of personal identity that bases identity on the story or narrative that gives meaning and substance to that person's life.

Negative liberty: The liberty of noninterference; the liberty of being free of any interference with one's life or person or property; the liberty of being left alone to use one's resources as one wishes, but with no expectation of aid.

Occasionalism: The dualist view that God controls all the acts of both mind and body, and keeps them in perfect order and harmony, so that their coordinated acts appear to interact though they actually do not. Cases in which the mind appears to cause the body to move are merely occasions when God causes both mental ideas and physical movement.

Ockham's Razor, principle of: A principle formulated by William of Ockham; specifically, the principle that all else being equal, the simplest hypothesis is more plausible than a more complicated hypothesis; or alternatively, the principle that theories should not posit entities beyond necessity. Sometimes called the Principle of Parsimony (and sometimes spelled "Occam").

Ontological argument: An argument for the existence of God, based on the idea that God is the only being whose existence is *necessary* (since the meaning of "God" implies that there can be no greater conceivable being, and an *existent* being is greater than a similar but *nonexistent* being).

Pascal's wager: An argument for belief in the existence of God based on Pascal's claim that we have more to gain by believing, so belief is a "better bet."

Political obligation: The obligation to obey the laws of one's government.

Positive liberty: The enhancement of individual freedom by providing resources (such as education) that will enlarge free choice and opportunity

Pragmatism: The philosophical position that maintains that the meaning of a concept is determined by the practical consequences of its application, and that the truth of a claim or theory is based on its usefulness in guiding us.

Predestination: The religious view that each person's salvation or damnation is decided by God's choice, long before that person's birth; human choice plays no role whatsoever in determining whether one is saved or damned.

Preestablished harmony: A version of mind–body dualism that claims there is no interaction between mind and body, between the mental and the physical; rather, God establishes a plan and an order that keeps minds and bodies running in perfect harmony.

Premise: In an argument, a premise is a statement that supports or provides justification for the conclusion.

Problem of evil: A problem that confronts believers in an omnipotent, omniscient, and benevolent God. If God has the power and wisdom to stop suffering and prevent evil, then how can God be considered kind and benevolent if He allows these to exist?

Qualia: The qualitative content of such psychological experiences as emotions, sensations, and perceptions; the special "feel" of psychological experiences.

Rationalism: The view that genuine knowledge (or at least the most important elements of knowledge) must be based purely on reason.

Rationalist compatibilism: The position that we are genuinely free and morally responsible only when we are following the path of the True and the Good; when we are doing the right thing for the right reasons. Freedom does not require open alternatives; genuine freedom means following the single true path.

Red herring: A popular alternative name for the irrelevant reason fallacy.

Reductio ad absurdum: Reduction to absurdity; that is, an argument form that draws out the implications of a position, shows that its implications lead to absurd results, and concludes that therefore the position must be false.

Relativism, cultural: The ethical view that ethical acts and principles are true relative to one's culture, and the right act is the act that is ethically approved by the culture one inhabits.

Relativism, sociological: The claim that different cultures have substantively different ethical systems.

Role responsibility: Responsibility for a role or office or task.

Skepticism: The view that we can never attain certainty; that knowledge is impossible, or at least doubtful.

Social contract (Theory of Government): The view that the legitimacy of government is derived entirely and exclusively from the consent of the governed.

Social contract ethics: In ethics, the view that ethical principles for any society are established by the agreement and consent of the persons living in that society.

Soft determinism:(sometimes called compatibilism): The view that determinism is true, but we still have free will and are morally responsible because determinism is compatible with free will and moral responsibility.

Strawman fallacy: The fallacy of distorting or exaggerating or misrepresenting an opponent's position in order to make it easier to attack.

Synthetic statement: In contrast to an *analytic* statement, a statement in which the predicate asserts something of the subject that is not already contained in the subject term; for example, "Penguins are excellent swimmers."

Teleological ethics: Ethical systems that focus on goals and outcomes more than on rules and principles; in contrast to deontological ethics.

Utilitarian ethics: An ethical theory that maintains that the right act is the act which produces the greatest balance of pleasure over suffering for all.

Valid: In *deductive* arguments, an argument in which the truth of the premises guarantees the truth of the conclusion; in a valid deductive argument, it is impossible for all the premises to be true and the conclusion to be false: *If* all the premises of a valid deductive argument are true, then its conclusion *must* be true.

Virtue ethics: An ethical theory that emphasizes the development of good character, rather than questions of what acts are right or wrong.

INDEX